BRIEF

PART 1 BASIC CONCEPTS OF OM AND VALUE CHAINS

PART 2 DESIGNING OPERATIONS AND SUPPLY CHAINS

PART 3 MANAGING OPERATIONS AND SUPPLY CHAINS

SUPPLEMENTS

CONTENTS

2E

Operations AND Supply Chain Management

David A. Collier • James R. Evans

Australia • Brazil • Canada • Mexico • Singapore • United Kingdom • United States

***Operations and Supply Chain Management*, 2nd Edition**
David A. Collier, James R. Evans

Senior Vice President, Higher Education & Skills Product: Erin Joyner

Product Director: Jason Fremder

Sr. Product Manager: Aaron Arnsparger

Sr. Learning Designer: Brandon Foltz

Sr. Content Manager: D. Jean Bora

Product Assistant: Margaret Russo

Marketing Manager: Christopher Walz

Intellectual Property Analyst: Ashley Maynard

Intellectual Property Project Manager: Kelli Besse

Production Service: SPi Global

Art Direction, Text and Cover Design: Chris Doughman

Cover Image: iStockPhoto.com/thitivong

For product information and technology assistance, contact us at **Cengage Customer & Sales Support, 1-800-354-9706** or **support.cengage.com.**

For permission to use material from this text or product, submit all requests online at **www.cengage.com/permissions.**

Library of Congress Control Number: 2019920622

Student Edition:
ISBN: 978-0-357-13169-5

Loose-leaf Edition:
ISBN: 978-0-357-13173-2

Cengage
200 Pier 4 Boulevard
Boston, MA 02210
USA

Cengage is a leading provider of customized learning solutions with employees residing in nearly 40 different countries and sales in more than 125 countries around the world. Find your local representative at **www.cengage.com.**

To learn more about Cengage platforms and services, register or access your online learning solution, or purchase materials for your course, visit **www.cengage.com**.

Printed at CLDPC, USA, 04-22

Supplements

David A. Collier was the Eminent Scholar, Alico Chair in Operations Management, at the Lutgert College of Business, Florida Gulf Coast University, Fort Myers, Florida. He retired in 2017. Dr. Collier holds a Bachelor of Science of Mechanical Engineering and a Masters of Business Administration from the University of Kentucky and Ph.D. in Production and Operations Management from The Ohio State University. Dr. Collier previously taught at the Fuqua School of Business at Duke University, the Colgate Darden Graduate School of Business at the University of Virginia, the Fisher College of Business at The Ohio State University, and at the University of Warwick in England.

Dr. Collier is the recipient of five awards for outstanding journal articles, has written and published eight invited book chapters, seven of his cases have been reprinted in major marketing and operations management textbooks, several of his articles have been reprinted in the *Harvard Business Review* 10 Must Reads series, and has over 80 refereed journal publications. He has published in journals such as *Management Sciences, Decision Sciences, Journal of Operations Management, Production & Operations Management, International Journal of Operations and Production Management, Business Horizons, Journal of Service Science,* and *International Journal of Service Industry Management.* Dr. Collier has over 11,000 reads and 3,000 citations according to ResearchGate.

He is the author of six books on service, quality, and operations management: *Service Management: The Automation of Services* (1985), *Service Management: Operating Decisions* (1987), *The Service/Quality Solution: Using Service Management to Gain Competitive Advantage* (1994), *Operations Management: Goods, Services and Value Chains* (2005), *Operations and Supply Chain Management* (2018 to current) and *OM6* (current).

Professor Collier was selected to the 1991 and 1992 Board of Examiners for Malcolm Baldrige National Quality Award. He has been a consultant and executive management instructor over his 41-year career for many organizations such as Chase Bank, AT&T, the United States Postal Service, and Emery Worldwide. He is on numerous Who's Who directories such as Who's Who of Emerging Leaders in America.

James R. Evans James R. Evans is Professor Emeritus of Operations, Business Analytics, and Information Systems in the Lindner College of Business at the University of Cincinnati, having retired after over 43 years on the faculty. He holds BSIE and

MSIE degrees from Purdue University and a Ph.D. in Industrial and Systems Engineering from Georgia Tech. He served as president of the Decision Sciences Institute 1997–1998 and 11 years on the Board of Examiners and Panel of Judges for the Malcolm Baldrige National Quality Award. He has been the editor of the *Quality Management Journal*, published by the American Society for Quality and served on editorial boards of numerous other journals. Dr. Evans has published 100 refereed papers in major academic journals and more than 50 editions of 20 textbooks. During the annual Quality Congress in May 2004, the American Society for Quality presented Dr. Evans and co-author Bill Lindsay with the Philip B. Crosby Medal for writing *The Management and Control of Quality, 5th edition*. The Crosby medal was presented "for authoring a distinguished book contributing significantly to the extension of the philosophy and application of the principles, methods, and techniques of quality management." He also received the 2018 Lindner Research Excellence Award from the College of Business at the University of Cincinnati and the 2019 Baldrige Foundation Leadership Award for Excellence in Education..

Operations and supply chain management (OSCM) has evolved into one of today's most important business disciplines. OSCM is an outgrowth of the disciplines of industrial engineering, strategic management, quality control, and management science. Although OSCM began with a strong focus in production and manufacturing, one cannot deny the fact that over 80 percent of U.S. jobs are now in the service sector and more than half of goods-producing industry jobs involve service processes. Consequently, most business graduates will work in the service sector, or in service-related aspects of manufacturing firms; thus, it is vital that any book in this area has a strong service orientation.

Operations and Supply Chain Management, 2E is written to help students understand the role of operations in both goods-producing and service-providing organizations. It has evolved from a series of books written by us, beginning with *Operations Management: Goods, Services, and Value Chains*, which was the first text to integrate goods and services from the perspective of the value chain, six editions of a shorter and more student-friendly text, *OM*, a 4LTR Press book published by Cengage Learning, and a subsequent re-branding of that title as *Operations and Supply Chain Management*, which provided a more extensive integration of supply chain management and Cengage MindTap technology. In this revision, we have strengthened the focus on supply chains and quantitative applications, added a new chapter on process and resource utilization, added many new solved problems, greatly expanded the number of questions and problems, added a new case to each chapter, and included a set of supplements for important quantitative topics.

Organization of the Book

This book is divided into three major parts and a set of supplements. Part 1 introduces the basic concepts, terminology, and models of operations and supply chain management. Part 2 focuses on the design of goods and services to support business strategy and the global value chains and processes that create and deliver them to customers. Part 3 addresses more tactical and day-to-day management issues of operating systems and supply chains. Part 4 contains recommended supplements that are intended to provide a basic introduction or review of key quantitative and analytics topics that are used throughout this book. A brief description of each chapter and supplement follows.

Part 1: Basic Concepts of OM and Value Chains

Chapter 1: Operations Management and Value Chains

This chapter introduces OM, explains what operations managers do, and provides brief tours of manufacturing and service companies; describes the differences between goods and services, the concepts of a customer benefit package, process, value, and value chains; and discusses the importance of sustainability, the role of business analytics in OM, the history of OM, and current and future challenges of OM.

Chapter 2: Measuring Performance in Operations and Value Chains

The chapter provides an in-depth discussion of performance measurement in value chains and the way in which they support operations from a strategic perspective. This includes key categories of organizational performance measures and how internal and external measures are related, the use of analytics in OM with an application to the value of a loyal customer, and four models of organizational performance: the Baldrige Performance Excellence framework, the balanced scorecard, the value chain model, and the Service-Profit Chain model.

Chapter 3: Operations Strategy

The chapter focuses on the importance of operations strategy for gaining competitive advantage. We address approaches for understanding customer wants and needs, ways to evaluate goods and services, key competitive priorities, sustainability and operations strategy, and Professor Terry Hill's strategy development framework with an application to McDonald's Corporation.

Chapter 4: Technology and Operations Management

The chapter focuses on the role of technology in goods-producing and service-providing organizations. Key manufacturing technologies such as Computer-Integrated Manufacturing Systems (CIMs), Computer-Aided Design and Engineering (CAD/CAE), and Flexible Manufacturing Systems (FMSs) are described. Technology in service industries and value chains, such as e-service and customer relationship management (CRM) are also addressed. Finally, benefits and challenges of technology, key decisions such as scalability, and applications of decision analysis are discussed.

Part 2: Designing Operations and Supply Chains

Chapter 5: Goods and Service Design

The chapter focuses on the design of goods and services and the processes that create and deliver them to customers. Topics include an integrated framework for goods and service design, quality function deployment (QFD), Taguchi loss functions, reliability, design for manufacturability and sustainability, service-delivery system design areas, and service encounter design. A case study of LensCrafters provides a broad view of how these ideas are implemented in practice.

Chapter 6: Supply Chain Design

The chapter addresses global supply chains, key decisions in supply chain design and the impact of blockchain technology, efficient and responsive supply chains, push and pull systems, vertical integration and outsourcing with break-even analysis, offshoring and reshoring, location decisions using the center of gravity method and optimization using the transportation model, and a case study of a global supply chain firm using these concepts.

Chapter 7: Process Selection, Design, and Improvement

The chapter addresses process choice decisions and types of processes used to produce goods and services (projects, job shops, flow shops, and continuous flow). It also discusses the product-process matrix, the service-positioning matrix, process design using hierarchical levels of work and process/value stream mapping, mistake-proofing concepts, and approaches to process improvement, including reengineering.

Chapter 8: Facility and Work Design

The chapter deals with facility layout and work design issues. It includes discussions of broad facility design issues, the four common types of facility layout patterns, assembly line balancing, and basic concepts of work measurement. It also addresses workplace safety, ergonomics, and workforce ethics in global supply chains.

Part 3: Managing Operations and Supply Chains

Chapter 9: Forecasting and Demand Planning

This chapter describes the importance of forecasting in operating systems and supply chains and presents basic quantitative methods for forecasting, including simple moving average, exponential smoothing models, and linear regression. Other topics include understanding the nature of time series, computing, forecast errors and measuring forecast accuracy, using tracking signals, and judgmental forecasting.

Chapter 10: Capacity Management

The chapter focuses on understanding, measuring, and making both long- and short-term capacity decisions. Topics covered include capacity decisions and economies of scale, the focused factory, measuring theoretical and effective capacity, safety capacity, computing capacity requirements for job shops with setup/changeover times, managing capacity by shifting and stimulating demand, revenue management, and learning curves.

Chapter 11: Process Analysis and Resource Utilization

The chapter provides an in-depth discussion of how to analyze processes, compute resource utilization and identify resource levels needed to achieve target utilizations, calculate process throughput, identify bottlenecks, and apply Little's law. In addition, this chapter discusses waiting line management and applications of single and multiple server queueing models and spreadsheet simulation and explains the logic and principles of the Theory of Constraints.

Chapter 12: Managing Inventories in Supply Chains

The chapter focuses on the principles of inventory management systems and quantitative approaches for managing inventories. These include ABC analysis, fixed-order-quantity and fixed-period inventory systems for deterministic and stochastic demand, economic order quantity, quantity discount, and single-period inventory models. Spreadsheet simulation is also illustrated for analyzing fixed-order-quantity inventory systems.

Chapter 13: Supply Chain Management and Logistics

The chapter focuses on the management of supply chains. It introduces the Supply Chain Operations Reference (SCOR) model, concepts of sourcing and purchasing, supplier relationships and value chain integration, logistics and transportation, vendor-managed inventory, and risk management in global supply chains. Emphasis is placed on measuring supply chain performance, and it discusses metrics such as inventory turnover, total supply chain costs, and the cash-to-cash conversion cycle. Other topics include supplier certification, sustainability in supply chains, manufactured goods recovery, and reverse logistics.

Chapter 14: Resource Management

The chapter describes generic frameworks for resource management in both goods-producing and service-providing organizations. Major topics include aggregate planning decisions and strategies, disaggregation of aggregate plans, applications of linear optimization for resource planning, master production planning, material requirements planning, multiple-level lot sizing, and capacity requirements planning.

Chapter 15: Operations Scheduling and Sequencing

The chapter introduces concepts of operations scheduling and sequencing with applications in both manufacturing and services. Included are heuristic approaches and optimization models for staff scheduling, appointment systems, single processor sequencing criteria and rules, S.M. Johnson's two-resource sequencing algorithm, Gantt charts, dispatching, and the Clarke-Wright vehicle routing and scheduling heuristic.

Chapter 16: Quality Management

The chapter explains basic concepts quality, the philosophies of Deming, Juran, and Crosby, the GAP model, ISO 9000, Six Sigma and the DMAIC process, the cost of quality, the Seven Quality Control tools, root cause analysis, Kaizen, and breakthrough improvement. Numerical examples illustrating metrics used in Six Sigma such as defects per million opportunities and sigma levels are included.

Chapter 17: Quality Control and SPC

This chapter addresses quality control systems and the role of statistical process control (SPC), emphasizing the construction and analysis of control charts for continuous and discrete data. Other topics discussed include common and special cause variation, quality at the source, quality control in services, practical issues in implementing SPC, and process capability indexes and analysis.

Chapter 18: Lean Operating Systems

The concepts of lean operating systems are introduced in goods-producing and service-providing organizations. This includes a discussion of the key principles of lean thinking, waste in organizations, and lean tools such as the 5Ss, batching and single-piece flow, and total productive maintenance. Also included are a discussion of Lean Six Sigma, lean "tours" of a manufacturing and a service organization, just-in-time and Kanban systems, and a comparison of the philosophies of lean thinking, quality management, and the Theory of Constraints.

Chapter 19: Project Management

The chapter addresses project management from both an organizational and a technical viewpoint. Tools and techniques for planning, scheduling, and controlling projects are illustrated. Topics include the project life cycle, the role of project managers, project networks, the Critical Path Method and PERT, contributors to project success or impediments, project control and Gantt charts, time and cost trade-offs, and project crashing decisions.

Part 4: Supplements

Supplement A: Probability and Statistics

The supplement provides a review of key concepts of probability and statistics used in the text. Topics include descriptive statistics, frequency distributions and histograms, author-supplied Excel templates, the Excel Data Analysis Regression tool, and sample size determination. The chapter also describes basic discrete and continuous probability distributions including the uniform, normal, Poisson, and exponential distributions, and computing expected values.

Supplement B: Decision Analysis

The supplement reviews concepts of decision analysis that are used in product selection, facility capacity expansion and location, inventory analysis, technology and process selection, and other areas of operations management. Topics include structuring decision problems, making decisions with and without event probabilities, and the expected value of perfect information. An Excel template is illustrated for performing these computations.

Supplement C: Break-Even Analysis

This supplement describes the use of break-even analysis with applications in profitability analysis, outsourcing decisions, and technology choice decisions that are discussed in the text. Both analytical equations and an Excel template are used. The Excel Goal Seek tool is illustrated for finding break-even points.

Supplement D: Linear Optimization

This supplement reviews the process of formulating linear optimization models and solving them with Excel Solver, which are used in several chapters in the text. It also describes how to interpret the Solver Answer and Sensitivity reports.

Supplement E: The Transportation and Assignment Problems

This supplement extends from Supplement D and explains the transportation and assignment problems, which are used in supply chain management and scheduling applications. It illustrates the formulation of the optimization models, how to implement them on spreadsheets, and how to solve them using Excel Solver.

Supplement F: Queuing Models

This supplement introduces basic concepts of queuing systems that have wide applicability in manufacturing and service organizations. The focus is on defining queuing terms and structures, probability distributions of arrival and service processes, performance metrics, and analytical models for single server and multiple server queues. Excel templates for these models are illustrated.

Supplement G: Simulation

This supplement reviews basic concepts of simulation modeling, generating random samples from probability distributions (drawing upon concepts in Supplement A) and implementing them in spreadsheets. A simple example of simulating a production-inventory system using Excel is described in detail, including the use of Excel data tables to perform multiple replications of the simulation model.

Features and Pedagogy to Enhance Learning

Each chapter begins with

1. a practical discussion or scenario to which students can easily relate, and which provides motivation for the practical importance of the chapter material, and
2. a set of Learning Objectives for the chapter.

Throughout each chapter are numerous feature boxes that highlight real organizations and provide practical insight into the concepts and applications of OSCM. Chapters with quantitative material have detailed solved problems that carefully illustrate the use of formulas, equations, calculations, Excel templates, and insights obtained from the results. These features assist student understanding and their ability to successfully answer end-of-chapter and MindTap problems and exercises.

At the end of each chapter can be found a summary of the chapter Learning Objectives and a list of Key Terms that were defined in the chapter, which students should know and understand. Questions and problems are provided in four categories:

- ***Review questions*** to check student's basic understanding of key concepts (all chapters),
- ***Discussion questions and experiential activities*** that require thoughtful discussion or hands-on experiences (all chapters),
- ***Computational problems and exercises*** that are intended to be solved manually in order to master the formulas and equations (chapters with quantitative content), and
- ***Excel-based problems*** that may be solved using spreadsheets or the supplied spreadsheet templates to perform more complex calculations or what-if analyses (chapters with quantitative content).

The number and scope of the questions and problems have been greatly expanded from the previous editions of our books. A set of 37 unique Excel templates created by one of the authors is available in MindTap. These templates allow students to enter data and easily calculate results. Student template worksheets are protected to avoid any corruption of formulas; unprotected templates are available to instructors. In addition, Excel worksheets with data sets for problems and cases are available in MindTap.

Each chapter also has three cases, which require students to thoughtfully apply the concepts and techniques in a broader context. The cases are drawn from a variety of industries such as manufacturing, banking, sports, health care, and professional engineering services. Two cases in each chapter are stand-alone, while the third, *Hudson Jewelers*, is an integrative case study that spans all chapters, focusing on the mining, production, cutting, distribution, and marketing of diamonds in global supply chains.

MindTap

OUTCOME-DRIVEN DIGITAL RESOURCES PROPEL STUDENTS FROM MEMORIZATION TO MASTERY. MindTap's learning and teaching resources equip you with complete ownership of your course. You can use these digital tools to challenge every student, build their confidence and empower them with the knowledge and skills to succeed in business today. MindTap includes all the resources that come with the textbook including all Excel templates used for Solved Problem examples and associated end-of-chapter Excel problems.

MindTap includes a variety of learning tools such as quizzes to check fundamental understanding, algorithmic problems with full solutions, feedback for practice, chapter review video summaries, problem walk-through videos that show step-by-step how to solve quantitative problems, and Excel-based problems that ask students to perform what-if analyses. MindTap showcases Excel Online integration powered by Microsoft, which helps students learn to be become better problem solvers using spreadsheets, while minimizing instructor grading time. For more information about the MindTap courseware that accompanies this text, please contact your Cengage learning consultant.

Instructor Resources

Many instructor resources are available on the instructor companion site, which can be found and accessed at www.cengage.com/decisionsciences/collier/oscm/2e. The companion site provides a detailed **Instructor Manual-Solutions Manual** for each chapter, with a brief summary of chapter content, answers or suggested answers for all questions and problems, and case solutions with tips for using the cases. (A separate document consolidates all case solutions for the integrative case, Hudson Jewelers.) From the site, instructors also have access to unprotected **Excel templates**, which may be used in class to help students understand the formulas and how they work, **PowerPoint slides** with a teaching outline that incorporates exhibits to complement instructor lectures and slides that now are fully accessible with alt-text descriptions included, a **MindTap Educator Guide** designed specifically for this product, as well as downloadable **Test Banks**.

In addition to the companion site resources, another instructor resource available to adopters is the *Cognero Test Bank*. Cengage testing powered by *Cognero*® is a flexible, online system that allows you to author, edit, and manage test bank content from multiple Cengage solutions, create multiple test versions in an instant, and deliver tests from your LMS, your classroom, or wherever you would like (contact your Cengage sales representative for more information).

Acknowledgments

We are indebted to our retired senior acquisitions editor Charles McCormick, Jr., whose vision of integrating goods and services into an operations management book brought us together. In addition, we thank our current Sr. Product Manager, Aaron Arnsparger and his colleagues, especially Jean Bora, Sr. Content Manager, Brandon Foltz, Sr. Learning Designer, Christopher Walz, Marketing Manager, and Mark Hopkinson, Sr. Digital Delivery Lead who oversaw the development, production, and marketing efforts for this product.

We hope you enjoy this book about an important body of knowledge that we both sincerely care about. As one unknown source once said, "Do not follow where the path may lead. Go instead where there is no path and leave a trail." We worked hard at trying to integrate and balance our focus on goods and services and provide innovative ways of thinking about operations and supply chain management concepts, models, and techniques. If any students or instructors have any positive feedback, suggestions for improvement, or discover any errors, please contact one of us.

David A. Collier, Eminent Scholar (Emeritus), Alico Chair in Operations Management, Lutgert College of Business, Florida Gulf Coast University, dac1354@gmail.com

James R. Evans, Professor Emeritus, Lindner College of Business, University of Cincinnati, James.Evans@UC.edu

Operations Management and Value Chains

1

Apple's significant profit margins are in large part due to a focus on its global supply chain and operational excellence.

Roman Tiraspolsky/Shutterstock.com

LEARNING OBJECTIVES

After studying this chapter, you should be able to:

1-1 Explain the concept and importance of operations management.

1-2 Describe what operations managers do.

1-3 Explain the differences between goods and services.

1-4 Define the concept of value and explain how the value of goods and services can be enhanced.

1-5 Describe a customer benefit package.

1-6 Explain the difference between value chains and supply chains, and identify three general types of processes in a business.

1-7 Contrast the three different frameworks for describing value chains.

1-8 Summarize the historical development of OM.

1-9 State the current and future key challenges facing OM.

Apple has mastered the art of blending physical goods with services to create value for its customers. Think iPod + iTunes, iPhone/iPad + apps, Apple stores + Genius Bar; well, you get the picture. Managing all operations involved—from the creation of goods and services through their delivery to the customer and postsale services—is one of Apple's core competencies.

"Operations expertise is as big an asset for Apple as product innovation or marketing," says Mike Fawkes, the former supply chain chief at Hewlett-Packard. "They've taken operational excellence to a level never seen before."

Managers and engineers often work at global supplier and manufacturer sites to refine their operations, and designers work with suppliers to create new tooling equipment. When the iPad 2 debuted, Apple employees monitored every handoff point—suppliers, production, loading dock, airport, truck depot, and distribution center—to make sure each unit was accounted for and of the highest quality.

Apple's retail stores give it a final operational advantage. The company can track demand by the store and by the hour, and adjust production forecasts daily. If it becomes clear that a given part will run out, teams are deployed and given approval to spend millions of dollars on extra equipment to undo the bottleneck. Apple's significant profit margins are in large part due to this focus on its global supply chain and operational excellence.[1]

WHAT DO YOU THINK?

Cite some other examples in which digital content has been combined with a physical good. How does this change the way companies must manage their operations?

1-1 Operations Management

Creating and delivering goods and services to customers depends on an effective system of linked facilities and processes, and the ability to manage them effectively around the world. Apple, for example, manages a large, global network of suppliers in countries such as Malaysia and Indonesia, and factories in the United States, China, and other countries to produce its physical goods, which must be coordinated with the development and production of software and other digital content, retail sales, and service and support. As the opening anecdote suggests, coordinating these goods-producing and service-providing processes can be challenging. **Operations management (OM)** *is the science and art of ensuring that goods and services are created and delivered successfully to customers.* OM includes the *design of* goods, services, and the processes that create them; the day-to-day *management* of those processes; and the continual *improvement* of these goods, services, and processes.

The way in which goods and services, and the processes that create and support them, are designed and managed can make the difference between a delightful or an unhappy customer experience. That is what OM is all about! Operations management is the only function by which managers can directly affect the value provided to all stakeholders—customers, employees, investors, and society (See the box, "What Do Operations Managers Do?").

Why is OM important? To answer this, we might first ask the question: What makes a company successful? In 1887, William Cooper Procter, grandson of the founder of Procter & Gamble, told his employees, "The first job we have is to turn out quality merchandise that consumers will buy and keep on buying. If we produce it efficiently and economically, we will earn a profit, in which you will share." Procter's statement—which is still as relevant today as it was over 100 years ago—addresses three issues that are at the core of operations management: *efficiency, cost*, and *quality*. Efficiency (a measure of how well resources are used in creating outputs), the cost of operations, and the quality of the goods and services that create customer satisfaction all contribute to profitability and ultimately the long-run success of a company. A company cannot be successful without people who understand how these concepts relate to each other, which is the essence of OM, and who can apply OM principles effectively in making decisions.

What Do Operations Managers Do?

Some key activities that operations managers perform include the following:

- Forecasting: predict the future demand for raw materials, finished goods, and services.
- Supply chain management: manage the flow of materials, information, people, and money from suppliers to customers.
- Facility layout and design: determine the best configuration of machines, storage, offices, and departments to provide the highest levels of efficiency and customer satisfaction.
- Technology selection: use technology to improve productivity and respond faster to customers.
- Quality management: ensure that goods, services, and processes will meet customer expectations and requirements.
- Purchasing: coordinate the acquisition of materials, supplies, and services.
- Resource and capacity management: ensure that the right amount of resources (labor, equipment, materials, and information) is available when needed.
- Process design: select the right equipment, information, and work methods to produce high-quality goods and services efficiently.
- Job design: decide the best way to assign people to work tasks and job responsibilities.
- Service encounter design: determine the best types of interactions between service providers and customers, and how to recover from service upsets.
- Scheduling: determine when resources such as employees and equipment should be assigned to work.
- Sustainability: decide the best way to manage the risks associated with products and operations to preserve resources for future generations.

1-2 OM in the Workplace

Many people who are considered "operations managers" have titles such as chief operating officer, hotel or restaurant manager, vice president of manufacturing, customer service manager, plant manager, field service manager, or supply chain manager. The concepts and methods of OM can be used in any job, regardless of the functional area of business or industry, to better create value for internal customers (within the organization) and for external customers (outside the organization). OM principles are used in accounting, human resources management, legal work, financial activities, marketing, environmental management, and every type of service activity. Thus, everyone should understand OM and be able to apply its tools and concepts. Following are some examples of how the authors' former students (who were not OM majors!) are using OM in their jobs.

After graduating from college, Shelly Decker and her sister embarked on an entrepreneurial venture to manufacture and sell natural soaps and body products. Shelly was an accounting and information systems major in college, but she was using OM skills every day:

- *Process design*: When a new product was to be introduced, the best way to produce it had to be determined. This involved charting the detailed steps needed to make the product.
- *Inventory management*: Inventory was tightly controlled to keep cost down and to avoid production that wasn't needed. Inventory was taken every four weeks and adjusted in the inventory management system accordingly.

- *Scheduling*: Production schedules were created to ensure that enough product was available for both retail and wholesale customers, taking into account such factors as current inventory and soap production capacity.
- *Quality management*: Each product was inspected and had to conform to the highest quality standards. If a product did not conform to standards (e.g., wrong color, improper packaging, improper labeling, improper weight, size, or shape), it was removed from inventory to determine where the process broke down and to initiate corrective action.

Without an understanding of OM, the company would never have gotten off the ground!

Tom James started as a senior software developer for a small software development company that creates sales proposal automation software. Tom uses OM skills in dealing with quality and customer service issues related to the software products, and he is also extensively involved in project management activities related to the development process, including identifying tasks, assigning developers to tasks, estimating the time and cost to complete projects, and studying the variance between the estimated and actual time it took to complete the project. He is also involved in continuous improvement projects; for example, he seeks to reduce development time and increase the efficiency of the development team. Tom was an information technology and management major in college.

United Performance Metals: The Life of an Operations Manager

United Performance Metals, formerly known as Ferguson Metals, located in Hamilton, Ohio, is a supplier of stainless steel and high-temperature alloys for the specialty metal market. The company's primary production operations include slitting coil stock and cutting sheet steel to customer specifications with rapid turnaround times from order to delivery. With only 78 employees, about half of whom are in operations, the director of operations and quality is involved in a variety of daily activities that draw upon knowledge of not only OM and engineering, but also finance, accounting, organizational behavior, and other subjects. He typically spends about 50 percent of his time working with foremen, supervisors, salespeople, and other staff discussing such issues as whether or not the company has the capability to accomplish a specific customer request, as well as routine production, quality, and shipping issues. The remainder of his time is spent investigating such issues as the technical feasibility and cost implications of new capital equipment or changes to existing processes, trying to reduce costs, seeking and facilitating design improvements on the shop floor, and motivating the workforce. The ability to understand customer needs, motivate employees, work with other departments, and integrate processes and technology are skills that all operations managers need.

AP Images/Mark Duncan

Coiled steel awaiting processing.

Maskalin/Alamy Stock Photo

Slitting coils into finished strips.

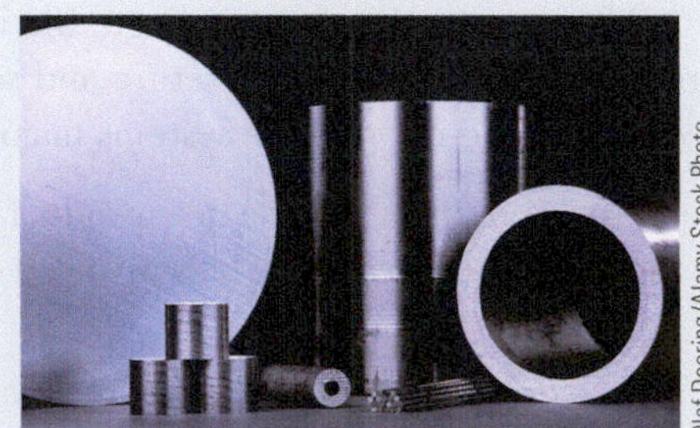
Olaf Doering/Alamy Stock Photo

Some of Ferguson's finished products.

Brooke Wilson began as a process manager for JPMorgan Chase in the credit card division. After several years of working as an operations analyst, he was promoted to a production supervisor position overseeing "plastic card production." Among his OM-related activities are:

- *Planning and budgeting*: Representing the plastic card production area in all meetings, developing annual budgets and staffing plans, and watching technology that might affect the production of plastic credit cards.
- *Inventory management*: Overseeing the management of inventory for items such as plastic blank cards; inserts such as advertisements; envelopes, postage, and credit card rules and disclosure inserts.
- *Scheduling and capacity*: Daily to annual scheduling of all resources (equipment, people, and inventory) necessary to issue new credit cards and reissue cards that are up for renewal, replace old or damaged cards, as well as cards that are stolen.
- *Quality*: Embossing the card with accurate customer information and quickly getting the card in the hands of the customer.

Brooke was an accounting major in college.

1-3 Understanding Goods and Services

Companies design, produce, and deliver a wide variety of goods and services that consumers purchase. *A* **good** *is a physical product that you can see, touch, or possibly consume.* Examples of goods include cell phones, appliances, food, flowers, soap, airplanes, furniture, coal, lumber, personal computers, paper, and industrial machines. *A* **durable good** *is one that does not quickly wear out and typically lasts at least three years.* Vehicles, dishwashers, and furniture are some examples. *A* **nondurable good** *is one that is no longer useful once it's used, or lasts for less than three years.* Examples are toothpaste, software, clothing and shoes, and food. Goods-producing firms are found in industries such as manufacturing, farming, forestry, mining, construction, and fishing.

A **service** *is any primary or complementary activity that does not directly produce a physical product.* Services represent the nongoods part of a transaction between a buyer (customer) and a seller (supplier).[2] Service-providing firms are found in industries such as banking, lodging, education, health care, and government. The services they provide might be a mortgage loan, a comfortable and safe place to sleep, a college degree, a medical procedure, or police and fire protection.

Designing and managing operations in a goods-producing firm is quite different from that in a service organization. Thus, it is important to understand the nature of goods and services, and particularly the differences between them.

Goods and services share many similarities. They are driven by customers and provide value and satisfaction to customers who purchase and use them. They can be standardized for the mass market or customized to individual needs. They are created and provided to customers by some type of process involving people and technology. Services that do not involve significant interaction with customers (e.g., credit card processing) can be managed much the same as goods in a factory, using proven principles of OM that have been refined over the years. Nevertheless, some very significant differences exist between goods and services that make the management of service-providing organizations different from goods-producing organizations and create different demands on the operations function.[3]

1. **Goods are tangible, whereas services are intangible.** Goods are consumed, but services are experienced. Goods-producing industries rely on machines and "hard technology" to perform work. Goods can be moved, stored, and repaired, and generally

require physical skills and expertise during production. Customers can often try them before buying. Services, on the other hand, make more use of information systems and other "soft technology," require strong behavioral skills, and are often difficult to describe and demonstrate. A senior executive of the Hilton Corporation stated, "We sell time. You can't put a hotel room on the shelf."[4]

2. **Customers participate in many service processes, activities, and transactions.** Many services require that the customer be present either physically, on a telephone, or online for service to commence. In addition, the customer and service provider often coproduce a service, meaning that they work together to create and simultaneously consume the service, as would be the case between a bank teller and a customer to complete a financial transaction. The higher the customer participation, the more uncertainty the firm has with respect to service time, capacity, scheduling, quality performance, and operating cost.

   A **service encounter** *is an interaction between the customer and the service provider.* Some examples of service encounters are making a hotel reservation, asking a grocery store employee where to find the pickles, or making a purchase on a website. Service encounters consist of one or more **moments of truth**—*any episodes, transactions, or experiences in which a customer comes into contact with any aspect of the delivery system, however remote, and thereby has an opportunity to form an impression.*[5] A moment of truth might be a gracious welcome by an employee at the hotel check-in counter, a grocery store employee who seems too impatient to help, or trying to navigate a confusing website. Customers judge the value of a service and form perceptions through service encounters. Therefore, employees who interact directly with customers or design service processes need to understand the importance of service encounters.

   Customers judge the value of a service and form perceptions through service encounters.

3. **The demand for services is more difficult to predict than the demand for goods.** Customer arrival rates and demand patterns for such service delivery systems as banks, airlines, supermarkets, call centers, and courts are very difficult to forecast. The demand for services is time-dependent, especially over the short term (by hour or day). This places many pressures on service firm managers to adequately plan staffing levels and capacity.

4. **Services cannot be stored as physical inventory.** In goods-producing firms, inventory can be used to decouple customer demand from the production process or between stages of the production process and ensure constant availability despite fluctuations in demand. Service firms do not have physical inventory to absorb such fluctuations in demand. For service delivery systems, availability depends on the system's capacity. For example, a hospital must have an adequate supply of beds for the purpose of meeting unanticipated patient demand, and a float pool of nurses when things get very busy. Once an airline seat, a hotel room, or an hour of a lawyer's day are gone, there is no way to recapture the lost revenue.

5. **Service management skills are paramount to a successful service encounter.** Employees who interact with customers require service management skills such as knowledge and technical expertise (operations), cross-selling other products and services (marketing), and good human interaction skills (human resources). **Service management** *integrates marketing, human resources, and operations functions to plan,*

create, and deliver goods and services, and their associated service encounters. OM principles are useful in designing service encounters and supporting marketing objectives.

6. **Service facilities typically need to be in close proximity to the customer.** When customers must physically interact with a service facility—for example, post offices, hotels, and branch banks—they must be in a location convenient to customers. A manufacturing facility, on the other hand, can be located on the other side of the globe, as long as goods are delivered to customers in a timely fashion. In today's Internet age, many services are only a few mouse clicks away.
7. **Patents do not protect services.** A patent on a physical good or software code can provide protection from competitors. The intangible nature of a service makes it more difficult to keep a competitor from copying a business concept, facility layout, or service encounter design. For example, restaurant chains are quick to copy new menu items or drive-through concepts.

These differences between goods and services have important implications to all areas of an organization, and especially to operations. These are summarized in Exhibit 1.1. Some are obvious, whereas others are more subtle. By understanding them, organizations can better select the appropriate mix of goods and services to meet customer needs and create the most effective operating systems to produce and deliver those goods and services.

EXHIBIT 1.1 How Goods and Services Affect Operations Management Activities

OM Activity	Goods	Services
Forecasting	Forecasts involve longer-term time horizons. Goods-producing firms can use physical inventory as a buffer to mitigate forecast errors. Forecasts can be aggregated over larger time frames (e.g., months or weeks).	Forecast horizons generally are shorter, and forecasts are more variable and time-dependent. Forecasting must often be done on a daily or hourly basis, or sometimes even more frequently.
Facility Location	Goods-producing facilities can be located close to raw materials, suppliers, labor, or customers/markets.	Service facilities must be located close to customers/markets for convenience and speed of service.
Facility Layout and Design	Factories and warehouses can be designed for efficiency because few, if any, customers are present.	The facility must be designed for good customer interaction and movement through the facility and its processes.
Technology	Goods-producing facilities use various types of automation to produce, package, and ship physical goods.	Service facilities tend to rely more on information-based hardware and software.
Quality	Goods-producing firms can define clear, physical, and measurable quality standards and capture measurements using various physical devices.	Quality measurements must account for customer's perception of service quality and often must be gathered through surveys or personal contact.
Inventory/Capacity	Goods-producing firms use physical inventory such as raw materials and finished goods as a buffer for fluctuations in demand.	Service capacity such as equipment or employees is the substitute for physical inventory.
Process Design	Because customers have no participation or involvement in goods-producing processes, the processes can be more mechanistic and controllable.	Customers usually participate extensively in service creation and delivery (sometimes called coproduction), requiring more flexibility and adaptation to special circumstances.
Job/Service Encounter Design	Goods-producing employees require strong technical and production skills.	Service employees need more behavioral and service management skills.
Scheduling	Scheduling revolves around the movement and location of materials, parts, and subassemblies and when to assign resources (i.e., employees, equipment) to accomplish the work most efficiently.	Scheduling focuses on when to assign employees and equipment (i.e., service capacity) to accomplish the work most efficiently without the benefit of physical inventory.
Supply Chain Management	Goods-producing firms focus mainly on the physical flow of goods, often in a global network, with the goal of maximizing customer satisfaction and profit, and minimizing delivery time, costs, and environmental impact.	Service-providing firms focus mainly on the flow of people, information, and services, often in a global network, with the goal of maximizing customer satisfaction and profit, and minimizing delivery time, costs, and environmental impact.

A similar classification of OM activities in terms of high/low customer contact was first proposed in the classic article by R. B. Chase, "Where Does the Customer Fit in a Service Operation?" (*Harvard Business Review*, November–December 1978, p. 139).

How to Increase Value?

To increase value, an organization must

(a) increase perceived benefits while holding price or cost constant;

(b) increase perceived benefits while reducing price or cost; or

(c) decrease price or cost while holding perceived benefits constant.

In addition, proportional increases or decreases in perceived benefits as well as price result in no net change in value. Management must determine how to maximize value by designing processes and systems that create and deliver the appropriate goods and services customers want to use, pay for, and experience.

1-4 The Concept of Value

Today's consumers demand innovative products, high quality, quick response, impeccable service, and low prices; in short, they want value in every purchase or experience. One of the most important points that we emphasize in this book is that the underlying purpose of every organization is to provide value to its customers and stakeholders.

***Value** is the perception of the benefits associated with a good, service, or bundle of goods and services in relation to what buyers are willing to pay for them.* The decision to purchase a good or service or a customer benefit package is based on an assessment by the customer of the perceived benefits in relation to its price. The customer's cumulative judgment of the perceived benefits leads to either satisfaction or dissatisfaction. One of the simplest functional forms of value is:

$$\text{Value} = \frac{\text{Perceived benefits}}{\text{Price (cost) to the customer}}$$

If the value ratio is high, the good or service is perceived favorably by customers, and the organization providing it is more likely to be successful.

The focus on value has forced many traditional goods-producing companies to add services and, increasingly, digital content to complement their physical goods. A goods-producing company can no longer be viewed as simply a factory that churns out physical goods, because customer perceptions of goods are influenced highly by such facilitating services as financing and leasing, shipping and installation, maintenance and repair, and technical support and consulting. Today we see digital content such as apps, streaming videos, and social networks becoming vital to create customer value. Coordinating the operational capability to design and deliver an integrated package of physical and digital goods and services is the essence of operations management.

1-5 Customer Benefit Packages

"Bundling" goods, services, and digital content in a certain way to provide value to customers not only enhances what customers receive, but can also differentiate the product from competitors. Such a bundle is often called a customer benefit package. *A **customer benefit package (CBP)** is a clearly defined set of tangible (goods-content) and intangible (service-content) features that the customer recognizes, pays for, uses, or experiences.* The CBP is a way to conceptualize and visualize goods and services by thinking broadly about how goods and services are bundled and configured together.

A CBP consists of a primary good or service coupled with peripheral goods and/or services, and sometimes variants. *A **primary good or service** is the "core" offering that attracts customers and responds to their basic needs.* For example, the primary service of a personal checking account is convenient financial transactions. ***Peripheral goods or services** are those that are not essential to the primary good or service, but enhance it.* A personal checking account might be supported and enhanced by such peripheral goods as a printed monthly account statement, designer checks and checkbooks, a special credit card, and such peripheral services as a customer service hotline and online bill payment. It is interesting to note that today, many business-to-business manufacturers such as custom machining or metal fabricators, think of their core offering as service—providing customized design assistance and ontime delivery—with the actual good as peripheral. Finally, *a* ***variant*** *is a CBP feature that departs from the standard CBP and is normally location or firm specific.*

EXHIBIT 1.2 A CBP Example for Purchasing a Vehicle

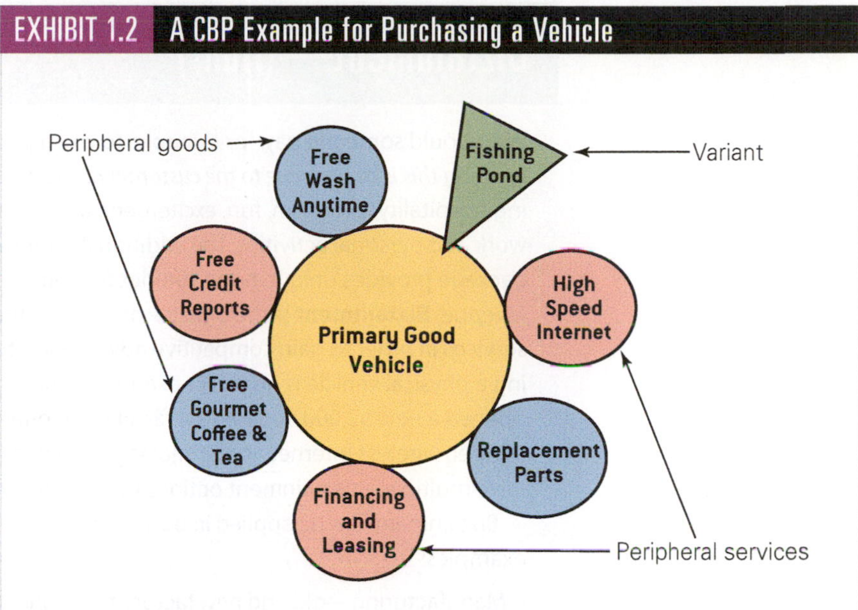

A CBP can easily be expressed in a graphical fashion, as shown in Exhibit 1.2. The CBP attributes and features (described in the circles) are chosen by management to fulfill certain customer wants and needs. For example, financing and leasing, which are peripheral services, meet the customer's wants and needs of personal financial security. In fact, if two vehicles have similar prices and quality levels, then the leasing program may be the key to which vehicle the customer buys. Vehicle replacement parts, a peripheral good, meet the customer's wants and needs of fast service and safety. A variant might be a fishing pond where kids can fish while parents shop for vehicles.

> Each good or service in the customer benefit package requires a process to create and deliver it to customers.

When defining a CBP, don't confuse the features determined by management with customers' wants and needs. For example, if a customer need is to ensure the safety of their valuables in a hotel, a CBP feature that management might select is a room safe. Thus, you would not put "safety of valuables" on a CBP diagram, but rather "room safe." A CBP diagram should reflect on the features management selects to fulfill certain customer wants and needs.

Finally, we may bundle a group of CBPs together. One example would be a combined land-cruise vacation to Alaska, which might consist of a bundle of CBPs such as the travel agency that books the package and optional land excursions from the ship; the land-tour operator that handles hotels, transportation, and baggage handling; and the cruise line that books air travel, and provides meals, and entertainment. Bundled CBPs raise some interesting issues about pricing strategies and partnerships among firms. For example, a firm might actually be able to charge a premium price for the bundled CBPs than if purchased separately, or alliances between hotels and airlines provide discounted vacation packages that are less expensive than if booked separately.

In most cases, many "goods" and "services" that we normally think of have a mixture of both goods and service content. Exhibit 1.3 illustrates a continuum of goods and service content with several examples. Toothpaste, for instance, is high in goods content, but when you purchase it, you are also purchasing some services, such as a telephone call center to field customer questions and complaints. Similarly, a bicycle might seem like a pure good, but it

Biztainment—(Huh?)[6]

Why would someone pay, for example, to crush grapes with her feet? *Might it be that the process of doing this is as valuable to the customer as the outcome itself?* Entertainment is the act of providing hospitality, escapism, fun, excitement, and/or relaxation to people as they go about their daily work and personal activities. The addition of entertainment to an organization's customer benefit package provides unique opportunities for companies to increase customer satisfaction and grow revenue. **Biztainment** is the practice of adding entertainment content to a bundle of goods and services in order to gain competitive advantage. The old business model of just selling and servicing a physical vehicle is gone. For example, a BMW automobile dealership in Fort Myers, Florida, opened a new 52,000-square-foot facility that offers a putting green, private work areas, a movie theater, wireless Internet access, massage chairs, a golf simulator, and a café, so that customers have multiple entertainment options during their visits.

Biztainment can be applied in both manufacturing and service settings. Consider the following examples:

- Manufacturing—old and new factory tours, showrooms, customer training and education courses, virtual tours, short films on how things are made, driving schools, history lessons on the design and development of a physical good
- Retail—on-line shopping with entertaining graphics (emoji), simulators, product demonstrations, climbing walls, music, games, contests, holiday decorations and walk-around characters, blogs, interactive store designs, aquariums, movie theaters, makeovers
- Restaurants—toys, themes, electronic menus, contests, games, characters, playgrounds, live music
- Agriculture—pick-your-own food, mazes, make-your-own wine, grape-stomping, petting zoos, farm tours
- Lodging—kids' spas, health clubs, casinos, cable television, arcades, massage, free on-line games, arts and crafts classes, pools, family games, wildlife, miniature golf
- Telecommunications—text and video messaging with funny graphics (emoji), music and TV downloads, cool ring tones, designer phones, cell phone apps

Some organizations that use entertainment as a means of enhancing the firm's image and increasing sales that you might be familiar with are the Hard Rock Café, Chuck E. Cheese, Benihana of Tokyo restaurants, Verizon, and many others. The data show the value of biztainment. For example, Build-A-Bear Workshop boasts an average of $600 per square foot in annual revenue, double the U.S. mall average.

often includes such services as safety instruction and maintenance. At the other extreme in Exhibit 1.3 are psychiatric services, which are much higher in service content but might include goods such as a bill, books, and medical brochures that support the service. Attending a symphony, play, or movie is essentially a pure service but may include program brochures and ticket stubs that offer discounts at local restaurants as peripheral goods.

Today, we are seeing more digital content being bundled with both goods and services. For example, General Electric manufactures locomotives and jet engines, yet their future is intelligent machines that make smart operating decisions and monitor themselves for maintenance and repair. Netflix sells digital content in the form of movies, and television shows and series. iTunes sells music.

Buying More Than a Car

People usually think that when they buy a new car, they are simply purchasing the vehicle. Far from it. Most automobiles, for example, bundle a good, the automobile, with many peripheral services. Such services might include the sales process, customized leasing, insurance, warranty programs, loaner cars when a major service or repair is needed, free car washes at the dealership, opportunities to attend a manufacturer's driving school, monthly newsletters sent by e-mail, and Web-based scheduling of oil changes and other service requirements. Such bundling is described by the customer benefit package framework.[7]

Gajus/Shutterstock.com

1-6 Value Chains

A **value chain** *is a network of facilities and processes that describes the flow of materials, finished goods, services, information, and financial transactions from suppliers, through the facilities and processes that create goods and services, and those that deliver them to the customer.* Value chains involve all major functions in an organization. This includes not only operations but also purchasing, marketing and sales, human resource management, finance and accounting, information systems and technology, distribution, and service and support. *A* **supply chain** *is the portion of the value chain that focuses primarily on the physical movement of goods and materials, and supporting flows of information and financial transactions through the supply, production, and distribution processes.* We will focus on supply chains in Chapters 6 and 12.

EXHIBIT 1.3 Examples of Goods and Service Content

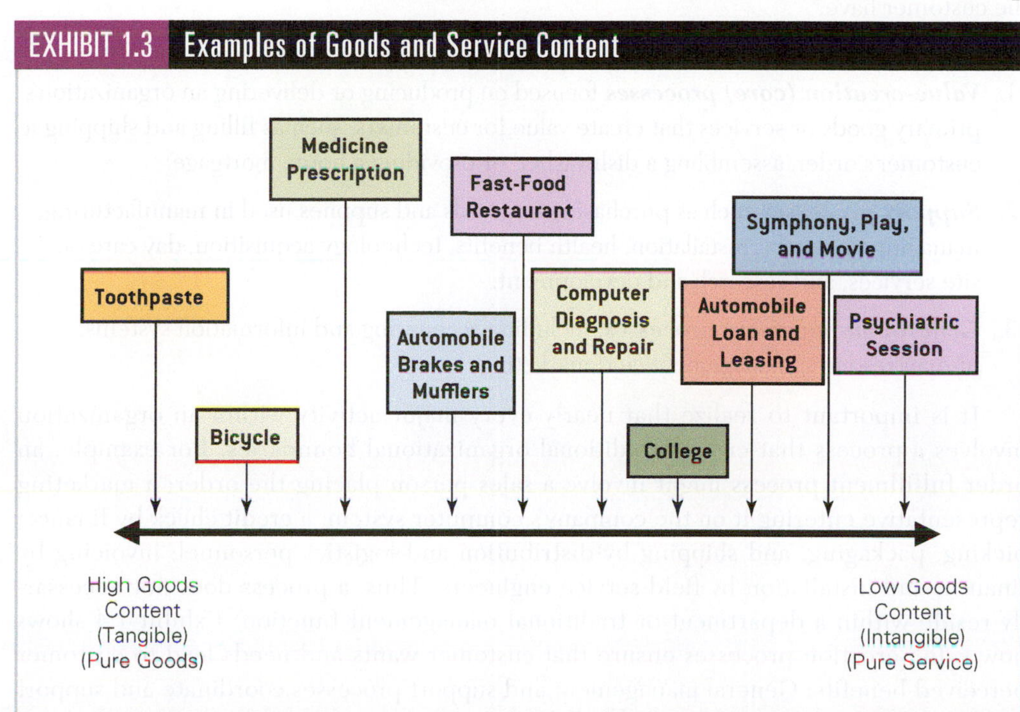

Many organizations use the terms "value chain" and "supply chain" interchangeably; however, we differentiate these two terms in this book. A value chain is broader in scope than a supply chain and is easier to apply to service-providing organizations as well as to goods-producing firms, as we shall see later in this chapter.

It is important for you to understand how operations management influences the design and management of value chains. Today's organizations face difficult decisions in balancing cost, quality, service, and sustainability objectives to create value for their customers and stakeholders, and in coordinating the many activities that take place within value chains. Modern firms increasingly deliver goods and services to multiple markets and operate in a global business environment. As a result, many companies have reconfigured their value chains and moved some operations out of the United States to keep costs competitive, remain profitable, and improve customer service. As one chief financial officer wrote in a *CFO Magazine* survey, "You cannot compete globally unless you use global resources."[8] Thus, we emphasize the importance of understanding the global business environment and local culture, and their impact on value chain design and operations.

1-6a Processes

Each good or service in the customer benefit package requires a process to create and deliver it to customers. *A* **process** *is a sequence of activities that is intended to create a certain result*, such as a physical good, a service, or information. A practical definition, according to AT&T, is that a process is how work creates value for customers.[9] Processes are the means by which goods and services are produced and delivered. For example, a car wash process might consist of the following steps: check the car in, perform the wash, inspect the results, notify the customer that the car is finished, quickly deliver the car back to the customer, and collect payment. In designing such a process, operations managers need to consider the process goals, such as speed of service, a clean car, no vehicle damage, and the quality of all service encounters. OM managers would ask questions such as: Should the car be cleaned inside as well as outside? How long should a customer expect to wait? What types of chemicals should be used to clean the car? What training should the employees who wash the cars and interact with the customer have?

Key processes in business typically include:

1. ***Value-creation (core) processes*** focused on producing or delivering an organization's primary goods or services that create value for customers, such as filling and shipping a customer's order, assembling a dishwasher, or providing a home mortgage.
2. ***Support processes*** such as purchasing materials and supplies used in manufacturing, managing inventory, installation, health benefits, technology acquisition, day care on-site services, and research and development.
3. ***General management processes***, including accounting and information systems, human resource management, and marketing.

It is important to realize that nearly every major activity within an organization involves a process that crosses traditional organizational boundaries. For example, an order fulfillment process might involve a sales-person placing the order; a marketing representative entering it on the company's computer system; a credit check by finance; picking, packaging, and shipping by distribution and logistics personnel; invoicing by finance; and installation by field service engineers. Thus, a process does not necessarily reside within a department or traditional management function. Exhibit 1.4 shows how value-creation processes ensure that customer wants and needs lead to customer perceived benefits. General management and support processes coordinate and support value creation and delivery.

EXHIBIT 1.4 How Primary, Support, Supplier, and Management Processes Are Related

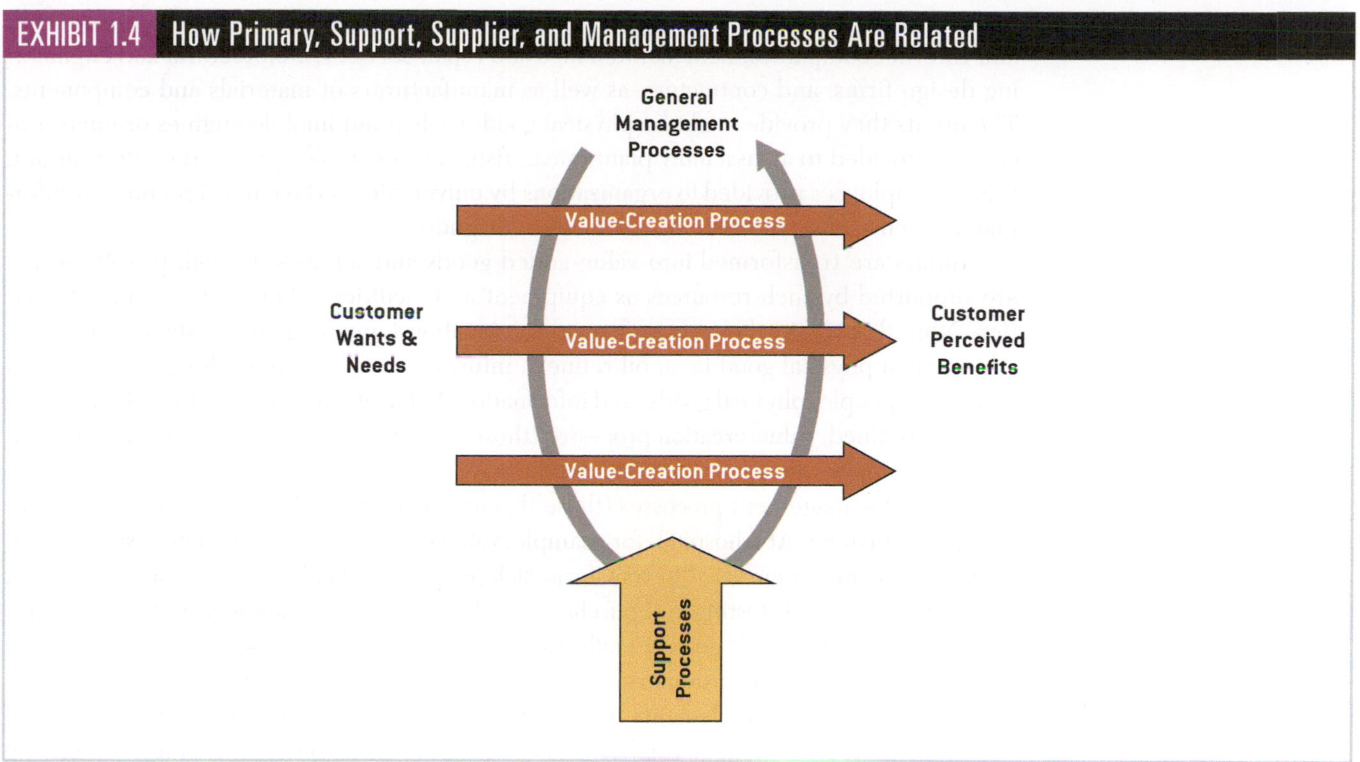

1-7 Value Chain Frameworks

We will describe a value chain from three different perspectives: an input-output framework, a preproduction and postproduction services framework, and a hierarchical supply chain perspective.

1-7a Value Chains: An Input-Output Framework

As shown in Exhibit 1.5, a value chain can be depicted as a "cradle-to-grave" input-output model of the operations function. The value chain begins with suppliers who provide inputs to a goods- or service-providing process or network of processes. Suppliers might be retail

EXHIBIT 1.5 An Input-Output Framework of a Value Chain

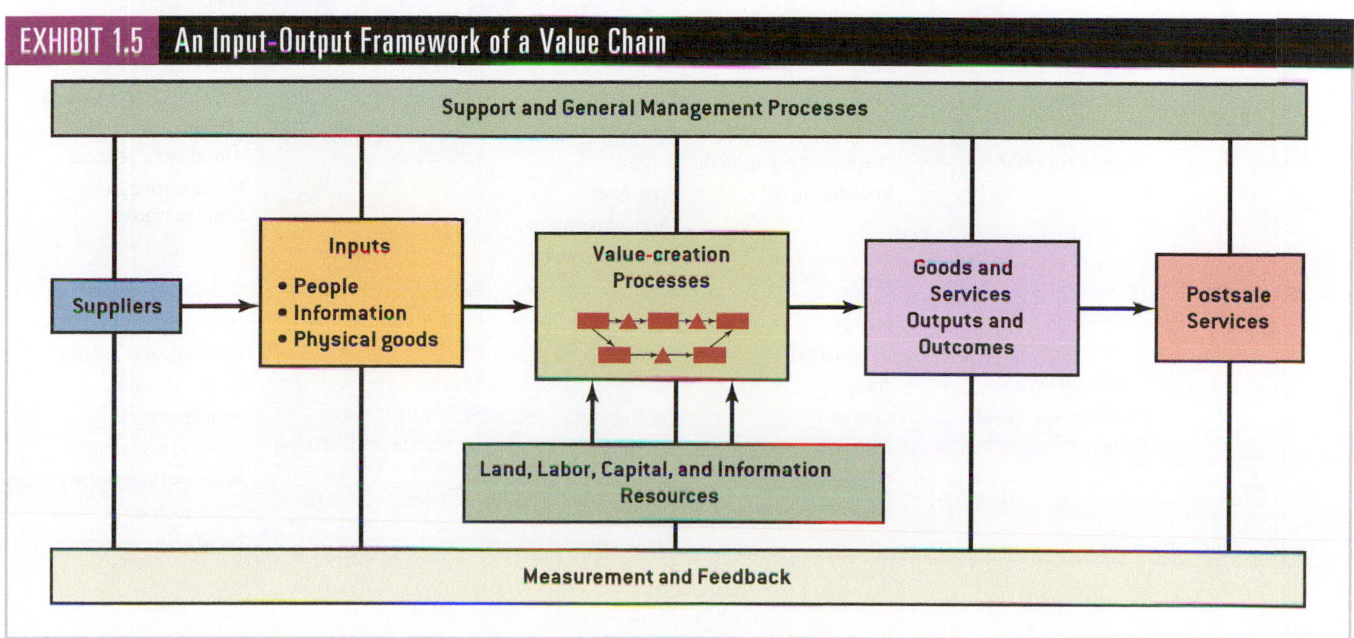

stores, distributors, employment agencies, dealers, financing and leasing agents, information and Internet companies, field maintenance and repair services, architectural and engineering design firms, and contractors, as well as manufacturers of materials and components. The inputs they provide might be physical goods such as automobile engines or microprocessors provided to an assembly plant; meat, fish, and vegetables provided to a restaurant; trained employees provided to organizations by universities and technical schools; or information such as market research or a medical diagnosis.

Inputs are transformed into value-added goods and services through processes that are supported by such resources as equipment and facilities, labor, money, and information. Note that what is being transformed can be almost anything—for instance, people in a hospital, a physical good in an oil refinery, information in an e-publishing business, or a mixture of people, physical goods, and information. Value chain processes include the three types we defined: value-creation processes (those that directly create and deliver goods and services), support processes (those "behind the scenes," but which support core processes), and general management processes (those that are needed for efficient and effective business performance). At a hospital, for example, value creation processes such as surgery and drug administration are used to transform sick people into healthy ones, whereas support processes such as lab testing and purchasing help to ensure that surgery and drug administration accomplish their goals. Finally, the value chain outputs—goods and services—are delivered or provided to customers and targeted market segments. Some examples of value chains that illustrate the elements in Exhibit 1.5 are shown in Exhibit 1.6. The success of the entire value chain depends on how it is designed and managed. This includes measuring performance (which will be addressed in Chapter 2) and using the feedback from measurements to improve all aspects of the value chain.

EXHIBIT 1.6 Examples of Goods and Service-Providing Value Chains

Organization	Suppliers	Inputs	Value-creation Process	Outputs	Customers and Market Segments
Auto assembly plant	Engine plant Tires Frame Axles Paint Seats	Labor Energy Auto parts Specifications	Welding Machining Assembly Painting	Automobiles Trucks	Economy Luxury Rental Trucking Ambulance Police
Hospital	Pharmaceutical companies Equipment suppliers Food suppliers Organ donors Medical suppliers	Patients Beds Staff Drugs Diagnostic equipment Knowledge	Admissions Lab testing Doctor diagnosis Food service Surgery Schedules Drug administration Rehabilitation	Healthy people Lab results Accurate bills Community health education	Heart clinics Pediatrics Emergency and trauma services Ambulatory services Medical specialties and hospital wards
State Government	Highway and building contractors Employment agencies Food suppliers Equipment suppliers Other governments	Labor Energy Information Trash Crimes Disputes Sick people Low- income people	Health care benefits Food stamps Legal services Prisons Trash removal Park services License services Police services Tax services	Good use of taxpayers' monies Safety net Security Reallocate taxes Clean, safe, and fun parks	Disabled people Low-income people Criminals and prisons Corporate taxes Boat licenses Building inspections Weekend vacationers Child custody services Legal court services

1-7b The Value Chain at Buhrke Industries Inc.

To illustrate the input-output perspective of a value chain, we highlight Buhrke Industries Inc., located in Arlington Heights, Illinois, which provides stamped metal parts to many industries, including automotive, appliance, computer, electronics, hardware, housewares, power tools, medical, and telecommunications. A simplified view of Buhrke's value chain is shown in Exhibit 1.7.

Buhrke's objective is to be a customer's best total value producer with on-time delivery, fewer rejects, and high-quality stampings. However, the company goes beyond manufacturing goods; it prides itself in providing the best service available as part of its customer value chain. Service is more than delivering a product on time. It's also partnering with customers by providing personalized service for fast, accurate response; customized engineering designs to meet customer needs; preventive maintenance systems to ensure high machine uptime; experienced, highly trained, long-term employees; and troubleshooting by a knowledgeable sales staff.

Suppliers and other value chain inputs include people, information, and physical goods—for example, engineering blueprints and specifications, rolled steel, factory equipment and lubricants, pallets and boxes, employment agencies, inbound shipping, and outside training and industrial marketing firms. Value-creation processes include tooling, inspection, production, finishing, and sometimes assembly into a complete subassembly. Outputs include the stamped metal parts and postsale service outcomes such as out-in-the-field consulting and troubleshooting by company employees. General management processes coordinate processes, often in different functional areas, while support processes include hiring, medical benefits, and accounting. As many as 100 processes are required for Buhrke to perform its work and create value for its customers.

The major stages of Buhrke's value chain, shown in Exhibit 1.7, begin with a customer request for a quotation. The estimating department processes such job parameters as specifications, metals, finishing or packaging services, the presses that will be used to run the job, and customer deadlines in developing a quote. Next, a sales engineer is assigned to monitor each stamping job from start to finish, so the customer may have the convenience of a single point of contact. Sales engineers work closely with the engineering staff to convey customer

EXHIBIT 1.7 The Value Chain at Buhrke Industries

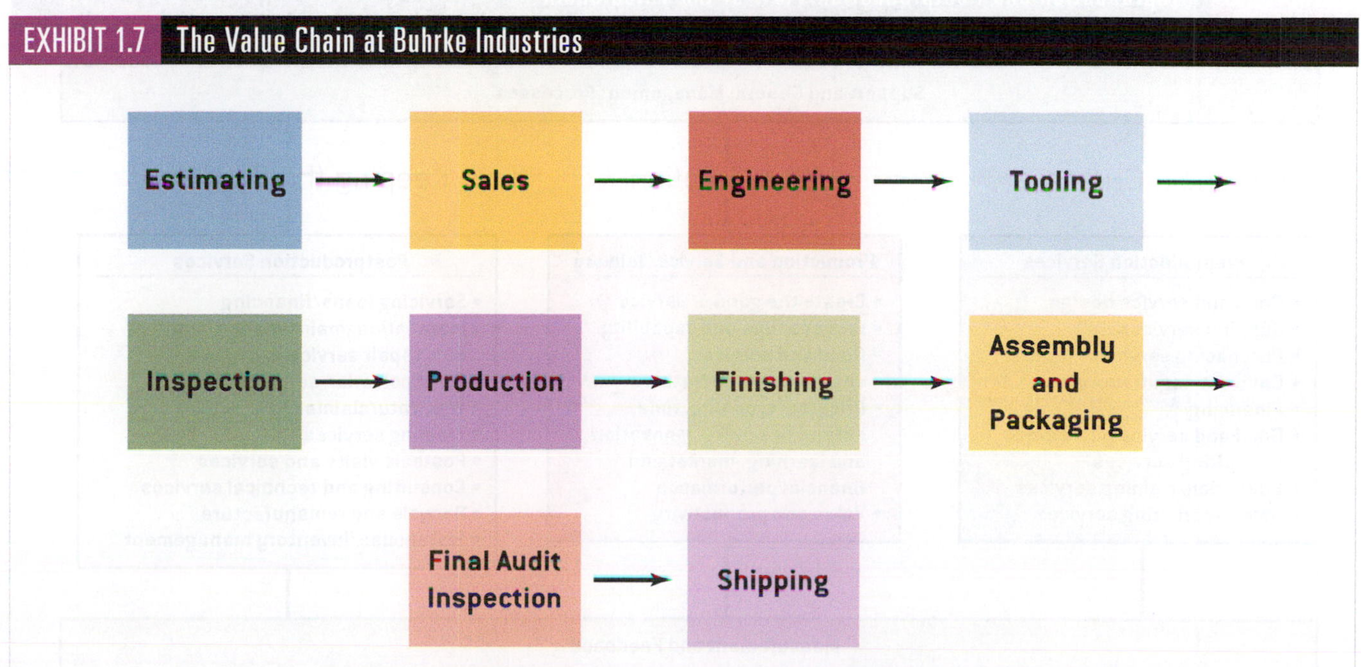

needs. Engineers then design the best tooling for the job, using computer-assisted design processes to ensure precise designs and timely completion. After a tool is designed and built, it is maintained in an on-site tool room. Buhrke's toolmakers have decades of experience constructing tools for metal stamping, and they are put on a strict maintenance regimen to ensure long life and consistent stampings.

Production of the metal parts is accomplished on a full range of presses, from 15 to 200 tons, with speeds of up to 1,500 parts per minute. Inspection of raw materials (inputs), work-in-process, and finished products (outputs) helps ensure zero defects. The company provides a full range of secondary and finishing operations, from heat-treating to powder coating to tapping, and to add value to customers. Customers do not need to ship stampings elsewhere or arrange for another service provider to finish the job.

At the customer's request, Buhrke will assemble the stampings with other components to deliver a complete subassembly. Buhrke will even procure parts for assembly, such as plastics that the company does not manufacture. Buhrke is also able to package finished stampings or subassemblies. Before stampings are boxed up and shipped (and even after the incoming inspection and in-process audits), Buhrke provides a final audit inspection. Finally, Buhrke offers the convenience of shipping the finished product where and when customers want. For further information and video tours of the plant, visit www.buhrke.com.

1-7c Value Chains: Preproduction and Postproduction Services Framework

A second view of the value chain can be described from the preservice and postproduction services framework as shown in Exhibit 1.8. Preproduction and postproduction services complete the ownership cycle for the good or service. Preproduction services include customized and team-oriented product design, consulting services, contract negotiations, product and service guarantees, customer financing to help purchase the product, training customers to use and maintain the product, purchasing and supplier services, and other types of front-end services. The focus here is on "gaining a customer."

EXHIBIT 1.8 Preproduction and Postproduction View of the Value Chain

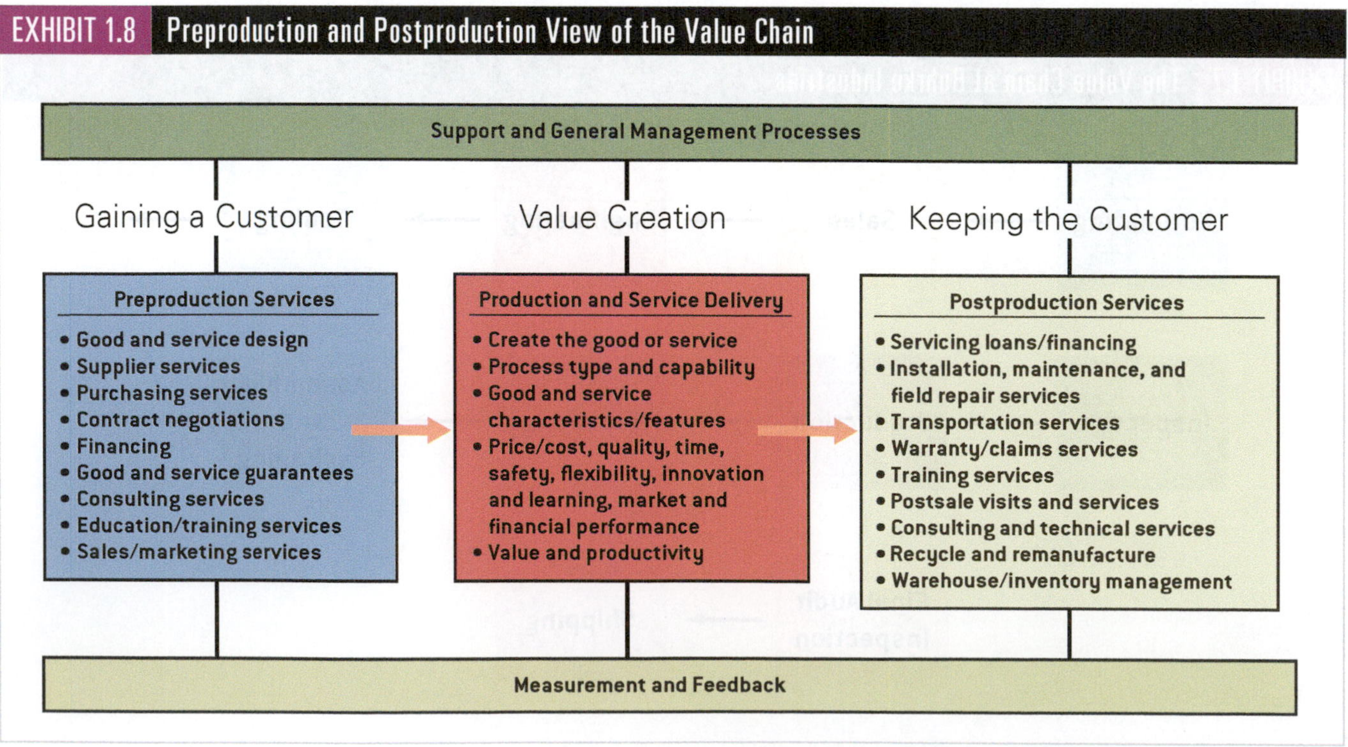

Support and General Management Processes
Gaining a Customer
Value Creation
Keeping the Customer
Preproduction Services
• Good and service design
• Supplier services
• Purchasing services
• Contract negotiations
• Financing
• Good and service guarantees
• Consulting services
• Education/training services
• Sales/marketing services
Production and Service Delivery
• Create the good or service
• Process type and capability
• Good and service characteristics/features
• Price/cost, quality, time, safety, flexibility, innovation and learning, market and financial performance
• Value and productivity
Postproduction Services
• Servicing loans/financing
• Installation, maintenance, and field repair services
• Transportation services
• Warranty/claims services
• Training services
• Postsale visits and services
• Consulting and technical services
• Recycle and remanufacture
• Warehouse/inventory management
Measurement and Feedback

Postproduction services include on-site installation or application services, maintenance and repair in the field, servicing loans and financing, warranty and claim services, warehouse and inventory management for the company and sometimes for its customers, training, telephone service centers, transportation delivery services, postsale visits to the customer's facility by knowledgeable sales and technical-support people, recycling and remanufacturing initiatives, and other back-end services. The focus here is on "keeping the customer."

This view of the value chain emphasizes the notion that service is a critical component of traditional manufacturing processes. Preproduction services for Ford Motor Company include engineering design, supplier, sales, and leasing processes, and postproduction services include financing, maintenance and repair, warranty and claims, and customer education and training programs. Service is a key differentiating factor in the eyes of customers for many manufacturing firms. Ford Motor Company is continuing to develop a competitive strategy where service is at the core of their global strategy. Note that the Buhrke Industries Inc. value chain can also be defined using the preservice and postservice perspectives.

Both perspectives enhance management's understanding of where and how they create value for customers. Automobile companies such as Ford Motor Company might use the preservice and postservice model to highlight service processes, and associated customer service encounters and experiences.

1-7d The Value Chain at Amazon

To illustrate this perspective of a value chain, we highlight Amazon.

Amazon.com, started in 1995 as an online bookstore, has evolved into the world's largest seller of a wide variety of products. It provides customer value by focusing on the complete customer experience that begins when a customer visits its website and continues through ongoing customer relationship management activities long after an individual order is processed. Exhibit 1.9 depicts Amazon's value chain from the perspective of the model shown in Exhibit 1.8.

Preproduction services that focus on gaining a customer include:

- *Product variety*—Amazon sells pretty much everything that you can imagine. Amazon manufactures its own products and services, such as the Kindle e-book reader and the Kindle Store. Amazon's virtual storefront provides much greater product selection than can be found in a typical "bricks-and-mortar" store.

EXHIBIT 1.9 A Value Chain Model of Amazon

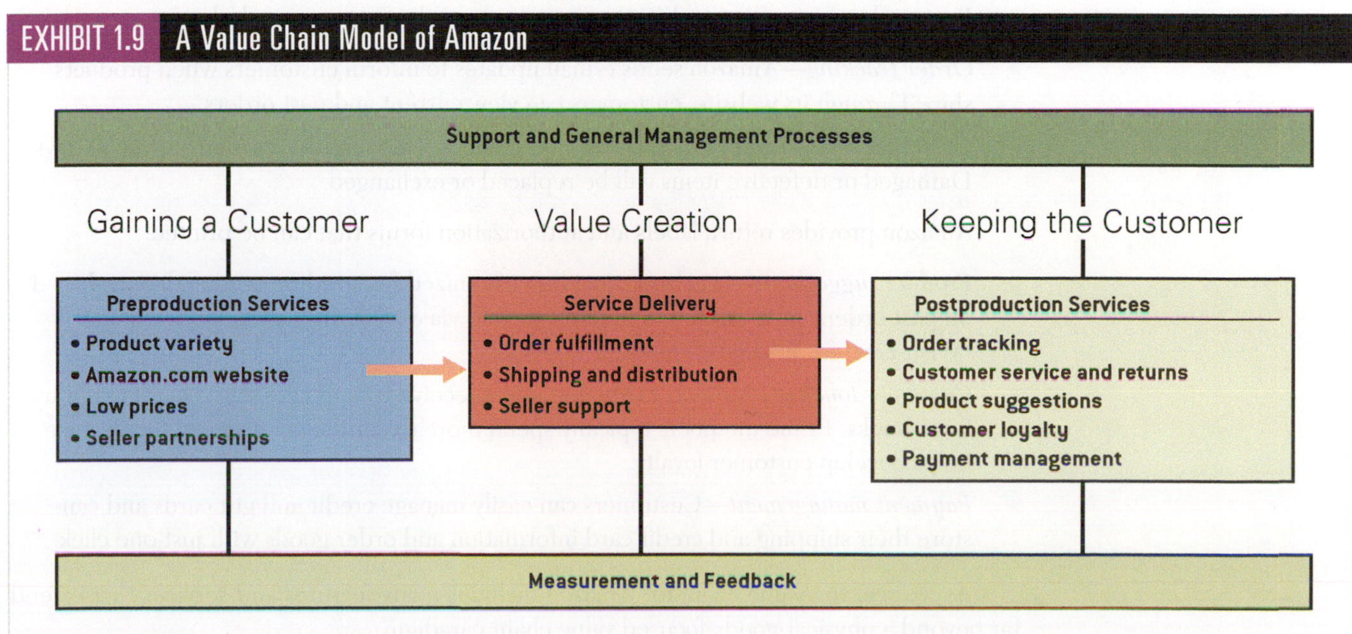

- *Amazon.com website*—Amazon's website facilitates the customer experience. Customers can conveniently shop by department, search products, see new releases, peruse their browsing history, access account information, manage orders and credit cards, and so on. From an efficiency perspective, order entry uses customer labor!
- *Low prices*—Amazon strives to offer the lowest prices possible. It does this through operations and supply chain management—continually improving efficiencies and leveraging economies of scale.
- *Seller and distributor partnerships*—Amazon partners with third-party sellers who would ordinarily be competitors, thus expanding its offerings and providing competitive prices and services to its customers. Amazon also partners with third-party transportation firms such as UPS and FedEx to deliver orders to customers.

Amazon creates and delivers value to customers through a set of key value-creation processes and location decisions. These include:

- *Order fulfillment*—Amazon's fulfillment centers are designed for efficient order picking and packaging, using information technology, bar code sorting, and order-matching processes to ensure accuracy. Its information system stores the locations of individual products and creates routes for order pickers.
- *Distribution center location*—Amazon has fulfillment centers close to major metropolitan markets. Being closer to customers not only provides faster service (e.g., same-day delivery) but also reduces transportation costs.
- *Shipping options*—Amazon offers free shipping for many orders over $35. Customers can split orders for faster service. For a fixed annual fee, Amazon Prime provides unlimited two-day shipping and optional next-day delivery for an additional, low price.
- *Customer pickup locations*—Amazon has opened pickup points at numerous locations such as college campuses (the first was opened at Purdue University) to make it easier for customers to receive products at a secure location and at times that are convenient.
- *Seller support*—Sellers are an important customer group. Amazon Services launched a new version of Amazon WebStore (http://webstore.amazon.com), providing business customers with tools to easily design, build, and manage their multichannel, e-commerce businesses using Amazon's technology.

Postproduction services, which focus on keeping the customer include:

- *Order tracking*—Amazon sends e-mail updates to inform customers when products ship. Through its website, customers can view current and past orders.
- *Customer service and returns*—New, unopened items can be returned within 30 days. Damaged or defective items will be replaced or exchanged.

Amazon provides return labels and authorization forms that can be printed.

- *Product suggestions*—Amazon provides customized featured recommendations based on past orders and searches on its website and via e-mail. Items can be saved on a "Wish List" for future reference.
- *Customer loyalty*—Amazon Prime members receive free movies and a lending library for e-books. Prime members typically spend more than other customers; this feature helps develop customer loyalty.
- *Payment management*—Customers can easily manage credit and gift cards and can store their shipping and credit card information and order goods with just one click.

As we see, the value chain for Amazon includes many features and services that extend far beyond a physical-goods-focused value chain paradigm.

1-7e Value Chains: Hierarchical Supply Chain Framework

Supply chains are the foundation of most value chains. For example, Hewlett-Packard (HP) ships thousands of computers and peripherals daily and spends some $50 billion, or about 64 percent of its revenue, on supply chain activities. Supply chain optimization "has a direct impact on customer satisfaction, stock price and profitability," says an HP senior vice president of supply chain.[10]

The basic purpose of a supply chain is to coordinate the flow of materials, services, and information among the elements of the supply chain to maximize customer value. The key functions generally include purchasing and procurement of materials and supplies, sales and order processing, operations, inventory and materials management, transportation and distribution, information management, finance, and customer service.

A goods-producing supply chain generally consists of suppliers, manufacturers, distributors, retailers, and customers arranged in a hierarchical structure, as illustrated in Exhibit 1.10. Raw materials and components are ordered from suppliers and must be transported to manufacturing facilities for production and assembly into finished goods. Finished goods are shipped to distributors who operate distribution centers.

Distribution centers (DCs) *are warehouses that act as intermediaries between factories and customers, shipping directly to customers or to retail stores where products are made available to customers*. At each factory, distribution center, and retail store, inventory generally is maintained to improve the ability to meet demand quickly. **Inventory** *refers to raw materials, work-in-process, or finished goods that are maintained to support production or satisfy customer demand.*

EXHIBIT 1.10 Typical Goods-Producing Supply Chain Structure

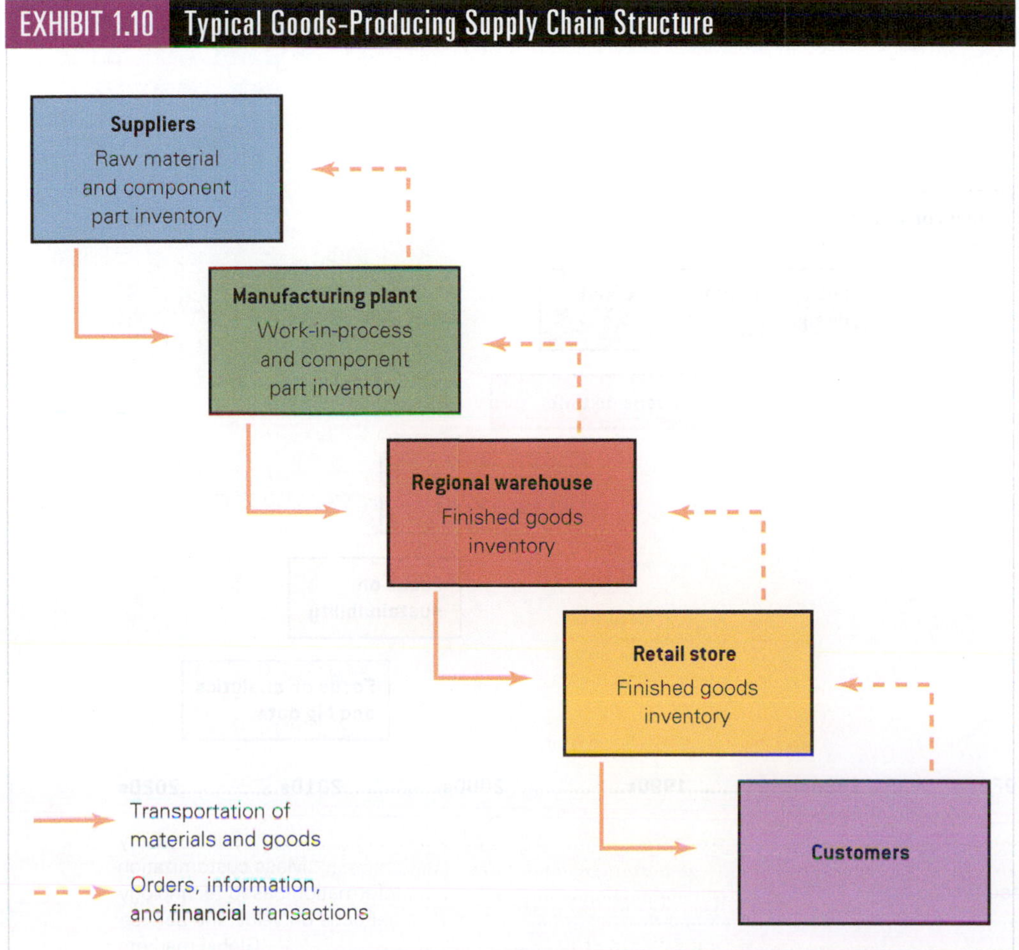

Lutsenko_Oleksandr/Shutterstock.com

HP ships computers, peripherals, and supplies each day, with more than 60 percent of its revenue spent on supply chain activities.

As inventory levels diminish, orders are sent to the previous stage upstream in the process for replenishing stock. Orders are passed up the supply chain, fulfilled at each stage, and shipped to the next stage.

Not all supply chains have each of the stages illustrated in Exhibit 1.10. A simple supply chain might be one that supplies fresh fish at a Boston restaurant. Being close to the suppliers (fisherman), the restaurateur might purchase fish directly from them daily and cut and fillet the fish directly at the restaurant. A slightly more complex supply chain for a restaurant in the Midwest might include processing and packaging by a seafood wholesaler and air transportation and delivery to the restaurant. For consumers who want to buy fish from a grocery store, the supply chain is more complex and would include wholesale delivery and storage by the retailer.

1-8 OM: A History of Change and Challenge

In the last century, operations management has undergone more changes than any other functional area of business and is the most important factor in competitiveness. That is one of the reasons why every business student needs a basic understanding of the field. Exhibit 1.11

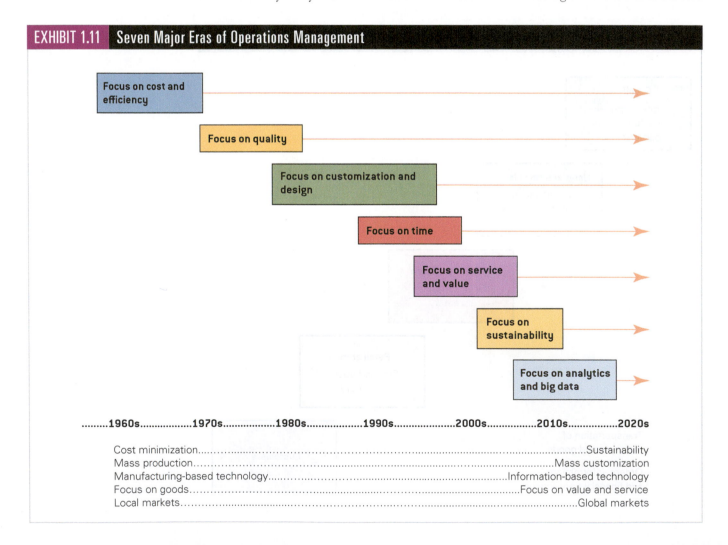

EXHIBIT 1.11 Seven Major Eras of Operations Management

Focus on cost and efficiency →

Focus on quality →

Focus on customization and design →

Focus on time →

Focus on service and value →

Focus on sustainability →

Focus on analytics and big data →

.........1960s.................1970s.................1980s..................1990s....................2000s................2010s................2020s

Cost minimization..Sustainability
Mass production..Mass customization
Manufacturing-based technology...Information-based technology
Focus on goods..Focus on value and service
Local markets..Global markets

is a chronology of major themes that have changed the scope and direction of operations management over the last half century. To better understand the challenges facing modern business and the role of OM in meeting them, let us briefly trace the history and evolution of these themes.

1-8a A Focus on Efficiency

During the Industrial Revolution, many inventions came into being that allowed goods to be manufactured with greater ease and speed, and led to the development of modern factories. In the 1940s, Toyota developed new ways of creating manufacturing efficiencies, which we study in Chapter 17. The development of computers and other forms of technology during the last 50 years has revolutionized operations.

1-8b The Quality Revolution

After World War II, Japanese companies embarked on a massive effort to train the workforce, using statistical tools developed at Western Electric and other innovative management tools to identify causes of quality problems and fix them. By the mid-1970s, the world discovered that Japanese goods had fewer defects, were more reliable, and better met consumer needs than did American goods. As a result, Japanese firms captured major shares of world markets in many different industries such as automobiles and electronics. Thereafter, quality became an obsession with top managers of nearly every major company and continues to be so today. In 1987, the U.S. government established the Malcolm Baldrige Award to focus national attention on quality.

1-8c Customization and Design

As the goals of low cost and high product quality became "givens," companies began to emphasize innovative designs and product features to gain a competitive edge. Inflexible mass-production methods that produced high volumes of standardized goods and services using unskilled or semiskilled workers and expensive, single-purpose equipment, though very efficient and cost-effective, were inadequate for the new goals of increased goods and service variety and continual product improvement. New types of operating systems emerged that enabled companies to manufacture goods and services better, cheaper, and faster than their competitors, while facilitating innovation and increasing variety.

1-8d Time-Based Competition

As information technology matured, time became an important source of competitive advantage. Quick response is achieved by continually improving and reengineering processes—that is, fundamentally rethinking and redesigning processes to achieve dramatic improvements in cost, quality, speed, and service. That task includes developing products faster than competitors, speeding ordering and delivering processes, rapidly responding to changes in customers' needs, and improving the flow of paperwork.

1-8e The Service Revolution

In 1955, about 50 percent of the U.S. workforce was employed in goods-producing industries and 50 percent in service-providing industries. Today, about four of every five U.S. jobs are in services, as summarized in Exhibit 1.12.

In addition, estimates are that at least 50 percent of the jobs in goods-producing industries are service- and information-related, such as human resources management, accounting, financial, legal, advertising, purchasing, engineering, and so on. Thus, today, about 90 percent of the jobs in

EXHIBIT 1.12 U.S. Employment by Economic Sector

	2012	2022 (projected)
Goods, excluding agriculture	12.6%	12.1%
Services	79.9%	80.9%
Agriculture, forestry, fishing, and hunting	1.5%	1.2%
Nonagriculture self-employed, and unpaid family workers	6.0%	5.8%

Source: U.S. Bureau of Labor Statistics.

the U.S. economy are in service-providing processes. This means that if you are employed in the United States, you will most likely work in a service- or information-related field.

1-8f Sustainability

In today's world, sustainability has become one of the most important issues that organizations face. **Sustainability** *refers to an organization's ability to strategically address current business needs and successfully develop a long-term strategy that embraces opportunities and manages risk for all products, systems, supply chains, and processes to preserve resources for future generations*. Sustainability can be viewed from three perspectives: environmental, social, and economic.

- **Environmental sustainability** *is an organization's commitment to the long-term quality of our environment*. Environmental sustainability is important because environmental concerns are placing increased pressure on all goods and service-providing organizations across the globe.
- **Social sustainability** *is an organization's commitment to maintain healthy communities and a society that improves the quality of life*. Social sustainability is important because every organization must protect the health and well-being of all stakeholders and their respective communities, treat all stakeholders fairly, and provide them with essential services.
- **Economic sustainability** *is an organization's commitment to address current business needs and economic vitality, and to have the agility and strategic management to prepare successfully for future business, markets, and operating environments*. Economic sustainability is important because staying in business for the long term, expanding markets, and providing jobs are vital to national economies.

These three dimensions of sustainability are often referred to as the "triple bottom line." Sustainability represents a broad and, to many, a new paradigm for organizational performance. Not only do sustainability practices lead to better public perception, they can improve productivity, eliminate waste, and help organizations become more competitive. OM plays a vital role in helping organizations accomplish these goals. Exhibit 1.13 provides examples of business practices that support these three dimensions. We will discuss the role of OM in achieving sustainability throughout the book.

1-8g Analytics and Big Data

Today, all organizations have access to an enormous amount of data and information. In OM, data are used to evaluate operations performance, quality, order accuracy, customer satisfaction, delivery, cost, environmental compliance, and many other areas of the business. Leveraging such data is fast becoming a necessity in creating competitive advantage. A new discipline has emerged in recent years called business analytics. **Business analytics** *is a process of transforming data into actions through analysis and insights in the context of organizational decision making and problem solving.*[11] Business analytics is used to understand past and current performance (descriptive analytics), predict the future by detecting patterns and relationships in data (predictive analytics), and identify the best decisions (prescriptive analytics).

EXHIBIT 1.13 Examples of Sustainability Practices

Environmental Sustainability

- **Waste management:** Reduce waste and manage recycling efforts
- **Energy optimization:** Reduce consumption during peak energy demand times
- **Transportation optimization:** Design efficient vehicles and routes to save fuel
- **Technology upgrades:** Develop improvements to save energy and clean and reuse water in manufacturing processes
- **Air quality:** Reduce greenhouse gas emissions
- **Sustainable product design:** Design goods whose parts can be recycled or safely disposed of

Social Sustainability

- **Product safety:** Ensure consumer safety in using goods and services
- **Workforce health and safety:** Ensure a healthy and safe work environment
- **Ethics and governance:** Ensure compliance with legal and regulatory requirements and transparency in management decisions
- **Community:** Improve the quality of life through industry-community partnerships

Economic Sustainability

- **Performance excellence:** Build a high-performing organization with a capable leadership and workforce
- **Financial management:** Make sound financial plans to ensure long-term organizational survival
- **Resource management:** Acquire and manage all resources effectively and efficiently
- **Emergency preparedness:** Have plans in place for business, environmental, and social emergencies

We will introduce and use various analytical techniques throughout this book. Supplements A–G at the end of this book provide introductions to the following topics:

- Probability and statistics (Supplement A)
- Decision Analysis (Supplement B)
- Break-Even Analysis (Supplement C)
- Linear Optimization (Supplement D)
- The Transportation and Assignment Models (Supplement E)
- Queueing Models (Supplement F)
- Simulation (Supplement G)

In addition, a unique set of Microsoft Excel spreadsheet templates that we will present throughout the text to facilitate the use of analytic techniques is available in MindTap. Exhibit 1.14 summarizes where the templates are used.

You have undoubtedly heard the term "big data." Big data refers to massive amounts of business data from a wide variety of sources, much of which is available in real time. A study by the McKinsey Global Institute noted that, "The effective use of big data has the potential to transform economies, delivering a new wave of productivity growth and consumer surplus. Using big data will become a key basis of competition for existing companies, and will create new competitors who are able to attract employees that have the critical skills for a big data world."[12]

Big data helps retailers make optimum inventory decisions to ensure that their warehouses are stocked with the right products at the right time. Data such as social media trends, purchasing patterns, and market changes help predict what products need to be stocked and where. Big data, such as weather and traffic data, also helps supply chains to improve routing and delivery decisions. Big data also helps improve manufacturing, process flow, quality, and preventive maintenance.

For services, big data is analyzed, for example, to create a custom ad focused on an individual's behavior and preferences. Big data analytics also supports service businesses such as virtual banking, remote medical diagnosis by artificial intelligence, self-driving vehicles, virtual movie actors, and National Basketball Association player and team performance. These systems are evolving at an exponential pace and transforming goods-producing and service-providing industries.

EXHIBIT 1.14 Summary of Excel Spreadsheet Templates Available in MindTap

Template	Chapter References	Description
Statistical Analysis	2	Computes basic statistical measures and a frequency distribution and histogram
VLC	2	Computes the value of a loyal customer (VLC)
Decision Analysis	4	Computes classic decision strategies with and without probabilities
Break-Even	4, 7	Computes a break-even point and optimal outsourcing decision
Taguchi	5	Computes the Taguchi loss function and economic tolerance
Systems Reliability	5	Computes reliabilities of series and parallel systems
Location Analysis	6	Computes total costs to determine least-cost location for production
Center of Gravity	6	Finds and plots the center of gravity
Little's Law	7	Computes flowtime, throughput, or work-in-process using Little's Law
Work Measurement	8	Computes normal and standard times for work measurement studies
Learning Curve	8	Computes and charts the time to produce the first 100 units for a learning curve
Moving Average	9	Calculates and plots moving average forecasts
Exponential Smoothing	9	Calculates and plots exponential smoothing forecasts
Work Order Capacity	10	Computes capacity requirements for multiple work orders
Service Capacity	10	Uses capacity measurement equation to compute capacity, service rate, or number of servers
Single Server Queue	11	Calculates measures for a single server queueing model
Multiple Server Queue	11	Calculates measures for a multiple server queueing model
Queue Simulation	11	Performs a single server queueing simulation for discrete arrival and service time distributions
ABC	12	Conducts ABC inventory analysis
EOQ	12	Finds the economic order quantity and plots the cost functions
Quantity Discount	12	Computes optimal order size for a quantity discount inventory model
FQS Safety Stock	12	Computes safety stock and reorder point for fixed-quantity inventory systems
FPS Safety Stock	12	Computes safety stock and reorder point for fixed-period inventory systems
Single-Period Inventory	12	Finds the optimal ordering quantity for a single-period inventory systems with uniform or normal demand
Inventory Simulation	12	Simulates a fixed quantity inventory situation
Total Supply Chain Cost	13	Evaluates total supply chain costs for supplier selection decisions
Agg. Plan-Level	14	Evaluates aggregate planning using a level production strategy
Agg. Plan-Chase	14	Evaluates aggregate planning using a chase production strategy
Aggregate Planning	14	General template for Aggregate Planning to seek minimum cost strategies using trial-and-error
Sequencing	15	Computes flowtime, lateness, and tardiness for job sequencing problems
Six Sigma	16	Computes DPU, DPMO, and sigma level
Pareto	16	Finds and plots a Pareto distribution
x-Bar and R-Chart	17	Plots an x-bar and R-chart for quality control
p-Chart	17	Plots a p-chart for quality control
c-Chart	17	Plots a c-chart for quality control
Process Capability	17	Computes process capability measures and a frequency distribution and histogram
Gantt Chart	18	Creates a visual chart depicting the schedule for a project

1-9 Current and Future Challenges

OM is continually changing, and all managers need to stay abreast of the challenges that will define the future workplace. Here are some issues facing contemporary OM:

- *Customers*. Consumers demand an increasing variety of high-quality goods with new and improved features that are delivered faster than ever—along with outstanding service and support. Being first to market means more now than ever before, and OM plays a vital role.
- *Technology*. Technology continues to evolve at a rapid pace. Applications in design and manufacturing as well as the use of information technology in services have provided the ability to develop innovative products and services and more effectively manage

and control extremely complex operations. Future transformative technologies, such as artificial intelligence, 3-D metal printing, the Internet of Things, nanotechnology, smart cities, genetic design, quantum computing, and others, are forthcoming. OM needs to continue to leverage and exploit these technology advances.

- *Workforce*. Today's workforce requires new skills, continual learning, more diversity, and better management. These tasks often fall on the shoulders of operations managers. Organizations will need to become more flexible with how and where their workforces operate in global value chains.
- *Globalization*. Globalization no longer means just an opportunity for organizations to enter new markets. We now live in an era of the "borderless marketplace." Today, firms have to contend with a growing number of competitors and sources of lower-cost labor. For example, labor costs are far cheaper outside the United States (where manufacturing labor averages about $40 per hour); in Asia, Mexico, and South America, labor costs range from $3 to $10 per hour. In addition, managing operations in countries with vastly different cultures can be problematic.
- *Sustainability*. Performance in global operations and supply chains use to mean a focus on cost, quality, and time. Today, sustainability is a fourth major performance area. Global sourcing managers, for example, must qualify suppliers on at least these four performance areas. A global supplier that is best at cost, quality, and delivery performance but uses child labor or pollutes community drinking water is not going to do business with the modern companies of today.
- *Optimizing supply chains*. Value chains now span across many continents. Companies today face many challenges in designing and optimizing their supply chains. These include determining where to best source raw materials, components, and finished goods. Sourcing abroad, of course, requires efficient transportation and scheduling, and also incurs risks related to intellectual property and supply chain disruptions from natural disasters and other factors. Coordinating this entire process to minimize total costs is a continuing challenge.

Operations and Supply Chain Management Professional Websites

If you want to check out careers and issues in operations, distribution, and supply chain management try these professional association websites:

- American Production & Inventory Control Society (APICS)—www.apics.org
- American Society for Quality (ASQ)—www.asq.org
- American Society of Transportation & Logistics (AST&L)—www.astl.org
- Council of Supply Chain Management Professionals (CSCMP)—www.cscmp.org
- European Logistics Associations (ELALOG)—www.elalog.edu
- Production Managers Association (PMA)—www.pma.org.uk
- Project Management Association (PMI)—www.pmi.org
- Reverse Logistics Association (RIA)—www.ria.org

Many of these associations have certification programs to document the participant's expertise and knowledge.

CHAPTER 1 LEARNING OBJECTIVE SUMMARIES

1.1 **Explain the concept and importance of operations management.** Creating and delivering goods and services to customers depends on an effective system of linked facilities and processes, and the ability to manage them effectively around the world. **Operations management (OM)** *is the science and art of ensuring that goods and services are created and delivered successfully to customers.* OM includes the *design* of goods, services, and the processes that create them; the day-to-day *management* of those processes; and the continual *improvement* of these goods, services, and processes. Three issues are at the core of operations management: *efficiency, cost*, and *quality*.

1.2 **Describe what operations managers do.** Many people who are considered "operations managers" have titles such as chief operating officer, hotel or restaurant manager, vice president of manufacturing, customer service manager, plant manager, field service manager, or supply chain manager. The concepts and methods of OM can be used in any job, regardless of the functional area of business or industry, to better create value for internal customers (within the organization) and for external customers (outside the organization). OM principles are used in accounting, human resources management, legal work, financial activities, marketing, environmental management, and every type of service activity. Some key activities that operations managers perform include: forecasting, supply chain management, facility layout and design, technology selection, quality management, purchasing, resource and capacity management, process design, job design, scheduling, and sustainability.

1.3 **Explain the differences between goods and services.** Companies design, produce, and deliver a wide variety of goods and services that consumers purchase. *A* **good** *is a can see, touch, or possibly consume. A* **service** *is any primary or complementary activity that does not directly produce a physical product.*

1.4 **Define the concept of value and explain how the value of goods and services can be enhanced.** The underlying purpose of every organization is to provide value to its customers and stakeholders. The decision to purchase a good or service or a customer benefit package is based on an assessment by the customer of the perceived benefits in relation to its price. The customer's cumulative judgment of the perceived benefits leads to either satisfaction or dissatisfaction. One of the simplest functional forms of value is:

$$\text{Value} = \frac{\text{Perceived benefits}}{\text{Price (cost) to the customer}}$$

1.5 **Describe a customer benefit package.** "Bundling" goods, services, and digital content in a certain way to provide value to customers not only enhances what customers receive, but can also differentiate the product from competitors. A customer benefit package consists of a primary good or service coupled with peripheral goods and/or services, and sometimes variants.

1.6 **Explain the difference between value chains and supply chains, and identify three general types of processes in a business.** Many organizations use the terms "value chain" and "supply chain" interchangeably; however, a value chain is broader in scope than a supply chain and is easier to apply to service-providing organizations as well as to goods producing firms.

Key processes in business typically include:

1. ***Value-creation processes*** focused on producing or delivering an organization's primary goods or services that create value for customers, such as filling and shipping a customer's order, assembling a dishwasher, or providing a home mortgage.
2. ***Support processes*** such as purchasing materials and supplies used in manufacturing, managing inventory, installation, health benefits, technology acquisition, day care on-site services, and research and development.
3. ***General management processes***, including accounting and information systems, human resource management, and marketing.

1.7 **Contrast the three different frameworks for describing value chains.**

- An input-output framework: Inputs are transformed into value-added goods and services through processes that are supported by such resources as equipment and facilities, labor, money, and information.
- A preproduction and postproduction services framework: Focuses on gaining customers (pre-) and keeping customers (post-)
- A hierarchical supply chain perspective: A goods-producing supply chain generally consists of suppliers, manufacturers, distributors, retailers, and customers arranged in a hierarchical structure.

1.8 **Summarize the historical development of OM.** Exhibit 1.11 offers a chronology of major themes that have changed the scope and direction of operations management over the last half-century.

1.9 **State the current and future challenges facing OM:**

- Customers
- Technology
- Workforce
- Globalization
- Sustainability
- Optimizing supply chains

KEY TERMS

- **Biztainment**
- **Business analytics**
- **Customer benefit package (CBP)**
- **Distribution center (DC)**
- **Durable good**
- **Economic sustainability**
- **Environmental sustainability**
- **Good**
- **Inventory**
- **Moment of truth**
- **Nondurable good**
- **Operations management (OM)**
- **Peripheral good or service**
- **Primary good or service**
- **Process**
- **Service**
- **Service encounter**
- **Service management**
- **Social sustainability**
- **Supply chain**
- **Sustainability**
- **Value**
- **Value chain**
- **Variant**

REVIEW QUESTIONS

1.1 1. Explain the concept and importance of operations management.

1.1 2. Describe how operations management is used in work throughout business organizations.

1.2 3. State three of the key activities that operations managers perform and briefly explain them.

1.3 4. Define a good and a service.

1.3 5. Explain how goods differ from services.

1.4 6. Define the concept of value.

1.4 7. How can an organization increase value to its customers?

1.5 8. Describe a customer benefit package.

1.5 9. What is a peripheral good or service? Provide some examples.

1.5 10. Define "biztainment" and provide an example.

1.6 11. Explain the difference between value chains and supply chains.

1.6 12. Define and explain the three major types of processes in business?

1.7 13. What is a distribution center?

1.7 14. Contrast the three different frameworks for describing value chains.

1.8 15. Define sustainability and explain its three dimensions.

1.8 16. What percent of U.S. economy jobs are in the service sector?

1.8 17. Describe the importance of data and business analytics in operations and supply chain management.

1.8 18. Summarize the historical development of OM.

1.9 19. Select one of the following challenges facing OM: customers, technology, workforce, globalization, sustainability, or optimizing supply chains, and explain its short- and long-term impact.

DISCUSSION QUESTIONS AND EXPERIENTIAL ACTIVITIES

1.1 20. Describe a customer experience you have personally encountered where the good or service or both were unsatisfactory (e.g., defective product, errors, mistakes, poor service, and service upsets). How might the organization have handled it better, and how could operations management have helped?

1.1 21. Search recent articles in your local newspaper and business magazines such as *Fortune*, *Business Week*, *Fast Company*, and so on and identify OM concepts and issues that are discussed. How do these fit into the classification in the box "What Do Operations Managers Do?" in this chapter?

1.2 22. Interview a manager at a local company about the work he or she performs. Identify (a) the aspects of the job that relate to OM (like the OM activities in the box "What Do Operations Managers Do?") and (b) examples of value-creation, support, and general management processes.

1.2 23. Evaluate how the activities described in the box "What Do Operations Managers Do?" can be applied to a student organization or fraternity to improve its effectiveness.

1.2 24. Interview a working friend or family member as to how they use operations management principles in their job and write a short paper summarizing your findings (maximum two pages).

1.3 25. Explain how the seven differences between goods and services would be applied to a major airline service. Provide airline examples that illustrate each difference.

1.3 26. Explain why a bank teller, nurse, or flight attendant must have service management skills. How do the required skills differ for someone working in a factory? What are the implications for hiring criteria and training?

1.3 27. Do you think you will be working in manufacturing or services when you graduate? What do you think will be the role of manufacturing in the U.S. economy in the future?

1.3 28. Choose one of the following services and explain, using specific examples, how each of the ways that services differ from manufactured goods apply.

a. A family practice medical office
b. A fire department
c. A restaurant
d. An automobile repair shop

1.5 29. Explain how the customer benefit package is enhanced from the customer's viewpoint by adding digital content to a physical good such as an automobile, cell phone, or appliance? How is value increased?

1.5 30. Draw the customer benefit package (CBP) for one of the items in the following list and explain how your CBP provides value to the customer. Make a list of a few example processes that you think would be necessary to create and deliver "each good or service" in the CBP you selected and briefly describe issues that must be considered in designing these processes.

- A trip to Disney World
- A new personal computer
- A credit card
- A fast-food restaurant
- A wireless mobile telephone
- A one-night stay in a hotel

1.6 31. Why is process thinking important in operations management? Thinking of yourself as an "operations manager" for your education, how could process thinking improve your performance as a student?

1.6 32. One of our former students, who had worked for Taco Bell, related a story of how his particular store developed a "60-second, 10-pack club" as an improvement initiative and training tool. The goal was to make a 10-pack of tacos in a minute or less, each made and wrapped correctly, and the total within one ounce of the correct weight. Employees received recognition and free meals for a day. Employees strove to become a part of this club, and more importantly, service times dropped dramatically. Techniques similar to those used to improve the taco-making process were used to improve other products. Explain how this anecdote relates to process thinking. What would the employees have to do to become a part of the club?

1.6 33. Review one of the operations and supply chain management professional websites and report what you find.

1.7 34. Select an organization you are familiar with and draw and describe its value chain using one of the three value chain frameworks (i.e., the input-output, preservice and post-services or the hierarchical model) described in this chapter.

1.8 35. Search the Web for either (a) an organization that has defined its sustainability strategy and policy, and give examples of how they are implementing it, or (b) an organization that has received negative or controversial media coverage for its ethical or sustainability practices. Write a paper describing what you found (maximum of two typed pages).

1.8 36. Describe new ways for how your college or university can apply the sustainability practices in Exhibit 1.13. Summarize your results in a short paper.

1.8 37. Discuss how the three perspectives of sustainability influence (or perhaps, should influence) your personal purchasing decisions. For example, do you consider whether apparel is made in safe and ethical factories? Should companies exploit their sustainability efforts for marketing purposes? Why or why not?

1.8 38. Research and write a short paper describing how business analytics has been applied to problems and decisions in operations management. Use the information in the box "What do Operations Managers Do?" to help your search process.

1.9 39. Select one of the OM challenges and investigate it in more detail. Prepare a 5–10-minute presentation on what you found.

1.9 40. Geoff Colvin of Fortune magazine discussed the concept of a "friction-free economy" in which labor, information, and money move cheaply and quickly through the firm's global supply chains.[13] (The term was actually coined by Bill Gates in 1997 and is now becoming a reality.) Research this concept and write a two-page paper that describes the impacts and challenges that a friction-free economy would have on operations management.

Mickey Mouse: To Talk or Not?

When Walt Disney created the Disney empire in the 1950s, he forbid its star characters such as Mickey Mouse and Pluto to talk. Mr. Disney thought it would be too difficult to control the service encounters between customers and the Disney characters, and it would ruin the "magic" of Disney. Therefore, Disney characters were trained to gesture and use only their body language to interact and entertain guests.

Today, during a meeting of (fictional) senior "imagineering" managers, Mr. Luke Tomas, V. P. of Costume Design, said, "Mr. Walt Disney would not like Mickey Mouse talking if he were alive." "But Luke, if Mickey speaks it gives us new ways to interact with our guests," responded Cindy Bridgetown, V.P. of Imagineering, and Luke's boss. "Cindy, we can't control the conversation if Mickey talks to guests. Kids and parents are going to get their feelings hurt one way or another. And it's too demanding on our employees."

Case Questions for Discussion:

1. Using the "What Do Operations Managers Do?" box in the chapter, what key activities most directly relate to the case situation?
2. Provide one good and bad example of a "moment of truth" if Mickey Mouse talks to customers.
3. Explain the advantages and disadvantages of talking Disney characters from a service perspective?

Zappos, A Subsidiary of Amazon

Zappos (www.zappos.com) is a Las Vegas–based online retailer that has been cited in *Fortune's* list of the Best Companies to Work For and *Fast Company's* list of the world's most innovative companies. In fact, its remarkable success resulted in Zappos being bought by Amazon for $850 million in 2009. Zappos was founded in San Francisco in 1999 and moved to Las Vegas for the cheap real estate and abundant call center workers. The company sells a large variety of shoes from nearly every major manufacturer and has expanded its offerings to handbags, apparel, sunglasses, watches, and electronics. Despite the crippling economic downturn, sales jumped almost 20 percent in 2008, passing the $1 billion mark two years ahead of schedule.

The company's first core value is "Deliver WOW through service," which is obvious if you've ever ordered from Zappos. It provides free shipping in both directions

Zappos provides free shipping in both directions on all purchases.

on all purchases. It often gives customers surprise upgrades for faster shipping. And it has a 365-day return policy. In 2003, Zappos made a decision about customer service: It views any expense that enhances the customer experience as a marketing cost because it generates more repeat customers through word of mouth. CEO Tony Hsieh never outsourced his call center because he considers the function too important to be sent to overseas. Job one for these frontliners is to delight callers. Unlike most inbound telemarketers, they don't work from a script. They're trained to encourage callers to order more than one size or color, because shipping is free in both directions, and to refer shoppers to competitors when a product is out of stock.

Most important, though, they're implored to use their imaginations. This means that a customer having a tough day might find flowers on his or her doorstep the next morning. One Minnesota customer complained that her boots had begun leaking after almost a year of use. Not only did the Zappos customer service representative send out a new pair—in spite of a policy that only unworn shoes are returnable—but she also told the customer to keep the old ones, and mailed a hand-written thank-you.[14] Over 95 percent of Zappo's transactions take place on the Web, so each actual customer phone call is a special opportunity. "They may only call once in their life, but that is our chance to wow them," Hsieh says.

Zappos uses a sophisticated computer system known as Genghis to manage its operations. This includes an order entry, purchasing, warehouse management, inventory, shipping, and e-commerce system. Genghis tracks inventory so closely that customers can check online how many pairs of size 12 Clarks Desert boots are available in the color sand. For employees, it automatically sends daily e-mail reminders to call a customer back, coordinates the warehouse robot system, and produces reports that can specifically assess the impact on margins of putting a particular item on sale.

Free shipping has become a customer expectation. Research has found that online customers abandon their virtual shopping carts up to 75 percent of the time at the end of their order entry process when they can't get free shipping. Other online retailers have copied the free-shipping policies of Zappos. L.L. Bean, for example, now provides free shipping and free returns with no minimum order amount.

Case Questions for Discussion:

1. Draw and describe the customer benefit package that Zappos provides. Goods? Services? Digital content? Who manufacturers the physical goods? Who is responsible for the quality and delivery of the physical goods?
2. Identify and describe the primary, support, and general management processes needed to execute a customer order at Zappos.
3. Describe how any three of the OM activities in the box "What Do Operations Managers Do?" impact the management of both the goods that Zappos sells and the services that it provides.
4. Explain how this case illustrates each of the seven major differences between goods-producing and service-providing businesses.

Integrative Case: Hudson Jewelers

The Hudson Jewelers case study in MindTap integrates material found in each chapter of this book.

Case Questions for Discussion:

1. Use one of the three value chain frameworks discussed in this chapter to characterize the diamond value chain. How does this value chain gain a customer? How does it create value? How does it keep a customer?
2. Research what major diamond producers are doing regarding social, environment, and financial sustainability practices. Study corporate annual reports, for example. Provide two or three examples.
3. Write a two-page paper on "blood diamonds" and/or "ethical diamonds." Define each and explain the positives and negatives for this social sustainability issue. What should be the role of diamond producers? What is the role of operations managers in this industry?

Measuring Performance in Operations and Value Chains | 2

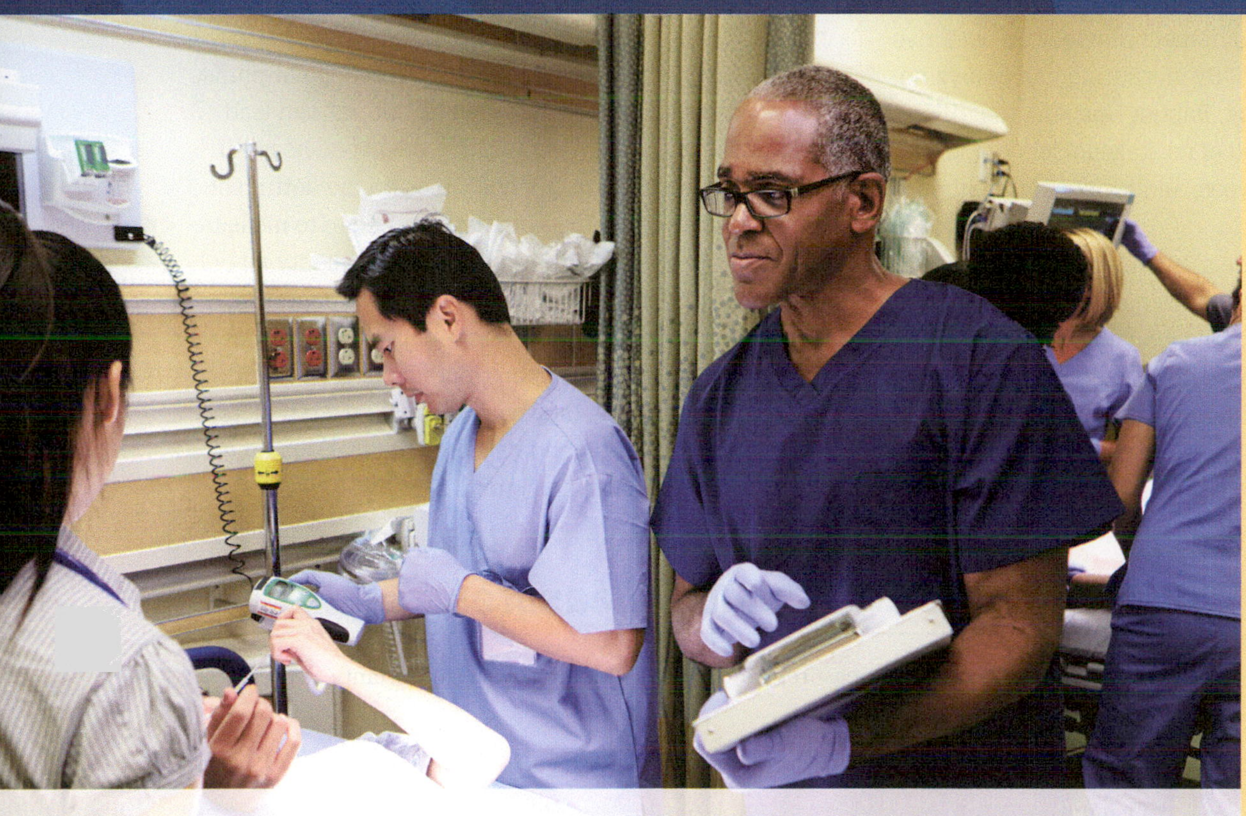

Monkey Business Images/Shutterstock.com

LEARNING OBJECTIVES

After studying this chapter, you should be able to:

2-1 Describe the types of measures used for decision making.

2-2 Explain the use of analytics in OM and how internal and external measures are related.

2-3 Explain how to design a good performance measurement system.

2-4 Describe four models of organizational performance.

Baptist Hospital, Inc. (BHI) is a subsidiary of Baptist Health Care with about 2,252 employees and includes two hospitals and an ambulatory care complex that delivers an array of outpatient and diagnostic services. Continuous improvement is an important aspect of BHI's culture, driven by peer, employee, physician, and patient surveys, as well as using the Malcolm Baldrige National Quality Award performance framework to gather information and identify opportunities for improvement.

BHI uses a variety of listening and learning approaches to determine customer needs, including surveys and Customer Value Analysis to determine patient loyalty attributes. Information gathered from the listening and learning activities is collected and analyzed using a customer relationship management database to identify the key requirements for each customer group and as input into strategic planning, service design, and FOCUSPDCA (a performance improvement process). BHI's information and knowledge management systems enable it to collect and integrate data from clinical systems, employees, patients, financial systems, decision support systems, and physicians for tracking overall organizational performance and for identifying opportunities for improvement. Reports are generated to support organizational performance and learning, financial performance, clinical outcomes (quality) improvement, customer satisfaction, team activities, and continuous improvement results.[1]

WHAT DO YOU THINK?

What measures do you think a company should use to evaluate its goods or services? Provide some examples.

Measurement *is the act of quantifying the performance of organizational units, goods and services, processes, people, and other business activities.* Measurement provides an objective basis for making decisions. By measuring and analyzing organizational performance, Baptist Hospital, Inc. (BHI) is able to better manage all of its stakeholders (patients, third-party payers, employees, and suppliers), leading to more successful outcomes.

Good measures provide a "scorecard" of performance, help identify performance gaps, and make accomplishments visible to the workforce, the stock market, and other stakeholders. For example, the ground-operations area of American Airlines is concerned primarily with the service passengers receive at airports.[2] The ground-operations area routinely measures several factors that customers have noted are important, such as waiting time at the ticket counter, time to opening the cabin door after gate arrival, bag-delivery time, and cabin cleanliness. The popular phrase "How you are measured is how you perform" can lead to improvements. For example, doctors at one hospital tended to rush through colonoscopies, to the detriment of the patients. After an administrator began to measure the length of the procedures and assign a quality rating, doctors' behavior changed and quality improved. However, the wrong kind of performance measure can be dangerous. In one company, engineers were measured on how quickly they could design new products. Unfortunately, those products were not what customers wanted, and revenues and profits quickly fell.

2-1 Types of Performance Measures

Organizational performance measures can be classified into several important categories:

- Financial
- Customer and market
- Quality
- Time
- Flexibility
- Innovation and learning
- Productivity and operational efficiency
- Sustainability

Within each of these categories are organizational-level measures that are of interest primarily to senior managers, as well as more specific measures that are used by operations managers. Together, these measures provide the means of assessing the effectiveness of operations along supply and value chains. Some of them are summarized in Exhibit 2.1.

2-1a Financial Measures

Financial measures, such as cost and revenue, often take top priority in for-profit organizations. For example, the banking industry monitors closely the costs associated with checking account transactions. Internet banking is being promoted because it has a distinct cost advantage: the estimated transaction costs typically are 1 percent of branch bank transaction costs. Traditional financial measures that companies use include revenue, return on investment, operating profit, pretax profit margin, asset utilization, growth, revenue from new goods and services, earnings per share, and other liquidity measures. Nonprofit organizations, such as the Red Cross,

EXHIBIT 2.1 The Scope of Business and Operations Performance Measurement

Performance Measurement Category	Typical Organizational-Level Performance Measures	Typical Operational-Level Performance Measures
Financial	Revenue and profit	Labor and material costs
	Return on assets	Cost of quality
	Earnings per share	Budget variance
Customer and market	Customer satisfaction	Customer claims and complaints
	Customer retention	Type of warranty failure/upset
	Market share	Sales forecast accuracy
Quality	Customer ratings of goods and services	Defects/unit or errors/opportunity
	Product recalls	Service representative courtesy
Time	Speed	Flow processing or cycle time
	Reliability	Percent of time meeting promised due date
Flexibility	Design flexibility	Number of engineering changes
	Volume flexibility	Assembly-line changeover time
Innovation and learning	New product development rates	Number of patent applications
	Employee satisfaction	Number of improvement suggestions implemented
	Employee turnover	Percent of workers trained on statistical process control
Productivity and operational efficiency	Labor productivity	Manufacturing yield
	Equipment utilization	Order fulfillment time
Sustainability	Environmental and regulatory compliance	Toxic waste discharge rate
	Product-related litigation	Workplace safety violations
	Financial audits	Percent of employees with emergency preparedness training

churches, and government agencies, focus more on minimizing costs and maximizing value to their target markets, customers, and society. Monitoring cost and adherence to budgets are important factors in their operational success.

2-1b Customer and Market Measures

You have probably completed customer satisfaction surveys at a restaurant or after an Internet purchase, or perhaps you have lodged a complaint. Through customer and market feedback, an organization learns how satisfied its customers and stakeholders are with its goods and services and performance. Other customer-focused performance measures include customer retention, gains and losses of customers and customer accounts, customer complaints, warranty claims, measures of perceived value, loyalty, positive referral, and customer relationship building.

Measures of customer satisfaction reveal areas that need improvement and show whether changes actually result in improvement. *A* ***customer-satisfaction measurement system*** *provides a company with customer ratings of specific goods and service features and indicates the relationship between those ratings and the customer's likely future buying behavior.* It tracks trends and reveals patterns of customer behavior from which the company can predict future customer needs and wants. It also tracks and analyzes complaints and other measures of dissatisfaction. At Federal Express, for instance, customers are asked to rate everything from billing to the performance of couriers, package condition, tracking and tracing capabilities, complaint handling, and helpfulness of employees. A restaurant might rate food appearance, taste, temperature, and portions, as well as cleanliness, staff friendliness, attentiveness, and perception of value.

eBay: If It moves, measure It

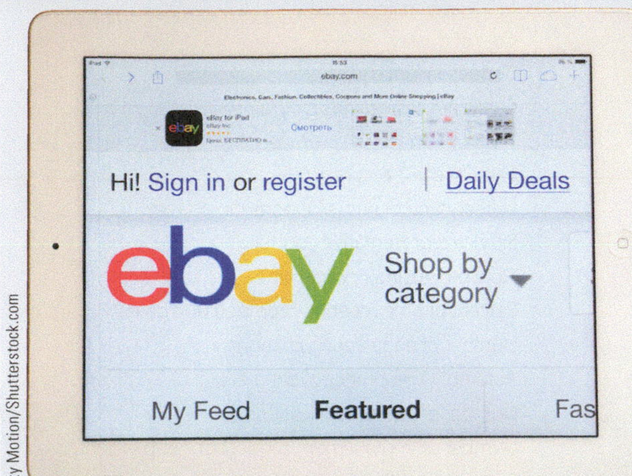

Sky Motion/Shutterstock.com

A saying around eBay's headquarters is, "If it moves, measure it."[3] eBay is just one of many Internet companies that pay close attention to measurements. Web metrics such as how many people visit a site, register to become users, length of time that visitors spend on the site, and how long it takes pages to load are commonly used and tracked closely by most Internet companies. eBay monitors these things, analyzes the data, and uses the results to make timely business decisions, for example, to provide customer incentives such as free listings to stimulate demand during slow periods. One unique measurement that eBay monitors is the "take rate"—the ratio of revenues to the value of goods traded on the site. How might they use this metric to improve customer service and profitability?

Marketplace performance indicators could include market share, measures of business growth, new product and geographic markets entered, and percentage of new product sales, as appropriate. For example, in a commodity market in which Cargill Kitchen Solutions competes (making various egg products for restaurants and schools from raw eggs), its performance drivers include the U.S. share of market and total pounds of egg products sold. In the highly competitive semiconductor industry, STMicroelectronics looks not only at sales growth but also at differentiated product sales.

2-1c Quality

Quality *measures the degree to which the output of a process meets customer requirements.* Quality applies to both goods and services. **Goods quality** *relates to the physical performance and characteristics of a good.* Goods quality is generally measured using instruments, technology, and data-collection processes. For example, the dimensions and weight of a good such as a laptop computer, its storage capacity, battery life, and actual speed are easy to measure. **Service quality** *is consistently meeting or exceeding customer expectations (external focus) and service-delivery system performance (internal focus) for all service encounters.* Many companies, including Amazon.com, Federal Express, and Nordstrom, have worked hard to provide superior service quality to their customers. Measuring service quality is paramount in such organizations.

Service-quality measures are based primarily on human perceptions of service collected from customer surveys, focus groups, and interviews. Research has shown that customers use five key dimensions to assess service quality[4]:

1. *Tangibles*—Physical facilities, uniforms, equipment, vehicles, and appearance of employees (i.e., the physical evidence).
2. *Reliability*—Ability to perform the promised service dependably and accurately.
3. *Responsiveness*—Willingness to help customers and provide prompt recovery to service upsets.

4. *Assurance*—Knowledge and courtesy of the service providers and their ability to inspire trust and confidence in customers.
5. *Empathy*—Caring attitude and individualized attention provided to customers.

These five dimensions help form the basis for quality measurement in service organizations. Note that all but the first pertain to behavioral characteristics at the service encounter level, which are more difficult to measure than physical and technical characteristics.

Every service encounter provides an opportunity for error. *Errors in service creation and delivery are sometimes called* **service upsets** *or* **service failures**. Service measures should be linked closely to customer satisfaction so that they form the basis for improvement efforts. For example, a restaurant manager might keep track of the number and type of incorrect orders or measure the time from customer order to delivery.

2-1d Time

Time relates to two types of performance measures—the *speed* of doing something (such as the time to process a customer's mortgage application) and the *variability* of the process. Speed can lead to a significant competitive advantage. Progressive Insurance, for example, boasts that it settles auto-insurance claims before competitors know there has been an accident![5] Speed is usually measured in clock time, whereas variability is usually measured by quantifying the variance around average performance or targets. A useful measure is **processing time**, *the time it takes to perform some task.* For example, to make a pizza, a worker needs to roll out the dough, spread the sauce, and add the toppings, which might take three minutes. **Queue time** *is a fancy word for* **wait time**, *the time spent waiting.*

An important aspect of measuring time is the variance around the average time, as unanticipated variability is what often leads to an unhappy customer experience. Variability is usually measured by statistics such as the standard deviation or mean absolute deviation. For example, suppose that one company takes 10 days to process a new life insurance application plus or minus one day, while another takes 10 days plus or minus five days. Which life insurance process will give the best service to its customers? Which firm would you rather do business with?

2-1e Flexibility

Flexibility *is the ability to adapt quickly and effectively to changing requirements.* As new products are being introduced faster and customers expect more customization, operations managers must design value chains that are highly flexible. Flexibility can relate either to adapting to changing customer needs or to the volume of demand. **Goods and service design flexibility** *is the ability to develop a wide range of customized goods or services to meet different or changing customer needs.* Examples of design flexibility include Dell's ability to provide a wide range of customized computer hardware to accommodate home users, small businesses, and large company's server needs, or a health club's ability to customize an individual client's workout or provide cardio rehabilitation classes for heart patients. Such flexibility requires a highly adaptable operations capability. Design flexibility is often evaluated by such measures as the rate of new product development or the percent of a firm's product mix that has been developed over the past three years.

Volume flexibility *is the ability to respond quickly to changes in the volume and type of demand.* This might mean rapid changeover from one product to another as the demand for certain goods increases or decreases, or the ability to produce a wide range of volumes as demand fluctuates. A hospital may have intensive-care nurses on standby in case of a dramatic increase in patient demand because of an accident or be able to borrow specialized diagnostic equipment from

FedEx: Measuring Service Performance

FedEx developed a composite measure of its service performance called the Service Quality Indicator (SQI), which is a weighted sum of 10 factors reflecting customers' expectations of company performance. These are listed below.

The weights reflect the relative importance of each failure. Losing a package, for instance, is more serious than delivering it a few minutes late. The index is reported weekly and summarized on a monthly basis. Continuous improvement goals for the SQI are set each year. SQI is really a measure of process effectiveness. Meeting SQI performance goals also can account for as much as 40 percent of a manager's performance evaluation!

Error Type	Description	Weight
1.	*Complaints reopened*—customer complaints (on traces, invoices, missed pickups, etc.) reopened after an unsatisfactory resolution	3
2.	*Damaged packages*—packages with visible or concealed damage or spoilage due to weather or water damage, missed pickup, or late delivery	10
3.	*International*—a composite score of performance measures of international operations	1
4.	*Invoice adjustments*—customer requests for credit or refunds for real or perceived failures	1
5.	*Late pickup stops*—packages that were picked up later than the stated pickup time	3
6.	*Lost packages*—claims for missing packages or with contents missing	10
7.	*Missed proof of delivery*—invoices that lack written proof of delivery information	1
8.	*Right date late*—delivery past promised time on the right day	1
9.	*Traces*—package status and proof of delivery requests not in the COSMOS IIB computer system (the FedEx "real-time" tracking system)	3
10.	*Wrong day late*—delivery on the wrong day	5

Source: Service Quality Indicators at FedEx (internal company document).

other hospitals when needed. Measures of volume flexibility would include the time required to change machine setups or the time required to "ramp up" to an increased production volume in response to surges in sales.

2-1f Innovation and Learning

Innovation *refers to the ability to create new and unique goods and services that delight customers and create competitive advantage.* Many goods and services are innovative when they first appear—think of the iPhone. However, competitors quickly catch up (e.g., Google's Android operating system and the latest Droid phones); thus, innovation needs to be a constant process for many companies and must be measured and assessed. **Learning** *refers to creating, acquiring, and transferring knowledge, and modifying the behavior of employees in response to internal and external changes.* For instance, when something goes wrong in one office or division, can the organization ensure that the mistake is not repeated again and does not occur in other offices or divisions? The importance of innovation and learning was well stated by Bill Gates, who said, "Microsoft is always two years away from failure."

Measures of innovation and learning focus on an organization's people and infrastructure. Key measures might include intellectual asset growth, patent applications, the number of "best practices" implemented within the organization, and the percentage of new products developed over the past few years in the product portfolio. Of particular importance are measures associated with an organization's human resource capabilities. These can relate to employee training and skills development, satisfaction, and work-system performance and effectiveness. Examples include absenteeism, turnover, employee satisfaction, training

> "Microsoft is always two years away from failure."
> —BILL GATES

A Powerful Productivity Metric for Herc Rentals Inc.

Herc Rentals (hercrentals.com) is a full-service equipment-rental firm with a large presence in North America. It employs about 5,000 people, and operates 270 company-owned facilities generating a couple of billion dollars in revenue. It rents equipment like air compressors, earthmoving machines, pumps, trucks, electric scissor lifts, and material handling equipment to a wide variety of customers. The advantages of renting are numerous and include reducing the renter's time and cost of managing the equipment, greater financial flexibility, and avoiding the inconvenience and cost of maintenance and repair.

One of several performance measures that drive the business is dollar utilization, which is determined by dividing annual rental revenue (output) by the cost of buying and maintaining the equipment (inputs). Each year, performance goals are set to increase this output-input productivity metric.

hours per employee, training effectiveness, and measures of improvement in job effectiveness. For instance, The Ritz-Carlton Hotel Company tracks percent turnover very closely, as this measure is a key indicator of employee satisfaction and the effectiveness of its selection and training processes.

2-1g Productivity and Operational Efficiency

Productivity *is the ratio of the output of a process to the input.* As output increases for a constant level of input, or as the amount of input decreases for a constant level of output, productivity increases. Thus, a productivity measure describes how well the resources of an organization are being used to produce output.

$$\text{Productivity} = \frac{\text{Quantity of Output}}{\text{Quantity of Input}} \quad [2.1]$$

The measures used for the quantity of output and quantity of input in Equation 2.1 need not be expressed in the same units.

Examples of productivity measures include units produced per labor hour, airline revenue per passenger mile, hotel revenue per full-time employee, meals served per labor dollar, and the number of students per teacher. Productivity measures are often used to track trends over time.

Operational efficiency *is the ability to provide goods and services to customers with minimum waste and maximum utilization of resources.* Some measures of operational efficiency might include the time it takes to fulfill orders, times to set up machinery and equipment, times to change from one product to another on an assembly line, manufacturing yields, and supply-chain performance, to name just a few.

2-1h Sustainability

The **triple bottom line (TBL or 3BL)** *refers to the measurement of environmental, social, and economic sustainability.* Environmental regulations usually require organizations to measure and report compliance, but many companies go beyond what is minimally required. Organizations track numerous environmental measures such as energy consumption, recycling and other resource conservation activities, air emissions, solid and hazardous waste rates, and so on. Social sustainability measures include consumer and workplace safety, community relations, and corporate ethics and governance. Measuring consumer and workplace safety is vital to all organizations, as the well-being of their customers and employees should be a major concern.

SOLVED PROBLEM 2.1: CALCULATING PRODUCTIVITY

Consider a division of Miller Chemicals that produces water purification crystals for swimming pools. The major inputs used in the production process are labor, raw materials, and energy. For Year 1, labor costs are \$180,000; raw materials cost \$30,000; and energy costs amount to \$5,000. Labor costs for Year 2 are \$350,000; raw materials cost \$40,000; and energy costs amount to \$6,000. Miller Chemicals produced 100,000 pounds of crystals in Year 1 and 150,000 pounds of crystals in Year 2.

Solution:

Using Equation 2.1, we have for Year 1:

$$\begin{aligned}\text{Productivity} &= \frac{\text{Quantity of Output}}{\text{Quantity of Input}}\\ &= \frac{100{,}000}{(\$180{,}000 + \$30{,}000 + \$5{,}000)}\\ &= 0.465\ \text{lb / dollar}\end{aligned}$$

For Year 2 we have:

$$\begin{aligned}\text{Productivity} &= \frac{\text{Quantity of Output}}{\text{Quantity of Input}}\\ &= \frac{150{,}000}{(\$350{,}000 + \$40{,}000 + \$6{,}000)}\\ &= 0.379\ \text{lb / dollar}\end{aligned}$$

We see that productivity has declined in the past year.

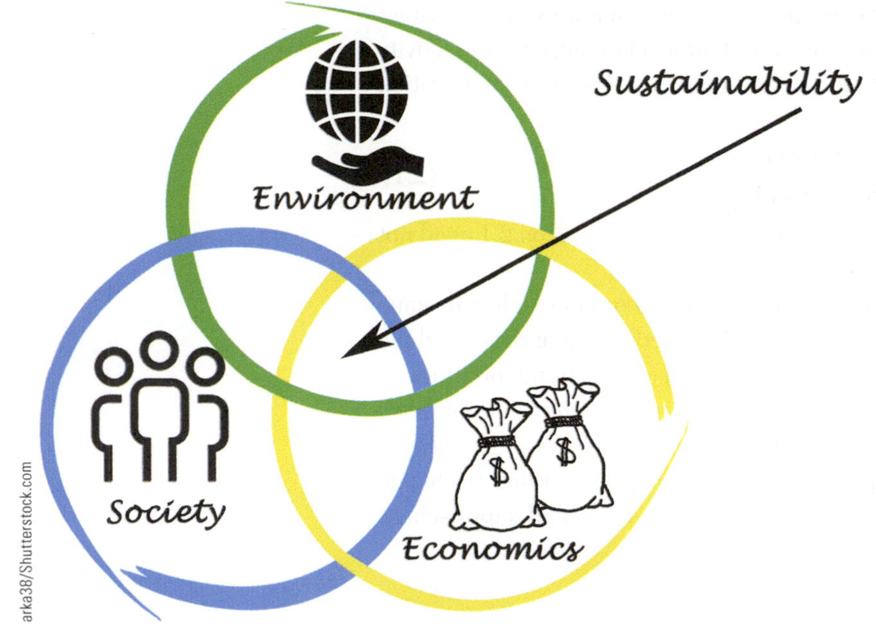

Federal and state agencies such as the Occupational Safety and Health Administration (OSHA) require organizations to track and report safety indicators, such as reportable accidents. Examples of safety-related performance measures include accident rates, the parts per million of toxic chemicals in a public water supply, or the security in a hotel room. Other social sustainability measures would be the number of ethical violations and community service hours. Finally, economic sustainability measures might include financial audit results, regulatory compliance, legal or governmental sanctions, donations to civic groups, fines for environmental violations, and measures of accomplishment of strategic initiatives, such as the percentage of action plans and project milestones completed on time.

2-2 Analytics in Operations Management

As we noted in Chapter 1, business analytics is helping operations managers analyze data more effectively and make better decisions. Business analytics include statistical analysis and decision modeling tools. Exhibit 2.2 summarizes these tools, which are used in many chapters in this book. The supplements provide a review of these tools, basic concepts, and examples to assist in understanding solved problems and in working end-of-chapter problems and exercises.

EXHIBIT 2.2 Business Analytics Tools in OM

Business Analytics Tools for OM	Focus	Applications
Statistical Analysis (Supplement A)	Collecting, organizing, analyzing, summarizing, interpreting, and presenting data.	Visualizing data using charts to examine performance trends; comparing results relative to other business units, competitors, or best-in-class benchmarks; understanding relationships among different measures.
Decision Analysis (Supplement B)	Identifying the best economic decision alternative with uncertain futures.	Product selection, facility capacity expansion and location, inventory analysis, and technology and process analysis.
Break-Even Analysis (Supplement C)	Identifying the best economic choice between two options that vary with volume.	Profitability analysis, outsourcing decisions, and technology choices.
Optimization (Supplements D and E)	Identifying the best decisions to maximize or minimize some objective while satisfying constraints and requirements.	Product mix, process selection, production planning, scheduling, and transportation and supply chain management.
Queueing Models (Supplement F)	Understand behavior of waiting line systems with random arrivals of customers and service times using analytical models.	Process design and analysis for manufacturing and service, resource utilization analysis, and bottleneck analysis.
Simulation (Supplement G)	Developing and analyzing a logical model of a system and conducting computer-based experiments to describe, explain, and predict system behavior.	Process design for manufacturing and service, inventory systems, complex waiting line analysis, and resource planning.

Statistics *involves collecting, organizing, analyzing, interpreting, and presenting data.* A statistic is a summary measure of data. **Descriptive statistics** *refers to methods of describing and summarizing data using tabular, visual, and quantitative techniques.* Statistics provides the means of gaining insight—both numerically and visually—into large quantities of data, understanding uncertainty and risk in making decisions, and drawing conclusions from sample data that come from very large populations. Operations managers use statistics to gauge production and quality performance to determine process and design improvements. Statistical methods allow us to gain a richer understanding of data by not only summarizing data succinctly but also finding unknown and interesting relationships among the data.

Decision modeling tools are used in operations and supply chain management to describe the behavior of production and service systems, predict performance, and prescribe the best courses of action. These include decision analysis, break-even analysis, optimization, queueing models, and simulation.

All of these tools are implemented on Excel spreadsheets. Spreadsheets are widely applied in all areas of business and used by nearly everyone. Spreadsheets provide a convenient way to manage and manipulate data, perform calculations, and display visual graphics simultaneously, using intuitive representations instead of abstract mathematical notation. They are a highly effective platform for developing and solving decision models and communicating results. You should be familiar with basic Excel skills, such as opening, saving, and printing files; using workbooks and worksheets; moving around a spreadsheet; selecting cells and ranges; inserting/deleting rows and columns; entering and editing text, numerical data, and formulas in cells; formatting data (number, currency, decimal places, etc.); Excel formulas and basic functions; relative and absolute addressing; and using Excel menus.

MindTap contains a wide variety of Excel templates that perform calculations to analyze and solve problems in many chapters of this book. The templates are designed so that you need only enter the data and information as instructed, and Excel takes care of the rest. Solved Problem 2.2 illustrates an example of using the *Statistical Analysis* template to compute basic descriptive statistics, frequency distributions, and histograms. The templates allow you to conduct trial-and-error "what-if?" analyses by changing data and assumptions to understand their impact on results.

In addition to the Excel templates provided with this book, several applications require you to develop logical models for optimization, queueing, and simulation problems using

SOLVED PROBLEM 2.2: USING THE STATISTICAL ANALYSIS EXCEL TEMPLATE

The La Ventana Window Company manufactures original equipment and replacement windows for residential building and remodeling applications. In a cutting process for a certain window model, specifications call for a dimension of 25.50 inches. If the dimension is larger than 25.52 inches, it will be too tight in assembly; and if it is 25.48 inches or less, it will be too loose and will not meet customer requirements. The plant manager collected a sample of 50 parts from this process and measured the dimensions, as shown below. What information do the data provide?

25.51	25.50	25.49	25.50	25.50	25.48	25.50	25.50	25.49	25.52
25.49	25.51	25.51	25.51	25.50	25.50	25.50	25.51	25.50	25.50
25.48	25.50	25.50	25.51	25.50	25.50	25.49	25.50	25.51	25.50
25.49	25.49	25.49	25.51	25.50	25.48	25.48	25.48	25.47	25.49
25.49	25.50	25.50	25.50	25.49	25.48	25.51	25.51	25.50	25.51

Solution:

Exhibit 2.3 shows the results of these quality measurements using the *Statistical Analysis* spreadsheet template. Simply enter the data in the data matrix and also enter the number of cells for the histogram and lower and upper limits for the histogram in the yellow cells in the spreadsheet. The spreadsheet will automatically adjust the frequency distribution and histogram. We see that the mean and median values are close to or at the target; however, the frequency distribution and histogram show that no values exceed 25.52, but seven values are 25.48 or less, perhaps suggesting the need for an adjustment to the process. The template is designed such that you can easily change the values from which the frequency distribution and histogram are constructed.

EXHIBIT 2.3 *Statistical Analysis* Spreadsheet Template Results for La Ventana Window Company Data

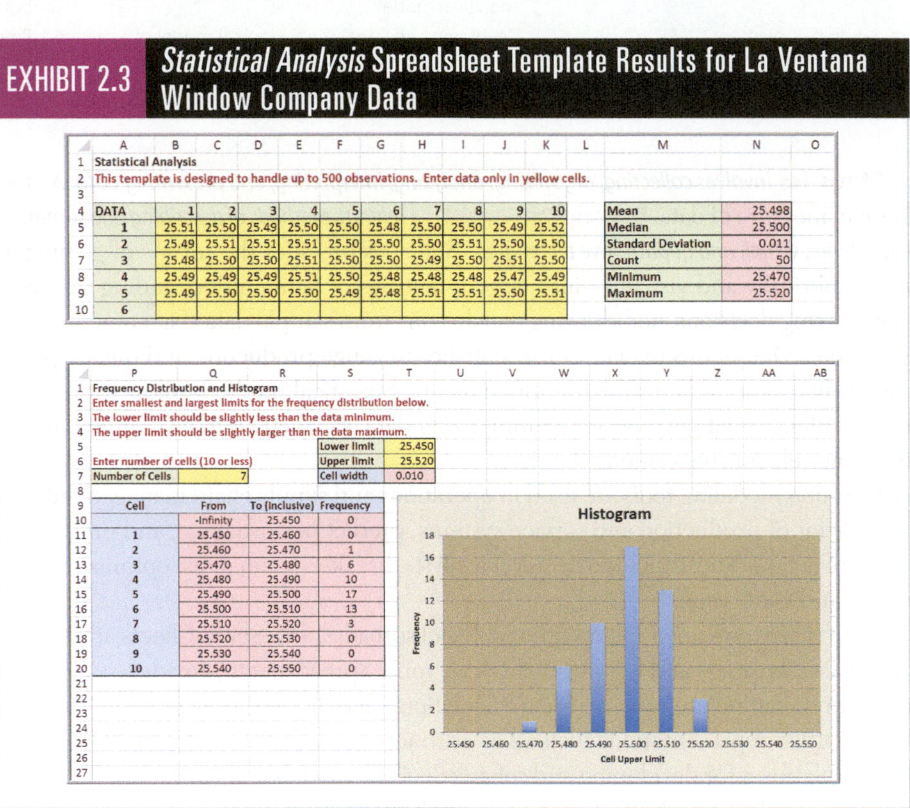

Statistical Analysis

This template is designed to handle up to 500 observations. Enter data only in yellow cells.

DATA	1	2	3	4	5	6	7	8	9	10
1	25.51	25.50	25.49	25.50	25.50	25.48	25.50	25.50	25.49	25.52
2	25.49	25.51	25.51	25.51	25.50	25.50	25.50	25.51	25.50	25.50
3	25.48	25.50	25.50	25.51	25.50	25.50	25.49	25.50	25.51	25.50
4	25.49	25.49	25.49	25.51	25.50	25.48	25.48	25.48	25.47	25.49
5	25.49	25.50	25.50	25.50	25.49	25.48	25.51	25.51	25.50	25.51
6										

Mean	25.498
Median	25.500
Standard Deviation	0.011
Count	50
Minimum	25.470
Maximum	25.520

Frequency Distribution and Histogram

Enter smallest and largest limits for the frequency distribution below.

The lower limit should be slightly less than the data minimum.

The upper limit should be slightly larger than the data maximum.

Enter number of cells (10 or less)

Number of Cells	7

Lower limit	25.450
Upper limit	25.520
Cell width	0.010

Cell	From	To (Inclusive)	Frequency
	-Infinity	25.450	0
1	25.450	25.460	0
2	25.460	25.470	1
3	25.470	25.480	6
4	25.480	25.490	10
5	25.490	25.500	17
6	25.500	25.510	13
7	25.510	25.520	3
8	25.520	25.530	0
9	25.530	25.540	0
10	25.540	25.550	0

Excel spreadsheets. Various Excel tools, such as Solver, Goal Seek, and data tables will be used to find solutions and analyze the models you develop. These are explained in the supplements and illustrated in solved problems where they are used.

2-2a Linking Internal and External Measures

Managers must understand the cause-and-effect linkages between key measures of performance. These relationships often explain the impact of (internal) operational performance on external results, such as profitability, market share, or customer satisfaction. For example, how do goods- and service-quality improvements impact revenue growth? How do improvements in complaint handling affect customer retention? How do increases or decreases in employee satisfaction affect customer satisfaction? How do changes in customer satisfaction affect costs and revenues?

The quantitative modeling of cause-and-effect relationships between external and internal performance criteria is called **Interlinking.**[6] Interlinking tries to quantify the performance relationships between all parts of the value chain—the processes ("how"), goods and services outputs ("what"), and customer experiences and outcomes ("why"). With interlinking models, managers can objectively make internal decisions that impact external outcomes, for example, determining the effects of adding resources or changing the operating system to reduce waiting time, and thereby increase customer satisfaction (see Exhibit 2.4).

As one example, the controls group of Johnson Controls, Inc., examined the relationship between satisfaction levels and contract renewal rates. They found that 91 percent of contract renewals came from customers who were either satisfied or very satisfied, and customers who gave a "not satisfied" rating had a much higher defection rate. By examining the data, they found that a 1-percentage-point increase in the overall satisfaction score was worth $13 million in service contract renewals annually. As a result, Johnson Controls made improving customer satisfaction a key strategic initiative.[7]

2-2b The Value of a Loyal Customer

Many organizations lose customers because of poor goods quality or service performance. This is often the result of operations managers failing to consider the economic impact of lost customers when they cut service staff or downgrade product designs. Likewise, many organizations do not understand the economic value of potential new customers when evaluating proposed goods or service improvements on a strict economic basis. Thus, they need an understanding of how customer satisfaction and loyalty affect the bottom line. One way to do this is to compute the economic value that good customers provide.

The **value of a loyal customer (VLC)** *quantifies the total revenue or profit each target market customer generates over the buyer's life cycle.* Understanding the effects of operational decisions on revenue and customer retention can help organizations more appropriately use their

EXHIBIT 2.4 Interlinking Internal and External Performance measures

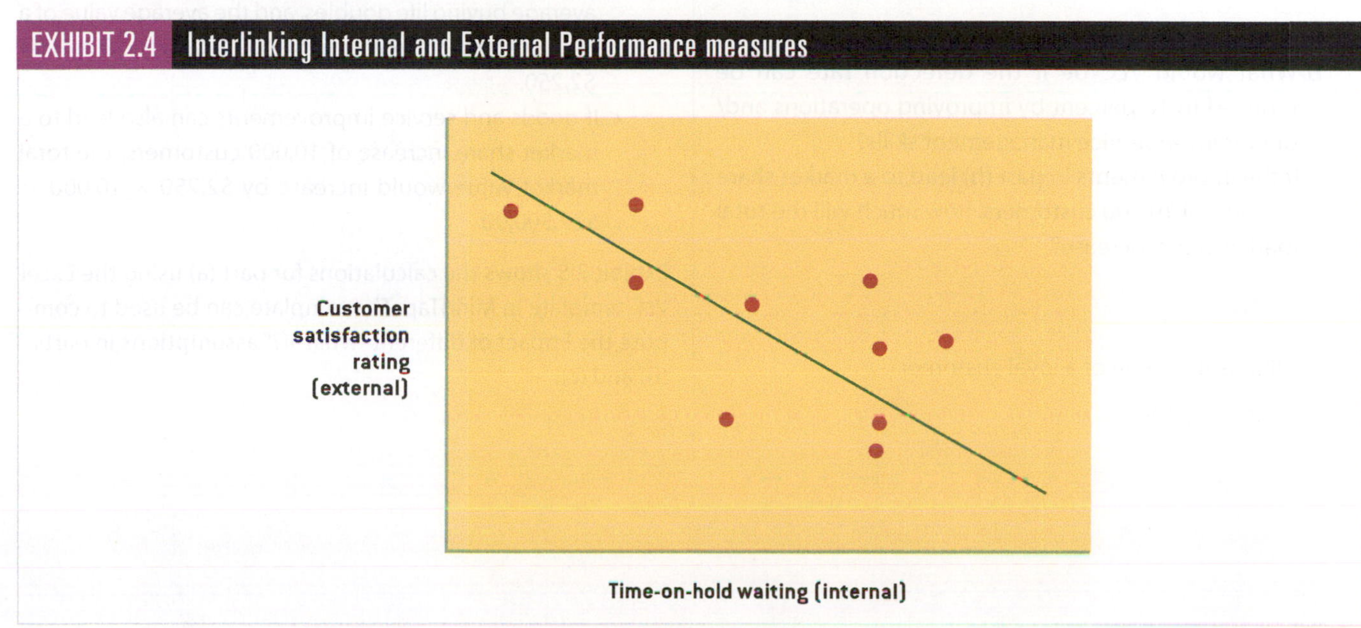

resources. Goods-producing and service-providing organizations both benefit from understanding the value of a loyal customer performance relationship. When one considers the fact that it costs three to five times more to acquire a new customer than keep an existing customer, it is clear why customer retention is often the focus of top management improvement initiatives and strategies.

VLC can be computed with the following equation:

$$VLC = P \times CM \times RF \times BLC \tag{2.2}$$

where

P = the revenue per unit
CM = contribution margin to profit and overhead expressed as a fraction (i.e., 0.45, 0.5, etc.)
RF = repurchase frequency = number of purchases per year
BLC = buyers' lifecycle computed as 1/defection rate, expressed as a fraction (1/0.2 = 5 years, 1/0.1 = years, etc.)

By multiplying the *VLC* times the absolute number of customers gained or lost, the total market value can be found. Solved Problem 2.3 illustrates how to use this formula to compute *VLC*.

SOLVED PROBLEM 2.3: COMPUTING THE VALUE OF A LOYAL CUSTOMER

Suppose that a computer manufacturer estimates that its annual customer retention rate is 80 percent, which means that 20 percent of customers who purchase a computer will not buy from it again (we call this the customer defection rate = 1 − customer retention rate).

Assume that fixed costs are 35 percent and the manufacturer makes a before-tax profit margin of 10 percent. Therefore, the incremental contribution to profit and overhead is 45 percent. We also assume that customers buy a new computer every two years, or 0.5 times per year, at an average cost of $1,000.

a. What is the value of a loyal customer?
b. What would VLC be if the defection rate can be reduced to 10 percent by improving operations and/or employee service management skills?
c. If the improvements in part (b) lead to a market share increase of 10,000 customers, how much will the total market value increase?

Solution:

a. What is the value of a loyal customer?

P = $1,000
CM = 0.45
RF = 0.5 (customers purchase a new machine every two years)
BLC = 1/0.2 = 5 (if 20 percent of customers do not return each year, then, on average, the buying life of a customer is five years)

Therefore, the average value of a loyal customer over his or her average buying life is $1,000 × 0.45 × 0.5 × 5 = $1,125.

b. If the defection rate can be reduced to 10 percent, the average buying life doubles, and the average value of a loyal customer increases to $1,000 × 0.45 × 0.5 × 10 = $2,250.
c. If goods and service improvements can also lead to a market share increase of 10,000 customers, the total market value would increase by $2,250 × 10,000 = $22,500,00.

Exhibit 2.5 shows the calculations for part (a) using the Excel *VLC* template in MindTap. The template can be used to compute the impact of different "what-if?" assumptions in parts (b) and (c).

EXHIBIT 2.5 Excel *VLC* template

	A	B	C	D
1	Value of a Loyal Customer			
2	Enter data only in yellow cells.			
3				
4	Revenue per unit	$1,000.00		
5	Percent contribution margin to profit and overhead	45%		
6	Repurchase frequency (purchases/year)	0.5		
7	Defection rate	0.2		
8				
9	Buyer's life cycle	5.00		
10	VLC	$1,125.00		

Operations managers can influence the VLC by increasing the contribution margin through reducing operating costs, increasing repurchase frequency by better customer service, and reducing customer defection rates by creating and delivering consistently excellent system performance. Process managers can use the VLC numbers to help justify improvement initiatives in job and process design, capacity and scheduling, and facility design.

2-3 Designing Measurement Systems in Operations

What makes a good performance measurement system for operations? Many organizations define specific criteria for selecting and deleting performance measures from the organization's information system. IBM Rochester, for example, asks the following questions:

- Does the measurement support our mission?
- Will the measurement be used to manage change?
- Is it important to our customers?
- Is it effective in measuring performance?
- Is it effective in forecasting results?
- Is it easy to understand/simple?
- Are the data easy/cost-efficient to collect?
- Does the measurement have validity, integrity, and timeliness?
- Does the measurement have an owner?

Good performance measures are actionable. **Actionable measures** *provide the basis for decisions at the level at which they are applied*—the value chain, organization, process, department, workstation, job, and service encounter. They should be meaningful to the user, timely, and reflect how the organization generates value to customers. Performance measures should support, not conflict with, customer requirements. For example, customers expect a timely response when calling a customer support number. A common operational measure is the number of rings until the call is picked up. If a company performs well on this measure, but puts the customer on hold or in a never-ending menu, then a conflict clearly exists.

Analytics for Managing Sports Teams

Professional and amateur sports are just beginning to take advantage of today's analytical methods and software capabilities in order to evaluate performance and return on investment. In basketball, for example, the "box score" documents traditional performance metrics such as points, field goal percentage, fouls, blocked shots, assists, steals, turnovers, minutes played, and offensive and defensive rebounds. Analytics in the form of shot charts, rebound charts, play-by-play data, and motion-capture video and analysis is used to supplement traditional data. Today, the critical question is how to effectively analyze such data in order to maximize performance and owners' returns for minimal cost.

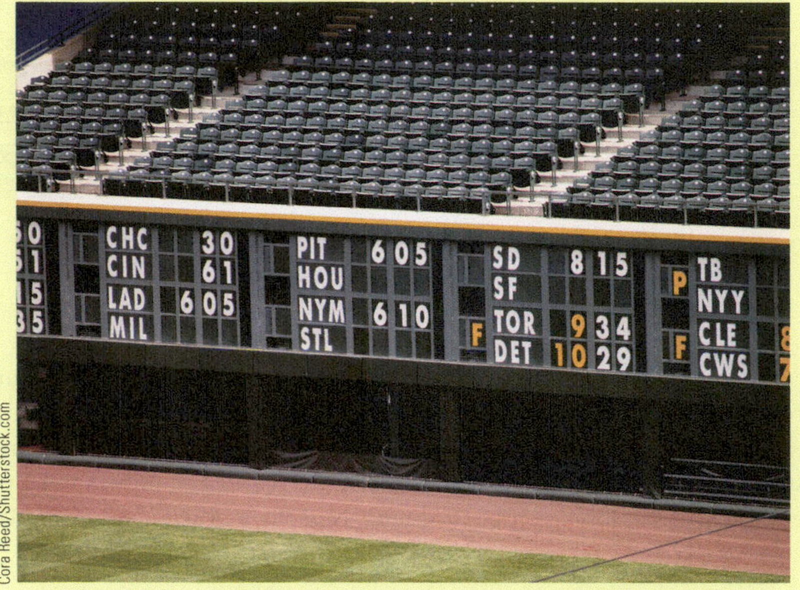

Cora Reed/Shutterstock.com

The popular book and film *Moneyball* demonstrated the use of analytics in sports management to the average sports fan. The book, published in 2003, before analytics became a buzzword in business, profiles how the Oakland Athletics baseball team used analytics to build a competitive team even with a limited budget, and compete with better-funded teams such as the New York Yankees, which spent nearly three times as much on player personnel. To promote the use of analytics in sports management, the Massachusetts Institute of Technology hosts the annual MIT Sloan Sports Analytics Conference that has been attended by students from over 150 different schools and representatives from over 50 professional sports teams.

2-4 Models of Organizational Performance

Four models of organizational performance—the Baldrige Performance Excellence framework, the balanced scorecard, the value chain model, and the Service-Profit Chain—provide popular frameworks for thinking about designing, monitoring, and evaluating performance. The first two models provide more of a "big picture" of organizational performance, whereas the last two provide more detailed frameworks for operations managers. Although OM focuses on execution and delivery of goods and services to customers, it is important to understand these "big-picture" models of organizational performance because operations managers must communicate with all functional areas. In addition, understanding these models helps you better appreciate the interdisciplinary nature of an organization's performance system, the role that operations plays, and why operations managers need interdisciplinary skills.

2-4a Malcolm Baldrige Performance Excellence Framework

The Baldrige Performance Excellence program, formerly known as the Malcolm Baldrige National Quality Award Program, was created to help stimulate American organizations to improve quality, productivity, and overall competitiveness, and to encourage the development of high-performance management practices through innovation, learning, and sharing of best practices. Organizations can receive awards in manufacturing, small business, service, education, health care, and not-for-profit categories. Baldrige recipients show exceptional results that outperform those of their competitors and peers. The program's website at www.nist.gov/baldrige/ provides a wealth of current information about the award, the performance criteria, award recipients, and other aspects of the program.

The Baldrige Performance Award

Although the award itself receives the most attention, the primary purpose of the program is to provide a framework for performance excellence through self-assessment to understand an organization's strengths and weaknesses, thereby setting priorities for improvement. This framework is shown in Exhibit 2.6. Integration plays a key role, emphasizing that no single piece of the system can operate independently. In this fashion, the seven categories represent a logical approach to planning, executing, and reviewing performance. The framework also defines the *Criteria for Performance Excellence*. The criteria are designed to provide a framework for managing an organization to achieve outstanding results. The seven categories are:

1. *Leadership*: This category addresses how senior leaders' personal actions guide and sustain the organization, the organization's governance system, and approaches for fulfilling ethical, legal, and societal responsibilities.
2. *Strategy*: This category focuses on how an organization develops strategic objectives and action plans, implements them, and changes them if circumstances require, and measures progress.
3. *Customers*: This category addresses how an organization engages its customers for long-term marketplace success, builds a customer-focused culture, listens to the voice of its customers, and uses this information to improve and identify opportunities for innovation.
4. *Measurement, Analysis, and Knowledge Management*: This category focuses on how an organization selects, gathers, analyzes, manages, and improves its data, information, and knowledge assets; how it manages its information technology; and how it reviews data and uses the results to improve its performance.
5. *Workforce*: This category addresses how an organization assesses workforce capability and capacity needs; builds a high-performance environment; and engages, manages, and develops its workforce to utilize its full potential in alignment with the organization's overall needs.
6. *Operations*: This category addresses how an organization designs, manages, improves, and innovates its work systems and work processes to deliver customer value, and achieve organizational success.
7. *Results*: This category examines an organization's performance and improvement in key business areas—product and process results, customer-focused results, workforce-focused results, leadership and governance results, and financial and market results.

In essence, the criteria framework represents a macro-level interlinking model that relates management practices to business results. For example, if senior managers understand their customers and create effective strategies (Categories 1–3), and then translate plans into actions through the workforce and operations (Categories 5 and 6), then positive results (Category 7) should follow. Category 4 provides the foundation for measuring and assessing results and continual improvements. Some simplify the theory of the Baldrige Award by saying that "leadership drives the system that creates results."

EXHIBIT 2.6 Baldrige Model of Organizational Performance

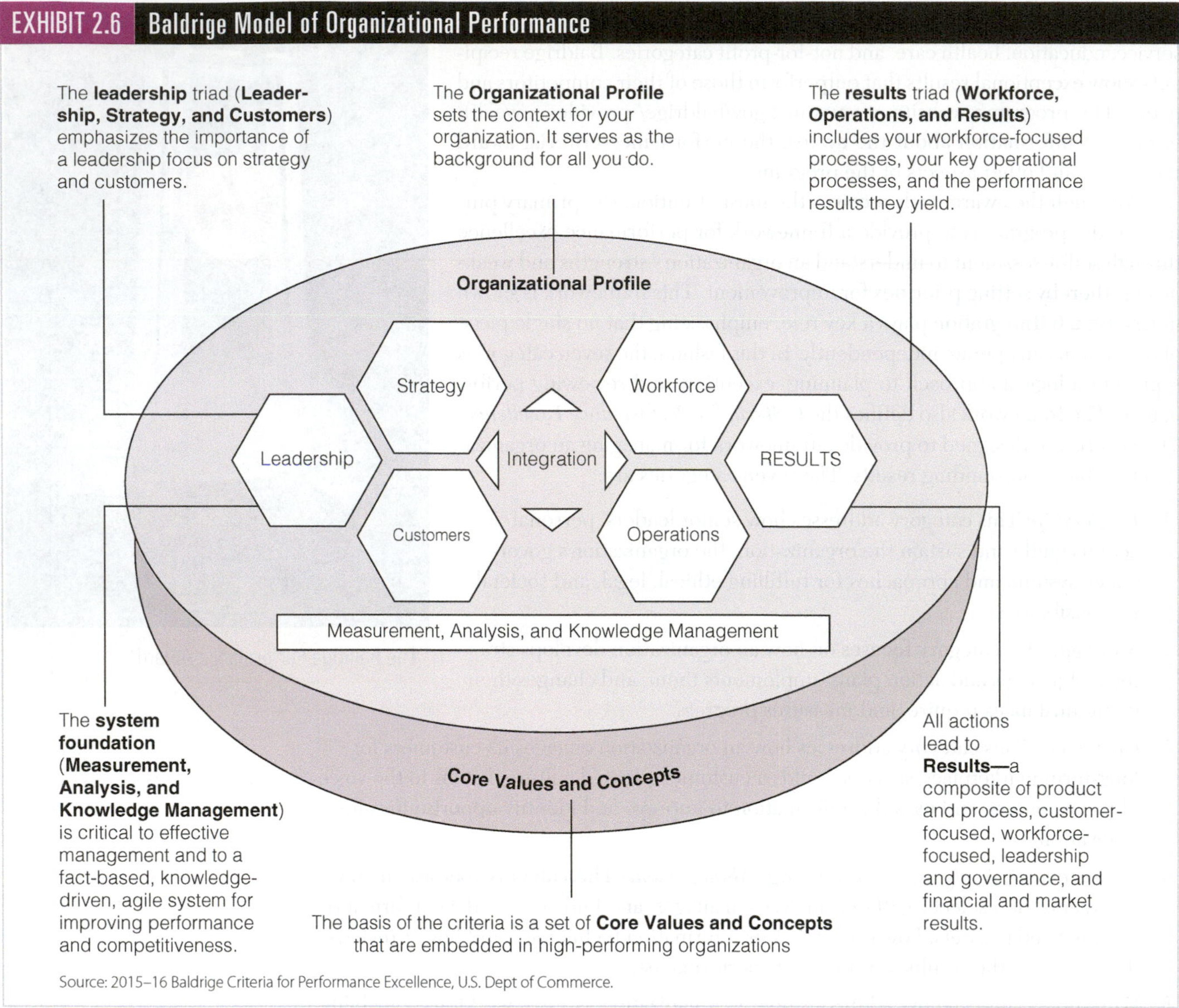

The **leadership** triad (**Leadership, Strategy, and Customers**) emphasizes the importance of a leadership focus on strategy and customers.
The **Organizational Profile** sets the context for your organization. It serves as the background for all you do.
The **results** triad (**Workforce, Operations, and Results**) includes your workforce-focused processes, your key operational processes, and the performance results they yield.
Organizational Profile
Strategy
Workforce
Leadership
Integration
RESULTS
Customers
Operations
Measurement, Analysis, and Knowledge Management
Core Values and Concepts
The **system foundation** (**Measurement, Analysis, and Knowledge Management**) is critical to effective management and to a fact-based, knowledge-driven, agile system for improving performance and competitiveness.
The basis of the criteria is a set of **Core Values and Concepts** that are embedded in high-performing organizations
All actions lead to **Results**—a composite of product and process, customer-focused, workforce-focused, leadership and governance, and financial and market results.

Source: 2015–16 Baldrige Criteria for Performance Excellence, U.S. Dept of Commerce.

2-4b The Balanced Scorecard

Robert Kaplan and David Norton of the Harvard Business School, in response to the limitations of traditional accounting measures, popularized the notion of the *balanced scorecard*, which was first developed at Analog Devices. Its purpose is "to translate strategy into measures that uniquely communicate your vision to the organization." Their version of the balanced scorecard, as shown in Exhibit 2.7, consists of four performance perspectives:

- *Financial Perspective*: Measures the ultimate value that the business provides to its shareholders. This includes profitability, revenue growth, stock price, cash flows, return on investment, economic value added (EVA), and shareholder value.
- *Customer Perspective*: Focuses on customer wants and needs and satisfaction as well as market share and growth in market share. This includes safety, service levels, satisfaction ratings, delivery reliability, number of cooperative customer–company design initiatives, value of a loyal customer, customer retention, percent of sale from new goods and services, and frequency of repeat business.
- *Innovation and Learning Perspective*: Directs attention to the basis of a future success—the organization's people and infrastructure. Key measures might include

Would You Fly on This Airline?

Imagine entering the cockpit of a modern jet airplane and seeing only a single instrument there. How would you feel about boarding the plane after the following conversation with the pilot?

Passenger: I'm surprised to see you operating the plane with only a single instrument. What does it measure?

Pilot: Airspeed. I'm really working on airspeed this flight.

Passenger: That's good. Airspeed certainly seems important. But what about altitude? Wouldn't an altimeter be helpful?

Pilot: I worked on altitude for the last few flights, and I've gotten pretty good at it. Now I have to concentrate on proper airspeed.

Passenger: But I notice you don't even have a fuel gauge. Wouldn't that be useful?

Pilot: You're right; fuel is significant, but I can't concentrate on doing too many things well at the same time. So on this flight I'm focusing on airspeed. Once I get to be excellent at airspeed, as well as altitude, I intend to concentrate on fuel consumption on the next set of flights.[8]

Concentrating on only one measure at a time is not a good idea, either for pilots or for modern organizations. World-class organizations normally use between 3 and 10 performance measures per process, depending on the complexity of goods and services, number of market segments, competitive pressures, and opportunities for failure.

EXHIBIT 2.7 The Balanced Scorecard Performance Categories and Linkages

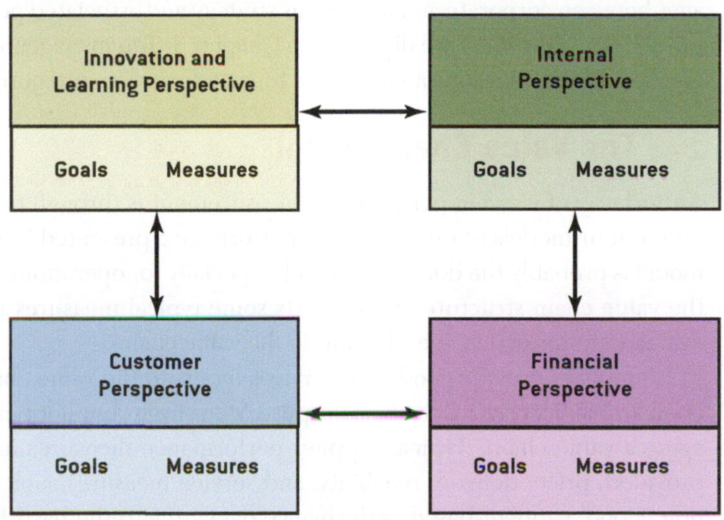

Source: Adapted from R. S. Kaplan and D. P. Norton, "The Balanced Scorecard—Measures That Drive Performance," *Harvard Business Review*, January–February 1992, p.72.

intellectual and research assets, time to develop new goods and services, number of improvement suggestions per employee, employee satisfaction, market innovation, training hours per employee, hiring process effectiveness, revenue per employee, and skills development.

- *Internal Perspective*: Focuses attention on the performance of the key internal processes that drive the business. This includes such measures as goods- and service-quality levels, productivity, flow time, design and demand flexibility, asset utilization, safety, environmental quality, rework, and cost.

PRO-TEC Coating Company: Keeping Performance in Balance

Martin Kucera/Shutterstock.com

PRO-TEC Coating Company is the industry leader in advanced high-strength steel coating and ultra-high-strength steel coating. PRO-TEC uses a balanced-scorecard (BSC) approach to help align the company's six key success factors (KSFs)—associate quality of life, customer service, technical innovation and product development, system reliability, good citizenship, and long-term viability—with its mission, vision, and values; its quality, safety, and environmental policies; company policy manuals; and procedure and work instruction manuals for its integrated Quality and Environmental System.

The BSC uses a stoplight color-coded designation (green, yellow, and red) that reflects the actual performance (good, marginal, or at-risk) against short-term targets. The at-risk BSC measures require action, and are reviewed at monthly plant management meetings. The BSC is also used for managing daily operations. For example, measures for safety and health, such as completion of housekeeping and quarterly safety audit items, mobile equipment inspections, and the weekly safety binder sign-off, are reviewed each Monday.[9]

The internal perspective is most meaningful to operations managers, as they deal with the day-to-day decisions that revolve around creating and delivering goods and services. The internal perspective includes all types of internal processes that we introduced in Chapter 1: value-creation processes, support processes, and general management or business processes.

The balanced scorecard is designed to be linked to an organization's strategy. The linkages between corporate and operations strategy and associated performance measures (called *competitive priorities*) are discussed in Chapter 3. Top management's job is to guide the organization, make trade-offs among these four performance categories, and set future directions.

2-4c The Value Chain Model

A third way of viewing performance measurement is through the value chain concept itself. Of the four models of organizational performance presented in this chapter, the value chain model is probably the dominant model, especially for operations managers. Exhibit 2.8 shows the value chain structure and suggests some typical measures that managers would use to evaluate performance at each point in the value chain.

Suppliers provide goods and services inputs to the value chain that are used in the creation and delivery of value chain outputs. Measuring supplier performance is critical to managing a value chain. Typical supplier performance measures include quality of the inputs provided, price, delivery reliability, and service measures such as rates of problem resolution. Good, supplier-based performance data are also the basis for cooperative partnerships between suppliers and their customers.

Operations managers have the primary responsibility to design and manage the processes and associated resources that create value for customers. Process data can reflect defect and error rates of intermediate operations, and also efficiency measures such as cost, flow time, delivery variability, productivity, schedule performance, equipment downtime, preventive maintenance activity, rates of problem resolution, energy and equipment efficiency, and raw material usage. For example, Motorola measures nearly every process in the company, including engineering design, order entry, manufacturing, human resources, purchasing, accounting, and marketing, for improvements in error rates and flow times. One of its key business objectives is to reduce total organizational flow time—the time from the point a customer expresses a need until the customer pays the company for the good or service.

EXHIBIT 2.8 Examples of Value Chain Performance Measurements

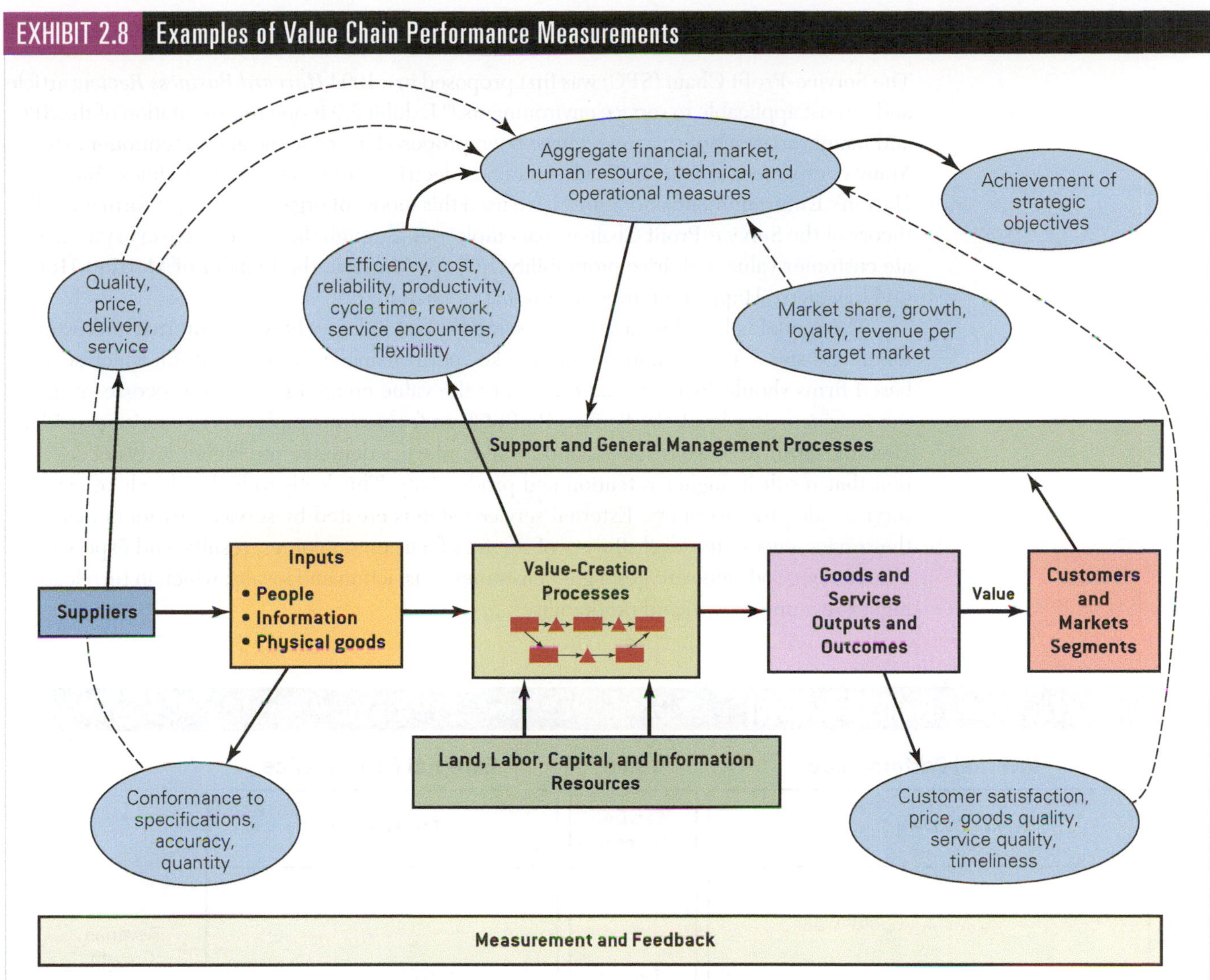

Measuring goods and services outputs and outcomes tell a company whether its processes are providing the levels of quality and service that customers expect. Organizations measure outputs and outcomes using measures such as unit cost, defects per million opportunities, and lead time. Through customer and market information, an organization learns how satisfied its customers and stakeholders are with its goods and services and performance and how best to configure the goods and services (i.e., customer benefit packages). Measures of customer satisfaction and retention reveal areas that need improvement and show whether changes actually result in improvement.

Measurement and feedback provide the means of coordinating the value chain's physical and information flows and for assessing whether the organization is achieving its strategic objectives. This is similar to the role of Category 4 (Measurement, Analysis, and Knowledge Management) in the Malcolm Baldrige framework. One objective of timely information sharing is to reduce or replace assets (employees, inventory, trucks, buildings, etc.) with smart and timely performance information. For example, General Electric sells lightbulbs in Walmart stores; these sales are recorded immediately at General Electric factories and production is scheduled to real-time sales data. Fewer resources are needed to achieve performance goals when "information replaces assets." That is, inventories are reduced, flow times are shorter, quality is better, and costs are lower.

2-4d The Service-Profit Chain

The Service-Profit Chain (SPC) was first proposed in a 1994 *Harvard Business Review* article and is most applicable to service environments.[10] Exhibit 2.9 is one representation of the SPC, and many variations of this model have been proposed in academic and practitioner articles. Many companies, such as Citibank, General Electric, Intuit, Southwest Airlines, Taco Bell, Harrah's Entertainment, and Xerox, have used this model of organizational performance. The theory of the Service-Profit Chain is that employees, through the service-delivery system, create customer value and drive profitability. As J. W. Marriott, the founder of Marriott Hotels, said long ago, "Happy employees create happy customers."

The model is based on a set of cause-and-effect linkages between internal and external measures, and in this fashion, defines the key performance measurements on which service-based firms should focus. Because much of the value created in service processes is at the service-encounter level, the Service-Profit Chain focuses on employees or service providers. Healthy, motivated, well-trained, and loyal employees demonstrate higher levels of satisfaction that result in higher retention and productivity. This leads to higher levels of external service value to customers. External service value is created by service providers mainly at the service-encounter level. Buyers of services focus on outcomes, results, and experiences. Ultimately, good value creates higher customer satisfaction and loyalty, which in turn leads to higher revenue growth and profitability.

EXHIBIT 2.9 The Service-Profit Chain Model

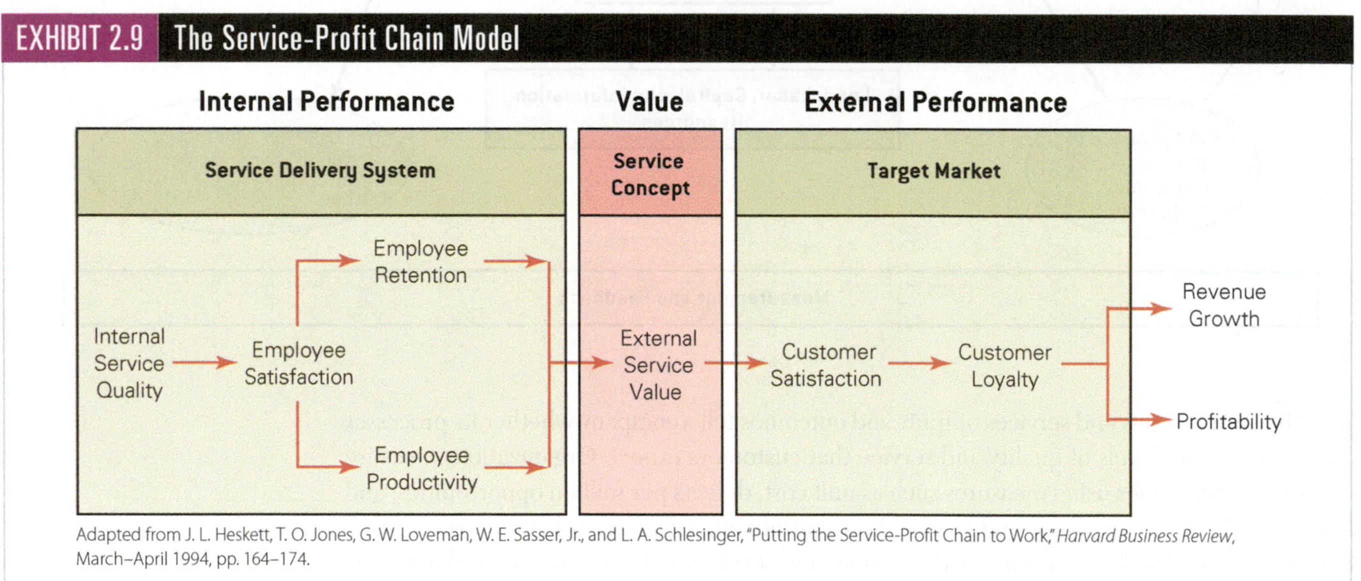

Adapted from J. L. Heskett, T. O. Jones, G. W. Loveman, W. E. Sasser, Jr., and L. A. Schlesinger, "Putting the Service-Profit Chain to Work," *Harvard Business Review*, March–April 1994, pp. 164–174.

CHAPTER 2 LEARNING OBJECTIVE SUMMARIES

2.1 **Describe the types of measures used for decision making.** Performance measures can be classified into several key categories:

- Financial
- Customer and market
- Quality
- Time
- Flexibility
- Innovation and learning
- Productivity and operational efficiency
- Sustainability

2.2 **Explain the use of analytics in OM and how internal and external measures are related.** Exhibit 2.2 summarizes key business analytics tools used in OM. These help to describe the behavior of production and service systems, predict performance, and prescribe the best courses of action. The quantitative modeling of cause-and-effect relationships between external and internal performance criteria is called Interlinking. Cause-and-effect linkages between key measures of performance often explain the impact of (internal) operational performance on external results, such as profitability, market share, or customer satisfaction. For example, how do goods- and service-quality improvements impact revenue growth? How do improvements in complaint handling affect customer retention? How do increases or decreases in processing time affect customer satisfaction? How do changes in customer satisfaction affect costs and revenues?

2.3 **Explain how to design a good performance measurement system.** Good performance measures are actionable. They should be meaningful to the user, timely, and reflect how the organization generates value to customers. Performance measures should support, not conflict with, customer requirements. IBM Rochester, for example, asks the following questions:

- Does the measurement support our mission?
- Will the measurement be used to manage change?
- Is it important to our customers?
- Is it effective in measuring performance?
- Is it effective in forecasting results?
- Is it easy to understand/simple?
- Are the data easy/cost-efficient to collect?
- Does the measurement have validity, integrity, and timeliness?
- Does the measure have an owner?

2.4 **Describe four models of organizational performance.** Four models of organizational performance—the Malcolm Baldrige Award framework, the balanced scorecard, the value chain model, and the service-profit chain—provide popular frameworks for thinking about designing, monitoring, and evaluating performance. The first two models provide more of a "big picture" of organizational performance, whereas the last two provide more detailed frameworks for operations managers. Exhibits 2.6–2.9 graphically illustrate these models.

KEY TERMS

- **Actionable measures**
- **Customer-satisfaction measurement system**
- **Descriptive statistics**
- **Flexibility**
- **Goods and service design flexibility**
- **Goods quality**
- **Innovation**
- **Interlinking**
- **Learning**
- **Measurement**
- **Operational efficiency**
- **Processing time**
- **Productivity**
- **Quality**
- **Queue time**
- **Service quality**
- **Service upsets (service failures)**
- **Statistics**
- **Triple bottom line (TBL or 3BL)**
- **Value of a loyal customer (VLC)**
- **Volume flexibility**
- **Wait time**

REVIEW QUESTIONS

2.1 1. Define measurement.

2.1 2. What are the eight performance measure categories for organizations?

2.1 3. What is a customer-satisfaction system?

2.1 4. Define goods quality and service quality.

2.1 5. What are five dimensions of service quality?

2.1 6. Define service upsets and give an example from personal experience.

2.1 7. The performance measure "time" relates to what two performance dimensions?

2.1 8. Define goods and service design flexibility and volume flexibility.

2.1 9. Define innovation and learning.

2.1 10. Define productivity and operational efficiency.

2.2 11. Define interlinking. Why is it important?

2.2 12. Define the value of a loyal customer. Why is it important?

2.2 13. How are the customer defection and customer retention rate related?

2.3 14. What are some of the questions IBM uses to evaluate performance measures?

2.3 15. Define actionable measures.

2.4 16. Explain the Baldrige Model of Organizational Performance.

2.4 17. What are the four performance categories of the balanced scorecard approach to performance measurement?

2.4 18. What are example performance metrics for suppliers, value-creation processes, and customers in the value chain model of organizational performance?

2.4 19. What is the primary theory of the service-profit chain model of organizational performance?

2.4 20. What are the implications of Marriott's quote "Happy employees create happy customers"? What does this mean for human resource management?

DISCUSSION QUESTIONS AND EXPERIENTIAL ACTIVITIES

2.1 21. What types of performance measurements might be used to evaluate a fraternity or student organization?

2.1 22. Select an organization you are familiar with or have an interest in and write a short two-page paper describing key performance metrics in that industry and firm using the format of Exhibit 2.1.

2.1 23. Interview managers at a local company to identify the key business measures (financial, market, supplier, employee, process, information, innovation, etc.) for that company. What quality indicators does that company measure? What cause-and-effect (interlinking) performance relationships would be of interest to the organization?

2.1 24. Research and write a short paper on how some organization applies the five dimensions of service quality.

2.2 25. Discuss some analytical or graphical approaches that organizations can use for analyzing performance data based on your experience and previous coursework.

2.3 26. Revenue or costs per passenger mile are two key performance measures in the airline industry. Research their use in this industry and prepare a one-page paper summarizing how they are used and why they are so important.

2.4 27. Under which perspective of the balanced scorecard would you classify each of the following measurements?

a. On-time delivery to customers
b. Time to develop the next generation of products
c. Manufacturing yield
d. Engineering efficiency
e. Quarterly sales growth
f. Percent of products that equal 70 percent of sales
g. Cash flow
h. Number of customer partnerships
i. Increase in market share
j. Unit cost of products

2.4 28. When the value of a loyal customer (VLC) market segment is high, should these customers be given premium goods and services for premium prices? If the VLC is low, should they be given less service? Explain.

COMPUTATIONAL PROBLEMS AND EXERCISES

These exercises require you to apply the formulas and methods described in the chapter. They should be solved manually.

2.1 29. Each day, a FedEx competitor processes approximately 70,000 shipments. Suppose that they use the same Service Quality Index as FedEx and identified the following numbers of errors during a 5-day week (see the "FedEx: Measuring Service Performance" box). These values are hypothetical and do not reflect any real company's actual performance.

Complaints reopened: 125
Damaged packages: 18
International: 102
Invoice adjustments: 282
Late pickup stops: 209
Lost packages: 2
Missed proof of delivery: 26
Right date late: 751
Traces: 115
Wrong day late: 15

Compute the Service Quality Indicator by finding the weighted sum of errors as a percentage of total shipments. How might such an index be used in other organizations such as a hotel or an automobile service facility?

2.1 30. Productivity measures for a manufacturing plant over a six-month period follow:

Month	Jan.	Feb.	Mar.	Apr.	May	June
Productivity	1.46	1.42	1.49	1.50	1.30	1.25

Using January as the base period, compute a productivity index for February to June, and comment on what those productivity indexes tell about the productivity trend.

2.1 31. A major airline is attempting to evaluate the effect of recent changes it has made in scheduling flights between New York City and Los Angeles. Data available are shown below:

	Number of Flights	Number of Passengers
Month prior to schedule change (January)	16	8,795
Month after schedule change (June)	27	15,653

Using January as the base period, compute a productivity index for January and June, and comment on what those productivity indexes tell about the productivity trend.

2.1 32. A hamburger factory produces 60,000 hamburgers each week. The equipment used costs $10,000 and will remain productive for four years. The labor cost per year is $13,500.

a. What is the productivity measure of "units of output per dollar of input" averaged over the four-year period?

b. We have the option of $13,000 equipment, with an operating life of five years. It would reduce labor costs to $11,000 per year. Should we consider purchasing this equipment (using productivity arguments alone)?

2.1 33. A computer software firm provides a $20' \times 30'$ office for its six systems analysts and plans to hire two additional analysts. To maintain a 100-square-foot working space per analyst, the firm's owner-manager is considering expansion. The cost of expansion is $40 per square foot with annual maintenance costs of $4 per square foot. The useful life of floor space is 20 years. By how much should employee productivity increase to justify the additional expenditure? The current salary of the systems analysts is $25,000.

2.1 34. A factory produces 10,000 desk staplers each week. The equipment used costs $50,000 and will remain productive for three years. The labor cost per year is $180,000.

a. What is the productivity measure of "units of output per dollar of input" averaged over the three-year period?

b. We have the option of buying $80,000 of new equipment, with an operating life of six years. It would reduce labor costs to $104,000 per year. Should we consider purchasing this equipment (using productivity arguments alone)?

2.1 35. A fast-food restaurant has a drive-through window and during peak lunch times can handle a maximum of 50 cars per hour with one person taking orders, assembling them, and acting as cashier. The average sale per order is $9.00. A proposal has been made to add two workers and divide the tasks among the three. One will take orders, the second will assemble them, and the third will act as cashier. With this system it is estimated that 70 cars per hour can be serviced. Use productivity arguments to recommend whether or not to change the current system.

2.1 36. The data shown below apply to the first two quarters of the current year. Using total-dollar measures of input and output, compare the total profit and productivity achieved for the two quarters. How does second-quarter productivity compare with the first-quarter productivity? Use partial-factor productivity to identify what might be done to improve productivity and profitability during the third quarter.

	First Quarter	Second Quarter
Unit selling price	$20.00	$21.00
Total units sold	10,000	8,500
Labor hours	9,000	7,750
Labor cost/hour	$10.00	$10.00
Material usage (lb)	5,000	4,500
Material cost/pound	$15.00	$15.50
Other costs	$20,000	$18,000

2.1 37. A manufacturing firm uses two measures of productivity:

a. Total sales/Total inputs
b. Total sales/Total labor inputs

Given the data for the last three years below, calculate the productivity ratios. How would you interpret the results? All figures are in dollars.

	Year 1	Year 2	Year 3
Sales	$110	$129	$124
Materials	62	73	71
Labor	28	33	28
Overhead	8	12	10

2.2 38. If the customer defection rate is 17.5 percent, what is the customer retention rate?

2.2 39. Estimate the value of a loyal customer of a loyal Volvo automobile owner? Assume the contribution margin is 0.32, the purchase price is $70,000, the repurchase frequency is every four years, and the customer defection rate is 30 percent.

2.2 40. What is the average value of a loyal customer (VLC) in a target market segment if the average purchase price is $70 per visit, the frequency of repurchase is every month, the contribution margin is 20%, and the average customer defection rate is 25%? If a continuous improvement goal is set of a 20% defection rate next year and 15% two years from now, what are the revised VLCs over their average buying life?

2.2 41. What is the average defection rate for grocery store shoppers in a local area of a large city if they spend $50 per visit, shop 52 weeks per year, the grocery store has a 16% gross contribution margin, and the value of a loyal customer is estimated at $2,000 per year?

2.2 42. What is the value of a loyal customer (VLC) in the small contractor target market segment who buys an electric drill on average every four years (or every 0.25 year) for $100, when the gross margin on the drill averages 50 percent, and the customer retention rate is 60 percent? What if the customer retention rate increases to 80 percent? What is a 1 percent change in market share worth to the manufacturer if it represents 100,000 customers? What do you conclude?

2.2 43. If a coffee shop's average transaction price is $4.00, their gross margin is 60 percent, the typical customer makes a purchase once a week or 52 weeks per year, and management estimates the value of a loyal customer over their buying life cycle as $520, what is the customer defection rate?

EXCEL-BASED PROBLEMS

For these problems, you may use Excel or the spreadsheet templates in MindTap to assist in your analysis.

2.2 44. A key hospital outcome measure of clinical performance is length of stay (LOS), that is, the number of days a patient is hospitalized. For patients at one hospital with acute myocardial infarction (heart attack), the length of stay over the past four years has consistently decreased. The hospital also has data for various treatment options such as the percentage of patients who received aspirin upon arrival and cardiac medication for Left Ventricular Systolic Dysfunction (LVSD). The data are shown below:

Year	Average LOS	Aspirin on arrival	LVSD medication
2007	4.35 days	95%	89%
2008	4.33 days	98%	93%
2009	4.12 days	99%	96%
2010	4.15 days	100%	98%

Illustrate the interlinking relationships by constructing scatter charts using Excel showing the LOS as a function of the other variables. What do these models tell you?

2.2 45. Customers call a call center to make room reservations for a small chain of 42 motels located throughout the southwestern part of the United States. Business analytics is used to determine how and if the following performance metrics are related: time by quarter, average time on hold (seconds) before a customer reaches a company customer service representative, percent of time the customer inquiry is solved the first time (called first pass quality) and customer satisfaction with the overall call center experience.

Quarter	Average Hold Time	Percent Solved First Time	Overall Customer Satisfaction Percent
Q1	22 seconds	89%	96%
Q2	34 seconds	80%	92%
Q3	44 seconds	78%	82%
Q5	67 seconds	85%	84%
Q6	38 seconds	87%	90%
Q7	70 seconds	76%	80%
Q8	86 seconds	67%	74%

Develop graphical interlinking models by constructing scatter charts using Excel showing the relationships between each pair of variables. What do results tell you?

2.2 46. Use the Excel template *VLC* to find the average value of a loyal customer (VLC) in a target market segment if the average purchase price is $75 per visit, the frequency of repurchase is six times per year, the contribution margin is 10 percent, and the average customer defection rate is 25 percent?

2.2 47. Using the base case data in question 46, use the Excel template *VLC* to analyze how the value of a loyal customer (VLC) will change if the average customer defection rate varies between 15 and 40 percent (in increments of 5 percent) and the frequency of repurchase varies between 3 and 9 times per year (in increments of 1 year). Sketch graphs (or use Excel charts) to illustrate the impact of these assumptions on the VLC.

2.2 48. What is the average defection rate for grocery store shoppers in a local area of a large city if they spend $45 per visit, shop 52 weeks per year, the grocery store has a 4 percent gross margin, and the value of a loyal customer is estimated at $3,500 per year? Use a trial-and-error approach with the Excel template *VLC* to find your answer.

2.2 49. What is a grocery store's contribution margin (CM) if the average purchase price is $86.55 per visit, the customer defection rate is 0.10, the VLC is $1,800, and 52 purchases are made per year? Use a trial-and-error approach with the Excel template *VLC* to find your answer.

2.2 50. Use the Excel template *VLC* to estimate the value of a loyal customer for a loyal Craftsman tool buyer. Assume the contribution margin is 0.25, the purchase price is $300 for a certain set of tools, and the repurchase frequency is every five years, and the customer defection rate is 10 percent. If the target market segment for this tool set is one million customers and this firm has a 27 percent market share, what is the VLC for this firm's target market?

2.2 51. A retail store sells a popular cosmetic called *Devine* and the store manager was given $100,000 by the corporate office to improve store performance any way she thinks best. The "base case" information is a price of $30 per bottle, a contribution margin of 0.50, a customer defection rate of 17 percent, and a repurchase frequency of three times a year. If these improvement funds could be used to (a) increase the contribution margin to 0.58 or (b) reduce the customer defection rate to 15 percent or (c) increase the repurchase frequency to four times per year, what is the best way to spend these improvement funds by answering the next two multiple choice questions? (*Assume all other variables remain at the base case level for each of the three improvement options.*)

Use the Excel template *VLC* to answer these questions and summarize your answers using the table below:

Price	Contribution Margin	Repurchase Frequency	Defection Rate	VLC in $
$30	0.50	3	17%	
$30	0.58	3	17%	
$30	0.50	3	15%	
$30	0.50	4	17%	

a. The value of a loyal customer (VLC) for improvement option (a) is _____?

b. The best way to use the $100,000 in improvement funds is Option _____?

2.2 52. The manager at Raphael's Four-Star Italian Restaurant wants to set the price of their premiere entrée. He estimates a loyal customer is worth $1,000. Based on survey data, the customer defection rate is 0.22, the repurchase frequency is once a month, and the restaurant's contribution margin is 18.5 percent. What is the price he should charge for the premiere entrée? Use the Excel template *VLC* to search for the solution.

2.2 53. A computer manufacturer currently has a 20 percent customer defection rate. Their accounting department estimates the incremental contribution to profit and overhead as 35 percent. Customers purchase computers every four years at an average cost of $1,200.00. In an effort to reduce the defection rate, the company is improving both the quality of its computers and its post-sale service. Use the Excel template *VLC* to determine the increase in the average value of a loyal customer if the defection rate drops to 5 percent.

Rapido Burrito

Rapido Burrito is a small, regional chain of quick service restaurants. Rather than wait in a cafeteria-style line, customers check boxes for their choice of ingredients, sauce, and so on paper menus at their table. The food is prepared quickly and then delivered to the tables.

Lately, one of the store managers has been hearing customer complaints, such as: "The tortillas are too thin"; "The food is not hot"; "Every time I get a burrito, it seems to be a different size"; and "I got the wrong ingredients on my burrito." Many complaints were submitted through the corporate website.

The district manager was most concerned with the comments about the consistency of size. One of the staff designed a customer survey using the questions in Exhibit 2.10, based on a 5-point Likert scale (5 = excellent, or strongly agree; 1 = poor or strongly disagree) for the first 10 questions. The last two questions were coded as a 1, 2, 3, or 4.

They administered the questionnaire to 25 random customers. The restaurant also gathered data on the weights of 50 samples of 3 burritos (a total of 150). Both the survey data and weight data are available on the Excel worksheet *Rapido Burrito Case Data* in MindTap.

Case Questions for Discussion:

1. What conclusions do you reach when you calculate descriptive statistics for the answers to each of the survey questions in the database?
2. If you average the responses to the first seven questions by customer, how closely are those averages correlated to the satisfaction score? Include a scatter chart in your analysis.
3. Analyze the data on burrito weights using descriptive statistical measures such as the mean and standard deviation, and tools such as a frequency distribution and a histogram. What do your results tell you about the consistency of the food servings?
4. What recommendations for decision making and improvement can you make to the store manager?

EXHIBIT 2.10 Customer Survey Questions

1. Was the menu easy to read?
2. Was the order prepared correctly?
3. Was the food tasty?
4. Was the food served hot?
5. Were employees courteous and polite?
6. Was the restaurant clean?
7. In your opinion, did you receive a good value for the price you paid?
8. What was your level of satisfaction?
9. How likely are you to dine with us again?
10. How likely are you to recommend us to your friends/family?
11. How often do you eat at Rapido Burrito? First time, less than once/month, one to three times a month, weekly?
12. What was the main ingredient in your burrito: chicken, beef, pork, or beans?

Greyhound Bank: Credit Card Division

Greyhound Bank operates in the United States and provides a full range of financial services for individuals and business. The credit card division is a profit center that has experienced a 10 percent annual growth rate over the last five years. These credit card services include producing and mailing the plastic credit cards to customers, preparing online and mailing monthly statements to customers, handling all customer requests such as stop payments and customer complaints, and preparation and distribution of summary online reports to all individual and corporate customers.

"Our internal operational measures seem to be good," Ms. Juanita Sutherland, the president of Greyhound's credit card division stated, "but the customer perceives our performance as poor based on marketing's recent customer survey. So, what's going on here? Can anyone at this meeting explain to me this mismatch between these two different sources of information? Is it an important problem or not?"

Mr. Luke C. Morris, the vice president of operations quickly responded, "Juanita, one reason there's a mismatch is that operations doesn't have a say in the customer survey's design or performance criteria. We don't ask the same questions or use the same criteria!"

"Wait a minute Luke. We often ask you operations folks for input into our customer survey design but the job usually gets shuttled to your newest MBA who doesn't have enough company knowledge to truly help us out," stated Mr. Bill Barlow, the corporate vice president of marketing, as he leaned forward on the conference room table.

"O.K.," Ms. Sutherland interjected, "I want you two to work on this issue and tell me in one week what to do." I've got another appointment so I must leave now but you two have got to work together and figure this thing out. I'm worried that we are losing customers!"

At a subsequent meeting between Mr. Morris and Mr. Barlow and their respective operations and marketing staffs, the following comments were made:

- "The trends in the marketing customer survey are helpful to everyone but the performance criteria simply do not match up well between marketing and operations."
- "Plastic card turnaround performance is very good based on the marketing survey data, but the wording of the customer survey questions on plastic card turnaround time is vague."
- "Operations people think they know what constitutes excellent service but how can they be sure?"
- "You'll never get marketing to let us help them design 'their' customer survey," said an angry operations supervisor. "Their marketing questions and what really happens are two different things."
- "We need a consistent numerical basis for knowing how well process performance matches up with external performance. My sample of data (see Exhibit 2.11) is a place to start."

EXHIBIT 2.11 Sample Internal and External Greyhound Credit Card Performance Data*

Month	Customer Satisfaction Percent (%)	New Applicant Processing Time (Days)	Plastic Production Turnaround Time (Days)
1	86.4	1.7	1.005
2	81.8	1.0	1.007
3	81.6	1.4	1.208
4	83.7	1.8	0.906
5	83.3	1.6	1.057
6	81.7	1.5	1.099
7	84.0	1.2	0.755
8	84.5	1.3	1.208
9	83.3	1.7	0.906
10	82.6	1.1	1.087
11	84.2	1.3	0.884
12	85.0	1.1	0.987
13	85.6	0.9	0.755
14	85.8	1.0	1.102
15	84.1	0.9	0.782

*These data are available in the Excel worksheet *Greyhound Case Data* in MindTap.

- "If your backroom operational performance measures really do the job, who cares about matching marketing and operations performance information. The backroom is a cost center, not a profit center!"

The meeting ended with a lot of arguing but not much progress. Both functional areas were protecting their "turf." How would you address Ms. Sutherland's questions?

Case Questions for Discussion:

1. What are the major problems facing the credit card division?
2. What steps are required to develop a good internal and external performance and information system?
3. How should internal and external performance data be related? Are these data related? What do charts and/or statistical data analysis tell you, if anything? (Use the data in Exhibit 2.11 to help answer these questions.)
4. Is the real service level what is measured internally or externally? Explain your reasoning.
5. What are your final recommendations?

Integrative Case: Hudson Jewelers

The Hudson Jewelers case study available in MindTap integrates material found in each chapter of this book.

Case Questions for Discussion:

1. What is the value of a loyal customer to Hudson Jewelers for a wealthy individual who visits Naples every February and buys jewelry for her extended family every other year? Assume the following:

Customer retention rate	=	80 percent
Contribution margin	=	0.55
Price per purchase	=	$200,000

2. Design an individual service plan for this "AAAA" customer.

Operations Strategy 3

Any change in strategic direction typically has significant consequences for the entire value chain and for operations.

Brian A Jackson/Shutterstock.com

LEARNING OBJECTIVES

After studying this chapter, you should be able to:

3-1 Explain how organizations seek to gain competitive advantage.

3-2 Explain approaches for understanding customer wants and needs.

3-3 Describe how customers evaluate goods and services.

3-4 Explain the five key competitive priorities.

3-5 Explain the role of OM, sustainability, and operations in strategic planning.

3-6 Describe Hill's framework for operations strategy.

Over the past two decades, the transformation to a digital society has caused many companies to redefine their strategy. Some have had to completely reinvent themselves. For example, the demise of film cameras caused Kodak to change to digital cameras. However, with stiff competition from Sony, Samsung, and others, Kodak ended up filing for Chapter 11 bankruptcy protection and has changed its strategy to focus on large commercial inkjet printers, digital printing presses, workflow software, and package printing. Likewise, Xerox, long known for its paper copy machines, has reinvented itself and branched out into new but risky business services, including commercial information technology, document outsourcing, finance, human resources (HR), transportation, and health care.

Changing a corporate strategy has many implications for operations and the entire value chain. Facilities may have to be reconfigured or new ones built; new technology may have to be acquired; new processes and jobs must be designed; and so on. Looking back at Exhibit 1.7, we also see that all aspects of preproduction services, production processes, and postproduction services will be affected.

WHAT DO YOU THINK?

How do you see the digital society affecting education? For example, what implications are emerging technologies, such as e-books and distance learning, having? Can you think of others?

3-1 Gaining Competitive Advantage

Competitive advantage *denotes a firm's ability to achieve market and financial superiority over its competitors.* In the long run, a sustainable competitive advantage provides above-average performance and is essential to the survival of the business. Creating a competitive advantage requires a fundamental understanding of two things. First, management must understand customer needs and expectations—and how the value chain can best meet these through the design and delivery of attractive customer benefit packages. Second, management must build and leverage operational capabilities to support desired competitive priorities.

Every organization has a myriad of choices in deciding where to focus its efforts—for example, on low cost, high quality, quick response, or flexibility and customization—and in designing its operations to support its chosen strategy. The opening scenario suggests that organizations have many strategic choices in designing and operating their domestic and global value chains. These choices should be driven by current and emerging customer needs and expectations. In particular, what happens in operations—on the front lines and on the factory floor—must support the strategic direction the firm has chosen.

Any change in a firm's customer benefit package, targeted markets, or strategic direction typically has significant consequences for the entire value chain and for operations.

Although it may be difficult to change the *structure* of the value chain, operations managers have considerable freedom in determining what components of the value chain to emphasize, in selecting technology and processes, in making human resource policy choices, and in making other relevant decisions to support the firm's strategic emphasis.

3-2 Understanding Customer Wants and Needs

Because the fundamental purpose of an organization is to provide goods and services of value to customers, it is important to first understand customer desires and also to understand how customers evaluate goods and services. However, a company usually cannot satisfy all customers with the same goods and services. Often, customers must be segmented into several natural groups, each with unique wants and needs. These segments might be based on buying behavior, geography, demographics, sales volume, profitability, or expected levels of service. By understanding differences among such segments, a company can design the most appropriate customer benefit packages, competitive strategies, and processes to create the goods and services to meet the unique needs of each segment.

To correctly identify what customers expect requires being "close to the customer." There are many ways to do this, such as having employees visit and talk to customers, having managers talk to customers, and doing formal marketing research. Marriott Corporation, for example, requires top managers to annually work a full day or more in the hotels as bellhops, waiters, bartenders, front-desk service providers, and so on, to gain a true understanding of customer wants and needs, and the types of issues that their hotel service providers must face in serving the customer. Good marketing research includes such techniques as focus groups, salesperson and employee feedback, complaint analysis, on-the-spot interviews with customers, videotaped service encounters, mystery shoppers, telephone hotlines, Internet monitoring, and customer surveys.

Basic customer expectations are generally considered the minimum performance level required to stay in business and are often called **order qualifiers**. For example, a radio and driver-side air bag are generally expected by all customers for an automobile. In the highly competitive pizza business, efficient delivery would be considered an order qualifier. However, the unexpected features that surprise, entertain, and delight customers by going beyond the expected often make the difference in closing a sale; these are called order winners. **Order winners** *are goods and service features and performance characteristics that differentiate one customer benefit package from another and win the customer's business*. Collision avoidance systems or a voice-activated music system in an automobile, for example, Papa John's Pizza focused on "better ingredients, better pizza" as the order winner to differentiate the business from the competitors. Over time, however, order winners eventually become order qualifiers as customers begin to expect them. Thus, to stay competitive, companies must continually innovate and improve their customer benefit packages.

3-3 Evaluating Goods and Services

Research suggests that customers use three types of attributes in evaluating the quality of goods and services: search, experience, and credence.[1] **Search attributes** *are those that a customer can determine prior to purchasing the goods and/or services*. These attributes include things like color, price, freshness, style, fit, feel, hardness, and smell. **Experience attributes** *are those that can be discerned only after purchase or during consumption or use*. Examples of these attributes are friendliness, taste, wearability, safety, fun, and customer satisfaction. **Credence attributes** *are any aspects of a good or service that the customer must believe in but cannot personally evaluate even after purchase and consumption*. Examples include the expertise of a surgeon or mechanic, the knowledge of a tax advisor, or the accuracy of tax preparation software.

This classification has several important implications for operations. For example, the most important search and experience attributes should be evaluated during design, measured during manufacturing, and drive key operational controls to ensure that they are built into the good with high quality. Credence attributes stem from the nature of services, the design of the service system, and the training and expertise of the service providers.

These three evaluation criteria form an evaluation continuum from easy to difficult, as shown in Exhibit 3.1. This model suggests that goods are easier to evaluate than services and that goods are high in search qualities, whereas services are high in experience and credence attributes. Of course, goods and services are usually combined and configured in unique ways, making for an even more complex customer evaluation process. Customers evaluate services in ways that are often different from goods. A few ways are summarized below along with significant issues that affect operations.

- Customers seek and rely more on information from personal sources than from non-personal sources when evaluating services prior to purchase. Operations must ensure that accurate information is available and that experiences with prior services and service providers result in positive experiences and customer satisfaction.
- Customers perceive greater risks when buying services than when buying goods. Because services are intangible, customers cannot look at or touch them prior to the

Listen to Your Customers—Creatively!

Rawpixel.com/Shutterstock.com

At IDEO, one of the world's leading design firms (it designed Apple's first mouse and stand-up toothpaste tubes as just two examples), design doesn't begin with a far-out concept or a cool drawing. It begins with a deep understanding of the people who might use whatever product or service eventually emerges from its work, drawing from anthropology, psychology, biomechanics, and other disciplines. When former Disney executive Paul Pressler assumed the CEO position at Gap, he met with each of Gap's top 50 executives, asking them such standard questions as "What about Gap do you want to preserve and why?," "What about Gap do you want to change and why?," and so on. But he also added one of his own: "What is your most important tool for figuring out what the consumer wants?" Some companies use unconventional and innovative approaches to understand customers. Texas Instruments created a simulated classroom to understand how mathematics teachers use calculators; and a manager at Levi Strauss used to talk with teens who were lined up to buy rock concert tickets. The president of Chick-fil-A spends at least one day each year behind the counter, as do all of the company's employees, and has camped out overnight with customers at store openings. At Whirlpool, when customers rate a competitor's product higher in satisfaction surveys, engineers take it apart to find out why. The company also has hundreds of consumers fiddle with computer-simulated products while engineers record the users' reactions on videotape.[2]

purchase decision. They experience the service only when they actually go through the process. This is why many are hesitant to use online banking or bill paying.

Dissatisfaction with services is often the result of customers' inability to properly perform or coproduce their part of the service. A wrong order placed on the Internet can be the result of customer error despite all efforts on the part of the company to provide clear instructions. The

EXHIBIT 3.1 How Customers Evaluate Goods and Services

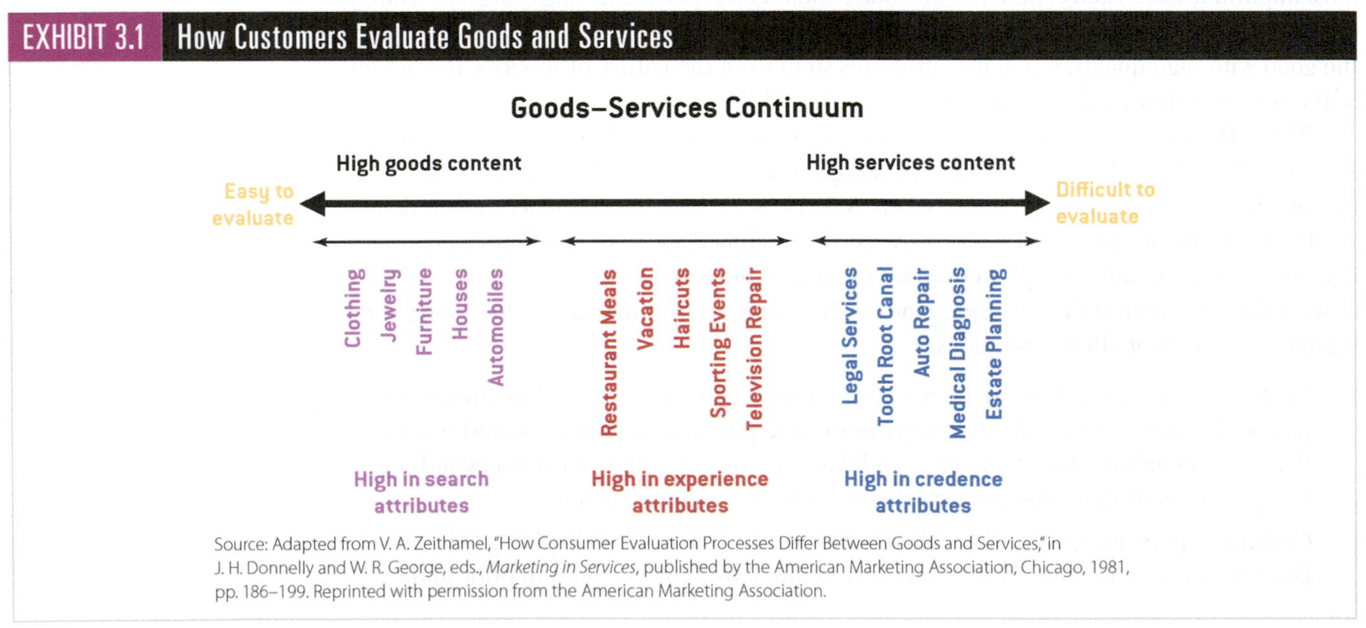

Source: Adapted from V. A. Zeithamel, "How Consumer Evaluation Processes Differ Between Goods and Services," in J. H. Donnelly and W. R. George, eds., *Marketing in Services*, published by the American Marketing Association, Chicago, 1981, pp. 186–199. Reprinted with permission from the American Marketing Association.

design of services must be sensitive to the need to educate customers on their role in the service process.

These insights help to explain why it is more difficult to design services and service processes than goods and manufacturing operations.

General Electric discovered that design determines 75 percent of its manufacturing costs.

3-4 Competitive Priorities

Every organization is concerned with building and sustaining a competitive advantage in its markets. A strong competitive advantage is driven by customer needs and aligns the organization's resources with its business opportunities. A strong competitive advantage is difficult to copy, often because of a firm's culture, habits, or sunk costs. Competitive advantage can be achieved in different ways such as outperforming competitors on price or quality, responding quickly to changing customer needs in designing goods and services, or providing rapid design or delivery.

Competitive priorities *represent the strategic emphasis that a firm places on certain performance measures and operational capabilities within a value chain.* Understanding competitive priorities and their relationships with customer benefit packages provides a basis for designing the value and supply chains that create and deliver goods and services. In general, organizations can compete on five key competitive priorities:

1. Cost
2. Quality
3. Time
4. Flexibility
5. Innovation

All of these competitive priorities are vital to success. For example, no firm today can sacrifice quality simply to reduce costs, or emphasize flexibility to the extent that it would make its goods and services unaffordable. However, organizations generally make trade-offs among these competitive priorities and focus their efforts along one or two key dimensions. For example, Amazon competes primarily on time, cost, and flexibility. Apple, on the other hand, competes on quality and innovation.

3-4a Cost

Many firms, such as Walmart, gain competitive advantage by establishing themselves as the low-cost leader in an industry. These firms achieve their competitive advantage through low prices. They do this through high volumes and the efficient design and operation of their supply chain. Although prices are generally set outside the realm of operations, low prices cannot be achieved without strict attention to cost and the design and management of operations.

General Electric, for example, discovered that design determines 75 percent of its manufacturing costs. Costs accumulate through the value chain, and include the costs of raw materials and purchased parts, direct manufacturing cost, distribution, post-sale services, and all supporting processes. Through good design and by chipping away at costs, operations managers help to support a firm's strategy to be a low-price leader. They emphasize achieving economies of scale and finding cost advantages from all sources in the value chain.

Southwest Airlines: Competing with Low Cost

Carlos Yudica/Shutterstock.com

The only major U.S. airline that has been continuously profitable over the last several decades is Southwest Airlines. Other airlines have had to collectively reduce costs by $18.6 billion, or 29 percent of their total operating expenses, to operate at the same level (cost per mile) as Southwest. The high-cost airlines such as United and American face enormous pressure from low-fare carriers such as Southwest Airlines. A long-time industry consultant, stated "The industry really is at a point where survival is in question." In recent years, airlines have reduced capacity, cut routes, and increased fees for peripheral services like baggage and food. We have also seen mergers, such as between Delta and Northwest and between United and Continental, to reduce system-wide costs.[3]

Low cost can result from high productivity and high-capacity utilization. More important, improvements in quality lead to improvements in productivity, which in turn lead to lower costs. Thus, a strategy of continuous improvement is essential to achieve a low-cost competitive advantage.

3-4b Quality

The role of quality in achieving competitive advantage was demonstrated by several research studies.[4] Researchers have found that:

- Businesses offering premium-quality goods usually have large market shares and were early entrants into their markets.
- Quality is positively and significantly related to a higher return on investment for almost all kinds of market situations.
- A strategy of quality improvement usually leads to increased market share, but at a cost in terms of reduced short-run profitability.
- Producers of high-quality goods can usually charge premium prices.

Exhibit 3.2 summarizes the impact of quality on profitability. The value of a good or service in the marketplace is influenced by the quality of its design. Improvements in performance, features, and reliability will differentiate the good or service from its competitors, improve a firm's quality reputation, and improve the perceived value of the customer benefit package. This allows the company to command higher prices and achieve an increased market share. This, in turn, leads to increased revenues that offset the added costs of improved design. Improved conformance in production leads to lower manufacturing and service costs through savings in rework, scrap, and warranty expenses. The net effect of improved quality of design and conformance is increased profits.

In many industries, strategies often lead to trade-offs between quality and cost; some company strategies sacrifice quality in order to develop a low-cost advantage. Such has been the case with new automobile start-ups, especially with Hyundai Motor Co. However, goods quality has evolved over the years and now is generally considered to be an order qualifier.

Operations managers deal with quality issues on a daily basis; these include ensuring that goods are produced defect-free or that service is delivered flawlessly. In the long run, it is the design of goods and service processes that ultimately defines the quality of outputs and outcomes.

Time reductions often drive simultaneous improvements in quality, cost, and productivity.

3-4c Time

Mike Flippo/Shutterstock.com

In today's society, time is perhaps the most important source of competitive advantage. Customers demand quick response, short waiting times, and consistency in performance. Many firms, such as CNN, FedEx, and Walmart, know how to use time as a competitive weapon to create and deliver superior goods and services.

Speeding up processes in supply chains improves customer response. Deliveries can be made faster, and more often on time. However, time reductions can only be accomplished by streamlining and simplifying processes to eliminate non-value-added steps such as rework and waiting time. This forces improvements in quality by reducing the opportunity for mistakes and errors. By reducing non-value-added steps, costs are reduced as well. Thus, time reductions often drive simultaneous improvements in quality, cost, and productivity. Designing processes and using technology efficiently to improve speed and time reliability are some of the most important activities for operations managers.

3-4d Flexibility

Success in globally competitive markets requires both design and demand flexibility. In the automobile industry, for example, new models are constantly being developed. Companies that can exploit flexibility by building several different vehicles on the same assembly line at one time, enabling them to switch output as demand shifts, will be able to sell profitably at lower volumes.

EXHIBIT 3.2 Interlinking Model of Quality and Profitability

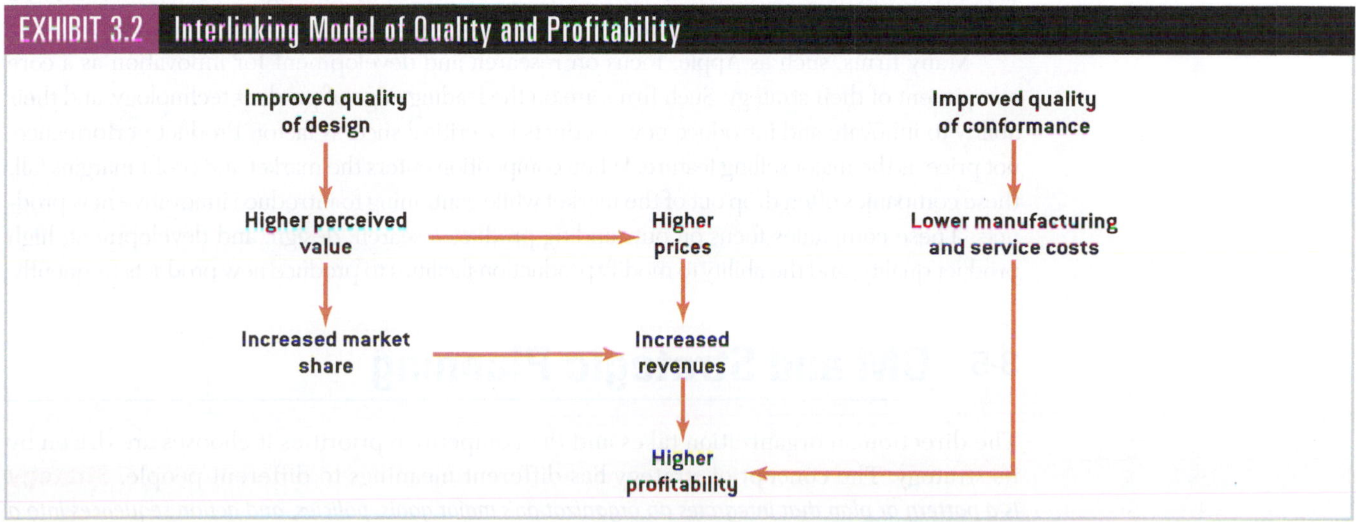

Trade-Offs Among Competitive Priorities

As fast-food menus get more complex and complaints about inaccurate orders increase, the amount of time customers spend waiting in line for their food is increasing. The average amount of time the typical consumer spends waiting in a drive-thru line jumped nearly 40 seconds in one year—to 219.97 seconds in 2014 from 180.83 seconds in 2013. While speed has been a competitive priority, the trend toward healthier items such as Cantina bowls at Taco Bell or fruit smoothies at McDonald's, require extra time to make and inspect. At the same time, fast-food chains are working harder to keep high levels of order accuracy.[6]

Flexibility is manifest in mass-customization strategies that are becoming increasingly prevalent today. **Mass customization** *is being able to make whatever goods and services the customer wants, at any volume, at any time for anybody, and for a global organization, from any place in the world.*[5] Some examples include Sign-tic company signs that are uniquely designed for each customer from a standard base sign structure; business consulting; Levi's jeans that are cut to exact measurements; personal Web pages; estate planning; Motorola pagers customized in different colors, sizes, and shapes; personal weight-training programs; and modular furniture that customers can configure to their unique needs and tastes. Customer involvement might occur at the design (as in the case of custom signs), fabrication (Levi's jeans), assembly (Motorola pagers), or postproduction (customer-assembled modular furniture) stages of the value chain. Mass customization requires companies to align their activities around differentiated customer segments and design goods, services, and operations around flexibility.

3-4e Innovation

Innovation *is the discovery and practical application or commercialization of a device, method, or idea that differs from existing norms.* Over the years, innovations in goods (such as telephones, automobiles, computers, optical fiber, satellites, and cell phones) and services (self-service, all-suite hotels, health maintenance organizations, and Internet banking) have improved the overall quality of life. Within business organizations, innovations in manufacturing equipment (computer-aided design, robots and automation, and smart tags) and management practices (customer satisfaction surveys, quantitative decision models, and the Malcolm Baldrige criteria) have allowed organizations to become more efficient and better meet customers' needs.

Many firms, such as Apple, focus on research and development for innovation as a core component of their strategy. Such firms are on the leading edge of product technology, and their ability to innovate and introduce new products is a critical success factor. Product performance, not price, is the major selling feature. When competition enters the market and profit margins fall, these companies often drop out of the market while continuing to introduce innovative new products. These companies focus on outstanding product research, design, and development; high product quality; and the ability to modify production facilities to produce new products frequently.

3-5 OM and Strategic Planning

The direction an organization takes and the competitive priorities it chooses are driven by its strategy. The concept of strategy has different meanings to different people. **Strategy** *is a pattern or plan that integrates an organization's major goals, policies, and action sequences into a cohesive whole.*[7]

Strategies Aren't Always Successful

In the early 1990s, Walmart embarked on a strategy that dictated that a third of new growth would come from abroad. Walmart's first store outside the United States was a Sam's Club that opened in Mexico City in 1991. Mexico would go on to become the company's most successful international market, followed by Canada, where it bought a struggling chain of stores in 1994 and turned it around. But as the company pursued more acquisitions to hit its aggressive targets, criticism followed. "It was growth for growth's sake," says Yarbrough. To some, the deals seemed more opportunistic than deliberate. Says former Walmart executive Bendel, "It's a little bit of an overstatement to say they had an international strategy—other than acquiring businesses in new markets."

As Walmart expanded in Germany in 1998, they learned a brutal lesson. Walmart insisted on bagging groceries for customers, which in Germany signaled a higher-end shopping experience and eroded Walmart's value proposition. Clerks were required to smile at customers, which was not socially acceptable in the country, Germans had trouble pronouncing the company's name, and the company clashed with unions. Eventually, they pulled out in 2006.[8]

Basically, a strategy is the approach by which an organization seeks to develop the capabilities required for achieving its competitive advantage. Effective strategies develop around a few key competitive priorities such as low cost or fast service time, which provide a focus for the entire organization and exploit an organization's **core competencies,** *which are the strengths that are unique to that organization*. Such strengths might be a particularly skilled or creative workforce, customer relationship management, clever bundling of goods and services, strong supply chain networks, extraordinary service, green goods and services, marketing expertise, or the ability to rapidly develop new products or change production output rates.

SOLVED PROBLEM 3.1

Define the customer benefit package (CBP) for a health club, recreation center, or gymnasium you frequent. (Check out the website of your favorite club, center, or gym for more information.) Use this information to help describe the organization's strategic mission, strategy, competitive priorities, and how it wins customers.

One example is depicted below.

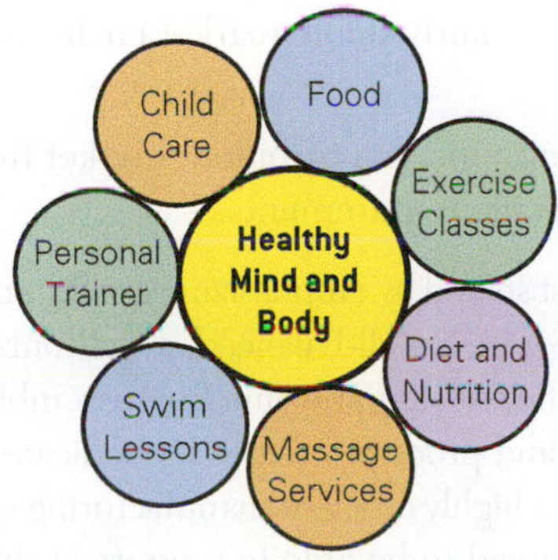

Mission: The mission of our health club is to offer many pathways to a healthy living style and body.
Strategy: We strive to provide our customers with superior:

- ways to improve and maintain the health and well-being of the body and mind
- friendly, professional staff that care about them
- clean facilities, equipment, uniforms, parking lot, food service, and the like
- customer convenience (location, food, communication, schedules, etc.)

Competitive #1 Priority: many pathways to healthy living and a healthy body (design flexibility); #2 Priority: friendly, professional staff and service encounters (service quality); #3 Priority: super clean (goods, facility, and environmental quality); #4 Priority: customer convenience in all respects (time); and #5 Priority: price (cost).
How to win customers? Providing a full-service health club with superior service, staff, and facilities. (Although you would not see this in company literature, this health club provides premium service at premium prices.)
Remember that each primary or peripheral good or service in the customer benefit package requires a process to create and deliver it to customers, and therefore OM skills are needed.

Strategic planning is the process of determining long-term goals, policies, and plans for an organization. The objective of strategic planning is to build a position that is so strong in selected ways that the organization can achieve its goals despite unforeseeable external forces that may arise. Strategy is the result of a series of hierarchical decisions about goals, directions, and resources; thus, most large organizations have three levels of strategy: corporate, business, and functional. At the top level, *corporate strategy* is necessary to define the businesses in which the corporation will participate and develop plans for the acquisition and allocation of resources among those businesses. The businesses in which the firm will participate are often called strategic business units (SBUs) and are usually defined as families of goods or services having similar characteristics or methods of creation. For small organizations, the corporate and business strategies frequently are the same.

The second level of strategy is generally called *business strategy* and defines the focus for SBUs. The major decisions involve which markets to pursue and how best to compete in those markets—that is, which competitive priorities the firm should pursue.

Finally, the third level of strategy is *functional strategy*, the means by which business strategies are accomplished. A functional strategy is the set of decisions that each functional area (marketing, finance, operations, research and development, engineering, etc.) develops to support its particular business strategy.

Our particular focus will be on *operations strategy*—how an organization's processes are designed and organized to produce the type of goods and services to support the corporate and business strategies.

3-5a Operations Strategy

An ***operations strategy*** *is the set of decisions across the value chain that supports the implementation of higher-level business strategies*. It defines how an organization will execute its chosen business strategies. Developing an operations strategy involves translating competitive priorities into operational capabilities by making a variety of choices and trade-offs for design and operating decisions. That is, operating decisions must be aligned with achieving the desired competitive priorities. For example, Progressive automobile insurance has developed a competitive advantage around superior customer service. To accomplish this, its operating decisions have included on-the-spot claims processing at accident sites; "Total Loss Concierge" service to help customers with unrepairable vehicles get a replacement vehicle; and the industry's first Web 2.0 site, with easier navigation, customization, and video content.

To illustrate how operations strategy can support competitive priorities, consider two types of business strategies for a manufacturer:

1. Produce a well-defined set of products in a fairly stable market environment as a low-cost leader.
2. Provide high product variety and customization in a turbulent market that requires innovative designs to meet customer-specific requirements.

In the first situation, the firm would be best served by emphasizing quality and cost reduction in their make-to-stock strategy. This would require a well-balanced, synchronized supply chain approach with strong supplier involvement, efficient assembly line final assembly processes, and high work standardization. Some equipment and processes might be dedicated to a particular product line or family of products. In this case, a highly efficient manufacturing system is needed.

In the second situation, the firm would need to be able to operate at different levels of production volume while also achieving high quality and flexibility. An operations strategy based on mass customization would be appropriate.

Product design would require constant innovation and shorter development cycles. Operations would need to be highly flexible in a make-to-order environment, producing batches of unique, customer-specified orders in low to moderate volumes, and using employees with high skill levels and diverse capabilities.

Operations and supply-chain strategy for service businesses is somewhat similar to manufacturers but differs in seven unique ways, as described in Chapter 1. In Section 3.6a, we discuss how operations strategy is reflected at McDonald's to achieve its competitive priorities.

How operations are designed and implemented can have a dramatic effect on business performance and achievement of the strategy. Therefore, operations require close coordination with functional strategies in other areas of the firm such as marketing and finance.

3-5b Sustainability and Operations Strategy

Sustainability is defined in previous chapters using three dimensions—environmental, social, and economic sustainability. Stakeholders such as the community, green advocacy groups, and the government drive environmental sustainability. Social sustainability is driven by ethics and human ideals of protecting the planet and its people for the well-being of future generations. Economic sustainability is driven by shareholders such as pension funds and insurance companies. Therefore, sustainability is an organizational strategy—it is broader than a competitive priority. Sustainability requires major changes in the culture of the organization (see box on General Electric).

> Sustainability is an organizational strategy—it is broader than a competitive priority.

Companies such as Apple, Kaiser Permanente, and Nike view sustainability as a corporate strategy. A majority of global consumers believe that it is their responsibility to contribute to a better environment and would pay more for brands that support this aim. Likewise, retailers and manufacturers are demanding greener products and supply chains. In 2007, Walmart Stores Inc. announced that it would transition toward selling only concentrated laundry detergents, which

New Strategies for Environmental Sustainability

Many durable products such as cell phones, televisions, and refrigerators contain hazardous materials and cannot be easily reused or recycled. As a result, organizations need to rethink strategically the environmental challenges that result from obsolete durable goods. Cell phones, for example, become obsolete quickly as a result of manufacturers making rapid improvements in design, and service providers offering new incentives. Some new strategies that have been suggested include:

- Creating better designs that focus on ease of disassembly and lower costs for refurbishing and recycling. This might include modular designs that make it easier to reuse parts than to recycle them, or to recover valuable materials more easily.
- Incorporating refurbishing and recycling activities into manufacturers' value chains. As many as 130 million phones are retired each year, with significant waste and environmental implications.
- Creating more secondary markets for refurbished phones. This can increase profits by enticing users of voice-only phones to upgrade to data plans if the price of the phones can be reduced.
- Developing new processes to collect and refurbish old phones. For example, ReCellular Inc. has partnered with Verizon, Motorola, Walmart, and others, but still it only captures 5 percent of retired phones, suggesting that the cell phone value chain has not matured.[9]

Bakalusha/Shutterstock.com

use much less water and therefore require less packaging and space for transport and storage. Every major supplier in the detergent industry was involved. Government actions are also driving these initiatives. The 2009 U.S. stimulus package earmarked $70 billion for the development of renewable and efficient energy technologies and manufacturing. The European Union has set targets for reducing emissions to 20 percent of 1990 levels by 2020.

Companies that have embraced sustainability pursue this strategy throughout their operations. For example, computer maker Dell Inc. has announced that it is committed to becoming "the greenest technology company on the planet." Such a strategy often requires considerable innovation in value chains, operations design, and day-to-day management. For example, Dell launched a program called Design for the Environment that seeks to minimize adverse impacts on the environment by controlling raw material acquisition, manufacturing processes, and distribution programs while linking green policies with consumer use and disposal. This framework encourages Dell's product designers to consider the full product life cycle, and it provides them with a platform for collaborating with suppliers, supply chain experts, and external recycling experts and other downstream partners to help them fully understand the environmental implications of their design decisions.[10]

Companies are also paying closer attention to ethical issues of outsourcing, particularly the human resource practices of off-shore suppliers, which may include unreasonable work hours or unsafe working conditions. Such issues are more difficult to monitor when control is relinquished to an off-shore manufacturer.

3-5c Global Supply Chains and Operations Strategy

Although not every organization operates in the global business environment, modern technology and distribution have made it feasible and attractive for both large and small companies to develop supply chains that span international boundaries. A **multinational enterprise** *is an organization that sources, markets, and produces its goods and services in several countries to minimize costs, and to maximize profit, customer satisfaction, and social welfare.* Examples of multinational enterprises include British Petroleum, General Electric, United Parcel Service, Siemens, Procter & Gamble, Toyota, and the International Red Cross. Their value chains provide the capability to source, market, create, and deliver their goods and services to customers worldwide. Multinational enterprises operate complex supply chains that challenge operations managers. In today's global business environment, good supply chain design can lead to major reductions in total supply chain costs and improvements in customer response time. (In Chapters 6 and 13, we provide more detail on global supply chain decisions, purchasing, sourcing, and global logistics.)

One operations strategy question that multinational firms must answer is "What is our supply chain strategy to meet slower growth in industrialized countries and more rapid growth in emerging economies?" For example, Harley-Davidson (HD) has rewritten its corporate and operations strategy, which drives changes in business and functional units, and process design. HD has a long-term strategy to grow their international business to 50 percent of their total annual sales volume by the late 2027. Sales had been declining since it peaked in 2006. HD already has motorcycle assembly plants in countries like India, but recently announced it was closing its Kansas City factory and moving work to another plant in York, New York and a new factory in Thailand. Asia is a fast-growing market, but high tariffs have reduced sales. Such decisions are controversial; however, HD sees no other viable option. Therefore, its supply chains are becoming more global and its operations strategy must change accordingly.

One area that requires change is HD's Supplier Code of Conduct. It must now operate in places like Asia, China, Europe, India, and Latin America. HDs strategy is to manufacture smaller bikes to increased foreign sales. It also wants to build more electric-powered bikes. These product design changes fit the new markets. To do this, their operations strategy and supplier relationships must change. New and smaller manufactured parts are sourced worldwide based on performance measures like high quality, fast delivery, and low costs. Without capable and high-quality manufactured parts, HD cannot meet its growth goals and fulfill its long-term strategy. Suppliers are also required to follow the laws of their host country, be responsible in sourcing of materials and services, honor patents and trademarks, and practice social, economic, and environmental sustainability.

Another area of HD's operations strategy—its sustainability initiatives and practices—has changed. A HD Sustainability Committee monitors social, legislative, and political trends around the world that could affect the company's supply chains and its processes. The committee assists senior management in setting corporate and operations strategy goals and to ensure they are aligned. This includes manufactured goods recovery and recycling described in Chapter 13 (see Section 13-6b).

HD's logistic functions and global dealer networks are undergoing major changes also. Harley-Davidson has partnered with UPS Supply Chain Solutions to help it deliver parts and bikes to a global network of dealers and factories. Prior to this partnership, HD found that supplier less-than-truckload shipments had increased freight costs far faster than the growth in sales.

The next section provides a framework for changing and aligning corporate, marketing, and operations strategy as Harley-Davidson is doing now.

3-6 A Framework for Operations Strategy

A useful framework for strategy development that ties corporate and marketing strategy to operations strategy was proposed by Professor Terry Hill at Templeton College, Oxford University, and is shown in Exhibit 3.3.[11] It was originally designed for goods-producing organizations; however, it can also be applied to service-providing firms. This framework defines the essential elements of an effective operations strategy in the last two columns—*operations design choices and building the right infrastructure*.

Operations design choices *are the decisions management must make as to what type of process structure is best suited to produce goods or create services*. It typically addresses six key areas—types of processes, value chain integration and outsourcing, technology, capacity and facilities, inventory and service capacity, and trade-offs among these decisions.

Infrastructure *focuses on the nonprocess features and capabilities of the organization and includes the workforce, operating plans and control systems, quality control, organizational structure, compensation systems, learning and innovation systems, and support services*. The infrastructure must support process choice and provide managers with accurate and timely information to make good decisions. These decisions lie at the core of organizational effectiveness, and suggest that the

General Electric: Green Starts at the Top

Jeffrey Immelt, the CEO of General Electric, proposed a green business strategy and plan to his 35 top executives in 2004, and they voted against it. Immelt refused to take no for an answer and overruled his executives. The result of his efforts is now defined in GE's highly successful Ecomagination initiative. Ecomagination (http://ge.ecomagination.com) is a business strategy designed to drive innovation and the growth of profitable environmental solutions while engaging stakeholders. GE invests in innovation through its R&D efforts and outside venture capital investments. The resulting goods and services enable GE and its customers to reduce emissions while generating revenue from their sale. Combining profits and energy savings, GE continues to invest in environmental solutions, perpetuating the cycle. Specific green and measurable targets have been established by year. For example, GE's greenhouse gas (GHG) target set in 2008 has been exceeded by 30 percent.

Roman Sotola/Shutterstock.com

EXHIBIT 3.3 Hill's Strategy Development Framework

Corporate Objectives	Marketing Strategy	How Do Goods and Services Qualify and Win Orders in the Marketplace?	Operations Strategy: Operations Design Choices	Operations Strategy: Infrastructure
• Growth • Economic sustainability (survival)[1] • Profit • Return on investment • Other market and financial measures • Social (welfare) sustainability[1] • Environmental sustainability[1]	• Goods and services markets and segments • Range • Mix • Volumes • Standardization versus customization • Level of innovation • Leader versus follower alternatives	• Safety • Price (cost) • Range • Flexibility • Demand • Goods and service design • Quality • Service • Goods • Environment • Social (community) • Brand image • Delivery • Speed • Variability • Technical support • Pre- and postservice support	• Type of processes and alternative designs • Supply chain integration and outsourcing • Technology • Capacity and facilities (size, timing, location) • Inventory • Trade-off analysis	• Workforce • Operating plans and control system(s) • Quality control • Organizational structure • Compensation system • Learning and innovation systems • Support services

Sources: Adapted from T. Hill, *Manufacturing Strategy: Text and Cases*, 3rd ed., Burr Ridge, IL: McGraw-Hill, 2000, p. 32; T. Hill, *Operations Management: Strategic Context and Managerial Analysis*, 2nd ed., Prigrame MacMillan, 2005, p. 50.

[1]Note: We have added sustainability criteria to Professor Hill's original framework.

integrative nature of operations management is one of the most important aspects of success. Operations design and infrastructure criteria and decisions in Prof. Hill's strategy framework define the value chain that supports environmental, social, and economic sustainability.

A key feature of this framework is the link between operations and corporate and marketing strategies. Clearly, it is counterproductive to design a customer benefit package and an operations system to produce and deliver it, and then discover that these plans will not achieve corporate and marketing objectives. This linkage is described by the four major decision loops illustrated in Exhibit 3.4. Decision loop #1 (shown in red) ties together corporate strategy—which establishes the organization's direction and boundaries—and marketing strategy—which evaluates customer wants and needs and targets market segments.

The output of red loop #1 is the input for green loop #2. Decision loop #2 (green) describes how operations evaluates the implications of competitive priorities in terms of process choice and infrastructure. The key decisions are "Do we have the process capability to achieve the corporate and marketing objectives per target market segment? Are our processes capable of consistently achieving order-winner performance in each market segment?"

Decision loop #3 (blue) lies within the operations function of the organization and involves determining if process choice decisions and capabilities are consistent with infrastructure decisions and capabilities. The fourth decision loop (yellow loop #4) represents operations' input into the corporate and marketing strategy. Corporate decision makers ultimately decide how to allocate resources to achieve corporate objectives.

3-6a Operations Strategy at McDonald's

McDonald's Corporation is the world's leading foodservice retailer, with sales of almost $23 billion in more than 32,000 restaurants in 117 countries, employing 1.6 million people.[12] The company's vision provides the basis for its strategy:

EXHIBIT 3.4 Four Key Decision Loops in Terry Hill's Generic Strategy Framework

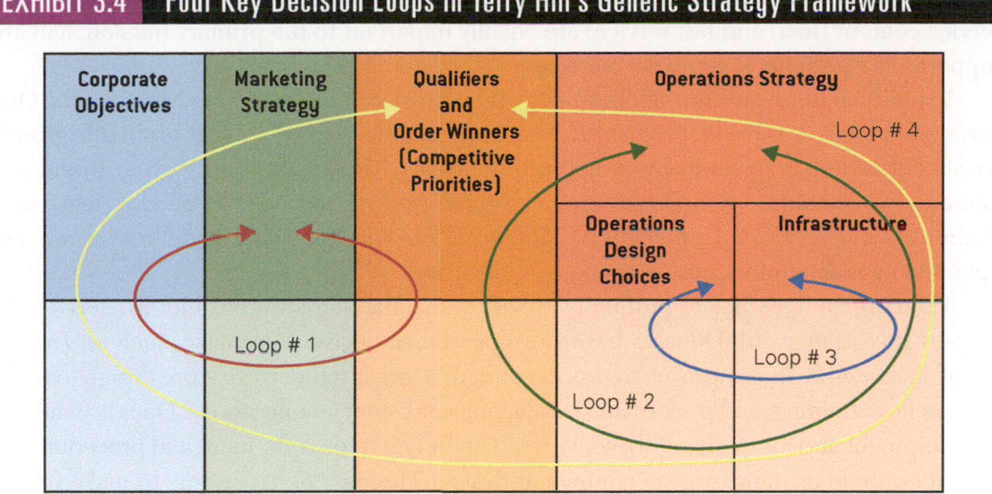

McDonald's vision is to be the world's best quick-service restaurant experience. Being the best means providing outstanding quality, service, cleanliness, and value, so that we make every customer in every restaurant smile. To achieve our vision, we focus on three worldwide strategies:

1. **Be the Best Employer**
   Be the best employer for our people in each community around the world.
2. **Deliver Operational Excellence**
   Deliver operational excellence to our customers in each of our restaurants.
3. **Achieve Enduring Profitable Growth**
   Achieve enduring profitable growth by expanding the brand and leveraging the strengths of the McDonald's system through innovation and technology.

McDonald's also defines its "Values in Action" policies, program, and practices, which is basically "doing the right thing." In its Corporate Responsibility Report, it defines the following four sustainability initiatives:

- *Build a sustainable McDonald's that involves all facets of our business.* For example, McDonald's is developing an environmental scorecard that drives greater awareness of resource use (energy, water, air emission, and waste), with the ultimate goal of reducing the environmental impact of its supply chains.
- *Commit to a three-pronged approach—reduce, reuse, and recycle.* For example, 82 percent of McDonald's packaging is made from renewable materials. In some global markets, McDonald's delivery trucks use their own reprocessed cooking oil for fuel.
- *Strive to provide eco-friendly workplaces and restaurants.* Better recycling efforts have diverted over 58 percent of waste normally targeted for a landfill to other recycling uses. Green facilities have been built in countries such as Brazil, Germany, and France.
- *Work with suppliers and outside experts to continuously improve purchasing decisions and evaluation of supplier performance regarding animal welfare.* Animal welfare scorecards and supplier audits in addition to better designs of animal-handling facilities are two examples of this initiative.

McDonald's also actively participates in social media platforms to share information about its sustainability policies and initiatives.

What is the CBP that McDonald's offers? Exhibit 3.5 shows the CBP, in which goods and service content (food and fast service) are equally important to the primary mission, and are supported by peripheral goods and services.

Exhibit 3.6 illustrates how Hill's strategy framework can be applied to McDonald's. One corporate objective is profitable growth. The marketing strategy to support profitable growth consists of adding both company-owned and franchised McDonald's and Partner Brand restaurants. McDonald's is committed to franchising as a key strategy to grow and leverage value chain capabilities. Over 75 percent of McDonald's restaurants worldwide are owned and operated by independent businesspeople—franchisees.

The core competency to profitable growth is maintaining low-cost and fast service. To support this strategy, McDonald's has many operational decisions to make, such as: Does it adopt an assembly-line approach to process design? Does it standardize store design to make process flow, training, and performance evaluation consistent among stores? Does it standardize equipment and job design work activities? The french fryer equipment and procedure are a good example of standardizing equipment design. There is "only one way to make french fries" in 32,000 stores worldwide, and this contributes to consistent goods quality, fast service, and a standardized training program. Likewise, ordering by the numbers and digital printouts of customer orders in the drive-through improves order accuracy and speed of service. Of course, the entire human resource function is built around the needs of the McDonald's value chain and operating systems. McDonald's has been identified as one of the best places to work by *Fortune* and *The American Economic Review*. Examples of supportive infrastructure include good hiring criteria, recognition and reward programs, training, and promotion criteria.

A second corporate objective is *operational excellence*. The ultimate objective of operational excellence is satisfied customers. Operational excellence includes value chain, process, equipment, and job efficiencies, as well as superior people-related performance—all focused to support the service-encounter level. McDonald's strategy is to deliver exceptional customer experiences through a combination of great-tasting food, outstanding service, being a good place to work, profitable growth, and consistent value. McDonald's service goals also include extended or 24-hour service to make McDonald's the most convenient food-service choice for customers. To put sparkle in McDonald's service, initiatives include training for the unexpected and keeping it simple.

EXHIBIT 3.5 McDonald's Customer Benefit Package

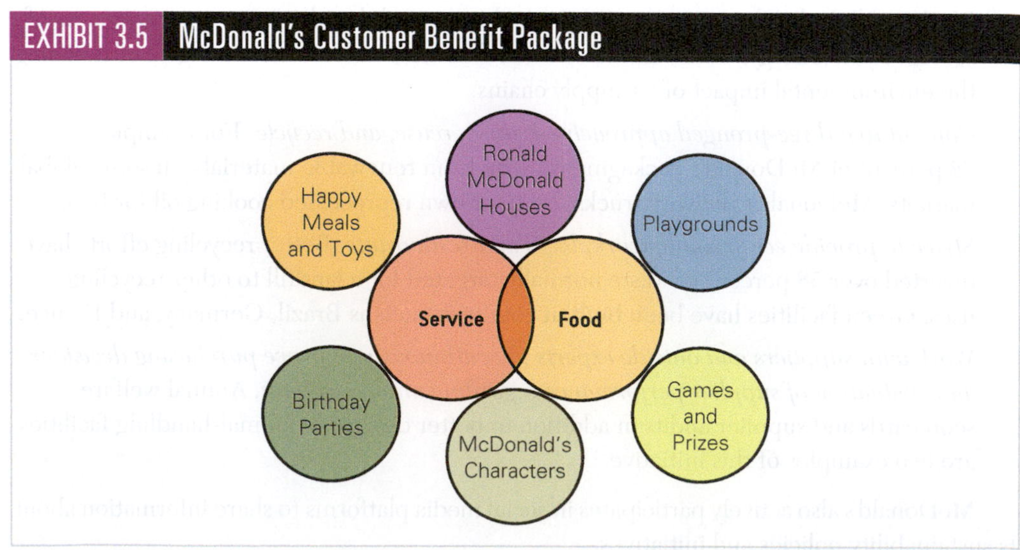

A third corporate objective is leveraging innovation and technology capabilities. In the United States, McDonald's has 40 distribution centers to support more than 12,000 restaurants and about 350 suppliers. More than 2,000 safety and quality checks surround McDonald's food as it moves through its supply chains (from farms to restaurants). Information technology is used to coordinate the activities of McDonald's value chain.

> The ultimate objective of operational excellence is satisfied customers. Operational excellence includes the value chain, process, equipment, and job efficiencies, as well as superior people-related performance—all focused to support the service-encounter level.

EXHIBIT 3.6 Applying the Hill's Strategy Development Framework to McDonald's

Corporate Objective Examples	Marketing Strategy Examples	How Do Goods and Services Qualify and Win Orders in the Marketplace?	Operations Strategy: Operating Design Choice Examples	Operations Strategy: Infrastructure Examples
Profitable Growth	Add worldwide 1,000 McDonald's restaurants using company-owned and franchised stores	Competitive priorities tie the corporate and marketing strategies to the operational strategy ⟷	• Flow shop process design • Standardized store design • Equipment design • Job design • Order-taking process • Capacity and facility size, location, and clusters	• Hiring process and criteria • First job training • Recognition and rewards • Training for the unexpected • Keeping it simple • Manager trainee program • Coaching and counseling • Teamwork • E-mail capabilities
Operational Excellence	Ideal store location, best training and employee well-being programs	• #1 Low prices • #2 Quick service (delivery speed) • #3 High service quality	• Global value chain coordination • Suppliers • Resource scheduling • Inventory placement and control • Distribution centers • Standardized operational and job procedures	• Operating plans and control system(s) • Shift management • Supplier relations and negotiation • Equipment maintenance • Online network capability • Distribution centers
Leverage Strengths through Innovation and Technology	Develop new food items, store and food mix Tie demand analysis to promotions	⟷ • #4 High goods quality	• Store equipment technology • Value chain information systems to tie stores, distribution centers, and suppliers together • New food products	• Quality control • Laboratory testing • Organizational structure • Compensation systems • Online network capability
Diversity	Long-standing commitment to a diverse workforce	• #5 Demand flexibility	• Training and franchising • Process performance • Career paths	• Learning and innovation systems • Hamburger University
Sustainability	Values in Action policies and initiatives	• #6 Brand image ⟷	• Greener supply chains • Recycling processes • Reduce energy use • Animal welfare	• Greener buildings • Ronald McDonald House • Mobile health centers • Youth camps

Susan Montgomery/Shutterstock.com

Ronald McDonald House in Ann Arbor, Michigan.

Another corporate objective is developing and maintaining a diverse workforce. Diversity at McDonald's means understanding, recognizing, and valuing the differences that make each person unique. Hamburger University, located in Oak Brook, Illinois, has trained over 275,000 managers in 22 different languages and also manages 10 international training centers in Australia, England, Japan, Germany, and elsewhere.

McDonald's supports its social responsibility objective with over 200 Ronald McDonald House Charities. Social responsibility activities also include funding immunization programs for 1 million African children, Olympic youth camps, disaster relief, and sponsored mobile health centers in underserved areas. Other corporate objectives not shown in Exhibit 3.6 include a high return on investment, exploring nontraditional locations for stores, and commitment to the environment.

Competitive priorities are derived from McDonald's vision statement and strategy. The ranking in Exhibit 3.6 reflects their importance. The competitive priorities tie the corporate and marketing strategies to the operations strategy. The competitive priorities provide direction on key operations-strategy issues listed in the last two columns of Exhibit 3.6.

CHAPTER 3 LEARNING OBJECTIVE SUMMARIES

3.1 **Explain how organizations seek to gain competitive advantage.** Creating a competitive advantage requires a fundamental understanding of two things. First, management must understand customer wants and needs—and how the value chain can best meet these needs through the design and delivery of customer benefit packages that are attractive to customers. Second, management must build and leverage operational capabilities to support desired competitive priorities.

3.2 **Explain approaches for understanding customer wants and needs.** To correctly identify what customers expect requires being "close to the customer." There are many ways to do this, such as having employees visit and talk to customers, having managers talk to customers, and doing formal marketing research. The Kano model helps to differentiate between basic customer needs, expressed needs, and the "wow" features that can often be order winners.

3.3 **Describe how customers evaluate goods and services.** Research suggests that customers use three types of attributes in evaluating the quality of goods and services: search, experience, and credence. This classification has several important implications for operations. For example, the most important search and experience attributes should be evaluated during design and measured during manufacturing, and drive key operational controls to ensure that they are built into the good with high quality. Credence attributes stem from the nature of services, the design of the service system, and the training and expertise of the service providers.

3.4 **Explain the five key competitive priorities.** Five key competitive priorities are the following:

1. Cost—Many firms gain competitive advantage by establishing themselves as the lowcost leader in an industry.
2. Quality—Quality is positively and significantly related to a higher return on investment for almost all kinds of market situations.
3. Time—Customers demand quick response, short waiting times, and consistency in performance.
4. Flexibility—Success in globally competitive markets requires a capacity for both design and demand flexibility.
5. Innovation—Many firms focus on research and development for innovation as a core component of their strategy.

3.5 **Explain the role of OM, sustainability, and operations in strategic planning.** Developing an operations strategy involves translating competitive priorities into operational capabilities by making a variety of choices and trade-offs in design and operating decisions. That is, operating decisions must be aligned with achieving the desired competitive priorities. For example, if corporate objectives are to be the low-cost and mass-market producer of a good, then adopting an assembly-line type of process can help achieve this corporate objective. How operations are designed and implemented can have a dramatic effect on business performance and achievement of the strategy. Therefore, operations require close coordination with functional strategies in other areas of the firm, such as marketing and finance. An operations strategy should exploit an organization's core competencies, such as a particularly skilled or creative workforce, customer relationship management, clever bundling of goods and services, strong supply chain networks, extraordinary service, marketing expertise, or the ability to rapidly develop new products or change production output rates. Many companies view sustainability as a corporate strategy. A majority of global consumers believe that it is their responsibility to contribute to a better environment and would pay more for brands that support this aim. Likewise, retailers and manufacturers are demanding greener products and supply chains. Companies that have embraced sustainability pursue this strategy throughout their operations.

3.6 **Describe Hill's framework for operations strategy.** Hill's framework defines the essential elements of an effective operations strategy in the last two columns—operations design choices and building the right infrastructure. These define the value chain that supports environmental, social, and economic sustainability. A key feature of this framework is the link between operations and corporate and marketing strategies. This linkage is described by the four major decision loops that link together the elements of the framework (see Exhibit 3.3). The integrative nature of operations management is one of the most important aspects of success.

KEY TERMS

- **Competitive advantage**
- **Competitive priorities**
- **Core competencies**
- **Credence attributes**
- **Experience attributes**
- **Infrastructure**
- **Innovation**
- **Mass customization**
- **Multinational enterprise**
- **Operations design choices**
- **Operations strategy**
- **Order qualifiers**
- **Order winners**
- **Search attributes**
- **Strategy**

REVIEW QUESTIONS

3.1 1. Explain how organizations seek to gain competitive advantage.

3.1 2. Define order qualifiers and order winners.

3.2 3. Explain approaches for understanding customer wants and needs.

3.2 4. Define search, experience, and credence attributes, and provide an example of each.

3.3 5. Describe how customers evaluate goods and services.

3.4 6. What are the five competitive priorities? Cite an example of an organization that demonstrates the competitive priority.

3.4 7. Define mass customization and provide two examples.

3.4 8. What is innovation? Provide two examples from well-known companies.

3.5 9. Define strategy. Explain how corporate, business, and functional strategies support overall strategy.

3.5 10. Provide some examples of core competencies, and explain the value to an organization of understanding its core competencies.

3.5 11. What is operations strategy? How can it support competitive priorities?

3.5 12. Explain the role of OM, sustainability, and operations in strategic planning.

3.6 13. Describe Hill's framework for operations strategy.

3.6 14. How does Dr. Hill's strategy framework tie corporate strategy to marketing and operations strategy?

3.6 15. How would you rank McDonald's competitive priorities in Exhibit 3.6?

3.6 16. Provide three examples of McDonald's management making choices on sustainability. (See Exhibit 1.13 in Chapter 1.)

DISCUSSION QUESTIONS AND EXPERIENTIAL ACTIVITIES

3.1 17. What might the competitive advantage be for each of the following companies?

a. eBay
b. Southwest Airlines
c. Starbucks
d. Apple
e. Facebook
f. Uber
g. 3M
h. Amazon
i. Bentley automobiles
j. Nordstrom

3.2 18. Select a business with which you are familiar and identify examples of order qualifiers and winners. You might also research the businesses on the Internet or visit the library.

3.3 19. Select a business with which you are familiar and identify examples of customers using search, experience, and credence quality to evaluate the good or service. You might also research the businesses on the Internet or visit the library.

3.3 20. Provide examples of search, experience, and credence attributes for a ride sharing service such as Uber or Lyft.

3.4 21. Choose an organization with which you are familiar that falls into *one* of the following categories:

- sporting goods store
- haircut salon
- college bar or restaurant
- pizza business
- a sports team
- wireless telephone service

Define the firm's strategic mission, strategy, and competitive priorities. What are the order qualifiers and winners? What would operations have to be good at to make this a successful business or organization?

3.4 22. How does a package delivery service such as UPS or FedEx use the competitive priority "time" to its competitive advantage? Research, then explain and provide examples in a short paper (maximum of two typed pages).

3.4 23. How does Walmart use the competitive priority "cost" to its competitive advantage? Research, then explain and provide examples in a short paper (maximum of two typed pages).

3.4 24. How does Procter & Gamble use the competitive priority "quality" to its competitive advantage? Research, then explain and provide examples in a short paper (maximum of two typed pages).

3.4 25. How does your cell phone provider use the competitive priority "flexibility" to its competitive advantage? Research, then explain and provide examples in a short paper (maximum of two typed pages).

3.4 26. Compare Lyft (www.lyft.com) and Uber (www.uber.com) strategies. Explain the similarities and differences in their missions, strategies, and competitive priorities, and how their operations strategies might differ. Use the Internet or business magazines to research the information you need. Report your findings in a short paper (maximum of two typed pages).

3.4 27. Explain the interlinking model of quality and profitability (Exhibit 3.2). How does it connect to business and operations strategy? Can you provide any examples of goods and services that support and add credibility to this model?

3.4 28. Is it possible for a world-class organization to achieve superiority in all five major competitive priorities—price (cost), quality, time, flexibility, and innovation? Explain your reasoning.

3.5 29. Why is sustainability a strategy and not a competitive priority? Explain your reasoning.

3.5 30. Identify two firms that endorse sustainability as part of their corporate strategy and discuss how sustainability is integrated into their strategies.

3.5 31. Research and write a short paper on a company that has a clear strategy based on social and ethical sustainability.

3.6 32. Apply Hill's strategy framework to a goods-producing or service-providing organization of your choice. This will require research to identify corporate objectives and competitive priorities. See the McDonald's example in the chapter for guidance and make sure that you emphasize OM concepts, capabilities, and execution. Report your findings in a short paper (maximum of two typed pages).

3.6 33. Identify two competing organizations (e.g., AT&T and Verizon, TaylorMade and Callaway golf club manufacturers, or Starbucks and Panera). Explain the differences in their missions, strategies, and competitive priorities, and how their operations strategies might differ. Use the Internet or business magazines to research the information you need. Report your findings in a short paper (maximum of two typed pages).

3.6 34. Research Apple and define its strategic mission, vision, corporate strategy, competitive priorities, and operations strategy. What can you say about Apple's strategy and practices regarding sustainability? You might use the Internet or visit the library. Report your findings in a short paper (maximum of two typed pages).

3.6 35. How do the "Veja Company: Sneakers with a Conscience" operations and supply chain decisions and practices support their mission and strategy? Provide examples and explain. Report your findings in a short paper (maximum of two typed pages).

The Greater Cincinnati Chamber of Commerce

Founded in 1839 to facilitate the growth and ease of commerce, the Greater Cincinnati Chamber of Commerce (www.cincinnatichamber.com) is a membership organization of approximately over 7,000 businesses and organizations in the region that surrounds Cincinnati, Ohio. The Chamber's stated purpose is to serve its members and region toward economic prosperity, and its vision are simple:

- *Our purpose: To grow the vibrancy and economic prosperity of our region.*
- *Our vision: We are the hottest city in America.*
- *Our core values: We are visionaries, collaborators, and makers of change. We lead inclusively with passion, integrity, and fun.*

The Chamber delivers a diverse range of products and services, including

- New Business Attraction
- Business Retention
- Elections and Voting
- Government Advocacy
- Education and Training Services
- Networking Events
- Awards and Recognitions
- Networking Opportunities
- Festivals and Events
- "Business Connections" membership directory
- Chamber newsletter(s)

While technically a not-for-profit organization, many Chamber services are expected to generate an excess of revenues over expenses, which is required to support a variety of non-revenue-producing Chamber programs. The management group defined a vision for the organization as follows: *Be the first place that businesses in the region go for solutions to the competitive challenges of growth.* Their growth statement is:

> *The Cincinnati Chamber drives growth by providing business resources and accelerators, immersive engagement opportunities and company cost-saving programs. We're equipped to help grow your talent pool, navigate the regional workforce ecosystem and expand your cultural thinking.*

The Chamber is organized in a series of product-focused departments. These departments interact directly with customer segments to develop and deliver Chamber products and services.

Support groups assist these line departments in product and service delivery functions that include Information Services, Administration, Human Resources, Marketing/Communications, and Finance. In addition, the Chamber's Membership/Member Relations department serves Chamber staff and members in providing information and access to Chamber products and services, including Chamber membership.

The Chamber has ongoing relationships with affiliate organizations that are housed within the Chamber's downtown Cincinnati office. Those affiliates include the Cincinnati Minority Supplier Development Council, the Cincinnati Minority Enterprise Business Mentoring Program, The Japan-America Society, and many more.

The Chamber developed the "Measurement Report Card" emphasizing measurement as the tool to drive effectiveness. This Measurement Report Card links the Strategic Plan, Program of Work, departmental and work group measures into one unified system. This Report Card incorporates a broadened set of measures, coupling financial goals with penetration and satisfaction data through the quarterly operations report.

Case Questions for Discussion:

1. Characterize the customer benefit package that the Chamber offers. What other peripheral goods might the Chamber provide to complement its services? How might this affect their strategy?
2. What sources of competitive advantage do you feel the Chamber has? Who do they compete with?
3. Critique their mission and strategy. What operational processes must they excel at to accomplish their mission and vision?
4. Rank order their competitive priorities.
5. In many areas, a Chamber of Commerce is primarily in the travel and tourism business. How does the Greater Cincinnati Chamber of Commerce appear to differentiate itself from these types of organizations?

Sustainable Lawn Care

"Chris, we make the highest-quality grass seed and fertilizer in the world. Our brands are known everywhere!" stated Caroline Ebelhar, the vice president of manufacturing for The Lawn Care Company. "Yeah! But the customer doesn't have a Ph.D. in organic chemistry to understand the difference between our grass seed and fertilizer compared to those of our competitors! We need to also be in the lawn-care application service business, and not just the manufacturer of super-perfect products," responded Chris Kilbourne, the vice president of marketing, as he walked out of Caroline's office. This ongoing debate among Lawn Care's senior management team had not been resolved, but the chief executive officer, Mr. Steven Marion, had been listening very closely. Soon they would have to make a major strategic decision.

The Lawn Care Company, a fertilizer and grass seed manufacturer with sales of almost $1 billion, sold some of its products directly to parks and golf courses. Customer service in this goods-producing company was historically very narrowly defined as providing "the right product to the right customer at the right time." Once these goods were delivered to the customer's premises and the customer signed the shipping documents, Lawn Care's job was done. For many park and golf course customers, a local subcontractor or the customers themselves applied the fertilizer and seed. These application personnel often did the job incorrectly, using inappropriate equipment and methods. The relationship among these non-lawn care application service personnel, The Lawn Care Company, and the customer also was not always ideal.

When claims were made against The Lawn Care Company because of damaged lawns or polluted lakes and streams, the question then became one of who was at fault. Did the quality of the physical product or the way it was applied cause the damage? Either way, the customers' lawns or waterways were in poor shape, and in some cases the golf courses lost substantial revenue if a green or hole was severely damaged or not playable. One claim filed by a green advocacy group focused on a fish kill in a stream near a golf course.

One of Lawn Care's competitors began an application service for parks and golf courses that routinely applied the fertilizer and grass seed for its primary customers. This competitor bundled the application service to the primary goods, fertilizer and grass seed, and charged a higher price for this service. The competitor delivered and applied the fertilizer on the same day to avoid the liability of storing toxic fertilizer outside on the golf course or park grounds. The competitor learned the application business in the parks and golf course target market segment and was beginning to explore expanding into the residential lawn-care application service target market. The Lawn Care Company sold the "highest-quality physical products" in the industry, but it was not currently in either the professional park and golf course or the residential "application service" lawn-care market segments. The Lawn Care Company considered its value chain to end once it delivered its products to the job site or non-lawn care application service. The competitor sold the customer "a beautiful lawn with a promise of no hassles." To the competitor, this included an application service bundled to grass seed and fertilizer.

Le Do/Shutterstock.com

Case Questions for Discussion:

1. Define Lawn Care's current strategic mission, strategy, competitive priorities, value chain, and how it wins customers. What are the order qualifiers and winners? Draw the major stages in its value chain without an application service.
2. What problems, if any, do you see with Lawn Care's current strategy, vision, customer benefit package and value chain design, and pre- and postservices?
3. Redo Questions (1) and (2) and provide a new or revised strategy and associated customer benefit package and value chain that is more appropriate for today's marketplace.
4. What does operations have to be good at to successfully execute your revised strategy?
5. What are your final recommendations?

Integrative Case: Hudson Jewelers

The Hudson Jewelers case study found in MindTap integrates material found in each chapter of this book.

Case Questions for Discussion:

1. Define and draw the customer benefit package and state Hudson Jewelers's strategy; rank order its competitive priorities, order qualifiers, and order winners; and state the ways they gain competitive advantage.
2. Evaluate a customer's retail store experience in terms of search, experience, and credence attributes. Provide some examples and explain why they can be classified as search, experience, and credence attributes.
3. Define in detail the attributes of "value" when buying and codesigning a $50,000 wedding ring. What creates a buying experience that would delight the customer?

Technology and Operations Management | 4

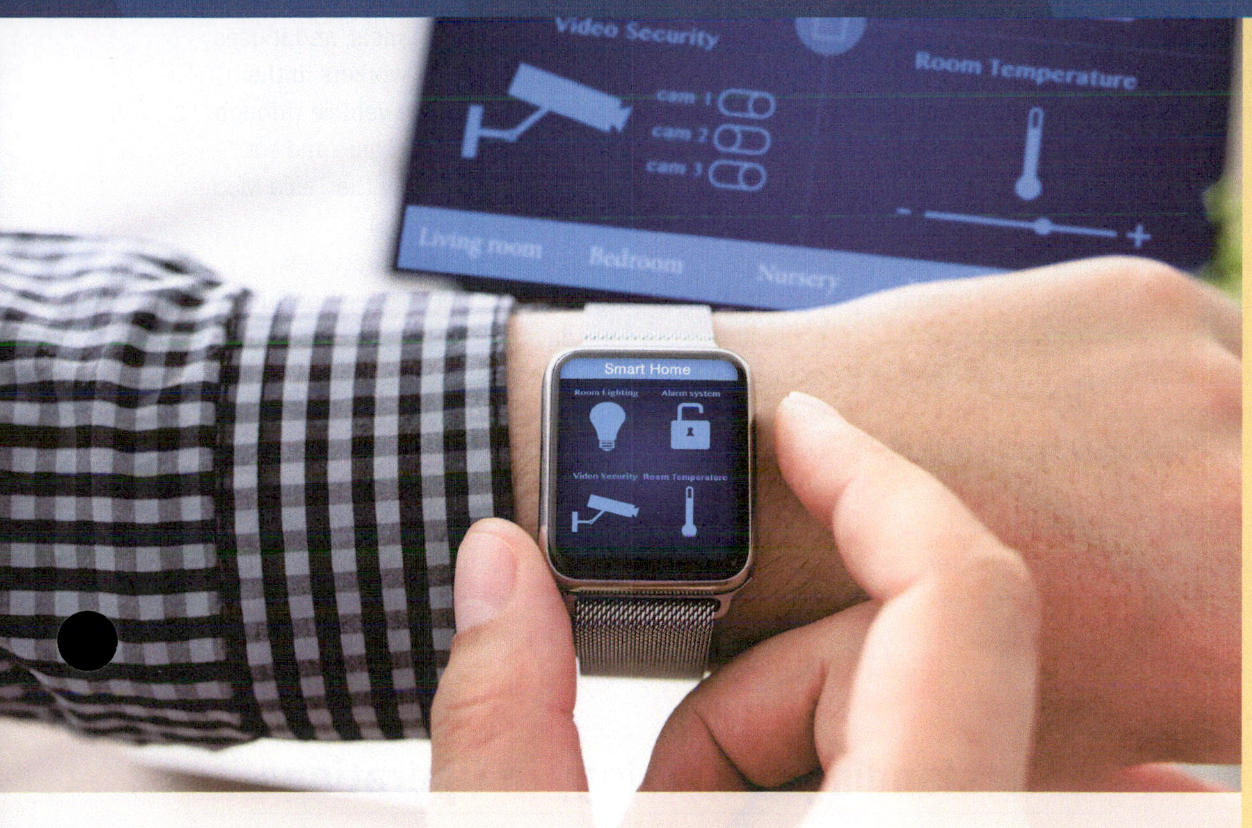

Denys Prykhodov/Shutterstock.com

LEARNING OBJECTIVES

After studying this chapter, you will be able to:

4-1 Describe different types of technology and their roles in manufacturing and service operations.

4-2 Explain how manufacturing and service technology and analytics strengthen the value chain.

4-3 Explain the benefits and challenges of using technology.

4-4 Describe key technology decisions and how analytics can assist in making technology decisions.

You may have heard a newer buzzword—the "Internet of Things (IoT)." This refers to physical products with embedded sensors that are connected to the Internet, such as smart watches and fitness devices, thermostats, lighting, security, and refrigerators, to name just a few. IoT sensors on commercial appliances can delight customers. A leaky refrigerator hose will immediately trigger a text message to your phone, encouraging you to get the problem fixed before the house floods. IoT sensors will monitor your grocery supplies, and send a resupply list as soon as you run short.

The IoT is changing operations management. Bar code scanners and RFID chips have been in use for years to track products in the supply chain and improve customer response. Electronic screwdrivers with embedded sensors help workers screw in fasteners with the right torque. Part bins have built-in scales that can alert workers if they grab the wrong part. Sensors in manufacturing equipment can automatically adjust ingredients, temperature, and pressure in chemical processes, thus improving product quality. They can be used to adjust the position of physical objects as they move down an assembly line so that they are positioned correctly and accurately for processing. Services will also be affected; tech experts make over 4 million house calls each year to help customers install connected devices. Companies that sell IoT products and have the expertise to support them will have an advantage over their competitors such as Amazon and Walmart. The IoT will require companies to overhaul their information technology (IT), supply-chain, and logistics systems.[1]

WHAT DO YOU THINK?

In what ways has technology benefited your life and work as a student?

Technology—both physical and information—has dramatically changed how work is accomplished in every industry, from mining to manufacturing, to education, to health care. Technology is the enabler that makes today's service and manufacturing systems operate productively and meet customer needs better than ever. Most of you probably cannot imagine living in a world without personal computers, the Internet, or wireless communications. However, new technology such as the electric car requires a rethinking of the customer benefit package, supply chain, and operations. With a limited range, the practicality of electric vehicles requires the ability to quickly charge batteries during longer trips. Tesla is building a nationwide network of 30-minute charging stations that will allow individuals to drive across the entire United States. It is also developing battery-swapping stations that can change the batteries faster than a typical gasoline fill-up. Tesla refuses to sell through independent dealers; it operates all its own showrooms and service centers to avoid the middleman price inflation and to build and maintain customer relationships. Its manufacturing plant has a high level of automation to manufacture body panels, and it uses an army of industrial robots to assist workers in the assembly process and to transport the vehicle through the plant. Robots even insert seats and glue and set windshields. (Search YouTube for "How the Tesla Model S Is Made" for a behind-the-scenes tour.)

Technological innovation in goods, services, manufacturing, and service delivery is a competitive necessity. In the early days of the Internet, Jack Welch, retired CEO of General Electric, for example, pushed GE to become a leader among traditional, old-economy companies in embracing the Internet after noticing his wife Christmas shopping on the Web. "I realized that if I didn't watch it, I would retire as a Neanderthal," he was reported as saying, "So I just started reading everything I could about it." He began by pairing 1,000 Web-savvy mentors with senior people to get his top teams up to Internet speed quickly.[2]

4-1 Understanding Technology in Operations

We may categorize technology into two basic groups. **Hard technology** *refers to equipment and devices that perform a variety of tasks in the creation and delivery of goods and services.* Some examples of hard technology are computers, microprocessors, optical switches, satellites, sensors, robots, automated machines, bar-code scanners, and radio-frequency identification (RFID) tags.

RFID tags are the modern successor to bar codes. RFID tags are tiny computer chips that can be placed on shipping containers, individual products, credit cards, prescription medicines, passports, livestock, and even people. They transmit radio signals to identify locations and track movements throughout the supply chain. They have many applications in both manufacturing and service industries. Retail, defense, transportation, and health care have begun requiring their suppliers to implement this technology. RFID can bring visibility and enhanced security to the handling and transportation of materials, baggage, and other cargo. RFID can help identify genuine products from counterfeit knock-offs, thus helping to lower overall product and operational costs.[3] They have also been used to monitor residents in assisted living buildings and track the movements of doctors, nurses, and equipment in hospital emergency rooms.

Soft technology *refers to the application of the Internet, computer software, and information systems to provide data, information, and analysis and to facilitate the creation and delivery of goods and services.* Some examples are database systems, artificial intelligence programs, and voice-recognition software. Both types are essential to modern organizations (see the box about Amazon.com later in this chapter). As described in the introduction to this chapter, the hybrid and ultimately the electric vehicle are good examples of integrating hard and soft technology.

Information technology (IT) provides the ability to integrate all parts of the value chain through better management of data and information. This leads to more effective strategic and operational decisions to design better customer benefit packages that support customers' wants and needs, achieve competitive priorities, and improve the design and operation of all processes in the value chain.

Increasingly, both hard and soft technology are being integrated across the organization, allowing managers to make better decisions and share information across the value chain. Such systems, often called integrated operating systems (IOSs), include computer-integrated manufacturing (CIM) systems, enterprise resource planning (ERP) systems, and customer relationship management (CRM) systems, all of which use technology to create better and more customized goods and services and deliver them faster at lower prices. We will discuss these systems in the following sections.

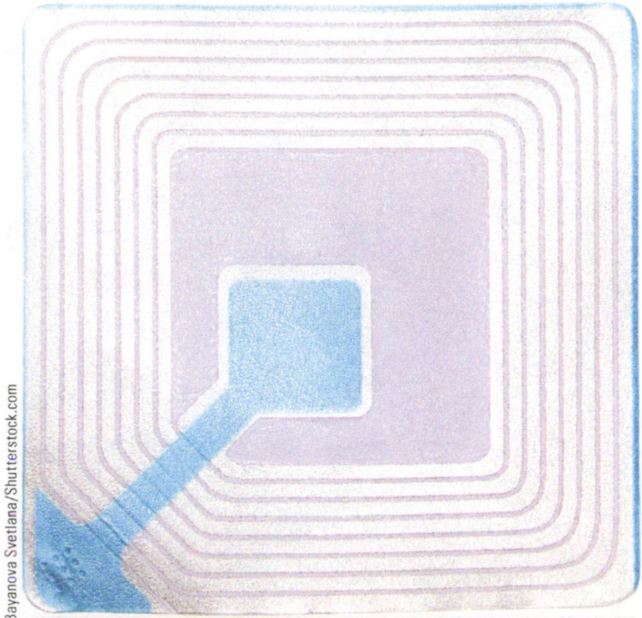

Bayanova Svetlana/Shutterstock.com

RFID tags such as this one are attached to objects and used to track and manage inventory and assets.

4-1a Manufacturing Technology

Although high-tech, automated manufacturing processes receive a lot of media attention, much of the technology used in small- and medium-sized manufacturing enterprises around the world is still quite basic. The box on making jigsaw puzzles illustrates simple, low-tech, manufacturing technology. Producing automobiles, jet engines, and other sophisticated products requires far more advanced methods. However, from an operations management standpoint, all organizations face common issues regarding technology:

- The right technology must be selected for the goods that are produced.
- Process resources, such as machines and employees, must be set up and configured in a logical fashion to support production efficiency.

Who's Making Steel Wire?

Voestalpine AG (www.voestalpine.com) opened a new steel rolling mill in Donawitz, Austria. It produces 500,000 tons of steel using 14 employees. Voestalpine's strategy was not to compete with major bulk steel producers but instead focus on high-value niche products such as steel wire. The Donawitz factory produces wire for use in shock absorbers and piston cases for vehicle manufacturers such as BMW and Mercedes-Benz. Using 1960s technical capabilities, a similar mill would employ over 1,000 people.

The red-hot metal moves along a 700-meter production line. Three technicians sit in a computer control room called the "pulpit" with banks of flatscreens on the wall monitoring performance. They control the factory. Another 300 people work in support roles like purchasing, logistics, machine maintenance, and accounting. Wolfgang Eder, the chief executive officer said, "In the long-run we will lose most of our classic blue-collar workers, people doing the hot and dirty jobs of coking plants and around the blast furnaces. This will all be automated."

During the last two decades, the steel industry worldwide has seen the number of worker-hours needed to produce a ton of steel decrease from 700 to 250 hours per ton.[4]

Nomad_Soul/Shutterstock.com

Drescher Paper Box: Making Jigsaw Puzzles

Drescher Paper Box in Buffalo, New York, formed in 1867, manufactures high-quality, laminated, cardboard jigsaw puzzles and board games and assembles them for retail stores. Drescher also produces cotton-filled jewelry boxes, candy boxes, business card boxes, and custom-made industrial boxes. Manufacturing jigsaw puzzles consists of three major steps: making the puzzle pieces, making the puzzle boxes, and final assembly. A printed picture is cut to size and laminated on a thick puzzle-board backing. Large presses are used to cut the puzzle into pieces, which are then bagged. The box-making process begins with blank cardboard. Boxes are scored and cut, then laminated with printed graphics. In the final assembly process, the puzzles are boxed and shrink-wrapped for shipment.

bogdan ionescu/Shutterstock.com

- Labor must be trained to operate the equipment.
- Process performance must be continually improved.
- Work must be scheduled to meet shipping commitments/customer promise dates.
- Quality must be ensured.

4-1b Computer-Integrated Manufacturing Systems (CIMSs)

Much of the technology used in manufacturing today is automated and linked with information technology. **Computer-integrated manufacturing systems (CIMSs)** *represent the union of hardware, software, database management, and communications to automate and control production activities, from planning and design to manufacturing and distribution.* CIMSs include many hard and soft technologies with a wide variety of acronyms, vendors, and applications and are essential to productivity and efficiency in modern manufacturing.

The roots of CIMSs began with **numerical control (NC)** *machine tools, which enable the machinist's skills to be duplicated by a programmable device (originally punched paper tape) that controls the movements of a tool used to make complex shapes.* **Computer numerical control (CNC)** *machines are NC machines whose operations are driven by a computer.*

Industrial robots were the next major advance in manufacturing automation. *A* **robot** *is a programmable machine designed to handle materials or tools in the performance of a variety of tasks.* Robots can be "taught" a large number of sequences of motions and operations and even to make certain logical decisions. Other typical applications are spray painting, machining, inspection, and material handling. Robots are especially useful for working with hazardous materials or heavy objects; for instance, in nuclear power plants robots are used to do work in highly radioactive areas. Robots are currently being developed to automate the sewing process in apparel factories. In services, robots help doctors complete intricate brain surgery by drilling very precise holes into the skull.

Integrated manufacturing systems began to emerge with computer-aided design/computer-aided engineering (CAD/CAE) and computer-aided manufacturing (CAM) systems. **CAD/CAE** *enables engineers to design, analyze, test, simulate, and "manufacture" products before they physically exist, thus ensuring that a product can be manufactured to specifications when it is released to the shop floor.* For example,

Nissan is cutting in half the time needed to take new cars from design to showroom, using computer-aided design software. The Nissan Note subcompact was rolled out to the Japanese market just 10.5 months after its design was finalized, in contrast to the 20.75 months that the process used to take.[5] **CAM** *involves computer control of the manufacturing process, such as determining tool movements and cutting speeds.*

Flexible manufacturing systems (FMSs) *consist of two or more computer-controlled machines or robots linked by automated handling devices such as transfer machines, conveyors, and transport systems. Computers direct the overall sequence of operations and route the work to the appropriate machine, select and load the proper tools, and control the operations performed by the machine.* More than one item can be machined or assembled simultaneously, and many different items can be processed in random order. Honda has been a pioneer in using FMSs and robotic technology. Its competitive priorities are moving toward design and demand flexibility so it is changing operating systems and technology to support these priorities. Honda assembly plants use flexible manufacturing cells where the robots can be reprogrammed to build different models of cars.[6] Today, many companies have achieved complete integration of CAD/CAE, CAM, and FMSs into what we now call computer-integrated manufacturing systems (CIMSs).

CIMS Facts

According to the National Research Council, companies with computer-integrated manufacturing system experience have been able to:

- decrease engineering design costs by up to 30 percent;
- increase productivity by 40 to 70 percent;
- increase equipment utilization by a factor of 2 to 3;
- reduce work-in-process and lead times by 30 to 60 percent; and
- improve quality by a factor of 3 to 4.

4-1c Advances in Manufacturing Technology

Innovations in technology have changed manufacturing in many industries. You have undoubtedly heard of 3-D printing, technically called additive manufacturing. This is the process of producing a three-dimensional solid object from a digital model file. "Additive" means that successive layers of material such as plastics, ceramics, or glass are built up rather than attained by traditional machining processes such as milling or drilling, which remove materials.

3-D printing technology has numerous applications. For example, industrial designers can quickly produce a physical model from a digital computer-aided design drawing; this is often called rapid prototyping and is used extensively in architecture, industrial design, and automotive, aerospace, and other manufacturing industries. It is used in the dental and medical industries for implants and prosthetics, and even in the fashion industry a contestant on the TV show "Project Runway" used it to create wearable fashion accessories! The technology is expanding the customer benefit package, allowing consumers to create custom products. For instance, Nokia introduced 3-D printing to make custom cases for mobile phones.

New types of industrial robots are being developed. Baxter developed one that can be trained like a human being and costs about half as much as the least expensive industrial robots currently on the market. With no coding whatsoever, the robot can be taught, and afterwards it will use common sense—if it drops something, it will pick it up. Robots like Baxter let smaller manufacturers work more efficiently, allowing real workers to put in work where it's actually needed instead of spending time on menial sorting tasks.[7]

Nanotechnology involves the manipulation of matter on atomic, molecular, and supramolecular scales, thus bringing with it super-precision manufacturing. Currently applied mostly in space

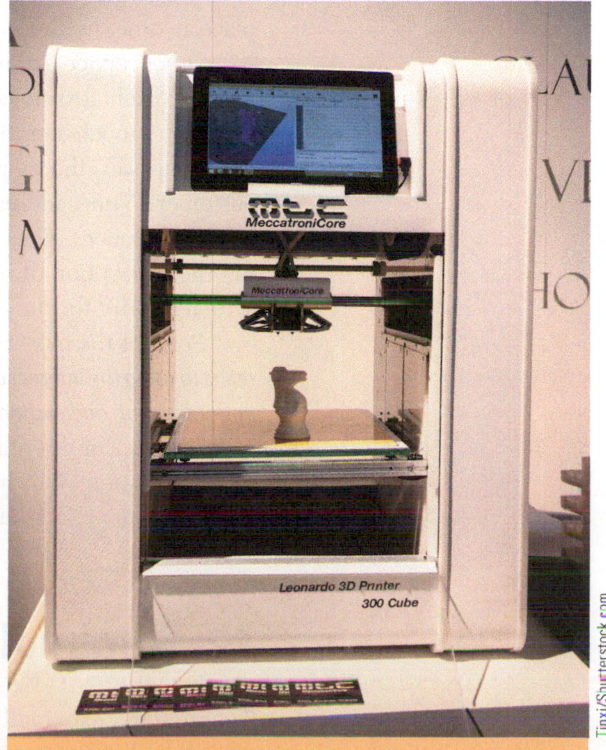

Tinxi/Shutterstock.com

3-D printers can be used to create both prototypes and working products.

Alcoa: 3-D Printing for Jet Engine Parts

Alcoa makes parts for gas turbines used in commercial jets that have to handle temperatures of up to 2,000°F and the stresses of aviation. Between tooling, development, and casting, it used to take Alcoa upward of a year to manufacture one of the nickel-alloy parts that go into an engine. With additive manufacturing, Alcoa has managed to cut in half the time required to develop the process and manufacture the part and cut the cost of the process by about 25 percent. Alcoa pairs computer-aided design, or CAD, with 3-D printing to construct the die from a computer file, layer by layer. A process that once took half a year could be completed in two to eight weeks, allowing the company to dramatically increase its output.[8]

technology and biotechnology, it is going to play an indispensable role in every manufacturing industry in the future. In many ways, it has already changed the world. Examples of application in nanotechnology include:

- Faster computer processing.
- Superconductive materials based on carbon nanotubes lifting magnetic cars and trains.
- Smaller memory cards that have more memory space.
- Clothes that last longer and keep the wearer cool in the summer.
- Bandages that heal wounds faster.[9]

All of these advances—and more that are on the horizon—will continue to make OM a challenging and exciting field.

4-1d Service Technology

You have undoubtedly encountered quite a bit of service technology in your own daily life. Technology is used in many services, including downloading music, banking, automated car washes, voice recognition in telephone menus, medical procedures, hotel and airline kiosks, and entertainment such as the robots used in Disney World's Hall of Presidents and Country Bear Jamboree attractions. One innovation that is being used by Stop & Shop, a grocery chain serving New England, is a portable device called EasyShop. EasyShop is a handheld terminal that allows loyalty card shoppers to scan items as they shop and receive targeted offers. Shoppers can also place an order at the deli department, for example, and then be alerted when the order is ready.[10]

Other service technologies are used behind the scenes in hotels, airlines, hospitals, and retail stores to facilitate service experiences. To speed order entry for pizza delivery, for instance, many firms use a touch-sensitive computer screen that is linked to a customer database. When a repeat customer calls, the employee need only ask for the customer's phone number to bring up the customer's name, address, and delivery directions (for a new customer, the information need only be entered once). The employee is able to address the customer immediately by name, enhancing the perception of service quality, and then enter the order quickly on the touch-sensitive screen to print for the kitchen, eliminating errors due to misreading of handwritten orders.[11]

Perhaps the most common service technology in use today involves the Internet. **E-service** *refers to using the Internet and technology to provide services that create and deliver time, place, information, entertainment, and exchange value to customers and/or support the sale of goods.* Many individuals use airline, hotel, and rental car websites or "one-stop" e-services like Microsoft Expedia in planning a vacation. The Internet of Things, digital personal assistants, and virtual reality offer new experiences for customers.

4-2 Technology in Value Chains

Technology, especially the Internet and e-communications, is changing the operation, speed, and efficiency of the value chain and presents many new challenges to operations managers. In many situations, electronic transaction capability allows all parts of the value chain to immediately recognize and react to changes in demand and supply. This requires tighter integration of many of the components of the value chain. In some cases, technology provides the capability to eliminate parts of the traditional value chain structure and streamline operations.

Kroger: Leveraging Two Seconds of Savings

Bar code scanners have been used in grocery stores for many years, requiring associates to scan items manually in the checkout lanes. Using a patented technology, the national grocery chain Kroger has been testing a new innovation called Advantage Checkout, designed to save customers time as well as to save the company operating costs and labor. Customers place items on a quick-moving conveyor belt. The items enter a tunnel lined with high-powered cameras to capture images of the products and scan the bar codes, then leave the tunnel on another conveyor to be bagged. The scanner can perform the function of several traditional or self-checkout lanes, takes up less floor space, and requires fewer workers. For a process that is done thousands of times in 2,400 stores, Kroger's CFO noted, "You can really leverage two seconds of savings that way."[12]

Business analytics plays a critical role in managing value chains, particularly for integrating and analyzing data throughout the value chain within an information systems framework. Netflix, for example, uses analytics everywhere, from marketing to operations to customer service. Netflix collects extensive data using surveys, website user testing, brand-awareness studies, and segmentation research. It uses analytics to help decide what price to pay for the rights to distribute new DVDs.[13] Using data on customer preferences, film ratings, and comparisons with people who have similar viewing and preference histories, Netflix predicts movies that a customer is likely to enjoy and creates personalized recommendations. This information also helps manage its film inventory by recommending older movies to balance demand for newer releases.[14]

Customer relationship management (CRM) *is a business strategy designed to learn more about customers' wants, needs, and behaviors in order to build customer relationships and loyalty, and ultimately enhance revenues and profits.* CRM exploits the vast amount of data that can be collected from consumers. For example, using a cell phone to make a voice call leaves behind data on whom you called, how long you talked, what time you called, whether your call was successful or it was dropped, your location, the promotion you may be responding to, and purchase histories.[15] Similarly, supermarkets, drugstores, and retail stores use "loyalty cards" that leave behind a digital trail of data about purchasing patterns. By better understanding these patterns and hidden relationships in data, stores can customize advertisements, promotions, coupons, and so on down to each individual customer and send targeted text messages and e-mail offers.

> Technology, especially the Internet and e-communications, is changing the operation, speed, and efficiency of the value chain and presents many new challenges to operations managers.

A typical CRM system includes market segmentation and analysis, customer service and relationship building, effective complaint resolution, cross-selling of goods and services, and pre- and postproduction processes such as preproduction order processing and postproduction field service. Of course, the value chain must be capable of delivering what the customer wants, and that is where sound operational analysis is required.

CRM helps firms gain and maintain competitive advantage by:

- segmenting markets based on demographic and behavioral characteristics;
- tracking sales trends and advertising effectiveness by customer and market segment;
- identifying which customers should be the focus of targeted marketing initiatives with predicted high customer response rates;
- forecasting customer retention (and defection) rates and providing feedback as to why customers leave the company;
- identifying which transactions are likely to be fraudulent;
- studying which goods and services are purchased together, and what might be good ways to bundle them (i.e., the customer benefit package);
- studying and predicting what Web characteristics are most attractive to customers and how the website might be improved; and
- linking the previous information to competitive priorities by market segment and process and value chain performance.

In recent years, cloud computing has improved the efficiency, productivity, and cost for organizations using information technology and CRM. Many now outsource CRM and other IT services; for instance, Netflix outsourced most of its Web technology work to Amazon.

4-3 Benefits and Challenges of Technology

Technology provides many benefits but at the same time poses some key challenges. A summary of the benefits and challenges of technology is given in Exhibit 4.1. Can you think of others?

One major benefit of technology has been its impact on sustainability. In Florida, for example, Card Sound Golf Club in Key Largo had an underground sensor system installed that allowed the club to cut in half the amount of fresh water it used to flush salt out of water used to irrigate the golf course. Many other golf courses are using this advanced sensor technology to reduce water consumption and keep their golf courses green—and not just in color.[16]

Intel suggests that the microprocessor is the "ultimate invention for achieving sustainability."[17] Microprocessor-based information and communication technology (ICT) provides sustainable economic, environmental, and social benefits on a national and global basis, often contributing to substantial economic gains through better productivity. These gains have significantly offset carbon usage, enabling more productivity, fewer miles traveled, and greater operational and material efficiencies. ICT is responsible for a phenomenon known as

EXHIBIT 4.1 Example Benefits and Challenges of Adopting Technology

Benefits	Challenges
• Creates new industries and job opportunities • Restructures old and less productive industries • Integrates supply and value chain players • Increases marketplace competitiveness and maintains the survival of the firm • Provides the capability to focus on smaller target market segments through mass customization • Improves/increases productivity, quality, customer satisfaction, speed, safety, and flexibility/customization—does more with less • Lowers cost • Raises world's standard of living • Monitors the environment and health of the planet	• Higher employee skill levels required, such as information technology and service management skills • Integration of old (legacy) and new technology and systems • Job shift and displacement • Less opportunity for employee creativity and empowerment • Protecting the employee's and customer's privacy and security • Fewer human service providers, resulting in customer ownership not being assigned, nonhuman service encounters, and inability of the customer to change decisions and return goods easily • Information overload • Global outsourcing and impact on domestic job opportunities • Enforcement of regulations and laws to support sustainability goals

dematerialization, by which the same or an increased quality and quantity of goods and/or services are created using fewer natural resources. ICT has also enabled flexible work options such as telecommuting, which not only yields environmental benefits but social benefits as well.

4-4 Technology Decisions and Implementation

Managers must make good decisions about introducing and using new technology. They must understand the relative advantages and disadvantages of using technologies and their impact on the workforce. Although technology has proven quite useful in eliminating monotony and hazardous work, and can help people develop new skills and talents, it can also rob them of empowerment and creativity. The goal of the operations manager is to provide the best synthesis of technology, people, and processes; this interaction is often called the *sociotechnical system.* Designing the sociotechnical system includes making decisions about job specialization versus enlargement, employee empowerment, training, decision support systems, teams and work groups, job design, recognition and reward, career advancement, and facility and equipment layout.

A key factor that affects technology decisions is scalability. **Scalability** *is a measure of the contribution margin (revenue minus variable costs) required to deliver a good or service as the business grows and volumes increase.* Scalability is a key issue in e-commerce. **High scalability** *is the capability to serve additional customers at zero or extremely low incremental costs.* For example, Monster.com is an online job posting and placement service that is largely information intensive. Customers can post their resumes on the Monster.com website and print out job advertisements and opportunities from their office or home computers at their expense. This service is highly scalable because its fixed costs are approximately 80–85 percent of total costs.

The incremental cost to serve an additional customer is very small, yet the revenue obtained from this customer remains high. If an organization establishes a business where the incremental cost (or variable cost) to serve more customers is zero, then the firm is said to be *infinitely scalable*. Online newspapers, magazines, and encyclopedias; e-banking services; and other information-intensive businesses have the potential to be infinitely scalable.

Process Innovations in Restaurants

Peter Bernik/Shutterstock.com

Letting customers order food, pay their bills, and provide feedback through tableside tablets is a quickly evolving trend in large chain restaurants such as Chili's, Applebee's, Olive Garden, Panera, and Pizzeria Uno. This technology is improving efficiency and customer satisfaction, and helps the organizations to better hear the voice of their customers. Each of the restaurant chains reported more efficient operations and more dollars spent per order. Tablets reduced the average time customers spent at tables by 10 minutes. Receipts printed at tables or sent via e-mail significantly reduce the time servers spend bouncing among tables. The faster a restaurant can turn its tables—move customers in and out—the higher its profits. In addition to the time factor, Panera's table-side tablets resulted in fewer order errors, and customer orders were $5 higher than average. The tablets are providing restaurants with customer feedback, ordering patterns, and other data that can be used to streamline service operations.[18]

> Although technology has proven quite useful in eliminating monotony and hazardous work, and can help people develop new skills and talents, it can also rob them of empowerment and creativity.

On the other hand, **low scalability** *implies that serving additional customers requires high incremental variable costs.* Many of the dot.com companies that failed around the year 2000 had low scalability and unsustainable demand (volumes) created by extraordinary advertising expenses and artificially low prices.

Many companies do not really understand how to implement technology effectively. The risk of a technology adoption failure is high. For instance, one major candy company installed three software packages just as retailers placed orders for Halloween candy. The software was incompatible with other systems, and candy piled up in warehouses because of missed or delayed deliveries. Such experiences are reminiscent of comparable failures of automated manufacturing technology encountered by the automobile and other industries during the 1970s. Reasons include rushing to the wrong technology, buying too much and not implementing it properly, and underestimating the time needed to make it work.

4-4a Analytical Methods for Technology Decisions

Making technology decisions is not always easy. Analytical methods based on data can provide more informed decisions, particularly when economics plays a key role. We will discuss two simple techniques for applying analytics—decision analysis and break-even analysis—and illustrate their application to technology decisions.

Decision Analysis for Technology Decisions **Decision analysis** *is the formal study of how people make decisions, particularly when faced with uncertain information, as well as a collection of techniques to support the analysis of decision problems.* Supplement B provides a short tutorial on decision analysis and explains how to structure decision problems analytically and choose the best decision. Solved Problems 4.1 and 4.2 apply these techniques to technology decisions. We suggest that you review this appendix before studying the solved problems.

SOLVED PROBLEM 4.1: MAKING A TECHNOLOGY CHOICE DECISION

Maling Manufacturing needs to purchase a new piece of machining equipment. The two choices are a conventional (labor-intensive) machine and an automated (computer-controlled) machine. Profitability will depend on a future unknown event—the demand volume. The following table presents an estimate of the net present value of profit over the next three years.

	Demand Volume	
Decision	**Low**	**High**
Conventional machine	$15,000	$21,000
Automated machine	$9,000	$35,000

Given the uncertainty associated with the demand volume, and no other information to work with, what decisions should the company make using the maximax, maximin, and minimax-regret criteria?

Solution:

For the maximax criterion (maximize the maximum profit), we have:

Decision	Maximum profit
Conventional (d_1)	$21,000
Automated (d_2)	$35,000

maximax decision = d_2

For the maximin criterion (maximize the minimum profit), we have:

Decision	Minimum profit
Conventional (d_1)	$15,000
Automated (d_2)	$9,000

maximin decision = d_1

Using the minimax regret criterion, we construct the opportunity loss matrix and find the decision that minimizes the maximum opportunity loss:

Opportunity Loss Matrix:

Decision	Low	High	Maximum
Conventional (d_1)	0	$14,000	$14,000
Automated (d_2)	$6,000	0	$ 6,000

minimax regret decision = d_2

Exhibit 4.2 shows the *Decision Analysis* Excel template in MindTap applied to this problem.

EXHIBIT 4.2 Excel *Decision Analysis* Template for Solved Problem 4.1

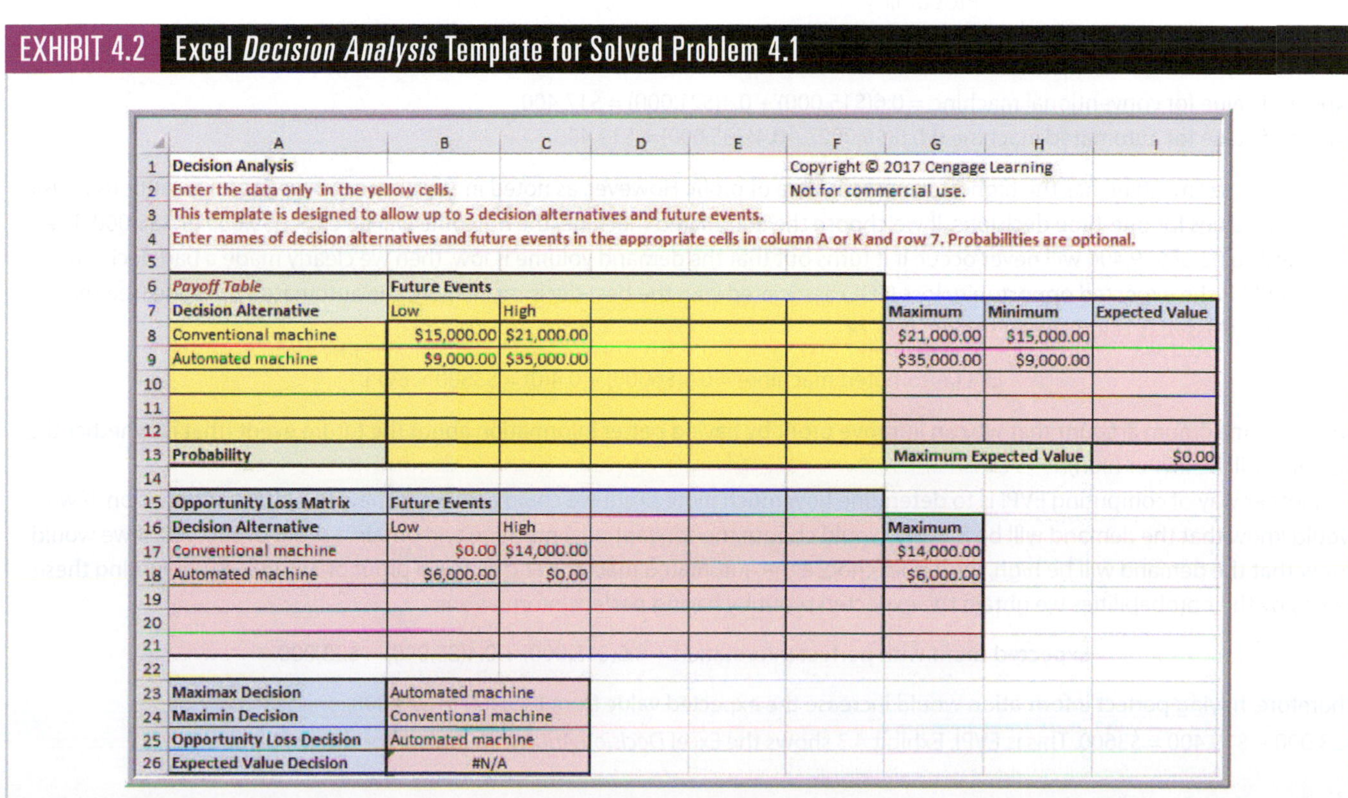

Decision Analysis — Copyright © 2017 Cengage Learning. Not for commercial use.

Enter the data only in the yellow cells.

This template is designed to allow up to 5 decision alternatives and future events.

Enter names of decision alternatives and future events in the appropriate cells in column A or K and row 7. Probabilities are optional.

Payoff Table	Future Events		Maximum	Minimum	Expected Value
Decision Alternative	Low	High			
Conventional machine	$15,000.00	$21,000.00	$21,000.00	$15,000.00	
Automated machine	$9,000.00	$35,000.00	$35,000.00	$9,000.00	
Probability			Maximum Expected Value		$0.00

Opportunity Loss Matrix	Future Events		Maximum
Decision Alternative	Low	High	
Conventional machine	$0.00	$14,000.00	$14,000.00
Automated machine	$6,000.00	$0.00	$6,000.00

Maximax Decision	Automated machine
Maximin Decision	Conventional machine
Opportunity Loss Decision	Automated machine
Expected Value Decision	#N/A

An aggressive, risk-taking manager would use the maximax criterion that would choose the decision that maximizes the maximum profit among all events—in this case, the automated machine. A conservative, risk-averse manager would use the maximin criterion that would choose the decision that will maximize the minimum possible profit among all events—in this case, the conventional machine. The minimax regret criterion chooses the decision that minimizes the maximum opportunity loss; this would be the automated machine. There is no optimal decision; the decision involves determining how much risk one is willing to take.

SOLVED PROBLEM 4.2: MAKING A TECHNOLOGY CHOICE DECISION WITH EVENT PROBABILITIES

In the Maling Manufacturing situation in Solved Problem 4.1, suppose that the company can obtain reasonable estimates of the probabilities that the future demand will be high or low. Based on their research, they estimate a 0.6 probability of a low demand volume and a 0.4 probability of a high demand volume. What is the expected value decision and expected value of perfect information (EVPI)?

Solution:

	Demand Volume	
Decision	**Low**	**High**
Conventional machine	$15,000	$21,000
Automated machine	$9,000	$35,000
Probability	0.6	0.4

The expected profits for each decision are:

Expected value for conventional machine = 0.6($15,000) + 0.4($21,000) = $17,400
Expected value for automated machine = 0.6($9,000) + 0.4($35,000) = $19,400

The automated machine has the highest expected value of profit. However, as noted in Supplement B we must be cautious in using expected values for one-time decisions. If we choose the automated machine, the outcome will be either $9,000 or $35,000. The expected value of $19,400 will never occur. If it turns out that the demand volume is low, then we clearly made a bad decision.

The EVPI is the expected opportunity loss (EOL) associated with the best decision, namely, the automated machine (see the opportunity loss matrix in Solved Problem 4.1), or

EOL(automated machine) = 0.6($6000) + 0.4(0) = $3600 = EVPI.

This is the maximum amount that we can improve profit by having better information about the future event (that is, whether the demand will be low or high).

Another way of computing EVPI is to determine how much more profit we could achieve by having perfect information. If we would know that the demand will be low, we would choose the conventional machine and obtain a profit of $15,000; if we would know that the demand will be high, we would choose the automated machine and obtain a profit of $35,000. By weighting these values by their probabilities we obtain the expected profit by having perfect information:

Expected profit with perfect information = 0.6($15,000) + 0.4(35,000) = $23,000.

Therefore, having perfect information would increase the expected value from $19,400 to $23,000, or an increase of $23,000 − $19,400 = $3600. This is EVPI. Exhibit 4.3 shows the Excel *Decision Analysis* template for this problem.

EXHIBIT 4.3 Excel *Decision Analysis* Template for Solved Problem 4.2

	A	B	C	D	E	F	G	H	I
1	Decision Analysis					Copyright © 2017 Cengage Learning			
2	Enter the data only in the yellow cells.					Not for commercial use.			
3	This template is designed to allow up to 5 decision alternatives and future events.								
4	Enter names of decision alternatives and future events in the appropriate cells in column A or K and row 7. Probabilities are optional.								
5									
6	*Payoff Table*	Future Events							
7	Decision Alternative	Low	High				Maximum	Minimum	Expected Value
8	Conventional machine	$15,000.00	$21,000.00				$21,000.00	$15,000.00	$17,400.00
9	Automated machine	$9,000.00	$35,000.00				$35,000.00	$9,000.00	$19,400.00
10									
11									
12									
13	Probability	0.60	0.40				Maximum Expected Value		$19,400.00
14									
15	Opportunity Loss Matrix	Future Events							
16	Decision Alternative	Low	High				Maximum		
17	Conventional machine	$0.00	$14,000.00				$14,000.00		
18	Automated machine	$6,000.00	$0.00				$6,000.00		
19									
20									
21									
22									
23	Maximax Decision	Automated machine							
24	Maximin Decision	Conventional machine							
25	Opportunity Loss Decision	Automated machine							
26	Expected Value Decision	Automated machine							
27	EVPI	$3,600.00							

Break-Even Analysis for Technology Decisions Break-even analysis is a simple approach to analyze profit or loss, or to make an economical choice between two options that vary with volume. Supplement C provides a short tutorial on break-even analysis, and we suggest that you review this before studying the solved problems.

SOLVED PROBLEM 4.3: EVALUATING TECHNOLOGY DECISIONS USING BREAK-EVEN ANALYSIS

Based on its initial decision analysis, Maling Manufacturing has decided to purchase an automated machine. However, two vendors, A and B, can provide the technology, but their costs differ. Maling Manufacturing has determined that if it purchased the machine from vendor A, it would cost $85,000, but the unit cost for each part, will only be $3.50. If they purchase from vendor B, the machine would cost $60,000 but the unit cost of each part would be $5.00 because of higher maintenance. They anticipate making 20,000 parts over the life of the machine; however, the actual value is uncertain. Which one should be chosen? How would the uncertainty about the number of parts needed affect this decision?

Solution:

a. Using formulas (C.1) and (C.7) in Supplement C, we have

$$\text{Total cost (TC)} = \text{Fixed cost (FC)} + \text{Unit cost (C)} \times \text{Quantity (Q)} \qquad (C.1)$$

$$TCA = FCA + CA \times Q = \$85,000 + \$3.50(20,000) = \$155,000$$
$$TCB = FCB + CB \times Q = \$60,000 + \$5.00(20,000) = \$160,000$$

$$\text{Cost difference (D)} = \text{Total cost vendor A (TCA)} - \text{Total cost vendor B (TCB)} \qquad (C.7)$$
$$D = TCA - TCB = \$155,000 - \$160,000 = -\$5,000$$

Therefore, the machine from vendor A is less expensive and should be chosen. Exhibit 4.4 shows the Excel *Break-Even* template from MindTap for these calculations.

EXHIBIT 4.4 Comparison of Vendor Costs Using the Excel *Break-Even* Template for Solved Problem 4.3

	G	H
4	Technology Choice Decision	
5	Quantity	20,000
6		
7	Option A	
8	Fixed cost	$85,000.00
9	Unit cost	$3.50
10		
11	Option B	
12	Fixed cost	$60,000.00
13	Unit cost	$5.00
14		
15	Total Cost Option A	$155,000.00
16	Total Cost Option B	$160,000.00
17	Cost difference (Option A - Option B)	-$5,000.00
18	Economical Decision	Option A

Because of the uncertainty in the number of parts they will need to make, finding the break-even point would help in making a rational decision. As explained in Supplement C, set the total costs equal to each other and solve for the break-even point:

$$\$85{,}000 + \$3.50Q^* = \$60{,}000 + \$5.00Q^*$$

$$\$25{,}000 = \$1.50Q^*$$

$$Q^* = 16{,}667 \text{ units}$$

Unless there is a substantial risk that the required production would fall below this value, the company should still choose vendor A. We could use the Excel *Goal Seek* tool as described in Supplement C to find the break-even point using the Excel template. This is shown in Exhibit 4.5.

EXHIBIT 4.5 Break-Even Point Using the Excel *Break-Even* Template for Solved Problem 4.3

	G	H
4	Technology Choice Decision	
5	Quantity	16,667
6		
7	Option A	
8	Fixed cost	$85,000.00
9	Unit cost	$3.50
10		
11	Option B	
12	Fixed cost	$60,000.00
13	Unit cost	$5.00
14		
15	Total Cost Option A	$143,333.33
16	Total Cost Option B	$143,333.33
17	Cost difference (Option A - Option B)	$0.00
18	Economical Decision	Break-even

SOLVED PROBLEM 4.4: A RENT-OR-BUY DECISION

The Physics Laboratory is trying to decide whether it should rent or purchase a copier machine. The cost of renting a machine would be \$200 per year including all service calls plus \$0.04 (4 cents) per page copied. The cost of purchasing a machine would be \$600 plus \$50 per year for a service contract in case the machine breaks down. There is no variable cost associated with purchasing the machine. The laboratory will have to purchase its own paper regardless of whether it rents or purchases the copier machine. For what quantities of copies will it be advantageous to rent the machine instead of purchasing it?

Solution:

This problem is similar to the outsourcing example in Supplement C. Purchasing is analogous to producing in-house, and renting is analogous to outsourcing. To determine whether it is advantageous to rent instead of purchasing, we need to find the break-even point. If Q = number of copies, then the cost of purchasing is \$600 + \$50 = \$650 (a fixed cost). The cost of renting is \$200 + \$0.04Q. The break-even point is found by solving

$$\$650 = \$200 + \$0.04Q^*$$
$$Q^* = \$450/\$0.04 = 11{,}250 \text{ pages}$$

If the number of copies is less than the break-even quantity of 11,250 pages, it is cheaper to rent than purchase. Exhibit 4.6 shows the use of the Excel *Break-Even* template after using Goal Seek to find the break-even quantity.

EXHIBIT 4.6 Portion of Excel *Break-Even* Template for Solved Problem 4.4

	D	E
4	Outsourcing Decision	
5	Quantity	11,250
6		
7	Produce In-House	
8	Fixed cost	\$650.00
9	Unit cost	
10		
11	Outsource	
12	Fixed cost	\$200.00
13	Unit cost	\$0.04
14		
15	Total In-House Production Cost	\$650.00
16	Total Outsourced Cost	\$650.00
17	Cost difference (In-House - Outsourced)	\$0.00
18	Economical Decision	Break-even

CHAPTER 4 LEARNING OBJECTIVE SUMMARIES

4.1 **Describe different types of technology and their role in manufacturing and service operations.** Some examples of hard technology are computers, computer chips and microprocessors, optical switches and communication lines, satellites, sensors, robots, automated machines, and RFID tags. Some examples of soft technology are database systems, artificial intelligence programs, and voice recognition software. Computer integrated manufacturing systems (CIMSs) play an important role in modern manufacturing.

All organizations face common issues regarding technology:

- The right technology must be selected for the goods that are produced.
- Process resources such as machines and employees must be set up and configured in a logical fashion to support production efficiency.
- Labor must be trained to operate the equipment.
- Process performance must be continually improved.
- Work must be scheduled to meet shipping commitments/customer promise dates.
- Quality must be ensured.

4.2 **Explain how manufacturing and service technology and analytics strengthen the value chain.** With all the new technology that has evolved, a new perspective and capability for the value chain has emerged—the *e-commerce view of the value chain.* This includes business-to-business (B2B), business-to-customer (B2C), customer-to-customer (C2C), and government-to-customer (G2C) value chains; some examples are GE Plastics, Federal Express, and eBay, respectively. Business analytics play a critical role in managing value chains, particularly for integrating and analyzing data throughout the value chain within an information systems framework. Two key information systems that drive value chain management are enterprise resource planning (ERP) and customer relationship management (CRM). ERP combines each department's information into a single, integrated system with a common database so that departments can easily share information and communicate with each other. A typical CRM system includes market segmentation and analysis, customer service and relationship building, effective complaint resolution, cross-selling of goods and services, and pre- and and postproduction processes such as preproduction order processing and postproduction field service.

4.3 **Explain the benefits and challenges of using technology.** Benefits and challenges are summarized in Exhibit 4.1. Benefits include new jobs, higher productivity and quality, improved competitiveness, mass customization, reduced cost, and better sustainability. Challenges include higher skill level requirements, integration with legacy systems, less employee-customer interaction, and job losses.

4.4 **Describe key technology decisions and how analytics can assist in making technology decisions** Managers must understand the relative advantages and disadvantages of using technologies and their impact on the workforce, such as job specialization versus enlargement, empowerment, training, teams and work groups, job design, recognition and reward, and career advancement, Scalability is a key factor that affects technology decisions. Analytical methods such as decision analysis and break-even analysis can help to understand the economics of alternative technologies and assist managers in making good decisions.

KEY TERMS

- **Computer-aided design/computer-aided engineering (CAD/CAE)**
- **Computer-aided manufacturing (CAM)**
- **Computer-integrated manufacturing systems (CIMSs)**
- **Computer numerical control (CNC)**
- **Customer relationship management (CRM)**
- **Decision analysis**
- **E-service**
- **Flexible manufacturing systems (FMSs)**
- **Hard technology**
- **High scalability**
- **Low scalability**
- **Numerical control (NC)**
- **Robot**
- **Scalability**
- **Soft technology**

REVIEW QUESTIONS

4.1 1. Describe different types of technology and their role in manufacturing and service operations.

4.1 2. Define hard and soft technology and give an example.

4.1 3. What is CAD/CAE? Provide one nontextbook example.

4.1 4. What is 3-D printing? Provide two examples.

4.2 5. Explain how manufacturing and service technology strengthen the value chain.

4.2 6. What is CRM? How does it help OM do its job?

4.2 7. What types of technology might a major hotel chain use to enhance the customer experience?

4.3 8. Explain the benefits and challenges of using technology.

4.4 9. Explain the concept of scalability. Identify one low and one highly scalable organization and explain why you categorize them as such.

4.4 10. How can decision analysis be used in making technology decisions?

4.4 11. How can break-even analysis help managers make decisions?

DISCUSSION QUESTIONS AND EXPERIENTIAL ACTIVITIES

4.1 12. *Bloomberg Businessweek* published an article titled "This Economic Model Organized Asia for Decades. Now It's Broken" (June 21, 2017; https://www.bloomberg.com/news/features/2017-06-21/this-economic-model-organized-asia-for-decades-now-it-s-broken). Research and explain the concept of the "Asian Jobs Ladder" and the disruptive role of automation. What conclusions can be reached?

4.1 13. Describe at least one application of modern technology in each of these service industries:

a. Financial services
b. Public and government services
c. Transportation services
d. Educational services
e. Hotel and motel services

How does your example application improve things, or does it?

4.1 14. Identify and describe (maximum of one typed page) a service encounter where technology helps create and deliver the service in total or in part. What hard and soft technology most likely is involved?

4.1 15. Research radio frequency identification devices (RFID) and provide examples of how they are or might be used to improve productivity in operations.

4.1 16. Investigate the current technology available for laptop computers, cell phones, or tablets. Select two different models and compare their features and operational characteristics, as well as manufacturer's support and service. Briefly explain how you might advise (a) a college student majoring in art and (b) a salesman for a high-tech machine tool company in selecting the best device for his or her needs (maximum of two typed pages).

4.1 17. Identify and describe (maximum of two typed pages) a business that uses ERP to manage its value chain (if possible, draw a picture of key elements of the value chain such as sourcing, production, shipping, sales, billing, and so on). What benefits and challenges does ERP bring to this business?

4.2 18. Explain how manufacturing and service technology and business analytics strengthen the value chain.

4.2 19. Discuss each of these statements. What might be wrong with each of them?

a. "We've thought about computer integration of all our manufacturing functions, but when we looked at it, we realized that the labor savings wouldn't justify the cost."

b. "We've had these computer-controlled robots on the line for several months now, and they're great! We no longer have to reconfigure the whole line to shift to a different product. I just give the robots new instructions, and they change operations. Just wait until this run is done and I'll show you."

c. "Each of my manufacturing departments is authorized to invest in whatever technologies are necessary to perform its function more effectively. As a result, we have state-of-the-art equipment throughout our factories—from CAD/CAM to automated materials handling to robots on the line. When we're ready to migrate to a CIM environment, we can just tie all these pieces together."

d. "I'm glad we finally got that CAD system," the designer said, a computer-generated blueprint in hand. "I was able to draw these plans and make modifications right on the computer screen in a fraction of the time it used to take by hand." "They tell me this new computer-aided manufacturing system will do the same for me," the manufacturing engineer replied. "I'll just punch in your specs and find out."

4.2 20. Describe a situation where self-service and technology help create and deliver the customer benefit package to the customer. Provide examples of how such a system can cause a defect, mistake, or service upset.

4.2 21. How can social media enhance the sale of a physical good? A service? Provide examples. Explain.

4.3 22. Research and write a short paper (maximum of two typed pages) on the impact of electric vehicles on the three dimensions of sustainability.

4.3 23. Identify and describe (maximum of two typed pages) two apps for your cell phone or electronic reader and how they improve your productivity and quality of life.

4.3 24. Research what jobs are most and least likely to be replaced by technology and automation.

4.3 25. Research and write a short paper (maximum of two typed pages) on the advantages and disadvantages of "technology transfer" when a firm partners with a firm in another country.

4.4 26. Research and write a short paper about how business analytics or advances in information systems influence the use of technology and decision making in operations management.

COMPUTATIONAL PROBLEMS AND EXERCISES

These exercises require you to apply the formulas and methods described in the chapter. The problems should be solved manually.

4.4 27. Southland Corporation's decision to produce a new line of recreational products has resulted in the need to choose one of two automated manufacturing systems based on proposals from two vendors, A and B. The economics of this decision depends on the market reaction to the new product line. The possible long-run demand has been defined as low, medium, or high. Based on detailed financial analyses of system costs as a function of volume and sales under each demand scenario, the following payoff table gives the projected profits in millions of dollars.

	Long-Run Demand		
Decision	**Low**	**Medium**	**High**
Vendor A	$150	$200	$200
Vendor B	$50	$200	$500

a. Determine the best decisions using the maximax, maximin, and opportunity loss decision criteria.

b. Assume that the best estimate of the probability of low long-run demand is 0.20, of medium long-run demand is 0.15, and of high long-run demand is 0.65. What is the best decision using the expected value criterion?

4.4 28. The Gorman Manufacturing Company must decide whether to purchase a component part from a supplier or to manufacture the component at its own plant. If demand is high, it would be to Gorman's advantage to manufacture the component. If demand is low, however, Gorman's unit manufacturing cost will be high because of underutilization of equipment. The projected profit in thousands of dollars for Gorman's make-or-buy decision is as follows.

	Demand		
Decision	**Low**	**Medium**	**High**
Manufacture component	$220	$40	$100
Purchase component	$210	$45	$70

a. Determine the best decisions using the maximax, maximin, and opportunity loss decision criteria.

b. Assume that the probability of low demand is 0.35, of medium demand is 0.35, and of high demand is 0.30. What is the best decision using the expected value criterion and what is the expected value of perfect information?

4.4 29. You need to expand your small business, Paddle Incorporated, that manufactures paddle board rackets. The fixed cost for the new technologically advanced equipment is $15,000. The variable cost to produce each unit using the new equipment is $10, and the selling price for the finished product is $25. What quantity needs to be produced and sold to break even?

4.4 30. The Vera Molding company has two alternatives for meeting a customer requirement for 9,000 units of a specialty molding. If done in-house, fixed cost would be $350,000 with variable cost at $30 per unit. Alternative two is to outsource for a total cost of $80 per unit.

a. What is the break-even quantity?

b. Should the firm make the 9,000 units in-house or outsource?

4.4 31. Luke's Ristorante wants to add a sea bass dinner to their menu. A small grill and oven would be added to the kitchen cooking area at a fixed cost of $9,000. The variable cost per fish dish is estimated to be $9.60 per entrée. If 600 fish dinners are sold per year to break even, what should be the price of the new fish entrée?

4.4 32. Meyers Window Company introduced a new window design but sales were below expectations. Sales in units last year were 800 units. Variable cost per unit averaged $105.72, the fixed cost was $42,000, and the selling price was $149.99.

a. What is the break-even quantity for this new window?

b. If sales stayed the same next year, how much would the variable cost have to be reduced to break even?

4.4 33. MovieFix is a video streaming company that sells to a potential audience of 300,000 customers. The selling price is $20 per month and its variable cost is $14.62 per month. What is the most the company should spend on annual fixed costs to acquire and maintain the firm's equipment if it serves 300,000 customers?

4.4 34. Pesto Restaurant must decide between two types of technology in its kitchen. Option A is to use an induction oven process with a fixed cost of $20,000 and a variable cost of $6.51 per meal. Option B is to use a gas-fired oven process with a fixed cost of $12,000 and a variable cost of $7.86 per meal. The average selling price per meal is $18.60.

a. What is the break-even quantity?

b. If the restaurant manager expects to sell 1,500 meals, which option, A or B, is best? Justify.

4.4 35. The selling price per box for Cynthia's Cookies is $19.95. Fixed costs are $65,000 and the variable cost per box is $9.88.

a. What is the break-even quantity?

b. If sales last year were 8,200 boxes, what was the net profit?

4.4 36. In Problem 35, Cynthia's Cookies must decide between two improvement options. Option 1 is spending $10,000 on a new online marketing campaign that is expected to increase last year's sales (units) by 20 percent. Option 2 is to reduce variable costs by 10 percent by spending $10,000 on equipment and process improvements. For Option 2, sales remain at 8,200 boxes. (The assumption here is that each option is equally costly to implement.) What option provides the higher profits?

EXCEL-BASED PROBLEMS

For these problems, you may use Excel or the spreadsheet templates in MindTap to assist in your analysis.

4.4 37. Edwards Machine Tools needs to purchase a new machine. The basic model is slower but costs less, while the advanced model is faster but costs more. Profitability will depend on future demand. The following table presents an estimate of profits over the next three years.

	Demand Volume		
Decision	Low	Medium	High
Basic model	$80,000	$100,000	$150,000
Advanced model	$40,000	$110,000	$220,000

Given the uncertainty associated with the demand volume, and no other information to work with, how would you make a decision? Use the Excel template *Decision Analysis* and explain your reasoning.

4.4 38. Suppose that in Problem 37 a forecasting study determines that the probabilities of demand volume are Low = 0.2, Medium = 0.2, and High = 0.6. Use the Excel template *Decision Analysis* to determine the expected value decision. How appropriate is it to use this criterion? Interpret EVPI, the expected value of perfect information.

4.4 39. A company is considering three vendors for purchasing a CRM system: Delphi Inc., CRM International, and Murray Analytics. The costs of the system are expected to depend on the length of time required to implement the system, which depends on such factors as the amount of customization required, integration with legacy systems, resistance to change, and so on. Each vendor has different expertise in handling these things, which affect the cost. The costs (in millions of $) are shown below for short, medium, and long implementation durations. Use the Excel template *Decision Analysis* to identify what vendor to select. Clearly explain your recommendation.

Decision Alternative	Short	Medium	Long
Delphi, Inc.	$4.00	$5.50	$8.00
CRM International	$6.00	$4.25	$6.50
Murray Analytics	$4.50	$5.00	$7.20

4.4 40. A hospital is evaluating whether to outsource or perform in-house a large set of blood and urine laboratory tests. The fixed cost of the laboratory equipment located in the hospital is $800,000 and the weighted average variable cost per test if performed in-house is $28.75. A third-party lab located three miles from the hospital will perform the same tests with more advanced and faster equipment. The lab distributes the results electronically to the hospital at a price of $31.00. If the annual volume last year was 250,000 tests, should the hospital do all lab tests in-house or outsource? Use the Excel template *Break-Even* to determine the best decision.

4.4 41. Suzy's Temporary Employee (STE) business, located in a big city, can do an online criminal background check in-house for $1.29 per search with a fixed cost of $29,000. A third-party online security firm offered to do a similar security search for $8.00 per person with an annual service contract with STE. If STE's forecast is 3,000 searches next year, should STE continue to do the search in-house or accept the third-party offer? Use the Excel template *Break-Even* to determine the best decision. What other criteria are important in making this decision?

4.4 42. A manager of Paris Manufacturing that produces computer hard drives is planning to lease a new automated inspection system. The manager believes the new system will be more accurate than the current manual inspection process. The firm has had problems with hard drive defects in the past and the automated system should help catch these defects before the drives are shipped to the final assembly manufacturer. The relevant information follows.

Option A: Current Manual Inspection System
 Annual fixed cost = $45,000
 Inspection variable cost per unit = $15 per unit
Option B: New Automated Inspection System
 Annual fixed cost = $165,000
 Inspection variable cost per unit = $0.55 per unit

a. Suppose annual demand is 8,000 units. Use the Excel template *Break-Even* to determine whether or not the firm should lease the new inspection system?
b. Use the Excel Goal Seek tool to find the break-even quantity.

4.4 43. Assume the cost factors given in Problem 42 have not changed. A marketing representative of *NEW-SPEC*, a firm that specializes in providing manual inspection processes for other firms, approached Paris Manufacturing and offered to inspect parts for $19 each with no fixed cost. They assured Paris Manufacturing the accuracy and quality of their manual inspections would equal the automated inspection system. Demand for the upcoming year is forecast to be 8,000 units. Should the manufacturer accept the offer? Use the Excel template *Break-Even* to make your recommendation.

RoboJet Car Wash

Drew Ebel was contemplating buying an automated car wash franchise as a family business. His wife Caroline, their two kids, Jasmine and Luke, and their dog, Lilly, were a close-knit family that were tired of the bureaucracy of corporate and government jobs. The dual-career family had saved $200,000 in cash. Drew, who was 62, could cash in some of his retirement accounts to free up another $200,000. These monies would be used for a down payment.

Drew and Caroline needed to develop a business plan stating the strategy and mission of their business, evaluate the economics of the business using break-even analysis, select a site and buy the property, and start up the business with an idea of providing superior customer service—a premium car washing experience using automation. Drew had a Bachelor's Degree in Mechanical Engineering and Caroline earned a Bachelor's Degree in Accounting. Drew and Caroline collected information on the cost of the franchise shown in Case Exhibit 4.1.

NeONBRAND/unsplash.com

SOURCE: Ryko [https://www.ryko.com/systems/softgloss-maxx/]

Car Wash Industry

In 1914, the first car washing assembly line was opened in Detroit, Michigan. People pushed Model-T cars through the wash stations in a circular route. By 1928, a people-powered chain conveyor pulled cars through a straight (serial) assembly line. The vehicles got dirty, especially on the roads of the era. By 1932, there were 32 carwashes in the United States. In the 1930s, car wash owners began to ask manufacturers if they could build automated brushes and other electro-mechanical car washing devices. In 1946, the first semiautomatic car wash system was developed with an overhead sprinkler system, three sets of manually operated brushes, and a conveyer powered by an electric motor pulling cars along a straight line. By the 1950s, automated car washing systems were developed by several manufacturers. Today, five people using a robotic car washing system do the work of over twenty people using 1950s technology. Once robots were able to vacuum and clean the interior of nonstandard vehicles and wipe down the exterior with no damage, one person could operate the entire car wash operation from a single computer console.

Available Information Collected to Date

Investment costs are shown in Exhibit 4.7. Variable costs are estimated to be $15.16 per vehicle per year. Variable costs included in this estimate account for four full-time employees plus the manager, environmental fees and disposal, office expense, insurance, and some accounting, attorney, routine maintenance, and advertising expenses. We assume that the car wash operates 300 days per year. The average price of a wash is $22 per car. Drew and Caroline had good estimates of price and variable costs, but were puzzled as to what was a good fixed cost estimate. Detailing vehicles, dent repair, and windshield repair are a separate on-site department. These services generate an estimated net profit of $130,000 per year.

The key factor in a successful car wash business is location. This includes site location, traffic density and patterns, and the demographics of the surrounding area. Based on ZIP code analysis, one promising location showed a high net worth for residents in the area. For that area, they estimated demand to be between 10,000 and 14,000 car washes per year. The closest full-service car wash business to this new location was 5.2 miles away.

EXHIBIT 4.7 RoboJet Car Wash—Investment Costs

Type of Investment	Cost and Related Information
Site (premium location in high traffic intersection)	$300,000 to $600,000
Equipment	
Automated car wash system	$300,000
Initial parts inventory	$5,000
Detailing, dent, and windshield repair equipment	$7,000
Other equipment (cash register, televisions for waiting area, telephone, online hookup)	$6,000
Building	
Car wash assembly line (tunnel) building	$250,000
Detailing garages	$50,000
Lobby and office complex	$45,000
Pole sign and advertising board(s)	$8,000
Licenses, inspections, building permits, incorporation fee, attorney, architect, engineer, environmental impact report, and utilities to property	$50,000
Start-up—Cash On Hand	$50,000 to $100,000
Property and building closing, title insurance, land survey, filing fees, appraisal, vending license and occupation fees, and environmental audits	$5,000
Total Investment Costs: $450,000 + 300,000 + 5,000 + 7,000 + 6,000 + 250,000 + 50,000 + 45,000 + 8,000 + 50,000 + 75,000 + 5,000	$1,251,000
*Mortgage (assuming investment cost of $1,251,000 − $400,000 down payment = $851,000 mortgage)	$6,000 per month

Drew and Caroline wondered what other characteristics make for a successful car wash service. Some car wash conveyors are designed with a capacity to process up to 100 cars per hour, but most car wash conveyors operated in the 30 cars per hour or less range. The speed of the conveyor can be changed in most car wash systems depending on demand, weather, and degree of dirt on vehicles. Keeping the robots operating is a struggle, and all car wash owners have stories of losing a high demand day of sales because of machine breakdowns and parts shortages.

Case Questions for Discussion:

Drew and Caroline had many issues they needed to address in their business plan. They also planned to visit automated conveyer car wash sites and talk to owners. Some of the questions on their mind include:

1. How might the strategy, mission, competitive priorities, and customer benefit package of this business affect their technology decisions?
2. What issues and problems should you anticipate with managing this business, particularly with respect to technology? What role does operations play in successfully handling these issues and problems?
3. What does a break-even analysis tell you about this business venture? What if they could reduce variable cost and/or increase the average price per wash?
4. Should Drew and Caroline go into this business?

Bracket International—The RFID Decision

Jack Bracket, the CEO of Bracket International (BI), has grown his business to sales last year of $78 million, with a cost of goods sold of $61 million. Average inventory levels are about $14 million. As a small manufacturer of steel shelving and brackets, the firm operates three small factories in Ohio, Kentucky, and South Carolina. BI's number one competitive priority is "service first," while high product quality and low cost are the number two and three priorities. Service at BI includes preproduction services such as customized engineering design, production services such as meeting customer promise dates and being flexible to customer-driven changes, and postproduction services such as shipping, distribution, and field service.

The Ohio and Kentucky factories are automated flow shops, whereas the South Carolina factory specializes in small custom orders and is more of a batch-processing job shop. All three factories use bar coding labels and scanning equipment to monitor and control the flow of materials. BI manually scans about 9,850 items per day at all three factories. An item may be an individual part, a roll of sheet steel, a box of 1,000 rivets, a pallet load of brackets, a box of quart oil cans, a finished shelf or bracket set ready for shipment, and so on. That is, whatever a bar code label can be stuck on is bar coded. A factory year consists of 260 days. One full-time BI employee works 2,000 hours per year with an average salary including benefits of $69,000.

Two recent sales calls have Mr. Bracket considering switching from the old bar coding system to a radio-frequency identification device (RFID) system. The RFID vendors kept talking about "on-demand" operational planning and control and how their RFID and software systems could speed up the pace of BI's workflows. One RFID vendor provided the following information:

- Bar code scan times for the sheet metal business (similar to BI) average 10 seconds per item and include employee time to find the bar code, pick up the item and/or position the item or handheld bar code reader so it can read the bar code, and in some cases physically reposition the item. Item orientation is a problem with manual bar coding.
- The 10-second bar code scan time does not include the employee walking to the bar coding area or equipment. It is assumed that the employee is in position to scan the item. The 10 seconds does not include the time to replace a scratched or defective bar code label. Replacing a damaged bar code tag, including changes to the computer system, may take up to five minutes.
- All three BI factories can be fitted with RFID technology (readers, item tags, and hardware-related software) for $620,000. In addition, new supply chain operating system software that takes advantage of the faster pace of RFID information is priced for all three factories at $480,000 and includes substantial training and debugging consulting services.
- RFID scan time is estimated to be 2/100ths of a second, or basically instantaneous.

- For the sheet metal business, bar code misreads average 2 percent (i.e., 0.02) over the year of total reads, and this is estimated to reduce to 0.2 percent (i.e., 0.002) for RFID technology. The 0.2 percent is due to damaged RFID tags or occasional radio-frequency interference or transmission problems. Misreads are a problem because items are lost and not recorded in BI's computer system. The vendor guessed that a single misread could cost a manufacturer on average $4 but noted this estimate could vary quite a bit.

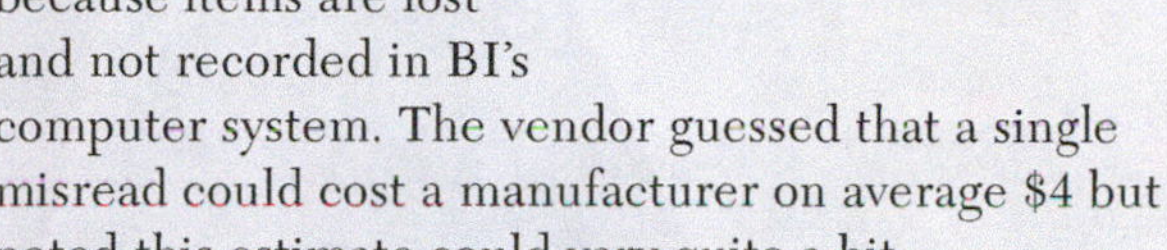

Kondor83/Shutterstock.com

- According to the RFID vendors, other benefits of RFID systems include readily located inventory, fewer required inventory audits, and reduced misplacements and theft. However, they did not have any information quantifying these benefits.

Bracket International recently had problems adapting quickly to changing customer requirements. BI had to deny a Wolf Furniture job order request because it could not react quickly enough to a change in job specifications and order size. Eventually, BI lost the Wolf Furniture business, which averaged about $2 million per year. Another BI customer, Home Depot, keeps talking about BI needing to be more flexible because Home Depot's on-demand point-of-sale systems require frequent changes to BI orders. Home Depot is BI's top customer, so every effort needs to be made to keep Home Depot happy.

Mr. Bracket doesn't think throwing away the bar coding system that works is a good idea. The BI employees are familiar with using bar coding technology, whereas the RFID technology seems hidden from employees. He also doesn't think the return on investment (ROI) on an RFID system is compelling. So why does he feel so guilty when the RFID vendors leave his office? Is he doing the right thing or not? He has an obligation to his trusted employees to do the right thing. Should he adopt RFID based purely on strategic and/or economic benefits? He writes down several questions he needs to investigate.

Case Questions for Discussion:

1. How does RFID compare to bar coding?
2. What is the economic payback in years for this possible RFID adoption? (Hint: There are two benefits that can be quantified—labor savings due to faster scan times and misread savings. Annual benefits divided by economic benefits equals payback.)
3. What are the risks of adopting a new technology too early? Too late?
4. What do you recommend Mr. Bracket do in the short and long terms? Explain your reasoning.

Integrative Case: Hudson Jewelers

The Hudson Jewelers case study found in MindTap integrates material found in each chapter of this book.

Case Questions for Discussion:

1. What are the advantages and disadvantages from the service provider's (jeweler's) perspective of using "design your own ring" 3-D/CAD technology at the retail store level? What are the risks from the customer's viewpoint?
2. Research jewelry retail store software programs and summarize their capabilities in terms of customer relationship management, accounting, point of sale, inventory management, payment systems, and customer loyalty programs. Provide references.

5 Goods and Service Design

LEARNING OBJECTIVES

After studying this chapter, you should be able to:

5-1 Describe the steps involved in designing goods and services.

5-2 Explain the concept and application of quality function deployment.

5-3 Describe how the Taguchi loss function, reliability, design for manufacturability, and design for sustainability are used for designing manufactured goods.

5-4 Define the five elements of service-delivery system design.

5-5 Describe the four elements of service-encounter design.

5-6 Explain how goods and service design concepts are integrated at LensCrafters.

Fuel efficiency and environmental concerns are important in developing nations as the number of vehicles on their streets continues to rise.

Frank Bienewald/LightRocket/Getty Images

In developing markets such as China and India, consumers can't afford large, expensive cars, much less drive them in overcrowded population centers. Fuel efficiency as well as environmental concerns are also important, as developing nations seek to cap carbon emissions even as the number of vehicles on their streets continues to rise. But these consumers are not willing to buy inferior cars that simply cost less. Rather, like most of us, they want low-cost vehicles that are designed to meet their needs and still have high quality, reliability, and style—in other words, have value. Consumers in India, for instance, need cars that maximize passenger room because they use their autos primarily as family vehicles to drive around town; by contrast, in the West, with its better roads and routine long-distance driving, cargo capacity matters more. Indian drivers are willing to pay a bit more for cars that offer the latest in comfort, safety, and utility, but not for cars with power windows and locks or fancy sound systems. Automatic transmissions are desirable in India and China—nobody wants to keep pressing the clutch and shifting gears in the inevitable stop-and-go traffic—but powerful engines are not. Succeeding in developing markets, therefore, requires rethinking from start to finish how new cars should be designed and built. It calls for a deep understanding of the unique needs of consumers and the ability to assemble the combination of power trains, bodies, features, and options that best match those desires—at affordable prices.[1]

WHAT DO YOU THINK?

How important are design and value in your purchasing decisions? Provide some examples for goods and services.

Perhaps the most important strategic decision that any firm makes involves the design and development of new goods and services, and the value chain structure and processes that make and deliver them. In fact, decisions about what goods and services to offer and how to position them in the marketplace often determine the ultimate growth, profitability, and success of the firm. Every design project—a new automobile or cell phone, a new online or financial service, even a new pizza—is a series of trade-offs: between technology and functionality, between ambition and affordability, between the desires of the people creating the object and the needs of the people using it.[2]

In today's world, the complexity of customer benefit packages requires a high level of coordination throughout the value chain. As the authors of the opening anecdote about automobile design note, design for value "involves a series of complex, varied, carefully thought-out decisions about which types of engines to use; which equipment should be standard; what safety add-ons to include; how parts and materials are engineered; and which designs are most attractive to the target customer base." At the other end of the value chain, sales and maintenance, and even financing, should also be examined for new ideas: Given limited dealer networks, might roving mechanics be sent out to perform regular maintenance? Could entire extended families enter into financing deals for new cars? Similar questions apply to the design of every good and service.

5-1 Designing Goods and Services

To design and improve goods and services, most companies use some type of structured process. The typical goods and services development processes are shown in Exhibit 5.1. In general, the designs of both goods and services follow a similar path. The critical differences lie in the detailed product and process design phases.

Steps 1 and 2—Strategic Mission, Analysis, and Competitive Priorities Strategic directions and competitive priorities should be consistent with and support the firm's mission and vision. These steps require a significant amount of research and innovation involving marketing, engineering, operations, and sales functions, and should involve customers, suppliers, and employees throughout the value chain. The data and information that result from this effort provide the key input for designing the final customer benefit package.

Step 3—Customer Benefit Package Design and Configuration Clearly, firms have a large variety of possible choices in configuring a customer benefit package (CBP). For example, when buying a new vehicle, an automobile dealer might include such options as leasing, free oil changes and/or maintenance, a performance driving school, free auto washes, service pickup and delivery, loaner cars, and so on.

Essentially, CBP design and configuration choices revolve around a solid understanding of customer needs and target markets, and the value that customers place on such attributes as the following:

- **Time**—Many grocery stores now offer self-service checkout to reduce customer waiting time. Manufacturers such as Dell use the Internet to acquire customer information for more responsive product design.
- **Place**—UPS has UPS Stores strategically located for customer convenience that also provide packaging services; many companies offer day-care centers on-site to provide convenience to their employees.

EXHIBIT 5.1 An Integrated Framework for Goods and Service Design

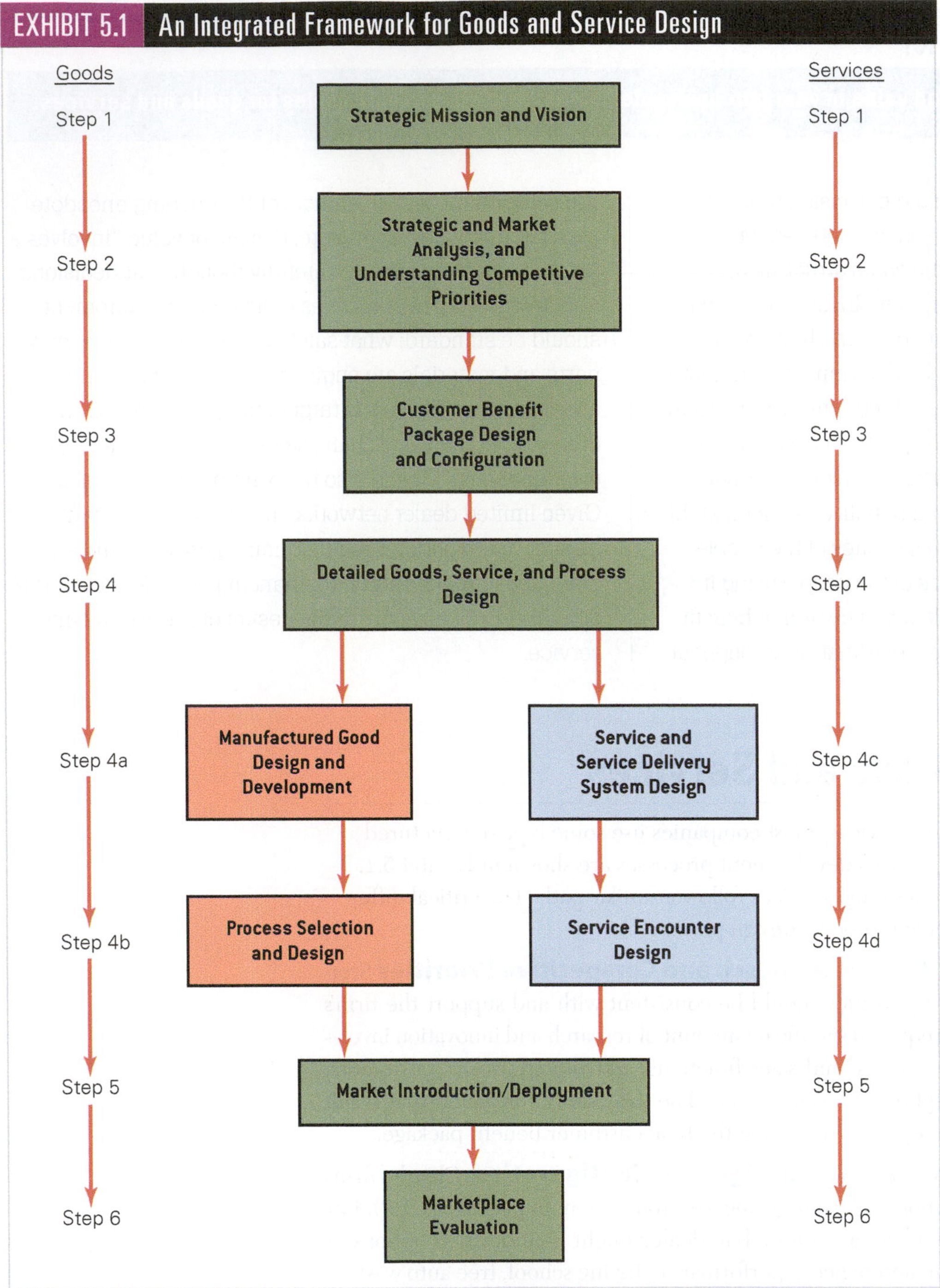

- **Information**—Bank of America provides an Internet search capability for the best home equity loan. A business dedicated to providing guitar music books and videos (www.ChordMelody.com) offers a telephone hot line to speak with a professional guitarist for questions on selecting the proper instructional and performance material.
- **Entertainment**—Some Dick's Sporting Goods Stores provide a rock-climbing wall for children while other family members shop. A pianist serenades shoppers at Nordstrom's department stores. Some minivans have built-in DVD players.
- **Exchange**—Retail stores such as Best Buy allow customers to travel to the store and buy the goods, purchase goods on their websites and have them delivered, or purchase goods on their websites and have them ready to be picked up at the store.
- **Form**—For manufactured goods, form is associated with the physical characteristics of the good and addresses the important customer need of aesthetics. An interior designer might use methods such as sketches, photographs, physical samples, or even computer-simulated renderings to show how a kitchen might be transformed.

A job-seeking service such as Monster.com provides pure information value, whereas buying an automobile or going on a vacation involves all six types.

Step 4—Detailed Goods, Services, and Process Design If a proposal survives the concept stage—and many do not—each good or service in the CBP, as well as the process that creates it, must be designed in more detail. This is where the designs of goods and services differ, as suggested by the alternate paths in Exhibit 5.1. The first three steps in Exhibit 5.1 are more strategic and conceptual in nature, whereas step 4 focuses on detailed design and implementation.

The design of a manufactured goods focuses on its physical characteristics—dimensions, materials, color, and so on. Much of this work is done by artists and engineers to translate customer requirements into physical specifications. This is the focus of step 4a in the exhibit. The process by which the good is manufactured (i.e., the configuration of machines and labor) can be designed as a separate activity (step 4b), with, of course, proper communication and coordination with the designers of the good.

The design of a service in steps 4c and 4d in Exhibit 5.1, however, cannot be done independently from the "process" by which the service is delivered. The process by which the service is created and delivered (i.e., "produced") is, in essence, the service itself! For example, the steps that a desk clerk follows to check in a guest at a hotel represent the process by which the guest is served and (hopefully) experiences a sense of satisfaction. Thus, service design must be addressed from two perspectives—the service delivery system and the service encounter—as noted in steps 4c and 4d in Exhibit 5.1.

> Every design project—a new automobile or cell phone, a new online or financial service, even a new pizza—is a series of trade-offs: between technology and functionality, between ambition and affordability, between the desires of the people creating the object and the needs of the people using it.

For both goods and services, this phase usually includes prototype testing. **Prototype testing** *is the process by which a model (real or simulated) is constructed to test the product's performance under actual operating conditions, as well as consumer reactions to the prototypes.* For example, at General Motors (GM), parts are designed and digitally analyzed using special software; one-third scale models are produced, assembled, and tested in a wind tunnel to evaluate the aerodynamics of automobile designs. Today, many companies use advanced technology to perform rapid prototyping—the process of building prototypes quickly to reduce product development cost and time to market. GM has a laboratory where 15 specialists take part orders from GM design centers all over the world, build them within hours, and then express ship them back, allowing designers and engineers to quickly evaluate them.[3]

Step 5—Market Introduction/Deployment In this step, the final bundle of goods and services—the customer benefit package—is advertised, marketed, and offered to customers. For manufactured goods, this includes making the item in the factory and shipping it to warehouses or wholesale and retail stores; for services, it might include hiring and training employees or staying open an extra hour in the evening. For many services it means building sites such as branch banks or hotels or retail stores.

Engines like this are designed and digitally analyzed as part of the prototype testing process.

LaRosa's Pizzeria: Understanding the Voice of the Customer

LaRosa's Pizzeria, a regional chain of informal Italian restaurants in the greater Cincinnati area, realized that customers know what they want. To gather information to help design a new restaurant configuration, LaRosa's went out to current and potential customers and noncustomers in nonmarket areas to acquire the voice of the customer. Here are some real examples of customers' experiences at other restaurants that LaRosa's clearly wanted to avoid:

- "So there I was, like herded cattle, standing on the hard concrete floor, cold wind blasting my ankles every time the door opened, waiting and waiting for our name to be called."
- "And then I saw a dirty rag being slopped around a dirty table."
- "I swear! The salad looked like the server ran down to the river bank and picked weeds and grass—I'm never going back!"
- "When they're that age, going to the bathroom is a full-contact sport—they're reaching and grabbing at everything, and you're trying to keep them from touching anything because the bathroom is so dirty."

Customer Satisfaction

Rawpixel.com/Shutterstock.com

In the last example, what the customer really was saying is "The bathroom tells me what the kitchen might be like. Do I really want to eat here?" Clean bathrooms turned out to be the most important customer requirement that the company learned from listening to the voice of the customer.

What are the implications of the other customer comments? Interestingly, none of these comments revolves totally around the physical good (food) itself; service-facility and service-encounter quality are clearly important customer requirements!

> The process by which the service is created and delivered (i.e., "produced") is, in essence, the service itself!

Step 6—Marketplace Evaluation The marketplace is a graveyard of missed opportunities: poorly designed goods and services and failed execution resulting from ineffective operations. The final step in designing and delivering a customer benefit package is to constantly evaluate how well the goods and services are selling, and customers' reactions to them.

5-2 Customer-Focused Design

The design of a good or service should reflect customer wants and needs, which are often termed customer requirements. *Customer requirements, as expressed in the customer's own words, are called the* **voice of the customer**. The design process must translate the voice of the customer into specific technical features that characterize a design and provide the "blueprint" for manufacturing or service delivery. Technical features are generally expressed in the language of designers and engineers; examples include the type and amount of materials, size and shape of parts, strength requirements, service procedures to follow, and employee behavior during service interactions. An effective approach for doing this is called *quality function deployment.* **Quality function deployment (QFD)** *is an approach to guide the design, creation, and marketing of goods and services by integrating the voice of the customer into all decisions.* QFD can be applied to a specific manufactured good or service, or to the entire CBP. The process is initiated with a matrix, which, because of its structure (as shown in Exhibit 5.2), is often called the *House of Quality*.

> The marketplace is a graveyard of missed opportunities: poorly designed goods and services and failed execution resulting from ineffective operations.

Building a House of Quality begins by identifying the voice of the customer and technical features of the design and listing them in the appropriate places in the diagram. As shown in Exhibit 5.2, the voice of the customer and the technical features create a matrix structure in the center of the diagram. By evaluating how each technical feature relates to each customer requirement (using a scale such as "very strong," "strong," "weak," or "no relationship"), designers can determine how well a design reflects the actual customer requirements. This might be based on expert experience, customer surveys, or other experiments. The lack of a relationship between a customer requirement and any of the technical features would suggest that the final good or service will have difficulty in meeting customer needs. Similarly, if a technical feature does not relate to any customer requirement, it may be unnecessary in the design. The roof of the House of Quality shows the interrelationships between any pair of technical features, and these relationships help in answering questions such as "How does a change in one product characteristic affect others?" This can help refine a design and evaluate trade-offs in design decisions.

To the right of the relationship matrix is an assessment of the importance of each customer requirement and how competitors' products compare with the proposed design in

EXHIBIT 5.2 The House of Quality

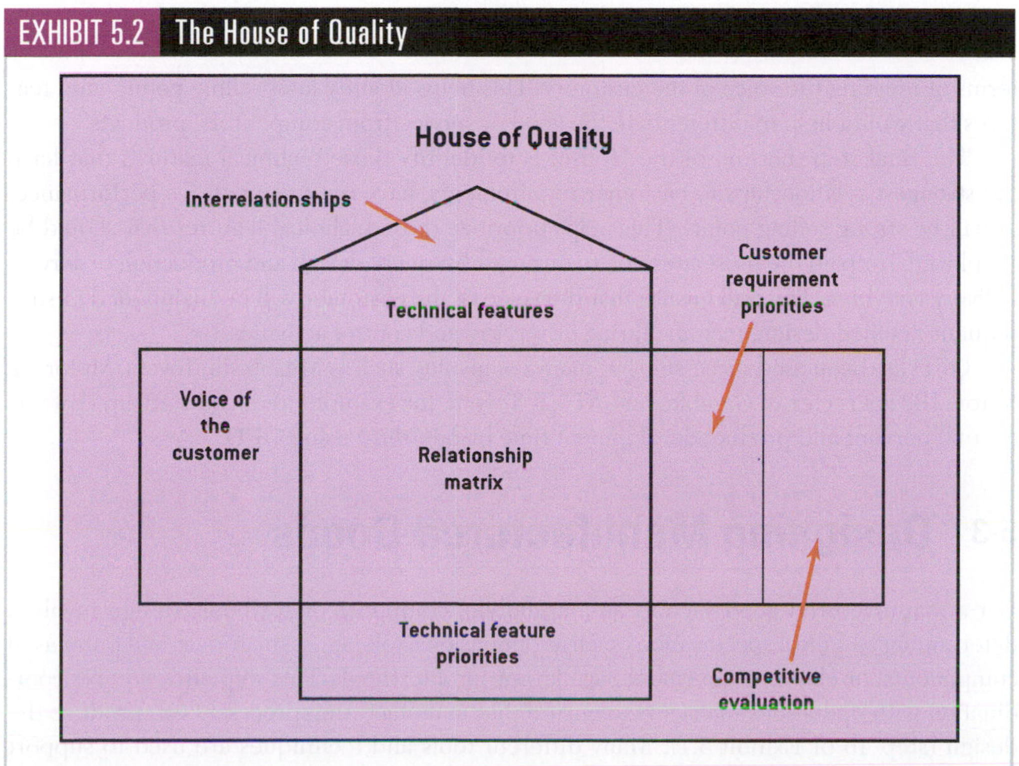

Using the House of Quality: Building a Better Pizza

A restaurant wants to develop a "signature" pizza. The voice of the customer in this case consists of four attributes. The pizza should be tasty, healthy, and visually appealing, and should provide good value. The "technical features" that can be designed into this particular product are price, size, amount of cheese, type of additional toppings, and amount of additional toppings. The symbols in the matrix in the exhibit at the right show the relationships between each customer requirement and technical feature. For example, taste bears a moderate relationship with amount of cheese and a strong relationship with type of additional toppings. In the roof, the price and size area seem to be strongly related (as size increases, the price must increase). The competitive evaluation shows that competitors are currently weak on nutrition and value, so those attributes can become key selling points in a marketing plan if the restaurant can capitalize on them. Finally, at the bottom of the house are targets for the technical features based on an analysis of customer-importance ratings and competitive ratings. The features with asterisks are the ones to be "deployed," or emphasized, in subsequent design and production activities.

House of Quality Example for a Pizza

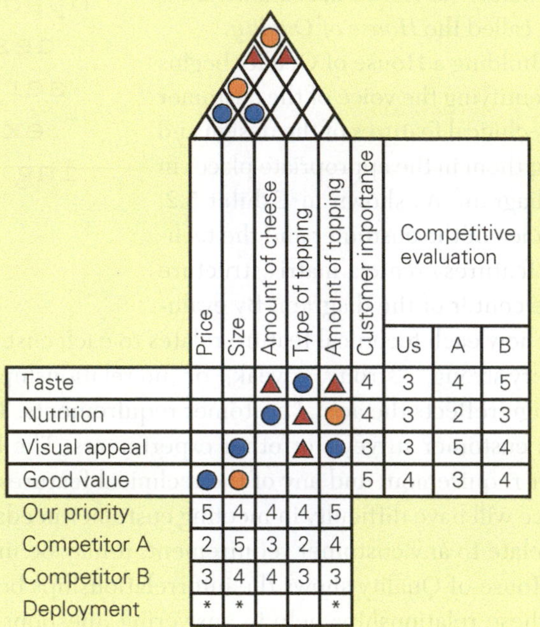

Legend: 1=low, 5=high
Very strong relationship
Strong relationship
Weak relationship

terms of meeting the voice of the customer. This helps identify key "selling points" and features that would help to differentiate the good or service from competitors' products.

The final step (bottom of the House) is to identify those technical features that have the strongest relationships to customer requirements, have poor competitive performance, or will be strong selling points. This helps prioritize those technical features that should be "deployed," or paid the most attention to during subsequent design and production or service delivery activities. This will ensure that the voice of the customer will be maintained in subsequent detailed design, manufacturing or service, and control activities.

QFD has been used successfully by many companies, such as Mitsubishi, Toyota, Motorola, Xerox, IBM, Procter & Gamble, and AT&T. Toyota, for example, reduced start-up costs by over 60 percent and product development time by one-third using QFD.

5-3 Designing Manufactured Goods

For a manufactured good such as an automobile, computer, or textbook, design involves determining technical specifications such as dimensions, tolerances, materials, and purchased components; or choice of fonts and page layout for a textbook. This step also requires coordination with operations managers to ensure that manufacturing processes can produce the design (step 4b of Exhibit 5.1). Many different tools and techniques are used to support product design activities; we review some of the most important ones in this section.

5-3a Tolerance Design and the Taguchi Loss Function

For most manufactured goods, design blueprints specify a target dimension (called the *nominal*), along with a range of permissible variation (called the *tolerance*); for example, 0.500 ± 0.020 cm. The nominal dimension is 0.500 cm but may vary anywhere in the range from 0.480 to 0.520 cm. This is sometimes called the *goal-post model* (see Exhibit 5.3). Tolerance design involves determining the acceptable tolerance. Narrow tolerances improve product functionality and performance, but tend to raise manufacturing costs because they usually require higher-precision technology. Wide tolerances, on the other hand, reduce costs, but may have a negative impact on product performance. Thus, designers must consider these trade-offs and should use sound scientific and engineering approaches to optimizing tolerances rather than simply setting them judgmentally.

Genichi Taguchi, a Japanese engineer, maintained that the traditional practice of setting design specifications is inherently flawed. The goal-post model assumes that any value within the tolerance range is acceptable, but those outside are not. In the previous example, what is the real difference between 0.479 and 0.481? Not much; the impact of either value on the performance characteristic of the product would be about the same, yet a part having the dimension of 0.481 would be acceptable, whereas the other would not be. In reality, neither value is close to the nominal specification. Taguchi argued that the smaller the variation from the nominal specification, the better the quality. In turn, products are more consistent and fail less frequently, and thus are less costly in the long run.

Taguchi measured quality as the variation from the target value of a design specification and then translated that variation into an economic "loss function" that expresses the cost of variation in monetary terms. This approach can be applied to both goods and services.

Taguchi proposed measuring the loss resulting from the deviation from the target by a quadratic function so that larger deviations cause increasingly larger losses. The loss function is

$$L(x) = k(x - T)^2 \qquad [5.1]$$

where

$L(x)$ is the monetary value of the loss associated with deviating from the target, T;

x is the actual value of the dimension; and

k is a constant that translates the deviation into dollars.

Exhibit 5.4 illustrates this Taguchi loss function. The constant, k, is estimated by determining the cost of repair or replacement if a certain deviation from the target occurs. Solved problems 5.1 and 5.2 show an example of the Taguchi loss function and how it can be used to set design tolerances.

EXHIBIT 5.3 Traditional Goal-Post View of Conforming to Specifications

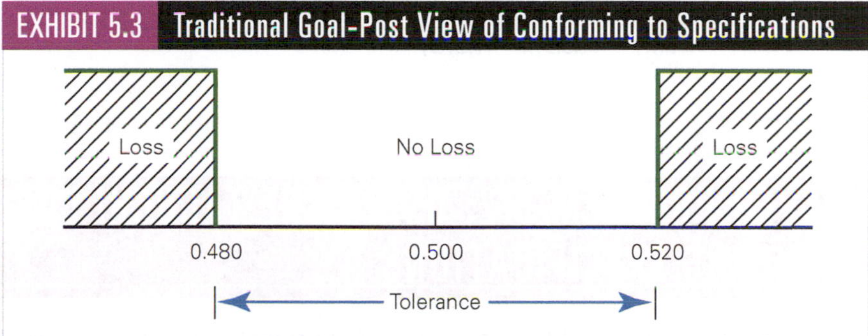

EXHIBIT 5.4 Nominal-Is-Best Taguchi Loss Function

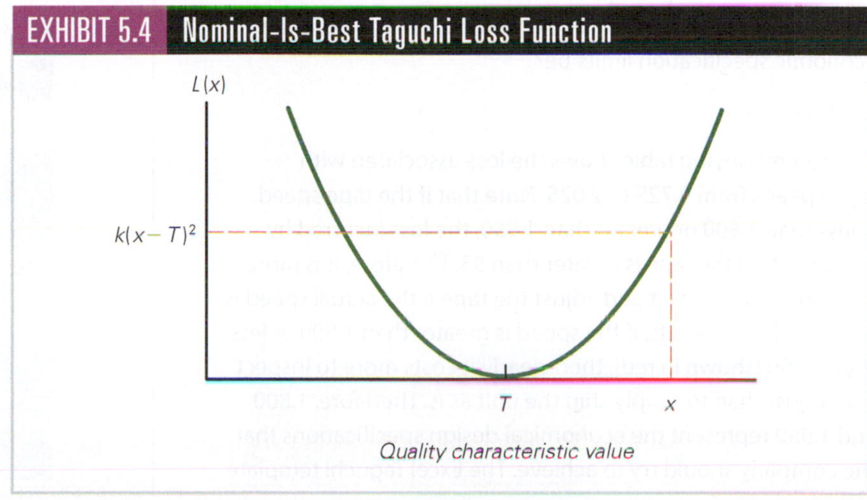

SOLVED PROBLEM 5.1: FINDING THE TAGUCHI LOSS FUNCTION

Cassette tapes are still used in some handheld recording devices and in less expensive portable musical instrument recording devices. The desired speed of a cassette tape is 1.875 inches per second. Any deviation from this value causes a change in pitch and tempo and thus poor sound quality. Suppose that adjusting the tape speed under warranty when a customer complains and returns a device costs a manufacturer $20. Based on past information, the company knows the average customer will return a device if the tape speed is off the target by at least 0.15 inch per second; in other words, when the speed is either 2.025 or 1.725. Find the Taguchi loss function.

EXHIBIT 5.5 Portion of Excel *Taguchi* Template

	A	B	C	D
1	**Taguchi Loss Function**			
2	Enter data only in yellow cells.			
3				
4	**Calculation of *k* for the Loss Function**			
5	**Deviation from target**	0.15		
6	**Loss associated with deviation**	$20.00		
7	**k**	$888.89		
8				
9	**Loss Calculation for a Specific *x***			
10	**Target specification, T**	1.875		
11	**Dimensional value, x**	1.925		
12	**k**	$888.89		
13	**Loss**	$2.22		

Solution:

The loss associated with a deviation of $(x-T) = 0.15$ from the target is $L(x) = \$20$. To find the loss function for any value of x, we substitute these values into Equation 5.1 and solve for k:

$$20 = k(0.15)^2$$
$$k = 888.9$$

and thus the loss function is

$$L(x) = 888.9(x - 1.875)^2$$

For example, if the actual speed is 1.925 inches per second, the Taguchi loss function estimates that the economic loss will be $L(1.9) = 888.89(1.925 - 1.875)^2 = \$2.22$. Some, but not all, customers might perceive poor sound quality for this small of a deviation and return the product for adjustment, so the average loss is smaller. Exhibit 5.5 shows a portion of the Excel *Taguchi* template in MindTap that can be used to perform these calculations.

SOLVED PROBLEM 5.2: USING THE TAGUCHI LOSS FUNCTION TO SET ECONOMIC SPECIFICATIONS

For the scenario in Solved Problem 5.1, suppose that a technician tests the tape speed prior to packaging and can adjust the speed to the target of 1.875 at a cost of $5. What should the economic specification limits be?

Solution:

The accompanying table shows the loss associated with tape speeds from 1.725 to 2.025. Note that if the tape speed is less than 1.800 or greater than 1.950, the loss incurred by not adjusting the tape is greater than $5. Therefore, it is more economical to inspect and adjust the tape if the actual speed is outside of these limits. If the speed is greater than 1.800 or less than 1.950 (shown in red), then clearly it costs more to inspect and adjust than to simply ship the unit as is. Therefore, 1.800 and 1.950 represent the economical design specifications that the company should try to achieve. The Excel Taguchi template computes these economic specifications using a break-even analysis approach in rows 15–19, as shown in Exhibit 5.6.

Tape Speed, *x*	*L(x)*
1.725	$20.00
1.740	$16.20
1.755	$12.80
1.770	$9.80
1.785	$7.20
1.800	$5.00
1.815	$3.20
1.830	$1.80
1.845	$0.80
1.860	$0.20
1.875	$0
1.890	$0.20
1.905	$0.80

Tape Speed, *x*	*L(x)*
1.920	$1.80
1.935	$3.20
1.950	$5.00
1.965	$7.20
1.980	$9.80
1.995	$12.80
2.010	$16.20
2.025	$20.00

EXHIBIT 5.6 Economic Design Specifications Using the Excel *Taguchi* Template

	A	B	C	D
1	**Taguchi Loss Function**			
2	**Enter data only in yellow cells.**			
3				
4	**Calculation of *k* for the Loss Function**			
5	**Deviation from target**	0.15		
6	**Loss associated with deviation**	$20.00		
7	**k**	$888.89		
8				
9	**Loss Calculation for a Specific *x***			
10	**Target specification, T**	1.875		
11	**Dimensional value, x**	1.925		
12	**k**	$888.89		
13	**Loss**	$2.22		
14				
15	**Economic Design Specifications**			
16	**Target specification, T**	1.875		
17	**k**	$888.89		
18	**Cost of inspection and adjustment**	$5.00		
19	**Break-Even Tolerance**	0.075		
20	**Lower specification limit**	1.800		
21	**Upper specification limit**	1.950		

5-3b Design for Reliability

Everyone expects their car to start each morning and their computer to work without crashing. **Reliability** *is the probability that a manufactured good, piece of equipment, or system performs its intended function for a stated period of time under specified operating conditions.* Reliability applies to services as well as manufacturing; a system could be a service process where each stage (work activity or station) is analogous to a component part in a manufactured good.

Reliability is a *probability*, that is, a value between 0 and 1. For example, a reliability of 0.97 indicates that, on average, 97 out of 100 times the item will perform its function for a given period of time under specified operating conditions. Often, reliability is expressed as a percentage simply to be more descriptive (97 percent reliable). Reliability can be improved by using better components or by adding redundant components. In either case, costs increase; thus, trade-offs must be made.

Automotive Gremlins

Have you even encountered mysterious noises and rattles in your engine or transmission? While some might attribute such mischievous behavior to gremlins, there is usually an engineering explanation. In transmissions, for example, which consist of many gears and other parts in a "stack-up" assembly, the lack of precision tolerances can lead to problems in performance such as gear clashes upon shifting and, eventually, premature failure. When the parts in the assembly are at the high end of the tolerance range, the stack-up becomes too tight; if they are at the low end of the tolerance range, the stack-up is too loose. In either case, drivers will notice the difference. This is why Taguchi advocated producing parts on the nominal specification with minimal variation.

Many manufactured goods consist of several components that are arranged in series but are assumed to be independent of one another, as illustrated in Exhibit 5.7. If one component or process step fails, the entire system fails. If we know the individual reliability, p_j, for each component, j, we can compute the total reliability of an n-component series system, R_s. If the individual reliabilities are denoted by $p_1, p_2, \ldots, p_n$ and the system reliability is denoted by R_s, then

$$R_s = (p_1)(p_2)(p_3)\cdots(p_n) \qquad [5.2]$$

Other designs consist of several parallel components that function independently of each other, as illustrated in Exhibit 5.8. The entire system will fail only if all components fail; this is an example of redundancy. The system reliability of an n-component parallel system is computed as

$$R_p = 1 - (1 - p_1)(1 - p_2)(1 - p_3)\cdots(1 - p_n) \qquad [5.3]$$

Many other systems are combinations of series and parallel components. To compute the reliability of such systems, you have to analyze the structure and use formulas 5.2 or 5.3 to replace series subsystems or parallel subsystems with equivalent single components until the final structure is either a simple series or parallel system. These formulas can help designers and engineers assess the reliability of proposed designs and optimize their performance. Solved Problems 5.3–5.6 illustrate the use of these formulas and an Excel template for reliability analysis.

EXHIBIT 5.7 Structure of a Serial System

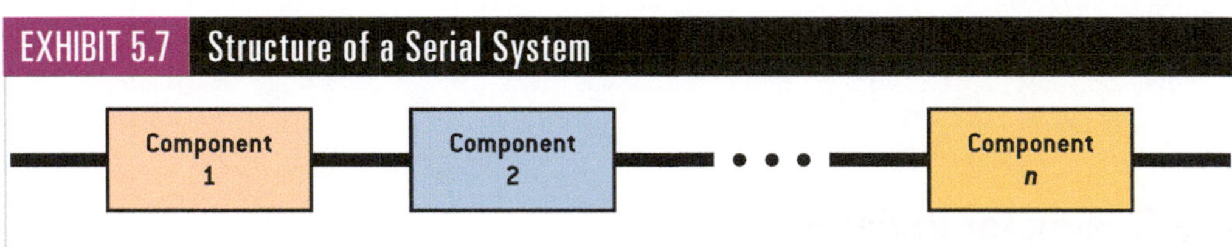

EXHIBIT 5.8 Structure of a Parallel System

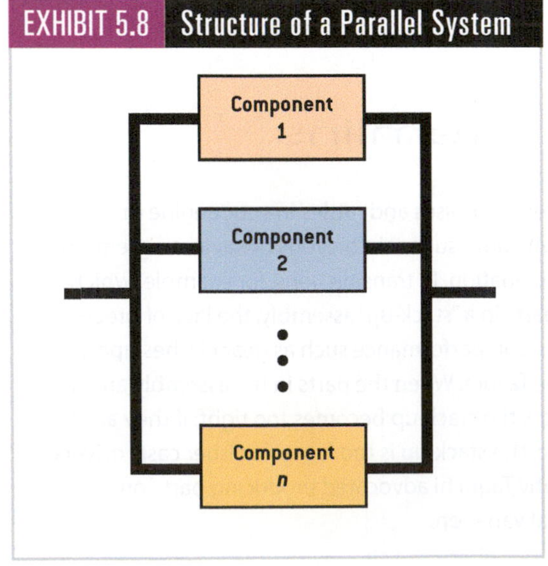

5-3c Design for Manufacturability

Many aspects of product design can adversely affect manufacturability and, hence, quality. Some parts may be designed with features difficult to fabricate repeatedly or with unnecessarily tight tolerances.[4] Some parts may lack details for self-alignment or features for correct insertion. In other cases, parts so fragile or so susceptible to corrosion or contamination may be damaged in shipping or by internal handling. Sometimes a design simply has more parts than are needed to perform the desired functions, which increases the chance of assembly error. Thus, problems of poor design may show up as errors, poor yield, damage, or functional failure in fabrication, assembly, test, transport, and end use.

Design for manufacturability (DFM) *is the process of designing a product for efficient production at the highest level of quality.* One way of doing this is through product simplification. **Product simplification** *is the process of trying to simplify designs to reduce complexity and costs and thus improve productivity, quality, flexibility, and customer satisfaction.* The simpler the design, the

SOLVED PROBLEM 5.3: COMPUTING RELIABILITY OF A SERIES SYSTEM

Consider a new laboratory blood analysis machine consisting of three major subassemblies: A, B, and C. The manufacturer is evaluating the preliminary design of this piece of equipment. The reliabilities of each subassembly are shown in Exhibit 5.9. What is the system reliability?

EXHIBIT 5.9 Subassembly Reliabilities

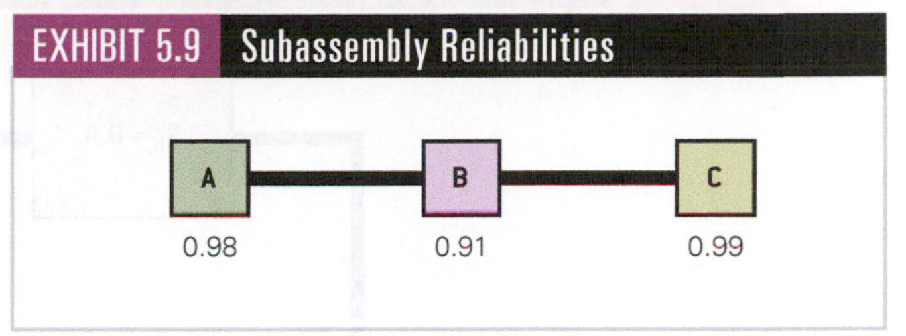

Solution:

Because this is a series system, we use Equation 5.2:

$$R_s = (0.98)\,(0.91)\,(0.99) = 0.883 \text{ or } 88.3 \text{ percent}$$

SOLVED PROBLEM 5.4: COMPUTING RELIABILITY OF A PARALLEL SYSTEM

The reliability of an electronic component in an automated machine tool is 0.91. The design engineer is considering creating a parallel (backup) system as shown in Exhibit 5.10. (Assume equipment software switches to the working component if one fails.) How much is reliability improved?

EXHIBIT 5.10 Parallel System

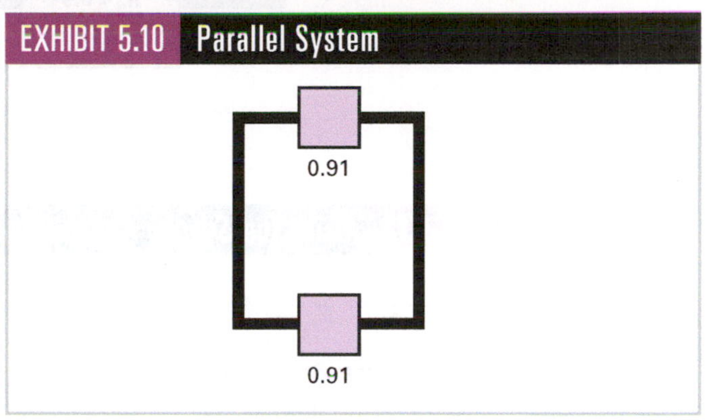

Solution:

Using Equation 6.3, the reliability of the parallel system is

$$R_p = 1 - (1 - 0.91)\,(1 - 0.91) = 1 - 0.0081 = 0.9919.$$

The reliability has increased from 91 percent to over 99 percent by adding the redundant component.

SOLVED PROBLEM 5.5: COMPUTING THE RELIABILITY OF A SERIES SYSTEM WITH A PARALLEL SUBSYSTEM

Exhibit 5.11 shows as series system with parallel redundancy for component B. What is the reliability of this system?

Solution:

First, compute the reliability of the parallel subsystem for component B using formula 5.3: $R_B = 1 - (1 - 0.9)^3 = 0.999$. We use the Excel template *System Reliability* available on MindTap to facilitate the calculations as shown in Exhibit 5.12. Replace this parallel system with a single component having this reliability, resulting in a series system shown in Exhibit 5.13. Next, compute the reliability of this equivalent series system using formula 5.2 or the Excel template as shown in Exhibit 5.14. $R_S = (0.99)(0.999)(0.96)(0.98) = 0.93$. The reliability of the original system is therefore 0.93.

EXHIBIT 5.11 A Series–Parallel System

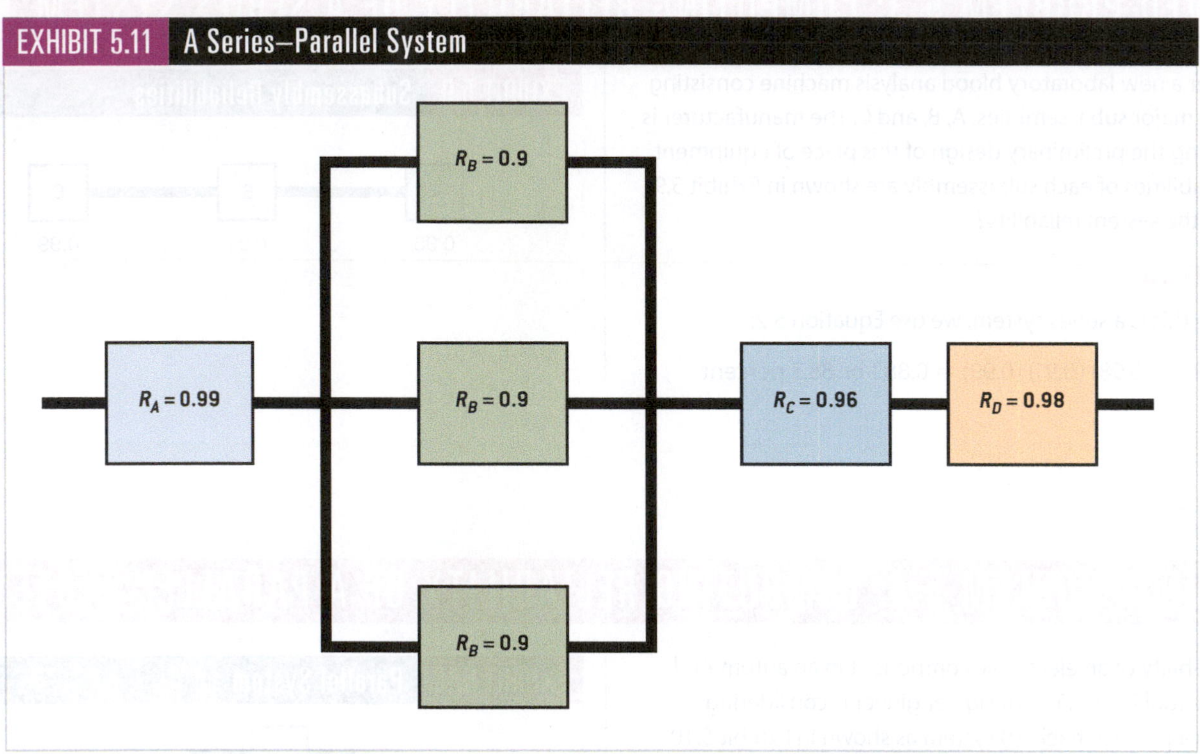

EXHIBIT 5.12 Using the *System Reliability* Excel Template for Component B

	A	B	C	D	E
1	System Reliability			Copyright © 2019 Cengage Learning	
2	Enter data only in yellow cells			Not for commercial use.	
3					
4	Series Systems			Parallel Systems	
5					
6	Component	Reliability		Component	Reliability
7	Component 1			Component 1	0.9
8	Component 2			Component 2	0.9
9	Component 3			Component 3	0.9
10	Component 4			Component 4	
11	Component 5			Component 5	
12	Component 6			Component 6	
13	Component 7			Component 7	
14	Component 8			Component 8	
15	Component 9			Component 9	
16	Component 10			Component 10	
17	System Reliablity	0.000000000		System Reliablity	0.9990000000

EXHIBIT 5.13 Equivalent Series System

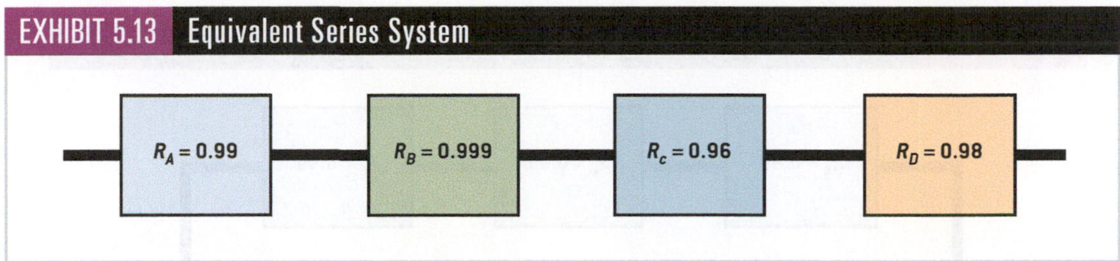

EXHIBIT 5.14 Using the *System Reliability* Template for the Equivalent Series System

	A	B	C	D	E
1	System Reliability			Copyright © 2019 Cengage Learning	
2	Enter data only in yellow cells			Not for commercial use.	
3					
4	Series Systems			Parallel Systems	
5					
6	Component	Reliability		Component	Reliability
7	Component 1	0.99		Component 1	
8	Component 2	0.999		Component 2	
9	Component 3	0.96		Component 3	
10	Component 4	0.98		Component 4	
11	Component 5			Component 5	
12	Component 6			Component 6	
13	Component 7			Component 7	
14	Component 8			Component 8	
15	Component 9			Component 9	
16	Component 10			Component 10	
17	System Reliablity	0.930460608		System Reliablity	0.0000000000

SOLVED PROBLEM 5.6: COMPUTING THE RELIABILITY OF A PARALLEL SYSTEM WITH SERIES SUBSYSTEMS

Exhibit 5.15 shows a parallel system that consists of two series subsystems. What is the reliability of this system?

Solution:

Convert each series subsystem to an individual component. Using the *System Reliability* template or formula 5.2, we see that $R_{ABC} = (0.95)(0.98)(0.99) = 0.92169$ and $R_{DE} = (0.99)(0.97) = 0.9603$. This results in the equivalent parallel system shown in Exhibit 5.16. The reliability of this parallel system is $R = (1 - 0.92169)(1 - 0.9603) = 0.9969$.

EXHIBIT 5.15 A Parallel System with Series Subsystems

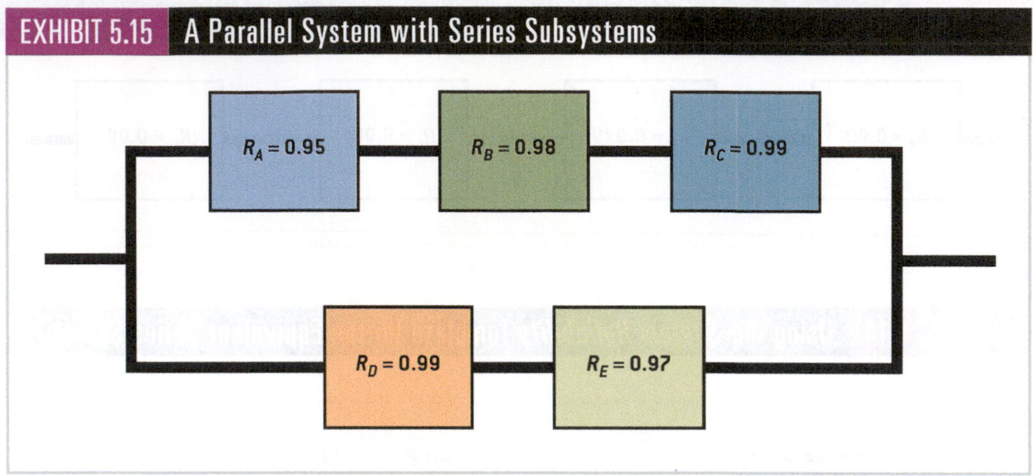

EXHIBIT 5.16 Equivalent Parallel System

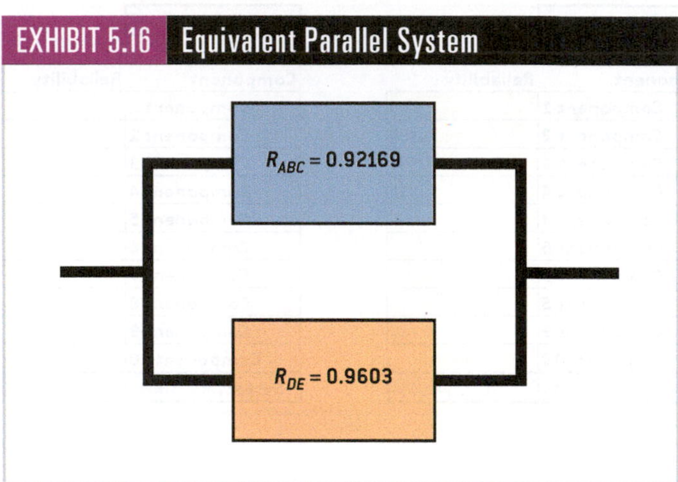

fewer opportunities for error, the faster the flow time, the better the chance of high process efficiency, and the more reliable the manufactured good or service process. For example, the redesign of the Cadillac Seville rear-bumper assembly reduced the number of parts by half and cut assembly time by 57 percent, to less than eight minutes, saving the company over $450,000 annually in labor costs.[5] Because many of the eliminated parts were squeak- and rattle-causing fasteners, nuts, bolts, and screws, the change also improved the quality of the car.

Toyota: Simple Design Simplifies Operations

Manufacturing complexity is driven by choices and options. For the Toyota Venza, simplicity is key. In effect, there is one model that is available in four versions: a four-cylinder engine with front-wheel drive or all-wheel drive, or a six-cylinder engine with the same. Not only does this design strategy give consumers a nicely equipped vehicle right from the get-go, but it also makes things comparatively easier at the Toyota Georgetown assembly plant by reducing the complexity of assembling a much larger variety of different models and options.[6]

5-3d Design for Sustainability

Environmental concerns are placing increased pressure on design. Pressures from environmental groups clamoring for "socially responsible" designs, states and municipalities that are running out of space for landfills, and consumers who want the most for their money have caused designers and managers to look carefully at the concept of Design for Environment.[7] **Design for Environment (DfE)** *is the explicit consideration of environmental concerns during the design of goods, services, and processes, and includes such practices as designing for recycling and disassembly*. For example, Energy Star dishwashers use advanced technology to get your dishes clean while using less water and energy. A dishwasher built in 1994 uses considerably more water per cycle than today's Energy Star–certified models and costs an extra $40 a year in electrical utility bills. In addition, an Energy Star dishwasher results in a reduction of 1,140 pounds of carbon dioxide that is released to the air due to less demand on electrical power and water plants. One aspect of designing for sustainability is designing products that can easily be repaired and refurbished or otherwise salvaged for reuse.

5-4 Service-Delivery System Design

As we illustrated in Exhibit 5.1, the design of services revolves around designing the service-delivery system and service encounters. **Service-delivery system design** *includes facility location and layout, the servicescape, service process and job design, and technology and information support systems*. Integrating all of these elements is necessary to design a service that provides value to customers and can create a competitive advantage. A poor choice on any one of these components, such as technology or job design, can degrade service system efficiency and effectiveness.

5-4a Facility Location and Layout

Location affects a customer's travel time and is an important competitive priority in a service business. Health clinics, rental car firms, post offices, health clubs, branch banks, libraries, hotels, emergency service facilities, retail stores, and many other types of service facilities depend on good location decisions. Starbucks Coffee shops, for example, are ubiquitous in many cities, airports, and shopping malls. The layout of a facility affects process flow, costs, and customer perception and satisfaction.

5-4b Servicescape

The **servicescape** *is all the physical evidence a customer might use to form an impression.*[8] *The servicescape also provides the behavioral setting where service encounters take place*. People around the world,

Pepsi: From Plastic- to Plant-Based Bottles

Pepsi introduced new soft-drink bottles made entirely from plant material such as switch grass, pine bark, and corn husks instead of oil-based plastic. The new bottles look, feel, and protect the drink inside exactly the same as Pepsi's current bottles. Pepsi is conducting tests of the bottles, and after it can be sure that it can successfully produce them on a large scale, Pepsi will begin to convert all of its products—billions of bottles each year—to the new design. Pepsi noted that the cost to research and design the new bottle was in the millions of dollars.[9]

HUZAIME/Shutterstock.com

for example, recognize the servicescape of McDonald's restaurants. The building design (golden arches), decorative schemes and colors, playground, menu board, packaging, employee uniforms, drive-through, and so on all support McDonald's competitive priorities of speed, consistency, cleanliness, and customer service. The standardization and integration of the servicescape and service processes enhance efficiency. McDonald's servicescape helps establish its brand image.

> McDonald's servicescape helps to establish its brand image.

A servicescape has three principal dimensions:[10]

1. *Ambient conditions*—made manifest by sight, sound, smell, touch, and temperature. These are designed into a servicescape to please the five human senses. For example, Starbucks decided to quit serving a warm breakfast in all Starbucks stores because the egg-and-cheese breakfast sandwiches were interfering with the aroma of the coffee in stores.
2. *Spatial layout and functionality*—how furniture, equipment, and office spaces are arranged. This includes building footprints and facades, streets, and parking lots. A law firm would probably design various conference areas for conversations to take place in a quiet and private setting; a children's hospital would probably include safe, enclosed play areas for kids.
3. *Signs, symbols, and artifacts*—the more explicit signals that communicate an image about a firm. Examples include mission statements and diplomas on a wall, a prominently displayed company logo on company vehicles, a trophy case of awards, letterhead, and company uniforms. Luxury automobile dealers offer free food and soft drinks instead of vending machines.

Some servicescapes, termed **lean servicescape environments**, *are very simple.* Online ticket outlets and Federal Express drop-off kiosks would qualify as lean servicescape environments, as both provide service from one simple design. *More complicated designs and service systems are termed* **elaborate servicescape environments.** Examples include hospitals, airports, and universities.[11]

5-4c Service Process and Job Design

Service process design *is the activity of developing an efficient sequence of activities to satisfy both internal and external customer requirements.* Service process designers

s_bukley/Shutterstock.com

Great Customer Service the Disney Way

Perhaps we should call it the "Disney Wow" because that's what the Disney organization seeks to do in creating outstanding customer service. They pay great attention to every detail of a customer's experience, from the overall servicescape to every service encounter with a cast member, all designed to create a "Wow!" in the customer's mind. For instance, guests who forget where they parked but remember their arrival time can be helped by a Disney employee because a record is kept of the time that each row in the parking lot is filled. Disney shares its knowledge with other organizations—for example, by working with the National Football League to create great experiences at the Super Bowl.

must concentrate on developing procedures to ensure that things are done right the first time, that interactions between customers and service providers are simple and quick, and that human error is avoided. Fast-food restaurants, for example, have carefully designed their processes for a high degree of accuracy and fast response time.[12] New hands-free intercom systems, better microphones that reduce ambient kitchen noise, and screens that display a customer's order are all focused on these requirements.

In many services, the customer and service provider coproduce the service, which makes service process and job design more uncertain and challenging. For example, customers can slow down or upset service providers and other customers at any time. Therefore, managers need to anticipate potential service upsets—including those caused by customers—and develop appropriate responses such as providing extra capacity, training service providers on proper behavior, and empowering them to deal with problems when they occur. Superior service management training is critical for excellent service process and job design.

A First-Class Servicescape

lev radin/Shutterstock.com

Emirates Airlines has introduced First-Class Private Suites on all of their A380 and A340-500 aircraft, and on most Boeing 777s. The suites provide an unparalleled servicescape for upper-echelon travelers. They include privacy doors, a personal mini-bar, seats that convert into a fully flat bed with mattress, a vanity table and mirror, up to 2,000 channels of the latest movies and TV shows on demand, and even an A380 Shower Spa.[13]

5-4d Technology and Information Support Systems

Hard and soft technologies are important factors in designing services to ensure speed, accuracy, customization, and flexibility. Nurses, airline flight attendants, bank tellers, police, insurance claims processors, dentists, auto mechanics and service-counter personnel, engineers, hotel room maids, financial portfolio managers, purchasing buyers, and waiters are just a few examples of job designs that are highly dependent on accurate and timely information.

5-5 Service-Encounter Design

Service-encounter design *focuses on the interaction, directly or indirectly, between the service provider(s) and the customer.* It is during these points of contact with the customer that perceptions of the firm and its goods and services are created. Service-encounter design and job design are frequently done in iterative improvement cycles.

The principal elements of service-encounter design are

- customer-contact behavior and skills;
- service-provider selection, development, and empowerment;
- recognition and reward; and
- service recovery and guarantees.

These elements are necessary to support excellent performance and create customer value and satisfaction.

5-5a Customer-Contact Behavior and Skills

Customer contact *refers to the physical or virtual presence of the customer in the service-delivery system during a service experience.* Customer contact is measured by the percentage of time the customer must be in the system relative to the total time it takes to provide the service. *Systems in which the percentage of customer contact is high are called* **high-contact systems;** *those in which it is low are called* **low-contact systems.**[14,15] Examples of high-contact systems are estate planning and hotel check-in; examples of low-contact systems are construction services and package sorting and distribution.

> Companies must carefully select customer-contact employees, train them well, and empower them to meet and exceed customer expectations.

Many low-contact systems, such as processing an insurance policy in the backroom, can be treated much like an assembly line, whereas service-delivery systems with high customer contact are more difficult to design and control. One reason for this is the variation and uncertainty that people (customers) introduce into high-contact service processes. For example, the time it takes to check a customer into a hotel can be affected by special requests (e.g., a king bed or handicapped-accessible room) and questions that customers might ask the desk clerk. Low-customer-contact systems are essentially free of this type of customer-induced uncertainty and therefore are capable of operating at higher levels of operating efficiency. High-customer-contact areas of the organization are sometimes described as the "front room or front office" and low-customer-contact areas as "back room or back office."

Customer-contact requirements *are measurable performance levels or expectations that define the quality of customer contact with representatives of an organization.* These might include such technical requirements as response time (answering the telephone within two rings), service management skills such as cross-selling other services, and/or behavioral requirements (using a customer's name whenever possible). Walt Disney Company, highly recognized for extraordinary customer service, clearly defines expected behaviors in its guidelines for guest service, which include making eye contact and smiling, greeting and welcoming every guest, seeking out guests who may need assistance, providing immediate service recovery, displaying approachable body language, focusing on the positive rather than rules and regulations, and thanking each and every guest.[16]

5-5b Service-Provider Selection, Development, and Empowerment

Companies must carefully select customer-contact employees, train them well, and empower them to meet and exceed customer expectations. Many companies begin with the recruiting process, selecting those employees who show the ability and desire to develop good customer relationships. Major companies such as Procter & Gamble seek people with excellent interpersonal and communication skills, strong problem-solving and analytical skills, assertiveness, stress tolerance, patience and empathy, accuracy and attention to detail, and computer literacy.

Empowerment *means giving people authority to make decisions based on what they feel is right, to have control over their work, to take risks and learn from mistakes, and to promote change.* At The Ritz-Carlton Hotel Company, no matter what their normal duties are, employees must assist a fellow service provider who is responding to a guest's complaint or wish if such assistance is requested. Ritz-Carlton employees can spend up to $2,000 to resolve complaints, with no questions asked. However, the actions of empowered employees should be guided by a common vision. That is, employees require a consistent understanding of what actions they may or should take.

5-5c Recognition and Reward

After a firm hires, trains, and empowers excellent service providers, the next challenge is how to motivate and keep them. Research has identified key motivational factors to be recognition, advancement, achievement, and the nature of the work itself. A good compensation system can help to attract, retain, and motivate employees. Other forms of recognition such as formal and informal employee and team recognition, preferred parking spots, free trips and extra vacation days, discounts and gift certificates, and a simple "thank you" from supervisors are vital to achieving a high-performance workplace.

5-5d Service Guarantees and Recovery

Despite all efforts to satisfy customers, every business experiences unhappy customers. *A* **service upset** *is any problem a customer has—real or perceived—with the service-delivery system and includes terms such as* service failure, error, defect, mistake, *and* crisis. Service upsets can adversely affect business if not dealt with effectively.

A **service guarantee** *is a promise to reward and compensate a customer if a service upset occurs during the service experience.* Many organizations—for example, Federal Express and Disney—have well-publicized service guarantees to gain competitive advantage. An *explicit service guarantee* is in writing and included in service provider publications and advertisements. Taco Bell and Hampton Inns use explicit service guarantees to differentiate themselves from competitors. *Implicit guarantees* are not in writing but are implied in everything the service

L.L. Bean: Service Guarantee

In 1916, Mr. L.L. Bean placed the following notice on the wall of his store—"I do not consider a sale complete until goods are worn out and customers still satisfied." Today, L.L. Bean's explicit service guarantee is "Our products are guaranteed to give 100 percent satisfaction in every way. Return anything purchased from us at any time if it proves otherwise. We do not want you to have anything from L.L. Bean that is not completely satisfactory." L.L. Bean continues by saying, "From kayaks to slippers, fly rods to sweaters, everything we sell at L.L. Bean is backed by the same rock solid guarantee of satisfaction. It's been that way since our founder sold his very first pair of Bean Boots in 1912. Whether you purchased your item on llbean.com, by mail, by phone or at one of our stores, visit any L.L. Bean retail store for fast and friendly service." L.L. Bean's website and call center give detailed instructions on returns and exchanges, including free shipping in some situations. L.L. Bean makes it as easy as possible for customers to invoke the service guarantee.[17]

Michael G McKinne/Shutterstock.com

provider does. Premium service providers such as The Ritz-Carlton Hotel Company and many engineering, consulting, and medical organizations use implicit service guarantees. Objectives of service guarantees include setting customer expectations prior to experiencing the service, setting employee performance expectations, reducing customer risk, allowing premium pricing, forcing operational improvement, building customer loyalty and brand image, and increasing sales and revenue.[18]

Service guarantees are carefully designed and offered prior to the customer experiencing the service. A good service guarantee includes determining what services to include, procedures for the customer and service provider to invoke the guarantee, and the best economic payout amount. Clearly, the best a firm can hope for is never to have to invoke a service guarantee; thus, the firm must design its processes and operational capability to minimize service upsets.

Nevertheless, service upsets occasionally occur. When this happens, companies need to recover the customer's trust and confidence. **Service recovery** *is the process of correcting a service upset and satisfying the customer.* Service recovery should begin immediately after a service upset occurs and when the customer is visibly upset; the longer customers wait, the angrier they might get. Service-recovery processes should be clearly documented, and employees should be trained and empowered to use them whenever necessary. Service providers need to listen carefully to determine the customer's feelings and then respond sympathetically, ensuring that the issue is understood. Then they should make every effort to resolve the problem quickly, provide a simple apology, and perhaps offer compensation such as free meals or discount coupons.

5-6 An Integrative Case Study of LensCrafters

To illustrate how goods and services are designed in an integrated fashion, we will study LensCrafters—a well-known provider of eyeglasses produced "in about an hour." We use the framework for goods and service design shown in Exhibit 5.17.

Steps 1 and 2—Strategic Mission, Market Analysis, and Competitive Priorities LensCrafters (www.lenscrafters.com) is an optical chain of about 860 special service shops with on-site eyeglass production capabilities in the United States, Canada, and Puerto Rico. All resources necessary to create and deliver "one-stop-shopping" and eyeglasses "in about an hour" are available in each store.

LensCrafters's mission statement is focused on being the best by

- creating customers for life by delivering legendary customer service;
- developing and energizing associates and leaders in the world's best workplace;
- crafting perfect-quality eyewear in about an hour; and
- delivering superior overall value to meet each customer's individual needs.[19]

EXHIBIT 5.17 One Example View of LensCrafters's Customer Benefit Package

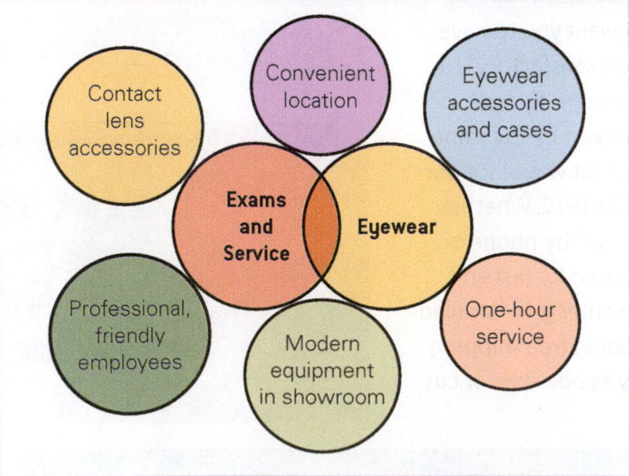

Step 3—Customer Benefit Package Design and Configuration Our perception of the LensCrafters customer benefit package is the integrated set of goods and services depicted in Exhibit 5.17. The primary good (eyewear) and the primary service (accurate eye exam and one-hour service) are of equal importance. Peripheral goods and services encircle the primary ones to create "a total LensCrafters' experience."

Steps 4a and b—Manufactured Good Design and Process Selection The manufacturing process is integrated into the service facility to provide rapid order response, yet not sacrifice quality. In this industry, it is unusual for customers to watch their eyeglasses being made, and this "service experience" is viewed as adding value. The equipment used in the labs is the most technologically advanced equipment in the industry. The eyewear is manufactured to specifications in a clean, modern, professionally run facility.

Other issues that LensCrafters would need to consider in designing its manufacturing processes are:

- How are eyeglass lenses and frames ordered? Are these materials ordered by individual stores or consolidated by region/district? How can the high quality of eyewear be ensured? What new materials are available?
- What items should be stored at the region/district warehouse and stores? What type of purchasing and inventory control systems should be used? How should supplier performance be evaluated?
- What eyewear-making equipment should be used? What is the latest technology? Which equipment is most flexible? Should the equipment be purchased or leased? How should it be maintained and by whom?
- What is the most efficient production procedure to make the goods and meet time schedules? Where should quality be checked in the manufacturing process?

Step 4c—Service-Delivery System Design The service-delivery system, as evidenced by the location and layout, servicescape, service processes, job designs, technology, and organizational structure, is combined into an integrated service-delivery system. LensCrafters's stores are located in high-traffic areas such as shopping centers and malls within 5 to 10 miles of the target market.

A typical store layout is shown in Exhibit 5.18. The servicescape is designed to convey an impression of quality and professionalism. The store is spacious, open, clean, and carpeted, with professional merchandise display areas, modern furniture in the retail area, modern equipment in the laboratory, technicians in white lab coats, shiny machines in the lab, and bright lights throughout. The store display cases, eye examination areas, and fitting stations are in the high-contact area where customers and service providers interact frequently. Optometry degrees, certifications, and licenses hanging on the wall provide physical evidence of employees' abilities.

A greeter directs each customer to the appropriate service area as he or she enters the store. The low contact area of a LensCrafters store—the optical laboratory—is separated from the retail area by large glass panels. The optical laboratory becomes a "showroom" where the customer's perception of the total delivery process is established.

The store is a service factory. The typical service process begins when a customer makes an appointment with an optician, and continues until the eyeglasses are received and paid for. Between these two events, the customer travels to the store, parks, receives a greeting from store employees, obtains an eye examination, selects frames, is measured for proper eyeglasses and frame fit, watches the eyeglasses being made in the laboratory, and receives a final fitting to make sure all is well. Information flow in the forms of prescriptions, bills, and receipts complements the physical flows of people and eyewear.

EXHIBIT 5.18 A Schematic View of a Typical LensCrafters's Store Layout

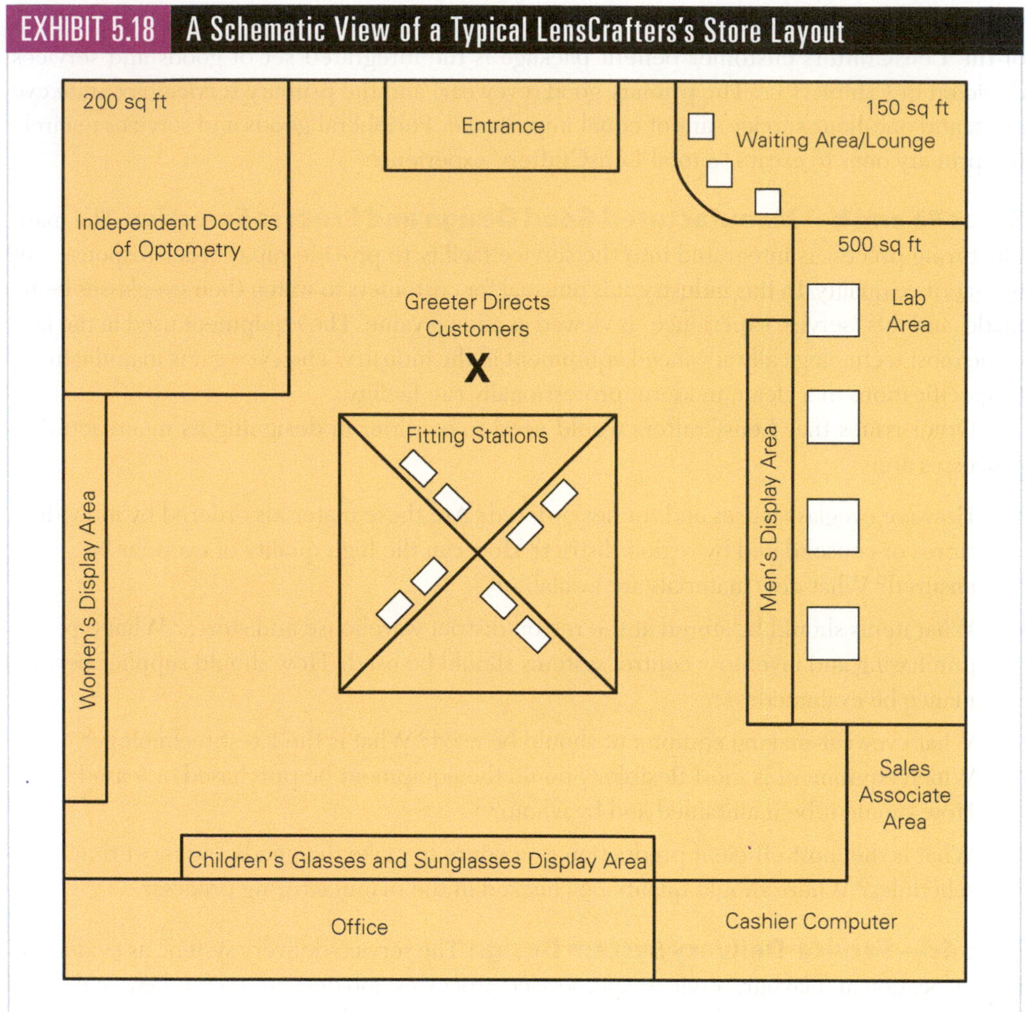

Step 4d—Service Encounter Design Each job at LensCrafters—sales associate, lab technician, and doctor of optometry—requires both technical skills and service management skills. Associates are well trained, friendly, and knowledgeable about their jobs. The lab technicians are certified in all work tasks and processes. Many associates are cross-trained.

At the service-encounter level, key issues that managers need to consider include the following:

- What human resource management processes and systems will ensure hiring the right people, training them properly, and motivating them to provide excellent service? What recognitions and rewards should be provided?
- How are associates trained to handle service upsets and service recovery?
- What standards should be set for grooming and appearance?
- What behavioral standards, such as tone of voice, physical mannerisms, and the language that associates use in customer interactions, should be set?
- How should employee performance be measured and evaluated?
- What can be done to make the one-hour wait a positive experience for customers?

LensCrafters reinforces its customer benefit package with a comprehensive, 90-day, unconditional service guarantee design defined as follows:

> Our glasses warranty protects you in case you change your mind. Maybe you bought red frames, only to decide they're not your color. Or you realize you should have gotten the anti-reflective coating. Or after wearing them for a few days, it becomes clear they're not comfortable. It doesn't matter what your reason is—you should love your purchase. So we give you peace of mind with every pair.
>
> *How does it work?* Our eyewear guarantee is simple. Just return your eyeglasses—in resalable condition—to LensCrafters within 90 days. We'll exchange them for a new pair or refund your money. We stand behind every pair.
>
> *What does "Unconditional" really mean?* The 90 days begins on the date you purchase your eyeglasses. If you exchange your purchase for a pair at a lower price, we'll refund the price difference. If you exchange your purchase for a pair at a higher price, you'll only pay the price difference. And we guarantee ONE-YEAR EYEWEAR PROTECTION.
>
> With purchase of our One-Year Eyewear Protection Plan, you can make sure your eyeglasses are covered, whether you need a repair or replacement.

Steps 5 and 6—Market Introduction/Deployment and Evaluation Although the company has been around for some time, it undoubtedly faces challenges in replicating its design concept in new locations. On a continuing basis, as technology and procedures change, LensCrafters will have to develop processes to introduce changes into all existing locations to maintain operational consistency and achieve its strategic objectives. For example, how might it react as competitors such as Walmart enter the optical industry?

As you see, LensCrafters's manufacturing and service design depends on a variety of operations management concepts, all of which are integrated and support a rather complex customer benefit package.

CHAPTER 5 LEARNING OBJECTIVE SUMMARIES

5.1 **Describe the steps involved in designing goods and services.** The steps are outlined in Exhibit 5.1, which highlights the differences in designing goods and services. These are summarized below.

Steps 1 and 2—Strategic Mission, Analysis, and Competitive Priorities

Step 3—Customer Benefit Package Design and Configuration

Step 4—Detailed Goods, Services, and Process Design

Step 5—Market Introduction/Deployment

Step 6—Marketplace Evaluation

5.2 **Explain the concept and application of quality function deployment.** QFD focuses on turning the voice of the customer into specific technical requirements that characterize a design and provide the "blueprint" for manufacturing or service delivery. The process is initiated with a matrix, which because of its structure is often called the House of Quality (see Exhibit 5.2).

5.3 **Describe how the Taguchi loss function, reliability, design for manufacturability, and design for sustainability are used for designing manufactured goods.** The Taguchi loss function is a reaction to the *goalpost model* of conforming to specifications. Taguchi's approach assumes that the smaller the variation about the nominal specification, the better is the quality. In turn, products are more consistent, and total costs are lower. The loss function is represented by

$$L(x) = k(x - T)^2 \quad [5.1]$$

Reliability is the probability that a manufactured good, piece of equipment, or system performs its intended function for a stated period of time under specified operating conditions. Many goods are configured using a series of components, parallel (redundant) components, or a combination of these. If the individual reliabilities are denoted by $p_1, p_2, p_3, \ldots, p_n$ and the system reliability is denoted by Rs, then for a series system,

$$R_s = (p_1)(p_2)(p_3)\cdots(p_n) \quad [5.2]$$

The system reliability of an n-component parallel system is computed as

$$R_p = 1 - (1 - p_1)(1 - p_2)(1 - p_3)\cdots(1 - p_n) \quad [5.3]$$

To compute the reliability of systems that include combinations of series and parallel components, first compute the reliability of the parallel components and treat the result as a single series component; then use the series reliability formula to compute the reliability of the resulting series system.

One way to improve reliability during design is to anticipate any product failures that may occur and then design the product to prevent such failures. Another useful approach is DFM, or design for manufacturability, which is intended to prevent product designs that simplify assembly operations but require more complex and expensive components, designs that simplify component manufacture while complicating the assembly process, and designs that are simple and inexpensive to produce but difficult or expensive to service or support. Sustainability concerns are being addressed through an approach called design for environment (DfE), which often includes designing goods that can be repaired or recycled.

5.4 **Define the five elements of service-delivery system design**. Service-delivery system design includes facility location and layout, the servicescape, service process and job design, and technology and information support systems.

5.5 **Describe the four elements of service-encounter design.** The principal elements of service-encounter design are customer-contact behavior and skills; service-provider selection, development, and empowerment; recognition and reward; and service guarantees and recovery. Service guarantees are offered prior to the customer buying or experiencing the service and help to minimize the risk to the customer. Service recovery normally occurs after a service upset and may require free meals, discount coupons, or a simple apology.

5.6 **Explain how goods and service design concepts are integrated at LensCrafters.** Managers at LensCrafters must understand both the goods and service sides of the business to be successful. Complex customer benefit packages (see Exhibit 5.17, which highlights both the goods and services that are integrated at LensCrafters) require complex operating systems. To design and manage LensCrafters' processes, an understanding of OM is a critical skill.

KEY TERMS

- **Customer-contact requirements**
- **Customer contact**
- **Design for Environment (DfE)**
- **Design for manufacturability (DFM)**
- **Elaborate servicescape environment**
- **Empowerment**
- **High-contact systems**
- **Lean servicescape environment**

- **Low-contact systems**
- **Product simplification**
- **Prototype testing**
- **Quality function deployment (QFD)**
- **Reliability**
- **Service-delivery system design**
- **Service-encounter design**
- **Service guarantee**
- **Service process design**
- **Service recovery**
- **Servicescape**
- **Service upset**
- **Voice of the customer**

REVIEW QUESTIONS

5.1 1. Explain the importance of new product design and development.

5.1 2. What are the six major steps in designing goods and services?

5.1 3. What is prototype testing? Why is it used?

5.2 4. Explain the concept and application of quality function deployment.

5.3 5. Describe the goal-post view of conforming to specifications.

5.3 6. Describe how the Taguchi loss function is used for designing manufactured goods.

5.3 7. Describe how reliability is used for designing manufactured goods.

5.3 8. Describe how design for manufacturability (DFM) and design for sustainability are used for designing manufactured goods.

5.3 9. What is the rationale for product and process simplification?

5.4 10. Explain the five elements of service-delivery system design.

5.5 11. What is customer contact?

5.5 12. Define high- and low-contact systems and provide examples of each.

5.5 13. Describe the four elements of service-encounter design.

5.5 14. Define a service guarantee and provide one example.

5.5 15. Define a service upset and provide one example from your personal experiences.

5.6 16. Explain how goods and service design concepts are integrated at LensCrafters.

DISCUSSION QUESTIONS AND EXPERIENTIAL ACTIVITIES

5.2 17. How might modern technology, such as the Internet, be used to understand the voice of the customer?

5.2 18. What lessons can be learned from the LaRosa's Pizzeria boxed example?

5.2 19. In building a House of Quality, what departments or functions should be involved in each step of the process?

5.3 20. Explain how the goal-post view of conforming to specifications differs from Taguchi's loss function. Would you rather buy an automobile where suppliers used the goal-post or Taguchi models? Why?

5.3 21. Research and write a short paper (maximum two typed pages) illustrating an example of how a company applies concepts of Design for Environment (DfE).

5.4 22. Choose a servicescape for a business with which you are familiar and list key physical attributes of the servicescape and their impact on customer service and value. Explain how the servicescape establishes the behavioral setting for your example.

5.4 23. Define lean and elaborate servicescapes and give an example not in the textbook.

5.4 24. Select a service at your school, such as financial aid, bookstore, curriculum advising, and so on. Propose a redesign of this service and its service delivery system. First, baseline the current service and system and then suggest how to redesign and improve it. Make use of chapter ideas as best you can.

5.5 25. Identify a job in an organization and describe how the four elements of service-encounter design are designed and managed for this job. (The job you select could be in a professional organization such as a dentist or tax advisor, or in a routine service organization such as a hotel check-in desk clerk or airline flight attendant.)

5.5 26. Propose an explicit service guarantee for a fast-food restaurant. Clearly explain why you included the features of your service guarantee (maximum of one page). Do you think that a restaurant would adopt it? Why or why not?

5.5 27. Identify a service-provider job and associated service encounters and design and write a job description for it. (Consider desired customer-contact skills and behaviors, education and training requirements, empowerment capabilities, hiring criteria, and so on.)

5.5 28. Is it easier to management a high- or low-customer-contact business? Explain.

5.5 29. Characterize the following goods and services on the low–high-customer-contact continuum and justify your answer in a sentence or two.

a. participating in a case study classroom discussion
b. listening and taking notes in a classroom lecture
c. machining an aluminum part in a factory
d. taking your automobile to the dealer for repair and waiting for service contact
e. playing golf in a foursome of friends
f. driving a truck and delivering the shipment at the loading dock
g. handling a customer's claim on a lost shipment over the telephone
h. approving medical claims in an insurance company

5.5 30. Find an example of a service guarantee and explain its strengths and weaknesses.

5.5 31. How would you rate the following service-encounter experience?

You are going on a trip to see a play in New York City. Your airline flight sits at the gate awaiting the pilot and co-pilot at 8 am in the morning. You sit and you sit. After one hour, all passengers are ask to leave the plane, take all carry-on bags, and are informed that the flight is cancelled. Neither the flight attendants nor airline gate personnel apologize. At the rebook counter, you are informed that you'll receive a full credit for this flight (i.e., zero cost to you). You take off on a substitute flight the same morning. It arrives in NYC at 2:35 pm. The replacement flight is on-time and all goes well. You arrive three hours and forty minutes after your original arrival time.

Describe your negative and positive reactions to this experience.

5.6 32. Do you think you will be working in manufacturing or services when you graduate? What do you think will be the role of manufacturing in the U.S. economy in the future?

COMPUTATIONAL PROBLEMS AND EXERCISES

These exercises require you to apply the formulas and methods described in the chapter. The problems should be solved manually.

5.2 33. Given the following customer requirements and technical requirements for an automobile, construct a partial House of Quality. Use your own preferences to denote relationship strengths.

Customer Requirements	Technical Requirements
good mileage	acceleration rate
fast response when passing	fuel economy
good handling	passing time

5.2 34. Develop a House of Quality for a manufactured good or service based on current or past work experience or something else you are familiar with. Some ideas might be a quick service oil change, a fast-food restaurant, a new car, or a fitness club.

5.2 35. The following exhibit shows a partially completed House of Quality for a proposed fitness center.

a. Examine the relationships in the roof of the House of Quality. Explain why they make sense (or if you think they do not, explain why). How would this assessment help in the design activity?

b. Complete the matrix in the body of the House of Quality. That is, examine each pair of customer and technical requirements and determine if there is a very strong relationship, a strong relationship, a weak relationship, or no relationship and fill in the appropriate symbols in the matrix.

c. Suppose that the most important customer requirements identified through surveys and focus groups are "Has programs I want," "Family activities available," "Equipment available when desired," "Easy to sign up for programs," and "Value for your money." "Staff available when needed" was ranked low, while the remaining were ranked moderate in importance. Based on this information, identify the most important technical requirements that should be addressed in subsequent design activities.

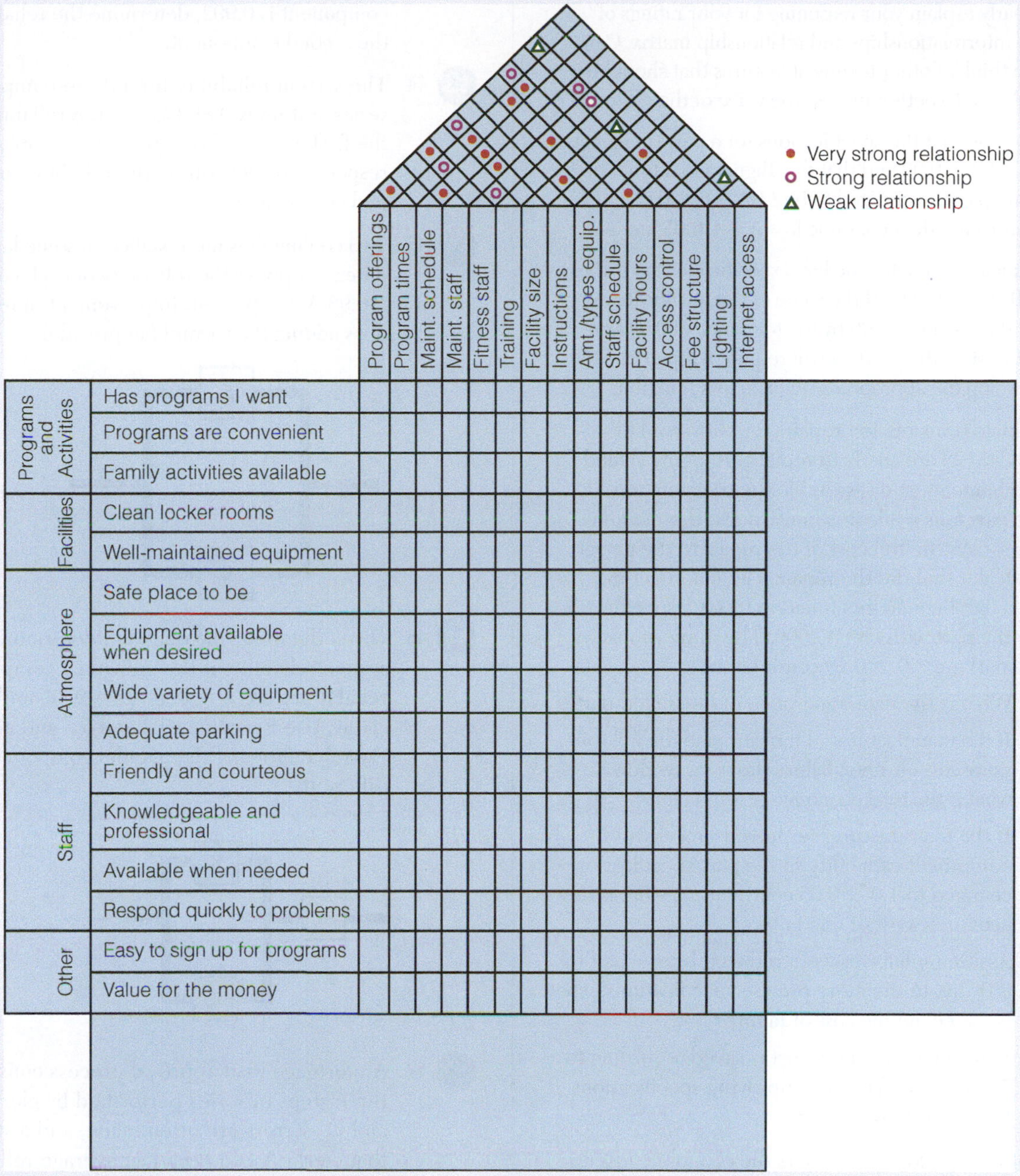

- Very strong relationship
- Strong relationship
- Weak relationship

		Program offerings	Program times	Maint. schedule	Maint. staff	Fitness staff	Training	Facility size	Instructions	Amt./types equip.	Staff schedule	Facility hours	Access control	Fee structure	Lighting	Internet access
Programs and Activities	Has programs I want															
	Programs are convenient															
	Family activities available															
Facilities	Clean locker rooms															
	Well-maintained equipment															
Atmosphere	Safe place to be															
	Equipment available when desired															
	Wide variety of equipment															
	Adequate parking															
Staff	Friendly and courteous															
	Knowledgeable and professional															
	Available when needed															
	Respond quickly to problems															
Other	Easy to sign up for programs															
	Value for the money															

5.2 36. Build a House of Quality (showing only the Voice of the customer, Technical features, Interrelationships, and Relationship matrix from Exhibit 5.2) for designing and producing chocolate chip cookies. The voice of the customer consists of the following:

a. Soft
b. Fresh
c. Bittersweet
d. Not burned
e. Large size
f. Moderate price
g. Lots of chocolate

The technical features identified are

a. baking temperature,
b. baking time,
c. type of chocolate,
d. proportion of chocolate,
e. size,
f. shape,
g. thickness,
h. batch size, and
i. amount of preservatives.

Clearly explain your reasoning for your ratings of the interrelationships and relationship matrix. Can you think of other technical features that should be included to better address the voice of the customer?

5.3 37. Suppose that the specifications for a part (in inches) are 6.00 ± 0.02 and that the Taguchi loss function for some part is estimated to be $L(x) = 6{,}800\ (x - T)^2$. Determine the economic loss if $x = 6.05$ inches.

5.3 38. A quality characteristic has a specification (in inches) of 0.200 ± 0.020. If the value of the quality characteristic exceeds 0.200 by the tolerance of 0.020 on either side, the product will require a repair of $150. Develop the appropriate Taguchi loss function.

5.3 39. Vehicle transmission repairs for part number TAC45123 are costly to replace. A highly skilled mechanic must disassemble the transmission. If the part fails while it is in warranty, the manufacturer pays the full cost of the repair to the garage or dealer that did the repair. The manufacturer uses the Taguchi loss function to set a specification for the part with $k = 40{,}000$. The dimensions for the part are 1.0 ± 0.10 centimeters.

a. What is the economic value of one failed part?

b. If the manufacturer of the part paid the full warranty cost on 1,862 failures last year worldwide, what is the total economic cost of failure?

c. If the manufacturer improved process and equipment capability so the part specifications changed to 1.0 ± 0.05 centimeters, what is the economic cost of one failure?

d. Assuming failures were reduced by one half to 931 due to the more precise specifications, what is the economic cost of failure?

e. How much warranty cost is saved according to Taguchi estimates by improving specifications from ±0.10 to ±0.05?

5.3 40. Cameras Galore, Inc. wants the economic loss due to a failed part to be no more than $300 with a target (T) specification of 4.5 centimeters and a $k = 12{,}000$. Using the Taguchi loss function, what is the value of x that meets these criteria?

5.3 41. The manufacturing of compact disks requires four sequential steps. The reliability of each of the steps is 0.96, 0.87, 0.92, and 0.89, respectively. What is the reliability of the process?

5.3 42. The service center for a brokerage company provides three functions to callers: account status, order confirmations, and stock quotes. The reliability was measured for each of these services over one month with these results: 90%, 80%, and 96%, respectively. What is the overall reliability of the call center?

5.3 43. The system reliability for a two-component parallel system is 0.99968. If the reliability of the first component is 0.992, determine the reliability of the second component.

5.3 44. The system reliability for a three-component series system is 0.893952. If the reliability of the first and third components is 0.96 and 0.97, respectively, determine the reliability of the second component.

5.3 45. Two cooling fans are installed in some laptop computers. Suppose the reliability of each cooling fan is 0.98. What percent improvement in reliability does adding the second fan provide?

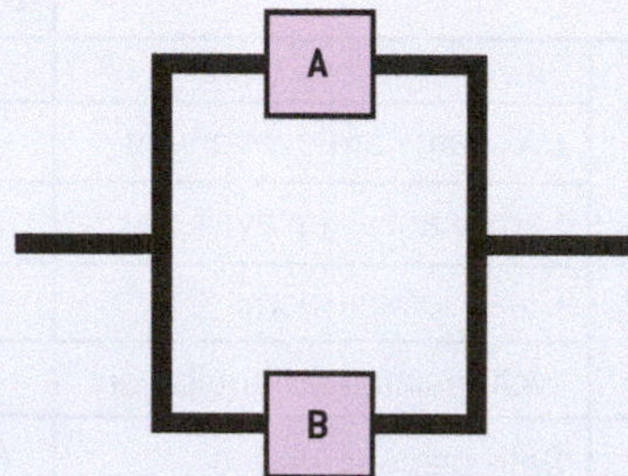

5.3 46. Given the following diagram, determine the total system reliability if the individual component reliabilities are A = 0.94, B = 0.82, and C = 0.87. (Hint: Use Equations 5.2 and 5.3 and note that the reliabilities of the parallel components are different.)

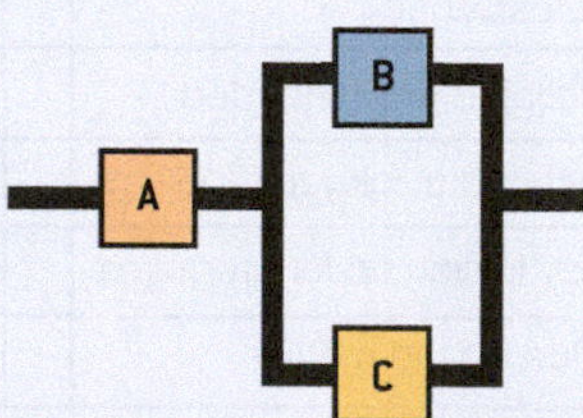

5.3 47. A mortgage loan approval process consists of three steps in series performed by clerks A, B, and C. Errors are often made, and a study found that clerks A and B had an average reliability of only 0.85, which results in the paperwork having errors, missing information, and so on. Clerk C who performs the final review catches nearly all mistakes and has a reliability of 0.99, but the work involved is causing a considerable backlog. After studying the process, the loan manager decided to add an additional clerk D with more experience to each of the first two steps to check the work, having a reliability of 0.95 as shown in the diagram on the next page.

a. How much does adding this redundancy improve the reliability of the original process?

b. If, in addition to adding clerks D, the reliability of clerks A and B can be improved to 0.95 through better training, how much can the reliability be improved?

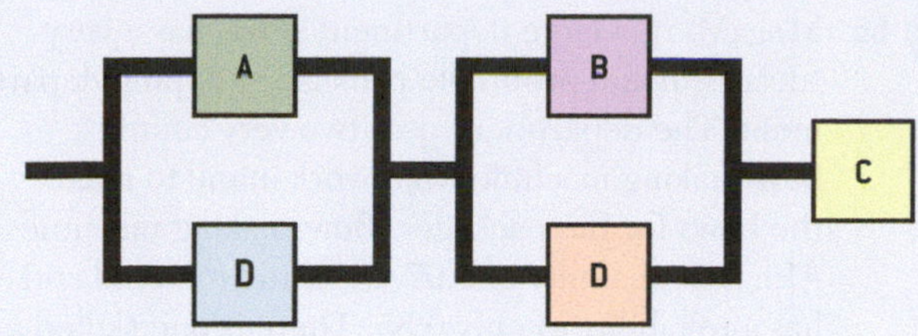

5.3 48. A simple electronic assembly consists of two components in a series configuration with reliabilities as shown in the figure below.

Engineers would like to increase the reliability by adding additional components in one of the two proposed designs shown below:

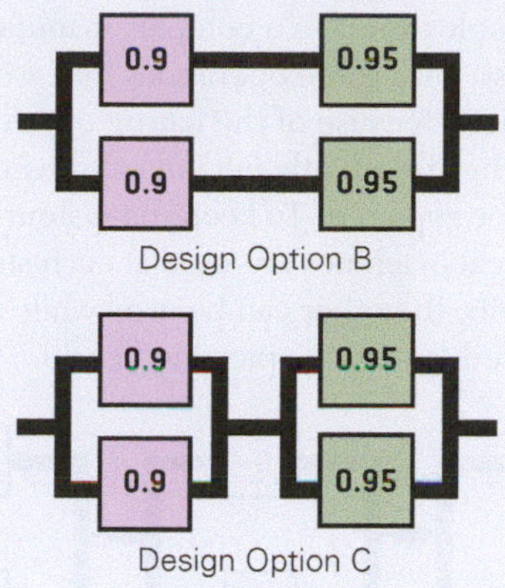

a. Find the reliability of the original design.

b. Explain how the configurations of the proposed designs differ.

c. Which proposed design has the best reliability?

EXCEL-BASED PROBLEMS

For these problems, you may use Excel or the spreadsheet templates in MindTap to assist in your analysis.

5.3 49. Assume the specifications for a part (in inches) are 5.00 ± 0.37, and the Taguchi loss function is estimated to be $L(x) = 9{,}300\ (x - T)^2$. Use the Excel template *Taguchi* to determine the estimated loss if the quality characteristic under study takes on a value of 5.50 inches.

5.3 50. Assume the specifications for a television remote control part (in inches) are 5.00 ± 0.10, and the Taguchi loss function is estimated to be $L(x) = 5{,}500\ (x - T)^2$. Determine the estimated loss per part if the quality characteristic (i.e., actual process performance) under study takes on a value of 4.91 inches. Use the Excel template *Taguchi* to find the total economic loss if a production order for 50,000 remotes is recalled due to this part being so close to the lower specification of 4.9.

5.3 51. A quality characteristic has a design specification (in cm.) of 0.200 ± 0.02. *If the actual process value of the quality characteristic is at the boundary of the tolerance on either side,* the product will require a repair of $30. Use the Excel template *Taguchi* to find the value of k and state the Taguchi loss function. What is the loss associated with $x = 0.205$?

5.3 52. For the situation in problem 51, what are the economic design specifications if the cost of inspection and adjustment is $7.50?

5.3 53. Suppose that the design specifications for a hydraulic cylinder are 10.00 ± 0.10 centimeters and that the Taguchi loss function is estimated to be $L(x) = 1{,}400\ (x - T)^2$. Use the Excel template *Taguchi* to answer the following questions:

a. Determine the estimated loss for a production order if the quality characteristic under study takes on a value of 10.04 and 100 parts are produced.

b. Assume the production process is recalibrated weekly and a new sample of cylinders after recalibration reveals an x-bar of 9.789. What action, if any, is need in this situation? Explain.

5.3 54. An electronic missile guidance system at Mguide Inc. consists of components A, B, C, and D, which have reliabilities of 0.98, 0.97, 0.91, and 0.95, respectively (see the following diagram).

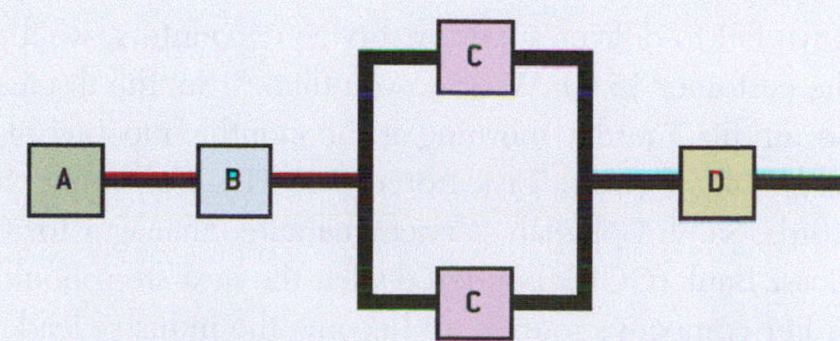

a. Use the Excel template *Systems Reliability* to compute the reliability of the entire system.

b. Suppose the customer requires a reliability of at least 0.98. Try to find a configuration that meets this requirement using the minimum number of components. Use the Excel template *Systems Reliability* to assist in your analysis.

5.3 55. Magnaplex Inc. has a complex manufacturing process, with three operations that are performed in series. Because of the nature of the process, machines frequently fall out of adjustment and must be repaired. To keep the system going, two identical machines are used at each stage; thus, if one fails, the other can be used while the first is repaired (see accompanying figure).

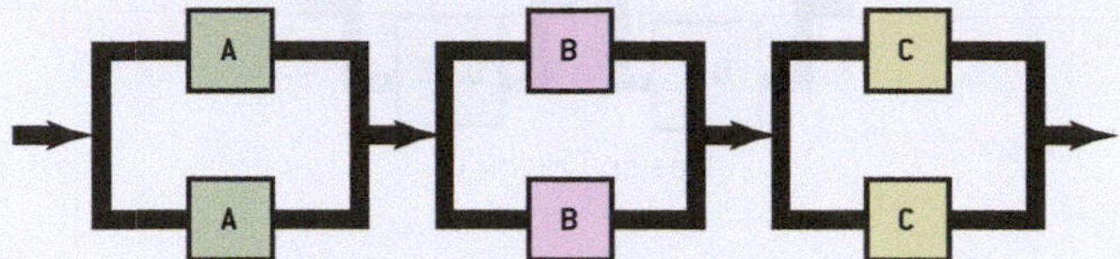

The reliabilities of the machines are as follows:

Machine	Reliability
A	0.85
B	0.92
C	0.90

Use the Excel template *Systems Reliability* to answer the following questions:

a. Analyze the system reliability, assuming only one machine at each stage (all the backup machines are out of operation).

b. How much is the reliability improved by having two machines at each stage?

5.3 56. MegaMart, a large department store, has a very successful and profitable package wrapping department. The department uses two very complex bow-making machines that work inline to make the bows for the packages. Bow-making machine #1 has a reliability of 0.97. Machine #2 is old and has a reliability of only 0.85. There is one skilled operator who knows how to operate the machines. She had been very reliable but recently has had increasing health problems that have caused her to miss work about 10 percent of the time. Use the Excel template *Systems Reliability* to answer the following questions:

a. What is the current reliability of the system, including the operator?

b. Management is considering either scrapping machine #2 and replacing it with a new machine, which has a reliability of 0.98 at a cost of $5,000, or training another operator to fill in when the first operator is absent, at a cost of $5,100. Management estimates that profits from the department would increase by $7,000 per year if the bow-making line operated at 100 percent of capacity. If management wants to pay off its investment in the first year, determine the expected net profit for each alternative and recommend which one will be the most profitable to management.

Gulf Coast Bank: Service Guarantees

"I know what we can do next; everything has been so successful so far," said Kay Ebelhar, marketing services division manager. "How about designing and offering a *courtesy service guarantee*? We will promise to greet customers, give them our undivided attention, and then thank them when they leave. As with our other service guarantees, if we fail to deliver superior service encounters, we'll give the customer $5.00! What do you think?" So, the discussion began this Tuesday morning at the monthly meeting of the Marketing Control Task Force (MCTF). Following these words, Sarah Coleman, service guarantee manager for Gulf Coast Bank (GCB), pondered what the next step should be in her company's journey to become the industry leader in customer service.

Four years ago, the bank undertook an extensive study to identify the needs of its target customers and analyze the actions of its competitors. Aided by extensive market research, management quickly realized that certain service features such as convenient location, interest rates paid on customer accounts, and extended branch bank hours had become a baseline level of performance (order qualifiers) from which nearly all competitors operated. GCB leaders determined that to gain a competitive advantage, they must provide customers with superior service, in addition to the baseline features. To achieve this, the MCTF was created.

The bank's service guarantee program has been in place for 10 months now. Since January, media campaigns have announced the service guarantees to the public and bank employees have received training about them. In this short amount of time, it has been difficult to evaluate the results of the service guarantee program. Sarah knows that the bank spent $860 for payouts during the 10 months for 300 branch banks and that there seemed to be no trend up or down in the monthly payout amounts. Sarah was the only one asking tough questions during MCTF meetings such as "Are service upsets and errors being reduced?," "Are employees motivated to provide exceptional service?," "Are the bank's processes and operational capability getting better so GCB can execute these service guarantee performance levels?," "Is a $5 payout per service upset adequate?," and "Is the bank's current service guarantee program a failure?"

A Gold Service Guarantee Program was developed with the intent of insuring that the bank would emerge as a leader in service quality within its market. It would also be a source of competitive advantage, and a fundamental component of their new corporate culture.

The initial phase of the Gold Service program consisted of a series of print, radio, and television advertising, as well as promotional campaigns geared toward customers and employees. During this "awareness phase," the goal was to create a general market awareness of Bourbon Bank's attention to superior service. Next came the "action phase," where the bank set out to show specifically what it meant to have excellent customer service. By implementing external programs for customers, as well as internal programs for employees, it could demonstrate the bank's commitment to following through with the ideals established in the previous phase. Media campaigns played a significant role in this phase too, and promotional videos were used internally to create service guarantee awareness and action.

Externally, the Gold Service Telephone Line was established to answer and resolve any customer question or problem (although the average speed of answer time at the bank's customer call center was increasing, not decreasing these past 10 months). Single-transaction express teller windows at all branch banks added friendly signs aimed at satisfying customers requiring simple transactions and quick response.

Internally, an extensive two-day training program for all 6,200 employees was developed to teach them how to live up to the attributes of the "customer service pledge." After training and signing the pledge, each employee received a paperweight inscribed with the pledge as a way of making "Gold Service" more meaningful and relevant to both customers and employees.

The bank initially introduced three specific guarantees. First, checking and savings account statements are guaranteed to be accurate. If there is a mistake, regardless of the reason, the customer receives $5.00. Second, customers are promised answers about their application for a home or automobile loan in the time frame specified by the customer. This guarantee is the personal commitment of the employee who takes the application to deliver an answer within the customer's specified time frame. If the employee does not, GCB will pay the customer $5.00. Finally, the bank promises that customers who call the Gold Service Telephone Line will not be transferred, asked to tell their story twice, or made to search for answers themselves. If they are, the employee will award the $5.00 payout on the spot. All payouts are credited to the customer's bank accounts.

A $5.00 payout is associated with each guarantee and is given to the customer at the time the guarantee is invoked. In addition, a service upset form is completed describing the incident. Either the employee or the customer can complete the form, but both must sign it to invoke the guarantee. The service upset form is then sent to a central location for tracking. Monthly, managers receive summary reports about the guarantee infractions in their area but the reports do not identify specific individuals who might be at fault. MCTF receives a summary of this report by the branch bank.

Sarah Coleman was the only member of the MCTF who had doubts about the success of the service guarantee program, but she was not about to push too hard—her job depended on the success of the program. Everyone else on the task force had jumped on the marketing bandwagon and hyped up the program as a solid success, even the president and CEO, Mr. Del Car. Privately, Sarah had many questions about this service guarantee initiative but all the banks were doing them.

Case Questions for Discussion:

1. What are the objectives of the service guarantee program?
2. Is a total payout of $860 over 10 months for 300 branches good or bad?
3. Are the bank's services and processes truly redesigned to meet the service guarantee promises?
4. Is GCB's service guarantee program well-designed and executed?
5. What are your final recommendations?

Tom's Auto Service

Tom's Auto Service (TAS) is a regional quick-service vehicle oil-change and lubricant-change service somewhat similar to Jiffy Lube and Tuffy Tire & Auto Service. TAS seeks to differentiate its 32 stores from competition by focusing on peripheral goods and services, the servicescape, and customer-friendly employees. The primary customer benefit package consists of friendly, professional employees who regularly interact with customers, providing oil, oil filters, air filters, tires, windshield wiper blades, and lubricants. Automotive associations also certify TAS mechanical and technical personnel, and their certificates are displayed in the customer waiting room. All technical work is guaranteed for 90 days. Employees are carefully interviewed for employment, and background checks are done on technical skills and criminal history. Video on-the-job-training is required of all new hires. All employees are trained to operate the store cash register and payment software. Store managers are responsible for the overall store operations and the customer waiting lounge.

StockLite/Shutterstock.com

The customer waiting area is larger and more comfortable at Tom's Auto Service than at most of their competitors.

Many other peripheral goods and services define TAS's customer benefit package. For example, the customer waiting rooms include several blends of fresh coffee and tea, sodas, current magazines, Wi-Fi, and a high-definition television. Customers receive vehicle maintenance brochures and discount coupons for their next visit. TAS also offers other services, such as cleaning the vehicle's windows outside and inside, vacuuming carpets, reviewing service history with the customer, and explaining the technical aspects of vehicle service if the customer asks or if a potential safety or mechanical problem is discovered.

The facility layout consists of four service bays, with a pit below three of the bays for draining and changing oil and lubricants. All necessary tools and equipment are provided for each bay. The customer waiting area is carpeted and larger than those of competitors, with comfortable sofas and chairs. A large window in the waiting area allows customers to see their vehicles being serviced in any of the bays. Employees are professionally dressed in clean blue uniforms, paid for by TAS, with their first names embroidered on them. To maintain a professional appearance, employees are required to wash their arms and hands after each service job.

A vehicle checklist is used to ensure completeness of the work and as a means of quality control. The standard time to complete a routine job is 18 minutes in the bay area, plus nine minutes for customer check-in and checkout. Other work, such as changing tires, takes longer. Store managers and assistant managers are trained and empowered to approve free service if the customer is dissatisfied for any reason.

TAS surveys customers regularly as a way of understanding customer satisfaction. Results from 206 customer surveys are summarized in Exhibit 5.19. Samples of good and bad written customer comments are shown in Exhibit 5.20. These results are over the past three months for nine randomly selected stores. Store managers never know when their store may be in the corporate survey results. The corporate vice presidents of marketing, human resource management, and operations were asked to analyze these data to determine what actions might be necessary to reward or improve performance.

The VP of operations, David Margate, decided to analyze this information. A final report to the CEO was due in two weeks. To assist Mr. Margate, answer the following questions.

Case Questions for Discussion:

1. Define and draw the customer benefit package, and state TAS's mission, strategy, and rank order of competitive priorities.
2. Identify and briefly describe the eight "design" features, described in Sections 5.4 and 5.5, of the (a) service-delivery system and (b) service encounters.
3. Identify and briefly describe five processes TAS stores use and their relative importance.
4. Given your analysis of the survey data, what opportunities for improvement, if any, do you recommend?
5. Summarize your final recommendations to the CEO.

EXHIBIT 5.19 TAS Customer Quarterly Example Survey Results ($n = 206$)

Survey Questions	Average Score on 1 (worst) to 5 (best) Scale
Store Managers	
1. Store managers monitor my vehicle's maintenance and repair very well.	4.36
2. Store managers understand my individual wants and needs.	3.87
3. Store managers always go over the vehicle check sheet with me prior to paying the bill.	4.40
Standards of Performance	
4. Cleaning the vehicle windows and vacuuming are extra services that I like.	4.66
5. Knowing the vehicle history makes me feel secure that I am doing the right thing in terms of vehicle maintenance and repair.	4.43

(Continued)

Survey Questions		Average Score on 1 (worst) to 5 (best) Scale
6.	My vehicle was fixed correctly (i.e., technically competent).	4.13
7.	Standards of performance at TAS are clearly visible inside the store, such as employee certifications and good equipment.	4.54
8.	Standards of performance at TAS are clearly advertised in the media and help me understand what to expect during vehicle service.	4.20
Employees		
9.	TAS employees are really good at what they do.	3.80
10.	Service personnel are polite, friendly, and clearly explain technical details if I ask.	4.01
11.	When problems come up, the mechanics are always helpful in correcting and explaining the issue/problem.	3.88
Facility		
12.	The facility is clean and well maintained.	4.84
13.	The customer waiting area is really nice and why I come here.	4.79
Overall Experience		
14.	The total time I spent in TAS was as expected.	4.59
15.	My service experience during each repeat visit is of consistent high quality and meets my expectations.	3.94
16.	TAS is clearly better than competitors.	4.45

EXHIBIT 5.20 Five Good and Five Bad Sample TAS Customer Written Comments

1. I come to TAS because of the outstanding vehicle technical knowledge and skills of the employees.
2. Believe it or not, I really like the coffee and enjoy reading the magazines in the waiting area.
3. The mechanics are very careful and conscientious when working on my car.
4. When I complained that there were streaks on my windows, they redid my windows and gave me a discount coupon for my next visit—real nice people.
5. Very fast and convenient service—I'll be back.
6. Store managers are super but the mechanics don't like to talk to us customers.
7. I won't come back; a mechanic kept staring at me!
8. I felt pressured to buy the air and fuel filters but they looked clean to me.
9. All the mechanics seem hurried while I was there.
10. The mechanic got grease on my fender and when I ask him to please clean it off, he shrugged and wiped it off with a cleaner.

Integrative Case: Hudson Jewelers

The Hudson Jewelers case study found in MindTap integrates material found in each chapter of this book.

Case Questions for Discussion:

1. Hudson Jewelers' current layout displays jewelry designs from the CAD system on a screen in the front of the store. However, customers have little privacy when designing jewelry there. What are the economic and non-economic advantages and disadvantages of the following options: (a) keep the current layout; (b) move the CAD system into a new private room; and (c) use option (b), buy a second CAD system, and build another private room. Data are provided in the case study.
2. Define (a) the servicescape for Hudson Jewelers using the three dimensions as subheadings, and (b) the nature of Hudson Jewelers' service encounters.
3. Propose a "service guarantee" for Hudson Jewelers. What exactly will you guarantee? Should it be explicit in writing, or simply an implicit, nonwritten guarantee? Or is it better not to do it at all? Explain and justify your logic.

6 | Supply Chain Design

LEARNING OBJECTIVES

After studying this chapter, you should be able to:

- **6-1** Explain the concept of a global supply chain, describe the key design decisions and explain the impact of blockchain technology on global supply chains.
- **6-2** Describe the key trade-offs that managers must consider in designing supply chains, and how to evaluate outsourcing and offshoring decisions.
- **6-3** Describe how Inditex/Zara designs and operates its supply chain.
- **6-4** Explain the types of decisions required and criteria used to locate facilities in supply chains, and be able to apply the center of gravity method.
- **6-5** Explain how the transportation model can be used to help optimize costs in supply chains.

For the Gap and other clothing manufacturers, the supply chain has significant implications for social responsibility and sustainability.

Sandratsky Dmitriy/Shutterstock.com

Many of you have probably shopped at apparel stores such as the Gap, Old Navy, or Banana Republic. Apparel supply chains typically begin at farms that grow raw materials such as cotton. Textile mills then weave the raw materials into fabrics for making T-shirts, jeans, and other clothing items. Factories then cut and sew the fabrics into finished goods, which are then transported to retail stores for sale to consumers. For clothing manufacturers, which rely greatly on manual labor, the supply chain has significant implications for social responsibility and sustainability.

The Gap is one company that takes this seriously. As they note: "Gap Inc. seeks to ensure that the people working at various points along the supply chain are treated with fairness, dignity, and respect—an aspiration that is born out of the belief that each life is of equal value, whether the person is sitting behind a sewing machine at a factory that produces clothes for Gap Inc., working at one of our stores, or wearing a pair of our jeans. We know that our efforts to improve the lives of people who work on behalf of our company help us run a more successful business. People who work a reasonable number of hours in a safe and healthy environment not only have a better quality of life, but they also tend to be more productive and deliver higher-quality products than those who work in poor conditions."[1]

WHAT DO YOU THINK?

What percentage of the clothes in your closet do you think are produced in other countries? What do you think the structures of the manufacturers' supply chains look like? Do clothing firms have a responsibility to improve work conditions and sustainability practices wherever they do business?

We introduced the concept of a supply chain in Chapter 1, noting that a supply chain is a key subsystem of a value chain that focuses primarily on the physical movement of goods and materials along with supporting information through the supply, production, and distribution processes. Organizations face numerous decisions in designing their supply chains. These decisions include the number, type, and location of manufacturing plants, distribution centers, retail stores, and customer service or technical support centers; the selection of suppliers; ways of managing information flow throughout the supply chain; and the integration of all the pieces into an effective, efficient system. The location of factories, distribution centers, and service facilities establishes the infrastructure for the supply chain and has a major impact on profitability.

Poor supply chain design can undermine the strategy of the firm and can easily result in lower revenue, market share, and profits. As a firm's product lines and markets change or expand, the design or redesign of supply chains becomes even more a critical issue. In addition, as companies merge and consolidate, they face many challenges and must reevaluate their supply chains and locations of facilities.

The location of factories, distribution centers, and service facilities establishes the infrastructure for the supply chain and has a major impact on profitability.

In this chapter, we focus on the design of the supply chain that sets the infrastructure for day-to-day operating decisions. In Chapter 12, we will focus on managing such tasks as sourcing and purchasing, supplier relationships, logistics and transportation, managing inventory, dealing with risk, and cost analysis in supply chains.

6-1 Global Supply Chains

Although not every organization operates in the global business environment, modern technology and distribution have made it feasible and attractive for both large and small companies to develop supply chains that span international boundaries. *A* **multinational enterprise** *is an organization that sources, markets, and produces its goods and services in several countries to minimize costs, and to maximize profit, customer satisfaction, and social welfare*. Examples of multinational enterprises include British Petroleum, General Electric, United Parcel Service, Siemens, Procter & Gamble, Toyota, and the International Red Cross. Their value chains provide the capability to source, market, create, and deliver their goods and services to customers worldwide.

Multinational enterprises operate complex supply chains that challenge operations managers. In today's global business environment, good supply chain design can lead to major reductions in total supply chain costs and improvements in customer response time.

6-1a Decisions in Supply Chain Design

Operations managers make numerous decisions in designing global supply chains. Some of the major decisions, which are not inclusive of all the issues and decisions that global supply chain executives face, are summarized in Exhibit 6.1. Many of these decisions are strategic

Johnson & Johnson Redesigns its Supply and Value Chain

J&J recognized they needed to redesign their value and supply chains in 2014. The changes took three years to design and implement. Changes included globalizing formulations and packaging to increase efficiencies and not leaving those decisions to individual markets. They also decreased the number of raw material suppliers by one-third and standardized formulations to make it easier to source ingredients. They improved the manufacturing processes to provide more flexibility in batch sizes, and consolidated packaging suppliers. Overall, the number of manufacturing plants was reduced from 27 to 13; packaging suppliers from 50 to 6; and chemical suppliers from 74 to 13. Water needed for cleaning was reduced by 20 percent. As a result, the supply chain now has much more agility and lower costs, and it has allowed J&J to more easily roll out the new products to China and other countries globally.[2]

and should support an organization's strategy, mission, and competitive priorities. Others, such as selecting transportation modes and measuring performance, are tactical and influence how supply chains are managed on a day-to-day basis; these issues are addressed in Chapter 13. We will briefly discuss each of these.

- **Strategy**—Supply chains should support an organization's strategy, mission, and competitive priorities. In Chapter 3, we provided an overall framework for developing corporate, marketing, and operations strategy and subsequent design decisions. Executives, for example, might choose a supply chain that is highly efficient versus one that is more flexible for its particular industry and market. Different types of supply chains may better fit the slower growth of industrialized countries or the more rapid growth of emerging economies. Can suppliers and customers trust our supply chains on issues like product quality and shipment data?
- **Control**—A second supply chain design decision is centralization versus decentralization. *The* **operational structure** *of a supply chain is the configuration of resources, such as suppliers, factories, warehouses, distributors, technical support centers, engineering design and sales offices, and communication links.* Different management skills are required for different operational structures. For example, Walmart's global supply chain, though very large, is focused on purchasing and distribution and is controlled from a centralized location in Bentonville, Arkansas. In contrast, General Electric's supply chain, which encompasses such diverse businesses as medical imaging, jet engines, and electrical power generation, are all quite different. Each business is a profit center with its own unique market and operating conditions. Consequently, the operational structure is decentralized globally.
- **Location**—The location of facilities in a supply chain has a significant impact on cost, customer service, and data reliability. Later in this chapter, we will discuss how to evaluate location decisions and present some simple approaches and quantitative models that aid in these decisions.
- **Sustainability**—Sustainability is a key issue in supply chains, and we often hear about this in the media (often quite negatively). We introduced the basic ideas of sustainability in Chapter 1. Sustainability issues, concepts, and methods are highlighted throughout this book. Upwards of 60 to 70 percent of a company's carbon footprint is found along their supply chains.

EXHIBIT 6.1 Eleven Example Supply Chain Design Decisions

1. **Strategy**. What competitive priorities should we emphasize? How do we build a sustainable supply change that suppliers and customers can trust? What is our supply chain strategy to meet the slower growth of industrialized countries and more rapid growth of emerging economies while considering cultural differences?
2. **Control**. Do we centralize or decentralized control of the supply chain? How do we secure supplier and customer payments along our supply chains? Who has access to the transaction data along the supply chain?
3. **Location**. Where do we locate facilities such as research and development offices, call centers, and warehouse and distribution centers in the supply chain to provide efficiencies and improve customer value?
4. **Sustainability**. How do we champion economic, environmental, and social sustainability goals and practices in global supply chains?
5. **Technology**. Do we share our technology and intellectual property with suppliers and partners in other countries? If so, how do we protect intellectual property, patents, and rights?
6. **Digital content**. How do we build and integrate digital content and e-commerce capabilities into goods and services and our supply chains? Are our collaborative tools and work with global customers and vendors secure?
7. **Sourcing**. From whom do we purchase raw materials, parts, and subassemblies? How do we track returns and recalls?
8. **Logistics and transportation**. What transportation modes (i.e., ship, air, rail, or truck) should we use to maximize service and minimize costs? How do we ensure the shipment arrived at its correct destination? What custom documents are missing while our shipment is held up at the seaport?
9. **Outsourcing**. What supply chain activities do we keep in-house or outsource to suppliers (either domestically or abroad)? Do we outsource to contract manufacturers or use third-party logistics providers? Should we outsource to a single supplier?
10. **Managing risk**. How do we address supply chain risks and disruptions? Was the payment misrouted? Who has our money? Is the shipment damaged? Did it arrive? Who owns the shipment now? What is our risk mitigation plan?
11. **Measuring performance**. What performance metrics to use in managing our supply chains? Are our supply chain's digital records and information flows secure? Are our supplier's digital records trustworthy? Does our supplier's income statement and balance sheet match throughout the world?

- **Technology**—Dealing with intellectual property is an important issue for multinational enterprises. Technology often provides a competitive edge, and licensing it to firms in other countries can lead to risks. Protecting and honoring patents from other countries is also a constant topic in global trade negotiations. And, as noted in Chapter 1, patents do not protect services.
- **Digital content**—Digital content in goods and services is becoming increasingly important. A product such as a car, appliance, jet engine, or cell phone is a bundle of physical goods and services that is often enhanced with other services by means of the "Internet of Things."
- **Sourcing**—Selecting suppliers from whom to purchase is a key design decision that also ties closely with the location decision. A key sourcing decision is whether to use a single source or multiple sources. A single supplier often provides economies of scale and the ability to form close partnerships; however, multiple suppliers lower the risk of a supply disruption.
- **Logistics and Transportation**—Transportation is more complex in global supply chains. Global shipments often require multiple modes of transportation, such as water shipping, air, rail, and truck. The transportation infrastructure may vary considerably in foreign countries. The coast of China, for example, enjoys much better transportation, distribution, and retail infrastructures than the interior of the country.

A single supplier often provides economies of scale and the ability to form close partnerships; however, multiple suppliers lower the risk of a supply disruption.

- **Managing Risks**—In Chapter 13, we discuss risk management of the supply chain. These risks are both strategic and tactical and require every company to develop a risk mitigation strategy and plan.
- **Measuring performance**—Almost every chapter contains concepts and methods for measuring performance at all levels of the organization. We focus on measuring supply chain performance in Chapters 2 and 13.

6-1b Blockchain Technology and Supply Chains

You have undoubtedly heard of bitcoin, the digital cryptocurrency. The technology underlying bitcoin is **blockchain**, *a distributed database network that holds records of digital data and events in a way that makes them tamper-resistant.* A blockchain records every transaction, which are distributed over multiple computers, making the transactions transparent and secure. One advantage of such a distributed system is no single individual or organization has total control. Today, IBM has developed blockchain open source code with over one thousand active users. Microsoft has over 5,000 blockchains on its servers.

Blockchain technology is in its infancy but it is already changing the efficiency and competitive priorities of supply chains. The goals of a blockchain-enriched supply chain are to be intelligent, collaborative, transparent, and secure while maximizing customer service at minimum costs. Organizations such as Nasdaq, IBM, Nike, British Airways, UPS, Citi, and Apple are experimenting with this new technology and potential supply chain enabler. As a good and/or service moves along the supply chain, the transactions are updated with full traceability back to the source. For example, De Beers uses blockchain technology to track diamonds from the point they are mined to when they are sold to consumers. This ensures that the company avoids "conflict" or "blood diamonds" and assures the consumers that they are buying the genuine article.[3]

The adoption of blockchain technology in supply chains impacts most of supply chain decisions we listed in Exhibit 6.1. Consider, for example, the degree of control. Full disclosure and accountability among value chain participants are no longer dependent on a single supplier, customer, or organization. The shared ledger of transactions is updated in real time for all to see immediately. The ledger documents the creation, movement, and arrival of assets.

Food Safety in Walmart's Supply Chain Using Blockchain

Walmart serves 260 million customers a week. One part of its blockchain testing project co-developed with IBM is handling recalls of food. Today, when one or more of Walmarts customers become ill due to contaminated food, it takes days, sometimes weeks, to identify the product, supplier, shipper, and where the food is located throughout Walmart's many supply chains.

Two products are being tested using blockchain. One is a USA-sourced packaged product, and the other is pork from China. If there's an issue with tainted food using blockchain it would take Walmart minutes or hours to track the supplier(s), shippers, warehouses, and retail stores involved. The vice president of food safety at Benton, Arkansas-based Walmart, Frank Yiannas, said, "With blockchain we believe that enhanced traceability is good. If the tests are successful, Walmart will expand them to multiple food items in both countries."[4]

The asset could be a manufactured part or a million dollar electronic payment. The transaction might be a purchase order, a payment for goods or services, a custom's inspection, or a shipping invoice. The distributed system is transparent, and therefore, builds trust. The goal is to achieve supply chain consensus around one dominate version of the truth recorded by blockchain technology.

Blockchain technology can also support decisions regarding sustainability and risk. Anyone along the supply chain can answer questions such as, "Was that shipment of lettuce truly grown organically?," How long did that container of lettuce sit on the loading dock?," and "What farm was the source of the *E. coli* contaminated lettuce?" See the accompanying box on Walmart.

Digital content, as noted in Exhibit 6.1, drives supply chain performance. Blockchain technology can support the Internet of Things. Electric utilities are examining blockchain to connect heat pumps, electric meters, and electric grid transformers. This supply chain data would be stored in a blockchain system to be analyzed by advanced analytics methods. Once area energy usage and patterns are evaluated, the information could be coupled with energy management and trading systems to maximize electrical grid efficiencies and keep costs low.

The logistics and transportation functions in a supply chain would be enabled by blockchain technology. For example, *Kouvola Innovation*, based in Finland, is helping firms outfit shipping containers with electronic devices that send out signals about the container's location, ambient temperature inside the container, and how much the container vibrates as it travels. This real time data flows to the cloud and a blockchain where everyone has access to the information. All supply chain players know the situation of the cargo at any time. This enhanced communication prevents thousands of duplicate e-mails and telephone calls about the status of the shipment. No one firm and its internal database controls the information.

While blockchain technology holds great promise for use in supply chains, one question that blockchain can't answer is whether the people and software using the data are trustworthy. Blockchain merely allows all players in the supply chain to see the same data in real time, even if it is inaccurate or fraudulent. Thus, organizations need to carefully evaluate its benefits and challenges.

6-2 Supply Chain Design Trade-Offs

Executives have many trade-offs to consider when designing a supply chain. We see many examples of different supply chain design structures in a variety of industries. For example, most major airlines and trucking firms such as United Airlines and UPS operate "hub-and-spoke" systems; some firms such as Apple and Nike depend on contract manufacturers to manufacture almost 100 percent of their physical goods; while others like Harley Davidson and Allen-Edmonds Shoe Corporation produce almost 100 percent of their manufactured goods in company-owned factories. Here, we discuss some key design trade-offs in supply chains.

6-2a Efficient and Responsive Supply Chains

Supply chains can be designed from two strategic-perspectives—providing high efficiency and low cost, or providing agile response. **Efficient supply chains** *are designed for efficiency and low cost by minimizing inventory and maximizing efficiencies in process flow.* A focus on efficiency works best for goods and services with highly predictable demand, stable product lines with long life cycles that do not change frequently, and low contribution margins. In designing an efficient supply chain, for example, an organization would seek to balance capacity and demand, resulting in low levels of inventory; might use only a few, large distribution centers (as opposed to small ones) to generate economies of scale; and use optimization models that minimize costs of routing products from factory through distribution centers to retail stores and customers. Examples of companies that run efficient supply chains are Procter & Gamble and Walmart.

On the other hand, **responsive supply chains** *focus on flexibility and responsive service and are able to react quickly to changing market demand and requirements*. A focus on flexibility and response is best when demand is unpredictable; product life cycles are short and change often because of product innovations; fast response is the main competitive priority; customers require customization; and contribution margins are high. Responsive supply chains have the ability to quickly respond to market changes and conditions faster than traditional supply chains; are supported by information technology that provides real-time, accurate information to managers across the supply chain; and use information to identify market changes and redirect resources to address these changes. Companies such as Apple and Nordstrom are examples of companies having responsive supply chains.

6-2b Push and Pull Systems

Two ways to configure and run a supply chain are as a push system or a pull system. A supply chain can be viewed from "left to right"—that is, materials, information, and goods are moved or pushed downstream from supplier to customer. A **push system** *produces goods in advance of customer demand using a forecast of sales and moves them through the supply chain to points of sale, where they are stored as finished-goods inventory*. Examples of push systems are "big-box" retailers such as Best Buy and department stores such as Macy's. A push system has several advantages, such as immediate availability of goods to customers and the ability to reduce transportation costs by using full-truckload shipments to move goods to distribution centers. However, some disadvantages exist. Forecasting can be difficult when customer demand changes quickly, which either can result in higher costs from excessive stock or out-of-stock conditions. Push systems work best when sales patterns are consistent and when there are few distribution centers and products.

In contrast, viewing the supply chain from "right to left" and transferring demand to upstream processes is sometimes referred to as a *demand chain* or *pull system*. A **pull system** *produces only what is needed at upstream stages in the supply chain in response to customer demand signals from downstream stages*. Physical goods are "pulled" by customer demand through each stage of the supply chain. That is, ideally, if we sell one unit, we make one unit; if we sell ten units, we make ten units; and so on. This minimizes inventory and production costs. Pull systems generally reduce the chances of having excessive inventory, but can result in shortages if customer demand suddenly increases or if schedules are missed. Pull systems are more effective when there are many production facilities, many points of distribution, and many products.

Dell, for example, introduced the idea of a make-to-order supply chain design to the computer industry and has long been recognized for outstanding practices in this area. Dell pulls component parts into its factories based on actual customer orders and carries no finished goods inventory, relying on information technology to drive its supply chain. This also provides the customer with the newest technology rather than a finished computer that has been sitting in a warehouse for months. Suppliers' component part delivery schedules must match Dell's factory assembly schedules, which in turn must be integrated with shipping schedules. Each factory worldwide is rescheduled every two hours, and at the same time updates are sent to all third-party suppliers and logistics providers.

Other examples of pull systems are airplane manufacturers such as Boeing, and manufacturers of custom machine tools. Pull systems are becoming easier to manage because of better information technology such as cloud computing. Having up-to-date data on sales, manufacturing, shipments en route, and so on can help to eliminate inventories and move toward more effective pull system configurations.

EXHIBIT 6.2 Supply Chain Push–Pull Systems and Boundaries

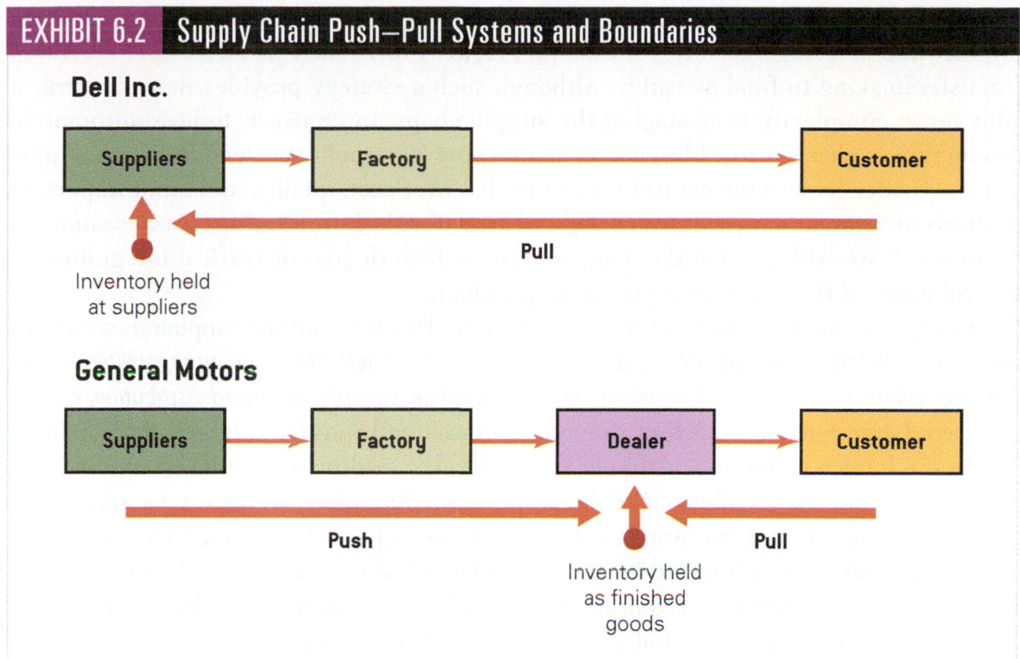

Many supply chains are combinations of push and pull systems. This can be seen in the simplified version of several supply chains in Exhibit 6.2. *The point in the supply chain that separates the push system from the pull system is called the* **push–pull boundary**. For a company like Dell, the push–pull boundary is very early in the supply chain, where suppliers store inventory for frequent deliveries to Dell factories. Dell also ships directly to the customer, skipping the distributors and retailers. General Motors stores finished goods closer to the customer, at dealers. General Motors pushes finished goods from its factories to the dealer. Dealers might install various options to customize the automobile for the customer. Customers pull the finished goods from the dealer. Thus, the push–pull boundary for General Motors is at the dealers.

The location of the push–pull boundary can affect a supply chain's responsivity. Many firms try to push as much of the finished product as possible close to the customer to speed up response and reduce work-in-process inventory requirements. **Postponement** *is the process of delaying product customization until the product is closer to the customer at the end of the supply chain.* An example is a manufacturer of refrigerators that have different door styles and colors. A postponement strategy would be to manufacture the refrigerator without the door and maintain inventories of doors at the distribution centers. When orders arrive, the doors can be quickly attached to the left or right side of the refrigerator and the unit can be shipped. This postponement approach allows customers to buy exactly what they need while manufacturers reduce their inventory and installation costs.

Although supply chains can have a profoundly positive effect on business performance, supply chain initiatives do not always work out as one would hope. Nike, for example, spent about $500 million on developing a global supply chain over the last couple of decades, and only now is it beginning to reap the benefits of this long, costly supply chain design and improvement initiative.

6-2c Vertical Integration and Outsourcing

One of the most important strategic decisions a firm can make about its supply chain is whether to vertically integrate or outsource key business processes and functions. **Vertical integration** *refers to the process of acquiring and consolidating elements of a value chain* *to achieve more control.* Some firms might consolidate all processes for a specific product or product line in a single facility; for example, Henry Ford's early factories did everything from steelmaking to final assembly. Although such a strategy provides more control, it adds more complexity to managing the supply chain. In contrast, today's automobile production is characterized by a complex network of suppliers. Decentralizing supply chain activities lessens the control that a firm has over cost, quality, and other important business metrics, and often leads to higher levels of risk. In the Inditex/Zara example in Section 6.3, we will see that the company uses a high degree of vertical integration to control many of the major stages of its supply chain.

Companies must decide whether to integrate backward (acquiring suppliers) or forward (acquiring distributors), or both. **Backward integration** *refers to acquiring capabilities toward suppliers, whereas* **forward integration** *refers to acquiring capabilities toward distribution, or even customers.* Large companies such as Motorola, Siemens, and Sony have the resources to build facilities in foreign countries and develop a high level of vertical integration. Their objective is to own or control most, if not all, of the supply chain. Many large chemical manufacturers, for example, such as DuPont, British Petroleum, Haimen Jiangbin, and GFS Chemicals, are buying raw material suppliers and integrating backward. At the same time, chemical companies in industrial countries are acquiring smaller and more profitable specialty manufacturers of chemicals and advanced materials, a form of forward integration. Recently, Delta Air Lines purchased a $150 million refinery in an effort to reduce its expenses for jet fuel—the largest expense for an airline, and also the most difficult to forecast and manage.

Outsourcing *is the process of having suppliers provide goods and services that were previously provided internally.* Outsourcing is the opposite of vertical integration in the sense that the organization is shedding (not acquiring) a part of its organization. The organization that outsources does not have ownership of the outsourced process or function. Some large U.S. banks and airlines, for example, have outsourced their telephone call service centers to third-party suppliers within or outside the United States.

The United States has experienced three waves of outsourcing:

- The first wave, several decades ago, involved the exodus of *goods-producing jobs* from the United States in many industries. Companies relied on foreign factories for the production of computer components, electronics, and many other goods. Gibson Guitars, for example, produces its Epiphone line in Korea.
- The second wave involved *simple service work* such as standard credit card processing, billing, keying information into computers, and writing simple software programs. Accenture, for example, has information technology and bookkeeping operations in Costa Rica.
- The third and current wave involves *skilled knowledge work* such as engineering design, graphic artists, architectural plans, call center customer service representatives, and computer chip design. For example, Fluor Corporation of Aliso Viejo, California, uses engineers and draftspeople in the Philippines, Poland, and India to develop detailed blueprints and specs for industrial construction and improvement projects.[5]

Many supply chains use contract manufacturing for their outsourcing strategy. *A* **contract manufacturer** *is a firm that specializes in certain types of goods-producing activities, such as customized design, manufacturing, assembly, and packaging, and works under contract for end users.* Outsourcing to contract manufacturers can offer significant competitive advantages such as access to advanced manufacturing technologies, faster product time-to-market, customization of goods in regional markets, and lower total costs resulting from economies of scale. The main disadvantage of using a contract manufacturer is that the client

Greatwide Logistics Services—A 3PL Provider

Greatwide Logistics Services, which was formed by consolidating nine regional 3PLs in the United States, works with six of the top 10 grocery retailers and wholesalers in the United States, as well as such customers as Walmart, Tyson, and Nordstrom. It uses business analytics to forecast demand and build models to leverage the capacity of its nationally centralized system, which uses satellites to track the locations of 5,000 truck tractors and over 10,000 trailers. By combining different customer needs and schedules, shipments can piggyback on another customer's shipment or use trucks on the return leg of a regular run. This leads to higher efficiency and cost savings for all customers. As one example, efficient routing and coordination of vendor delivery dates have led to a 21 percent reduction in transportation costs for one private-label spice manufacturer.[6]

Biz Idea Production/Shutterstock.com

firm gives up control and its technology to the contract manufacturer. We will discuss break-even analysis for outsourcing decisions in the next section. Finally, the degree of vertical integration forward or backward in the supply chain is an important decision for executives of the firm.

Many firms also use **third-party logistics (3PL) providers**—*businesses that provide integrated services that might include packaging, warehousing, inventory management, and transportation.* 3PLs can leverage business intelligence and analytics to create efficiencies and economies of scale in the supply chain (see the box on Greatwide Logistics Services). Zappos is a good example of using 3PLs for customer deliveries, returns, and some inbound shipping from Asian factories. Toshiba used to have repair locations across the country, whereas UPS warehoused its parts. UPS suggested that Toshiba move its repair technicians into UPS facilities, which resulted in a 24-hour turnaround for computer repairs. It also saved transportation costs, lowered inventories, and reduced the carbon footprint. 3PLs provide many services that help integrate and coordinate different parts of a supply chain.[7]

6-2d The Economics of Outsourcing Decisions

Outsourcing decisions are often based on economics—is it less expensive to manufacture a product or perform a service in-house or to outsource the work to an external supplier? If a company decides to do the work in-house, it typically incurs fixed costs associated with equipment, setting up a production line, or training, as well as a variable cost per unit. Fixed costs do not vary with volume and often include costs of a building, buying or leasing equipment, and administrative costs. Variable costs are a function of the quantity produced and might include labor, transportation, and materials costs. However, the variable cost per unit will normally be more if the work is outsourced to an external supplier. This decision can be made using break-even analysis (see Supplement C Break-Even Analysis) by comparing the costs for a given production quantity, or finding the break-even point. Solved Problem 6.1 illustrates how break-even analysis can be used to address this.

SOLVED PROBLEM 6.1: USING BREAK-EVEN ANALYSIS FOR OUTSOURCING DECISIONS

A firm is evaluating the alternative of manufacturing a part that is currently being outsourced from a supplier. For in-house manufacturing, the annual fixed cost is \$45,000 and the unit cost per part is \$130. Currently, the unit cost of purchasing the part from the supplier is \$160. The demand forecast is 1,200 units.

a. Compute the costs of manufacturing in-house and outsourcing. What decision should the firm make?
b. Determine the break-even quantity for which the firm would be indifferent between manufacturing the part in-house or outsourcing it. Explain the decision rule based on the break-even quantity.
c. What is the maximum price per part the manufacturer should be willing to pay to the supplier if the forecast is 800 parts?

Solution:

a. Define FCI as the fixed cost of in-house manufacturing, CI as the unit cost of manufacturing in-house, FCO the fixed cost of outsourcing, and CO the unit cost of outsourcing. Then FCI = \$45,000, CI = \$130, and CO = \$160. Note that there is no fixed cost associated with outsourcing. Using formulas (C.5)–(C.7) in Supplement C, we have

Total cost in-house (TCI)
= Fixed cost in-house (FCI) + Unit cost in-house (CI) × Quantity (Q)
= \$45,000 + \$130 × 1200
= \$201,000

Total cost to outsourcing (TCO)
= Fixed cost outsourcing (FCO) + Unit cost outsourcing (CO) × Quantity (Q)
= \$0 + \$160 x 1200
= \$168,000

Cost difference (D) = Total cost in-house (TCI) − Total cost outsourcing (TCO)
= \$201,000 − \$168,000
= \$33,000

That is, manufacturing in-house costs \$33,000 more than outsourcing. Therefore, the firm should outsource the part.

We may also use the *Break-Even* Excel template in MindTap. As shown in Exhibit 6.3, it is more economical to outsource.

b. Using formula (C.8) in Supplement C, the break-even quantity (Q^*) is

$$Q^* = \frac{\text{FCO} - \text{FCI}}{\text{CI} - \text{CO}} = \frac{0 - \$45{,}000}{\$130 - \$160} = 1{,}500 \text{ parts}$$

Whenever the anticipated quantity needed is greater than 1,500, the firm should produce the part in-house; otherwise, it should outsource. Because the demand is 1,200, the best decision is to outsource.

c. To find the maximum price per part the manufacturer should be willing to pay to the supplier if the forecast is 800 parts, we can use the break-even formula (C.8):

$$\begin{aligned}
Q^* &= [\text{FCO} - \text{FCI}]/[\text{CI} - \text{CO}] \\
Q^* \times (\text{CI} - \text{CO}) &= \text{FCO} - \text{FCI} \\
800 \times (\$130 - \text{CO}) &= \$0 - \$45{,}000 \\
\$104{,}000 - 800 \times \text{CO} &= -\$45{,}000 \\
-800 \times \text{CO} &= -\$149{,}000 \\
\text{CO} &= \$186.25
\end{aligned}$$

We may also use the Excel Goal Seek tool in the Break-Even template as described in Supplement C. The result is shown in Exhibit 6.4.

EXHIBIT 6.3 ***Break-Even* Template Results**

	D	E
4	**Outsourcing Decision**	
5	**Quantity**	1,200
6		
7	**Produce In-House**	
8	**Fixed cost**	\$45,000.00
9	**Unit cost**	\$130.00
10		
11	**Outsource**	
12	**Fixed cost**	
13	**Unit cost**	\$140.00
14		
15	**Total In-House Production Cost**	\$201,000.00
16	**Total Outsourced Cost**	\$168,000.00
17	**Cost difference (In-House - Outsourced)**	\$33,000.00
18	**Economical Decision**	Outsource

EXHIBIT 6.4 Results From Using the Goal Seek Tool

	D	E
4	**Outsourcing Decision**	
5	**Quantity**	800
6		
7	**Produce In-House**	
8	**Fixed cost**	$45,000.00
9	**Unit cost**	$130.00
10		
11	**Outsource**	
12	**Fixed cost**	
13	**Unit cost**	$186.25
14		
15	**Total In-House Production Cost**	$149,000.00
16	**Total Outsourced Cost**	$149,000.00
17	**Cost difference (In-House - Outsourced)**	$0.00
18	**Economical Decision**	Break-even

6-2e Offshoring and Reshoring

Offshoring *is the building, acquiring, or moving of process capabilities from a domestic location to another country location while maintaining ownership and control.* Offshoring differs from outsourcing in that the firm maintains ownership of the facility in another country.

Offshoring decisions involve determining what value creation, support, and/or general management processes should move to other countries. For example, a company might move a soda-bottling factory from the United States to India. The company benefits from lower wages, avoiding country trade tariffs, and access to local markets and customers. Recently, we have seen a number of foreign firms offshore and build factories in the United States. For example, the British company Rolls-Royce makes jet engine parts in the United States for assembly in Europe and Asia, taking advantage of lower energy costs and a more stable economic environment; Mercedes, BMW, Lexus, and others produce vehicles in the United States, Mexico, and Canada to be closer to customers.

Some global trade experts recommend keeping some primary processes or key parts of a manufacturing process out of foreign lands to protect the firm's core competencies. We can pose four possible scenarios. In the first scenario, all key processes remain in the home country, even though the firm sells its products overseas. An example would be Harley-Davidson. The second scenario represents a low degree of offshoring in which some noncritical support processes are moved overseas. Examples would be Microsoft and American Express.

A third scenario is for a company to offshore many of its primary as well as support processes while keeping its management processes consolidated at the corporate headquarters as Coca-Cola and FedEx do. Finally, truly global multinational firms such as Procter & Gamble, General Electric, and Honda locate all of their key processes across the globe for more effective coordination and local management. The global alignments, of course,

Allen-Edmonds Shoe Corporation: Not Everyone Offshores

At a time when more than 98 percent of all shoes sold in the United States are made in other countries, Allen-Edmonds Shoe Corp. is a lonely holdout against offshoring. Moving to China could have saved the company as much as 60 percent. However, John Stollenwerk, chief executive, will not compromise on quality and believes that Allen-Edmonds can make better shoes and serve customers faster in the United States. An experiment in producing one model in Portugal resulted in lining that wasn't quite right and stitching that wasn't as fine. Stollenwerk noted "We could take out a few stitches and you'd never notice it—and then we could take out a few more. Pretty soon you've cheapened the product, and you don't stand for what you're about."[8] Instead, Allen-Edmonds invested more than $1 million to completely overhaul its manufacturing process into a leaner, more efficient system that could reduce the cost of each pair of shoes by 5 percent. One year after implementing its new production processes, productivity was up 30 percent; damages were down 14 percent; and order fulfillment neared 100 percent, enabling the company to serve customers better than ever.[9]

may change over time. The third and fourth scenarios might leave the firm vulnerable to protecting trade secrets or losing first-hand knowledge of how to manufacture their own products.

The decision to offshore involves a variety of economic and noneconomic issues. Exhibit 6.5 summarizes the key issues in these decisions. When many manufacturers began offshoring to Asia in the early 1990s, they were focused strictly on low labor cost. This cost differential is narrowing. In addition, offshoring can create numerous problems, especially for small businesses who don't have the resources that larger firms do. For instance, the logistics of shipping from Asia can be complex. Travel expenses for executives and other employees needed to teach or monitor operations can mount up. Quality and production schedules are

EXHIBIT 6.5 Things to Consider when Making Offshoring Decisions

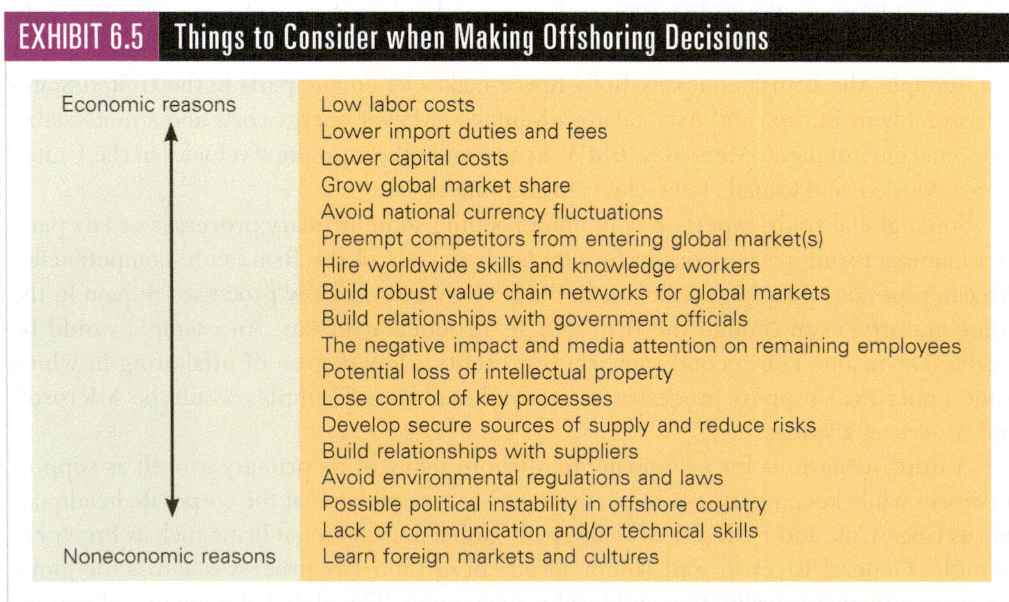

more difficult to control, as is enforcing intellectual property rights. Some foreign manufacturers, for example, began using inferior materials or parts despite contractual agreements. When all these factors are considered, some argue that the total cost of production in the United States is actually cheaper. As a result, many firms are bringing operations back to the United States.[10]

Reshoring *is the process of moving operations back to a company's domestic location*. For example, American Giant, an apparel company that makes popular sweatshirts, moved its sourcing back to the United States from India and found that it is easier to manage the supply chain. When solvents caused blotting on T-shirts at the Los Angeles factory, the issue was fixed in just a few hours with only about 10 yards of fabric wasted; had the company been sourcing fabric from India, it could have taken weeks, resulting in a loss of thousands of yards of fabric.[11] A nonprofit organization, the Reshoring Initiative (www.reshorenow.org) seeks to revitalize U.S. manufacturing by helping companies better understand the total cost of offshoring, so they can make more informed decisions. However, as an executive at General Electric noted, "You can't just move the production back to the U.S. You have to think about how you build and design it more efficiently, because otherwise you run into the same problems you had when you offshored." (Such problems might include managing operations and quality, for instance.) In addition, companies often struggle to rebuild their supplier base and find the right employees when they reshore.[12]

6-3 A Global Supply Chain Example: Inditex/Zara

To gain a better understanding of global supply chains and supply chain design decisions, we present a case study of Inditex and its flagship brand, Zara. Then we briefly show how Inditex/Zara made supply chain design decisions similar to those described in Exhibit 6.1.

Inditex (www.inditex.com) is a global fashion retailer based in La Coruna, Spain. Its most-recognized brand is Zara, with approximately 6,900 stores in over 85 countries speaking 45 different languages. To be successful in fashion, companies must continually provide the latest products and capitalize on tomorrow's trends, not yesterday's (as they say on "Project Runway": "In fashion, one day you're in; the next day you're out!"). What makes Zara unique is a value chain model that focuses on two basic rules: "Give customers what they want, and get it to them faster than anyone else."[13] As an example, Zara delivers new items to its stores twice weekly, taking less than two weeks from design to delivery! To accomplish this, the company must understand changing consumer trends and have the agility to rapidly produce and deliver appealing products that will sell before consumer tastes change again. This requires a highly responsive supply chain that seamlessly links market sensing, design, and production processes with customers.

Exhibit 6.6 illustrates the key elements of Inditex's global supply chain, which uses over 5,300 factories located in over 50 countries. It sources locally when possible; in Spain, for example, over 60 percent of its suppliers are located near textile and garment factories. However, they also outsource to over 1,600 suppliers worldwide.

Their supply chain design can also be viewed as more of a pull system, because point-of-sale data drives many flexible production processes. Zara uses a high degree of vertical integration to control many of the major stages of its supply chain. They employ exhaustive controls over product design, the selection and quality of raw materials, and end-of-product-life recycling initiatives. Inditex uses 28 third-party laboratories around the world to test its raw materials and dyes, products, and processes to ensure customer safety and comfort, and environmental well-being.

EXHIBIT 6.6 Inditex's Global Value Chain

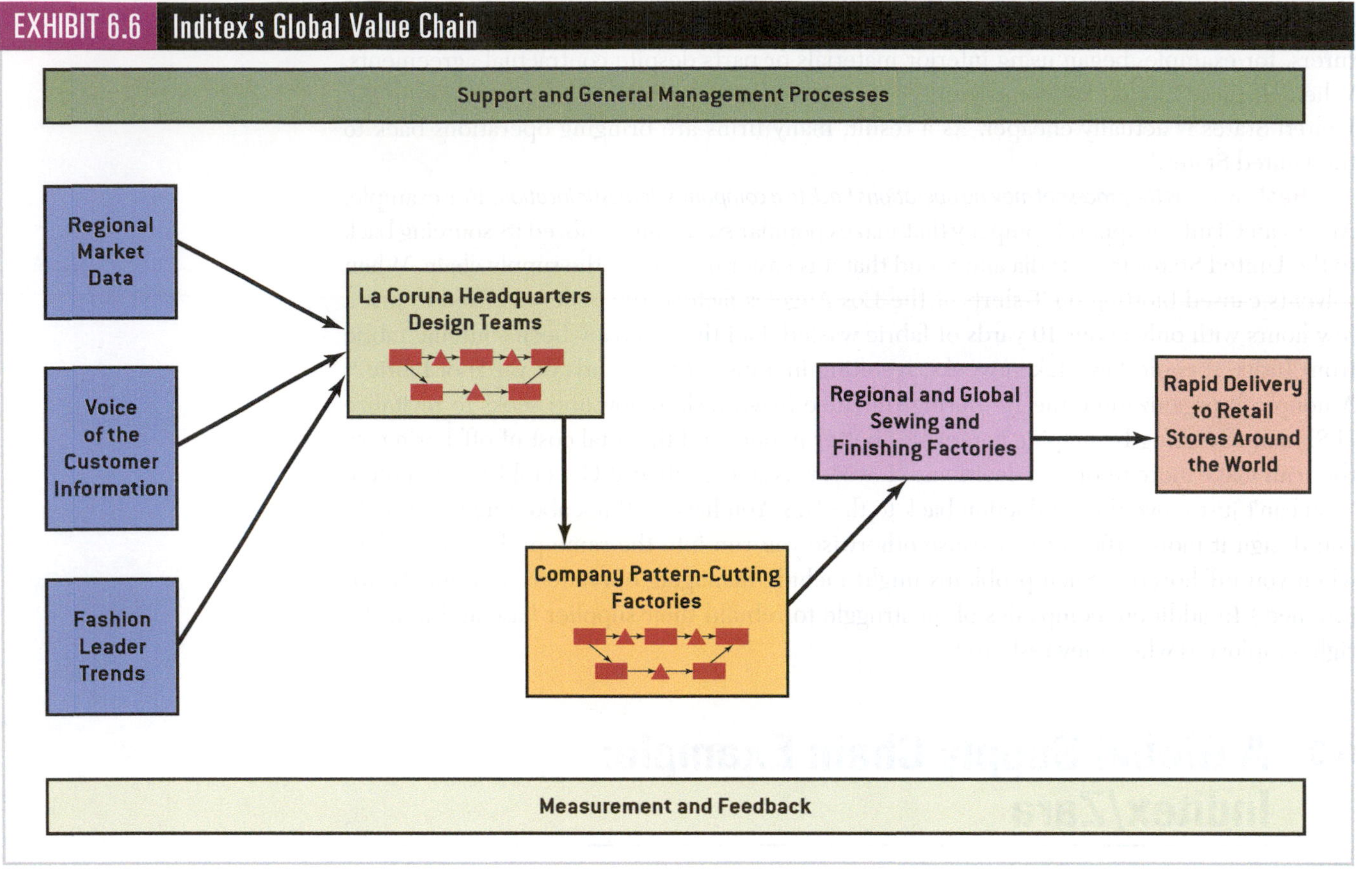

Business analytics is used to monitor and predict customer-buying behavior and supply chain performance. To avoid overstocks of items that don't sell, the company initially sends only a few orders for new styles but can quickly deliver more if they become hot-selling items. Store managers report this information daily through point-of-sale information. Marketing analysts then study the data and the voice of the customer (acquired by the sales staff), monitor trends from fashion leaders in Paris and Milan, and even track blogs to ensure that their goods meet different customer needs in each region. Inditex's products appear in multiple social media channels, in its commercials, and in over 20 corporate videos on topics like design, social responsibility, customer service, logistics, and fashion.

Design information is communicated to a team of in-house designers who quickly develop new designs and send them to factories to be manufactured. So, instead of producing up to six months in advance of the selling season, Inditex observes what goods are selling, makes more of them, and eliminates those that aren't selling, without having to keep and discount outdated inventory.

> Inditex's business model is based on the premise that all its processes must be sustainable and responsible.

Zara uses its own highly automated pattern-cutting factories and subcontracts labor-intensive sewing and finishing work to more than 300 small regional facilities in Spain, Portugal, and Morocco (called "proximity sourcing"); it also outsources some production to Asian factories. More than half of its production is performed close to its design and distribution centers in about a dozen company-owned factories. This approach is similar to "lean manufacturing" and exploits the principles of the Toyota production system, which we will describe in Chapter 17. In contrast, most other fashion retailers outsource all their manufacturing to Asia to reduce labor costs, resulting in slow supply chains that require the designers to make early style and volume commitments well ahead of the selling season. Although proximity sourcing is more costly, the ability of Inditex's supply chain to quickly change styles, ramp up manufacturing, and deliver goods to its stores allows them to capitalize on the hottest trends and offset the labor costs by increased revenue.

Inbound transportation to warehouse hubs is normally by air, ship, and truck. Outbound shipments to all retail stores twice weekly are delivered by truck and air cargo. In fact, its supply chain can deliver most goods in 24 hours in Europe and the United States, and in 48 hours in Asia and Latin America. Air transportation is used for most high-fashion and hot-selling items. Automated warehouses move clothing quickly to retail stores. One of their supply chain management principles is the "traceability" of all raw materials and finished goods from suppliers to factories to warehouses and to each retail store.

Sustainability and risk management are also important components of Inditex's supply chain. In its 2012 annual report the company states:

> Inditex's business model is based on the premise that all its processes must be sustainable and responsible. This concept of sustainability in Inditex not only covers the entire value chain but also considered the focal point of all its strategic decisions. In this regard, it is understood to be a responsibility that is shared by all Inditex's members of staff.... All of these [suppliers], as well as each factory where production is carried out, must be explicitly bound by the values of social and environmental responsibility that defines Inditex, through the Department of Corporate Social Responsibility, the Department of the Environment and the commercial and purchasing teams.... Inditex guarantees its customers products that meet the most exacting health and safety standards.[14]

The company's animal welfare policies and production standards, for example, are world class regarding animal skins, fur, and wool, and how the animals are to be treated. As part of Inditex's governing structure, the firm has a Committee of Risks that constantly evaluates supply chain risks such as shipping disruptions, chemical and dye spills and accidents, and data security breaches.

Zara's global supply chain addresses many of the key supply chain decisions described in Exhibit 6.1. For example:

- Zara defined a clear ***strategy*** and makes ***sourcing*** and facility ***location*** decisions based on its strategy. Zara favors keeping key operational activities such as suppliers and warehouses close to its factories,
- Although the firm ***outsources*** when appropriate, it maintains a high degree of supply chain ***control***. They have resisted the industry trend to transfer their fast-fashion production approach to developing countries.
- The firm exploits ***technology*** and business analytics to run its factories and design clothing faster than competitors, and uses ***digital content*** for marketing and promoting its products and philosophy.
- Air ***transportation*** is an integral part of quickly creating and delivering what the customer wants.
- They carefully manage ***supply chain risks*** associated with over- or undersupply. If a new design item, for example, does not sell within a few weeks of being in the stores, they cancel all orders and pursue a new design.
- The firm clearly works to champion ***sustainability*** wherever it can.
- Finally, Zara measures the **performance** of its supply chain through traceability of raw materials and finished goods.

6-4 Location Decisions

The principal goal of a supply chain is to provide customers with accurate and quick response to their orders at the lowest possible cost. This requires a network of facilities that are located strategically in the supply chain. Facility networking and location focuses on determining the best network structure and geographical locations for facilities to maximize service and revenue, and to minimize costs. These decisions can become complex, especially for a global supply chain, which must consider shipping costs between all demand and supply points in the network, fixed operating costs of each distribution and/or retail facility, revenue generation per customer location, facility labor and operating costs, and construction costs.

Larger firms have more complex location decisions. They might have to position a large number of factories and distribution centers advantageously with respect to suppliers, retail outlets, *and* each other. Rarely are these decisions made simultaneously. Typically, factories are located with respect to suppliers and a fixed set of distribution centers, or distribution centers are located with respect to a fixed set of factories and markets. A firm might also choose to locate a facility in a new geographic region not only to provide cost or service efficiencies but also to create cultural ties between the firm and the local community.

Location is also critical in services. A great servicescape and facility layout can seldom overcome a poor location decision, simply because customers may not have convenient access, which is one of the most important requirements for a service facility. Service facilities such as post offices, branch banks, dentist offices, and fire stations typically need to be in close proximity to the customer. In many cases, the customer travels to the service facility, whereas in others, such as mobile X-ray and imaging centers or "on-call" computer-repair services, the service travels to the customer.

Many service organizations operate large numbers of similar facilities. **Multisite management** *is the process of managing geographically dispersed service-providing facilities*. For example, McDonald's has over 30,000 restaurants worldwide plus hundreds of food-processing factories and distribution centers. Federal Express has over 1 million pickup and delivery sites worldwide, plus hundreds of sorting and distribution facilities. Some major banks have over 5,000 branch banks, plus thousands of ATM locations. Supply chains are vital to multisite management, and in each of these cases it can be difficult to design a good supply chain.

Criteria for locating these facilities differ depending on the nature of the service. For example, service facilities that customers travel to, such as public libraries and urgent-care facilities, seek to *minimize the average or maximum distance or travel time required* from among the customer population. For those that travel to customer locations, such as fire stations, the location decision seeks to minimize response time to customers.

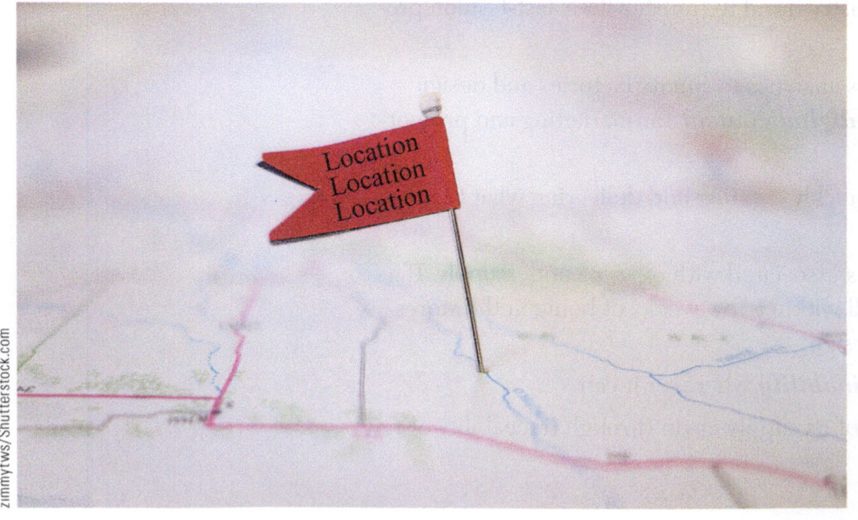

zimmytws/Shutterstock.com

6-4a Critical Factors in Location Decisions

Location decisions in supply and value chains are based on both economic and noneconomic factors. For example, although the Gap, Banana Republic, and Old Navy are part of the same corporation, each firm locates its factories differently. The Gap makes its goods in Mexico to provide more agility in supplying the North American market; Old Navy sources in China to keep costs down; and Banana Republic has facilities in Italy in order to be close to fashion innovations. Exhibit 6.7 is a list of some important location factors for site selection. Economic factors include facility costs such as construction, utilities, insurance, taxes, depreciation, and maintenance; operating costs, including fuel, direct labor, and administrative personnel; and transportation costs associated with moving goods and services from their origins to the final destinations, or the opportunity cost of customers coming to the facility. Audi, for instance, is building its first plant in North America—in Mexico—to exploit free-trade agreements that allow them to ship cars duty free to the United States and better manage exchange-rate fluctuations.

Location Drives Amazon's Operations Center of Excellence Decision

Amazon announced they were opening an Operations Center of Excellence in downtown Nashville, Tennessee, that will provide 5,000 full time jobs. Among their reasons for choosing this location were the following:

- Nashville is at the heart of population centers, and you can reach half of the U.S. population within a single-day drive.
- It's centrally located between two of the largest logistics providers in the country: FedEx in Memphis, and the *UPS Worldport* in Louisville, Kentucky.
- Being in the central time zone makes it easier to access to both East and West Coast customers.
- Nashville has a lot of supply chain talent, with universities such as Vanderbilt and Middle Tennessee State, which has a concentration in supply chain management.
- Its relatively low cost of living can attract employees from out of town.[15]

Economic criteria are not always the most important factors in such decisions. Sometimes location decisions are based upon strategic objectives such as preempting competitors from entering a geographical region. New facilities also require large amounts of capital investment and, once built, cannot easily be moved. Moreover, location decisions also affect the management of operations at lower levels of the organization. For instance, if a manufacturing facility is located far from sources of raw materials, it may take a considerable amount of time to deliver an order, and there will be more uncertainty as to the actual time of delivery. Noneconomic factors in location decisions include the availability of labor, transportation services, and utilities; climate, community environment, and quality of life; and state and local legal and political factors. These must be balanced with economic factors in arriving at a location decision that meets financial as well as customer and operational needs.

EXHIBIT 6.7 Example Location Factors for Site Selection

Location Factors	Transportation Factors	Utilities Factors	Climate, Community Environment, and Quality-of-Life Factors	State and Local Legal and Political Factors
Customer access	Minimize distance traveled (i.e., convenience)	Fuel availability	Housing and roads	Payroll taxes
Demand and markets	Closeness to markets	Waste disposal	K–12 schools	Local and state tax structure
Sourcing	Closeness to sources of supply	Water supply	Climate and living conditions	Taxation climate and policies
Ability to retain labor force	Adequacy of transportation modes (i.e., air, truck, train, water)	Power supply	Universities and research facilities	Opportunity for highway advertising
Availability of adequate labor skills	Costs of transportation	Local energy costs	Community attitudes	Tax incentives and abatements
Labor rates	Visibility of the facility from the highway	Communications capability	Health care facilities	Zoning laws
Location of competitors	Parking capability	Price/cost	Property costs	Health and safety laws
Volume of traffic around location (i.e., traffic congestion)	Inbound and outbound driving time for employees and customers	Utility regulatory laws and practices	Cost of living	Regulatory agencies and policies

6-4b Location Decision Process

Facility location is typically conducted hierarchically and involves the following four basic decisions where appropriate.

Global Location Decision Many companies must cope with issues of global operations such as time zones, foreign languages, international funds transfer, customs, tariffs, and other trade restrictions, packaging, international monetary policy, and cultural practices. The global location decision involves evaluating the product portfolio, new market opportunities, changes in regulatory laws and procedures, production and delivery economics, sustainability, and the cost to locate in different countries. With this information, the company needs to determine whether it should locate domestically or in another country; what countries are most amenable to setting up a facility (and what countries to avoid); and how important it is

SOLVED PROBLEM 6.2: MAKING AN ECONOMICAL LOCATION DECISION

The following data are related to the operating costs of three possible locations for Fountains Manufacturing:

	Location 1	Location 2	Location 3
Fixed costs	$165,000	$125,000	$180,000
Direct material cost per unit	$8.50	$8.40	$8.60
Direct labor cost per unit	$4.20	$3.90	$3.70
Overhead per unit	$1.20	$1.10	$1.00
Transportation cost per unit	$0.80	$1.10	$0.95

Which location would minimize the total costs, given annual production of 50,000 units?

Solution:

Compute the total cost associated with annual production. For example, the direct material cost at location 1 is ($8.50)(50,000 units) = $425,000, summarized as follows:

Total Costs	Location 1	Location 2	Location 3
Fixed costs	$165,000	$125,000	$180,000
Direct material	$425,000	$420,000	$430,000
Direct labor	$210,000	$195,000	$185,000
Overhead	$60,000	$55,000	$50,000
Transportation	$40,000	$55,000	$47,500
Total	$900,000	$850,000	$892,500

Based on total manufacturing and distribution costs, location 2 would be best. Exhibit 6.8 shows the Excel *Location Analysis* template in MindTap that can be used to perform these calculations.

EXHIBIT 6.8 Excel *Location Analysis* Template

	A	B	C	D	E	F	G	H
1	Location Analysis							
2	Enter data only in yellow cells. The template is designed for up to 5 locations.							
3								
4	Data	Location 1	Location 2	Location 3	Location 4	Location 5		
5	Fixed Costs	$165,000.00	$125,000.00	$180,000.00				
6	Direct material cost/unit	$8.50	$8.40	$8.60				
7	Direct labor cost/unit	$4.20	$3.90	$3.70				
8	Overhead/unit	$1.20	$1.10	$1.00				
9	Transportation cost/unit	$0.80	$1.10	$0.95				
10								
11	Annual Production	50000						
12								
13	Total Costs	Location 1	Location 2	Location 3	Location 4	Location 5		
14	Fixed Costs	$165,000.00	$125,000.00	$180,000.00				
15	Direct material cost	$425,000.00	$420,000.00	$430,000.00				
16	Direct labor cost	$210,000.00	$195,000.00	$185,000.00				
17	Overhead	$60,000.00	$55,000.00	$50,000.00				
18	Transportation cost	$40,000.00	$55,000.00	$47,500.00				
19	Total	$900,000.00	$850,000.00	$892,500.00				
20								
21	Least-cost location	Location 2						

to establish a local presence in other regions of the world. The decision by Mercedes-Benz to locate in Alabama was based on the fact that German labor costs were about 50 percent higher than labor costs in the southern United States; the plant also gives the company better inroads into the American market and functions as a kind of laboratory for future global-manufacturing ventures.

Regional Location Decision The regional location decision involves choosing a general region of a country, such as the northeast or south. Factors that affect the regional decision include size of the target market, the locations of major customers and sources of materials and supply; labor availability and costs; degree of unionization; land, construction, and utility costs; quality of life; and climate.

Community Location Decision The community location decision involves selecting a specific city or community in which to locate. In addition to the factors cited previously, a company would consider managers' preferences, community services and taxes (as well as tax incentives), available transportation systems, banking services, and environmental impacts. Mercedes-Benz settled on Vance, Alabama, after considering sites in 30 different states. Alabama pledged $250 million in tax abatements and other incentives, and the local business community came up with $11 million. The community also submitted a plan for how it would help the families of German workers adjust to life in that community.

Local Site Location Decision The site location decision involves the selection of a particular location within the chosen community. Site costs, proximity to transportation systems, utilities, payroll and local taxes, sustainability issues, and zoning restrictions are among the factors to be considered.

Researchers at the University of Tennessee developed a tool to help organizations assess their supply chain location decisions, identifying the strengths, weaknesses, opportunities, and threats of the different regions in the world. Called the EPIC framework, it provides the structure for assessing various regions around the globe for supply chain readiness from economic (E), political (P), infrastructural (I), and competence (C) perspectives. The framework measures and assesses the levels of "maturity" held by a geographic region, with specific respect to its ability to support supply chain activities. The four EPIC dimensions are then assessed using a set of variables associated with each dimension. Exhibit 6.9 summarizes the key variables and supply chain network design issues in the EPIC framework.[16]

6-4c The Center-of-Gravity Method

Supply chain design and location decisions are quite difficult to analyze and make. Many types of quantitative models and approaches, ranging from simple to complex, can be used to facilitate these decisions. We introduce a simple quantitative approach; however, in practice, more sophisticated models are generally used.

The **center-of-gravity method** *determines the x and y coordinates (location) for a single facility.* Although it does not explicitly address customer service objectives, it can be used to assist managers in balancing cost and service objectives. The center-of-gravity method takes into account the locations of the facility and markets, demand, and transportation costs in arriving at the best location for a single facility. It would seem reasonable to find some "central" location, between the goods-producing or service-providing facility and customers, at which to locate the new facility. But distance alone should not be the principal criterion, as the demand (volume, transactions, etc.) from one location to another also affects the costs. To incorporate distance and demand, the center of gravity is defined as the location that minimizes the weighted distance between the facility and its supply and demand points.

The first step in the procedure is to place the locations of existing supply and demand points on a coordinate system. The origin of the coordinate system and scale used are arbitrary, as long as the relative distances are correctly represented. Placing a grid over an ordinary map

EXHIBIT 6.9 EPIC Framework

Dimension	Key Variables	Supply Chain Network Design Issues/SCND
Economy	GDP and GDP Growth Rate	Retail store location
		Supply network—node location
		Retail store location
	Population Size	Sales channel—direct sales stores vs. distributors
		Ecommerce vs. retail store
	Foreign Direct Investment	Manufacturing location
	Exchange Rate Stability & CPI	Manufacturing location
	Balance of Trade	Sourcing & manufacturing location
Politics	Ease of Doing Business	Retail store location
		Supply network—node location
		Sourcing & manufacturing location
	Legal & Regulatory Framework	Retail store location
		Supply network—node location
		Sourcing & manufacturing location
	Risk of Political Stability	Retail store location
		Supply network–node location
		Sourcing & manufacturing location
	Intellectual Property Rights	R&D center
		E-commerce vs. retail store
		Decisions on product design
Infrastructure	Transportation Infrastructure	Logistics network design
	Utility Infrastructure (Electricity)	Sourcing, manufacturing, and logistics location
	Telecommunication & Connectivity	Sourcing, manufacturing, and logistics location
		Retail store location
Competence	Labor Relations	Sourcing, manufacturing, and logistics location
	Education Level	R&D center
		E-commerce vs. retail store
		Design school and champion
		Sourcing, manufacturing, and logistics location
		Retail store location
	Logistics Competence	Sourcing, manufacturing, and logistics location
		E-commerce vs. retail store (e.g., courier services)
	Customs & Security	Sourcing, manufacturing, and logistics location

is one way to do that. The center of gravity is determined by Equations 6.4 and 6.5, and can easily be implemented on a spreadsheet.

$$C_x = \Sigma X_i W_i / \Sigma W_i \quad [6.4]$$

$$C_y = \Sigma Y_i W_i / \Sigma W_i \quad [6.5]$$

where

C_x = x coordinate of the center of gravity
C_y = y coordinate of the center of gravity
X_i = x coordinate of location i
Y_i = y coordinate of location i
W_i = volume of goods or services moved to or from location i

The center-of-gravity method is often used to locate service facilities. For example, in locating a waste disposal facility, the location coordinates can be weighted by the average amount of waste generated from residential neighborhoods and industrial sites. Similarly, to locate a library, fire station, hospital, or post office, the population densities will define the appropriate weights in the model.

SOLVED PROBLEM 6.3: FINDING THE CENTER OF GRAVITY

Taylor Paper Products is a producer of paper stock used in newspapers and magazines. Taylor's demand is relatively constant, and thus can be forecast rather accurately. The company's two factories are located in Hamilton, Ohio, and Kingsport, Tennessee. The company distributes paper stock to four major markets: Chicago, Pittsburgh, New York, and Atlanta. The board of directors has authorized the construction of an intermediate warehouse to service those markets. Coordinates for the factories and markets are shown in the Excel template in Exhibit 6.10. For example, we see that location 1, Hamilton, is at the coordinate (58, 96); therefore, $X_1 = 58$ and $Y_1 = 96$. Hamilton and Kingsport produce 400 and 300 tons per month, respectively. Demand at Chicago, Pittsburgh, New York, and Atlanta is 200, 100, 300, and 100 tons per month, respectively. With that information, using Equations 6.4 and 6.5, the center of gravity coordinates are computed as follows:

$$C_x = \frac{58(400) + 80(300) + 30(200) + 90(100) + 127(300) + 65(100)}{400 + 300 + 200 + 100 + 300 + 100} = 76.3$$

$$C_y = \frac{96(400) + 70(300) + 120(200) + 110(100) + 130(300) + 40(100)}{400 + 300 + 200 + 100 + 300 + 100} = 98.1$$

The Excel *Center-of-Gravity* template on MindTap uses these formulas to find the best location. By overlaying a map on the chart, we see that the location is near the border of southern Ohio and West Virginia. Managers now can search that area for an appropriate site.

EXHIBIT 6.10 Excel *Center-of-Gravity* Template

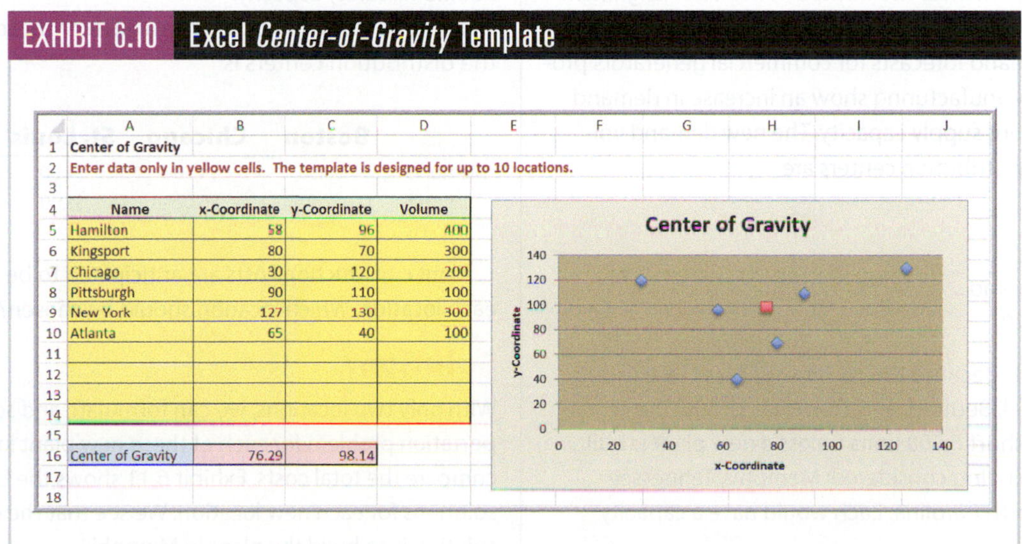

Center of Gravity

Enter data only in yellow cells. The template is designed for up to 10 locations.

Name	x-Coordinate	y-Coordinate	Volume
Hamilton	58	96	400
Kingsport	80	70	300
Chicago	30	120	200
Pittsburgh	90	110	100
New York	127	130	300
Atlanta	65	40	100
Center of Gravity	76.29	98.14	

6-5 Supply Chain Optimization

Supply chain optimization *is the process of ensuring that a supply chain operates at the highest levels of efficiency and effectiveness.* This includes minimizing the total costs of manufacturing and transportation, which might consider sourcing, distribution, and placement of inventory throughout the supply chain. Various optimization approaches are used to model complex transportation configurations and conduct "what-if" analyses to evaluate alternative supply chain strategies. Some typical uses of such a system are investigating the "what-if" effects of changes in demand and volume; changes in transportation modes and costs; transportation and labor strikes, natural disasters, and energy shortages; plant-capacity expansion proposals; new product lines; deletion of product lines; price changes and discounts; emerging global or local markets; transportation using public versus private carriers; and facility size, type, mix, and location(s). Supply chain optimization models can become very complex and requires sophisticated software to solve large, practical problems.

Supplement E introduces the **transportation model**—*a linear optimization model that seeks to minimize the cost of shipping from sources such as factories to destinations such as warehouses or customer zones.* This model is the basis for more advanced supply chain optimization models. Solved Problem 6.4 shows how this can be used.

SOLVED PROBLEM 6.4: A TRANSPORTATION MODEL FOR SUPPLY CHAIN OPTIMIZATION

This example draws upon the Foster Manufacturing transportation model in Supplement E: The Transportation and Assignment Problems. You should review this material first.

Long-term demand forecasts for commercial generators produced by Foster Manufacturing show an increase in demand that exceeds current supply capacity. The new demand volumes at the four distribution centers are

Boston: 8,000,
Chicago: 6,500,
St. Louis: 3,500, and
Lexington: 2,000,

which total 20,000. Because the current supply at its existing plants in Cleveland, Bedford, and York total 13,500, the company will be short 6,500 units unless a new plant is built. Two locations are being considered: Memphis, Tennessee and Charlotte, North Carolina. Each would have a capacity of 8,000 units to cover the forecasted demand and provide additional safety capacity.

The unit cost of shipping from each of these locations to the distribution centers is

	Boston	Chicago	St. Louis	Lexington
Memphis	$8.50	$4.50	$4.00	$4.00
Charlotte	$7.50	$6.00	$5.00	$4.50

Plant construction costs are anticipated to be the same for each location. Which location should be chosen?

Solution:

With only two locations, we can formulate and solve a transportation problem for each of these new plant locations and compare the total costs. Exhibit 6.11 shows the Excel Solver solutions for each new location. We see that the minimum cost solution is to build the plant in Memphis.

EXHIBIT 6.11 Excel Solver Solutions for Foster Manufacturing

	A	B	C	D	E	F	G	H	I	J	K
1	Foster Manufacturing										
2											
3	Data	Boston	Chicago	St. Louis	Lexington	Supply					
4	Cleveland	$3.00	$2.00	$7.00	$6.00	5000					
5	Bedford	$7.00	$5.00	$2.00	$3.00	6000					
6	York	$2.00	$5.00	$4.00	$5.00	2500					
7	Memphis	$8.50	$4.50	$4.00	$4.00	8000					
8	Demand	8000	6500	3500	2000						
9											
10											
11	Model										
12											
13	Decision variables	Boston	Chicago	St. Louis	Lexington		Supply Constraints	Cleveland	Bedford	York	Memphis
14	Cleveland	5000	0	0	0		Amount Shipped From	5000	6000	2500	6500
15	Bedford	500	0	3500	2000						
16	York	2500	0	0	0		Demand Constraints	Boston	Chicago	St. Louis	Lexington
17	Memphis	0	6500	0	0		Amount Shipped To	8000	6500	3500	2000
18											
19							Total cost	$65,750.00			

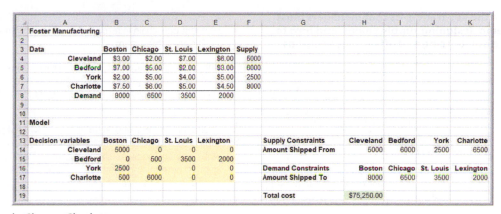

a. Choose Memphis

	A	B	C	D	E	F	G	H	I	J	K
1	Foster Manufacturing										
2											
3	Data	Boston	Chicago	St. Louis	Lexington	Supply					
4	Cleveland	$3.00	$2.00	$7.00	$6.00	5000					
5	Bedford	$7.00	$5.00	$2.00	$3.00	6000					
6	York	$2.00	$5.00	$4.00	$5.00	2500					
7	Charlotte	$7.50	$6.00	$5.00	$4.50	8000					
8	Demand	8000	6500	3500	2000						
9											
10											
11	Model										
12											
13	Decision variables	Boston	Chicago	St. Louis	Lexington		Supply Constraints	Cleveland	Bedford	York	Charlotte
14	Cleveland	5000	0	0	0		Amount Shipped From	5000	6000	2500	6500
15	Bedford	0	500	3500	2000						
16	York	2500	0	0	0		Demand Constraints	Boston	Chicago	St. Louis	Lexington
17	Charlotte	500	6000	0	0		Amount Shipped To	8000	6500	3500	2000
18											
19							Total cost	$75,250.00			

b. Choose Charlotte

CHAPTER 6 LEARNING OBJECTIVE SUMMARIES

6.1 **Explain the concept of a global supply chain, describe the key design decisions and explain the impact of blockchain technology on global supply chains.** Global supply chains are complex supply chains operated by multinational enterprises. Their value chains can source, market, create, and deliver goods and services to customers worldwide. Key design decisions include:

- Strategy (what competitive priorities should we emphasize?)
- Control (do we centralize or decentralize control of the supply chain?)
- Location (where do we locate facilities?)
- Sustainability (how do we champion economic, environmental, and social sustainability goals and practices in global supply chains?)
- Technology (do we share our technology and intellectual property with suppliers and partners in other countries?)
- Digital content (how do we build and integrate digital content and e-commerce capabilities into goods and services and our supply chains?)
- Sourcing (from whom do we purchase raw materials, m pars, and subassemblies?)
- Logistics and transportation (what transportation modes should we use to maximize service and minimize costs?)
- Outsourcing (what supply chain activities do we keep in-house or outsource to suppliers?)
- Managing risk (how do we address supply chain risks and disruptions?)
- Measuring performance (what performance metrics to use in managing our supply chains?)

Blockchain technology impacts most of these supply chain decisions. The goals of a blockchain-enriched supply chain are to be intelligent, collaborative, transparent, and secure while maximizing customer service at minimum costs.

6.2 **Describe the key trade-offs that managers must consider in designing supply chains, and how to evaluate outsourcing and offshoring decisions.**

- Efficient supply chains are designed for efficiency and low cost by minimizing inventory and maximizing efficiencies in process flow. P&G and Walmart are two companies that run efficient supply chains.
- Responsive supply chains are able to react quickly to changing market demand and requirements, because of their flexibility and responsive service. Apple and Nordstrom are two companies that have responsive supply chains.
- Push systems produce goods in advance of customer demand using a forecast of sales and moves them through the supply chain to points of sale. Best Buy and Macy's are push systems.
- Pull systems produce only what is needed at upstream stages in the supply chain in response to customer demand downstream. Dell uses this system.

Outsourcing: The company that outsources does not have ownership of the outsourced process and function. The simplest outsourcing decision is "make versus buy," based on economics, using break-even analysis.

Offshoring: The building, acquiring, or moving of process capabilities from a domestic location to another country location while maintaining ownership and control. Decisions to offshore involved determining what value creation, support, and/or general management processes should move.

6.3 **Describe how Inditex/Zara designs and operates its supply chain.** See Section 6-3 and in particular, Exhibit 6.6, which illustrates the key elements of Inditex's global supply chain.

6.4 **Explain the types of decisions required and criteria used to locate facilities in supply chains, and be able to apply the center of gravity method.** Exhibit 6.7 summarizes the location factors for site selection. Four key decisions are choosing the global location, regional location, community location, and local site location. The center-of-gravity method applies Equations 6.4 and 6.5 to determine a central location for a single facility based on demand as well as distance between existing locations.

6.5 **Explain how the transportation model can be used to help optimize costs in supply chains.** The transportation model is a linear optimization model that arises in planning the distribution of goods and services from several supply points to several demand locations. With a variety of shipping routes and differing transportation costs for routes, the objective is to determine how many units should be shipped from each origin to each destination so that all destination demands are satisfied with minimum total transportation costs.

KEY TERMS

- **Backward integration**
- **Blockchain**
- **Center-of-gravity method**
- **Contract manufacturer**
- **Efficient supply chains**

- **Forward integration**
- **Multinational enterprise**
- **Multisite management**
- **Offshoring**
- **Operational structure**
- **Outsourcing**
- **Postponement**
- **Pull system**
- **Push system**
- **Push–pull boundary**
- **Reshoring**
- **Responsive supply chains**
- **Supply chain optimization**
- **Third-party logistics (3PL) providers**
- **Transportation model**
- **Vertical integration**

REVIEW QUESTIONS

6.1 1. Explain the concept of a global supply chain and describe the key design decisions.

6.1 2. Define operational structure and provide an example of centralized control and decentralized control.

6.2 3. Define efficient and responsive supply chains and explain how they differ.

6.2 4. Define push and pull supply chains and explain how they differ.

6.2 5. Describe the ideas of vertical, forward, and backward integration.

6.2 6. What is a contract manufacturer. Provide some examples of contract manufacturers used by Apple.

6.2 7. What is a third-party logistics (3PL) provider? How does Amazon use 3PL providers?

6.2 8. How can break-even analysis be used to help managers make outsourcing decisions?

6.3 9. Define outsourcing, offshoring, and reshoring and explain how they differ.

6.4 10. Describe how Inditex/Zara designs and operates its supply chain.

6.4 11. Define multisite management and provide one example of a company that must handle this challenge.

6.4 12. Explain the types of decisions required and criteria used to locate facilities in supply chains.

6.4 13. Explain how the center of gravity method works.

6.4 14. Identify and explain the four EPIC dimensions to help location facilities around the world.

6.5 15. Explain supply chain optimization and how the transportation model can be used to help optimize costs in supply chains.

DISCUSSION QUESTIONS AND EXPERIENTIAL ACTIVITIES

6.1 16. One study that focused on the impact of China trade on the U.S. textile industry noted that 19 U.S. textile factories were closed and 26,000 jobs lost in the early 2000s. If these factories had not closed, it would have cost U.S. consumers $6 billion more in higher textile prices. Assuming these facts are true, offer an argument for or against off-shoring U.S. jobs.

6.1 17. How does globalization impact the supply chain design process?

6.1 18. If a small U.S. business with sales of $300 million wanted to expand into global markets, develop a check sheet with a list of twenty questions (and decisions) they might have to answer (make) regarding their supply chain(s). Be ready to present to the class.

6.1 19. Explain why it is important for operations managers to understand the local culture and practices of the countries in which a firm does business. What are some of the potential consequences if they don't?

6.1 20. Research a U.S. company that recently moved a corporate headquarters or factory or research and development center from the United States to another country. What were the advantages and disadvantages for the company in their offshoring decision? Develop a government-based incentive system to keep this offshoring from happening. Be ready to present to the class.

6.2 21. Research the topic of "reshoring" in the United States and evaluate its impact. Develop an incentive system for U.S. firms to bring work back to the United States. Be ready to present to the class.

6.4 22. Define the principal criteria that might be used for locating each of the following facilities:

- hospital
- chemical factory
- fire station
- coffee shop
- regional automobile parts

6.4 23. Select a firm such as Taco Bell (www.tacobell.com), Bank of America (www.bankofamerica.com), Walmart (www.walmart.com), or another service-providing organization of interest to you and write a short analysis and list of location and multisite management decisions that the firm faces.

6.5 24. How can satellite-based global positioning systems improve the performance of supply chains in the following industries: (a) trucking, (b) farming and food distribution, (c) manufacturing, and (d) ambulance service?

6.5 25. Find an article describing the application of optimization models in supply chain design and summarize how the models are used and the benefits that resulted from them. A good journal to search is *Interfaces*, which should be available in your school library, or *Analytics Magazine* (analytics-magazine.org), which is available to the public.

COMPUTATIONAL PROBLEMS AND EXERCISES

These exercises require you to apply the formulas and methods described in the chapter. The problems should be solved manually.

6.2 26. A company has two alternatives for meeting a customer requirement for 880,000 units of a part used in office printers. If done in-house, fixed cost would be $1,400,000 with variable cost at $1.90 per unit. Alternative two is to outsource for a total cost of $3.50 per unit. Determine the break-even point and determine if they should make the item in-house or outsource it.

6.2 27. A hospital is evaluating whether to outsource or perform in-house a large set of blood and urine laboratory tests. The fixed cost of the laboratory located in the hospital is $800,000 and the weighted average variable cost per test if performed in-house is $28.75. A third-party lab located one city block from the hospital will perform the same tests and distribute the results electronically to the hospital at a price of $32.00. If the annual volume last year was 250,000 tests, should the hospital outsource or make-in-house?

6.2 28. Industrial Products, Inc. has two alternatives for manufacturing 12,000 industrial 100-horse power electric motors per year. If done in-house, fixed cost would be $2,100,000 with variable cost at $6,800 per unit. Alternative two is to outsource for a total cost of $7,300 per unit.

a. What is the break-even quantity?

b. Should the firm make-in-house or outsource?

6.4 29. Using the information about customer vehicle traffic to and from a proposed new sports stadium (not built yet), find the best location for the stadium that minimizes total distance travelled using the center-of-gravity method.

Zip Code Location Options	Coordinates of Location x	y	Vehicles per Stadium Event
1	4	6	2,500
2	12	11	1,200
3	10	10	4,200
4	7	9	2,900

Use the center-of-gravity method to determine an ideal location for a service center.

 30. Microserve provides computer repair service on a contract basis to customers in five sections of the city. The five sections, the number of service contracts in each section, and the x and y coordinates of each section are as follows:

Section	No. of Contracts	Coordinates x	y
Parkview	90	8.0	10.5
Mt. Airy	220	6.7	5.9
Valley	50	12.0	5.2
Norwood	300	15.0	6.3
Southgate	170	11.7	8.3

Use the center-of-gravity method to determine an ideal location for a service center.

 31. Using the following information about material volume shipped from a factory to four retail outlets, find the best location for the factory using the center of gravity method.

Retail Outlet	Location Coordinates x, y	Material Movement
1	18, 6	1,000
2	12, 15	2,100
3	7, 10	1,900
4	7, 20	3,200

Use the center-of-gravity method to determine an ideal location for a service center.

 32. A supply chain manager faced with choosing among four possible locations has assessed each location according to the following criteria, where the weights reflect the importance of the criteria. How can he use this information to choose a location? Can you develop a quantitative approach to do this?

Criteria	Weight	Location 1	2	3	4
Raw material availability	0.15	G	P	OK	VG
Infrastructure	0.1	OK	OK	OK	OK
Transportation costs	0.35	VG	OK	P	OK
Labor relations	0.2	G	VG	P	OK
Quality of life	0.2	G	VG	P	OK

VG = Very good 5 pts; G = Good 4 pts; OK = Acceptable 3 pts ; P = Poor 1 pt.

 33. Supreme Auto Parts produces components for motorcycle engines. It has plants in Amarillo, Texas, and Charlotte, North Carolina, and supply factories in Detroit and Atlanta. Use the following production and cost data for a major component to formulate a transportation model to determine the best distribution plan. Do not attempt to solve.

Plant	Freight Costs Detroit	Atlanta	Capacity	Unit Cost
Amarillo	\$12	\$8	1,200	\$125
Charlotte	\$9	\$3	3,000	\$140
Demand	2,000	900		

EXCEL-BASED PROBLEMS

For these problems, you may use Excel Solver or the spreadsheet templates in MindTap to assist in your analysis.

 34. A university currently has a recycling program for paper waste. The fixed cost of running this program is \$15,000 per year. The variable cost for picking up and disposing of each ton of recyclable paper is \$40. If the work is outsourced to a recycling company, the cost would be \$65 per ton.

a. If the forecasted demand is 750 tons, what should the university do? Use the *Break-Even* Excel template to find your answer.

b. Find the break-even point using the Excel Goal Seek tool.

 35. Marine International manufactures an aquarium pump and is trying to decide whether to produce the filter system in-house or sign an outsourcing contract with Bayfront Manufacturing to make the filter system. Marine's expertise is producing the pumps themselves but they are considering producing the filter systems also. To establish a filter system production area at Marine International, the fixed costs is \$300,000 per year and they estimate their variable cost of production in-house at \$12.25 per filter system. If Marine outsources the production of the filter system to Bayfront, Bayfront will charge Marine \$30 per filter system. Use the *Break-Even* Excel template to determine if Marine International should outsource the production of the filter system to Bayfront if the demand is 25,000 pumps a year?

6.2 36. A firm is evaluating the alternative of manufacturing a part that is currently being outsourced from a supplier. The relevant information is provided below:

For in-house manufacturing:

Annual fixed cost = $80,000
Variable cost per part = $140

For purchasing from supplier:

Purchase price per part = $160

a. For this information, use the *Break-Even* Excel template to find the best decision if the demand is 5,000.

b. Determine the break-even quantity for which the firm would be indifferent between manufacturing the part in-house or outsourcing it. Use the Excel Goal Seek tool.

6.2 37. Refer to the information provided in Question 36 to answer the following questions using the *Break-Even* Excel template.

a. If demand is forecast to be 3,500 parts, should the firm make the part in-house or purchase it from a supplier?

b. The marketing department forecasts that the upcoming year's demand will be 3,500 parts. A new supplier offers to make the parts for $156 each. Should the company accept the offer?

c. What is the maximum price per part the manufacturer should be willing to pay to the supplier if the forecast is 3,500 parts?

6.4 38. Given the location information and volume of material movements from a supply point (warehouse) to several retail stores for Bourbon Hardware, find the optimal location for the supply point using the *Center of Gravity* Excel template.

Retail Outlet	Location Coordinates x	y	Material Movements
1	20	5	1,200
2	18	15	2,500
3	3	16	1,600
4	3	4	1,100
5	10	20	2,000

6.4 39. The Davis national drugstore chain prefers to operate one outlet in a town that has four major market segments. The number of potential customers in each segment along with the coordinates are as follows:

Market Segment	Location Coordinates x	y	Number of Customers
1	2	18	2,000
2	15	17	600
3	2	2	1,500
4	14	2	3,400

Find the best location using the *Center of Gravity* Excel template.

6.4 40. For the Davis drugstore chain in Problem 39, suppose that after five years, half the customers from segment 1 are expected to move to segment 2. Where should the drugstore shift, assuming the same criteria are adopted? Use the *Center of Gravity* Excel template to answer this question.

6.4 41. Cunningham Products is evaluating five possible locations to build a distribution center. Data estimated from the accounting department are provided below. The annual production is estimated to be 30,000 units.

Data for Problem 41	Location 1	Location 2	Location 3	Location 4	Location 5
Fixed costs	$75,000.00	$110,000.00	$95,000.00	$125,000.00	$110,000.00
Direct material cost/unit	$4.14	$4.65	$5.05	$4.50	$4.50
Director labor cost/unit	$12.45	$13.80	$11.80	$15.60	$13.75
Overhead/unit	$2.25	$2.60	$1.95	$2.75	$2.10
Transportation cost/unit	$0.50	$0.65	$0.30	$0.83	$0.67

a. Use the *Location Analysis* Excel template to determine the location that provides the least cost.

b. How would your answer change as the production volume increases?

6.5 **42.** Milford Lumber Company ships construction materials from three wood-processing plants to three retail stores. The shipping cost, monthly production capacities, and monthly demand for framing lumber are given below (these data are available in the Excel worksheet *Milford Lumber* on MindTap). Formulate a linear optimization model for this problem, implement your model on a spreadsheet, and use Excel Solver to find a solution that minimizes total distribution costs. See Supplement E for a discussion of modeling and solving transportation problems.

Plant	Store A	Store B	Store C	Capacity
1	$4.50	$3.10	$2.00	280
2	$5.10	$2.60	$3.80	460
3	$4.10	$2.90	$4.00	300
Demand	250	600	150	

6.5 **43.** Consider the following transportation problem data for Baker Industries (these data are available in the Excel worksheet *Baker Industries* on MindTap):

	Distribution Center			
Plant	Los Angeles	San Francisco	San Diego	Supply
San Jose	$4	$10	$6	100
Las Vegas	$8	$16	$6	300
Tucson	$14	$18	$10	300
Demand	200	300	200	

Use the techniques explained in Supplement E: The Transportation Problem to address the following:

a. Formulate the linear optimization model to minimize total cost.

b. Implement your model on a spreadsheet and use Excel Solver to find an optimal solution.

c. How would the optimal solution differ if we must ship 150 units on the Tucson to San Diego route? Explain how you can modify the model to incorporate this new information.

6.5 **44.** Arnoff Enterprises manufactures the central processing unit (CPU) for a line of personal computers. The CPUs are manufactured in Seattle, Columbus, and New York and shipped to warehouses in Pittsburgh, Mobile, Denver, Los Angeles, and Washington, DC for further distribution. The data below show the number of CPUs available at each plant and the number of CPUs required by each warehouse (these data are available in the Excel worksheet *Arnoff Enterprises* on MindTap). The shipping costs (dollars per unit) are also shown.

	Warehouse					
Plant	Pittsburgh	Mobile	Denver	Los Angeles	Washington	Supply
Seattle	$10	$20	$5	$9	$10	9,000
Columbus	$2	$10	$8	$30	$6	4,000
New York	$1	$20	$7	$10	$4	8,000
Demand	3000	5000	4000	6000	3000	

a. Formulate a linear optimization model for this problem, implement your model on a spreadsheet, and use Excel Solver to find a solution to determine the number of CPUs that should be shipped from each plant to each warehouse to minimize the total transportation cost.

b. The Pittsburgh warehouse has just increased its order by 1,000 units, and Arnoff has authorized the Columbus plant to increase its production by 1,000 units. Do you expect this development to lead to an increase or a decrease in the total transportation cost? Solve for the new optimal solution.

6.5 **45.** Forbelt Corporation has a one-year contract to supply motors for all refrigerators produced by the Ice Age Corporation. Ice Age manufactures the refrigerators at four locations around the country: Boston, Dallas, Los Angeles, and St. Paul. Plans call for these numbers (in thousands) of refrigerators to be produced at the four locations.

Boston	50
Dallas	70
Los Angeles	60
St. Paul	80

Forbelt has three plants that are capable of producing the motors. The plants and their production capacities (in thousands) follow.

Denver	100
Atlanta	100
Chicago	150

Because of varying production and transportation costs, the profit Forbelt earns on each lot of 1,000 units depends on which plant produced it and to which destination it was shipped. The accounting department estimates of the profit per unit (shipments are made in lots of 1,000 units) are as follows:

	Shipped to			
Produced at	**Boston**	**Dallas**	**Los Angeles**	**St. Paul**
Denver	$7	$11	$8	$13
Atlanta	$20	$17	$12	$10
Chicago	$8	$18	$13	$16

Given profit maximization as a criterion, Forbelt would like to determine how many motors should be produced at each plant and how many should be shipped from each plant to each destination to minimize total transportation costs. Formulate a linear optimization model, implement it on a spreadsheet, and use Excel Solver to find an optimal solution.

Bookmaster: Value Chain Design

"I'm going to Bookmaster to buy a book," Luke Chris yelled as he walked out of his apartment. "I'll be back in about ninety minutes," he continued as his roommate lay on the sofa after a hard night of partying. As he drove to the bookstore he caught a red stoplight at the first highway intersection. He always hated this intersection because the light took four minutes to complete a cycle. After seven traffic lights he arrived at the book store parking lot only to find a city bus blocking the driveway entrance, so he parked on the street and walked about one thousand feet to the store entrance. At the store door, he encountered a lady in a wheel chair exiting the store so he patiently held the doors opens for her and her friend. After his 30-minute ordeal to get to the store he went up to the information booth, waited until the current customer completed their query, and then asked Millie, the customer relations associate (CRA), if they had the book. After a quick search on the store's computer she said, "Yes, we have copies. The book is $89.95."

"I'll take you to the book," Millie said with a smile. Upon wandering the aisles of books, she came to the shelf where the book should be residing. But after a careful search, the book was missing. The store computer said they had two copies but they were not on the shelf as expected. After an extended search only one Bookmaster store across town had this book.

"Do you want to drive over there and get it," Millie asked again with a smile. "Or would you like me to order it for you? It only takes a couple of days to get the book over to this store." "No, I don't want to drive over to that store—it's 15 miles away," Luke said with a sigh.

Kzenon/Shutterstock.com

As Luke began to walk out of the store Millie asked, "Why don't I check to see if an e-book exists?" After examining the computer Millie said, "Yes, this book is in digital form. It costs $9.95 as an e-book." "Thanks, Millie, But I'll go back home and see if I can download it to my computer. I don't have an e-reader yet—they're too expensive—I'm a starving pre-med student. I could read it on my cell phone but the screen is small," Luke said as he began the difficult journey driving back to his apartment. "Yes, many students read textbooks on their cell phone but it destroys their eyesight," Millie proclaimed. "True, so I'll have to read it on my personal computer," Luke said with a smile. (Pause)

"Uh, Uh, Millie, do you go to school here?" Luke asked. "Yeah, I'm a sophomore in the business school," she replied. "Any chance we could meet for lunch sometime?" Luke asked with a lump in his throat. "Sure, here's my cell number," as she handed Luke a piece of crumbled up paper with her number on it. Luke walked out of the store thinking he would never have met Millie if he downloaded the book in his apartment.

Case Questions for Discussion:

1. Draw the "bricks and mortar" process stages of the value chain by which hard copy books are created, produced, distributed, and sold in retail stores. How does each player in the value chain make money? (Hint: You can use the exhibits in previous chapters, such as Exhibit 1.4, to help you identify major stages in the value chain. The value chain begins with suppliers.)
2. Draw the process stages for creating and downloading an e-book today. How does each player in this new electronic/digital value chain make money?
3. Compare and contrast value chain design and structure in the previous two questions from customer and management viewpoints. What are the advantages and disadvantage to each value chain design?
4. What is the role of operations in each of these value chain designs and structures?

Boston Red Sox Spring Training Decision

"Whew, I'm glad the town hall meeting is over. The audience was hostile!" Tom Bourbon commented as he was escorted by a police officer to his car in the high school parking lot. The officer replied. "There were over 1,000 people in the gymnasium, sir, and they were in an uproar. Let's get you out of here safely."

Tom and the other City Council members had just finished a town hall meeting open to the public to discuss four alternative locations for a new $80 million baseball stadium in Lee County, Florida. The City Council originally evaluated 16 sites and had arrived at the final four locations. The new 10,000-seat ballpark also includes practice fields, batting cages, and weight rooms. The stadium facility design and layout is to mimic the regular season Fenway Park in Boston, Massachusetts. However, the new park planned on "going green" by reducing energy consumption, allocating a carpooling parking lot close to the stadium to reduce patron traffic congestion and transportation costs and fuel use, and changing some of its work practices.

The five board members of City Council have to make a location decision in three weeks if they are to meet the contractual requirements of previous agreements. Once the stadium for spring training was complete, the Red Sox would sign a 30-year lease. Two economic impact studies indicated the stadium would generate $25 to $40 million annually to the local economy and support thousands of jobs in airports, hotels, restaurants, and retail stores.

The four possible locations were described as follows:

- Site A includes 241 acres and is big enough to build a sports village; it is located next to a shopping mall (denoted as 1 in Exhibit 6.12) and within 4 miles of Florida Gulf Coast University and an 8,000-seat indoor arena for events such as hockey and basketball games in a second shopping mall (denoted as 2 in Exhibit 6.12). The land cost to the City Council is $18 million.
- Site B includes 209 acres and is located between the two shopping malls 1 and 2. The site is about 2 miles from Florida Gulf Coast University. The land cost to the City Council is $22 million.
- Site C includes 2,000 acres of wetlands and habitat for animals. The area is within 3 miles of shopping mall 2 and Florida Gulf Coast University. The developer planned to donate 100 acres to the city, so the stadium land cost is free. The developer also offered to place 20 acres in a nature preserve for every acre that is developed for commercial purposes.
- Site D includes 106 acres located close to the airport and about 8 miles from the shopping mall 2 and Florida Gulf Coast University. The airport also includes a research park that hopes to attract high-tech industries and jobs. The land to the City Council is $22 million.

Exhibit 6.12 provides the coordinates for the population centers and the four possible locations. The populations for the five population centers are as follows: 1 (290,000), 2 (95,000),

3 (145,000), 4 (80,000), and 5 (120,000). Exhibit 6.13 summarizes the cost and judgments of the five City Council members for each site. It was thought that locating the Red Sox stadium close to the existing retail malls, restaurants, hotels, Florida Gulf Coast University, and the 8,000-seat indoor arena would create a retail and leisure service cluster where all could benefit. In the 10-month off-season for the Red Sox stadium, for example, local, regional, and national baseball clinics and tournaments could be played using this cluster of assets. Another viewpoint argued that locating the stadium next to the airport would encourage commercial development in this area, including the airport's research park.

Matt Trommer/Shutterstock.com

EXHIBIT 6.12 Location Grid for Boston Red Sox Spring Training Stadium Finalists

12 miles

I-75

Population Center 1

Population Center 2

Site D

Airport

Population Center 3

Site A

North

Shopping Mall 1

Site B

FGCU

Shopping Mall 2

Population Center 5

Population Center 4

Site C

0 1 2 3 4 5 6 7 8 9 10 11 12 miles

EXHIBIT 6.13 Site Cost Estimates and Rankings for Boston Red Sox Spring Training Stadium Finalists

Cost/Criteria	Site A	Site B	Site C	Site D
Stadium land cost	$18 million	$22 million	$0 million	$22 million
Additional utility cost	$1 million	$0.5 million	$3 million	$0.5 million
New road cost	$2 million	$0.5 million	$15 million	$2 million
Gain environmental group(s) endorsement	Almost	No	No	Yes
Traffic access and congestion	Good	Poor	Poor	Moderate
Utility, road, environment, and construction permits ready to go (shortest permit time)	Ready	Mostly Ready	Not Ready	Ready
Long-term economic growth and development around site (1 lowest to 5 highest/best)	4	3	4	5
Chance to preserve a huge area of the county	Moderate	Low	High	Low

Case Questions for Discussion:

You just finished your college's spring semester and have been working for the City Council as a summer intern. Your major is Information Systems & Operations Management (ISOM), and you want to earn a good recommendation from your summer intern boss. Your boss asks you to build an electronic spreadsheet model that scores, weights, and evaluates each quantitative and qualitative criterion and arrives at a summary score for each stadium site. To organize your analysis, you decide to answer the following questions:

1. Using the center-of-gravity model and Exhibit 6.12, compute the center of gravity for the population of the county. Show all computations, explain, and justify. Based solely on this criterion, where is the best stadium location?
2. Using a weighted scoring model of your own design, what are the summary scores for each stadium site for the qualitative criteria in Exhibit 6.13? (You must decide how to scale and weight each criterion and whether to include or not include cost estimates.) Show all calculations and explain your approach. You might wish to use Excel to perform these calculations. The data in Exhibit 6.12 are available in the Excel worksheet *Red Sox Case Data* on MindTap.
3. How will you combine these results (your center-of-gravity results, cost, and qualitative criteria analyses)? How might you compute a summary score for each site using all three criteria? Explain and justify.
4. Research and explain at least three ways a sports stadium can "go green," including at least one work practice for stadium employees. Do jobs and processes have to change too? Explain the role of OM.
5. What is your final stadium recommendation? Explain and justify.

Integrative Case: Hudson Jewelers

The Hudson Jewelers case study available in MindTap integrates material found in each chapter of this book.

Case Questions for Discussion:

1. Explain whether the global diamond supply chain a push system or a pull system, and whether the global diamond supply chain is an efficient or responsive system for make-to-order and make-to-stock jewelry. Provide some examples to justify your reasoning.
2. Research the extent of vertical integration in the global (seven-stage) diamond supply chain? Provide examples of forward and backward integration and the extent to which this is practiced in today's value chain. In this industry, what is the impact of vertical integration?

7 Process Selection, Design, and Improvement

LEARNING OBJECTIVES

After studying this chapter, you should be able to:

7-1 Describe the four types of processes used to produce goods and services.

7-2 Explain the logic and use of the product-process matrix.

7-3 Explain the logic and use of the service-positioning matrix.

7-4 Describe how to apply process and value stream mapping for process design.

7-5 Explain the concept of mistake proofing in process and product design for both goods and services.

7-6 Explain how to improve process designs using process and value stream maps.

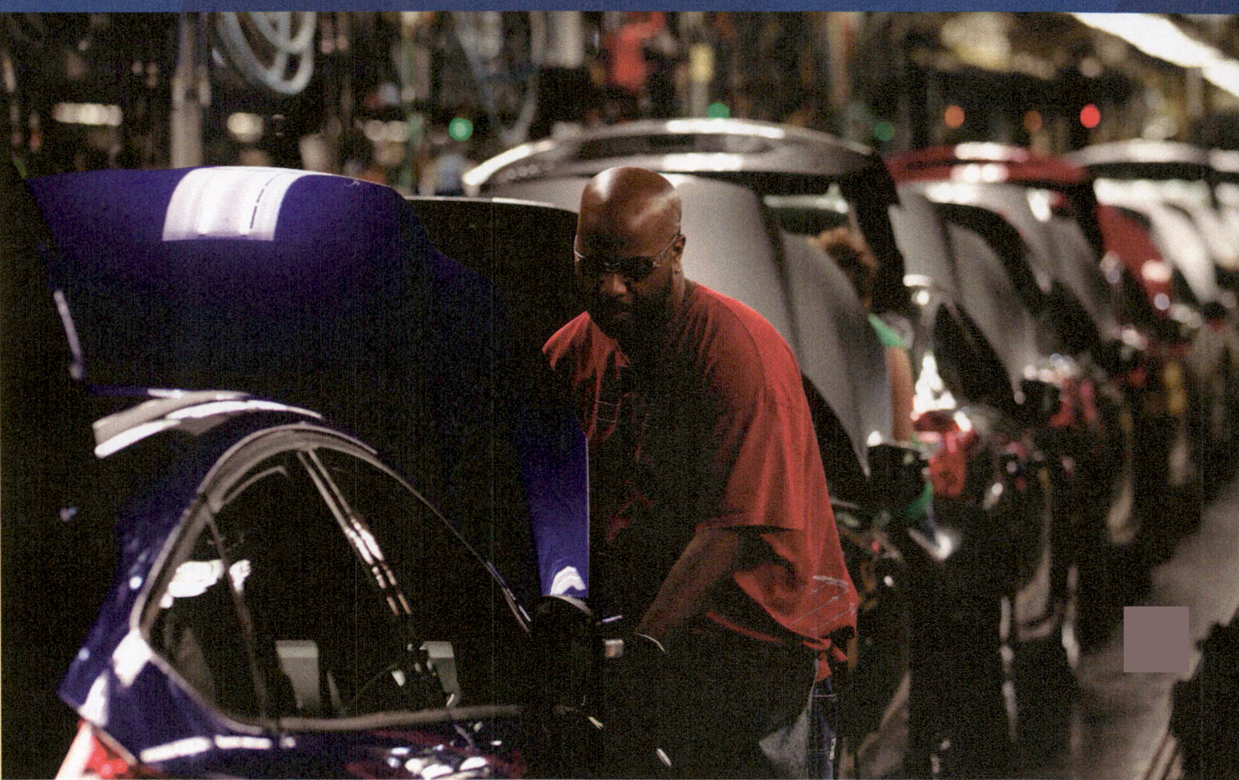

This Ford plant in Wayne, Michigan, is the first to make gas, electric, hybrid, and plug-in hybrid vehicles on the same production line.

Jeff Kowalsky/Bloomberg/Getty Images

Japanese automakers such as Toyota and Honda have used flexible manufacturing for decades. Some production lines can build six different models. Until recently, American factories were designed to produce only one. This is changing, as Ford retooled an inflexible sport utility vehicle (SUV) factory in Wayne, Michigan, to become an environmentally friendly workplace with flexible manufacturing capability. The factory will be the first facility in the world capable of building a wide range of vehicles—gas-powered, electric, hybrid, and plug-in hybrid—all on the same production line. This allows rapid change to different models as consumer wants and needs change.

To accomplish this, Ford's manufacturing team had to redesign and program most of the 696 robots to weld a variety of parts and get them to move in additional directions, recognize panels for different vehicles, grasp each at the right points, and know exactly how to weld them. Vehicles on the line ride on "skillets" that automatically raise and lower to the ideal height at each station for the task and model. The factory's integrated stamping facility allows the stamping and welding of all large sheet metal parts on-site. It also employs an efficient, synchronous material flow in which parts and other components move in kits to each operator, providing employees with the tools they need in the sequence they will need them.

The factory is not only flexible but environmentally friendly—it runs on a blend of renewable and conventional electricity. For example, it has 10 electric vehicle charging stations that recharge electric switcher trucks, which transport parts between adjacent facilities, and the factory recycles everything from packing materials to water bottles.[1]

WHAT DO YOU THINK?

Describe a situation that you have encountered in which a process was either well designed and enhanced your customer experience, or poorly designed and resulted in dissatisfaction.

Choosing appropriate processes and designing them to work effectively with each other is vital for an effective and efficient value chain and cannot be taken lightly. As the introductory example suggests, process design is an important operational decision that affects the cost of operations, customer service, and sustainability. Companies are just beginning to consider the environmental impact of their processes and those of their customers. See the box feature on Global Logistics and Sustainability and Solved Problem 7.1.

Process design is an important operational decision that affects the cost of operations, customer service, and sustainability.

7-1 Process Choice Decisions

Firms generally produce either in response to customer orders and demand or in anticipation of them. This leads to three major types of goods and services: custom, option-oriented, and standard.[2] **Custom,** *or* **make-to-order, goods and services** *are generally produced and delivered as one of a kind or in small quantities, and are designed to meet specific customers' specifications.* Examples include ships, Internet sites, weddings, taxi service, estate plans, buildings, and surgery. Because custom goods and services are produced on demand, the customer must wait for them, often for a long time because the good or service must be designed, created, and delivered.

Option, *or* **assemble-to-order, goods and services** *are configurations of standard parts, subassemblies, or services that can be selected by customers from a limited set.* Common examples are Dell computers, Subway sandwiches, machine tools, and travel agent services. Although the customer chooses how the goods and services are configured, any unique technical specifications or requirements cannot generally be accommodated.

In the future, process managers will not only need to quantify the trade-offs among cost, quality, time, and other priorities, but also the carbon footprint of their processes.

Standard, *or* **make-to-stock, goods and services** *are made according to a fixed design, and the customer has no options from which to choose.* Appliances, shoes, sporting goods, credit cards, online Web-based courses, and bus service are some examples. Standard goods are made in anticipation of customer demand and stocked in inventory, and therefore are usually available, although in some cases the proper color or size might be out of stock.

Process Choice and Sustainability

One example of a company that is focusing on sustainable processes is Alfa Laval, a Swedish company that provides goods and services to the energy, food, refrigeration and cooling, water, and pharmaceutical industries in over 100 countries. Carbon dioxide emissions from transporting Alfa Laval's products accounted for approximately 2 percent of its total emissions. Its Global Transport Department analyzed over 100,000 transactions to identify opportunities to reduce emissions by shifting from airfreight to surface (mainly ocean) transportation. The advantage of airfreight had been that the inventory levels could be minimized and a fast response to changing customer needs could be assured. However, a thorough cost-benefit analysis confirmed that increased inventory costs using surface shipping were more than outweighed by the carbon dioxide reduction and freight cost savings. The move from air to surface shipping meant redesigning and switching the ordering process for 32,000 order lines per year. Switching to sea freight also required an inventory buildup at distribution centers to ensure that delivery performance to end customers would not suffer, along with major changes to Alfa Laval's processes. The process changes resulted in a reduction of approximately 12 percent in inventory, carbon dioxide emissions, and similar freight shipping savings.[3]

s_oleg/Shutterstock.com

SOLVED PROBLEM 7.1: COMPUTING ENVIRONMENTAL SAVINGS

Clear Water Pool Service (CWPS) provides the maintenance for over 7,000 pools in southwest Florida. In 2010, CWPS purchased vehicle routing and scheduling software and a GPS truck locator system. Before the use of the "smart system," CWPS's vans and trucks drove 1.26 million miles to service these pools on monthly and weekly appointment schedules. After one year of using the "smart system," CWPS reduced total miles driven to 1.03 million miles by using better vehicle routes from site to site, and using fewer vehicles. CWPS's vehicles average 20 miles per gallon. Unleaded gasoline has 8.91 kilograms (19.643 lb) of carbon dioxide (CO_2) per gallon, and 1 metric ton equals 1,000 kilograms (kg), according to government sources.

a. Find the number of gallons of gasoline saved annually.
b. How many metric tons of CO_2 did not go into the Earth's atmosphere because of CWPS using smart vehicle scheduling and locator technology?

Solution:

a. By dividing number of miles saved by miles per gallon, we get the number of gallons of gasoline saved annually:

$$(1{,}260{,}000 - 1{,}030{,}000\ 3\ \text{miles/year})/(20\ \text{miles per gallon}) = 11{,}500\ 3\ \text{gallons saved/year.}$$

b. By multiplying the number of gallons saved/year by 8.91 and dividing by 1,000, we get metric tons of CO_2 released into the atmosphere:
(11,500 gallons saved/year)(8.91 kg of CO_2 per gallon)/ 1,000 kg CO_2 per metric ton = 102.5 metric tons of CO_2 not released into the atmosphere due to better vehicle routing and scheduling.

We note that manufacturing systems often use the terms *make-to-order, assemble-to-order,* and *make-to-stock* to describe the types of systems used to manufacture goods. The terminology is not as standardized in service industries, although the concepts are similar.

Four principal types of processes are used to produce goods and services:

1. Projects.
2. Job shop processes.
3. Flow shop processes.
4. Continuous flow processes.

Projects *are large-scale, customized initiatives that consist of many smaller tasks and activities that must be coordinated and completed to finish on time and within budget.* Some examples of projects are legal defense preparation, construction, and software development. Projects are often used for custom goods and services, and occasionally for standardized products such as "market homes" that are built from a standard design.

Job shop processes *are organized around particular types of general-purpose equipment that are flexible and capable of customizing work for individual customers.* Job shops produce a wide variety of goods and services, often in small quantities. Thus, they are often used for custom or option type products. In job shops, customer orders are generally processed in batches, and different orders may require a different sequence of processing steps and movement to different work areas.

Flow shop processes *are organized around a fixed sequence of activities and process steps, such as an assembly line, to produce a limited variety of similar goods or services.* An assembly line is a common example of a flow shop process. Many large-volume, option-oriented and standard goods and services are produced in flow shop settings. Some common examples are automobiles, appliances, insurance policies, checking account statements, and hospital laboratory work. Flow shops tend to use highly productive, specialized equipment and computer software.

Continuous flow processes *create highly standardized goods or services, usually around the clock in very high volumes.* Examples of continuous flow processes are automated car washes, paper and steel mills, paint factories, and many electronic, information-intensive services such as credit card authorizations and security systems. The sequence of work tasks is very rigid and the processes use highly specialized, automated equipment that is often controlled by computers with minimal human oversight.

> It is important to understand product life cycles because when goods and services change and mature, so must the processes and value chains that create and deliver them.

Exhibit 7.1 summarizes these different process types and their characteristics.

A **product life cycle** *is a characterization of product growth, maturity, and decline over time.* It is important to understand product life cycles because when goods and services change and mature, so must the processes and value chains that create and deliver them.

The traditional product life cycle (PLC) generally consists of four phases—*introduction, growth, maturity,* and *decline and turnaround.* A product's life cycle has important implications in terms of process design and choice. For example, new products with low sales volume might be produced in a job shop process; however, as sales grow and volumes increase, a flow shop process might be more efficient. As another example, a firm might introduce a standard product that is produced with a flow shop process, but as the market matures, the product might become more customized. In this case, a job shop process might be more advantageous.

Rethinking Airplane Manufacturing Processes

Airplane manufacturing is typically performed on a project basis where volumes are lower and airlines demand more customization. However, as demand is rising rapidly, Boeing is rethinking this paradigm. Boeing plans to use newer, more standardized manufacturing techniques for its new 777X jetliner, paving the way for significant savings as it gradually feeds the changes back into existing assembly lines. The approach will draw increasingly on lessons learned from outside the aerospace industry. Boeing hired an executive from Toyota who observed, "If we can develop a system where we have direct deliveries to our lines and in an orientation which our operators will use to simply secure instead of handling parts, we have tremendous opportunities." Improving the sequencing of parts reduces inventory, eases cash flow, and requires less space, thus lowering overhead. One Boeing executive noted: "We've gone to a single moving line, and even though it goes one inch per half-hour, it's a moving line and it is the same concept as Toyota. We (put everything that is needed in kits). We make it very visible. We deliver things right to the side, and before we had mechanics running all over the factory getting parts."[4]

Jordan Tan/Shutterstock.com

EXHIBIT 7.1 Characteristics of Different Process Types

Type of Process	Characteristics	Goods and Services Examples	Type of Product
PROJECT	One of a kind	Space shuttle, cruise ships, small business tax service, consulting	
	Large scale, complex	Dams, bridges, skyscrapers	
	Resources brought to the site	Skyscrapers, weddings, consulting	
	Wide variation in specifications or tasks	Custom jewelry, surgery, Web pages	
JOB SHOP	Significant setup and/or changeover time	Automobile engines, auto body repair, major legal cases	Custom or Make-to-Order
	Low to moderate volume	Machine tools, beauty salons	
	Batching (small to large jobs)	Orders from small customers, mortgages, tourist tour groups	
	Many process routes with some repetitive steps	Shoes, hospital care, commercial loans	
	Customized design to customer's specifications	Commercial and Web-based printing	
	Many different products	Heavy equipment, financial services	
	High workforce skills	Legal services, consulting	
FLOW SHOP	Little or no setup or changeover time	Insurance policies	Option or Assemble-to-Order
	Dedicated to a small range of goods or services that are highly similar	Cafeterias, airline frequent flyer programs	
	Similar sequence of process steps	Refrigerators, stock trades	
	Moderate to high volumes	Toys, furniture, lawnmowers	
CONTINUOUS FLOW	Very high volumes in a fixed processing sequence	Gasoline, paint, memory chips, check posting	Standardized or Make-to-Stock
	Not made from discrete parts	Grain, chemicals	
	High investment in equipment and facility	Steel, paper, power-generating facilities	
	Dedicated to a small range of goods or services	Automated car wash	
	Automated movement of goods or information between process steps	Credit card authorizations, electric utilities	
	24-hour/7-day continuous operation	Steel, electronic funds transfer, broadcasting	

What often happens in many firms is that product strategies change, but managers do not make the necessary changes in the process to reflect the new product characteristics.

Two approaches to help understand the relationships between product characteristics for goods and services and process choice decisions are the product-process matrix and service-positioning matrix, which we introduce in the following sections.

7-2 The Product-Process Matrix

The product-process matrix was first proposed by Hayes and Wheelwright and is shown in Exhibit 7.2.[5] *The* **product-process matrix** *is a model that describes the alignment of process choice with the characteristics of the manufactured good.* The most appropriate match between type of product and type of process occurs along the diagonal in the product-process matrix. As one moves down the diagonal, the emphasis on both product and process structure shifts from low volume and high flexibility to higher volumes and more standardization. If product and process characteristics are not well matched, the firm will be unable to achieve its competitive priorities effectively.

EXHIBIT 7.2 Product-Process Matrix

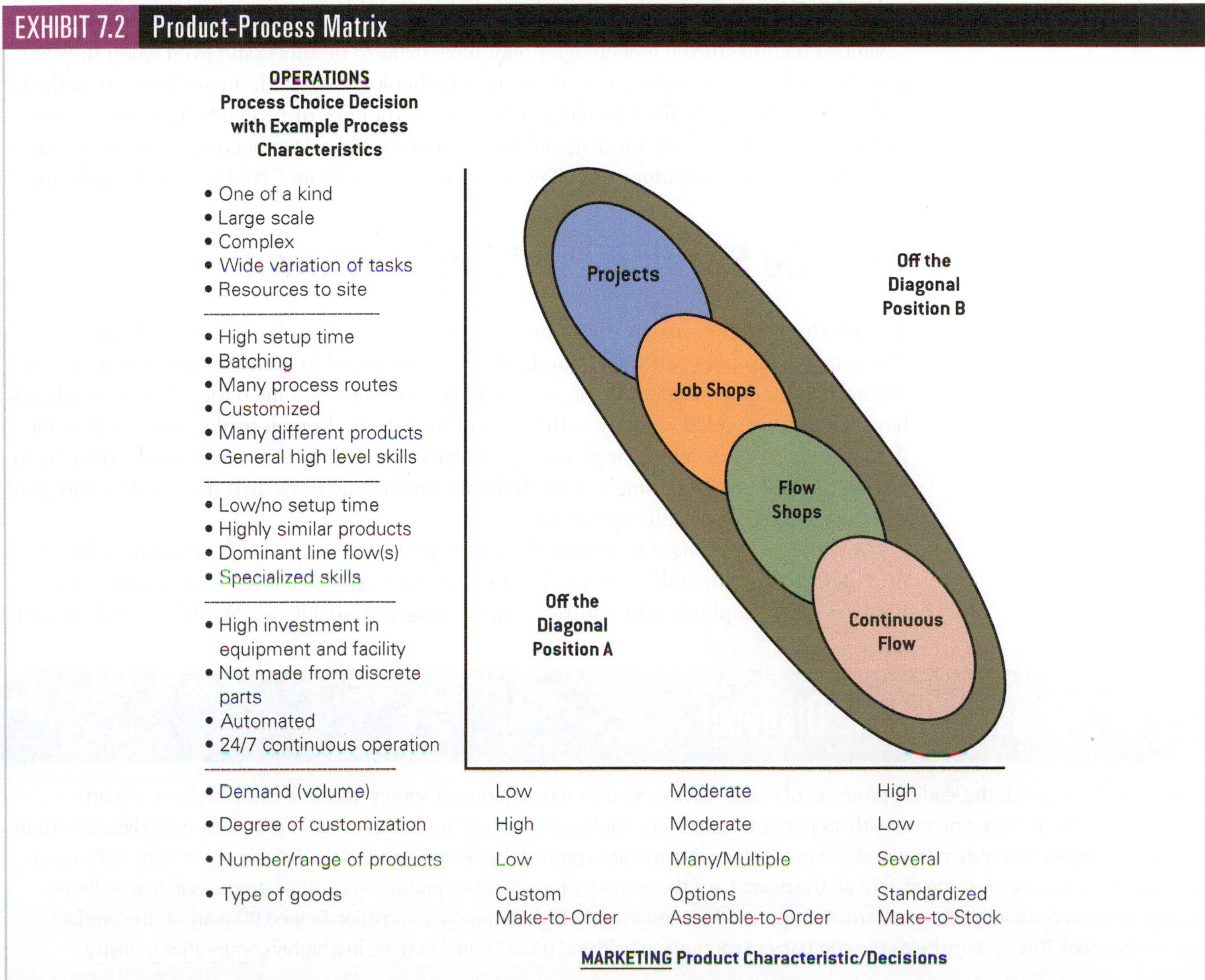

For example, consider a firm that manufactures only a few products with high volumes and low customization using a flow shop process structure. This process choice best matches the product characteristics. However, suppose that as time goes on and customer needs evolve, marketing and engineering functions develop more product options and add new products to the mix. This results in a larger number and variety of products to make, lower volumes, and increased customization. The firm finds itself "off the diagonal" and in the lower left-hand corner of the matrix (denoted by Position A in Exhibit 7.2). There is a mismatch between product characteristics and process choice. If the firm continues to use the flow shop process, it may find itself struggling to meet delivery promises and incur unnecessary costs because of low efficiencies.

On the other hand, by selectively and consciously positioning a business off the diagonal of the product-process matrix (often called a "positioning strategy"), a company can differentiate itself from its competitors. However, it must be careful not to get too far off the diagonal, or it must have a market where high prices absorb any operational inefficiencies. For example, Rolls-Royce produces a small line of automobiles, using a process similar to a job shop rather than the traditional flow shop of other automobile manufacturers. Each car requires about 900 hours of labor. For Rolls-Royce this strategy has worked, but its target market is willing to pay premium prices for premium quality and features.

The theory of the product-process matrix has been challenged by some who suggest that advanced manufacturing technologies may allow firms to be successful even when they position themselves off the diagonal. These new technologies provide manufacturers with the capability to be highly flexible and produce lower volumes of products in greater varieties at lower costs. Therefore, off-diagonal positioning strategies are becoming more and more viable for many organizations and allow for "mass-customization" strategies and capabilities.[6]

7-3 The Service-Positioning Matrix

The product-process matrix does not transfer well to service businesses and processes.[7,8] The relationship between volume and process is not found in many service businesses. For example, to meet increased volume, service businesses such as retail outlets, banks, and hotels have historically added capacity in the form of new stores, branch banks, and hotels to meet demand but they do not change their processes. These limitations are resolved by introducing the *service-positioning matrix.* To better understand it, we first discuss the concept of a pathway in a service-delivery system.

A **pathway** *is a unique route through a service system.* Pathways can be customer driven or provider driven, depending on the level of control that the service firm wants to ensure. Pathways can be physical in nature, as in walking around Disney World or a golf course;

Becton Dickinson: Off the Diagonal

Becton Dickinson (BD) is the leading producer of needle devices for the medical industry. Spring-loaded IV catheters have 12 parts, assembled in an automated process with 48 steps carried out at incredibly fast speeds. Instead of using one long assembly line, BD's Utah plant uses a production system that makes it relatively easy to modify a product by altering or adding subassembly stations. BD's manufacturing process choice is somewhat of off the diagonal of the product-process matrix, producing multiple products in high volumes in more-or-less a continuous flow pattern. A simple product design and a high degree of automation helped BD work off the product-process diagonal. This strategy helps the company to continue to hold and grow its market share in a highly competitive industry.

procedural, as in initiating a transaction via the telephone with a brokerage firm; or purely mental and virtual, as in doing an Internet search. **Customer-routed services** *are those that offer customers broad freedom to select the pathways that are best suited for their immediate needs and wants from many possible pathways through the service delivery system.* The customer decides what path to take through the service-delivery system with only minimal guidance from management. Searching the Internet to purchase an item or visiting a park are examples.

Provider-routed services *constrain customers to follow a very small number of possible and pre-defined pathways through the service system.* An automatic teller machine (ATM) is an example. A limited number of pathways exist—for example, getting cash, making a deposit, checking an account balance, and moving money from one account to another. Mailing and processing a package using the U.S. Postal Service, Federal Express, or UPS is another example of a provider-routed service.

Designs for customer-routed services require a solid understanding of the features that can delight customers, as well as methods to educate customers about the variety of pathways that may exist and how to select and navigate through them.

The service-positioning matrix (SPM), as shown in Exhibit 7.3, is roughly analogous to the product-process matrix for manufacturing. The SPM focuses on the service-encounter level

EXHIBIT 7.3 The Service-Positioning Matrix

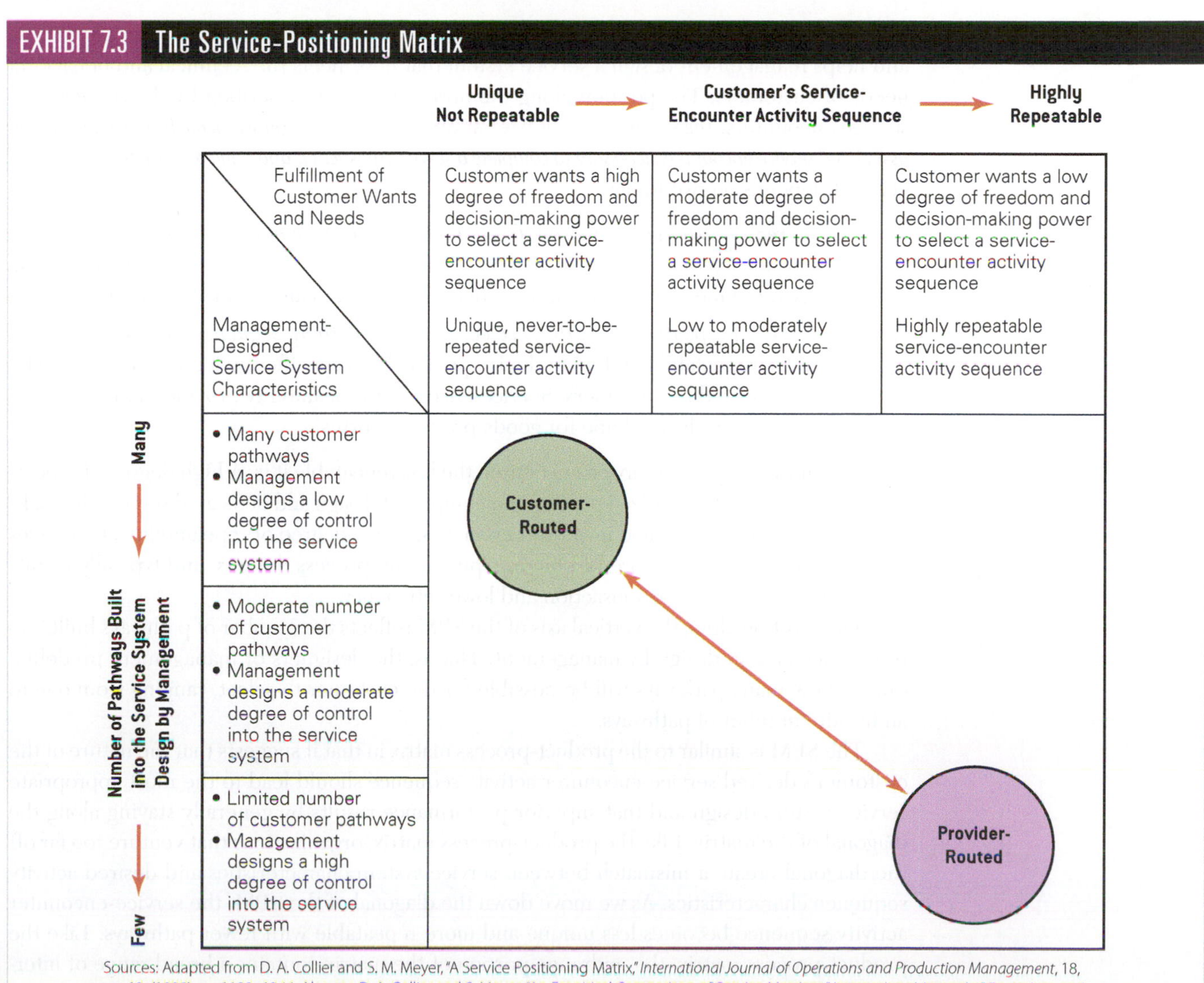

Unique
Not Repeatable
Customer's Service-Encounter Activity Sequence
Highly Repeatable
Fulfillment of Customer Wants and Needs
Management-Designed Service System Characteristics
Customer wants a high degree of freedom and decision-making power to select a service-encounter activity sequence
Unique, never-to-be-repeated service-encounter activity sequence
Customer wants a moderate degree of freedom and decision-making power to select a service-encounter activity sequence
Low to moderately repeatable service-encounter activity sequence
Customer wants a low degree of freedom and decision-making power to select a service-encounter activity sequence
Highly repeatable service-encounter activity sequence
Many
Number of Pathways Built into the Service System Design by Management
Few
• Many customer pathways
• Management designs a low degree of control into the service system
• Moderate number of customer pathways
• Management designs a moderate degree of control into the service system
• Limited number of customer pathways
• Management designs a high degree of control into the service system
Customer-Routed
Provider-Routed

Sources: Adapted from D. A. Collier and S. M. Meyer, "A Service Positioning Matrix," *International Journal of Operations and Production Management*, 18, no. 12, (1998) pp. 1123–1244. Also see D. A. Collier and S. Meyer, "An Empirical Comparison of Service Matrices," *International Journal of Operations and Production Management*, 20, no. 5–6 (2000), pp. 705–729.

Apple: New Design Requires New Processes

When Apple introduced a redesigned line of MacBooks that featured precision unibody enclosures milled from an extruded block of aluminum that improved rigidity and durability, and also resulted in a thinner design, it needed to develop an entirely new process. The process started with an extruded block of aluminum that was carved out using computer numerical control (CNC) machines, similar to processes used in the aerospace industry. The aluminum sheets were cut into blocks that underwent 13 separate milling operations. Apple used CNC to precision-cut keyboard holes from the face of the slab, mill out the "thumbscoop" that provides enough of a recession to open the display lid, machine out complex patterns from the inside, and perforate the speaker grill holes using lasers. Once the inside was precision cut, the edges were rounded and polished. The material machined from the aluminum block was collected and recycled.[9]

and helps management design a service system that best meets the technical and behavioral needs of customers. The position along the horizontal axis is described by the sequence of service encounters. *The* **service-encounter activity sequence** *consists of all the process steps and associated service encounters necessary to complete a service transaction and fulfill a customer's wants and needs.* It depends on two things:

1. *The degree of customer discretion, freedom, and decision-making power in selecting the service-encounter activity sequence.* Customers may want the opportunity to design their own unique service-encounter activity sequence, in any order they choose.
2. *The degree of repeatability of the service-encounter activity sequence.* Service-encounter repeatability refers to the frequency that a specific service-encounter activity sequence is used by customers. Service-encounter repeatability provides a measure analogous to product volume for goods-producing firms.

The more unique the service encounter, the less repeatable it is. A high degree of repeatability encourages standardized process and equipment design and dedicated service channels, and results in lower costs and improved efficiency. A low degree of repeatability encourages more customization and more flexible equipment and process designs, and typically results in higher relative cost per transaction and lower efficiency.

The position along the vertical axis of the SPM reflects the number of pathways built into the service system design by management. That is, the designers or management predefine exactly how many pathways will be possible for the customer to select, ranging from one to an infinite number of pathways.

The SPM is similar to the product-process matrix in that it suggests that the nature of the customer's desired service-encounter activity sequence should lead to the most appropriate service system design and that superior performance results by generally staying along the diagonal of the matrix. Like the product-process matrix, organizations that venture too far off the diagonal create a mismatch between service system characteristics and desired activity sequence characteristics. As we move down the diagonal of the SPM, the service-encounter activity sequence becomes less unique and more repeatable with fewer pathways. Like the product-process matrix, the midrange portion of the matrix contains a broad range of intermediate design choices.

7-4 Process Design

The goal of process design is to create the right combination of equipment, labor, software, work methods, and environment to produce and deliver goods and services that satisfy both internal and external customer requirements. Process design can have a significant impact on cost (and hence profitability), flexibility (the ability to produce the right types and amounts of products as customer demand or preferences change), and the quality of the output.

We can think about work at four hierarchical levels:

1. Task.
2. Activity.
3. Process.
4. Value chain.

A ***task*** *is a specific unit of work required to create an output.* Examples are inserting a circuit board into an iPad subassembly or typing the address on an invoice. *An* ***activity*** *is a group of tasks needed to create and deliver an intermediate or final output.* Examples include all the tasks necessary to build an iPad; for example, connecting the battery and assembling the cover pieces, or inputting all the information correctly on an invoice, such as the items ordered, prices, discounts, and so on. An example of a process would be manufacturing an iPad or fulfilling a customer order. The value chain for an iPad would include acquiring the materials and components, manufacturing and assembly, distribution, retail sales, and face-to-face and Web-based customer support.

Exhibit 7.4 shows an example for the production of antacid tablets. The value chain shows an aggregate view focused on the *goods-producing processes* (supporting services such as engineering, shipping, accounts payable, advertising, and retailing are not shown). The next level in the hierarchy of work is at the *production process* level where tablets are made. The third level focuses on the *mixing workstation* (or *work activities)* where the ingredients are unloaded into mixers. The mixer must be set up for each batch and cleaned for the next batch because many different flavors, such as peppermint, strawberry-banana, cherry, and mandarin orange, are produced using the same mixers. The fourth and final level in the work hierarchy is the *flavoring tasks,* which are defined as three tasks, each with specific procedures, standard times per task, and labor requirements. These three tasks could be broken down into even more detail if required.

7-4a Process and Value Stream Mapping

Understanding process design objectives focuses on answering the question: What is the process intended to accomplish? An example process objective might be "to create and deliver the output to the customer in 48 hours." Another key question to consider is: What are the critical customer and organizational requirements that must be achieved?

Designing a goods-producing or service-providing process requires six major activities:

1. Define the purpose and objectives of the process.
2. Create a detailed process or value stream map that describes how the process is currently performed (sometimes called a current state or baseline map). Of course, if you are designing an entirely new process, this step is skipped.
3. Evaluate alternative process designs. That is, create process or value stream maps (sometimes called future state maps) that describe how the process can best achieve customer and organizational objectives.
4. Identify and define appropriate performance measures for the process.

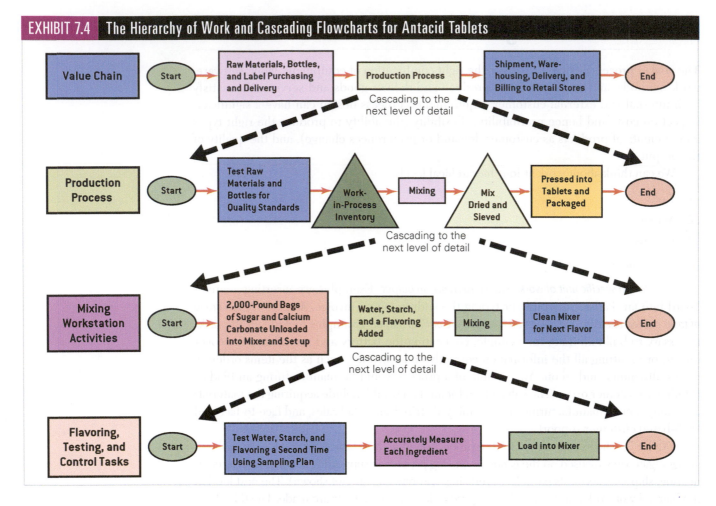

EXHIBIT 7.4 The Hierarchy of Work and Cascading Flowcharts for Antacid Tablets

Value Chain: Start → Raw Materials, Bottles, and Label Purchasing and Delivery → Production Process → Shipment, Warehousing, Delivery, and Billing to Retail Stores → End

Cascading to the next level of detail

Production Process: Start → Test Raw Materials and Bottles for Quality Standards → Work-in-Process Inventory → Mixing → Mix Dried and Sieved → Pressed into Tablets and Packaged → End

Cascading to the next level of detail

Mixing Workstation Activities: Start → 2,000-Pound Bags of Sugar and Calcium Carbonate Unloaded into Mixer and Set up → Water, Starch, and a Flavoring Added → Mixing → Clean Mixer for Next Flavor → End

Cascading to the next level of detail

Flavoring, Testing, and Control Tasks: Start → Test Water, Starch, and Flavoring a Second Time Using Sampling Plan → Accurately Measure Each Ingredient → Load into Mixer → End

5. Select the appropriate equipment and technology.
6. Develop an implementation plan to introduce the new or revised process design. This includes developing process performance criteria and standards to monitor and control the process.

Still Waiting for Your Luggage?

Airlines have been working to redefine their customer benefit packages. Since 2010, Alaska Airlines has offered a 20-minute baggage guarantee:

> If your bags are not at baggage claim within 20 minutes of your plane's arrival at the gate, we'll offer you a $25 Discount Code for use on a future Alaska Airlines flight, or 2,500 Alaska Airlines Mileage Plan™ Bonus Miles. In the rare instance that we don't meet our 20-minute guarantee, just get ahold of us within 2 hours of your flight's arrival for your discount code or Miles. You can reach out to us on Twitter @alaskaair, call our customer service center, or simply come and speak with one of our Customer Service Agents at the airport.

Could your preferred airline do this without improving their operations and baggage-handling processes?[10]

monticello/Shutterstock.com

A **process map (flowchart)** *describes the sequence of all process activities and tasks necessary to create and deliver a desired output or outcome.* It documents how work either is or should be accomplished, and how the transformation process creates value. We usually first develop a "baseline" map of how the current process operates in order to understand it and identify improvements for redesign.

Process maps delineate the boundaries of a process. *A* **process boundary** *is the beginning or end of a process.* The advantages of a clearly defined process boundary are that it makes it easier to obtain senior management support, assign process ownership to individuals or teams, identify key interfaces with internal or external customers, and identify where performance measurements should be taken. Thus, each of the levels in Exhibit 7.4 represents a process map defining different process boundaries. Exhibit 7.5 shows a flowchart for an automobile repair process using the typical symbols used for process maps. Process maps clearly delineate the process boundaries.

In service applications, flowcharts generally highlight the points of contact with the customer and are often called *service blueprints* or *service maps*. Such flowcharts often show the separation between the back office and the front office with a "line of customer visibility," such as the one shown in Exhibit 7.5.

Non-value-added activities such as transferring materials between two nonadjacent workstations, waiting for service, or requiring multiple approvals for a low-cost electronic transaction simply lengthen processing time, increase costs, and often increase customer frustration. Eliminating non-value-added activities in a process design is one of the most important responsibilities of operations managers. This is often accomplished using value stream mapping, a variant of more generic process mapping.

> Eliminating non-value-added activities in a process design is one of the most important responsibilities of operations managers.

The **value stream** *refers to all value-added activities involved in designing, producing, and delivering goods and services to customers.* A value stream map (VSM) shows the process flows in a manner similar to an ordinary process map; the difference lies in that value stream maps highlight value-added versus non-value-added activities and include costs associated with work activities for both value- and non-value-added activities.

To illustrate this, consider a process map for the order fulfillment process in a restaurant, as shown in Exhibit 7.6. From the times on the process map, the "service standard" order posting and fulfillment time is an average of 30 minutes per order (5 + 1 + 4 + 12 + 3 + 5). The restaurant's service guarantee requires that if this order posting and fulfillment time is more than 40 minutes, the customer's order is free of charge.

Evgeny Litvinov/Shutterstock.com

The chef's time is valued at $30 per hour, oven operation at $10 per hour, precooking order waiting time at $5 per hour, and postcooking order waiting time at $60 per hour. The $60 estimate reflects the cost of poor quality for a dinner waiting too long that might be delivered to the customer late (and cold).

Exhibit 7.7 illustrates a value stream map for the order posting and fulfillment process in Exhibit 7.6. Exhibit 7.7 is one of many formats for value stream mapping. Here, non-value-added time is 33.3 percent (10/30 minutes) of the total order posting and fulfillment time, and non-value-added cost

EXHIBIT 7.5 Automobile Repair Flowchart

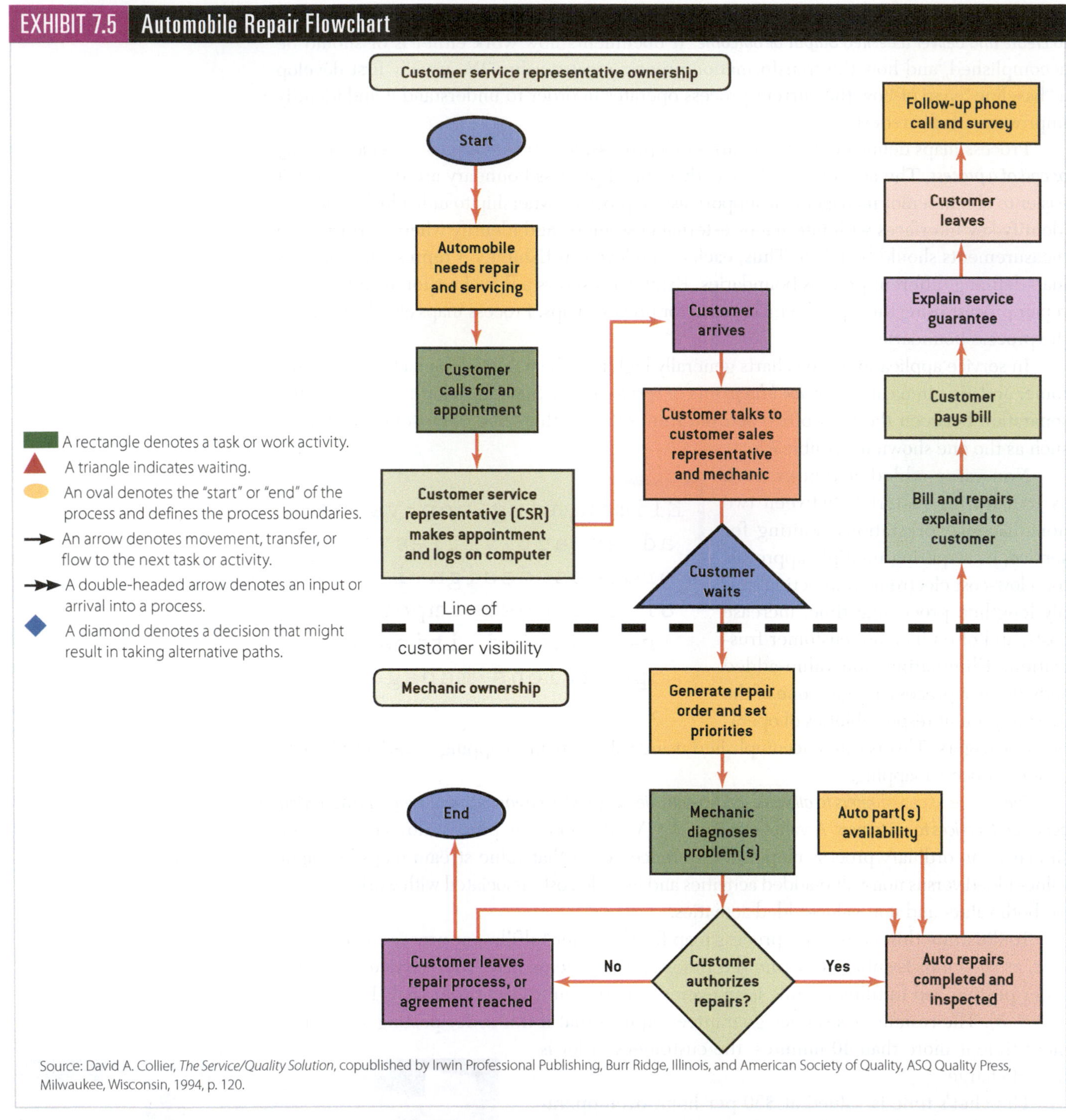

Source: David A. Collier, *The Service/Quality Solution*, copublished by Irwin Professional Publishing, Burr Ridge, Illinois, and American Society of Quality, ASQ Quality Press, Milwaukee, Wisconsin, 1994, p. 120.

is 31.7 percent ($5.417/$17.087) of total cost. Suppose that a process improvement incorporates wireless technology to transmit food orders to the kitchen and notify the waiter when the order is ready so that the waiting time can be reduced from 10 minutes to 4 minutes on the front and back ends of the process. Hence, the total processing time is reduced from 30 to 24 minutes (a 20 percent improvement). Costs are reduced by $3.25 with a three-minute wait time reduction on the front and back ends of the process. Therefore, cost per order goes from $17.087 to $13.837 (a 19 percent improvement). Increasing the speed of this part of the restaurant delivery process may also allow for a higher seat turnover during peak demand periods, thus helping to increase total revenue and contribute to profit and overhead.

EXHIBIT 7.6 Restaurant Order Posting and Fulfillment Process

Start
Order Arrival Rate
Waiter places customer meal order on order board—assume zero time
Order waits 5 minutes
Chef picks up order and checks "is it accurate?" 1 minute
Yes
No—recheck with waiter
Chef stages raw material— 4 minutes
Chef prepares side dishes 12 minutes
Ovens— 10 minutes
A
A
Chef assembles order— 3 minutes
Prepared order waits for pickup— 5 minutes
Waiter picks up customer order— assume zero time
END

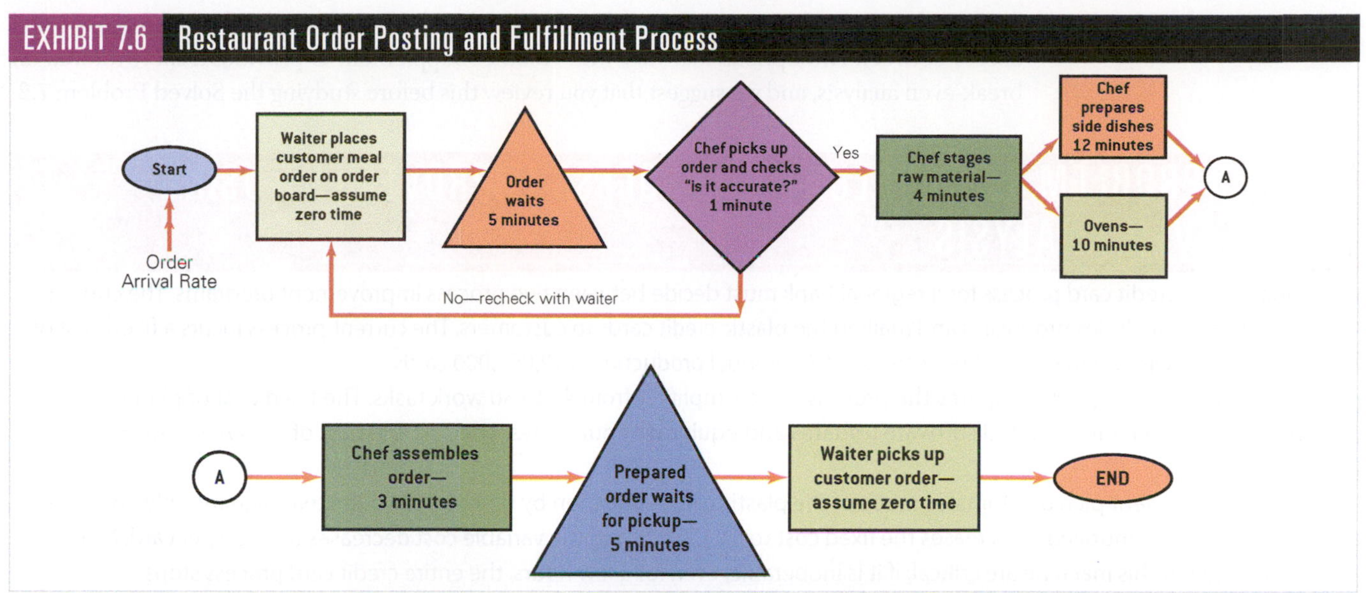

EXHIBIT 7.7 Value Stream Map for Restaurant Order Posting and Fulfillment Process

Value-Added Activities (VA)
Non-Value-Added Activities (NVA)
Order waits on order board @ (5 minutes per order) × (1 hr/60 min) × ($5 per hour) = $0.417
Chef picks up order and checks "Is it accurate?" @ (1 minute per order) × (1 hr/60 min) × ($30 per hour) = $0.50
If order is accurate, chef stages raw materials @ (4 minutes per order) × (1 hr/60 min) × ($30 per hour) = $2.00
Chef cooks meal using ovens @ (12 minutes per order) × (1 hr/ 60min) × ($30 per hour) = $6.00 labor cost (10 minutes per order) × (1 hr/60 min) × ($10/hour oven cost) = $1.67 equipment cost
Total labor + Oven cost = $7.67
Chef assembles order @ (3 minutes per order) × (1 hr/60 minutes) × ($30 per hour) = $1.50
Prepared order waits for waiter to pick up customer's order @ (5 minutes per order) × (1 hr/60 min) × ($60 per hour) = $5.00

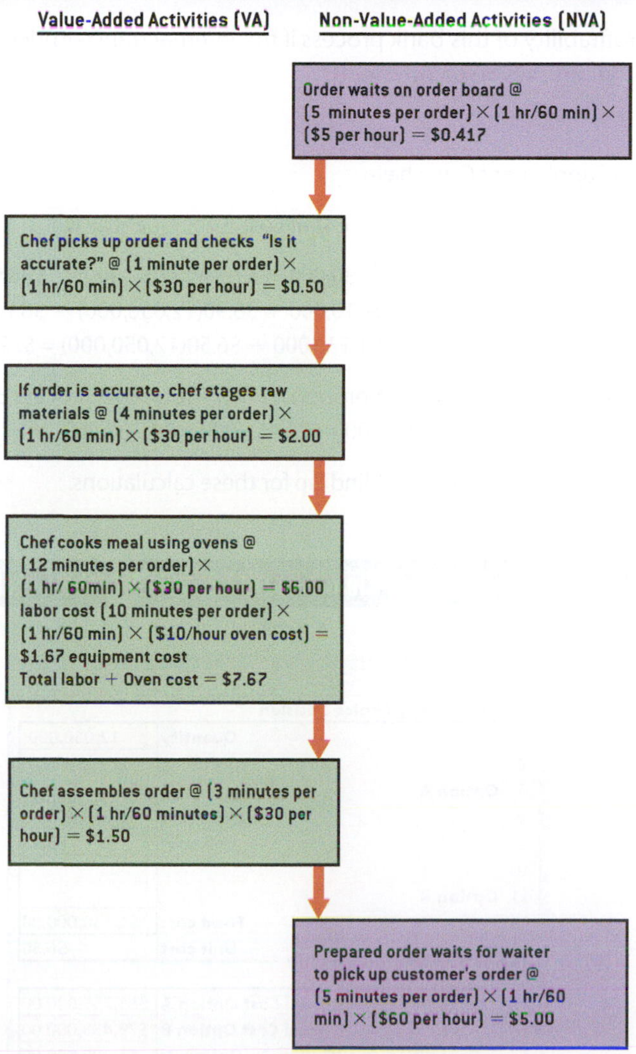

Total Time = 20 minutes (VA time) + 10 minutes (NVA time) = 30 minutes
Total Cost = $11.67 (VA cost) + $5.417 (NVA cost) = $17.087

Break-even analysis is a simple approach to analyze profit or loss, or to make an economical choice between two options that vary with volume. Supplement C provides a short tutorial on break-even analysis, and we suggest that you review this before studying the Solved Problem 7.2.

SOLVED PROBLEM 7.2: EVALUATING PROCESS IMPROVEMENT USING BREAK-EVEN ANALYSIS

The manager of a credit card process for a regional bank must decide between two process improvement programs. The current credit card process includes producing and mailing the plastic credit cards to customers. The current process incurs a fixed cost of $480,000 per year with a variable cost per card of $7.34. Annual production is 12,050,000 cards.

Process improvement plan A requires the process to be simplified from 42 to 30 work tasks. The fixed cost of plan A increases to $610,000 due to added software updates and equipment purchases. The variable cost of plan A is expected to be $6.90 per card.

Process improvement plan B automates much of the plastic card production by buying a machine that requires only one operator and is computer controlled. It increases the fixed cost to $1,130,000 and the variable cost decreases to $6.50 per card. Maintenance and repair of this machine are critical; if it is inoperable, even for a few hours, the entire credit card process stops.

a. What is the total cost of the current process and the two improvement plans A and B?

b. What do you recommend the bank do?

c. What is the internal profitability of this bank process if the internal transfer price is two percent higher than the variable cost per card for the option you recommend?

Solution:

a. Using formulas (C.1) and (C.7) in Supplement C, we have

$$\text{Total cost (TC)} = \text{Fixed cost (FC)} + \text{Unit cost (C)} \times \text{Quantity (Q)} \tag{C.1}$$

$$TC_{Current} = FC_C + C_C \times Q = \$480{,}000 + \$7.34(12{,}050{,}000) = \$88{,}927{,}000$$
$$TC_A = FC_A + C_A \times Q = \$610{,}000 + \$6.90(12{,}050{,}000) = \$83{,}755{,}000$$
$$TC_B = FC_B + C_B \times Q = \$1{,}130{,}000 + \$6.50(12{,}050{,}000) = \$79{,}455{,}000$$

$$\text{Cost difference (D)} = \text{Total cost process A } (TC_A) - \text{Total cost process B } (TC_B) \tag{C.7}$$
$$D = \$83{,}755{,}000 - \$79{,}455{,}000 = \$4{,}300{,}000$$

Exhibit 7.8 shows the Excel *Break-Even* template from MindTap for these calculations.

EXHIBIT 7.8 Comparison of Process Improvement Plan A and B Costs Using the Excel *Break-Even* Template

	G	H
4	Technology Choice Decision	
5	Quantity	12,050,000
6		
7	Option A	
8	Fixed cost	$610,000.00
9	Unit cost	$6.90
10		
11	Option B	
12	Fixed cost	$1,130,000.00
13	Unit cost	$6.50
14		
15	Total Cost Option A	$83,755,000.00
16	Total Cost Option B	$79,455,000.00
17	Cost difference (Option A - Option B)	$4,300,000.00
18	Economical Decision	Option B

b. What do you recommend the bank do?

Process improvement plan B is least expensive at $79,455,000 and should be chosen; the best economical decision is also provided in the Excel template. In addition, Plans A or B have a lower total costs than the cost of the current process, which is $88,927,000. The manager should make sure that machine maintenance and repair services are readily available and possibly in-house. If in-house, fixed and/or variable costs may increase and require the computations to be redone.

c. What is the internal profitability of this bank process if the internal transfer price is two percent higher than the variable cost per card for the option you recommend?

Internal transfer price for plan B = $6.50*1.02 = $6.63 per card

Using the Excel template shown in Exhibit 7.9, the internal profitability of adopting process improvement plan B = $436,500

EXHIBIT 7.9 Profitability of Process Improvement Plan B Using the Excel *Break-Even* Template

	A	B
4	Profitability Analysis	
5	Quantity	12,050,000
6		
7	Cost	
8	Fixed cost	$1,130,000.00
9	Unit cost	$6.50
10		
11		
12	Revenue	
13	Unit revenue	$6.63
14		
15	Total Cost	$79,455,000.00
16	Total Revenue	$79,891,500.00
17	Net Profit	$436,500.00
18	Profit or Loss	Profit

7-5 Mistake-Proofing Processes

Human beings tend to make mistakes inadvertently. Typical mistakes in production are omitted steps in a process, setup errors, missing parts, wrong parts, or incorrect adjustments. Such errors can arise from the following factors:

- Forgetfulness due to lack of reinforcement or guidance.
- Misunderstanding or incorrect identification because of the lack of familiarity with a process or procedures.
- Lack of experience.
- Absentmindedness and lack of attention, especially when a process is automated.

Blaming workers not only discourages them and lowers morale, but usually does not address the source of the problems, which is usually in the system.

Preventing mistakes can be done in three ways:

1. *Designing potential defects and errors out of the process.* Clearly, this approach is the best because it eliminates any possibility that the error or defect will occur and will not result in rework, scrap, or wasted time.
2. *Identifying potential defects and errors and stopping a process before they occur.* Although this approach prevents defects and errors, it does result in some non-value-added time.
3. *Identifying defects and errors soon after they occur and quickly correcting the process.* This can avoid large amounts of costly defects and errors in the future, but does result in some scrap, rework, and wasted resources.

Good design can eliminate many defects and errors, but still cannot account for the human factor.

Poka-yoke (POH-kah YOH-kay) *is an approach for mistake-proofing processes using automatic devices or simple methods to avoid human error*. Poka-yoke is focused on two aspects: (1) prediction, or recognizing that a defect is about to occur and providing a warning and (2) detection, or recognizing that a defect has occurred and stopping the process.

Many applications of poka-yoke are deceptively simple, inexpensive to implement, and are often quite creative. Some examples are given next:

- Many machines have sensors that would be activated only if the part was placed in the correct position.
- A device on a drill counts the number of holes drilled in a work piece; a buzzer sounds if the work piece is removed before the correct number of holes has been drilled.
- Computer programs display a warning message if a file that has not been saved is to be closed.
- Passwords set for web accounts are entered twice.

Poka-Yoke for Consumer Safety

Many poka-yokes are designed for consumer safety. For example, you can't start a lawn mower unless the handle bar is held. In some automobiles, you cannot enter information for GPS directions while the vehicle is in motion. Collision avoidance systems use radar to determine whether the car is approaching another vehicle too fast. If it senses that a collision might occur, it activates a buzzer and a warning light. If the driver doesn't slow down, then the seatbelt retracts and the brakes are applied lightly. If it determines that a collision will occur, then both the seatbelt retraction and the brakes are strongly applied.[11]

ambrozinio/Shutterstock.com

- Orders for critical aircraft parts use pre-fit foam forms that only allow the correct part to be placed in them, ensuring that the correct parts are shipped.
- Associates at Amazon sort products into bins that weigh them and compare the weight to the order; if there is an inconsistency, the associate is prompted to verify the items.

Richard B. Chase and Douglas M. Stewart suggest that the same concepts can be applied to services.[12] The major differences are that service mistake-proofing must account for the customers' activities as well as those of the producer, and for interactions between the customer and provider. Chase and Stewart classify service poka-yokes by the type of error they are designed to prevent: server errors and customer errors. Server errors result from the task, treatment, or tangibles of the service. Customer errors occur during preparation, the service encounter, or during resolution. The following list summarizes the typical types of service errors and related poka-yokes.

- *Task errors* include doing work incorrectly, work not requested, work on the wrong order, or working too slowly. Some examples of poka-yoke devices for task errors are computer prompts, color-coded cash register keys, measuring tools such as a French-fry scoop, and signaling devices. Hospitals use trays for surgical instruments that have indentations for each instrument, preventing the surgeon from leaving one of them in the patient. Simple checklists are often used; for example, LifeWings, a company that applies flight-tested safety lessons from the aviation industry to medicine, works with medical teams to create standardized lists of activities for every procedure.[13]
- *Treatment errors* arise in the contact between the server and the customer, such as lack of courteous behavior, and failure to acknowledge, listen, or react appropriately to the customer. A bank encourages eye contact by requiring tellers to record the customer's eye color on a checklist as they start the transaction. To promote friendliness at a fast-food restaurant, trainers provide the four specific cues for when to smile: when greeting the customer, when taking the order, when telling about the dessert special, and when giving the customer change. They encourage employees to observe whether the customer smiled back, a natural reinforcer for smiling.
- *Tangible errors* are those in physical elements of the service, such as unclean facilities, dirty uniforms, inappropriate temperature, and document errors. Hotels wrap paper strips around towels to help the housekeeping staff identify clean linen and show which ones should be replaced. Spell-checkers in word processing software help reduce document misspellings (provided they are used!).
- *Customer errors in preparation* include the failure to bring necessary materials to the encounter, to understand their role in the service transaction, and to engage the correct service. A computer manufacturer provides a flowchart to specify how to place a service call. By guiding the customers through three yes-or-no questions, the flowchart prompts them to have the necessary information before calling.
- *Customer errors during an encounter* can be due to inattention, misunderstanding, or simply a memory lapse, and include failure to remember steps in the process or to follow instructions. Poka-yoke examples include height bars at amusement rides that indicate rider size requirements, beepers that signal customers to remove cards from ATM machines, and locks on airplane lavatory doors that must be closed to turn on the lights. Some cashiers at restaurants fold back the top edge of credit card receipts, holding together the restaurant's copies while revealing the customer's copy.
- *Customer errors at the resolution stage* of a service encounter include failure to signal service inadequacies, to learn from experience, to adjust expectations, and to execute appropriate post-encounter actions. Hotels might enclose a small gift certificate to encourage guests to provide feedback. Strategically placed tray-return stands and trash receptacles remind customers to return trays in fast-food facilities.

7-6 Process Improvement

Few processes are designed from scratch. Many process design activities involve redesigning an existing process to improve performance. Management strategies to improve process designs usually focus on one or more of the following:

- *increasing revenue* by improving process efficiency in creating goods and services and delivery of the customer benefit package;
- *increasing agility* by improving flexibility and response to changes in demand and customer expectations;
- *increasing product and/or service quality* by reducing defects, mistakes, failures, or service upsets;
- *decreasing costs* through better technology or elimination of non-value-added activities;
- *decreasing process flow time* by reducing waiting time or speeding up movement through the process and value chain; and
- *decreasing the carbon footprint of the task, activity, process, and/or value chain.*

Process and value stream maps are the foundation for improvement activities. Typical questions that need to be evaluated during process analysis include:

1. Are the steps in the process arranged in logical sequence?
2. Do all steps add value? Can some steps be eliminated, and should others be added in order to improve quality or operational performance? Can some be combined? Should some be reordered?
3. Are capacities of each step in balance; that is, do bottlenecks exist for which customers will incur excessive waiting time?
4. What skills, equipment, and tools are required at each step of the process? Should some steps be automated?
5. At which points in the system (sometimes called process fail points) might errors occur that would result in customer dissatisfaction, and how might these errors be corrected?
6. At which point or points in the process should performance be measured? What are appropriate measures?
7. Where interaction with the customer occurs, what procedures, behaviors, and guidelines should employees follow that will present a positive image?
8. What is the impact of the process on sustainability? Can we quantify the carbon footprint of the current process?

Sometimes, processes grow so complex that it is easier to start from a "clean sheet" rather than try to improve incrementally. **Reengineering** *has been defined as "the fundamental rethinking and radical redesign of business processes to achieve dramatic improvements in critical, contemporary measures of performance, such as cost, quality, service, and speed."*[14]

Reengineering was spawned by the revolution in information technology and involves asking basic questions about business processes: Why do we do it? Why is it done this way? Such questioning often uncovers obsolete, erroneous, or inappropriate assumptions. Radical redesign involves tossing out existing procedures and reinventing the process, not just incrementally improving it. The goal is to achieve quantum leaps in performance. All processes and functional areas participate in reengineering efforts, each requiring knowledge and skills in operations management.

Some good examples of reengineering are provided below:

- Intel Corporation had previously used a 91-step process costing thousands of dollars to purchase ballpoint pens—the same process used to purchase forklift trucks! The improved process was reduced to eight steps.
- In rethinking its purpose as a customer-driven, retail service company, rather than a manufacturing company, Taco Bell eliminated the kitchen from its restaurants. Meat and beans are cooked outside the restaurant at central commissaries and reheated. Other food items such as diced tomatoes, onions, and olives are prepared off-site. This innovation saved about 11 million hours of work and $7 million per year over the entire chain.[15]

Metro Health Hospital: Process Mapping Improves Pharmacy Service

Metro Health Hospital in Grand Rapids, Michigan, applied process mapping, reducing the lead time for getting the first dose of a medication to a patient in its pharmacy services operations. The lead time was measured from the time an order arrived at the pharmacy to its delivery on the appropriate hospital floor. A process-improvement team carefully laid out all the process steps involved and found that the pharmacy had a 14-stage process with some unnecessary steps, resulting in a total lead time of 166 minutes. During the evaluation process, the pharmacy calculated that technicians were spending 77.4 percent of their time locating products; when a pharmacist needed a technician for clinical activities, the technician was usually off searching for a drug. The team outlined several non-value-added steps in the process, only one of which was out of the pharmacy's control (i.e., the time it took to transport the ordered medication, once filled, to the appropriate floor). Overall, the pharmacy at Metro realized a 33 percent reduction in time to get medications to patients, and reduced the number of process steps from 14 to 9 simply by removing non-value-added steps. Patients have experienced a 40 percent reduction in pharmacy-related medication errors, and the severity of those errors has decreased.[16]

CHAPTER 7 LEARNING OBJECTIVE SUMMARIES

7.1

Describe the four types of processes used to produce goods and services. Four principal types of processes are used to produce goods and services (see Exhibit 7.1):

1. projects,
2. job shop processes,
3. flow shop processes, and
4. continuous flow processes.

7.2

Explain the logic and use of the product-process matrix. The most appropriate match between type of product and type of process occurs along the diagonal in the product-process matrix (see Exhibit 7.2). As one moves down the diagonal, the emphasis on both product and process structure shifts from low volume and high flexibility to higher volumes and more standardization.

7.3

Explain the logic and use of the service-positioning matrix. The SPM focuses on the service-encounter level and helps management design a service system that best meets the technical and behavioral needs of customers (see Exhibit 7.3). The position along the horizontal axis is described by the sequence of service encounters. The SPM is similar to the product-process matrix in that it suggests that the nature of the customer's desired service-encounter activity sequence should lead to the most appropriate service system design and that superior performance results from generally staying along the diagonal of the matrix. As in the product-process matrix, organizations that venture too far off the diagonal create a mismatch between service system characteristics and desired activity sequence characteristics. As we move down the diagonal of the SPM, the service-encounter activity sequence becomes less unique and more repeatable with fewer pathways. Like the product-process matrix, the midrange portion of the matrix contains a broad range of intermediate design choices.

7.4

Describe how to apply process and value stream mapping for process design. Designing a goods-producing or service-providing process requires six major activities:

1. Define the purpose and objectives of the process.
2. Create a detailed process or value stream map that describes how the process is currently performed.
3. Evaluate alternative process designs.
4. Identify and define appropriate performance measures for the process.
5. Select the appropriate equipment and technology.
6. Develop an implementation plan to introduce the new or revised process design. A process map documents how work either is, or should be, accomplished, and how the transformation process creates value. We usually first develop a "baseline" map of how the current process operates in order to understand it and identify improvements for redesign. In service applications, flowcharts generally highlight the points of contact with the customer and are often called *service blueprints or service maps.* Such flowcharts often show the separation between the back office and the front office with a "line of customer visibility." A value stream map (VSM) shows the process flows in a manner similar to an ordinary process map; however, the difference lies in that value stream maps highlight value-added versus non-value-added activities and include costs associated with work activities for both value-added and non-value-added activities (see Exhibits 7.4 to 7.7).

7.5

Explain the concept of mistake proofing in product and process design for both goods and services. Preventing mistakes can be done in three ways:

1. Designing potential defects and errors out of the process.
2. Identifying potential defects and errors and stopping a process before they occur.
3. Identifying defects and errors soon after they occur and quickly correcting the process.

The best approach is the first, since it eliminates any possibility that the error or defect will occur and will not result in rework, scrap, or wasted time. Poka-yoke is an approach for mistake-proofing processes using automatic devices or simple methods to avoid human error. For services, mistake-proofing must account for the customers' activities as well as those of the producer, and for interactions between the customer and provider.

7.6

Explain how to improve process designs and analyze process maps. Management strategies to improve process designs include *increasing revenue* by improving process efficiency in creating goods and services and delivery of the customer benefit package; *increasing agility* by improving flexibility and response to changes in demand and customer expectations; *increasing product and/or service quality* by reducing defects, mistakes, failures, or service upsets; *decreasing costs* through better technology or elimination of non-value-added activities; *decreasing process* flow time by reducing waiting time or speeding up movement through the process and value chain.

Reengineering examines processes from a "clean sheet" approach and involves asking basic questions such as: Why do we do it? and Why is it done this way? The goal is to achieve quantum leaps in performance.

For process maps, key improvement questions include the following:

- Are the steps in the process arranged in logical sequence?
- Do all steps add value? Can some steps be eliminated, and should others be added in order to improve quality or operational performance? Can some be combined? Should some be reordered?
- Are capacities of each step in balance; that is, do bottlenecks exist for which customers will incur excessive waiting time?
- What skills, equipment, and tools are required at each step of the process? Should some steps be automated?
- At which points in the system might errors occur that would result in customer dissatisfaction, and how might these errors be corrected?
- At which point or points should performance be measured?
- Where interaction with the customer occurs, what procedures, behaviors, and guidelines should employees follow that will present a positive image?

KEY TERMS

- **Activity**
- **Continuous flow processes**
- **Custom, or make-to-order, goods and services**
- **Customer-routed services**
- **Flow shop processes**
- **Job shop processes**
- **Option, or assemble-to-order, goods and services**
- **Pathway**
- **Process boundary**
- **Process map (flowchart)**
- **Product-process matrix**
- **Product life cycle**
- **Projects**
- **Provider-routed services**
- **Reengineering**
- **Service-encounter activity sequence**
- **Standard, or make-to-stock, goods and services**
- **Task**
- **Value stream**

REVIEW QUESTIONS

7.1 1. Define custom, option, and standard goods and services and give a new example of each. How does the type of goods and services affect process choice?

7.1 2. Describe the four types of processes used to produce goods and services.

7.1 3. What is the (traditional) product life cycle? How does it relate to process design and selection? Explain how firms make money when their goods or services follow the traditional product life cycle.

7.2 4. Explain the logic and use of the product-process matrix.

7.3 5. Define a service encounter activity sequence and give three examples.

7.3 6. Define a pathway and give an example.

7.3 7. Explain the differences between customer-routed services and provider-routed services and give an example of each.

7.3 8. Explain the logic and use of the service-positioning matrix.

7.4 9. What is a process map? How is it used in process design?

7.4 10. What are the advantages of clearly defining the process boundaries?

7.4 11. Explain the concept of the hierarchy of work. How is it useful in process design activities?

7.4 12. What is the value stream? How does a value stream map differ from an ordinary process map?

7.4 13. Describe how to apply process and value stream mapping for process design.

7.5 14. Why do people make inadvertent mistakes? How does poka-yoke help prevent such mistakes?

7.5 15. Describe the types of errors that service poka-yokes are designed to prevent.

7.6 16. What are the possible objectives to improving a process?

7.6 17. How can process maps be used for improvement?

7.6 18. What is reengineering? How does it differ from other approaches to process improvement?

DISCUSSION QUESTIONS AND EXPERIENTIAL ACTIVITIES

7.1 19. What type of process—project, job shop, flow shop, and continuous flow—would most likely be used to produce the following? Explain your reasoning.

   a. Personal computers
   b. Weddings
   c. Paper
   d. Paper books
   e. Tax preparation

7.1 20. What type of process—project, job shop, flow shop, and continuous flow—would most likely be used to produce the following?

   a. Gasoline
   b. Air-conditioners
   c. Specialized machine tools
   d. Ships
   e. Producing many flavors of ice cream

7.1 21. List some common processes that you perform as a student. How can you use the knowledge from this chapter, such as identifying bottlenecks, to improve them?

7.2 22. Use the product-process matrix to explain the implications for Boeing in changing from a project focus to more of a flow shop process as explained in the box "Rethinking Airplane Manufacturing Processes." Limit your discussion to one typed page.

7.3 23. Provide some examples of customer- and provider-routed services that you have encountered that are different from those described in this chapter. Can you identify any improvements to these processes?

7.3 24. Design a process for one of the following activities:

a. Preparing for an exam
b. Writing a term paper
c. Planning a vacation

7.4 25. Discuss how sustainability might be incorporated into a process or value chain improvement initiative. Try to find an example and summarize it in a manner similar to that in the box feature on Alfa Laval.

7.4 26. What sustainability issues are present in the example restaurant order fulfillment process example (Exhibits 7.6 and 7.7)? What other restaurant processes need to include sustainability criteria in their design and day-to-day management?

7.4 27. Draw a flowchart for a process of interest to you, such as a quick oil-change service, a factory process you might have worked in, ordering a pizza, renting a car or truck, buying products on the Internet, or applying for an automobile loan. Identify the points where something (people, information) waits for service or is held in work-in-process inventory, the estimated time to accomplish each activity in the process, and the total flow time. Evaluate how well the process worked and what might be done to improve it.

7.4 28. Develop a value stream map for the process you flowcharted in question 27 to identify the value-added and non-value-added activities. How can you estimate costs and/or revenue for the process steps?

7.5 29. Identify several sources of errors as a student or in your personal life. Develop some poka-yokes that might prevent them.

COMPUTATIONAL PROBLEMS AND EXERCISES

These exercises require you to apply the formulas and methods described in the chapter. The problems should be solved manually.

7.1 30. Carbon dioxide emissions associated with a one-night stay in a hotel room are calculated at 29.53 kg of CO_2 per room day for an average hotel. The 200 rooms of your hotel are all occupied for two days during a college football game.

a. How much CO_2 did the guests and hotel release into the atmosphere?
b. What work, leisure activities, and processes in the hotel generate CO_2 emissions? Provide three examples and explain how carbon dioxide is emitted.

7.1 31. A JetAir 304 airplane emits 22 kilograms of carbon dioxide per hour while flying. Today, the plane flew for 8.2 hours on six flights. This emission rate doesn't include the time on the ground running its engines and other airport gate and airport emissions.

a. How much carbon dioxide did the JetAir 304 airplane release into the atmosphere today?
b. What work, leisure activities, and processes in the airline and airport generate CO_2 emissions? Provide three examples and explain how carbon dioxide is emitted.

7.1 32. In Solved Problem 7.1 on Clear Water Pool Service (CWPS), CWPS replaced a fleet of pool service vans with hybrid/electric- and gasoline-driven systems. This reduced the number of gallons of gasoline used to 6,000 gallons per year. How many metric tons of carbon dioxide did not go into Earth's atmosphere because CWPS changed to hybrid-powered vehicles?

7.1 33. Assume you are the chief operating officer of the fast food chain with 5,500 stores in North America. Each store operates 360 days a year and has one heated dryer in the ladies and men's restrooms. Each dryer operates 200 times per day per restroom. One pound is 453.6 grams. To dry your hands in a retail store restroom requires zero carbon dioxide emissions if you let your hands drip dry. If you use one standard size paper towel, 10 grams of CO2 were generated to manufacturer the towel. If you use a standard heated electric dryer 20 grams of CO2 are used to generate this energy and operate the dryer.

a. How many pounds of carbon dioxide are released in the atmosphere from the heated electric hand dryers in the fast-food chain's stores?

b. Given your answer in (a), how would you have customers dry their hands in the chain's fast-food stores? What other criteria might be important?

7.1 34. Worthington Machining must decide whether to purchase Process A with specialized metal folding equipment needing two employees to operate it or Process B with general purpose folding equipment requiring five employees. Process A requires a fixed cost of $1,430,000 and a variable cost of $14.32 per metal panel. Process B requires a fixed cost of $820,000 and a variable cost of $20.05. Process A is more automated than Process B.

a. What is the break-even quantity between these two processes?

b. If predicted demand for next year is 120,000 panel folds, what process do you recommend? What is the cost savings?

7.1 35. Given the information in problem 34, what do you recommend if Worthington Machining can buy folded metal panels of identical size at a price of $27.25 per panel?

7.1 36. A college textbook publisher sells a certain e-book for $40.00. For the current process, the publisher has fixed cost of $355,000 and a variable cost per book of $30.00.

a. What is the break-even quantity for this book?

b. If the variable cost increased 10 percent due to poor operating performance, what is the new break-even quantity?

c. If through better process efficiency the fixed cost decreases by ten percent and the variable cost decreases to $27.90, what is the revised break-even quantity?

7.1 37. The police department of a major city needs a faster process to do criminal background checks. They eliminated several vendors and their products because they required too much retraining and major changes in search process steps. The police department review committee thought many of these searches might not hold up in court due to process and verification changes. The two finalist required few changes in the non-online process. Process A resulted in a fixed cost of $1,100,000 and a variable cost per search of $1.34. Process B required a fixed cost of $925,000 and a variable cost per search of $1.45.

a. What is the break-even quantity between these two processes?

b. If predicted demand for next year is one million searches, what process do you recommend? What is the cost savings?

7.1 38. Dot's Restaurant must decide between two technology processes in their kitchen. They only serve dinner after 4 p.m. on a small island called Sanibel. The restaurant is open 250 days per year. Dot and her husband, Ham, are retired. They became bored playing golf five times a week and decided to open this boutique restaurant. Process A uses an induction oven and microwave process with a fixed cost of $44,000 and a variable cost of $4.19 per meal. Process B uses a gas fired oven process with heating lamps with a fixed cost of $28,000 and a variable cost of $5.86 per meal. Process A speeds up cooking and delivery time. The average selling price per meal is $31.38.

a. What is the break-even quantity?

b. If the restaurant manager expects to sell 10,000 meals, which option, A or B, is best? Justify.

c. Is the restaurant profitable if they purchase the process option you recommend in part (b)?

7.4 39. Refer to Exhibit 7.7, the restaurant value stream map, and recompute the total value-added and non-value-added time and cost given the following new information. If a restaurant uses iPads to place orders and notify waiters when the customer's order is ready, the time on the order board (now an electronic order board) decreases from five to one minute, and the prepared order wait time decreases from five to three minutes. How might speeding up the order and delivery process affect customer satisfaction? Explain.

EXCEL-BASED PROBLEMS

For these problems, you may use Excel or the spreadsheet templates in MindTap to assist in your analysis.

7.1 40. Samoset Fans, Inc. manufacturers its fan blades in-house. The owner, Betty Dice, doesn't outsource any fan parts except fan motors—all other fans parts are made in-house. Their current process and its equipment are getting old. Maintenance and repair costs are increasing at eight percent per year. She and her company team are evaluating two new processes. The first process has an annual fixed cost of $720,000 and a variable cost of $17 per fan blade. The second process is more automated and requires an annual fixed cost of $1,300,000 and a variable cost of $13 per fan blade. The internal transfer cost of a fan blade is $20, and this helps the firm determine the total manufactured cost of a completed fan. Use the Excel template *Break-Even* in MindTap to answer the following questions:

a. What is the break-even quantity between these two processes?

b. If predicted demand for next year is 150,000 blades, what process do you recommend? What is the cost savings?

c. What volume of demand does Samoset Fans, Inc need to make an internal profit on fan blades of $100,000, assuming they installed the process you recommend in part (b)?

7.1 41. Rework computational problem 34 (Worthington Machining) using the *Break-Even* Excel template in MindTap to answer the following questions:

a. What is the break-even quantity between these two processes?

b. If predicted demand for next year is 120,000 panel folds, what process do you recommend? What is the cost savings?

7.1 42. Rework computational problem 36 (college textbook publisher) using the *Break-Even* template in MindTap and answer the following questions:

a. What is the break-even quantity for this book?

b. If the variable cost increased 10 percent due to poor operating performance, what is the new break-even quantity?

c. If through better process efficiency the fixed cost decreases by ten percent and the variable cost decreases to $27.90, what is the revised break-even quantity?

7.1 43. An automated car wash called Jet Express outside a large Texas city on the beltway is deciding whether to build and install one dedicated vehicle wash line or have two parallel wash lines. There are no other cash washes at this intersection and there will be none because all the land is developed. The second line allows for some economies of scale in total cost. The monthly fixed cost of one wash line is $15,000 per month or $180,000 per year. This includes the mortgage payment, taxes on the building, and wash equipment. The variable cost for this single line is $16 per vehicle. The fixed cost for two wash lines is $26,000 per month or $312,000 per year, and the variable cost to operate two lines is $13 per vehicle because some wash crews can work both lines. The price of the average interior and exterior car wash is $25. Use the Excel template *Break-Even* in MindTap to answer the following questions:

a. What is the break-even quantity for one and two automated wash line?

b. Annual forecasts of demand for this site ranges from 20,000 to 40,000 per year. What would you recommend?

7.1 44. The deli at a Metro Supermarket experiences constant and continuous demand. Staffing is a problem for store managers but several of the employees suggested they buy more deli cutting machines and weighing scales and place them side-by-side. Currently, three slicing machines and two weighing scales are randomly scattered behind the counter. The deli is a job shop with demanding requirements, such as what weight of product the customer wants, how thick or thin to slice the cheese and meat, how the customer wants them wrapped and packaged, and so on. Customer priority is determined by selecting a number to determine your turn for service. The employees are constantly retracing their steps, and they go to cold food storage lockers and display cases and walk between different slicing and weighing equipment. They also have backroom work tasks to perform in stocking shelves and cold storage lockers and cleaning equipment and floors. Customers can "see" the deli so it must be clean! Employee turnover is high in this demanding job shop work environment.

The fixed cost includes three parts. First, the fixed costs associated with buying three more slicing machines and four more weighing scales is $11,000. The current fixed cost of existing equipment is $7,000. The supermarket accounting department also sets the fixed cost of the building deli area and cold storage lockers at a $36,000. The predicted variable cost of the produce plus operating six slicing machines and six scales including labor costs is $18.15 per customer order. The average deli order costs the customer $19.65. Use the Excel template *Break-Even* in MindTap to answer the following questions:

a. What is the break-even quantity in customer orders per year?

b. How many orders does the deli fill per day at the break-even quantity if the supermarket is open 360 days a year?

c. What type of process is the deli shop within the supermarket? Explain. Justify.

d. If demand was 52,000 orders filled by the deli last year, how much money did the deli contribute to profits for the supermarket?

e. If you were store manager, would you add the extra machines? Would you raise deli prices?

Custom Drapes, Inc.

Lilly Hillcrest started a custom drapery business in Naples, Florida in 2014. Her market segment is for owners of homes over one million dollars. Her prices are high, but the customer receives exceptional personal service and a service guarantee on all work. Customer service and the quality of their work are the top competitive priorities of Custom Drapes (CD).

Custom draperies require Lilly and her employees to visit the customer's home and evaluate the home's layout, light, and color palette to decide what type of draperies might work best. Two of Lilly's staff are interior designers specializing in drapery window treatments. Next the customer and employee select the fabric. Fabric books contain millions of fabric colors, weaves, and designs. The customer and designer must also decide on many other drape design characteristics, such as pleated folds, flat panels, classic tab and rod drapes, goblet pleats, linings, and valance designs. The number of custom combinations now is in the billions, with many opportunities for errors. For high-end customers, the drapes for one wall can be over $100,000.

The next step is for an employee to take measurements of the venue where the drapes are to be installed. These specifications can range from a half-dozen to several dozen measurements. Once the customer order is approved, a work order is released to CD's in-house factory. Purchase orders are sent to the supplier(s) for the fabric and thread. Each work order is hand cut, sewed, and pressed using industrial sewing and stream pressing machines. CD groups sewing machines in one area of the factory alongside stainless steel work tables. Each order requires a new setup to install thread, set and calibrate the machine, and position the fabric. The sewing machines can accommodate a wide variety of thread weights and types of fabric, such as silk or cotton. The employees are cross-trained and skilled at sewing and pleating different fabrics. These skilled backroom employees inspect their own work, and three employees must sign off on a complete order. Eighteen percent of the factory work requires rework during production.

Their average customer order requires 36 square yards of fabric for two pleated panels on each side of a window or sliding glass door with a ceiling height of eleven feet. Each window treatment may be a separate order (i.e., a lot size of one) given the order specifications. If the fabric is the same, customer orders for an entire home are batched.

Larger drapery manufacturers use automated cutting and sewing systems to produce standard drapes sold in most retail stores. They use tens of millions of square yards of fabric per year to produce their panels. Most large drapery and curtain manufacturers are located in Asia.

The automated systems include computer-aided design software, large fabric and conveyor tables, huge spools of different types and colors of thread and fabric, and automated sewing equipment. Even small systems need thousands of square feet of production space. The bigger manufacturers sell their drapes through furniture stores worldwide without direct customer contact. Their order completion times are double CD's lead times.

In the last few years, more regional furniture stores have asked CD to manufacture draperies for them. These standardized draperies would be in certain sizes and lengths and sold in the stores. The furniture stores would select the style and fabric, and CD would manufacture them. Lilly summarized these proposed standard orders on her computer's spreadsheet as producing 32 different drapery panels in order quantities ranging from 1,000 to 10,000 drapery panels. This mix of standard orders totaled 112,568 panels.

Lilly was considering purchasing a small, used computerized curtain panel system for $490,000 and building a new building to house the equipment. The building would cost $2.5 million dollars including kitchen, security, and other factory equipment. The new factory would be built behind the current custom factory on land Lilly owned. The variable cost to manufacture a typical standard drape panel using this system would be $78.90, and the panel would be sold for $100.

1. Rank in order the competitive priorities for CD's custom jobs. Rank in order the competitive priorities for the standard drapery business.
2. What is the break-even quantity (in panels) if Lilly builds the facility and buys the equipment to produce standard panels?
3. Should Custom Draperies accept the proposals to manufacture 32 different drapery panels in order sizes up to 10,000 panels? What are the implications? If the answer is yes, what other operations and logistics decisions are necessary to support this growth initiative? If your answer is no, justify and explain.
4. What are the strategic growth options for Custom Draperies?
5. What are your final recommendations?

Hickory Medical Clinic

The Hickory Medical Clinic recently conducted a patient satisfaction survey. Using a scale of 1–5, with 1 being "very dissatisfied" and 5 being "very satisfied," the clinic compiled a check sheet for responses that were either 1 or 2, indicating dissatisfaction with the performance attributes. Exhibit 7.10 shows the count of patients that scored the process attribute as a 1 (very dissatisfied) or 2 (dissatisfied) out of 100 patients surveyed.

EXHIBIT 7.10 The Number of Patient's Dissatisfied with the Process

Making an Appointment	Check-in/Check-out	Care and Treatment
Ease of getting through on the phone—10	Courtesy and helpfulness of the receptionist—7	Respect shown by nurses/assistants—0
Friendliness of the telephone receptionist—5	Amount of time to register—1	Responsiveness to phone calls related to care—5
Convenience of office hours—7	Length of wait to see a physician—13	How well the physician listened—3
Ease of getting a convenient appointment—12	Comfort of registration waiting area—4	Confidence in the physician's ability—1
		Explanation of medical condition and treatment—2

Doctors have extremely busy schedules. They have surgeries to perform, and many are teaching faculty at the local medical school. Many surgeries are emergencies or take longer than expected, resulting in delays of getting back to the clinic. In the clinic, one or two telephone receptionists answer calls for three different surgical departments, which include 20 or more doctors. The receptionist's job is to schedule appointments, provide directions, and transfer calls to the proper doctor's administrative (department) scheduler. This generally requires putting the patient on hold. Often, the receptionist must take a hand-written message and personally deliver it to the department's scheduler because the phone line is always busy. However, the receptionist cannot leave his or her desk without someone else to cover the phones. A student intern examined the processes for answering phone calls and registering patients. The flowcharts she developed are shown in Exhibits 7.11 and 7.12. (An encounter form captures the patient check-in information.)

EXHIBIT 7.11 Current Hickory Medical Clinic Process for Answering Phone Calls

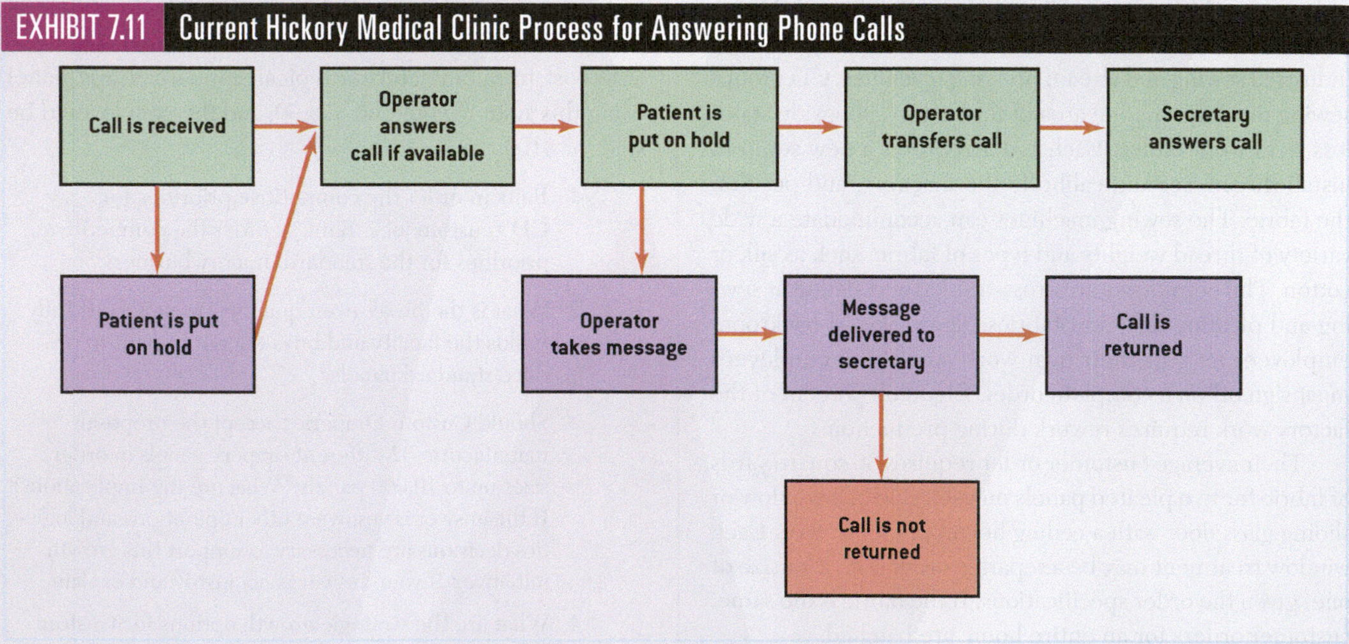

EXHIBIT 7.12 Current Hickory Medical Clinic Patient Registration Process

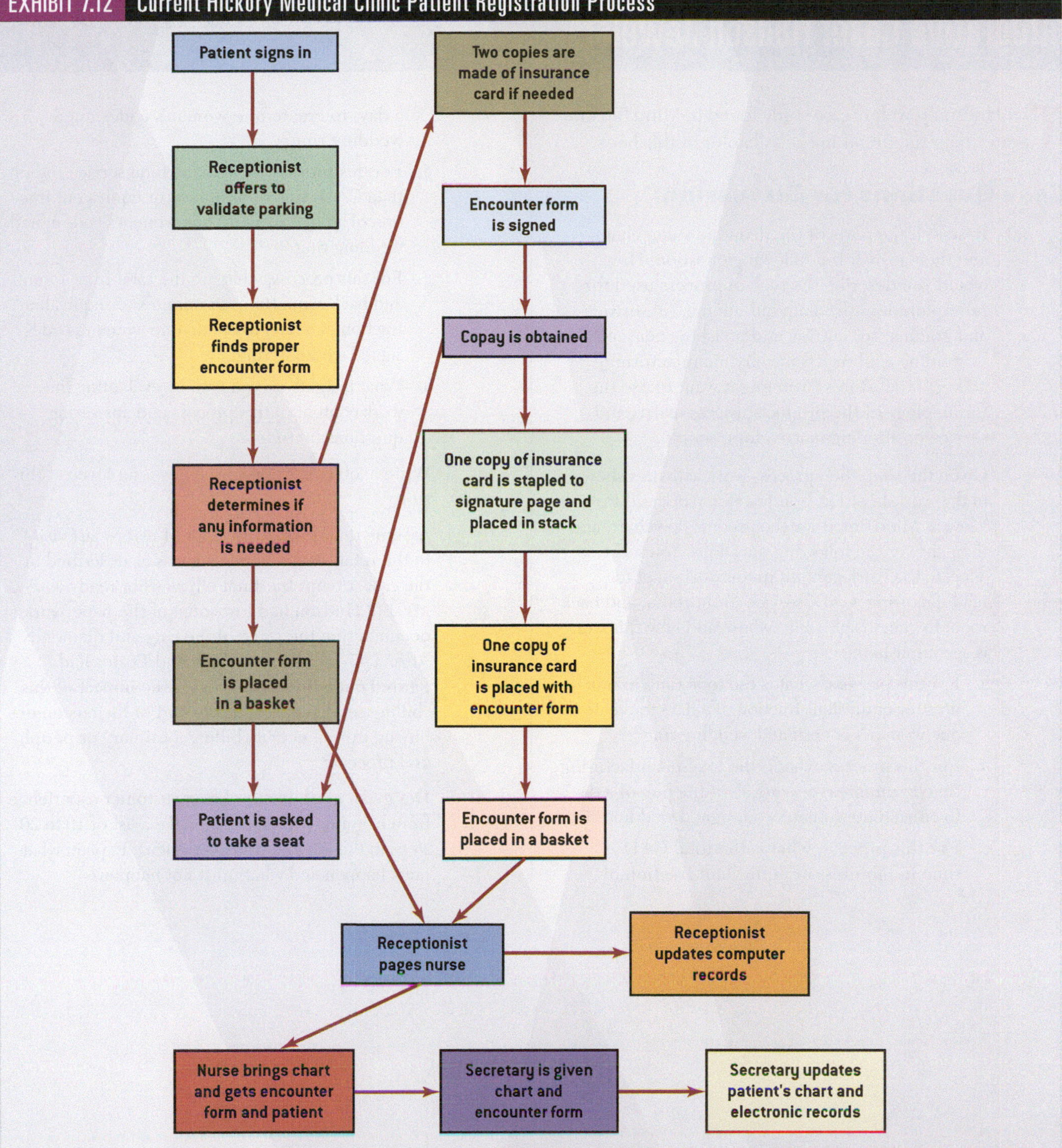

Case Questions for Discussion:

1. What conclusions do you reach from the satisfaction survey results? What implications would this have for a better process design?
2. Propose some process improvements to the flowcharts and develop new flowchart(s) of the redesigned process(es). Cite key advantages and disadvantages of your flowchart(s).
3. How should the organization implement the new process plans?

Integrative Case: Hudson Jewelers

The Hudson Jewelers case study found in MindTap integrates material found in each chapter of this book.

Case Questions for Discussion:

1. Research the parts of the diamond value chain and then answer the following question: How would you describe the type of process used for (a) exploration, (b) diamond mining, (c) sorting and grading, (d) cutting and polishing centers, (e) trading centers, (f) jewelry manufacturing, and (g) retail stores? You might want to use the terminology of the product-process matrix and service positioning matrix, for example.
2. Given the simplified process work activities shown in the worksheet Hudson Jeweler Work and Process Flow in MindTap, draw the process flowchart, and then answer the following questions. You must allocate the work content in the worksheet to manufacturing, CAD, service, front room, and back room to gain insights into where and how this work is accomplished.
   a. For this process, what is the total time in minutes (or equivalent fraction of a day) to create one woman's codesigned wedding ring?
   b. For this process, what is the total manufacturing time in minutes (or equivalent fraction of a day) to create one woman's codesigned wedding ring?
   c. For this process, what is the total CAD time in minutes (or equivalent fraction of a day) to create one woman's codesigned wedding ring?
   d. For this process, what is the total service (other than CAD) time in minutes (or equivalent fraction of a day) to create one woman's codesigned wedding ring?
   e. For this process, what are the total front room and back room times in minutes (or equivalent fraction of a day) to create one woman's codesigned wedding ring?
   f. What insights do you gain by evaluating the work content of this process and answering questions (a) to (e)?
3. Write a job description for a new employee at this store.
4. Assume that during Lilly's and Lester's last visit to the retail store everything was as described in the case, except the final bill was not ready and Mr. Bill Hudson had lost some of the paperwork documenting the price of the ring and diamonds. After a 45-minute wait, Lilly and Lester had figured out a final bill. What is the impact of this "billing service upset" at the end of the customer's buying experience? Is billing a primary or peripheral process?
5. Design an ideal diamond-ring customer experience from beginning to end (i.e., make a list of 10 to 20 steps in the job and process design). Explain what must happen and what must not happen.

Facility and Work Design | 8

Facility and workplace design can play a role in creating a satisfying customer experience.

895Studio/Shutterstock.com

LEARNING OBJECTIVES

After studying this chapter, you should be able to:

8-1 Identify the objectives of facility design and describe four layout patterns and when they should be used.

8-2 Explain how to design product layouts using assembly-line balancing.

8-3 Explain the concepts of process layout.

8-4 Explain the concepts and approaches used in work measurement.

8-5 Describe issues related to the design of workplaces and jobs.

Vytec (www.vytec.com) is a leading manufacturer of vinyl siding for homes and businesses. Vytec makes 50 different product lines (called profiles) of siding, soffits, and accessories. Each profile is typically produced in 15 colors, creating 750 stock-keeping units. The finished siding is packaged in a carton that holds 20 pieces that are usually 12 feet long. The cartons are stacked in steel racks (called beds). Each bed holds 30 to 60 cartons, depending on the bed's location in the warehouse. Vytec's main warehouse is more than 200,000 square feet.

Over time, demand for each siding profile changes; some are added and others discontinued. One problem the warehouse faces periodically is the need to redo the location and capacity of beds in the warehouse. Using basic layout principles, high-demand siding profiles are located closest to the shipping dock to minimize travel and order-picking time. Although management would like to find a permanent solution to this stock placement problem in the warehouse, continuous changes in demand and product mix necessitate a new warehouse design every few years.[1]

WHAT DO YOU THINK?

Think of a facility in which you have conducted business—for instance, a restaurant, bank, or automobile dealership. How did the physical environment and layout enhance or degrade your customer experience?

Once processes are selected and designed, organizations must design the infrastructure to implement these processes. This is accomplished through the design of the physical facilities and work tasks that must be performed. The physical design of a factory needs to support operations as efficiently as possible, as we can see in the Vytec example. Facility and work design are important elements of an organization's infrastructure and key strategic decisions that affect cost, productivity, responsiveness, and agility.

A good layout should support the ability of operations to accomplish its mission.

In both goods-producing and service-providing organizations, facility layout and work design influence the ability to meet customer wants and needs, enhance sustainability, and provide value. A poorly designed facility can lock management into a noncompetitive situation and be very costly to correct. For many service organizations, the physical facility and workplace are vital parts of service design (see the box, Facility Layouts in Fitness Centers). It can also play a significant role in creating a satisfying customer experience, particularly when customer contact is high. Facility design must be integrated with and support job and process design.

8-1 Facility Layout

Facility layout *refers to the specific arrangement of physical facilities.* Facility layout studies are necessary whenever (1) a new facility is constructed; (2) there is a significant change in demand or throughput volume; (3) a new good or service is introduced to the customer benefit package; or (4) different processes, equipment, and/or technology are installed. The objectives of layout studies are to minimize delays in materials handling and customer movement, maintain flexibility, use labor and space effectively, promote high employee morale and customer satisfaction, minimize energy use and environmental impact, provide for good housekeeping and maintenance, and enhance sales as appropriate in manufacturing and service facilities. Essentially, a good layout should support the ability of operations to accomplish its mission.

Four major layout patterns are commonly used in configuring facilities: product layout, process layout, cellular layout, and fixed-position layout.

8-1a Product Layout

A **product layout** *is an arrangement based on the sequence of operations that is performed during the manufacturing of a good or delivery of a service.* Exhibit 8.1 shows a typical product layout used in wine-making. Product layouts support a smooth and logical flow where all goods or services move in a continuous path from one process stage to the next, using the same sequence of

Facility Layouts in Fitness Centers

Many readers belong to a fitness center, or perhaps have one at their schools. Fitness centers use different layouts, similar to what we might see in manufacturing. Typically, you will see a ***process layout*** that groups free weights, stretching areas, cardio equipment, and strength machines in common areas. If strength machines are arranged in a logical fashion for "circuit training" (where you typically exercise big muscles first), then we have elements of a ***product layout***. We might also see a ***cellular layout***—for instance, when all leg machines, all chest and shoulder machines, and so on are grouped together within a process layout. Cybex, a manufacturer of fitness equipment, offers a "gym planner" application by which one can drag and drop Cybex equipment, furniture, and accessories to design a personal training studio or fitness center (http://www.cybexintl.com/solutions/gymplanner.aspx).

fiphoto/Shutterstock.com

work tasks and activities. You have seen a product layout if you have ever eaten at Subway or Chipotle; the ingredients are arranged in a specific order as you build your sandwich or burrito. Other examples include credit card processing, paper manufacturing, insurance policy processing, and automobile assembly.

> Facility design must be integrated with and support job and process design.

Advantages of product layouts include higher output rates, lower work-in-process inventories, less materials handling, higher labor and equipment utilization, and simple planning and control systems. However, several disadvantages are associated with product layouts. For instance, a breakdown of one piece of equipment can cause the entire process to shut down. In addition, because the layout is determined by the good or service, a change in product design or the introduction of new products may require major changes in the layout; thus, flexibility can be limited. Therefore, product layouts are less flexible and expensive to change. They also usually require more costly, specialized equipment. Finally, and perhaps most important, the jobs in a product-layout facility, such as those on a mass-production line, may provide little job satisfaction. This is primarily because of the high level of division of labor often required, which usually results in monotony. However, this can be avoided by cross-training and frequently rotating job responsibilities (see the box on Cargill Kitchen Solutions later in this chapter).

EXHIBIT 8.1 Product Layout for Wine Manufacturer

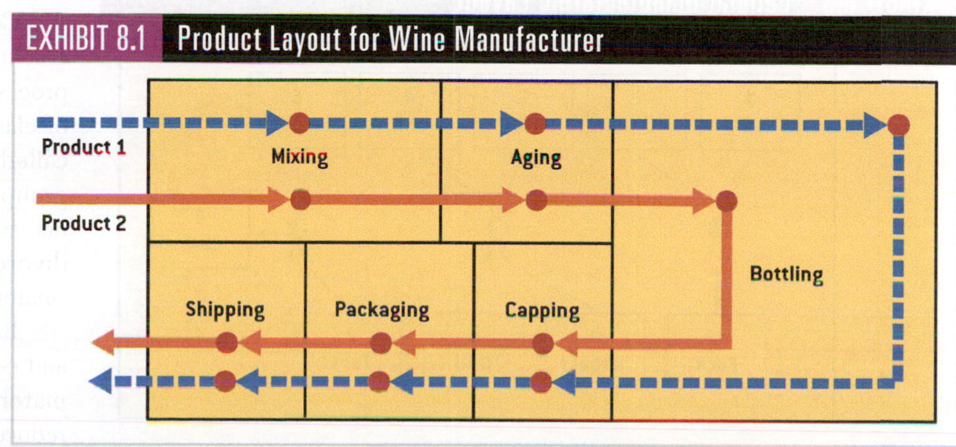

8-1b Process Layout

A **process layout** *consists of a functional grouping of equipment or activities that do similar work.* For example, all drill presses or fax machines may be grouped together in one department, and all milling or data entry machines in another. Depending on the processing they require, tasks may be moved in different sequences among departments (see Exhibit 8.2). Job shops are an example of facilities that use process layouts because they typically handle a wide variety of customized orders. Legal offices, shoe manufacturing, jet engine turbine blades, and hospitals also use process layouts.

Compared to product layouts, process layouts provide more flexibility and generally require a lower investment in equipment. If a piece of equipment fails, it generally does not affect the entire system. Also, the diversity of jobs inherent in a process layout can lead to increased worker satisfaction. Some of the limitations of process layouts are low equipment utilization, high materials-handling costs, more complicated planning and control systems, and higher worker skill requirements.

8-1c Cellular Layout

In a **cellular layout,** *the design is not according to the functional characteristics of equipment, but rather is based on self-contained groups of equipment (called cells) needed for producing a particular set of goods or services.* The cellular concept was developed at the Toyota Motor Company.

An example of a manufacturing cell is shown in Exhibit 8.3. In this exhibit we see a U-shaped arrangement of machines that is typical of cellular manufacturing. The cell looks similar to a product layout but operates differently. Within the cell, materials move clockwise or counterclockwise from one operation to the next. The cell is designed to operate with one, two, or three employees, depending on the needed output during the day (Exhibit 8.3 shows how three operators might be assigned to machines). Each operator is responsible for loading the parts on the individual machine, performing the processing operation, unloading the parts, and moving them to the next operation. Working in parallel, they increase the output from the cell.

EXHIBIT 8.2 Process Layout for a Machine Shop

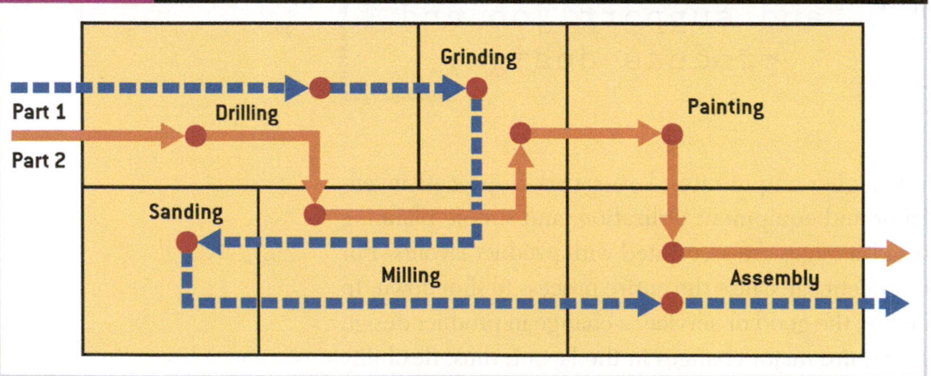

Part 1
Part 2
Drilling
Grinding
Painting
Sanding
Milling
Assembly

EXHIBIT 8.3 Cellular Manufacturing Layout

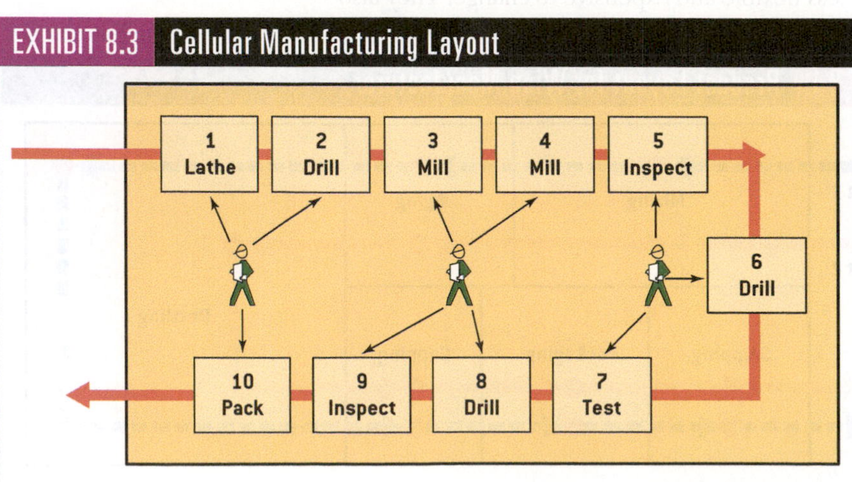

Cellular layouts facilitate the processing of families of parts with similar processing requirements. The procedure of classifying parts into such families is called *group technology*. Services also group work analogous to manufacturers, such as legal (labor law, bankruptcy, divorce, etc.) or medical specialties (maternity, oncology, surgery, etc.).

Because the workflow is standardized and centrally located in a cellular layout, materials-handling requirements are reduced, enabling workers to concentrate on production rather than on moving parts between machines. Quicker response to quality problems within cells can improve the overall level of quality. Because machines are closely linked within a cell, additional floor space becomes available for other productive uses. Because workers have greater responsibility in a cellular manufacturing system, they become more aware of their contribution to the final product; this increases their morale and satisfaction and, ultimately, quality and productivity.

Cellular Manufacturing at Louis Vuitton

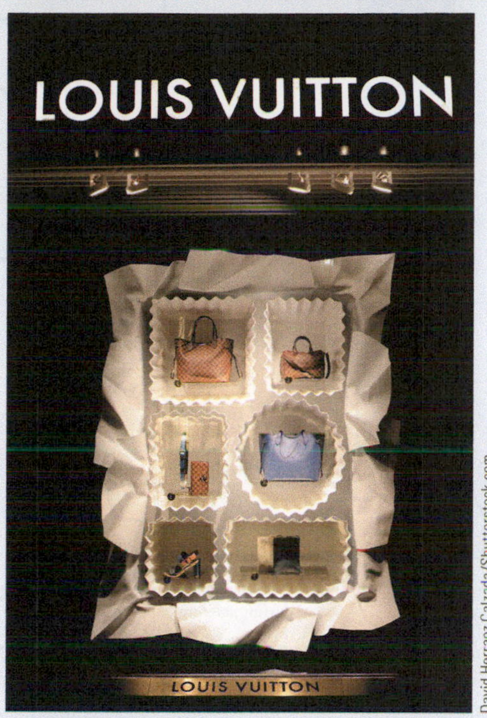

David Herraez Calzada/Shutterstock.com

Louis Vuitton is one of the world's most recognizable luxury brands and has grown significantly in recent years. When Vuitton was building a new factory in Marsaz, France, it had to find ways to increase production in its existing factories. Luxury bags are produced in low volume, but the production process can benefit from recognizing the common features across items and making sure that work is coordinated. By reorganizing teams of about 10 workers in U-shaped clusters, Vuitton was able to free up 10 percent more floor space in its factories and was able to hire 300 new people without increasing facility size. At Vuitton's shoe factory in Italy, robots now fetch the foot molds around which a shoe is made, instead of workers walking back and forth from their workstations to the shelves, resulting in a considerable gain in time.[2]

8-1d Fixed-Position Layout

A ***fixed-position layout*** *consolidates the resources necessary to manufacture a good or deliver a service, such as people, materials, and equipment, in one physical location.* Rather than moving work-in-process from one work center to another, it remains stationary. The production of large items such as heavy machine tools, airplanes, buildings, locomotives, and ships is usually accomplished in a fixed-position layout. This fixed-position layout is synonymous with the "project" classification of processes. Service-providing firms also use fixed-position layouts; examples include major hardware and software installations, sporting events, and concerts. Fixed-position layouts usually require a high level of planning and control compared with other types of layouts.

Exhibit 8.4 summarizes the relative features of product, process, cellular, and fixed-position layouts. It is clear that the basic trade-off in selecting among these layout types is flexibility versus productivity.

8-1e Facility Layout in Service Organizations

Service organizations use product, process, cellular, and fixed-position layouts to organize different types of work. For example, looking back at Exhibit 5.12, which shows the typical LensCrafters facility layout, we see the customer-contact area is arranged in a process layout.

EXHIBIT 8.4 Comparison of Basic Layout Patterns

Characteristic	Product Layout	Process Layout	Cellular Layout	Fixed-Position Layout
Demand volume	High	Low	Moderate	Very low
Equipment utilization	High	Low	High	Moderate
Automation potential	High	Moderate	High	Moderate
Setup/changeover requirements	High	Moderate	Low	High
Flexibility	Low	High	Moderate	Moderate
Type of equipment	Highly specialized	General purpose	Moderate specialization	Moderate specialization

EXHIBIT 8.5 Product Layout for a Pizza Kitchen

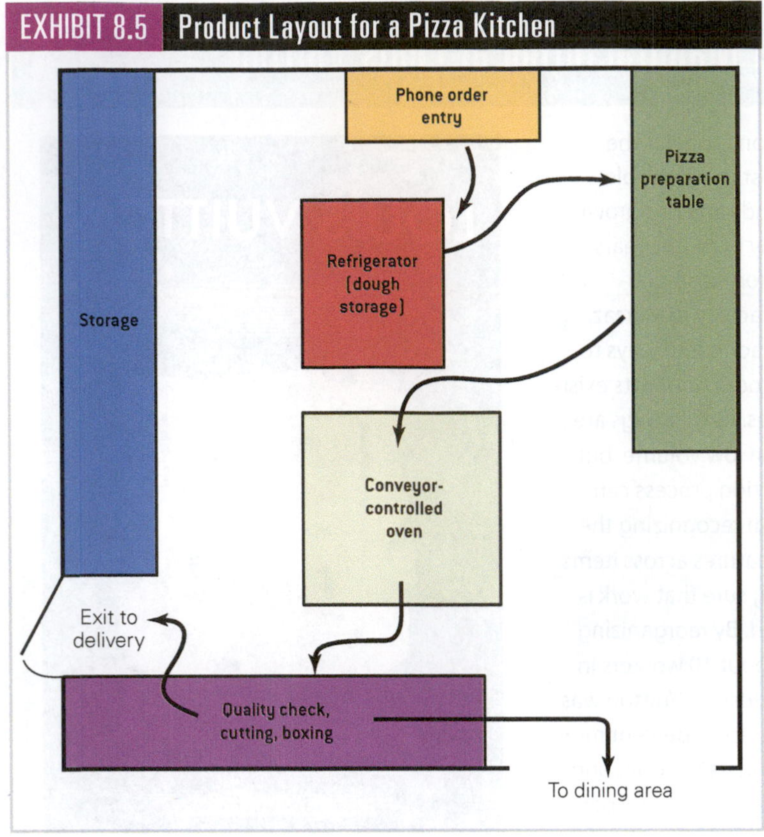

In the lab area, however, where lenses are manufactured, a cellular layout is used. (Also, see the box titled "Facility Layouts in Fitness Centers.")

In service organizations, the basic trade-off between product and process layouts concerns the degree of specialization versus flexibility. Services must consider the volume of demand, range of the types of services offered, degree of personalization of the service, skills of employees, and cost. Those that need the ability to provide a wide variety of services to customers with differing requirements usually use a process layout. For example, libraries place reference materials, serials, and microfilms into separate areas; hospitals group services by function also, such as maternity, oncology, surgery, and X-ray; and insurance companies have office layouts in which claims, underwriting, and filing are individual departments.

Service organizations that provide highly standardized services tend to use product layouts. For example, Exhibit 8.5 shows the layout of the kitchen at a small pizza restaurant that has both dine-in and delivery.

The design of service facilities requires the clever integration of layout with the servicescape and process design to support service encounters. At Victoria's Secret, the layout of a typical store is defined by different zones, each with a certain type of apparel, such as women's sleepwear and intimate apparel, and personal-care products. Display case placement in the store is carefully planned. A companion store, Victoria's Secret Perfume, which specializes in fragrances, color cosmetics, skincare, and personal accessories, is often placed next to and connected to a Victoria's Secret store to increase traffic and sales in both stores.

Sorbis/Shutterstock.com

8-2 Designing Product Layouts

Product layouts in flow shops generally consist of a fixed sequence of workstations. Workstations are generally separated by buffers (queues of work-in-process) to store work waiting for processing, and are often linked by gravity conveyors (which cause parts to simply roll to the end and stop) to allow easy transfer of work.

An example is shown in Exhibit 8.6. Such product layouts, however, can suffer from two sources of delay: flow-blocking delay and lack-of-work delay. **Flow-blocking delay** *(or blocking delay) occurs when a work center completes a unit but cannot release it because the in-process storage at the next stage is full*. The worker must remain idle until storage space becomes available. **Lack-of-work delay** *occurs whenever one stage completes work and no units from the previous stage are awaiting processing*. Lack-of-work delay is often described as "starving" the immediate successor workstation. Such delays cause bottlenecks, which we defined in Chapter 7, limiting the throughput of the entire process. It is important to identify any bottlenecks if process improvements are to be made.

These sources of delay can be minimized by attempting to "balance" the process by designing the appropriate level of capacity at each workstation. This is often done by adding additional workstations in parallel. Product layouts might have workstations in series, in parallel, or in a combination of both. Thus, many different configurations of workstations and buffers are possible, and it is a challenge to design the right one.

An important type of product layout is an assembly line. *An* **assembly line** *is a product layout dedicated to combining the components of a good or service that has been created previously*. Assembly lines were pioneered by Henry Ford and are vital to economic prosperity and are the backbone of many industries such as automobiles and appliances; their efficiencies lower costs and make goods and services affordable to mass markets. Assembly lines are also important in many service operations such as processing laundry, insurance policies, mail, and financial transactions.

8-2a Assembly-Line Balancing

The sequence of tasks required to assemble a product is generally dictated by its physical design. Clearly, you cannot put the cap on a ballpoint pen until the ink has been inserted. However, for many assemblies that consist of a large number of tasks, there are many ways to group tasks together into individual workstations while still ensuring the proper sequence of work. **Assembly-line balancing** *is a technique to group tasks among workstations so that each workstation has—in the ideal case—the same amount of work*. Assembly-line balancing focuses on organizing work efficiently in flow shops.

For example, if it took 90 seconds per unit to assemble an alarm clock, and the work was divided evenly among three workstations, then each workstation would be assigned 30 seconds of work content per unit. Here, there is no idle time per workstation, and the output of the first workstation immediately becomes the input to the next workstation. Technically, there is no bottleneck workstation, and the flow of clocks through the assembly line is constant and continuous. In reality, this is seldom possible, so the objective is to minimize the imbalance among workstations while trying to achieve a desired output rate. A good balance results in achieving throughput necessary to meet sales commitments and minimize the cost of operations. Typically, one either

> Assembly-line balancing focuses on organizing work efficiently in flow shops.

EXHIBIT 8.6 A Typical Manufacturing Workstation Layout

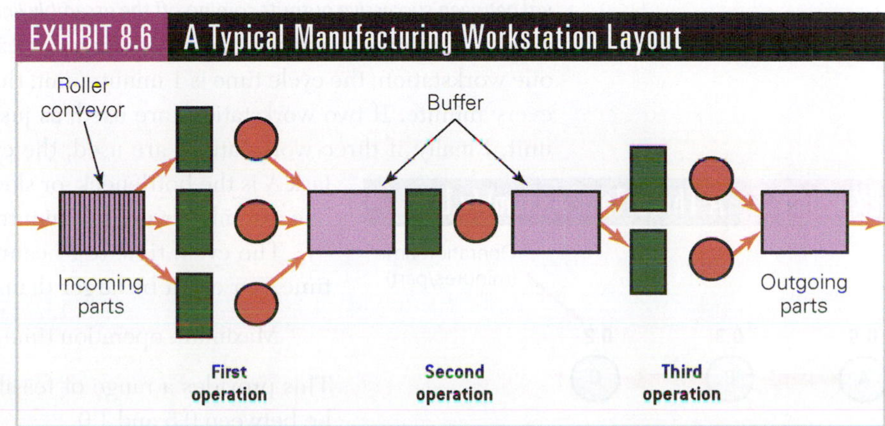

minimizes the number of workstations for a given production rate or maximizes the production rate for a given number of workstations.

To begin, we need to know three types of information:

1. The set of tasks to be performed and the time required to perform each task.
2. The precedence relations among the tasks—that is, the sequence in which tasks must be performed.
3. The desired output rate or forecast of demand for the assembly line.

The first two can be obtained from an analysis of the design specifications of a good or service. The third is primarily a management policy issue, because management must decide whether to produce exactly to the forecast, overproduce and hold inventory, subcontract, and so on.

To illustrate the issues associated with assembly-line balancing, let us consider an activity consisting of three tasks, as shown in Exhibit 8.7. Task A is first, takes 0.5 minute, and must be completed before task B can be performed. After task B, which takes 0.3 minute, is finished, task C can be performed; it takes 0.2 minute. Because all three tasks must be performed to complete one part, the total time required to complete one part is $0.5 + 0.3 + 0.2 = 1.0$ minute.

Suppose that one worker performs all three tasks in sequence. In an 8-hour day, he or she could produce (1 part/1.0 min) (60 minutes per hour) (8 hours per day) = 480 parts/day. Hence, the capacity of the process is 480 parts/day.

Alternatively, suppose that three workers are assigned to the line, each performing one of the three tasks. The first operator can produce 120 parts per hour, as his or her task time is 0.5 minute. Thus, a total of (1 part/0.5 min) (60 minutes per hour) (8 hours per day) = 960 parts/day could be sent to operator 2. Because the time operator 2 needs for his or her operation is only 0.3 minute, he or she could produce (1 part/0.3 min) (60 minutes per hour) (8 hours per day) = 1,600 parts/day. However, operator 2 cannot do so because the first operator has a lower production rate. The second operator will be idle some of the time waiting on components to arrive. Even though the third operator can produce (1 part/0.2 min) (60 minutes per hour) (8 hours per day) = 2,400 parts/day, we see that the maximum output of this three operator assembly line is 960 parts per day. That is, workstation 1 performing task A is the bottleneck in the process.

A third alternative is to use two workstations. The first operator could perform operation A while the second performs operations B and C. Because each operator needs 0.5 minute to perform the assigned duties, the line is in perfect balance, and 960 parts per day can be produced. We can achieve the same output rate with two operators as we can with three, thus saving labor costs. How work tasks and activities are grouped into workstations is important in terms of process capacity (through-put), cost, and time to do the work.

An important concept in assembly-line balancing is the cycle time. **Cycle time** *is the interval between successive outputs coming off the assembly line*. These could be manufactured goods or service-related outcomes. In the three-operation example shown in Exhibit 8.7, if we use only one workstation, the cycle time is 1 minute/unit; that is, one completed assembly is produced every minute. If two workstations are used, as just described, the cycle time is 0.5 minute/unit. Finally, if three workstations are used, the cycle time is still 0.5 minute/unit, because task A is the bottleneck, or slowest operation. The line can produce only one assembly every 0.5 minute.

EXHIBIT 8.7 A Three-Task Assembly Line

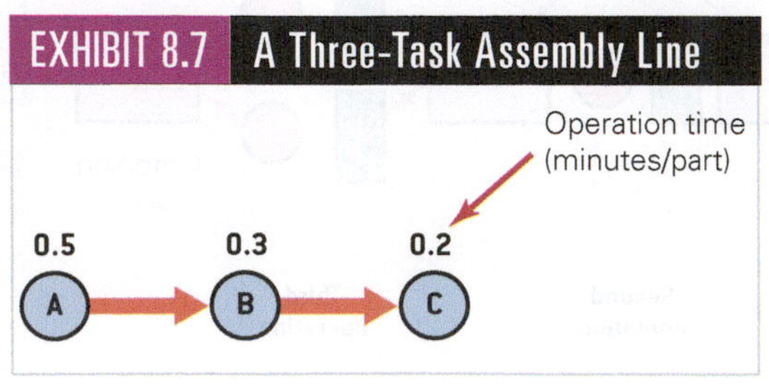

The cycle time (CT) cannot be smaller than the largest operation time, nor can it be larger than the sum of all operation times (Σt). Thus,

$$\text{Maximum operation time} \le CT \le \text{Sum of operation times} \qquad [8.1]$$

This provides a range of feasible cycle times. In the example, CT must be between 0.5 and 1.0.

Cycle time is related to the output required to be produced in some period of time (R) by the following equation:

$$CT = A/R \quad [8.2]$$

where A = available time to produce the output. R is normally the demand forecast. Thus, if we specify a required output (demand forecast), we can calculate the maximum cycle time needed to achieve it. Note that if the required cycle time is smaller than the largest task time, then the work content must be redefined by splitting some tasks into smaller elements.

For a given cycle time, we may also compute the theoretical minimum number of workstations required:

$$\text{Minimum number of workstations required} = \text{Sum of task times/Cycle time} = \Sigma t/CT \quad [8.3]$$

When this number is a fraction, the theoretical minimum number of workstations should be rounded up to the next highest integer. For example, for a cycle time of 0.5, we would need at least 1.0/0.5 = 2 workstations.

The following equations provide additional information about the performance of an assembly line:

$$\text{Total time available} = (\text{Number of workstations})(\text{Cycle time}) = (N)(CT) \quad [8.4]$$

$$\text{Total idle time} = (N)(CT) - \Sigma t \quad [8.5]$$

$$\text{Assembly-line efficiency} = \Sigma t/(N \times CT) \quad [8.6]$$

$$\text{Balance delay} = 1 - \text{Assembly-line efficiency} \quad [8.7]$$

The total time available computed by Equation 8.4 represents the total productive capacity that management pays for. Idle time is the difference between total time available and the sum of the actual times for productive tasks as given by Equation 8.5. Assembly-line efficiency, computed by Equation 8.6, specifies the fraction of available productive capacity that is used. One minus efficiency represents the amount of idle time that results from imbalance among workstations and is called the *balance delay*, as given by Equation 8.7.

SOLVED PROBLEM 8.1: COMPUTING ASSEMBLY LINE PERFORMANCE MEASURES

Bass Fishing Inc. assembles fishing reels in an assembly line using six workstations. Management wants an output rate of 300 reels per day (with a 7.5-hour workday). The sum of the task times is eight minutes/reel. Find the cycle time, total time available, total idle time, assembly line efficiency, and balance delay.

Solution:

Use Equations 8.2–8.7.

Cycle time = $CT = A/R$ = [(7.5 hours/day)(60 minutes/hour)]/(300 reels/day) = 450/300 = 1.5 minutes/reel

Total time available = (number of workstations)(cycle time) = $(N)(CT)$ = (6)(1.5) = 9.0 minutes

Total idle time = $(N)(CT) - \Sigma t$ = (6)(1.5) − 8 = 1 minute/reel

Assembly-line efficiency = $\Sigma t/(N \times CT)$ = 8/(6 × 1.5) = 0.889, or 88.9%

Balance delay = 1 − Assembly-line efficiency = 1 − 0.889 = 0.111, or 11.1%

Management is paying for eight minutes of work and one minute of idle time per reel.

In Solved Problem 8.1, suppose that we use seven workstations. The total time available is 7(1.5) = 10.5 minutes; the total idle time is 10.5 − 8 = 2.5 minutes; and the line efficiency is reduced to 8/10.5 = 0.76. One objective of assembly-line balancing is to maximize the line efficiency. Note that if we use only six workstations, the total time available is 5(1.5) = 7.5 minutes. Because this is less than the sum of the task times, it would be impossible to achieve the desired output rate of 300 reels per day.

8-2b Line-Balancing Approaches

Balancing the three-task example in the previous section was quite easy to do by inspection. With a large number of tasks, the number of possible workstation configurations can be very large, making the balancing problem very complex. Decision rules, or heuristics, are used to assign tasks to workstations. Because heuristics cannot guarantee the best solution, one often applies a variety of different rules in an attempt to find a very good solution among several alternatives. For large line-balancing problems, such decision rules are incorporated into computerized algorithms and simulation models.

To illustrate a simple, yet effective, approach to balancing an assembly line, suppose that we are producing an in-line skate, as shown in Exhibit 8.8. The target output rate is 360 units per week. The effective workday (assuming one shift) is 7.2 hours, considering breaks and lunch periods. We will assume that the facility operates five days per week.

Eight tasks are required to assemble the individual parts. These, along with task times, are

1. Assemble wheels, bearings, and axle hardware (2.0 min).
2. Assemble brake housing and pad (0.2 min).
3. Complete wheel assembly (1.5 min).
4. Inspect wheel assembly (0.5 min).
5. Assemble boot (3.5 min).
6. Join boot and wheel subassemblies (1.0 min).
7. Add line and final assembly (0.2 min).
8. Perform final inspection (0.5 min).

We can use the task times to compute a range of feasible cycle times. This is done by assuming that (1) only one workstation is used for the entire assembly, and (2) each task is assigned to a unique workstation. For instance, if we use only one workstation for the entire assembly and assign all tasks to it, the cycle time is 9.4 minutes. Alternatively, if each task is assigned to a unique workstation, the cycle time is 3.5, the largest task time. Thus, feasible cycle times must be between 3.5 and 9.4 minutes.

EXHIBIT 8.8 A Typical In-Line Skate

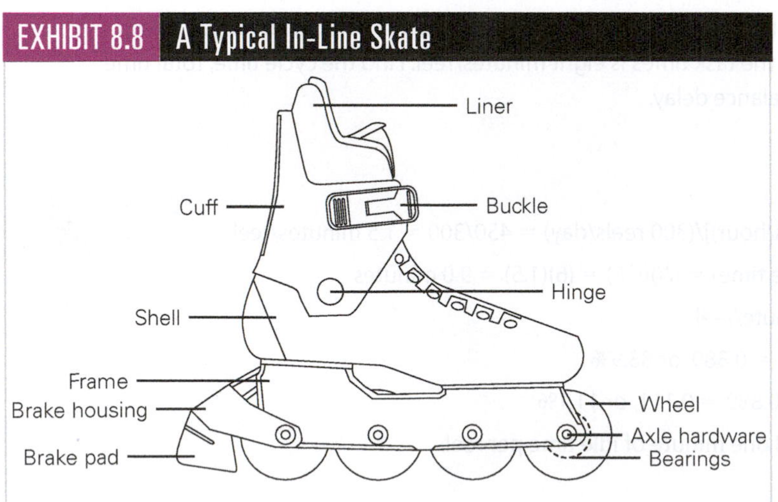

However, the cycle time depends on how many units we need to produce and how much time is available. For a target output rate, we can use Equations 8.2 and 8.3 to find the theoretical minimum number of workstations needed for balancing the assembly line. Solved Problem 8.2 shows how to do this.

The eight tasks need not be performed in this exact order; however, it is important to ensure that certain precedence restrictions are met. For example, you cannot perform the wheel assembly

SOLVED PROBLEM 8.2: COMPUTING THE MINIMUM NUMBER OF WORKSTATIONS REQUIRED

Suppose that we need to produce 360 units per week by operating one shift per day for five days per week. The effective workday (assuming one shift) is 7.2 hours, considering breaks and lunch periods. What is the minimum number of workstations needed?

Solution:

First, use Equation 8.2 to find the appropriate cycle time:

$CT = A/R$ = [(7.2 hours/shift)(60 min/hour]/[(360 units/week)/(5 shifts/week)] = 6.0 minutes/unit

The theoretical minimum number of workstations is found using Equation 8.3:

$\Sigma t/CT = 9.4/6.0 = 1.57$ or, rounded up, 2 workstations.

(task 3) until both tasks 1 and 2 have been completed, but it does not matter whether task 1 or task 2 is performed first because they are independent of each other. These types of relationships are usually developed through an engineering analysis of the product. We can represent them by an arrow diagram, shown in Exhibit 8.9. The arrows indicate what tasks must precede others. Thus, the arrow pointing from tasks 1 and 2 to task 3 indicate that tasks 1 and 2 must be completed before task 3 is performed; similarly, task 3 must precede task 4. The numbers next to each task represent the task times.

This precedence network helps visually determine whether a workstation assignment is *feasible*—that is, meets the precedence restrictions. For example, in Exhibit 8.9 we might assign tasks 1, 2, 3, and 4 to one workstation, and tasks 5, 6, 7, and 8 to a second workstation, as illustrated by the shading. This is feasible because all tasks assigned to workstation 1 are completed before those assigned to workstation 2. However, we could not assign tasks 1, 2, 3, 4, and 6 to workstation, 1, and tasks 5, 7, and 8 to workstation 2, because operation 5 must precede operation 6.

The problem is to assign the eight work activities to workstations without violating precedence or exceeding the cycle time of 6.0. Different rules may be used to assign tasks to workstations. For example, one line-balancing decision rule example is to assign the task with the *longest task time first* to a workstation if the cycle time would not be exceeded. The longest-task-time-first decision rule assigns tasks with long task times first, because shorter task times are easier to fit in the line balance later

Cycle Times and Economic Cycles

When the global economic crisis hit a few years ago, demand for automobiles fell dramatically. As a result, automobile manufacturers needed to reduce production. One way they did so was to change the cycle time for their auto assembly plants. For example, General Motors announced that the factory making the Chevrolet Silverado and GMC Sierra pickup trucks would operate only one shift and change its line speed from 55 to 24 trucks per hour. "We don't need excess inventory out there," GM spokesman Chris Lee said. He also said, "We adjust up and down to the market."[3]

EXHIBIT 8.9 Precedence Network and Workstation Assignment

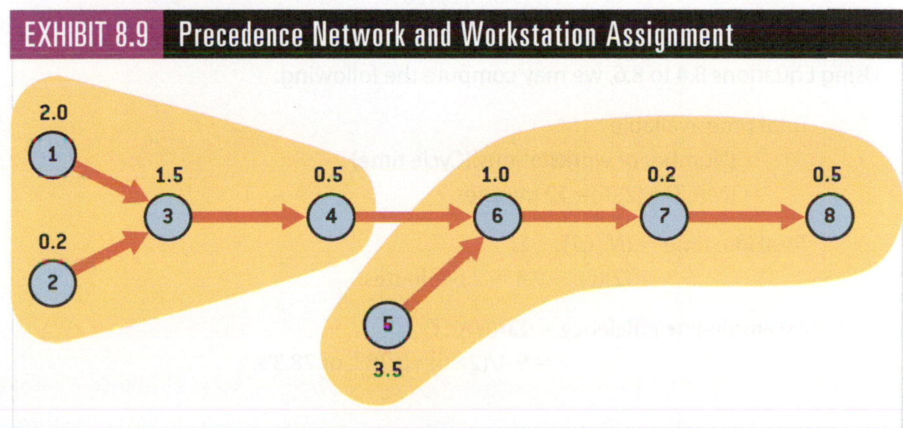

in the procedure. Another rule might be to assign the shortest task first. These rules attempt to minimize the amount of idle time at workstations, but they are heuristics and do not guarantee optimal solutions.

The longest-task-time rule can be formalized as follows:

1. Choose a set of "assignable tasks"—those for which all immediate predecessors have already been assigned.
2. Assign the assignable task with the *longest* task time first. Break ties by choosing the lowest task number.
3. Construct a new set of assignable candidates. If no further tasks can be assigned, move on to the next workstation. Continue in this way until all tasks have been assigned.

In the assembly line configuration in Solved Problem 8.3, efficiency is not very high because the precedence relationships constrained the possible line-balancing solutions. The target efficiency for most assembly lines is 80 to 90 percent, but this is

SOLVED PROBLEM 8.3 BALANCING THE IN-LINE SKATE ASSEMBLY LINE

Use the longest task time first line-balancing decision rule to balance the in-line skate assembly line problem depicted in Exhibit 8.9.

Solution:

We will call the first workstation "A" and determine which tasks can be assigned. In this case, tasks 1, 2, and 5 are candidates, as they have no immediate predecessors. Using the decision rule—*choose the activity with the longest task time first*—we therefore assign task 5 to workstation A.

Next, we determine a new set of tasks that may be considered for assignment. At this point, we may only choose among tasks 1 and 2 (even though task 5 has been assigned, we cannot consider task 6 as a candidate because task 4 has not yet been assigned to a workstation). Note that we can assign both tasks 1 and 2 to workstation A without violating the cycle time restriction.

At this point, task 3 becomes the only candidate for assignment. Because the total time for tasks 5, 1, and 2 is 5.7 minutes, we cannot assign task 3 to workstation A without violating the cycle time restriction of 6.0 minutes. In this case, we move on to workstation B.

At workstation B, the only candidate we can assign next is task 3. Continuing, we can assign tasks 4, 6, 7, and 8 in that order and still be within the cycle time limit. Because all tasks have been assigned to a workstation, we are finished. This assembly-line balance is summarized as follows:

Workstation	Tasks	Total Time	Idle Time
A	1, 2, 5	5.7	0.3
B	3, 4, 6, 7, 8	3.7	2.3
	Total	9.4	2.6

Using Equations 8.4 to 8.6, we may compute the following:

Total time available

$= \text{(Number of workstations)(Cycle time)}$

$= (N)(CT) = (2)(6) = 12 \text{ minutes}$

Total idle time $= (N)(CT) - \Sigma t$

$= (2)(6) - 9.4 = 2.6 \text{ minutes}$

Assembly-line efficiency $= \Sigma t/(N \times CT)$

$= 9.4/(2 \times 6) = 0.783.$ or 78.3%

highly dependent on things like the degree of automation, inspection stations, workforce skills, complexity of the assembly, and so on. One option is to redefine the work content for the assembly task in more detail if this is possible, by breaking down the tasks into smaller elements with smaller task times and rebalancing the line, hoping to achieve a higher efficiency.

In the real world, assembly-line balancing is quite complicated because of the size of practical problems as well as constraints that mechanization or tooling place on work tasks. Also, in today's manufacturing plants, there is virtually no such thing as a single-model assembly line. In the automotive industry, many model combinations and work assignments exist. Such mixed-model assembly-line-balancing problems are considerably more difficult to solve. Simulation modeling is frequently used to obtain a "best set" of assembly-line-balancing solutions and then engineers, operations managers, and suppliers evaluate and critique these solutions to find the best design.

8-3 Designing Process Layouts

In designing process layouts, we are concerned with the arrangement of departments or work centers relative to each other. Two major approaches are commonly used. The first focuses on the costs associated with moving materials or the inconvenience that customers might experience in moving between physical locations. This approach is widely used in manufacturing. In general, work centers with a large number of moves between them should be located close to one another. This approach usually starts with an initial layout and data on the historical or forecasted volume between departments and the materials-handling costs. The centroid of each department, which is the geometric center of the shape, is used to compute distances and materials-handling costs for a particular layout. In an effort to improve the current solution, exchanges between the locations of two or three departments at a time are made, and the new total cost is calculated. If the total cost has been reduced, then this solution is used to examine other location changes in an effort to reduce the total cost.

The second approach is used when it is difficult to obtain data on costs or volumes moved between departments. This approach is useful in many service applications such as offices, laboratories, retail stores, and so on. Rather than using materials-handling costs as the primary criterion, the user constructs a preference table that specifies how important it is for two departments to be close to one another. An example of such "closeness ratings" follows:

A Absolutely necessary
B Especially important
C Important
D Ordinary closeness okay
E Unimportant
F Undesirable

Using these ratings, the approach attempts to optimize the total closeness rating of the layout.

Computer graphics and design software are providing a major advance in layout planning. They allow interactive design of layouts in real time and can eliminate some of the disadvantages, such as irregularly shaped departments, that often result from manual design on a block grid. Despite the capabilities of the computer, no layout program will provide optimal solutions for large, realistic problems. Like many practical solution procedures in management science, they are heuristic; that is, they can help the user to find a very good, but not necessarily the optimal, solution.

8-4 Work Measurement

To effectively design facilities, workplaces, and jobs, managers need to determine the times to perform various tasks and work activities. How long it takes to perform a task depends on the worker's pace, operating conditions, and work method used. **Work measurement** *is a systematic procedure for the analysis of work, and determination of standard times required to perform key tasks in a process. A* **standard time** *is a reasonable estimate of the amount of time needed to perform a task based on an analysis of the work by a trained industrial engineer or other operations expert.* Work measurement is used for

- estimating work-force and equipment capacity,
- identifying task times for assembly line balancing,
- establishing budgets,
- determining what new work procedures will cost,
- evaluating time and cost tradeoffs among process design alternatives,
- establishing wage-incentive systems,
- monitoring and evaluating employee performance and productivity, and
- providing accurate information for scheduling and sequencing.

Without accurate time standards, it is impossible to perform these tasks.

Work measurement relies on time studies. *A* **time study** *is the development of a standard time by observing a task with the use of a stopwatch and analyzing the data.* A time study consists of the following steps:

1. *Define each task that comprises a job or work activity.* Often, small tasks are grouped together.
2. *Measure and record the time needed to perform each task for multiple samples.* A trained observer with a stopwatch usually does this. Multiple observations are used to smooth out variations in performing the tasks. Sample sizes can be determined statistically (see Supplement A: Probability and Statistics).
3. *Rate the employee's performance of each task.* This means determining if a worker is performing a task at a normal pace—one that can be consistently performed by an average employee without undue fatigue—or faster or slower than normal. This is measured by a performance rating factor (PRF). A PRF of 100 percent (or 1.0) is a normal pace.
4. *Compute the normal time for each task.* Normal time is the expected time required to perform some work activity at a normal pace, under normal operating conditions, and using a prescribed method.
5. *Determine allowances for fatigue, personal time, unavoidable delays, and so on.*
6. *Determine the standard time by adjusting for the allowance.*

Normal times are calculated using the following equation:

$$\begin{aligned}\text{Normal Time} &= \text{Observed time (OT)} \times \text{Performance Rating Factor (PRF)}\\ &= \text{OT} \times \text{PRF}\end{aligned} \quad [8.8]$$

Allowances *include time for labor fatigue and personal needs, equipment breakdowns, rest periods, information delays, and so on.* Most allowance factors are in the range of 10 to 20 percent. By adjusting the normal time for allowances, we determine the standard time. It is computed using the following equation:

$$\text{Standard time} = \text{Normal time} \times (1 + \text{Allowance Factor}) \quad [8.9]$$

Solved Problem 8.4 illustrates how to compute standard times. In Solved Problem 8.5, we show how to use an Excel template to perform a work measurement study.

SOLVED PROBLEM 8.4: COMPUTING STANDARD TIME

Suppose that work study analyst A rates an employee at PRF = 1.2 and an observed time of 2.5 minutes per unit, B rates the same employee at PRF = 1.0 and an observed time of 2.2 minutes per unit, and C rates the same employee at PRF = 0.9 and an observed time of 2.1 minutes per unit. What should the standard time be, assuming an allowance factor of 20 percent?

Solution:

The normal time for each analyst is found using Equation 8.8:

Normal Time = Observed time (OT) × Performance Rating Factor (PRF) = OT × PRF

Analyst	OT	PRF	Normal Time
A	2.5	1.2	3.00
B	2.2	1.0	2.20
C	2.1	0.9	1.89

Averaging these values, we use a normal time of 7.09/3 = 2.363 minutes per unit. If the allowance factor is 20 percent, then the standard time is found using Equation 8.9:

Standard time = Normal time × (1 + Allowance Factor) = 2.363 × 1.2 = 2.836 minutes per unit.

SOLVED PROBLEM 8.5: A WORK MEASUREMENT STUDY FOR A FAUCET ASSEMBLY

We will consider a simple manual assembly process of assembling a faucet stem that consists of four parts: a housing, stem, washer, and screw. An observational study of the assembly process identified six work elements in the assembly process and the performance rating factors:

1. Get housing and stem (PRF = 1.0).
2. Screw in stem (PRF = 1.1).
3. Get and insert washer (PRF = 1.0).
4. Get and insert screw (PRF = 1.0).
5. Tighten screw (PRF = 0.97).
6. Place completed assembly in tray (PRF = 1.0).

Ten observations of this assembly task were taken and shown in Exhibit 8.10 using continuous timing. **Continuous timing** *involves starting the clock at the beginning of each observation and recording the cumulative time at the completion of each work task.* This is easier to do with a stopwatch than trying to reset it for every work element. The actual task times for each work element can be found by subtracting successive cumulative times. Take the first observation. The first work element, "Get housing and stem," was completed in 0.03 minutes; this is the actual time to perform this task. The second work element, "Screw in stem," was completed in a cumulative time of 0.13 minutes; thus, the actual time for this task was 0.13 – 0.03 = 0.10 minutes. We also assume a five percent personal allowance, five percent fatigue allowance, and 10 percent delay of materials allowance. Thus, the total allowance factor is 20 percent.

What is the standard time for this assembly task? How many assemblies can be expected to be completed each work day, assuming an eight-hour day with one hour off for lunch and breaks?

Solution:

An Excel template for work measurement is available in MindTap that can be used for a typical work measurement study when continuous timing is used. Exhibit 8.11 shows its application for the faucet stem assembly study. The work element times for all observations are added and averaged to obtain the mean time for each work element. Performance ratings are given in column C. By multiplying the performance-rating factor by the average observed time, we obtain the normal time for each work task and add them. Next the allowances are determined to compute the standard time.

The standard time for the faucet assembly job is 0.660 minutes per faucet assembly. Thus, an assembler of faucet-stem assemblies can be expected to produce at a standard rate of 1/.660 parts per minute, or about 91 parts per hour. In an eight-hour workday, with one hour off for lunch and breaks, an assembler can produce (91 parts per hour)(7 hours) = 637 faucet stem assemblies per workday.

EXHIBIT 8.10 Assembly Task Time Observations (minutes)

Get housing and stem									
0.03	0.03	0.02	0.03	0.04	0.03	0.04	0.04	0.03	0.03
Screw in stem									
0.13	0.15	0.14	0.16	0.13	0.12	0.14	0.16	0.15	0.13
Get and insert washer									
0.24	0.25	0.26	0.29	0.23	0.21	0.24	0.26	0.27	0.22
Get and insert screw									
0.32	0.33	0.36	0.38	0.33	0.30	0.32	0.33	0.37	0.31
Tighten screw									
0.48	0.50	0.54	0.53	0.50	0.45	0.51	0.52	0.58	0.49
Place assembly in tray									
0.51	0.53	0.58	0.56	0.54	0.49	0.54	0.55	0.62	0.52

EXHIBIT 8.11 Excel Template *Work Measurement*

	A	B	C	D	E	F	G	H	I	J	K	L	M	N	O	P	Q	R	S	T
1	Work Measurement											Copyright © 2017 Cengage Learning								
2	Enter data only in yellow-shaded cells. This template is designed for up to 10 work elements.											Not for commercial use.								
3																				
4																	Normal		Allowances	20%
5		Work element	Rating	Observation	1	2	3	4	5	6	7	8	9	10	Sum	Average	Time			
6	1	Get housing and stem	1.00	Cumulative time	0.03	0.03	0.02	0.03	0.04	0.03	0.04	0.04	0.03	0.03					Standard Time	0.66
7				Element time	0.03	0.03	0.02	0.03	0.04	0.03	0.04	0.04	0.03	0.03	0.32	0.03	0.032			
8	2	Screw in stem	1.10	Cumulative time	0.13	0.15	0.14	0.16	0.13	0.12	0.14	0.16	0.15	0.13						
9				Element time	0.10	0.12	0.12	0.13	0.09	0.09	0.10	0.12	0.12	0.10	1.09	0.11	0.120			
10	3	Get and insert washer	1.00	Cumulative time	0.24	0.25	0.26	0.29	0.23	0.21	0.24	0.26	0.27	0.22						
11				Element time	0.11	0.10	0.12	0.13	0.10	0.09	0.10	0.10	0.12	0.09	1.06	0.11	0.106			
12	4	Get and insert screw	1.00	Cumulative time	0.32	0.33	0.36	0.38	0.33	0.30	0.32	0.33	0.37	0.31						
13				Element time	0.08	0.08	0.10	0.09	0.10	0.09	0.08	0.07	0.10	0.09	0.88	0.09	0.088			
14	5	Tighten screw	0.97	Cumulative time	0.48	0.50	0.54	0.53	0.50	0.45	0.51	0.52	0.58	0.49						
15				Element time	0.16	0.17	0.18	0.15	0.17	0.15	0.19	0.19	0.21	0.18	1.75	0.18	0.170			
16	6	Place assembly in tray	1.00	Cumulative time	0.51	0.53	0.58	0.56	0.54	0.49	0.54	0.55	0.62	0.52						
17				Element time	0.03	0.03	0.04	0.03	0.04	0.04	0.03	0.03	0.04	0.03	0.34	0.03	0.034			
18	7			Cumulative time																
19				Element time																
20	8			Cumulative time																
21				Element time																
22	9			Cumulative time																
23				Element time																
24	10			Cumulative time																
25				Element time																
26																Sum	0.550			

8-5 Workplace and Job Design

Not only is it important to effectively design the overall facility layout, but it is equally important to focus on the design of individual workstations and the jobs performed by the workforce. A well-designed workplace should allow for maximum efficiency and effectiveness as the work task or activity is performed, and may also need to facilitate service management skills, particularly in high-contact, front-office environments.

8-5a Workplace Design

Key questions that must be addressed in designing the workplace include:

1. *Who will use the workplace?* Will the workstation be shared? How much space is required? Workplace designs must take into account different physical characteristics of individuals, such as differences in size, arm length, strength, and dexterity. For offices, layouts range from open formats to encourage collaboration and relationship building to isolated cubicles and offices with walls and few windows. As described in Chapter 5, defining the office servicescape and service-encounter design are also important.
2. *How will the work be performed?* What tasks are required? How much time does each task take? How much time is required to set up for the workday or for a particular job? How might the tasks be grouped into work activities most effectively? This includes knowing what information, equipment, items, and procedures are required for each task, work activity, and job.
3. *What technology is needed?* Employees may need to use a computer or have access to customer records and files, special equipment, intercoms, tablets, and other forms of technology.
4. *What must the employee be able to see?* Employees might need special fixtures for blueprints, test procedures, sorting paper, antiglare computer screens, and so on.
5. *What must the employee be able to hear?* Employees may need to communicate with others, wear a telephone headset all day, be able to listen for certain sounds during product and laboratory testing, or be able to hear warning sounds.
6. *What environmental and safety issues need to be addressed?* What protective clothing or gear should the employee wear? What is an acceptable noise level? Are all employees trained on emergency evacuation procedures and plans?

To illustrate some of these issues, let us consider the design of the pizza-preparation table for a pizza restaurant. The objective of a design is to maximize throughput—that is, the number of pizzas that can be made—minimize errors in fulfilling customer orders; and minimize total flow time and customer waiting and delivery time. In slow-demand periods, one or two employees may make the entire pizza. During periods of high demand, such as weekends and holidays, more employees may be needed. The workplace design would need to accommodate this.

An example of a pizza-preparation workstation is shown in Exhibit 8.12. Ingredients should be put on the pizzas in the following order: sauce, vegetables (mushrooms, peppers, onions, etc.), cheese, and, finally, meat. Because cheese and meat are the highest-cost items and also greatly affect taste and customer satisfaction, the manager requires that those items be weighed to ensure that the proper amounts are included. All items are arranged in the order of

Operations managers who design jobs for individual workers need to understand how the physical environment can affect people.

EXHIBIT 8.12 Pizza-Preparation Workplace Design

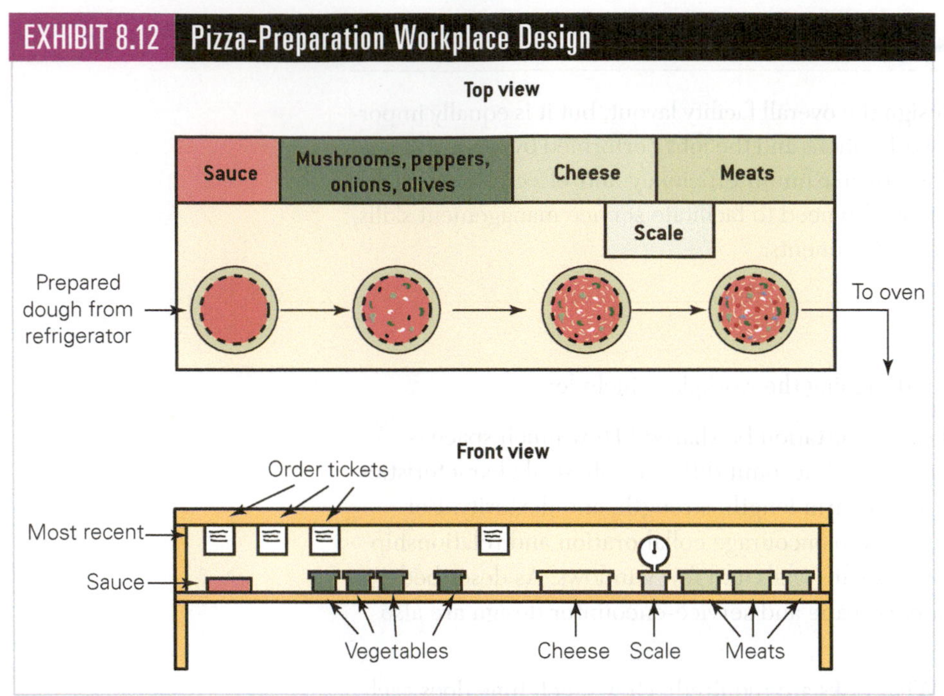

assembly within easy reach of the employee and, as the front view illustrates, order tickets are hung at eye level, with the most recent orders on the left to ensure that pizzas are prepared on a first-come-first-served basis.

In office cubicles, e-mails, telephone calls, cell phones, pagers, and the like interrupt office workers so much that some companies have established "information-free zones" within the office. If you work in one of these zones, all of these interruption devices are turned off or blocked from operating so employees can focus on their work. Companies think information-free zones improve employee attention spans and productivity.

8-5b Job Design

The physical design of a facility and the workplace can influence significantly how workers perform their jobs as well as their psychological well-being. Thus, operations managers who design jobs for individual workers need to understand how the physical environment can affect people. *A* ***job*** *is the set of tasks an individual performs.* ***Job design*** *involves determining the specific job tasks and responsibilities, the work environment, and the methods by which the tasks will be carried out to meet the goals of operations.*

Two broad objectives must be satisfied in job design. One is to meet the firm's competitive priorities—cost, efficiency, flexibility, quality, and so on; the other is to make the job safe, satisfying, and motivating for the worker. Resolving conflicts between the need for technical and economic efficiency and the need for employee satisfaction is the challenge that faces operations managers in designing jobs. Clearly, efficiency improvements are needed to keep a firm competitive. However, it is also clear that any organization with a large percentage of dissatisfied employees cannot be competitive.

What is sought is a job design that provides for high levels of performance and at the same time a satisfying job and work environment. This is true for manufacturing jobs such as working on an assembly line, as well as for service jobs such as working in a lawyer's office or medical clinic.

The relationships between the technology of operations and the social/psychological aspects of work has been understood since the 1950s. It is known as the *sociotechnical approach* to job design and provides useful ideas for operations managers. Sociotechnical approaches to work design provide opportunities for continual learning and personal growth for all employees. ***Job enlargement*** *is the horizontal expansion of the job to give the worker more variety—although not necessarily more responsibility.* Job enlargement might be accomplished, for example, by giving a production-line worker the task of building an entire product rather than a small subassembly, or by job rotation, such as rotating nurses among hospital wards or flight crews on different airline routes.

Cargill Kitchen Solutions: Innovative Job Design

Cargill Kitchen Solutions manufactures and distributes more than 160 different types of egg-based food products to more than 1,200 U.S. food-service operations such as quick-service restaurants, schools, hospitals, convenience stores, and food processors. Although production efficiency requires a product layout design in which each production department is organized into specific work or task areas, Cargill Kitchen Solutions has several innovative strategies to design its work systems to also provide a highly satisfying work environment for its employees. The company uses a rotation system whereby workers rotate to another workstation every 20 minutes. This minimizes stress injuries, fights boredom, reinforces the concept of "internal customers," and provides a way of improving and reinforcing learning. Cargill Kitchen Solutions has led its industry with this workplace design approach since 1990, and OSHA standards were developed that mirror this rotation system.[4]

Job enrichment *is vertical expansion of job duties to give the worker more responsibility*. For instance, an assembly worker may be given the added responsibility of testing a completed assembly, so that he or she acts also as a quality inspector. A highly effective approach to job enrichment is to use teams. Some of the more common ones are:

- natural work teams, which perform entire jobs, rather than specialized, assembly-line work;
- virtual teams, in which members communicate by computer, take turns as leaders, and join and leave the team as necessary; and
- self-managed teams (SMTs), which are empowered work teams that also assume many traditional management responsibilities.

Virtual teams, in particular, have taken on increased importance in today's business world. Information technology provides the ability to assemble virtual teams of people located in different geographic locations.[5] For example, product designers and engineers in the United States can work with counterparts in Japan, transferring files at the end of each work shift to provide an almost continuous product development effort.

Teams not only enrich jobs; they also provide numerous benefits for quality and productivity. For example, it has been noted that medical errors are reduced when doctors and other health care professionals work together in teams. Honda reorganized its product development organization so that sales, manufacturing, research and development, and purchasing associates work together as a team to improve decisions and make them more quickly.

8-5c Safety, Ergonomics, and the Work Environment

> Safety is one of the most important aspects of workplace design, particularly in today's society.

Safety is one of the most important aspects of workplace design, particularly in today's society. To provide safe and healthful working conditions and reduce hazards in the work environment, the Occupational Safety and Health Act (OSHA) was passed in 1970. It requires employers to furnish to each of their employees a place of employment free from recognized hazards that cause or are likely to cause death or serious physical harm. Business and industry must abide by OSHA guidelines or face potential fines and penalties.

Safety is a function of the job, the person performing the job, and the surrounding environment. The job should be designed so that it will be highly unlikely that a worker can injure him- or herself. At the same time, the worker must be educated in the proper use of equipment and the methods designed for performing the job. Finally, the surrounding environment must be conducive to safety. This might include nonslip surfaces, warning signs, buzzers, mirrors, and clearly marked exit signs.

Ergonomics *is concerned with improving productivity and safety by designing workplaces, equipment, instruments, computers, workstations, and so on that take into account the physical capabilities of people.* The objective of ergonomics is to reduce fatigue, the cost of training, human errors, the cost of doing the job, and energy requirements while increasing accuracy, speed, reliability, and flexibility.

Finally, it is important to pay serious attention to the work environment, not only in factories but in every facility where work is performed, such as offices, restaurants, hospitals, and retail stores. A Gallup study showed that the less satisfied workers are with the physical aspects of their work environment, such as temperature, noise, or visual surroundings, the more likely they are to be dissatisfied with their jobs.[6] The study also found that workers who can personalize their workspaces to make it feel like their own were more productive and engaged in their work. Research has shown that bringing the outdoor environment into the workplace lowers stress, and that sunlight improves creativity. The famed architect Frank Gehry used these ideas in Facebook's headquarters, incorporating skylights and a rooftop garden in designing the facility.[7]

8-5d Workforce Ethics and Global Supply Chains

Global supply chains bring a host of new issues related to the design of work. Workers in many countries are bullied, and forced to work excessive hours, for wages on which they can barely survive. Some suppliers have been known to falsify records or substitute inferior materials. Many firms now take ethical work practices much more seriously than before, particularly after many embarrassing revelations of poor working conditions in supply chains were highly publicized.

Ethical trade means that retailers, brands, and their suppliers take responsibility for improving the working conditions of the people who make the products they sell. Most of these workers are employed by supplier companies around the world, many of them based in poor countries where laws designed to protect workers' rights are inadequate or not enforced.

Doing so is simply good business. A study conducted by Software Advice found that, on average, consumers said they would pay 27 percent more for a product normally priced at $100 if it was produced under auspicious (favorable) working conditions. What's more, when asked which of three ethical initiatives would make them more likely to purchase a product, consumers were nearly evenly split among improved working conditions (34 percent), reduced environmental impact (32 percent), and more involvement in the community (31 percent).[8]

The Ethical Trading Initiative (ETI) is a leading alliance of companies, trade unions, and nongovernmental organizations that promotes respect for workers' rights around the globe. Their vision is a world where all workers are free from exploitation and discrimination, and enjoy conditions of freedom, security, and equity. ETI seeks to ensure the following:

1. Employment is freely chosen.
2. Freedom of association and the right to collective bargaining are respected.
3. Working conditions are safe and hygienic.
4. Child labor shall not be used.

5. Living wages are paid.
6. Working hours are not excessive.
7. No discrimination is practiced.
8. Regular employment is provided.
9. No harsh or inhumane treatment is allowed.[9]

These workplace conditions support social sustainability, as described in Exhibit 1.12. Companies must keep track of where their products are being made, and of the working conditions of the people who make them. This is typically done by audits, often by global sourcing managers. Many companies such as Apple and Nike are identifying new buying practices that support rather than undermine suppliers' ability to provide decent pay and conditions for their workers.

CHAPTER 8 LEARNING OBJECTIVE SUMMARIES

8.1 **Identify the objectives of facility design and describe four layout patterns and when they should be used.** Four major layout patterns are commonly used in designing and building processes: product layout, process layout, cellular layout, and fixed-position layout. Product layouts support a smooth and logical flow where all goods or services move in a continuous path from one process stage to the next using the same sequence of work tasks and activities. Job shops are an example of firms that use process layouts to provide flexibility in the products that can be made and the utilization of equipment and labor. Cellular layouts facilitate the processing of families of parts with similar processing requirements. The production of large items such as heavy machine tools, airplanes, buildings, locomotives, and ships is usually accomplished in a fixed-position layout. This fixed-position layout is synonymous with the "project" classification of processes.

Service organizations use product, process, cellular, and fixed-position layouts to organize different types of work. Those that need the ability to provide a wide variety of services to customers with differing requirements usually use a process layout. Service organizations that provide highly standardized services tend to use product layouts.

8.2 **Explain how to design product layouts using assembly-line balancing.** Assembly-line balancing seeks to achieve the throughput necessary to meet sales commitments and minimize the cost of operations. Typically, one either minimizes the number of workstations for a given production rate or maximizes the production rate for a given number of workstations.

To begin, we need to know three types of information:

1. the set of tasks to be performed and the time required to perform each task;
2. the precedence relations among the tasks—that is, the sequence in which tasks must be performed; and
3. the desired output rate or forecast of demand for the assembly line. The cycle time (*CT*) must satisfy:

maximum operation time $\leq CT \leq$ sum of operation times [8.1]

Cycle time (*CT*) is related to the output required to be produced in some period of time (R) by the following equation:

$$CT = A/R \quad [8.2]$$

where A = available time to produce the output and R = demand forecast. For a given cycle time:

Minimum number of workstations required = Sum of task times/ Cycle time = $\Sigma t/CT$ [8.3]

Additional formulas for assembly line performance:

Total time available = (Number workstations)(Cycle time) = $(N)(CT)$ [8.4]

Total idle time = $(N)(CT) = \Sigma t$ [8.5]

Assembly-line efficiency = $\Sigma t/(N = CT)$ [8.6]

Balance delay = 1 − Assembly-line efficiency [8.7]

One line-balancing decision rule example is to assign the task with the *longest task time first* to a workstation if the cycle time would not be exceeded. The longest-task-time-first decision rule assigns tasks with long task times first, because shorter task times are easier to fit in the line balance later in the procedure. In the real world, assembly-line balancing is quite complicated because of the size of practical problems, as well as constraints that mechanization or tooling place on work tasks.

8.3 **Explain the concepts of process layout.** In designing process layouts, we are concerned with the arrangement of departments or work centers relative to each other. Costs associated with moving materials or the inconvenience that customers might experience in moving between physical locations are usually the principal design criteria for process layouts. In general, work centers with a large number of moves between them should be located close to one another.

8.4 **Explain the concepts and approaches used in work measurement.** Work measurement is a systematic procedure for the analysis of work, and determination of standard times required to perform key tasks in a process. A standard time is a reasonable estimate of the amount of time needed to perform a task based on an analysis of the work by a trained industrial engineer or other operations expert. Work measurement relies on time studies. A time study is the development of a standard time by observing a task with the use of a stopwatch and analyzing the data. The standard time is computed as:

Standard time = Normal time × (1 + Allowance Factor)

where

Normal Time = Observed time (OT) × Performance Rating Factor (PRF)

8.5 **Describe issues related to the design of workplaces and jobs.** Key questions that must be addressed at the workstation level include the following:

1. Who will use the workplace? Will the workstation be shared? How much space is required?
2. How will the work be performed? What tasks are required? How much time does each task take? How much time is required to set up for the workday or for a particular job? How might the tasks be grouped into work activities most effectively?
3. What technology is needed?
4. What must the employee be able to see?
5. What must the employee be able to hear?
6. What environmental and safety issues need to be addressed? What protective clothing or gear should the employee wear?

Two broad objectives must be satisfied in job design. One is to meet the firm's competitive priorities—cost, efficiency, flexibility, quality, and so on; the other is to make the job safe, satisfying, and motivating for the worker. Resolving conflicts between the need for technical and economic efficiency and the need for employee satisfaction is the challenge that faces operations managers in designing jobs

Some of the more common approaches to job enrichment are

- natural work teams, which perform entire jobs, rather than specialized, assembly-line work;
- virtual teams, in which members communicate by computer, take turns as leaders, and join and leave the team as necessary; and
- self-managed teams (SMTs) are empowered work teams that also assume many traditional management responsibilities. Virtual teams, in particular, have taken on increased importance in today' business world.

KEY TERMS

- **Allowances**
- **Assembly-line balancing**
- **Assembly line**
- **Cellular layout**
- **Continuous timing**
- **Cycle time**
- **Ergonomics**
- **Facility layout**
- **Fixed-position layout**
- **Flow-blocking delay**
- **Job**
- **Job design**
- **Job enlargement**
- **Job enrichment**
- **Lack-of-work delay**
- **Normal time**
- **Process layout**
- **Product layout**
- **Standard time**
- **Time study**
- **Work measurement**

REVIEW QUESTIONS

8.1 1. What are the objectives of facility and work design? How can it help support strategic directions?

8.1 2. Under what conditions are facility layout studies conducted?

8.2 3. What is a "flow blocking delay" and a "lack of work delay"? What types of designs can help to reduce these two sources of delay?

8.2 4. What is an assembly line? Define the "assembly-line balancing problem" and explain what information is needed to solve it.

8.2 5. When might you have to rebalance an assembly line? Explain.

8.3 6. Explain the concepts of designing process layouts.

8.3 7. What is a "closeness rating," and how can computer analysis support layout decisions?

8.3 8. Explain how to design product layouts using assembly-line balancing.

8.4 9. What is work measurement? How can it be used to improve organizational performance?

8.4 10. Explain the concept of normal time. How can an operations manager verify whether the time to perform a task is indeed "normal"?

8.4 11. How does standard time differ from normal time? How are standard times used in operations management?

8.4 12. What is time study? Describe the basic procedure for conducting a time study.

8.5 13. Define job design, job enlargement, and job enrichment, and give a non-textbook example of each.

8.5 14. Why is safety important?

8.5 15. Define ergonomics and give an example of a good or bad experience.

8.5 16. Describe the Ethical Trading Initiative (ETI) and how it fits with sustainability.

8.5 17. What key questions should be asked when designing workplaces?

8.5 18. Describe the human issues related to workplace design.

DISCUSSION QUESTIONS AND EXPERIENTIAL ACTIVITIES

8.1 19. What are the advantages and disadvantages of each of the major types of layout patterns? Provide one example of each type of layout for goods-producing and service-providing firms.

8.1 20. Discuss the type of facility layout that would be most appropriate for:

a. printing books,
b. performing hospital laboratory tests,
c. manufacturing home furniture,
d. a hospital,
e. a photography studio, and
f. a library.

8.1 21. Describe the layout of a typical fast-food franchise such as McDonald's. What type of layout is it? How does it support productivity? Do different franchises (e.g., Burger King or Wendy's) have different types of layouts? Why?

8.1 22. Research and write a short paper illustrating how an organization uses one of the following types of facility layouts:

- Product layout
- Process layout
- Cellular layout
- Fixed-position layout

8.1 23. Visit a manufacturer or service organization and critique their facility design. What are the advantages and disadvantages? How does the layout affect process flows, customer service, efficiency, and cost? Describe the basic types of materials-handling systems commonly used in manufacturing.

8.1 24. Many company cafeterias are changing from the traditional cafeteria (process) layout to a product layout in which food items are arranged into stations (salads, Italian, cold sandwiches, roast beef and ham, etc.). What types of layouts are these? Discuss the advantages and disadvantages of each type of layout.

8.1 25. What type of layout is typically used in a home kitchen? Can you suggest an alternative layout that might have some different advantages?

8.3 26. How is assembly line efficiency related to unit cost? Explain.

8.4 27. Do you think the following jobs require standard times? Explain your reasoning.

- Carpet installers
- Software programmers
- Cable TV installers
- Hotel maids
- Bank tellers
- Airline flight attendants
- Dentists
- Medical doctors
- Restaurant reservations
- Telephone call center representatives

8.5 28. What do you think of Cargill Kitchen Solutions' 20-minute job rotation approach? Would you want to work in such an environment, or one in which you performed the same tasks all day. Why?

8.5 29. Research and write a short paper (one-page maximum) on the advantages and disadvantages of virtual teams in today's digital environment.

8.5 30. What is the role of ergonomics in job design? What factors do you think are the most important?

8.5 31. List the ergonomic features of your automobile's interior and discuss any improvements that you can identify.

8.5 32. How might sustainability issues be incorporated into the design of facilities and workplaces? Provide examples and explain your reasoning.

8.5 33. Research and write a short report (maximum of two typed pages) on green facility design making sure that you incorporate some of the key topics in this chapter.

COMPUTATIONAL PROBLEMS AND EXERCISES

These exercises require you to apply the formulas and methods described in the chapter. The problems should be solved manually.

8.1 34. Peter's Paper Clips uses a three-stage production process: cutting wire to prescribed lengths, inner bending, and outer bending. The cutting process can produce at a rate of 200 pieces per minute; inner bending, 160 pieces per minute; and outer bending, 150 pieces per minute. Determine the hourly capacity of each process stage and the number of machines needed to meet an output rate of 20,000 units per hour. How does facility layout impact your numerical analysis and process efficiency? Explain.

8.2 35. Bass Fishing, Inc. assembles fishing nets with aluminum handles in an assembly line using four workstations. Management wants an output rate of 200 nets per day using a 7.5-hour work day. The sum of the task times is 7.00 minutes/net.

a. What is the cycle time?

b. What is assembly-line efficiency?

c. What is total idle time?

8.2 36. Use the activities and precedence relations in Exhibit 8.13 to do the following:

a. Draw a precedence diagram for this assembly line.

b. Balance the assembly line for an eight-hour-shift output of 30 pieces.

c. Determine maximum and minimum cycle times.

EXHIBIT 8.13 Data for Problem 36

Activity	Predecessors	Time per Piece (min.)
A	none	7
B	none	2
C	A	6
D	A	10
E	B	3
F	B	2
G	D, E	12
H	C	2
I	F	3
J	H, G, I	9

8.2 37. An assembly line with 30 activities is to be balanced. The total amount of time to complete all 30 activities is 60 minutes. The longest activity takes 2.4 minutes and the shortest takes 0.3 minutes. The line will operate for 480 minutes per day.

a. What are the maximum and minimum cycle times?

b. How much daily output will be achieved by each of those cycle times?

8.2 38. In problem 37, suppose the line is balanced using 14 workstations and a finished product can be produced every 4.5 minutes.

a. What is the production rate in units per day?

b. What is the assembly line efficiency?

8.2 39. A small assembly line for the assembly of power steering pumps needs to be balanced. Exhibit 8.14 is the precedence diagram. The cycle time is determined to be 1.5 minutes. How would the line be balanced by choosing the assignable task having the *longest* task time first?

EXHIBIT 8.14 Precedence Diagram for Problem 39

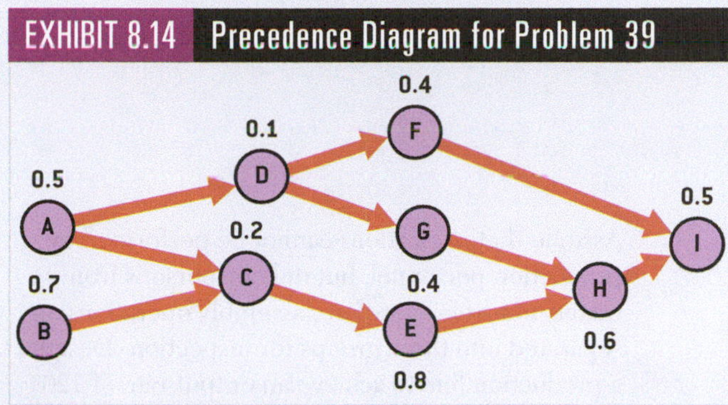

8.2 40. For the assembly line described in problem 39, how would the line be balanced by choosing the assignable task having the *shortest* task time first?

8.2 41. To make one particular model of a personal digital assistant (PDA) on an assembly line, the work content is defined by the ten tasks below.

Work Task	Time (seconds)	Immediate Predecessor(s)
1	3.0	None
2	2.0	None
3	1.5	1,2
4	5.0	3
5	3.5	4
6	3.0	4
7	2.5	5,6
8	4.0	7
9	2.0	8
10	5.5	9
Total	32.0 seconds	

a. Draw the precedence diagram for this assembly line.

b. What is the cycle time if you want to produce 4,500 PDAs per workday assuming 7.5 hours per day?

c. What is the theoretical minimum number of workstations to balance this line?

d. Using the largest task time first decision rule with the shortest task time rule being used for breaking ties, balance this assembly line. (Make sure you do not violate precedent relationships and the total work per workstation must be less than or equal to six seconds.)

e. Compute process efficiency and evaluate the resulting balance in part d.

f. Comment on the results

8.2 **42.** For the in-line skate assembly example in this chapter, suppose the times for the individual operations are as follows:

Task	Time (sec.)
1	20
2	10
3	30
4	10
5	30
6	20
7	10
8	20

Assume that inspections cannot be performed by production personnel, but only by persons from quality control. Therefore, assembly operations are separated into three groups for inspection. Design a production line to achieve an output rate of 120 per hour and 90 per hour.

8.2 **43.** For the in-line skate example described in problem 42, design a production line to achieve an output rate of 90 per hour.

8.2 **44.** You have been asked to set up an assembly line to assemble a computer mouse. The precedence network is shown in Exhibit 8.15; task times in minutes are given beside each task. There are 480 minutes of assembly time per shift and the company operates one shift each day. The required output rate is forecasted to be 60 units per shift.

EXHIBIT 8.15 Precedence Network for Problem 44

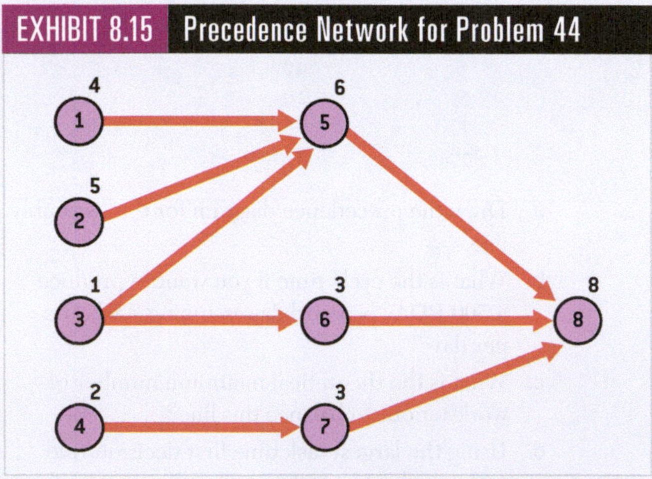

a. Balance the assembly line using the *longest processing time* rule. State the tasks associated with each workstation, total time, and idle time.

b. What is the assembly-line efficiency?

c. Is your assembly-line balance solution good or bad? What criteria do you use to make this assessment? Explain.

8.2 **45.** Balance the assembly line in Exhibit 8.16 for (a) a shift output of 40 pieces and (b) a shift output of 20 pieces. Assume an 8-hour shift, and use the rule: choose the assignable task with the *longest processing time*. Compute the line efficiency for each case.

EXHIBIT 8.16 Precedence Diagram for Problem 45

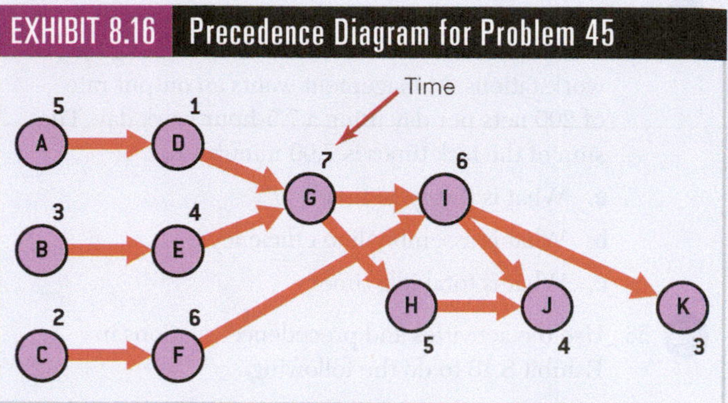

8.4 **46.** The Florida Appliance Company is installing an assembly line to produce vacuum cleaners, and you, as an operations manager, are responsible for balancing the line. The tasks to be performed are listed below, along with their task times in seconds and immediate predecessors.

Task	Time (sec)	Immediate Predecessor(s)
A	60	—
B	40	A
C	30	B
D	20	B
E	40	B
F	60	C
G	70	D
H	50	F, G
I	20	E
J	60	H, I

a. Draw the precedence diagram for this assembly line.

b. The company is planning to operate two shifts per day, eight hours per shift. If the desired output rate of the line is 480 units per day, what is the cycle time?

c. Balance the assembly line using the longest task time first processing rule.

d. What is the efficiency of your balance?

8.4 **47.** Using a rating factor of 1.00, compute the normal time for drilling a hole in a steel plate if these are the observed times (in minutes):

0.240	0.250	0.290	0.240	0.270
0.250	0.245	0.190	0.200	0.230

8.4 **48.** A part-time employee who rolls out dough balls at a pizza restaurant was observed over a 40-hour period for a work-sampling study. During that time, she prepared 550 pieces of pizza dough. The analyst made 50 observations and found the employee not working four times. The overall performance rating was 1.10. The allowance for the job is 15 percent. Based on these data, what is the standard time in minutes for preparing pizza dough?

EXCEL-BASED PROBLEMS

For these problems, you may use Excel or the spreadsheet templates in MindTap to assist in your analysis.

8.4 49. Nine observations from a work measurement study using continuous timing are shown below. Allowances are determined as: personal, five percent; fatigue, five percent; delay, five percent. Use the *Work Measurement* Excel template to determine the standard time for this operation.

Work	Observation									
Element	1	2	3	4	5	6	7	8	9	Performance Rating
A	0.09	0.12	0.08	0.11	0.10	0.09	0.13	0.12	0.13	105%
B	0.23	0.18	0.21	0.20	0.24	0.22	0.26	0.25	0.25	100%
C	0.46	0.49	0.46	0.44	0.47	0.47	0.49	0.46	0.48	90%
D	0.61	0.66	0.62	0.59	0.69	0.67	0.67	0.66	0.70	85%
E	0.70	0.74	0.72	0.68	0.79	0.80	0.76	0.78	0.81	100%
F	1.00	1.02	0.98	0.99	1.08	1.09	1.02	1.06	1.09	110%

8.4 50. Five observations from a work measurement study are shown below. Continuous timing was not used, but the times in minutes for each work element were recorded individually. Assume a total allowance of 20 percent. Use the *Work Measurement* Excel template to determine the standard time for this operation.

	Observation					
Work Element	1	2	3	4	5	Performance Rating
Get casting	0.21	0.21	0.21	0.20	0.25	0.95
Load in fixture	0.27	0.28	0.25	0.25	0.27	0.90
Drill	1.04	1.06	1.00	1.04	1.04	1.00
Unload	0.21	0.18	0.25	0.22	0.20	0.95
Inspect	0.25	0.26	0.24	0.25	0.20	0.80
Place in bin	0.12	0.11	0.10	0.13	0.12	1.10

Employee 842 versus The State

"He filed a lawsuit against us, Luke," stated Mike Verssa, the Vice President of Operations for the State Human Resources Commission (SHRC). "Luke, you are his manager. What happened? He claims you raised his daily productivity quota for processing invoices from 200 to 300."

"Mr. Verssa, I did raise his quota to more closely match the other employees. This employee is always late for work, plays games on the computer, violates our dress code, and is generally disliked by his peer employees. He never makes our standard output quotes. We had our best people retrain him but it doesn't help. He should be fired," responded Luke Davis, the employee's immediate supervisor. "Is there any logic or numerical basis for you increasing his quota?" Mike asked Luke. "Yes, we hired an outside consultant to do a work measurement study on this employee. We benchmarked the employee's performance against four other employees doing the identical jobs. The four employees were chosen at random. I'll dig it out and get it to you," Luke replied.

Luke reviewed the work measurement study for employee 842 and gave it to Mike Verssa. Exhibits 8.17 and 8.18 document the tasks to compute a normal time for each of the four benchmark employees. The data was collected using a continuous timing method. An allowance factor of 20 percent is assumed for all state employees working at SHRC. The workday was 7 hours plus a 1-hour lunch break. The sample size was large with a statistical significance level of less than 0.01. Employee 842 also participated in the work measurement study by the same thirty-party consultant. His normal time was 1.722 minutes per invoice.

Case Questions for Discussion:

1. After reviewing the work study, who's case is justified—the state or the employee? Explain your reasoning.
2. What other issues should be considered?
3. Would you present these data in court? Why or why not?
4. What are your final recommendations?

EXHIBIT 8.17 Work Measurement Samples for Two SHRC Employees A and B

Cumulative Time (CT) Select Time (T) Tasks		All times in (minutes. hundredths of seconds) Sample #A	Rating Factor	Normal Time		Sample #B	Rating Factor	Normal Time
Sorting/Matching	T	13.09	1.00	13.09	T	22.60	1.10	24.86
	CT	13.09			CT	22.60		
Keying	T	28.45	1.00	28.45	T	23.40	1.10	25.74
	CT	41.54			CT	46.00		
End of Day Activities	T	24.23	1.00	24.23	T	13.94	1.10	15.33
	CT	65.77		65.77	CT	59.94		65.93
Total Time		65.77		65.77		59.94		65.93
Number Processed		52.00		52.00		54.00		54.00
Normal Time/Invoice				1.265				1.221

EXHIBIT 8.18 Work Measurement Samples for Two SHRC Employees C and D

Task		Sample #C	Rating Factor	Normal Time		Sample #D	Rating Factor	Normal Time
Sorting/Matching	T	8.44	1.10	9.28	T	7.43	1.20	8.92
	CT	8.44			CT	7.43		
Keying	T	14.26	1.10	15.69	T	5.55	1.20	6.66
	CT	22.70			CT	12.98		
End of Day Activities	T	6.47	1.10	7.12	T	15.52	1.20	18.62
	CT	29.17		32.09	CT	28.50		34.20
Total Time		29.17		32.09		28.50		34.20
Number Processed		32.00		32.00		39.00		39.00
Normal Time/Invoice				1.003				0.877

BankUSA: Cash Movement

"Del, every wire transfer request is processed first-come-first-served. Some of these wires are for millions of dollars, while others are under $100," said Betty Kelly, a 28-year-old manager of Cash Movement (CM). She continued, "I'm also concerned that all wires regardless of dollar amount go through the same quality checkpoints and whether we are staffed correctly."

Betty left her boss Del Carr's office with many related issues on her mind. As Betty sat down in her office chair, Steve Breslin, supervisor of outgoing wires, said, "Betty, last week we processed a wire for $80,000 incorrectly to Houston Oaks Bank, and now they won't give it back. What should we do?" "Steve, give me the information, and I'll call the bank now," said Betty. The rest of Betty's day was spent recovering this money and discussing several personnel issues.

The Cash Movement (CM) operating unit is responsible for transferring money for BankUSA and any of its customers. Over 80 percent of all transaction requests are for individual customers, and the remaining requests are for commercial (business) customers. For example, a customer will sell stock and request that cash funds be sent to another institution such as a mutual fund, credit union, or another bank. The customer will request his or her local customer investment manager (CIM) to transfer money into or out of the account. The CIM will then request by e-mail or fax that Cash Movement process the transaction. All wires must be settled on the same day.

The average demand for outgoing wires is 306 wires per day for a 7.5-hour workday. Therefore, the cycle time for this demand rate using Equation 8.2 is computed as follows:

$$
\begin{aligned}
CT = A/R &= [(7.5 \text{ hours/day})(60 \text{ minutes/hour})] \\
&\quad \div (306 \text{ wires/day}) \\
&= (450 \text{ minutes/day})/(306 \text{ wires/day}) \\
&= 1.47 \text{ minutes/wire}
\end{aligned}
$$

Cash Movement employs 21 people, with three managers, 11 associates in outgoing wires, two associates in incoming wires, three associates in checks, and two associates in other areas. The average annual salary per associate is $30,000 with an additional 30 percent for benefits and overhead costs. Overhead costs include the cost of leasing/renting the building, operation of common areas such as the cafeteria and meeting rooms, utilities, insurance, and photocopy services.

jamnoon028/Shutterstock.com

Process workflow is documented in Exhibit 8.19, with 47 detailed steps consolidated into 16 logical workgroups/activities. The processing times in the last column are based on stopwatch time studies. The weighted average time per outgoing wire is 7.05 minutes. A total of 11 people work in this process. The assembly line could be balanced using the original 47 steps if the times per step were given (they are not), but Betty thought she would begin by trying to balance the line using a more aggregate grouping of work with 16 workgroup activities. The 16 work activities are performed in a series or sequentially, but how they are grouped does make a difference.

The first stage is external to the internal Cash Movement process and involves the front-room interaction between the customer (client) and the CIM. Here, an electronic transfer request can range from a few minutes to hours trying to help the customer decide what to do, and may include a visit to the customer's home or office. This external work activity is not part of the internal process assembly-line balance. The process begins at work activity 1 and ends at work activity 16.

A wire transfer request can "fail" in several ways, with cost consequences to the bank. For example, if the wire is processed incorrectly or is not completed on time, the customer's transaction may fail. The effect of a failed transaction includes the customer being upset, customers leaving the bank forever, customers referring friends and relatives to other banks, and the possible financial loss of processing

EXHIBIT 8.19 Outgoing Wire Process Steps and Standard Times

Process Steps (47 detailed steps Aggregated into 16 steps)	Workgroup Activity Number	% Work through This Stage	Processing Times per Client Transfer Request (minutes)
Client Requests		100%	16 minutes (2 to 120 minutes) This front-room step is not part of the outgoing wire backroom process, so ignore it.
Steps 1 to 3 (client and customer investment manager interaction, accurate collection of process input information, submit to backroom outgoing wire process for transaction execution)			
Logging (Begin Outgoing Wire Process)			
Steps 4 and 5 (receive request and verify)	1	100%	0.8 minute
Steps 6, 11, and back to 4 and 5 (incorrect or missing information—rework)	2	3%	10 minutes
Step 7 (confirm if >$50,000)	3	100%	0.8 minute
Steps 8 to 10 (separate into different batches and forward)	4	100%	0.1 minute
Verify the Receipt of Fax (Wire Request)			**First Quality Control Checkpoint**
(Steps 4 to 7 above)			
Direct Wire Input			
Steps 12 and 13 (receive batches and key into system—batches are variable but a typical batch is about 30 wires, which takes about 30 minutes to key into the computer)	5	100%	1 minute
Steps 14 to 16 (run remote report and tape and see if total dollar amounts match—verify)	6	100%	0.1 minute
Steps 17 to 19 (tape and remote report do not match—rework manually by checking each wire against each computer file—done by someone other than keyer)	7	3%	10 minutes
Verify the Accuracy of Wire Request			**Second Quality Control Checkpoint**
(Steps 12 to 19 above with a focus on keying the wire)	8	100%	0.5 minute
Steps 20 and 23 (receive and verify the wire's accuracy a second time in the computer—done by someone else)			
Verify the Accuracy of the Keyed Wire			**Third Quality Control Checkpoint**
(Steps 20 and 23 above, with a focus on the wire in the computer)	9	100%	1 minute
Steps 24 and 28 (release the wire)	10	5%	3 minutes
Steps 25 to 27 (if wire incorrect, cancel wire, and rekey—back to step 12)	11	70%	0.1 minute
Step 29 (if CM needs to debit a customer's account, do steps 30 to 32, and batch and run tape)	12	30%	0.1 minute
Step 29 (if CM does not need to debit a customer's account, do step 33—wire is complete and paperwork filed)			
Verify the Wire Was Sent Correctly			**Fourth Quality Control Checkpoint**
(Steps 29 to 33)			
Steps 34 to 36 (taking money out of the customer's trust account and putting it in a Cash Management internal account)	13	100%	0.75 minute
Verify That Appropriate Funds Were Taken from the Customer's Account			**Fifth Quality Control Checkpoint**
(Steps 34 to 36—done by someone else)			
Step 37 (if totals on tape match totals on batch, go to steps 38 to 44)	14	97%	0.1 minute
Step 37 (if totals do not match, find the error by examining the batch of wires; then go to steps 39 to 43)	15	35	10 minutes
Steps 45 to 47 (verify and file wire information)	16	100%	0.75 minute

the transaction the next business day at a new security price. BankUSA may have to compensate the customer for a failed transaction in terms of customer losses due to lost interest earnings on daily price changes plus processing fees. The average processing fee is $50 per wire. Moreover, any failed transaction must be researched and reprocessed, which constitutes "internal failure costs." Research and reprocessing costs per wire are estimated at $200. CM processes about 1,500 outgoing wires per week, with about one error every two weeks. Errors happen due to CM mistakes but also are caused by other BankUSA departments, other financial institutions, and customers themselves. The information flow of this electronic funds transfer system is sometimes quite complex, with BankUSA having only partial control of the value chain.

Specific types of errors include the same wire being sent out twice; wire not sent out at all; wire sent with inaccurate information on it, including dollar amount; or wire sent to the wrong place. No dollar amount has been assigned to each type of failure. The largest risk to Cash Movement is to send the money twice or to send it to the wrong institution. If CM catches the error the same day the wire is sent, the wire is requested to be returned that day. If a wire is sent in duplication, the receiving institution must receive permission from the customer to return the money to BankUSA. This results in lost interest and the possibility of long delays in returning the money or BankUSA having to take legal action to get the money back. For international transaction requests that are wired with errors, the cost of getting the money back is high. These costs are potentially so high, up to several hundred thousand dollars, that five quality control steps are built into the cash management process, as shown in Exhibit 8.14. All wires, even low dollar amounts, are currently checked and rechecked to ensure completeness and accuracy.

As Betty, the manager of Cash Movement, drove home, she wondered when she would ever get the time to analyze these issues. She remembered taking a college course in operations management and studying the topic of assembly-line balancing (she majored in finance), but she wondered if this method would work for services. She decided to begin her analysis by answering the following questions.

Case Questions for Discussion:

1. What is the best way to group the work represented by the 16 workgroups for an average demand of 306 outgoing wires per day? What is your line balance if peak demand is 450 wires per day? What is assembly-line efficiency for each line-balance solution?
2. How many people are needed for the outgoing wire process using assembly-line-balancing methods versus the current staffing level of 11 full-time-equivalent employees?
3. How many staff members do you need for the outgoing wire process if you eliminate all rework?
4. What are your final recommendations?

Integrative Case: Hudson Jewelers

The Hudson Jewelers case study available in MindTap integrates material found in each chapter of this book.

Case Question for Discussion:

1. Design and draw the layout for your high-end jewelry store. Critique its strengths and weaknesses. (Make use of concepts in Chapters 4, 5, 7, and 8.)

9 Forecasting and Demand Planning

LEARNING OBJECTIVES

After studying this chapter, you should be able to:

- 9-1 Describe the importance of forecasting to the value chain.
- 9-2 Explain basic concepts of forecasting and time series.
- 9-3 Explain how to apply simple moving average and exponential smoothing models.
- 9-4 Describe how to apply regression as a forecasting approach.
- 9-5 Explain the role of judgment in forecasting.
- 9-6 Describe how statistical and judgmental forecasting techniques are applied in practice.

Disney theme parks must forecast guest volumes and resource (labor, equipment, facility) utilizations in order to provide an enjoyable guest experience.

Matt Stroshane/Bloomberg/Getty Images

Forecasting is a key operations planning activity at Walt Disney World Resort. Analysts must forecast the attendance at each theme park, and this influences park hours and other strategic plans. Forecasts are also generated for more specific activities such as guest arrivals at Disney hotels, park entry turnstiles, restaurants, and merchandise locations. All these forecasts are incorporated into a labor demand planning system that matches staffing schedules with anticipated demand. Forecasts are also used to predict wait times for rides and set return times in the parks' FASTPASS1 system. These applications of analytics are focused on one goal—to enhance the guest experience![1]

WHAT DO YOU THINK?

Think of a pizza delivery franchise located near a college campus. What factors that influence demand do you think should be included in trying to forecast demand for pizzas?

Forecasting *is the process of projecting the values of one or more variables into the future*. Good forecasts are needed in all organizations to drive analyses and decisions related to operations. Forecasting is a key component in many types of integrated operating systems, such as supply chain management, customer relationship management, and revenue management systems.

Poor forecasting can result in poor inventory and staffing decisions, resulting in part shortages, inadequate customer service, and many customer complaints. In the telecommunications industry, competition is fierce; and goods and services have very short life cycles. Changing technology, frequent price wars, and incentives for customers to switch services increase the difficulty of providing accurate forecasts.

Many firms integrate forecasting with value chain and capacity management systems to make better operational decisions.

Many firms integrate forecasting with value chain and capacity management systems to make better operational decisions. National Car Rental, for example, is using data analysis and forecasting methods in its value chain to improve service and reduce costs. Instead of accepting customer demand as it is and trying to plan resources to meet the peaks and valleys, its models help shift demand to low-demand periods and better use its capacity. The proactive approach to spring break peak demand helps plan and coordinate rental office and call center staffing levels and schedules, vehicle availability, advertising campaigns, and vehicle maintenance and repair schedules. Many commercial software packages also tie forecasting modules into supply chain and operational planning systems.

9-1 Forecasting and Demand Planning

Organizations make many different types of forecasts. Consider a consumer products company, such as Procter & Gamble, that makes many different goods in various sizes. Top managers need long-range forecasts expressed in total sales dollars for use in financial planning and for sizing and locating new facilities. At lower organizational levels, however, managers of the various product groups need aggregate forecasts of sales volume for their products in units that are more meaningful to them—for example, pounds of a certain type of soap—to establish production plans. Finally, managers of individual manufacturing facilities need forecasts by brand and size—for instance, the number of 64-ounce boxes of Tide detergent—to plan material usage and production schedules. Similarly, airlines need long-range forecasts of demand for air travel to plan their purchases of airplanes, and short-term forecasts to develop seasonal routes and schedules; university administrators require enrollment forecasts; city planners need forecasts of population trends to plan highways and mass transit systems; and restaurants need forecasts to be able to plan for food purchases.

Accurate forecasts are needed throughout the value chain, as illustrated in Exhibit 9.1, and are used by all functional areas of an organization, such as accounting, finance, marketing, operations, and distribution. Forecasting is typically included in comprehensive value

DIRECTV: Forecasting New Technology Adoption

When DIRECTV planned to launch its business in the early 1990s, it needed to forecast subscriptions of satellite television over a five-year horizon. As was noted, "The most critical forecast is the forecast prior to product launch." DIRECTV needed a forecast that would answer the following questions: How many of the homes in the United States would subscribe to satellite television, and when would they subscribe? The forecast was developed using a quantitative model that describes the adoption pattern of many new products and technologies.

txking/Shutterstock.com

DIRECTV's management made use of the forecast in several important ways:

- The forecast for the first year that indicated very rapid consumer acceptance of direct broadcast satellite systems supported DIRECTV's decision to launch a second million-dollar satellite sooner than originally planned. The second satellite permitted DIRECTV to carry a greater variety of programming.
- DIRECTV management used the forecast to solicit funding and to develop partnerships with equipment manufacturers such as Sony, programming providers like Disney, and national retailers such as Radio Shack.

A comparison of the actual number of subscribers and the forecast over the first five years indicated that the forecast closely predicted the trends in actual values.[2]

chain and demand-planning software systems. These systems integrate marketing, inventory, sales, operations planning, and financial data. For example, the SAP Demand Planning module enables companies to integrate planning information from different departments or organizations into a single demand plan. Some software vendors are beginning to use the

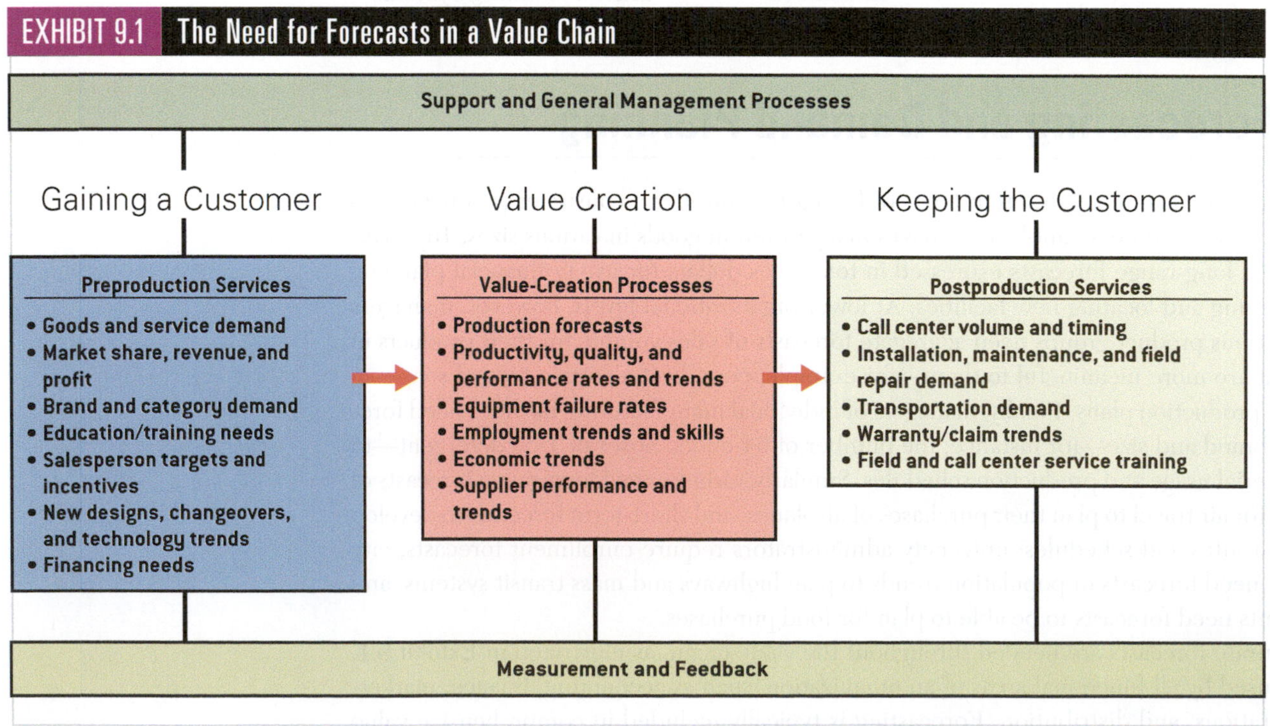

EXHIBIT 9.1 The Need for Forecasts in a Value Chain

terms *demand planning* or *demand chain* instead of supply chain. This highlights the fact that customers' wants and needs define the customer benefit package, and that customer demand pulls goods and services through the supply chain.

9-2 Basic Concepts in Forecasting

Before diving into the process of developing forecasting models, it is important to understand some basic concepts that are used in model development. These concepts are independent of the type of model and provide a foundation for users to make better use of the models in operations decisions.

9-2a Forecast Planning Horizon

Forecasts of future demand are needed at all levels of organizational decision making. *The* **planning horizon** *is the length of time on which a forecast is based.* Long-range forecasts cover a planning horizon of 1 to 10 years and are necessary to plan for the expansion of facilities and to determine future needs for land, labor, and equipment. Intermediate-range forecasts over a 3- to 12-month period are needed to plan workforce levels, allocate budgets among divisions, schedule jobs and resources, and establish purchasing plans. Short-range forecasts focus on the planning horizon of up to three months and are used by operations managers to plan production schedules and assign workers to jobs, determine short-term capacity requirements, and aid shipping departments in planning transportation needs and establishing delivery schedules.

Forecasts of future demand are needed at all levels of organizational decision making.

The **time bucket** *is the unit of measure for the time period used in a forecast.* A time bucket might be a year, quarter, month, week, day, hour, or even a minute. For a long-term planning horizon, a firm might forecast in yearly time buckets; for a short-range planning horizon, the time bucket might be an hour or less. Customer call centers, for example, forecast customer demand in 5-, 6-, or 10-minute intervals. Selecting the right planning horizon length and time bucket size for the right situation is an important part of forecasting.

9-2b Data Patterns in Time Series

Statistical methods of forecasting are based on the analysis of historical data, called a time series. *A* **time series** *is a set of observations measured at successive points in time or over successive periods of time.* A time series provides the data for understanding how the variable that we wish to forecast has changed historically. For example, the daily ending Dow Jones stock index is one example of a time series; another is the monthly volume of sales for a product. To explain the pattern of data in a time series, it is often helpful to think in terms of five characteristics: *trend, seasonal, cyclical, random variation*, and *irregular (one-time) variation*. Different time series may exhibit one or more of these characteristics. Understanding these characteristics is vital to selecting the appropriate forecasting model or approach.

A **trend** *is the underlying pattern of growth or decline in a time series.* Although data generally exhibit random fluctuations, a trend shows gradual shifts or movements to relatively higher or lower values over a longer period of time. This gradual shifting over time is usually due to such long-term factors as changes in performance, technology, productivity, population, demographic characteristics, and customer preferences.

Trends can be increasing or decreasing and can be linear or nonlinear. Exhibit 9.2 shows various trend patterns. Linear increasing and decreasing trends are shown in Exhibit 9.2(a) and (b), and nonlinear trends are shown in Exhibit 9.2(c) and (d).

Seasonal patterns *are characterized by repeatable periods of ups and downs over short periods of time.* Seasonal patterns may occur over a year; for example, the demand for cold beverages is low during the winter, begins to rise during the spring, peaks during the summer months, and then begins to decline in the autumn. Manufacturers of coats and jackets, however, expect the opposite yearly pattern. Exhibit 9.3 shows an example of natural gas usage in a single-family home over a two-year period, which clearly exhibits a seasonal pattern.

We generally think of seasonal patterns occurring within one year, but similar repeatable patterns might occur over the weeks during a month, over days during a week, or hours during a day. For instance, pizza delivery peaks on the weekends, and grocery store traffic is higher during the evening hours. Likewise, customer call center volume might peak in the morning and taper off throughout the day. Different days of the week might have different seasonal patterns.

> Selecting the right planning horizon length and time bucket size for the right situation is an important part of forecasting.

Cyclical patterns *are regular patterns in a data series that take place over long periods of time.* A common example of a cyclical pattern is the movement of stock market values during "bull" and "bear" market cycles.

Random variation (*sometimes called* **noise**) *is the unexplained deviation of a time series from a predictable pattern such as a trend, seasonal, or cyclical pattern.*

EXHIBIT 9.2 Example Linear and Nonlinear Trend Patterns

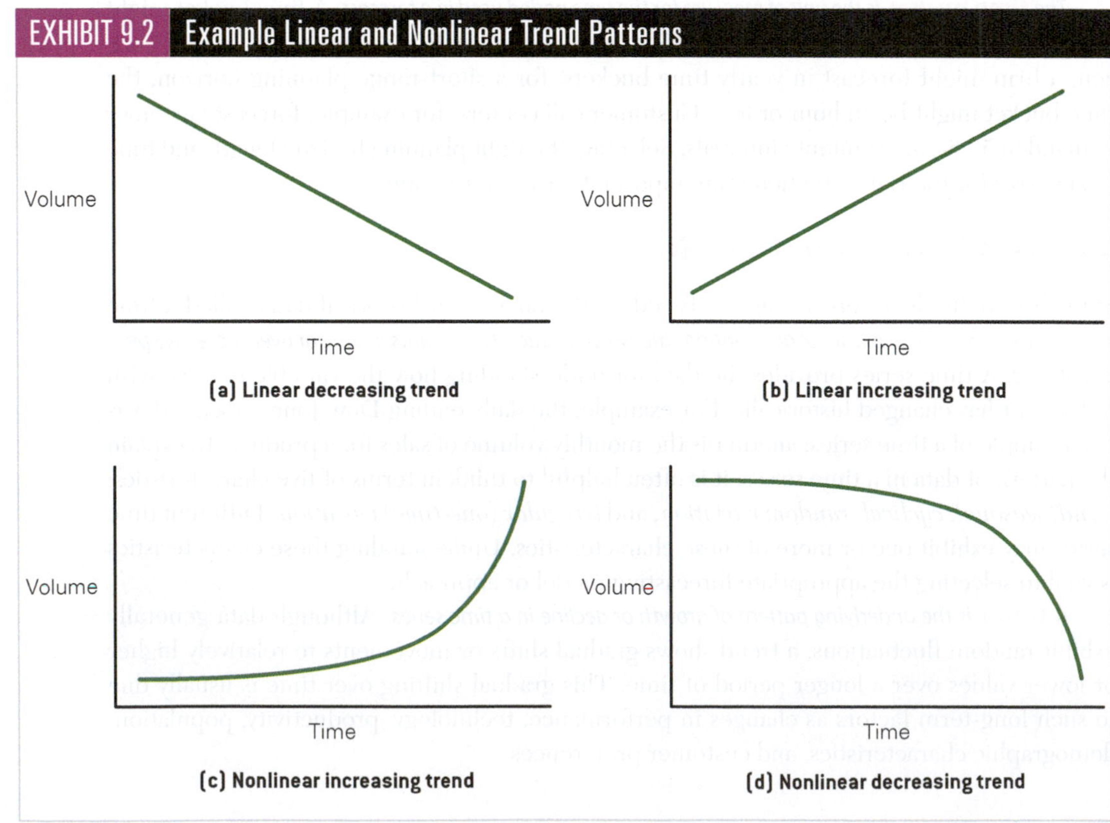

EXHIBIT 9.3 Seasonal Pattern of Home Natural Gas Usage

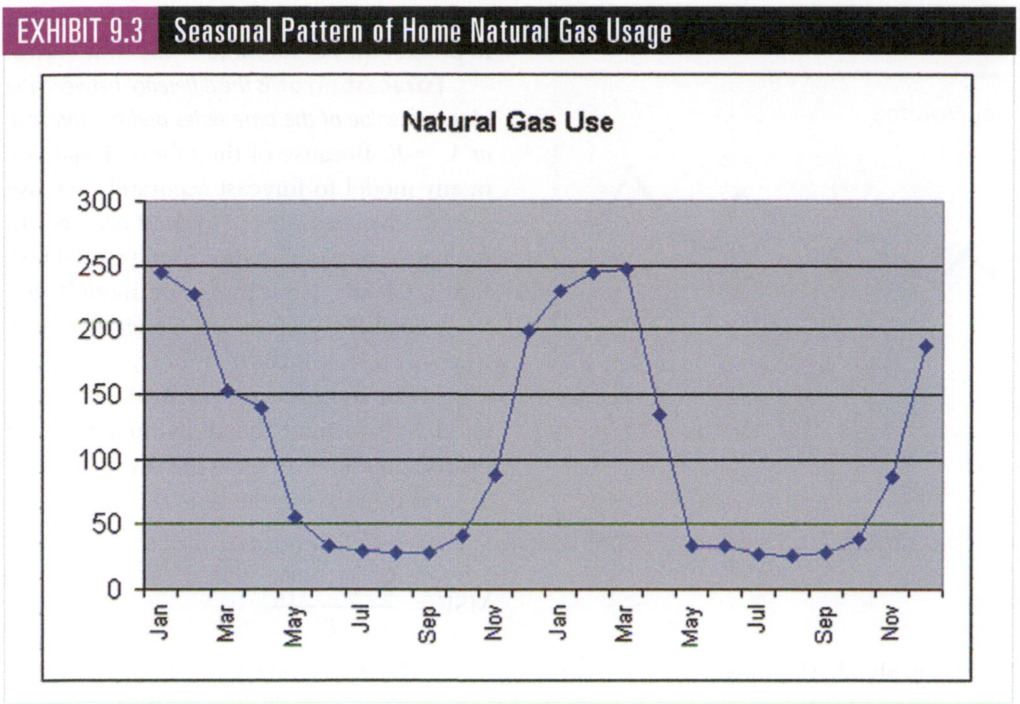

Random variation is caused by short-term, unanticipated, and nonrecurring factors and is unpredictable. Because of random variation, forecasts are never 100 percent accurate.

Irregular variation *is a one-time variation that is explainable.* For example, a hurricane can cause a surge in demand for building materials, food, and water. After the 9/11 terrorist attacks on the United States, many forecasts that predicted U.S. financial trends and airline passenger volumes had to be discarded due to the effects of this one-time event.

An example of a time series is given in the spreadsheet in Exhibit 9.4. These data represent the call volumes over 24 quarters from a call center at a major financial institution. The data are plotted on a chart in Exhibit 9.5. We can see both an increasing trend over the entire six years along with seasonal patterns within each of the years. For example, during the first three quarters of each year, call volumes increase, followed by a rapid decrease in the fourth quarter as customers presumably turn their attention to the holiday season. To develop a reliable forecast for the future, we would need to take into account both the long-term trend and the annual seasonal pattern.

EXHIBIT 9.4 Call Center Volume (This Excel spreadsheet is available in the Excel worksheet *Exhibit 9.4* in MindTap.)

	A	B	C	D
1	**Call Center Volume**			
2	**Period**	**Year**	**Quarter**	**Call Volume**
3	1	1	1	362
4	2	1	2	385
5	3	1	3	432
6	4	1	4	341
7	5	2	1	382
8	6	2	2	409
9	7	2	3	498
10	8	2	4	387
11	9	3	1	473
12	10	3	2	513
13	11	3	3	582
14	12	3	4	474
15	13	4	1	544
16	14	4	2	582
17	15	4	3	681
18	16	4	4	557
19	17	5	1	628
20	18	5	2	707
21	19	5	3	773
22	20	5	4	592
23	21	6	1	627
24	22	6	2	725
25	23	6	3	854
26	24	6	4	661

9-2c Forecast Errors and Accuracy

All forecasts are subject to error, and understanding the nature and size of errors is important to making good decisions. We denote the historical values of a time series by $A_1, A_2, \ldots, A_t$. In general, A_t represents the value of the time series for period t. We will let F_t represent the forecast value for period t. When we make this forecast, we will not know the actual value of the time series in period t, A_t. However, once A_t becomes known,

EXHIBIT 9.5 Chart of Call Volume

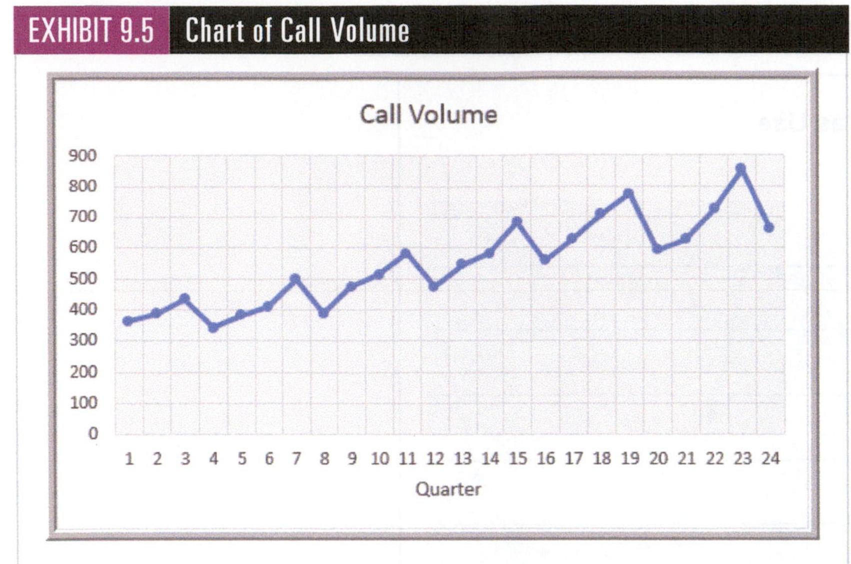

we can assess how well our forecast was able to predict the actual value of the time series.

Forecast error *is the difference between the observed value of the time series and the forecast, or* $A_t - F_t$. Because of the inherent inability of any model to forecast accurately, we use quantitative measures of forecast accuracy to evaluate how well the forecasting model performs. Clearly, we want to use models that have small forecast errors. Generally, three types of forecast error metrics are used.

Mean square error, or MSE, is calculated by squaring the individual forecast errors and then averaging the results over all T periods of data in the time series.

$$\text{MSE} = \frac{\Sigma(A_t - F_t)^2}{T} \quad [9.1]$$

MSE is probably the most commonly used measure of forecast accuracy. (Sometimes the square root of MSE is computed; this is called the *root mean square error, RMSE.*)

Another common measure of forecast accuracy is the mean absolute deviation (MAD), computed as

$$\text{MAD} = \frac{\Sigma|A_t - F_t|}{T} \quad [9.2]$$

EXHIBIT 9.6 Forecast Error of Example Time-Series Data (This spreadsheet is available in the Excel worksheet *Exhibit 9.6* in MindTap.)

	A	B	C	D	E	F	G	H	I	J	K	L
1	**Forecast Error of Example Time-Series Data**											
2	**Period**	**Year**	**Quarter**	**Call Volume**	**Forecast Ft**	**Error (At - Ft)**		**Squared Error**		**Absolute Deviation**		**Percentage Error**
3	1	1	1	362	343.8	18.20		331.24		18.2		5.03%
4	2	1	2	385	361.6	23.40		547.56		23.4		6.08%
5	3	1	3	432	379.4	52.60		2766.76		52.6		12.18%
6	4	1	4	341	397.2	-56.20		3158.44		56.2		16.48%
7	5	2	1	382	415	-33.00		1089.00		33		8.64%
8	6	2	2	409	432.8	-23.80		566.44		23.8		5.82%
9	7	2	3	498	450.6	47.40		2246.76		47.4		9.52%
10	8	2	4	387	468.4	-81.40		6625.96		81.4		21.03%
11	9	3	1	473	486.2	-13.20		174.24		13.2		2.79%
12	10	3	2	513	504	9.00		81.00		9		1.75%
13	11	3	3	582	521.8	60.20		3624.04		60.2		10.34%
14	12	3	4	474	539.6	-65.60		4303.36		65.6		13.84%
15	13	4	1	544	557.4	-13.40		179.56		13.4		2.46%
16	14	4	2	582	575.2	6.80		46.24		6.8		1.17%
17	15	4	3	681	593	88.00		7744.00		88		12.92%
18	16	4	4	557	610.8	-53.80		2894.44		53.8		9.66%
19	17	5	1	628	628.6	-0.60		0.36		0.6		0.10%
20	18	5	2	707	646.4	60.60		3672.36		60.6		8.57%
21	19	5	3	773	664.2	108.80		11837.44		108.8		14.08%
22	20	5	4	592	682	-90.00		8100.00		90		15.20%
23	21	6	1	627	699.8	-72.80		5299.84		72.8		11.61%
24	22	6	2	725	717.6	7.40		54.76		7.4		1.02%
25	23	6	3	854	735.4	118.60		14065.96		118.6		13.89%
26	24	6	4	661	753.2	-92.20		8500.84		92.2		13.95%
27						**Sum**		**87910.60**	**Sum**	**1197**	**Sum**	**218.13%**
28						**MSE**		**3662.94**	**MAD**	**49.88**	**MAPE**	**9.09%**

SOLVED PROBLEM 9.1: COMPUTING FORECAST ERROR

Consider the call volume time series in Exhibit 9.4. Suppose that a forecasting method provided the forecasts in column E of the spreadsheet in Exhibit 9.6. Columns F through L compute MSE, MAD, and MAPE.

To compute MSE, we first find the errors between the observations and the forecasts. For example, in period 1, the observation $A_1 = 362$, and the forecast $F_1 = 343.8$. The forecast error is $A_1 - F_1 = 362 - 343.8 = 18.2$, which is computed in cell F2. In column H, we square the error and compute $(A_t - F_t)^2$ for each period t. We add these values in cell H26 and then divide by the number of periods (24) to compute MSE in cell H27 using formula (9.1). Therefore, MSE is 87,910.6/24 = 3,662.94.

To compute MAD, we find the absolute deviation between the observation and the forecast, $|A_t - F_t|$, for each period in column J. We add these in cell J27 and then divide by the number of observations in cell J28 using Equation 9.2. Thus, MAD = 1,197/24 = 49.88.

Finally, to compute MAPE, we find the absolute percentage error for each period by dividing the error in column F by the value of the observation in column D and taking the absolute value; that is, $|(A_t - F_t)/A_t|$. Then divide the sum of these values by the number of observations in cell L28 using Equation 9.3. Thus, MAPE = 218.13%/24 = 9.09%. Using MAPE, the forecast differs from actual call volume on average by plus or minus 9.09 percent.

This measure is simply the average of the sum of the absolute deviations for all the forecast errors.

A third measure of forecast error is the mean absolute percentage error (MAPE):

$$\text{MAPE} = \frac{\Sigma|(A_t - F_t)/A_t| \times 100}{T} \quad [9.3]$$

This is simply the average of the percentage error for each forecast value in the time series.

A major difference between MSE and MAD is that MSE is influenced much more by large forecast errors than by small errors (because the errors are squared). The values of MAD and MSE depend on the measurement scale of the time-series data. For example, forecasting profit in the range of millions of dollars would result in very large values, even for accurate forecasting models. On the other hand, a variable like market share, which is measured as a fraction, will always have small values of MAD and MSE. Thus, the measures have no meaning except in comparison with other models used to forecast the same data. MAPE is different in that the measurement scale factor is eliminated by dividing the absolute error by the time-series data value. This makes the measure easier to interpret. The selection of the best measure of forecasting accuracy is not a simple matter; indeed, forecasting experts often disagree on which measure should be used. However, MSE generally is the most popular.

9-3 Statistical Forecasting Models

Forecasting methods can be classified as either statistical or judgmental. **Statistical forecasting** *is based on the assumption that the future will be an extrapolation of the past.* Many different techniques exist; which technique should be used depends on the variable being forecast and the time horizon. Statistical methods can generally be categorized as *time-series methods*, which extrapolate historical time-series data, and *regression methods*, which extrapolate historical time-series data but can also include other potentially causal factors that influence the behavior of the time series.

Widely varying statistical forecasting models have been developed, and we cannot discuss all of them. However, we present some of the basic and more popular approaches used in OM applications.

9-3a Simple Moving Average

The simple moving average concept is based on the idea of averaging random fluctuations in a time series to identify the underlying direction in which the time series is changing. A **moving average (MA) forecast** *is an average of the most recent "k" observations in a time series.* Thus, the forecast for the next period ($t + 1$), which we denote as F_{t+1}, for a time series with t observations is

$$F_{t+1} = \Sigma(\text{most recent "}k\text{" observations})/k$$
$$= (A_t + A_{t-1} + A_{t-2} + \cdots + A_{t-k+1})/k \qquad [9.4]$$

MA methods work best for short planning horizons when there is no major trend, seasonal, or business cycle patterns—that is, when demand is relatively stable and consistent. As the value of k increases, the forecast reacts slowly to recent changes in the time series because older data are included in the computation. As the value of k decreases, the forecast reacts more quickly. If a significant trend exists in the time-series data, moving-average-based forecasts will lag actual demand, resulting in a bias in the forecast. Solved Problem 9.2 illustrates the calculations for moving average forecasts.

The number of data values to be included in the moving average is often based on managerial insight and judgment. Thus, it should not be surprising that for a particular time series, different values of k lead to different measures of forecast accuracy.

9-3b Single Exponential Smoothing

Single exponential smoothing (SES) *is a forecasting technique that uses a weighted average of past time-series values to forecast the value of the time series in the next period.* SES forecasts are based on averages using and weighting the most recent actual demand more than older demand data.

SOLVED PROBLEM 9.2: COMPUTING MOVING AVERAGES

Exhibit 9.7 shows the number of gallons of milk sold each month at Gas-Mart, a local convenience store. Compute the forecasts for months four and five using a two-, three-, and four-month moving average, and find the MSE for each.

Solution:

Let's examine the three-month case. In Equation 9.4, $k = 3$. The moving average calculation for the first three months of the milk-sales time series, and thus the forecast for month 4, is

$$F_4 = \frac{172 + 217 + 190}{3} = 193.00$$

Because the actual value observed in month 4 is 233, we see that the forecast error in month 4 is $233 - 193 = 40$.

The calculation for the second three-month moving average (F_5) is

$$F_5 = \frac{217 + 190 + 233}{3} = 213.33$$

This provides a forecast for month 5. The error associated with this forecast is $179 - 213.33 = -34.33$. A complete summary of these moving average calculations is shown in Exhibit 9.7. The mean square error for these forecasts is 1,457.33.

You should be able to follow the calculations for the two- and four-month moving averages. Exhibit 9.8 shows the Excel *Moving Average* template available in MindTap for $k = 3$.

EXHIBIT 9.7 Milk-Sales Moving Average Forecasts (This spreadsheet is available in the Excel worksheet *Exhibit 9.8* in MindTap.)

Gas-Mart Monthly Milk Sales

Month	Sales	2-Month MA	Error	3-Month MA	Error	4-Month MA	Error		Squared Errors 2-Month MA	3-Month MA	4-Month MA
1	172										
2	217										
3	190	194.5	-4.50						20.25		
4	233	203.5	29.50	193.00	40.00				870.25	1600.00	
5	179	211.5	-32.50	213.33	-34.33	203.00	-24.00		1056.25	1178.78	576.00
6	162	206	-44.00	200.67	-38.67	204.75	-42.75		1936.00	1495.11	1827.56
7	204	170.5	33.50	191.33	12.67	191.00	13.00		1122.25	160.44	169.00
8	180	183	-3.00	181.67	-1.67	194.50	-14.50		9.00	2.78	210.25
9	225	192	33.00	182.00	43.00	181.25	43.75		1089.00	1849.00	1914.06
10	250	202.5	47.50	203.00	47.00	192.75	57.25		2256.25	2209.00	3277.56
11	151	237.5	-86.50	218.33	-67.33	214.75	-63.75		7482.25	4533.78	4064.06
12	218	200.5	17.50	208.67	9.33	201.50	16.50		306.25	87.11	272.25
								Sum	16147.75	13116.00	12310.75
								MSE	1614.78	1457.33	1538.84

EXHIBIT 9.8 *Moving Average* Excel Template for Three-Month Moving Average Forecasts (This template is available in MindTap.)

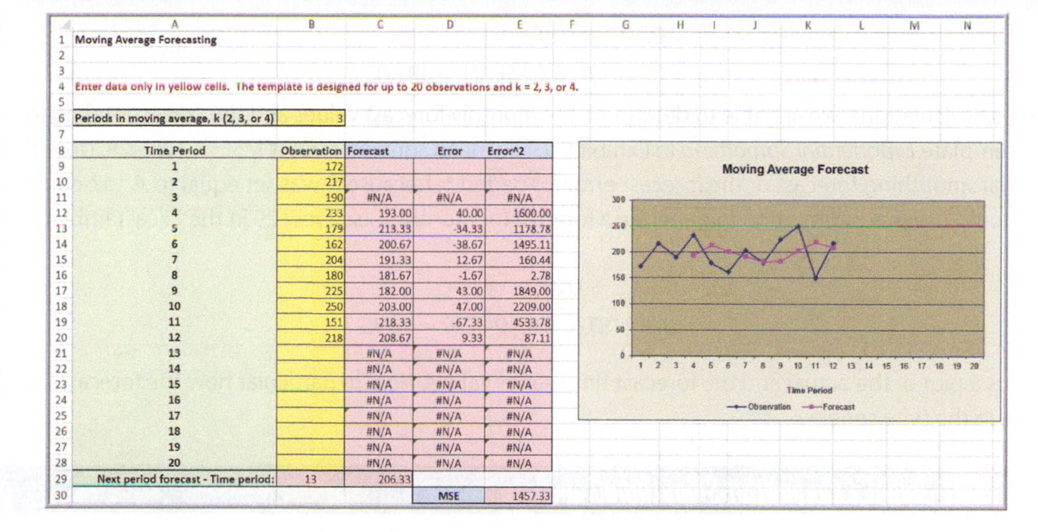

Moving Average Forecasting

Enter data only in yellow cells. The template is designed for up to 20 observations and k = 2, 3, or 4.

Periods in moving average, k (2, 3, or 4): 3

Time Period	Observation	Forecast	Error	Error^2
1	172			
2	217			
3	190	#N/A	#N/A	#N/A
4	233	193.00	40.00	1600.00
5	179	213.33	-34.33	1178.78
6	162	200.67	-38.67	1495.11
7	204	191.33	12.67	160.44
8	180	181.67	-1.67	2.78
9	225	182.00	43.00	1849.00
10	250	203.00	47.00	2209.00
11	151	218.33	-67.33	4533.78
12	218	208.67	9.33	87.11
13		#N/A	#N/A	#N/A
14		#N/A	#N/A	#N/A
15		#N/A	#N/A	#N/A
16		#N/A	#N/A	#N/A
17		#N/A	#N/A	#N/A
18		#N/A	#N/A	#N/A
19		#N/A	#N/A	#N/A
20		#N/A	#N/A	#N/A
Next period forecast - Time period:	13	206.33		
			MSE	1457.33

SES methods do not try to include trend or seasonal effects. The basic exponential smoothing model is

$$\begin{aligned} F_{t+1} &= \alpha A_t + (1 - \alpha)F_t \\ &= F_t + \alpha(A_t - F_t) \end{aligned} \qquad [9.5]$$

where α is called the *smoothing constant* ($0 \leq \alpha \leq 1$). To use this model, set the forecast for period 1, F_1, equal to the actual observation for period 1, A_1. Note that F_2 will also have the same value.

Using the two preceding forms of the forecast equation, we can interpret the simple exponential smoothing model in two ways. In the first model shown in Equation 9.5, the forecast for the next period, F_{t+1}, is a weighted average of the forecast made for period t, F_t, and the actual observation in period t, A_t. The second form of the model in Equation 9.5, obtained by simply rearranging terms, states that the forecast for the next period, F_{t+1}, equals the forecast for the last period, F_t, plus a fraction, α, of the forecast error made in period t, $A_t - F_t$. Thus, to make a forecast once we have selected the smoothing constant, we need only know the previous forecast and the actual value. Solved Problem 9.3 illustrates the application of single exponential smoothing.

SOLVED PROBLEM 9.3: USING SINGLE EXPONENTIAL SMOOTHING

Consider the milk-sales time series presented in Exhibit 9.7. Compute exponential smoothing forecasts using $\alpha = 0.2$.

Solution:

To begin, the exponential smoothing forecast for period 2 is equal to the actual value of the time series in period 1. Thus, with $A_1 = 172$, we will set $F_1 = 172$ to get the computations started. Using Equation 9.5 for $t = 1$, we have

$$F_2 = 0.2A_1 + 0.8F_1$$
$$= 0.2(172) + 0.8(172) = 172.00$$

For period 3 we obtain

$$F_3 = 0.2A_2 + 0.8F_2$$
$$= 0.2(217) + 0.8(172) = 181.00$$

By continuing these calculations, we are able to determine the monthly forecast values and the corresponding forecast errors shown in the Excel template *Exponential Smoothing* in Exhibit 9.9. The mean squared error is MSE = 1285.28. Note that we have not shown an exponential smoothing forecast or the forecast error for period 1, because F_1 was set equal to A_1 to begin the smoothing computations. You could use this information to generate a forecast for month 13 (see row 29 in the Excel template) as

$$F_{13} = 0.2A_{12} + 0.8F_{12}$$
$$= 0.2(218) + 0.8(194.59) = 199.27$$

Exhibit 9.9 also shows a plot of the actual and the forecast time-series values. Note in particular how the forecasts "smooth out" the random fluctuations in the time series.

EXHIBIT 9.9 Excel *Exponential Smoothing* Template

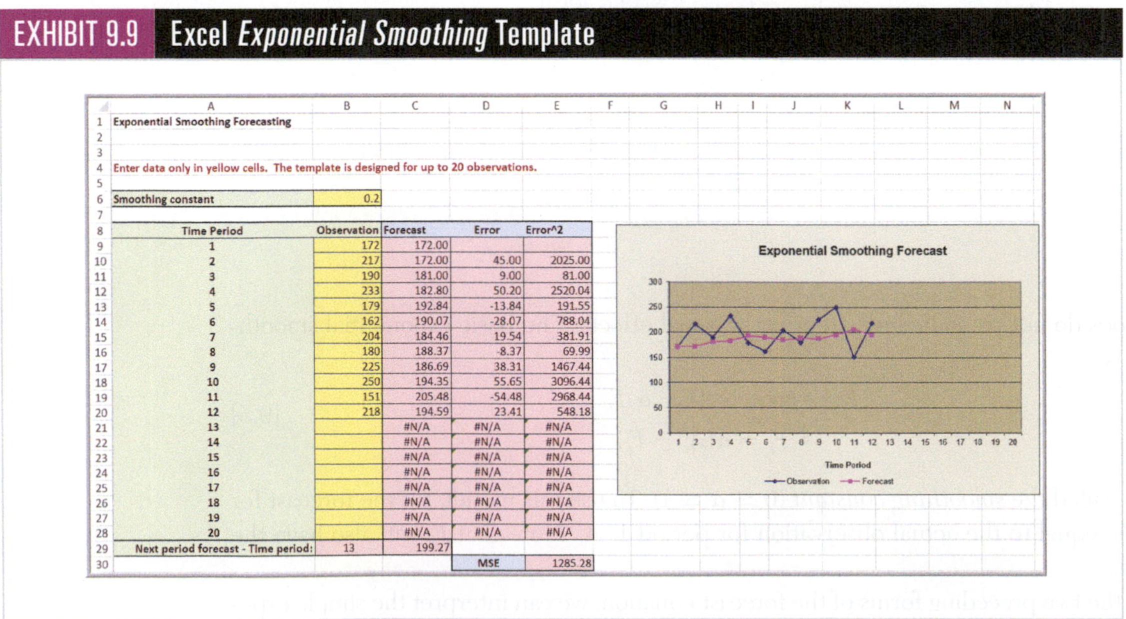

Exponential Smoothing Forecasting

Enter data only in yellow cells. The template is designed for up to 20 observations.

Smoothing constant: 0.2

Time Period	Observation	Forecast	Error	Error^2
1	172	172.00		
2	217	172.00	45.00	2025.00
3	190	181.00	9.00	81.00
4	233	182.80	50.20	2520.04
5	179	192.84	-13.84	191.55
6	162	190.07	-28.07	788.04
7	204	184.46	19.54	381.91
8	180	188.37	-8.37	69.99
9	225	186.69	38.31	1467.44
10	250	194.35	55.65	3096.44
11	151	205.48	-54.48	2968.44
12	218	194.59	23.41	548.18
13		#N/A	#N/A	#N/A
14		#N/A	#N/A	#N/A
15		#N/A	#N/A	#N/A
16		#N/A	#N/A	#N/A
17		#N/A	#N/A	#N/A
18		#N/A	#N/A	#N/A
19		#N/A	#N/A	#N/A
20		#N/A	#N/A	#N/A
Next period forecast - Time period:	13	199.27		
			MSE	1285.28

By repeated substitution for F_t in Equation 9.5, it is easy to demonstrate that F_{t+1} is a decreasingly weighted average of all past time-series data. Thus, exponential smoothing models "never forget" past data as long as the smoothing constant is strictly between 0 and 1. In contrast, MA methods "completely forget" all the data older than k periods in the past.

Typical values for α are in the range of 0.1 to 0.5. Larger values of α place more emphasis on recent data. If the time series is very volatile and contains substantial random variability, a small value of the smoothing constant is preferred. The reason for this choice is that since much of the forecast error is due to random variability, we do not want to overreact and adjust the forecasts too quickly. For a fairly stable time series with relatively little random variability, larger values of the smoothing constant have the advantage of quickly adjusting the forecasts when forecasting errors occur and therefore allowing the forecast to react faster to changing conditions. Similar to the MA model, we can experiment to find the best value for the smoothing constant to minimize the mean square error or one of the other measures of forecast accuracy.

The smoothing constant is approximately related to the value of k in the moving average model by the following relationship:

$$\alpha = 2/(k + 1) \qquad [9.6]$$

Therefore, an exponential smoothing model with $\alpha = 0.5$ is roughly equivalent to a moving average model with $k = 3$.

One disadvantage of exponential smoothing is that if the time series exhibits a positive trend, the forecast will lag the actual values and, similarly, will overshoot the actual values if a negative trend exists. It is good practice to analyze new data to see whether the smoothing constant should be revised to provide better forecasts. If values of α greater than 0.5 are needed to develop a good forecast, other types of forecasting methods might be more appropriate.

9-3c Finding the Best Forecasting Model

We usually do not know whether a moving average model or exponential smoothing model will work best. Sophisticated statistical software can identify the best parameters and models automatically. However, with Excel, the only way is to experiment with different models using historical data and comparing error metrics. The Excel forecasting templates we have illustrated allow you to easily change the value of k for moving averages or the value of α for exponential smoothing and compare MSE. Solved Problem 9.4 provides an example.

SOLVED PROBLEM 9.4: COMPARING FORECASTING MODELS

A retail store records customer demand during each sales period. Use the following demand data to develop three-period and four-period moving average forecasts and single exponential smoothing forecasts with $\alpha = 0.5$. Using MSE, which method provides the better forecast?

Period	Demand	Period	Demand
1	86	7	91
2	93	8	93
3	88	9	96
4	89	10	97
5	92	11	93
6	94	12	95

Using the Excel *Moving Average* template, we find that the MSE for a three-period moving average is 5.98, the MSE for a four-period moving average is 6.21, and the MSE for the exponential-smoothing model is 9.65. Therefore, among these three models, the three-period moving average is best. Exhibit 9.10 shows the results for this model using the Excel template. We encourage you to experiment with different values of α using the *Exponential Smoothing* template to see if you can improve the forecast accuracy.

EXHIBIT 9.10 Excel *Moving Average* Template

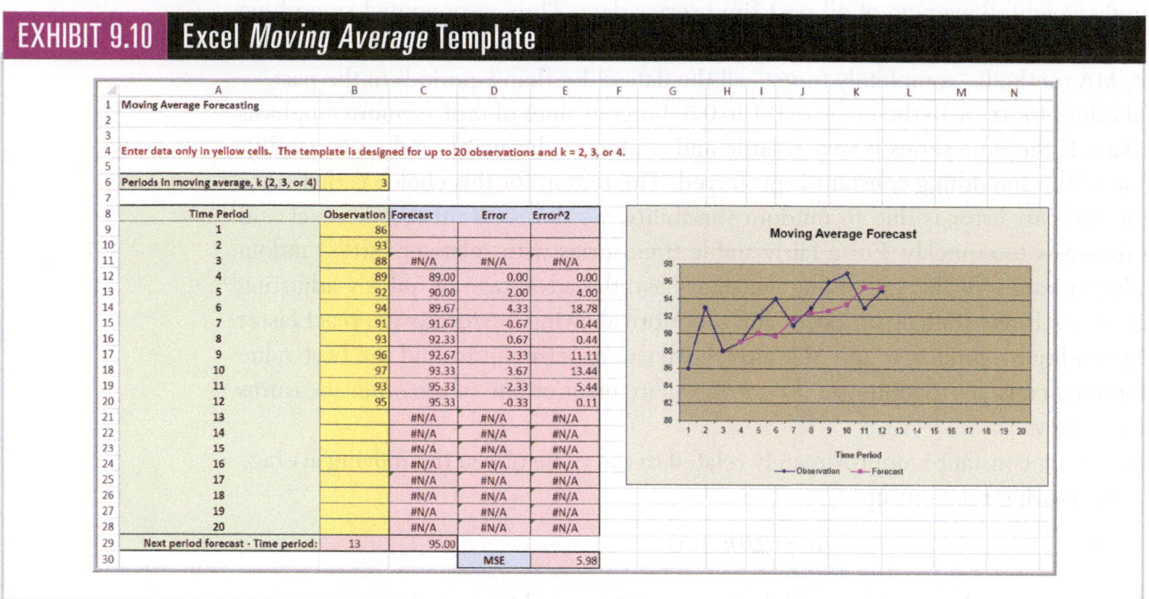

Moving Average Forecasting

Enter data only in yellow cells. The template is designed for up to 20 observations and k = 2, 3, or 4.

Periods in moving average, k (2, 3, or 4)	3

Time Period	Observation	Forecast	Error	Error^2
1	86			
2	93			
3	88	#N/A	#N/A	#N/A
4	89	89.00	0.00	0.00
5	92	90.00	2.00	4.00
6	94	89.67	4.33	18.78
7	91	91.67	-0.67	0.44
8	93	92.33	0.67	0.44
9	96	92.67	3.33	11.11
10	97	93.33	3.67	13.44
11	93	95.33	-2.33	5.44
12	95	95.33	-0.33	0.11
13		#N/A	#N/A	#N/A
14		#N/A	#N/A	#N/A
15		#N/A	#N/A	#N/A
16		#N/A	#N/A	#N/A
17		#N/A	#N/A	#N/A
18		#N/A	#N/A	#N/A
19		#N/A	#N/A	#N/A
20		#N/A	#N/A	#N/A
Next period forecast - Time period:	13	95.00		
			MSE	5.98

9-4 Regression as a Forecasting Approach

Regression analysis *is a method for building a statistical model that defines a relationship between a single dependent variable and one or more independent variables, all of which are numerical.* Regression analysis has wide applications in business; however, we will restrict our discussion to simple applications in forecasting. Supplement A: *Probability and Statistics*, provides a review of regression analysis and an application of Excel's Data Analysis regression tool. We will first consider only simple regression models in which the value of a time series (the dependent variable) is a function of a single independent variable, time.

A simple regression model for forecasting uses the linear function

$$Y_t = a + bt \qquad [9.7]$$

where Y_t represents the value of the dependent variable, and t represents time. If we can identify the best values for a and b, which represent the intercept and slope of the straight line that best fits the time series, we can forecast the value of Y for the next time period, $t + 1$ by computing $Y_{t+1} = a + b(t+1)$.

Simple linear regression finds the best values of a and b using the *method of least squares*. The method of least squares minimizes the sum of the squared deviations between the actual time-series values (A_t) and the estimated values of the dependent variable (Y_t).

9-4a Excel's Add Trendline Option

Excel provides a very simple tool to find the best-fitting regression model for a time series. In Excel, first, click the chart to which you wish to add a trendline to display the *Chart Tools* menu. Click *Add Chart Element* from the *Design* tab and select *Trendline*. You may choose among a linear and a variety of nonlinear functional forms to fit the data. Selecting an appropriate nonlinear form requires some advanced knowledge of functions and mathematics, so we will restrict our discussion to the linear case. Choose *Linear*. Then right-click on the trendline to display the *Format Trendline* options (see Exhibit 9.11). Check the boxes for *Display Equation on chart* and *Display R-squared value on chart*. The R^2 value is a measure of how much variation in the dependent variable is explained by the independent variable (time). The maximum value for R^2 is 1.0; therefore, a high value suggests that the model will be a good predictor. Excel will display the results on the chart you have selected; you may move the equation and R^2-value for better readability by dragging them to a different location. An easier way to do all this is to simply click on the data series in the chart to select the series, and then add a trendline by clicking on the right mouse button (try it!).

EXHIBIT 9.11 Format Trendline Dialog Box

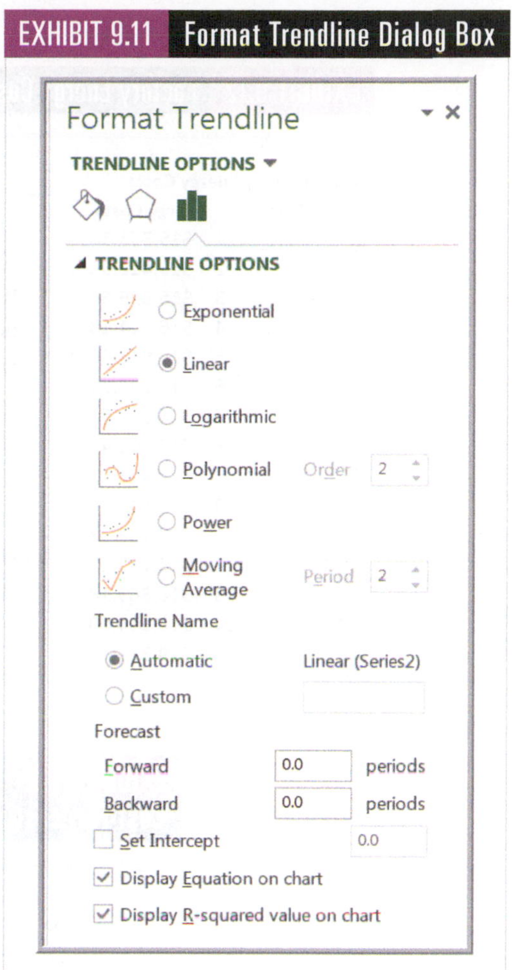

9-4b Causal Forecasting Models with Multiple Regression

In more advanced forecasting applications, other independent variables such as economic indexes or demographic factors that may influence the time series can be incorporated into a regression model. **multiple linear regression model** *A linear regression model with more than one independent variable is called a* **multiple linear regression model**. We illustrate the use of multiple linear regression for forecasting with causal variables in Solved Problem 9.6.

SOLVED PROBLEM 9.5: USING TRENDLINES FOR FORECASTING

Exhibit 9.12 shows total energy costs over the past 15 years at a manufacturing plant. The plant manager needs to forecast costs for the next year to prepare a budget for the VP of finance. The chart suggests that energy costs appear to be increasing in a fairly predictable linear fashion, and that energy costs are related to time by a linear function. Find a trendline and forecast the energy cost for the next year.

Solution:

Exhibit 9.13 shows the trendline added to the chart. The model is

Energy cost = \$15,112 + 280.66(Time)

Thus, to forecast the cost for the next year (16), we compute

Energy cost = \$15,112 + 280.66(16) = \$19,602.56

We could forecast further out into the future if we wished, but the uncertainty of the accuracy of the forecast will be higher. Note that the R^2 value is 0.97; this suggests that the model is a good predictor of energy cost.

EXHIBIT 9.12 Factory Energy Costs (This is available in the Excel worksheet *Exhibit 9.12* in MindTap.)

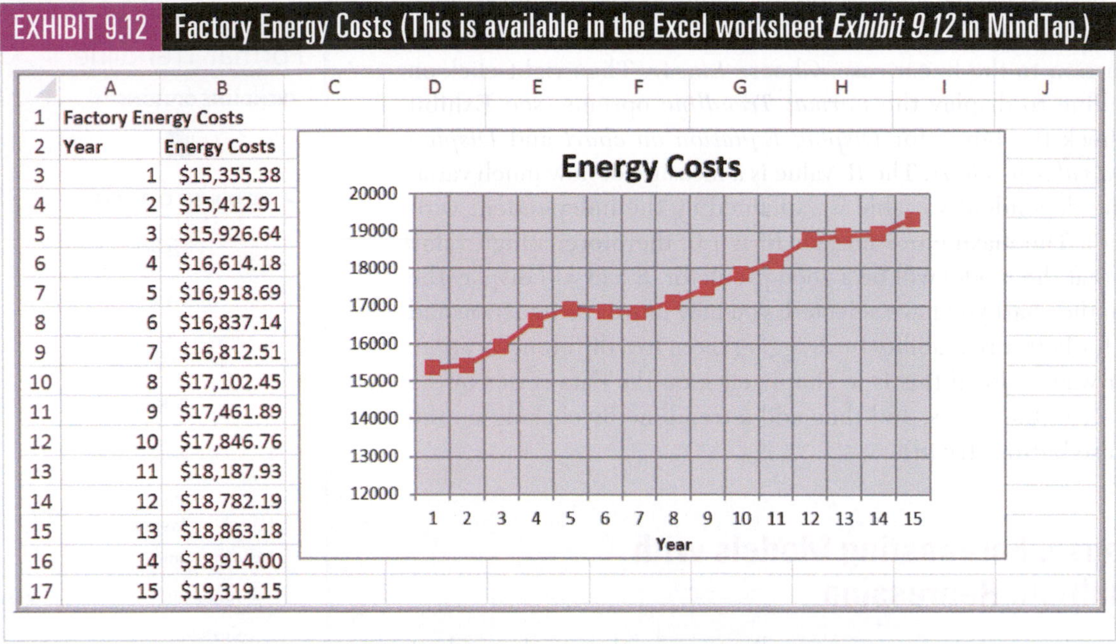

	A	B
1	Factory Energy Costs	
2	Year	Energy Costs
3	1	$15,355.38
4	2	$15,412.91
5	3	$15,926.64
6	4	$16,614.18
7	5	$16,918.69
8	6	$16,837.14
9	7	$16,812.51
10	8	$17,102.45
11	9	$17,461.89
12	10	$17,846.76
13	11	$18,187.93
14	12	$18,782.19
15	13	$18,863.18
16	14	$18,914.00
17	15	$19,319.15

EXHIBIT 9.13 Least-Squares Regression Model for Energy Cost Forecasting

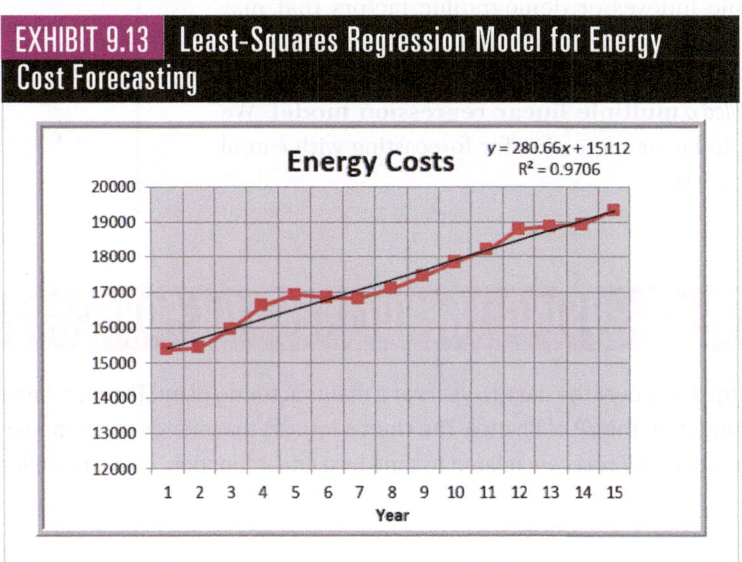

SOLVED PROBLEM 9.6: USING MULTIPLE REGRESSION TO FORECAST GASOLINE SALES

Exhibit 9.14 shows the sales of gasoline over 10 weeks during June through August along with the average price per gallon. Develop a forecasting model using multiple linear regression and forecast sales for week 11 and compare the results to a simple linear regression model using a trendline.

Solution:

Exhibit 9.15 shows a chart of the gasoline-sales time series with a fitted trendline. During the summer months, it is not unusual to see an increase in sales as more people go on vacations. The chart shows that the sales appear to increase over time with a linear trend, making linear regression an appropriate forecasting technique.

The fitted regression line is

$$\text{Sales} = 6{,}382 + (1{,}084.7)(\text{Week})$$

The R^2-value of 0.6842 means that about 68 percent of the variation in the data is explained by time. Using the model, we would predict sales for week 11 as

$$\begin{aligned}\text{Sales} &= 6{,}382 + (1{,}084.7)(11) \\ &= 18{,}313.7\end{aligned}$$

However, we also see that the average price per gallon changes each week, and this may influence consumer sales. Therefore, the sales trend might not simply be a factor of steadily increasing demand but might also be influenced by the average price. Thus, to forecast gasoline sales (i.e., the dependent variable) we propose a multiple regression model using two independent variables (weeks and price):

$$\text{Sales} = \beta_0 + (\beta_1)(\text{Week}) + (\beta_2)(\text{Price})$$

Using the Excel Data Analysis tool for regression, we obtain the results shown in Exhibit 9.16. The regression model is

$$\text{Sales} = 47{,}747.81 + (640.71)(\text{Week}) - (19{,}550.6)(\text{Price})$$

This makes sense because as price increases, sales should decrease. Notice that the R^2-value is higher when both variables are included, explaining almost 86 percent of the variation in the data. The *p*-values for both variables are small, indicating that they are statistically significant variables in predicting sales.

Based on trends in crude oil prices, the company estimates that the average price for the next week will drop to $1.80. Then, using this model we would forecast the sales for week 11 as

$$\begin{aligned}\text{Sales} &= 47{,}747.81 + (640.71)(11) - (19{,}550.6)(\$1.80) \\ &= \$19{,}604.54\end{aligned}$$

EXHIBIT 9.14 Gasoline Sales Data (This is available in the worksheet *Exhibits 9.14–9.16* in MindTap.)

	A	B	C
1	Gasoline Sales		
2			
3	Gallons Sold	Week	Price/Gallon
4	10420	1	$1.95
5	7388	2	$2.20
6	7529	3	$2.12
7	11932	4	$1.98
8	10125	5	$2.01
9	15240	6	$1.92
10	12246	7	$2.03
11	11852	8	$1.98
12	16967	9	$1.82
13	19782	10	$1.90
14		11	$1.80

Multiple regression provides a technique for building forecasting models that not only incorporate time but other potential causal variables.

Notice that this is higher than the pure time-series forecast because the price per gallon is estimated to fall in week 11 and result in a somewhat higher level of sales. The multiple regression model provides a more realistic and accurate forecast than simply extrapolating the historical time series. Exhibits 9.15 and 9.16 are also available in the Excel worksheet *Exhibits 9.14–9.16* in MindTap.

EXHIBIT 9.15 Chart of Sales versus Time

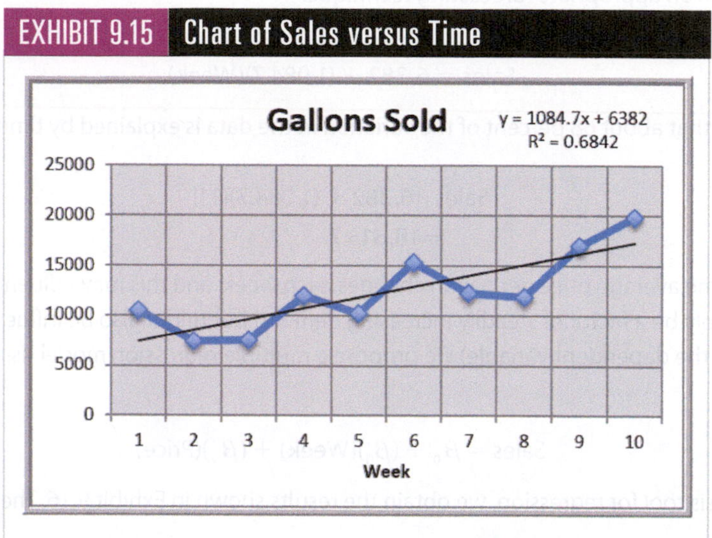

EXHIBIT 9.16 Multiple Regression Results

	A	B	C	D	E	F	G
1	SUMMARY OUTPUT						
2							
3	*Regression Statistics*						
4	Multiple R	0.925735067					
5	R Square	0.856985415					
6	Adjusted R Square	0.816124105					
7	Standard Error	1702.532878					
8	Observations	10					
9							
10	ANOVA						
11		*df*	*SS*	*MS*	*F*	*Significance F*	
12	Regression	2	121585603.5	60792801.75	20.97302837	0.001106194	
13	Residual	7	20290327.4	2898618.2			
14	Total	9	141875930.9				
15							
16		*Coefficients*	*Standard Error*	*t Stat*	*P-value*	*Lower 95%*	*Upper 95%*
17	Intercept	47766.65379	14279.32308	3.345162338	0.012332162	14001.42013	81531.88745
18	Week	640.2462516	241.8696978	2.647070954	0.033082057	68.31529851	1212.177205
19	Price/Gallon	-19557.96493	6725.840727	-2.907884043	0.022728987	-35462.05102	-3653.878833

9-5 Judgmental Forecasting

Judgmental forecasting *relies upon opinions and expertise of people in developing forecasts*. When no historical data are available, only judgmental forecasting is possible. But even when historical data are available and appropriate, they cannot be the sole basis for prediction. The demand for goods and services is affected by a variety of factors such as global markets and cultures, interest rates, disposable income, inflation, and technology. Competitors' actions and government regulations also have an impact. Thus, some element of judgmental forecasting is always necessary. One interesting example of the role of judgmental forecasting occurred during a national recession. All economic indicators pointed toward a future period of low demand for manufacturers of machine tools. However, the forecasters of one such company recognized that recent government regulations for automobile pollution control would require the auto industry to update its current technology by purchasing new tools. As a result, this machine tool company was prepared for the new business.

Several approaches are used in judgmental forecasts. **Grassroots forecasting** *is asking those who are close to the end consumer, such as salespeople, about the customers' purchasing plans*. A more complicated approach is called the Delphi method. *The* **Delphi method** *consists of forecasting by expert opinion by gathering judgments and opinions of key personnel based on their experience and knowledge of the situation.* In the Delphi method, a group of people, possibly from both inside and outside the organization, is asked to make a prediction, such as industry sales for the next year. The experts are not consulted as a group so as not to bias their predictions—for example, because of dominant personalities in the group—but make their predictions and justifications independently. The responses and supporting arguments of each individual are summarized by an outside party and returned to the experts along with further questions. Experts whose opinions fall in the midrange of estimates as well as those whose predictions are extremely high or low (i.e., outliers) might be asked to explain their predictions. The process iterates until a consensus is reached by the group, which usually takes only a few rounds. Other common approaches to gathering data for judgmental forecasts are surveys using questionnaires, telephone contact, and personal interviews.

9-6 Forecasting in Practice

In practice, managers use a variety of judgmental and quantitative forecasting techniques. Statistical methods alone cannot account for such factors as sales promotions, competitive strategies, unusual economic or environmental disturbances, new product introductions, large one-time orders, labor union strikes, and so on. Many managers begin with a statistical forecast and adjust it to account for such factors. Others may develop independent judgmental and statistical forecasts and then combine them, either objectively by averaging or in a subjective manner. It is impossible to provide universal guidance as to which approaches are best, for they depend on many things, such as the presence or absence of trends and seasonality, the number of data points available, length of the forecast time horizon, and the experience and knowledge of the forecaster.

The first step in developing a practical forecast is to understand its purpose. For instance, if financial personnel need a sales forecast to determine capital investment strategies, a long (two- to five-year) time horizon is necessary. For such forecasts, using aggregate groups of items is usually more accurate than using individual-item forecasts added together. These forecasts would probably be measured in dollars. In contrast, production personnel may need short-term forecasts for individual items as a basis for procurement of materials and scheduling. In this case, dollar values would not be appropriate; rather, forecasts should be made in terms of units of production. The level of aggregation often dictates the appropriate method. Forecasting the total amount of soap to produce over the next planning period is certainly different from forecasting the amount of each individual product to produce. Aggregate forecasts are generally much easier to develop, whereas detailed forecasts require more time and resources.

The choice of a forecasting method depends on other criteria as well. Among them are the time span for which the forecast is being made, the needed frequency of forecast updating, data requirements, the level of accuracy desired, and the quantitative skills needed. The

Ten Practical Principles of Forecasting

A group of international experts published a set of principles to guide best practices in forecasting, yet it has been found that many organizations fall short in applying these principles.

1. Use quantitative rather than qualitative methods.
2. Limit subjective adjustments of quantitative forecasts.
3. Adjust for events expected in the future.
4. Ask experts to justify their forecasts in writing.
5. Use structured procedures to integrate judgmental and quantitative methods.
6. Combine forecasts from approaches that differ.
7. If combining forecasts, begin with equal weights.
8. Compare past performance of various forecasting methods.
9. Seek feedback about forecasts.
10. Use multiple measures of forecast accuracy.[3]

time span is one of the most critical criteria. Different techniques are applicable for long-range, intermediate-range, and short-range forecasts. Also important is the frequency of updating that will be necessary. For example, the Delphi method takes considerable time to implement and thus would not be appropriate for forecasts that must be updated frequently.

Forecasters should also monitor a forecast to determine when it might be advantageous to change or update the model. *A tracking signal provides a method for doing this by quantifying* ***bias****—the tendency of forecasts to consistently be larger or smaller than the actual values of the time series.* The tracking method used most often is to compute the cumulative forecast error divided by the value of MAD at that point in time; that is,

$$\text{Tracking signal} = \frac{\Sigma(A_t - F_t)}{\text{MAD}} \qquad [9.8]$$

Typically, tracking signals between plus and minus 4 indicate that the forecast is performing adequately. Values outside this range indicate that you should reevaluate the model used.

CHAPTER 9 LEARNING OBJECTIVE SUMMARIES

9.1 **Describe the importance of forecasting to the value chain.** Accurate forecasts are needed throughout the value chain and are used by all functional areas of an organization, such as accounting, finance, marketing, operations, and distribution. Poor forecasting can result in poor inventory and staffing decisions, resulting in part shortages, inadequate customer service, and many customer complaints. In the telecommunications industry, competition is fierce, and goods and services have very short life cycles. Forecasting is typically included in comprehensive value chain and demand-planning software systems. These systems integrate marketing, inventory, sales, operations planning, and financial data.

9.2 **Explain basic concepts of forecasting and time series.** Long-range forecasts cover a planning horizon of 1 to 10 years and are necessary to plan for the expansion of facilities and to determine future needs for land, labor, and equipment. Intermediate-range forecasts over a 3- to 12-month period are needed to plan workforce levels, allocate budgets among divisions, schedule jobs and resources, and establish purchasing plans. Short-range forecasts focus on the planning horizon of up to 3 months and are used by operations managers to plan production schedules and assign workers to jobs, to determine short-term capacity requirements, and to aid shipping departments in planning transportation needs and establishing delivery schedules.

Different time series may exhibit one or more of the following characteristics: *trend, seasonal, cyclical, random variation,* and *irregular (one-time) variation.* All forecasts are subject to error, and understanding the nature and size of errors is important to making good decisions. Generally, three types of forecast error metrics are used: mean square error, mean absolute deviation, and mean absolute percentage deviation. See Equations 9.1–9.3 in the formula card.

9.3 **Explain how to apply simple moving average and exponential smoothing models.** The simple moving average concept is based on the idea of averaging random fluctuations in a time series to identify the underlying direction in which the time series is changing.

$$F_{t+1} = \Sigma(\text{most recent "}k\text{" observations})/k$$
$$= (A_t + A_{t-1} + A_{t-2} + \cdots + A_{t-k+1})/k \quad [9.4]$$

Moving average (MA) methods work best for short planning horizons when there are no major trend, seasonal, or business cycle patterns; that is, when demand is relatively stable and consistent. As the value of k increases, the forecast reacts slowly to recent changes in the time series because older data are included in the computation. As the value of k decreases, the forecast reacts more quickly. If a significant trend exists in the time series data, moving-average-based forecasts will lag actual demand, resulting in a bias in the forecast.

Single exponential smoothing (SES) forecasts are based on averages using and weighting the most recent actual demand more than older demand data. SES methods do not include trend or seasonal effects. The basic exponential smoothing model is

$$F_{t+1} = \alpha A_t + (1 - \alpha)F_t$$
$$= F_t + \alpha(A_t - F_t) \quad [9.5]$$

Typical values for α are in the range of 0.1 to 0.5. Larger values of α place more emphasis on recent data. If the time series is very volatile and contains substantial random variability, a small value of the smoothing constant is preferred. The reason for this choice is that because much of the forecast error is due to random variability, we do not want to overreact and adjust the forecasts too quickly. For a fairly stable time series with relatively little random variability, larger values of the smoothing constant have the advantage of quickly adjusting the forecasts when forecasting errors occur, therefore allowing the forecast to react faster to changing conditions.

9.4 **Describe how to apply regression as a forecasting approach.** Simple regression models forecast the value of a time series (the dependent variable) as a function of a single independent variable, time.

$$Y_t = a + bt \quad [9.7]$$

In more advanced forecasting applications, other independent variables, such as economic indexes or demographic factors that may influence the time series, can be incorporated into a regression model. An example is

$$\text{Sales} = \beta_0 + (\beta_1)(\text{Week}) + (\beta_2)(\text{Price})$$

Multiple regression models often provide a more realistic and accurate forecast than simply extrapolating the historical time series.

9.5 **Explain the role of judgment in forecasting.** When no historical data are available, only judgmental forecasting is possible. The demand for goods and services is affected by a variety of factors, such as global markets and cultures, interest rates, disposable income, inflation, and technology. Competitors' actions and government regulations also have an impact. Thus, some element of judgmental forecasting is always necessary.

The major reasons given for using judgmental methods rather than quantitative methods are (1) greater accuracy, (2) ability to incorporate unusual or one-time events, and (3) the difficulty of obtaining the data necessary for quantitative techniques. Also, judgmental methods seem to create a feeling of "ownership" and add a commonsense dimension.

CHAPTER 9 LEARNING OBJECTIVE SUMMARIES

9.6 **Describe how statistical and judgmental forecasting techniques are applied in practice.** In practice, managers use a variety of judgmental and quantitative forecasting techniques. Statistical methods alone cannot account for such factors as sales promotions, competitive strategies, unusual economic or environmental disturbances, new product introductions, large onetime orders, labor union strikes, and so on. Many managers begin with a statistical forecast and adjust it to account for such factors. Others may develop independent judgmental and statistical forecasts and then combine them, either objectively by averaging or in a subjective manner.

The choice of a forecasting method depends on other criteria, such as the time span for which the forecast is being made, the needed frequency of forecast updating, data requirements, the level of accuracy desired, and the quantitative skills needed.

Forecasters should also monitor a forecast to determine when it might be advantageous to change or update the model. The tracking method used most often is to compute the cumulative forecast error divided by the value of MAD at that point in time; that is,

$$\text{Tracking signal} = \frac{\Sigma(A_t - F_t)}{\text{MAD}} \quad [9.8]$$

Typically, tracking signals between plus or minus 4 indicate that the forecast is performing adequately. Values outside this range indicate that you should reevaluate the model.

KEY TERMS

- **Bias**
- **Cyclical patterns**
- **Delphi method**
- **Forecast error**
- **Forecasting**
- **Grassroots forecasting**
- **Irregular variation**
- **Judgmental forecasting**
- **Moving average (MA) forecast**
- **Multiple linear regression model**
- **Planning horizon**
- **Random variation (noise)**
- **Regression analysis**
- **Seasonal patterns**
- **Single exponential smoothing (SES)**
- **Statistical forecasting**
- **Time bucket**
- **Time series**
- **Trend**

REVIEW QUESTIONS

9.1 1. Define forecasting and explain why is it important.

9.1 2. How is forecasting used throughout the value chain?

9.2 3. Describe the different time horizons used in forecasting and provide examples of each.

9.2 4. What is a time series? Explain the four characteristics that time series may exhibit and provide some practical examples.

9.2 5. Explain the importance of selecting the proper planning horizon in forecasting.

9.2 6. Define forecast error. Explain how to calculate the three common measures of forecast accuracy.

9.3 7. Explain how to compute single moving average forecasts.

9.3 8. Explain how to determine the number of data values (k) in a moving average forecast.

9.3 9. Explain how to apply simple moving average and exponential smoothing models.

9.4 10. Describe how to apply regression as a forecasting approach.

9.5 11. Explain the role of judgment in forecasting.

9.6 12. Describe how statistical and judgmental forecasting techniques are applied in practice.

9.6 13. What is bias in forecasting? Explain the importance of using tracking signals to monitor forecasts.

DISCUSSION QUESTIONS AND EXPERIENTIAL ACTIVITIES

9.1 14. Discuss some forecasting issues that you encounter in your daily life. How do you make your forecasts?

9.1 15. Suppose that you were thinking about opening a new restaurant. How would you go about forecasting demand and sales?

9.1 16. If a manager asked you whether to use time-series forecasting models or regression-based forecasting models, what would you tell him or her?

9.2 17. Looking back at the chapters you have studied so far, discuss how good forecasting can improve operations decisions in these areas.

9.5 18. Interview a current or previous employer about how he or she makes forecasts. Document in one page what you discovered, and describe it using the ideas discussed in this chapter.

9.5 19. Research and write a short paper (two pages maximum) that summarizes the capabilities of commercial software available for forecasting. How does such software compare with using Excel?

9.5 20. Search the Internet for some time-series data that relates to sustainability, for example, environmental emissions. What types of patterns do these data exhibit? Apply forecasting techniques in this chapter to forecast ten years into the future.

COMPUTATIONAL PROBLEMS AND EXERCISES

These exercises require you to apply the formulas and methods described in the chapter. The problems should be solved manually.

9.2 21. Compute MSE, MAD, and MAPE (Equations 9.1 to 9.3) for the following customer satisfaction data:

Month	Customer Satisfaction Score	Forecast
1	88.4	84.0
2	87.2	86.6
3	90.1	89.1
4	92.7	88.7
5	91.5	89.9

9.2 22. ProScript sells writing software that edits and proofs manuscripts. The last six months of data are shown below:

Month	Demand	Forecast
16	230	200
17	197	185
18	222	210
19	240	228
20	252	239

Compute MSE, MAD, and MAPE (Equations 9.1 to 9.3) for these data.

9.3 23. Cynthia's Design Studios had sales the last four months of $13,700, $15,400, $17,100, and $18,800. Sales are related to how many designers Cynthia has on-duty. The sales forecast helps her decide on the proper staffing levels.

a. What is the forecast for the fifth month using a two-period moving average?

b. What is the forecast for the fifth month using $\alpha = 0.9$ in an exponential smoothing model with $A_4 = \$18,800$ and $F_4 = \$16,913$ to get things started.

9.3 24. Ink cartridges for the Burke Model 901 printer the last four weeks are as follows:

Week	1	2	3	4
Units Sold	112	95	125	118

a. What is the three-week moving average for the fifth week?

b. What is the four-week moving average for the fifth week?

c. Actual sales for week five were 126. With this information, what is the four-week moving average forecast for week six?

d. What can you conclude about this demand pattern?

9.3 25. A manufacturer uses a moving average to predict how many replacement parts for Part #8119 they should produce per month. Past demand is as follows:

Month	Demand (units)
1	302
2	288
3	325
4	401
5	430
6	456

What are the forecasts for month seven using two-, four-, and six-period moving averages? What can we learn from the answers?

9.3 26. Exotic Wines, Inc. wants to use exponential smoothing with $\alpha = 0.25$ to forecast demand in bottles sold. The demand the last four months are 2,321, 3,097, 2,845, and 3,812 bottles. The forecast for bottles was 2,321 bottles for the second month. What is the forecast for the fifth month?

9.3 27. A small airplane company called Just In Time flies between cities in Florida. It is trying to decide whether to add one extra plane to its fleet next year. Passenger demand that last four quarters are as follows: Q1 = 4,403, Q2 = 4,008, Q3 = 3,750, and Q4 = 4,508 passengers. The forecast for passengers in the second month was 4,403 passengers.

a. What is the forecast for the fifth month using exponential smoothing with $\alpha = 0.1$?

b. Given only what you learned in a, should the airline add another plane?

9.4 28. A linear regression model is Units = 3,014 − 0.639*Week. For week 38, what is the forecast for the number of units?

9.4 29. Ham's Used Cars sells cars with an upward trend based on time and the degree of bad weather. Weather is scored with 1 being bad weather and 5 being great weather. Using the following multiple regression model, Sales (units of used cars) = 0.92 + 0.44*Week + 1.04*Weather, what is the forecast of used car sales for week 9 with bad weather?

9.5 30. What is the tracking signal for the end of period 39 when actual demand is 800 units and the forecast is 700 units in period 39. The algebraic sum of the forecast errors at the end of period 38 was -111 units. Assume that MAD is computed at the end of period 39 to be 2.11. What does this tracking signal mean?

EXCEL-BASED PROBLEMS

For these problems, you may use Excel or the spreadsheet templates in MindTap to assist in your analysis.

9.3 31. Canton Supplies, Inc., is a service firm that employs approximately 100 people. Because of the necessity of meeting monthly cash obligations, the chief financial officer wants to develop a forecast of monthly cash requirements. Because of a recent change in equipment and operating policy, only the past seven months of data are considered relevant. The change in operations has had a great impact on cash flow. What forecasting model do you recommend? Use the *Moving Average* and *Exponential Smoothing* Excel templates or other Excel tools to help you answer this question.

Month	Cash Required ($1,000)	Month	Cash Required ($1,000)
1	190	5	230
2	212	6	240
3	218	7	200
4	260		

9.3 32. The Costello Music Company has been in business five years. During that time, its sales of electric organs has grown from 12 to 76 units per year. Fred Costello, the firm's owner, wants to forecast next year's organ sales. The historical data follow:

Year	1	2	3	4	5
Sales	12	28	34	50	76

a. Construct a chart for this time series on a spreadsheet.

b. What forecasting method do you recommend and why? Use appropriate Excel templates and tools to justify your recommendation.

c. Use your recommendation to obtain a forecast for Years 6 and 7.

9.3 33. The historical sales for a certain model of a single serve coffee maker in units is January, 26; February, 21; March, 20; April, 23; May, 17; and June, 20. Using a two-month moving average, determine the forecast for July using the *Moving Average* Excel template. If July experienced a demand of 15, what is the forecast for August?

9.3 34. The manufacturer of gas outdoor grills provides sales data for the last three years as follows:

	Quarter Number (in thousands)			
Year	1	2	3	4
1	20	40	50	20
2	30	60	60	50
3	40	50	70	50

Use the *Exponential Smoothing* Excel template to develop single exponential smoothing models with $\alpha = 0.2, 0.4$, and 0.6. Compare these models using MSE and identify the best one.

9.3 35. For the coffee maker sales data in problem 33, use the *Exponential Smoothing* Excel template with $\alpha = 0.2$ to compute the exponential smoothing forecasts for February through July.

9.3 36. Forecasts and actual sales of digital music players at Just Say Music are as follows:

Month	Forecast	Actual Sales
March	150	170
April	220	229
May	205	192
June	256	241
July	250	238
August	260	210
September	270	225
October	280	179

a. Plot the data on a spreadsheet and provide insights about the time series.

b. What is the forecast for November, using a two-period moving average?

c. What is the forecast for November, using a three-period moving average?

d. Compute MSE for the two- and three-period moving average models using the *Moving Average* Excel template and compare your results.

9.3 37. For the actual sales data at Just Say Music in problem 36, find the best single exponential smoothing model by evaluating the MSE for α from 0.1 to 0.9, in increments of 0.1. How does this model compare with the best moving average model found in problem 36?

9.3 38. To plan factory staffing levels, Luke's Surfboards, needs to forecast sales for the next two quarters. Sales of surfboards for the last five years are shown below in millions of dollars. These data are available in the worksheet *C9 Excel P38 Data* in MindTap.

Year, Quarter	Time (X)	Sales $ (Y)
1, Q1	1	2
1, Q2	2	4
1, Q3	3	5
1, Q4	4	4
2, Q1	5	3
2, Q2	6	5
2, Q3	7	7
2, Q4	8	5
3, Q1	9	4
3, Q2	10	8
3, Q3	11	9
3, Q4	12	6
4, Q1	13	5
4, Q2	14	8
4, Q3	15	10
4, Q4	16	6
5, Q1	17	6
5, Q2	18	7
5, Q3	19	9
5, Q4	20	7

a. Use the *Moving Average* Excel template to find the best moving average model with $k = 2, 3, 4$, and 5 periods.

b. Using the best moving average model found in (a), what are the quarterly forecasts for year six, assuming that actual sales in each quarter will equal forecasted sales?

c. If actual sales for quarter 1, 2, and 3 for Year 6 were $8.4, $7.6, and $9.2 million, what is the sales forecast for the fourth quarter?

9.3 39. A restaurant wants to forecast its weekly sales. Historical data (in dollars) for fifteen weeks are shown below and can be found in the Excel worksheet *C9 Excel P39 Data* in MindTap. Use Excel and the *Moving Average* template to answer the following questions. (Note: You may copy the data from the worksheet to the template.)

Week	Sales (dollars)
1	1623
2	1533
3	1455
4	1386
5	1209
6	1348
7	1591
8	1332
9	1245
10	1521
11	1421
12	1502
13	1656
14	1614
15	1332

a. Plot the data and provide insights about the time series.

b. What is the forecast for week 16, using a two-period moving average?

c. What is the forecast for week 16, using a three-period moving average?

d. Compare MSE for the two- and three-period moving average models to determine the best model.

9.3 40. For the restaurant sales data in problem 39, use the *Exponential Smoothing* Excel template in MindTap to find the best exponential smoothing model by evaluating the MSE for α from 0.1 to 0.9, in increments of 0.1. How does this model compare with the best moving average model found in problem 39?

9.3 41. Consider the quarterly sales data for Kilbourne Health Club shown below.

	Quarter				Total
Year	**1**	**2**	**3**	**4**	**Sales**
1	4	2	1	5	12
2	6	4	4	14	28
3	10	3	5	16	34
4	12	9	7	22	50
5	18	10	13	35	76

These data are available in a simpler format in the Excel worksheet *C9 Excel P41* in MindTap.

a. Use the *Moving Average* Excel template to develop a four-period moving average model and compute MAD, MAPE, and MSE for your forecasts.

b. Use the *Exponential Smoothing* Excel template to find a good value of α for a single exponential smoothing model and compare your results to part (a) using only MSE.

9.3 42. The number of component parts used in a production process each of the last 10 weeks is as follows.

Week	Parts	Week	Parts
1	200	6	210
2	350	7	280
3	250	8	350
4	360	9	290
5	250	10	320

a. Use the *Moving Average* Excel template to develop moving average models with two, three, and four periods. Compare them using MSE to determine which is best. From the results below, the four-period forecast is the best.

b. Using Equation 9.6, what is the best alpha value (smoothing constant) to begin your analysis using exponential smoothing based on the results of part (a)?

9.3 43. The monthly sales of a new business software package at a local discount software store were as follows:

Week	1	2	3	4	5	6	7	8	9	10
Sales	460	415	432	450	488	512	475	502	449	486

a. Plot the data on a spreadsheet and provide insights about the time series.

b. Use the *Moving Average* Excel template to find the best number of weeks to use in a moving average forecast based on MSE.

c. Use the *Exponential Smoothing Excel* template to find the best single exponential smoothing model to forecast these data

9.3 44. Using the factory energy cost data in Exhibit 9.11, find the best moving average and exponential smoothing models using the *Moving Average* and *Exponential Smoothing* Excel templates. Compare their forecasting ability with the regression model developed in the chapter. Which model would you choose and why?

9.3,4 45. The historical demand for the Panasonic Model 304 Pencil Sharpener is January, 80; February, 100; March, 60; April, 80; and May, 90 units.

a. Using a four-month moving average and the *Moving Average* Excel template, what is the forecast for June?

b. Develop a linear regression model using Excel and compute a forecast for June, July, and August.

c. Compare these results and explain the implications of the regression model.

9.4 46. The president of a small manufacturing firm is concerned about the continual growth in manufacturing costs in the past several years. The data series of the cost per unit for the firm's leading product over the past eight years are given as follows:

Year	Cost/Unit	Year	Cost/Unit
1	\$20.00	5	\$26.60
2	\$24.50	6	\$30.00
3	\$28.20	7	\$31.00
4	\$27.50	8	\$36.00

a. Plot this time series on a spreadsheet. Does a linear trend appear to exist?

b. Use Excel to develop a simple linear regression model for these data. What average cost increase has the firm been realizing per year?

9.3,6 47. A chain of grocery stores had the following weekly demand (cases) for a particular brand of laundry soap:

Week	1	2	3	4	5	6	7	8	9	10
Demand	31	22	33	26	21	29	25	22	20	26

a. Use the *Moving Average* Excel template to develop three- and four-period moving average forecasts, and compute MSE for each. Which provides the better forecast? What would be your forecast for week 11?

b. Use the *Exponential Smoothing* Excel template to develop an exponential smoothing forecast using the smoothing constant value determined by Equation 9.6.

c. Compute the tracking signal for a three- and four-period moving average model on a spreadsheet. Is there any evidence of bias?

9.6 48. Two experienced managers are resisting the introduction of a computerized exponential smoothing system, claiming that their judgmental forecasts are much better than any computer could do. Their past record of predictions is as follows:

Week	Actual Demand	Manager's Forecast
1	4,000	4,500
2	4,200	5,000
3	4,200	4,000
4	3,000	3,800
5	3,800	3,600
6	5,000	4,000
7	5,600	5,000
8	4,400	4,800
9	5,000	4,000
10	4,800	5,000

These data are available in the Excel worksheet *C9 Excel P48* in MindTap.

Compare the manager's judgmental forecasts to those obtained using time series models. Are the manager's judgmental forecasts performing satisfactorily? (Use appropriate Excel templates and compute error metrics for the manager's forecasts on a spreadsheet.)

United Dairies, Inc.

United Dairies, Inc. supplies milk to independent grocers in Collier County, Florida. Milk is perishable so forecast accuracy is critical in predicting the number of gallons of milk sold per month. Sales data in gallons for the past twelve months is shown in Exhibit 9.17 (these data are available in the worksheet *United Dairies Case Data* in MindTap). The demand indicates a seasonal pattern because in the winter months (months 1 to 3 and 12) the population of the county increases dramatically as people from the northern United States, Canada, and Europe spend their winters there to avoid the harsh weather.

EXHIBIT 9.17 United Dairies Milk Demand (gallons)

Month	Milk (gallons)
1	3,750
2	3,480
3	3,450
4	3,000
5	2,900
6	3,050
7	2,750
8	2,520
9	2,800
10	3,000
11	3,200
12	3,240

Case Questions for Discussion:

1. What moving average or exponential smoothing model would you recommend to forecast demand? Clearly show your results and explain your conclusions.
2. What might the economic impact be of over or under forecasting here for this perishable commodity?

BankUSA: Forecasting Help Desk Demand by Day

Production Perig/Shutterstock.com

"Hello, is this the investment management help desk?" said a tired voice on the other end of the telephone line at 7:42 a.m. "Yes, how can I help you?" said Thomas Bourbon, customer service representative (CSR). "I've got a problem. My best customer, with assets of over $10 million in our bank, received his monthly trust account statement. He says we computed the market value of one of his stocks inaccurately by using the wrong share price, which makes his statement $42,000 too low. I assured him we would research the problem and get back to him by the end of the day. Also, do you realize that I waited over four minutes before you answered my call?" said the trust administrator, Chris Miami. "Mr. Miami, give me the customer's account number and the stock in question, and I'll get back to you within the hour. Let's solve the customer's problem first. I apologize for the long wait," said Bourbon in a positive and reassuring voice.

The Help Desk supports fiduciary operations activities worldwide by answering questions from company employees, such as portfolio managers, stock traders, backroom company process managers, branch bank managers, accountants, and trust account administrators. These internal customers originate over 98 percent of the volume of Help Desk inquiries. Over 50 different internal processes and organizational units call the Help Desk. Some external customers such as large estate and trust administrators are tied directly to their accounts via the Internet and occasionally call the Help Desk directly.

The Help Desk is the primary customer contact unit within fiduciary operations, employing 14 full-time customer service representatives (CSRs), three CSR support employees, and three managers, for a total of 20 people. The three CSR support employees work fulltime on research in support of the CSRs answering the telephone.

The Help Desk handles about 2,000 calls a week, and the pressure to reduce unit cost is ongoing. Forecast accuracy is a key input to better staffing decisions that minimize costs and maximize service. The accompanying table shows the number of calls per day (call volume). These data are available in the Excel worksheet *BankUSA Case Data* in MindTap.

The senior manager of the Help Desk, Dot Gifford, established a team to try to evaluate short-term forecasting. The Help Desk staffing team consists of Gifford, Bourbon, Miami, and a new employee, David Hamlet, who has an undergraduate major in operations management from a leading business school. This four-person team is charged with developing a long-term forecasting procedure for the Help Desk. Gifford asked the team to make an informal presentation of their analysis in 10 days. The primary job of analysis has fallen on Hamlet, the newly hired operations analyst. It's his chance to make a good first impression on his boss and colleagues.

Day	Call Volume
1	204
2	336
3	295
4	251
5	280
6	300
7	398
8	418
9	309
10	471
11	522
12	502
13	449
14	452
15	420
16	500

Case Questions for Discussion:

1. What are the service management characteristics of the CSR job?
2. Define the mission statement and strategy of the Help Desk. Why is the Help Desk important? Who are its customers?
3. How would you handle the customer affected by the inaccurate stock price in the bank's trust account system? Would you take a passive or proactive approach? Justify your answer.
4. Using the data on call volume in the table, how would you forecast short-term demand?

Integrative Case: Hudson Jewelers

The Hudson Jewelers case study found in MindTap integrates material found in each chapter of the book.

Case Question for Discussion:

1. The worksheet *Hudson Jeweler Demand Case Data* in MindTap provides the number of visits over one year from January to December (52 weeks). Chart the data in Excel and explain the characteristics of the time series. How would you forecast future demand for customer visits? What criteria will you use to determine a "good" forecast? What methods would you use, and why? What is your final recommendation with respect to a forecasting method?

10 Capacity Management

LEARNING OBJECTIVES

After studying this chapter, you should be able to:

- **10-1** Explain the concept of capacity.
- **10-2** Describe how to compute and use capacity measures.
- **10-3** Describe long-term capacity expansion strategies.
- **10-4** Describe short-term capacity adjustment strategies.
- **10-5** Explain the concepts and applications of learning curves.

Capacity decisions can have a profound impact on business performance.

Sheila Fitzgerald/Shutterstock.com

In April of 2016 Tesla unveiled its low-cost Model 3 electric car. Over 325,000 potential buyers put up a deposit in the first week. While Tesla added new production capacity to increase production of its higher-cost Model S by some 35,000 vehicles to about 100,000 in 2015, the Model 3 will bring some significant capacity challenges. Jay Baron, CEO of the Center for Automotive Research in Ann Arbor observed: "They have to speed up production, and you're talking four or five times faster than they produce now. On top of all that you need more people. You need more stations on the assembly line."[1]

WHAT DO YOU THINK?

Have you ever experienced problems with a service because of inadequate labor or equipment capacity?

Capacity *is the capability of a manufacturing or service system, such as a facility, process, workstation, or piece of equipment, to accomplish its purpose or to produce output in a period of time.*

Some examples are the ability to make enough hamburgers during a weekday lunch hour to meet customer demand at a quick service restaurant or the ability to handle emergency room patients with a waiting time of 20 minutes or less. Having sufficient capacity to meet customer demand and provide high levels of customer service is vital to a successful business and long-term economic sustainability.

Capacity decisions cannot be taken lightly and can have profound impacts on business performance, as the introduction suggests. For example, while Tesla's factory was optimized for its model S luxury vehicle, the company will now require new assembly lines and scale up its production capacity. This also means that they will need to hire additional workers, engineers, and staff to support not only its value-creation processes, but also support processes such as scheduling, quality, training, and supplier development. In addition, it will need to expand its network of retail and service centers across the country.

10-1 Understanding Capacity

Capacity can be viewed in one of two ways:

1. as the rate of production output per unit of time; or
2. as units of resource availability.

For example, as an output rate, the capacity of an automobile plant might be the number of automobiles capable of being produced per week and the capacity of a paper mill as the number of tons it can produce per year. As a resource availability measure, the capacity of a hospital would be measured by the number of beds available, and the capacity of "cloud" storage would be measured in gigabytes.

Operations managers must decide on the appropriate levels of capacity to meet current (short-term) and future (long-term) demand. Exhibit 10.1 provides examples of such capacity decisions. Short-term capacity decisions usually involve adjusting schedules or staffing levels. Longer-term decisions typically involve major capital investments. To satisfy customers in the long run, capacity must be at least as large as the average demand. However, demand for many goods and services typically varies over time. A process may not be capable of meeting peak demand at all times, resulting in either lost sales or customers who must wait until the good or service becomes available. At other periods of time, capacity may exceed demand, resulting in idle processes or facilities, or buildups in physical inventories. This is illustrated in Exhibit 10.2.

EXHIBIT 10.1 Examples of Short- and Long-Term Capacity Decisions

Short-Term Capacity Decisions	Long-Term Capacity Decisions
• Amount of overtime scheduled for the next week	• Construction of a new manufacturing plant
• Number of emergency room nurses on call during a downtown festival weekend	• Expanding the size and number of beds in a hospital
• Number of call center workers to staff during the holiday season	• Number of branch banks to establish in a new market territory

10-1a Capacity Decisions and Economies of Scale

Capacity decisions are often influenced by economies and diseconomies of scale. **Economies of scale** *are achieved when the average unit cost of a good or service decreases as the capacity and/or volume of throughput increases.* For example, the design and construction cost per room of building a hotel decreases as the facility gets larger because the fixed cost is allocated over more rooms, resulting in a lower unit room cost. This lends support to building larger facilities with more capacity.

Capacity decisions are often influenced by economies and diseconomies of scale.

EXHIBIT 10.2 The Demand versus Capacity Problem Structure

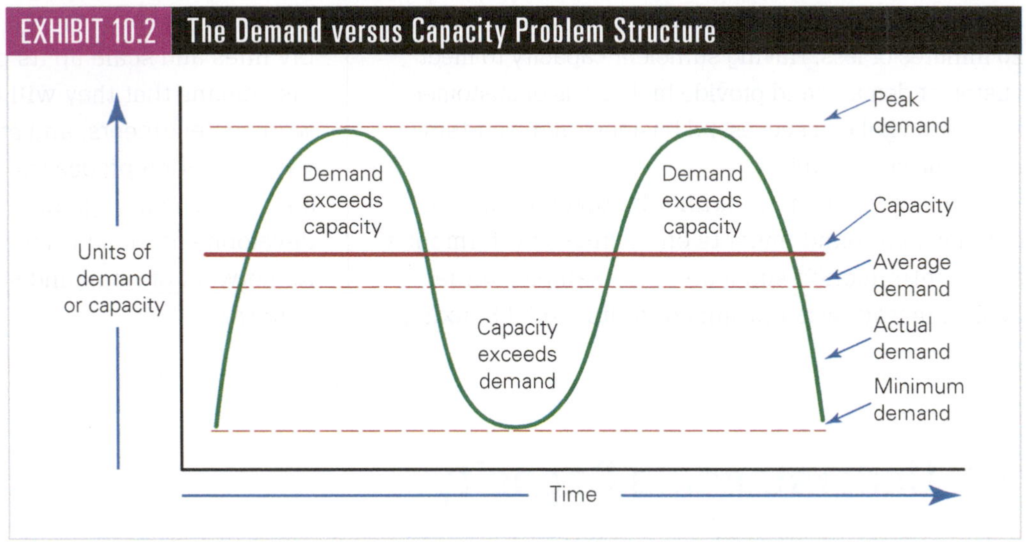

Diseconomies of scale *occur when the average unit cost of the good or service begins to increase as the capacity and/or volume of throughput increases.* In the hotel example, as the number of rooms in a hotel continues to increase, the average cost per unit begins to increase because of larger amounts of overhead and operating expenses required by higher levels of such amenities as restaurants, parking, and recreational facilities. This suggests that some optimal amount of capacity exists where costs are at a minimum. The pressure on global automakers for improving economies of scale is evident by Daimler and Nissan announcing plans to share the costs of developing small-car technology, including engines. They will swap 3.1 percent stakes in their companies with plans to generate $5.3 billion in savings over 5 years.[3]

As a single facility adds more and more goods and/or services to its portfolio, the facility can become too large and "unfocused." At some point, diseconomies of scale arise, and unit costs increase because dissimilar product lines, processes, people skills, and technology exist in the same facility. In trying to manage a large facility with too many objectives and missions,

Clogged Courts

Court systems in most major cities are strained past their capacity with case backlogs and long delays, often resulting in freeing criminals before they go to trial or incarcerating defendants who are subsequently acquitted for long periods of time. Civil cases can be stuck in court systems for years. Some court systems are turning to technology and OM principles to address these capacity issues. For example, better computers and software for judges allow them to scan conviction and sentencing documents right from their courtrooms rather than recess to their chambers. Police departments are also scanning reports, allowing prosecutors faster access to information. Improved scheduling, such as blocking time for certain types of cases that are backlogged and hiring part-time retired judges, can help also. Can you think of other OM practices that might help?[2]

BCFC/Shutterstock.com

key competitive priorities such as delivery, quality, customization, and cost performance can begin to deteriorate. This leads to the concept of a focused factory.

*A **focused factory** is a way to achieve economies of scale, without extensive investments in facilities and capacity, by focusing on a narrow range of goods or services, target market segments, and/or dedicated processes to maximize efficiency and effectiveness.* The focused factory argues to "divide and conquer" by adopting smaller, more focused facilities dedicated to (1) a few key products, (2) a specific technology, (3) a certain process design and capability, (4) a specific competitive priority objective such as next-day delivery, and (5) particular market segments or customers and associated volumes.

10-2 Capacity Measurement

Capacity measures are used in many ways in long-term planning and short-term management activities. For example, managers need to plan capacity contingencies for unanticipated demand and plan routine equipment and labor requirements.

Capacity can be measured in various ways. ***Theoretical capacity** is the maximum rate of output that can be produced in a period of time under ideal operating conditions.* Usually, we can determine the amount that can be produced in a short period of time, such as a minute, hour, or shift, and extrapolate the maximum rate of output that can be produced over a longer period of time using simple logic. Solved Problem 10.1 provides a simple example.

However, theoretical capacity cannot always be achieved. Preventive maintenance or unanticipated events such as material delays, equipment breakdowns, employee absences, or worker fatigue will reduce the theoretical capacity. ***Effective capacity** is the actual capacity that can reasonably be expected to be achieved in the long run under normal operating conditions.* Setup time is an important factor in determining effective capacity. Short setup times clearly increase capacity and improve flexibility by allowing rapid changeovers to different models or products on manufacturing or assembly lines. Much work has gone into seeking ways to reduce setup times in manufacturing.

Capacity provides the ability to satisfy demand. Clearly, from a practical perspective, capacity-planning decisions should be based on effective capacity rather than theoretical capacity, as ideal operating conditions are nearly impossible to sustain. To satisfy customers in the long run, effective capacity must be at least as large as the average demand. However, demand for many goods and services typically vary over time. A process may not be capable of meeting peak demand at all times, resulting in either lost sales or customers that must wait until the good or service becomes available. At other periods of time, capacity may exceed demand, resulting in idle processes or facilities or buildups in physical inventories.

To account for variation in customer demand and effective capacity, some amount of safety capacity is normally planned in order to meet customer demand. **Safety capacity** (often

SOLVED PROBLEM 10.1: MEASURING THEORETICAL CAPACITY

An automobile transmission-assembly factory operates two shifts per day, five days per week. During each shift, with ideal operating conditions, 400 transmissions can be completed. What is the theoretical monthly capacity of this factory?

Solution:

The number of shifts/month is calculated as 2 shifts/day × 5 days per week × 4 weeks/month) = 40 shifts per month. Therefore, the theoretical monthly capacity is

$$\begin{aligned}\text{Capacity} &= (400 \text{ transmissions/shift}) \times (40 \text{ shifts/month})\\ &= 16{,}000 \text{ transmissions/month}\end{aligned}$$

called the capacity cushion) *is an amount of capacity reserved for unanticipated events such as demand surges, materials shortages, and equipment breakdowns.* This is defined by Equation 10.1.

$$\text{Theoretical capacity} = \text{Safety capacity} + \text{Effective capacity} \quad [10.1]$$

For example, in Solved Problem 10.1, suppose that the effective capacity averages 15,000 transmissions/month because of unplanned maintenance. Then using Equation 10.1, the safety capacity that must be reserved is

$$\begin{aligned}\text{Safety capacity} &= \text{Theoretical capacity} - \text{Effective capacity}\\ &= 16{,}000 \text{ transmissions/month} - 15{,}000 \text{ transmissions/month}\\ &= 1{,}000 \text{ transmission/month}\end{aligned}$$

This might be ensured by adding overtime, such as an additional night or Saturday shift. For a factory, safety capacity might be computed over a year, whereas for an individual workstation, it might be updated monthly. Safety capacity for flowshops and assembly lines is normally in the 1 to 10 percent range.

Many organizations deal with jobs that have different characteristics, such as volumes, setup times, and processing times. This is typical for job shops in manufacturing that produce custom products or services such as market research, law offices, laboratories, and medical organizations. For such organizations, it is important to be able to compute the capacity that is required to perform the work.

A **work order** *is a specification of work to be performed for a customer or a client.* It generally includes the quantity to be produced, the processing requirements, and resources needed. For any production situation, setup time can be a substantial part of total system capacity and therefore must be included in evaluating capacity. Some services, such as hospital surgeries, may require a new setup for each unit (i.e., the order size is one). For example, setup time for a surgery might include sterilizing equipment, cleaning and disinfecting the surgical suite, and preparing equipment for the next procedure. Equation 10.2 provides a general expression for evaluating the capacity required to meet a given production volume for one work order, i.

$$\text{Capacity required}\,(C_i) = [\text{Setup time}\ (S_i) + \text{Processing time}\ (P_i)] \times \text{Order size}\ (Q_i) \quad [10.2]$$

where

C_i = capacity requirements in units of time (e.g., minutes, hours, days) for work order i

S_i = setup or changeover time for work order i as a fixed amount that does not vary with volume

P_i = processing time for each unit of work order i (e.g., hours/part, minutes/transaction, etc.)

Q_i = size of order i in numbers of units

If we sum the capacity requirements over all work orders, we can compute the total capacity required. Solved Problem 10.2 provides an example.

Manufacturing work orders normally assume that one setup is necessary for each work order, and therefore the setup time is spread over the single work order quantity. That is, setup time is independent of order size. In this case, we use the following equation:

$$C_i = S_i + [P_i \times Q_i] \quad [10.3]$$

Note that in Equation 10.3, the setup time is not multiplied by the order size, whereas it is in Equation 10.2. It is important to understand the differences between service and manufacturing applications.

SOLVED PROBLEM 10.2: COMPUTING CAPACITY REQUIREMENTS FOR WORK ORDERS

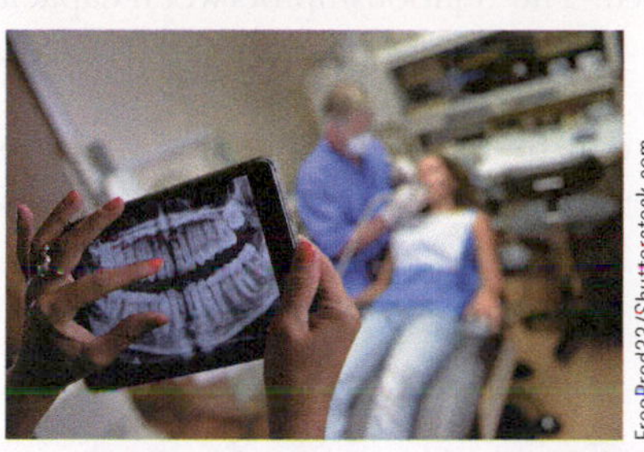

FreeProd33/Shutterstock.com

A typical dentist's office has a complicated mix of dental procedures and significant setup times; thus, it is similar to a job shop. Suppose a dentist works a nine-hour day with one hour for lunch and breaks. During the first six months the practice is open, he does all the work, including cleaning and setting up for the next dental procedure. Setup and processing times for three procedures are shown in Exhibit 10.3. Also shown are the number of appointments and demand for each type.

On a particular day, there are two scheduled first appointments for single tooth crowns (see last column of Exhibit 10.3), one second appointment for a single tooth crown, four tooth-whitening appointments, three first appointments for a partial denture, and two third appointments for a partial denture. Is there sufficient capacity to perform all the work?

We may use Equation 10.2 to compute the capacity requirements. Exhibit 10.4 shows the results using the Excel *Work Order Capacity* template in MindTap. Note that this template applies only to situations using Equation 10.2. We see that a total of 610 minutes of work are scheduled during a 480-minute workday. Therefore, there is a capacity shortage of 130 minutes. The dentist will either have to work two hours longer or reschedule some patients.

From this analysis, we see that 21.3 percent of his total capacity is used to set up and change over from one dental procedure to the next. If a dental assistant or technician is hired to do this work (assuming that this can be done off-line while the dentist continues to work on other patients), revenue would increase by about 20 percent. If setup times could be reduced by 50 percent, the total setup time would be 65 minutes instead of 130 minutes, and the capacity shortage would only be 65 minutes, requiring only one hour of overtime.

EXHIBIT 10.3 Dental Office Procedures and Times for Today

Dental Procedure	Number of Appointments	Setup or Changeover Time (Minutes)	Processing Time (Minutes)	Demand (No. of Patients Scheduled)
Single tooth crown	1st	15	90	2
	2nd	10	30	1
Tooth whitening	1st	5	30	4
Partial denture	1st	20	30	3
	2nd	10	20	0
	3rd	5	30	2

EXHIBIT 10.4 Dental Office Demand-Capacity Analysis Using the Excel *Work Order Capacity* Template*

	A	B	C	D	E	F	G	H
1	**Capacity Measurement**							
2	Enter data only in yellow cells. The template is designed for up to 10 work orders.							
3								
4						Total	Total	
5	Work Order	Setup Time	Processing Time	Order Size		Setup Time	Processing Time	Total Time
6	Single tooth crown 1st appt.	15	90	2		30.00	180.00	210.00
7	Single tooth crown 2nd appt	10	30	1		10.00	30.00	40.00
8	Tooth whitening	5	30	4		20.00	120.00	140.00
9	Partial dewnture 1st appt.	20	30	3		60.00	90.00	150.00
10	Partial denture 2nd appt.	10	20	0		0.00	0.00	0.00
11	Partial denture 3rd appt.	5	30	2		10.00	60.00	70.00
12								
13								
14								
15								
16								
17					Total	130.00	480.00	610.00
18					Percentage	21.31%	78.69%	100.00%

*Assumes one setup time per dental procedure to set up and clean the equipment and room before the next patient arrives.

In many situations, we need to determine the number of servers, which could be pieces of equipment or people, to meet a capacity need when the service rate (units produced per time period) is known. The relationship between capacity, service rate, and number of servers is

$$\text{Capacity} = \text{Service Rate} \times \text{Number of Servers} \qquad [10.4]$$

This equation can be used to determine the effective capacity or to find the number of servers required to achieve a certain level of capacity. Solved Problem 10.3 illustrates an example.

SOLVED PROBLEM 10.3: CAPACITY MEASUREMENT WITH KNOWN SERVICE RATES

A college of business has an IT support staff in its computer lab. Consultants receive numerous requests for questions and help. Each request takes an average of five minutes, and there are an average of 25 requests per hour.

a. Suppose that there are three consultants. How many students can the support staff handle each hour?
b. If the lab is expanded, and the college anticipates 120 requests per hour, how many consultants will be needed?

Solution:

a. Using Equation 10.4, and noting that each consultant can complete 12 requests/hour, we have

$$\begin{aligned}\text{Capacity} &= \text{Service Rate} \times \text{Number of Servers}\\ \text{Capacity (requests/hour)} &= \text{(12 requests/hour/consultant)} \times \text{3 consultants}\\ &= \text{36 requests/hour}\end{aligned}$$

b. Again, using Equation 10.4, we have

$$\begin{aligned}\text{120 requests/hour} &= \text{(12 requests/hour/consultant)} \times \text{Number of consultants}\\ \text{Number of consultants required} &= \text{(120 requests/hour)/(12 requests/hour/consultant)}\\ &= \text{10 consultants}\end{aligned}$$

An Excel template, *Service Capacity*, is available in MindTap. Exhibit 10.5 illustrates its use for this example.

EXHIBIT 10.5 Excel *Service Capacity* Template

	A	B	C	D	E
1	**Service Capacity**		Copyright © 2019 Cengage Learning		
2			Not for commercial use.		
3	**Enter any two of the three values only in the yellow cells**				
4	**and the spreadsheet will calculate the third.**				
5					
6	**Capacity**	120			
7	**Service Rate**	12			
8	**Number of Servers**				
9					
10	**Capacity**				
11	**Service Rate**				
12	**Number of Servers**	10.00			

10-2a Using Capacity Measures for Operations Planning

Capacity needs must be translated into specific requirements for equipment and labor. To illustrate this, we present a simple example. Fast Burger Inc. is building a new restaurant near a college football stadium. The restaurant will be open 16 hours per day, 360 days per year. Managers have concluded that the restaurant should have the capacity to handle a peak hourly demand of 100 customers. This peak hour of demand happens two hours before every home football game. The average customer purchase is

1 burger (4-ounce hamburger or cheeseburger)

1 bag of french fries (4 ounces)

1 soft drink (12 ounces)

AriN/Shutterstock.com

Consequently, management would like to determine how many grills, deep fryers, and soft drink spouts are needed. Observe how Equation 10.4 is used throughout this example.

A 36 × 36-inch grill cooks 48 ounces of burgers every 10 minutes, and a single-basket deep fryer cooks 2 pounds of french fries in 6 minutes, or 20 pounds per hour. Finally, one soft drink spout dispenses 20 ounces of soft drink per minute, or 1,200 ounces per hour. These effective capacity estimates are based on the equipment manufacturer's studies of actual use under normal operating conditions.

To determine the equipment needed to meet peak hourly demand, Fast Burger must translate expected demand in terms of customers per hour into needs for grills, deep fryers, and soft drink spouts. First note that the peak hourly demand for burgers, french fries, and soft drinks are as follow:

Product	Peak Hourly Demand (ounces)
Burgers	400
French fries	400
Soft drinks	1,200

Because the capacity of a grill is (48 oz/10 minutes)(60 minutes/hour) = 288 ounces/hour, the number of grills needed to satisfy a peak hourly demand of 400 ounces of burgers is

$$\begin{aligned} \text{Number of grills} &= 400/288 \\ &= 1.39\,\text{grills} \end{aligned}$$

To determine the number of single-basket deep fryers needed to meet a peak hourly demand of 400 ounces of french fries, we must first compute the hourly capacity of the deep fryer.

$$\begin{aligned} \text{Capacity of deep fryer} &= (20\ \text{lb/hour})(16\ \text{oz/lb}) \\ &= 320\ \text{oz/hour} \end{aligned}$$

Hence, the number of single-basket deep fryers needed is 400/320 = 1.25.

Finally, the number of soft drink spouts needed to satisfy peak demand of 1,200 ounces is

$$\text{Number of soft drink spouts needed} = 1{,}200/1{,}200 = 1.0$$

After reviewing this analysis, the managers decided to purchase two 36 × 36-inch grills. Grill safety capacity is 2.0 − 1.39 = 0.61grills or 175.7 oz/hour [(0.61) × (48 oz/10 min) × (60 min/hour), or about 44 hamburgers per hour. Management decided this excess safety capacity was justified to handle demand surges and grill breakdowns. With two grills the managers reduced their risk of being unable to fill customer demand. If they installed two french fryer machines, they would have 0.75 excess machines, and that was thought to be wasteful. However, they realized that if the one french fryer machine broke down they would not be able to cook enough fries, so they decided to purchase two deep fryers.

Management decided to go with a two-spout soft drink system. Although their analysis showed a need for only one soft drink spout, the managers wanted to provide some safety capacity, primarily because they felt the peak hourly demand for soft drinks might have been underestimated and customers tend to refill their drinks in this self-service situation.

The managers of Fast Burger Inc. must also staff the new restaurant for peak demand of 100 customers/hour. Assume front-counter service personnel can take and assemble orders at the service rate of 15 customers per hour. The minimum number of front-service counter people that should be assigned to this peak demand period is (100 customers/hour)/(15 customers/hour/server) = 6.67 servers. To provide additional safety capacity to account for variations in order sizes, for example, Fast Burger management decides to assign eight people to the front-service counter during this peak demand period.

The management at Fast Burger now has an equipment and labor capacity plan for this peak-demand period. Notice that equipment capacity, which is difficult to increase in the short-term, is high, whereas labor is more easily changed. This equipment and labor capacity strategy must also be coupled with good forecasting of demand—the subject of the next chapter.

10-3 Long-Term Capacity Strategies

In developing a long-range capacity plan, a firm must make a basic economic trade-off between the cost of capacity and the opportunity cost of not having adequate capacity. Capacity costs include both the initial investment in facilities and equipment and the annual cost of operating and maintaining them, much of which are fixed costs. The cost of not having sufficient capacity is the opportunity loss incurred from lost sales and reduced market share. Having too much capacity, particularly if demand falls, can be devastating. For example, International Paper recently closed its Franklin paper mill in Virginia. The mill had a capacity of 600,000 tons per year, but demand had fallen 30 percent and was forecasted to continue falling, much of it a result of new technologies such as e-mail, Kindles and iPads, and electronic transactions.[4] Too little capacity, on the other hand, can squeeze profit margins or leave a firm vulnerable to competitors if it cannot satisfy customer orders.

Long-term capacity planning must be closely tied to the strategic direction of the organization—what products and services it offers. For example, many goods and services are seasonal, resulting in unused capacity during the off-season. Many firms offer **complementary goods and services**, *which are goods and services that can be produced or delivered using the same resources available to the firm, but whose seasonal demand patterns are out of phase with each other.* Complementary goods or services balance seasonal demand cycles and therefore use the excess capacity available, as illustrated in Exhibit 10.6. For instance, demand for lawnmowers peaks in the spring and summer; to balance manufacturing capacity, the producer might also produce leaf blowers and vacuums for the autumn season and snowblowers for the winter season.

EXHIBIT 10.6 Seasonal Demand and Complementary Goods or Services

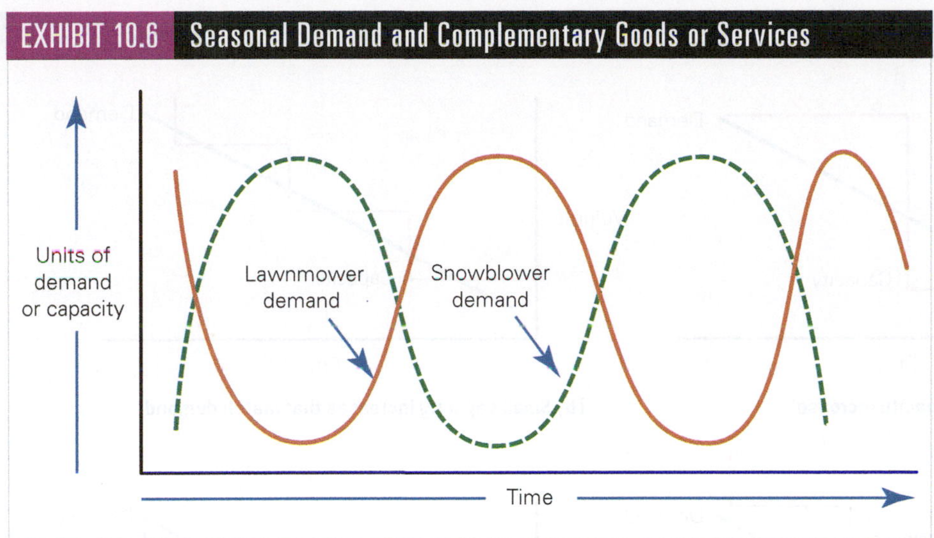

10-3a Capacity Expansion

Capacity requirements are rarely static; changes in markets and product lines and competition will eventually require a firm to either plan to increase or reduce long-term capacity. Such strategies require determining the *amount, timing*, and *form* of capacity changes. To illustrate capacity expansion decisions, let us make two assumptions: (1) capacity is added in "chunks," or discrete increments; and (2) demand is steadily increasing.

Four basic strategies for expanding capacity over some fixed time horizon are shown in Exhibit 10.7 (these concepts can also be applied to capacity reduction):

1. One large capacity increase (Exhibit 10.7a)
2. Small capacity increases that match demand (Exhibit 10.7b)
3. Small capacity increases that lead demand (Exhibit 10.7c)
4. Small capacity increases that lag demand (Exhibit 10.7d)

The strategy in Exhibit 10.7(a) involves one large increase in capacity over a specified period. The advantage of one large capacity increase is that the fixed costs of construction and operating system setup needs to be incurred only once, and thus the firm can allocate these costs over one large project. However, if aggregate demand exhibits steady growth, the facility will be underutilized. The alternative is to view capacity expansion incrementally as in Exhibit 10.7(b), (c), and (d).

Exhibit 10.7(b) illustrates the strategy of matching capacity additions with demand as closely as possible. This is often called a *capacity straddle strategy*. When capacity is above the demand curve, the firm has excess capacity; when it is below, there is a shortage of capacity to meet demand. In this situation, there will be short periods of over- and underutilization of resources. Exhibit 10.7(c) shows a capacity-expansion strategy with the goal of maintaining sufficient capacity to minimize the chances of not meeting demand. Here, capacity expansion leads or is ahead of demand, and hence is called a *capacity lead strategy*. Because there is always excess capacity, safety capacity to meet unexpected demand from large orders or new customers is provided.

Finally, Exhibit 10.7(d) illustrates a policy of a *capacity lag strategy* that results in constant capacity shortages. Such a strategy waits until demand has increased to a point where additional capacity is necessary. It requires less investment and provides for high capacity

EXHIBIT 10.7 Capacity Expansion Options

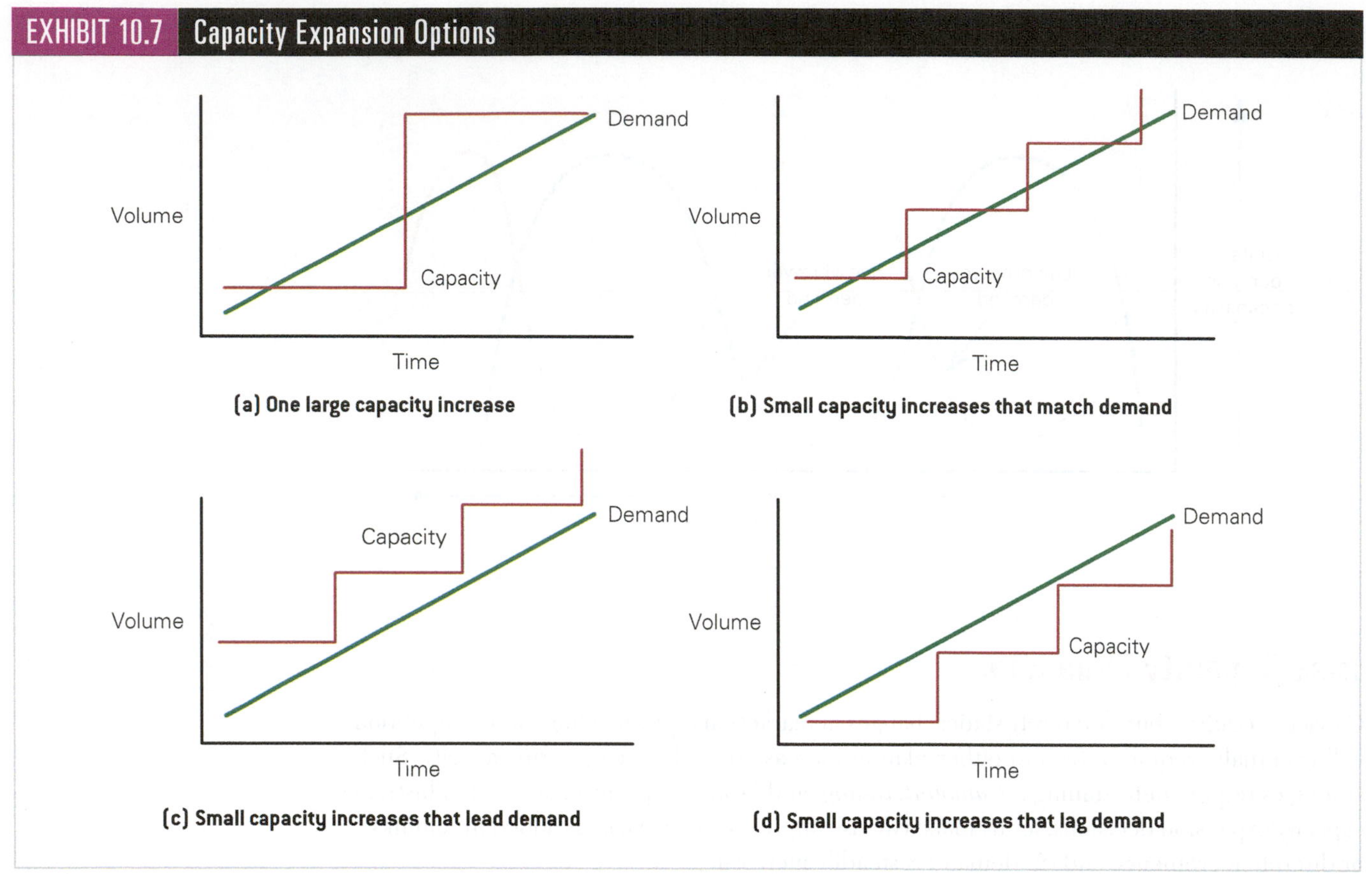

Briggs & Stratton: Managing Capacity

Briggs & Stratton is the world's largest producer of air-cooled gasoline engines for outdoor power equipment. The company designs, manufactures, markets, and services these products for original equipment manufacturers worldwide. These engines are primarily aluminum alloy gasoline engines ranging from 3 through 25 horsepower. Briggs & Stratton is a leading designer, manufacturer, and marketer of portable generators, lawnmowers, snow throwers, pressure washers, and related accessories. It also provides engines for manufacturers of other small engine-driven equipment such as snowmobiles, go-karts, and jet skis.

Jaggat Rashidi/Shutterstock.com

The complementary and diverse original equipment markets for Briggs & Stratton engines allow factory managers to plan equipment and labor capacities and schedules in a much more stable operating environment. This helps minimize manufacturing costs, stabilize workforce levels, and even out volumes so that assembly lines can be used in a more efficient fashion.[5]

utilization and thus a higher rate of return on investment. However, it may also reduce long-term profitability through overtime, subcontracting, and productivity losses that occur as the firm scrambles to satisfy demand. In the long run, such a policy can lead to a permanent loss of market position.

10-4 Short-Term Capacity Management

If short-term demand is stable and sufficient capacity is available, then managing operations to ensure that demand is satisfied is generally easy. However, when demand fluctuates above and below average capacity levels as was illustrated in Exhibit 10.2, firms have two basic choices. First, they can adjust capacity to match the changes in demand by changing internal resources and capabilities. The second approach is to manage capacity by shifting and stimulating demand.

10-4a Managing Capacity by Adjusting Short-Term Capacity Levels

When short-term demand exceeds capacity, a firm must temporarily increase its capacity, or it will be unable to meet all of the demand. Similarly, if demand falls well below capacity, then idle resources reduce profits. Short-term adjustments to capacity can be done in a variety of ways and are summarized as follows:

- *Add or share equipment:* Capacity levels that are limited by machine and equipment availability are more difficult to change in the short run because of high capital expense. However, leasing equipment as needed can accomplish this in a cost-effective manner. Another way is through innovative partnership arrangements and capacity sharing. For example, a consortium of several hospitals might be set up in which each hospital focuses on a particular specialty and shares services.
- *Sell unused capacity:* Some firms might sell idle capacity, such as computer storage space and computing capacity, to outside buyers and even to competitors. For example, hotels often develop partnership arrangements to accommodate their competitors' guests when they are overbooked.
- *Change labor capacity and schedules:* Labor capacity can usually be managed easily through short-term changes in workforce levels and schedules. Overtime, extra shifts, temporary employees, and outsourcing are common ways of increasing capacity. Adjusting workforce schedules to better coincide with demand patterns is another. Many quick-service restaurants employ large numbers of part-time employees with varying work schedules.
- *Change labor skill mix:* Hiring the right people who can learn quickly and adjust to changing job requirements and cross-training them to perform different tasks provides the flexibility to meet fluctuating demand. In supermarkets, for example, it is common for employees to work as cashiers during busy periods and to assist with stocking shelves during slow periods.
- *Shift work to slack periods:* Another strategy is to shift work to slack periods. For example, hotel clerks prepare bills and perform other paperwork at night, when check-in and checkout activity is light. This allows more time during the daytime hours to service customers. Manufacturers often build up inventory during slack periods and hold the goods for peak demand periods.

Firms can adjust capacity to match changes in demand by changing internal resources and capabilities, or manage capacity by shifting and stimulating demand.

10-4b Managing Capacity by Shifting and Stimulating Demand

Some general approaches to influence customers to shift demand from periods without adequate capacity to periods with excess capacity, or to fill times with excess capacity, include the following:

- *Vary the price of goods or services:* Price is the most powerful way to influence demand. For example, hotels might offer cheaper rates on the weekend; airlines might offer better prices for midweek flights; a restaurant might cut its meal prices in half after 9:00 p.m. In a similar fashion, manufacturers typically offer sales and rebates of overstocks to stimulate demand, smooth production schedules and staffing requirements, and reduce inventories.
- *Provide customers with information:* Many call centers, for example, send notes to customers on their bills or provide an automated voice message recommending the best times to call. Amusement parks such as Disney World use signs and literature informing customers when certain rides are extremely busy.
- *Advertising and promotion:* After-holiday sales are heavily advertised in an attempt to draw customers to periods of traditionally low demand. Manufacturer or service coupons are strategically distributed to increase demand during periods of low sales or excess capacity.
- *Add peripheral goods and/or services:* Movie theaters offer rentals of their auditoriums for business meetings and special events at off-peak times. Fast-food chains offer birthday party planning services to fill up slow demand periods between peak meal times. Extended hours also represent a peripheral service; many supermarkets remain open 24/7 and encourage customers to shop during late-night hours to reduce demand during peak times.
- *Provide reservations:* A **reservation** *is a promise to provide a good or service at some future time and place.* Typical examples are reservations for hotel rooms, airline seats, and scheduled surgeries and operating rooms. Reservations reduce the uncertainty for both the good or service provider and the customer. With advance knowledge of when customer demand will occur, operations managers can better plan their equipment and workforce schedules and rely less on forecasts.

> During the first year of RMS implementation, revenues at National Car Rental increased by $56 million.

If You Make a Reservation, Show up or Pay!

Walt Disney World's better restaurants established a policy whereby if you make a dinner reservation and do not cancel at least 24 hours in advance, they will charge your credit card $10 per person. This no-show policy applies to 19 Disney park restaurants. The most upscale Disney restaurant charges $25 per person. Restaurant (service) capacity is perishable, and Disney handles the risks of idle service capacity by overbooking and/or charging fees for abrupt cancellations and no-shows![6]

Africa Studio/Shutterstock.com

The Mysteries of Hotel Revenue Management

How can the cost of the same hotel room, at the same property, vary dramatically from one day to the next? Historically, hotels have just looked at how many reservations they have or what competitors are charging.

Today, they use analytics to decide how to price rooms based on the market they are in, special events or holidays that may affect demand, room differences, popularity on different days of the week, and the guest mix at any point in time, and even weather forecasts. Like most hotel brands, Best Western revenue managers rely on analytical methodology that includes forecasting demand, scanning websites like Expedia.com to see what their competitors are charging, and comparing their own booking trends. For example, properties might pay more for a standard room with a king-size bed on a weekday for solo business travelers, while a room with two queen beds may be priced higher on weekends when more families are traveling.[7]

Paul Velgos/Shutterstock.com

10-4c Revenue Management Systems (RMS)

Many types of organizations manage perishable assets, such as a hotel room, an airline seat, a rental car, a sporting event or concert seat, a room on a cruise line, the capacity of a restaurant catering service or electric power generation, or broadcast advertising space. For such assets, which essentially represent service capacity, high utilization is the key to financial success.

A **revenue management system (RMS)** *consists of dynamic methods to forecast demand, allocate perishable assets across market segments, decide when to overbook and by how much, and determine what price to charge different customer (price) classes.* These four components of RMS—forecasting, allocation, overbooking, and pricing—must work in unison if the objective is to maximize the revenue generated by a perishable asset. The ideas and methods surrounding RMS are often called yield management. Revenue management systems integrate a wide variety of decisions and data into a decision support system used mainly by service-providing businesses.

The earliest revenue management systems focused solely on overbooking—how many perishable assets to sell in excess of physical capacity to optimally tradeoff the cost of an unsold asset versus the loss of goodwill of having more arrivals than assets. Modern RMS software simultaneously makes changes in the forecast, allocation, overbooking, and pricing decisions in a real-time operating system. Forecasts are constantly being revised. Allocation involves segmenting the perishable asset into target market categories, such as first, business, and coach classes in an airline flight. Each class is defined by its size (number of seats), price, advance purchase restrictions, and booking policies. Allocation is

> If you don't sell or use the ticket, the revenue-generating opportunity for that seat cannot be recaptured—it is lost forever.

a real-time, ongoing method that does not end until there is no more opportunity to maximize revenue (the night or concert is over, the airplane takes off). As happens with forecasts, bookings and time move forward; the target market categories are redefined; and prices change in an attempt to maximize revenue.

Many organizations have exploited RMS technology. Marriott improved its revenues by \$25–\$35 million by using RMS methods. Royal Caribbean Cruise Lines obtained a revenue increase in excess of \$20 million for one year.[8] During the first year of RMS implementation, revenues at National Car Rental increased by \$56 million.[9]

Theater seats provide another good example of managing a perishable asset. Revenue management systems are often used to manage theater, stadium, and concert seats. If you don't sell or use the ticket, the revenue-generating opportunity for that seat cannot be recaptured—it is lost forever.

10-5 Learning Curves and Capacity Requirements

*The **learning curve** concept is that direct labor unit cost decreases in a predictable manner as the experience in producing the unit increases.* For most people, for example, the longer you play a musical instrument or a video game, the better and faster you become. The same is true in assembly operations, which was recognized in the 1920s at Wright-Patterson Air Force Base in the assembly of aircraft. Studies showed that the number of labor-hours required to produce the fourth plane was about 80 percent of the amount of time spent on the second; the eighth plane took only 80 percent as much time as the fourth; the sixteenth plane 80 percent of the time of the eighth, and so on. The decrease in production time as the number produced increases is illustrated in Exhibit 10.8. As production doubles from x units to 2x units, the time per unit of the $2x^{th}$ unit is 80 percent of the time of the xth unit. This is called an 80 percent learning curve. In general, *a **p-percent learning curve** characterizes a process in which the time of the $2x^{th}$ unit is p percent of the time of the xth unit.* Learning curves exhibit a steep initial decline and then level off as employees become more proficient in their tasks.

Learning curves can be used to estimate labor-hours for repetitive work and are therefore useful in computing capacity requirements in both the short- and long-term. These estimates can be used to plan staffing levels, price products, estimates costs, establish budgets, and help managers negotiate with supply chain suppliers and customers.

Mathematically, the learning curve is represented by the function

$$y = ax^{-b} \tag{10.5}$$

EXHIBIT 10.8 An 80 Percent Learning Curve

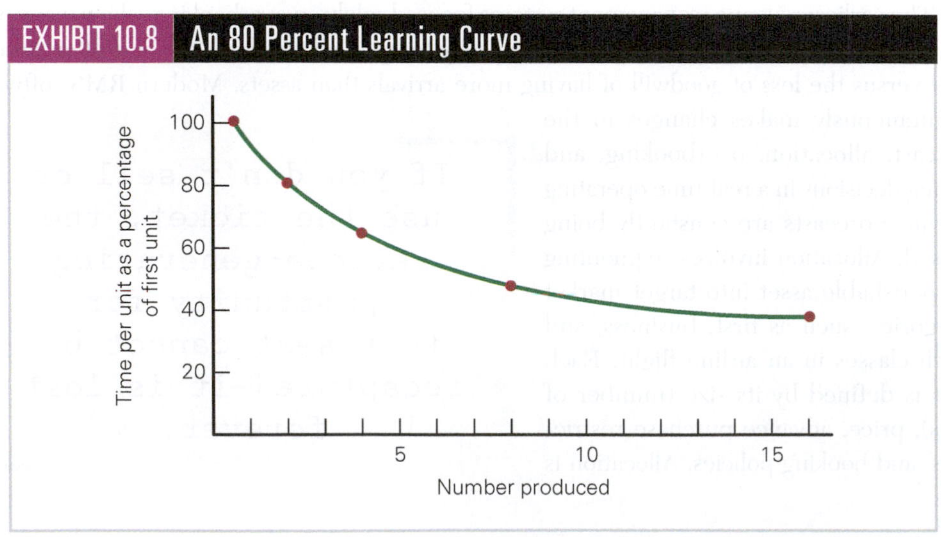

where
x = number of units produced,
a = hours required to produce the first unit,
y = time to produce the xth unit, and
b = constant that defines a $100p$ percent learning curve (i.e., if $p = 0.8$, then we have an 80% learning curve).

An Excel template, *Learning Curve*, is available in MindTap for computing and displaying learning curves. You need only enter the time of the first unit and the percent learning curve. Using formula (10.5), the template computes the time for 100 units, as well as the cumulative time and cumulative average time for each unit. It also provides a chart of the time for each unit and the cumulative average time for each unit.

SOLVED PROBLEM 10.4: COMPUTING A LEARNING CURVE

Suppose that the time for the first unit is 3,500 minutes, and we estimate a 90% learning curve. How much time will the 10th unit take? What is the cumulative time for producing 50 units?

Solution:

Using the *Learning Curve* Excel template, we obtain the results shown in Exhibit 10.9 (a portion of the template results for the first 50 units) and Exhibit 10.10 (a chart of the unit time and cumulative average time. We see that the 10th unit 2,466 minutes to complete and the cumulative time for producing the first 50 units will be 112,497 units. The cumulative average time for the first 50 units is 2249.9, meaning that the average time for units 1–50 was 2249.9. As learning improves, managers can adjust their capacity requirements based on the results.

EXHIBIT 10.9 Portion of *Learning Curve* Excel Template

	A	B	C	D	E	F	G	H	I
1	Learning Curve								
2	Enter the data only in the yellow cells. This template is designed to compute the production time for the first 100 units.								
3	A chart of the unit time and cumulative average time is given to the right of the tables.								
4	Enter the % learning curve as a whole number, e.g., 80 or 90.								
5									
6	First unit	3500							
7	% learning curve	90%							
8									
9	b	0.1520							
10									
11	Unit	Time	Cumulative Time	Cum. Avg. Time		Unit	Time	Cumulative Time	Cum. Avg. Time
12	1	3500	3500	3500.0		26	2133.0	64129.3	2466.5
13	2	3150.0	6650.0	3325.0		27	2120.8	66250.1	2453.7
14	3	2961.7	9611.7	3203.9		28	2109.1	68359.2	2441.4
15	4	2835.0	12446.7	3111.7		29	2097.9	70457.0	2429.6
16	5	2740.5	15187.2	3037.4		30	2087.1	72544.1	2418.1
17	6	2665.5	17852.7	2975.5		31	2076.7	74620.8	2407.1
18	7	2603.8	20456.5	2922.4		32	2066.7	76687.6	2396.5
19	8	2551.5	23008.0	2876.0		33	2057.1	78744.6	2386.2
20	9	2506.2	25514.3	2834.9		34	2047.8	80792.4	2376.2
21	10	2466.4	27980.7	2798.1		35	2038.8	82831.1	2366.6
22	11	2430.9	30411.6	2764.7		36	2030.0	84861.2	2357.3
23	12	2399.0	32810.6	2734.2		37	2021.6	86882.8	2348.2
24	13	2370.0	35180.6	2706.2		38	2013.4	88896.2	2339.4
25	14	2343.4	37524.0	2680.3		39	2005.5	90901.7	2330.8
26	15	2319.0	39843.0	2656.2		40	1997.8	92899.5	2322.5
27	16	2296.4	42139.4	2633.7		41	1990.3	94889.8	2314.4
28	17	2275.3	44414.6	2612.6		42	1983.0	96872.8	2306.5
29	18	2255.6	46670.2	2592.8		43	1975.9	98848.8	2298.8
30	19	2237.1	48907.4	2574.1		44	1969.1	100817.8	2291.3
31	20	2219.8	51127.2	2556.4		45	1962.3	102780.2	2284.0
32	21	2203.4	53330.5	2539.5		46	1955.8	104736.0	2276.9
33	22	2187.8	55518.4	2523.6		47	1949.4	106685.4	2269.9
34	23	2173.1	57691.5	2508.3		48	1943.2	108628.6	2263.1
35	24	2159.1	59850.6	2493.8		49	1937.1	110565.7	2256.4
36	25	2145.7	61996.3	2479.9		50	1931.2	112496.8	2249.9

EXHIBIT 10.10 Learning Curve Chart

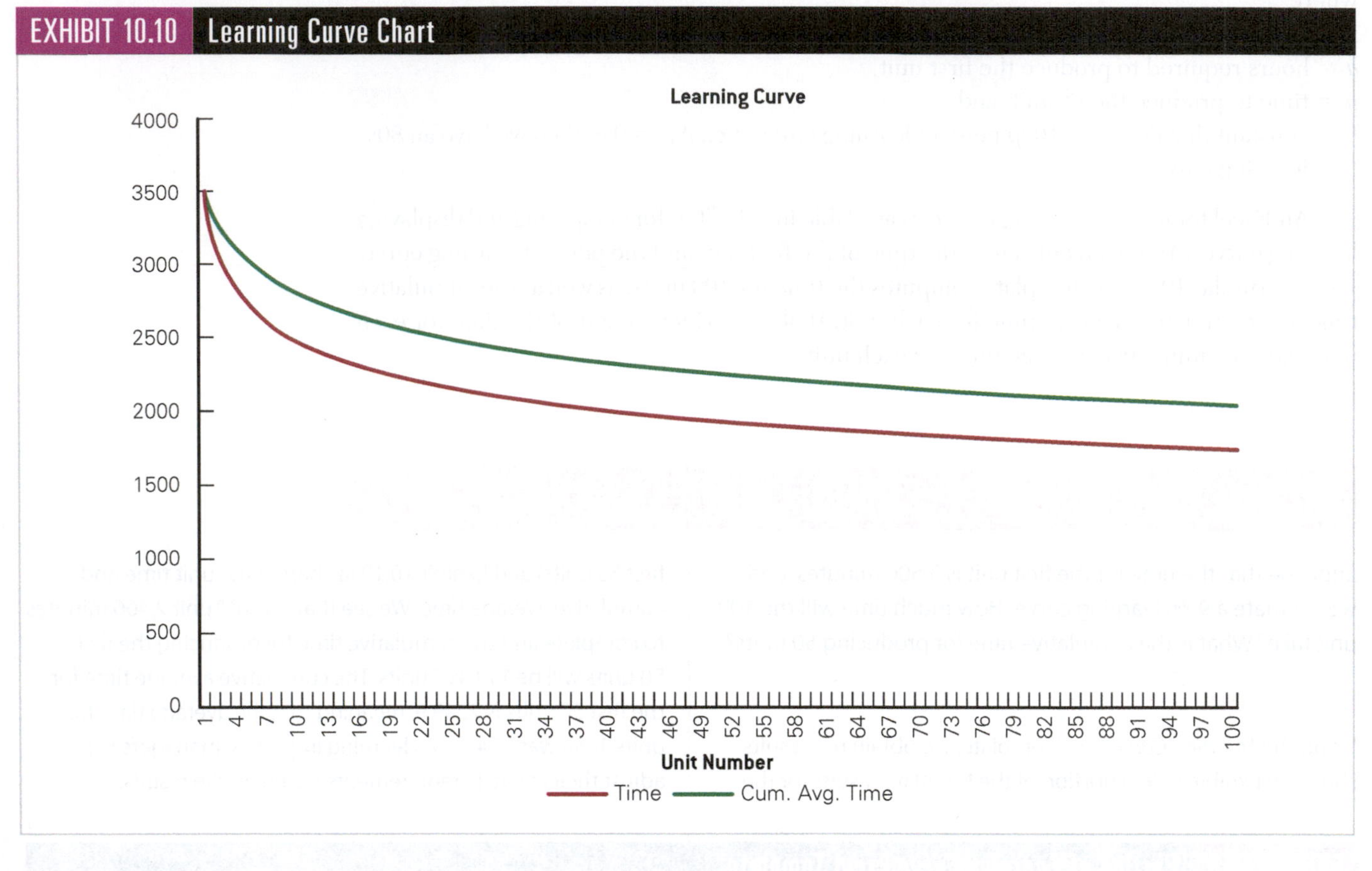

For goods-producing industries, learning curve phenomena can be found in the production of locomotives, airplanes, electric power generating turbines, and ships. For services, we might find it in consulting projects, tax preparation, and repetitive surgeries, such as hip replacements. Defense industries (e.g., the aircraft and electronics industries), which introduce many new and complex products, use learning curves to estimate labor requirements and capacity, determine costs and budget requirements, and plan and schedule production. Eighty-percent learning curves are generally accepted as a standard, although the ratio of machine work to manual assembly affects the curve percentage. Obviously, no learning takes place if all assembly is done by machine. As a rule of thumb, if the ratio of manual to machine work is 3 to 1 (three-fourths manual), then 80 percent is a good value; if the ratio is 1 to 3, then 90 percent is often used. An even split of manual and machine work would suggest the use of an 85 percent learning curve. The learning factor may also be estimated from past histories of similar parts or products.

A broader extension of the learning curve is the experience curve. *The* **experience curve** *states that the cost of doing any repetitive task, work activity, or project decreases as the accumulated experience of doing the job increases.* The terms improvement curve, experience curve, and manufacturing progress function are often used to describe the learning phenomenon in the aggregate context. Marketing research, software design, developing engineering specifications for a water plant, accounting and financial auditing of the same client, implementing a software integration project, and so on are examples of this broader view. The idea is that each time experience doubles, costs decline by 10 to 30 percent. Costs must always be translated into constant dollars to eliminate the inflation effect.

CHAPTER 10 LEARNING OBJECTIVE SUMMARIES

10.1

Explain the concept of capacity. Capacity can be viewed in one of two ways:

1. as the rate of output per unit of time, or
2. as units of resource availability.

Operations managers must decide on the appropriate levels of capacity to meet current (short-term) and future (long-term) demand.

As a single facility adds more and more goods and/or services to its portfolio, the facility can become too large and "unfocused." At some point, diseconomies of scale arise, and unit cost increases because dissimilar product lines, processes, people skills, and technology exist in the same facility. The focused factory endeavors to " divide and conquer" by adopting smaller, more focused facilities dedicated to a (1) few key products, (2) a specific technology, (3) a certain process design and capability, (4) a specific competitive priority objective such as next-day delivery, and (5) particular market segments or customers and associate volumes.

10.2

Describe how to compute and use capacity measures. Theoretical capacity is the maximum rate of output that can be produced in a period of time under ideal operating conditions. Usually, we can determine the amount that can be produced in a short period of time, such as a minute, hour, or shift, and extrapolate the maximum rate of output that can be produced over a longer period of time using simple logic. Effective capacity is the actual capacity that can reasonably be expected to be achieved in the long run under normal operating conditions. Safety capacity (often called the capacity cushion), is an amount of capacity reserved for unanticipated events such as demand surges, materials shortages, and equipment breakdowns. This is defined by Equation 10.1.

$$\text{Theoretical capacity} = \text{Safety capacity} + \text{Effective capacity} \quad [10.1]$$

Many organizations deal with jobs that have different characteristics, such as volumes, setup times, and processing times. A work order is a specification of work to be performed for a customer or a client. It generally includes the quantity to be produced, the processing requirements, and resources needed. A general expression for evaluating the capacity required to meet a given production volume for one work order, *i*, is

$$\text{Capacity required } (C_i) = \text{Setup time } (S_i) + [\text{Processing time } (P_i) \times \text{Order size } (Q_i)] \quad [10.2]$$

where

C_i = capacity requirements in units of time (for instance, minutes, hours, days) for work order *i*.
S_i = setup or changeover time for work order *i* as a fixed amount that does not vary with volume.
P_i = processing time for each unit of work order *i* (e.g., hours/part, minutes/transaction, etc.).
Q_i = size of order i in numbers of units.

If we sum the capacity requirements over all work orders, we can compute the total capacity required:

$$\Sigma C_i = \Sigma[S_i + (P_i \times Q_i)] \quad [10.3]$$

10.3

Describe long-term capacity expansion strategies. In developing a long-range capacity plan, a firm must make a basic economic trade-off between the cost of capacity and the opportunity cost of not having adequate capacity. Capacity costs include both the initial investment in facilities and equipment, and the annual cost of operating and maintaining them. The cost of not having sufficient capacity is the opportunity loss incurred from lost sales and reduced market share.

Four basic strategies for expanding capacity over some fixed time horizon are: one large capacity increase; small capacity increases that match average demand; small capacity increases that lead demand; and small capacity increases that lag demand (see Exhibit 10.6).

10.4

Describe short-term capacity adjustment strategies. When demand fluctuates above and below average capacity levels, firms can adjust capacity to match the changes in demand by changing internal resources and capabilities, or manage capacity by shifting and stimulating demand. Short-term adjustments to capacity can be done in a variety of ways, such as adding or sharing equipment, selling unused capacity, changing labor capacity and schedules, changing the labor skill mix, and shifting work to slack periods. Some general approaches to influence customers to shift demand are varying the price of goods or services, providing customers with information, advertising and promotion, adding peripheral goods and/or services, and providing reservations. Revenue management systems help organizations maximize revenue by adjusting prices to influence demand.

10.5

Explain the concepts and applications of learning curves. The learning curve concept is that direct labor unit cost decreases in a predictable manner as the experience in producing the unit increases. In general, a p-percent learning curve characterizes a process in which the time of the $2x^{th}$ unit is p percent of the time of the xth unit. Learning curves exhibit a steep initial decline and then level off as employees become more proficient in their tasks. Learning curves can be used to estimate labor-hours for repetitive work and are therefore useful in computing capacity requirements in both the short- and long-term. These estimates can be used to plan staffing levels, price products, estimates costs, establish budgets, and help managers negotiate with supply chain suppliers and customers.

Eighty-percent learning curves are generally accepted as a standard, although the ratio of machine work to manual assembly affects the curve percentage. Obviously, no learning takes place if all assembly is done by machine. As a rule of thumb, if the ratio of manual to machine work is 3 to 1 (three-fourths manual), then 80 percent is a good value; if the ratio is 1 to 3, then 90 percent is often used. An even split of manual and machine work would suggest the use of an 85 percent learning curve. The learning factor may also be estimated from past histories of similar parts or products.

KEY TERMS

- **Capacity**
- **Complementary goods and services**
- **Diseconomies of scale**
- **Economies of scale**
- **Effective capacity**
- **Experience curve**
- **Focused factory**
- **Learning curve**
- **p-percent learning curve**
- **Reservation**
- **Revenue management system (RMS)**
- **Safety capacity (capacity cushion)**
- **Theoretical capacity**
- **Work order**

REVIEW QUESTIONS

10.1 1. Explain the concept of capacity.

10.1 2. How are capacity decisions influenced by economies and diseconomies of scale?

10.1 3. What is a focused factory? How can it make a more efficient use of capacity?

10.2 4. Summarize the different ways in which capacity can be measured.

10.2 5. Why is safety capacity important? Provide some examples of safety capacity in manufacturing and service organizations.

10.2 6. Explain how safety capacity and planned capacity are related.

10.2 7. Define a work order and provide examples in goods-producing and service-providing industries.

10.2 8. What is setup time? Why is it important in determining capacity?

10.2 9. How are total time, setup time, and processing time related?

10.3 10. Discuss four strategies used for capacity expansion. What are the risks and benefits of each strategy?

10.3 11. Why do firms often incorporate complementary goods and services into their product lines?

10.4 12. Discuss various ways for managing short-term capacity.

10.4 13. What advantages do reservations have?

10.4 14. Why do service organizations use revenue management systems (RMS)? What are the advantages and disadvantages?

10.5 15. Explain the concept of learning curves. Why are they important in managing operations?

10.5 16. Explain the experience curve and how it differs from the traditional learning curve.

DISCUSSION QUESTIONS AND EXPERIENTIAL ACTIVITIES

10.1 17. Provide and discuss some examples of economies and diseconomies of scale in a college environment.

10.1 18. Research and write a short paper (two pages maximum) on organizations that have successfully used the focused factory concept.

10.1 19. Can you identify a focused factory in a service facility? Explain.

10.1 20. Provide some examples of short- and long-term capacity decisions different from Exhibit 10.1.

10.2 21. Define useful capacity measures for a(n)

   a. brewery.
   b. airline.
   c. movie theater.
   d. pizza restaurant.
   e. amusement park.

10.3 22. How might a college or university with growing enrollment use the capacity expansion strategies in Exhibit 10.6? Discuss the pros and cons of each of these.

10.4 23. Briefly describe a business you are familiar with and explain how it might use each of the five ways to adjust its short-term capacity levels.

10.4 24. Research and write a short paper (two pages maximum) on two examples of revenue management applications not in the text and explain how they help organizations.

10.5 25. What types of jobs are best suited to apply learning curves? How would you determine this?

COMPUTATIONAL PROBLEMS AND EXERCISES

These exercises require you to apply the formulas and methods described in the chapter. The problems should be solved manually.

26. An order fulfillment process normally operates two shifts a day, six days per week. Under ideal conditions, 380 orders can be processed per shift. What is the effective weekly theoretical capacity?

27. Baker Manufacturing Company forecasts the following demand for a product (in thousands of units) over the next five years.

Year	1	2	3	4	5
Forecast Demand	114	129	131	134	133

Currently the manufacturer has eight machines that operate on a two-shift (eight hours each) basis. Twenty days per year are available for scheduled maintenance of equipment. Assume there are 250 workdays in a year. Each manufactured good takes 26 minutes to produce.

a. What is the effective capacity of the factory?

b. Given the five-year forecast, how much extra capacity is needed each year?

c. Does the firm need to buy more machines? If so, how many? When?

28. Hickory Manufacturing Company forecasts the following demand for a product (in thousands of units) over the next five years.

Year	1	2	3	4	5
Forecast Demand	60	79	81	84	84

Currently the manufacturer has seven machines that operate on a two-shift (eight hours each) basis. Twenty days per year are available for scheduled maintenance of equipment with no process output. Assume there are 250 workdays in a year. Each manufactured good takes 25 minutes to produce.

a. What is the effective capacity of the factory?

b. Given the five-year forecast, how much extra capacity is needed each year?

c. Does the firm need to buy more machines? If so, how many? When?

29. The consumer loan division of a major bank wants to determine the size of the staff it would need to process up to 200 loan applications per day. It is estimated that each loan officer can process a loan application in approximately 20 minutes and works seven hours each day. How many loan officers would be needed to handle that volume of business?

30. The roller coaster at Treasure Island Amusement Park consists of 16 cars, each of which can carry up to three passengers. According to a time study, each run takes 2.5 minutes, and the time to unload and load riders is 3.5 minutes. What is the theoretical capacity of the system in number of passengers per hour?

31. The quad chair lift at Whiteface Mountain Ski Resort carries four skiers in each chair to the top of the intermediate slope in four minutes based on timing a large sample of skiers. The time between loading skiers on successive chairs is 15 seconds.

a. What is the effective capacity of the system in number of skiers per hour?

b. If only one skier gets on the chair being loaded approximately 10 percent of the time, will the capacity of the system be affected? Explain.

c. Frequently it is necessary to stop the chair lift temporarily to assist beginning skiers in safely getting on and off. How could the resort's operations manager assess the effect of this practice on the lift capacity?

32. The basic pizza-making process consists of (1) preparing the pizza, (2) baking it, and (3) cutting and boxing (or transferring to a platter for dine-in service). It takes five minutes to prepare a pizza, eight minutes to bake it, and one minute to cut and box or transfer. If the restaurant has only one preparer, what is the theoretical capacity of each stage of the pizza-making process in pizzas per hour? What if two preparers are available?

33. A lab performs two type of blood tests, A and B. The time per setup (in minutes), processing time (in seconds), and order size (number of tests) is given below. Each test requires a new setup. Determine the total capacity required for this lab in minutes.

Blood Test	Setup Time (Minutes)	Processing Time (Seconds)	Order Size (Tests)
A	7.5	84	700
B	6.0	54	500

10.2 34. Medical Solutions, Inc. has the following claims it must complete in the next week (40 hours). The jobs are as follows:

Claim Type	Number of Claims to Process (Work Order Quantity)	Setup (Changeover) Time per Claim Type (hours)	Processing Time per Claim (hours)
Cancer Treatment	18	3	0.9
Spinal Injury	12	1	1.6
Hip Replacement	9	2	0.7

All claims of the same type are processed together. Is 40 hours enough capacity? (Hint: use Equation 10.3.). If not, what short-term capacity solution would you recommend?

10.2 35. Abbott Manufacturing produces plastic cases for solar photovoltaic panels and has decided to combine orders from customers to increase work order size, and thereby, make one large production run per model type. Plastic injection molding machines are used to make these parts, and it is time consuming to clean and re-setup the machines between production runs. Each molding machine and operator works one nine-hour shift with a one-hour lunch break and one-half hour for operator breaks.

Consolidated Work Orders	Work Order Quantity	Setup (Changeover) Time per Work Order (minutes)	Processing Time per Panel (seconds)
Model XVT-5 Case	9,500 panels	90	2.05
Model UYT-3 Case	7,500	75	1.78
Model KLY-6 Case	10,800	150	4.31

What is the total workload (demand) in hours for this work order mix? How many machines will it take to do this work in one, two, or three days? How might this process be improved?

10.2 36. Bennington Products makes four products on three machines. The production schedule for the next six months is as follows:

Production Schedule						
Product	Jan	Feb	Mar	Apr	May	Jun
1	200	0	200	0	200	0
2	100	100	100	100	100	100
3	50	50	50	50	50	50
4	100	0	100	0	100	0

The number of hours (hours/product/machine) each product requires on each machine is as follows:

	Product			
Machine	1	2	3	4
1	0.25	0.15	0.15	0.25
2	0.33	0.20	0.30	0.50
3	0.20	0.30	0.25	0.10

Setup times are roughly 20 percent of the operation times. The machine hours available during the six months are as follows:

Machine	Jan	Feb	Mar	Apr	May	Jun
1	120	60	60	60	60	60
2	180	60	180	60	180	60
3	120	60	120	60	120	60

Determine whether there is enough capacity to meet the product demand. Make sure you state any assumptions.

10.2 37. As the assistant manager of a restaurant, how many servers will you need given the following information for Saturday night's dinner menu?

- Demand (dinners served) = 100 dinners per hour
- Service rate per server = 16 dinners/hour

What assumptions might be needed in this problem?

10.2 38. We know the following data for Albert's fabricating production area:

Number of machines = 5

Number of working days in year = 340

Processing time per unit = 60 minutes

a. What is the annual capacity with a single eight-hour shift?

b. What is the annual capacity with two shifts?

10.2 39. Given the following data for Alice's assembly shop:

Number of machines = 6

Number of working days in year = 340

Processing time per unit = 40 minutes

a. What is the annual capacity with a single eight-hour shift?

b. What is the annual capacity with two shifts?

10.2 40. Worthington Hills grocery store has five regular checkout lines and one express line (12 items or less). Based on a sampling study, it takes 11 minutes on the average for a customer to go through the regular line and four minutes to go through the express line. The store is open from 9 a.m. to 9 p.m. daily.

a. What is the store's maximum capacity (customers processed per day)?

b. What is the store's capacity by day of the week if the five regular checkout lines operate according to the schedule below (the express line is always open)?

Hours/ Day	Mon	Tue	Wed	Thur	Fri	Sat	Sun
9–12 a.m.	1	1	1	1	3	5	2
12–4 p.m.	2	2	2	2	3	5	4
4–6 p.m.	3*	3	3	3	5	3	2
6–9 p.m.	4	4	4	4	5	3	1

* A 3 means 3 regular checkout lines are open on Monday from 4 to 6 p.m.

10.2 41. Tony's Income Tax Service is determining its staffing requirements for the next income tax season. Income tax preparers work 50 hours per week from January 15 through April 15 (assume four weeks per month). There are two major tasks: preparation of short forms and preparation of long forms. The time normally needed to prepare a short form is 15 minutes; long forms takes 50 minutes if all customer records are in order. Fifteen percent of customers using the long form have complicated problems that require approximately one-half hour of additional work. The usual mix of customers requiring long versus short forms is 40 to 60 percent. Preparers work at 85 percent efficiency, meaning that only 85 percent of their time is productive. Tony expects 1,000, 3,500, and 5,000 customers for each of the three months, respectively. How many preparers are needed each month to meet that demand?

10.2 42. A state department of transportation district is responsible for 300 miles of highway. During a winter storm, salt trucks spread an average of 400 pounds of salt per mile and travel at an average speed of 25 mph. Because of nonproductive travel time, the average efficiency of the trucks (i.e., the productive time spent salting the roads) is 60 percent. How many seven-ton trucks will be needed to complete the process of salting all roads within two hours?

EXCEL-BASED PROBLEMS

For these problems, you may use Excel or the spreadsheet templates in MindTap to assist in your analysis.

43. A hotel hosts banquets for conferences in a large ballroom with tables of eight. Servers must get the meals from the kitchen, bring them out to the tables, and then place the meals on the tables. It takes four minutes to get the meals, bring them out to the tables, and then 15 seconds to serve each guest. Use the *Service Capacity* Excel template to answer the following questions.

a. If 20 servers are available, how many tables can be served in 20 minutes?

b. The hotel wants to be able to serve 140 tables in 20 minutes. How many servers are needed?

10.2 44. A plant manufactures three products, A, B, and C. A drill press is required to perform one operation for each product. The plant operates one eight-hour shift 20 days per month. The operation times for each product follow:

Product	A	B	C
Operation Time (minutes/unit)	5.0	1.85	7.0

Determine the amount of equipment needed to produce 10,000 units per month. Use the *Service Capacity* Excel template. (Hint: be sure to compute the correct service rates.)

45. Operating at an 80 percent learning rate, the first unit took 72 hours to produce. Use the Learning Curve Excel template to determine how long the 32nd unit will take. What is the cumulative average time for the one-hundredth unit?

46. Suppose a manufacturer of copiers has concluded that a 75 percent learning curve applies to the time a beginning service technician takes to install copy machines. Use the *Learning Curve* Excel template to answer the following questions:

a. If the time required to install the first copy machine is estimated to be four hours, what is an estimate of the time required by a new technician to install the second and third copiers?

b. If the learning rate changes to 60 or 95 percent, what is an estimate of the time required by a new technician to install the second and third copiers?

10.5 47. Yacht Superior manufactures boats for a yacht rental firm. They are in negotiation for the total price for 50 Model C314 yachts. Based on past experience, the learning rate for their employees and system is 75 percent and they estimate the first unit will require 2,750 labor hours. Use the *Learning Curve* Excel template to determine how long the fiftieth unit will take and what is the cumulative average time for the fiftieth unit. How can this learning-curve information help Yacht Superior plan labor, equipment, and facility capacity, and help price the total contract?

10.5 48. A manufacturer has committed to supply 16 units of a particular product in four months (i.e., 16 weeks) at a price of $30,000 each. The first unit took 1,000 hours to produce. Even though the second unit took only 750 hours to produce, the manufacturer is anxious to know

a. if the delivery commitment of 16 weeks will be met,

b. whether enough labor is available (currently 500 hours is available per week), and

c. whether or not the venture is profitable.

Use the *Learning Curve* Excel template to answer these questions. Assume the material cost per unit equals $22,000; labor equals $10 per labor-hour, and overhead is $2,000 per week.

10.5 49. Linda Bryant recently started a small home-construction company. In an effort to foster high quality, rather than subcontracting individual work, she has formed teams of employees who are responsible for the entire job. She has contracted with a developer to build 20 homes of similar type and size. She has four teams of workers. The first homes were built in an average of 145 days. Use the *Learning Curve* Excel template to find out how long will it take to complete the contract if an 85 percent learning curve applies.

Appleton Pulp and Paper Mill

Appleton Corporation is one of the largest forest-products companies in the world, converting trees into three basic product groups: (1) building materials, such as lumber and plywood; (2) white paper products, including printing and writing grades of white paper; (3) brown paper products, such as liner-board and corrugated containers. Given the highly competitive markets within the forest-products industry, survival dictates that Appleton maintains its position as a low-cost producer of quality products. That requires an ambitious capital program to improve the timber base and to build modern, cost-effective timber conversion facilities.

An integrated pulp and paper mill is a facility in which wood chips and chemicals are processed to produce paper products or dried pulp. First, wood chips are cooked and bleached in the pulp mill; the resulting pulp is piped directly into storage tanks, as shown in Exhibit 10.11. From the storage tanks the pulp is sent to either the paper mill or a dryer. Any excess pulp not allocated to the paper mill or dryer is stored in the storage tanks until the next day. In the paper mill, the pulp is converted to finished paper products. Alternatively, the pulp is sent to a dryer, and the dried pulp is then sold to paper mills that do not have the capability of producing their own pulp. The profit margin is higher for dried pulp, so it is important to fully utilize the dryer capacity. The total system is a large facility costing several hundred million dollars.

The pulp mill has a capacity of 800 tons per day (TPD), the paper mill has a capacity of 600 TPD of pulp use, and the dryer can handle 200 TPD. However, all of the equipment in the mill is subject to downtime for maintenance and reliability breakdowns. The pulp mill is assumed to have an average of 10 percent downtime. The actual downtime varies between 0 and 20 percent each day. For example, one

EXHIBIT 10.11 Pulp and Paper Process

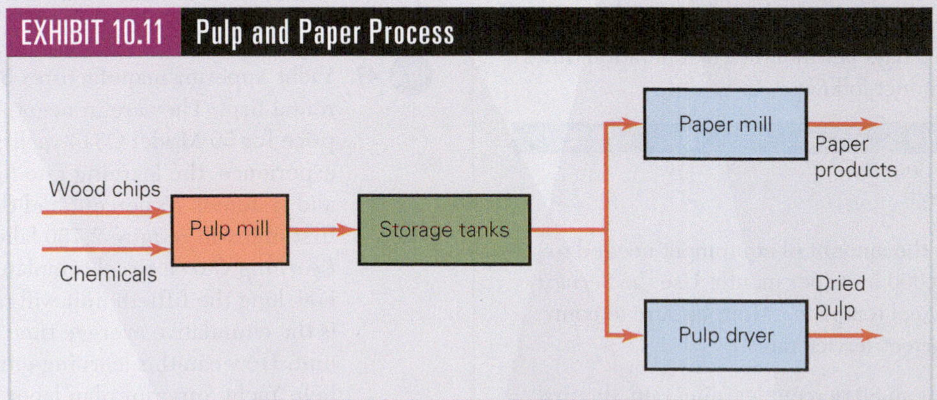

day the pulp mill might be down 2 percent of the time, the next day 20 percent, and so on. In the paper mill, downtime averages 5 percent of the total working hours and may vary between 0 and 10 percent each day. Dryer downtime averages 15 percent and may vary from 0 to 30 percent each day. (Such situations can be modeled as uniform probability distributions; see Supplements A, *Probability and Statistics*, and G, *Simulation*.) Because of downtime, any pulp that has been allocated to the paper mill or dryer but cannot be produced is discarded.

Storage tank capacity is limited to 800 TPD. If the storage tanks become full, pulp mill production stops for the day. On any day, once all pulp has been produced or the storage tanks become full, the pulp is sent to the paper mill or dryer for processing. Production at the pulp mill resumes the next day.

Case Questions for Discussion:

For all questions, develop and use a spreadsheet simulation model for your analysis. Use the approaches described in Supplements A and G to develop the probability distributions and implement the simulation model.

1. At the beginning of day one, 75 tons are remaining in the storage tank. At the current capacities (base case), what is the average amount of pulp lost at the dryer and paper mill over a month (30-days)?
2. What will happen to the estimated amount of pulp lost per month if (treat each question independently of the others)
   a. the pulp mill capacity decreases to 700 from the base case?
   b. pulp mill capacity increases to 900 from the base case?
   c. pulp mill capacity increases to 1,000 or more from the base case?
   d. the paper mill capacity increases to 700 from the base case?
   e. storage tank capacity increases to 1,000 from the base case?
   f. dryer capacity is increased to 300 from the base case? Explain what effect this has on paper mill production.
3. What is the impact of improving reliability to the point where downtime is zero at all facilities?
4. Using the results from question 2, summarize the impact of increasing capacities at the pulp mill, paper mill, dryer, and storage tank from the base case.

David Christopher, Orthopedic Surgeon

David Christopher received his medical degrees from the University of Kentucky and the University of Virginia. He did his residency and early surgeries at Duke University Medical Center. Eight years ago he set up his own orthopedic surgery clinic in Atlanta, Georgia. Today, one other doctor has joined his clinic in addition to 12 support personnel such as X-ray technicians, nurses, accounting, and office support. The medical practice specializes in all orthopedic surgery, except it does not perform spinal surgery. The clinic has grown to the point where both orthopedic surgeons are working long hours, and Dr. Christopher is wondering whether he needs to hire more surgeons.

Rocketclips, Inc./Shutterstock.com

Both surgeons are working long hours, and Dr. Christopher is wondering whether he needs to hire more surgeons.

An orthopedic surgeon is trained in the preservation, investigation, and restoration of the form and function of the extremities, spine, and associated structures by medical, surgical, and physical means. He or she is involved with the care of patients whose musculoskeletal problems include congenital deformities; trauma; infections; tumors; metabolic disturbances of the musculoskeletal system; deformities; injuries; and degenerative diseases of the spine, hands, feet, knee, hip, shoulder, and elbows in children and adults. An orthopedic surgeon is also concerned with primary and secondary muscular problems and the effects of central or peripheral nervous system lesions of the musculoskeletal system. Osteoporosis, for example, results in fractures, especially in the hips, wrists, and spine. Treatments have been very successful in getting the fractures to heal.

Dr. Christopher collected the data in Exhibit 10.9 as an example of the clinic's typical workweek. Both surgeons work 11 hours each day, with 1 hour off for lunch, or 10 effective hours. All surgeries are performed from 7:00 a.m. to 12:00 noon, 4 days a week. After lunch, the surgeons see patients in the hospital and at the clinic from 1:00 p.m. to 6:00 p.m. Over the weekend and on Fridays, the surgeons rest, attend conferences and professional meetings, and sometimes do guest lectures at a nearby medical school. The doctors want to leave a safety capacity each week of 10 percent for unexpected problems with scheduled surgeries and emergency patient arrivals.

The setup and changeover times in Exhibit 10.12 reflect time allowed between each surgery for the surgeons to clean themselves up, rest, review the next patient's medical record for any last-minute issues, and prepare for the next surgery. Dr. Christopher feels these changeover times help ensure the quality of their surgery by giving them time between operations. For example, standing on a concrete floor and bending over a patient in a state of concentration places great stress on the surgeon's legs and back. Dr. Christopher likes to sit down for a while between surgeries to relax. Some surgeons go quickly from one patient to the next; however, Dr. Christopher thinks this practice of rushing could lead to medical and surgical errors. Dr. Christopher wants answers to the following questions.

Case Questions for Discussion:

1. What is the clinic's current weekly workload?
2. Should the clinic hire more surgeons, and if so, how many?
3. What other options and changes could be made to maximize patient throughput and surgeries, and therefore revenue, yet not compromise the quality of medical care?
4. What are your final recommendations? Explain your reasoning.

EXHIBIT 10.12 Orthopedic Surgeon One-Week Surgery Workload (These data are available in the Excel worksheet *Orthopedic Surgeon Case Data* in MindTap)

Orthopedic Surgery Procedure	Surgeon Changeover Time (Minutes)	Surgery Time (Minutes)	Surgeon Identity	Demand (No. of Patients Scheduled Weekly)
Rotator cuff repair	20	45	B	2
Cartilage knee repair	20	30	B	1
Fracture tibia/fibula	20	60	B	1
Achilles tendon repair	20	30	B	3
ACL ligament repair	20	60	B	3
Fractured hip	20	80	A	0
Fractured wrist	20	60	A	2
Fractured ankle	20	70	A	1
Hip replacement	30	150	A	2
Knee replacement	30	120	A	3
Shoulder replacement	40	180	B	1
Big toe replacement	20	90	B	0

Integrative Case: Hudson Jewelers

The Hudson Jewelers case study available in MindTap integrates material found in each chapter of this book.

Case Question for Discussion:

1. Explain how capacity is measured at the following stages of the diamond value chain: (a) mining, (b) cutting and polishing, (c) jewelry manufacturing for custom and standard jewelry, and (d) the retail store? (There can be multiple measures so make sure you define the unit of measure.)

Process Analysis and Resource Utilization

11

aldomurillo/E+/Getty Images

LEARNING OBJECTIVES

After studying this chapter, you should be able to:

11-1 Describe how to compute resource utilization and use the equations for practical applications.

11-2 Be able to identify process bottlenecks and calculate throughput.

11-3 Explain how to apply Little's Law to process analyses.

11-4 Understand the key concepts and mathematics of waiting line management and queueing models.

11-5 Explain how simulation can be used to model queues and evaluate performance.

11-6 Explain the principles and logic of the Theory of Constraints.

When former Cincinnati city manager Valerie Lemmie started her job, she asked building inspectors whether the city had a "one-stop shop" for building permits. They said, "Sure. You stop here once, you stop there once, and you stop there once." What she found out was that a permit stops 473 times on its way from the initial application to final approval. After spending a week at city hall and taking notes on every step of the process, a consultant hired to analyze the Department of Buildings and Inspections ended up with about 30 feet of flowcharts that depicted the building permit process. Although Ms. Lemmie conceded that improvement wouldn't be easy, an assistant noted that a lot of people wanted to know how they could do their jobs better. "They know everything that's wrong with it probably more than anyone else. And more than anyone else, they need to be part of the solution."[1]

WHAT DO YOU THINK?

Can you think of any processes that you encounter at your college or university that seem very complex or require excessive waiting?

In Chapter 7, we discussed process selection, design, and improvement. However, designing and improving processes to achieve excellent customer service also requires an understanding of job and work design, forecasting workloads, and capacity issues that we learned about in Chapters 8–10.

In the opening scenario, the building permit process was plagued with unnecessary and non-value-added work, inefficient resource utilization, and excessive waiting that caused process times to balloon. Analyzing manufacturing and service processes, understanding how resources are used, identifying and managing bottlenecks, and managing customer wait times are important tasks for operations managers. These topics are the focus of this chapter. Excellent customer service is a function of good day-to-day operations and process selection, design, improvement, and analysis.

Excellent customer service is a function of good day-to-day operations and process selection, design, improvement, and analysis.

11-1 Resource Utilization

Idle machines, trucks, people, computers, warehouse space, and other resources used in a process simply drain away potential profit. **Utilization** *is the fraction of time a workstation or individual is busy over the long run.* It is difficult to achieve 100 percent utilization. For example, utilization in most job shops ranges from 65 to 90 percent. In flow shops, it might be between 80 and 95 percent, and for most continuous flow processes, above 95 percent. Job shops require frequent machine changeovers and delays, whereas flow shops and continuous flow processes keep equipment more fully utilized. Service facilities have a greater range of resource utilization. Movie theaters, for example, average 5 to 20 percent utilization when seat utilization is computed over an entire month. Most airlines and hotels find seat and room utilization, respectively, above 50 percent.

11-1a Computing Resource Utilization

Two ways of computing resource utilization are

$$\text{Utilization } (U) = \frac{\text{Resources Used}}{\text{Resources Available}} \qquad [11.1]$$

$$\text{Utilization } (U) = \frac{\text{Demand Rate}}{\text{Service Rate} \times \text{Number of Servers}} \qquad [11.2]$$

Equation 11.1 computes utilization as the proportion of available resources that are being used. Equation 11.2 computes utilization based on the ratio of the demand rate to effective service capacity based on the service rate and number of servers. If a manager knows any two of the three variables in Equation 11.1 or any three of the four variables in Equation 11.2, then the remaining variable can be found. For both equations, the dimensions of the numerator and denominator (time periods, units, etc.) must be the same, as utilization is a dimensionless quantity.

The demand rate and service rate in Equation 11.2 represent averages over a time period; for example, a service rate of five customers per hour or a demand rate of 28 customers per hour. For a process design to be feasible, the calculated utilization over the long run cannot exceed 100 percent. Solved Problems 11.1 and 11.2 illustrate the use of these equations to compute resource utilization. Note that in our discussion of capacity in Chapter 10, the denominators of these equations represent capacity. Therefore, utilization is simply the ratio of resources used or demand rate to the capacity; that is, the fraction of capacity that is being used.

We may use these equations to identify process design options to achieve a target utilization. For example, we might want to know how many resources must be available in Equation 11.1, or how many servers we might need if we know the demand rate and service rate in Equation 11.2 to achieve a target utilization. We can find these using simple algebra to solve for the unknown quantities.

SOLVED PROBLEM 11.1: USING EQUATION 11.1 TO COMPUTE RESOURCE UTILIZATION

A hotel has 80 rooms. If, on a given day, 65 rooms are occupied, what is the utilization of hotel rooms?

Solution:

Use Equation 11.1,

$$\text{Utilization } (U) = \frac{\text{Resources Used}}{\text{Resources Available}}$$

The utilization of the hotel rooms is

$$U = \frac{65 \text{ rooms}}{80 \text{ rooms}} = \frac{65}{80} = 0.8125\text{, or } 81.25\%$$

SOLVED PROBLEM 11.2: USING EQUATION 11.2 TO COMPUTE RESOURCE UTILIZATION

a. Suppose that an inspection station for assembled printers receives 40 printers/hour and has two inspectors, each of whom can inspect 30 printers per hour. What is the utilization of the inspection station?
b. Suppose that the demand is estimated to be 100 printers per hour. What is the utilization if three, four, or five inspectors are available?
c. If the demand for printer inspections is 150 printers per hour, how many inspectors would be needed to achieve a utilization of at least 80 percent?

Solution:

a. Using Equation 11.2 where servers represent inspectors,

$$\text{Utilization } (U) = \frac{\text{Demand Rate}}{\text{Service Rate} \times \text{Number of Servers}}$$

We have

$$U = \frac{40 \text{ printers/hour}}{30 \text{ printers/hour/inspector} \times 2 \text{ inspectors}}$$

$$= \frac{40}{60} = 0.667\text{, or } 66.7\%$$

Note that the service rate of both inspectors working together is 60 printers/hour. Because the demand rate is smaller, the inspectors would, on average, be idle one-third of the time.

b. With three, four, or five inspectors, the utilization would be

$$\text{Three inspectors: } U = \frac{100}{30 \times 3} = \frac{100}{90} = 1.11 \text{ or } 111\%$$

$$\text{Four inspectors: } U = \frac{100}{30 \times 4} = \frac{100}{120} = 0.833 \text{ or } 83.3\%$$

$$\text{Five inspectors: } U = \frac{100}{30 \times 5} = \frac{100}{150} = 0.666 \text{ or } 66.7\%$$

For three inspectors, the utilization exceeds 100 percent; therefore, the work would eventually pile up because the effective capacity would not be able to handle the demand. With four inspectors, utilization is 83.3 percent, while with five inspectors it is 66.7 percent. Recommending four inspectors is a good feasible solution.

c. With a demand of 150 printers/hour and a target utilization of 80 percent, we use Equation 11.2 to solve for the number of inspectors:

$$0.8 \leq \frac{150 \text{ printers/hour}}{30 \text{ printers/hour/inspector} \times \text{Number of inspectors}}$$

$$0.8 \times 30 \times \text{Number of inspectors} \leq 150$$

$$\text{Number of inspectors} \leq \frac{150}{24} = 6.25$$

Because we want the utilization to be 0.8 or greater, we used an inequality in the equation, noting that the right-hand side is the actual utilization based on the number of servers, which should be greater than or equal to 0.8. Because the number of inspectors must be a whole number, we round down to 6. The actual utilization is

$$U = \frac{150}{30 \times 6} = 0.83$$

11-2 Process Throughput and Bottlenecks

We identified four hierarchical levels of work in Chapter 7: task, activities, processes, and value chains. Most work is performed in a series of work activities in a process. For example, in manufacturing, a job moves from one machine center to the next; likewise, many services, such as processing insurance claims, consist of several different work activities performed by different specialists. *The number of units or tasks that are completed per unit time from a process is called* **throughput**. Throughput might be measured as parts per day, transactions per minute, or customers per hour, depending on the context.

> Total process output is at the throughput rate of the bottleneck.

A logical question to consider is how much throughput can be achieved for an entire process. Like the old adage that a chain is only a strong as its weakest link, process throughput is limited by the smallest output rate of the work activities that comprise the process. A **bottleneck** *is the work activity that effectively limits the throughput of the entire process.* Solved Problem 11.3 illustrates an example of identifying bottlenecks.

Identifying and breaking process bottlenecks is an important part of process design and improvement, and will increase the speed of the process, reduce waiting and work-in-process inventory, enhance customer service, and use resources more efficiently. Analysis of bottlenecks can provide useful insights for evaluating and choosing alternative process designs.

Tracking Hospital Patient Flow[2]

Hannibal Regional Hospital uses radio frequency identification technology (RFID) to track patients throughout its ambulatory care unit. Patient badges are embedded with a RFID chip that communicates via antennas throughout the hospital. The hospital unit includes a surgical suite and areas for blood transfusions, injections, and radiology. The objective was to better understand patient flow and where and how long they wait in each process stage. "You cannot manage what you cannot measure," states Judy Patterson, director of preoperative services at the 91-bed hospital.

Patient tracking results found that 20 percent of outpatient treatment was being handled after official hospital hours. The solution was scheduling physicians and patients in blocks of time, identifying and breaking process bottlenecks, and tracking patient arrival times. Therefore, physicians must use their time more efficiently and be more aware of when patients arrive. Two results of these changes in scheduling and physician behavior were that patient processing time decreased and physician utilization increased.

Future uses of RFID technology include using it to track equipment such as portable X-ray machines, scopes, surgical tools, and high-tech cameras. In one test situation, the technology was used to track epidural pumps in the birthing unit to solve a recurring problem. "We often had trouble finding the pumps late at night," Patterson says.

SOLVED PROBLEM 11.3: IDENTIFYING BOTTLENECKS

The process for renewing a driver's license at the Archer County Courthouse is as follows. First, the clerk fills out the application; then the clerk takes the driver's picture; and finally, a typist enters the information into the computer system and processes the new license. It takes an average of five minutes to fill out an application, one minute to take a picture, and seven minutes to process the new license. There are two clerks and three typists. How many licenses can be processed in one hour if both the clerks and typists have an 80 percent target utilization?

Solution:

The service rate for clerks is 5 + 1 = 6 minutes per license. Converting this to an hourly rate, we have 10 licenses/hour/clerk. The clerks work independently; hence the effective service rate of the two clerks is 20 licenses/hour.

Using Equation 11.2, we find the number of licenses/hour (i.e., the demand rate) that can be processed by the clerks:

$$\text{Utilization } (U) = \frac{\text{Demand Rate}}{\text{Service rate} \times \text{Number of Servers}}$$

$$0.8 = \frac{\text{Number of licenses/hour}}{\text{10 licenses/hour/clerk} \times \text{2 clerks}}$$

$$\text{Number of licenses/hour} = 0.8 \times (10 \times 2) = 16$$

Typists require seven minutes/license, or 60/7 = 8.57 licenses/hour/typist. Using Equation 11.2 and a utilization rate of 0.80, the number of licenses/hour that can be processed by the typists is:

$$0.8 = \frac{\text{Number of licenses/hour}}{\text{8.57 licenses/hour/typist} \times \text{3 typists}}$$

$$\text{Number of licenses/hour} = 0.8 \times 25.71 = 20.57$$

We see that the throughput of the system is limited by the work activity of the clerks, so the total process output is 16 licenses/hour. Therefore, the clerks are the bottleneck resource.

In Chapter 7, we discussed an example of a restaurant order posting and fulfillment process (see Exhibit 7.6). The process consisted of five work activities:

- Work activity 1: Chef decides if order is accurate
- Work activity 2: Chef stages raw materials
- Work activity 3: Chef prepares side dishes
- Work activity 4: Oven operation
- Work activity 5: Chef assembles order

Exhibit 11.1 shows a portion of the process in Exhibit 7.6 for these work activities. Note that activities 3 and 4 are performed in parallel, with the chef preparing side dishes while the meal cooks in the oven.

Exhibit 11.2 provides an analysis of the output rates and utilizations for each work activity using one chef and two ovens. Consider work activity 3. The output per time period for this activity is

$$\frac{\text{1 chef} \times \text{60 minutes/hour}}{\text{12 minutes per order}} = \text{5 orders/hour,}$$

which is simply the denominator of Equation 11.2.

The resource utilization in line five of Exhibit 11.2 is computed using Equation 11.2 as:

$$\text{Utilization } (U) = \frac{\text{Demand Rate}}{\text{Service Rate} \times \text{Number of Servers}}$$

$$U = \frac{\text{20 orders/hour}}{\text{5 orders/hour} \times \text{1 chef}} = \text{4.0, or 400\%}$$

The output rates and utilizations for the other work activities are computed in a similar fashion.

EXHIBIT 11.1 Restaurant Order Fulfillment Process

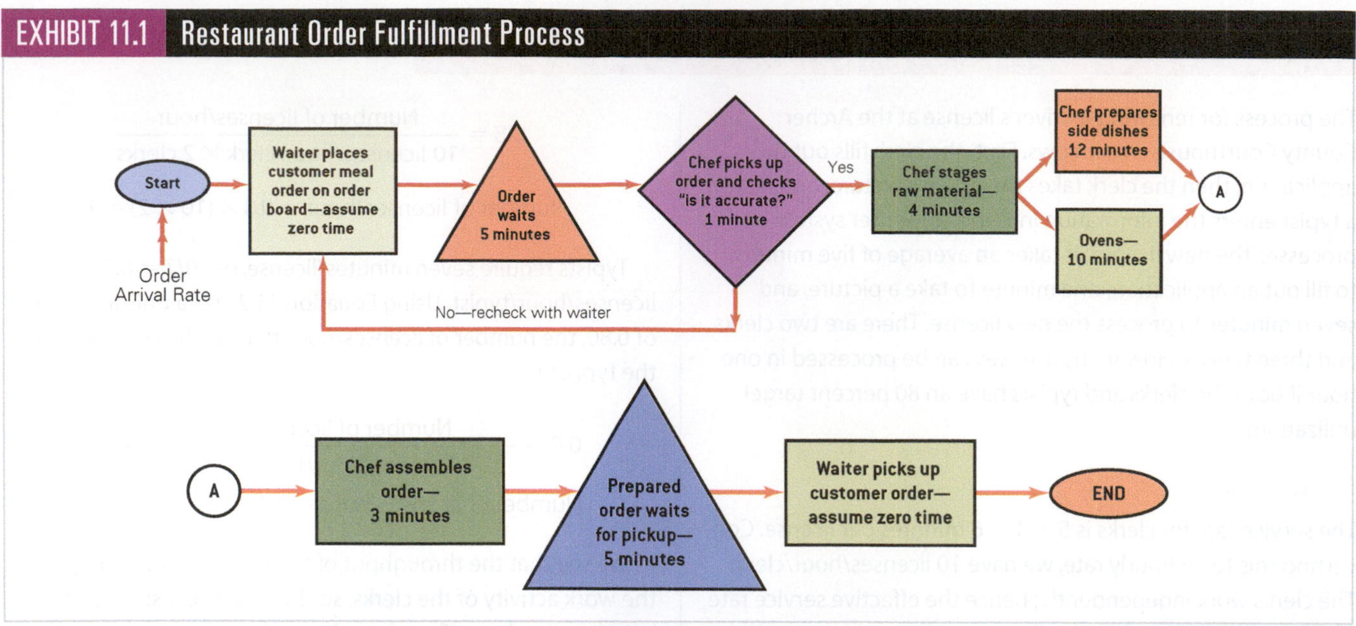

EXHIBIT 11.2 Utilization Analysis of Restaurant Fulfillment Process (1 Chef and 2 Ovens)

	Work Activity #1 (Chef decides if order is accurate)	Work Activity #2 (Chef stages raw materials)	Work Activity #3 (Chef prepares side dishes)	Work Activity #4 (Oven operation)	Work Activity #5 (Chef assembles order)
Order arrival rate (given)	20 orders/hr	20 orders/hr	20 orders/hr	20 orders/hr	20 orders/hr
Time per order	1 minute	4 minutes	12 minutes	10 minutes	3 minutes
Number of resources	1 chef	1 chef	1 chef	2 ovens	1 chef
Output per time period	60 orders/hr	15 orders/hr	5 orders/hr	12 orders/hr	20 orders/hr
Resource utilization with 1 chef and 2 ovens	33%	133%	400%	167%	100%

As we noted earlier, whenever the utilization is greater than 100 percent, the work (orders) will endlessly back up in front of that resource. Work activity 3 has a chef utilization rate of 400 percent and a corresponding output rate of only five orders per hour, which is the highest utilization and lowest output rate among all work activities. Clearly, it is the most constraining activity in this process and represents the bottleneck. The process is constrained by labor resource availability, and more resources are needed.

The only way to improve the output rate of the process is to increase the output rate of the bottleneck activity. Identifying and breaking process bottlenecks is an important part of process analysis and improvement and will increase the throughput, reduce work-in-process inventory, and use resources more efficiently.

A logical question to consider is how many chefs are needed to bring the utilization down below 100 percent at work activity 3? This can be found by using Equation 11.2 as follows:

$$U = 1.0 \geqslant \frac{20 \text{ orders/hour}}{5 \text{ orders/hour} \times \text{number of chefs}}$$

$$5 \text{ orders/hour} \times \text{number of chefs} \times 1.00 \geqslant 20 \text{ orders/hour}$$

$$\text{Number of chefs} \geqslant \frac{20}{5} = 4$$

EXHIBIT 11.3 Revised Utilization Analysis of Restaurant Fulfillment Process (4 Chefs and 2 Ovens)

	Work Activity #1 (Chef decides if order is accurate)	Work Activity #2 (Chef stages raw materials)	Work Activity #3 (Chef prepares side dishes)	Work Activity #4 (Oven operation)	Work Activity #5 (Chef assembles order)
Resource utilization with 4 chefs and 2 ovens	8.33%	33%	100%	167%	25%

With four chefs, the resource utilizations are recomputed for all labor intensive work activities in Exhibit 11.3. For example, the utilization of the chefs for work activity 1 is computed as

$$U = \frac{20 \text{ orders/hour}}{60 \text{ orders/hour} \times 4 \text{ chefs}} = 0.0833, \text{ or } 8.33\%$$

We see that while the utilizations of the labor-intensive work activities have been reduced, work activity 4, the oven, is now the bottleneck, with a utilization of 167%. The process has switched from being labor (chef) constrained to equipment (oven) constrained. To determine how many ovens to have, we solve Equation 11.2:

$$U = 1.00 \geqslant \frac{20 \text{ orders/hour}}{6 \text{ orders/hour} \times \text{number of ovens}}$$

$$6 \text{ orders/hour} \times \text{number of ovens} \times 1.00 \geqslant 20 \text{ orders/hour}$$

$$\text{Number of ovens} \geqslant 20/6 = 3.33$$

The utilization of four ovens would be

$$U = \frac{20 \text{ orders/hour}}{6 \text{ orders/hour} \times 4 \text{ ovens}} = 0.83 \text{ or } 83\%.$$

Exhibit 11.4 shows the summary of the analysis with four chefs and four ovens. Again, work activity 3 has the slowest output rate (20 orders/hour) and the highest utilization and remains the bottleneck. The only way to improve throughput is to hire more chefs or increase the speed at which they work (i.e., reduce the chefs' time per order so as to increase the output rate).

Exhibit 11.5 shows a process flowchart with output rates in Exhibit 11.4. The work activity with the smallest output rate (activity 3 with 20 orders/hour) is the bottleneck. Exhibit 11.6 shows a funnel analogy of the bottleneck for this process. Work activity 5 must wait for work coming from work activity 3 before it can complete the order. Therefore, work activity 5 is "starved" for work.

Solved Problem 11.4 illustrates a similar problem of identifying bottlenecks and exploring options to increase throughput.

EXHIBIT 11.4 Revised Utilization Analysis of Restaurant Fulfillment Process (4 Chefs and 4 Ovens)

	Work Activity #1 (Chef decides if order is accurate)	Work Activity #2 (Chef stages raw materials)	Work Activity #3 (Chef prepares side dishes)	Work Activity #4 (Oven operation)	Work Activity #5 (Chef assembles order)
Order arrival rate (given)	20 orders/hr	20 orders/hr	20 orders/hr	20 orders/hr	20 orders/hr
Time per order	1 minute	4 minutes	12 minutes	10 minutes	3 minutes
Number of resources	4 chefs	4 chefs	4 chefs	4 ovens	4 chefs
Output per time period	240 orders/hr	60 orders/hr	20 orders/hr	24 orders/hr	80 orders/hr
Resource utilization with 4 chefs and 4 ovens	8.33%	33%	100%	83%	25%

EXHIBIT 11.5 Restaurant Fulfillment Process Output Rates with 4 Chefs and 4 Ovens

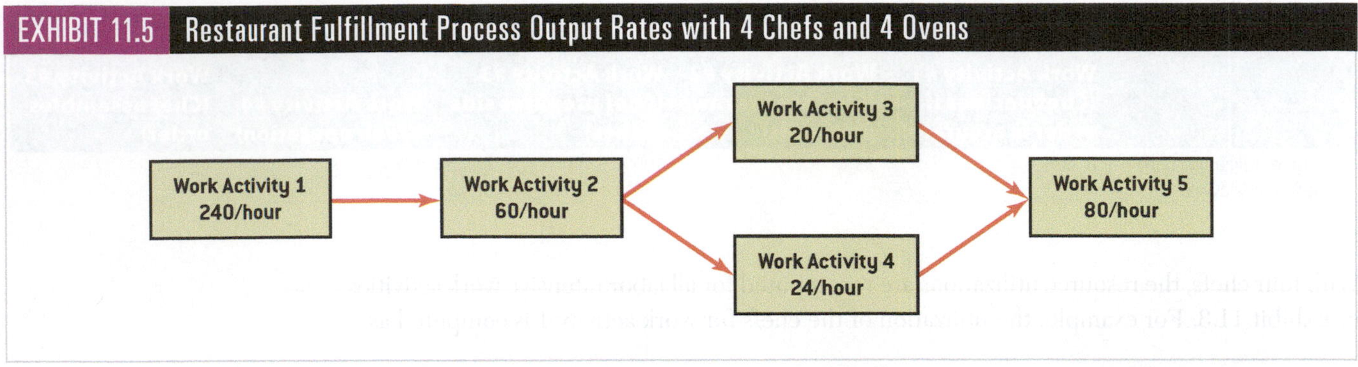

EXHIBIT 11.6 Funnel Analogy of Bottleneck Work Activities for the Restaurant

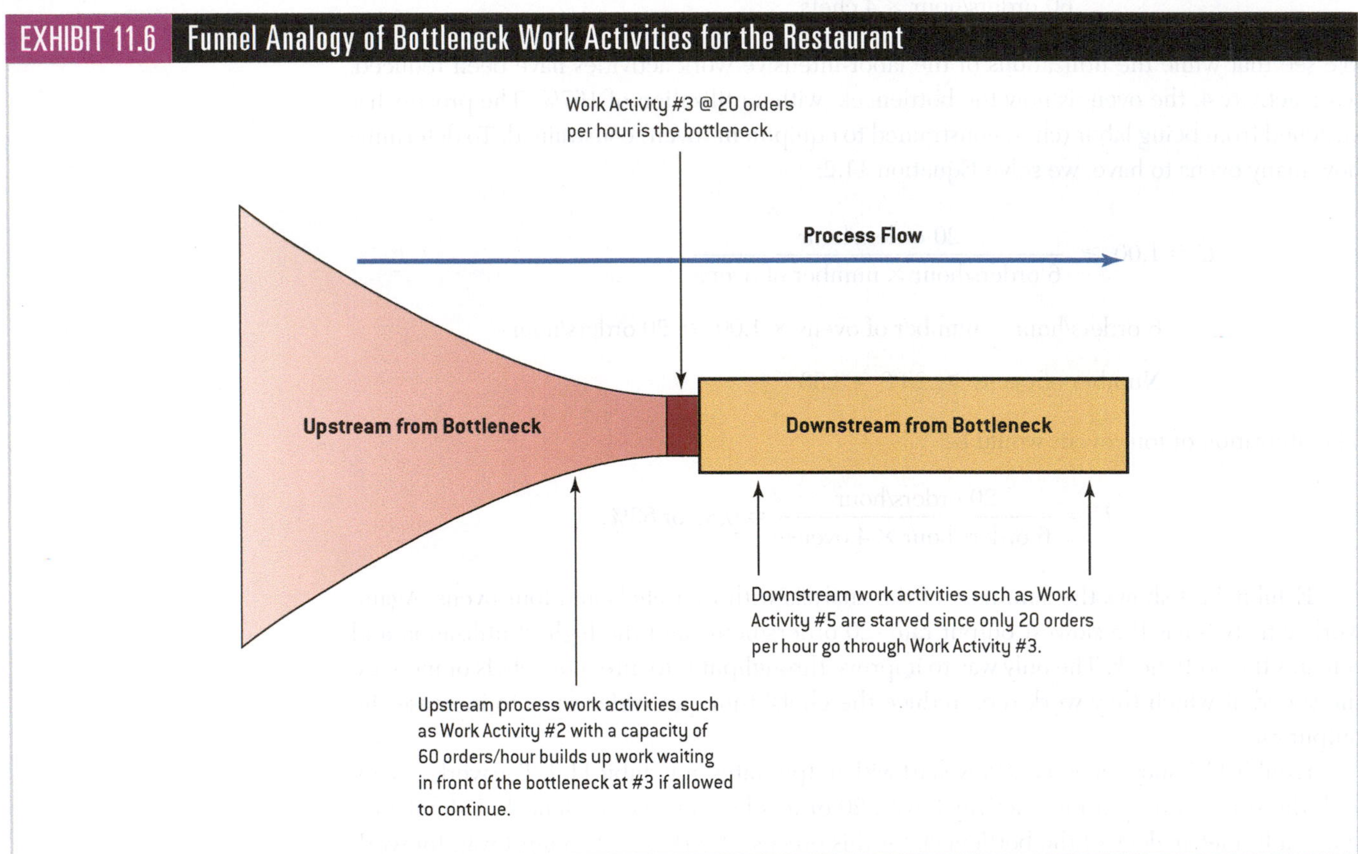

SOLVED PROBLEM 11.4: EVALUATING AND IMPROVING BOTTLENECKS

Processing automobile insurance claims involves the four work activities shown in Exhibit 11.7. The numbers in parentheses are the times in minutes to complete and process one claim. Demand averages 20 claims per hour, and each claim must be processed by each work activity. An administrative clerk performs work activity A; a coding specialist, B; a claims analyst, C; and a claims reviewer, D.

a. How many administrative clerks should be hired, assuming a target utilization of at least 80 percent?

b. What is the labor utilization of all four labor resources if two employees are available for each work activity?

c. What is output rate in claims per hour for each work activity (based on the assumption of two employees per activity) and the throughput for this process? What is the bottleneck activity?

d. Given the staffing levels described in (c), how can total process throughput be increased? Identify several practical options and analyze them numerically.

EXHIBIT 11.7 Process Flow for Solved Problem 11.4

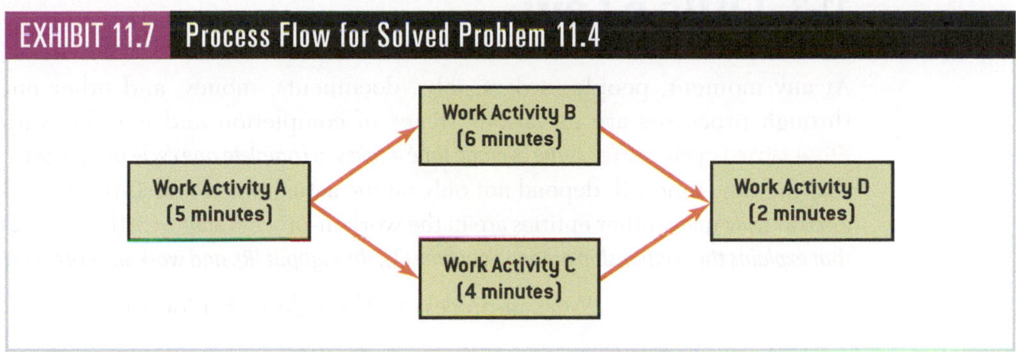

Solution:

In our calculations, we first convert the service rates to claims/hour:

Administrative clerks:

service rate = 5 minutes/claim, or 12 claims/hour

Coding specialists:

service rate = 6 minutes/claim, or 10 claims/hour

Claim specialists:

service rate = 4 minutes/claim, or 15 claims/hour

Claim reviewers:

service rate = 2 minutes/claim, or 30 claims/hour

In all calculations, we use Equation 11.2:

$$\text{Utilization } (U) = \frac{\text{Demand Rate}}{\text{Service Rate} \times \text{Number of Servers}}$$

a. Let N be the number of clerks. Then to ensure a target utilization of 0.80, we have

$$0.80 \leqslant \frac{20}{12 \times N}$$
$$9.6N \leqslant 20$$
$$N \leqslant 2.08 \text{ or 2 clerks}$$

b. Administrative clerks:

$$U = \frac{\text{20 claims/hour}}{\text{12 claims/hour} \times \text{2 clerks}} = 0.833 \text{ or } 83.3\%$$

Coding specialists:

$$U = \frac{\text{20 claims/hour}}{\text{10 claims/hour} \times \text{2 coding specialists}} = 1.00 \text{ or } 100\%$$

Claim specialists:

$$U = \frac{\text{20 claims/hour}}{\text{15 claims/hour} \times \text{2 claim specialists}} = 0.667 \text{ or } 66.7\%$$

Claim reviewers:

$$U = \frac{\text{20 claims/hour}}{\text{30 claims/hour} \times \text{2 claim reviewers}} = 0.333 \text{ or } 33.3\%$$

c. The output rate for each work activity is simply the denominator of Equation 11.2:

Activity A: 12 claims/hour/clerk × 2 clerks
= 24 claims/hour

Activity B: 10 claims/hour/coder × 2 coders
= 20 claims/hour

Activity C: 15 claims/hour/specialist × 2 specialists
= 30 claims/hour

Activity D: 30 clams/hour/reviewer × 2 reviewers
= 60 claims/hour.

Process throughput is limited by the bottleneck, which is activity B, 20 claims/hour.

d. One improvement option is to add a third coder, with an increase in labor cost. This increases the output rate for activity B to 10 claims/hour/coder × 3 coders = 30 claims/hour. All other resource levels and output rates remain the same. The bottleneck is now work activity A with an output rate of 24 claims/hour, a 20 percent increase.

Other options to increase process throughput include speeding up the service rates, adding resources, or transferring labor resources among the work activities. For example, if it is possible to speed up the clerks' service rate to 15 claims/hour from 12 claims/hour and transfer one of the reviewers to coding, we have the following output rates:

Activity A = 15 claims/hour/clerk × 2 clerks
= 30 claims/hour

Activity B = 10 claims/hour/coder × 3 coders
= 30 claims/hour

Activity C = 15 claims/hour/specialist × 2 specialists
= 30 claims/hour

Activity D = 30 clams/hour/reviewers × 1 reviewer
= 30 claims/hour

Each activity now has an equal output rate, so process throughput is now 30 claims/hour and the bottleneck has disappeared. In this fashion, we have eliminated the additional labor cost of adding a third coder.

11-3 Little's Law

At any moment, people, orders, jobs, documents, money, and other entities that flow through processes are in various stages of completion and may be waiting in queues. **Flow time (cycle time)** *is the average time it takes to complete one cycle of a process.* It makes sense that the flow time will depend not only on the actual time to perform the tasks required but also on how many other entities are in the work-in-process stage. **Little's Law** *is a simple equation that explains the relationship among flow time (T), throughput (R), and work-in-process (WIP):*

$$\text{Work-in-process} = \text{Throughput} \times \text{Flow time}$$

or

$$\text{WIP} = R \times T \qquad [11.3]$$

Little's Law provides a simple way of evaluating average process performance. If we know any two of the three variables, we can compute the third using Little's Law. Little's Law can be applied to many different types of manufacturing and service operations. See Solved Problems 11.5 to 11.8. Solved Problem 11.8 shows a practical financial application of Little's Law .

SOLVED PROBLEM 11.5: COMPUTING WORK-IN-PROCESS USING LITTLE'S LAW

Suppose that a voting facility processes an average of 50 people per hour (throughput) and that, on average, it takes 10 minutes for each person to complete the voting process (flow time). How many voters, on average, are voting?

Solution:

Using Equation 11.3, we can compute the average number of voters in process (work-in-process):

$$\begin{aligned} \text{Work-in-process (WIP)} &= R \times T \\ &= 50 \text{ voters/hr} \times (10 \text{ minutes}/60 \text{ minutes per hour}) \\ &= 8.33 \text{ voters} \end{aligned}$$

Therefore, on average, we would expect to find about eight or nine voters inside the facility. Exhibit 11.8 shows the use of the Excel template *Little's Law* in MindTap for solving this problem. Note that the flow time is converted to hours for consistent dimensions.

EXHIBIT 11.8 Using Little's Law Template to Compute Work-in-Process

	A	B	C	D	E
1	Little's Law		Copyright © 2017 Cengage Learning		
2			Not for commercial use.		
3	Enter any two of the three values only in the yellow cells				
4	and the spreadsheet will calculate the third.				
5					
6	Throughput (R)	50			
7	Flow time (T)	0.16666667			
8	Work-in-process (WIP)				
9					
10	Throughput (R)				
11	Flow time (T)				
12	Work-in-process (WIP)	8.33			

Little's Law explains the relationship among work-in-process, throughput, and flowtime on an aggregate basis using long-term averages. While this provides useful insight for designing and managing processes, it does not capture the randomness in arrival and service rates and dynamic behavior that often exists in manufacturing and service systems. Queueing models, which we discuss next, address these issues.

SOLVED PROBLEM 11.6: COMPUTING THROUGHPUT USING LITTLE'S LAW

Suppose that the loan department of a bank takes an average of six days (0.2 months) to process an application (flowtime) and that an internal audit found that about 100 applications are in various stages of processing at any one time (work-in-process). What is the throughput?

Solution:

In Little's Law, $T = 0.2$ and WIP = 100 applications. Using Equation 11.3, we calculate the throughput of the department as

$$R = \text{WIP}/T = 100 \text{ applications}/0.2 \text{ months}$$
$$= 500 \text{ applications per month}$$

Exhibit 11.9 shows the use of the spreadsheet template.

EXHIBIT 11.9 Using Little's Law Template to Compute Throughput

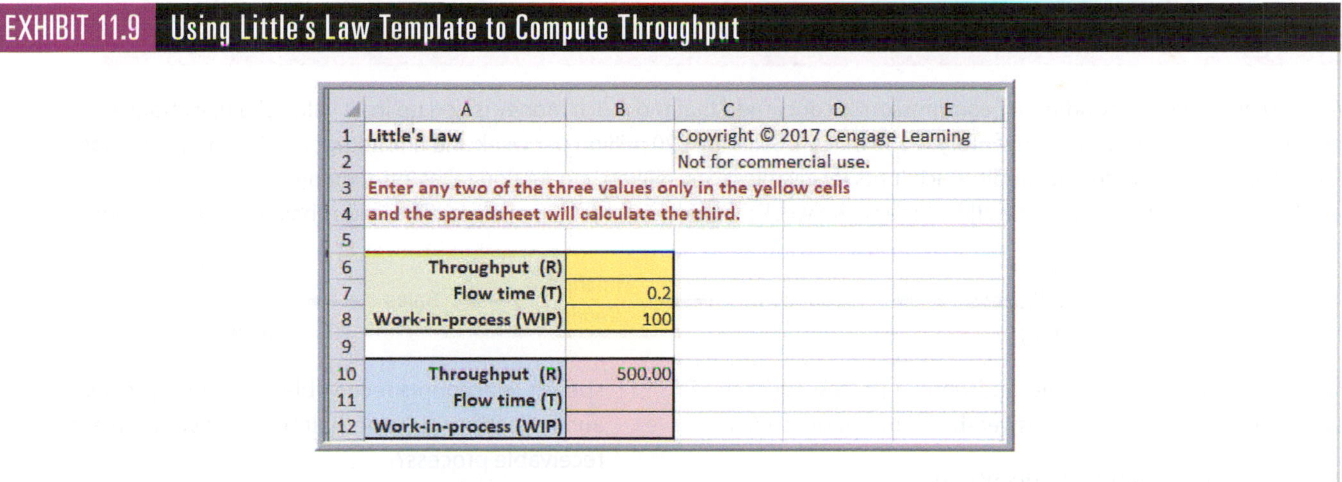

	A	B	C	D	E
1	Little's Law		Copyright © 2017 Cengage Learning		
2			Not for commercial use.		
3	Enter any two of the three values only in the yellow cells				
4	and the spreadsheet will calculate the third.				
5					
6	Throughput (R)				
7	Flow time (T)	0.2			
8	Work-in-process (WIP)	100			
9					
10	Throughput (R)	500.00			
11	Flow time (T)				
12	Work-in-process (WIP)				

SOLVED PROBLEM 11.7: COMPUTING FLOW TIME USING LITTLE'S LAW

Suppose that a restaurant makes 400 pizzas per week, each of which uses 1/2 pound of dough, and that it typically maintains an inventory of 70 pounds of dough. What is the average time that the dough is in inventory waiting to be used?

Solution:

In this case, $R = 200$ pounds per week of dough and WIP = 70 pounds, and we want to compute the flow time. Using Little's Law, the flow time is

$$T = \text{WIP}/R = 70/200$$
$$= 0.35 \text{ weeks, or about 2.5 days}$$

This information can be used to verify the freshness of the dough. Exhibit 11.10 shows the use of the spreadsheet template.

EXHIBIT 11.10 Using Little's Law Template to Compute Flow Time

	A	B	C	D	E
1	Little's Law		Copyright © 2017 Cengage Learning		
2			Not for commercial use.		
3	Enter any two of the three values only in the yellow cells				
4	and the spreadsheet will calculate the third.				
5					
6	Throughput (R)	200			
7	Flow time (T)				
8	Work-in-process (WIP)	70			
9					
10	Throughput (R)				
11	Flow time (T)	0.35			
12	Work-in-process (WIP)				

SOLVED PROBLEM 11.8: APPLYING LITTLE'S LAW TO A VALUE CHAIN

A manufacturer of air conditioner compressors is concerned that too much money is tied up in its value chain. Average raw material and work-in-process inventory is $50 million. Sales are $20 million per week and finished-goods inventory averages $30 million. The average outstanding accounts receivable is $60 million. Production takes, on average, one week to produce a compressor and the typical sales flow time is two weeks. Assume 50 weeks in one year. The value chain is depicted below:

Identify throughput, flow time, and work-in-process for each step in the value chain, and answer the following questions:

a. What is the flow unit in this system?
b. What is the total flow time of a throughput dollar?
c. What is the average dollar inventory in the value chain?
d. Which of the three processes—production, sales, or accounts receivable—is the best candidate for freeing up dollars for the air conditioner manufacturer?
e. What is the target level of average accounts receivable inventory if management can reduce the time a dollar spends in accounts receivable inventory (processing and collections) by one-half by improving the accounts receivable process?
f. What else does this analysis demonstrate?

Solution:

Exhibit 11.11 shows the throughput, flow time, and work-in-process for each step in the value chain. The numbers in squares are given in the problem and the numbers in ovals are computed.

EXHIBIT 11.11 Flow Time Analysis of the Air Conditioner Compressor Value Chain

WIP = $R \times T$	Raw Material & WIP Inventory	Production	Finished Goods Inventory	Sales Process	Accounts Receivable Inventory
Inventory (WIP)	$50m	$20m	$30m	$40m	$60m
Throughput Rate (R)	$1,000m/yr	$1,000m/yr	$1,000m/yr	$1,000m/yr	$1,000m/yr
Flow Time (T)	0.05 years	0.02 years	0.03 years	0.04 years	0.06 years

a. The flow unit is one throughput dollar ($).
b. First, review the calculations in Exhibit 11.11. If we add the flow times for each process in the value chain we obtain 0.05 + 0.02 + 0.03 + 0.04 + 0.06 = 0.20 years, or 10 weeks.
c. The answer using Exhibit 11.11 is $50m + $20m + $30m + $40m + $60m = $200m.
d. Clearly, accounts receivable ties up $60m in cash and takes an average of 0.06 years, or three weeks, to process and collect the money. The fact is a dollar tied up in accounts receivable is just as valuable as a dollar tied up in production or inventory.
e. WIP = $R \times T$ = $1,000m/year × 0.03 year = $30m instead of $60m. This improvement initiative frees up monies for other purposes or to reduce cash flow and debt needs.
f. Accounts receivable accounts for 30 percent (3/10) of the total flow time and total cash to operate the business ($60m/$200m). See Exhibit 11.11.

11-4 Managing Waiting Lines

A ***queue*** *is a waiting line.* Queues are common in both manufacturing and service processes when uncertainty exists in demand and service rates. Jobs wait for processing at machines and workstations, and customers wait in queues for service at banks, grocery stores, and other establishments. Understanding queues allows us to analyze current and alternative process designs to understand their behavior, predict process performance, and better allocate resources. Queueing models help managers understand key performance measures such as waiting times, queue lengths, and machine or server idle times so that they can manage resources more effectively and provide better customer satisfaction.

11-4a Queueing System Characteristics

A ***queueing system*** *consists of customers that arrive for service, one or more servers that provide the service, and a queue (waiting line) of entities that wait for service if the server is busy.* Customers need not be people but can be machines awaiting repair, airplanes waiting to take off, subassemblies waiting for a machine, computer programs waiting for processing, or telephone calls awaiting a customer service representative. Servers might be people such as clerks, customer service representatives, or repairpersons; and servers may also be airport runways, machine tools, repair bays, ATMs, or computers. In many cases, a queue is a physical line, as you experience in a bank or grocery store. In other situations, a queue may not even be visible or even in one location, as with computer jobs waiting for processing or credit card transactions waiting to be processed electronically.

Customers, servers, and queues in a queueing system can be arranged in various ways. Three common queueing configurations are

1. *One or more parallel servers fed by a single queue* as illustrated in Exhibit 11.12a (customers are indicated by circles and servers are represented by squares). This is the typical configuration used by many banks and airline ticket counters.
2. *Several parallel servers fed by their own queues* (see Exhibit 11.12b). Most supermarkets and discount retailers use this type of system.
3. *A combination of several queues in series*. This structure is common when multiple processing operations exist, such as in manufacturing facilities and many service systems. For instance, an assembly line is a set of workstations arranged in a serial structure—the output of one station becomes the input of another station. Another example is a drive-through at a restaurant that may have a queue of cars placing orders followed by a queue of cars at the pickup window. Exhibit 11.13 shows an example of queues in series for a typical voting facility.

EXHIBIT 11.12 Parallel Servers with (a) A Single Queue and (b) Multiple Queues

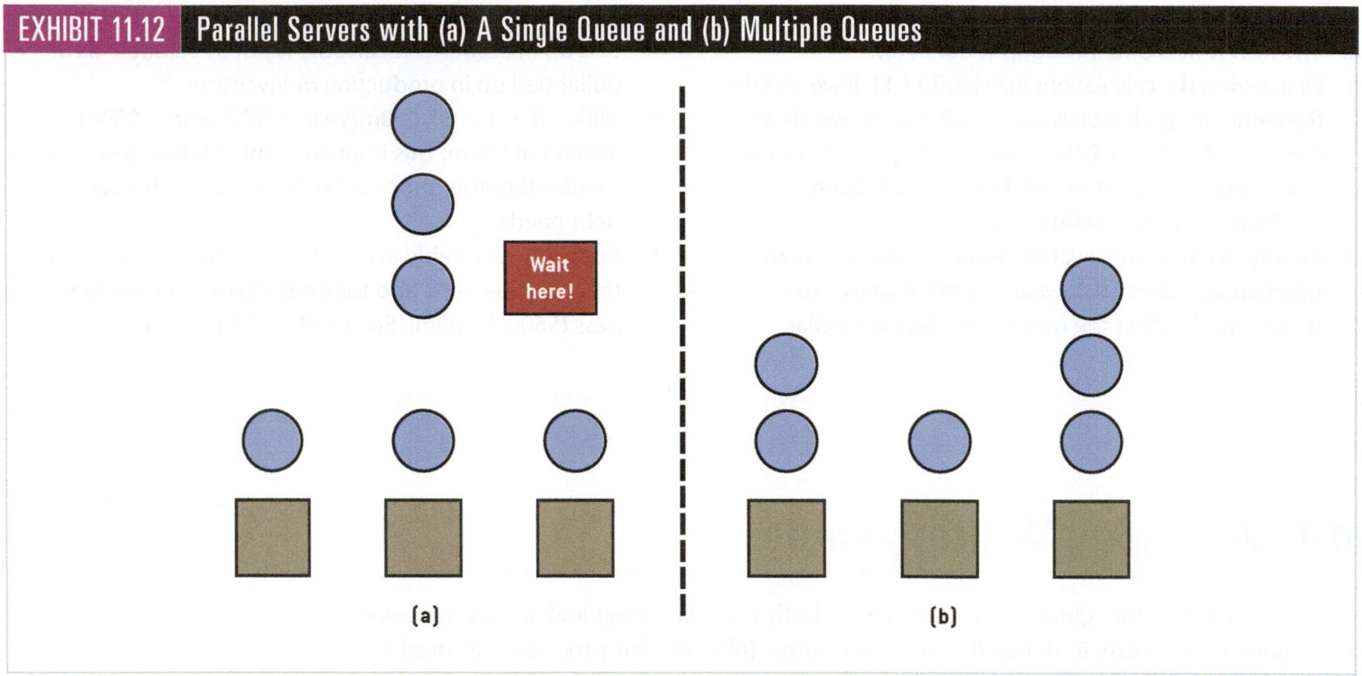

EXHIBIT 11.13 Queues in Series in a Typical Voting Facility

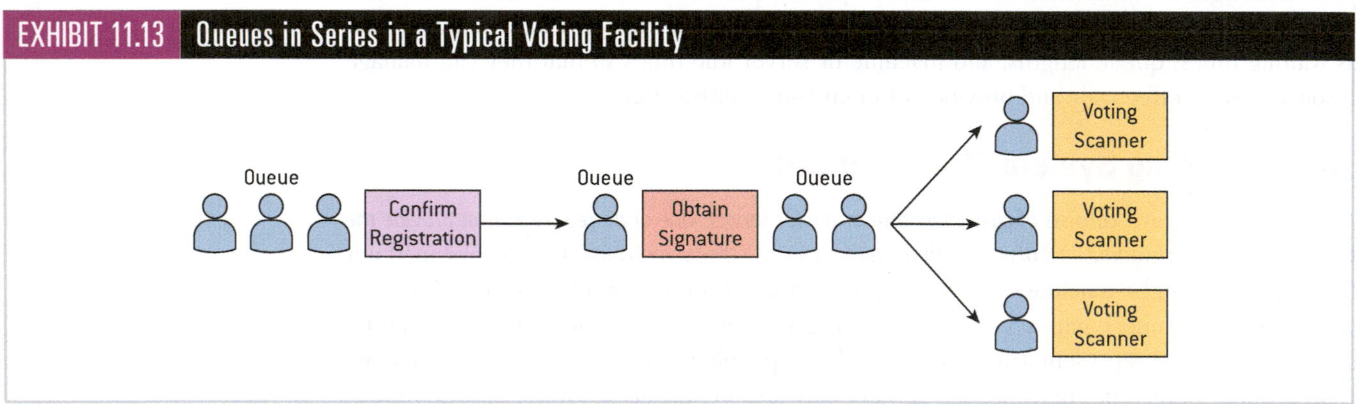

Choosing the right queueing system configuration is an important element of process design. For instance, customers in a multiple queue configuration become frustrated when a person enters a line next to them and receives service first. People expect to be treated fairly; in queueing situations that means "first-come, first-served"(FCFS).

In the mid-1960s, a major New York bank was one of the first to switch to a serpentine line (one line feeding into several servers). Previously, the bank used multiple parallel lines. American Airlines copied this at their airport counters and most other firms followed suit. Other types of services, such as the U.S. Postal Service, have migrated to single serpentine lines. Studies have shown that customers are happier when they wait in a serpentine line, rather than in parallel lines.

Fast-food franchises like Wendy's and Burger King have used single lines for many years.[3] Burger King found that multiple parallel lines create stress and anxiety whereas using a single serpentine line allows customers to focus on what they want to order and not be distracted by which line is shorter. Other companies like McDonald's, however, have stayed with multiple lines but have added automated kiosks for self-service ordering. Some McDonald's executives felt that the multiple-line system accommodates higher volumes of customers more quickly, despite time studies that have proven a single serpentine line to be faster. But the perception of a long single line may cause customers to leave, and consumer perception is what really counts.

Queueing theory *is the analytical study of waiting lines.* Typical performance measures that are computed using queueing theory include

1. The probability that the system is empty (i.e., the probability of 0 units in both the queue and in service).
2. The average number of units waiting for service in the queue.
3. The average number of units in the system (queue and in service).
4. The average time a unit spends waiting for service (time in queue).
5. The average time a unit spends in the system (waiting time plus service time).
6. The probability that an arriving unit has to wait for service.
7. The probability of n units in the system (queue and in service).

Such performance measures can help to improve process designs. For example, if a manager can predict that a certain configuration will result in unacceptable waiting lines from the customers' perspective, then he or she might decide to add additional resources to serve the customers. However, designing the process to avoid waiting can be costly to the service provider. Managers must weigh the benefits of shorter waiting times against these costs in process design decisions. Understanding and managing queues are vital to providing superior customer service and achieving long-run profitability.

Supplement F provides a detailed explanation of analytical queueing models and Excel templates that compute these performance measures. We suggest that you review this before proceeding. We will illustrate how these models and templates can be used in practical OM applications.

11-4b Using Queueing Theory for Process Analysis

Analyzing queueing systems can be performed with analytical models or simulation models. Analytical models are simpler to use and can provide good estimates of the average long-run behavior of queueing systems.

The simplest queueing model, called a *single server queueing model*, has the following characteristics and assumptions:

1. The waiting line has a single server.
2. The pattern of arrivals follows a Poisson probability distribution.
3. The service times follow an exponential probability distribution.
4. The queue discipline is FCFS.
5. Arriving customers must join the queue and cannot leave while waiting.

Solved Problem 11.9 illustrates the single server model. If we know the mean arrival rate, λ (the average number of arrivals in a specified period of time), for the Poisson distribution and the mean service rate, μ (the average number of units that can be served in a specified period of time), then we can compute performance measures listed earlier using the equations in Supplement F or the *Single Server Queue* spreadsheet template available in MindTap.

SOLVED PROBLEM 11.9: A SINGLE SERVER QUEUEING MODEL

The reference desk of a large library receives requests for assistance at a mean rate of 10 requests per hour, and it is assumed that the desk has a mean service rate of 12 requests per hour.

a. What is the probability that the reference desk is idle?
b. What is the average number of requests that will be waiting for service?
c. What is the average number of requests in the system?
d. What is the average waiting time for a request for assistance?
e. What is the average time that a customer spends in the library?
f. What is the probability that an arriving customer has to wait for service?
g. What is the probability that three customers are either waiting or in service at the reference desk at the same time?

Solution:

Using Equations F.1–F.7 for the single server queueing model in Supplement F we compute the following:

a. $P_0 = 1 - \frac{\lambda}{\mu} = 1 - \frac{10}{12} = 0.167$ [F.1]

b. $L_q = \frac{\lambda^2}{\mu(\mu - \lambda)} = \frac{10^2}{12(12 - 10)} = 4.1667$ customers [F.2]

c. $L = L_q + \frac{\lambda}{\mu} = 4.1667 + \frac{10}{12} = 5.000$ customers [F.3]

d. $W_q = \frac{L_q}{\lambda} = \frac{4.1667}{10}$ [F.4]

$= 0.417$ hours, or about 25 minutes

e. $W = W_q + \frac{1}{\mu}$

$= 0.4167$ hours $+ 1/12$ hours [F.5]

$= 0.5$ hours or 30 minutes

f. $P_w = \frac{\lambda}{\mu} = \frac{10}{12} = 0.8333$ [F.6]

g. Using Equation F.7, we have

$P_3 = (\lambda/\mu)^3 P_0 = (10/12)^3(0.167) = 0.096$

Exhibit 11.14 shows these calculations using the *Single Server Queue* Excel template available in MindTap.

EXHIBIT 11.14 *Single Server Queue* Excel Template Results for Solved Problem 11.9

	A	B	C	D	E
1	Single Server Queueing Model	Copyright © 2017 Cengage Learning			
2	Enter the data only in the yellow cells.	Not for commercial use.			
3					
4	Lambda	10			
5	Mu	12			
6					
7	Probability system is empty	0.167			
8	Average number waiting for service in the queue	4.167			
9	Average number in system (queue and in service)	5.000			
10	Average time waiting for service (time in queue)	0.417			
11	\verage waiting time in system (waiting time plus service time)	0.500			
12	Probability arrival has to wait	0.833			
13	n =	3			
14	Probability of n units in the system (queue and in service)	0.096			

Queueing models can be used to evaluate job and process designs and appropriate staffing levels. Solved Problem 11.10 illustrates an example.

In many practical situations, such as those shown in Exhibit 11.12a, we have multiple servers in which customers wait in a single serpentine line and move to the next available server.

SOLVED PROBLEM 11.10: USING QUEUEING MODELS TO EVALUATE PROCESS AND JOB STAFFING LEVELS

A fast-food franchise operates a drive-up window. Orders are placed at an intercom station at the back of the parking lot. The employee at the window takes the orders, assembles them, processes the payment, and delivers them to the customers. After placing an order, the customer pulls up and waits in line at the drive-up window until the cars in front have been served. By hiring a second person to help process orders, the manager hopes to improve service. With one person, the average service time for a drive-up customer is two minutes; with two people working together, the average service time can be reduced to one minute, 15 seconds. Note that the drive-up window operation is still a single server waiting line because only one customer is served at a time. Cars arrive at the rate of 24 per hour.

a. Determine the average waiting time when one employee is working the drive-up window. What percentage of time will that person not be occupied serving customers?
b. Determine the average waiting time when two employees are working at the drive-up window. What percentage of time will no one be occupied serving drive-up customers?
c. Would you recommend hiring a second employee to work the drive-up window? Justify your answer.

Solution:

a. In using the single server queueing model, the arrival and server rates must both be measured in units per time period. Because the average service time with one order-taker is two minutes, the average service rate is 60/2 = 30 cars per hour. Exhibit 11.15 shows the results using the Excel *Single Server Queue* template. The average waiting time is 0.133 hours, or about eight minutes. The probability that the system is empty is 0.200; thus, the server will be idle 20 percent of the time.
b. It is important to understand that with two employees, we still have a single server model. The "server" is the drive-up window, not the employees! With two employees, the average service time is one minute and 15 seconds, or 1.25 minutes. Therefore, the average service rate is 60/1.25 = 48 cars per hour. Exhibit 11.16 shows the results using the Excel *Single Server Queue* template. The average waiting time drops to 0.021 hours, or 1.26 minutes. Because the service rate is much faster with two servers, the probability that the system is empty increases to 0.500. This means that the two employees will be idle half the time.
c. Although employee idle time increases to 50 percent and labor costs double, customer waiting time decreases from eight minutes to 1.26 minutes. In addition, we see that the average number waiting for service drops from 3.2 to 0.5, and the probability that an arriving customer has to wait also drops from 0.8 to 0.5. These improvements provide much better customer service and could lead to higher revenues, which may offset the additional cost of labor.

EXHIBIT 11.15 Queueing Performance Results for One Employee

	A	B	C	D	E
1	**Single Server Queueing Model**	Copyright © 2017 Cengage Learning			
2	**Enter the data only in the yellow cells.**	Not for commercial use.			
3					
4	**Lambda**	24			
5	**Mu**	30			
6					
7	**Probability system is empty**	0.200			
8	**Average number waiting for service in the queue**	3.200			
9	**Average number in system (queue and in service)**	4.000			
10	**Average time waiting for service (time in queue)**	0.133			
11	**\verage waiting time in system (waiting time plus service time)**	0.167			
12	**Probability arrival has to wait**	0.800			
13	**n =**	3			
14	**Probability of n units in the system (queue and in service)**	0.102			

EXHIBIT 11.16 Queueing Performance Results for Two Employees

	A	B	C	D	E
1	Single Server Queueing Model	Copyright © 2017 Cengage Learning			
2	Enter the data only in the yellow cells.	Not for commercial use.			
3					
4	Lambda	24			
5	Mu	48			
6					
7	Probability system is empty	0.500			
8	Average number waiting for service in the queue	0.500			
9	Average number in system (queue and in service)	1.000			
10	Average time waiting for service (time in queue)	0.021			
11	Average waiting time in system (waiting time plus service time)	0.042			
12	Probability arrival has to wait	0.500			
13	n =	3			
14	Probability of n units in the system (queue and in service)	0.063			

A *multiple server queueing model* can properly evaluate such a queueing system structure. (In Exhibit 11.12b each server has a distinct queue, such as with highway tollbooths, bank teller windows, or supermarket checkout lines. The situation is Exhibit 11.12b cannot be handled easily using analytical models and we will not address this situation.)

In a multiple server model, we assume the following:

1. The waiting line has two or more identical servers that serve customers from a single queue.
2. The arrivals follow a Poisson probability distribution with a mean arrival rate of λ.
3. The service times have an exponential distribution.
4. The mean service rate, μ, is the same for each server.
5. The arrivals wait in a single line and then move to the first open server for service.
6. The queue discipline is first-come, first served (FCFS).
7. Arriving customers must join the queue and cannot leave while waiting.

Supplement F explains the mathematical equations used to compute the performance measures and illustrates the use of the *Multiple Server Queue* Excel template available in MindTap. Solved Problem 11.11 provides one example of the multiple server model.

SOLVED PROBLEM 11.11: A MULTIPLE SERVER QUEUEING MODEL

In Solved Problem 11.9, we analyzed the performance of a reference desk in a large library. The average customer waiting time was 25 minutes with an average of 4.167 customers waiting for service. The probability a customer must wait was 0.833. These performance results are quite high and represent poor service.

The library might consider adding additional reference librarians and service stations to provide better service. Thus, a multiple server queue model is appropriate and like Exhibit 11.12b. The mean arrival rate is still 10 requests per hour, and we assume that each reference librarian has the same service rate of 12 requests per hour. Should the library consider adding additional reference librarians? If so, how many?

Solution:

Exhibit 11.17 shows the results using the *Multiple Server Queue* Excel template. In comparing the results with Exhibit 11.13, we

EXHIBIT 11.17 Multiple Server Queuing Results

	A	B	C	D	E	F	G	H
1	**Multiple Server Queueing Model**			Copyright © 2017 Cengage Learning				
2	**Enter the data only in the yellow cells.**			Not for commercial use.				
3								
4	**Lambda**	10						
5	**Mu**	12						
6								
7	**Number of servers**	2	3	4	5	6	7	8
8	**Probability system is empty**	0.412	0.432	0.434	0.435	0.435	0.435	0.435
9	**Average number waiting for service in the queue**	0.175	0.022	0.003	0.000	0.000	0.000	0.000
10	**Average number in system (queue and in service)**	1.008	0.856	0.836	0.834	0.833	0.833	0.833
11	**Average time waiting for service (time in queue)**	0.018	0.002	0.000	0.000	0.000	0.000	0.000
12	**\verage waiting time in system (waiting time plus service time)**	0.101	0.086	0.084	0.083	0.083	0.083	0.083
13	**Probability arrival has to wait**	0.245	0.058	0.011	0.002	0.000	0.000	0.000

see that with two reference librarians, the average number of customers waiting for service drops from 4.167 to 0.175, and the average waiting time drops from 0.417 to 0.018 hours, or from 25 minutes to one minute. The probability that a customer has to wait goes from 0.833 to 0.245. Having more than two servers will not significantly improve the results and only cost more. Two librarian servers greatly improves customer service.

11-4c Economic Analysis of Queueing Alternatives

Operations managers face important decisions in designing queueing systems. A typical decision is determining the number of servers to use. In Solved Problem 11.11, we based this decision on the performance measures of the queueing model, but did not consider any costs. However, cost often plays an important role.

We can develop a simple model for the total cost of waiting for service (TC_W) as a function of the number of servers as well as the average number of customers in the system:

$$TC_W = C_s k + C_W L \qquad [11.4]$$

where C_W = the waiting cost per hour per customer, C_s = the hourly cost associated with each server, L = average number of customers in the system(queue and in service), and k = number of servers.

Clearly, the waiting-time cost cannot be accurately determined; managers must estimate a reasonable value that might reflect the potential loss of future revenue or customer dissatisfaction as appropriate. This is called the *imputed cost of waiting*. Equation 11.4 can then be used to compare alternatives and choose the best one.

SOLVED PROBLEM 11.12: USING AN ECONOMIC MODEL FOR A QUEUEING DECISION

Consider the library scenarios described in Solved Problems 11.9 and 11.11. Suppose C_W is estimated to be \$20 per hour, or \$0.33 per minute. Librarians are paid \$30 per hour, or \$0.50 per minute. Using Equation 11.4, the total cost per minute is

$$TC_W = C_s k + C_W L = 0.50k + 0.33L$$

Using the data from Solved Problems 11.9 and 11.11, we can compare the costs for having one, two, or three librarians as follows:

System	k	Labor Cost/min.	L	Waiting Cost/min.	Total Cost/min.
Single server	1	$0.50(1) = $0.50	5	$0.33(5) = $1.65	$2.15
Two-server	2	$0.0.50(2) = $1.00	1.008	$0.33(1.008) = $0.33	$1.33
Three-server	3	$0.0.50(3) = $1.50	0.856	$0.33(0.856) = $0.28	$1.78

The system having the lowest cost is the two-server system; therefore, the best decision is to hire one additional librarian.

11-5 Simulation Models for Analyzing Queueing Processes

Analytical queueing models rely on mathematical assumptions that limit their use. As explained in Supplement F, analytical queueing models make strict assumptions about arrival rates and service times. They assume a Poisson probability distribution for arrivals (demand) and an exponential distribution for service times (rates). But the actual arrival pattern may not match a Poisson distribution, or for that matter, any common probability distribution. Actual service times may not match the assumption and shape of an exponential probability distribution.

Simulation can be used to analyze processes that cannot be evaluated well analytically. They can use actual probability distributions for both demand and service rates (called empirical distributions). Simulation models are also better equipped to capture the dynamic behavior of queues over time. Often, analytical and simulation models are used in combination; an analytical model is used to get the first operating system performance estimates, and then simulation provides detailed analysis over many more time periods.

Supplement G provides an overview of basic concepts of simulation and how simulation models can be implemented on spreadsheets. We suggest that you review this before proceeding. In this section we provide a simple example of using simulation for analyzing a queueing process.

Lincoln Savings Bank is considering adding a drive-up window to better service customers, especially during peak times. The process is simple, and Exhibit 11.18 describes the logic of the system's operation. Drivers enter the system and approach the drive-up window. If cars are already at the window, the new arrival must wait in line until the drivers ahead have been serviced. Otherwise, the driver proceeds to the window, processes his or her transactions, and leaves.

EXHIBIT 11.18 Operation of Lincoln Savings Bank Drive-Up System

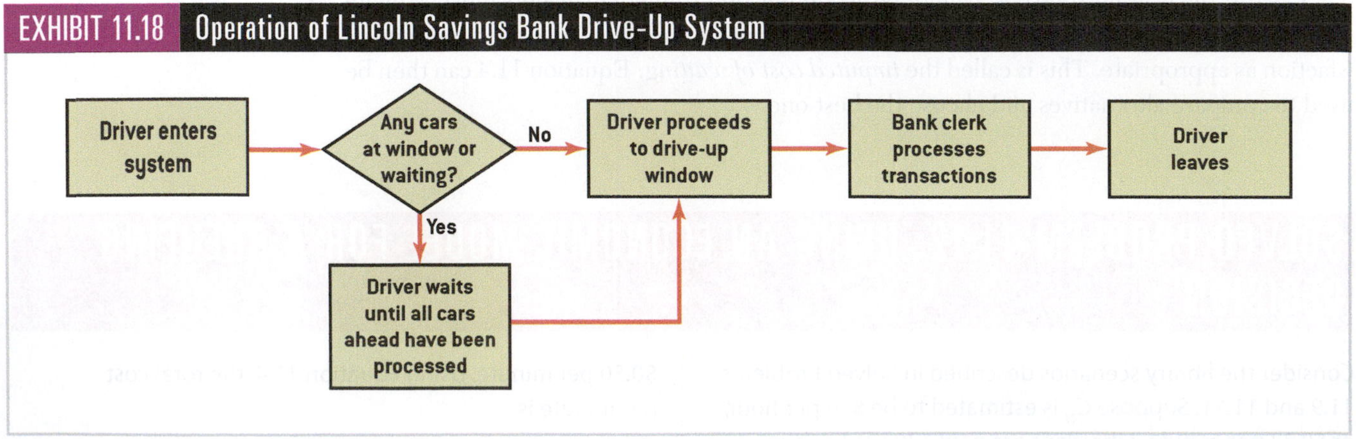

In modeling this system, we count the number of arrivals and determine whether or not a customer is being serviced during each one-minute interval. Then we consider what happens during the next one-minute interval, and so forth. *A simulation model that increments time in fixed intervals like this is referred to as a* **fixed-time simulation model**. During this process, we keep track of such information as the number of cars waiting, the number of arrivals, whether the window is busy or not, and when services are completed. These statistics form the basis for the simulation results, which will be analyzed by the branch manager.

From a study of traffic flow, the bank estimated the probability distribution of customer arrivals as shown in Exhibit 11.18 for the peak business period on Saturday mornings. As the data show, there is a 0.55 probability of no customer arriving during a given one-minute period, a 0.25 probability of one customer arriving, and so on. Historical data also show that the time to service a customer ranges from one to four minutes. Using these data, the bank estimated the probability distribution of service time, also shown in Exhibit 11.19.

An Excel template, *Queue Simulation*, for simulating a single server queueing model using discrete probability distributions for arrivals and service times is available in MindTap. Supplement G describes how to generate random values on a spreadsheet from discrete probability distributions, and you should review this before continuing so that you input the data correctly. The template simulates 100 time periods. Exhibit 11.20 show the use of this template for the Lincoln Savings Bank problem.

The logic of the spreadsheet model is rather complex, but is easy to understand. Essentially, the model determines the number of arrivals in each period using the arrival distribution, and determines if a server is available at that time period based on whether any previous customers are still waiting or are being served. If the server is free, the model generates a random service time, and computes how many other customers are waiting and whether a service was completed at the end of that time period. For example, in time period 1, no arrivals occur. In time period 2, one arrival occurs. Because the server is available, the first arrival goes immediately into service while the other waits. The service time is three minutes, so the first customer's transaction will be completed at the end of time period 4. In time period 3, two additional customers arrive. Because the server is busy, both must wait. In time period 4, one customer arrives and waits also. At the beginning of time period 5, the first waiting customer from period 2 goes into service and has a service time of one minute. This customer will complete service at the end of period 5, and the next waiting customer will be served at the beginning of period 6. You should be able to continue to trace the logic in this fashion.

Exhibit 11.21 shows a chart of the number waiting from one simulation run (called a replication) for 100 minutes of operation. As you can see, the number of customers waiting is relatively stable for the first hour but then begins to grow significantly. Such behavior could not be predicted using Equations 11.2 or 11.3 or analytical queueing models. Exhibit 11.22 shows the results from two additional simulation runs (simply recalculate the spreadsheet). Although there are fluctuations in the number waiting over time, the queue still eventually builds up. Multiple simulations are generally needed to fully understand a system's behavior.

EXHIBIT 11.19 Probability Distributions for Arrivals and Service Times

Number of Customers Arriving	Probability	Service Time (minutes)	Probability
0	0.55	1	0.50
1	0.25	2	0.30
2	0.10	3	0.15
3	0.10	4	0.05
	1.00		1.00

EXHIBIT 11.20 Portion of *Queue Simulation* Excel Template

	A	B	C	D	E	F	G	H
1	Single Server Queueing Simulation				Copyright © 2017 Cengage Learning			
2	Enter the data only in the yellow cells.				Not for commercial use.			
3	This template is designed to allow up to 8 random number intervals							
4	for the arrival and service time distributions.							
5								
6	Arrival Distribution				Service Time Distribution			
7	Random Number		Number of		Random Number		Service	
8	Interval		Arrivals		Interval		Time	
9	0	0.55	0		0	0.5	1	
10	0.55	0.8	1		0.5	0.8	2	
11	0.8	0.9	2		0.8	0.95	3	
12	0.9	1	3		0.95	1	4	
13								
14								
15								
16								
17								
18		Random	Number of	Server	Random	Service	Number	Service
19	Time Period	Number	Arrivals	Available?	Number	Time	Waiting	Completion?
20							0	
21	1	0.348	0	YES			0	NO
22	2	0.783	1	YES	0.924	3	0	NO
23	3	0.849	2	NO			2	NO
24	4	0.667	1	NO			3	YES
25	5	0.991	3	YES	0.094	1	5	YES
26	6	0.257	0	YES	0.638	2	4	NO
27	7	0.580	1	NO			5	YES
28	8	0.645	1	YES	0.599	2	5	NO
29	9	0.941	3	NO			8	YES
30	10	0.443	0	YES	0.656	2	7	NO

EXHIBIT 11.21 Number Waiting During 100 Minutes of Operation

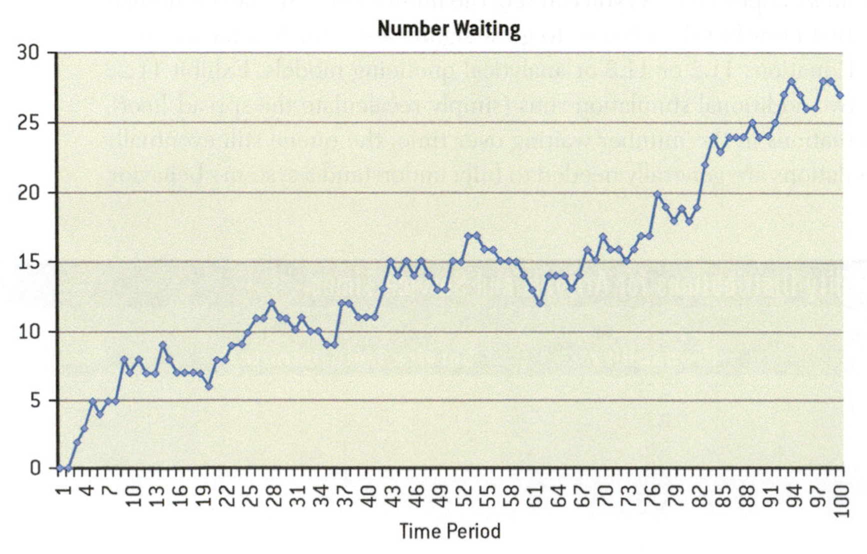

EXHIBIT 11.22 Queueing Behavior for Replications of the Simulation

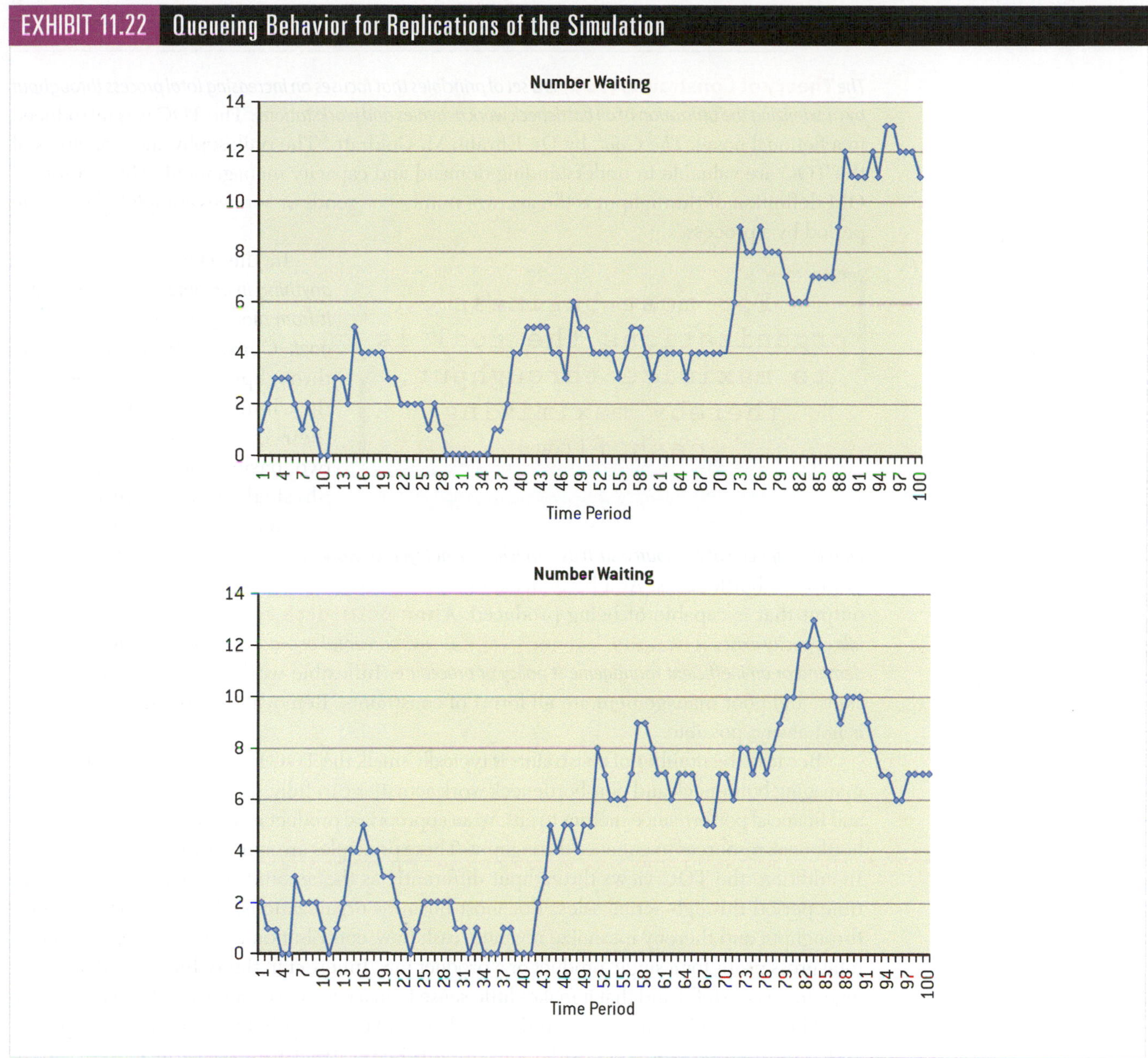

Because the simulation results indicate that a single drive-up window cannot handle the amount of business anticipated during peak periods, the manager might investigate the effect of adding a second drive-up window. Simulation would be an ideal way to study this alternative before committing money for construction. However, building a simulation model for this situation on a spreadsheet is more difficult than for the single-server case. Commercial simulation modeling software can handle this situation easily.

Recall that a primary objective of simulation is to describe the behavior of a real system. Do these results agree with what the bank manager would actually observe? Maybe. In the actual system, a customer will either park the car and transact business inside the bank or go to another bank. Or they will leave and return at another time if the line is too long. An important step in any simulation study is the validation of the simulation model, that is, showing that it accurately represents the real-world system it is designed to simulate.

11-6 The Theory of Constraints

The **Theory of Constraints (TOC)** *is a set of principles that focuses on increasing total process throughput by maximizing the utilization of all bottleneck work activities and workstations.* The TOC was introduced in a fictional novel, *The Goal,* by Dr. Eliyahu M. Goldratt.[4] The philosophy and principles of the TOC are valuable in understanding demand and capacity management. The traditional OM definition of throughput is the average number of goods or services completed per time period by a process.

> For most business organizations the goal is to maximize throughput, thereby maximizing cash flow.

In the TOC, a **constraint** *is anything in an organization that limits it from moving toward or achieving its goal.* Constraints determine the throughput of a facility because they limit production output to their own capacity. There are two basic types of constraints: physical and nonphysical. *A* **physical constraint** *is associated with the capacity of a resource such as a machine, employee, or workstation.* Physical constraints result in process bottlenecks. At a bottleneck, the input exceeds the capacity, restricting the total output that is capable of being produced. *A* **non-bottleneck work activity** *is one in which idle capacity exists. A* **nonphysical constraint** *is environmental or organizational, such as low product demand or an inefficient management policy or procedure.* Inflexible work rules, inadequate labor skills, and poor management are all forms of constraints. Removing nonphysical constraints is not always possible.

Because the number of constraints is typically small, the TOC focuses on identifying them, managing bottleneck and non-bottleneck work activities carefully, linking them to the markets and financial performance metrics to ensure an appropriate product mix, and scheduling the non-bottleneck resources to enhance throughput. These principles are summarized in Exhibit 11.23. In addition, the TOC views throughput differently as the amount of money generated per time period through actual sales. For most business organizations, the goal is to maximize throughput and thereby maximize revenue, cash flow, contribution to profit and overhead, or total gross profit for a single product or a product mix. Inherent in this definition is that excess inventory is wasteful and that it makes little sense to make a good or service until it can be sold.

The TOC helps managers understand the relationship between demand, capacity, and resource utilization. Consider the three process structures shown in Exhibit 11.24.

EXHIBIT 11.23 Basic Principles of the Theory of Constraints

Non-bottleneck Management Principles	Bottleneck Management Principles
Move jobs through non-bottleneck workstations as fast as possible until the job reaches the bottleneck workstation.	Only the bottleneck workstations are critical to achieving process and factory objectives and should be scheduled first.
At non-bottleneck workstations, idle time is acceptable if there is no work to do, and therefore resource utilizations may be low.	An hour lost at a bottleneck resource is an hour lost for the entire process or factory output.
Use smaller order (also called lot or transfer batches) sizes at non-bottleneck workstations to keep work flowing to the bottleneck resources and eventually to the marketplace to generate sales.	Work-in-process buffer inventory should be placed in front of bottlenecks to maximize resource utilization at the bottleneck.
An hour lost at a non-bottleneck resource has no effect on total process or factory output and incurs no real cost.	Use large order sizes at bottleneck workstations to minimize setup time and maximize resource utilization.
	Bottleneck workstations should work at all times to maximize throughput and resource utilization so as to generate cash from sales and achieve the company's goal.

In Exhibit 11.24(a), a bottleneck workstation is feeding non-bottleneck workstations. Because the non-bottleneck workstation capacity of 160 units is higher than the bottleneck workstation with a capacity of 80 units, all output from the bottleneck is quickly moved through the two-stage process to meet demand and is sold. No work-in-process inventory accumulates in front of the downstream non-bottleneck workstations. The resource utilization at the bottleneck is computed using Equation 11.1:

$$\text{Utilization} = \text{Resources Used/Resources Available}$$
$$= 80 \text{ units}/80 \text{ units} = 1.0 \text{ or } 100\%$$

Likewise, the utilization at the non-bottleneck workstation, if it only makes what is needed, is 50% (80/160).

Using TOC logic, it is acceptable for the non-bottleneck workstations to be idle as long as everything possible is being done to maximize throughput and utilization at the bottleneck workstations. This is a radical change from the conventional wisdom to

> An hour lost at a bottleneck resource is an hour lost for the entire process or factory output.

EXHIBIT 11.24 Theory of Constraint Principles Applied to Different Process Structures

	Bottleneck →	Non-bottleneck →	Demand
Demand (units/hour)	80	80	80
Available hours	160	160	
Processing hours/unit	2	1	
Capacity (units)	80	160	
Resource (workstation) Utilization %	100.0%	50.0%	

(a) Managing a bottleneck feeding a non-bottleneck workstation

	Non-bottleneck →	Bottleneck →	Demand
Demand (units/hour)	80	80	80
Available hours	160	160	
Processing hours/unit	1	2	
Capacity (units)	160	80	
Resource (workstation) Utilization %	50.0%	100.0%	

(b) Managing a non-bottleneck feeding a bottleneck workstation

	Non-bottleneck →	Bottleneck →	Assembly, Ship, and Demand
Demand (units/hour)	80	80	80
Available hours	160	160	
Processing hours/unit	1	2	
Capacity (units)	160	80	
Resource (workstation) Utilization %	50.0%	100.0%	

(c) Managing parallel bottleneck and non-bottleneck workstations feeding assembly and shipping work stations

maximize utilization of all workstations. Operations managers have traditionally thought that everyone had to be busy all the time or something was wrong. TOC argues that by maximizing resource utilization for all non-bottleneck workstations, the system creates excess inventory that may not be sold. In addition, maximizing non-bottleneck utilization increases operating expenses and purchasing costs.

In the process structure in Exhibit 11.24(b), a non-bottleneck workstation feeds a bottleneck workstation. The non-bottleneck workstation producing at full capacity (i.e., 100% utilization) creates 160 units; however, the bottleneck workstation can use only 80 units, so 80 units accumulate in front of the bottleneck as work-in-process inventory. There is no need for the non-bottleneck workstation to produce more than 80 units, so the target utilization should be 50%, or perhaps a little higher to provide some safety capacity against uncertainty.

The third process structure shown in Exhibit 11.24(c) defines a bottleneck and non-bottleneck workstation working in parallel, supplying their output to a downstream work station such as an assembly or shipping workstation. Again, there is no need for the non-bottleneck workstation to produce more than 80 units, so the utilization should be targeted at about 50%, as previously described.

SOLVED PROBLEM 11.13: USING THE THEORY OF CONSTRAINTS

Tucson Electric manufacturers electric motor armatures using several production cells. Two of the production cells are shown in Exhibit 11.25. Machinist A and polisher A work on larger armatures. Machinist B and polisher B work on smaller armatures. Exhibit 11.26 documents the selling price and net contribution to profit and overhead for the two finished armatures.

EXHIBIT 11.25 Tucson Electric Production Cell

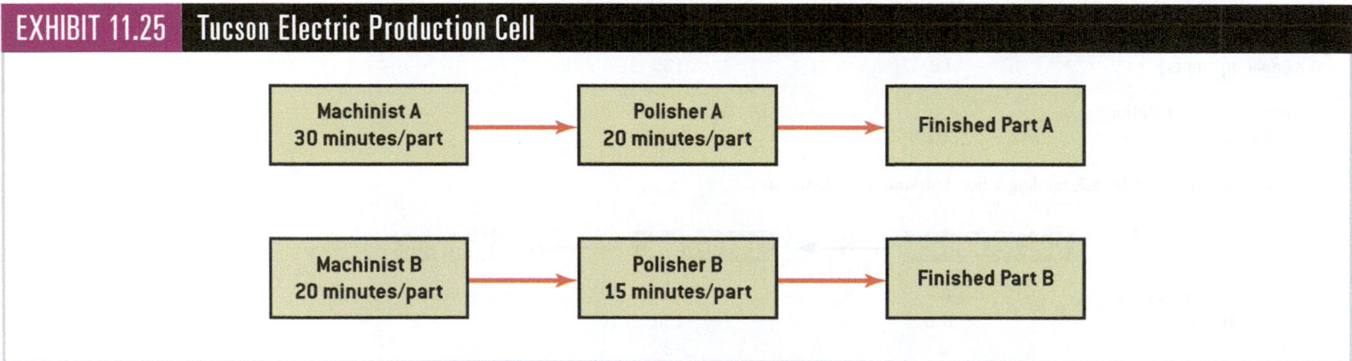

EXHIBIT 11.26 Net Contribution to Profits and Overhead of Two Electric Motor Armatures

Finished Product	A	B
Contract Selling Price	$26	$17
Value-Added Manufacturing Cost	$16	$12
Net Contribution to Profit and Overhead	$10	$5

a. Where are the bottlenecks in this process? Cite one TOC principle from Exhibit 11.22 that explains your answer.
b. What workstation(s) in Exhibit 11.24 would you expect to have the most idle time (i.e., lowest workstation utilization)?
c. Compute the total revenue and contribution to profit and overhead per hour for each armature by applying the TOC logic to the problem?
d. Given your answers in part (c), which armature would you try to sell based on the criteria of total revenue per hour and total contribution to profit and overhead (P&OH) per hour?
e. How should marketing and operations react to the TOC?

Solution:

a. The bottlenecks are the machinist workstations for both processes A and B. The machinist workstation would starve the downstream polisher machine workstations.

Machinist A = 60 minutes/hour divided by 30 minutes/armature = 2.0 armatures/hour
Polisher A = 60 minutes/hour divided by 20 minutes/armature = 3.0 armatures/hour
Machinist B = 60 minutes/hour divided by 20 minutes/armature = 3.0 armatures/hour
Polisher B = 60 minutes/hour divided by 15 minutes/armature = 4.0 armatures/hour

Note in Exhibit 11.22 that "An hour lost at a bottleneck resource (in this case the machinist) is an hour lost for the entire process or factory output."

b. Use Equation 11.1: Utilization = Resources Used/Resources Available. For the polisher A, Utilization = 20/30 = 0.666 or 66.7%. Notice that polisher A is starved for work and 33.3% of the time is idle. For polisher B, Utilization = 15/20 = 0.75 or 75.0%. Notice polisher B is starved for work and 25% of the time is idle.

c.

Finished Product	Process Bottleneck	Bottleneck Workstation Output Rate	Net Contribution to P&OH per Unit	Total Revenue per Hour	Total Contribution to P&OH per Hour
A	Machinist A	2 units/hour	$10	2 × $26 = $52/hour	2 × $10 = $20
B	Machinist B	3 units/hour	$ 5	3 × $17 = $51/hour	3 × $5 = $15

d. For total revenue per hour, there is only a $1/unit difference between selling A or B. But for the financial criterion, contribution to profit and overhead, there is a $5/unit difference between A and B. Notice that both are based on the process bottlenecks. That is, the value of a scarce resource, in this case, machinist A and B's time. It is also possible that the sales commission structure at Tucson Electric places equal weight on selling A and B. Yet, based on the TOC and bottleneck analysis, the firm makes more contribution to profit and overhead by selling A, not B.

e. Traditionally, marketing focused on increasing sales revenue and market share. Operations and logistics managers focus on minimizing costs and resources. Both functional areas need to be trained in the TOC to improve sales incentives and overall company financial performance. Many firms train managers in the TOC in several functional areas such as marketing, operations, engineering, and finance. Then they better understand and coordinate their function's measurement systems and practices.

The TOC has been used successfully in many companies. As the TOC evolved, it has been applied not only to manufacturing but to other areas such as distribution, marketing, and human resource management. Binney and Smith, maker of Crayola crayons, and Procter & Gamble both use the TOC in their distribution efforts. Binney and Smith had high inventory levels yet poor customer service. By using the TOC to better position its distribution inventories, it was able to reduce inventories and improve service. Procter & Gamble reported $600 million in savings through inventory reduction and elimination of capital improvement through the TOC. A government organization that produces publications of labor statistics for the state of Pennsylvania used the TOC to better match work tasks to workers to reduce idle labor and overtime requirements and to increase throughput, job stability, and profitability.

> Great customer service does not happen by chance; it is built into the very fabric of job, process, and supply chain design and improvement.

Kreisler Manufacturing Corporation: Using the TOC

Kreisler Manufacturing Corporation is a small, family-run company that makes metal components for airplanes. Its clients include Pratt & Whitney, General Electric, Rolls Royce, and Mitsubishi. After learning about the TOC, managers identified several areas of the factory, including the Internal Machine Shop and Supplier Deliveries, as bottlenecks, and began to focus on maximizing throughput at these bottlenecks. Setups were videotaped to see exactly what was happening. It was discovered that 60 percent of the time it took to complete a setup involved the worker looking for materials and tools. To remove this constraint, Kreisler assembled all the necessary materials and tools for setup into a prepackage "kit," thus cutting 60 percent off the setup time.

Kreisler also created a "visual factory" by installing red, yellow, and green lights on every machine. If a workstation is being starved or production stops, the operator turns on the red light. If there is a potential crisis or a risk of starving the constraint workstation, the worker turns on the yellow light. If all is running smoothly, the green light is on. Giving the machine operator control over these signals instilled a sense of ownership in the process and caught the attention and interest of everyone in the factory. In the early stages of implementing the TOC, there were many red lights; today they are green. By applying the TOC, on-time deliveries increased to 97 percent from 65 percent, and 15 percent of the factory's "hidden capacity" was revealed and freed up. In addition, WIP inventory was reduced by 20 percent and is expected to be reduced by another 50 percent.[12]

Ulrich Baumgarten/Getty Images

CHAPTER 11 LEARNING OBJECTIVE SUMMARIES

11.1 **Describe how to compute resource utilization and use the equations for practical applications. Utilization** *is the fraction of time a workstation or individual is busy over the long run.* Two ways of computing resource utilization are

$$\text{Utilization } (U) = \frac{\text{Resources Used}}{\text{Resources Available}} \quad [11.1]$$

$$\text{Utilization } (U) = \frac{\text{Demand Rate}}{\text{Service Rate} \times \text{Number of Servers}} \quad [11.2]$$

Equation 11.1 computes utilization as the proportion of available resources that are being used. Equation 11.2 computes utilization based on the ratio of the demand rate to effective service capacity based on the service rate and number of servers.

If a manager knows any two of the three variables in Equation 11.1 or any three of the four variables in Equation 11.2, then the remaining variable can be found. For both equations, the dimensions of the numerator and denominator (time periods, units, etc.) must be the same, as utilization is a dimensionless quantity.

11.2 **Be able to identify process bottlenecks and calculate throughput.** *A* **bottleneck** *is the work activity that effectively limits the throughput of the entire process. The number of units or tasks that are completed per unit time from a process is called* **throughput**. Throughput might be measured as parts per day, transactions per minute, or customers per hour, depending on the context. We identify bottleneck by identifying the work activity that has the smallest throughput. Identifying and breaking process bottlenecks is an important part of process design and improvement, and will increase the speed of the process, reduce waiting and work-in-process inventory, enhance customer service, and use resources more efficiently.

11.3 **Explain how to apply Little's Law to process analyses. Flow time (cycle time)** *is the average time it takes to complete one cycle of a process.* It makes sense that the flow time will depend not only on the actual time to perform the tasks required but also on how many other entities are in the work-in-process stage. **Little's Law** *is a simple equation that explains the relationship among flow time (T), throughput (R), and work-in-process (WIP):*

$$\text{Work-in-process} = \text{Throughput} \times \text{Flow time}$$

or

$$WIP = R \times T \quad [11.3]$$

Little's Law provides a simple way of evaluating average process performance. If we know any two of the three variables, we can compute the third using Little's Law.

11.4 **Understand the key concepts and mathematics of waiting line management and queueing models.** *A* **queue** *is a waiting line.* Understanding queues allows us to analyze current and alternative process designs to understand their behavior, predict process performance, and better allocate resources. Queueing models help managers understand key performance measures such as waiting times, queue lengths, and machine or server idle times so that they can manage resources more effectively and provide better customer satisfaction. *A* **queueing system** *consists of customers that arrive for service, one or more servers that provide the service, and a queue (waiting line) of entities that wait for service if the server is busy.*

Queueing theory *is the analytical study of waiting lines.* Typical performance measures that are computed using queueing theory include

1. The probability that the system is empty (i.e., the probability of 0 units in both the queue and in service).
2. The average number of units waiting for service in the queue.
3. The average number of units in the system (queue and in service).
4. The average time a unit spends waiting for service (time in queue).
5. The average time a unit spends in the system (waiting time plus service time).
6. The probability that an arriving unit has to wait for service.
7. The probability of n units in the system (queue and in service).

Equations F.1–F.7 in Supplement F provide the calculations for these measures for a single server queueing model.

11.5 **Explain how simulation can be used to model queues and evaluate performance.** Simulation can be used to analyze processes that cannot be evaluated well analytically. They can use actual probability distributions for both demand and service rates (called empirical distributions). Simulation models are also better equipped to capture the dynamic behavior of queues over time. Often, analytical and simulation models are used in combination; an analytical model is used to get the first operating system performance estimates, and then simulation provides detailed analysis over many more time periods.

11.6 **Explain the principles and logic of the Theory of Constraints.** *The* **Theory of Constraints (TOC)** *is a set of principles that focuses on increasing total process throughput by maximizing the utilization of all bottleneck work activities and workstations.* In the TOC, *a* **constraint** *is anything in an organization that limits it from moving toward or achieving its goal.* Constraints determine the throughput of a facility because they limit production output to their own capacity. There are two basic types of constraints: physical and nonphysical. *A* **physical constraint** *is associated with the capacity of a resource such as a machine, employee, or workstation.* Physical constraints result in process bottlenecks. At a bottleneck, the input exceeds the capacity, restricting the total output that is capable of being produced. *A* **non-bottleneck work activity** *is one in which idle capacity exists. A* **nonphysical constraint** *is environmental or organizational, such as low product demand or an inefficient management policy or procedure.* The TOC focuses on identifying constraints, managing bottleneck and non-bottleneck work activities carefully, linking them to the markets and financial performance metrics to ensure an appropriate product mix, and scheduling the non-bottleneck resources to enhance throughput. Exhibit 11.22 summarizes the basic principles of the TOC.

KEY TERMS

- **Bottleneck**
- **Constraint**
- **Fixed-time simulation model**
- **Flow time (cycle time)**
- **Little's Law**
- **Non-bottleneck work activity**
- **Nonphysical constraint**
- **Physical constraint**
- **Queue**
- **Queueing theory**
- **Queueing system**
- **Theory of Constraints (TOC)**
- **Throughput**
- **Utilization**

REVIEW QUESTIONS

11.1 1. Define utilization and explain two ways computing resource utilization.

11.2 2. What is throughput and how is it measured?

11.2 3. What is a bottleneck? Explain why is it important.

11.2 4. What are some ways to improve throughput in a process?

11.2 5. Define flow time.

11.3 6. Explain Little's Law and illustrate how it can be used by providing a numerical example.

11.4 7. What is a queue, and why is it important to understand it?

11.4 8. What does a queueing system consist of?

11.4 9. Describe common queueing configurations.

11.4 10. What is queueing theory? Summarize the performance measures that are computed in queueing models.

11.4 11. List the characteristics and assumptions of a single server queueing model.

11.4 12. List the characteristics and assumptions of a multiple server queueing model.

11.4 13. How can economic analysis be used in making queueing system design decisions?

11.5 14. What are the advantages of using simulation to analyze queueing models?

11.6 15. What are the basic principles of the Theory of Constraints (TOC)? How do these principles impact costs?

DISCUSSION QUESTIONS AND EXPERIENTIAL ACTIVITIES

11.1 16. Identify one example of a resource with a very low average utilization rate and a second example with a very high average utilization rate. Consider both service and manufacturing organizations. Write a short (one page typed) paper that describes these situations and their capacity implications.

11.2 17. Select a service process and draw the flowchart using no more than 10 process steps. The service process can be based on your work experience, such as in accounting or human resource management, or a familiar process such as a quick-service automobile oil change, buying an automobile, getting a telephone installed in your home or apartment, ordering a home delivery pizza, and using the Internet. (If a facility layout helps explain the overall service design then include the layout.) Discuss where bottlenecks are likely to occur. If you can obtain data, estimate the throughput for the process.

11.3,4 18. What are the analogies between Little's Law and a single server queueing model?

11.4 19. In what queueing situations might you apply only analytical models? Only simulation models? Can you think of a situation where you might apply both types of models to a real-world problem?

11.4 20. Identify and describe a queueing system of interest to you. Draw a picture of the system.

11.6 21. How would you apply the TOC to a quick-service automobile oil change process? Explain.

11.6 22. Research and write a short paper (two pages maximum) on how an organization has applied the TOC.

11.6 23. Explain how actual resource utilization might be only 40 percent at a non-bottleneck workstation by applying the TOC.

COMPUTATIONAL PROBLEMS AND EXERCISES

These exercises require you to apply the formulas and methods described in the chapter. The problems should be solved manually.

11.1 24. A 30,000-seat college football stadium is used 18 times for games, concerts, and graduation ceremonies. Each event averages six hours and assumes the stadium is full for each event. The stadium is available 365 days a year from 6 a.m. to midnight. What is the seat utilization? Can you think of one or two other assets that have such low resource utilization?

11.1 25. As the assistant manager of a restaurant, how many servers will you need given the following information for Saturday night's dinner menu:

- Demand (dinners served) = 100 dinners per hour
- Server target utilization = 85%
- Service rate per server = 16 dinners/hour

What does the service rate per server assume? Explain.

11.1 26. An automobile-emissions center tests 50 autos per hour. Each inspector can inspect one auto every four minutes. If the center wanted a target utilization of 90 percent, how many inspectors would they require?

11.1 27. A big city automobile quick-service oil change shop can process 20 autos per hour over its multiple bays. Each mechanic can change the oil and do other related tasks at a rate of one car every 30 minutes. If the center wanted a target labor utilization of 90 percent, how many oil-changing mechanics would they require?

11.1 28. The consumer loan division of a major bank wants to determine the size of the staff it would need to process up to 200 loan applications per day. It estimated that each loan officer can process a loan application in approximately 20 minutes. If the utilization of a loan officer is 0.8 (80 percent) and each loan officer works seven hours each day, how many loan officers would be needed to handle that volume of business?

11.1 29. A plant manufactures three products, A, B, and C. A drill press is required to perform one operation for each product. Machine operators work at 75 percent utilization, and the machines have 95 percent utilization. The plant operates one eight-hour shift 20 days per month. The operation times for each product follow:

Product	A	B	C
Operation Time (minutes/product)	5.0	1.85	7.0

Determine the amount of equipment and number of machine operators needed to produce 10,000 units per month.

11.1 30. The demand for intensive care services in an urban hospital is nine patients per hour on Mondays while intensive care nurses can handle four patients per hour. What is nurse (labor) utilization if five intensive care nurses are scheduled to be on duty for Monday? What are the advantages and disadvantages of this resource schedule for Mondays from the patient's and management's perspective?

11.1 31. A telephone call center uses three customer service representatives (CSRs) during the 8:30 to 9:00 a.m. time period. The standard service rate is 3.0 minutes per telephone call per CSR. Assuming a target labor utilization rate of 80 percent, how many calls can these three CSRs handle during this half-hour period?

11.1 32. What is the implied service rate at a bank teller window if customer demand is 26 customers per hour, two bank tellers are on duty, and their labor utilization is 90 percent?

11.1 33. What is the implied service rate per service counter employee at an airport automobile rental counter if customer demand is 36 customers per hour, two service counter employees are on duty, and their labor utilization is 90 percent?

11.1 34. After two years in your first job, you are promoted to call center manager for a major hotel chain. The expected service rate is 3.0 minutes per telephone call per customer service representative (CSR). With three telephone CSRs on-duty during the 6:30 to 7:00 a.m. time period, and assuming a 90 percent target CSR labor utilization rate, how many telephone calls can these three CSRs handle during this time period?

11.1 35. The production process shown in Exhibit 11.27 consists of five stages. The numbers in parentheses are the times in minutes to complete one unit before it moves on to the next stage. The demand rate is 36 units per hour.

a. How many workers are needed at each stage if management wants a utilization of at least 90 percent?

EXHIBIT 11.27 Process Flow for Problem 35

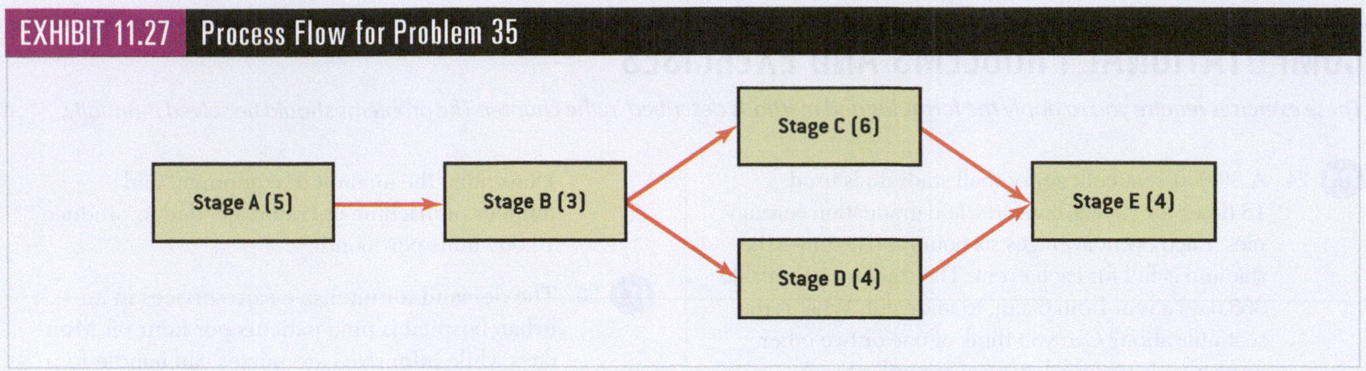

b. Suppose that the number of workers at each stage are as follows:

Stage	Number of Workers
A	3
B	3
C	5
D	2
E	4

What is the output rate at each stage?

c. Where is the bottleneck in this process?

11.1,2 36. Marion Health Clinic sees patients on a walk-in basis only. On average, 10 patients per hour enter the clinic. All patients register at the registration window with a registration clerk (RC), which takes three minutes. After registration, but before being seen by a nurse practitioner (NP), the registration records clerk (RRC) pulls the patient's records from the records room, which takes six minutes. At his or her turn, each patient then sees a NP, who checks weight, temperature, and blood pressure. This work activity takes five minutes. The NP determines if the patient must see a doctor (MD) or can be handled by a physician's assistant (PA). There is one MD, one PA, one NP, one RRC, one BC, and one RC in the system at the current time.

The NP sends 40 percent of the patients to the PA and 60 percent to the MD. The PA takes on average six minutes per patient, whereas the MD takes 15 minutes. After the patient sees the PA and/or MD, the patient pays the bill or processes insurance information with the billing clerk (BC), which takes five minutes per patient. Then the patient exits the process.

a. Draw a process flow diagram, label everything, and place the times and percentages given in the problem on the diagram.

b. What is the throughput in patients per hour of each stage in the process?

c. What are the labor utilization rates for the MD, NP, PA, BC, RRC, and RC? Are these values appropriate? If not, how might you redesign the process? Where is the bottleneck?

d. The PA often discovers the patient should see a MD, so the patient is sent to the MD after seeing the PA 50 percent of the time. How does this change affect your answers to the questions above?

11.1,2 37. A car rental company at a major airport has 70 percent of its fleet of 200 cars rented each day on average. Cars are rented for an average of four days. How many rentals are processed each day on average?

11.1,2 38. Due to county and state budget cuts Archer County Courthouse now has only two clerks and two typists and expects to process 40 drivers/hour (see Solved Problem 11.3). What is the current labor utilization of each labor type, and where is the bottleneck in this three-stage process? What is the impact of your analysis on customer service? How might the job and process design be improved?

11.2 39. For Solved Problem 11.3 on processing driver's licenses at the Archer County Courthouse in this chapter, if 40 drivers are to be processed each hour, how many clerks and typists should be hired assuming a 90 percent target utilization rate?

11.2 40. How can you improve throughput for the process in part (b) of problem 35? Assume that all 17 workers have the ability to perform the work at each stage but that no additional workers may be hired.

11.2 41. A medical equipment testing and calibration service is depicted in Exhibit 11.28. The customer usually brings the equipment to the service center. The service process requires service technicians to perform three process steps #1 to #3. Each technician is cross-trained so they can perform any of the three steps. The inspector does step #4 alone. After step #4, two parallel work activities are performed. That is, a shipping clerk packs the work (step #7), while simultaneously, a billing clerk prepares the

EXHIBIT 11.28 Flow Chart of the Medical Equipment Testing and Calibration Service Process

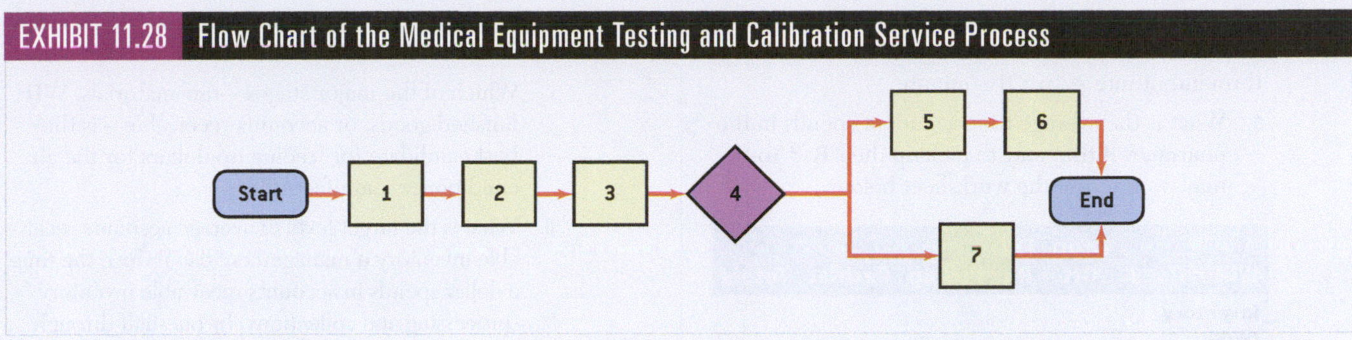

invoice (step #5), and the customer is contacted by phone for pick-up (step #6). The average throughput is three equipment units per hour.

The table below shows the work content of the process steps, activity times in minutes per unit, shared and non-shared work activities, and the type of resource required. There are three service technicians on duty, one inspector, one billing clerk, and one shipping clerk.

Activity	Activity Time (minutes)	Activity Performed By
Start	—	
1	8	Service technician
2	17	Service technician
3	25	Service technician
4	12	Inspector
5	3	Billing clerk
6	7	Billing clerk
7	25	Shipping clerk
End	—	

a. What is the service rate for the service technician?

b. What is the labor utilization rate (%) for the billing clerk?

c. What is the labor utilization rate (%) for the service technician?

d. What job represents the bottleneck in this process?

11.3 42. An accounting firm is capable of processing 20 EZ tax forms per day, and the average number of forms on-hand in the office is 64 forms. What is the average processing time per EZ tax form?

11.3 43. What is the average time a loaf of sliced bread stays in an urban sandwich shop if the restaurant uses 46 loaves per day and they maintain an average inventory of 150 loaves?

11.3 44. The Wilcox Student Health Center has just implemented a new computer system and service process to "improve efficiency." The process flowchart and analysis framework is also provided. As pharmacy manager, you are concerned about waiting time and its potential impact on college students who "get no respect." All prescriptions (Rxs) go through the process shown in Exhibit 11.29.

Assume that students arrive to drop off Rxs at a steady rate of two Rxs per minute, with an average of one Rx per student. The average number of students in process (assume waiting and being serviced) at each station is *drop off*—five students, *pick up*—three students and *pay cashier*—six students.

The fill Rx station typically has 40 Rxs in process and waiting on average. Because of this perceived long wait, 95 percent of the students decide to come back later for pick up. They come back an average of three hours later. If the students choose to stay, each name is called as soon as the Rx is filled, and the student then enters the pick-up line. Assume that the system is operating at a steady state.

EXHIBIT 11.29 Pharmacy Process

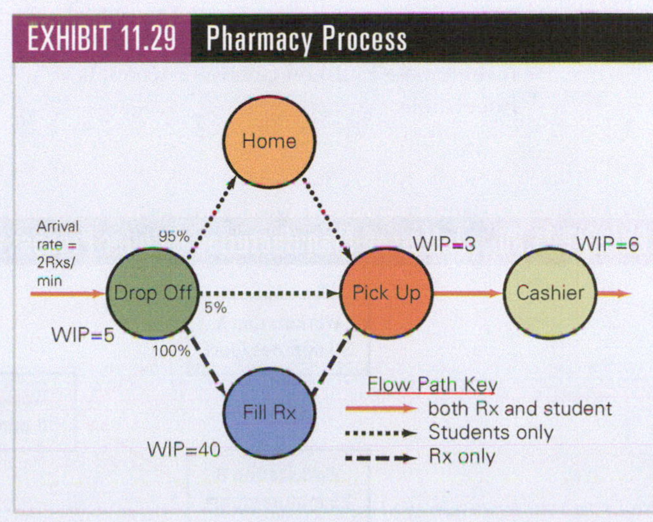

People and information flow with the assumption of one Rx per student. Demand (arrival) or throughput rate = two Rxs/minute

a. What is the average time a student spends in the pharmacy if they stay to pick up their Rx? You may want to use the worksheet below.

WIP = $R \times T$	Drop Off	Fill Rx	Pickup	Cashier	Totals
Inventory (WIP)					
Throughput Rate (R)					
Flow Time (T)					

b. How many minutes does the student spend in the pharmacy if he or she picks up the Rx three hours later (i.e., the student goes home after dropping the Rx off)?

c. What is the average time in minutes that all students spend in the pharmacy?

d. What is the average time in minutes that the Rx spends in the process? Count time from entering the drop-off line to completing payment.

11.3 45. A manufacturer of air conditioner compressors is concerned that too much money is tied up in its value chain. Average raw material inventory is \$50 million and work-in-process (WIP) production inventory is \$20 million. Sales are \$20 million per week and finished goods inventory averages \$30 million. The average outstanding accounts receivable is \$60 million. Assume 50 weeks in one year. The value chain is shown below:

a. What is the flow time of a throughput dollar? (Hint: Use a WIP = $R^{\circ}T$ and the worksheet format as shown in problem 44 to organize your solution.)

Raw Material Inventory → Production (WIP) Inventory → Finished Goods → Accounts Receivable

b. What is the average dollar inventory in the value chain?

c. Which of the major stages—raw materials, WIP, finished goods, or accounts receivable—is the best candidate for freeing up dollars for the air conditioner manufacturer?

d. What is the target level of average accounts receivable inventory if management can reduce the time a dollar spends in accounts receivable inventory (processing and collections) by one-half through improving the accounts receivable process?

e. What else does this flow-time analysis problem demonstrate?

11.4 46. An airport limousine service has one employee work the airport counter. A customer arrives on the average of once every three minutes, and it takes on average two minutes to process the transaction.

a. What is the probability that the system is empty?

b. What is the probability that a customer must wait for service?

c. What is the average number of customers waiting for service in the queue?

d. What is the average wait time in the queue?

e. What is the probability of five customers in the system (queue and in-service)?

11.6 47. Jefferson Manufacturing machines parts for assembly in air compressors. The process is shown in Exhibit 11.30.

a. Where is the bottleneck workstation? Cite one TOC principle from Exhibit 11.22 that explains your answer.

b. What is the longest throughput time for the entire work cell?

c. If Jefferson Manufacturing works a 40-hour week, can this production cell meet a demand of 80 parts/week? Cite one TOC principle from Exhibit 11.23 that explains your answer.

d. Where should the operations manager spend his or her firm's improvement funds?

EXHIBIT 11.30 Jefferson Manufacturing Cellular Process One

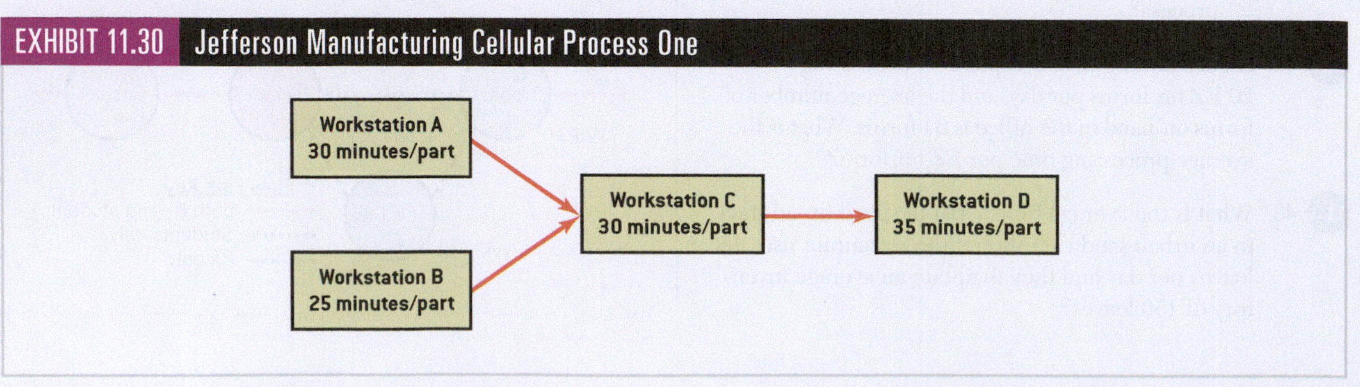

EXHIBIT 11.31 Jefferson Manufacturing Cellular Process Two

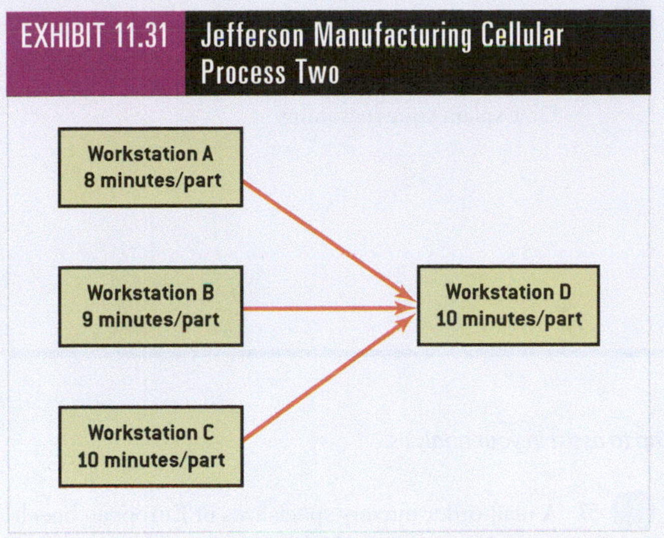

11.6 48. Jefferson Manufacturing in problem 47 has another cellular layout and process shown in Exhibit 11.31.

a. Where is the bottleneck workstation? Cite one TOC principle from Exhibit 11.23 that explains your answer.

b. Where should the manager position extra inventory in this production cell according to the TOC?

c. If Jefferson Manufacturing works a 45-hour week, how many parts per week can this production cell produce? Cite one TOC principle from Exhibit 11.23 that explains your answer.

11.6 49. Rambler Manufacturing produces three clutch plates for small automobiles at its factory in Columbus, Ohio. The three processes shown in Exhibit 11.32 are composed of common and different work activities to manufacture the clutch plates. Exhibit 11.33 provides information on each clutch plate's selling price, value-added manufactured cost, and net contribution to profit and overhead per unit. The value-added cost is the sum of raw materials, purchased units, and equipment and labor work on the clutch plate.

a. For each clutch plate process, where is the bottleneck workstation and what would you expect to see if you visited the process? Cite one TOC principle from Exhibit 11.23 that explains your answer.

b. What workstation would you expect the most idle time (i.e., lowest workstation utilization)? Cite one TOC principle from Exhibit 11.23 that explains your answer.

c. What is the total revenue and contribution to profit and overhead per hour for each clutch plate applying the TOC logic to the problem?

d. Given your answers in part (c), which clutch plate would you try to sell based on total revenue per hour and total contribution to profit and overhead per hour criteria?

e. If you could recommend one, and only one, process improvement, what would it be? Explain.

EXHIBIT 11.32 Three Process Flows (Production Lines) for Rambler Manufactured Clutch Plates

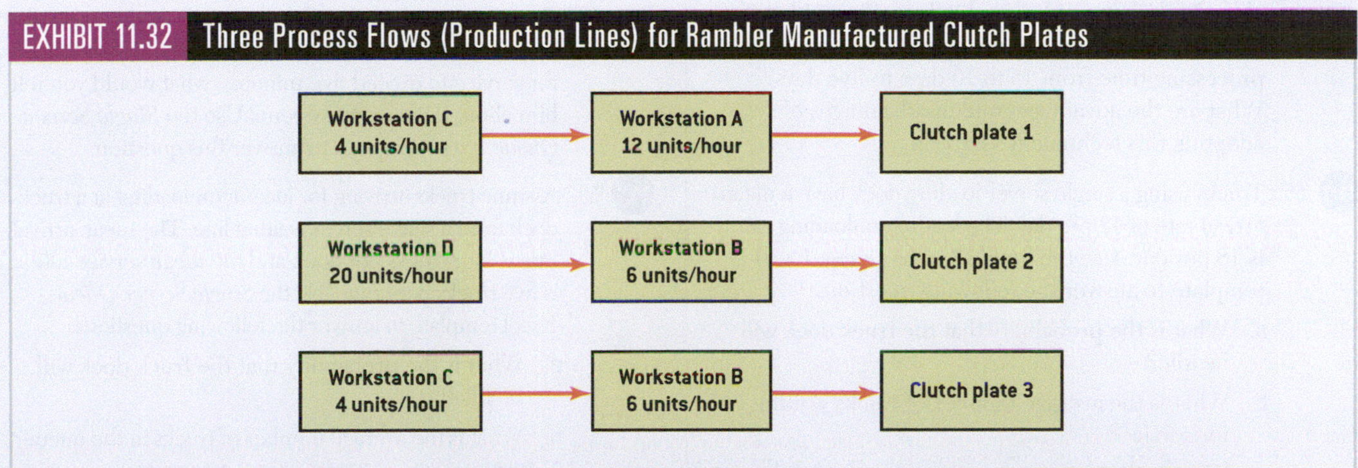

EXHIBIT 11.33 Net Contribution to Profits and Overhead of Three Clutch Plates

Clutch Plate Number	1	2	3
Selling Price	$100	$135	$175
Value-Added Manufacturing Cost	$48	$98	$110
Net Contribution to Profit and Overhead	$52	$38	$65

11.6 50. For Rambler Manufacturing in problem 49, suppose that sales of clutch plates 1, 2, and 3, respectively are 180, 300, and 200 units for the week, and workstation C works two shifts for a total of 90 hours this week. What is the workload in hours for the week on workstation C and what is workstation C's utilization? Can workstation C fulfil the week's sales?

11.6 51. For Rambler Manufacturing in problems 49 and 50, would you rather invest the same amount of money to double the throughput rate of workstation B or C? Explain your reasoning.

EXCEL-BASED PROBLEMS

For these problems, you may use Excel or the Excel templates in MindTap to assist in your analysis.

11.3 52. A manufacturer's average WIP inventory for Part #2934 is 995 parts. The workstation produces parts at the rate of 225 parts per day. Use the Excel template *Little's Law* to find the average time a part spends in this workstation.

11.3 53. An express checkout line at a grocery store takes an average of three minutes to ring-up a customer's order. On average six customers are in the checkout line. Use the Excel template *Little's Law* to find the average number of customers per hour that are processed in the checkout line.

11.3 54. An accounts receivable manager processes 200 checks per day with an average processing time of 15 working days. Use the Excel template *Little's Law* to find the average number of accounts receivable checks being processed in her office. What if through information technology she reduces the processing time from 15 to 10 days to five days? What are the advantages and disadvantages of adopting this technology? Explain.

11.4 55. Trucks using a single server loading dock have a mean arrival rate of 12 per day. The loading/unloading rate is 18 per day. Use the *Single Server Queue* Excel template to answer the following questions:

a. What is the probability that the truck dock will be idle?

b. What is the average number of trucks waiting for service?

c. What is the average time a truck waits for the loading or unloading service?

d. What is the probability that a new arrival will have to wait?

e. What is the probability that three trucks are waiting for service?

11.4 56. Arrivals to a single server queue occur at an average rate of three per minute. Use the appropriate Excel function to develop the probability distribution for the number of arrivals for $x = 0$ through 10.

11.4 57. A mail-order nursery specializes in European beech trees. New orders, which are processed by a single shipping clerk, have a mean arrival rate of six per day and a mean service rate of eight per day. Use the *Single Server Queue* Excel template to answer the following questions:

a. What is the average time an order spends in the queue waiting for the clerk to begin service?

b. What is the average time an order spends in the system?

c. How many orders, on average, are in the queue and system?

11.4 58. Pete's Market is a small local grocery store with one checkout counter. Shoppers arrive at the checkout lane at an average rate of 15 customers per hour and the average order takes three minutes to ring up and bag. If Pete does not want the average time waiting for service to exceed five minutes, what would you tell him about the current system? Use the *Single Server Queue* Excel template to answer this question.

11.4 59. Assume trucks arriving for loading/unloading at a truck dock from a single server waiting line. The mean arrival rate is four trucks per hour, and the mean service rate is five trucks per hour. Use the *Single Server Queue* Excel template to answer the following questions:

a. What is the probability that the truck dock will be idle?

b. What is the average number of trucks in the queue?

c. What is the average number of trucks in the system?

d. What is the average time a truck spends in the queue waiting for service?

e. What is the average time a truck spends in the system?

f. What is the probability that an arriving truck will have to wait?

g. What is the probability that more than two trucks are waiting for service?

11.4 60. Marty's Barber Shop has one barber. Customers arrive at a rate of 2.2 per hour, and haircuts are given at an average rate of five customers per hour. Use the *Single Server Queue* Excel template to answer the following questions:

a. What is the probability that the barber is idle?
b. What is the probability that one customer is receiving a haircut and no one is waiting?
c. What is the probability that one customer is receiving a haircut and one customer is waiting?
d. What is the probability that one customer is receiving a haircut and two customers are waiting?
e. What is the probability that more than three customers are waiting?
f. What is the average time a customer waits for service?

11.4 61. Keuka Park Savings and Loan currently has one drive-up teller window. Cars arrive at a mean rate of 10 per hour. The mean service rate is 12 cars per hour. Use the *Single Server Queue* Excel template to answer the following questions:

a. What is the probability that the service facility will be idle?
b. If you were to drive up to the facility, how many cars would you expect to see waiting and being serviced?
c. What is the average time waiting for service?
d. What is the probability an arriving car will have to wait?
e. What is the probability that more than four vehicles are waiting for service?
f. As a potential customer of the system, would you be satisfied with these waiting-line characteristics? How do you think managers could go about assessing its customers' feelings about the current system?

11.4 62. Fore and Aft Marina is a new marina planned for a location on the Ohio River near Madison, Indiana. Assume that Fore and Aft decides to build one docking facility and expects a mean arrival rate of five boats per hour and a mean service rate of 10 boats per hour. Use the *Single Server Queue* Excel template to answer the following questions:

a. What is the probability that the boat dock will be idle?
b. What is the average number of boats that will be waiting for service?
c. What is the average time a boat will wait for service?
d. What is the average time a boat will spend at the dock?
e. What is the probability that more than two boats are waiting for service?
f. If you were the owner, would you be satisfied with this level of service?

11.4 63. Long lines of patients wait for CAT scanning service in a hospital. Patients arrive for scans at a rate of 1.8 per hour. The average processing time for CAT service is 27 minutes per patient. Your summer internship is in the hospital where you are assigned to help analyze the bottleneck situation. One tool that you think can help evaluate the situation is a single server queueing model. Use the *Single Server Queue* Excel template to answer the following questions:

a. What is the probability that the system is empty?
b. What is the probability that a customer must wait for service?
c. What is the average number of customers waiting for service in the queue?
d. What is the average wait time in the queue?
e. What is the average time spent in the system?
f. Given these results, what might be your recommendations?

11.4 64. The City Beverage Drive-Thru is considering a two-server system. Cars arrive at the store at the mean rate of six per hour. The service rate for each server is 10 per hour. Use the *Multiple Server Queue* Excel template to answer the following questions:

a. What is the probability that both servers are idle?
b. What is the average number of cars waiting for service?
c. What is the average time waiting for service?
d. What is the average time in the system?
e. What is the probability of having to wait for service?

11.4 65. Big Al's Car Wash has two wash bays. Each bay can wash 15 cars per hour. Cars arrive at the carwash at the rate of 15 cars per hour on the average, join the waiting line, and move to the next open bay when it becomes available. Use the *Multiple Server Queue* Excel template to answer the following questions:

a. What is the average time waiting for a bay?
b. What is the probability that a customer will have to wait?
c. As a customer of Big Al's, do you think the system favors the customer? If you were Al, what would be your attitude toward this service level?

11.4 66. The district manager of a fast-food restaurant chain was receiving numerous complaints about customers waiting too long at the counter to place and receive their order. During the peak hour of store operation, the district manager's audit team found that customers arrived at an average rate of one customer every minute. The standard firm service time was 2.5 minutes per customer. The store had three cash registers (service channels) open during this audit time, but four were available (i.e., one was idle). The fourth cash register was not opened because the store manager did not schedule an extra employee to work that day. Use the *Multiple Server Queue* Excel template to answer the following questions:

a. What is the probability that the system is empty?

b. What is the probability that a customer must wait for service?

c. What is the average number of customers waiting for service in the queue?

d. What is the average wait time in the queue?

e. How would opening the fourth cash register have impacted service?

11.4 67. Kurelis Interior Design provides home and office decorating assistance. In normal operation an average of 2.5 customers arrive per hour. One design consultant is available to answer customer questions and make product recommendations. The consultant averages 10 minutes with each customer. Use the *Single Server Queue* or *Multiple Server Queue* Excel templates as appropriate to answer the following questions:

a. Compute operating characteristics for the customer-waiting line.

b. Service goals dictate that an arriving customer should not wait for service more than an average of five minutes. Is this goal being met? What action do you recommend?

c. Should they hire a second consultant?

d. If the consultant can reduce the average time spent with customers to eight minutes, will the service goal be met?

11.4 68. Keuka Park Savings and Loan currently has one drive-up teller window. Cars arrive at a mean rate of 10 per hour. The mean service rate is 12 cars per hour per window. To improve its customer service, Keuka Park Savings and Loan wants to investigate the effect of a second drive-up teller window. What effect would adding a second (new) teller window have on the system? Does this system appear acceptable? Use the *Single Server Queue* or *Multiple Server Queue* Excel templates as appropriate for your analysis.

11.4 69. Trosper Tire Company has decided to hire a new mechanic to handle all tire changes for customers ordering new tires. Two mechanics are available for the job. One mechanic has limited experience and can be hired for $22 per hour. It is expected that this mechanic can service an average of three customers per hour. A mechanic with several years of experience is also being considered for the job. This mechanic can service an average of four customers per hour but must be paid $30 per hour. Assume that customers arrive at the Trosper garage at the rate of two per hour. Use the *Single Server Queue* Excel template to answer the following questions:

a. Compute waiting-line operating characteristics for each mechanic.

b. If the company assigns a customer-waiting cost of $20 per hour, what are total costs of using a less or more experienced mechanic? What do you recommend?

11.4 70. Kurelis Interior Design (see problem 67) provides home and office decorating assistance. On average, their high-end customers spend $36,000 on interior design fees plus $186,000 for furniture. In normal operation an average of 2.5 customers arrive per hour. One design consultant is available to answer customer questions and make product recommendations. The consultant averages 10 minutes with each customer. Compare the economics of remaining with one consultant (option one) or hiring a second consultant (option two) given the following information. The high-end customer does not like to wait, so customer-waiting time is valued at $5.00 per minute. Consultants are paid $25 including benefits. Use the *Single Server Queue* or *Multiple Server Queue* Excel templates as appropriate.

11.4 71. An airport limousine service has one employee work the airport counter. A customer arrives on the average of once every three minutes, and it takes on average two minutes to process the transaction. Use the *Single Server Queue* Excel template to answer the following questions:

a. What is the probability a customer has to wait for service?

b. What is the average time customers wait in the queue?

c. The target service standard for the limousine service is a probability of customers having to wait less than 10 percent. How many employees should be working to meet this target service level?

d. If 10 more customers per hour would be gained from competing transportation firms by increasing the number of employees to the answer in (c), what is system performance? Is it less than a 10 percent chance target service standard?

11.4 72. A medical clinic has two administrators handling all processing of insurance claims in a shared office. Administrator A handles only private insurance claims and processing. Administrator B handles only Medicare claims. On average, it takes about the same time (15 minutes) to process private or Medicare claims. Medicare patients arrive at the counter at a rate of three per hour, while private insurance patients arrive at a rate of two per hour. Use the *Single Server Queue* or *Multiple Server Queue* Excel templates as appropriate to answer the following questions:

a. What is the average waiting time for each type of patient (claim) given the current job design?

b. What is the average waiting time for both types of patients if each administrator could handle either transaction?

c. What do you recommend the medical clinic do with regard to insurance claim processing and job design?

The University Rare Book Library Process

A rare book library at a University of England in England houses first edition (FE), original manuscript (OM), and authors' journals (AJ). Some of these rare books are worth hundreds of thousands of dollars, and most are worth more than $5,000. People from all over the world visit the library to use its unique collection of rare books, and they seldom if ever are allowed to remove books from the library. Only certified librarians are able to collect the requested books and manuscripts from the bookshelves, as many of them are very fragile.

The rare book process involves the creation of value by the speed and reliability of the process (time utility); the safekeeping of human knowledge (place and information utility); the preservation of old books (form utility); and, to some rare book experts, the joy of seeing and reading the thoughts of people from different ages (entertainment utility). The output or outcome of the process is intangible—no physical goods are created here—just information, entertainment, historical research, and knowledge transfer.

The goal of the librarian is to design a structured process with many checks and balances to ensure the security of the rare books, yet create professional service encounters. The process flowchart for examining rare books in a library is shown in Exhibit 11.34. Note the line of visibility that separates the front-office activities from the back-office activities. Here, library patrons must follow a very small number of predefined pathways through the service delivery system. Customers have little freedom or power to depart from the standard pathways and service encounter activity sequences; the process is highly repeatable; and management control is high.

Assume the throughput rate defined by Exhibit 11.34 is 40 library patrons per hour. All library patrons must remain in the visitor's area until they register with one of the head

Joseph Sohm/Shutterstock.com

librarians. On average, there are 10 people waiting in the visitor's area. The head librarians verify that the patron has accounts in good standing with the library; this activity averages three minutes. After registering, the patron moves to a reference waiting area. On average, 12 people are waiting to be serviced in this second waiting area.

A special librarian then takes the request from the patron and guides him or her to one of three smaller waiting areas in the library: first editions, manuscripts, and authors' journals. This first special librarian activity averages 4 minutes and is the first of two activities carried out by the special librarian. One special librarian handles one customer at a time. On average, 50 percent of the patrons ask to see first editions, 40 percent ask for original manuscripts, and 10 percent ask for authors' journals. When patrons arrive at one of the three smaller waiting areas, they wait for the special librarian to perform the second activity, which is finding and retrieving the item. The library staff estimates, on average, that five people are waiting to be served for first-edition books, three people waiting to be served for an original manuscript, and

EXHIBIT 11.34 Process Flowchart for the University Rare Book Library

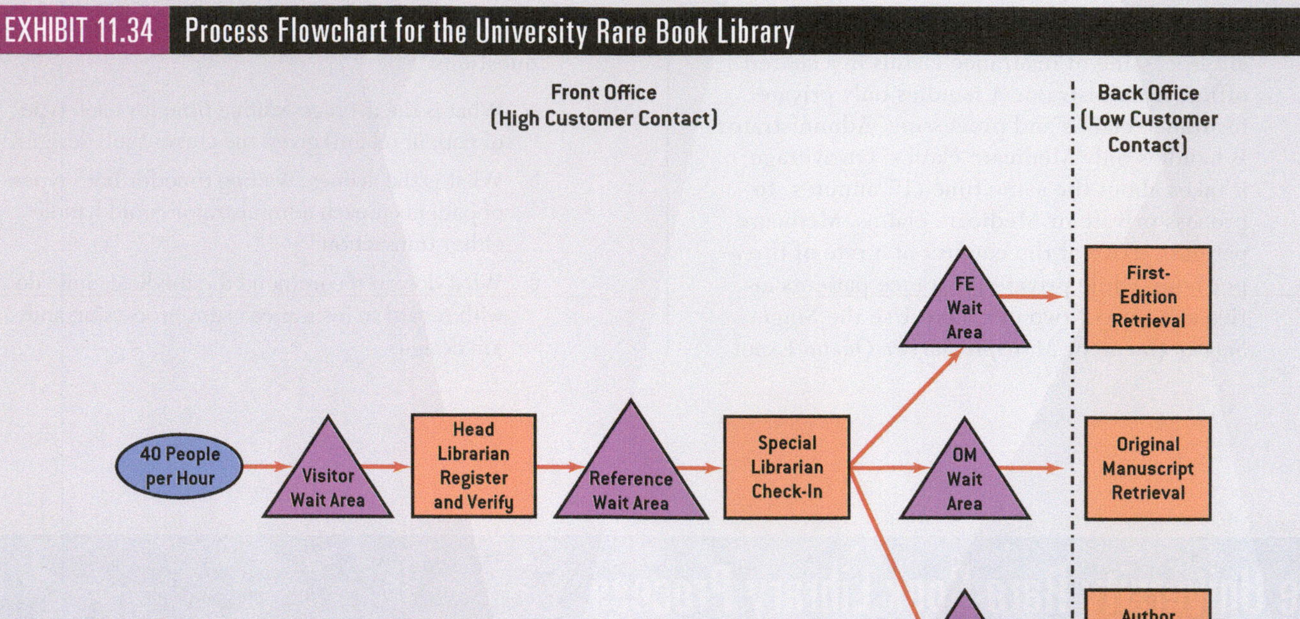

EXHIBIT 11.35 Worksheet for the University Rare Book Library Using Little's Law

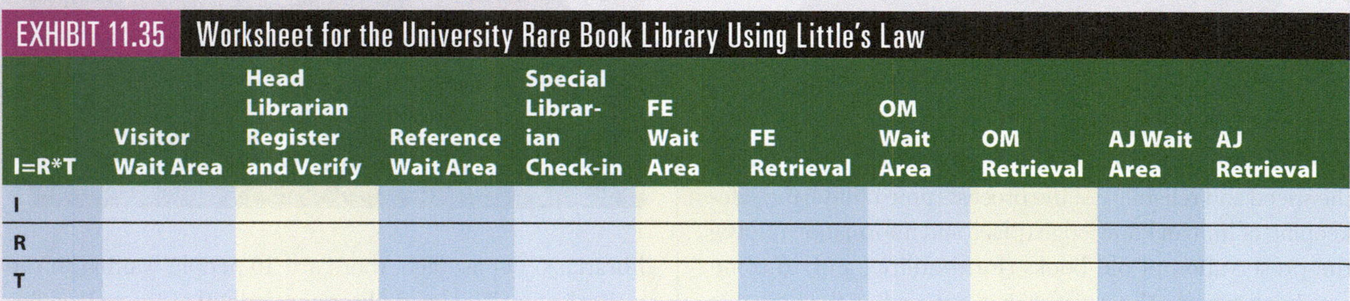

I=R*T	Visitor Wait Area	Head Librarian Register and Verify	Reference Wait Area	Special Librar-ian Check-in	FE Wait Area	FE Retrieval	OM Wait Area	OM Retrieval	AJ Wait Area	AJ Retrieval
I										
R										
T										

one person is waiting to be served for an authors' journal. The special librarians take an average of four minutes to fill a first-edition book retrieval, and six minutes to fill an original manuscript or author's journal retrieval. Worksheet Exhibit 11.35 may be helpful in answering questions about the process.

Case Questions for Discussion:

1. How many minutes, on average, does it take for a first-edition patron to get the requested book from time of entry into the library? (State all assumptions and show the calculations.)
2. How many minutes, on average, does it take for the average library patron to get the requested book from time of entry into the library? (State all assumptions and show the calculations.)
3. How many patrons, on average, are there in the total library service delivery system? (State all assumptions and show the calculations.)
4. If the following numbers of employees work at each activity, what is labor utilization for each job activity? Head librarian: two employees, three minutes per activity; special librarian check-in: three employees, four minutes per activity; first-edition retrieval: two employees, four minutes per activity; original manuscript retrieval: two employees, six minutes per activity; and authors' journal retrieval: one employee, six minutes per activity.
5. What labor resource is the bottleneck?
6. What do you recommend to break the bottleneck(s)? Explain and justify your reasoning.

Bourbon County Court

"Why don't they buy another copying machine for this office? I waste a lot of valuable time fooling with this machine when I could be preparing my legal cases," noted Mr. H.C. Morris, as he waited in line. The self-service copying machine was located in a small room immediately outside the entrance of the courtroom. Mr. Morris was the county attorney. He often copied his own papers, as did other lawyers, to keep his legal cases and work confidential. This protected the privacy of his clients as well as his professional and personal ideas about the cases.

He also felt awkward at times standing in line with secretaries, clerks of the court, other attorneys, police officers and sheriffs, building permit inspectors, and the dog warden—all trying, he thought, to see what he was copying. The line for the copying machine often extended out into the hallways of the courthouse.

Mr. Morris mentioned his frustration with the copying machine problem to Judge Hamlet and his summer intern, Dot Gifford. Ms. Gifford was home for the summer and working toward a joint MBA/JD degree from a leading university.

"Mr. Morris, there are ways to find out if that one copying machine is adequate to handle the demand. If you can get the Judge to let me analyze the situation, I think I can help out. We had a similar problem at the law school with word processors and at the business school with student lab microcomputers."

The next week Judge Hamlet gave Dot the go-ahead to work on the copying machine problem. He asked her to write a management report on the problem with recommendations so he could take it to the Bourbon County Board of Supervisors for their approval. The board faced deficit spending last fiscal year, so the tradeoffs between service and cost must be clearly presented to the board.

Dot's experience with analyzing similar problems at school helped her know what type of information and data was needed. After several weeks of working on this project, she developed the information contained in Exhibits 11.36 to 11.38.

Dot was not quite as confident in evaluating this situation as others because the customer mix and associated labor costs seemed more uncertain in the county courthouse. In the law school situation, only secretaries used the word processing terminals; in the business school situation, students were the ones complaining about long waiting times to get on a microcomputer terminal. Moreover, the professor guiding these two past school projects had suggested using queueing models for one project and simulation for the other project. Dot was never clear on how the method of analysis was chosen. Now, she wondered which

EXHIBIT 11.36 Bourbon County Court—Customer Arrivals per Hour (These Data Are Available in the Worksheet *Bourbon County Court Case Data* in MindTap.)

	Customer Arrivals in One Hour		Customer Arrivals in One Hour		Customer Arrivals in One Hour		Customer Arrivals in One Hour		Customer Arrivals in One Hour
1	5	11	10	21	3	31	11	41	14
2	9	12	17	22	9	32	8	42	7
3	7	13	18	23	11	33	9	43	4
4	13	14	14	24	10	34	8	44	7
5	7	15	11	25	12	35	6	45	7
6	7	16	16	26	4	36	8	46	2
7	7	17	5	27	8	37	14	47	4
8	11	18	6	28	9	38	12	48	7
9	8	19	8	29	9	39	11	49	2
10	6	20	13	30	9	40	15	50	8

*A sample of customer arrivals at the copying machine was taken for five consecutive nine-hour work days plus five hours on Saturday for a total of fifty observations. The mean arrival rate is 8.92 arrivals per hour.

EXHIBIT 11.37 Bourbon County Court—Copying Service Times (These Data Are Available in the Worksheet *Bourbon County Court Case Data* in MindTap.)

Obs. No.	Hours per Job	Obs. No.	Hours per Job
1	0.0700	26	0.0752
2	0.1253	27	0.0752
3	0.0752	28	0.1002
4	0.2508	29	0.0388
5	0.0226	30	0.0978
6	0.1504	31	0.0752
7	0.0501	32	0.1002
8	0.0250	33	0.0250
9	0.0150	34	0.0752
10	0.2005	35	0.0501
11	0.1253	36	0.0301
12	0.1754	37	0.0752
13	0.0301	38	0.0501
14	0.1002	39	0.0075
15	0.0752	40	0.0602
16	0.3009	41	0.2005
17	0.0752	42	0.0501
18	0.0376	43	0.0150
19	0.0501	44	0.0501
20	0.0226	45	0.0527
21	0.1754	46	0.1203
22	0.0700	47	0.1253
23	0.1253	48	0.1053
24	0.0752	49	0.1253
25	0.2508	50	0.0301

*A sample of customers served at the copying machine was taken for five consecutive nine-hour work days plus five hours on Saturday for a total of fifty observations. The average service time is 0.0917 hours per copying job or 5.499 minutes per job. The equivalent service rate is 10.91 jobs per hour (i.e., 10.91 jobs/hour = (60 minutes/hour)/5.5 minutes/job).

EXHIBIT 11.38 Bourbon County Court—Cost and Customer Mix

Resource Category	Mix of Customers in Line (%)	Cost or Average Direct Wages per Hour
Lease and maintenance cost of copying machine per year @250 days/year	N/A	$18,600
Average hourly copier variable cost (electric, ink, paper, etc.)	N/A	$5/hour
Secretaries	50%	$18.75
Clerks of the court	20%	$22.50
Building inspectors and dog warden	10%	$28.40
Police officers and sheriffs	10%	$30.80
Attorneys	10%	$100.00

*The mix of customers standing in line was collected at the same time as the data in the other case exhibits. Direct wages do include employee benefits but not work opportunity costs or ill-will costs, etc.

methodology she should use for the Bourbon County Court situation.

To organize her thinking, Dot listed a few of the questions she needed to address as follows:

1. Assuming a Poisson arrival distribution and an exponential service time distribution, apply queueing models to the case situation and evaluate the results.
2. What are the economics of the situation using queueing model analysis?
3. What are your final recommendations using queueing model analysis.
4. *Advanced Question:* Do the customer arrival and service empirical (actual) distributions in the case match the theoretical distributions assumed in queueing models?

Integrative Case: Hudson Jewelers

The Hudson Jewelers case study found in MindTap integrates material found in each chapter of this book.

Case Questions for Discussion:

1. What is the average number of customers per hour that can be served for Activity B (CAD Demo & Jewelry Concept) if two employees are in the store? Assume each employee works at 100% utilization.
2. Given the seasonal nature of demand at Hudson Jewelers provided in the Excel file *Hudson Jeweler Demand Case Data* in MindTap, how would you estimate the mean arrival and service rates for Friday to be used in a queueing model? What does the queueing analysis tell you? By developing a histogram of the demand (customer arrival) rate, does demand match the queueing model assumed Poisson distribution?

12 Managing Inventories in Supply Chains

LEARNING OBJECTIVES

After studying this chapter, you should be able to:

12-1 Explain the importance of inventory, types of inventories, and key decisions and costs.

12-2 Describe the major characteristics that impact inventory decisions.

12-3 Describe how to conduct an ABC inventory analysis.

12-4 Explain how a fixed-order-quantity inventory system operates and how to use the economic order quantity (EOQ), quantity discount, and safety stock models.

12-5 Explain how a fixed-period inventory system operates.

12-6 Describe how to apply the single-period inventory model.

12-7 Conduct and analyze simulation models for fixed-order-quantity systems with uncertain demand and lead times using the Excel Inventory Simulation template.

Rent the Runway builds relationships with well-known designers to ensure that their company offers the most in-demand items for every season.

FashionStock.com/Shutterstock.com

"We're not in the fashion business. We're in the fashion-technology-engineering-supply-chain-operations-reverse logistics-dry cleaning-analytics business."[1]

That's how Rent the Runway characterizes itself. Rent the Runway is a company that allows customers to rent high-fashion dresses for either 4 or 8 days at approximately 10 percent of the retail price of a dress. By building relationships with well-known designers, the company ensures that they have the most beautiful, in-demand items for every season. Customers can view the selection of dresses (nearly 65,000 dresses and accessories are available) and their availability through a website, and receive style and fit advice from Rent the Runway consultants and customer reviews. Dresses are shipped to customers and returned by mail. The company processes orders through its 150,000-square-foot fulfillment center. They use a proprietary, high-speed, "reverse-logistics" system that allows them to turn items around in record time, usually within 1 day. As they note, "No other company on Earth has the infrastructure to process as fast." Finally, Rent the Runway exploits analytics by gathering huge amounts of data from every click, delivery, return, and step along the way to improve its decisions and make everything they do faster, smarter, easier, and nimbler.

WHAT DO YOU THINK?

Can you cite any experiences in which the lack of appropriate inventory at a retail store has caused you as the customer to be dissatisfied?

Inventory *is any asset held for future use or sale.* The unique business model that Rent the Runway has cannot be implemented without highly effective inventory management systems. For example, decisions about the number of dresses that will comprise Rent the Runway's seasonal rental inventory must be made shortly after preseason fashion shows, which are several months in advance of the rental season. The firm runs the risk of having too many, not enough, or the wrong styles. Wrong decisions can impact profitability significantly. The availability of inventory can also affect the company's reputation and customer retention, and failing to rent to a customer because the rental unit was damaged by a previous customer can result in a challenging customer service encounter. Managing inventories must also be coordinated with other aspects of its operations and supply chain. For example, Rent the Runway recognized that ensuring quick inventory turnaround times is a core competency and brought its laundry operation in-house.[2]

Top management needs to understand the role that inventories play in a company's financial performance, operational efficiency, and customer satisfaction, and strike the proper balance in meeting strategic objectives.

Many manufacturing firms maintain large amounts of inventory; this is costly and wasteful. The old concept of keeping warehouses and stockrooms filled to capacity with inventory has been replaced with the idea of producing finished goods as late as possible prior to shipment to the customer. Better information technology and applications of analytics have allowed dramatic reductions in inventory.

The expenses associated with financing and maintaining inventories are a substantial part of the cost of doing business (i.e., cost of goods sold). Managers are faced with the dual challenges of maintaining sufficient inventories to meet demand while at the same time incurring the lowest possible cost. **Inventory management** *involves planning, coordinating, and controlling the acquisition, storage, handling, movement, distribution, and possible sale of raw materials, component parts and subassemblies, supplies and tools, replacement parts, and other assets that are needed to meet customer wants and needs.*

12-1 Understanding Inventory

Generally, inventories are physical goods used in operations and include raw materials, parts, subassemblies, supplies, tools, equipment or maintenance, and repair items. For example, a small pizza business must maintain inventories of dough, toppings, sauce, and cheese, as well as supplies such as boxes, napkins, and so on. Hospitals maintain inventories of blood and other consumables, and retail stores such as Best Buy maintain inventories of finished goods—televisions, appliances, and computers—for sale to customers. In some service organizations, inventories are not physical goods that customers take with them, but capacity available for serving customers, such as hotel rooms or airline seats.

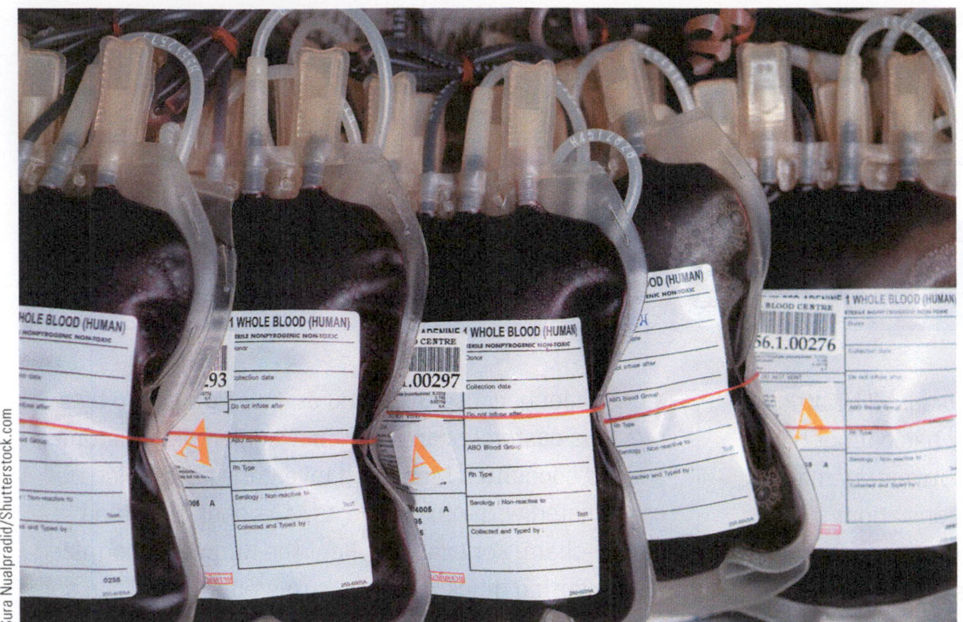

Sura Nualpradid/Shutterstock.com

One of the difficulties of inventory management is that every function in an organization generally views inventory objectives differently. Marketing and operations prefer high inventory levels to provide the best possible customer service and process efficiency, whereas financial personnel seek to minimize inventory investment and thus would prefer small inventories. Top management needs to understand the role that inventory plays in a company's financial performance, operational efficiency, and customer satisfaction, and strike the proper balance in meeting strategic objectives.

12-1a Key Definitions and Concepts

Many different types of inventories are maintained throughout the value chain—before, during, and after production—to support operations and meet customer demands (see Exhibit 12.1). **Raw materials, component parts, subassemblies, and supplies** *are inputs to manufacturing and service-delivery processes.* **Work-in-process (WIP) inventory** *consists of partially finished products in various stages of completion that are awaiting further processing.* For example, a pizza restaurant might

EXHIBIT 12.1 Role of Inventory in the Value Chain

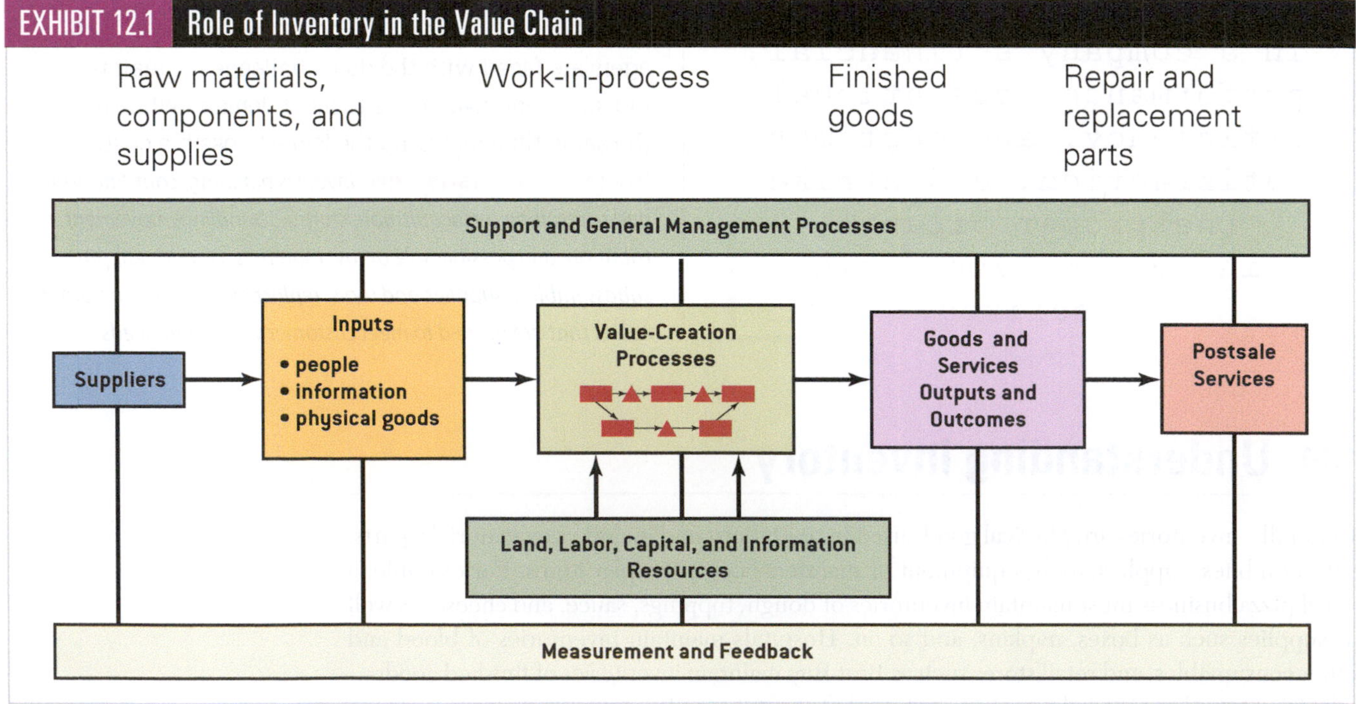

prepare a batch of pizzas with only cheese and sauce and add other toppings when orders are placed. WIP inventory also acts as a buffer between workstations in flow shops or departments in job shops to enable the operating process to continue when equipment might fail at one stage or supplier shipments are late. **Finished-goods inventory** *is completed products ready for distribution or sale to customers.* Finished goods might be stored in a warehouse or at the point of sale in retail stores. Finished-goods inventories are necessary to satisfy customers' demands quickly without having to wait for a product to be made or ordered from the supplier.

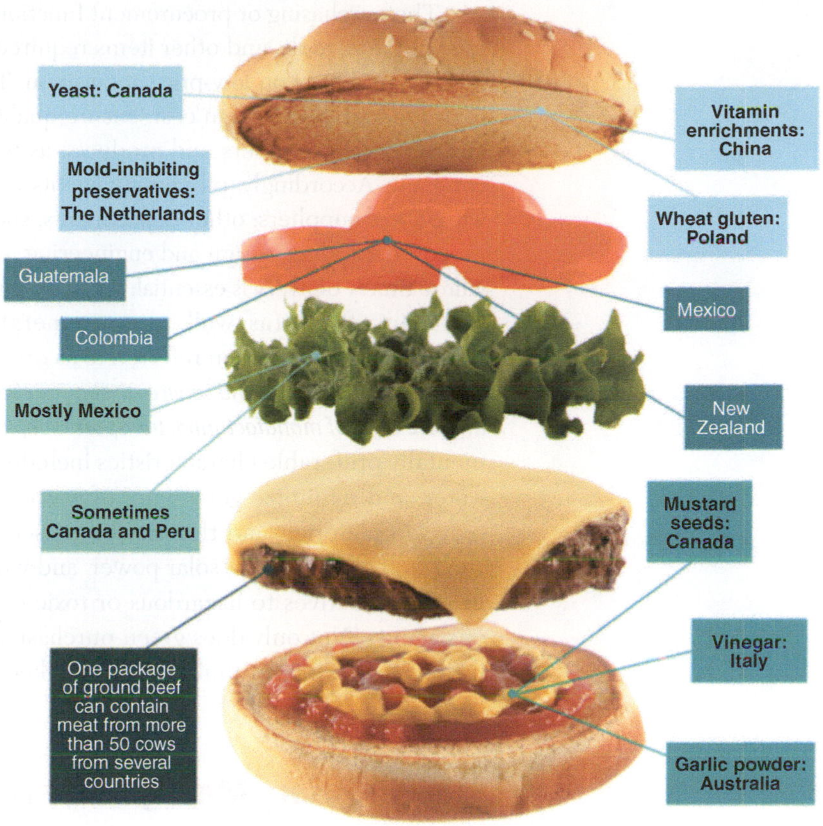

High levels of WIP and finished-goods inventories can be undesirable. Large WIP can hide such problems as unreliable machines, late supplier shipments, or defective parts; and large amounts of finished goods inventory can quickly become obsolete when technology changes or new products are introduced.

Customer demand is most often highly variable and uncertain. Lack of sufficient inventory can cause production lines to shut down or customers to become dissatisfied and purchase goods and services elsewhere. To reduce the risk associated with not having enough inventory, firms often maintain additional stock beyond their normal estimates.

TheCrimsonMonkey/E+/Getty Images

12-1b Managing Inventories in Global Supply Chains

Today's global supply chains present significant challenges to inventory management. The components and materials used in nearly any product are often purchased from suppliers across the globe and shipped through complex supply chains. This is even more important for perishable goods. For example, a common cheeseburger at a fast-food restaurant may consist of wheat gluten from Poland, preservatives from the Netherlands, tomatoes from Latin America, lettuce from Mexico or New Zealand, mustard seeds from Canada, vinegar from Italy, garlic powder from Australia, and ground beef from more than 50 cows from several countries. Purchasing, tracking, and managing such a variety of items in global supply chains requires good technology, processes, and information technology (IT) support. Technology such as radio-frequency identification (RFID) chips can increase inventory accuracy to better than 98 percent—much higher than the current industry average of 65 percent—and allows firms to track individual containers. With thousands of products and materials, hundreds of suppliers, and numerous orders and shippers, an accurate information system is essential. Enterprise resource planning (ERP) systems (which we will discuss in Chapter 14), such as those sold by SAP and Oracle, provide the infrastructure to effectively manage all of this information. Using cloud computing simplifies data management, improves the availability and accessibility of data, and allows companies to share information among many suppliers.

The purchasing or procurement function is responsible for acquiring raw materials, component parts, tools, and other items required from outside suppliers. In the past, purchasing focused primarily on low-price acquisition. Today, however, purchasing must focus on global sourcing and total system cost; ensure quality, delivery performance, and technical support; and seek new suppliers and products, as well as be able to evaluate their potential to the company. Accordingly, purchasing agents must maintain good relations and communication with global suppliers; other departments, such as accounting and finance, where budgets are prepared; product design and engineering, where material specifications are set; production, where timely delivery is essential; and with the legal department, where contracts are reviewed.

Many firms (as well as consumers) subscribe to **environmentally preferable purchasing (EPP),** often referred to as **green purchasing,** *which is the affirmative selection and acquisition of products and services that most effectively minimize negative environmental impacts over their life cycle of manufacturing, transportation, use, and recycling or disposal.* Examples of environmentally preferable characteristics include products and services that conserve energy and water, and minimize generation of waste and releases of pollutants; products made from recycled materials and that can be reused or recycled; energy from renewable resources such as biobased fuels, solar power, and wind power; alternate fuel vehicles; and products using alternatives to hazardous or toxic chemicals, radioactive materials, and biohazardous agents. Not only does green purchasing conserve resources and the environment, but it improves safety, stimulates new markets for recycled materials, and provides potential cost savings.[3]

12-1c Inventory Management Decisions and Costs

Inventory managers deal with two fundamental decisions:

1. When to order items from a supplier or when to initiate production runs if the firm makes its own items.
2. How much to order or produce each time a supplier or production order is placed.

Inventory management is all about making trade-offs among the costs associated with these decisions.

Inventory costs can be classified into four major categories:

1. Ordering or setup costs.
2. Inventory-holding costs.
3. Shortage costs.
4. Unit cost of the SKUs.

Ordering costs or **setup costs** *are incurred as a result of the work involved in placing orders with suppliers or configuring tools, equipment, and machines within a factory to produce an item.* Order and setup costs do not depend on the number of items purchased or manufactured, but rather on the number of orders placed.

Inventory-holding or **inventory-carrying costs** *are the expenses associated with carrying inventory.* Holding costs are typically defined as a percentage of the dollar value of inventory per unit of time (generally 1 year). They include costs associated with maintaining storage facilities, such as gas and electricity, taxes, insurance, and labor and equipment necessary to handle, move, and retrieve inventory items, plus the opportunity cost of capital represented by holding inventory, normally for 1 year. However, from an accounting perspective, it is difficult to precisely allocate such costs to an individual stock-keeping unit (SKU). Essentially, holding costs reflect the opportunity cost associated with using the funds invested in inventory for alternative uses and investments.

Smart Fitting Rooms Help Inventory Management

Bloomingdale's, a division of Macy's, uses modern technology to help solve a common problem that has cost apparel retailers dearly in sales: frustrated customers who give up and leave rather than take the time to acquire the right piece of clothing. At several stores, Bloomingdale's has designed "smart fitting rooms" with Apple iPads that connect to the complex inventory-management systems it uses to keep track of millions of items. With the iPads, a customer or a store associate can scan the item in question to find which colors and sizes are in stock, as well as see ratings and reviews by other customers. The tablets also recommend items that would complement the scanned original. And, with a tap, a customer can summon an associate.

The initiative is part of a bigger push by Macy's Inc. to become more competitive. Macy's is way ahead of other retailers in terms of using unsold inventory from physical stores to fill online orders (rather than sell it on clearance), as well as offering store pickup for orders placed online.[4]

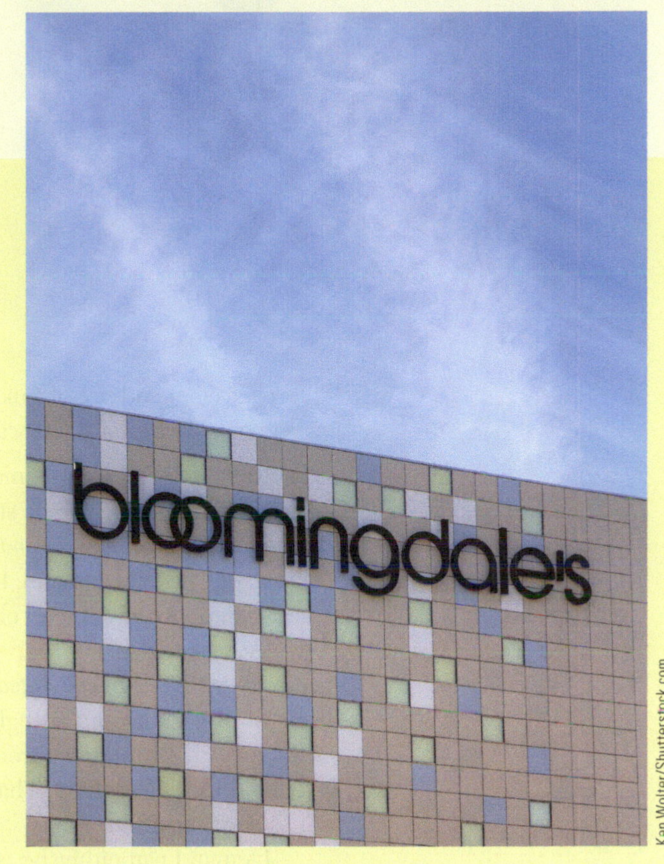

Ken Wolter/Shutterstock.com

Shortage or **stockout costs** *are costs associated with inventory being unavailable when needed to meet demand.* These costs can reflect backorders, lost sales, or service interruptions for external customers, or costs associated with interruptions to manufacturing and assembly lines for internal customers. **Unit cost** *is the price paid for purchased goods or the internal cost of producing them.* In most situations, the unit cost is a "sunk cost" because the total purchase cost is not affected by the order quantity. However, the unit cost of SKUs is an important purchasing consideration when quantity discounts are offered; it may be more economical to purchase large quantities at a lower unit cost to reduce the other cost categories and thus minimize total costs.

12-2 Inventory Characteristics

Various inventory situations are possible.[5] For instance, a self-serve gasoline station maintains an inventory of only a few grades of gasoline, whereas a large appliance store may carry several hundred different items. Demand for gasoline is relatively constant, whereas the demand for air conditioners is highly seasonal and variable. If a gasoline station runs out of gas, a customer will go elsewhere. However, if an appliance store does not have a particular item in stock, the customer may be willing to order the item and wait for delivery or go to another appliance store. Because the demand and inventory characteristics of the gasoline station and appliance store differ significantly, the proper control of inventories requires different approaches.

HomeStudio/Shutterstock.com

One of the first steps in analyzing an inventory problem should be to describe the essential characteristics of the environment and inventory system that follow.

Number of Items Most firms maintain inventories for a large number of items, often at multiple locations. To manage and control these inventories, each item is often assigned a unique identifier, called a stock-keeping unit, or SKU. *A* ***stock-keeping unit (SKU)*** *is a single item or asset stored at a particular location.* For example, each color and size of a man's dress shirt at a department store and each type of milk (whole, 2 percent, skim) at a grocery store would be a different SKU.

Nature of Demand Demand can be classified as independent or dependent, constant or uncertain, and dynamic or static. ***Independent demand*** *is demand for an SKU that is unrelated to the demand for other SKUs and needs to be forecasted.* This type of demand is directly related to customer (market) demand. Inventories of finished goods such as toothpaste and electric fans have independent demand characteristics.

SKUs are said to have ***dependent demand*** *if their demand is directly related to the demand of other SKUs and can be calculated without needing to be forecasted.* For example, a chandelier may consist of a frame and six lightbulb sockets. The demand for chandeliers is an independent demand and would be forecasted, whereas the demand for sockets is dependent on the demand for chandeliers. That is, for a forecast of chandeliers we can calculate the number of sockets required.

Demand can either be constant over some period of time (or assumed to be constant), or we can assume that it is uncertain. Sometimes we might simply assume that demand is constant in order to make our models easier to solve and analyze, perhaps by using historical averages or statistical point estimates of forecasts. When such an assumption is unwarranted, we can characterize demand using a probability distribution. For example, we might assume that the daily demand for milk is constant at 100 gallons, or we might assume that it is normally distributed with a mean of 100 and a standard deviation of 10. Models that incorporate uncertainty are generally more difficult to build and analyze.

Demand, whether deterministic or stochastic, may also fluctuate or remain stable over time. *Stable demand is usually called* ***static demand,*** *and demand that varies over time is referred to as* ***dynamic demand.*** For example, the demand for milk might range from 90 to 110 gallons per day, every day of the year. This is an example of static demand because the parameters of the probability distribution do not change over time. However, the demand for airline flights to Orlando, Florida, will probably have different means and variances throughout the year, reaching peaks around Thanksgiving, Christmas, spring break, and in the summer, with lower demands at other times. This is an example of dynamic demand.

Number and Duration of Time Periods In some cases, the selling season is relatively short, and any leftover items cannot be physically or economically stored until the next season. For example, Christmas trees that have been cut cannot be stored until the following year; similarly, other items such as seasonal fashions are sold at a loss simply because there is no storage space or it is uneconomical to keep them for the next year. In other situations, firms are concerned with planning inventory requirements over an extended number of time periods—for example, monthly over a year—in which inventory is held from one time period to the next. The type of approach used to analyze "single-period" inventory problems is different from the approach needed for the "multiple-period" inventory situation.

A lost sale has an associated opportunity cost, which may include loss of goodwill and potential future revenue.

Lead Time *The* **lead time** *is the time between placement of an order and its receipt.* Lead time is affected by transportation carriers, buyer order frequency and size, and supplier production schedules, and may be deterministic or stochastic (in which case it may be described by some probability distribution).

Stockouts *A* **stockout** *is the inability to satisfy the demand for an item.* When stockouts occur, the item is either back-ordered or a sale is lost. *A* **backorder** *occurs when a customer is willing to wait for the item; a* **lost sale** *occurs when the customer is unwilling to wait and purchases the item elsewhere.* Backorders result in additional costs for transportation, expediting, or perhaps buying from another supplier at a higher price. A lost sale has an associated opportunity cost, which may include loss of goodwill and potential future revenue.

Stockouts Matter

According to the Food Marketing Institute and Grocery Manufacturers of America, stockouts in the fast-moving consumer goods sector are as high as 8.3 percent, with promotional products even higher. As a result, retailers lose around 4 percent of their sales because consumers will buy the item elsewhere, substitute the product with another brand, or just forget about it.[6]

12-3 ABC Inventory Analysis

One useful method for defining inventory value is ABC analysis. It is an application of the *Pareto principle*, named after an Italian economist who studied the distribution of wealth in Milan during the 1800s. He found that a "vital few" controlled a high percentage of the wealth. ABC analysis consists of categorizing inventory items or SKUs into three groups according to their total annual dollar usage.

1. "A" items account for a large dollar value but a relatively small percentage of total items.
2. "C" items account for a small dollar value but a large percentage of total items.
3. "B" items are between A and C.

Typically, A items comprise 60 to 80 percent of the total dollar usage but only 10 to 30 percent of the items, whereas C items account for 5 to 15 percent of the total dollar value and about 50 percent of the items. There is no specific rule on where to make the division between A, B, and C items; the percentages used here simply serve as a guideline. Total dollar usage or value is computed by multiplying item usage (volume) times the item's dollar value (unit cost). Therefore, an A item could have a low volume but high unit cost, or a high volume and low unit cost.

ABC analysis gives managers useful information to identify the best methods to control each category of inventory. Class A items require close control by operations managers. Class C items need not be as closely controlled and can be managed using automated computer systems. Class B items are somewhere in the middle. Solved Problem 12.1 illustrates the use of an Excel template to perform an ABC inventory analysis.

SOLVED PROBLEM 12.1: ABC INVENTORY ANALYSIS

Consider the data for 20 inventoried items of a small company, depicted in columns A through C in the Excel *ABC* template available in MindTap shown in Exhibit 12.2. Conduct an ABC analysis for these data.

Solution:

For each item, enter the projected annual usage or forecast (in units) and the unit cost. The projected annual dollar usage in column D is found by multiplying the projected annual usage by the unit cost. The right side of the spreadsheet computes the cumulative dollar usage, cumulative percent of total dollar usage, and cumulative percent of items. To apply the Pareto principle, we must next sort the data in columns A through D by the projected annual dollar usage, largest first. To do this, right-click on any of the numerical values in column D (except for the total in row 29), and select *Sort* > *Sort Largest to Smallest* (or *Descending*, depending on Excel version) from the menu that appears. The result is shown in Exhibit 12.3. Analysis of Exhibit 12.3 indicates that about 70 percent of the total dollar usage is accounted for by the first five items; that is, only 25 percent of the items. In addition, the lowest 50 percent of the items account for only about 5 percent of the total dollar usage. Exhibit 12.4 shows a simple histogram of the ABC analysis classification scheme for this set of data.

EXHIBIT 12.2 Excel *ABC* Template Before Sorting

	A	B	C	D	E	F	G	H	I
1	**ABC Inventory Analysis**								
2									
3	**Enter data only in yellow cells; the template is designed for up to 20 items.**								
4	**After entering the data, right click on any value in column D; choose Sort > Sort Largest to Smallest.**								
5									
6		**Projected**		**Projected**		**Cumulative**	**Cumulative**	**Cumulative**	
7	**Item**	**Usage**		**Dollar Usage**		**Dollar**	**Percent**	**Percent**	
8	**Number**	**Annual**	**Unit Cost**	**Annual**		**Usage**	**of Total**	**of Items**	
9									
10	1	15000	$5.00	$75,000.00		$75,000	2.80%	5%	
11	2	6450	$20.00	$129,000.00		$204,000	7.61%	10%	
12	3	5000	$45.00	$225,000.00		$429,000	16.00%	15%	
13	4	200	$12.50	$2,500.00		$431,500	16.10%	20%	
14	5	20000	$35.00	$700,000.00		$1,131,500	42.21%	25%	
15	6	84	$250.00	$21,000.00		$1,152,500	43.00%	30%	
16	7	800	$80.00	$64,000.00		$1,216,500	45.38%	35%	
17	8	300	$5.00	$1,500.00		$1,218,000	45.44%	40%	
18	9	10000	$35.00	$350,000.00		$1,568,000	58.50%	45%	
19	10	2000	$65.00	$130,000.00		$1,698,000	63.35%	50%	
20	11	5000	$25.00	$125,000.00		$1,823,000	68.01%	55%	
21	12	3250	$125.00	$406,250.00		$2,229,250	83.17%	60%	
22	13	9000	$0.50	$4,500.00		$2,233,750	83.33%	65%	
23	14	2900	$10.00	$29,000.00		$2,262,750	84.42%	70%	
24	15	800	$15.00	$12,000.00		$2,274,750	84.86%	75%	
25	16	675	$200.00	$135,000.00		$2,409,750	89.90%	80%	
26	17	1470	$100.00	$147,000.00		$2,556,750	95.39%	85%	
27	18	8200	$15.00	$123,000.00		$2,679,750	99.97%	90%	
28	19	1250	$0.16	$200.00		$2,679,950	99.98%	95%	
29	20	2500	$0.20	$500.00		$2,680,450	100.00%	100%	
30									
31			Total	$2,680,450.00					

EXHIBIT 12.3 Excel *ABC* Template After Sorting

	A	B	C	D	E	F	G	H	I
1	**ABC Inventory Analysis**								
2									
3	**Enter data only in yellow cells; the template is designed for up to 20 items.**								
4	**After entering the data, right click on any value in column D; choose Sort > Sort Largest to Smallest.**								
5									
6		**Projected**		**Projected**		**Cumulative**	**Cumulative**	**Cumulative**	
7	**Item**	**Usage**		**Dollar Usage**		**Dollar**	**Percent**	**Percent**	
8	**Number**	**Annual**	**Unit Cost**	**Annual**		**Usage**	**of Total**	**of Items**	
9									
10	5	20000	$35.00	$700,000.00		$700,000	26.12%	5%	
11	12	3250	$125.00	$406,250.00		$1,106,250	41.27%	10%	
12	9	10000	$35.00	$350,000.00		$1,456,250	54.33%	15%	
13	3	5000	$45.00	$225,000.00		$1,681,250	62.72%	20%	
14	17	1470	$100.00	$147,000.00		$1,828,250	68.21%	25%	
15	16	675	$200.00	$135,000.00		$1,963,250	73.24%	30%	
16	10	2000	$65.00	$130,000.00		$2,093,250	78.09%	35%	
17	2	6450	$20.00	$129,000.00		$2,222,250	82.91%	40%	
18	11	5000	$25.00	$125,000.00		$2,347,250	87.57%	45%	
19	18	8200	$15.00	$123,000.00		$2,470,250	92.16%	50%	
20	1	15000	$5.00	$75,000.00		$2,545,250	94.96%	55%	
21	7	800	$80.00	$64,000.00		$2,609,250	97.34%	60%	
22	14	2900	$10.00	$29,000.00		$2,638,250	98.43%	65%	
23	6	84	$250.00	$21,000.00		$2,659,250	99.21%	70%	
24	15	800	$15.00	$12,000.00		$2,671,250	99.66%	75%	
25	13	9000	$0.50	$4,500.00		$2,675,750	99.82%	80%	
26	4	200	$12.50	$2,500.00		$2,678,250	99.92%	85%	
27	8	300	$5.00	$1,500.00		$2,679,750	99.97%	90%	
28	20	2500	$0.20	$500.00		$2,680,250	99.99%	95%	
29	19	1250	$0.16	$200.00		$2,680,450	100.00%	100%	
30									
31			**Total**	$2,680,450.00					

EXHIBIT 12.4 ABC Histogram for the Results from Exhibit 12.3

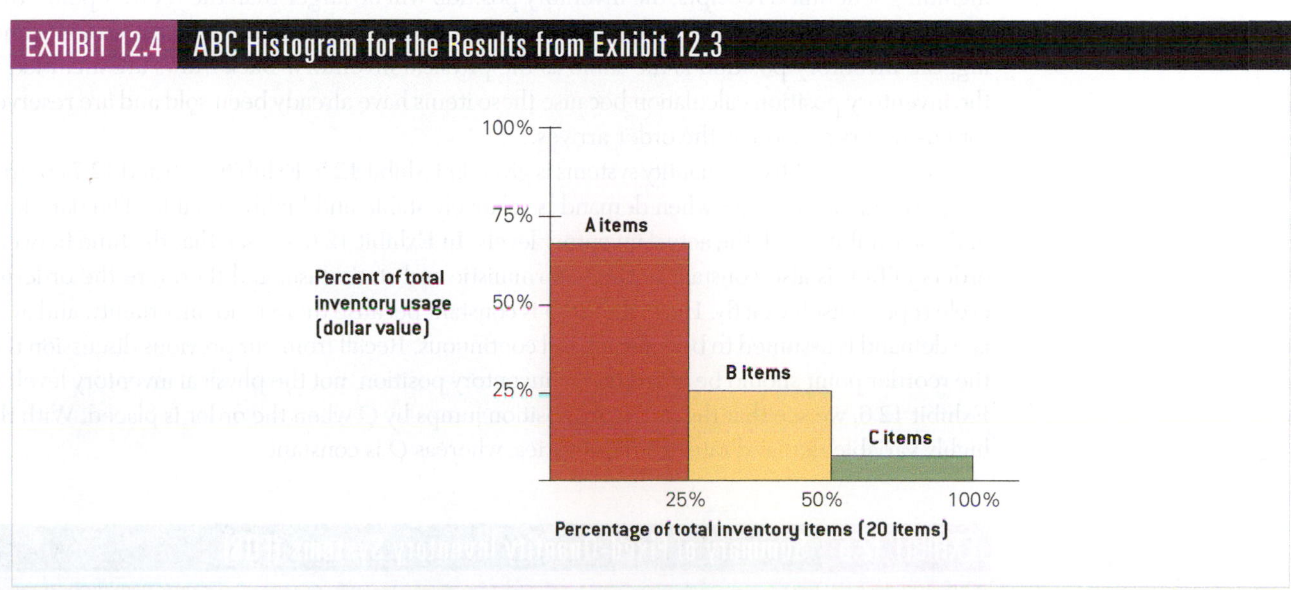

12-4 Managing Fixed-Quantity Inventory Systems

In a **fixed-quantity system (FQS),** *the order quantity or lot size is fixed; that is, the same amount, Q, is ordered every time*. The order quantity (Q) can be any quantity of product, such as a box, pallet, or container, as determined by the vendor or shipping standards; it does not have to be determined economically (see economic order quantity in the next section). FQSs are used extensively in the retail industry. For example, most department stores have cash registers that are tied into a computer system. When the clerk enters the SKU number, the computer recognizes that the item is sold, recalculates the inventory position, and determines whether a purchase order should be initiated to replenish the stock. If computers are not used in such systems, some form of manual system is necessary for monitoring daily usage. This requires substantial clerical effort and commitment by the users to fill out the proper forms when items are used and is often a source of errors, so it is not recommended.

A more appropriate way to manage an FQS is to continuously monitor the inventory level and place orders when the level reaches some "critical" value. The process of triggering an order is based on the inventory position. **Inventory position (IP)** *is defined as the on-hand quantity (OH) plus any orders placed but which have not arrived (called scheduled receipts, SR), minus any backorders (BO), or*

$$IP = OH + SR - BO \qquad [12.1]$$

When the inventory position falls at or below a certain value, r, called the *reorder point*, a new order is placed. *The* **reorder point** *is the value of the inventory position that triggers a new order*. Why not base the reordering decision on the physical inventory level—that is, just the on-hand quantity—instead of a more complex calculation? The answer is simple. When an order is placed but has not been received, the physical stock level will continue to fall below the reorder point before the order arrives. If the ordering process is automated, the computer logic will continue to place many unnecessary orders simply because it will see the stock level being less than r, even though the original order will soon arrive and replenish the stock. By including scheduled receipts, the inventory position will be larger than the reorder point, thus preventing duplicate orders. Once the order arrives and no scheduled receipts are outstanding, the inventory position is the same as the physical inventory. Backorders are included in the inventory position calculation because these items have already been sold and are reserved for customers as soon as the order arrives.

A summary of fixed-quantity systems is given in Exhibit 12.5. Exhibits 12.6 and 12.7 contrast the performance of FQS when demand is relatively stable and highly variable. The dark lines in these exhibits track the actual inventory levels. In Exhibit 12.6, we see that the time between orders (TBO) is also constant in the deterministic and static case, and therefore the ordering cycle repeats itself exactly. Here, the TBO is constant because there is no uncertainty, and average demand is assumed to be constant and continuous. Recall from our previous discussion that the reorder point should be based on the inventory position, not the physical inventory level. In Exhibit 12.6, we see that the inventory position jumps by Q when the order is placed. With the highly variable demand rate, the TBO varies, whereas Q is constant.

EXHIBIT 12.5 Summary of Fixed-Quantity Inventory Systems (FQS)

Ordering decision rule	A new order is triggered whenever the inventory position for the item drops to or past the reorder point. The size of each order is Q units.
Key characteristics	The order quantity Q is always fixed.
	The time between orders (TBO) is constant when the demand rate is stable.
	The TBO can vary when demand is variable.

EXHIBIT 12.6 Fixed-Quantity System (FQS) Under Stable Demand

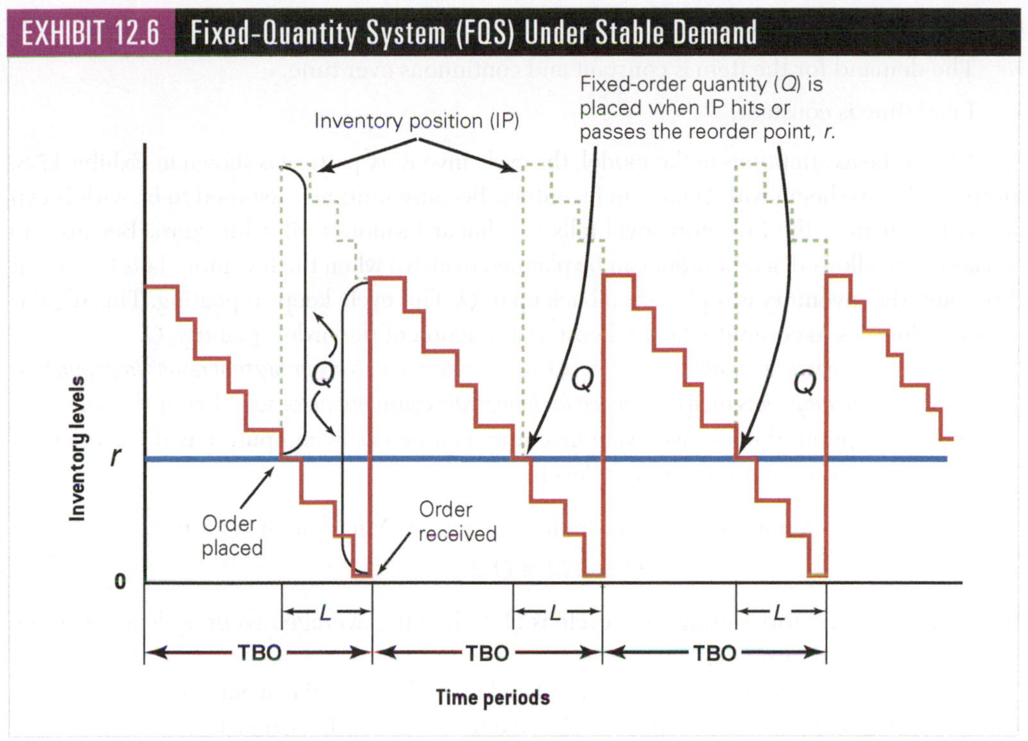

EXHIBIT 12.7 Fixed-Quantity System (FQS) with Highly Variable Demand

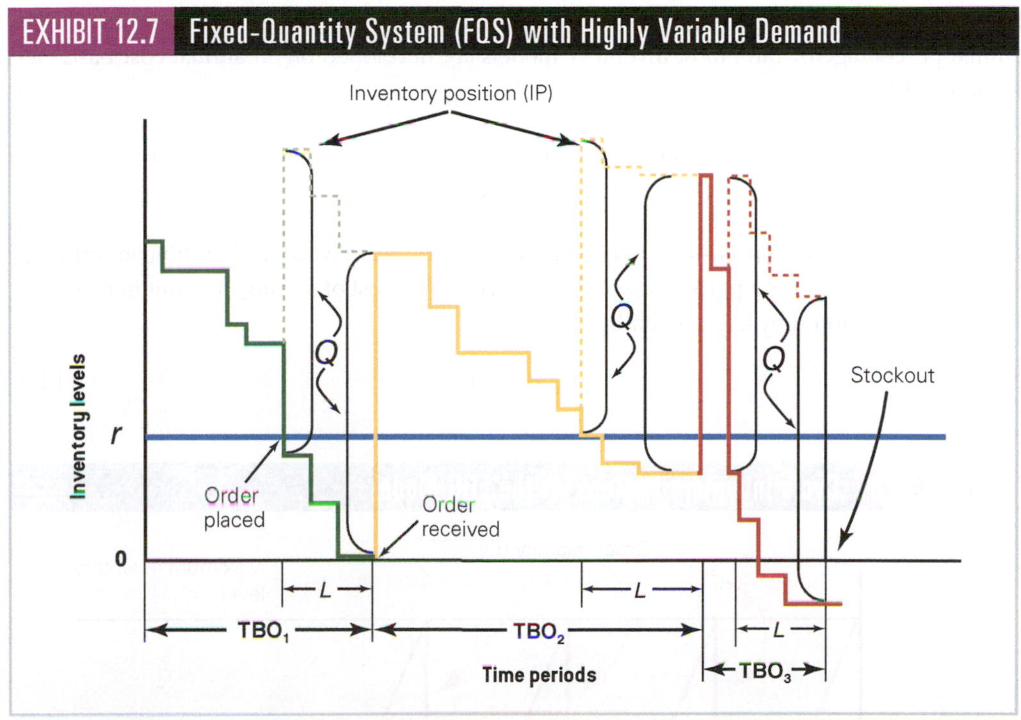

12-4a The EOQ Model

The **economic order quantity (EOQ)** *model is a classic economic model developed in the early 1900s that minimizes the total cost, which is the sum of the inventory-holding cost and the ordering cost.* Several key assumptions underlie the quantitative model we will develop:

- Only a single item (SKU) is considered.
- The entire order quantity (Q) arrives in the inventory at one time.
- Only two types of costs are relevant—order/setup and inventory-holding costs.

- No stockouts are allowed.
- The demand for the item is constant and continuous over time.
- Lead time is constant.

Under the assumptions of the model, the cycle inventory pattern is shown in Exhibit 12.8. Suppose that we begin with Q units in inventory. Because units are assumed to be withdrawn at a constant rate, the inventory level falls in a linear fashion until it hits zero. Because no stockouts are allowed, a new order can be planned to arrive when the inventory falls to zero; at this point, the inventory is replenished back up to Q. This cycle keeps repeating. This regular pattern allows us to compute the total cost as a function of the order quantity, Q.

Cycle inventory *(also called* **order** *or* **lot size inventory***) is inventory that results from purchasing or producing in larger lots than are needed for immediate consumption or sale.* From the constant demand assumption, the average cycle inventory can be easily computed as the average of the maximum and minimum inventory levels:

$$\begin{aligned}\text{Average cycle inventory} &= (\text{Maximum inventory} + \text{Minimum inventory})/2 \\ &= (Q + 0)/2 = Q/2\end{aligned} \qquad [12.2]$$

If the average inventory during each cycle is $Q/2$, then the average inventory level over any number of cycles is also $Q/2$.

The inventory-holding cost can be calculated by multiplying the average inventory by the cost of holding one item in inventory for the stated period (see Equation 12.5). The period of time selected for the model is up to the user; it can be a day, week, month, or year. However, because the inventory-holding costs for many industries and businesses are expressed as an annual percentage or rate, most inventory models are developed on an annual cost basis (see Equation 12.4). Let

I = annual inventory-holding charge expressed as a percent of unit cost

C = unit cost of the inventory item or SKU

I includes two types of costs—cost of capital (money) plus any inventory-handling and storage costs, both expressed as a percentage of the item cost. The cost of storing one unit in inventory for the year, denoted by C_h, is given by

$$C_h = I \times C \qquad [12.3]$$

EXHIBIT 12.8 Cycle Inventory Pattern for the EOQ Model

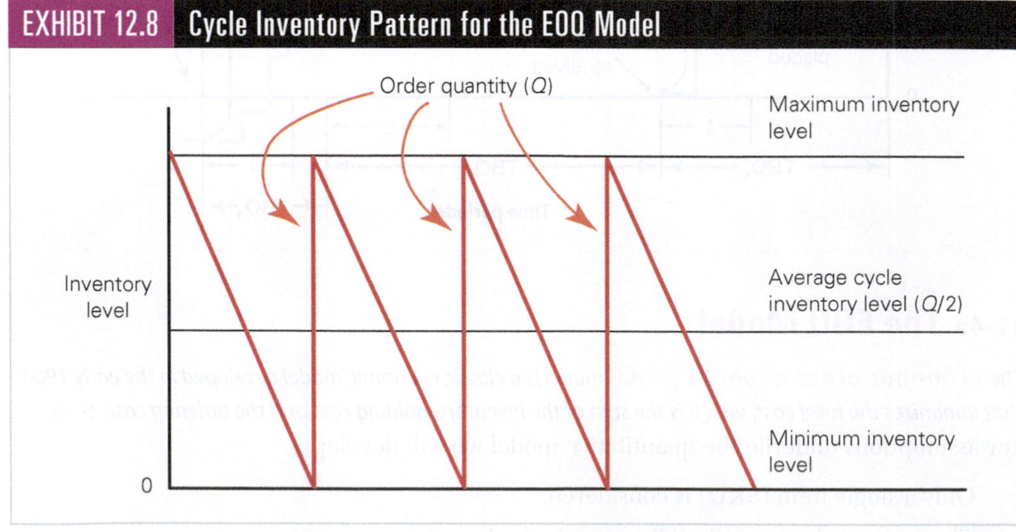

Thus, the general equation for annual inventory-holding cost is

$$\text{Annual inventory-holding cost} = \begin{pmatrix}\text{Average}\\ \text{inventory}\end{pmatrix}\begin{pmatrix}\text{Annual holding}\\ \text{cost}\\ \text{per unit}\end{pmatrix} = \frac{1}{2}QC_h \qquad [12.4]$$

The second component of the total cost is the ordering cost. Because the inventory-holding cost is expressed on an annual basis, we need to express ordering costs as an annual cost also. Letting D denote the annual demand for the product, we know that by ordering Q items each time we order, we have to place D/Q orders per year. If C_0 is the cost of placing one order, the general expression for the annual ordering cost is shown in Equation 12.5.

$$\begin{matrix}\text{Annual}\\ \text{ordering}\\ \text{cost}\end{matrix} = \begin{pmatrix}\text{Number of}\\ \text{orders}\\ \text{per year}\end{pmatrix}\begin{pmatrix}\text{Cost}\\ \text{per}\\ \text{order}\end{pmatrix} = \frac{D}{Q}C_0 \qquad [12.5]$$

Thus, the total annual cost is the sum of the inventory-holding cost given by Equation 12.4 plus the order or setup cost given by Equation 12.5:

$$TC = \frac{1}{2}QC_h + \frac{D}{Q}C_0 \qquad [12.6]$$

The next step is to find the order quantity, Q, that minimizes the total cost expressed in Equation 12.6. By using differential calculus, we can show that the quantity that minimizes the total cost, denoted by Q^*, is given by Equation 12.7. Q^* is referred to as the *economic order quantity*, or *EOQ*.

$$Q^* = \sqrt{\frac{2DC_0}{C_h}} \qquad [12.7]$$

Finally, we need to determine *when* to place an order for Q^* units. The reorder point, r, depends on the lead time and the demand rate. Because we assume that demand is constant in the EOQ model, the reorder point is found by multiplying the fixed demand rate, d (units/day, units/month, etc.), by the length of the lead time, L (in the same units, e.g., days or months). Note that it is easy to convert the annual demand D (in units/year) to a demand rate, d, having the same time units as the lead time.

$$\begin{aligned} r &= \text{Lead time demand} \\ &= \text{demand rate} \times \text{lead time} \qquad [12.8] \\ &= d \times L \end{aligned}$$

Note that in the total cost model (Equation 12.6), both the annual inventory holding cost and the annual ordering cost vary only with the order quantity, Q. If any fixed costs contribute to the total annual inventory cost, TC, such as the annual cost of purchasing inventory ($C \times D$), they would not impact the EOQ. Solved Problem 12.2 provides an example of applying the EOQ model.

SOLVED PROBLEM 12.2: COMPUTING AN ECONOMIC ORDER QUANTITY

The sales of a popular mouthwash at Merkle Pharmacies over the past 6 months have averaged 2,000 cases per month, which is the current order quantity. Merkle's cost is $12.00 per case. The company estimates its cost of capital to be 12 percent. Insurance, taxes, breakage, handling, and pilferage are estimated to be approximately 6 percent of item cost. Thus, the annual inventory-holding costs are estimated to be 18 percent of item cost. Because the cost of one case is $12.00, the cost of holding one case in inventory for 1 year, using Equation 12.4, is $C_h = (IC) = 0.18(\$12.00) = \$2.16$ per case per year.

The cost of placing an order is estimated to be \$38.00 per order regardless of the quantity requested in the order. From this information, we have

$$D = 24{,}000 \text{ cases per year.}$$
$$C_0 = \$38 \text{ per order.}$$
$$I = 18 \text{ percent.}$$
$$C = \$12.00 \text{ per case.}$$
$$C_h = IC = \$2.16.$$

Find the economic order quantity and the total cost associated with it, and compare the cost to the current purchasing policy of ordering 2,000 cases per month. What should the reorder point be?

Solution:

Thus, the minimum-cost economic order quantity (EOQ) as given by Equation 12.7 is

$$\text{EOQ} = \sqrt{\frac{2(24{,}000)(38)}{2.16}} = \text{919 cases rounded to a whole number}$$

For the data used in this problem, the total-cost model based on Equation 12.6 is

$$TC = \frac{1}{2}Q(\$2.16) + \frac{24{,}000}{Q}(\$38.00)$$
$$= \$1.08Q + 912{,}000/Q$$

For the EOQ of 919, the total cost is calculated to be (1.08)(919) + (24,000/919)(\$38.00) = \$1,984.90.

We can compare this total cost using EOQ with the current purchasing policy of $Q = 2{,}000$. The total annual cost of the current order policy is

$$TC = 1.08(2{,}000) + 912{,}000/2{,}000$$
$$= \$2{,}616.00$$

Thus, the EOQ analysis has resulted in a \$2,616.00 − \$1,984.90 = \$631.10 savings, or 24.1 percent cost reduction. Notice also that the total ordering costs (\$992) are equal to the total inventory-holding costs (\$992) for the EOQ. In general, this will always be true for the EOQ model. Exhibit 12.9 shows the Excel *EOQ Model* template available in MindTap, which finds the EOQ and optimal costs, and charts the cost functions. You can see the curve is relatively flat around the minimum-total-cost solution. The Sensitivity Analysis section allows you to compare the EOQ with any other order quantity.

To find the reorder point, suppose that the lead time to order a case of mouthwash from the manufacturer is $L = 3$ days. Considering weekends and holidays, Merkle operates 250 days per year. So, on a daily basis, the deterministic annual demand of 24,000 cases corresponds to a daily demand of $d = 24{,}000/250 = 96$ cases. per day. Thus, using Equation 12.8, we anticipate

EXHIBIT 12.9 ***EOQ Model* Excel Template**

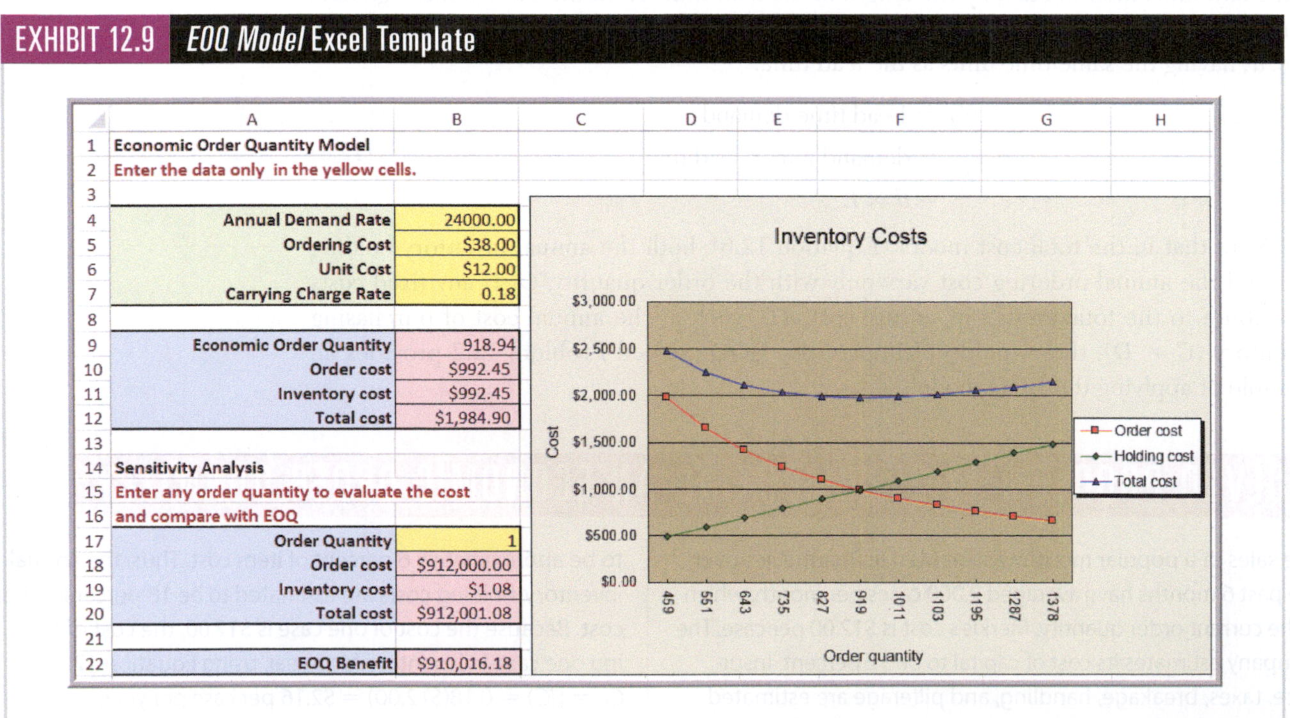

	A	B
1	Economic Order Quantity Model	
2	Enter the data only in the yellow cells.	
3		
4	Annual Demand Rate	24000.00
5	Ordering Cost	\$38.00
6	Unit Cost	\$12.00
7	Carrying Charge Rate	0.18
8		
9	Economic Order Quantity	918.94
10	Order cost	\$992.45
11	Inventory cost	\$992.45
12	Total cost	\$1,984.90
13		
14	Sensitivity Analysis	
15	Enter any order quantity to evaluate the cost	
16	and compare with EOQ	
17	Order Quantity	1
18	Order cost	\$912,000.00
19	Inventory cost	\$1.08
20	Total cost	\$912,001.08
21		
22	EOQ Benefit	\$910,016.18

that $r = d \times L = 96 \times 3 = 288$ cases to be sold during the 3-day lead time. Therefore, Merkle should order a new shipment from the manufacturer when the inventory level reaches 288 cases. Also note that the company will place $D/Q = 24{,}000/919 = 26.12$, or approximately 26 orders per year. With 250 working days per year, an order would be placed every (250 days per year)/(26.1 orders per year) = 9.6 days per order. This represents the average time between orders (TBO) of 9.6 days in Exhibit 12.6.

12-4b Quantity Discount Model

Many suppliers offer discounts for purchasing larger quantities of goods or services. This often occurs because of economies of scale, shipping larger loads, from not having to break apart boxes of items, or simply as an incentive to increase total revenue. You might have noticed such incentives at stores like Amazon, where books or other items are often advertised in discounted bundles—for example, two books by the same author for a lower price than buying them individually. For services, discounts might be based on the number of transactions, vehicles rented, website counts and hits, and gigabytes or terabytes used. Loyalty programs like those used by hotels and airlines are a form of providing discounts to customers based on volume.

To incorporate quantity discounts in the basic EOQ model requires us to include the purchase cost of the item in the total cost equation. We did not include the purchase cost of the item in the EOQ model because it does not affect the optimal order quantity. Because the annual demand is constant, the total annual purchase cost remains the same no matter what the individual order quantities are. However, when the unit price varies by order quantity, as would be the case with price breaks for quantity discounts, we need to incorporate that into the model. For instance, a company might offer several discount categories. As an example, suppose that for every item ordered up to 1,000, a base unit price applies; if the order is for 1,001 to 2,000 items, a discounted unit price (of, perhaps, two percent) applies; for every additional item ordered beyond 2,000, a larger discount (say, four percent) applies. We cannot use the EOQ formula, because different purchase costs result in different holding cost rates, and a calculated EOQ may not even fall within the appropriate discount category.

To compute the optimal order quantity, a three-step procedure is used:

Step 1. Compute Q^* using the EOQ formula for the unit cost associated with each discount category.

Step 2. For Q^*s that are too small to qualify for the assumed discount price, adjust the order quantity upward to the nearest order quantity that will allow the product to be purchased at the assumed price. If a calculated Q^* for a given price is larger than the highest order quantity that provides the particular discount price, that discount price need not be considered further, since it cannot lead to an optimal solution.

Step 3. For each of the order quantities resulting from steps 1 and 2, compute the total annual cost using the unit price from the appropriate discount category. The total annual cost can be found by adding the purchase cost (annual demand, D, times the unit cost, C) to the holding and order costs as shown in Equation [12.9]:

$$TC = \frac{Q}{2}C_h + \frac{D}{Q}C_0 + DC \qquad [12.9]$$

The order quantity yielding the minimum total annual cost is the optimal order quantity. Solved Problem 12.3 illustrates this procedure using the example in Solved Problem 12.2.

SOLVED PROBLEM 12.3: FINDING THE OPTIMAL ORDER SIZE FOR QUANTITY DISCOUNTS

Merkle Pharmacies (see Solved Problem 12.2) can obtain discounts from the manufacturer of mouthwash by ordering larger quantities than the economic order quantity of 919 cases:

Discount Category	Order Size	Discount	Unit Cost
1	0 to 3,999	0	$12.00
2	4,000 to 12,999	3%	$11.64
3	12,000 and over	5%	$11.40

The annual demand is 24,000 units, the carrying charge rate is 18 percent, and the order cost is $38.00. What is the optimal order size to minimize total inventory and purchase costs?

Solution:

The five-percent discount looks attractive; however, the 12,000-case order quantity is substantially more than the EOQ recommendation of 919 cases. The purchase discount might be outweighed by the larger holding costs that would have to be incurred if this quantity was ordered. Using the three-step procedure, we do the following:

Step 1: Using the EOQ formula [12.9] for each discount category using the appropriate unit costs, we find:

Discount Category	EOQ
1	919
2	933
3	943

Step 2: Adjust the order quantities for discount categories 2 and 3 to the minimum order sizes required for the discount:

Discount Category	Adjusted Order Size
1	919
2	4,000
3	12,000

Step 3: Use formula [12.9] to compute the total annual cost using the unit price for each discount category. Note that the holding cost, C_h, depends on the actual unit cost, so it is different for each category.

$$TC = \frac{Q}{2}C_h + \frac{D}{Q}C_o + DC$$

Discount Category	Adjusted Order Size	Holding Cost	Order Cost	Purchase Cost	Total Cost
1	919	$ 999.52	$992.38	$288,000	$289,984.90
2	4,000	$ 4,190.40	$228.00	$279,360	$283,778.40
3	12,000	$12,571.20	$ 76.00	$279,360	$292,007.20

The minimum total cost occurs for discount category 2. Therefore, the optimal decision is to order 4,000 units at the three-percent discount rate. Note that the sum of the inventory and ordering costs with $Q^* = 4{,}000$ is $4,190.40 + 228.00 = $4,418.40. This portion of the total cost is substantially more than the $1,984.90 cost associated with the 919-unit order size. In effect, the quantity-discount savings of three percent per unit is so great that we are willing to operate the inventory system with a substantially higher inventory level and substantially higher inventory-holding cost. Provided space is available to handle larger inventories, purchasing in larger quantities to obtain discounts is economically sound. The Excel *Quantity Discount* template in Exhibit 12.10, available in MindTap, performs the necessary calculations.

Exhibit 12.11 shows a chart of total inventory costs as a function of order size. You can see a saw tooth-type pattern over the categories.

EXHIBIT 12.10 Excel *Quantity Discount* Template

	A	B	C	D	E	F	G	H	I	J	K
1	Quantity Discount Inventory Model			Copyright © 2019 Cengage Learning							
2	Enter the data only in the yellow cells.			Not for commercial use.							
3											
4	Annual demand	24000		Discount	Minimum						
5	Cost per unit	$12.00		Category	Order Size	Discount (%)	Unit Cost				
6	Carrying charge	18%		1	0	0%	$12.00				
7	Order cost	$38.00		2	4000	3%	$11.64				
8				3	12000	5%	$11.40				
9				4							
10				6							
11											
12			Adjusted			Unit		Annual	Annual	Annual	Total
13	Discount		Order		Unit	Holding	Order	Holding	Ordering	Purchase	Annual
14	Category	EOQ	Size	Discount	Cost	Cost	Quantity	Cost	Cost	Cost	Cost
15	1	919	919	0%	$12.00	$2.16	919	$992.52	$992.38	$288,000.00	$289,984.90
16	2	933	4000	3%	$11.64	$2.10	4000	$4,190.40	$228.00	$279,360.00	$283,778.40
17	3	943	12000	5%	$11.40	$2.05	12000	$12,571.20	$76.00	$279,360.00	$292,007.20
18	4										
19	5										
20										Minimum cost	$283,778.40
21										Optimal order size	4000

EXHIBIT 12.11 Chart of Inventory Costs for Discount Categories

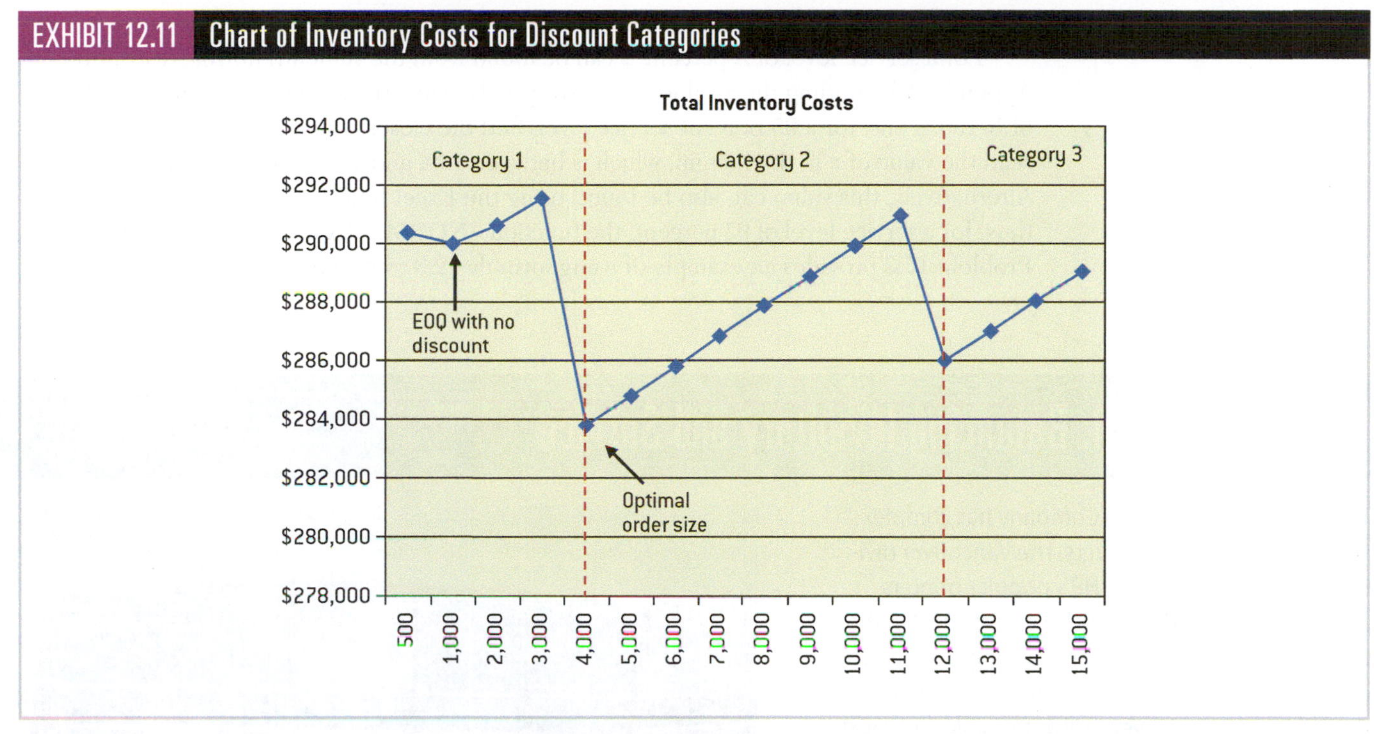

12-4c Safety Stock and Uncertain Demand in a Fixed-Order-Quantity System

Stockouts occur whenever the lead-time demand exceeds the reorder point. When demand is uncertain, using EOQ based only on the average demand will result in a high probability of a stockout. One way to reduce this risk is to increase the reorder point by adding additional stock—called safety stock—to the average lead time demand. **Safety stock** *is additional, planned on-hand inventory that acts as a buffer to reduce the risk of a stockout.*

To determine the appropriate reorder point, we first need to know the probability distribution of the lead-time demand, which we often assume to be normally distributed. The appropriate reorder point depends on the risk that management wants to take of incurring a stockout. *A* ***service level*** *is the desired probability of not having a stockout during a lead-time period.* For example, a 95 percent service level means that the probability of a stockout during the lead time is 0.05. Choosing a service level is a management policy decision.

When demand is uncertain, then the reorder point is the average demand during the lead time, μ_L plus the additional safety stock. The average demand during the lead time is found by multiplying the average demand per unit of time by the length of the lead time expressed in the same time units. When a normal probability distribution provides a good approximation of lead-time demand, the general expression for reorder point is

$$r = \mu_L + z\sigma_L \qquad [12.10]$$

where μ_L = average demand during the lead time

σ_L = standard deviation of demand during the lead time

z = the number of standard deviations necessary to achieve the acceptable service level

The term "$z\sigma_L$" represents the amount of safety stock.

For a service level of X percent, z can be found from the standard normal distribution in Appendix A by finding the z-value that corresponds to an area under the normal distribution of X/100. Thus, for a 95 percent service level, find the closest value in the table to 0.95, and read the value of z in the margin, which is between 1.64 and 1.65 (the actual value is 1.645). Alternatively, this value can also be found using the Excel function =NORM.S.INV(X/100), thus, for a service level of 95 percent, the function =NORM.S.INV(0.95) yields 1.645. Solved Problem 12.3 provides an example of using formula 12.9 to find the reorder point.

Hewlett-Packard: Balancing Inventory and Service

Ken Wolter/Shutterstock.com

The Hewlett-Packard (HP) Company has complex supply chains for its products. The Vancouver division manufactures one of HP's popular printers and ships them to distribution centers (DCs) in the United States, the Far East, and Europe. Because the printer industry is highly competitive, HP dealers like to carry as little inventory as possible, but must supply goods to end-users quickly. Consequently, HP operates under a lot of pressure to provide high levels of availability at the DCs for the dealers. DCs operate as inventory stocking points with large safety stocks to meet a target off-the-shelf fill rate, where replenishment of goods comes from manufacturing. HP developed a quantitative model to compute cost-effective target inventory levels considering safety stock to meet fill rate requirements. The model helped improve inventory investment by over 20 percent. What would the HP chief financial officer think of this result?[7]

SOLVED PROBLEM 12.4: COMPUTING THE REORDER POINT FOR A FIXED ORDER QUANTITY SYSTEM WITH UNCERTAIN DEMAND

Southern Office Supplies Inc. distributes office supplies to customers in the Southeast. One popular SKU is laser printer paper. Ordering costs are \$45.00 per order. One ream of paper costs \$3.80, and Southern uses a 20 percent annual inventory-holding cost rate. Thus, the inventory-holding cost is $C_h = IC = 0.20(\$3.80) = \$0.76$ per ream per year. The average annual demand is 15,000 reams, or about $15{,}000/52 = 288.5$ reams per week, and historical data shows that the standard deviation of weekly demand is about 71. The lead time from the manufacturer is 2 weeks. Compute the reorder point and the total annual cost. How much safety stock is maintained?

Solution:

To determine the reorder point, begin by using Equations 12.11 and 12.12. The average demand during the lead time (μ_L) is $(288.5)(2) = 577$ reams, and the standard deviation of demand during the lead time (σ_L) is approximately $71\sqrt{2} = 100$ reams. If Southern's managers desire a service level of 95 percent, we use the normal distribution tables in Appendix A or the Excel function =NORM.S.INV(0.95) to identify the standard normal *z*-value of 1.645. Therefore, the reorder point with safety stock using Equation 12.10, *r*, is

$$r = \mu_L + z\sigma_L = 577 + 1.645(100)$$
$$= 742 \text{ reams}$$

If we apply the EOQ model using the average annual demand, we find that the optimal order quantity would be

$$Q^* = \sqrt{\frac{2DC_o}{C_h}} = \sqrt{\frac{2(15{,}000)(45)}{0.75}} = 1{,}333 \text{ reams}$$

Using this EOQ, Southern can anticipate placing approximately 11 orders per year ($D/Q = 15{,}000/1{,}333$), slightly more than a month apart. Using Equation 12.7, the total annual cost is \$1,012.92. The safety stock is $742 - 577 = 165$ units.

The reorder point without any additional safety stock, using Equation 12.8, is $2(288.5) = 577$. Considering safety stock, a policy of ordering 1,333 reams whenever the inventory position reaches the reorder point of 742 will minimize inventory costs and incur a risk of at most a 5 percent probability of stockout during a lead-time period. Exhibit 12.12 shows the Excel *FQS Safety Stock* template available in MindTap for performing these calculations.

EXHIBIT 12.12 Excel *FQS Safety Stock* Template

	A	B	C	D	E
1	Fixed Order Quantity Inventory System				
2	with Uncertain Demand				
3	Enter the data only in the yellow cells.				
4					
5	Average Annual Demand	15000.00			
6	Ordering Cost	\$45.00			
7	Unit Cost	\$3.80			
8	Carrying Charge Rate	0.20			
9	Lead time (weeks)	2.00			
10	Standard deviation of weekly demand	71.00			
11	Service level	0.95			
12					
13	Economic Order Quantity	1332.78			
14	Order cost	\$506.46			
15	Inventory cost	\$506.46			
16	Total cost	\$1,012.92			
17					
18	Average demand during lead time	576.92			
19	Standard deviation during lead time	100.41			
20	z-value	1.64			
21	Safety stock	165			
22	Reorder point	742			

In many cases, we do not know the mean and standard deviation of demand during the lead time, but only for some other length of time such as a day or week. Suppose that μ_t and σ_t are the mean and standard deviation of demand for some time interval t, and that the lead time L is expressed in the same units (days, weeks, etc.). If the distributions of demand for all time intervals are identical to and independent of each other, we can use basic statistical results to find μ_L and σ_L based on μ_t and σ_t as follows:

$$\mu_L = \mu_t L \quad [12.11]$$

$$\sigma_L = \sigma_t \sqrt{L} \quad [12.12]$$

12-5 Managing Fixed-Period Inventory Systems

An alternative to a fixed-order-quantity system is **a fixed-period system (FPS)**—*sometimes called a periodic review system—in which the inventory position is checked only at fixed intervals of time, T, rather than on a continuous basis*. At the time of review, an order is placed for sufficient stock to bring the inventory position up to a predetermined maximum inventory level, M, sometimes called the replenishment level, or "order-up-to" level.

There are two principal decisions in an FPS:

1. The time interval between reviews.
2. The replenishment level.

We can set the length of the review period judgmentally based on the importance of the item or the convenience of review. For example, management might select to review noncritical SKUs every month and more critical SKUs every week. We can also incorporate economics using the EOQ model.

The EOQ model provides the best "economic time interval" for establishing an optimal policy for an FPS system under the model assumptions. This is given by

$$T = Q^*/D \quad [12.13]$$

where Q^* is the economic order quantity. The optimal replenishment level without any safety stock is computed by

$$M = d(T + L) \quad [12.14]$$

where d = average demand per time period (days, weeks, months, etc.), L is the lead time in the same time units, and M is the demand during the lead time plus review period. When demand is stochastic, managers can add appropriate safety stock to the optimal replenishment level to ensure a target service level.

A summary of fixed-period systems is given in Exhibit 12.13. Exhibit 12.14 shows the system operation graphically. In Exhibit 12.14, at the time of the first review, a rather large

EXHIBIT 12.13 Summary of Fixed-Period Inventory Systems

Managerial Decisions	Review Period (T) and Replenishment Level (M)
Ordering decision rule	Place a new order every T periods, where the order quantity at time t is $Q_t = M - IP_t$, and IP_t is the inventory position at the time of review, t.
Key characteristics	The review period, T, is constant, and placing an order is time-triggered.
	The order quantity, Q_t, varies at each review period.
	M is chosen to include the demand during the review period and lead time, plus any safety stock.
	Stockouts can occur when demand is stochastic and can be addressed by adding safety stock to the expected demand during time $T + L$.

EXHIBIT 12.14 Operation of a Fixed-Period System (FPS)

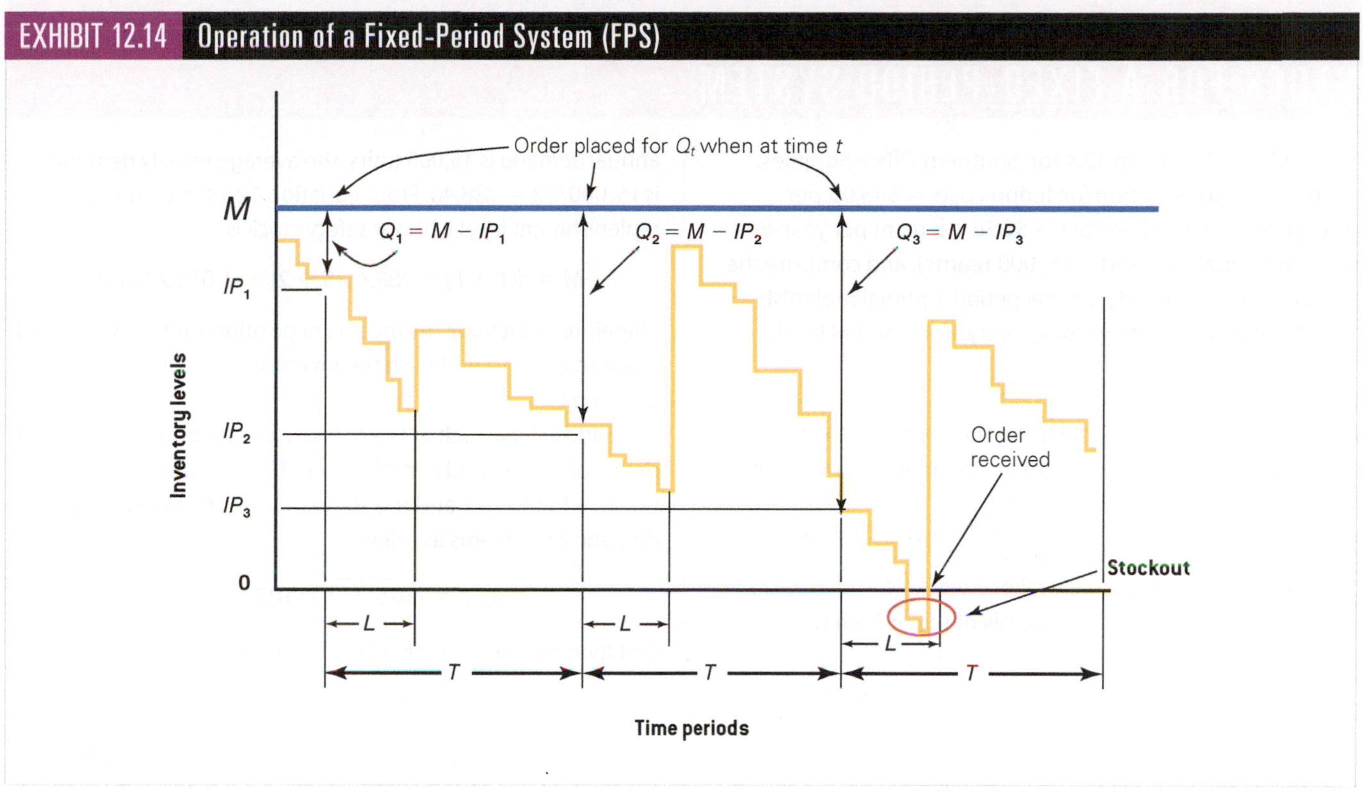

amount of inventory (IP_1) is in stock, so the order quantity (Q_1) is relatively small. Demand during the lead time was small, and when the order arrived, a large amount of inventory was still available. At the third review cycle, the stock level is much closer to zero because the demand rate has increased (steeper slope). Thus, the order quantity (Q_3) is much larger. During the lead time, demand was high and some stockouts occurred. Note that when an order is placed at time T, it does not arrive until time $T + L$. Thus, in using an FPS, managers must cover the risk of a stockout over the time period $T + L$, and therefore, must carry more inventory.

To add safety stock to the replenishment level (M) in an FPS, we can use the same statistical principles as with the FQS. We must compute safety stock over the period $T + L$, so the replenishment level is computed as follows:

$$M = \mu_{T+L} + z\sigma_{T+L} \quad [12.15]$$

$$\mu_{T+L} = \mu_t(T+L) \quad [12.16]$$

$$\sigma_{T+L} = \sigma_t\sqrt{T+L} \quad [12.17]$$

Solved Problem 12.5 provides an example of using these formulas for a fixed-period inventory system.

The choice of which system to use—FQS or FPS—depends on a variety of factors, such as how many total SKUs the firm must monitor, whether computer or manual systems are used, availability of technology and human resources, the nature of the ABC profile, and the strategic focus of the organization, such as customer service or cost minimization. Thus, the ultimate decision is a combination of technical expertise and subjective managerial judgment. Many other advanced inventory models are available (see the box, "There's More to Inventory Modeling"), but the FQS and FPS provide the foundation for these.

SOLVED PROBLEM 12.5: COMPUTING REPLENISHMENT LEVEL AND SAFETY STOCK FOR A FIXED-PERIOD SYSTEM

Refer to Solved Problem 12.4 for Southern Office Supplies. Use the same information (ordering costs = \$45.00 per order, inventory-holding cost = \$0.76 per ream per year, and average annual demand = 15,000 reams), and compute the economic order quantity, review period, optimal replenishment level without safety stock, safety stock, and M level.

Solution:

We can apply the EOQ model using the average annual demand, and find that the optimal order quantity would be

$$Q^* = \sqrt{\frac{2DC}{C_h}} = \sqrt{\frac{2(15,00)(45)}{0.76}} = 1,333 \text{ reams}$$

Data indicate that it usually takes 2 weeks ($L = 2$ weeks) for Southern to receive a new supply of paper from the manufacturer.

Using Equation 12.13 we compute the review period as

$$T = Q^*/D = 1,333/15,000 = .0889 \text{ years}$$

If we assume 52 weeks/year, then $T = 52(.0889) = 4.6$ weeks, which is approximately 5 weeks. Whether to round T up or down is a management decision. Because the average annual demand is 15,000 units, the average weekly demand is $15,000/52 = 288.46$. From Equation 12.14, the optimal replenishment level without safety stock is

$$M = d(T + L) = 288.46(5 + 2) = 2,019.22 \text{ units}$$

Therefore, we review the inventory position every 5 weeks and place an order to replenish the inventory up to an *M* level of 2,019 units.

To add safety stock to the *M* level, we compute the standard deviation of demand over the period $T + L$ using Equations 12.15 to 12.17 and the standard deviation of weekly demand of 71 reams as follows:

$$\sigma_{T+L} = 71\sqrt{5 + 2} = 187.8 \text{ reams}$$

and then the safety stock with a 95 percent service level is

$$z\sigma_{T+L} = 1.645(187.8) = 309 \text{ reams}$$

The *M* level with safety stock and a 95 percent service level is $M = 2,019 + 309 = 2,328$ reams. Exhibit 12.15 shows the Excel *FPS Safety Stock* template available in MindTap for performing these calculations.

EXHIBIT 12.15 Excel *FPS Safety Stock* Template

	A	B	C	D	E
1	Fixed Period Inventory System with Uncertain Demand				
2	Enter the data only in the yellow cells.				
3					
4	Average Annual Demand	15000.00			
5	Ordering Cost	\$45.00			
6	Unit Cost	\$3.80			
7	Carrying Charge Rate	0.20			
8	Lead time (weeks)	2.00			
9	Standard deviation of weekly demand	71.00			
10	Service level	0.95			
11					
12	Economic Order Quantity	1332.78			
13	Order cost	\$506.46			
14	Inventory cost	\$506.46			
15	Total cost	\$1,012.92			
16					
17	Review period (weeks, rounded up)	5			
18	Optimal replenishment level without safety stock	2019.23			
19	Standard deviation of demand during T+L	187.85			
20	z-value	1.64			
21	Safety stock	309			
22	M-Level	2328			

There's More to Inventory Modeling

The inventory models we discussed are the basic models for managing inventories. Many other models have been developed to assist managers in other situations. For example, there are cases in which it may be desirable—from an economic point of view—to plan for and allow shortages. This situation is most common when the value per unit of the inventory is very high, and hence the inventory-holding cost is high. An example is a new-car dealer's inventory. Most customers do not find the specific car they want in stock, but are willing to backorder it. Another example is when interactions among multiple SKUs must be considered. For example, limited warehouse capacity might restrict the amount of inventory that may be stored, and EOQs might not be appropriate. Another situation is when managers might limit the dollar value of inventory investment at any one time. For both of these situations, quantitative models have been developed for finding optimal inventory order policies.

Kevin_Hsieh/Shutterstock.com

12-6 Single-Period Inventory Model

The single-period inventory model applies to inventory situations in which one order is placed for a good in anticipation of a future selling season where demand is uncertain. At the end of the period the product has either sold out, or there is a surplus of unsold items to sell for a salvage value. Single-period models are used in situations involving seasonal or perishable items that cannot be carried in inventory and sold in future periods.

One example is the situation faced by clothing stores that must place orders as far as 6 months in advance of their selling seasons; other examples would be ordering dough for a pizza restaurant, which stays fresh for only 3 days, and purchasing seasonal holiday items such as Christmas trees. In such a single-period inventory situation, the only inventory decision is how much of the product to order at the start of the period. Because newspaper sales are a typical example of the single-period situation, the single-period inventory problem is sometimes referred to as the *newsvendor problem*.

The newsvendor problem can be solved using a technique called *marginal economic analysis*, which compares the cost or loss of ordering one additional item with the cost or loss of not ordering one additional item. The costs involved are defined as

c_s = the cost per item of overestimating demand (salvage cost); this cost represents the loss of ordering one additional item and finding that it cannot be sold.

c_u = the cost per item of underestimating demand (shortage cost); this cost represents the opportunity loss of not ordering one additional item and finding that it could have been sold.

The optimal order quantity is the value of Q^* that satisfies Equation 12.18:

$$P(\text{demand} \le Q^*) = \frac{c_u}{c_u + c_s} \qquad [12.18]$$

This formula can be used for any probability distribution of demand, such as a uniform or a normal distribution. Solved Problems 12.6 and 12.7 illustrate how to find optimal order quantities for uniform and normal probability distribution assumptions.

SOLVED PROBLEM 12.6: SINGLE-PERIOD INVENTORY MODEL WITH UNIFORM DEMAND

Let us consider a buyer for a department store who is ordering fashion swimwear about 6 months before the summer season. The store plans to hold an August clearance sale to sell any surplus goods by July 31. Each piece costs \$40 per pair and sells for \$60 per pair. At the sale price of \$30 per pair, it is expected that any remaining stock can be sold during the August sale. We will assume that a uniform probability distribution for demand ranging from 350 to 650 items, shown in Exhibit 12.16, describes the demand. Note that the expected demand is 500. Determine the optimal order quantity.

Solution:

The retailer will incur the cost of overestimating demand whenever it orders too much and has to sell the extra items available after July. Thus, the cost per item of overestimating demand is equal to the purchase cost per item minus the August sale price per item; that is, $C_s = \$40 - \$30 = \$10$. In other words, the retailer will lose \$10 for each item that it orders over the quantity demanded. The cost of underestimating demand is the lost profit (opportunity loss) due to the fact that it could have been sold but was not available in inventory. Thus, the per-item cost of underestimating demand is the difference between the regular selling price per item and the purchase cost per item; that is, $c_u = \$60 - \$40 = \$20$. The optimal order size Q must satisfy this condition:

$$P(\text{demand} \leq Q^*) = \frac{c_u}{c_u + c_s} = \frac{20}{20 + 10} = \frac{20}{30} = \frac{2}{3}$$

Because the demand distribution is uniform, the value of Q^* is two-thirds of the way from 350 to 650. Thus, $Q^* = 550$ swimwear SKUs. Note that whenever $c_u \leq c_s$, the formula leads to the choice of an order quantity more likely to be less than demand; hence a higher risk of a stockout is present. However, when $c_u > c_s$, as in the example, the optimal order quantity leads to a higher risk of a surplus.

Exhibit 12.17 shows the Excel *Single-Period Inventory* template available in MindTap for this example.

EXHIBIT 12.16 Probability Distribution for Single-Period Model

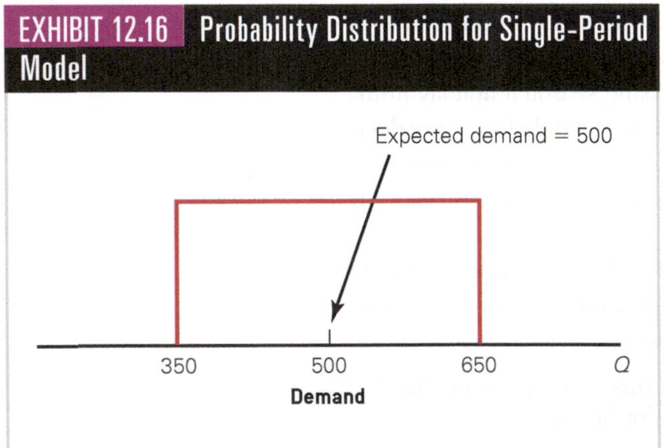

EXHIBIT 12.17 Excel *Single-Period Inventory* Template Using a Uniform Distribution

	A	B
1	Single Period Inventory Model	
2	Enter the data only in the yellow cells.	
3		
4	Item cost	\$40.00
5	Selling price	\$60.00
6	Sale price	\$30.00
7		
8	Cs	\$10.00
9	Cu	\$20.00
10	P(demand <= Q*)	0.67
11		
12	Uniform Distribution	
13	Minimum	350.00
14	Maximum	650.00
15	Optimal order quantity Q*	550.00
16		
17	Normal Distribution	
18	Mean	
19	Standard deviation	
20	Optimal order quantity Q*	

SOLVED PROBLEM 12.7: SINGLE PERIOD INVENTORY MODEL WITH NORMAL DEMAND

Consider the same scenario in Solved Problem 12.6, except that demand is normally distributed with a mean of 500 units and a standard deviation of 50 units. Determine the optimal order quantity.

Solution:

No matter what type of demand distribution is assumed, the same process applies. We find the value of Q^* that satisfies Equation 12.18. In this case, the optimal order quantity, Q^*, must still satisfy the requirement that $P(\text{demand} \leq Q^*) = 2/3$. Exhibit 12.18 shows the normal distribution for this situation. From Appendix A, the z-value corresponding to the shaded area of 0.67 is $z = 0.44$. Then Q^* is:

$$Q^* = \mu + 0.44\sigma = 500 + 0.44(50) = 522$$

EXHIBIT 12.18 Normal Distribution for Determining Q^*

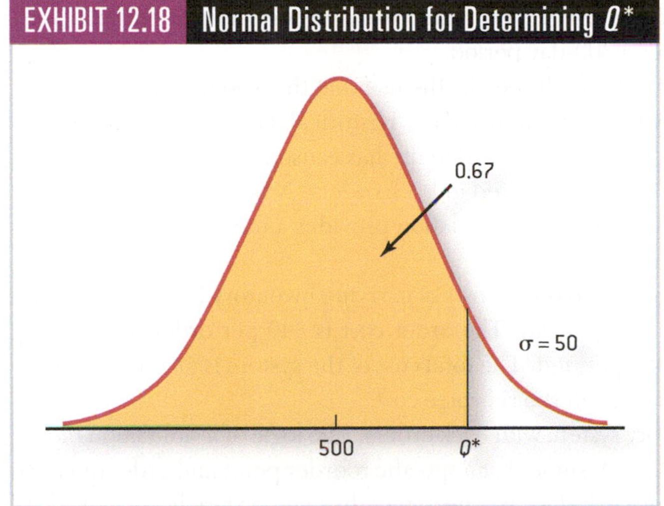

Alternatively, Q^* can be found using the Excel function =NORM.INV(*probability, mean, standard deviation*); thus =NORM.INV(0.67, 500, 50) = 522. Exhibit 12.19 shows the Excel *Single Period Inventory* template for this example.

EXHIBIT 12.19 Excel *Single Period Inventory* Template Using a Normal Distribution

	A	B
1	Single Period Inventory Model	
2	Enter the data only in the yellow cells.	
3		
4	Item cost	$40.00
5	Selling price	$60.00
6	Sale price	$30.00
7		
8	Cs	$10.00
9	Cu	$20.00
10	P(demand <= Q*)	0.67
11		
12	Uniform Distribution	
13	Minimum	
14	Maximum	
15	Optimal order quantity Q*	
16		
17	Normal Distribution	
18	Mean	500.00
19	Standard deviation	50.00
20	Optimal order quantity Q*	521.54

12-7 Simulation Modeling of Inventory Systems

Simulation is used extensively to improve process flows and supply chain effectiveness. In this section we demonstrate the use of simulation in making simple inventory-policy decisions. We will describe the logic of simulating a fixed-order-quantity system with backorders and use the Excel *Inventory Simulation* template available in MindTap. Supplement G provides an overview of basic concepts of simulation and how simulation models can be implemented on spreadsheets. We recommend that you review this before proceeding.

EXHIBIT 12.20 Historical Demand Data for Scott Audio Systems

Units Sold	Number of Days	Relative Frequency
0	150	0.50
1	75	0.25
2	45	0.15
3	15	0.05
4	15	0.05

EXHIBIT 12.21 Purchasing Lead Time

Lead time (days)	Frequency	Relative Frequency
1	6	0.20
2	3	0.10
3	12	0.40
4	6	0.20
5	3	0.10

Scott Audio Systems is a retail firm that carries high-quality audio equipment. Demand for one of its products varies, and can only be estimated using historical data. Exhibit 12.20 shows the frequencies of sales over a 300-day period.

The inventory problem is further complicated by the fact that the lead time in purchasing from the manufacturer varies between one and five days. Historical data on lead times for 30 orders is shown in Exhibit 12.21. The lead time variability has caused the store to run out of inventory on several occasions, which has resulted in back orders. Note that we have uncertainty in both the daily demand the lead time. Simulation provides a means of incorporating these uncertainties into a useful model.

An analysis of interest, insurance, and other costs of carrying inventory led to an estimate for the holding cost of $0.20 per unit per day. The order cost is $40 per order. Finally, the shortage cost is estimated to be $100 per unit. The total cost of the system is given by the sum of the ordering cost, the holding cost, and the shortage cost.

This is a fixed-quantity inventory system with back orders. The logic of a simulation model for one day is shown in Exhibit 12.22. Assume that a specific reorder point and order quantity have been selected. At the start of each day, we check whether any orders have arrived. If so, the current inventory on-hand is increased by the quantity received. We will assume that orders are received and inventory on-hand is updated at the start of each day.

Next, we generate a value for the daily demand using the relative frequency distribution in Exhibit 12.20. If there is sufficient inventory on-hand to meet the daily demand, the stock level is decreased by the amount of the daily demand. In addition, the inventory position (inventory on-hand plus scheduled receipts minus back orders—see Equation 12.1) is also decreased by the daily demand. If, however, inventory on-hand is not sufficient to satisfy all the demand, we satisfy as much of the demand as possible. Any unsatisfied demand will result in a backorder, for which we compute a shortage cost.

After the daily order has been processed, the next step is to determine if the inventory position has reached the reorder point and a new order should be placed. If an order is placed, the company incurs an ordering cost and a lead time must be randomly generated to reflect the time between the order placement and the receipt of the goods. Finally, an inventory-holding cost—20 cents for each unit in the daily ending inventory—is computed. The total daily cost is the sum of the shortage cost, ordering cost, and inventory-holding costs. The average cost/day is found by averaging the total costs in column T.

EXHIBIT 12.22 Simulation Logic for One Day's Operation

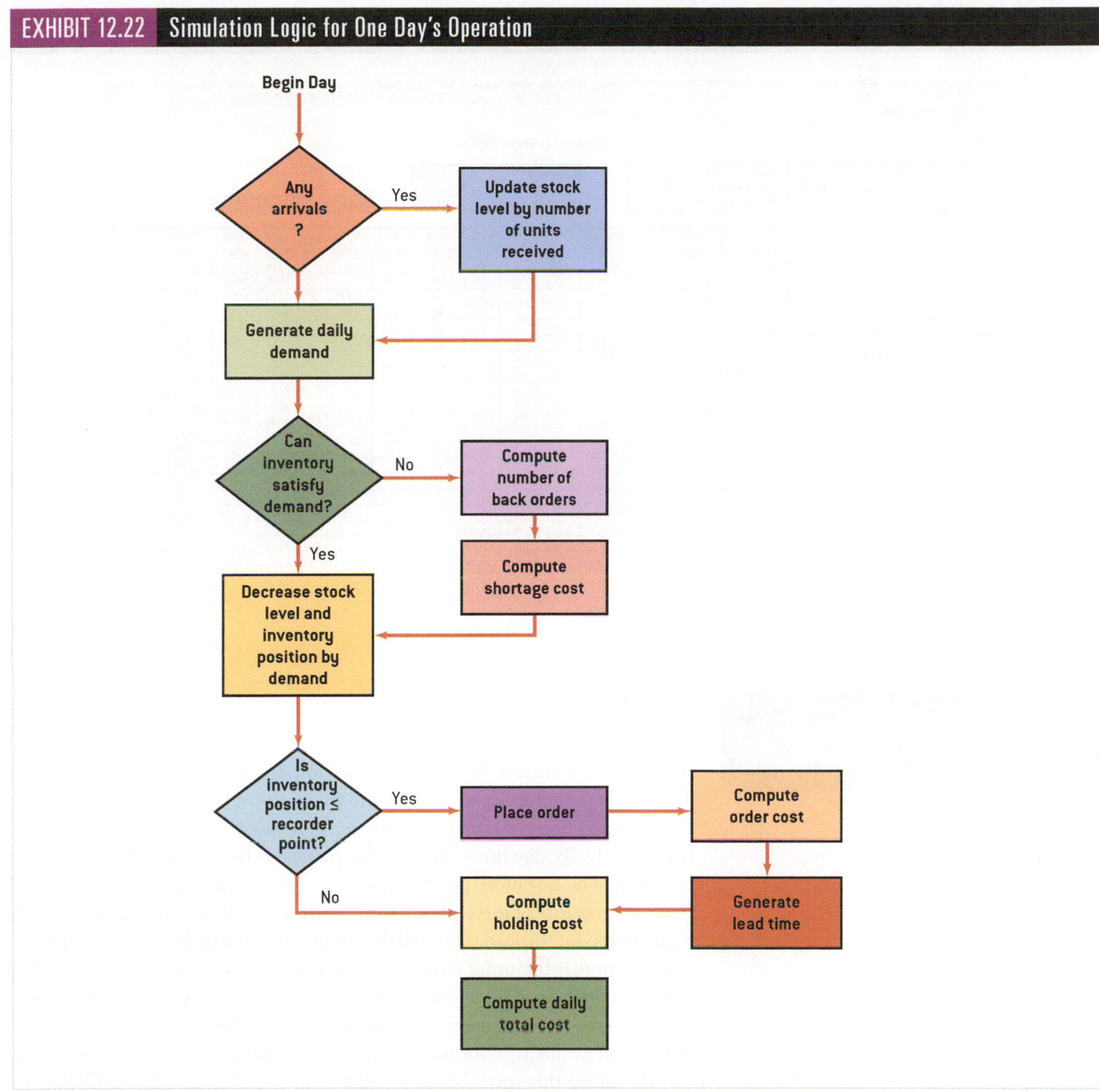

Because of the dynamic nature of the simulation process; that is, modeling the sequence of events that occur over time, we need to perform these calculations over a sufficient number of days to obtain meaningful results. How long to run a simulation model is essentially a statistical question similar to choosing a sample size for a confidence interval, for example. The longer a simulation model is run, the less the variability in results. The Excel template *Inventory Simulation* (available in MindTap) implements the logic in Exhibit 12.22 and uses the approaches described in Supplement G to generate random values from the demand and lead time distributions to simulate 50 days of operation. Exhibit 12.23 shows a portion of this spreadsheet for the first 20 days of the simulation.

To help you understand the logic, at the start of day one, five units are in inventory and no orders arrive (thus, the inventory position is also five). A random number, 0.225, is used to

EXHIBIT 12.23 Portion of Excel Template *Inventory Simulation*

Inventory Simulation

Enter the data only in the yellow cells.

This template is designed to allow up to 8 random number intervals for the demand and lead time distributions.

Copyright © 2017 Cengage Learning
Not for commercial use.

Demand Distribution		
Random Number Interval		Demand
0	0.5	0
0.5	0.75	1
0.75	0.9	2
0.9	0.95	3
0.95	1	4

Lead Time Distribution		
Random Number Interval		Lead Time
0	0.2	1
0.2	0.3	2
0.3	0.7	3
0.7	0.9	4
0.9	1	5

Order Quantity	5
Reorder Point	3
Initial Inventory	5

Order Cost	$40.00
Holding Cost	$0.20
Back Order Cost	$100.00

Average cost/day	$10.28

Day	Beg Inv	Order Rec'd	Units Rec'd	Random Number	Dmd	End Inv	Back Order	Order Placed?	Inv Pos	Random Number	Lead time	Hold Cost	Order Cost	Short Cost	Total Cost
1	5		0	0.225	0	5	0	NO	5			$1.00	$0.00	$0.00	$1.00
2	5		0	0.431	0	5	0	NO	5			$1.00	$0.00	$0.00	$1.00
3	5		0	0.867	2	3	0	YES	8	0.747	4	$0.60	$40.00	$0.00	$40.60
4	3		0	0.169	0	3	0	NO	8			$0.60	$0.00	$0.00	$0.60
5	3		0	0.697	1	2	0	NO	7			$0.40	$0.00	$0.00	$0.40
6	2		0	0.898	2	0	0	NO	5			$0.00	$0.00	$0.00	$0.00
7	0	YES	5	0.661	1	4	0	NO	4			$0.80	$0.00	$0.00	$0.80
8	4		0	0.057	0	4	0	NO	4			$0.80	$0.00	$0.00	$0.80
9	4		0	0.332	0	4	0	NO	4			$0.80	$0.00	$0.00	$0.80
10	4		0	0.041	0	4	0	NO	4			$0.80	$0.00	$0.00	$0.80
11	4		0	0.877	2	2	0	YES	7	0.821	4	$0.40	$40.00	$0.00	$40.40
12	2		0	0.447	0	2	0	NO	7			$0.40	$0.00	$0.00	$0.40
13	2		0	0.538	1	1	0	NO	6			$0.20	$0.00	$0.00	$0.20
14	1		0	0.048	0	1	0	NO	6			$0.20	$0.00	$0.00	$0.20
15	1	YES	5	0.531	1	5	0	NO	5			$1.00	$0.00	$0.00	$1.00
16	5		0	0.231	0	5	0	NO	5			$1.00	$0.00	$0.00	$1.00
17	5		0	0.979	4	1	0	YES	6	0.918	5	$0.20	$40.00	$0.00	$40.20
18	1		0	0.618	1	0	0	NO	5			$0.00	$0.00	$0.00	$0.00
19	0		0	0.337	0	0	0	NO	5			$0.00	$0.00	$0.00	$0.00
20	0		0	0.008	0	0	0	NO	5			$0.00	$0.00	$0.00	$0.00

EXHIBIT 12.24 Results for 20 Replications of the Inventory Simulation Model

Data Table Replication	
1	$25.97
2	$14.63
3	$14.32
4	$ 8.43
5	$10.49
6	$ 7.70
7	$28.11
8	$21.13
9	$20.68
10	$15.04
11	$20.67
12	$25.39
13	$ 6.96
14	$ 5.69
15	$15.86
16	$34.13
17	$39.37
18	$32.54
19	$21.14
20	$15.10
Average	$19.17

find the daily demand (in this case, zero) from the demand distribution table. Total daily cost consists of holding the five units at a unit cost of $0.20. On days two and three, the random numbers generate demands of zero and two, respectively. By day three, the reorder point has been reached, so an order is placed. The inventory position now increases by the amount of the order (ending inventory of three plus five units on order). A random number, 0.747, is generated for the lead time, and determines that the order will arrive in four days. Note that the order cost is now included in the total daily cost for day three. On day seven, this order arrives, bringing the physical inventory back up to four (after subtracting the demand of one on day seven). You should be able to follow the logic for the rest of the spreadsheet. Note, however, that if you download this spreadsheet template example, the numbers will change whenever the spreadsheet is recalculated.

The output from the simulation is the average total cost per day for using one particular order quantity and reorder point combination. Cell R4 computes the average daily cost over the 50 days of the simulation. For the results shown in Exhibit 12.23, the average cost/day is $10.28. Because of the randomness embedded in the model, recalculating the spreadsheet will result in a different result. However, we can use a data table as explained in Supplement G to replicate the simulation model multiple times and find a distribution of the average cost/day. Exhibit 12.24 shows the results from a data table for 20 replications of the spreadsheet. While there is considerable variability among the simulations, the overall average cost/day was $19.17.

The objective is to find the combination of order quantity and reorder point that will result in the lowest possible average cost/day. We will ask you to do this in a problem at the end of this chapter.

CHAPTER 12 LEARNING OBJECTIVE SUMMARIES

12.1 **Explain the importance of inventory, types of inventories, and key decisions and costs.** Inventories may be physical goods used in operations, and include raw materials, parts, subassemblies, supplies, tools, equipment or maintenance, and repair items. In some service organizations, such as airlines and hotels, inventories are not physical goods that customers take with them, but provide capacity available for serving customers. Inventory managers deal with two fundamental decisions:

1. When to order items from a supplier or when to initiate production runs if the firm makes its own items; and
2. How much to order or produce each time a supplier or production order is placed. Inventory management is all about making trade-offs among the costs associated with these decisions. Inventory costs can be classified into four major categories: ordering or setup costs, inventory-holding costs, shortage costs, and unit cost of the SKUs.

12.2 **Describe the major characteristics that impact inventory decisions.** One of the first steps in analyzing an inventory problem should be to describe the essential characteristics of the environment and inventory system:

1. *Number of items.* To manage and control these inventories, each item is often assigned a unique identifier, called a stock-keeping unit (SKU).
2. *Nature of demand.* Demand can be classified as independent or dependent, deterministic or stochastic, and dynamic or static.
3. *Number and size of time periods.* The type of approach used to analyze "single-period" inventory problems is different from the approach needed for the "multiple-period" inventory situation.
4. *Lead time.* Lead time is affected by transportation carriers, buyer order frequency and size, and supplier production schedules and may be deterministic or stochastic (in which case it may be described by some probability distribution).
5. *Stockouts.* Backorders result in additional costs for transportation, expediting, or perhaps buying from another supplier at a higher price. A lost sale has an associated opportunity cost, which may include loss of goodwill and potential future revenue.

12.3 **Describe how to conduct an ABC inventory analysis.** ABC analysis consists of categorizing inventory items or SKUs into three groups according to their total annual dollar usage.

1. "A" items account for a large dollar value but a relatively small percentage of total items.
2. "C" items account for a small dollar value but a large percentage of total items.
3. "B" items are between A and C.

Class A items require close control by operations managers. Class C items need not be as closely controlled and can be managed using automated computer systems. Class B items are somewhere in the middle.

12.4 **Explain how a fixed-order-quantity inventory system operates and how to use the EOQ, quantity discount, and safety stock models.** A way to manage a fixed-order-quantity system (FQS) is to continuously monitor the inventory level and place orders when the level reaches some "critical" value. The process of triggering an order is based on the inventory position. When the inventory position falls at or below a certain value, *r*, called the *reorder point*, a new order is placed (see Exhibits 12.5 and 12.6).

The total annual cost for the EOQ model is

$$TC = \frac{1}{2}QC_h + \frac{D}{Q}C_0. \qquad [12.6]$$

The order quantity that minimizes the total cost, denoted by Q^*, is

$$Q^* = \sqrt{\frac{2DC_0}{C_h}} \qquad [12.7]$$

The reorder point depends on the lead time and the demand rate. One approach to choosing the reorder point is to use the *average demand during the lead time* (μL). If d is the demand per unit of time (day, week, etc.), and L is the lead time expressed in the same units of time, then the demand during the lead time is calculated as $r = d\,L$.

To incorporate quantity discounts in the basic EOQ model requires us to include the purchase cost of the item in the total cost equation. To compute the optimal order quantity, a three-step procedure is used:

Step 1. Compute Q^* using the EOQ formula for the unit cost associated with each discount category.

Step 2. For Q^*s that are too small to qualify for the assumed discount price, adjust the order quantity upward to the nearest order quantity that will allow the product to be purchased at the assumed price. If a calculated Q^* for a given price is larger than the highest order quantity that provides the particular discount price, that discount price need not be considered further, since it cannot lead to an optimal solution.

Step 3. For each of the order quantities resulting from steps 1 and 2, compute the total annual cost using the unit price from the appropriate discount category. The total annual cost can be found by adding the purchase cost (annual demand, D, times the unit cost, C) to the holding and order costs as shown in Equation [12.9]:

$$TC = \frac{Q}{2}C_h + \frac{D}{Q}C_0 + DC \qquad [12.9]$$

When demand is uncertain, we may reduce the risk of a stockout by adding additional stock—called safety stock—to the average lead-time demand, thus increasing the reorder point. Choosing the appropriate amount of safety stock depends on the risk that management wants to take of incurring a stockout. This is specified by the service level—the probability of not having a stockout during a lead-time period. For normally distributed demand, the reorder point is $r = \mu_L + z\sigma_L$, where μ_L = average demand during the lead time, σ_L = standard deviation of demand during the lead time, and z = the number of standard deviations necessary to achieve the acceptable service level.

CHAPTER 12 LEARNING OBJECTIVE SUMMARIES

12.5 **Explain how a fixed-period inventory system operates.** For a fixed-period inventory system, at the time of review, an order is placed for sufficient stock to bring the inventory position up to a predetermined maximum inventory level, *M*, sometimes called the *replenishment level*, or *"order-up-to" level.* We can set the length of the review period judgmentally based on the importance of the item or the convenience of review. The EOQ model provides the best "economic time interval" for establishing an optimal policy for an FPS system under the model assumptions. This is given by $T = Q^*/D$. The optimal replenishment level is computed by $M = d(T + L)$, where d = average demand per time period, L is the lead time, and *M* is the demand during the lead time plus review period (see Exhibits 12.13 and 12.14). Safety stock can also be added to *M*, if desired.

12.6 **Describe how to apply the single-period inventory model.** The single-period inventory model applies to inventory situations in which one order is placed for a good in anticipation of a future selling season where demand is uncertain. At the end of the period, the product has either sold out or there is a surplus of unsold items to sell for salvage value.

The news-vendor problem can be solved using a technique called *marginal economic analysis*, which compares the cost or loss of ordering one additional item with the cost or loss of not ordering one additional item. The costs involved are defined as

- c_s = the cost per item of overestimating demand (salvage cost); this cost represents the loss of ordering one additional item and finding that it cannot be sold.
- c_u = the cost per item of underestimating demand (shortage cost); this cost represents the opportunity loss of not ordering one additional item and finding that it could have been sold.

The optimal order quantity is the value of Q* that satisfies

$$P(\text{demand} \le Q^*) = \frac{c_u}{c_u + c_s} \qquad [12.18]$$

12.7 **Conduct and analyze simulation models for fixed-order-quantity systems with uncertain demand and lead times using the Excel *Inventory Simulation* template.** A fixed order quantity simulation model can be developed on a spreadsheet by following the logic in the flowchart in Exhibit 12.22. The *Inventory Simulation* Excel template implements this logic for input values of the order quantity, reorder point, initial inventory, inventory costs, and discrete probability distributions of demand and lead time (see Exhibit 12.23). Data tables (see Supplement G) can be used to replicate the simulation model multiple times to find a distribution of the average cost/day. By experimenting with different values of the order quantity and reorder point, we can seek the lowest possible inventory cost.

KEY TERMS

- Backorder
- Cycle inventory or order (lot size) inventory
- Dependent demand
- Dynamic demand
- Economic order quantity (EOQ)
- Environmentally preferable purchasing (EPP) or green purchasing
- Finished-goods inventory
- Fixed-period system (FPS)
- Fixed-quantity system (FQS)
- Independent demand
- Inventory
- Inventory management
- Inventory position (IP)
- Inventory-holding or inventory-carrying costs
- Lead time
- Lost sale
- Ordering costs or setup costs
- Raw materials, component parts, subassemblies, and supplies
- Reorder point
- Safety stock
- Service level
- Shortage or stockout costs
- Static demand
- Stock-keeping unit (SKU)
- Stockout
- Unit cost
- Work-in-process (WIP) inventory

REVIEW QUESTIONS

12.1 1. Define inventory and provide some examples.

12.1 2. Explain the importance of inventory, types of inventories, and key decisions and costs.

12.1 3. How does inventory affect a firm's financial performance?

12.1 4. Define environmentally preferable purchasing or green purchasing.

12.1 5. Define and explain the different types of inventory costs that managers must consider in making replenishment decisions. How can these costs be determined in practice?

12.1 6. How does order cost differ from setup cost?

12.2 7. What is a SKU? Provide some examples in both goods and services.

12.2 8. Explain the difference between independent and dependent demand, deterministic and stochastic demand, and static and dynamic demand. Provide an example of an inventory item for each combination of these demand types (e.g., independent, stochastic, and static, and so on).

12.2 9. Define lead time. What factors affect lead time?

12.2 10. Describe the two different types of stockouts that firms often face. What must be done to prevent them?

12.2 11. Describe the major characteristics that impact inventory decisions.

12.3 12. Describe how to conduct an ABC inventory analysis. ABC analysis consists of categorizing inventory items or SKUs into three groups according to their total annual dollar usage.

12.4 13. Define inventory position. Why is inventory position used to trigger orders in a FQS rather than the actual stock level?

12.4 14. Define cycle inventory and explain how it is computed.

12.4 15. What is the EOQ model? What assumptions are necessary to apply it? How do these assumptions change the nature of the cycle inventory pattern graphically?

12.4 16. Explain how the total annual inventory cost is expressed in the EOQ model.

12.4 17. Discuss the sensitivity of the EOQ model's optimal solution to changes in the model parameters. Why is this important?

12.4 18. How are optimal lot sizes for a quantity discount model computed?

12.4 19. Define service level. Why is it not necessarily desirable to attempt to attain a 100-percent service level?

12.4 20. Explain how a fixed-order-quantity inventory system operates and how to use the EOQ and safety stock models.

12.5 21. Explain how a fixed-period inventory system operates.

12.6 22. Describe how to apply the single period inventory model.

12.6 23. Provide three examples of where the single period model would apply in practice.

DISCUSSION QUESTIONS AND EXPERIENTIAL ACTIVITIES

12.1 24. List some products in your personal or family "inventory." How do you manage them? (For instance, do you constantly run to the store for milk after it is gone? Do you throw out a lot of milk because of spoilage?) How might the ideas in this chapter change your way of managing these SKUs?

12.1 25. Discuss some of the issues that a small pizza restaurant might face in inventory management. Would a pizza restaurant use a fixed-order quantity or period system for fresh dough (purchased from a bakery on contract)? What would be the advantages and disadvantages of each in this situation?

12.1 26. Find two examples of using RFID technology to monitor and control SKUs and explain the advantages and disadvantages of adopting such technology.

12.1 27. Interview a manager at a local business about his or her inventory and materials-management system, and prepare a report summarizing its approaches. Does the system use any formal models? Why or why not? How does the manager determine inventory-related costs?

12.1 28. Provide examples of perishable inventory. How does fresh fruit differ from a concert seat even though both are perishable?

12.1 29. Find, describe, and draw an organization's supply chain and identify the types of inventory in it and, if possible, their purpose and how they are monitored and controlled. (The example could be a place you worked such as a call center, restaurant, factory, retail store, hotel, school, or medical office.)

12.4 30. Does the EOQ increase or decrease if estimates of setup (order) costs include fixed, semi-variable, and pure variable costs while inventory-holding costs include only pure variable costs? Vice versa? What are the implications? Explain.

12.4 31. The Lemma Company manufactures and sells ten products. Managers find ways to reduce the setup and inventory-holding costs by one-half. What effect will this have on the EOQs for the ten products?

12.4 32. Why are quantity discounts often given by suppliers? How do these affect the customer's inventory decisions?

12.5 33. Why does the fixed-period model have to cover the time period of T + L, while the fixed-order quantity model must cover only the time period L? Why is this important?

12.7 34. When is simulation useful in analyzing inventory systems?

COMPUTATIONAL PROBLEMS AND EXERCISES

These exercises require you to apply the formulas and methods described in the chapter. The problems should be solved manually.

12.4 35. What is the inventory position if the on-hand quantity is 462 units, scheduled receipts are 200 units, and 130 units are on backorder?

12.4 36. If the order quantity is 220 units, inventory-carrying costs are 24 percent year, and each unit costs $18, what is the average cycle inventory? How much does it cost to carry this cycle inventory year?

12.4 37. What are the z-values for service levels of 80, 85, 90, 95, and 99 percent, assuming demand is normally distributed?

12.4 38. Rapallo Sneakers, Inc. sells a pair of LG sneakers for $40. Due to the recent fitness craze, these shoes are in high demand: 45 pairs of shoes are sold per week. The ordering cost is $40 per order, and the annual holding cost is 20 percent of the selling price. If the store operates 50 weeks a year, what can you say about the size of the current order quantity of 250 pairs?

12.4 39. Using the information for Rapallo Sneakers, Inc. in Problem 38, how much could be saved by ordering the EOQ?

12.4 40. Alice opens an aquarium store in a lively shopping mall and finds business to be booming, but she often stocks out of key items customers want. She decides to experiment with inventory-control methods, such as using a fixed-order quantity (FQS) and/or fixed-order period (FPS) systems. The FLUVAL 303 Pump, a high margin and profitable pump, is one of her best sellers, but it stocks out frequently. You collect the following data with respect to this pump's sales.

Demand = five units week	Store open 50 weeks/year
Order cost = $40/order	Lead-time = three weeks
Item cost = $80/pump	Std. deviation in weekly demand = 6
Inventory-holding cost = 15 percent year	Service level = 96 percent

a. What is inventory-carrying (holding) cost pump year?
b. What is the economic order quantity ?
c. What is the average number of orders per year if using the EOQ?
d. What is the reorder point without safety stock?
e. What is the safety stock quantity?
f. What is the reorder point with safety stock?
g. If the current order quantity used by Alice is 20 pumps per order, how much money can she save by adopting an EOQ ordering policy?

12.4 41. If the EOQ = 80 units, annual demand = 500 units, and there are 50 weeks in a year, what is the fixed-order interval for a fixed-period system?

12.4 42. Cynthia Baker, manager of a large medical supply house that operates 50 weeks per year and six days per week, has decided to implement a fixed-period inventory system for all class A items. One such item has the following characteristics:

Demand = 10,000 units/year
Order cost = $50/order
Holding cost = $4/unit/year

If Cynthia wishes to minimize total cost (thereby approximating the EOQ), what should the review period (i.e., the number of workdays between orders) be?

12.4 43. Brenda opened a pool and spa store in a lively shopping mall and finds business to be booming but she often stocks out of key items customers want. She decides to experiment with inventory control methods, such as using a continuous review (fixed-order quantity) and/or periodic review (fixed-order period) system. The 28-ounce bottle of Super Algaecide (SA) is a high margin SKU, but it stocks out frequently. Ten SA bottles come in each box, and she orders boxes from a vendor 160 miles away. Brenda is busy running the store and seldom has time to review store inventory status and order the right quantity at the right time. She collected the following data:

Demand = 10 boxes per week	Store open 48 weeks/year
Order cost = \$40/order	Lead-time = 4 weeks
Item cost = \$80/box	Std. deviation in weekly demand = 6
Inventory holding cost = 15 percent per year	Service level = 90 percent

a. What is the economic order quantity (EOQ) rounded to the next highest number?

b. What is the reorder point for SA with safety stock?

c. What is the average number of orders per year using the EOQ?

12.4 44. Brenda, in problem 43, wants to consider setting up a fixed-period inventory system for the 28-ounce bottle of Super Algaecide (SA) SKU. At the beginning of the current week, D. J. Kole, the materials manager, checked the inventory level and found
55 units on-hand. There were no scheduled receipts and 25 units were on backorder.

a. What is the review period (T) rounded up to a whole number?

b. What is stock replenishment level with safety stock (M)?

c. How many units should be ordered?

12.4 45. TV Galore is a new specialty store that sells television sets, video games, and other television-related products. A new Japanese-manufactured game sells cost \$400. Because such games have a short life cycle and can be considered somewhat perishable, inventory-carrying cost is high. It is at an annual rate of 25 percent of SKU value. Ordering costs are estimated to be \$80 per order. Annual demand is forecast at 900 units next year. The standard deviation of daily demand is seven units, the desired service level is 95 percent, the lead time is five weeks, and assume 52 weeks per year.

a. Set up a fixed-order-quantity system computing the EOQ, reorder point with safety stock, and total order and inventory carrying costs.

b. Setup a fixed-period system computing the review period (T) and the replenishment level (M) with safety stock. Round the review period to the next highest number.

c. How much more does it cost to carrying inventory in a FPS than a FQS using only dL versus $d(T + L)$ and safety stock = $z\sigma_L$ versus $z\sigma_{T+L}$?

12.4 46. After one year you are promoted to assistant manager and realize current inventory management practices are not systematic with too much stock of some SKUs and too little of others. Your retail store operates 52 weeks per year and one SKU you stock is a high-end cell phone. The company's current order quantity is 250 cell phones per order. You collect the following information about this cell phone and want to set up a fixed-order quantity (FQS) to impress higher-level managers and get promoted again!

Demand	12.5 cell phones per week
Lead time	four weeks
Order cost	\$20/order
Holding cost	\$1.20/cell phone/year
Cycle service level	95 percent
Standard deviation of weekly demand	6 cell phones

Current on-hand inventory is 35 cell phones, with a scheduled receipt for 20 cell phones and no backorders.

a. What is the economic order quantity (EOQ)?

b. What is the reorder point with safety stock?

c. Based on the FQS information calculated previously, should an order be placed and if so, for how many cell phones?

d. What is the total annual cost savings using the EOQ you computed previously versus the current ordering policy of $Q = 250$ cell phones?

e. If you change to a fixed-period system (FPS) and all other information remains the same, what is the review period (T)?

f. What is the replenishment level (M) with safety stock for this FPS?

12.4 47. JAZ Medical Supplies is implementing a new economic order quality (EOQ) inventory-control system and needs a good estimate of the cost to process a purchase order (PO); i.e, the order cost C_o. It takes four total labor hours to process a PO. The average number of SKUs on a PO is four. The average wage for people working in the purchasing department is $22 per hour plus employee benefits of $3 per hour. Fixed costs for the purchasing department are $300,000 per year assuming 2,000 hours per employee per year workweek. Given this information, what is a good estimate of C_o per SKU to use in an EOQ model?

12.4 48. Bishop Manufacturing is implementing an economic order quality (EOQ) inventory-control system and needs a good estimate of the cost to process a purchase order (PO). It takes five total labor hours to process a PO. The average number of stock keeping units (SKUs) on a PO is 2.2. The average wage for people working in the purchasing department is $22 per hour plus employee benefits of $3 per hour. Fixed-costs for the purchasing department are $250,000 per year assuming a 2,000 hour per employee per year work week. What is a good estimate of the cost to order one SKU?

12.4 49. Given the weekly demand data in Exhibit 12.25 illustrate the operation of a fixed-order-quantity inventory system with a reorder point of 75, an order quantity of 100, and a beginning inventory of 125. Lead time is one week. All orders are placed at the end of the week. Using Equation 12.1, what is the average inventory and number of stockouts?

EXHIBIT 12.25 Problem 49 Demand Data

Week	Demand
1	25
2	30
3	20
4	40
5	40
6	25
7	50
8	35
9	30
10	40
11	20
12	25

12.4 50. Exhibit 12.26 gives the daily demand of a certain oil filter at an auto supply store. Illustrate the operation of a fixed-order-quantity inventory system by graphing the inventory level versus time if $Q = 40$, $R = 15$, and the lead time is three days. The beginning inventory on day one is 30 units. Assume that orders are placed at the end of the day and that they arrive at the beginning of the day. Therefore, if an order is placed at the end of day five, it will arrive at the beginning of day nine. Assume that 30 items are on hand at the start of day one. Use Equation 12.1 to evaluate the inventory position and when to place orders.

EXHIBIT 12.26 Problem 50 Oil Filter Demand Data

Day	Demand
1	6
2	8
3	5
4	4
5	5
6	6
7	1
8	1
9	3
10	8
11	8
12	6
13	7
14	0
15	2
16	4
17	7
18	3
19	5
20	9
21	3
22	6
23	1
24	9
25	1

12.4 51. The reorder point is defined as the demand during the lead time for the item. In cases of long lead times, the lead-time demand and thus the reorder point may exceed the economic order quantity, Q^*. In such cases the inventory position will not equal the inventory on hand when an order is placed, and the reorder point may be expressed in terms of either inventory position or inventory on hand. Consider the EOQ model with $D = 5{,}000$, $C_o = \$32$, $C_h = \$2$, and 250 working days per year. Identify the reorder point in terms of inventory position and in terms of inventory on hand for each of these lead times.

a. five days
b. 15 days
c. 25 days
d. 45 days

12.4 52. The XYZ Company purchases a component used in the manufacture of automobile generators directly from the supplier. XYZ's generator production, which is operated at a constant rate, will require 1,200 components per month throughout the year. Assume ordering costs are $25 per order, item cost is $2.00 per component, and annual inventory-holding costs are charged at 20 percent. The company operates 250 days per year, and the lead time is five days.

a. Compute the EOQ, total annual inventory-holding and ordering costs, and the reorder point.

b. Suppose XYZ's managers like the operational efficiency of ordering in quantities of 1,200 items and ordering once each month. How much more expensive would this policy be than your EOQ recommendation? Would you recommend in favor of the 1,200-item order quantity? Explain. What would the reorder point be if the 1,200-item quantity were acceptable?

12.4 53. The maternity ward of a hospital sends one baby blanket home with each newborn baby. The following information is available for the baby blankets:

Demand = 80 blankets/week
Standard deviation in weekly demand = seven blankets
Desired cycle service level = 96 percent
Delivery lead time (L) = two weeks (delivery of the blankets, not the babies!)
Annual holding cost = $2.00
Ordering cost = $8.00/order
Cost of one blanket = $6.00
The hospital is open 52 weeks each year.

a. As the new maternity ward manager, you decide to improve the current ordering methods used for items which are stocked in the maternity ward. Calculate the economic order quantity for baby blankets.

b. Baby blankets are currently ordered in quantities of 200. How much would the maternity ward save in total annual relevant costs by changing to the EOQ?

c. You decide that a fixed-order quantity system will be used for ordering the blankets. Describe and calculate what must be known for implementing such a system.

12.4 54. Nation-Wide Bus Lines is proud of the six-week driver-training program it conducts for all new Nation-Wide drivers. The program costs Nation-Wide $22,000 for instructors, equipment, and so on, and is independent of the number of new drivers in the class as long as the class size remains less than or equal to 35. The program must provide the company with approximately five new fully trained drivers per month. After completing the training program, new drivers are paid $1,800 per month but do not work until a full-time driver position is open. Nation-Wide views the $1,800 as a holding cost necessary to maintain a supply of newly trained drivers available for immediate service. Viewing new drivers as inventory SKUs, how large should the training classes be in order to minimize Nation-Wide's total annual training and new-driver idle-time costs? How many training classes should the company hold each year? What is the total annual cost of your recommendation?

12.4 55. A product with an annual demand of 1,000 SKUs has C_o = $30 and C_h = $8. The demand exhibits some variability such that the lead-time demand follows a normal distribution, with a mean of 25 and a standard deviation of five.

a. What is the recommended order quantity?

b. What is the reorder point and safety stock level if the firm desires at most a two-percent probability of a stockout on any given order cycle?

c. If the manager sets the reorder point at 30, what is the probability of a stockout on any given order cycle? How many times would you expect to stockout during the year if this reorder point was used?

12.4 56. The B&S Novelty and Craft Shop in Bennington, Vermont, sells a variety of quality, handmade items to tourists. It will sell 300 hand-carved miniature replicas of a colonial soldier each year, but the demand pattern during the year is uncertain. The replicas sell for $20 each, and B&S uses a 15-percent annual inventory-holding cost rate. Ordering costs are $5 per order, and demand during the lead time follows a normal distribution, with a mean of 15 and a standard deviation of six.

a. What is the recommended order quantity?

b. If B&S is willing to accept a stockout roughly twice a year, what reorder point would you recommend? What is the probability that B&S will have a stockout in any one order cycle?

c. What is the safety stock level and annual safety stock costs for this product?

12.4 **57.** Apply the EOQ model to the quantity-discount situation shown in the data below:

Discount Category	Order Size	Discount	Unit Cost
1	0 to 99	0 percent	$10.00
2	100 or more	3 percent	$ 9.70

Assume that $D = 500$ units per year, $C_o = \$40$, and the annual inventory-holding cost is 20 percent. What order quantity do you recommend?

12.4 **58.** Allen's Shoe Stores carries a basic black dress shoe for men that sells at an approximate constant rate of 500 pairs of shoes every three months. Allen's current buying policy is to order 500 pairs each time an order is placed. It costs $30 to place an order, and inventory-carrying costs have an annual rate of 20 percent. With the order quantity of 500, Allen's obtains the shoes at the lowest possible unit cost of $28 per pair. Other quantity discounts offered by the manufacturer are listed below:

Order Quantity	Price Per Pair
0–99	$36
100–199	$32
200–299	$30
300 or more	$28

What is the minimum-cost order quantity for the shoes? What are the annual savings of your inventory policy over the policy currently being used?

12.5 **59.** For the data given in Exhibit 12.26 for problem 50, illustrate the operation of a fixed-period-inventory system with a replenishment (M) level of 40, a review period of five days, a lead time of 3 days, and use Equation 12.1. Assume that orders are placed at the end of the day and that they arrive at the beginning of the day. Therefore, if an order is placed at the end of day five, it will arrive at the beginning of day nine. Here, the order quantity varies while the review period and lead time remain fixed. Note that you need columns for day, beginning inventory, demand, ending inventory, order placed, inventory position, and order received.

12.5 **60.** Crew Soccer Shoes Company is considering a change of their current inventory-control system for soccer shoes. The information regarding the shoes is given below:

Demand = 100 pairs/week
Lead time = three weeks
Order cost = $35/order
Holding cost = $2.00/pair/year
Cycle service level = 95 percent
Standard deviation of weekly demand = 50
Number of weeks per year = 52

a. The company decides to use a fixed-order quantity system. What would be the reorder point and the economic order quantity?

b. In this system, at the beginning of the current week, the materials manager, Luke Thomas, checked the inventory level of shoes and found 300 pairs. There were no scheduled receipts and no back orders. Should he place an order? Explain your answer.

c. If the company changes to a fixed-period system and reviews the inventory every two weeks ($T = 2$), how much safety stock is required?

12.5 **61.** Wildcat Tools is a distributor of hardware and electronics equipment. Their socket wrench inventory needs better management. The information regarding the wrenches is given below.

Demand—50 wrenches per month
Lead time—One month
Order cost—$20/order
Holding cost—$2.40/wrench/year
Backorder cost—$15/backorder
Cycle-service level—90 percent
Standard deviation of monthly demand—20 wrenches
Current on-hand inventory is 65 wrenches, with no scheduled receipts and no backorders.

a. The company decides to use a continuous review system. What is the recommended reorder point, safety stock, and the economic order quantity?

b. Based on the information calculated in (a), should an order be placed? If yes, how much should be ordered?

c. The company wants to investigate the fixed-period system with a twice-per-month review (P = two weeks or 0.5 months), how much safety stock is required?

12.5 **62.** Tune Football Helmets Company is considering changing the current inventory-control system for football helmets. The information regarding the helmets is given below:

Demand = 200 units/week
Lead time = two weeks
Order cost = $60/order
Holding cost = $1.50/unit/year
Cycle service level = 95 percent
Standard deviation of weekly demand = 60
Number of weeks per year = 52

a. The firm decides to use a fixed-period system to control the inventory and to review the inventory every two weeks. At the beginning of the current week, D. J. Jones, the materials manager, checked the inventory level of helmets and found 450 units. There were no scheduled receipts and no back orders. How many units should be ordered?

b. If the firm changes to a fixed-quantity system, what would the reorder point and the economic order quantity be?

EXCEL-BASED PROBLEMS

For these problems, you may use Excel or the spreadsheet templates available in MindTap to assist in your analysis.

12.3 63. The Welsh Corporation uses 13 key components in one of its manufacturing plants. The data are provided in the worksheet *C12 Excel P63 Data* in MindTap. Use the *ABC* Excel template in MindTap to perform an ABC analysis. Explain your decisions and logic.

12.3 64. Use the *ABC* Excel template in MindTap to perform an ABC analysis for the data provided in the worksheet *C12 Excel P64 Data* in MindTap. Clearly explain why you classified items as A, B, or C.

12.3 65. Use the *ABC* Excel template in MindTap to perform an ABC analysis for the data provided in the worksheet *C12 Excel P65 Data* in MindTap. Clearly explain why you classified items as A, B, or C.

12.4 66. A&M Industrial Products purchases a variety of parts used in small industrial tools. Inventory has not been tightly controlled, and managers think that costs can be substantially reduced. The items in the worksheet *C12 Excel P66* in MindTap comprise the inventory of one product line. Use the *ABC* Excel template in MindTap to perform an ABC analysis of this inventory situation.

12.4 67. Mama Mia's Pizza purchases its pizza delivery boxes from a printing supplier. Mama Mia's delivers on-average 225 pizzas each month (assume deterministic demand). Boxes cost 43 cents each, and each order costs $12.50 to process. Because of limited storage space, the manager wants to charge inventory holding at 25 percent of the cost. The lead time is seven days, and the restaurant is open 360 days per year, assuming 30 days per month. Use the *EOQ Model* Excel template in MindTap to determine the economic order quantity, reorder point assuming no safety stock, number of orders per year, and total annual cost.

12.4 68. Refer to the situation in problem 67. Suppose the manager of Mama Mia's current order quantity is 400 boxes. How much can be saved by adopting an EOQ versus their current Q = 400? Use the *EOQ Model* Excel template in MindTap to find your answer.

12.4 69. Super K Beverage Company distributes a soft drink that has a constant annual demand rate of 4,600 cases. A 12-pack case of the soft drink costs Super K $2.25. Ordering costs are $20 per order, and inventory-holding costs are charged at 25 percent of the cost per unit. There are 250 working days per year, and the lead time is four days. Use the *EOQ Model* Excel template in MindTap to find the economic order quantity and total annual cost, and compute the reorder point.

12.4 70. Environmental considerations, material losses, and waste disposal can be included in the EOQ model to improve inventory-management decisions. Assume that the annual demand for an industrial chemical is 1,200 lb, item cost is $5/lb, order cost is $40, inventory-holding cost rate (percent of item cost) is 18 percent. Use the *EOQ Model* Excel template in MindTap to answer the following:

a. Find the EOQ and total cost assuming no waste disposal.

b. Now assume that eight percent of the chemical is not used and disposed of, with a disposal cost of $0.75/lb. Find the EOQ and total cost when disposal costs are incorporated into the model. (Hint: Add to the holding cost the disposal cost times the percent of product that is disposed of. This calculation must be done manually.)

c. What implications do these results have for sustainability practices?

12.4 71. High Tech, Inc. is a virtual store that stocks a variety of cell phones in their warehouse. Customer orders are placed, picked and packaged, and then shipped to the customer. A fixed-order quantity inventory-control system (FQS) helps monitor and control these SKUs. The following information is for one of the cell phones that they stock, sell, and ship:

Average demand	12.5 cell phones per week
Lead time	3 weeks
Order cost	$20/order
Unit cost	$8.00
Carrying charge rate	0.25
Number of weeks	52 weeks per year
Standard deviation of weekly demand	3.75 cell phones
SKU service level	95 percent
Current on-hand inventory	35 cell phones
Scheduled receipts	20 cell phones
Backorders	2 cell phones

Use the *EOQ Model* or *FQS Safety Stock* Excel templates in MindTap, as appropriate, to answer the following:

a. What is the economic order quantity?
b. What are the total annual order and inventory-holding costs for the EOQ?
c. What is the reorder point without safety stock?
d. What is the reorder point with safety stock?
e. Based on the previous information, should a fixed-order quantity be placed, and if so, for how many cell phones?

12.4 72. Berta's Shoe Company is considering a change of their current inventory-control system for soccer shoes. The information regarding the shoes is given below:

Average demand = 250 pairs/week
Lead time = three weeks
Order cost = $75/order
Unit cost = $21.50
Carrying charge rate = 0.20
Desired service level = 95 percent
Standard deviation of weekly demand = 40
Number of weeks per year = 52

The company decides to use a fixed-order-quantity system. Use the *FQS Safety Stock* Excel template in MindTap to find the economic order quantity and reorder point to provide a 95 percent service level. Explain how the system will operate.

12.4 73. Handyman Hardware orders power mowers from a major Midwestern manufacturer. The following quantity discount schedule applies to 21-inch, self-propelled, electric start power mowers:

Order Size	Discount	Unit Cost
0 to 199	0	$180
200 to 499	5%	$171
500 or more	8%	$165.60

Annual demand is 1000 units, ordering cost is $20 per order, and annual inventory-carrying charge rate is 10 percent. Use the *Quantity Discount* Excel template in MindTap to determine the best order quantity.

12.4 74. A manufacturer procures a subassembly from a supplier. The annual demand is 120,000 units, cost per unit is $6, inventory-carrying charge rate is 10 percent, and the order cost is $200. For orders between 10,000 but less than 30,000, a three percent discount is applied, and for orders exceeding 30,000, a five percent discount is applied. What is the optimal order quantity? Use the *Quantity Discount* Excel template in MindTap to find your answer.

12.4 75. Find the optimal order quantity for an annual demand of 10,000 units, a cost per unit of $3, an inventory-carrying charge rate of 20 percent, and an order cost of 32 percent. For orders between 100 and 1999 units, the supplier gives a two percent discount, and for orders of 2000 units or more, the supplier gives a three percent discount. Use the *Quantity Discount* Excel template in MindTap to find the optimal order size, and explain how the adjusted order sizes for the discount categories were determined.

12.5 76. The Greyhound Company is considering changing its current inventory-control system for electronic picture frames. The information regarding one e-frame is given below:

Demand = 200 units/week
Lead time = three weeks
Order cost = $60/order
Unit cost = $80
Carrying charge rate = 0.075
Desired service level = 90 percent
Inventory position (IP) = 450
Standard deviation of weekly demand = 40
Number of weeks per year = 52

Use the *FPS Safety Stock* Excel template in MindTap to compute T and M for a fixed-period inventory system model with and without safety stock. Explain how this system would operate.

12.6 77. Suzie's Sweetshop makes special boxes of Valentine's Day chocolates. Each costs $15 in material and labor and sell for $30. After Valentine's Day, Suzie reduces the price to $10.00 and sells any remaining boxes. Historically, she has sold between 50 and 100 boxes. Determine the optimal number of boxes to make using the *Single Period Inventory* Excel template in MindTap. How would her decision change if she can only sell all remaining boxes at a price of $5?

12.6 78. For Suzie's Sweetshop scenario in problem 77, suppose that demand is normally distributed with a mean of 75 and a standard deviation of eight. How will her optimal order quantity change? Use the *Single Period Inventory* Excel template in MindTap to find your answer.

12.6 79. The J&B Card Shop sells calendars featuring a different colonial picture for each month. The once-a-year order for each year's calendar arrives in September. From past experience the September-to-July demand for the calendars can be approximated by a normal distribution with $\mu = 300$ and standard deviation = 20. The calendars cost $6.50 each, and J&B sells them for $15 each. Use the *Single Period Inventory* Excel template in MindTap to answer the following:

a. Suppose that J&B throws out all unsold calendars at the end of July. How many calendars should be ordered?

b. If J&B sells any surplus calendars for $1 at the end of July and can sell all of them at this price, how many calendars should be ordered?

12.7 80. Use the *Inventory Simulation* Excel template in MindTap for the Scott Audio Systems example in section 12-7 to determine the best order quantity-reorder point combination with the smallest average cost/day for all combinations of reorder points five, seven, and nine, and order quantities 10, 20, and 30. What is the best combination? You need only change the input values in the template, but recalculate each combination ten times using a data table to average out variations in the simulations. Once you set up the data table, it will automatically update as the input values are changed.

12.7 81. Daniel's Auto Parts is a small wholesale distributor of automobile after-market items. For one particular part, an analysis of historical sales resulted in the distribution of daily demand shown below:

Daily Demand	Probability
0	0.1770
1	0.0770
2	0.3850
3	0.2731
4	0.0879

When a new supply of the part is ordered, the lead-time distribution is shown below (for example, if the lead time is three, the order arrives on the third day after the order is placed):

Lead time (days)	Probability
3	0.10
4	0.75
5	0.10
6	0.05

Other information obtained from company records includes the following:

1. Order cost is $25.00 per order.
2. Back order cost is $10.00 per stockout.
3. Unit storage cost is $0.75 per day.

Use the *Inventory Simulation* Excel template in MindTap to identify the best reorder point and reorder level that will result in the lowest average cost/day using a data table with 20 replications. It will require some trial and error to hone in on the best parameters. Start with the reorder point between five and ten, and the order quantity between ten and 20.

Margate Hospital

Cost-containment activities have become particularly important to hospital operations managers, stimulated by major revisions in health care reimbursement policies and significant growth in marketing activities by private sector health care organizations. Recognizing that poor inventory control policies reflect ineffective use of organizational assets, many hospital managers have sought to institute more systematic approaches to the control of supply inventories.

At Margate Hospital, analysts collected data of 20 disposable SKUs in a pulmonary therapy unit. These data are shown in Exhibit 12.27 (these data are available in the worksheet *Margate Hospital Case Data* in MindTap). Three of the SKUs are designated as critical to patient care. The hospital administrator wants to develop better inventory management policies for these items.

Case Questions for Discussion:

1. Using the case data, propose a breakdown for an ABC analysis, and clearly outline how each category of items might be managed by the hospital. (Use the Excel *ABC* template in MindTap.)
2. How do you recommend managing these ABC and critical inventory categories?
3. Can you think of any other inventory management systems besides health care where some SKUs might be defined as "critical"?

EXHIBIT 12.27 Margate Hospital Study Data

SKU	Total Annual Usage	Average Unit Cost	
1	212	$24.00	
2	210	$2.00	
3	117	$50.00	
4	77	$28.00	
5	60	$58.00	
6	48	$55.00	
7	33	$73.00	
8	27	$210.00	Critical
9	19	$74.00	
10	18	$45.00	Critical
11	12	$33.00	
12	7	$65.00	
13	4	$41.00	
14	4	$20.00	
15	3	$72.00	Critcal
16	3	$61.00	
17	3	$8.00	
18	2	$134.00	
19	1	$34.00	
20	1	$29.00	

Hardy Hospital

Caroline Highgrove, Hardy Hospital's director of materials management, glanced at the papers spread across her desk. She wondered where the week had gone. On Monday, the director of university operations, Drew Paris, had asked Caroline to look into the purchasing and supplies systems for the hospital. Drew specifically wanted Caroline to evaluate the current materials-management system, identify ways to reduce costs, and recommend a final plan of action. Drew explained that the university was under pressure to cut expenses, and hospital inventory did not seem to be under control.

As Caroline reviewed her notes, she was struck by the variations in order sizes and order frequencies for the hospital's stock-keeping units (SKUs). For some SKUs, inventory ran out before new orders came in, whereas for other SKUs, excessively high stock levels were being carried. The university and hospital's computerized materials-management system was about a decade old and generally worked well; however, employees often ignored or did not update key information. Thus, data integrity was a major problem in this information system.

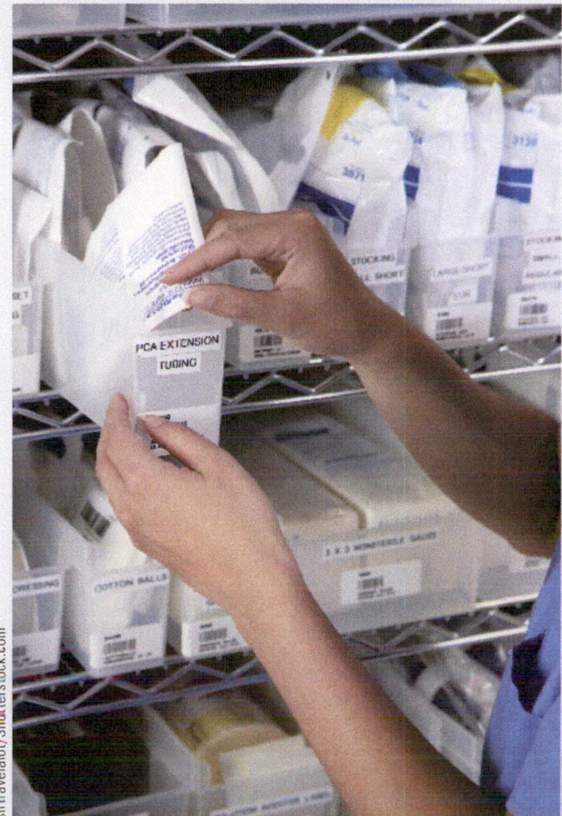

sirtravelalot/Shutterstock.com

Regular stock items were characterized by their long-standing and frequent use throughout the hospital.

Hospital and university supply orders were classified as either *regular stock* or *special order*. The hospital was the originator of almost all special orders. *Regular stock items*, such as bed sheets, uniforms, and syringes, were characterized by their long-standing and frequent use throughout the university and hospital, and by a low risk of obsolescence. When a department needed a regular stock item, that department generally ordered (requisitioned) the item. If the item was in stock, it would be delivered to the department by the next delivery date.

When the university did not normally stock an item, individual hospital departments could special-order them. Special-order items were supposed to be those of an experimental nature or critical to patient health care, but not used frequently. Hospital departments requiring these special items bypassed the university purchasing system. Once a special order was placed, the hospital department informed university purchasing so that it could eventually authorize payment on the vendor's invoice. Hospital department coordinators, doctors, or head nurses were responsible for initiating and/or authorizing special orders. In total, these special orders required a significant amount of work that took department coordinators and head nurses away from their duties. University purchasing kept no records on the hospital's special-order inventories or for the 215 secondary hospital stocking points such as exam rooms and moveable carts.

One department's head nurse explained that many departments were afraid of running out of regular stock items. University purchasing didn't understand the importance and nature of hospital inventory, and they were slow to respond. The nurse cited the months-long period university purchasing process needed to place new items on the regular stock list, and the long lead times sometimes involved in receiving orders requisitioned from the university's approved vendor list.

Because the university was a state institution, strict bidding and purchasing procedures had to be followed for both regular stock and special orders. For example, three written bids were required for an individual order of $2,000

EXHIBIT 12.28 Hardy Hospital Strike Disinfectant Data*

		Case Size		Cost per Case	Order Lead Time
Strike Disinfectant**		4 gallons		$84.20	2 weeks
Beginning SKU Balance	96	Week	1		
Receipt	200	Week	7		
Ending Balance	110	Week	16		

*These inventory balances are for the central hospital storeroom only. The receipt is a reasonable estimate of the current order quantity (Q).

**In gallons, not cases.

or more. The processing of these bids often took up to 2 months. For orders between $800 and $1,999, three telephone bids were necessary. In these situations, purchases could be made only from the lowest bidder. Orders under $800, or items on the state contract list, could be ordered over the phone, without any bids. State contract list items were those for which statewide needs had been combined and one contract left to cover all of them.

Caroline had gathered information on the costs of ordering and storing hospital supplies. For order costs, she estimated that, on average, the purchasing, account payables, and receiving personnel spent three hours processing a single purchase order. A single purchase order typically included four SKUs (i.e., each SKU on a purchase order was called a line item). The average hospital storeroom's wage was $18.50 an hour; with employee benefits and associated overhead, the cost of one worker-hour came to $24.

For inventory-holding costs, the university warehouse and hospital storeroom used 36,750 square feet of storage space. The university stored an average of $4.15 million in hospital supplies in this space. Records indicated that the average annual variable and semivariable cost for storage space this year would be $4.60 per square foot. Five warehouse workers and storeroom associates were required to handle the hospital's supplies. These individuals each earned $32,000 a year; benefits and overhead rates for these employees were the same as for other personnel, about 20 percent. Other warehouse costs, including obsolescence and taxes, were expected to reach $400,000 this year. The hospital operated 52 weeks per year. Also, the state recently had floated a bond issue at 8.9 percent, and Caroline thought that might be a good estimate of the cost of money to finance inventory, but she wasn't sure what other costs to include in inventory-holding costs.

After reviewing her notes on the hospital's materials-management situation, Caroline decided to take a closer look at some individual regular stock items. She sorted through the papers on her desk and found 30 SKUs of interest. She wanted to analyze all 30 SKUs but decided to begin with one SKU widely used in the hospital—Strike Disinfectant. Data on this SKU are shown in Exhibits 12.28 and 12.29.

EXHIBIT 12.29 Hardy Hospital Aggregate Strike Disinfectant Weekly Demand as Measured by Hospital Requisitions

Week	Strike*
1	31
2	27
3	1
4	12
5	11
6	8
7	4
8	15
9	15
10	16
11	10
12	9
13	8
14	5
15	10
16	4
Total	186
Mean	11.63
Standard Deviation	8.02
Cycle Service Level	97%

*Strike Disinfectant demand is quoted in gallons.

Case Questions for Discussion:

1. What are good estimates of order cost and inventory-holding cost? (State all assumptions and show all computations.)

2. What is the EOQ and reorder point with safety stock for Strike Disinfectant given your answer to question 1?
3. Compute the total order and inventory-holding costs for a fixed-quantity system (FQS) and compare to the current order Q's. Can you save money by adopting an FQS?
4. What are your final recommendations, including what you would recommend regarding regular and special orders, the state bidding system, and overall control of the university materials-management system? Explain the reasoning for your recommendations.

Integrative Case: Hudson Jewelers

The Hudson Jewelers case study found in MindTap integrates material found in each chapter of this book.

Case Questions for Discussion:

1. Research global supply and demand for diamonds and how it affects prices. What role do "diamond reserves" (inventory) play in determining prices? Explain. What do you think the demand-supply curves for diamonds looks like? Try to sketch it out.
2. What are the detailed components of inventory holding costs in this situation? What other factors might influence holding costs, such as security costs, obsolescence costs, and others. What is your estimate of inventory carrying costs as a percentage of item value? Explain your reasoning.

13 Supply Chain Management and Logistics

LEARNING OBJECTIVES

After studying this chapter, you should be able to:

13-1 Explain the basic concepts of supply chain management.

13-2 Describe the activities associated with logistics.

13-3 Describe the types of risks supply chains face and ways to mitigate them.

13-4 Describe how e-commerce has changed the role of supply chains.

13-5 List and describe the important metrics used to measure supply chain performance, and be able to evaluate total supply chain costs and cash-to-cash conversion cycles.

13-6 Describe how organizations are incorporating sustainability issues in managing their supply chains, and explain how manufactured goods recovery and reverse logistics work.

Nokia, now a global leader in technology connecting people and things, demonstrates its new virtual reality camera, Ozo, at a tech event. The company improves its supply chain by promoting the flow of information with suppliers and customers, and developing collaborative relationships with suppliers.

ANTTI AIMO-KOIVISTO/AFP/Getty Images

Nokia Corp, a Finnish company, was founded in 1865 as a paper mill. Nokia did not start manufacturing phones until 1982. By making this strategic decision, Nokia became a global leader in telecommunications by 1998. Industry experts have been fascinated by Nokia's ability to manage and adapt its supply chain over almost 150 years. Since 1995, Nokia's supply chain management approach has been to create the most efficient supplier network in order to offer the best solutions and meet customer expectations. The pillars for the company's success include:

- creating value-based partnerships with suppliers backed by factual information
- leadership
- flexibility
- trust

A research paper published in the *International Journal of Physical Distribution & Logistics Management* explained that Nokia improves its supply chain by promoting the flow of information with suppliers and customers, developing collaborative relationships with suppliers, designing for postponement, building inventory buffers by maintaining a stockpile of inexpensive but key components, having a dependable logistics system or partnership, and drawing up contingency plans and developing crisis management teams. Today, Nokia is a global leader in technologies that connect people and things.[1]

WHAT DO YOU THINK?

How do supply chains relate to your personal life? Explain and provide examples.

In Chapter 6, we focused on the structure and design of supply chains. In this chapter, we address the day-to-day issues that supply chain managers must deal with to ensure that supply chains accomplish their purpose in creating and delivering goods to customers. **Supply chain management (SCM)** *is the management of all activities that facilitate the fulfillment of a customer order for a manufactured good to achieve customer satisfaction at reasonable cost.* To stay competitive, "retailers need to know where things are at all times so they can redirect shipments, rebalance inventories and respond to new demands on the fly."[2]

As the opening discussion about Nokia suggests, effective supply chain management is critical to a company's success and its ability to meet customer needs. A report from AMR Research, Inc. suggests that companies that excel in supply chain operations also perform better in other financial measures of success. As one executive at AMR Research stated, "value chain performance translates into productivity and market-share leadership. … [S]upply chain leadership means more than just low costs and efficiency—it requires a superior ability to shape and respond to shifts in demand with innovative products and services."[3]

13-1 Managing Supply Chains

Managing a supply chain requires numerous operational activities, including working closely with suppliers, purchasing, transportation, inventory management, managing risks that may disrupt the supply chain, measuring supply chain performance, and ensuring sustainability.

An important component of supply chain management is called logistics. **Logistics** *is the management of transportation activities and the flow of materials within a supply chain to ensure adequate customer service at reasonable cost.* The logistics function is responsible for selecting transportation carriers; managing company-owned fleets of vehicles, distribution centers, and warehouses; controlling efficient interplant movement of materials and goods within the supply chain; and ensuring that goods are delivered to customers. Logistics play a key role both externally and internally. Externally, the logistics function is critical to satisfy customers' needs and expectations. Internally, it leads to efficiency in supply chain performance, enabling the company to operate with lower inventory levels and costs, and improve customer service. Because many

Supply Chains to Admire

Supply Chain Insights (www.supplychaininsights.com) provides professional advice for supply chain leaders on practices and technologies that make the biggest difference to corporate performance. The company developed the Supply Chains to Admire (TM) research methodology to better understand supply chain excellence. Some organizations that have been recognized for outstanding supply chain performance that have better operating margins and return on invested capital include Nike, Whole Foods, Estee Lauder, General Mills, Audi, Intel, and Samsung. Their website contains numerous videos that illustrate and explain how supply chain leadership is practiced in these companies and the results that they have achieved.

supply chains are global, most logistic managers must also deal with complex regulations, trade laws, tariffs, and multiple modes of transportation.

While purchasing has traditionally been an independent function, purchasing and logistics are often consolidated, and managers of these functions may have the title of global sourcing manager or specialist, distribution manager, commodity manager, virtual sourcing manager, transportation manager, or vice president of logistics.

13-1a The SCOR Model

The Supply Chain Operations Reference (SCOR) model *is a framework for understanding the scope of supply chain management (SCM) that is based on five basic functions involved in managing a supply chain: plan, source, make, deliver, and return.* (see the box on the SCOR model), which are the key processes that create value to customers.[4] These processes include many of the OM functions that we have already discussed, such as measurement, strategy, forecasting, capacity management, and inventory management, and those in subsequent chapters, such as scheduling and quality management. The unique characteristic of SCOR is that, whereas managers typically focus on activities within the span of their purchasing, manufacturing, and distribution processes, SCOR requires a clear understanding of the interactions among all parts of the system. For example, supply chain managers must use forecasting and information technology to better match production levels with demand and reduce costs; tightly integrate design, development, production, delivery, and marketing; and provide more customization to meet increasingly demanding customers. The SCOR framework can also help managers identify important performance metrics to manage and monitor their processes.

A supply chain is an integrated system of processes that requires much coordination and collaboration among its various players. Every company is part of a long chain (in fact, many long chains) of customers and suppliers. Each company is a customer to its suppliers and a supplier to its customers, so it does not make sense to think of a company as only one or the other. This promotes a systems perspective of supply chains rather than viewing organizations as disconnected from other elements of the supply chain. Exhibit 13.1 illustrates how the SCOR model may be used in a chain of customer–supplier relationships. Each major player (the company, its suppliers, its customers, suppliers' suppliers, and customers' customers) would typically manage its own supply chain using the SCOR framework—in essence, chaining these functions within a broader supply chain.

The SCOR Model

The Supply Chain Operations Reference (SCOR) model is a framework for understanding the scope of supply chain management (SCM) that is based on five basic functions involved in managing a supply chain: plan, source, make, deliver, and return.

1. *Plan*—Developing a strategy that balances resources with requirements and establishes and communicates plans for the entire supply chain. This includes management policies and aligning the supply chain plan with financial plans.
2. *Source*—Procuring goods and services to meet planned or actual demand. This includes identifying and selecting suppliers, scheduling deliveries, authorizing payments, and managing inventory.
3. *Make*—Transforming goods and services to a finished state to meet demand. This includes production scheduling, managing work-in-process, manufacturing, testing, packaging, and product release.
4. *Deliver*—Managing orders, transportation, and distribution to provide the goods and services. This entails all order management activities from processing customer orders to routing shipments, managing goods at distribution centers, and invoicing the customer.
5. *Return*—Processing customer returns; providing maintenance, repair, and overhaul; and dealing with excess goods. This includes return authorization, receiving, verification, disposition, and replacement or credit.

13-1b Sourcing and Purchasing

Suppliers are vital to supply chains, because they provide the materials and components needed for production to ultimately meet customer demand. If these are not delivered on time, in the proper quantity, and with the right level of quality, the entire supply chain could break down. For manufacturing, one of the first questions that supply chain managers must ask is where to obtain ("source") raw materials, manufactured components, and

EXHIBIT 13.1 APICS* Supply Chain Council's SCOR Model for Supply Chains

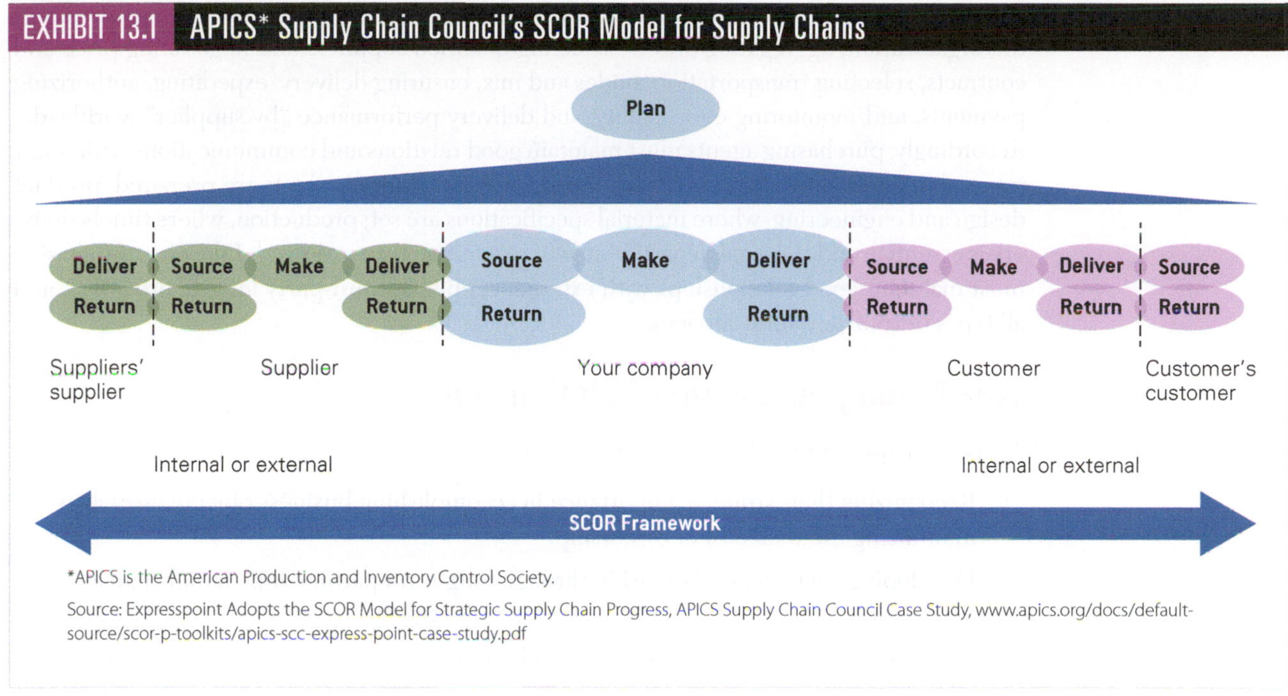

*APICS is the American Production and Inventory Control Society.

Source: Expresspoint Adopts the SCOR Model for Strategic Supply Chain Progress, APICS Supply Chain Council Case Study, www.apics.org/docs/default-source/scor-p-toolkits/apics-scc-express-point-case-study.pdf

subassemblies. For services, sourcing options might include employment agencies, equipment maintenance and repair companies, information systems providers, third-party logistic firms, engineering services, health care services, and retirement providers.

The best companies link sourcing decisions to their business strategy, use business analytics tools, and focus on the "total cost of ownership," not simply the cost of purchasing. In today's business environment, as we noted in Chapter 1, sourcing decisions are global; companies rely on goods and services obtained from many different countries and regions, and manufacturing operations are often distributed across the globe. Global sourcing seeks to balance various economic factors such as purchasing costs, transportation costs, taxes, and tariffs with delivery performance and quality requirements.

Purchasing (procurement) *is the function responsible for acquiring raw materials, component parts, tools, services, and other items required from external suppliers*. Purchasing can have a significant impact on total supply chain costs. For example, at Gillette, each division used to purchase supplies such as cardboard, aluminum, steel, and plastic independently. In fact, no one knew exactly how much the company spent on supplies worldwide. By coordinating division purchasing, the company saved hundreds of millions of dollars.

Because materials are one of the largest sources of cash outlay in any manufacturing firm, their acquisition requires careful management. For goods-producing firms, the purchasing department acts as an interface between suppliers and the production function. For service firms such as hotels, education, airlines, and health care, purchasing buys the goods necessary to perform their services. In addition, purchasing must buy services from organizations like temporary employment agencies, insurance and financial firms, laundry and landscape businesses, security companies, information technology corporations, and external education and training providers.

The principal goal of purchasing is to support its key internal customers. Thus, purchasing must do much more than simply buy according to the quoted line-item purchase prices. Purchasing must ensure quality, delivery performance, low cost, and technical support. Moreover, purchasing must continually seek new suppliers and products, and be able to evaluate their strategic, market, and economic potential to the company.

The responsibilities of a purchasing department include learning the material needs of the organization, aggregating orders, selecting qualified suppliers and negotiating price and contracts, selecting transportation modes and mix, ensuring delivery, expediting, authorizing payments, and monitoring cost, quality, and delivery performance "by supplier" worldwide. Accordingly, purchasing agents must maintain good relations and communications with other internal departments, such as accounting and finance, where budgets are prepared; product design and engineering, where material specifications are set; production, where timely delivery is essential; and the legal department, where contracts are reviewed. Likewise, purchasing must maintain good relationships with external suppliers, third-party logistic providers, and all types of transportation services.

13-1c Managing Supplier Relationships

Three principles for working with suppliers are:

1. Recognizing their strategic importance in accomplishing business objectives such as minimizing the total cost of ownership.
2. Developing a win–win relationship through long-term partnerships rather than as adversaries.
3. Establishing trust through openness and honesty, and therefore, leading to mutual advantages.

Dell, for instance, creates strong partnerships with global suppliers responsible for delivering thousands of parts. Keyboards are sourced in Mexico, soundcards in France, and power supplies, disk drives, and chips in Asia. The selection of suppliers is based on cost, quality, speed of service, and flexibility; and performance is tracked using a supplier "report card." Boeing, which spent $36 billion on 17,525 suppliers in 52 countries in one year, created a forum in which it meets with supplier representatives every other month, with a goal of improving the supplier performance measurement process and its tools.

When close relationships are developed, the total number of suppliers can be reduced, because there is no need for competition among suppliers for the same products. With larger contracts, suppliers benefit from economies of scale and customers benefit from volume discounts. Suppliers' involvement in early product design stages often allow customers to find out about new materials, parts, and technologies before their competitors. Moreover, with long-term contracts, suppliers are more willing to invest in process and system improvements. Many customers even provide assistance in making such improvements. In return, they receive better products and service.

13-1d Supply and Value Chain Integration

Supply chain integration *is the process of coordinating the physical flow of materials to ensure that the right parts are available at various stages of the supply chain, such as manufacturing and assembly plants*. Some firms, such as Walmart, manage supply chain integration themselves. Others make use of third-party "system integrators" such as Exel (www.exel.com) to manage the process. Exel manages supply chain activities across industries and geographic regions to reduce costs, accelerate product movement, and allow manufacturers and retailers to focus on their core business. Exel is able to deliver services and solutions such as consulting, e-commerce, transport, global freight, warehousing, home delivery, labeling, and co-packing, on a local, regional, or global basis.

From a broader perspective, drawing upon the value chain concepts in Chapter 1, we may define **value chain integration** *is the process of managing information, physical goods, and services to ensure their availability at the right place, at the right time, at the right cost, at the right quantity, and with the highest attention to quality*. For goods-producing firms, it requires consolidating information systems among suppliers, factories, distributors, and customers; managing the supply chain and scheduling factories; and studying new ways to use technology. Value chain integration includes improving internal processes for the client, as well as external processes that tie together suppliers, manufacturers, distributors, and customers. Other benefits are lower total value chain costs to the client, reduced inventory obsolescence, better global communication among all parties, access to new technologies, and better customer service.

Value chain integration in services—where value is in the form of low prices, convenience, and access to special, time-sensitive deals and travel packages—takes many forms. For example, third-party integrators for the leisure and travel industry value chains include Orbitz, Expedia, Priceline, and Travelocity. They manage information to make these value chains more efficient and create value for their customers. Many financial services use information networks provided by third-party information technology integrators such as AT&T, Sprint, IBM, and Verizon to coordinate their value chains. Hospitals also use third-party integrators for both their information and physical goods, such as managing patient billing and hospital inventories.

Electronic data interchange and Internet links streamline information flow between global customers and suppliers and increase the velocity of supply chains. Many firms now use cloud-based software for managing inventories in supply chains and synchronizing marketing and supply chain functions. Trucking companies track their trucks via global positioning system (GPS) technology as they move across the country, and many use in-vehicle navigational systems.

Firms such as MetLife, Marriott Hotels, General Electric, FedEx, Dow Chemical, Enterprise Rent-A-Car, and Bank of America have exploited technology effectively in their supply chain management activities. In many situations, electronic transaction capability allows all parts of the supply chain to immediately know and react to changes in demand and supply. This requires tighter integration of many components of the supply chain. In some cases, technology provides the capability to eliminate parts of the traditional supply chain structure and streamline operations.

13-2 Logistics

Logistics managers have two primary responsibilities:

1. *Purchasing transportation services.*
   - Selecting appropriate modes of shipment and mix of specific carriers.
   - Contracting with suppliers for domestic and global transportation services.
   - Negotiating transportation rates, and shipping, insurance, and liability contracts.
   - Managing international trade agreements, custom laws, and import/export fees.
   - Using business analytics to evaluate different shipping options.
2. *Managing inventories and the movement of materials and goods through the supply chain.*
   - Managing the flow of goods through warehouses, and sometimes, shipping directly to retail stores and customers.
   - Tracing shipments in transit and expedite them when necessary.
   - Coordinating shipments with airports, rail yards, and seaport docks.
   - Issuing and auditing freight bills.
   - Filing claims for damaged goods.

13-2a Transportation Services

> Transportation costs can add up to 10 percent to the total cost of the product as it moves through the supply chain.

The selection of transportation services is a complex decision, as varied services are available—rail, trucks, air, water, and pipeline. Each has advantages and disadvantages depending on the volume, size, and weight of the items being transported. Transportation costs can add up to 10 percent to the total cost of the product as it moves through the supply chain.

Rail transport provides a good balance between costs, delivery speed, tonnage capacity, and environmental sustainability. A typical train can carry 10,000 tons of freight. It is best over long hauls, in bad weather, and is somewhat immune to vehicle traffic congestion. Rail transit is generally slow and is used primarily for shipping large volumes of relatively low-value items over long distances. However, rail cars often encounter long delays and are less dependable than other forms of transportation. In addition, routes are inflexible and do not offer door-to-door service.

Trucks are the most flexible of all transportation modes with the capability for door-to-door pickup and delivery. Perishable goods such as fruit and flowers can be quickly moved to the buyer. Transportation costs are higher than rail, and it is used most often for short distances and smaller shipments. Weight and size constraints limit the capability of trucks for carrying certain loads, but their scheduled service is more dependable than that of rail. Weather, traffic congestion, and driver errors can limit this transportation mode. Full-truckload (FTL) and less-than-full truckload (LTL) shipments are critical to making a profit on a load. *A* ***backhaul*** *is when a truck delivers its load and also carries freight on the return journey.* Without backhaul business, the capacity utilization of the truck is low and non-revenue producing.

Sheila Fitzgerald/Shutterstock.com

Megaships like the *Benjamin Franklin*, shown here in Oakland, California, can carry as many as 18,000 containers.

International shipping relies on air and water. *Air shipments* have the highest transportation cost, are very fast for long distances, but are limited in how much weight they can carry. A 747 airplane designed to only carry freight can carry up to 100 metric tons. Airfreight is most often used to transport high-value items such as flowers, heart valves, seafood, electronics, and smaller manufactured parts. Routes are limited and must be supplemented with other modes of transportation to get products to customers.

Ships and barges are generally limited to transporting large quantities of bulky items—historically, raw materials such as coal and iron, but recently, items such as furniture and other manufactured products from overseas. For example, a 40-foot container can hold up to 1,600 bicycles, 3,000 flat-packed furniture kits, 130,000 T-shirts, or 15,000 small automobile parts. Today we are seeing "megaships"—tankers and freight carriers that can hold millions of gallons of oil or over 7,000 shipping containers; the CMA CGM *Benjamin Franklin* can carry 18,000 20-foot containers. The cost to ship one T-shirt from Asia to the United States using the *Benjamin Franklin* is about 2 cents.[5]

Weather can disrupt maritime shipments, and this mode requires high initial investment. They are slow, but inexpensive from a unit cost basis. Like air, they require other modes of transportation to get to customer locations.

Pipelines carry water, petroleum, natural gas, and sometimes a slurry of minerals or commodities. Pipelines have limited use and accessibility and are used primarily for such products as oil and natural gas. Initial investment costs are high, but once in operation the cost to transport per mile is very low. Preventive maintenance adds to the cost of operations, while packaging costs are zero. An important goal of managing a pipeline is not harming the environment (i.e., environmental sustainability).

Domestically, most consumer items are shipped via rail, trucks, and air. The critical factors in selecting a transportation mode are (1) speed, (2) accessibility, (3) cost, and (4) capability. Supply chain managers often combine these modes of transportation (called *intermodal transportation*) in a global supply chain such as transporting by ship and container to a seaport, loading the containers onto a train for transport to a large, "break bulk" warehouse, and

The Last Mile of Package Delivery

The Quadrobot U1 four-wheel electric vehicle looks like a gray toaster. About 2,000 vehicles will begin delivering packages with the Chinese Postal Service. The U1s are capable of various degrees of self-driving capabilities including being driven by a human driver if necessary. The vehicle is designed to deliver mail and small packages to neighborhoods and downtowns. "The last mile" of the shipping and delivery process are particularly troublesome for labor-intensive delivery trucks. Traffic congestion, ambiguous addresses, narrow streets, and country roads make local delivery a time-consuming and costly process.

The goal is for autonomous delivery vehicles to do this work without a human driver. The delivery person simply rides and loads and unloads mail and small packages to doorways while the vehicle itself does the driving. The U1 is not a substitute for major highway or heavier package deliveries. Another aspect of the U1 is its modular design. The electric motors, steering, batteries, and gears are packaged into the lower portion of the vehicle like a thick mattress. The U1 is designed for modular assembly and replacement with simple bolts and glue. The idea is for final assembly to be inexpensive and simple. China is building several U1 assembly line factories and one is planned for the United States. Quadrobot is also studying the U1 for use as a roving food vending vehicle that is positioned around the neighborhood or downtown area.[6]

delivering to individual retail stores by truck. New approaches to transportation, such as Amazon's use of personal vehicles to deliver packages and innovative technologies (see the box "The Last Mile of Package Delivery") are revolutionizing supply chains.

13-2b Managing Inventories in Supply Chains

Inventories support the supply chain by providing materials and goods where and when they are needed—at every stage of the supply chain—for production and to customers. Inventories provide buffers between production operations to help keep machines and operations running. Inventories also protect against disruptions in supply and sudden, unpredictable, surges in demand. Careful management of inventory is critical to supply chain time-based performance in order to respond effectively to customers.

Many companies rely on suppliers to help manage inventory in a supply chain. **Vendor-managed inventory (VMI)** *is where the vendor (supplier) monitors and manages inventory for the customer.* VMI essentially outsources the inventory management function in supply chains to suppliers. For example, a supplier such as a consumer goods manufacturer might manage the inventory for a grocery store. VMI allows the vendor to view inventory needs from the customer's perspective and use this information to optimize its own production operations, better control inventory and capacity, and reduce total supply chain costs. VMI also allows vendors to make production decisions using downstream customer demand data. One disadvantage of VMI is that it does not account for substitutable products from competing manufacturers and often results in higher customer inventories than necessary.

The performance of a supply chain often suffers from a phenomenon known as the *bullwhip effect*, in which inventories exhibit wild swings up and down. This has been observed across most industries and increases cost and reduces service to customers. The bullwhip effect results from order amplification in the supply chain. **Order amplification** *is a phenomenon that occurs when each member of a supply chain "orders up" to buffer its own inventory.*[7] In the case of a distributor, this might mean ordering extra finished goods; for a manufacturer, this might mean ordering extra raw materials or parts. Order amplification can be seen in Exhibit 13.2, which shows orders as compared to sales for an HP inkjet printer. The amplitude of sales over time is smaller than the variation in the order quantity. In this case, the distributor is ordering extra quantities as a hedge against the uncertainty in delivery or other factors such as sudden surges in demand.

EXHIBIT 13.2 Order Amplification at Hewlett Packard for an Inkjet Printer

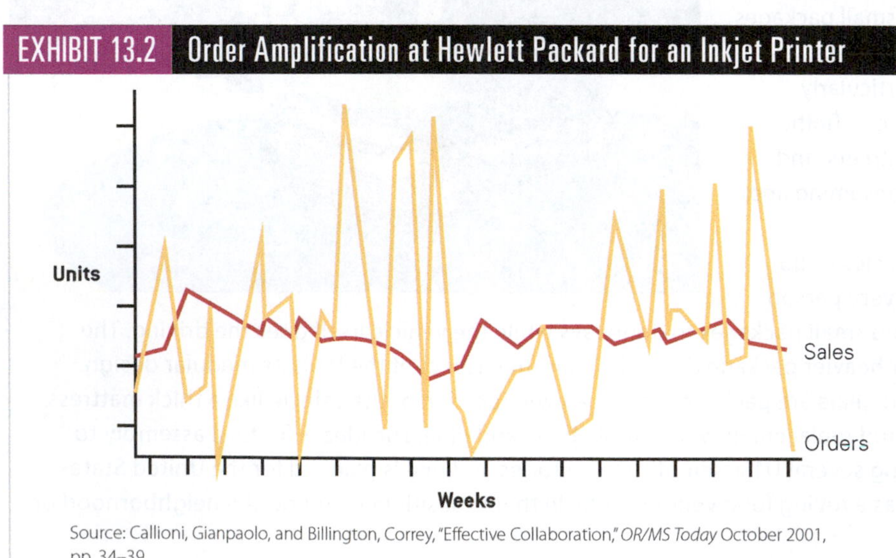

Source: Callioni, Gianpaolo, and Billington, Correy, "Effective Collaboration," *OR/MS Today* October 2001, pp. 34–39.

Many firms are taking steps to counteract this bullwhip phenomenon by modifying the supply chain infrastructure and operational processes. For example, instead of ordering based on observed fluctuations in demand at the next stage of the supply chain (which are amplified from other stages downstream), all members of the supply chain should use the same demand data from the point of the supply chain closest to the customer. Modern technology such as point-of-sale data collection, electronic data interchange, and RFID chips can help provide such data. Other strategies include using smaller order sizes,

Order Amplification at Procter & Gamble

Keith Homan/Shutterstock.com

Procter & Gamble (P&G) observed that frequent promotions sent costs spiraling. At one point, the company made 55 daily price changes on some 80 brands, which necessitated rework on every third order. Often, special packaging and handling were required. Ordering peaked during the promotions as distributors stockpiled huge quantities of goods (known as forward buying), which resulted in excessive overtime in the factories followed by periods of underutilization. Factories ran at 55 to 60 percent of rated efficiency with huge swings in output. These fluctuations strained the distribution system as well, loading up warehouses during slow periods and overworking the transportation systems at peak times.

P&G stabilized its pricing resulting in much smoother demand rates. Retailers automatically order products as they sell them; when 100 cases of Cheer detergent leave a retailer's warehouse, an order is placed for 100 more. Both P&G and retailers saved money. Plant efficiency rates increased to over 80 percent across the company; at the same time, North American inventories dropped 10 percent.[8]

stabilizing price fluctuations, and sharing information on sales, capacity, and inventory data among the members of the supply chain.

Order amplification increases as one moves back up the supply chain away from the retail customer. For example, small increases in demand by customers will cause distribution centers to increase their inventory. This leads to more frequent or larger orders to be placed with manufacturing. Manufacturing, in turn, will increase its purchasing of materials and components from suppliers. Because of lead times in ordering and delivery between each element of the supply chain, by the time the increased supply reaches the distribution center, customer demand may have leveled off or even dropped, resulting in an oversupply. This will trigger a reduction in orders back through the supply chain, resulting in undersupply later in time. Essentially, the time lags associated with information and material flow cause a mismatch between the actual customer demand and the supply chain's ability to satisfy that demand as each component of the supply chain seeks to manage its operations from its own perspective. This results in large oscillations of inventory in the supply chain network and characterizes the bullwhip effect.

13-3 Risk Management in Supply Chains

Companies face a multitude of risks in managing supply chains. Risks in domestic supply chains are often minimal; however, risks in global supply chains are much greater. These include production problems with suppliers that result in material shortages, labor strikes, unexpected transportation delays, delays from customs inspection or port operations, political instability in foreign countries, natural disasters, and even terrorism. Good supply chain managers must anticipate and mitigate these risks to ensure that the supply chain will be

Japanese Earthquake Disrupts Global Supply Chains

pryzmat/Shutterstock.com

On March 11, 2011, a devastating earthquake and tsunami in Japan caused ripples among global supply chains, particularly in the automotive industry. As Japan is an important source for automotive parts, graphic chips, and other high-tech components, the disaster caused General Motors to shut down a Louisiana factory that makes pickup trucks. North American Toyota plants experienced shortages of 150 critical parts and reduced operations to 30 percent of normal capacity. Companies scrambled to find suppliers in other countries such as China, Taiwan, and South Korea. As one consultant noted, "It's not just the assembly plant that needs to run; it's not just the direct supplier. I've got to understand the steel plant; I've got to understand every piece at a second tier, a third tier and a fourth tier below that. We've never had to do that before." Subsequently, Toyota announced that it was working to create a robust supply chain that would recover within two weeks in the event of a similar disaster.[9]

able to create and deliver its goods and services worldwide. Should they occur, they must take action to deal with the consequences and get the supply chain up and running again. For example, cybersecurity intrusions can greatly disrupt global supply chains. Supply chain managers must have backup plans, and multiple avenues of communication to keep supply chains operating effectively.

The consequences of supply chain disruptions can be significant. One research study analyzed more than 800 supply chain disruptions that took place between 1989 and 2000. Firms that experienced major supply chain disruptions saw a 93 percent decrease in sales, 33 to 40 percent lower shareholder returns, 13.5 percent higher share price volatility, 107 percent decline in operating income, and 114 percent ROA decline over a three-year period.[10]

Firms that experienced major supply chain disruptions saw a 93 percent decrease in sales, 33 to 40 percent lower shareholder returns, 13.5 percent higher share price volatility, 107 percent decline in operating income, and 114 percent ROA decline over a three-year period.

Risk management *involves identifying risks that can occur, assessing the likelihood that they will occur, determining the impact on the firm and its customers, and identifying steps to mitigate the risks.* Examples of short- and long-term risks that supply chains may face, and ways by which they can be mitigated, are summarized in Exhibits 13.3 and 13.4. Tactical risks are those that influence the day-to-day management of operations, while strategic risks can impact the design of the entire supply chain. Low- and mid-level managers, as well as front-line employees, can often address tactical risks. However, strategic risks must be addressed by top-level managers. Many of the ways to mitigate risks in Exhibits 13.3 and 13.4 are simply good OM practices, and are addressed throughout this book. Together, these methods of operations and supply chain management define a toolkit to improve performance and mitigate supply chain risks.

EXHIBIT 13.3 Tactical Supply Chain Risks and Possible Management Actions

Tactical Risks	Ways to Mitigate Tactical Risks
Inventory Risks • Inventory and warehouse stockouts • Inventory backorders • Imbalances between work centers	• Add safety stock • Change order quantities • Reduce lead times • Carry extra capacity • Add more inventory buffers between stages (work-in-progress)
Capacity Risks • Equipment shortage • Production capacity shortage • Overproduction • Equipment breakdowns • Employee shortages, strikes, and layoffs	• Lease/share extra equipment • Schedule overtime • Multiple suppliers • Schedule under time • Frequent preventive maintenance • Add temporary and backup (float pool) workers
Logistics and Scheduling Risks • Supplier quality problems • Supplier delivery problems • Long lead times for order cycles • Poor transportation infrastructure by country	• Add safety stock • Change order quantities • Increase lead times • Extra local warehouse space • Increase quality control inspections • Hire new and/or multiple contract manufacturer(s) and supplier(s) • Partnerships with local transportation firms • Emergency and/or backup plans to ship by air, truck, ship, or rail by alternative shippers

EXHIBIT 13.4 Strategic Supply Chain Risks and Possible Management Actions

Strategic Risks	Ways to Mitigate Strategic Risks
Global Economic Risks • Population and wealth forecasts by country • Monetary exchange rates and market size • Regulations, taxes, and tariff laws by county • Natural disasters such as earthquakes, tsunamis, volcanoes, hurricanes, and droughts. • Workforce skills, pay, and availability	• Franchise and company-owned store mix • Virtual versus direct sales channel mix • Facility locations (headquarters, R&D, factory, warehouse, service centers, distribution hubs, call centers, etc.) • Disaster and emergency plans and pre-deployment of resources • Multicountry sourcing of suppliers • Championing social sustainability in host country
Government Risks • Intellectual/patent rights and protection • Man-made disasters such as wars, chemical spills, transportation accidents, political revolutions, government instability, and terrorist attacks. • Government tariffs	• Global legal team to defend infringement • Facility locations (headquarters, R&D, factory, warehouse, service centers, distribution hubs, call centers, etc.) • Disaster and emergency plans and pre-deployment of resources • Multicountry outsourcing to contract manufacturers and suppliers
Product Risks • Product modifications due to cultural differences • Major forecasting errors by product by country • Chronic inventory and/or capacity shortages • Goods and service (product) obsolescence	• Better strategic planning and demand forecasting capability (i.e., hire experts, upgrade software and hardware data mining technology including social networks) • Cooperative plans to share resources • Hire more contract manufacturers and suppliers (outsourcing) • Hedging inventory
Security Risks • E-commerce system downtime • Cybersecurity • Theft, fraud, and payoff practices by country	• Technology upgrades and backup systems and sites • Sourcing (hiring) criteria for workforce • Corporate value and mission statements

13-4 Supply Chains in E-Commerce

E-commerce has greatly influenced the design and management of supply chains. There are many types of supply chains other than business to customer (B2C). Other major e-commerce relationships and supply chain structures include B2B—business to business; C2C—customer to customer; G2C—government to customer; G2G—government to government; and G2B—government to business. For example, GE Plastics (www.geplastics.com) used the Internet to completely change how plastics are designed, ordered, researched, and delivered for B2B customers. The entire GE Plastics website represents a value-added, information-intensive set of services—e-services—that facilitate the sale of goods (chemicals, plastics, resins, polymers, and the like). GE Polymerland (www.gepolymerland.com) allows other companies to buy, design, interact, research, and participate in a global auction service for many types of chemicals and plastics. The "buy" button reveals many value-added services, such as how to place an order, order status, shipment tracking, pricing, and inventory availability.

Federal, state, and local government value chains (i.e., G2C, G2G, and G2B) use e-commerce to provide better service for citizens, control waste and fraud, and minimize costs. Electronic tax filing and direct-deposit monthly Social Security checks are two examples. Food stamps are now in the form of electronic credit cards, and student loan applications must be electronically filed.

The e-commerce view of the supply chain is shown in Exhibit 13.5. *An* **intermediary** *is any entity—real or virtual—that coordinates and shares information between buyers and sellers.* Some firms, such as General Electric, Walmart, and Procter & Gamble, use e-commerce to communicate directly with suppliers and retail stores, and thereby skip traditional bricks-and-mortar intermediaries. **Return facilitators** *specialize in handling all aspects of customers returning a manufactured good or delivered service and requesting their money back, repairing the manufactured good and returning it to the customer, and/or invoking the service guarantee.* UPS Supply Chain Solutions (SCS), a subsidiary of the giant delivery company United Parcel Service (UPS), is a third-party logistics provider that can act as a return facilitator. UPS-SCS focuses on all aspects of the supply chain, including order processing, shipping, repair of defective or damaged goods, and even staffing customer service phone centers.

EXHIBIT 13.5 E-Commerce View of the Supply Chain

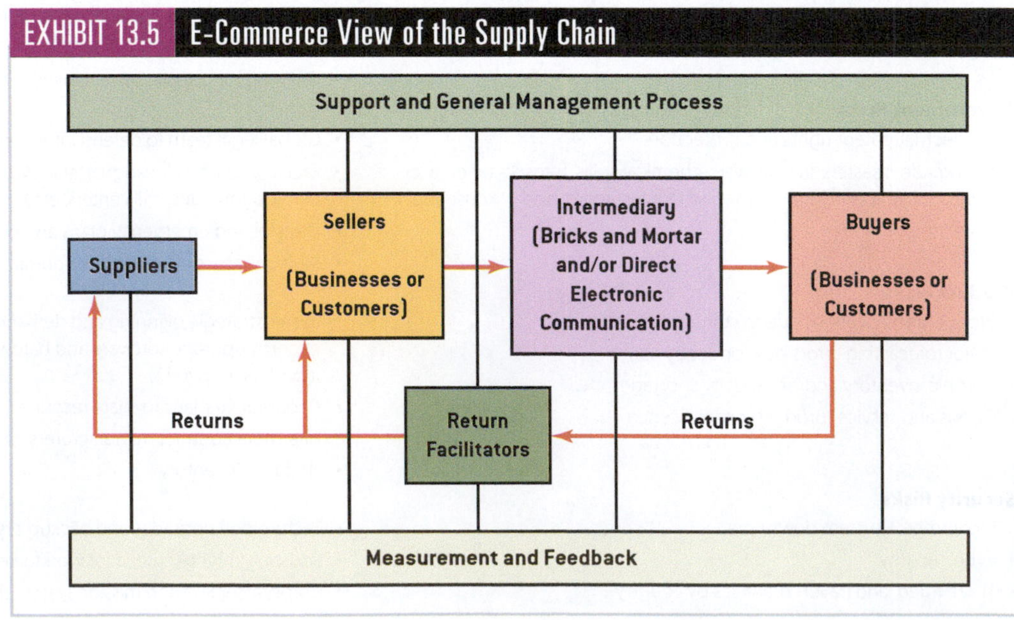

Zappos, for example, is a firm that provides its customers with a virtual platform that sells shoes and other clothing items. Their company mission is to "WOW customers with service." Thus, poor-quality goods or late customer delivery are unacceptable. Their supply chain is similar to Exhibit 13.5, consisting of suppliers, a virtual order platform, third-party shippers, and return facilitators. They don't own the factories or actually produce the physical goods, but outsource 100 percent of their physical goods to contract manufacturers in Asia. The performance of Zappos's global sourcing agents is critical to its success. Their Genghis global supply chain information system helps them manage their supply chains and suppliers. Their return processes include free shipping from the customer back to Zappos, disassembling the return shipping package and inspecting it, crediting the customer's financial account, refurbishing or discarding the product, or restocking items in their warehouse. UPS and Federal Express are the return facilitators.

13-5 Measuring Supply Chain Performance

Supply chain managers use numerous metrics to evaluate performance and identify improvements to the design and operation of their supply chains. Business analytics is used to create a visual dashboard for supply chain managers to gain insights into the relationships between these metrics.

Supply chain metrics typically balance customer requirements as well as internal supply chain efficiencies, and fall into several categories, as summarized in Exhibit 13.6.

- *Delivery reliability* is often measured by perfect order fulfillment. A "perfect order" is defined as one that is delivered meeting all customer requirements such as delivery date, condition of goods, accuracy of items, and correct invoice.
- *Responsiveness* is often measured by order fulfillment lead time or by perfect delivery fulfillment. Customers today expect rapid fulfillment of orders and having promised delivery dates met.
- *Customer-related measures* focus on the ability of the supply chain to meet customer wants and needs. Customer satisfaction is often measured by a variety of attributes on a perception scale that might range from "Extremely Dissatisfied" to "Extremely Satisfied."

EXHIBIT 13.6 Common Metrics Used to Measure Supply Chain Performance

Metric Category	Metric	Definition
Delivery reliability	Perfect order fulfillment	The number of perfect orders divided by the total number of orders
Responsiveness	Order fulfillment lead time	The time to fill a customer's order
	Perfect delivery fulfillment	The proportion of deliveries that were not just complete but also on time
Customer-related	Customer satisfaction	Customer perception of whether customers receive what they need when they need it, as well as such intangibles as convenient time of delivery, product and service quality, helpful manuals, and after-sales support
Supply chain efficiency	Average inventory value	The total average value of all items and materials held in inventory
	Inventory turnover	How quickly goods are moving through the supply chain?
	Inventory days' supply	How many days of inventory are in the supply chain or part of the supply chain?
Sustainability	Carbon dioxide emissions	The tons of CO_2 emissions generated per manufactured good or service process
	Energy reduction	How many kWh are needed before or after the change to the product, facility, equipment, process, or value chain?
Financial	Total supply chain costs	Total costs of order fulfillment, purchasing, maintaining inventory, distribution, technical support, and production
	Warranty/returns processing costs	The cost associated with repairs or restocking goods that have been returned
	Cash-to-cash conversion cycle	The average time to convert a dollar spent to acquire raw materials into a dollar collected for a finished good

- *Supply chain efficiency measures* include average inventory value, inventory turnover, and inventory days' supply. Average inventory value tells managers how much of the firm's assets are tied up in inventory. Inventory turnover (*IT*) is the ratio of the cost of goods sold divided by the average inventory value. Inventory turnover is computed using one of the following formulas:

$$\text{Inventory turnover } (IT) = \text{Sales/Average inventory} \tag{13.1}$$

$$\text{Inventory turnover } (IT) = \text{Cost of goods sold/Average inventory value} \tag{13.2}$$

Equation [13.1] is based on physical units of inventory, while Equation [13.2] uses dollar valuation. Note that inventory turnover can be computed over any time period such as months, quarters, or years. The cost of goods sold is the cost to produce the goods and services and normally does not include selling, general, administrative, research, engineering, and development expenses. Solved Problem 13.1 provides an example of computing inventory turnover using both of these equations.

"Good" values of inventory turnover depend on the industry, type of production process, and characteristics of the product such as volume, degree of customization, and amount of technology. Supermarkets, for instance, turn their inventory over 100 times per year; customized medical testing equipment has an inventory turnover rate of only 2 or 3. Most firms turn their inventory over 5 to 10 times per year. Careful examination of Equation 13.2 suggests that to achieve such high inventory turnover rates, average inventory value must be very low, which is an important objective for many firms. This also reduces the need to finance inventories and reduces the chances of inventory obsolescence.

Inventory days' supply (*IDS*) is calculated as follows:

$$\text{Inventory days' supply } (IDS) = \frac{\text{Average total inventory}}{\text{Cost of goods sold per day}} \tag{13.3}$$

SOLVED PROBLEM 13.1: COMPUTING INVENTORY TURNOVER

A retailer sells 4,000 units of a product each month. The average inventory on hand each month is 500 units.

a. What is the inventory turnover? What is the inventory turnover if the average on-hand inventory is 8,000 units?
b. A manufacturer has a cost of goods sold of $10,600,000 and an average inventory value of $3,600,000 over one year. What is the inventory turnover?

Solution:

a. Using Equation 13.1,

Inventory turnover = Sales/Average inventory
= 4,000/500
= 8

Assuming four weeks per month, this means that the retailer sells and replaces its inventory eight times per month, or twice each week. Equivalently, it sells 500 units in half a week.

If the average on hand inventory is 8,000 units, then IT = 4,000/8,000 = 0.5. In this case, it takes two months to turn over inventory and results in a much higher inventory holding cost.

b. Using Equation 13.2,

Inventory turnover = Cost of goods sold/Average inventory value
= $10,600,000/$3,600,000
= 2.94 times per year.

This means that the manufacturer sells and replaces its inventory approximately three times each year. Equivalently, it takes 365/2.94 = 124 days to sell $3,600,000 worth of inventory.

where the cost of goods sold per day is computed as

$$\text{Cost of goods sold per day} = \frac{\text{Annual cost of goods sold}}{\text{Operating days per year}} \qquad [13.4]$$

Solved Problem 13.2 illustrates an example.

- *Sustainability measures* show how supply chain performance affects the environment. These might include recycle versus original product manufacturing costs, water discharge quality, carbon dioxide emissions, and energy reductions. The goal is a carbon-neutral supply chain.
- *Financial measures* show how supply chain performance affects the bottom line. These might include total supply chain costs, costs of processing returns and warranties, and the cash-to-cash conversion cycle.

By tracking such measures and using the results to better control and improve supply chain performance, key organizational financial measures such as return on assets, cost of goods sold, revenue, and cash flow can be affected. For example, a reduction in average inventory value will improve return on assets; improved supplier performance can reduce the cost of goods sold; better customer satisfaction can increase revenues; and reduced lead times can have a positive impact on cash flow. Thus, senior managers should recognize the value of good supply chain design and management and provide resources to improve it.

13-5a Total Supply Chain Costs

Perhaps the most important financial measure for supply chain performance in Exhibit 13.6 is *total supply chain cost*. Supply chain managers must consider not only the direct cost of procurement, but also costs of transportation, tariffs and fees, inventory, and management oversight. Tariffs and fees may be imposed by a country involved in the creation and delivery of the product along the supply chain and can add to the cost of outsourcing globally. The North American Free Trade Agreement (NAFTA) signed in 1994 by Mexico, Canada, and the United States eliminates barriers to trade such as tariffs, and other countries in Asia are also seeking to eliminate them. In 2018, the United States, Mexico, and Canada reached an agreement to replace this with a new United States-Mexico-Canada agreement, which will replace NAFTA upon ratification. Management oversight costs include the cost of negotiating contracts, performing delivery and quality audits, monitoring shipments, travel to and from supplier facilities, problem resolution, and business-to-business sales relationship costs.

SOLVED PROBLEM 13.2: COMPUTING INVENTORY DAYS' SUPPLY

Suppose that the annual cost of goods sold is \$10,600,000, the average inventory value is \$3,600,000, and the firm operates 250 days per year. Then, using Equations 13.3 and 13.4, we have:

$$\begin{aligned} \text{Cost of goods sold per day} &= \$10{,}600{,}000/250 \\ &= \$42{,}400 \text{ per day.} \\ IDS &= \$3{,}600{,}000/\$42{,}400 \\ &= 84.9 \text{ days' supply.} \end{aligned}$$

This suggests that perhaps too much costly inventory is being maintained. Although the time period used in these calculations is typically days, modern technology allows this metric to be evaluated in terms of hours of inventory supply, and some supply chain managers are doing this.

Tariffs - Pros and Cons?

From 1790 to 1860, tariffs on imports generated ninety percent of the U.S. federal revenue. Later, tariffs were largely abandoned and generated less than one percent of total federal revenue. Tariffs are collected by Customs and Border Protection agents at over 300 ports of entry in the United States. Tariffs discourage imports by making them more expensive.

A few advantages of import tariffs include protecting domestic industries, and saving jobs from foreign competition, raising revenue, reducing the federal deficit, preventing the dumping of low-cost products into the domestic economy, and influencing the import nation's international trade practices and behavior. An example of the latter is fighting over the sharing of new technology to gain access to national markets. Disadvantages of tariffs include more expensive goods and services, less competitive pressure on domestic firms to improve, potential retaliation from other countries, discouragement of foreign investment, negative impact on country relationships, and making the economy of the country that impose the tariffs less efficient over the long-term.

Supply chain managers must include these costs and risks in their analyses as they redesign global supply chains and manage day-to-day operations and logistics.[11]

Supply chain managers seek to optimize the total system cost; this usually involves analytic modeling and analysis. We may calculate total supply chain costs using the following:

$$\text{Total supply chain cost } (TSCC) = \text{Procurement cost} + \text{Oversight cost} + \text{Transportation cost} + \text{Order cycle Inventory cost} + \text{Pipeline inventory cost}$$

or

$$TSCC = P \times D + O \times D + C_t \times D + C_o \times (D/Q) + (Q/2) \times C_h + d \times L \times C_h$$

By combining terms, we may express this as:

$$TSCC = D \times (P + O + C_t) + C_o \times (D/Q) + (Q/2) \times C_h + d \times L \times C_h \quad [13.5]$$

where

P = *Unit price of procurement*
O = *Management oversight costs per unit*
C_t = *Cost per unit for transportation including import and export tariffs and fees*
D = *Annual demand forecast (units)*
Q = *Order quantity (units)*
C_o = *Order cost per order*
C_h = *Annual inventory holding cost per unit*
L = *Lead time (days)*
d = *Average daily demand (units/day)*

In this formula, $P \times D$ represents the total annual cost of procuring the item, $O \times D$ is the total annual cost of management oversight, and $C_t \times D$ is the total annual transportation cost including tariffs and fees. From Chapter 12, we saw that the annual order cost is expressed in Equation 12.5 as $C_o \times (D/Q)$, and the annual inventory holding costs from Equation 12.4 is $(Q/2) \times C_h$. Finally, the average annual pipeline inventory *cost* $= d \times L \times C_h$. **Pipeline inventory** *is inventory that has been ordered but is in transit*. Note that $d \times L$ is the average number of units in transit; thus, $(dL)C_h$ is the average annual holding cost for this inventory. For example, suppose that a computer manufacturer orders an average of 10,000 keyboards each week and it takes four weeks to ship from a factory in Asia to the United States. The average daily demand is 10,000/7, and the lead time is 28 days; therefore, the pipeline inventory is $(10,000/7)(28) = 40,000$ units. Although pipeline inventory is not physically available to the user or customer, it must be accounted for to plan production and future replenishment orders.

SOLVED PROBLEM 13.3: COMPUTING TOTAL SUPPLY CHAIN COSTS

A global sourcing manager for Delta Automotive wants to compute the total supply chain costs for different order sizes for an automobile part purchased from three different global suppliers. The data for this problem is shown in Exhibit 13.7, and the annual demand $D = 400,000$ units. The supplier prices and transportation costs are predicated on an order quantity of 40,000 units (note that this is not the EOQ). Unit price discounts are given for larger order quantities that reflect economies of scale. Which supplier and order quantity provides the lowest total supply chain cost? Assume that parts are transported from Mexico to the United States by truck, by a combination of ships and trucks from Japan and China, and 250 working days per year.

Solution:

Exhibit 13.8 shows the calculation of total supply chain costs using Equation 13.5 for each supplier for the 40,000-unit order quantity using the *Total Supply Chain Cost* Excel template available in MindTap. We see that the Mexican supplier has the lowest cost. If the model is evaluated for the discounted prices and a 100,000-unit order quantity, you will find that the total cost is less for all three suppliers; however, you will see that the Chinese supplier will have the lowest total cost. This is summarized in the table below:

Total Supply Chain Costs	Order Quantity (Q)	
	40,000 units	**100,000 units**
Japanese Supplier	\$3,682,850	\$3,579,600
Mexican Supplier	\$3,568,200	\$3,526,300
Chinese Supplier	\$3,894,700	\$3,490,100

The Mexican supplier offers only a 2.6 percent discount in unit price [(\$7.60 − \$7.40)/\$7.60] when Q = 40,000 versus $Q = 100,000$. However, despite the fact that the unit transportation cost is much higher, the Chinese supplier offers a 15.7 percent procurement discount [(\$7.00 − \$5.90)/\$7.00] for $Q = 100,000$. Based strictly on minimizing total supply chain costs, Delta Automotive should outsource to the Chinese supplier with $Q = 100,000$ units. Delta Automotive saves \$78,100 (\$3,568,200 − \$3,490,100). In practice, the final decision would consider not only total supply chain costs but also the risks noted in Exhibits 13.3 and 13.4.

EXHIBIT 13.7 Cost Parameters for Selecting a Global Supplier and Order Quantity with Total Annual Demand (D) 5 400,000 Units

Global Supplier	Price Per Unit (P) at Q = 40,000	Price Per Unit (P) at Q = 100,000	Management Oversight Cost Per Unit (O)	Transportation & Tariff Cost Per Unit (C_t)	Order Cost Per Order (C_o)	Annual Holding Cost/Unit (C_h)	Lead Time in Days
Japanese Supplier	\$7.65	\$7.30	\$0.55	\$0.60	\$625	\$1.35	60
Mexican Supplier	\$7.60	\$7.40	\$0.65	\$0.35	\$400	\$1.35	45
Chinese Supplier	\$7.00	\$5.90	\$1.25	\$0.75	\$850	\$1.35	120

EXHIBIT 13.8 ***Total Supply Chain Cost* Excel Template for Q = 40,000**

	A	B	C	D	E	F
1	Total Supply Chain Cost Analysis	Copyright © 2017 Cengage Learning				
2	Enter the data only in the yellow cells.	Not for commercial use.				
3	The template is designed for up to five suppliers.					
4						
5	Supplier	Japanese	Mexican	Chinese		
6	Procurement cost/unit, P	$7.65	$7.60	$7.00		
7	Management oversight cost/unit, O	$0.55	$0.65	$1.25		
8	Unit transportation cost Ct	$0.60	$0.35	$0.75		
9	Order cost/order, C_o	$625.00	$400.00	$850.00		
10	Holding cost per unit, C_h	$1.35	$1.35	$1.35		
11	Lead time, L	60	45	120		
12						
13	Annual Demand, D	400000				
14	Order Quantity, Q	40000				
15	Average number of orders/year (D/Q)	10.00				
16	Average daily demand (D/250)	1600.00				
17						
18						
19	Total procurement cost	$3,060,000.00	$3,040,000.00	$2,800,000.00		
20	Total management oversight cost	$220,000.00	$260,000.00	$500,000.00		
21	Total annual transportation cost	$240,000.00	$140,000.00	$300,000.00		
22	Annual order cost	$6,250.00	$4,000.00	$8,500.00		
23	Annual holding cost	$27,000.00	$27,000.00	$27,000.00		
24	Average annual pipeline inventory cost	$129,600.00	$97,200.00	$259,200.00		
25	Total supply chain costs	$3,682,850.00	$3,568,200.00	$3,894,700.00		

13-5b The Cash-to-Cash Conversion Cycle

One of the more useful financial metrics for evaluating supply chain performance is the cash-to-cash conversion cycle, which identifies cash flows from the time costs are incurred (such as raw material inventory) to when it is paid (accounts receivable). The cycle is computed as inventory days' supply (*IDS*) plus accounts receivable days' supply (*ARDS*) minus accounts payable days' supply (*APDS*). The following formulas are used:

Inventory days' supply (*IDS*) = Average total inventory/Cost of goods sold per day (defined previously in Equations 13.3 and 13.4)

$$ARDS = \text{Accounts receivable value/Revenue per day} \quad [13.6]$$

$$APDS = \text{Accounts payable value/Revenue per day} \quad [13.7]$$

$$\text{Revenue per day } (R/D) = \text{Total revenue/Operating days per year} \quad [13.8]$$

Finally, the cash-to-cash conversion cycle is computed as:

$$\text{Cash-to-cash conversion cycle} = IDS + ARDS - APDS \quad [13.9]$$

Solved Problem 13.4 illustrates the cash-to-cash conversion cycle calculations.

13-5c Supplier Evaluation and Certification

Evaluating and measuring supplier performance plays an important role in supply chain management. For instance, Boeing created a forum in which it meets with supplier representatives every other month, with a goal of improving the supplier performance measurement process and its tools. Many companies segment suppliers into categories based on their importance to the business and manage them accordingly. At Corning, Level 1 suppliers, who provide raw materials, cases, and hardware, are deemed critical to business success and are managed by teams that include representatives from engineering, materials control, purchasing, and the supplier company. Level 2 suppliers provide specialty materials, equipment, and services, and are managed by internal customers. Level 3 suppliers provide commodity items and are centrally managed by purchasing.[12]

Many companies also use some type of supplier certification process. These processes are designed to rate and certify suppliers who provide quality materials in a cost-effective and timely manner. For example, the Pharmaceutical Manufacturers Association defines a **certified supplier** *as one that, after extensive investigation, is found to supply material*

SOLVED PROBLEM 13.4: EVALUATING THE CASH-TO-CASH CONVERSION CYCLE

Evaluate the cash-to-cash conversion cycle for a company that has annual sales of $3.5 million, annual cost of goods sold of $2.8 million, 250 operating days a year, total average on-hand inventory of $460,000, accounts receivable equal to $625,000, and accounts payable of $900,100. What can you conclude about the company's operating practices?

Solution:

Using Equations 13.3, 13.4 and 13.6 through 13.9., we compute the following:

$$CGS/D = \frac{\text{Annual cost of goods sold}}{\text{Operating days per year}} = \frac{\$2,800,000}{250}$$
$$= \$11,200 \text{ per day}$$

$$R/D = \frac{\text{Total revenue (sales)}}{\text{Operating days per year}} = \frac{\$3,500,000}{250}$$
$$= \$14,000 \text{ per day}$$

$$IDS = \frac{\text{Average total inventory}}{\text{Cost of goods sold per day}} = \frac{\$460,000}{\$11,200}$$
$$= 41.1 \text{ days}$$

$$ARDS = \frac{\text{Accounts receivable value}}{\text{Revenue per day}} = \frac{\$625,000}{\$14,000}$$
$$= 44.6 \text{ days}$$

$$APDS = \frac{\text{Accounts payable value}}{\text{Revenue per day}} = \frac{\$900,100}{\$14,000}$$
$$= 64.3 \text{ days}$$

Cash-to-cash conversion cycle = $IDS + ARDS - APDS =$ $41.1 + 44.6 - 64.3 = 21.4$. This is illustrated in the following figure:

From this analysis, the firm must borrow funds to finance its inventory. Its inventory and accounts receivable cycles add up to 85.7 days, yet it must pay its bill, on average, in

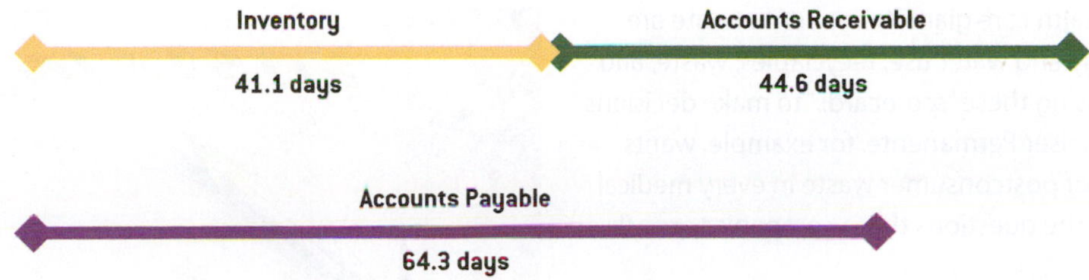

64.3 days. The firm receives the customer's payments (accounts receivable), on average, 21.4 days "after" it must pay its bills to suppliers (accounts payable), so it must borrow funds to finance inventory. If by improving inventory and/or accounts receivable systems and practices the firm can shorten the 85.7 days to 64.3 days, theoretically it should not have to borrow funds to support its inventory levels. All of these numbers should be compared to industry and competitor performance standards.

of such quality that routine testing on each lot received is unnecessary. Certification provides recognition for high-quality suppliers, which motivates them to improve continuously and attract more business. Target, for instance, purchases goods from more than 3,000 factories around the world. Every factory must meet their global social compliance requirements and must pass unannounced audits. Target evaluates the quality of the products being made, as well as the documentation, capability, and capacity of the factories. The factories are expected to address any corrective action recommendations or risk being dropped as a supplier.[13]

Supplier certification is driven by performance measurement and rating processes. For example, at Boeing, suppliers are rated on delivery—the percentage of pieces the supplier delivered on time to Boeing during a 12-month period; general performance—a comprehensive assessment of a supplier's business management performance from Boeing experts who assess supplier performance in the areas of management, scheduling, technical issues, cost and quality; and quality—either the percentage of pieces accepted, during a 12-month period, cost of product nonconformance subtracted from the price of products received during a 12-month period, or a scorecard criteria of quality indicators jointly selected by Boeing and the supplier. These ratings are translated in one of five performance categories: gold, silver, bronze, yellow, and red. Suppliers are eligible to receive the annual Boeing Performance Excellence Award if they achieve silver or gold performance ratings for the entire performance year.[14]

13-6 Sustainability in Supply Chains

In the past, supply chain performance was focused on cost, time, and quality performance. Today, sustainability is one of the key goals of supply chains (see the box "Getting Suppliers to Become Lean and Sustainable"). A large amount of harmful emissions and pollutants emanate from the supply chain. Research has suggested that upward of 60 to 70 percent of a company's carbon footprint is found along their supply chain.[15] Therefore, part of a supply chain manager's job today is to measure, monitor, and constantly try to improve environmental performance.

Getting Suppliers to Become Lean and Sustainable

Procter & Gamble and health care giant Kaiser Permanente are rating suppliers on energy and water use, recyclables, waste, and greenhouse gases, and using these "scorecards" to make decisions on which suppliers use. Kaiser Permanente, for example, wants to know the percentage of postconsumer waste in every medical product it buys. Some of the questions these companies are asking of suppliers include:

- What percent of energy consumed is generated from renewable resources? (Kaiser Permanente)
- How many metric tons of hazardous and nonhazardous waste are produced? (Procter & Gamble)

As the chief procurement officer at Kaiser Permanente stated, "We're sending a message to vendors loud and clear."[16]

Olivier Le Moal/Shutterstock.com

13-6a Green Sustainable Supply Chains

A **green sustainable supply chain** *is one that uses environmentally friendly inputs and transforms these inputs through change agents—whose byproducts can improve or be recycled within the existing environment.* This results in outputs that can be reclaimed and reused at the end of their life cycle, thus creating a sustainable supply chain.[17] Something as simple as reducing the amount of cardboard or filler by designing "smart packages" can save companies money and reduce landfill waste and energy usage.

In selecting suppliers, for example, supply chain managers might consider whether the supplier publishes an annual sustainability report, how the supplier ensures that its processes are free from environmentally harmful pollutants, whether the supplier has plans for reclaiming product components at the end of their life cycles, and whether the supplier has efficient recycling programs.

As one example, Apple is focusing on a goal of becoming completely powered by renewable energy. It is also targeting 100 percent renewable energy for its supply chain, launching a solar power operation in China and targeting net-zero deforestation for the forests that provide paper for its product packaging. In 2014, Apple achieved the goal of running its U.S. operations—offices, retail stores, and data centers—on 100 percent renewable energy. Worldwide, 87 percent of the company's facilities were renewably powered, using solar, wind, biogas, fuel cells, geothermal, and hydropower. Apple wants to eliminate its footprint from forests as well as power by making sure all its paper comes from sustainably managed forests. The best way to do that is to own the forest and the supply chain—a prime example of supply chain integration—instead of buying pulp or paper from outside vendors.[18]

> Research has suggested that upward of 60 to 70 percent of a company's carbon footprint is found along their supply chain.

An example of outstanding social sustainability performance and practices is the Vega Company (www.veja-store.com) founded in 2005. Vega's business model begins with suppliers followed by production and distribution, and ends with customers. Vega works with cotton, rubber, and leather suppliers, mainly in Brazil, to minimize their impact on

Sustainable Supply Chain Practices

Companies such as UPS and FedEx move a multitude of goods using trucks, airplanes, and trains. They use a lot of fuel, and these companies are challenged not only to save high energy costs but to reduce their carbon footprint. Customers today are more sensitive to environmental impact and are demanding better stewardship from the companies they deal with. UPS, for example, has been using low-emission rail transport since 1966 and selects the lowest-carbon route for customer shipments.[19] They also evaluate customers' supply chains for their environment impact and suggest improvements in transportation, inventory management, and shipping decisions. FedEx works with its suppliers to understand the environmental impacts of materials they use, and seeks to reduce those impacts.[20] Both UPS and FedEx often work with customers to analyze and improve their supply chains to enhance efficiency and reduce their customers' environmental footprint. These companies also exploit business analytics to improve routing their vehicles to reduce fuel consumption, and have introduced hybrid and electric vehicles in their fleets.

the environment while making a profit. Example practices of their sustainability business model include teaching Brazilian cotton farmers how to grow organic cotton with no pesticides; sourcing leather that uses eco-tanning methods with vegetable extracts instead of toxic metals such as chromium; sourcing directly from farmers eliminating warehouse and distributor intermediaries; supporting the production of natural rubber from trees to preserve Amazon forests and paying these farmers higher wages and creating better working conditions and family and community services. Other sustainable practices are described in the box on Sustainable Supply Chain Practices.

13-6b Manufactured Goods Recovery and Reverse Logistics

Many companies are developing options to recover manufactured goods that may be discarded or otherwise unusable. This is often called *manufactured goods recovery*, and consists of one or more of the following:

- *Reuse or resell* the equipment and its various component parts directly to customers once the original manufactured good is discarded. Furniture, appliances, and clothes are examples of the reuse and resell recovery option.
- *Repair* a manufactured good by replacing broken parts so it operates as required. Personal computers, vehicle parts, and shoes are examples of physical goods that may need to be repaired.
- *Refurbish* a manufactured good by updating its looks and/or components—for example, cleaning, painting, or perhaps replacing parts that are near failure. Products may have scratches, dents, or other forms of "cosmetic damage" that do not affect the performance of the unit. Refurbished products cannot be sold as new in the United States, which is why they are relabeled as refurbished or refreshed units even if they are as good as new. Often the equipment is returned to the manufacturer, which then fixes and certifies the unit and sells it at a discount.
- *Remanufacture* a good by completely disassembling it and repairing or replacing worn-out or obsolete components and modules. Honda, for example, remanufactures vehicle steering mechanism controls for sale as dealer-authorized replacement parts with the same warranty as new parts.
- *Cannibalize* parts for use and repair of other equipment of the same kind, such as automobiles, locomotives, and airplanes. Cannibalization can normally occur only with equipment that uses interchangeable parts, such as with automobiles and airplanes.
- *Recycle* goods by disassembling them and selling the parts or scrap materials to other suppliers. Aluminum soda cans, for example, are often melted and formed into new aluminum sheets and cans.
- *Incineration or landfill disposal* of goods that are not economical to repair, refurbish, remanufacture, or recycle.

For products that are of high enough value, it is normally more cost-effective to remanufacture or refurbish the product, and convert damaged inventory into saleable goods, thus recapturing value on products that would otherwise be lost in disposition. In addition, efficiencies associated with manufactured goods recovery can yield increases in customer loyalty and retention through an enhanced public and sustainable image; boost revenue; reduce operating costs; provide customers with replaceable parts, typically at lower prices than totally new parts; and improve the new customer's uptime.

Reverse logistics *refers to managing the flow of finished goods, materials, or components that may be unusable or discarded through the supply chain from customers toward either suppliers, distributors, or* *manufacturers for the purpose of reuse, resale, or disposal*. This reverse flow is opposite to the normal operating supply chain where the raw materials and parts are assembled into finished goods and then delivered to wholesalers, retailers, and ultimately customers. As a result, reverse logistics "closes the loop" in the supply chain and combined with the forward supply chain, is often called a closed loop system. In many firms, the forward supply chain operates independently of reverse logistics activities, sometimes with different owners and players.

Reverse logistics includes the following activities:

- *Logistics:* authorizing returns, receiving, sorting, testing, refurbishing, cannibalizing, repairing, remanufacturing, recycling, restocking, reshipping, and disposing of materials.
- *Marketing/sales*: remarketing and selling the recovered good for reuse or resale to wholesalers and retailers.
- *Accounting/finance:* approving warranty repairs, tracking reverse logistic revenue and costs, billing, and paying appropriate suppliers and third-party vendors.
- *Call center service*: managing service center calls all along the supply chain to coordinate work activities such as collecting items from many diverse sources for recovery operations.
- *Legal/regulatory compliance*: constantly monitoring compliance with local, state, federal, and country laws, import and export regulations including environmental, and service contract commitments.

An example of manufactured goods recovery within a reverse logistics supply chain is shown in Exhibit 13.9. Best Buy, Sears, and Target have all used reverse logistics to find buyers for defective, broken, or returned products that would otherwise end up in landfills. KPMG research found that companies can recover 0.3 percent of annual sales with a good reverse logistics system. Best Buy, for example, would make an extra $100 million at this 0.3 percent rate. As another example, Patagonia recaptures all of the fiber from its outdoor clothes and those of competitors,

EXHIBIT 13.9 Example of a Manufactured Goods Recovery (Reverse Logistics) Supply Chain

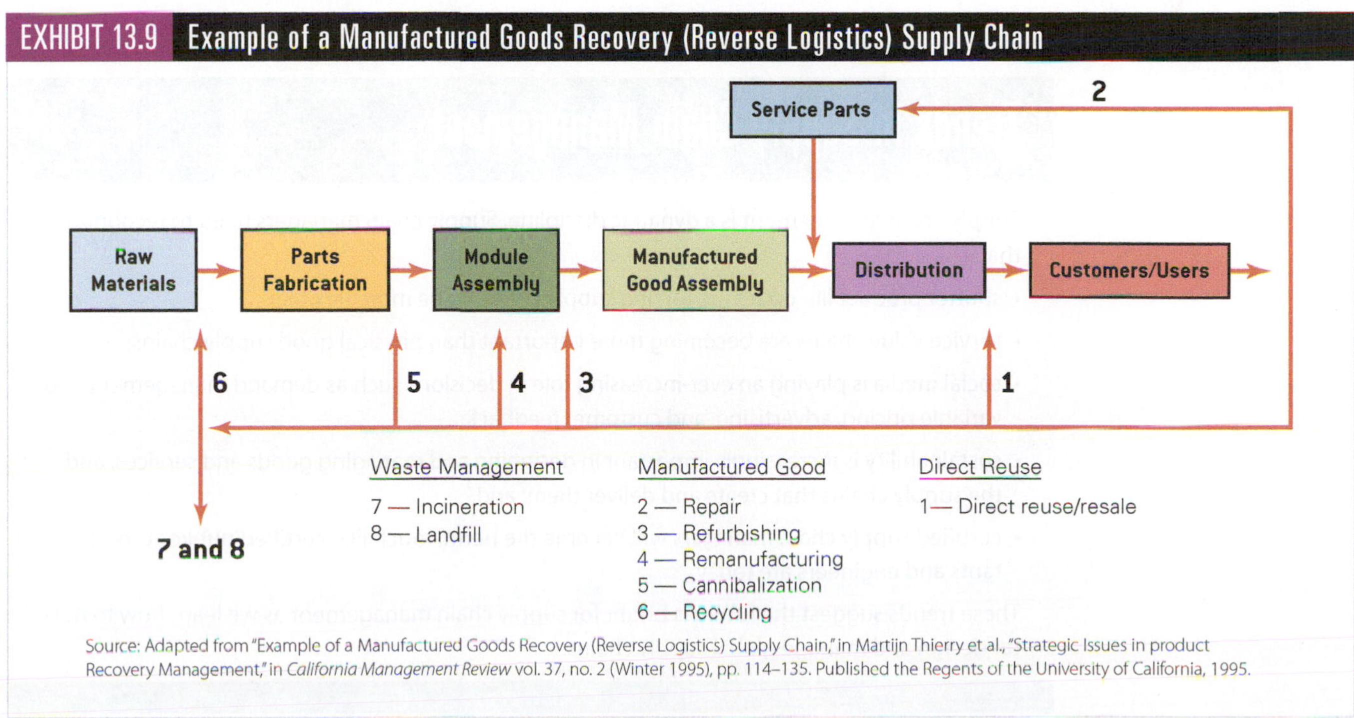

Source: Adapted from "Example of a Manufactured Goods Recovery (Reverse Logistics) Supply Chain," in Martijn Thierry et al., "Strategic Issues in product Recovery Management," in *California Management Review* vol. 37, no. 2 (Winter 1995), pp. 114–135. Published the Regents of the University of California, 1995.

as customers drop off worn duds at distribution centers or mail them in. Ninety percent of this recycled fiber is spun into new clothing; the rest is sold to a cement additive company.

Supply chain managers must evaluate the trade-offs between adopting different recovery options for a particular physical good. For example, how does the total cost of remanufacturing compare to cannibalizing parts or subassemblies? In addition, the manager must consider social and environmental sustainability criteria and issues in the final analysis of manufactured goods recovery.

Free Returns and Shipping Are Not Free

As online shopping surges, so do promises by stores like Target and Amazon of free shipping and returns. Target is redesigning its stores with a separate entrance for shoppers returning items. Nordstrom's now has a "Drop and Shop" service in some urban stores to return items bought online. Online shoe retailer Zappos has no time limit on when customers must return unwanted items. Happy Returns, a reverse logistics company, is building a network of return bars in shopping centers and malls. It plans to develop partnerships with many online retailers.

The key idea of returns is to reduce consumer risk when purchasing items online. In many situations, moving an item backwards in the supply chain is more costly than moving new products forward in the supply chain. Returned items can be resold as new, refurbished, repaired, or recycled. The cost of returns averages between 7 and 10 percent of the cost of goods sold, and it is increasing. While many companies also offer free shipping, the cost of shipping impacts the bottom line and is often included in the price to the consumer. Some goods on Amazon have higher prices than other retailers that do not provide free shipping, but when the shipping costs are included, the prices are comparable. So, free returns and shipping are not free.

Trends in Supply Chain Management

Supply chain management is a dynamic discipline. Supply chain managers need to recognize that

- shorter product life cycles are forcing supply chains to be more flexible;
- service value chains are becoming more important than physical good supply chains;
- social media is playing an ever-increasing role in decisions such as demand management and variable pricing, advertising, and customer feedback;
- sustainability is increasingly important in designing and managing goods and services, and the supply chains that create and deliver them; and
- certified supply chain managers will become the norm, much like certified public accountants and engineers are today.

These trends suggest the future is bright for supply chain management as we learn how to better design and manage global supply chains.

CHAPTER 13 LEARNING OBJECTIVE SUMMARIES

13.1 **Explain the basic concepts of supply chain management.** The basic purpose of a supply chain is to coordinate the flow of materials, services, and information among the elements of the supply chain to maximize customer value. The key functions generally include sales and order processing, transportation and distribution, operations, inventory and materials management, finance, and customer service. A goods-producing supply chain generally consists of suppliers, manufacturers, distributors, retailers, and customers. Raw materials and components are ordered from suppliers and must be transported to manufacturing facilities for production and assembly into finished goods. Finished goods are shipped to distributors that operate distribution centers.

13.2 **Describe the activities associated with logistics.** The primary responsibilities of logistics managers include:

1. Purchasing transportation services;
2. Managing the transportation of materials and goods through the supply chain;
3. Managing inventories.

Transportation costs can add up to 10 percent to the total cost of the product as it moves through the supply chain: rail, trucks, air, ships and barges, and pipelines are all methods of transport. Careful management of inventory is critical to time-based supply chain performance in order to respond effectively to customers.

13.3 **Describe the types of risks supply chains face and ways to mitigate them.** Risks in domestic supply chains are often minimal; however, risks in global supply chains are much greater. These include production problems with suppliers that result in material shortages, labor strikes, unexpected transportation delays, delays from customs inspection or port operations, political instability in foreign countries, natural disasters, and even terrorism. Examples of short- and long-term risks that supply chains may face, and ways by which they can be mitigated, are summarized in Exhibits 13.3 and 13.4. Tactical risks are those that influence the day-to-day management of operations, while strategic risks can impact the design of the entire supply chain. Low- and mid-level managers, as well as front line-employees, can often address tactical risks. However, strategic risks must be addressed by top-level managers.

13.4 **Describe how e-commerce has changed the role of supply chains.** The e-commerce view of the supply chain is shown in Exhibit 13.5. An intermediary is any entity—real or virtual—that coordinates and shares information between buyers and sellers. Some firms, such as General Electric, Walmart, and Procter & Gamble, use e-commerce to communicate directly with suppliers and retail stores, and thereby skip traditional bricks-and-mortar intermediaries. Return facilitators specialize in handling all aspects of customers returning a manufactured good or delivered service and requesting their money back, repairing the manufactured good and returning it to the customer, and/or invoking the service guarantee.

13.5 **List and describe the important metrics used to measure supply chain performance, and be able to evaluate total supply chain costs and cash-to-cash conversion cycles.** Supply chain managers use numerous metrics to evaluate performance and identify improvements to the design and operation of their supply chains. These include delivery reliability, responsiveness, customer-related measures, supply chain efficiency, and financial measures.

Total supply chain cost (TSCC) = Procurement cost + Oversight cost + transportation Cost + Order cycle inventory cost + Pipeline inventory cost or

$$TSCC = D \times (P + O + C_t) + C_o \times (D/Q) + (Q/2) \times C_h + d \times L \times C_h \quad [13.5]$$

where:

P = Unit price of procurement

O = Management oversight costs per unit

C_t = Cost per unit for transportation including import and exporttariffs and fees.

D = Annual demand forecast (units)

Q = Order quantity (units)

C_o = Order cost per order

C_h = Annual inventory holding cost per unit

L = Lead time (days)

d = Average daily demand (units/day)

The cash-to-conversion cycle is computed as inventory days' supply (IDS) plus accounts receivable days' supply (ARDS) minus accounts payable days' supply (APDS). The following formulas are used:

Inventory days' supply (IDS) =
Average total inventory/ Cost of goods sold per day [13.3]

Cost of goods sold per day (CGS/D) =
Cost of goods sold value/ Operating days per year [13.4]

$ARDS$ = Accounts receivable value/ Revenue per day [13.6]

$APDS$ = Accounts payable value/ Revenue per day [13.7]

Revenue per day (R/D) =
Total revenue/ Operating days per year [13.8]

Finally, the cash-to-cash conversion cycle is computed as:

Cash-to-cash conversion cycle = $IDS + ARDS - APDS$ [13.9]

CHAPTER 13 LEARNING OBJECTIVE SUMMARIES

13.6 **Describe how organizations are incorporating sustainability issues in managing their supply chains, and explain how manufactured goods recovery and reverse logistics work.** Companies move goods using trucks, airplanes, and trains. They are challenged not only to avoid high energy costs but also to reduce their carbon footprint. Many work to analyze and improve their supply chains to enhance efficiency and reduce their customers' environmental footprint.

These companies also exploit business analytics to improve routing their vehicles to reduce fuel consumption, and have introduced hybrid and electric vehicles in their fleets.

Manufactured goods recovery consists of one or more of the following:

- *Reuse or resell* the equipment and its various component parts.
- *Repair* a manufactured good by replacing broken parts so it operates as required.
- *Refurbish* a manufactured good by updating its looks and/or components.
- *Remanufacture* a good by completely disassembling it and repairing or replacing worn-out or obsolete components and modules.
- *Cannibalize* parts for use and repair of other equipment of the same kind, such as automobiles, locomotives, and airplanes.

KEY TERMS

- **Backhaul**
- **Certified supplier**
- **Green sustainable supply chain**
- **Intermediary**
- **Logistics**
- **Order amplification**
- **Pipeline inventory**
- **Purchasing (procurement)**
- **Return facilitators**
- **Reverse logistics**
- **Risk management**
- **Supply chain integration**
- **Supply chain management (SCM)**
- **Supply Chain Operations Reference (SCOR) model**
- **Value chain integration**
- **Vendor-managed inventory (VMI)**

REVIEW QUESTIONS

13.1 1. What is supply chain management? How does it differ from logistics?.

13.1 2. Explain the SCOR model. Why is it useful in managing supply chains?

13.1 3. Explain the role of the purchasing function.

13.1 4. What are the three key principles that should be used in working with suppliers?

13.1 5. Explain supply chain and value chain integration.

13.2 6. List the activities associated with logistics.

13.2 7. Cite and explain one advantage and one disadvantage of each of the following transportation modes: air, rail, truck, ships and barges, and pipelines.

13.2 8. What is vendor-managed inventory?

13.2 9. Explain the bullwhip effect in supply chains.

13.3 10. Describe the types of risks supply chains face and ways to mitigate them.

13.4 11. Describe how e-commerce has changed the role of supply chains.

13.5 12. List and describe the important metrics used in supply chain performance and be able to evaluate total supply chain costs.

13.5 13. Describe the components of cash-to-cash conversion cycle analyses. What are the implications of positive and negative cash flows?

13.5 14. What is a certified supplier? Why is supplier certification important?

13.6 15. Describe how organizations are incorporating sustainability issues in managing their supply chains, and explain how manufactured goods recovery and reverse logistics work.

DISCUSSION QUESTIONS AND EXPERIENTIAL ACTIVITIES

13.1 16. Draw a supply chain flowchart similar to Exhibit 13.1 using the SCOR Model for a business you have worked in or have experience with. Describe how the supply chain works. If you have little or no work experience, then do the assignment for a restaurant or business you frequent (maximum of two typed pages).

13.1 17. Research the job of a global sourcing manager and describe the job duties, travel requirements, and skill set (maximum of two typed pages).

13.3 18. Select three types of supply chain risks and explain in-depth how supply chain managers can help mitigate these risks. That is, develop an action plan to mitigate these risks (maximum of two typed pages).

13.6 19. Research and find a "return facilitator." Describe what they do and how they make money (maximum of two typed pages).

13.6 20. Research and find a good or service supply chain with a quantifiable carbon footprint. Write a short paper (maximum of two typed pages) on the topic, and if possible, how the carbon footprint was computed. Cite your sources.

13.6 21. Research and find a physical good that is biodegradable or carbon neutral. Be prepared to present your findings to the class in a two- to five-minute discussion.

13.6 22. Research what type(s) of reverse logistics program(s) your city, county, or state government supports and write a short paper describing how it works (and a simple flowchart if possible). What percentage of total waste ends up in a landfill? (maximum of two typed pages).

COMPUTATIONAL PROBLEMS AND EXERCISES

These exercises require you to apply the formulas and methods described in the chapter. The problems should be solved manually.

13.5 23. Keto Grocery Store sells 400 gallons of milk each month. The average on-hand inventory is 50 gallons. What is the inventory turnover? What does it mean?

13.5 24. Over the past year, Keto Grocery Store had a cost of goods sold of $24,500,000 and an average value of inventory of $1,100,500. What is its inventory turnover? What does it mean?

13.5 25. A big box electronics store sells 250 65-inch televisions during the year. The store maintains an average inventory of five units. What is its inventory turnover? What implications does this have for inventory management?

13.5 26. A manufacturer of large industrial electric motors has a cost of goods sold of $111,690,000 and an average inventory value of $14,609,300. What is its inventory turnover? What does it mean?

13.5 27. Bragg Johnson, materials manager at Johnson & Sons, has determined that a certain product experienced 3.8 turns last year, with an annual sales volume (at cost) of $975,000. What was the average inventory value for this product last year? What would be the average inventory level if inventory turns could be increased to 6.0?

13.5 28. Andrew Manufacturing held an average inventory of $1.1 million (raw materials, work-in-process, finished goods) last year. Its sales were $8.0 million, and its cost of goods sold was $5.8 million. The firm operates 260 days a year. What is the inventory days' supply? What target inventory level is necessary to reach a 20- and 10-day inventory days' supply during the next two years?

13.5 29. Based on the following information, how many days of supply of inventory is the firm holding (assume 250 days of operation per year)? Interpret your answer if the industry average inventory days' supply is 30 days.

Sales	$8,300,000
Cost of goods sold	$7,200,000
Gross profit	$1,100,000
Overhead costs	$600,000
Net profit	$500,000
Total inventory	$2,600,000
Fixed assets	$3,000,000
Long-term debt	$2,700,000

13.5 30. Claiken Incorporated is a supplier of axles for light trucks. They held an average axle inventory of $1.6 million last year, with a cost of goods sold of $21.0 million. What is the inventory turnover for axles? A customer wants them to increase its inventory turnover rate to 20 by implementing better inventory and operating practices. What average axle inventory level is needed to meet this 20-turn target?

13.5 31. What are total purchase and oversight costs if annual demand is 1,000,000 units, the purchase price is $2.42, and the management oversight costs to monitor and expedite the trans-Pacific shipment are $0.16 per unit?

13.5 32. What is the pipeline inventory value if average daily demand is 82 units, the lead time is 20 days, and annual inventory carrying costs is $12?

13.5 33. What are order cycle costs if annual demand is 8,000 units, the order quantity is 1,000 units, and annual order cost is $97? What if the order size changes to 500 units or 8,000 units?

13.5 34. What is the annual transportation cost if annual demand is 240,000 units and the cost to transship a unit is $0.80 per unit?

13.5 35. Given the information in Exhibit 13.10, compute the procurement, oversight, transportation, order cycle inventory, pipeline inventory costs, and total supply chain costs for an air conditioner coil purchased from the supplier Entity, Inc. The order size is Q = 5,000 units and the supply chain operates 365 days a year.

13.5 36. Given the information in Exhibit 13.11, what are the procurement, oversight, transportation, order cycle inventory, pipeline inventory costs, and total supply chain costs for using the supplier Ebert, Inc. Ebert manufactures small speakers for automobiles in its factory in the Philippines. The order size is Q = 10,000 units and the supply chain operates 300 days a year.

13.5 37. Consider the following performance data for Modular Computers, Inc (MCI).
Sales = $34 million, cost of goods sold = $30 million, total average inventory = $428,000, accounts receivable = $2,100,000, accounts payable = $2,900,000, and operating 365 days per year. Compute the cash-to-cash conversion cycle. What does it mean?

13.5 38. As an operations management consultant, you have been asked to evaluate a furniture manufacturer's cash-to-cash conversion cycle under the following assumptions: sales of $23.5 million, cost of goods sold of $20.8 million, 50 operating weeks a year, total average on-hand inventory of $2,150,000, accounts receivable equal to $2,455,000, and accounts payable of $3,695,000. What do you conclude? What recommendations can you make to improve performance?

13.5 39. Using the data in Problem 38, assume the operating manager reduces total average inventory on-hand by 21 percent by using better operations and supply chain methods. What is the revised cash-to-cash conversion cycle in weeks? What does this change in the cash-to-cash conversion cycle mean?

EXHIBIT 13.10 Model 78CDV2 Air Conditioner Coil

Certified Supplier	Annual Demand (D)	Price per Unit (P)	Oversight Cost per Unit (O)	Transport Cost per Unit (C_t)	Order Cost (C_o)	Cost to Store One Unit One Year (C_h)	Oder Lead Time in Days (L)
Entity, Inc.	80,000	$11.80	$1.05	$4.90	$255	$5.00	45

EXHIBIT 13.11 Automobile Speakers from Ebert, Inc.

Certified Supplier	Annual Demand (D)	Price per Unit (P)	Oversight Cost per Unit (O)	Transport Cost per Unit (C_t)	Order Cost (C_o)	Cost to Store One Unit One Year (C_h)	Oder Lead Time in Days (L)
Ebert, Inc.	300,000	$9.48	$0.25	$2.12	$400	$6.40	45

EXCEL-BASED PROBLEMS

For these problems, you may use Excel or the spreadsheet templates in MindTap to assist in your analysis.

13.5 40. Given the information in Exhibit 13.12 for the Edwin Company, use the *Total Supply Chain Cost* Excel template to find the costs associated with the supply chain. The order size is Q = 2,500 units and the supply chain operates 250 days a year.

EXHIBIT 13.12 Supply Chain Cost Data for Edwin Company

Annual Demand (D)	Price per Unit (P)	Oversight Cost per Unit (O)	Transport Cost per Unit (C_t)	Order Cost (C_o)	Cost to Store One Unit One Year (C_h)	Oder Lead Time in Days (L)
580,000	$9.60	$0.85	$6.70	$225	$15.00	30

13.5 41. Given the information in Exhibit 13.13 for Rockland, Inc., use the *Total Supply Chain Cost* Excel template to compute the costs associated with the supply chain. The order quantity is 20,000 units, and the supply chain operates 250 days a year. What if the supplier asks you to increase your order quantity to $Q = 50{,}000$ for a price discount of two percent, would you accept the new deal? Explain.

13.5 42. A major automobile manufacturer located in Georgetown, Kentucky, has two certified vendors that produce brake pads with the information shown in Exhibit 13.14. New Albany Manufacturing is located in Columbus, Ohio, and LaPlaya Manufacturing is located in Monterrey, Mexico. The automobile assembly factory is assumed to operate 250 days per year.

a. Use the *Total Supply Chain Cost* Excel template to compute the supply chain costs associated with each supplier if the annual demand is 1,000,000 brake pads.

b. What supplier and order quantity do you recommend based on total costs?

c. List other criteria you might use to make the final supplier decision.

d. What will you tell the supplier that is not awarded the brake pad order?

13.5 43. Given the information in Exhibit 13.15 and a budget of $5,000,000, what is the most that Loyola Machining can pay for each manufactured unit? Assume one year is 250 working days and the order size is 6,500 units. Use the *Total Supply Chain Cost* Excel template for your analysis.

13.5 44. Fans-and-More, Inc. assemble controllers for ceiling fans. Exhibit 13.16 provides information on a plastic case for fan infrared controllers produced by one of their suppliers, Byannan, Inc. The plastic case is made using injection molding machines. Byannan requires a minimum order quantity of 100,000 units. The supply chain is assumed to operate 250 days a year.

a. Use the *Total Supply Chain Cost* Excel template to find the total supply chain cost.

b. Due to political and loading dock unrest in Byannan's home country, you must decide whether to increase order sizes and carry more inventory to support fan sales. A fan with no controller is not a sellable stock-keeping-unit. What order size is best? What do you recommend Fans-and-More do?

EXHIBIT 13.13 Supply Chain Data for Rockland, Inc.

Annual Demand (D)	Price per Unit (P)	Oversight Cost per Unit (O)	Transport Cost per Unit (C_t)	Order Cost (C_o)	Cost to Store One Unit One Year (C_h)	Oder Lead Time in Days (L)
250,000	$6.41	$0.35	$3.27	$200	$8.20	20

EXHIBIT 13.14 Automobile Manufacturer's Two Certified Supplier Decision

Certified Supplier	Order Size (Q)	Price per Unit (P)	Oversight Cost per Unit (O)	Transport Cost per Unit (C_t)	Order Cost (C_o)	Cost to Store One Unit One Year (C_h)	Oder Lead Time in Days (L)
New Albany Mfg.	50,000	$11.80	$0.00	$0.90	$155	$1.45	45
LaPlaya Mfg.	100,000	$ 10.85	$0.46	$1.25	$195	$1.10	100

EXHIBIT 13.15 Supply Chain Costs for Loyola Machining

Annual Demand (D)	Price per Unit (P)	Oversight Cost per Unit (O)	Transport Cost per Unit (C_t)	Order Cost (C_o)	Cost to Store One Unit One Year (C_h)	Oder Lead Time in Days (L)
650,000	?	$0.11	$3.25	$300	$9.00	20

EXHIBIT 13.16 Supply Chain Costs for Fan-and-More, Inc.

Annual Demand (D)	Price per Unit (P)	Oversight Cost per Unit (O)	Transport Cost per Unit (C_t)	Order Cost (C_o)	Cost to Store One Unit One Year (C_h)	Oder Lead Time in Days (L)
1,500,000	$0.86	$0.06	$0.11	$315	$0.32	120

LCC Medical Manufacturing, Inc.

LCC Medical Manufacturing, located in Punta Gorda, Florida, produces medical devices for orthopedic surgery including replacement parts for human knees, hips, and elbows, and surgical tools. One component LCC outsources is the metal tibial component. This part has a metal stem that is inserted into the tibial lower leg bone. LCC is evaluating three Tier 1 suppliers to manufacture the component part in a certain size. Annual demand for this stock-keeping-unit (SKU) is 20,000 units per year, and we assume 250 working days in a year. Other information is shown in Exhibits 13.17 and 13.18.

Case Questions for Discussion:

1. What is the total supply chain and logistics cost for each supplier when $Q = 5{,}000$, $Q = 10{,}000$, and $Q = 20{,}000$?
2. What supplier and order quantity do you recommend based on total supply chain costs?
3. Given your total supply chain cost analysis and the qualitative criteria in Exhibit 13.18, using a weighted scoring model of your own design, what are your summary scores for each supplier? (You may decide how to scale each criterion, the weight of each criterion, and whether to include costs or not.)
4. What are your final recommendations?

EXHIBIT 13.17 LCC Medical Manufacturing Economic Outsourcing Information for a Surgical Kit

(Tier 1 Supplier)	Price per Unit (P) @ $Q = 5{,}000$	Price per Unit (P) @ $Q = 10{,}000$	Price per Unit (P) @ $Q = 20{,}000$	Management Oversight Cost (O) per Unit	Transport Mode Cost (C_t) per Unit	Order Costs (C_o)	Cost to Store One Unit per Year (C_h)	Order Lead Time (L) in Days
Xiajing	$1.25	$0.95	$0.70	$0.35	$0.25	$655	$0.90	120
MedicUSA	$1.70	$1.60	$1.55	$0.15	$0.15	$260	$0.80	90
Werkzeug	$1.60	$1.35	$1.30	$0.20	$0.20	$350	$0.70	120

EXHIBIT 13.18 LCC Medical Manufacturing Qualitative Sourcing Criteria for a Surgical Kit

	Rank Order (1 – worst, 5 – best)		
Supplier Selection Criteria	**Xiajing**	**Medic USA**	**Werkzeug**
Delivery reliability	3	5	4
Product quality	3	4	5
Single supplier risks (sole sourcing)	High	Moderate	Moderate
Product and customs uncertainty (obsolescence, fees, work stoppages, etc.)	3	5	4
Sustainability practices (green supplier)	2	3	5

J&L Packaging, Inc.: Cash-to-Cash Conversion Cycle

Jake and Lilly Gifford founded J&L Packaging, Inc. (J&LP) in 1995 after graduating from the University of Cincinnati. Jake earned a degree in robotics and mechanical engineering, while Lilly graduated with a degree in computer science. They met at the university while working on an information systems course project and married immediately after graduation. Their privately held firm manufactured cardboard packaging and boxes for computer devices such as personal computers, keyboards, replacement hard drives, servers, and so on. Many of their packages were high-end boxes with glossy finishes and the company's logo on the box. Last year, J&LP's sales were $106 million.

J&LP provided many services with their products, such as box and packaging design engineering and consulting, embossing and foil guidance, barcode advice, cartons that fold and collapse for easy storage, and a variety of colors and box strengths. In 2010, J&LP began to research the sustainability issues regarding boxes in the reverse logistics supply chain. Their research lead to a change in production technologies to accommodate up to 100 percent recycled fiber content and solar panels on the roofs of their two U.S. factories. They also hired an engineer to lead the company's efforts to become a "Green Cycle"-certified manufacturer.

J&LP recently purchased and installed an ISOWA FALCON state-of-the-art, four-color, high-speed flexo box machine with an extensive zero defects quality control system. This box cutting and fabrication machine is manufactured in Kasugai, Japan, by the ISOWA Corporation (www.isowa.com). There are several videos of this automated machine in operation on YouTube, for example, https://www.youtube.com/watch?=XofTns666Aw.

J&LP's financial information for last year follows. It is assumed the business operates 300 days per year. One note in J&LP financial statement states that the $4,906,000 of inventory does not include $886,000 in inventory allowances for excess, cancelled orders, and obsolete inventories. The note goes on to say, "Inventory management remains an area of focus as we balance the need to maintain strategic inventory levels to ensure competitive lead times versus the risk of inventory obsolescence because of changing technology and customer requirements. The box and packaging business is a dynamic industry that must quickly accommodate customer requirements, changes in forecasts, and new findings from research and development on product features and options." The following data (in thousands of dollars $) is provided.

Sales	
• Manufactured Goods	$87,475
• Services	$18,619
• Total	$106,094
Cost of Sales	
• Manufactured Goods	$25,818
• Services	$ 5,907
• Total	$31,725
Operating Expenses	
• Research and Development	$17,619
• Sales and Marketing	$23,132
• Other	$ 6,182
• Total	$46,933
Obsolete Inventories	$ 886
Inventories	$ 4,906
Accounts Receivable	$ 7,593
Accounts Payable	$ 9,338

Case Questions for Discussion:

1. Should we consider services in the cash-to-cash conversion cycle computations?
2. How will you handle the $886,000 in obsolete inventory?
3. What is the total cash-to-cash conversion cycle for J&L Packaging, Inc. for last year?
4. What are your conclusions and final recommendations?

Integrative Case: Hudson Jewelers

The Hudson Jewelers case study found in MindTap integrates material found in each chapter of the book.

Case Questions for Discussion:

1. Research short- and long-term risks in the global diamond supply chains and write a short paper (maximum of three pages) defining these risks and describing how they are mitigated by major diamond-producing corporations.
2. Obtain the annual report of a major diamond producer such as DeBeers, ALROSA, Rio Tinto, or BHP Billiton, and perform a cash-to-cash conversion cycle analysis of their business. What conclusions do you reach? Explain the implications of the analysis for the firm.

Resource Management | 14

The Mayo Clinic needs annual forecasts of patient visits by week to allocate resources effectively.

Keith Levit/Design Pics/Getty Images

LEARNING OBJECTIVES

After studying this chapter, you should be able to:

- **14-1** Describe the overall frameworks for resource planning in both goods-producing and service-providing organizations.
- **14-2** Explain options for aggregate planning.
- **14-3** Explain the three basic strategies for aggregate planning.
- **14-4** Describe the applications of linear optimization models for resource planning.
- **14-4** Describe ways to disaggregate aggregate plans using master production scheduling and material requirements planning.
- **14-5** Explain the concept and application of capacity requirements planning.

The Mayo Clinic in Rochester, Minnesota serves regional, national, and international patients. The clinic's goal is to provide the majority of patients with access to the health services they require within one week. This requires careful attention to the management of resources. To allocate clinical resources efficiently and effectively, the Mayo Clinic starts with annual forecasts of outpatient visits per year per clinic by week. Managers use these forecasts to determine patient appointment demand, staff capacity, schedules, and budgets. The most expensive resources in outpatient clinics are typically physicians. Individual physician's calendars define times when they are available to see patients for scheduled visits. Before setting expectations for individual physician's calendars, managers estimate the aggregate number of physician hours required in a particular week. To enable advance bookings of patients, and to give patients time to make travel plans, the design of a physician's calendars begins 12 weeks in advance. At regular intervals, physicians release their calendars so appointment schedulers can book future patient appointments.[1]

WHAT DO YOU THINK?

Think about planning a party or some student-related function. What resources would you need to pull it off, and how might you plan to ensure that you had everything at the right time and in the right quantity?

The Mayo Clinic example illustrates the challenges that managers face in dealing with limited and valuable resources. Every industry—service and manufacturing—must carefully manage these resources, particularly in the face of changing and uncertain demand. **Resource management** *deals with the planning, execution, and control of all the resources that are used to produce goods or provide services in a value chain.* Resources include materials, equipment, facilities, information, technical knowledge and skills, and of course, people. Typical objectives of resource management are to (1) maximize profits and customer satisfaction; (2) minimize costs; or (3) for not-for-profit organizations such as government and churches, maximize benefits to their stakeholders.

Resources include materials, equipment, facilities, information, technical knowledge and skills, and, of course, people.

14-1 Resource Planning Framework for Goods and Services

A generic framework for resource planning is shown in Exhibit 14.1. This framework is broken down into three basic levels. Level 1 represents aggregate planning. **Aggregate planning** *is the development of a long-term output and resource plan in aggregate units of measure.* Aggregate plans define output levels over a planning horizon of one to two years, usually in monthly or quarterly time buckets. They normally focus on product families or total capacity requirements rather than individual products or specific capacity allocations. Aggregate plans also help to define budget allocations and associated resource requirements.

Aggregate planning is driven by demand forecasts. High-level forecasts are often developed for aggregate groups of items (see the Nestlé box). For instance, a consumer-products company like Procter & Gamble might produce laundry soap in a variety of sizes. However, it might forecast the total demand for the soap in dollars over some future time horizon, regardless of product size. Aggregate planning would then translate these forecasts into monthly or quarterly production plans.

In Exhibit 14.1, Level 2 planning is called disaggregation. **Disaggregation** *is the process of translating aggregate plans into short-term operational plans that provide the basis for weekly and daily schedules and detailed resource requirements.* To disaggregate means to break up or separate into more detailed pieces. Disaggregation specifies more-detailed plans for the creation of individual goods and services or the allocation of capacity to specific time periods. For goods-producing firms, disaggregation takes Level 1 aggregate planning decisions and breaks them down into such details as order sizes and schedules for individual subassemblies and resources by week and day.

To illustrate aggregate planning and disaggregation, consider a producer of ice cream who might use long-term forecasts to determine the total number of gallons of ice cream to produce each quarter over the next two years. This projection provides the basis for determining how many employees and other resources such as delivery trucks would be needed throughout

EXHIBIT 14.1 Framework for Resource Management Planning for Goods and Services

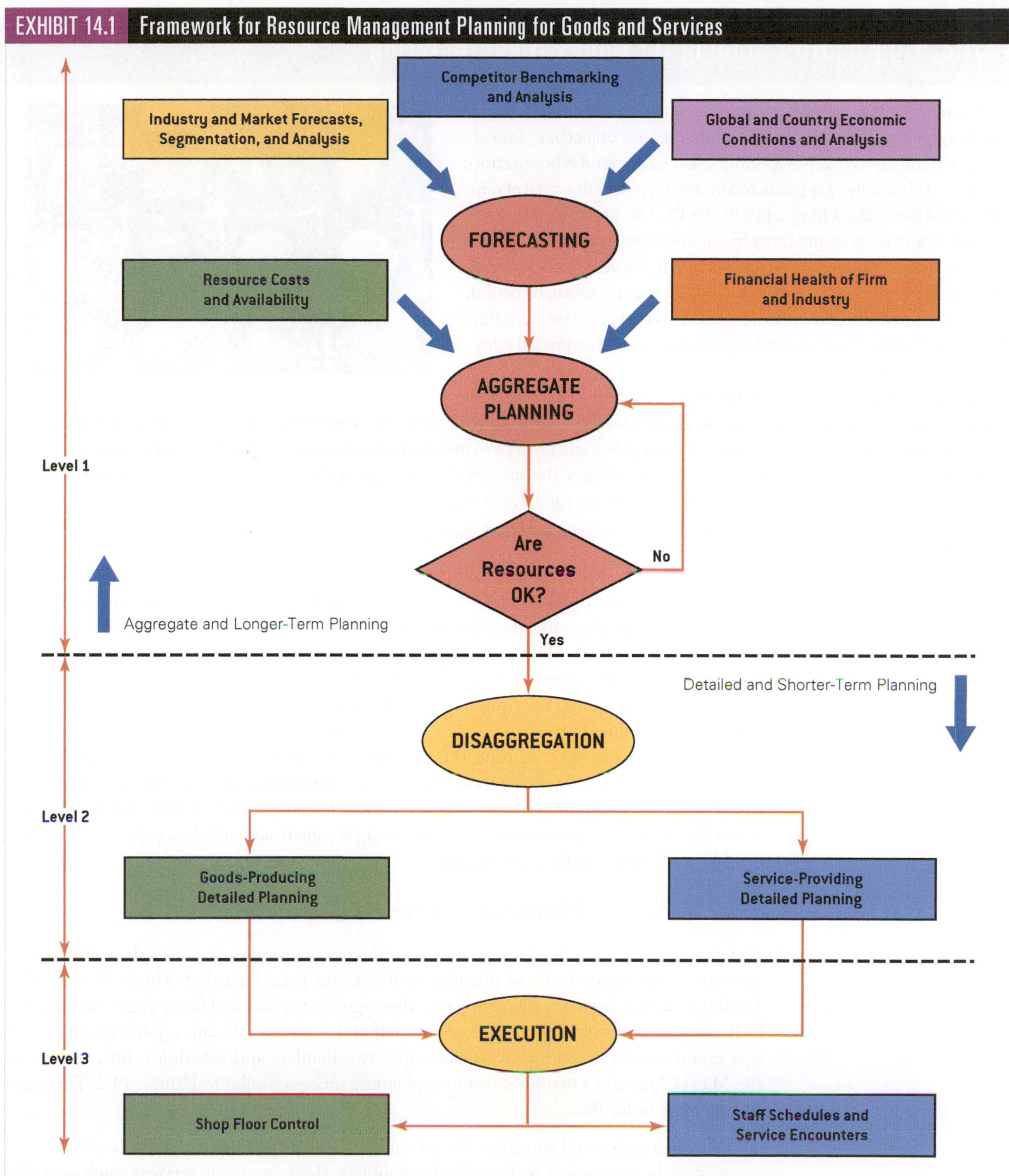

the year to support this plan. Disaggregation of the plan would involve developing targets for the number of gallons of each flavor to produce (which would sum to the aggregate planned number for each quarter); purchasing requirements for cream, chocolate, and other ingredients; work schedules and overtime plans; and so on.

Néstlé: Aggregate Planning for Candy Manufacturing

K. Jensen/Shutterstock.com

Aggregate plans at a company that was acquired by Néstlé are focused on quality, personnel, capital, and customer service objectives.[2] One of its major brand items that has a highly seasonal demand is boxed chocolates. Boxed chocolates are produced in three types, with a total of nine distinct end items: Black Magic, in 2 lb., 1½ lb., 1 lb., and ½ lb. boxes; Rendezvous, in a 14 oz. box; and Dairy Box, in the same four sizes as Black Magic. Forecasting is accomplished by dividing the year into 13 periods of four weeks each. Sales planning provides an item forecast, by period, for the full 13 periods. This estimate is updated every four weeks, reflecting the latest information on available inventories and estimated sales for the next 13 periods.

Aggregate planning is performed by first converting all items to a poundage figure. The planning task is to calculate levels of production that will best meet the quality, personnel, capital, and customer service restrictions. It is a stated company policy and practice to maintain a stable workforce. Short-term capacity can be increased with overtime and/or with part-time employees. The amount of inventory investment has become a major concern, and inventory levels must be kept low to meet restrictions on capital investment.

As another example, an airline might use long-term passenger forecasts to develop monthly aggregate plans based on the number of passenger miles each month. This aggregate plan would also specify the resource requirements in terms of total airline capacity, flight crews, and so on. Disaggregation would then create detailed, point-to-point flight schedules, crew work assignments, food purchase plans, aircraft maintenance schedules, and other resource requirements.

Level 3 focuses on executing the detailed plans made at Level 2, creating detailed resource schedules and job sequences. **Execution** *refers to moving work from one workstation to another, assigning people to tasks, setting priorities for jobs, scheduling equipment, and controlling processes*. Level 3 planning and execution in manufacturing is sometimes called *shop floor control* and is addressed further in the next chapter.

14-1a Resource Planning in Service Organizations

Resource management for most service-providing organizations generally does not require as many intermediate levels of planning as it does for manufacturing. This is illustrated in Exhibit 14.2. Service firms frequently take their aggregate plans and disaggregate them down to the execution level as detailed frontline staff and resource schedules, job sequences, and service-encounter execution. Physician capacity, calendars and schedules, for example, at the Mayo Clinic use a two-level resource planning process similar to Exhibit 14.2. There are several reasons for this:

- Most manufactured goods are discrete and are "built up" from many levels of raw materials, component parts, and subassemblies. However, many services, such as credit card authorizations, a telephone call, a movie, or arriving at a bank teller window, are instantaneous or continuous and are not discrete. Hence, there is no need for multiple levels of planning for some services.
- Services do not have the advantage of physical inventory to buffer demand and supply uncertainty, so they must have sufficient service capacity on duty at the right time

EXHIBIT 14.2 Two Levels of Disaggregation for Many Service Organizations

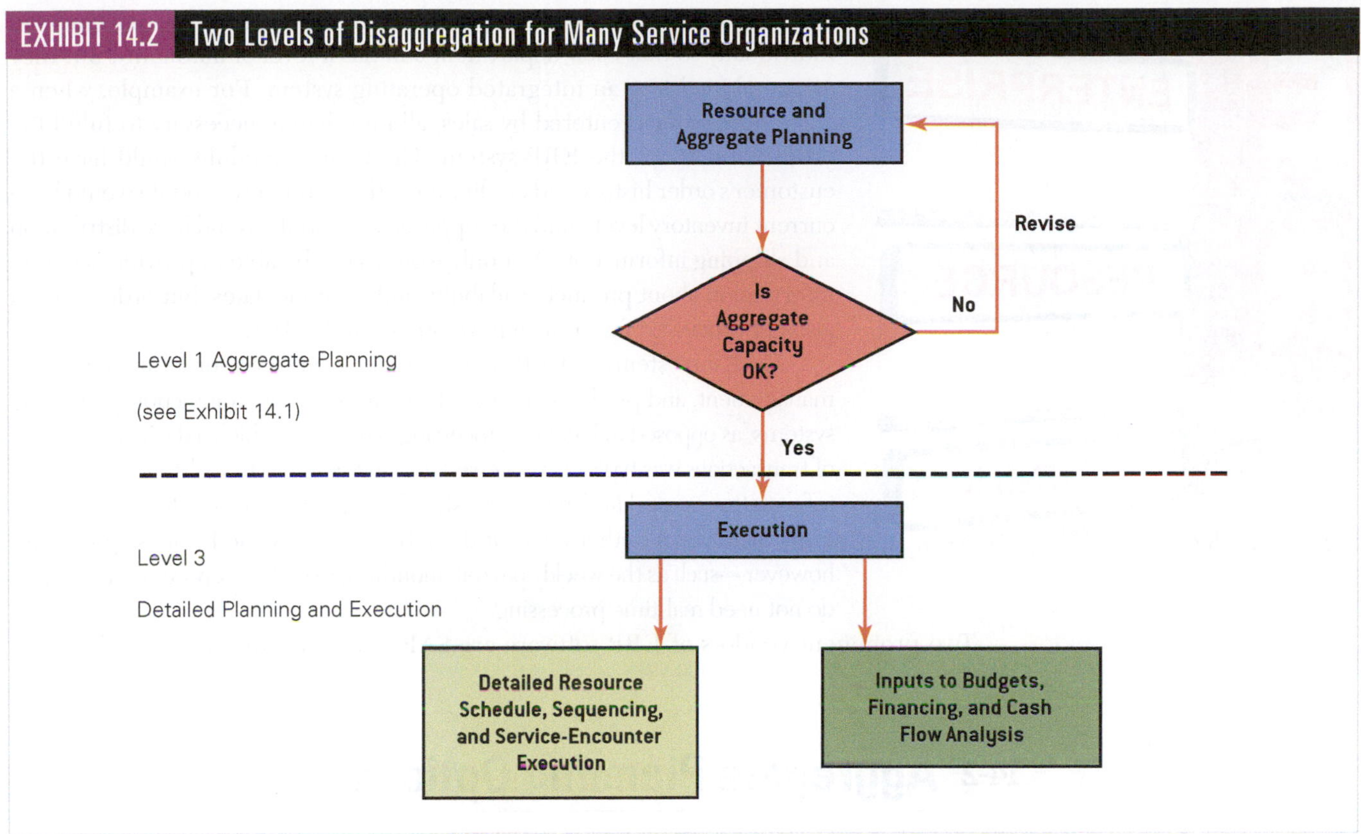

in the right place to provide good service to customers, making short-term demand forecasting and resource scheduling absolutely critical.

Some services, however, use the three levels of planning similar to manufacturing firms. For example, many service facilities, such as fast-food restaurants, need to be close to the customer, requiring them to be scattered within a geographical area. In these cases, the firm creates aggregate plans at the corporate level and then disaggregates them by region or district (geographically). This is similar to Level 2 intermediate planning in manufacturing. Regional and district offices further disaggregate these plans and budgets given the intermediate-level budgets and resource constraints. Level 3 resource planning and execution occurs at the store level, where local forecasts, food and other supply orders, staff work shifts and schedules, and service encounters are created.

14-1b Enterprise Resource Planning

Enterprise resource planning (ERP) is an important information systems tool for managing resources across the value chain. **ERP systems** *integrate all aspects of a business—accounting, customer relationship management, supply chain management, manufacturing, sales, human resources—into a unified information system, and they provide more timely analysis and reporting of sales, customer, inventory, manufacturing, human resource, and accounting data.* Traditionally, each department of a company, such as finance, human resources, and manufacturing, has individual information systems optimized to the needs of that department. If the sales department wants to know the status of a customer's order, for example, someone would typically have to call manufacturing or shipping. ERP combines each department's information into a single, integrated system with a common database so that departments can easily share information and communicate with each other.

nasirkhan/Shutterstock.com

ERP systems usually consist of different modules that can be implemented individually so that each department still has a level of autonomy, but they are combined into an integrated operating system. For example, when a customer's order is entered by sales, all information necessary to fulfill the order is built into the ERP system. The finance module would have the customer's order history and credit rating; the warehouse module would have current inventory levels; and the supply chain module would have distribution and shipping information. Not only would sales be able to provide accurate information about product availability and shipping dates, but orders would also get processed faster, with fewer errors and delays.

Most subsystems of ERP systems, such as customer ordering, inventory management, and production scheduling, are real-time, transaction-processing systems, as opposed to batched processing systems, in which a day's entire batch of transactions was typically processed during the night. In real-time processing, information is updated continuously, allowing the impacts to be reflected immediately in all other areas of the ERP system. Some business processes, however—such as the weekly payroll, monthly accounting reports, and billing—do not need real-time processing.

Two prominent vendors of ERP software are SAP (www.sap.com) and Oracle (www.oracle.com).

14-2 Aggregate Planning Options

Managers have a variety of options in developing aggregate plans in the face of fluctuating demand: workforce changes, inventory smoothing, and adjustments to facilities, equipment, and transportation. These are summarized in Exhibit 14.3. The choice of strategy depends on corporate policies, practical limitations, and cost factors.

Demand Management Marketing strategies can be used to influence demand and to help create more feasible aggregate plans. For example, pricing and promotions can increase or decrease demand or shift it to other time periods. In services, recall that demand is time dependent, and there is no option to store the service. A hotel manager, for example, may advertise a low weekend rate to the local market in an attempt to increase short-term revenue and contribution to profit and overhead. Thus, demand management strategies are crucial for good aggregate planning and capacity utilization.

> Managers have a variety of options in developing aggregate plans when demand fluctuates.

Production-Rate Changes One means of increasing the output rate without changing existing resources is through planned overtime. Alternatively, hours can be reduced during slow periods through planned undertime. However, reduced overtime pay or sitting idle can seriously affect employee morale. Subcontracting during periods of peak demand may also alter the output rate. This would probably not be a feasible alternative for some companies, but it is effective in industries that manufacture a large portion of their own parts, such as the machine-tool industry. When business is brisk, components can be subcontracted; when business is slow, the firm may act as a subcontractor to other industries that may be working at their capacity limit. In that way, a stable workforce is maintained.

Workforce Changes Changing the size of the workforce is usually accomplished through hiring and layoffs. Both have disadvantages. Hiring additional labor usually results in higher costs for the personnel department and for training. Layoffs result in severance pay and additional unemployment insurance costs, as well as low employee morale.

In many industries, changing workforce levels is not a feasible alternative. In firms that consist primarily of jobs with low skill requirements, however, it may be cost-effective. The toy industry is a good example. Accurate forecasts for the winter holiday season cannot be made until wholesale buyers have placed orders, usually around mid-year. Toy companies maintain a minimal number of employees until production is increased for the holidays. Then they hire a large number of part-time workers in order to operate at maximum capacity.

Inventory Changes In planning for fluctuating demand, inventory is often built up during slack periods and held for peak periods. However, this increases carrying costs and may necessitate more warehouse space. A related strategy is to carry back orders or to tolerate lost sales during peak demand periods. But this may be unacceptable if profit margins are low and competition is high.

Facilities, Equipment, and Transportation Facilities, equipment, and transportation generally represent long-term capital investments. Short-term changes in facilities and equipment are seldom used in traditional aggregate planning methods because of the capital costs involved. However, in some cases, it might be possible to rent additional equipment such as industrial forklifts, small machines, trucks, or warehouse space to accommodate periods of high demand.

EXHIBIT 14.3 Example Aggregate Planning Variables and Revenue/Cost Implications

Aggregate Planning Decision Options	Revenue/Cost Implications
Demand Management	
• Pricing strategies	• Increased revenue and lower unit costs
• Promotions and advertising	• Economies of scale
Production Rate	
• Overtime	• Higher labor costs and premiums
• Undertime	• Idle time/lost opportunity costs
• Subcontracting	• Overhead costs and some loss of control
Workforce	
• Hiring	• Acquisition and training costs
• Layoffs	• Separation costs
• Full- and part-time labor mix	• Labor cost and productivity changes
Inventory	
• Anticipation (build) inventories	• Inventory-carrying costs
• Allow stockouts	• Lost sales (revenue) and customer loyalty costs
• Plan for backorders	• Backorder costs and customer waiting costs
Facilities, Equipment, and Transportation	
• Open/closed facilities and hours	• Variable and fixed costs
• Resource utilization	• Speed and reliability of service and delivery
• Carbon emissions	• Low- to high-utilization impact on unit costs
• Mode (truck, rail, ship, air)	• Inbound and outbound costs per mode
• Capacity and resource utilization	• Number of full or partial loads

Dmitry Yashkin/Shutterstock.com

14-3 Strategies for Aggregate Production Planning

To develop an aggregate plan, we begin with a forecast of demand for some time horizon, which is typically a quarter or a year. *An* **aggregate production plan** *specifies the production level for each time period within the horizon, such as a week or month.*

We will assume that we are planning for n time periods. Let

P_t = production in time period t,
D_t = demand in period t, and
I_t = inventory at the end of period t.

The governing equation that defines the relationship among production, inventory, and demand at each time period is

Ending inventory in period $t - 1$ + Production in period t − Demand in period t = Ending inventory in period t

or

$$I_{t-1} + P_t - D_t = I_t \qquad [14.1]$$

Note that the ending inventory in period $t - 1$ is available at the beginning of period t. So if we know the production and demand for each period, the ending inventory is easily determined.

The fundamental question is to determine how much to produce in each time period to meet the anticipated demands at minimum cost. Three options are:

1. *Level production strategy*. A **level production strategy** *plans for the same production rate in each time period.* A level strategy avoids changes in the production rate and working within normal capacity restrictions. Labor and equipment schedules are stable and repetitive, making it easier to execute the plan. The Excel *Agg Plan—Level* template in MindTap provides a spreadsheet for implementing a level production strategy for a one-year time horizon and monthly time periods.
2. *Chase demand strategy*. A **chase demand production strategy** *sets the production rate equal to the demand in each time period.* Although inventories will be reduced and lost sales will be eliminated, many production-rate changes will dramatically change resource levels (the number of employees, machines, etc.). The Excel *Agg Plan—Chase* template in MindTap provides a spreadsheet for implementing a chase demand production strategy for a one-year time horizon and monthly time periods.
3. *Minimum cost strategy*. A minimum cost strategy seeks to determine production levels for each time period that minimizes the total cost. Although it might seem obvious to simply produce to the anticipated level of sales (the chase demand strategy), it may be advantageous to produce more than needed in earlier time periods when production costs may be lower and store the excess production as inventory for use in later time periods, thereby letting lower production costs offset the costs of holding the inventory. Optimization techniques can identify the minimum cost strategy. Supplement D provides an introductory review of linear optimization, including formulating models and solving them using Excel Solver.

Solved problem 14.1 illustrates the level and chase demand strategies. In Solved Problem 14.2, we show how to use linear optimization to find a minimum cost strategy.

SOLVED PROBLEM 14.1: EVALUATING LEVEL AND CHASE DEMAND STRATEGIES

F&J Enterprises needs to determine an aggregate plan for the next three months. Demand forecasts are

Month 1: 250
Month 2: 350
Month 3: 150

The production cost per unit varies each month because of contractual arrangements with suppliers. It is $10 in month 1, $13 in month 2, and $11.50 in month 3. Each unit held in inventory at the end of a month costs $0.80. Because of the company's commitment to customer service, no shortages are allowed. Initial inventory at the beginning of month 1 is 0 units.

a. Find a level production strategy that avoids any shortages.
b. Evaluate a chase demand production strategy.

Solution:

a. Using Equation 14.1, we have

Month 1: $0 + P_1 - 250 = I_1$
Month 2: $I_1 + P_2 - 350 = I_2$
Month 3: $I_2 + P_3 - 150 = I_3$

Total cost $= (10P_1 + 13P_2 + 11.5P_3) + 0.80(I_1 + I_2 + I_3)$

One way of avoiding shortages is to produce the maximum demand each month (350 units):

Month 1: $I_1 = 0 + 350 - 250 = 100.$
Month 2: $I_2 = 100 + 350 - 350 = 100.$
Month 3: $I_3 = 100 + 350 - 150 = 300.$

Total cost $= \$10 \times 350 + \$13 \times 350 + \$11.5 \times 350 + 0.80 \times (100 + 100 + 300) = \$12{,}075 + \$400 = \$12{,}475.$

However, a better level production strategy is to produce 300 units per month:

Month 1: $I_1 = 0 + 300 - 250 = 50.$
Month 2: $I_2 = 50 + 300 - 350 = 0.$
Month 3: $I_3 = 0 + 300 - 150 = 150.$

Total cost $= \$10 \times 300 + \$13 \times 300 + \$11.5 \times 300 + 0.80 \times (50 + 0 + 150) = \$10{,}350 + \$160 = \$10{,}510.$

b. For a chase demand strategy, $P_1 = 250, P_2 = 350, P_3 = 150.$

Month 1: $I_1 = 0 + 250 - 250 = 0.$
Month 2: $I_2 = 0 + 350 - 350 = 0.$
Month 3: $I_3 = 0 + 150 - 150 = 0.$

Total cost $= \$10 \times 250 + \$13 \times 350 + \$11.5 \times 150 + 0.80 \times (0 + 0 + 0) = \$8{,}775.$

SOLVED PROBLEM 14.2 FINDING A MINIMUM COST STRATEGY USING OPTIMIZATION

Find a minimum cost strategy for F&J Enterprises (Solved Problem 14.1) by building and solving a linear optimization model.

Solution:

A linear optimization model can be formulated by minimizing total cost and ensuring that Equation 14.1 holds for each month and that all variables are nonnegative. The objective function is

Minimize Total cost $= 10P_1 + 13P_2 + 11.5P_3 + 0.80(I_1 + I_2 + I_3)$

We will write the constraints so that the net production must equal the demand for each month as follows:

$P_1 - I_1 = 250$
$I_1 + P_2 - I_2 = 350$
$I_2 + P_3 - I_3 = 150$

$P_t, I_t \geq 0$ for t = 1, 2, 3

Exhibit 14.4 shows the Excel model that can be solved using Excel Solver. The decision variables are in cells B12:D13. In row 15, we compute the net production for each month. For example, cell B15 is $P_1 - I_1$, and cell C15 is $I_1 + P_2 - I_2$. In the Solver model, these must equal the demand for each month.

Exhibit 14.5 shows the minimum cost solution of $8,005. Note that production in month 1 exceeds demand because the low production cost outweighs the cost of holding additional inventory.

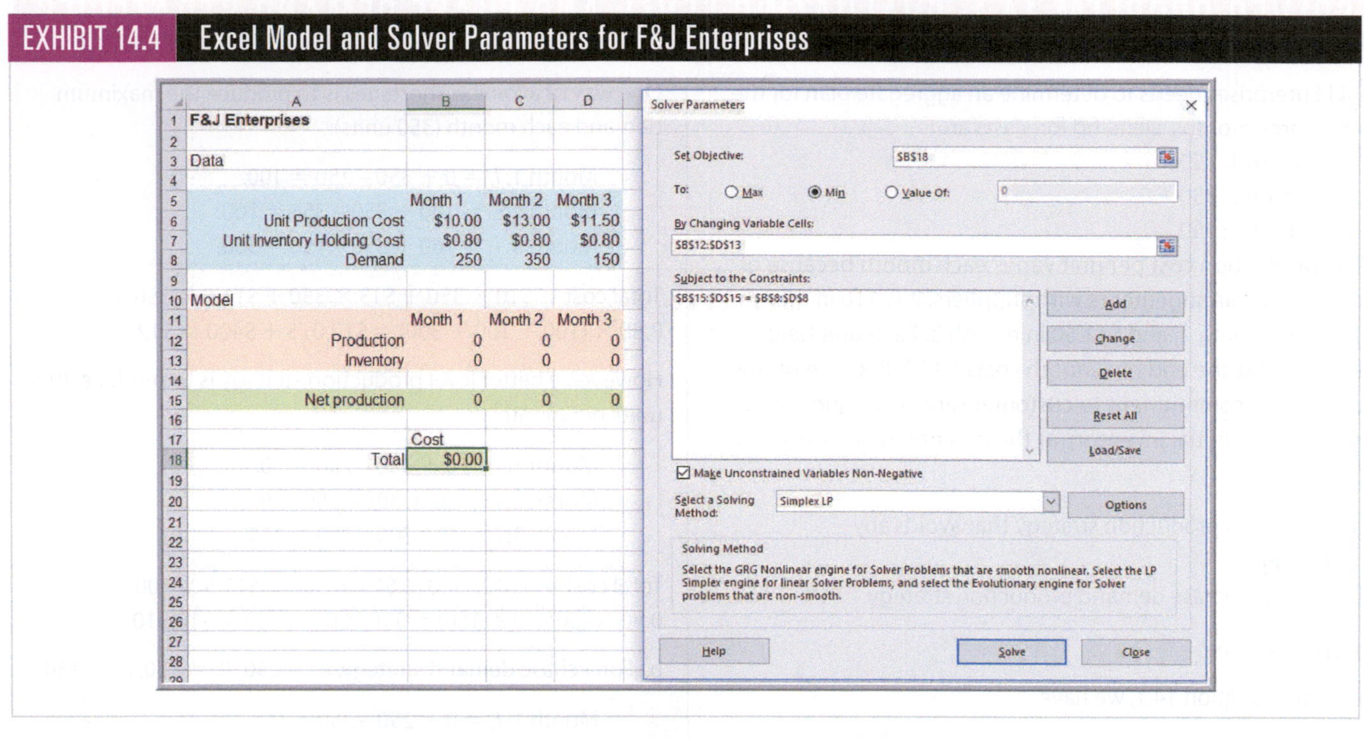

EXHIBIT 14.4 Excel Model and Solver Parameters for F&J Enterprises

EXHIBIT 14.5 Solver Solution

	A	B	C	D
1	F&J Enterprises			
2				
3	Data			
4				
5		Month 1	Month 2	Month 3
6	Unit Production Cost	$10.00	$13.00	$11.50
7	Unit Inventory Holding Cost	$0.80	$0.80	$0.80
8	Demand	250	350	150
9				
10	Model			
11		Month 1	Month 2	Month 3
12	Production	600	0	150
13	Inventory	350	0	0
14				
15	Net production	250	350	150
16				
17		Cost		
18	Total	$8,005.00		

14.3a Excel Templates for Aggregate Planning

When aggregate planning problems involve large numbers of decision variables and costs of production, inventory, lost sales, overtime, undertime, and rate changes, optimization models can be very complex and difficult to formulate. Good solutions can often be found by trial-and-error approaches using spreadsheets. The Excel templates *Agg Plan—Level*, *Agg Plan—Chase*, and *Aggregate Planning* in MindTap provide the ability to conduct trial-and-error evaluations of aggregate planning options for a one-year time horizon and monthly time periods for each of the three major strategies we have discussed. Solved Problem 14.3 illustrates the use of these strategies and templates for an aggregate planning problem.

SOLVED PROBLEM 14.3: DEVELOPING AN AGGREGATE PLAN

Golden Beverages produces two varieties of root beer in one of its plants—Old Fashioned and Foamy Delite. Golden Beverages operates as a continuous flow factory and must plan future production for a demand forecast that fluctuates quite a bit over the year, with seasonal peaks in the summer and winter holiday season. Exhibit 14.6 shows a monthly aggregate demand forecast for the next year. Notice that demand is in barrels per month—an aggregate unit of measure for both products. Golden Beverages has a normal production capacity of 2,200 barrels per month and a current inventory of 1,000 barrels. The production cost per barrel is \$70, holding cost per barrel per month is \$1.40, lost sales cost is \$90 per barrel, overtime cost is \$6.50 per barrel, undertime cost is \$3 per barrel, and a production rate change from one month to the next costs \$5 per barrel. How should Golden Beverages plan its overall production for the next 12 months in the face of such fluctuating demand? Compare the level production and chase demand strategies, and try to develop a minimum cost strategy.

EXHIBIT 14.6 Monthly Demand for Golden Beverages

Month	Demand
January	1,500
February	1,000
March	1,900
April	2,600
May	2,800
June	3,100
July	3,200
August	3,000
September	2,000
October	1,000
November	1,800
December	2,200

Solution:

In the *Agg Plan—Level* spreadsheet template, all data are entered in column B. In cell B12, enter the level production rate. Exhibit 14.7 shows the level production strategy using a level production rate of 2,200 barrels per month (entered in cell B12). To calculate the ending inventory for each month, we use Equation 14.1.

$$\text{Ending inventory} = \text{Beginning inventory} + \text{Production} - \text{Demand} \qquad [14.1]$$

For example, ending inventory for January is 1,000 + 2,200 − 1,500 = 1,700 and for February is 1,700 + 2,200 − 1,000 = 2,900.

For this solution, however, ending inventory builds up to a peak of 3,200 barrels in March, resulting in high inventory holding costs. The template also displays a chart of the cumulative demand and cumulative product availability (Exhibit 14.8). Whenever the cumulative product availability is at least as great as the cumulative demand, then the production schedule can satisfy the demand. However, we see that in August the cumulative demand exceeds the cumulative product availability and lost sales of 500 barrels occur due to inventory shortages. The total cost for this plan is \$1,920,440.

Exhibit 14.8 shows the production strategy for a level production rate of 2,300 barrels per month. If the level production rate exceeds the normal production rate in cell B10, then overtime will occur; if it is less than the normal production rate, then undertime will occur. From the chart, we see that lost sales no longer occur; however, overtime costs amount to \$7,800. With the higher inventory costs, the total cost is larger than that with a level production rate of 2200 units. You can experiment with the rate to understand the tradeoffs among costs, inventory levels, lost sales, and so on.

A chase demand strategy for Golden Beverages using the *Agg Plan—Chase* template is shown in Exhibit 14.9 with a total cost of \$1,835,050. The template assigns the production for each month in cells D16:D27 based on the demand, adjusted for initial inventory. Thus, in January, production is only 500 because the initial inventory from the previous December is 1000. As compared with the level production strategies, the cost of the chase demand strategy is less. Notice that no inventory carrying or lost sales costs are incurred, but substantial overtime, undertime, and rate-change costs are required. However, these offset the inventory costs. Because the cumulative demand is equal to the cumulative product availability for each month, the cumulative demand series is hidden.

Finally, to seek a minimum cost strategy, use the *Aggregate Planning* template, which allows you to select production levels for each month in cells D16:D27. After some experimentation and trial-and-error, we developed the solution shown in Exhibit 14.10. This eliminated any lost sales and kept ending inventory to low levels. The total cost of this plan is \$1,822,464, which is the best among the three strategies, but may not be the minimum cost.

EXHIBIT 14.7 Level Production Strategy for Rate = 2,200

	A	B	C	D	E	F	G
1	Aggregate Planning - Level Production Strategy		Copyright © Cengage Learning				
2	Enter the data only in the yellow cells.		Not for commercial use.				
3							
4	Production cost ($/unit)	$70.00					
5	Inventory holding cost ($/unit/month)	$1.40					
6	Lost sales cost ($/unit)	$90.00					
7	Overtime cost ($/unit)	$6.50					
8	Undertime cost ($/unit)	$3.00					
9	Rate change cost ($/unit)	$5.00					
10	Normal production rate (units)	2200					
11	Ending inventory (previous Dec.)	1000					
12	Level Production Rate	2200					
13							
14					Cumulative		
15			Cumulative		Product	Ending	Lost
16	Month	Demand	Demand	Production	Availability	Inventory	Sales
17	January	1500	1,500	2,200	3,200	1,700	0
18	February	1000	2,500	2,200	5,400	2,900	0
19	March	1900	4,400	2,200	7,600	3,200	0
20	April	2600	7,000	2,200	9,800	2,800	0
21	May	2800	9,800	2,200	12,000	2,200	0
22	June	3100	12,900	2,200	14,200	1,300	0
23	July	3200	16,100	2,200	16,400	300	0
24	August	3000	19,100	2,200	18,600	0	500
25	September	2000	21,100	2,200	21,300	200	0
26	October	1000	22,100	2,200	23,500	1,400	0
27	November	1800	23,900	2,200	25,700	1,800	0
28	December	2200	26,100	2,200	27,900	1,800	0
29	Average	2,175.00			Maximum	3,200	
30							
31		Production	Inventory	Lost Sales	Overtime	Undertime	Rate Change
32	Month	Cost	Cost	Cost	Cost	Cost	Cost
33	January	$154,000.00	$2,380.00	$0.00	$0.00	$0.00	$0.00
34	February	$154,000.00	$4,060.00	$0.00	$0.00	$0.00	$0.00
35	March	$154,000.00	$4,480.00	$0.00	$0.00	$0.00	$0.00
36	April	$154,000.00	$3,920.00	$0.00	$0.00	$0.00	$0.00
37	May	$154,000.00	$3,080.00	$0.00	$0.00	$0.00	$0.00
38	June	$154,000.00	$1,820.00	$0.00	$0.00	$0.00	$0.00
39	July	$154,000.00	$420.00	$0.00	$0.00	$0.00	$0.00
40	August	$154,000.00	$0.00	$45,000.00	$0.00	$0.00	$0.00
41	September	$154,000.00	$280.00	$0.00	$0.00	$0.00	$0.00
42	October	$154,000.00	$1,960.00	$0.00	$0.00	$0.00	$0.00
43	November	$154,000.00	$2,520.00	$0.00	$0.00	$0.00	$0.00
44	December	$154,000.00	$2,520.00	$0.00	$0.00	$0.00	$0.00
45	Totals	$1,848,000.00	$27,440.00	$45,000.00	$0.00	$0.00	$0.00
46							
47	Total cost	$1,920,440.00					

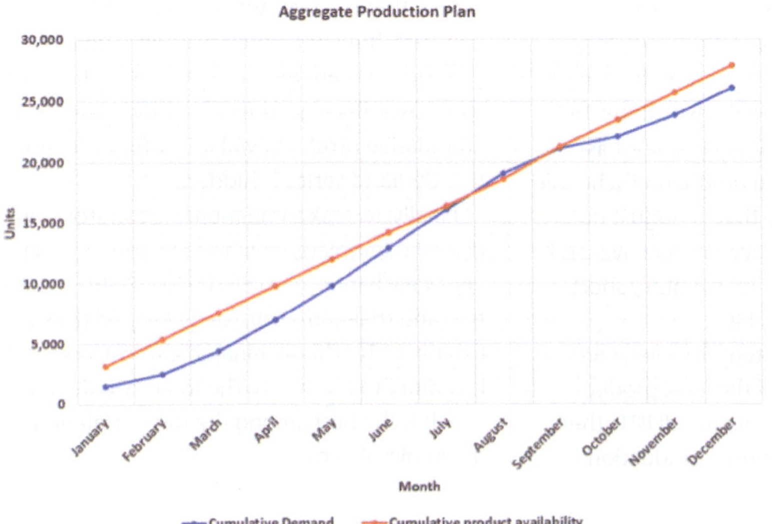

EXHIBIT 14.8 Level Production Strategy for Rate = 2300

	A	B	C	D
1	Aggregate Planning - Level Production Strategy		Copyright © Cengage Learning	
2	Enter the data only in the yellow cells.		Not for commercial use.	
3				
4	Production cost ($/unit)	$70.00		
5	Inventory holding cost ($/unit/month)	$1.40		
6	Lost sales cost ($/unit)	$90.00		
7	Overtime cost ($/unit)	$6.50		
8	Undertime cost ($/unit)	$3.00		
9	Rate change cost ($/unit)	$5.00		
10	Normal production rate (units)	2200		
11	Ending inventory (previous Dec.)	1000		
12	Level Production Rate	2300		

	Month	Demand	Cumulative Demand	Production	Cumulative Product Availability	Ending Inventory	Lost Sales
17	January	1500	1,500	2,300	3,300	1,800	0
18	February	1000	2,500	2,300	5,600	3,100	0
19	March	1900	4,400	2,300	7,900	3,500	0
20	April	2600	7,000	2,300	10,200	3,200	0
21	May	2800	9,800	2,300	12,500	2,700	0
22	June	3100	12,900	2,300	14,800	1,900	0
23	July	3200	16,100	2,300	17,100	1,000	0
24	August	3000	19,100	2,300	19,400	300	0
25	September	2000	21,100	2,300	21,700	600	0
26	October	1000	22,100	2,300	24,000	1,900	0
27	November	1800	23,900	2,300	26,300	2,400	0
28	December	2200	26,100	2,300	28,600	2,500	0
29	Average	2,175.00			Maximum	3,500	

	Month	Production Cost	Inventory Cost	Lost Sales Cost	Overtime Cost	Undertime Cost	Rate Change Cost
33	January	$161,000.00	$2,520.00	$0.00	$650.00	$0.00	$500.00
34	February	$161,000.00	$4,340.00	$0.00	$650.00	$0.00	$0.00
35	March	$161,000.00	$4,900.00	$0.00	$650.00	$0.00	$0.00
36	April	$161,000.00	$4,480.00	$0.00	$650.00	$0.00	$0.00
37	May	$161,000.00	$3,780.00	$0.00	$650.00	$0.00	$0.00
38	June	$161,000.00	$2,660.00	$0.00	$650.00	$0.00	$0.00
39	July	$161,000.00	$1,400.00	$0.00	$650.00	$0.00	$0.00
40	August	$161,000.00	$420.00	$0.00	$650.00	$0.00	$0.00
41	September	$161,000.00	$840.00	$0.00	$650.00	$0.00	$0.00
42	October	$161,000.00	$2,660.00	$0.00	$650.00	$0.00	$0.00
43	November	$161,000.00	$3,360.00	$0.00	$650.00	$0.00	$0.00
44	December	$161,000.00	$3,500.00	$0.00	$650.00	$0.00	$0.00
45	Totals	$1,932,000.00	$34,860.00	$0.00	$7,800.00	$0.00	$500.00
46							
47	Total cost	$1,975,160.00					

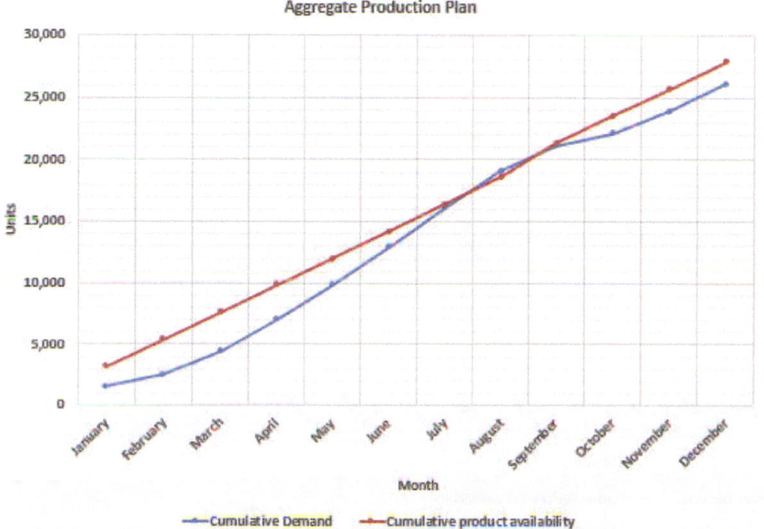

EXHIBIT 14.9 Chase Demand Strategy for Golden Beverages

	A	B	C	D
1	**Aggregate Planning - Chase Demand Strategy**		Copyright © Cengage Learning	
2	Enter the data only in the yellow cells.		Not for commercial use.	
3				
4	**Production cost ($/unit)**	$70.00		
5	**Inventory holding cost ($/unit/month)**	$1.40		
6	**Lost sales cost ($/unit)**	$90.00		
7	**Overtime cost ($/unit)**	$6.50		
8	**Undertime cost ($/unit)**	$3.00		
9	**Rate change cost ($/unit)**	$5.00		
10	**Normal production rate (units)**	2200		
11	**Ending inventory (previous Dec.)**	1000		

	A	B	C	D	E	F	G
13–15	**Month**	**Demand**	**Cumulative Demand**	**Production**	**Cumulative Product Availability**	**Ending Inventory**	**Lost Sales**
16	January	1500	1,500	500	1,500	0	0
17	February	1000	2,500	1,000	2,500	0	0
18	March	1900	4,400	1,900	4,400	0	0
19	April	2600	7,000	2,600	7,000	0	0
20	May	2800	9,800	2,800	9,800	0	0
21	June	3100	12,900	3,100	12,900	0	0
22	July	3200	16,100	3,200	16,100	0	0
23	August	3000	19,100	3,000	19,100	0	0
24	September	2000	21,100	2,000	21,100	0	0
25	October	1000	22,100	1,000	22,100	0	0
26	November	1800	23,900	1,800	23,900	0	0
27	December	2200	26,100	2,200	26,100	0	0
28	Average	2,175.00			Maximum	0	

	A	B	C	D	E	F	G
30–31	**Month**	**Production Cost**	**Inventory Cost**	**Lost Sales Cost**	**Overtime Cost**	**Undertime Cost**	**Rate Change Cost**
32	January	$35,000.00	$0.00	$0.00	$0.00	$5,100.00	$8,500.00
33	February	$70,000.00	$0.00	$0.00	$0.00	$3,600.00	$2,500.00
34	March	$133,000.00	$0.00	$0.00	$0.00	$900.00	$4,500.00
35	April	$182,000.00	$0.00	$0.00	$2,600.00	$0.00	$3,500.00
36	May	$196,000.00	$0.00	$0.00	$3,900.00	$0.00	$1,000.00
37	June	$217,000.00	$0.00	$0.00	$5,850.00	$0.00	$1,500.00
38	July	$224,000.00	$0.00	$0.00	$6,500.00	$0.00	$500.00
39	August	$210,000.00	$0.00	$0.00	$5,200.00	$0.00	$1,000.00
40	September	$140,000.00	$0.00	$0.00	$0.00	$600.00	$5,000.00
41	October	$70,000.00	$0.00	$0.00	$0.00	$3,600.00	$5,000.00
42	November	$126,000.00	$0.00	$0.00	$0.00	$1,200.00	$4,000.00
43	December	$154,000.00	$0.00	$0.00	$0.00	$0.00	$2,000.00
44	Totals	$1,757,000.00	$0.00	$0.00	$24,050.00	$15,000.00	$39,000.00
45							
46	Total cost	$1,835,050.00					

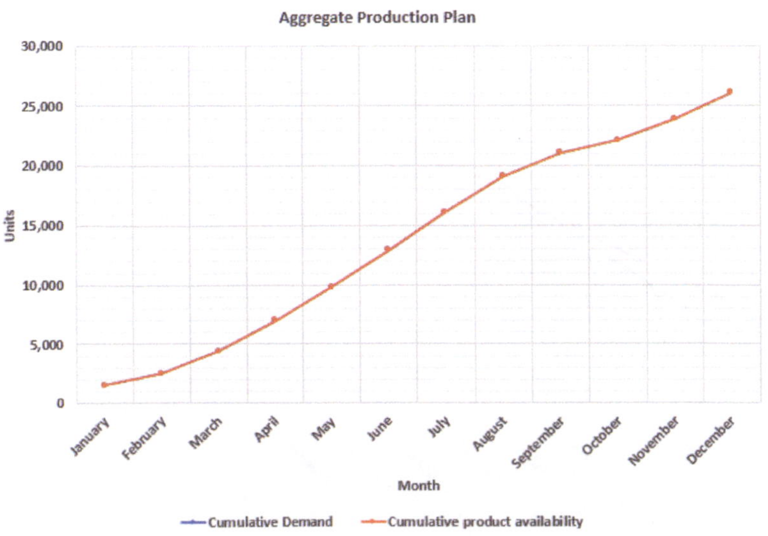

EXHIBIT 14.10 *Aggregate Planning* Template for Seeking a Minimum Cost Strategy

Aggregate Planning | Copyright © 2019 Cengage Learning | Not for commercial use.

Enter the data only in the yellow cells. This template is designed so that you can experiment with production levels in column D to identify good solutions.

Production cost ($/unit)	$70.00
Inventory holding cost ($/unit/month)	$1.40
Lost sales cost ($/unit)	$90.00
Overtime cost ($/unit)	$6.50
Undertime cost ($/unit)	$3.00
Rate change cost ($/unit)	$5.00
Normal production rate (units)	2200
Ending inventory (previous Dec.)	1000

Month	Demand	Cumulative Demand	Production	Cumulative Product Availability	Ending Inventory	Lost Sales
January	1500	1,500	750	1,750	250	0
February	1000	2,500	750	2,500	0	0
March	1900	4,400	2249	4,749	349	0
April	2600	7,000	2251	7,000	0	0
May	2800	9,800	2800	9,800	0	0
June	3100	12,900	3150	12,950	50	0
July	3200	16,100	3150	16,100	0	0
August	3000	19,100	3000	19,100	0	0
September	2000	21,100	2000	21,100	0	0
October	1000	22,100	1667	22,767	667	0
November	1800	23,900	1666	24,433	533	0
December	2200	26,100	1667	26,100	0	0
Average	2,175			Maximum	667	

Month	Production Cost	Inventory Cost	Lost Sales Cost	Overtime Cost	Undertime Cost	Rate Change Cost
January	$52,500.00	$350.00	$0.00	$0.00	$4,350.00	$7,250.00
February	$52,500.00	$0.00	$0.00	$0.00	$4,350.00	$0.00
March	$157,430.00	$488.60	$0.00	$318.50	$0.00	$7,495.00
April	$157,570.00	$0.00	$0.00	$331.50	$0.00	$10.00
May	$196,000.00	$0.00	$0.00	$3,900.00	$0.00	$2,745.00
June	$220,500.00	$70.00	$0.00	$6,175.00	$0.00	$1,750.00
July	$220,500.00	$0.00	$0.00	$6,175.00	$0.00	$0.00
August	$210,000.00	$0.00	$0.00	$5,200.00	$0.00	$750.00
September	$140,000.00	$0.00	$0.00	$0.00	$600.00	$5,000.00
October	$116,690.00	$933.80	$0.00	$0.00	$1,599.00	$1,665.00
November	$116,620.00	$746.20	$0.00	$0.00	$1,602.00	$5.00
December	$116,690.00	$0.00	$0.00	$0.00	$1,599.00	$5.00
Totals	$1,757,000.00	$2,588.60	$0.00	$22,100.00	$14,100.00	$26,675.00

Total cost	$1,822,463.60

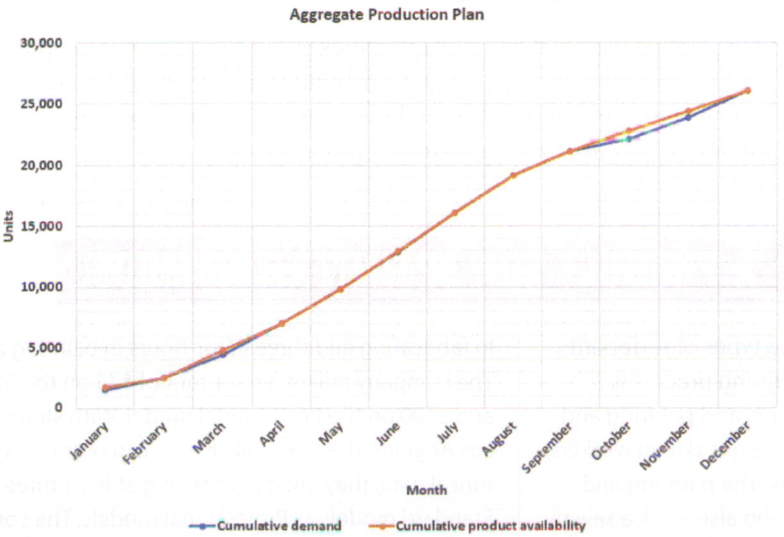

How Can We Use Aggregate Planning for a Tennis Club?

Services face many of the same issues in planning and managing resources as do manufacturing firms. Consider a 145-acre oceanfront resort located in Myrtle Beach, South Carolina, that is owned and operated by a major corporation. The tennis club and four courts are located next to the Sport & Health Club. All courts are lighted for night play, and there is no more room to build additional tennis courts. The demand for tennis lessons is highly seasonal, with peak demand in June, July, and August. In the summer months, when resort rooms are 98 to 100 percent occupied, requests for lesson time far exceed capacity, and owner and hotel guest complaints increase dramatically. The manager of the health club might consider a chase resource strategy with a base full-time tennis staff of two people and the use of part-time staff for much of the year. Or she might consider a level strategy with four full-time staff and no part-time staff.

14-4 Using Optimization Models for Resource Management

We have seen how to develop linear optimization models for aggregate planning. There are other applications of linear optimization for production planning that focus on product mix decisions, process selection, aggregate planning with multiple products, and many other scenarios. The spreadsheet models in the solved problems are available in MindTap.

14-4a Product Mix Models

Product mix models seek to determine quantities of different products to produce and sell in order to maximize contribution to profit. Constraints might include resource limitations such as production time, labor availability, and material availability, and marketing requirements such as minimum and maximum amounts to produce.

SOLVED PROBLEM 14.4: A PRODUCT MIX OPTIMIZATION MODEL

Beach Bum Surfboards manufactures two types of surfboards, Standard and Professional. The manufacturing process is performed in two departments: fabrication, and painting and finishing. The fabrication department has eight skilled workers, each of whom works seven hours per day. The painting and finishing department has four workers, who also work a seven-hour shift. Each Standard model requires four hours of labor in the fabricating department and 1.5 hours of labor in painting and finishing. The Professional model requires five labor-hours in fabricating and three labor-hours in painting and finishing. The company makes a net profit of \$75 on the Standard model and \$100 on the Professional model. With stores in Hawaii and Los Angeles, they can sell all they can produce. Based on historical data, they anticipate selling at least three times as many Standard models as Professional models. The company wants to determine how many of each model should be produced on a daily basis to maximize profit. Formulate and solve a linear optimization model.

Solution:

Define the decision variables:

S = number of Standard surfboards to produce each day
P = number of Professional surfboards to produce each day

The objective function is to maximize profit, which is the profit per unit times the number of units produced:

Maximize 75 \$/unit $\times$ S units + 100 \$/unit $\times$ P units
$= 75S + 100P$

Constraints reflect the limited labor in each department and the ratio of standard to professional models that the company anticipates selling.

Fabrication Department:

4 hours/unit $\times$ S units + 5 hours/unit $\times$ P units
$\leq$ 8 workers/shift $\times$ 7 hours/shift or $4S + 5P \leq 56$

Painting and Finishing Department:

1.5 hours/unit $\times$ S units + 3 hours/unit $\times$ P units
$\leq$ 4 workers/shift $\times$ 7 hours/shift or $1.5S + 3P \leq 28$

Marketing mix – Number of Standard models must be at least three times the number of as Professional models:

$S \geq 3P$, or $S - 3P \geq 0$

Nonnegativity:

$S, P \geq 0$

Exhibit 14.11 shows the Excel spreadsheet and Solver model (Excel worksheet Beach Bum Surfboards, available in MindTap). The optimal solution is to produce 9.88 standard models and 3.29 professional models per day with a profit of \$1070.59. Remember that linear optimization assumes that fractional values of decision variables are allowed, so the solution would have to be modified for practical implementation. For example, we might round the answers to produce 10 standard models and three professional models. Rounding, however, may result in an infeasible solution, in which case, we would need to restrict the variables to be integer when using Solver. If we check the constraints with the rounded values, we have

Fabrication Department:

$= 4(10) + 5(3) = 55 \leq 56$

Painting and Finishing Department:

$= 1.5(10) + 3(3) = 24 \leq 28$

Marketing mix – Number of Standard models must be at least three times the number of as Professional models:

$10 - 3(3) = 1 \geq 0$

In this case, all constraints are satisfied. For most practical problems with high volumes of production, rounding will have little effect.

EXHIBIT 14.11 Solver Model and Solution for Beach Bum Surfboards

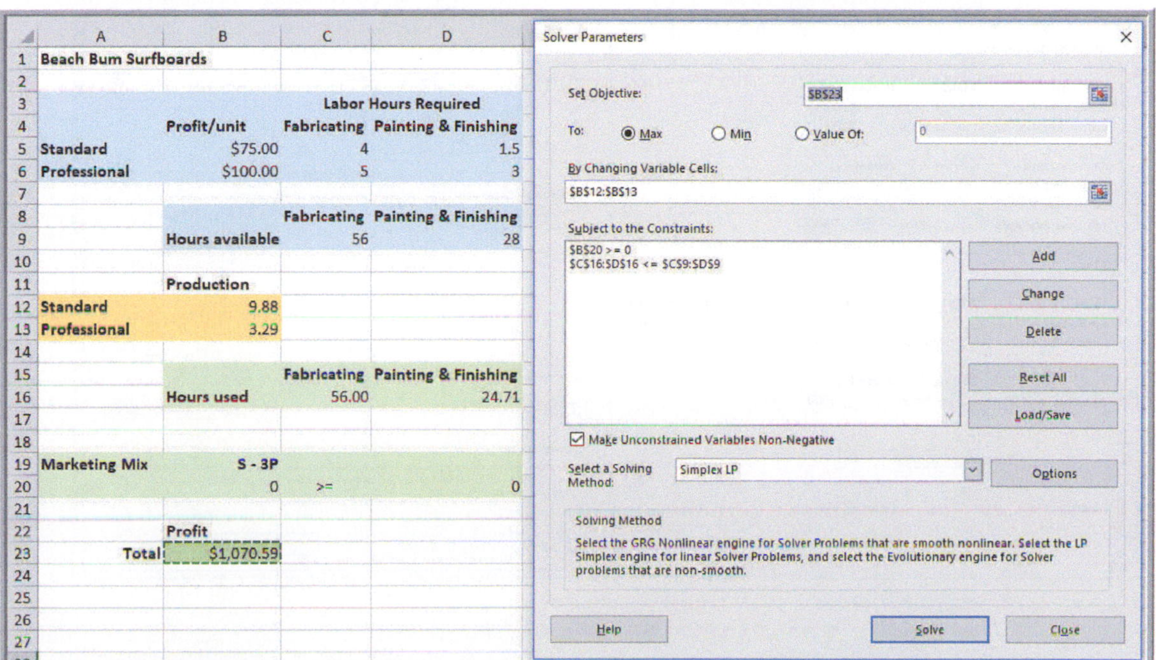

14-4b Process Selection Models

Process selection models seek to determine quantities of a product to make using alternative processes, such as manufacturing in-house or purchasing from a supplier, or using machines with different capabilities. The objective is usually to minimize cost, and typical constraints are meeting demand requirements and resource limitations. Solved Problem 14.5 illustrates an example.

SOLVED PROBLEM 14.5: A MAKE-OR-BUY OPTIMIZATION MODEL

A machine tool manufacturer uses two types of electronic controllers in its products. They have the capability to produce these in-house, but have limited resources. Thus, they may have to purchase some of them from an external supplier to fulfill demand. The cost to make controller A is \$225, and it can be purchased from a supplier for \$300. The cost to make controller B is \$195, with a purchase cost of \$250. The company needs at least 400 units of controller A and 350 units of controller B for the next month. The controllers require two processes: wiring and final assembly. Controller A requires 30 minutes to wire and 18 minutes to assemble, while controller B requires 20 minutes to wire and 15 minutes to assemble. The company has determined that 9000 minutes of labor for wiring and 7500 minutes of labor for assembly will be available. How many controllers should be produced in-house and how many should be purchased from the supplier to minimize cost?

Solution:

Let

X_{AM} = number of controllers A to make
X_{AP} = number of controllers A to purchase
X_{BM} = number of controllers B to make
X_{BP} = number of controllers B to purchase

The objective function is to minimize total cost:

$$\text{Minimize } 225\,X_{AM} + 300\,X_{AP} + 195\,X_{BM} + 250\,X_{BP}$$

Demand constraints:

$$X_{AM} + X_{AP} \geq 400$$
$$X_{BM} + X_{BP} \geq 350$$

Labor limitations:

$$30X_{AM} + 20X_{BM} \leq 9{,}000 \text{ wiring minutes}$$
$$18X_{AM} + 15X_{BM} \leq 7{,}500 \text{ assembly minutes}$$

Non-negativity:

All variables ≥ 0

Exhibit 14.12 shows the Excel spreadsheet and Solver model (Excel *worksheet Make-or-Buy Solver Model, available in MindTap*). The optimal solution is to make 66.67 units of controller A in-house, and purchase 333.33 units from the supplier, and to make all 350 units of controller B in-house. The total cost is \$183,250.

EXHIBIT 14.12 Solver Model and Solution for Make-or-Buy Model

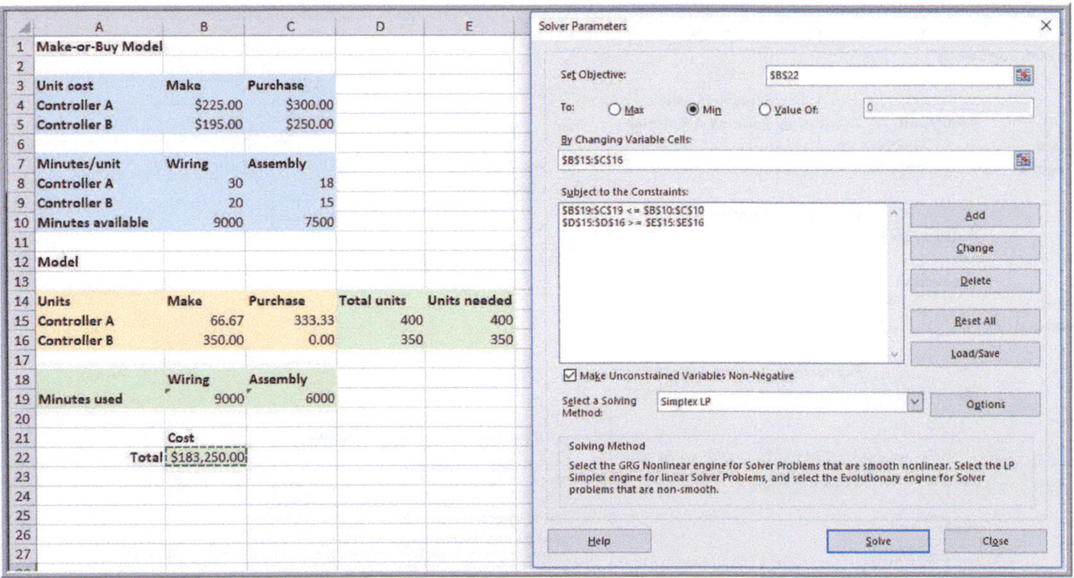

14-4c Capacity Constrained Production Planning With Multiple Products

We have seen how to develop linear optimization models for simple aggregate planning problems for a single product with material balance constraints (Equation 14.1). However, in many practical situations, we need to deal with multiple products and other capacity limitations. Solved Problem 14.6 illustrates an example for such a situation.

SOLVED PROBLEM 14.6: A MULTIPLE PRODUCT PRODUCTION PLANNING OPTIMIZATION MODEL

Romard Electronics produces two electronic components for an airplane-engine manufacturer. The order shown in Exhibit 14.13 has just been received for the next three-month period. Additional information on available production, labor, and storage capacity is given in Exhibit 14.14. Production and storage space requirements are provided in Exhibit 14.15.

EXHIBIT 14.13 Three-Month Demand Schedule for Romard Electronics Company

	April	May	June
Component 322A	1,000	3,000	5,000
Component 802B	1,000	500	3,000

EXHIBIT 14.14 Machine, Labor, and Storage Capacities

	Machine Capacity (hours)	Labor Capacity (hours)	Storage Capacity (Square feet)
April	400	300	10,000
May	500	300	10,000
June	600	300	10,000

EXHIBIT 14.15 Production and Storage Requirements for Components 322A and 802B

	Machine (hours/unit)	Labor (hours/unit)	Storage (sq.ft./unit)
Component 322A	0.10	0.05	2
Component 802B	0.08	0.07	3

Component 322A costs \$20 per unit to produce and component 802B costs \$10 per unit to produce. The company has determined that on a monthly basis, inventory-holding costs are eight percent of the cost of the product. The inventories at the beginning of the three-month scheduling period are 500 units for component 322A and 200 units for component 802B. The company wants to ensure a minimum inventory level at the end of the three-month period of at least 400 units of component 322A and at least 200 units of component 802B. Develop and solve a linear optimization model to minimize the total cost.

Solution:

Decision variables:

Let

x_{im} = the number of units produced of product *i* in month *m*.

I_{im} denote the inventory level of product *i* at the end of month *m*

For these variables, $i = 1$ refers to component 322A, $i = 2$ to component 802B, $m = 1$ to April, $m = 2$ to May, and $m = 3$ to June.

Objective function:

The production cost part of the objective function is

$$20x_{11} + 20x_{12} + 20x_{13} + 10x_{21} + 10x_{22} + 10x_{23}$$

Note that in this problem the production cost per unit is the same each month, and thus we need not include production costs in the objective function; that is, no matter what production schedule is selected, the total production costs will remain the same. However, we will include them so that the value of the objective function will include all the relevant costs associated with the problem.

The inventory cost is $0.015 \times \$20 = \$0.30$ per unit for component 322A, and $0.015 \times \$10 = \$0.15$ per unit for component 802B. Then, the inventory-holding cost portion of the objective function can be written as:

$$0.30I_{11} + 0.30I_{12} + 0.30I_{13} + 0.15I_{21} + 0.15I_{22} + 0.15I_{23}$$

The complete objective function is

$$\text{Minimize } 20x_{11} + 20x_{12} + 20x_{13} + 10x_{21} + 10x_{22} + 10x_{23} + 0.30I_{11} + 0.30I_{12} + 0.30I_{13} + 0.15I_{21} + 0.15I_{22} + 0.15I_{23}$$

Constraints:

First, we must guarantee that enough product is available to meet customer demand each month. We can use Equation 14.1 that we introduced earlier in this chapter:

Ending inventory in period $t - 1$ + Production in period t − Demand in period t = Ending inventory in period t

For the first month (April), we have

$$500 + x_{11} - I_{11} = 1{,}000$$

and

$$200 + x_{21} - I_{21} = 1{,}000$$

We can re-write these as:

$$x_{11} - I_{11} = 500$$

and

$$x_{21} - I_{21} = 800$$

Similarly, for the second and third months, we have

$$\text{Month 2:} \quad I_{11} + x_{12} - I_{12} = 3{,}000$$
$$I_{21} + x_{22} - I_{22} = 500$$
$$\text{Month 3:} \quad I_{12} + x_{13} - I_{13} = 5{,}000$$
$$I_{22} + x_{23} - I_{23} = 3{,}000$$

The constraints for minimum inventory levels at the end of the third month are

$$I_{13} \geq 400 \text{ and } I_{23} \geq 200$$

To reflect the machine, labor, and storage capacities, the following constraints are necessary:

Machine capacity:

$$0.10x_{11} + 0.08x_{21} \leq 400 \text{ (month 1)}$$
$$0.10x_{12} + 0.08x_{22} \leq 500 \text{ (month 2)}$$
$$0.10x_{13} + 0.08x_{23} \leq 600 \text{ (month 3)}$$

Labor capacity:

$$0.05x_{11} + 0.07x_{21} \leq 300 \text{ (month 1)}$$
$$0.05x_{12} + 0.07x_{22} \leq 300 \text{ (month 2)}$$
$$0.05x_{13} + 0.07x_{23} \leq 300 \text{ (month 3)}$$

Storage capacity:

$$2I_{11} + 3I_{21} \leq 10{,}000 \text{ (month 1)}$$
$$2I_{12} + 3I_{22} \leq 10{,}000 \text{ (month 2)}$$
$$2I_{13} + 3I_{23} \leq 10{,}000 \text{ (month 3)}$$

Finally, all variables must be non-negative.

Exhibit 14.16 shows the Excel spreadsheet and Solver model (Excel worksheet Romard Electronics in MindTap). The optimal solution is to produce 500 units of component 322A in April, 3000 in May, and 5400 in June, and carry no inventory except for the minimum requirement in June; and to produce 1928.6 units of component 802B in April, 2142.9 in May, and 428.6 in June. Because of the capacity limitations, the company is required to produce more than the demand of component 802B in April and May and carry inventory. The minimum total cost is $226.920, of which $223,000 is production and $3,920 is inventory.

EXHIBIT 14.16 Solver Model and Solution for Romard Electronics

	A	B	C	D	E	F	G	H	I
1	Romard Electronics								
2									
3	Data					Model			
4									
5	Demand	April	May	June		Units produced	April	May	June
6	Component 322A	1000	3000	5000		Component 322A	500.0	3000.0	5400.0
7	Component 802B	1000	500	3000		Component 802B	1928.6	2142.9	428.6
8									
9	Capacities	Machine hours	Labor hours	Square feet of storage		Ending inventories	April	May	June
10	April	400	300	10000		Component 322A	0.0	0.0	400.0
11	May	500	300	10000		Component 802B	1128.6	2771.4	200.0
12	June	600	300	10000					
13						Net Production	April	May	June
14	Requirements	machine hours/unit	Labor hours/unit	Storage (sq. ft./unit)		Component 322A	1000	3000	5000
15	Component 322A	0.1	0.05	2		Component 802B	1000	500	3000
16	Component 802B	0.08	0.07	3					
17						Capacity usage	Machine hours	Labor hours	Square feet of storage
18	Costs	Component 322A	Component 802B			April	204.3	160.0	3385.7
19	Unit production cost	$20.00	$10.00			May	471.4	300.0	8314.3
20	Carrying charge	8%	8%			June	574.3	300.0	1400.0
21	nventory holding/unit	$1.60	$0.80						
22									
23	Inventory Data	Initial inventory April	Min. required June				Cost	Production	Inventory
24	Component 322A	500	400			Total	$226,920.00	$223,000.00	$3,920.00
25	Component 802B	200	200						

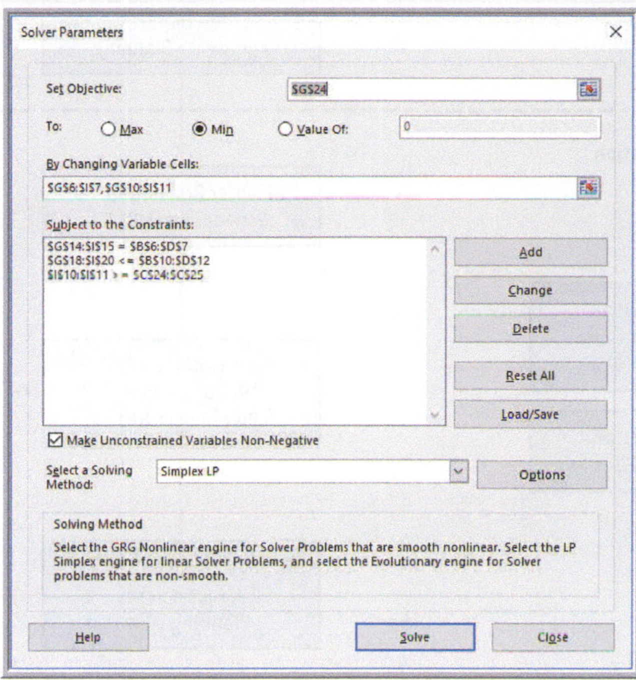

14-5 Disaggregation in Manufacturing

For manufacturing firms, Exhibit 14.17 shows a typical system for disaggregating aggregate plans into executable operations plans. Three important techniques in this process are master production scheduling (MPS), materials requirements planning (MRP), and capacity requirements planning (CRP).

14-5a Master Production Scheduling

A **master production schedule (MPS)** *is a statement of how many finished items are to be produced and when they are to be produced.* An example of a portion of an MPS with an eight-week planning horizon is shown in Exhibit 14.18. Typically, the master schedule is developed for weekly time periods over a 6- to 12-month horizon. The purpose of the master schedule is to translate the aggregate plan into a separate plan for individual finished goods. It also provides a means for evaluating alternative schedules in terms of capacity requirements, provides input to the MRP system, and helps managers generate priorities for scheduling by setting due dates for the production of individual items.

For make-to-order industries, order backlogs provide the needed customer-demand information; thus, the known customer orders (called *firm orders*) determine the MPS. In some industries where a few basic subassemblies and components are assembled in many different combinations to produce a large variety of end products, the MPS is usually developed for the basic subassemblies and not for the ultimate finished goods. Therefore, a different plan and schedule are needed to assemble the final finished good.

EXHIBIT 14.17 Disaggregation Framework for Manufacturing Plans and Schedules

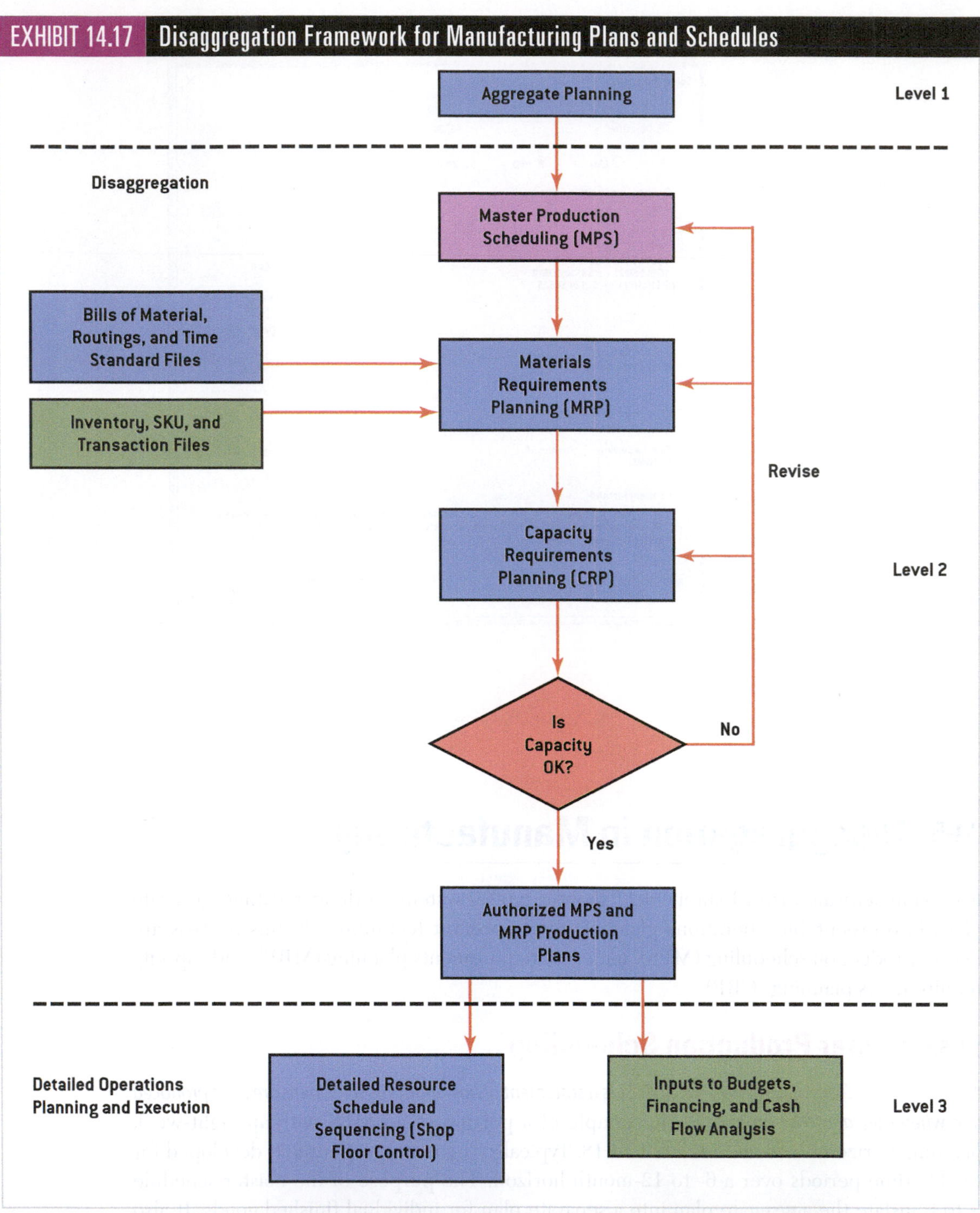

EXHIBIT 14.18 Eight-Week Master Production Schedule Example

		Week 1	2	3	4	5	6	7	8	
	Model A		200		200		350			MPS Planned Quantities
	Model B	150	100		190			120		
	·	·	·	·	·	·	·		·	
	·	·	·	·	·	·	·		·	
Totals	·	·	·	·	·	·	·		·	
Aggregate	X			75		75	75		60	
Production Plans (Units)		500	800	350	600	280	750	420	300	

A **final assembly schedule (FAS)** *defines the quantity and timing for assembling subassemblies and component parts into a final finished good.*

14-5b Materials Requirements Planning

To produce a finished product, many individual parts or subassemblies must be manufactured or purchased and then assembled together. Fixed-order-quantity and fixed-period inventory systems (see Chapter 12) were used long ago for planning materials in manufacturing environments. However, these systems did not capture the dependent relationships between the demand for finished goods and their raw materials, components, and subassemblies. This insight led to the development of materials requirements planning.

Materials requirements planning (MRP) *is a forward-looking, demand-based approach for planning the production of manufactured goods and ordering materials and components to minimize unnecessary inventories and reduce costs.* MRP projects the requirements for the individual parts or subassemblies based on the demand for the finished goods as specified by the MPS. The primary output of an MRP system is a time-phased report that gives (1) the purchasing department a schedule for obtaining raw materials and purchased parts, (2) the production managers a detailed schedule for manufacturing the product and controlling manufacturing inventories, and (3) accounting and financial functions production information that drives cash flow, budgets, and financial needs.

MRP depends on understanding three basic concepts: (1) the concept of dependent demand, (2) the concept of time phasing, and (3) lot sizing to gain economies of scale.

Dependent demand *is demand that is directly related to the demand of other SKUs and can be calculated without needing to be forecasted.* The concept of dependent demand is best understood by examining the bill of materials. A *bill of materials (BOM)* defines the hierarchical relationships between all items that comprise a finished good, such as subassemblies, purchased parts, and manufactured in-house parts. Some firms call the BOM the product structure. A BOM may also define standard times and alternative routings for each item.

For labor-intensive services, the analogy to the BOM is a bill of labor (BOL). *A* **bill of labor (BOL)** *is a hierarchical record analogous to a BOM that defines labor inputs necessary to create a good or service.* For example, a BOL for surgery includes the doctors and supporting surgery technicians and nurses. A broader concept is a *bill of resources (BOR)*, where the labor, information (e.g., X-rays, blood tests), equipment, instruments, and parts are all defined in a BOM format to support each specific type of surgery. Exhibit 14.19 shows the structure of a typical BOM.

End items *are finished goods scheduled in the MPS or FAS that must be forecasted.* These are the items at Level 0 of the BOM. For example, item A in Exhibit 14.19 is an end item. *A* **parent item** *is manufactured from one or more components.* Items A, B, D, F, and H are parents in Exhibit 14.19. End items are composed of components and subassemblies. **Components** *are any items (raw materials, manufactured parts, purchased parts) other than an end item that goes into a higher-level parent item(s).* Items B, C, D, E, F, G, H, and I are all components in the BOM in Exhibit 14.19. *A* **subassembly** *always has at least one immediate parent and also has at least one immediate component.* Subassemblies (sometimes called *intermediate items*) reside in the middle of the BOM; items B, D, F, and H in Exhibit 14.19 are examples. BOMs for simple assemblies might be flat, having only two or three levels, whereas more complex BOMs may have up to 15 levels.

> MRP depends on understanding three basic concepts: (1) the concept of dependent demand, (2) the concept of time phasing, and (3) lot sizing to gain economies of scale.

To understand the nature of dependent demand, assume that we wish to produce 100 units of end item A in Exhibit 14.19. Exhibit 14.20 shows the calculations for each of the items in the BOM, taking into account on-hand inventory. For each unit of A,

EXHIBIT 14.19 Example of a Bill of Materials and Dependent Demand

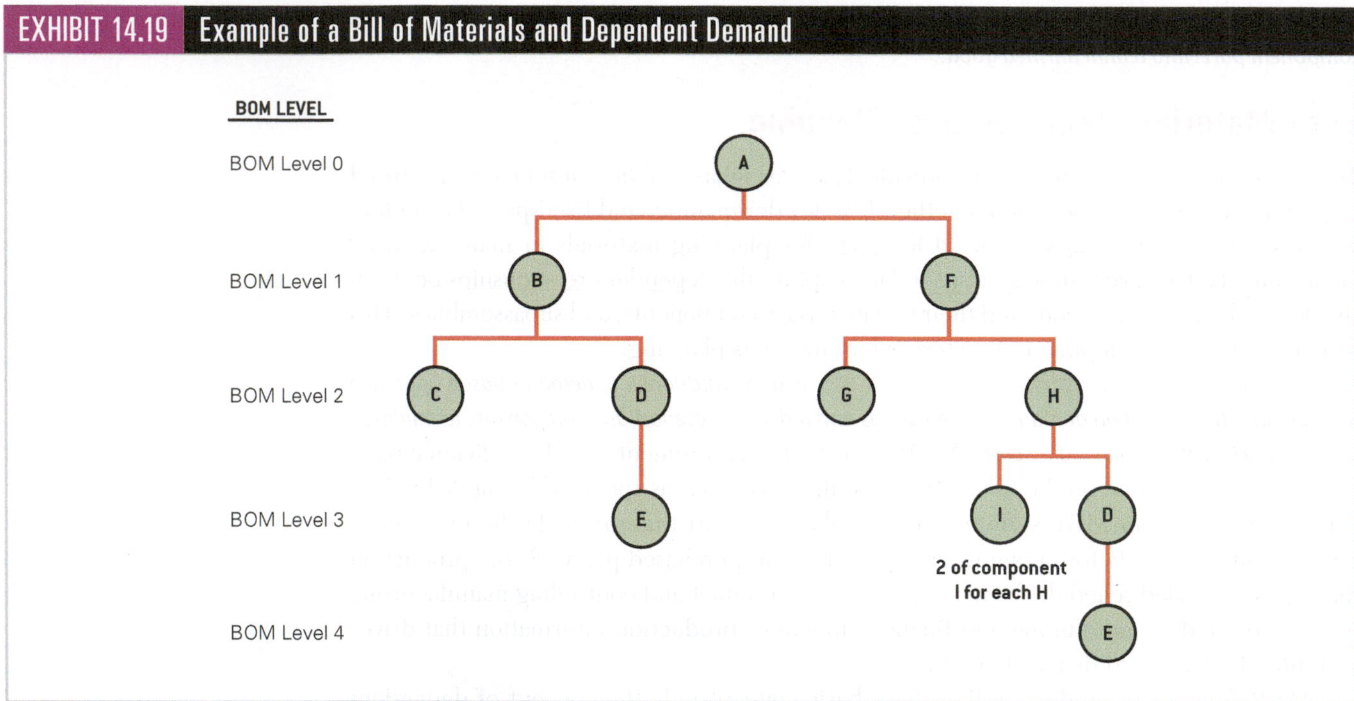

EXHIBIT 14.20 Dependent Demand Calculations

Item	On-Hand Inventory	Dependent Demand Calculations
A	0	100 − 0 = 100
B	33	100 − 33 = 67
C	12	67 − 12 = 55
D	47	67 + 50 − 47 = 70
E	10	70 − 10 = 60
F	20	100 − 20 = 80
G	15	80 − 15 = 65
H	30	80 − 30 = 50
I	7	50 × 2 − 7 = 93

we need one unit of items B and F. We have 33 units on hand for subassembly B, so we need to make only 100 − 33 = 67 units of B. Similarly, we have 20 units of F available and therefore require an additional 100 − 20 = 80 units. Next, at Level 2 of the BOM, for each unit of B, we need one unit of components C and D; and for each F, we need one unit of components G and H. Because we need to produce only an additional 67 units of B, and we have 12 units of component C on hand, we need to produce an additional 67 − 12 = 55 units of C.

Check the remaining calculations in Exhibit 14.20. Note that item D is a common subassembly that is used in both subassemblies B and H. Thus, we must include the requirements of item B (67 units) and item H (50 units) in computing the number of Ds to produce: 67 + 50 − 47 = 70 units.

Dependent demand also occurs in service businesses, but few managers recognize it. Many service organizations such as restaurants and retail stores offer repeatable, highly structured services and have high goods content of 50 percent or more. Therefore, the logic of dependent demand can be used to plan the goods-content portion of the customer benefit package. For example, meals in a restaurant can be thought of as end items. The service required to assemble an order can be defined in terms of the bill of materials (BOM) and lead times.

14-5c Time Phasing and Lot Sizing in MRP

Although the dependent demand calculations as described in the previous section provide the number of components or subassemblies needed in the BOM, they do not specify when orders should be placed or how much should be ordered. Because of the hierarchy of the BOM, there is no reason to order something until it is required to produce a parent item. Thus, all dependent demand requirements do not need to be ordered at the same time, but rather are *time phased* as necessary. In addition, orders might be consolidated to take advantage of

Using Production Planning Concepts in the Operating Room

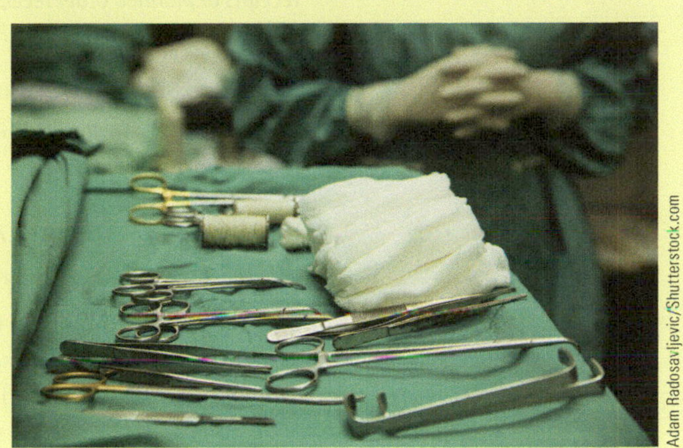
Adam Radosavljevic/Shutterstock.com

A 374-bed hospital with nine operating rooms in Houston, Texas, uses bills of materials and master production scheduling to plan surgeries and the surgical kits needed for a seven-day planning horizon. Bills of labor (BOL) are used to schedule surgeons, nurses, and orderlies. The bill of materials (BOM) file contains the materials, instruments, and supplies needed for various surgical procedures. End items are specific surgery procedures with a lot size of one. The concept and methods of dependent demand are alive and well in this surgery suite![3]

ordering economies of scale—this is called *lot sizing*. **MRP explosion** *is the process of using the logic of dependent demand to calculate the quantity and timing of orders for all subassemblies and components that go into and support the production of the end item(s).* In this section we will illustrate the process of time phasing.

Time buckets *are the time-period size used in the MRP explosion process and usually are one week in length.* Although small buckets such as one day are good for scheduling production over a short time horizon, they may be too precise for longer-range planning. Thus, larger buckets such as months are often used as the planning horizon gets longer. We assume that all time buckets are one week in length.

An MRP record consists of the following:

- **Gross requirements (GR)** *are the total demand for an item derived from all of its parents.* This is the quantity of the component needed to support production at the next-higher level of assembly. Gross requirements can also include maintenance, repair, and sparepart components that are added to the dependent demand requirements.
- **Scheduled or planned receipts (S/PR)** *are orders that are due or planned to be delivered.* A scheduled receipt was released to the vendor or shop in a previous time period and now shows up as a scheduled receipt. (In some of our examples, we assume, for simplicity, that all scheduled receipts are zero.) A planned order receipt is defined later. If the order is for an outside vendor, it is a *purchase order*. If the order is produced in-house, it is a *shop or manufactured order*.
- A **planned order receipt (PORec)** *specifies the quantity and time an order is to be received.* When the order arrives, it is recorded, checked into inventory, and available for use. It is assumed to be available for use at the beginning of the period.
- A **planned order release (PORel)** *specifies the planned quantity and time an order is to be released to the factory or a supplier.* It is a planned order receipt offset by the item's lead time. Planned order releases generate the gross requirements for all components in the MRP logic.
- **Projected on-hand inventory (POH)** *is the expected amount of inventory on hand at the beginning of the time period considering on-hand inventory from the previous period plus scheduled*

receipts or planned order receipts minus the gross requirements. The formula for computing the projected on-hand inventory is defined by Equation 14.2 as follows:

Projected on-hand in period t (POH_t) = On-hand inventory in period $t-1$ (OH_{t-1}) + Scheduled or planned receipts in period t (S/PR_t) − Gross requirements in period t (GR_t)
or

$$POH_t = OH_{t-1} + S/PR_t - GR_t \quad [14.2]$$

Lot sizing *is the process of determining the appropriate amount and timing of ordering to reduce costs*. It can be uneconomical to set up a new production run or place a purchase order for the demand in each time bucket. Instead, it is usually better to aggregate orders and achieve economies of scale. Many different lot sizing rules have been proposed. Some are simple, heuristic rules, whereas others seek to find the best economic trade-off between the setup costs associated with production and the holding costs of carrying inventory. We discuss three common lot sizing methods for MRP—lot-for-lot (LFL), fixed-order quantity (FOQ), and periodic-order quantity (POQ).

To illustrate these, we will consider the production of a simple product (A) whose bill of materials and inventory records are given in Exhibits 14.21 and 14.22. Note that item B is a common component for both items A and C; therefore, we cannot compute the gross requirements for item B until the planned order releases for items A and C have been determined.

Suppose that the MPS calls for 150 units of product A to be completed in week 4; 300 units in week 5; 50 units in week 6; and 200 units in week 7. We assume that the lead time is one week. The MPS in Exhibit 14.23 shows the demand for product A. The planned order releases are offset by one week to account for the lead time.

EXHIBIT 14.21 Bill of Materials

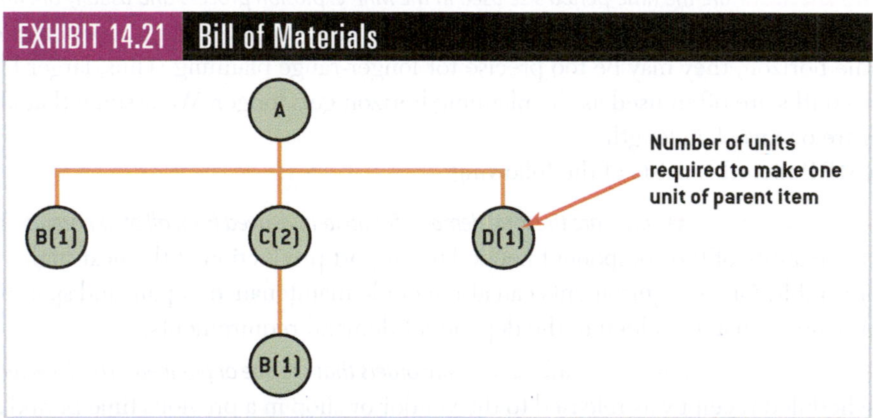

EXHIBIT 14.22 Item Inventory File

	Item	Item	It Item
Data category	B	C	D
Lead time (weeks)	1	2	1
Beginning (on-hand) inventory	100	10	40
Scheduled receipts	None	200 (week 2)	50 (week 3)

EXHIBIT 14.23 Example MPS

MPS	Lead Time = 1 week for Assembly						
Week	1	2	3	4	5	6	7
Product A—end item	0	0	0	150	300	50	200
Planned order release	0	0	150	300	50	200	0

EXHIBIT 14.24 MRP Record for Item C Using the Lot-for-Lot (LFL) Rule

Item C (two units of C are needed for one unit of A) Description **Lot size: LFL** **Lead time: 2 weeks**

Week		1	2	3	4	5	6	7
Gross requirements		0	0	300	600	100	400	0
Scheduled receipts			200					
Projected OH inventory	**10**	10	210	0	0	0	0	0
Planned order receipts		0	0	90	600	100	400	0
Planned order releases		**90**	**600**	**100**	**400**			

First consider item C. The MRP explosion is given in Exhibit 14.24. Notice from the BOM in Exhibit 14.21 that two units of item C are needed to produce one unit of end item A. Therefore, the gross requirements for item C in Exhibit 14.24 are directly derived from the planned order releases in the MPS in Exhibit 14.23 (150 × 2 = 300 units in period 3; 300 × 2 = 600 units in period 4; etc.).

Lot-for-Lot Rule *An ordering schedule that covers the gross requirements for each week is called* **lot-for-lot (LFL)**. In other words, we simply place orders each week to ensure that enough inventory is available to prevent shortages. If LFL is used for all dependent items, it clearly shows the true nature of dependent demand. Notice that LFL requires four planned orders, and the average inventory during this planning horizon is 10 + 210 + 760 + 60 + 10 + 610 + 610 = 2,270/7 = 324.3 units/week. The LFL rule minimizes the amount of inventory that needs to be carried; however, it ignores the costs associated with purchase orders or production setups. Thus, this rule is best applied when inventory-carrying costs are high and setup/order costs are low.

The projected on-hand quantity assumes the receipt of the planned order or scheduled receipt (S/PR_t) and is computed using Equation 14.2. LFL always tries to drive inventory levels to zero. We must compute the planned order release for item C before we can do the same for item B.

For example, using Equation 14.2 we compute the following:

$$POH_1 = OH_0 + S/PR_1 - GR_1 = 10 + 0 - 0 = 10$$
$$POH_2 = OH_1 + S/PR_2 - GR_2 = 10 + 200 - 0 = 210$$
$$POH_3 = OH_2 + S/PR_3 - GR_3 = 210 + 90 - 300 = 0$$
$$POH_4 = OH_3 + S/PR_4 - GR_4 = 0 + 600 - 600 = 0$$
$$POH_5 = OH_4 + S/PR_5 - GR_5 = 0 + 100 - 100 = 0$$
$$POH_6 = OH_5 + S/PR_6 - GR_6 = 0 + 400 - 400 = 0$$
$$POH_7 = OH_6 + S/PR_7 - GR_7 = 0 + 0 - 0 = 0$$

The planned order releases in Exhibit 14.24 are planned but have not yet been released. *The* **action bucket** *is the current time period.* When a planned order release reaches the action bucket, analysts evaluate the situation and release the order to the appropriate provider—supplier or in-house work center. In Exhibit 14.24, for example, only the planned order of 90 units of item C is in the action bucket for current time period of week 1. Therefore, the planned order needs to be released in week 1 and will show up the next week in the scheduled receipts row. Clearly, the total number of MRP calculations is enormous in multiproduct situations with many components, making a computer essential. Action notices are usually computer generated and provide a variety of information to help inventory planners make decisions about order releases delaying scheduled receipts, and expediting when necessary.

Fixed-Order-Quantity Rule *The* **fixed-order-quantity (FOQ)** *rule uses a fixed order size for every order or production run.* This is similar to the fixed-order-quantity approach for independent demand items. The FOQ can be a standard-size container or pallet load, or can be determined economically using the economic order quantity formula in Chapter 12. In the rare case where the FOQ does not cover the gross requirements, the order size is increased to equal the larger quantity, and FOQ defaults to LFL.

The rationale for the FOQ approach is that large lot sizes result in fewer orders and setups and therefore reduce the costs associated with ordering and setup. This allows the firm to take advantage of price breaks by suppliers and production economies of scale, and to avoid less-than-truckload shipments (which are usually more expensive than full truckloads). However, this creates larger average inventory levels that must be held at a cost, and it can distort the true dependent demand gross requirements for lower-level components. Thus, the FOQ model is best applied when inventory-carrying costs are low and setup/order costs are high.

We will illustrate this rule for item B in Exhibit 14.21. Exhibit 14.25 shows the MRP explosion. Note that component part commonality increases the dependent demand requirements, as shown in the gross requirements row. For example, the 700-unit gross requirement in period 4 is due to the planned order release in the MPS for 300 units of item A in week 4 (see Exhibit 14.23) plus the planned order release for parent item C of 400 units in week 4 (see Exhibit 14.24).

Suppose that the FOQ is chosen using the EOQ as $\sqrt{2 \times 10{,}000 \text{ units} \times 864/\$1} = \sqrt{640{,}000} = 800 \text{ units}$. Using Equation 14.2, we compute the following projected on-hand inventories for each period:

$$
\begin{aligned}
POH_1 &= OH_0 + S/PR_1 - GR_1 = 100 + 0 - 90 = 10\\
POH_2 &= OH_1 + S/PR_2 - GR_2 = 10 + 800 - 600 = 210\\
POH_3 &= OH_2 + S/PR_3 - GR_3 = 210 + 800 - 250 = 760\\
POH_4 &= OH_3 + S/PR_4 - GR_4 = 760 + 0 - 700 = 60\\
POH_5 &= OH_4 + S/PR_5 - GR_5 = 60 + 0 - 50 = 10\\
POH_6 &= OH_5 + S/PR_6 - GR_6 = 10 + 800 - 200 = 610\\
POH_7 &= OH_6 + S/PR_7 - GR_7 = 610 + 0 - 0 = 610
\end{aligned}
$$

Notice that FOQ results in three planned orders, and an average inventory is $10 + 210 + 760 + 60 + 10 + 610 + 610 = 2{,}270/7 = 324.3$ units/week. To understand the difference with LFL, we encourage you to compare these results to the LFL approach.

EXHIBIT 14.25 Item B Fixed-Order-Quantity (FOQ) Lot Sizing and MRP Record

Item B **Lot size: 800 units**
Description **Lead time: 1 week**

Week		1	2	3	4	5	6	7
Gross requirements		90	600	250	700	50	200	0
Scheduled receipts								
Projected OH inventory	**100**	10	210	760	60	10	610	610
Planned order receipts		0	**800**	**800**	0	0	**800**	0
Planned order releases		**800**	**800**			**800**		

Periodic-Order-Quantity Rule The **periodic-order quantity (POQ)** *orders a quantity equal to the gross requirement quantity in one or more predetermined time periods minus the projected on-hand quantity of the previous time period.* For example, a POQ of two weeks orders exactly enough to cover demand during a two-week period and therefore may result in a different quantity every order cycle. The POQ might be selected judgmentally—for example, "order every 10 days"—or be determined using an economic time interval, which is the EOQ divided by annual demand (D). For example, if $EOQ/D = 0.1$ of a year, and assuming 250 working days per year, then POQ = 25 days, or about every five weeks. A POQ for a one-week time period is equivalent to LFL. Using this rule, the projected on-hand inventory will equal zero at the end of the POQ time interval.

Some MRP users only use the simple LFL rule; others apply other lot sizing approaches to take advantage of economies of scale and reduce costs.

We illustrate this rule for item D using a POQ = two weeks. The result is shown in Exhibit 14.26. Using Equation 14.2, we compute the following:

$$POH_1 = OH_0 + S/PR_1 - GR_1 = 40 + 0 - 0 = 40$$
$$POH_2 = OH_1 + S/PR_2 - GR_2 = 40 + 0 - 0 = 40$$
$$POH_3 = OH_2 + S/PR_3 - GR_3 = 40 + 50 + 360 - 150 = 300$$
$$POH_4 = OH_3 + S/PR_4 - GR_4 = 300 + 0 - 300 = 0$$
$$POH_5 = OH_4 + S/PR_5 - GR_5 = 0 + 250 - 50 = 200$$
$$POH_6 = OH_5 + S/PR_6 - GR_6 = 200 + 0 - 200 = 0$$
$$POH_7 = OH_6 + S/PR_7 - GR_7 = 0 + 0 - 0 = 0$$

The first time that POH becomes negative "without" a planned order receipt is in week 3 (40 + 50 − 150 = −60). Therefore, if we order 60 units to cover week 3 requirements plus 300 units to cover week 4 requirements, we have an order quantity of 360 units. The next time the POH is negative "without" a planned order receipt is week 5 (0 + 0 − 50 = −50). This requires us to order 50 units to cover week 5 requirements plus 200 units to cover week 6 requirements. For this example, POQ results in two planned orders of 360 and 250 units. The average inventory is 40 + 40 + 300 + 0 + 200 + 0 + 0 = 580/7 = 82.9 units/week.

The POQ approach results in moderate average inventory levels compared to FOQ because it matches order quantities to time buckets. Furthermore, it is easy to implement because inventory levels can be reviewed according to a fixed schedule. However, POQ creates high average inventory levels if the POQ becomes too long, and it can distort true dependent demand gross requirements for lower-level components. An economic-based POQ model is best applied when inventory-carrying costs and setup/order costs are moderate.

As you see, lot sizing rules affect not only the planned order releases for the particular item under consideration but also the gross requirements of all lower-level component items. Some MRP users only apply the simple LFL rule; others apply other lot sizing approaches to take advantage of economies of scale and reduce costs. Exhibit 14.27 summarizes the MRP explosion for the BOM in Exhibit 14.21.

Steve Cukrov/Shutterstock.com

EXHIBIT 14.26 Item D Periodic-Order Quantity (POQ) Lot Sizing and MRP Record

Item D **Lot size: POQ=2 weeks**
Description **Lead time: 1 week**

Week		1	2	3	4	5	6	7
Gross requirements				150	300	50	200	
Scheduled receipts				50				
Projected OH inventory	**40**	40	40	300	0	200	0	0
Planned order receipts		0	0	360	0	250	0	0
Planned order releases			**360**		**250**			

EXHIBIT 14.27 Summary of MRP Explosion for Bill of Materials in Exhibit 14.21

MPS **Lead time = 1 week for assembly**

Week		1	2	3	4	5	6	7
Product A—end item		0	0	0	150	300	50	200
Planned order releases		0	0	150	300	50	200	0

Item C (two units of C are needed for one unit of A) **Lot size: LFL**
Description **Lead time: 2 weeks**

Week		1	2	3	4	5	6	7
Gross requirements		0	0	300	600	100	400	0
Scheduled receipts			200					
Projected OH inventory	**10**	10	210	0	0	0	0	0
Planned order receipts		0	0	90	600	100	400	0
Planned order releases		**90**	**600**	**100**	**400**			

Item B **Lot size: 800 units**
Description **Lead time: 1 week**

Week		1	2	3	4	5	6	7
Gross requirements		90	600	250	700	50	200	0
Scheduled receipts								
Projected OH inventory	**100**	10	210	760	60	10	610	610
Planned order receipts		0	**800**	**800**	0	0	**800**	0
Planned order releases		**800**	**800**			**800**		

Item D **Lot size: POQ = 2 weeks**
Description **Lead time: 1 week**

Week		1	2	3	4	5	6	7
Gross requirements				150	300	50	200	
Scheduled receipts				50				
Projected OH inventory	**40**	40	40	300	0	200	0	0
Planned order receipts		0	0	360	0	250	0	0
Planned order releases			**360**		**250**			

14-6 Capacity Requirements Planning

Capacity requirements planning (CRP) *is the process of determining the amount of labor and machine resources required to accomplish the tasks of production on a more detailed level, taking into account all component parts and end items in the materials plan.* For example, in anticipation of a big demand for pizzas on Super Bowl Sunday, one would have to ensure that sufficient capacity for dough making, pizza preparation, and delivery is available to handle the forecasted demand.

Capacity requirements are computed by multiplying the number of units scheduled for production at a work center by the unit resource requirements and then adding in the setup time. These requirements are then summarized by time period and work center. To illustrate CRP calculations, suppose the planned order releases for a component are as follows:

Time period	1	2	3	4
Planned order release	30	20	40	40

Assume the component requires 1.10 hours of labor per unit in Work Center D and 1.5 hours of setup time. We can use Equation 11.2 from Chapter 11 to compute the total hours required (called *work center load*) on Work Center D:

$$\text{Capacity required}\,(C_i) = \text{Setup time}\,(S_i) + \text{Processing time}\,(P_i) \times \text{Order size}\,(Q_i)$$

The capacity requirement in period 1 is 1.5 hours + (1.10 hours/unit)(30 units) = 34.5 hours. Similarly, in period 2 we have 1.5 hours + (1.10 hours/unit)(30 units) = 23.5 hours, and in periods 3 and 4 we have 1.5 hours + (1.10 hours/unit)(40 units) + 45.5 hours. The total load on Work Center D is 149 hours during these four weeks, or 37.25 hours per week if averaged.

Such information is usually provided in a *work center load report*, as illustrated in Exhibit 14.28. If sufficient capacity is not available, decisions must be made about overtime, transfer of personnel between departments, subcontracting, and so on. The master production schedule may also have to be revised to meet available capacity by shifting certain end items to different time periods or changing the order quantities. For example, the workload in Exhibit 14.28 in periods 3 and 4 could be scheduled to period 2 to fill the idle time and avoid overtime in periods 3 and 4. However, additional inventory-carrying costs would be incurred. So, as you see, leveling out work center load involves many cost trade-offs. This closed-loop, iterative process provides a realistic deployment of the master schedule to the shop floor.

EXHIBIT 14.28 Work Center D Example Load Report

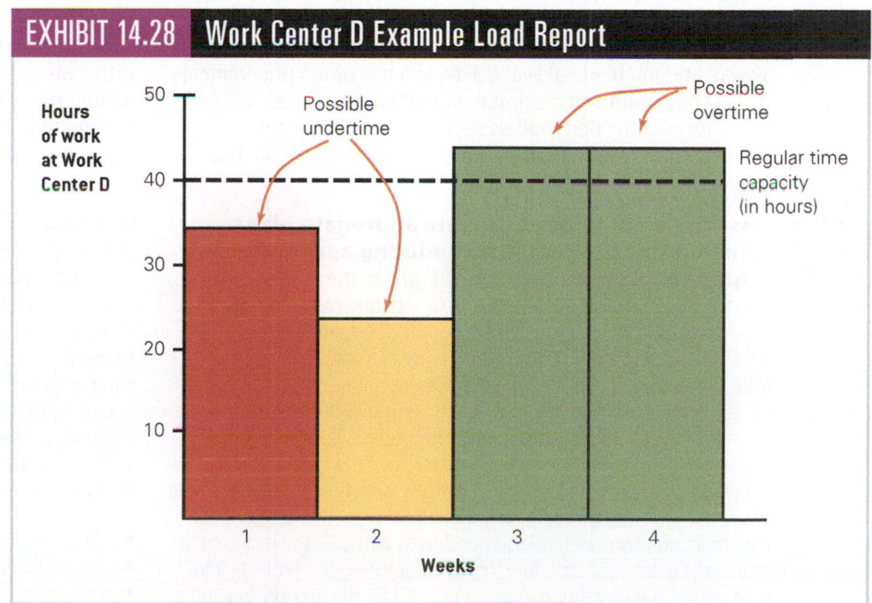

CHAPTER 14 LEARNING OBJECTIVE SUMMARIES

14.1 **Describe the overall frameworks for resource planning in both goods-producing and service-providing organizations.** Level 1 represents aggregate planning. Aggregate plans define output levels over a planning horizon of one to two years, usually in monthly or quarterly time buckets. They normally focus on product families or total capacity requirements rather than individual products or specific capacity allocations. Aggregate plans also help to define budget allocations and associated resource requirements.

Level 2 planning is called disaggregation. To disaggregate means to break up or separate into more detailed pieces. Disaggregation specifies more detailed plans for the creation of individual goods and services or the allocation of capacity to specific time periods. For goods-producing firms, disaggregation takes Level 1 aggregate planning decisions and breaks them down into such details as order sizes and schedules for individual subassemblies and resources by week and day.

Level 3 focuses on executing the detailed plans made at Level 2, creating detailed resource schedules and job sequences. Level 3 planning and execution in manufacturing is sometimes called *shop floor control*. Resource management for most service-providing organizations generally does not require as many intermediate levels of planning as it does for manufacturing.

14.2 **Explain options for aggregate planning.** Managers have a variety of options in developing aggregate plans in the face of fluctuating demand:

- Demand management: Marketing strategies can be used to influence demand and help create more feasible aggregate plans.
- Production-rate changes: One means of increasing the output rate without changing existing resources is through planned overtime. Alternatively, hours can be reduced during slow periods through planned undertime.
- Workforce changes: Changing the size of the workforce is usually accomplished through hiring and layoffs.
- Inventory changes: In planning for fluctuating demand, inventory is often built up during slack periods and held for peak periods. A related strategy is to carry back orders or to tolerate lost sales during peak-demand periods.
- Facilities, equipment, and transportation: Short-term changes in facilities and equipment are seldom used in traditional aggregate planning methods because of the capital costs involved.

14.3 **Explain the three basic strategies for aggregate planning.** A level strategy avoids changes in the production rate, working within normal capacity restrictions. Labor and equipment schedules are stable and repetitive, making it easier to execute the plan. An alternative to a level production strategy is to match production to demand every month (chase demand strategy). Although inventories will be reduced and lost sales will be eliminated, many production rate changes will dramatically change resource levels (the number of employees, machines, etc). Finally, we can use a minimum cost strategy that seeks to determine production levels for each time period that minimizes the total cost. All of these strategies can easily be evaluated using a spreadsheet.

14.4 **Describe the applications of linear optimization models for resource planning.** Product mix models seek to determine quantities of different products to produce and sell in order to maximize contribution to profit. Constraints might include resource limitations such as production time, labor availability, and material availability, and marketing requirements such as minimum and maximum amounts to produce.

Process selection models seek to determine quantities of a product to make using alternative processes, such as manufacturing or outsourcing, or using machines with different capabilities. The objective is usually to minimize cost, and typical constraints are meeting demand requirements and resource limitations.

Simple aggregate planning problems for a single product with material balance constraints can be modeled using linear optimization. In many practical situations, models must incorporate multiple products and other capacity limitations , resulting in more complex optimization models.

14.5 **Describe ways to disaggregate aggregate plans using master production scheduling and material requirements planning.** The purpose of the master schedule is to translate the aggregate plan into a separate plan for individual finished goods. It also provides a means for evaluating alternative schedules in terms of capacity requirements, provides input to the MRP system, and helps managers generate priorities for scheduling by setting due dates for the production of individual items.

MRP projects the requirements for the individual parts or subassemblies based on the demand for the finished goods as specified by the MPS. The primary output of an MRP system is a time-phased report that gives (1) the purchasing department a schedule for obtaining raw materials and purchased parts, (2) the production managers a detailed schedule for manufacturing the product and controlling manufacturing inventories, and (3) the accounting and financial functions production information that drives cash flow, budgets, and financial needs. MRP depends on understanding three basic concepts: (1) the concept of dependent demand, (2) the concept of time phasing, and (3) lot sizing to gain economies of scale.

The concept of dependent demand is best understood by examining the bill of materials. Because of the hierarchy of the BOM, there is no reason to order something until it is required to produce a parent item. Thus, all dependent demand requirements do not need to be ordered at the same time, but rather are time phased as necessary (see the LFL MRP time-phased record as an example). In addition, orders might be consolidated to take advantage of ordering economies of scale—this is called lot sizing. An MRP record (for example, Exhibit 14.24) consists of the following:

- Gross requirements (GR)
- Scheduled or planned receipts (S/PR)
- Projected on-hand inventory (POH)
- Planned order receipt (PORec)
- Planned order release (PORel)

CHAPTER 14 LEARNING OBJECTIVE SUMMARIES

There are three common lot sizing methods for MRP—lot-for-lot (LFL), fixed-order quantity (FOQ), and periodic-order quantity (POQ). Lot sizing rules affect not only the planned order releases for the particular item under consideration, but also the gross requirements of all lower-level component items. Some MRP users only use the simple LFL rule; others apply different lot sizing approaches to take advantage of economies of scale and reduce costs.

14.6 **Explain the concept and application of capacity requirements planning.** Capacity requirements are computed by multiplying the number of units scheduled for production at a work center by the unit resource requirements and adding the setup time. These requirements are then summarized by time period and work center. Such information is usually provided in a work center load report. If sufficient capacity is not available, decisions must be made about overtime, transfer of personnel between departments, subcontracting, and so on. The master production schedule may also have to be revised to meet available capacity by shifting certain end items to different time periods or changing the order quantities.

KEY TERMS

- **Action bucket**
- **Aggregate planning**
- **Aggregate production plan**
- **Bill of labor (BOL)**
- **Capacity requirements planning (CRP)**
- **Chase demand production strategy**
- **Components**
- **Dependent demand**
- **Disaggregation**
- **End item**
- **ERP systems**
- **Execution**
- **Final assembly schedule (FAS)**
- **Fixed-order quantity (FOQ)**
- **Gross requirements (GR)**
- **Level production strategy**
- **Lot sizing**
- **Lot-for-lot (LFL)**
- **Master production schedule (MPS)**
- **Materials requirements planning (MRP)**
- **MRP explosion**
- **Parent item**
- **Periodic-order quantity (POQ)**
- **Planned order receipt (PORec)**
- **Planned order release (PORel)**
- **Projected on-hand inventory (POH)**
- **Resource management**
- **Scheduled or planned receipts (S/PR)**
- **Subassembly**
- **Time buckets**

REVIEW QUESTIONS

14.1 1. Define resource management and explain its objectives and the effects of poor resource management in the value chain.

14.1 2. What is aggregate planning? Why is it used?

14.1 3. Describe the overall frameworks for resource planning in both goods-producing and service-providing organizations.

14.2 4. Explain options for aggregate planning.

14.3 5. Describe how to evaluate level production and chase demand strategies for aggregate planning.

14.4 6. Explain practical applications of optimization models for resource management.

14.5 7. What is a master production schedule? How does it differ from a final assembly schedule? Explain how one is constructed.

14.5 8. What is materials requirements planning? Of what value is it to organizations?

14.5 9. Explain the concept of dependent demand.

14.5 10. What is a bill of materials? Sketch a small example. What is the analogy of the BOM in services?

14.5 11. Define end-item, parent item, component parts, and subassembly. Identify these items in a bill of material.

14.5 12. Explain the concepts of time phasing and MRP explosion.

14.5 13. Describe ways to disaggregate aggregate plans using master production scheduling and material requirements planning.

14.5 14. Explain the pros and cons for LFL, FOQ, and POQ lot sizing methods.

14.6 15. Explain the concept and application of capacity requirements planning.

DISCUSSION QUESTIONS AND EXPERIENTIAL ACTIVITIES

14.1 16. Discuss some examples of real-life organizations that use demand management as a resource planning strategy.

14.1 17. Identify a goods-producing or service-providing organization and discuss how it might make aggregate planning decisions using the variables described in Exhibit 14.3.

14.2 18. Research and write a short paper (two pages maximum) describing how organizations use aggregate planning options in Exhibit 14.3.

14.3 19. Provide an argument for or against adopting a chase strategy for a major airline call center.

14.3 20. Interview a production manager at a nearby goods-producing company to determine how the company plans its production for fluctuating demand. What approaches does the company use?

14.5 21. Draw a simple bill-of-materials (BOM) for an automobile given the following requirements: (a) clearly label the end item and each component, (b) the BOM must contain no more than ten items, (c) the BOM must contain at least three levels (you may count the end-item level zero).

14.5 22. Construct a BOM for your college curriculum, thinking of core courses, electives, and so on as components of the end item. How might MRP concepts apply?

14.5 23. How do the concepts of master production scheduling and material requirements planning translate to a service organization? Provide an example.

14.5 24. How should managers choose an appropriate lot-sizing rule? Should they be chosen strictly on an economic basis, or should intangible factors be considered. Why?

COMPUTATIONAL PROBLEMS AND EXERCISES

These exercises require you to apply the formulas and methods described in the chapter. The problems should be solved manually.

14.3 25. The forecast demand for fudge for the next four months is 120, 160, 20, and 70 pounds.

a. What is the recommended production rate if a level strategy is adopted with no backorders or stock outs? What is the ending inventory for Month 4 under this plan?

b. What is the level production rate with no ending inventory in month 4?

14.3 26. Rapallo Corporation manufactures industrial vacuum cleaners with forecasted sales for the next five weeks as follows: Week 1 = 2,000 units, Week 2 = 2,500, Week 3 = 3,000, Week 4 = 3,000, and Week 5 = 3,500. Beginning inventory equals 13,000 units and the firm wants to maintain this level at the end of week 5.

a. What weekly production rate is necessary?

b. What is the ending inventory level over time using your answer in part a?

c. Suppose management wants to reduce its inventory level to 3,000 units by the end of week 5 because the chief financial officer is upset about the cost to carry so much inventory. How does the production plan and rate change?

14.3 27. Jet skis and snowmobiles are assembled by Mobile Incorporated. Because both end-items use the same small engine, you can aggregate demand for the engine assembly. Develop an aggregate plan that uses a level production strategy each quarter and the information that follows. What is the total cost? Assume lost sales are backordered and filled during the next quarter. Summarize the plan, its costs, and consequences using manual computations.

Initial Inventory Level	1,000 units
Regular Time	$15
Lost Sales Cost/Unit	$24
Inventory Carry Cost per unit	$3

Quarter	1	2	3	4	Totals	Beginning Inventory
Jet Ski Engine	10,000	15,000	16,000	3,000	44,000	600
Snowmobile Engine	9,000	7,000	19,000	10,000	45,000	400
Total Engines	19,000	22,000	35,000	13,000	89,000	1,000
Average Demand Rate/Quarter			22,000 units			
Regular Time Production Rate			22,000 units			

14.4 28. Metal Fabricators, Inc. manufactures gas grill tanks, Model # 1420, for four original equipment manufacturers (OEMs). Demand is forecast to be as follows: Quarter 1 – 2,800 tanks, Quarter 2—3,400, Quarter 3—3,600, and Quarter 4—2,900. Due to a hedging program for sheet steel and increases in international tariffs, production cost per quarter vary as follows: Quarter 1—$23.50 per tank, Quarter 2—$28.00, Quarter 3—$25.90, and Quarter 4—$29.00. Due to production contracts with the OEMs, no shortages are allowed. Beginning inventory for Quarter 1 is 300 tanks. At the end of each quarter, inventory holding costs are $4.25 per tank. Formulate this as a linear optimization model but do not solve (see Supplement D).

14.4 29. A lawn chair company, Leisure Furniture, manufactures two types of deck and lanai reclining chairs. Contribution to profits and overhead for Model A chairs are $35 and for Model B chairs $26. One independent process cuts and sews the weather proof fabric. A second process bends and welds the metal tube frame. The fabric process requires 2.2 hours for Model A and 3.1 for Model B with 300 production hours available. The metal frame process requires 1.8 hours for each Model A chair and 1.3 hours for Model B with 250 production hours available. Storage space is limited, and the chairs require a lot of space. One Model A chair requires 12 cubic feet of storage space, and a Model B chair needs 10 cubic feet of storage space. The warehouse adjacent to the factory has a total space for storing finished chairs of 150,000 cubic feet. Formulate this as a linear optimization model but do not solve (see Supplement D).

14.4 30. The Silver Star Bicycle Company will be manufacturing men's and women's models of its Easy-Pedal 10-speed bicycle during the next two months, and the company would like a production schedule indicating how many bicycles of each model should be produced in each month. Current demand forecasts call for 150 men's and 125 women's models to be shipped during the first month and 200 men's and 150 women's models to be shipped during the second month. Additional data are shown in Exhibit 14.29.

Each month, 3,000 hours of manufacturing labor and 1,000 hours of assembly labor are available. The company charges monthly inventory at the rate of two percent of the production cost based on the inventory levels at the end of the month. Silver Star would like to have at least 25 units of each model in inventory at the end of the two months. Formulate this as a linear optimization model but do not solve (see Supplement D).

14.5 31. Given the bill of material for the printer cartridge (A) in Exhibit 14.30; a gross requirement to build 200 units of A; an on-hand inventory level for end-item A of 80 units; and assuming zero lead-times for all items A, B, C, D, and E, compute the net requirements for each item. Assume all on-hand quantities for items B, C, D, and E are zero.

EXHIBIT 14.29 Data for Problem 30, Silver Star Bicycle Company

Model	Production Costs	Labor Required for Manufacturing (hours)	Labor Required for Assembly (hours)	Current Inventory
Men's	$40	10	3	20
Women's	$30	8	2	30

EXHIBIT 14.30 Bill of Material for Problems 31, 32, and 33

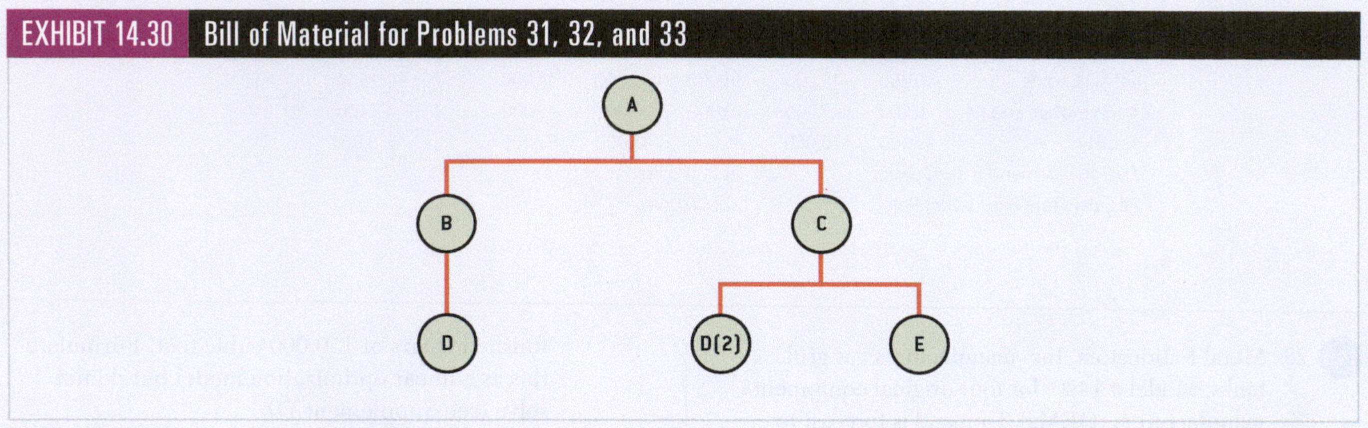

14.5 32. Given the bill of material for the printer cartridge in problem 31 and Exhibit 14.30, and the following on-hand quantities, compute the net requirements for each item. The gross requirement for A is still 200 units.

Item	On-Hand Inventory
A	40
B	50
C	100
D	70
E	25

14.5 33. Consider the same bill of material in Exhibit 14.30 and information in Problem 31 including the on-hand component quantities. Assume that two of component B are needed for each A and that the gross requirement for A is 220 units. Compute the net requirements for each item assuming zero lead times.

14.5 34. Given the bill of material in Exhibit 14.31, if the gross requirements to build 250 units and an on-hand inventory for A of 40 units, what are the net requirements for all items? All component parts have zero on-hand inventory except item D with 200 units. Assume all lead times are zero.

EXHIBIT 14.31 Bill of Material for Problem 34

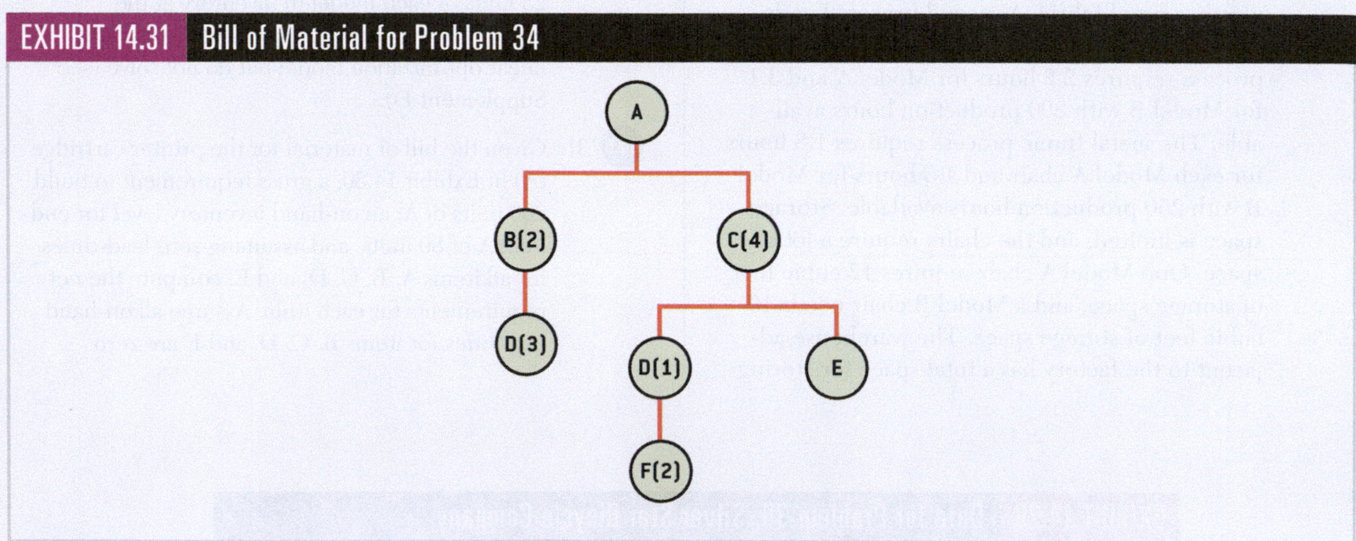

14.5 35. Given the information below, complete the MRP record and explain what it tells the inventory analyst to do.

Lot Size Rule: Fixed Q = 100 units
Safety Stock = 0 units
Lead Time = three weeks
Current On-Hand Quantity = 80 units

Weeks	1	2	3	4	5	6	7	8
Gross Requirement	20	0	60	0	100	80	0	60
Scheduled Receipts		100						
Projected On-Hand 80								
Planned Receipts								
Planned Order Release								

14.5 36. Each bank teller workstation is forecast to process 400 transactions (the end item) on Friday. The bank is open from 9:00 a.m. to 7:00 p.m. on Friday with 90 minutes for lunch and breaks. Three teller windows are open on Friday. A work-study analysis reveals that the breakdown of the transaction mix is 40% deposits, 45% withdrawals, and 15% transfers between accounts. A different form is used for each type of transaction so there is one deposit slip per deposit, one withdrawal slip per withdrawal, and two transfer slips per transfer.

The forecast is for 400 customer transactions during 8.5 hours on Friday at each of three teller stations. Deposit, withdrawal, and transfer slips are "dependent" upon forecast for the end-item (customer transactions).

a. How many transfer slips are needed on Friday?

b. How many withdrawal slips are needed on Friday?

c. Deposit slips are delivered every second day. If the on-hand balance of deposit slips is 50 at this bank, how many deposit slips should be ordered?

d. What is the end-item and component part in this bank example?

e. What are the implications of having too many or too few deposit, withdrawal, and transfer slips? Explain.

14.5 37. Irene's Kitchen & Catering Service sells three kinds of cakes—single, double, and triple layers. The product mix is 30% single layer, 50% double layer, and 20% triple layer. The bills of material are as follows:

Single Layer Cake	Double Layer Cake	Triple Layer Cake
Cake mix—1.16 lbs	Cake mix—1.75 lbs.	Cake mix—3.65 lbs.
Butter—0.5 cups	Butter—.75 cups	Butter—1 cup
Eggs—3	Eggs—4	Eggs—5

a. Irene's forecast for cakes for the next three months is 40 cakes a day or 2,880 cakes (40 cakes/day × 24 workdays/month × 3 months). How much cake mix does she need?

b. How much butter is needed?

c. How many eggs are needed?

14.5 38. The BOM for product A is shown in Exhibit 14.32 and data from the inventory records are shown in the table. In the master production schedule for product A, the MPS quantity row (showing completion dates) calls for 250 units in week 8. The lead time for production of A is two weeks. Develop the materials requirements plan for the next eight weeks for Items B, C, and D.

EXHIBIT 14.32 Bill of Material for Problem 38

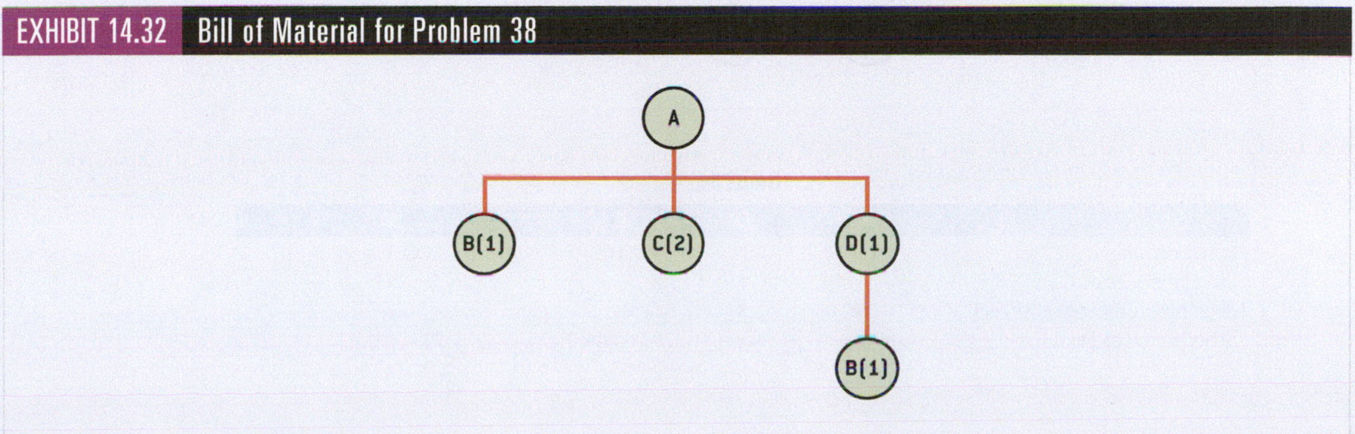

Data Category	B	C	D
Lot-sizing rule	P = 2	FOQ = 1,000	LFL
Lead time	2 weeks	1 week	2 weeks
Scheduled receipts	100 (week 1)	0	0
Beginning (on-hand) Inventory	0	100	0

MPS Product A – Lead Time = 2 weeks							
Week 1	2	3	4	5	6	7	8
Product A							250
Planned Order Release					250		

39. An orthopedic surgeon specializes in three types of surgery—hip, knee, and ankle replacements. The surgery mix is 40% hip replacements, 50% knee replacement, and 10% ankle replacement. Partial bills of materials for each type of surgery are as follows:

Hip Replacement	Knee Replacement	Ankle Replacement
Surgical Kit's #203 & #428	Surgical Kit #203	Surgical Kit #108
Hip Part Package #A	Knee Part Package #V	Ankle Part Package #P
Patient's Blood Type – 6 pints	Patient's Blood Type – 4 pints	Patient's Blood Type – 3 pints

a. In the next week, she is scheduled to do five hip replacements, three knee replacements, and one ankle replacement. How many surgical kits and part packages of each type should the hospital have available next week?

b. How many total pints of blood are needed next week?

c. Design a "mistake-proof" system to ensure each patient gets the correct blood type.

d. What are the implications of a shortage (stock out) of a surgical kit or part package discovered several hours before the operation? What if a part package has a missing part that is not discovered until surgery begins?

40. Consider the master production schedule, BOM shown in Exhibit 14.33, and inventory data shown below. Complete the MPS and MRP explosion and identify what actions, if any, you would take given this requirements plan.

Master Production Schedule Weeks	1	2	3	4	5	6	7	8
Customer req. "A"		5		8			10	
Customer req. "B"						5		10

Lead time for Product "A" 1 week.
Lead time for Product "B" 2 weeks.

EXHIBIT 14.33 Bill of Material for Problem 40

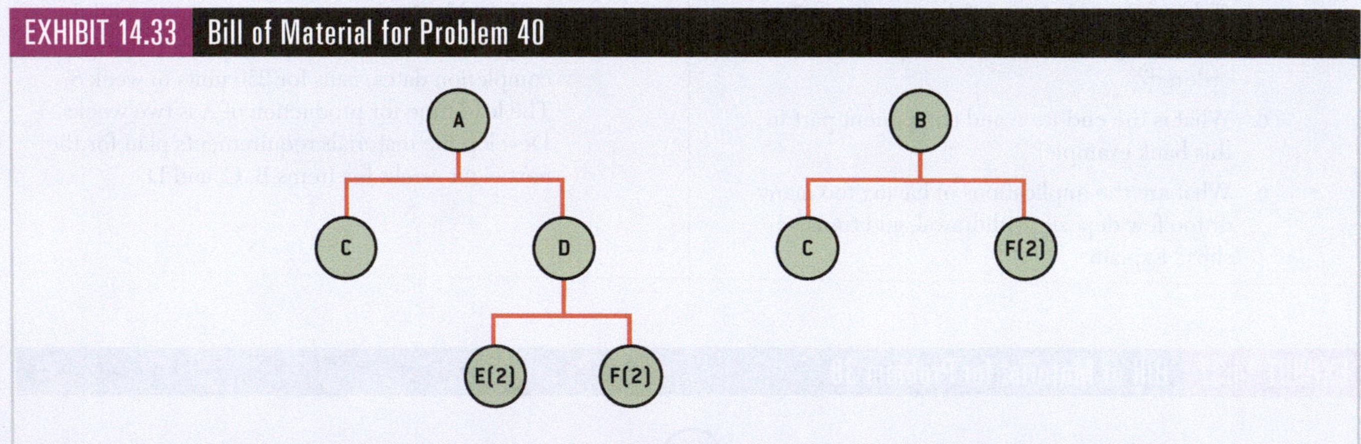

Item File

	C	D	E	F
Lot sizing rule	LFL	LFL	FOQ (25)	POQ (P = 2)
Lead time (weeks)	3	1	3	1
Beginning (on-hand) inventory	5	8	19	3
Scheduled receipts	8 in week 1	None	25 in week 3	20 in week 1

a. Develop a material requirement plan for the next seven weeks for items B and C.

b. Will any action notices be generated? If so, what are they and explain why they must be generated.

14.5 41. The MPS for product A calls for 100 units to be completed in week 4 and 200 units in week 7 (the lead time is one week). Spare part demand for Item B is 10 units per week. The bill of materials for product A is shown in Exhibit 14.34, and the inventory records are shown below.

	Item	Item
Data category	B	C
Lot sizing rule	FOQ = 500	LFL
Lead time (weeks)	2	3
Beginning (on-hand) inventory	100	10
Scheduled receipts	none	200 (week 2)

EXHIBIT 14.34 Bill of Material for Problem 41

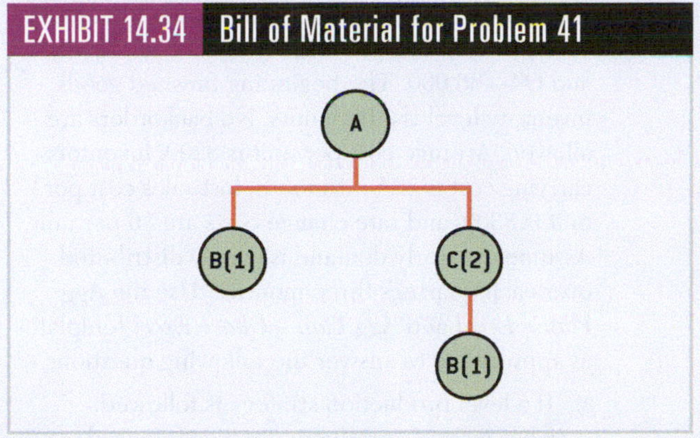

a. Develop a material requirement plan for the next 7 weeks for items B and C.

b. Will any action notices be generated? If so, what are they and explain why they must be generated.

14.5 42. Garden Manufacturing is a small, family-owned garden tool manufacturer located in Florence, South Carolina. The bills of materials for models A and B of a popular garden tool are shown in Exhibit 14.35 and other additional component information is provided. There is considerable component part commonality between these two models, as shown by the BOM.

The MPS calls for 100 units of Tool A to be completed in week 5 and 200 units of Tool A to be completed in week 7. End-item A has a two-week lead time. The MPS calls for 300 units of Tool B to be completed in week 7. End-item B has a one-week lead time. Do an MRP explosion for all items required to make these two garden tools. What actions, if any, should be taken immediately, and what other potential problems do you see?

	Item			
Data Category	**C**	**D**	**E**	**F**
Lot sizing rule	FOQ = 400	LFL	POQ = 4	LFL
Lead time	1 week	2 weeks	2 weeks	1 week
Scheduled receipts	450 (week 1)	50 (week 1)	None	None
Beginning inventory	100	70	50	900

EXHIBIT 14.35 Bill of Material for Problem 42

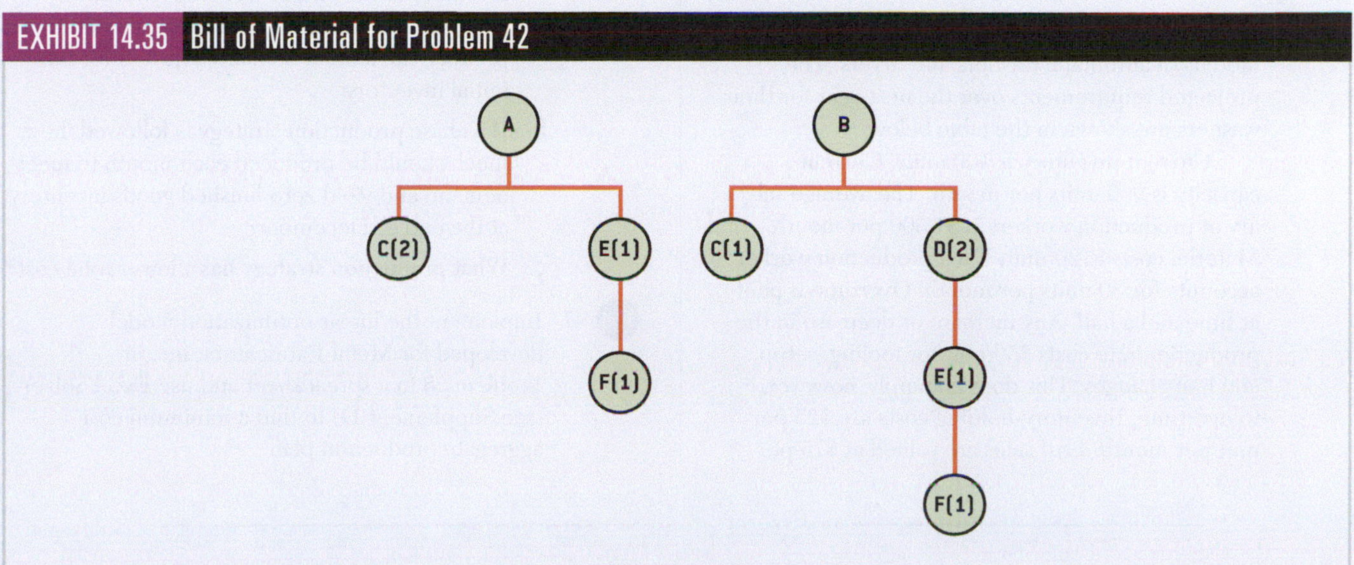

EXCEL-BASED PROBLEMS

For these problems, you may use Excel Solver or the spreadsheet templates in MindTap to assist in your analysis.

43. Chapman Pharmaceuticals, a large manufacturer of drugs, has this aggregate demand forecast (in thousands of liters) for a liquid cold medicine.

Month	Demand
January	200
February	120
March	75
April	40
May	15
June	7
July	5
August	10
September	30
October	70
November	120
December	180

The firm has a normal production rate of 90 thousand liters per month, and the initial inventory is 100 thousand liters. Inventory-holding costs are $30 per 1,000 liters per month, regular-time production costs are $400 per 1,000 liters. Overtime costs an additional 20 percent, and undertime costs an additional 12 percent. Assume that there are no lost sales or rate change costs. Use the *Agg Plan – Level and Agg Plan – Chase* Excel templates to compute the costs of a level production rate of 90 thousand liters per month and a chase demand production plan.

14.3 44. The Westerbeck Company manufactures several models of automatic washers and dryers. The projected requirements over the next year for their washers are shown in the table below.

Current inventory is 100 units. Current capacity is 960 units per month. The average salary of production workers is $1,300 per month. Material costs $120/unit. Each production worker accounts for 30 units per month. Overtime is paid at time and a half. Any increase or decrease in the production rate costs $50/unit for tooling, setup, and line changes. This does not apply, however, to overtime. Inventory-holding costs are $25 per unit per month. Lost sales are valued at $75 per unit. Compare the costs of level and chase demand production plans using the *Agg Plan – Level* and *Agg Plan – Chase* Excel templates. For the level strategy, compare the normal production rate of 960 units per monte with the average monthly demand rounded to a whole number.

Month	J	F	M	A	M	J	J	A	S	O	N	D
Requirement	800	1,030	810	900	950	1,340	1,100	1,210	600	580	890	1,000

14.3 45. Use the Excel template *Aggregate Planning* to try to find the best production strategy for the Westerbeck Company in Problem 44 to minimize the total cost. How much can you improve on the level and chase demand strategies?

14.3 46. Kings Appliance Manufacturers makes toasters and wants to evaluate a level strategy against a chase strategy. The quarterly demand forecasts are: Q1—12,000, Q2—15,000, Q3—18,000, and Q4—33,000. The beginning finished goods inventory level is 3,000 units. No backorders are allowed. Average cost per unit is $200, inventory-carrying cost is $2/unit/month, lost sales cost per unit is $300, and rate change costs are $6 per unit. Assume quarterly demand is evenly distributed over each quarter's three months. Use the *Agg Plan – Level* and *Agg Plan – Chase Excel* templates as appropriate to answer the following questions.

a. If a level production strategy is followed, what monthly production rate is required to meet demand and yield zero finished goods inventory at the end of December? Hint: Compute the monthly production needed to produce the annual demand adjusted for the initial inventory.

b. If a chase production strategy is followed, how much should be produced each month to meet demand and yield zero finished goods inventory at the end of December?

c. What production strategy has a lower total cost?

14.4 47. Implement the linear optimization model developed for Metal Fabricators, Inc. in Problem 28 in a spreadsheet and use Excel Solver (see Supplement D) to find a minimum cost aggregate production plan.

14.4 48. Implement the linear optimization model developed for Leisure Furniture in Problem 29 in a spreadsheet and use Excel Solver (see Supplement D) to determine the optimal production quantities of each type of chairs to produce to maximize revenue.

14.4 49. Implement the linear optimization model developed for the Silver Star Bicycle Company in Problem 30 in in a spreadsheet and use Excel Solver (see Supplement D) to determine a production plan that minimizes production and inventory costs and satisfies the labor-smoothing, demand, and inventory requirements. What inventories will be maintained, and how much labor is used each month in manufacturing and assembly?

Rocker Industries (A)

Rocker Industries (RI) produces recreational in-line skates (see Exhibit 14.36). Demand is seasonal, peaking in the summer months, with a smaller peak demand during December. For one of their more popular models that is being introduced with some cosmetic upgrades, RI has forecasted the following demand in pairs of skates for the next year (these data are available in the worksheet *Rocker Industries Case Data* in MindTap):

Month	Demand (pairs)
January	300
February	550
March	900
April	1,500
May	2,500
June	3,000
July	1,400
August	1,000
September	600
October	400
November	700
December	1,800

EXHIBIT 14.36 In-Line Skate

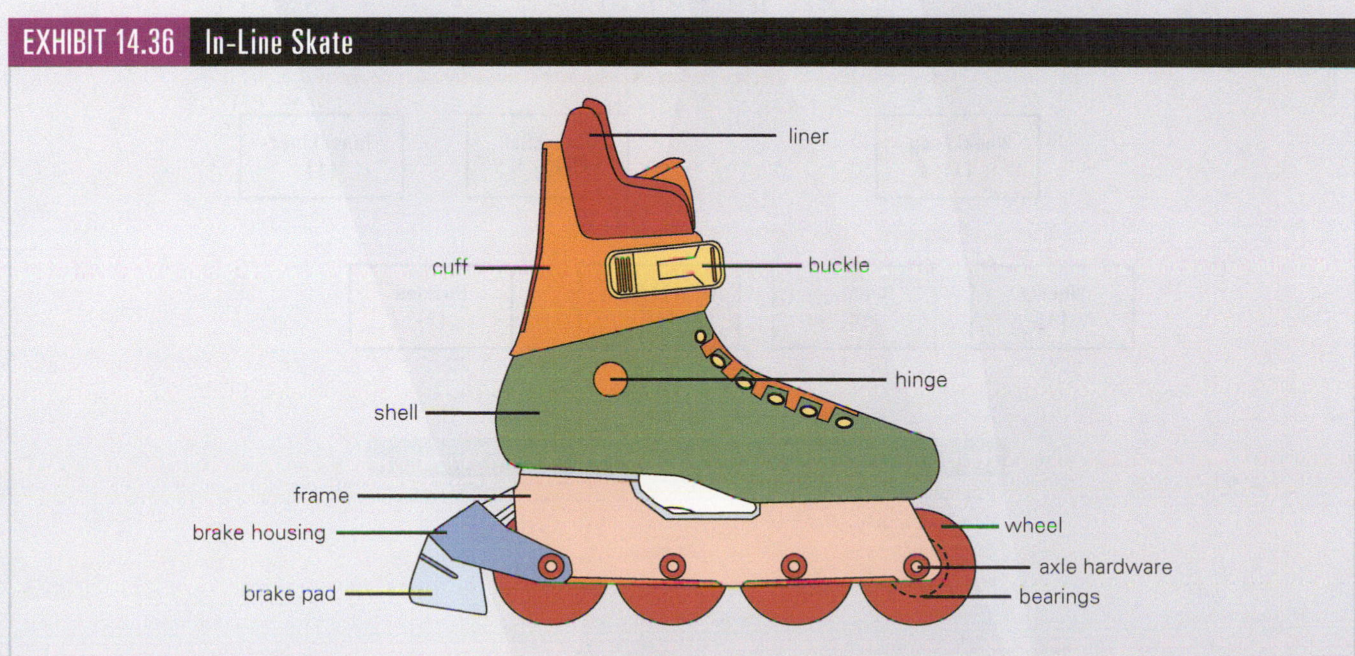

The manufacturing cost is $80 for each pair of skates, including materials and direct labor. Inventory holding cost is charged at 20 percent of the manufacturing cost per month. Because this is an "on-demand" good, customers will most likely buy another model if it is not available, thus, the lost sales cost is the marginal profit, which is the manufacturer markup of 100 percent or $80. The normal production rate is 1,000 pairs per month. However, changing the production rate requires administrative costs and is computed to be $1 per unit. Overtime can be scheduled at a cost computed to be $10 per pair. Assume beginning inventories are zero. Because Rocker Industries produces a variety of other products, labor can be shifted to other work, so undertime cost is not relevant.

Case Questions for Discussion:

1. Rocker Industries would like to evaluate level and chase demand strategies. Your report should not only address financial impacts, but potential operational and managerial impacts of the different strategies.
2. Rocker Industries would like to know the lowest cost aggregate plan. Use the *Aggregate Planning* Excel template to search for the best solution.

Rocker Industries (B)

The BOM, current inventory, and lead time (in months) for the in-line skates in Rocker Industries (A) case is shown in Exhibit 14.37. Using the chase demand strategy, you developed in Rocker Industries (A), develop a complete MRP week-by-week schedule using lot-for-lot (LFL) to meet production requirements for the first quarter of the year (January to March). Assume for simplicity that there are four weeks per month.

EXHIBIT 14.37 In-Line Skate Bill of Material and Related Information

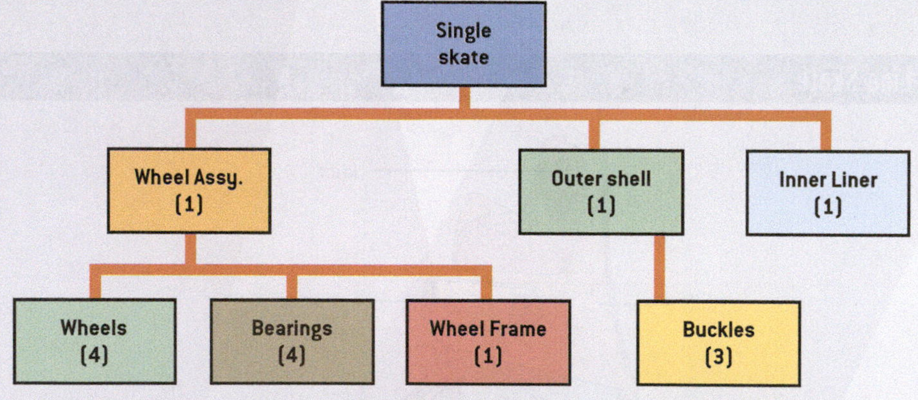

Item	Inventory	Lead time
Pair skates	50	1 weeks
Wheel assembly	100	2
Outer shell	25 pairs	3
Inner liner	0 pairs	3
Wheels	1500	1
Bearings	3000	1
Wheel frame	600	2
Buckles	5000	1

Case Questions for Discussion:

Use the MRP schedule to address the following questions.

1. When must the process of ordering and producing in-line-skates to meet demand for these three months begin?
2. What are the cost and capacity implications from the planned schedule of order releases?
3. What would be the effect on part planned order releases if a level aggregate plan was used instead of a chase strategy? (You do not have to redo the MRP explosion; simply explain the impact.)
4. What would be the pros and cons of reducing part lead times by one-half?
5. Do you see any opportunities to use lot sizing to batch order quantities? Select one part and explain/justify.
6. What other insights do you see? Is this a good planned order release schedule?

Blue Note Mortgage*

The process of obtaining a mortgage for a house or condominium is more complex than most people think. It starts with an application that contains all pertinent information about the borrower that the lender will need. The bank or mortgage company then initiates a process that leads to a loan decision. It is here that key information about the borrower is provided by third-party providers. This information includes a credit report, verification of income, verification of assets, verification of employment, and an appraisal of the property, among others. The result of the processing function is a complete loan file that contains all the information and documents needed to underwrite the loan, which is the next step in the process.

Brian A Jackson/Shutterstock.com

Underwriting is where the loan application is evaluated for its risk. Underwriters evaluate whether the borrower can make payments on time, can afford to pay back the loan, and has sufficient collateral in the property to back up the loan. In the event the borrower defaults on the loan, the lender can sell the property to recover the amount of the loan. But if the amount of the loan is greater than the value of the property, the lender cannot recoup their money. If the underwriting process indicates that the borrower is creditworthy, has the capacity to repay the loan, and that the value of the property in question is greater than the loan amount, then the loan is approved and will move to closing. Closing is the step where the borrower signs all the appropriate papers agreeing to the terms of the loan.

Beverly Frydann, the manager of a loan-processing department, needs to know how many employees will be needed over the next several months to process a certain number of loan files per month so she can better plan capacity. Staffing changes are expensive and time-consuming. Thus, it is quite important to understand staffing requirements well in advance. In many cases, the time to hire and train new employees can be 90 to 180 days, so it is not always possible to react quickly to changes in staffing needs. Hence, advance planning is vital so that Beverly can make good decisions about overtime or reductions in work hours, or adding or reducing temporary or permanent staff.

Suppose that there are different types of products that require processing. A product could be a 30-year, fixed-rate mortgage, 7/1 ARM, FHA loan, or a construction loan. Each of these loan types vary in their complexity and require different levels of documentation and, consequently, have different times to complete. Assume that the manager forecasts 750 loan applications in May, 825 in June, 900 in July, and 775 in August. Each employee works productively for 7 hours each day, and there are 22 working days in May, 20 in June, 22 in July, and 22 in August. Beverly also knows,

*We express our appreciation to Mr. Craig Zielazny of BlueNote Analytics, LLC, for providing the background for this case.

based on historical loan data, the percentage of each product type and how long it takes to process one loan of each type. These data are presented in Exhibit 14.38.

EXHIBIT 14.38 Loan Processing Data

Products	Product Mix (%)	Hours Per File
Product 1	22	3.60
Product 2	17	2.00
Product 3	13	1.70
Product 4	12	5.50
Product 5	10	4.00
Product 6	9	3.00
Product 7	7	2.00
Product 8	5	2.00
Product 9	3	1.50
Product 10	2	4.00
Total	100	

Beverly would like to predict the number of full-time equivalent (FTE) staff needed each month to ensure that all loans can be processed. Determine how to calculate the FTE required in order to provide sufficient resources to meet all production requirements.

Case Questions for Discussion:

1. Develop a spreadsheet model that Beverly can use to easily update the product mix for other months with different numbers of working days.
2. Use the model to determine how many FTE staff are required in May through August.
3. What types of aggregate planning strategies might Beverly use in this situation?

Integrative Case: Hudson Jewelers

The Hudson Jewelers case study available in MindTap integrates material found in each chapter of the book.

Case Question for Discussion:

1. Customer demand (weekly visits) at Hudson Jewelers is highly seasonal, as shown in the worksheet *Hudson Jeweler Demand Case Data* in MindTap (these data were used in Chapter 9 for forecasting). In the context of aggregate planning options (Section 14.2 and Exhibit 14.2), what types of decisions concerning resources does this service business have to make? Write a short paper of no more than two typed pages on these issues.

Operations Scheduling and Sequencing

15

Nursing staff are among the service providers who often present complex scheduling challenges for organizations.

Monkey Business Images/Shutterstock.com

LEARNING OBJECTIVES

After studying this chapter, you should be able to:

- **15-1** Explain the concepts of scheduling and sequencing.
- **15-2** Describe staff scheduling and appointment system decisions.
- **15-3** Explain sequencing performance criteria and rules for sequencing on a single processor.
- **15-4** Explain the process of dispatching and typical priority rules that are used.
- **15-5** Describe how to solve two-resource sequencing problems.
- **15-6** Explain the need for monitoring schedules using Gantt charts.
- **15-7** Describe how to use the Clarke–Wright method for vehicle routing and scheduling.

Jean Rowecamp, clinical coordinator of nursing services, was faced with a deluge of complaints by her nursing staff about their work schedules and complaints by floor supervisors about inadequate staffing. The nurses complained they were having too many shift changes each month. Supervisors said they had too many nurses during the days and not enough at night and on the weekends. It seemed that nothing she did would satisfy everyone. The nurses were unionized, so she couldn't schedule them for more than seven consecutive working days, and the nurses required at least 16 hours between shift changes. Nurses were constantly making "special requests" for personal time off, despite the negotiated procedures for bidding for shifts and vacation times. Jean lamented that she became an administrator and longed for the days before she had these responsibilities.

WHAT DO YOU THINK?

As a student, how do you schedule your homework, school projects, and study activities? What criteria do you use?

Creating schedules is not easy. The chapter-opening nursing example highlights the complexity of scheduling in service organizations. For example, union workforce rules and special requests can complicate the scheduling process. And in contrast with manufacturing, wide fluctuations in demand during the course of a day or week makes scheduling quite difficult. Nevertheless, good schedules have to be developed to provide high levels of patient care and to minimize costs.

Scheduling and sequencing are fairly common activities that operations managers perform every day in every business. They are fundamental to all three levels of aggregation and disaggregation planning that we described in the previous chapter. Good schedules and sequences lead to efficient execution of manufacturing and service plans and better customer service. It's one thing to promise great customer service and another to actually achieve it. For example, having the right number of employees at a call center at different times of the day and week will ensure that customers do not have to wait long. Good scheduling of jobs in a factory will ensure that customers receive their orders as promised, and increase productivity and efficiency.

15-1 Understanding Scheduling and Sequencing

Scheduling *refers to the assignment of start and completion times to particular jobs, people, or equipment.* For example, fast-food restaurants, hospitals, and call centers need to schedule employees for work shifts; doctors, dentists, and stockbrokers need to schedule patients and customers; airlines must schedule crews and flight attendants; sports organizations must schedule teams and officials; court systems must schedule hearings and trials; factory managers need to schedule jobs on machines and preventive maintenance work; and salespersons need to schedule customer deliveries and visits to potential customers. Many schedules are repeatable over the long term, such as those for retail store staff and assembly-line employees. Others might change on a monthly, weekly, or even daily basis, as might be the case with call center employees, nurses, or salespeople.

A concept related to scheduling is sequencing. **Sequencing** *refers to determining the order in which jobs or tasks are processed.* For example, triage nurses must decide on the order in which emergency patients are treated; housekeepers in hotels must sequence the order of rooms to clean; operations managers who run an automobile assembly line must determine the sequence by which different models are produced; and airport managers must sequence outgoing flights on runways. Note that in all these situations, processing takes place using a common resource with limited capacity. Thus, the sequence will ultimately determine how well the resource is used to achieve an objective such as meeting demand or customer due dates. Generally, a sequence specifies a schedule, and we will see this in various examples later in this chapter.

Scheduling and sequencing in back-office or low-contact service processes are similar to those for goods-producing processes. The same scheduling and sequencing concepts and methods used in manufacturing are beneficial in low-contact service processes.

It is not uncommon for a manufacturing facility to have hundreds of workstations or machine centers and to process thousands of different parts. Managers of such facilities also need daily or even hourly updates on the status of production to meet the information

Telling Umpires Where to Go

One of the authors of this book used to develop annual schedules for umpires in the American Baseball League. Some of the critical factors were to ensure that umpire crews were not assigned to consecutive series with the same team if possible; that the number of times a crew was assigned to a team was balanced over the course of the season; that travel sequences be rational and realistic; and that a variety of constraints be met. For example, one could not schedule a crew for a day game in another city after working a night game on the previous day. In addition, crews need time to rest and travel between game assignments. It also makes more sense move the crew to nearby cities rather than shuttling back and forth across the country.

Aspen Photo/Shutterstock.com

needs of supply chain managers, sales and marketing personnel, and customers. Similarly, service managers often manage dozens of part-time workers with varying work availability times (think of a fast-food restaurant manager near a college campus), or ever-changing workloads and demands (think of a hospital nurse administrator). The complexity of these situations dictates that effective scheduling systems be computerized, not only for generating schedules but also for retrieving information so that a salesperson can check the status of a customer's order or project a delivery date. Thus, implementing scheduling systems requires good information technology support.

15-2 Scheduling Applications and Approaches

Scheduling applies to all aspects of the value chain—planning and releasing orders in a factory, determining work shifts for employees, and making deliveries to customers. Many problems, such as staff scheduling, are similar across different organizations. Quite often, however (as with the baseball umpiring situation or scheduling classrooms and teachers at a university), unique situational factors require a unique solution approach. Many organizations use spreadsheets, desktop software packages, or Web-based tools for scheduling. Customized scheduling spreadsheets use readily available software such as Microsoft Excel, but may be rather expensive to develop. Commercial spreadsheet templates are simple to use and are generally inexpensive.

Scheduling applies to all aspects of the value chain—planning and releasing orders in a factory, determining work shifts for employees, and making deliveries to customers.

Software to Schedule Anywhere

One provider of small business software offers an online employee scheduling system called ScheduleAnywhere (ScheduleAnywhere.com). This service allows managers to schedule employees from any computer with Internet access, whether at work, at home, or on the road. ScheduleAnywhere gives users the power to schedule employees from any computer with Internet access; create schedules by position, department, location, and so on; view schedule information in a 1-day, 7-day, 14-day, or 28-day format; enter staffing requirements and view shift coverage; see who's scheduled and who's available; automatically rotate or copy employee schedules; preschedule time-off requests; avoid scheduling conflicts; and give employees read/write or read-only access to schedules.[1]

Alexander Chaikin/Shutterstock.com

Desktop and Web-based software packages are more powerful and have optimization capabilities. Typical features include the ability to schedule days on and days off for both full- and part-time employees, create alternative schedules to compare costs, and handling multiple shifts.

Many software packages have been developed for specific industries, such as call centers, law enforcement, and health care. Each industry has unique problem structures and decision variables. Concerro (formerly known as BidShift), for example, is a Web-based software package specifically designed for scheduling nurses. Over 170 hospitals have signed up to use this system; they estimate savings of $1 to $4 million per year, along with improved employee morale and quality of patient care.[2] In this section, we present two common applications of scheduling that are prevalent in operations management.

15-2a Staff Scheduling

Staff scheduling problems are prevalent in service organizations because of high variability in customer demand. Examples include scheduling call center representatives, hotel housekeepers, tollbooth operators, nurses, airline reservation clerks, police officers, fast-food restaurant employees, and many others.

Staff scheduling attempts to match available personnel with the needs of the organization by

1. accurately forecasting demand and translating it into the quantity and timing of work to be done;
2. determining the staffing required to perform the work by time period;
3. determining the personnel available and the full- and part-time mix; and
4. matching capacity to demand requirements, and developing a work schedule that maximizes service and minimizes costs.

The first step requires converting demand to a capacity measure—that is, the number of staff required. For instance, we might determine that for every $400 of sales forecast, we need one additional full-time employee. The second step determines the quantity and timing of the work to be done in detail, usually by hour of the day, and sometimes in 5- to 10-minute time intervals. Determining the staffing required must take into account worker productivity factors, personal allowances, sickness, vacations, no-shows, and so on.

Step 4 focuses on the matching of capacity to demand requirements; this is the essence of scheduling. Different approaches are required for different situations because of the nature of constraints. If service demands are relatively level over time, as in the case of hotel housekeepers, it is usually easy to schedule personnel on standard weekly work shifts. If the workload varies greatly within a shift, as is the case for telephone customer service representatives, the problem becomes one of scheduling shifts to meet the varying demand.

15-2b Scheduling Consecutive Days Off

Many organizations need to create staffing schedules to meet fluctuating demand over some period of time, typically a week. We will illustrate a relatively common problem of scheduling employees over a week so that they have two consecutive days off in the face of fluctuating requirements.[3]

The scheduling procedure can be described as follows:

1. List the minimum number of employees required for each day of the week.
2. Locate a set of at least two consecutive days having the smallest requirements. To do this, simply find the day with the smallest requirement, the next-smallest, and so on, until there are at least two consecutive days.
3. Circle the requirements for those two consecutive days. When there are several alternatives, we do one of two things. First, try to choose a pair of days with the lowest total requirement. If there are still ties, we are to choose the first available pair that makes the most sense to the scheduler.
4. Assign employee 1 to work on all days that are *not* circled and write down the schedule. Then subtract 1 from the requirement for each day that employee will work, as long as the requirement is a positive number.
5. Repeat the process using the new set of requirements for the next employee until all requirements become zero.

Solved Problem 15.1 provides an example.

SOLVED PROBLEM 15.1: CREATING A STAFFING SCHEDULE

T. R. Accounting Service is developing a workforce schedule for three weeks from now and has forecasted demand and translated it into the following minimum employee requirements for the week:

Day	**Mon.**	**Tue.**	**Wed.**	**Thur.**	**Fri.**	**Sat.**	**Sun.**
Minimum employees required	8	6	6	6	9	5	3

The requirements are for full-time accountants who do accounting work such as end-of-month financial statements, tax record organization, and federal, state, and local tax payments. T. R., the owner of the accounting service, wants to schedule the employees so that each employee has two consecutive days off and all demand requirements are met.

Solution:

Using the procedure described, first locate a *set of at least two consecutive days with the smallest requirements*. Sunday and Saturday, for example, have requirements of 3 and 5, respectively, whereas all others are greater than 5. We then circle the requirements for those two consecutive days. Thus, we have the following for employee 1:

Day	**Mon.**	**Tue.**	**Wed.**	**Thur.**	**Fri.**	**Sat.**	**Sun.**
Requirements	8	6	6	6	9	⑤	③

We assign accountant 1 to work on all days that are not circled, that is, Monday through Friday. Then we subtract 1 from the requirement for each day that accountant will work. This gives us the following requirements that remain:

Day	**Mon.**	**Tue.**	**Wed.**	**Thur.**	**Fri.**	**Sat.**	**Sun.**
Requirements	7	5	5	5	8	5	3

The procedure is repeated with this new set of requirements for accountant 2.

Day	**Mon.**	**Tue.**	**Wed.**	**Thur.**	**Fri.**	**Sat.**	**Sun.**
Requirements	7	⑤	⑤	⑤	8	⑤	③

In this case, we have many options. We choose to use Saturday and Sunday as days off for accountant 2, since this pair has the smallest total requirement of 8. We subtract 1 from each working day's requirement, yielding the following:

Day	**Mon.**	**Tue.**	**Wed.**	**Thur.**	**Fri.**	**Sat.**	**Sun.**
Requirements	6	4	4	4	7	5	3

Circling the smallest requirements until we obtain at least two consecutive days again yields the following for employee 3:

Day	**Mon.**	**Tue.**	**Wed.**	**Thur.**	**Fri.**	**Sat.**	**Sun.**
Requirements	6	④	④	④	7	5	③

Notice that Sunday is not adjacent to Tuesday, Wednesday, or Thursday, so we cannot use Sunday in the schedule. Remember we are looking for consecutive pairs of days. Let's choose the Tuesday–Wednesday pair. The remaining requirements are as follows:

Day	**Mon.**	**Tue.**	**Wed.**	**Thur.**	**Fri.**	**Sat.**	**Sun.**
Requirements	5	4	4	3	6	4	2

Continuing with this procedure, we obtain the sequence of requirements shown in Exhibit 15.1 (with circled numbers representing the lowest-requirement pair selected). The final accountant schedule is shown in Exhibit 15.2. Even though some requirements are exceeded, such as Thursday with a demand for six accountants yet we schedule eight, the solution minimizes the number of employees required.

EXHIBIT 15.1 Scheduling Procedure for T. R. Accounting Service

Employee Number	Mon.	Tue.	Wed.	Thur.	Fri.	Sat.	Sun.
4	5	4	4	3	6	④	②
5	4	3	③	②	5	4	2
6	3	2	3	2	4	③	①
7	②	①	2	1	3	3	1
8	2	1	①	⓪	2	2	0
9	①	⓪	1	0	1	1	0
10	1	⓪	⓪	0	0	0	0

EXHIBIT 15.2 Final Accountant Schedule

Employee Number	Mon.	Tue.	Wed.	Thur.	Fri.	Sat.	Sun.
1	X	X	X	X	X		
2	X	X	X	X	X		
3	X			X	X	X	X
4	X	X	X	X	X		
5	X	X			X	X	X
6	X	X	X	X	X		
7			X	X	X	X	X
8	X	X			X	X	X
9			X	X	X	X	X
10	X			X	X	X	X
Total	8	6	6	8	10	6	6

A more difficult problem that we do not address is that of determining a schedule of rotating shifts so that employees do not always have the same two days off. Over a predetermined longer cycle such as a quarter, all employees rotate through all possible days off. This makes for a fair and more equitable staff schedule, but it is complicated and beyond the scope of this book.

Many software packages are available to help with staff scheduling. However, scheduling is so integrated with the practices and culture of the organization that these standardized software packages normally need to be modified to work well in specific operating environments. Accurate input data and the user's understanding of how the software techniques develop the schedules are other challenges when adopting off-the-shelf scheduling software.

15-2c Optimization Models for Staff Scheduling

Optimization models are often used for staff scheduling problems. We recommend that you review Supplement D, Linear Optimization, and Supplement E, The Transportation and Assignment Problems, before proceeding. We will show how to develop optimization models for some simple staff scheduling problems.

Some organizations, such as call centers, hospitals, and quick service restaurants, might create schedules for a shorter time frame, such as a day. In a typical situation, the number of employees needed will vary each hour. For instance, a quick service restaurant that is open from 7:00 a.m. until midnight would typically need more employees during breakfast, lunch, and dinner times than at other times during the day. In a simple scenario, employees might work eight-hour shifts but may start at different times. For example, shift 1 might start at 7:00 a.m. and finish at 3:00 p.m. Shift 2 might go from 10:00 a.m. until 6:00 p.m., shift 3 from 3:00 p.m. until 11:00 p.m., and shift 4 from 5:00 p.m. until midnight. Note that these shifts overlap. For instance, between 10:00 a.m. and 3:00 p.m. we have employees from both shift 1 and shift 2 working; between 1:00 p.m. and 6:00 p.m., employees from shifts 2 and 3 are working; and from 4:00 p.m. through 9:00 p.m., employees form shifts 3 and 4 are working. The decision is how many employees are needed for each shift to ensure that the hourly requirements are met, while minimizing the total number of employees required.

This can be formulated as a simple integer optimization problem. An integer optimization model is one in which some or all variables must be whole numbers, whereas in the linear optimization model the variables are continuous. Define X_1, X_2, X_3, and X_4 as the number of employees assigned to work shifts 1, 2, 3, and 4, respectively. Clearly, we cannot assign a fractional number of employees, so we must ensure that the variables are integers. Fortunately, this is very easy to do using Excel Solver.

Let R(7 a.m.), R(8 a.m.), ... R(11 p.m.) be the number of employees needed from 7:00–8:00 a.m., 8:00–9:00 a.m., and so on up to 11:00 p.m. to midnight. The objective is to minimize the total number of employees:

$$\text{Min } X_1 + X_2 + X_3 + X_4$$

For each hour, we need to ensure that the total number of employees who work that hour is at least as large as the minimum requirements. For example, only employees starting at 7:00 a.m. will cover the 7, 8, and 9 a.m. hours; thus, we have the following constraints:

$$X_1 \geqslant R(7\text{ a.m.})$$
$$X_1 \geqslant R(8\text{ a.m.})$$
$$X_1 \geqslant R(9\text{ a.m.})$$

From 10:00 a.m. until 1:00 p.m., employees from both the first and second shifts are working. This results in the following constraints:

$$X_1 + X_2 \geqslant R(10\text{ a.m.})$$
$$X_1 + X_2 \geqslant R(11\text{ a.m.})$$
$$X_1 + X_2 \geqslant R(12\text{ p.m.})$$

From 1:00 p.m. until 4:00 p.m., employees from the second and third shifts are working. Therefore:

$$X_2 + X_3 \geq R(1 \text{ p.m.})$$
$$X_2 + X_3 \geq R(2 \text{ p.m.})$$
$$X_2 + X_3 \geq R(3 \text{ p.m.})$$

From 4:00 p.m. until 9:00 p.m., employees from the third and fourth shifts are working. The constraints are as follows:

$$X_3 + X_4 \geq R(4 \text{ p.m.})$$
$$X_3 + X_4 \geq R(5 \text{ p.m.})$$
$$X_3 + X_4 \geq R(6 \text{ p.m.})$$
$$X_3 + X_4 \geq R(7 \text{ p.m.})$$
$$X_3 + X_4 \geq R(8 \text{ p.m.})$$

Finally, from 9:00 p.m. until midnight, only employees from the fourth shift are working. We have

$$X_4 \geq R(9 \text{ p.m.})$$
$$X_4 \geq R(10 \text{ p.m.})$$
$$X_4 \geq R(11 \text{ p.m.})$$

All the variables must also be integers (whole numbers).

This model can be implemented on a spreadsheet and solved using Excel Solver. Solved Problem 15.2 illustrates an example.

SOLVED PROBLEM 15.2: AN OPTIMIZATION MODEL FOR STAFF SCHEDULING

Administrators at University Hospital can project the minimum number of nurses to have on hand for the various times of day. The hospital operates 24/7. Nurses start work at the beginning of one of the four-hour shifts shown below and work for eight hours (i.e., nurses starting shift 1 work shifts 1 and 2; those starting shift 2 work shifts 2 and 3, and so on). How many nurses should be assigned to start each shift to minimize the total number of nurses needed?

Shift	Time	Nurses Required
1	12:00 a.m. to 4:00 a.m.	4
2	4:00 a.m. to 8:00 a.m.	6
3	8:00 a.m. to 12:00 p.m.	12
4	12:00 p.m. to 4:00 p.m.	9
5	4:00 p.m. to 8:00 p.m.	7
6	8:00 p.m. to 12:00 a.m.	5

Solution:

Define $X_1, \ldots X_6$ as the number of nurses starting at the beginning of shifts 1 through 6, respectively. The objective is

$$\text{Minimize } X_1 + X_2 + X_3 + X_4 + X_5 + X_6$$

To ensure that the requirements are met for each shift, we have the following constraints:

$$X_6 + X_1 \geq 4$$
$$X_1 + X_2 \geq 6$$
$$X_2 + X_3 \geq 12$$
$$X_3 + X_4 \geq 9$$
$$X_4 + X_5 \geq 7$$
$$X_5 + X_6 \geq 5$$

All variables are integers.

The Excel model (with the optimal solution) and formulas are shown in Exhibits 15.3 and 15.4. This spreadsheet, *Solved Problem 15.2,* is available in MindTap. Exhibit 15.5 shows the Solver model used to find the optimal solution. In the spreadsheet, the decision variables are defined in cells B4 through B9, and the objective function to minimize is in cell B10. The constraints are that the total number of nurses assigned to each shift (cells C4 through C9) must be greater than or equal to the number required (cells E4 through E9) for each shift. In Solver, these are defined by the constraint \$B\$4: \$B\$9 ≥ \$E\$4:\$E\$9. To guarantee that the variables are whole numbers, select the *Add* button, and in the *Add Constraint* dialog, choose the decision variable range as the *Cell Reference*, and select *int* from the drop-down box ("integer" is automatically entered in the *Constraint* box) as shown in Exhibit 15.6. Then solve the model to obtain the results shown in Exhibit 15.3.

EXHIBIT 15.3 Excel Model and Solution for Solved Problem 15.2

	A	B	C	D	E	F
1	**Solved Problem 15.2**					
2						
3	Shift	Nurses Starting In This Shift	Total Nurses During Shift		Nurses Required	Excess
4	1	4	4	>=	4	0
5	2	5	9	>=	6	3
6	3	7	12	>=	12	0
7	4	2	9	>=	9	0
8	5	5	7	>=	7	0
9	6	0	5	>=	5	0
10	Total	23				

EXHIBIT 15.4 Excel Formulas for Solved Problem 15.2

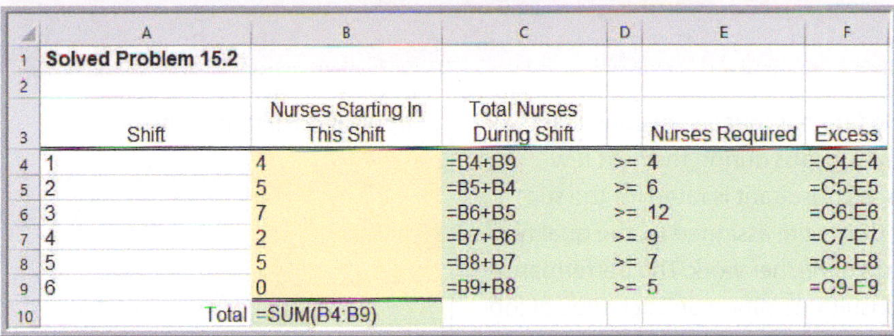

	A	B	C	D	E	F
1	**Solved Problem 15.2**					
2						
3	Shift	Nurses Starting In This Shift	Total Nurses During Shift		Nurses Required	Excess
4	1	4	=B4+B9	>=	4	=C4-E4
5	2	5	=B5+B4	>=	6	=C5-E5
6	3	7	=B6+B5	>=	12	=C6-E6
7	4	2	=B7+B6	>=	9	=C7-E7
8	5	5	=B8+B7	>=	7	=C8-E8
9	6	0	=B9+B8	>=	5	=C9-E9
10	Total	=SUM(B4:B9)				

EXHIBIT 15.5 Solver Model for Solved Problem 15.2

Solver Parameters

Set Objective: $B$10

To: ○ Max ◉ Min ○ Value Of: 0

By Changing Variable Cells:

$B$4:$B$9

Subject to the Constraints:

$B$4:$B$9 = integer
$C$4:$C$9 >= $E$4:$E$9

Add | Change | Delete | Reset All | Load/Save

☑ Make Unconstrained Variables Non-Negative

Select a Solving Method: Simplex LP | Options

Solving Method

Select the GRG Nonlinear engine for Solver Problems that are smooth nonlinear. Select the LP Simplex engine for linear Solver Problems, and select the Evolutionary engine for Solver problems that are non-smooth.

Help | Solve | Close

EXHIBIT 15.6 Solver *Add Constraint* Dialog for Integer Variables

Add Constraint

Cell Reference: Model!$B$4:$B$9 int Constraint: integer

Add Cancel OK

Another application of optimization modeling for staff scheduling is assigning staff to jobs, projects, or events. For many applications, the assignment model, which we discuss in Supplement E: The Transportation and Assignment Problems, can be used. Solved Problem 15.3 provides an example.

SOLVED PROBLEM 15.3 : AN OPTIMIZATION MODEL FOR ASSIGNING EMPLOYEES TO JOBS

An international consulting firm has four senior consultants available to work on consulting jobs during the next few months. Over the years each consultant is rated for the success of the consulting job they were assigned to, the quality of work, and the clients ratings of his/her work. The performance scores summarize each consultant's rating on each type of job and are shown in the table below. What assignment of senior consultants to client jobs maximizes the sum of the quality scores?

	Consulting Job Number			
Consultant	**1**	**2**	**3**	**4**
Mary	75	95	80	65
Luke	80	90	75	60
Alice	85	75	70	75
Tom	85	80	70	55

Solution:

For this problem, we develop an assignment model (see Supplement E). Let $X_{ij} = 1$ if consultant i (Mary = 1, Luke = 2, Alice = 3, and Tom = 4) is assigned to consulting job j. The optimization model is

$$\begin{aligned}\text{Maximize Quality Score} = {} & 75X_{11} + 80X_{21} + 85X_{31} \\ & + 85X_{41} + 95X_{12} + 90X_{22} \\ & + 75X_{32} + 80X_{42} + 80X_{13} \\ & + 75X_{23} + 70X_{33} + 70X_{43} \\ & + 65X_{14} + 60X_{24} + 75X_{34} + 55X_{44}\end{aligned}$$

Supply (Consultant) Constraints:

$$X_{11} + X_{12} + X_{13} + X_{14} \leq 1$$
$$X_{21} + X_{22} + X_{23} + X_{24} \leq 1$$
$$X_{31} + X_{32} + X_{33} + X_{34} \leq 1$$
$$X_{41} + X_{42} + X_{43} + X_{44} \leq 1$$

Demand (Job) Constraints:

$$X_{11} + X_{21} + X_{31} + X_{41} = 1$$
$$X_{12} + X_{22} + X_{32} + X_{42} = 1$$
$$X_{13} + X_{23} + X_{33} + X_{43} = 1$$
$$X_{14} + X_{24} + X_{34} + X_{44} = 1$$

Nonnegativity:

$$X_{ij} \geq 0 \quad \text{for } i = 1,\ldots,4 \quad \text{and} \quad j = 1,\ldots,4$$

Exhibit 15.7 shows the spreadsheet model and solution (don't forget to choose Max in the Solver dialog!). This spreadsheet, *Solved Problem 15.3*, is available in MindTap. Mary is assigned to job 3, Luke to job 2, Alice to job 4, and Tom to job 1. The total quality score is 330.

EXHIBIT 15.7 Spreadsheet Model and Solution for Solved Problem 15.3

	A	B	C	D	E	F
1	Solved Problem 15.3					
2						
3				Job		
4	Consultant	1	2	3	4	Supply
5	Mary	75	95	80	65	1
6	Luke	80	90	75	60	1
7	Alice	85	75	70	75	1
8	Tom	85	80	70	55	1
9	Demand	1	1	1	1	
10						
11	Model					
12				Job		
13	Consultant	1	2	3	4	
14	Mary	0	0	1	0	
15	Luke	0	1	0	0	
16	Alice	0	0	0	1	
17	Tom	1	0	0	0	
18						
19	Consultant Constrain	Mary	Luke	Alice	Tom	
20	Job assigned	1	1	1	1	
21						
22	Job Constraints	1	2	3	4	
23	Consultant assigned	1	1	1	1	
24						
25		Cost				
26	Total	330				

15-2d Appointment Systems

Appointments can be viewed as a reservation of service time and capacity. Using appointments provides a means to maximize the use of time-dependent service capacity and reduce the risk of no-shows. Appointment systems are used in many businesses, such as consulting, tax preparation, music instruction, and medical, dental, and veterinarian practices. Indirectly, appointments reduce the cost of providing the service because the service provider is idle less each workday. An appointment system must try to accommodate customers and forecast their behavior, such as the no-show rate or a difficult customer who demands more processing time.

Four decisions to make regarding designing an appointment system are the following:

1. *Determine the appointment time interval*, such as 1 hour or 15 minutes. Some professional services such as dentists and physicians use smaller appointment intervals and then take multiples of it, depending on the type of procedure thought to be required by the patient.
2. Based on an analysis of each day's customer mix, *determine the length of each workday and the time off duty*. Once the on- and off-duty days for the year (annual capacity) are determined, and assuming a certain customer mix and overbooking rate (see step 3), the service provider can forecast expected total revenues for the year.
3. *Decide how to handle overbooking* for each day of the week. Often, customers do not show up as scheduled. If the no-show percentage is low—say, 2 percent—then there may be no need to overbook. However, once the no-show percentage reaches 10 percent or more, overbooking is usually necessary to maximize revenue and make effective use of perishable and expensive time.
4. *Develop customer appointment rules* that maximize customer satisfaction. For example, some service providers leave one appointment interval open at the end of each workday. Others schedule a 60-minute lunch interval but can squeeze in a customer during lunch if necessary. Telephone and electronic appointment reminders are another way to help maximize service-provider utilization.

15-3 Sequencing

Sequencing in a job shop in which several different goods or services are processed—each of which may have a unique routing among process stages—is generally very complex. However, some special cases lend themselves to simple solutions. These special cases provide understanding and insight into more complicated scheduling problems. Sequencing is necessary when several activities (manufacturing goods, servicing customers, delivering packages, etc.) use a common resource. The resource might be a machine, a customer service representative, or a delivery truck. Sequencing can be planned, in which case it creates a schedule. For example, if a student plans to begin homework at 7:00 p.m. and estimates that it will take 60 minutes to complete an OM assignment, 45 minutes to read a psychology chapter, and 40 minutes to do statistics homework, then sequencing the work from most favorite to least favorite—OM, psychology, and statistics—creates the schedule:

Assignment	Start Time	End Time
OM	7:00	8:00
Psychology	8:00	8:45
Statistics	8:45	9:25

15-3a Sequencing Jobs on a Single Processor

The simplest sequencing problem is that of processing a set of jobs on a single processor. This situation occurs in many firms. For example, in a serial manufacturing process, a bottleneck workstation controls the output of the entire process. Thus, it is critical to schedule the bottleneck equipment efficiently. In other cases, such as in a chemical plant, the entire plant may be viewed as a single processor. Single processors for service situations include processing patients through an X-ray or CAT-scanning machine, trucks through a loading/unloading dock, or financial transactions through a control workstation.

Airlines Struggle with Boarding Sequencing

Airlines have tinkered with different boarding systems almost since the days of Orville and Wilbur Wright, who tossed a coin to decide who would fly first aboard their biplane. Slow boarding creates delays, which mean missed connections, unhappy customers, and extra costs. Researchers from Northern Illinois University once figured that every extra minute that a plane stands idle at the gate adds $30 in costs. About one in four U.S. flights runs at least 15 minutes late. Multiply that by thousands of flights each day, and it quickly adds up for the industry. Plenty of people have offered ideas for improvement, but no perfect method has ever emerged. Most airlines let first-class and other elite customers board first. After that, some carriers fill the rear rows and work toward the front. Others fill window seats and work toward the aisle. Some use a combination of the two. Airlines have also tried other tricks, like letting people board early if they do not have aisle-clogging, carry-on bags. One of the latest ideas is to have airline employees take carry-on bags at the gate and put them in the bins above passengers' assigned seats. Tests at Delta saw some improvement. Can you think of other ways to improve air boarding?[4]

In selecting the most appropriate sequencing rule, a manager must first consider the criteria on which to evaluate schedules. These criteria are often classified into three categories:

1. process-focused performance criteria,
2. customer-focused due-date criteria, and
3. cost-based criteria.

The applicability of the various criteria depends on the availability of data. Later we will show how these performance measures are applied to various sequencing rules.

Process-focused performance criteria pertain only to information about the start and end times of jobs and focus on shop performance such as equipment utilization and work-in-process (WIP) inventory. Two common measures are flow time and makespan. **Flow time** *is the amount of time a job spends in the shop or factory.* Low flow times reduce WIP inventory. Flow time is computed using Equation 15.1.

$$F_i = S_i + P_i \qquad [15.1]$$

where

F_i = flow time of job i
S_i = start time of job i
P_i = processing time of job i

Makespan *is the time needed to process a given set of jobs.* A short makespan aims to achieve high equipment utilization and resources by getting all jobs out of the shop quickly. Makespan is computed using Equation 15.2.

$$M = C_L - S_F \qquad [15.2]$$

where

M = makespan of a group of jobs
C_L = completion time of the last job in the group
S_F = start time of the first job in the group

We will assume that jobs arrived in numerical order (that is, 1, 2, 3, ..., and so on) and that all jobs will begin processing at time zero. If jobs arrive intermittently over time, the problem is much more complex. This situation will be discussed briefly later in this chapter.

SOLVED PROBLEM 15.4: COMPUTING FLOW TIME AND MAKESPAN

Suppose an insurance underwriting work area has five commercial insurance jobs to quote that have these processing times and due dates:

Job	Processing Time (P_i)
1	4 hours
2	7 hours
3	2 hours
4	6 hours
5	3 hours

If the jobs are sequenced in first-come-first served (FCFS) order, 1-2-3-4-5, compute the flow time, tardiness, and lateness for each job, as well as the makespan for the entire set of jobs.

Solution:

The flow time and makespan of each job are calculated using Equations 15.1, 15.3, and 15.4, as shown in the table below:

Job Sequence (i)	Start Time (S_i)	Processing Time (P_i)	Flow Time ($S_i + P_i$)
1	0	4	0 + 4 = 4 hours
2	4	7	4 + 7 = 11 hours
3	11	2	11 + 2 = 13 hours
4	13	6	13 + 6 = 19 hours
5	19	3	19 + 3 = 22 hours

Because all jobs are ready at time zero, no matter what sequence is chosen, the makespan is the same, because the time to process all the jobs is the sum of the processing times, or in this example, 22 hours.

Due-date criteria pertain to a customer's required due dates or internally determined shipping dates. Common performance measures are lateness and tardiness, or the number of jobs tardy or late. **Lateness** *is the difference between the completion time and the due date (either positive or negative).* **Tardiness** *is the amount of time by which the completion time exceeds the due date.* (Tardiness is defined as zero if the job is completed before the due date, and therefore no credit is given for completing a job early.) In contrast to process-focused performance criteria, these measures focus externally on customer satisfaction and service. They are calculated using Equations 15.3 and 15.4.

$$L_i = F_i - D_i \quad [15.3]$$

$$T_i = \text{Max}(0, L_i) \quad [15.4]$$

where

L_i = lateness of job i
D_i = due date of job i
T_i = tardiness of job i

SOLVED PROBLEM 15.5: COMPUTING LATENESS AND TARDINESS

For the commercial insurance example in Solved Problem 15.4, suppose the jobs have the following due dates:

Job	Processing Time (P_i)	Due Date (D_i)
1	4	15
2	7	16
3	2	8
4	6	21
5	3	9

If the jobs are sequenced in the order 1-2-3-4-5, compute the tardiness and lateness for each job.

Solution:

The flow time, tardiness, and lateness for each job are calculated using Equations 15.1, 15.3, and 15.4, as shown in the table below:

Job	Due Date (D_i)	Flow Time (F_i)	Lateness ($L_i = F_i - D_i$)	Tardiness [Max(0, L_i)]
1	15	4	4 − 15 = −11	0
2	16	11	11 − 16 = −5	0
3	8	13	13 − 8 = 5	5
4	21	19	19 − 21 = −2	0
5	9	22	22 − 9 = 13	13

We see that jobs 1, 2, and 4 are completed early, while jobs 3 and 5 are late. Job 5, in particular, is late by 13 hours—nearly two eight-hour working days.

A third type of performance criteria is cost based. Typical cost includes inventory, changeover or setup, processing or run, and material handling costs. This cost-based category might seem to be the most obvious criteria, but it is often difficult to identify the relevant cost categories, obtain accurate estimates of their values, and allocate costs to manufactured parts or services correctly. In most cases, costs are considered implicitly in process performance and due-date criteria.

15-3b Sequencing Rules

Three of the most popular sequencing rules for processing a set of jobs on a single processor jobs are

1. first come, first served (FCFS);
2. shortest processing time (SPT); and
3. earliest due date (EDD).

These rules are often applied when a fixed set of jobs needs to be sequenced at one point in time. In using one of these rules, a manager would sequence the jobs according to the chosen criterion. Different sequencing rules lead to very different results and performance. The FCFS rule is used in many service delivery systems but does not consider any job or customer performance criteria such as processing times or due dates. We used this rule in the previous solved problems.

Different sequencing rules lead to very different results and performance.

For the single-processor sequencing problem, the STP rule finds a *minimum average flow time* sequence. Solved Problem 15.6 provides an example.

SOLVED PROBLEM 15.6: APPLYING THE SPT SEQUENCING RULE

We will use the commercial insurance problem:

Job	Processing Time (P_i)
1	4
2	7
3	2
4	6
5	3

Find the flow times using the SPT rule, and compare the average flow time with the sequence 1-2-3-4-5.

Solution:

The SPT sequence is 3-5-1-4-2. The flow times are shown in the table below:

Job Sequence (i)	Start Time (S_i)	Processing Time (P_i)	Flow Time ($S_i + P_i$)
3	0	2	0 + 2 = 2 hours
5	2	3	2 + 3 = 5 hours
1	5	4	5 + 4 = 9 hours
4	9	6	9 + 6 = 15 hours
2	15	7	15 + 7 = 22 hours

The average flow time using the SPT rule is (2 + 5 + 9 + 15 + 22)/5 = 10.6 hours per job. For the sequence 1-2-3-4-5 (see Solved Problem 15.4), the average flow time is (4 + 11 + 13 + 19 + 22)/5 = 13.8 hours per job. We see that the SPT sequencing rule has a smaller average flow time, which is actually the minimum.

The EDD rule minimizes the maximum number of tardy jobs but doesn't perform as well on average flow time, WIP inventory, or resource utilization. To apply the EDD rule, we simply sequence the jobs in order of the earliest due dates. Solved Problem 15.7 illustrates this approach.

SOLVED PROBLEM 15.7: SEQUENCING BY EDD

Use the scenario in Solved Problem 15.5. Compute the flow times, lateness, and tardiness for the EDD sequence, as well as the average flow time.

Solution:

The processing times and due dates for five commercial insurance jobs were

Job	Processing Time (P_i)	Due Date (D_i)
1	4	15
2	7	16
3	2	8
4	6	21
5	3	9

Using the EDD rule, we would sequence the jobs in the order 3-5-1-2-4. The performance measures are computed in the table below:

Job	Due Date (D_i)	Processing Time (P_i)	Flow Time (F_i)	Lateness ($L_i = F_i - D_i$)	Tardiness [Max(0, L_i)]
3	8	2	0 + 2 = 2	−6	0
5	9	3	2 + 3 = 5	−4	0
1	15	4	5 + 4 = 9	−6	0
2	16	7	9 + 7 = 16	0	0
4	21	6	16 + 6 = 22	1	1

The average flow time is (2 + 5 + 9 + 16 + 22)/5 = 10.8 hours per job. Three jobs are early, and only one job is late.

15-3c An Excel Template for Sequencing

An Excel template, *Sequencing*, is available in MindTap to evaluate sequencing rules for a single processor. You may enter processing times, due dates, and sequences for up to 10 jobs. The template computes the average flowtime, lateness, and tardiness, as well as the number of tardy jobs and maximum tardiness. This template may be used to solve problems and compare the performance of different sequences. Solved Problem 15.8 shows one example.

SOLVED PROBLEM 15.8: USING THE EXCEL *SEQUENCING* TEMPLATE

Five tax analysis jobs are waiting to be processed by Martha at T. R. Accounting Service. Use the Excel template to compare the performance measures for the FCFS, SPT, and EDD sequencing rules. Which rule do you recommend? Why?

Job	Processing Time (days)	Due Date
1	7	11
2	3	10
3	5	8
4	2	5
5	6	17

Solution:

Exhibits 15.8 through 15.10 show the results for the FCFS, SPT, and EDD sequences using the Excel template. These are summarized in the table below with the best values for each criterion in color:

Performance Criteria	Sequence 1-2-3-4-5	SPT Sequence	EDD Sequence
Average Flow Time	15.4	**11.2**	11.8
Average Lateness	4.2	**1.0**	1.6
Average Tardiness	5.0	2.8	**2.4**
Number of Tardy Jobs	3	**2**	**2**
Maximum Tardiness	12.0	12.0	**6.0**

EXHIBIT 15.8 Excel *Sequencing* Template for Calculating FCFS Sequence Performance Measures

	A	B	C	D	E	F	G	H	I	J	K
1	Sequencing	Copyright © Cengage Learning									
2		Not for commercial use.									
3	Enter data only in yellow-shaded cells. Up to 10 jobs may be sequenced.						Average	Average	Average	Number of	Maximum
4							Flowtime	Lateness	Tardiness	Tardy Jobs	Tardiness
5	Number of Jobs	5					14.40	4.20	5.00	3	12.00
6											
7	Job	Processing Time	Due Date		Sequence	Processing Time	Due Date	Flowtime	Lateness	Tardiness	
8	1	7	11		1	7	11	7	-4	0	
9	2	3	10		2	3	10	10	0	0	
10	3	5	8		3	5	8	15	7	7	
11	4	2	5		4	2	5	17	12	12	
12	5	6	17		5	6	17	23	6	6	
13	6										
14	7										
15	8										
16	9										
17	10										

EXHIBIT 15.9 Excel *Sequencing* Template for Calculating SPT Sequence Performance Measures

	A	B	C	D	E	F	G	H	I	J	K
1	Sequencing	Copyright © Cengage Learning									
2		Not for commercial use.									
3	Enter data only in yellow-shaded cells. Up to 10 jobs may be sequenced.						Average	Average	Average	Number of	Maximum
4							Flowtime	Lateness	Tardiness	Tardy Jobs	Tardiness
5	Number of Jobs	5					11.20	1.00	2.80	2	12.00
6											
7	Job	Processing Time	Due Date		Sequence	Processing Time	Due Date	Flowtime	Lateness	Tardiness	
8	1	7	11		4	2	5	2	-3	0	
9	2	3	10		2	3	10	5	-5	0	
10	3	5	8		3	5	8	10	2	2	
11	4	2	5		5	6	17	16	-1	0	
12	5	6	17		1	7	11	23	12	12	
13	6										
14	7										
15	8										
16	9										
17	10										

EXHIBIT 15.10 Excel *Sequencing* Template for Calculating EDD Sequence Performance Measures

	A	B	C	D	E	F	G	H	I	J	K
1	Sequencing	Copyright © Cengage Learning									
2		Not for commercial use.									
3	Enter data only in yellow-shaded cells. Up to 10 jobs may be sequenced.						Average	Average	Average	Number of	Maximum
4							Flowtime	Lateness	Tardiness	Tardy Jobs	Tardiness
5	Number of Jobs	5					11.80	1.60	2.40	2	6.00
6											
7	Job	Processing Time	Due Date		Sequence	Processing Time	Due Date	Flowtime	Lateness	Tardiness	
8	1	7	11		4	2	5	2	-3	0	
9	2	3	10		3	5	8	7	-1	0	
10	3	5	8		2	3	10	10	0	0	
11	4	2	5		1	7	11	17	6	6	
12	5	6	17		5	6	17	23	6	6	
13	6										
14	7										
15	8										
16	9										
17	10										

From the summary table, choosing the best rule is not an easy decision. The FCFS rule does not provide any advantages. The SPT rule minimizes average flow time and average lateness (which also measures jobs that are early), but job 1 is extremely late by 12 days. The EDD rule minimizes the maximum tardiness and average tardiness. Jobs 1 and 5 are tardy by six days. Both the SPT and EDD rules have the smallest number of tardy jobs. If tardiness is of major concern, then the EDD sequence is the best, but if flow time and lateness are more important, then the SPT sequence is best. Notice the FCFS rule does not perform well, yet it is often used in manufacturing and service situations to process jobs and customers.

15-4 Dispatching Rules for Job Shop Scheduling

Real-life scheduling problems in job shops are often very large and complex. In the most general job shop situation, we must sequence n jobs on m machines, and each job may have a unique routing. If so, there are up to $(n!)^m$ possible schedules. For example, when $n = 5$ and $m = 4$, there are more than 200 million sequences! For such problems, we must resort to simple rules of thumb driven by sound logic.

In addition, scheduling in real manufacturing environments is dynamic—jobs are continually being created, eliminated, and changed and unforeseen events, such as machine breakdowns, occur that invalidate previously developed schedules. Hence, sequencing decisions must be made over time. **Dispatching** *is the process of selecting jobs for processing and authorizing the work to be done.*

In goods-producing businesses, dispatching is part of "shop floor control." In service-providing businesses, dispatching can be done in the front or back offices. An example of dispatching in the front office might be giving one customer priority over another in a bank or supermarket. An example in the back office would be rerouting delivery trucks to new destinations based on real-time updates on customer needs and current delivery performance.

Companies like Mobil Oil Corporation, for example, have computer-based systems for dispatching and processing customer orders for gasoline. Their dispatching process assigns orders to terminals and delivery trucks, adjusts order quantities to fit truck compartments, loads trucks to their maximum legal weight, routes trucks, and sequences deliveries with the objectives of minimizing the cost of delivered product, balancing the workload among the company trucks, and adhering to all laws and proper loading rules.

When new jobs arrive in an intermittent fashion, resulting in a constantly changing mix of jobs needing to be sequenced, dispatching rules assign priorities to whatever jobs are available at a specific time and then update the priorities when new jobs arrive. If SPT were used in a dynamic environment, a job with a large processing time might never get processed. In this case, some time-based exception rules (such as "if a job waits more than 40 hours, schedule it next") must be used to avoid this problem. Typical priority dispatching rules that are used include

- fewest number of operations remaining (FNO), and
- least work remaining (LWR)—the sum of all processing times for operations not yet performed.

SOLVED PROBLEM 15.9: USING THE FNO DISPATCHING RULE

Lynwood Manufacturing is a small job shop with a lathe (M), drill press (D), milling machine (M), and grinder (G). Jobs arrive as customers place orders. Let us assume that three jobs arrive with the work characteristics given below:

Job	Arrival Time	Processing Sequence (Processing Time in minutes)
1	0	L(10), D(20), G(35)
2	15	D(25), G(30), L(20), M(15)
3	20	D(10), M(25)

How should a dispatcher make scheduling decisions using the FNO rule?

Solution:

At time zero, job 1 is immediately scheduled on the lathe, and is finished on the lathe at time 10. At this time, it moves to the drill press, begins processing at time 10, and will be completed at time $10 + 20 = 30$. Job 2 arrives at time 15 and its first operation is on the drill press. Because job 1 is still on the drill press at this time, job 2 must wait. At time 20, job 3 arrives and must also wait at the drill press. When job 1 is completed at time 30 and moves to the grinder, the dispatcher must decide which of the waiting jobs—job 2 or job 3—should be scheduled next on the drill press. If the FNO dispatching rule is chosen, then the decision would be to schedule job 3 next, as it only has two operations remaining, whereas job 2 has four.

As you can see from Solved Problem 15.9, we must keep track of a lot of information about the status of each machine and job over time. This makes dispatching quite complicated, and it is best performed with the help of appropriate software. Simulation is often used to evaluate dispatching rules.

15-5 Two-Resource Sequencing Problem

In this section, we consider a flow shop with only two resources or workstations. We assume that each job must be processed first on Resource #1 and then on Resource #2. Processing times for each job on each resource are known. Let's look at an example.

Hirsch Products manufactures certain custom parts that first require a shearing operation (Resource #1) and then a punch-press operation (Resource #2). Hirsch currently has orders for five jobs, which have processing times (days) estimated as follows:

Job	Shear (days)	Punch-Press (days)
1	4	5
2	4	1
3	10	4
4	6	10
5	2	3

The jobs can be sequenced in any order but they must be sheared first. Therefore, we have a flow shop situation where each job must first be sequenced on the shear operation and then on the punch-press operation.

Suppose the jobs are sequenced in the order 1-2-3-4-5. This sequence can be represented by a Gantt chart showing the scheduled times for each job on each machine along a horizontal time axis (see Exhibit 15.11). This shows, for instance, that job 1 is scheduled on the shear for the first four days, job 2 for the next four days, and so on. We construct a Gantt chart for a given sequence by scheduling the first job as early as possible on the first machine (shear). Then, as soon as the job is completed, it can be scheduled on the punch press, provided that no other job is currently in progress. First, note that all jobs follow each other on the shearing machine. Because of variations in processing times, however, the punch press, the second operation, is often idle while awaiting the next job. The makespan is 37 days, and the flow times in days for the jobs are as follows:

Job	1	2	3	4	5
Flow Time (days)	9	10	22	34	37

In contrast to sequencing jobs on a single resource, the makespan can vary for each different sequence. Therefore, for the two-resource sequencing problem, it makes sense to try to find a sequence with the smallest makespan.

S.M. Johnson developed the following algorithm (known as *Johnson's Rule*) in 1954 for finding a minimum makespan schedule for a two-resource sequencing problem.[5]

1. List the jobs and their processing times on Resources #1 and #2.
2. Find the job with the shortest processing time (on either resource).
3. If this time corresponds to Resource #1, sequence the job first; if it corresponds to Resource #2, sequence the job last.
4. Repeat steps 2 and 3, using the next-shortest processing time and working inward from both ends of the sequence until all jobs have been scheduled.

Solved Problem 15.10 provides an example of using this procedure for Hirsch Products.

EXHIBIT 15.11 Gantt Job Sequence Chart for Hirsch Product Sequence 1-2-3-4-5

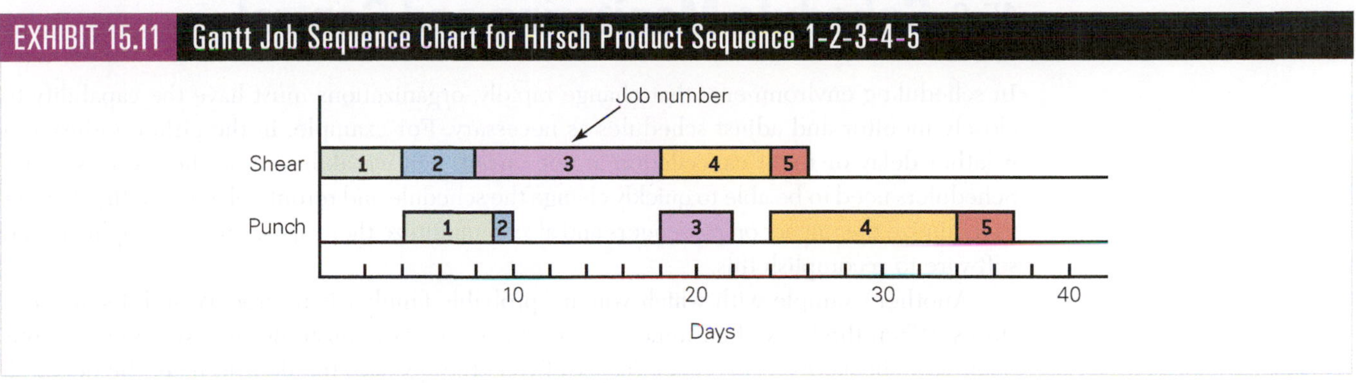

SOLVED PROBLEM 15.10: APPLYING JOHNSON'S RULE

Apply Johnson's Rule to find the minimum makespan sequence for the Hirsch Products scenario.

Solution:

First, identify the job with the shortest processing time (step 2 of Johnson's Rule). As shown below, this is job 2 on the punch-press.

Job	Shear (days)	Punch-Press (days)
1	4	5
2	4	(1)
3	10	4
4	6	10
5	2	3

Because the minimum time for job 2 is on the second machine, we schedule it last, according to step 3 of Johnson's Rule.

___ ___ ___ ___ 2

Next, we find the second-shortest processing time. It is two days, for job 5 on machine 1. Therefore, job 5 is scheduled first.

5 ___ ___ ___ 2

In the next step, we have a tie of four days between job 1 on the shear and job 3 on the punch press. When a tie occurs, either job can be chosen. If we pick job 1, we have the following sequence:

5 1 ___ ___ 2

Continuing with Johnson's rule, the last two steps yield the complete sequence.

5 1 ___ 3 2

5 1 4 3 2

The Gantt chart for this sequence is shown in Exhibit 15.12. Compared to the sequence 1-2-3-4-5, the makespan is reduced from 37 to 27 days, and the average flow time is also improved from 22.4 to 18.2 days. As noted, the total idle time on the punch press is now only four days, resulting in a punch press resource utilization of 23/27, or 85.2 percent, and we gain 10 days to schedule other jobs. If the sequencing problem structure fits the assumptions of Johnson's rule, it is a powerful algorithm. Again, commonsense scheduling is seldom as good as Johnson's rule.

EXHIBIT 15.12 Gantt Job Sequence Chart for Hirsch Product Sequence 5-1-4-3-2

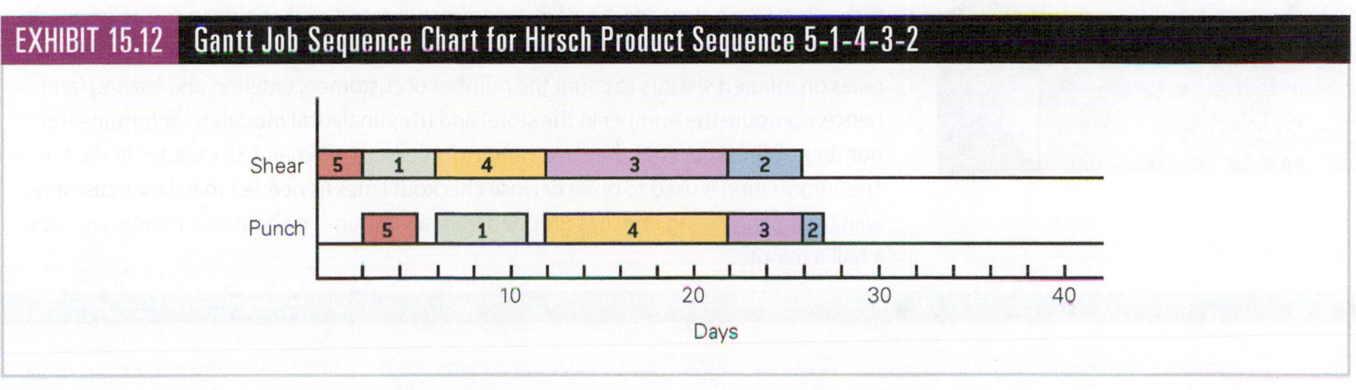

15-6 Schedule Monitoring and Control

In scheduling environments that change rapidly, organizations must have the capability to closely monitor and adjust schedules as necessary. For example, in the airline industry, a weather delay or flight cancellation at one airport can wreak havoc on the entire system. Schedulers need to be able to quickly change the schedule and reroute planes and flight crews to minimize the impact on passengers and also to minimize their costs. They use sophisticated software to accomplish this.

Another example with which you are probably familiar is in grocery and department stores. When the lines of customers at the checkouts grow, customer-focused organizations open new checkouts, bringing employees from other jobs on the floor to meet the demand. The box on Kroger describes some interesting technology they use to manage such situations.

Similar issues arise in manufacturing. Material shortages can occur; equipment malfunctions can cause delays in processing at individual workstations; inventory shipments may be late; items may be defective or damaged; and so on. Schedules must be changed when these things occur. Therefore, reschedules are a normal part of scheduling.

Short-term capacity fluctuations also necessitate changes in schedules. Factors affecting short-term capacity include absenteeism, labor performance, equipment failures, tooling problems, labor turnover, and material shortages. They are inevitable and unavoidable. Some alternatives available to operations managers for coping with capacity shortages are overtime, short-term subcontracting, alternate process routing, and reallocations of the workforce, as described in the previous chapter.

Gantt (bar) charts are useful tools for monitoring planned schedules, and an example is shown in Exhibit 15.13. The dark shaded areas indicate completed work. This chart shows, for example, that job 4 has not yet started on machine 2, job 1 is currently behind schedule on machine 3, and jobs 2 and 5 are ahead of schedule. Perhaps needed material has not yet been delivered for job 4, or perhaps machine 3 has had a breakdown. In any event, it is up to production-control personnel to revise the schedule or to expedite jobs that are behind schedule. Many other types of graphical aids are useful and commercially available.

Kroger: Managing Queues Using Scheduling Technology

Sean Pavone/Shutterstock.com

You probably don't like to wait in line at a grocery store, especially when the shopper in front of you has a basket full of items! Kroger, headquartered in Cincinnati, Ohio, is a national chain of grocery stores that has addressed this issue using some innovative technology. Kroger uses technology to forecast demand so that managers can better anticipate future needs before the lines grow too long. Their system, called Que Vision, relies on infrared sensors to count the number of customers entering and leaving (and hence, compute the number in the store) and uses analytical models to determine the number of checkout lines they need and to forecast the demand 30 minutes in the future. This information is used to open or close checkout lanes as needed to balance customer waiting times. Waiting time has dropped from an average of about four minutes to under a half a minute.

EXHIBIT 15.13 Gantt Chart Example for Monitoring Schedule Progress

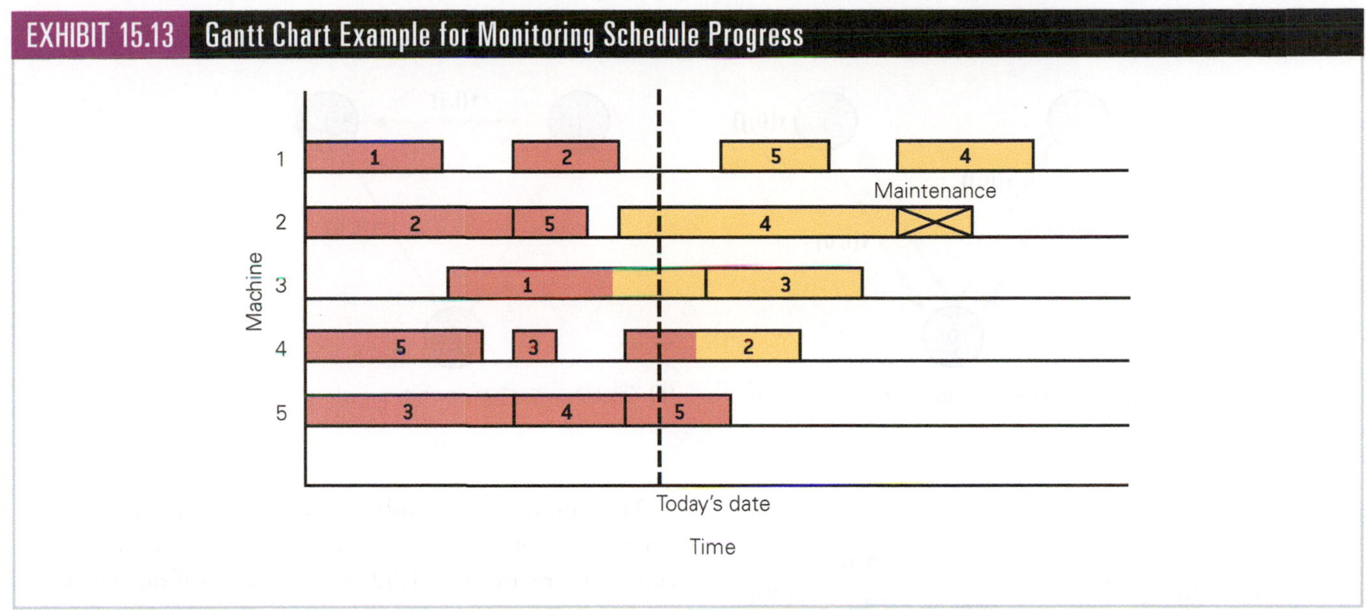

15-7 Vehicle Routing and Scheduling

A common scheduling problem in logistics involves determining routes from a central depot or warehouse to many customers. Examples would be delivering cases of soft drinks to convenience stores, or delivering packages via UPS or FedEx home delivery. Generally, time (such as limited working hours) or vehicle capacity restrictions preclude the use of using only one route from the depot to all customers.

One assumption is that by minimizing total delivery time or distance traveled the firm is also reducing operating costs (i.e., fuel, maintenance, number of vehicles) and greenhouse gas emissions. Environmental sustainability (explained in Exhibit 1.12) includes air quality and energy and transportation optimization. Applications such as Google Maps and GPS allow managers to carefully plan their dispatching and routing of company vehicles.

Vehicle Routing Software[6]

Many different companies have developed software to find optimal assignments of customers to vehicles, as well as the optimal sequence and schedule of customers served by each vehicle, in order to minimize transportation costs while satisfying feasibility constraints as to when and where stops are visited, what can be loaded in each vehicle, and what routes drivers can take. Routing software is used to plan deliveries from central locations, pick-ups from shippers, routes of service fleets, and even bus and taxi schedules. Modern software now uses cloud-based solutions, allowing customers to manage data better and provide better features. Many companies also use telematics systems to communicate with drivers using apps running on smart phones and tablets.

EXHIBIT 15.14 Combining Customers *i* and *j* on the Same Route

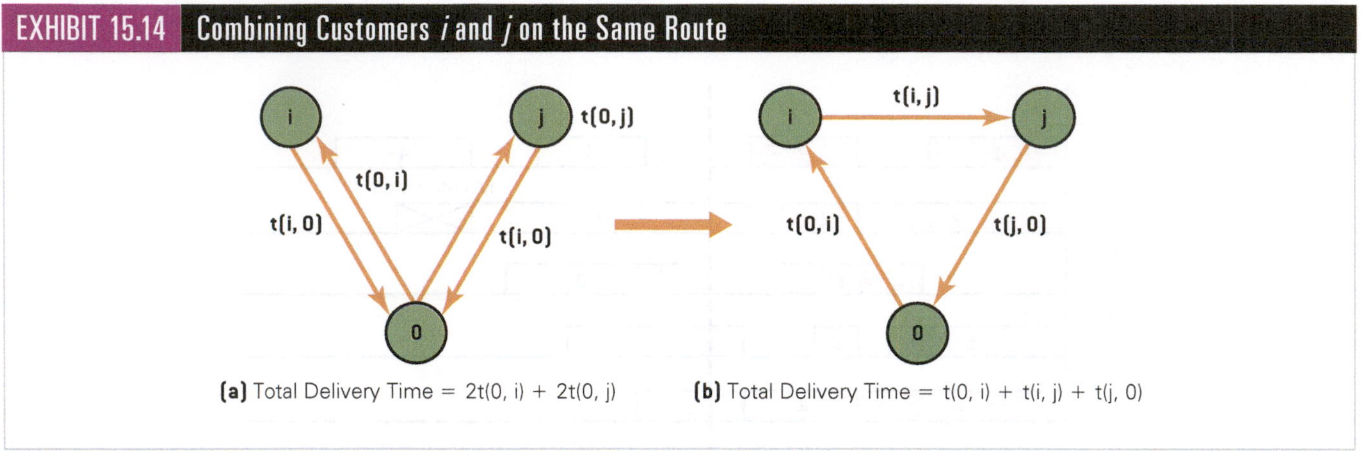

View Apart/Shutterstock.com

The number of possible routes can quickly increase as more delivery sites (customers) are added to the situation. For example, there are $(n - 1)!/2$ possible routes if one vehicle is to visit n delivery sites. Consider a simple example of a residential pool maintenance company visiting 12 customer pools in a day with one truck. Assuming the route from customer A to B is the same as from customer B to A, we divide by two: $(12-1)!/2 = 19{,}958{,}400$ possible routes! One pool maintenance firm in southwest Florida services over 7,000 pools; at their headquarters is a large screen with a map of their service area and all truck locations identified by GPS. IBM vehicle dispatching and routing software plan each truck's daily route.

Complete enumeration of all possible routes impractical. Linear optimization (see Supplement D) can be used to find good route plans, but the models are quite complex.. Heuristic methods try to provide a good solution (not necessarily an optimal solution) using rules and methods that help analysts solve the problem faster than if all possible options were computed.

15-7b The Clarke-Wright Method for Vehicle Routing

A simple technique that finds very good solutions for simple vehicle routing problems is the *Clarke–Wright Method*. This procedure starts by assuming that each customer is serviced individually from the depot, and then seeks to combine customers into longer routes to reduce the total travel time and remain within capacity restrictions.

Here is the main idea behind the procedure. Suppose that $t(i,j)$ is the travel time between customers i and j. We let "0" represent the central depot. We assume that $t(i,j) = t(j,i)$, that is, the distance from i to j is the same as from j to i. If we service each customer separately from the depot, then the total delivery time would be $2t(0,i) + 2t(0,j)$. If, however, we combine customers i and j on the same route, then the total time is $t(0,i) + t(i,j) + t(j,0)$. This is shown in Exhibit 15.14. This combined route is better than the individual routes if

$$t(0,i) + t(i,j) + t(j,0) < 2t(0,i) + 2t(0,j)$$

$$0 < 2t(0,i) - t(0,i) + 2t(0,j) - t(0,j) - t(i,j)$$

or

$$0 < t(0,i) + t(0,j) - t(i,j) = s(i,j)$$

The term $s(i,j)$ represents the savings associated with combining the customers on the same route. If the savings value is positive, then it is beneficial to combine them, as long as the combined requirements do not exceed the time or vehicle capacity restrictions.

Formally, the Clarke–Wright Method is implemented as follows.

1. Compute the savings $s(i, j)$ for all pairs of customers i and j.
2. Find the pair of customers with the largest savings, and determine if there is sufficient capacity to link these customers together. If so, construct a new route by combining them. If not, try the next largest savings, and so on.
3. Continue to apply step 2 as long as the next largest savings is positive. When all positive savings have been considered, stop.

Solved Problem 15.11 shows how this procedure can be used.

SOLVED PROBLEM 15.11: APPLYING THE CLARKE-WRIGHT METHOD

A chain of convenience stores has five locations in one city. Each week, cases of soft drinks must be delivered from a central warehouse to the stores. The table below shows the travel time in minutes between the locations, as well as to and from the warehouse ("0"). Assume that only one delivery vehicle is available and can load a maximum of 80 cases.

	Delivery Time						Demand (Cases required)
i/j	**0**	**1**	**2**	**3**	**4**	**5**	
0	—	20	51	50	15	90	—
1		—	10	55	30	53	46
2			—	50	60	38	33
3				—	60	10	30
4					—	12	75
5						—	30

We compute the savings between each pair of customers $s(i,j)$ as follows:

$$s(1,2) = t(0,1) + t(0,2) - t(1,2) = 20 + 51 - 10 = 61$$
$$s(1,3) = t(0,1) + t(0,3) - t(1,3) = 20 + 50 - 55 = 15$$
$$s(1,4) = t(0,1) + t(0,4) - t(1,4) = 20 + 15 - 30 = 5$$
$$s(1,5) = t(0,1) + t(0,5) - t(1,5) = 20 + 90 - 53 = 57$$
$$s(2,3) = t(0,2) + t(0,3) - t(2,3) = 51 + 50 - 50 = 51$$
$$s(2,4) = t(0,2) + t(0,4) - t(2,4) = 51 + 15 - 60 = 6$$
$$s(2,5) = t(0,2) + t(0,5) - t(2,5) = 51 + 90 - 38 = 103$$
$$s(3,4) = t(0,3) + t(0,4) - t(3,4) = 50 + 15 - 60 = 5$$
$$s(3,5) = t(0,3) + t(0,5) - t(3,5) = 50 + 90 - 10 = 130$$
$$s(4,5) = t(0,4) + t(0,5) - t(4,5) = 15 + 90 - 12 = 93$$

The savings in minutes are summarized in the table below:

i/j	**1**	**2**	**3**	**4**	**5**
1	—	61	15	5	57
2		—	51	6	103
3			—	5	130
4				—	93

The largest savings is 130 for customers 3 and 5. If these customers are combined on the same route, the total cases on this route would be 30 + 30 = 60, which is less than the capacity of 80; therefore, combine them, resulting in the route 0-3-5-0. The total distance of the route is 50 + 10 + 90 = 150.

New solution:

Routes	Travel Time	Cases on Route	Capacity Available
0-1-0	40	46	80 − 46 = 34
0-2-0	102	33	80 − 33 = 47
0-4-0	30	75	80 − 75 = 5
0-3-5-0	150	60	80 − 60 = 20
Total	322		

Note that the total travel time was reduced by the amount of the savings (452−322 =130).

The next largest savings is 103, between customers 2 and 5. However, if we add customer 2 on the route 0-3-5-0, the total cases for this customer (33) would exceed the available capacity (20); therefore, we do not consider this option. Similarly, the next largest savings of 93 for customers 4 and 5 would also exceed the capacity. The next largest savings is 61 for customers 1 and 2. We can combine them, resulting in the third iteration of the heuristics:

Routes	Travel Time	Cases on Route	Capacity Available
0-1-2-0	81	79	80 − 79 = 1
0-4-0	30	75	80 − 75 = 5
0-3-5-0	150	60	80 − 60 = 20
Total	261		

At this point, we can no longer add customer 4 to any route, so the procedure ends. The solution requires three routes: 0-1-2-0, 0-4-0, and 0-3-5-0. It is assumed that one delivery truck goes back to the central warehouse to complete each route

The initial solution is to service all customers individually from the warehouse:

Routes	Travel Time	Cases on Route	Capacity Available
0-1-0	40	46	80 − 46 = 34
0-2-0	102	33	80 − 33 = 47
0-3-0	100	30	80 − 30 = 50
0-4-0	30	75	80 − 75 = 5
0-5-0	180	30	80 − 30 = 50
Total	452		

separately. The total delivery time is reduced by 42.3 percent [(452 – 261)/452]. Sustainability benefits also accrue from reduced carbon dioxide emissions. If we assume that each route can be serviced by different delivery vehicles that depart at the same time, then all deliveries will be completed by the time corresponding to the longest route; in this case, 150. Of course, this does not consider the capital and operating costs of multiple vehicles. This is beyond the logic of the Clarke–Wright heuristic but could be incorporated in a spreadsheet model for financial analysis.

CHAPTER 15 LEARNING OBJECTIVE SUMMARIES

15.1 **Explain the concepts of scheduling and sequencing.** Scheduling and sequencing are common activities that operations managers perform every day in every business. They are fundamental to all three levels of aggregation and disaggregation planning that we described in the previous chapter. Good schedules and sequences lead to efficient execution of manufacturing and service plans. Some examples of scheduling: fast-food restaurants, hospitals, and call centers need to schedule employees for work shifts; doctors, dentists, and stockbrokers need to schedule patients and customers; airlines must schedule crews and flight attendants; sports organizations must schedule teams and officials; court systems must schedule hearings and trials; factory managers need to schedule jobs on machines and preventive maintenance work; and salespersons need to schedule customer deliveries and visits to potential customers. Some examples of sequencing: Triage nurses must decide on the order in which emergency patients are treated; housekeepers in hotels must sequence the order of rooms to clean; operations managers who run an automobile assembly line must determine the sequence by which different models are produced; and airport managers must sequence outgoing flights on runways.

15.2 **Describe staff scheduling and appointment system decisions.** Staff scheduling problems are prevalent in service organizations because of high variability in customer demand. Staff scheduling attempts to match available personnel with the needs of the organization by:

1. accurately forecasting demand and translating it into the quantity and timing of work to be done;
2. determining the staffing required to perform the work by time period;
3. determining the personnel available and the full- and part-time mix; and
4. matching capacity to demand requirements, and developing a work schedule that maximizes service and minimizes costs.

A simple problem of scheduling personnel with consecutive days off in the face of fluctuating requirements can be solved easily by hand. Solved Problem 15.1 provides an example.

Appointments can be viewed as a reservation of service time and capacity. Using appointments provides a means to maximize the use of time-dependent service capacity and reduce the risk of no shows. An appointment system must try to accommodate customers and forecast their behavior, such as the no-show rate or a difficult customer who demands more processing time.

Four decisions to make regarding designing an appointment system are the following:

1. Determine the appointment time interval.
2. Determine the length of each workday and the time off duty.
3. Decide how to handle overbooking.
4. Develop customer appointment rules that maximize customer satisfaction.

15.3 **Explain sequencing performance criteria and rules for sequencing on a single processor.** Sequencing criteria are often classified into three categories:

1. Process-focused performance criteria pertain only to information about the start and end times of jobs and focus on shop performance such as equipment utilization and WIP inventory. Two common measures are flow time and makespan.
2. Due date criteria pertain to customers' required due dates or internally determined shipping dates. Common performance measures are lateness and tardiness, or the number of jobs tardy or late.
3. Cost-based performance criteria include inventory, changeover or setup, processing or run, and material-handling costs. In most cases, costs are considered implicitly in process performance and due-date criteria.

Three of the most popular sequencing rules for prioritizing jobs are:

- First come, first served (FCFS)
- Shortest processing time (SPT)
- Earliest due date (EDD)

The SPT rule tends to minimize average flow time and WIP inventory and maximize resource utilization. The EDD rule minimizes the maximum of jobs past due but doesn't perform well on average flow time, WIP inventory, or resource utilization. The FCFS rule is used in many service-delivery systems and does not consider any job or customer criterion. FCFS focuses only on the time of arrival for the customer or job.

15.4 **Explain the process of dispatching and typical priority rules that are used.** Dispatching is the process of selecting jobs for processing and authorizing the work to be done. When new jobs arrive in an intermittent fashion, resulting in a constantly changing mix of jobs needing to be sequenced, dispatching rules assign priorities to whatever jobs are available at a specific time and then update the priorities when new jobs arrive. Typical priority dispatching rules that are used include

- fewest number of operations remaining (FNO), and
- least work remaining (LWR)—the sum of all processing times for operations not yet performed.

CHAPTER 15 LEARNING OBJECTIVE SUMMARIES

15.5 **Describe how to solve two-resource sequencing problems.** S.M. Johnson developed an algorithm for finding a minimum makespan schedule for a two-resource sequencing problem.

1. List the jobs and their processing times on Resources #1 and #2.
2. Find the job with the shortest processing time (on either resource).
3. If this time corresponds to Resource #1, sequence the job first; if it corresponds to Resource #2, sequence the job last.
4. Repeat steps 2 and 3, using the next-shortest processing time and working inward from both ends of the sequence until all jobs have been scheduled.

15.6 **Explain the need for monitoring schedules using Gantt charts.** In scheduling environments that change rapidly, such as at airlines, grocery stores, and manufacturing facilities, organizations must have the capability to closely monitor and adjust schedules as necessary.

Short-term capacity fluctuations also necessitate changes in schedules. Factors affecting short-term capacity include absenteeism, labor performance, equipment failures, tooling problems, labor turnover, and material shortages. They are inevitable and unavoidable. Gantt (bar) charts are useful tools for monitoring schedules.

15.7 **Describe how to use the Clarke–Wright method for vehicle routing and scheduling.** This procedure assumes each customer is serviced individually from a depot and then combines customers into longer routes to reduce total travel time. The method computes savings *s (i,j)* for all customers i and j; finds the pair of customers with the largest savings, and determines if there is sufficient capacity to link them together. If so, it constructs a new route combining them. If not, it tries the next largest savings then continues to move down the list for as long as the next largest savings is positive. (See Solved Problem 15.11 in chapter.)

KEY TERMS

- **Dispatching**
- **Flow time**
- **Lateness**
- **Makespan**
- **Scheduling**
- **Sequencing**
- **Tardiness**

REVIEW QUESTIONS

15.1 1. Define scheduling and sequencing. Provide examples from your experiences.

15.1 2. Explain how scheduling affects customer service and costs. Provide an example.

15.2 3. What are the four major decisions made by staff scheduling?

15.2 4. Why are appointment systems used? What decisions are necessary to design an appointment system?

15.3 5. Describe some practical examples of the single-resource sequencing problem.

15.3 6. Define flow time, makespan, tardiness, and lateness, and explain how they are computed.

15.3 7. What are the advantages and disadvantages of the SPT and EDD sequencing rules?

15.4 8. What is dispatching? Explain how priority dispatching rules are used.

15.5 9. Summarize the procedure (steps) used for the two-resource sequencing problem (Johnson's Sequencing Rule).

15.6 10. What is a Gantt chart and why is it important?

15.6 11. Why must schedules be closely monitored and often revised?

15.7 12. What are the objectives of vehicle routing and scheduling?

DISCUSSION QUESTIONS AND EXPERIENTIAL ACTIVITIES

15.1 13. Discuss how you decide to schedule your school assignments. Do your informal scheduling rules correspond to any of those in this chapter?

15.1 14. How does your college or university schedule classes? What criteria are used?

15.1 15. Discuss scheduling and sequencing issues in municipal services such as garbage collection, school-bus routing, or snowplowing. What types of criteria and approaches might be used?

15.1 16. Interview an operations or logistics manager at a nearby manufacturing or service company to find out about scheduling problems the company faces and how they are addressed.

15.2 17. Write a one-page paper listing the advantages and disadvantages of using part-time employees to help meet demand.

15.2 18. Explain why appointments are necessary for many professional services. (Hint: How do services differ from goods as described in Chapter 1?) List and explain some key issues and decisions that must be addressed in designing appointment systems.

15.2 19. Why is staff scheduling in a service environment a difficult task? What can managers do to ensure that staff schedules are effective and efficient?

15.2 20. Research software available to organizations to create staff schedules. What features do these types of software have? Prepare a one-page report.

15.7 21. Explain how modern vehicle routing and dispatching software and systems can support sustainability goals and objectives.

15.7 22. Do an Internet search of "vehicle-routing software" and "vehicle routing." Write a two-page report of the capabilities, advantages, and disadvantages of these vehicle-routing and dispatching systems. Provide one or two examples of real-world applications of these systems and the benefits.

COMPUTATIONAL PROBLEMS AND EXERCISES

These exercises require you to apply the formulas and methods described in the chapter. The problems should be solved manually.

15.2 23. A hospital emergency room needs the following numbers of nurses:

Day	M	T	W	T	F	S	S
Min. number	4	3	2	4	7	8	5

Each nurse should have two consecutive days off. How many full-time nurses are required, and what is a good nurse schedule?

15.2 24. A supermarket has the following minimum personnel requirements during the week. Each employee is required to have two consecutive days off. How many regular employees are required, and what is a good schedule?

Day	M	T	W	T	F	S	S
Min. Personnel	3	4	5	3	5	6	5

15.3 25. Five jobs are to be processed on one machine. If the jobs are processed in the FCFS order 1-2-3-4-5, compute the start time and flow time for each job:

Job	1	2	3	4	5
Processing time	8	3	5	9	4

15.3 26. These six jobs are to be scheduled on a single machine:

Job	1	2	3	4	5	6
Processing Time (min.)	100	130	210	90	150	80

a. Suppose the jobs are processed in FCFS numerical order. Compute the makespan, flow time for each job, and overall average flow time.

b. In what order would the jobs be processed using the SPT rule? Compute the average flow-time after each job is completed. Compare this answer with your answer to part a.

15.3 27. On Tuesday morning at 8 a.m., an IT analyst found four project "tickets" in her inbox that arrived overnight. The estimated times to complete the projects and the due dates requested are given below. If the projects are processed in a FCFS order (1-2-3-4), compute the flow time, lateness, and tardiness for each project. Convert the due dates to minutes past 8 a.m.

Project	1	2	3	4
Processing time (minutes)	45	20	90	60
Due date	10 a.m.	9 a.m.	noon	9:30 a.m.

15.3 28. Five patients arrived at the radiology department in a hospital and are waiting for X-rays.

Patient	1	2	3	4	5
Processing time (minutes)	25	20	30	40	15

Use the SPT rule to create a schedule. Compute the start time and flow time for each patient.

15.3 29. A workstation has one maintenance mechanic to repair failed machines. We can think of the mechanic as the processor (scarce resource) and the machines awaiting repair as the jobs. Let us assume that six machines are down, with estimated repair times given here, and that no new machines fail.

Job (fix machine #)	1	2	3	4	5	6
Processing time (hours)	10	3	7	2	9	6

Compute the flow time for each job using both the FCFS rule and the SPT rule, and compare the average flow times.

15.3 30. Five customers brought in computers to be repaired to a small shop. Estimated repair times (in days) and dates promised are given below. Due dates were set based on available technicians; however, one technician had a medical emergency and will be unavailable for at least two weeks so processing times were adjusted.

Customer job	1	2	3	4	5
Processing time (days)	4	5	1	7	3
Due date (days)	3	5	2	10	6

Use the EDD rule, and compute the start time, completion time, flow time, lateness, and tardiness for each job.

15.4 31. At Lynwood Manufacturing, (see Solved Problem 15.9), suppose the dispatcher uses the LWR instead of FNO. Which job (job 2 or job 3) will be scheduled next on the drill press at time 30?

15.5 32. A manufacturing process involving machined components consists of two operations done on two different machines. The status of the queue at the beginning of a particular week is as follows:

Job Number	Number of components	Scheduled Time on Machine 1 (min. per piece)	Scheduled Time on Machine 2 (min. per piece)
101	200	2.5	2.5
176	150	1.5	0.5
184	250	1.0	2.0
185	125	2.5	1.0
201	100	1.2	2.4
213	100	1.2	2.2

The processing on machine 2 must follow processing on machine 1. Schedule these jobs to minimize the makespan. Illustrate the schedule you arrive at with a bar chart.

15.5 33. On Monday morning, Baxter Industries has the following jobs waiting for processing in two departments, milling, and drilling, in that order.

	Time Required (hours)	
Job	Mill	Drill
216	4	7
327	8	10
462	10	3
519	5	6
258	9	12
617	2	7

a. Develop a minimum makespan schedule using Johnson's rule.

b. Construct a Gantt chart for the minimum makespan schedule.

15.5 34. Dan's Auto Detailing business performs two major activities: exterior cleanup, and interior detailing. Based on the size of car and condition, time estimates for six cars on Monday morning are as shown in the accompanying table.

	Car Number					
	1	2	3	4	5	6
Exterior	50	35	90	65	45	80
Interior	30	40	20	45	25	55

a. Sequence the cars so that *all exterior detailing is done first* and total completion time is minimized.

b. Draw a Gantt chart and evaluate the idle time.

15.7 35. The Naples Newspaper completes production of its daily edition by 5 a.m. A truck picks up pallets loaded with newspapers and delivers them to five neighbor sites, where carriers sort and fold the papers for individual routes. The mileage is shown in the following table. Currently, the truck picks up the number of pallets required by each customer at the factory, delivers them, and then returns to the factory to get the papers for the next customer (i.e., current route 0-1-0-2-0-3-0-4-0). The truck always returns to Scottsville and gets 10 miles per gallon using diesel fuel. A truck can carry up to 16 pallets. A gallon of diesel fuel is $3.00. The newspaper operates 365 days per year.

a. How many miles does the truck travel each day using the current route? What is the total number of miles traveled annually?

b. Use the Clarke-Wright Method to find a more efficient route.

c. How many miles, gallons, and dollars can be saved per year by adopting the current versus shorter route found by the Clarke-Wright Method?

d. How many pounds of gas are emitted into the atmosphere and saved per year using the shortest truck route versus the current truck route? Assume that one gallon of gas generates 15 pounds of carbon dioxide and other global-warming gases from the truck's tailpipe.

	Factory (0)	Scottsville (1)	Hudson (2)	Bonita (3)	Walker (4)	Pallets Demanded
Factory (0)	—	20	11	4	7	
Scottsville (1)		—	10	5	12	10
Hudson (2)			—	9	3	6
Bonita (3)				—	14	4
Walker (4)					—	8

EXCEL-BASED PROBLEMS

For these problems, you may use Excel Solver or the spreadsheet templates in MindTap to assist in your analysis.

36. For the scenario described in section 15.2c, suppose the number of employees needed for each hour are as shown in the following table.

Hour	Number of employees needed
7 a.m.	8
8 a.m.	10
9 a.m.	10
10 a.m.	7
11 a.m.	5
12 p.m.	4
1 p.m.	6
2 p.m.	6
3 p.m.	5
4 p.m.	8
5 p.m.	8
6 p.m.	12
7 p.m.	15
8 p.m.	10
9 p.m.	9
10 p.m.	7
11 p.m.	4

Develop and solve the optimization model on a spreadsheet and use Solver to find the number of employees to assign to the four work shifts to minimize the total number of employees.

15.2 37. The minimum number of part-time employees needed at a quick service restaurant for each two-hour block is shown in the following table.

Time Block	Minimum number required
1: 7-9 a.m.	12
2: 9-11 a.m.	6
3: 11-1 p.m.	15
4: 1-3 p.m.	10
5: 3-5 p.m.	5
6: 5-7 p.m.	13
7: 7-9 p.m.	9
8: 9-11 p.m.	6

Part time college students work four-hour shifts (e.g., 7–11 a.m., 9 a.m. to 1 p.m., and so on, starting at each two-hour block, with the last shift from 7 p.m. to 11 p.m.). Formulate an optimization model to determine how many employees are needed for each shift in order to minimize the total number of employees overall, implement it on a spreadsheet, and use Excel Solver to find an optimal solution.

38. David Chris is running the season's final basketball tournament for Youth Boosters. He is trying to schedule the referee crews for each game. The following table shows the number of times in the past that each crew has refereed a game for that team. David wants to assign crews to games that avoids placing crews with teams they have refereed before. Develop and solve an assignment model using Excel Solver to determine how referee crews

should be assigned to teams to minimize the sum of the number of times the crews have previously been paired with that team.

	Referee Crew Number					
Team	**1**	**2**	**3**	**4**	**5**	**6**
A	2	2	0	3	2	1
B	3	1	2	1	1	0
C	0	1	2	1	0	2
D	2	0	0	2	1	3
E	0	2	1	1	1	2
F	1	2	1	0	0	3

15.3 **39.** An earth moving machine had five jobs in the same area it must complete as soon as possible. Sequence the jobs using (a) FCFS order 1-2-3-4-5, and (b) the SPT rule. Use the *Sequencing* Excel template to compute performance measures for both sequences. What sequence is better?

Job	1	2	3	4	5
Processing time (hours)	10	8	16	25	20

15.3 **40.** Mike Reynolds has four assignments due in class tomorrow, and his class times are as follows.

Class	Time
Marketing 304	8 a.m.
OM 385	10 a.m.
Finance 216	1 p.m.
Psychology 200	3:30 p.m.

Each class lasts one hour, and Mike has no other classes. It is now midnight, and Mike estimates that the finance, OM, marketing, and psychology assignments will take him six, three, four, and two hours, respectively. Use the Excel *Sequencing* template to determine how he should schedule the work. Can he complete all of it on time?

15.3 **41.** Tony's Income Tax Service personnel can estimate the time required to complete customers' tax returns by using the following time standards assuming all information is available:

IRS Form	Standard Time (min.)
1040 short	10
1040 long	15
Schedule A	15
Schedule B	5
Schedule G	10
Schedule C	15
Schedule SE	5
Form 2106	10

One morning, five customers are waiting, needing the following forms filled out. They arrived in the order A-B-C-D-E.

Customer	Forms
A	1040 long, schedules A and B
B	1040 long, schedules A, B, SE, and 2106
C	1040 short
D	1040 long, schedules A, B, and G
E	1040 long, schedules A, B, C, and 2106

Use the Excel *Sequencing* template to answer the following questions:

a. If these customers are processed on a FCFS basis, what is the flow time for each and the average flowtime?

b. If SPT is used, how will these performance metrics differ?

15.3 **42.** Four blood samples have arrived in your laboratory with the following information:

Job	Processing Time (minutes)	Due Date
1	7	18
2	3	7
3	5	12
4	2	9

Use the Excel *Sequencing* template for the following:

a. Sequence the jobs using the SPT rule.

b. Sequence the jobs using the EDD rule.

c. Compare average flow time, average and maximum lateness, average and maximum tardiness, and makespan for these two sequencing rules and compare the results.

15.3 **43.** A bank's mortgage department must process the following six jobs to maximize client satisfaction. What sequencing rule should you use? For the rule you selected, find the best sequence using the Excel *Sequencing* template.

Mortgage	Processing Time (days)	Due Date
1	17	50
2	9	17
3	20	71
4	12	25
5	22	37
6	19	60

15.3 **44.** A manufacturing firm makes custom orthopedic parts for human knee, hip, and shoulder replacements. Because shipping the custom part(s) prior to the scheduled surgery date is essential, compare the SPT and EDD rules, and recommend the best sequencing rule for this situation. Use the Excel *Sequencing* template to evaluate each rule.

Customer	Processing Time (days)	Due Date
1	6	20
2	8	17
3	11	30
4	12	25

45. An insurance claims work area has five claims waiting for processing as follows:

Job	Processing Time	Due Date (D_j)
1	22	35
2	18	40
3	20	32
4	15	28
5	17	30

Use the Excel *Sequencing* template to find the average flowtime, average and maximum tardiness, and average lateness for the following sequences: SPT sequence, EDD sequence, and the sequence 2-1-5-3-4. What sequencing rule do you recommend and why?

46. Eight jobs have arrived in the following order:

Job	Processing Time	Due Date
1	7	21
2	3	7
3	5	8
4	2	5
5	6	17
6	9	16
7	14	38
8	4	12

Find and compare the performance measures for the following sequencing rules using the Excel *Sequencing* template:

a. Process in the order they have arrived
b. Shortest processing time
c. Earliest due date

47. In this chapter, we noted that the EDD rule minimizes the maximum job tardiness and maximum lateness, while the SPT rule minimizes the average flowtime. However, neither of these rules minimize the average lateness or average tardiness.
Use the Excel *Sequencing* template to answer the following using the data below:

a. Try to find a sequence that minimizes the average lateness.
b. Try to find a sequence that minimizes the average tardiness.
c. Can you generalize your logic into a rule or procedure that will accomplish these objectives most of the time?

Job	Processing Time	Due Date
1	7	21
2	3	7
3	5	8
4	2	5
5	6	17
6	9	16
7	14	38
8	4	12

48. An attorney's office operates with a single copier. At the beginning of a particular day the following jobs are waiting for processing. All jobs must be distributed to clients or in court by 9:00 a.m., and it is now 7:30 a.m.

Job	Job Content
1	500 regular size papers
	250 legal size papers
2	100 regular size papers
	400 legal size papers
3	1,000 regular size papers
4	1,500 legal size papers
5	1,200 regular size papers
	300 legal size papers

Regular size paper takes an average of 1.0 second per page to complete, while the legal-size paper takes 1.2 seconds per page. These times include allowances for stapling, bundling, move, and changeover time. The due date for each job is 90 minutes from now or 5,400 seconds. If processing is always by job, calculate the average flowtime, lateness, and tardiness for this group of jobs using FCFS (1-2-3-4-5) and SPT sequencing rules. Can all jobs be completed by 9:00 a.m.? Use the Excel *Sequencing* template to perform your analysis.

Luke's Balloon Shop

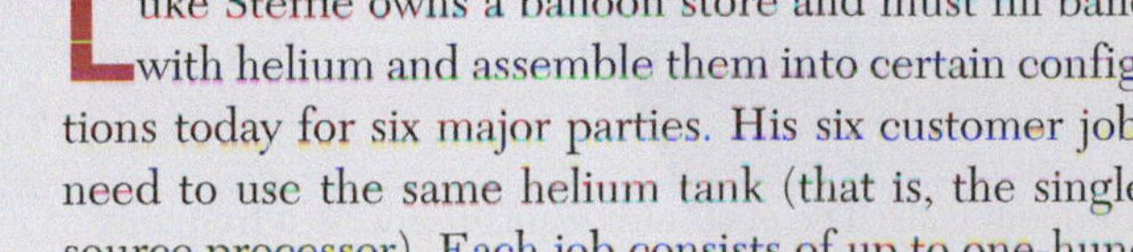

Luke Steffie owns a balloon store and must fill balloons with helium and assemble them into certain configurations today for six major parties. His six customer jobs all need to use the same helium tank (that is, the single-resource processor). Each job consists of up to one-hundred balloons. Luke is wondering the best way to sequence these jobs. Client (job) number five is his top customer. Luke's assistant store manager, Cindy Cheshire, wants to process them in sequential order (i.e., 1, 2, 3, 4, 5, and 6). Because the balloons lose air quickly, the company waits until the day of the parties to fill them. The workload is hectic. Business is booming and growing about 15 percent per year in their store location. The job processing time estimates are as follows:

Job	1	2	3	4	5	6
Processing time (min.)	240	130	210	90	170	165
Due dates (6 a.m. to midnight in minutes from opening)	240	360	480	240	720	780

Case Questions for Discussion:

1. Compute the average flow time, lateness, and tardiness for this group of jobs using Ms. Cheshire's sequential order of 1 (first), 2, 3, 4, 5, and 6 (last).
2. In what order would the jobs be processed using the SPT rule? Compute the average flow time, lateness, and tardiness for this group of jobs.
3. Compare the answers in Questions 1 and 2.
4. What are your short-term recommendations for this set of six jobs? Explain your reasoning.
5. What are your long-term recommendations with respect to sequencing jobs at Luke's store? Explain your reasoning.

Midwest Frequent Flyer Call Center

"I'm an accounting major, not an operations expert," yelled just-promoted Bob Barthrow, the executive vice president of the Midwest Frequent Flyer Call Center, during a senior-level management meeting. "Bob, Horizon Airlines (HA) is going to stop doing business with us if we don't provide better call center service. We need to maximize service and minimize costs! So, find a solution to HA's service problems or we are all out of a job," stated Adam Bishop, the CEO of Midwest Call Center Services (MCCS).

ESB Professional/Shutterstock.com

Bob retreated to his office and closed the door. As he sat in his chair, he thought about the many meetings he had participated in where managers promised great customer service but could not deliver it. Upon further reflection, he came to the conclusion that to promise great customer service you first must know how to analyze resource capacity and develop good schedules. He pulled out his old college operations management textbook and began reading. He also did a Google search on the topic and found several articles to read. He planned on building an electronic spreadsheet analysis of the situation.

Small and mid-sized airlines outsourced a variety of peripheral services to MCCS, such as billing and credit card management, baggage and customer flight claims management, reservations, loyalty programs, and call center management. HA accounted for 9 percent of MCCS revenues. HA customers had no idea the HA frequent flyer program was outsourced to MCCS. MCCS managed separate call centers for several airlines, each with its own dedicated staff and office space. MCCS customer service representatives (CSRs) who worked in the HA call center were trained by both MCCS and individual airlines such as HA. MCCS provided all CSRs with service management training and mentors, and CSR performance was electronically monitored. HA trained the CSRs by including airline tours and free flights so the CSRs would know the airline and its culture, and especially its frequent flyer program. HA CSRs were trained to handle 20 service upsets most likely to be described by incoming customer calls.

HA and GCCS categorized incoming calls into four categories as follows:

1. Redeem calls: The customer wants to redeem frequent flyer points for future airline flights.

2. Problem resolution: The customer wants to correct point debits and credits, flights, personal information, and so on.
3. Manage accounts: The customer wants to split, combine, transfer, delete, rename, and/or update the frequent flyer account(s).
4. Travel advice: The customer asks for travel advice. MCCS and HA provide "limited travel consulting service and advice." MCCS CSRs are trained to be nice yet tell the customer they do not provide full travel service, and refer customers to other travel agencies.

Average standard times for HA's call mix is shown in Exhibit 15.15. Bob wanted to get a standard service rate in the same units of measure used for other airlines, and that was calls per CSR per 30 minutes. Average HA-MCCS call center demand rounded to the nearest integer for the last 10 Mondays is shown in Exhibit 15.16. Bob thought a planned (target)

EXHIBIT 15.15 Midwest Frequent Flyer Call Mix

Type of HA Call	Standard Time Per Call (Seconds)	Percentage of Total Call (%)
Redeem	115	61%
Problem Resolution	175	25%
Manage Accounts	240	8%
Travel Advice	180	6%

EXHIBIT 15.16 Midwest Frequent Flyer Call Center Demand Data (These data are available in the Excel worksheet *MCCS Case Data* in MindTap.)

Time Period	Number of Calls Taken	Number of Abandon Calls by Customer*	Number of Busy Signal Calls Not Taken+	Total Calls
6:30	15	0	0	15
7:00	16	0	0	16
7:30	45	4	0	49
8:00	60	5	0	65
8:30	62	6	2	70
9:00	71	4	1	76
9:30	77	5	0	82
10:00	84	11	4	99
10:30	75	8	3	86
11:00	81	4	3	88
11:30	69	6	1	76
12:00	79	2	0	81
12:30	66	3	2	71
1:00	80	4	3	87
1:30	76	8	6	90
2:00	92	6	7	105
2:30	85	7	5	97
3:00	73	4	3	80
3:30	78	2	3	83
4:00	67	4	4	75
4:30	62	2	0	64
5:00	54	1	0	55
5:30	51	1	1	53
6:00	37	0	0	37
6:30	48	3	2	53
7:00	42	0	0	42
7:30	32	0	0	32
8:00	26	2	0	28
8:30	22	1	0	23
9:00	19	0	0	19
Totals	1,744	103	50	1,897
Average	58.1	3.4	1.7	63.2
Std Deviation	22.9	2.8	2.0	26.6
Minimum	15	0	0	15
Maximum	92	11	7	105

*An abandon call means the customer gets into the MCCS call center system but then hangs up for some undetermined reason. A customer who gets a busy signal because all incoming trunk phone lines are busy cannot get into the MCCS system and therefore hangs up.

EXHIBIT 15.17 Midwest Current CSR Staff Schedule (This is available in the Excel worksheet *MCCS Current Staff Schedule* in MindTap.)

Exhibit 13.23 HA-GCCS CSR Staff Schedule.xlsx - Microsoft Excel

	A	B	C	D	E	F	G	H	I	J	K	L	M	N	O	P	Q
1																	
2	Service Rep	6:30	7:00	7:30	8:00	8:30	9:00	9:30	10:00	10:30	11:00	11:30	12:00	12:30 PM	1:00	1:30	2:00
3	1	X--------	----------	----------	----------	----------	(----)------	----------	----------	(Lunch)	(Lunch)	----------	----------	----------	-----(----)	----------	----------
4	2	X--------	----------	----------	----------	----------	-----(----)	----------	----------	----------	(Lunch)	(Lunch)	----------	----------	----------	(----)------	----------
5	3			X--------	----------	----------	----------	(----)------	----------	----------	----------	(Lunch)	(Lunch)	----------	----------	(----)------	----------
6	4				X--------	----------	----------	-----(----)	----------	----------	----------	----------	(Lunch)	(Lunch)	----------	-----(----)	--------
7	5				X--------	----------	----------	----------	----------	----------	----------	(----)------	----------	(Lunch)	(Lunch)	----------	(----)------
8	6						X--------	----------	----------	----------	----------	-----(----)	----------	(Lunch)	(Lunch)	----------	-----(----)
9	7									X--------	----------	----------	(----)------	----------	(Lunch)	(Lunch)	----------
10	8									X--------	----------	----------	-----(----)	----------	----------	(Lunch)	(Lunch)
11	9										X--------	----------	----------	----------	(----)------	(Lunch)	(Lunch)
12	10																
13	11																
14	12																
15	13																
16	Avail CSR (Min)	60	60	90	150	150	150	150	180	210	210	180	180	180	150	135	180
17	Current # CSRs	2	2	3	5	5	5	5	6	7	7	6	6	6	5	4.5	6
18	Target # CSRs																
19	Short/Excess (-/+)																
20																	
21	Service Rep	2:30	3:00	3:30	4:00	4:30	5:00	5:30	6:00	6:30	7:00	7:30	8:00	8:30	9:00	Totals	
22	1																
23	2																
24	3	----------	----------														
25	4	----------	----------	----------													
26	5	----------	----------	----------													
27	6	----------	----------	----------	----------	----------											
28	7	-----(----)	----------	----------	----------	----------	----------	----------	----------								
29	8	----------	----------	----------	----------	(----)------	----------	----------	----------	----------							
30	9	----------	----------	----------	----------	-----(----)	----------	----------	----------	----------							
31	10	X--------	----------	----------	----------	----------	(Dinner)	(Dinner)	----------	----------	----------	(----)------	----------	----------	----------		
32	11	X--------	----------	----------	(----)------	----------	(Dinner)	(Dinner)	----------	----------	----------	-----(----)	----------	----------	----------		
33	12	X--------	----------	----------	-----(----)	----------	----------	----------	(Dinner)	(Dinner)	----------	----------	----------	----------	----------		
34	13	X--------	----------	----------	----------	----------	(----)------	----------	(Dinner)	(Dinner)	----------	----------	----------	----------	----------		
35	Avail CSR (Min)	315	330	300	210	210	135	150	150	120	120	90	120	120	120	#REF!	
36	Current # CSRs	10.5	11	10	7	7	4.5	5	5	4	4	3	4	4	4	#REF!	
37	Target # CSRs																
38	Short/Excess (-/+)																
39																	

Sheet1 Sheet2 Sheet3

Ready 100%

CSR labor utilization of 90 percent provided adequate safety capacity. The current HA-MCCS CSR staff schedule is shown in Exhibit 15.17. Full-time employee (FTE) policies require at least a 7-hour workday plus 1 hour for lunch or dinner and at least one 15-minute break per workday. Any workday less than FTE is considered part-time employment (PTE).

He planned to use a four-step analysis approach, with Step 1 being demand analysis. Exhibit 15.16 provided these data. Step 2 was to compute and explain the logic of setting a standard service time in calls/CSR/30 minutes. Step 3 involved analyzing resource (i.e., staff) capacity using the following equation:

$$\text{Utilization} = \frac{\text{Demand rate}}{\text{Service rate} \times \text{Number of servers}}$$

(Hint: This equation was introduced in Chapter 11.) Step 4 required a revised detailed staff schedule to meet demand to be developed given the target number of CSRs per time period for a given service rate, and an assumption for the target labor utilization. He planned to explain and justify all of his logic and assumptions in a written report to be presented to other managers and his direct reports.

Bob also found a year-old study on the cost of poor service for another airline serviced by MCCS, which found the cost of an abandon (customer hangs up for undetermined reason) or busy signal call to be estimated at \$21. This was his best estimate of the cost per call for poor customer service.

Bob knows his accounting principles, but if he is to be promoted, he must also demonstrate to management that he can analyze a process and successfully manage it. Use the following case questions to help Bob prepare a report.

Case Questions for Discussion:

1. Analyze the case data and *current* schedule, and answer the following "baseline" questions. What's labor utilization for each 30-minute period given the current staffing plan? Is the main problem lack of staff capacity or poor scheduling, or both? Can you support your answer with numerical analysis?
2. What is the cost of abandoned and busy signal calls for a typical Monday? Annually? (Make and state assumptions as needed.)
3. Develop a better CSR staff schedule (see Excel current staff schedule in Exhibit 15.17) if needed, and decide whether the company should hire more CSRs or lay off a few. Will you use part-time employees? If so, explain why and justify your reasoning.
4. What are your final recommendations?

Integrative Case: Hudson Jewelers

The Hudson Jewelers case study may be found in MindTap, and integrates material found in each chapter of this book.

Case Questions for Discussion:

1. Develop a staff schedule between the hours of 9 a.m. and 8 p.m. for week 8, which had 587 visits (see the worksheet *Hudson Jeweler Demand Case Data* in MindTap). Assume the maximum service rate is ten customers per hour per store employee. You will have to allocate the demand over the day and time periods. You may use the Excel worksheet *Hudson Jeweler Staffing Schedule Worksheet* that is available in MindTap or create your own.
2. What are the advantages and disadvantages of your store-staffing schedule?
3. Would you hire non-family employees to staff this single store? Explain your reasoning.

16 | Quality Management

LEARNING OBJECTIVES

After studying this chapter, you should be able to:

- **16-1** Explain the concepts and definitions of quality.
- **16-2** Describe the quality philosophies and principles of Deming, Juran, and Crosby.
- **16-3** Explain the GAP model and its importance.
- **16-4** Describe the concepts and philosophy of ISO 9000.
- **16-5** Describe the philosophy and methods of Six Sigma.
- **16-6** Explain the categories of cost-of-quality measurement.
- **16-7** Describe how to apply the Seven QC Tools.
- **16-8** Explain the concepts of kaizen and breakthrough improvement.

In 2014, GM shop forepersons performed thousands of service recalls to install kits consisting of ignition switches, ignition cylinders, and key sets for older-model, small cars subject to a safety recall.

Bloomberg/Getty Images

In February 2014, General Motors (GM) issued a sweeping recall of millions of vehicles suspected of having a faulty switch that automatically turns the engine off and prevents air bags from deploying—while the car is in motion. At least 100 people died, and others were hospitalized. The defect was first detected in 2001 and surfaced again in 2004; GM rejected a proposal to fix the problem because it would be too costly and take too long, and an engineer advised the company to redesign its key head, but this was also rejected. GM admitted that its employees were wrong to delay issuing a recall for about a decade after problems with the ignition switch were first discovered. The company's CEO termed the delay a "fundamental failure" after a probe found "a pattern of incompetence and neglect" throughout the company. Ultimately, the total cost of recalls exceeded $4 billion.[1]

The economic welfare and survival of businesses and nations depends on the quality of the goods and services they produce, which in turn depends fundamentally on the quality of the workforce and management practices that define their organization. High quality of goods and services provides an organization with a competitive edge; reduces costs due to returns, rework, scrap, and service upsets; increases productivity, profits, and other measures of success; and, most important,

WHAT DO YOU THINK?

What quality issues have you personally encountered or heard about in the news lately?

generates satisfied customers who reward the organization with continued patronage and favorable word-of-mouth advertising. And, as the introduction illustrates, high quality is vital to safety in all goods and services, and organizations bear the responsibility to ensure the quality of their products and take appropriate steps when poor quality is discovered. High quality is required in nearly every product to name a few, banking, medical care, toys, cell phones, and automobiles.

Quality must be addressed throughout the value chain, beginning with suppliers and extending through operations and postsale services.

Today, the high quality of goods and services is simply expected by consumers and business customers. Quality must be addressed throughout the value chain, beginning with suppliers and extending through operations and postsale services. **Quality management** *refers to systematic policies, methods, and procedures used to ensure that goods and services are produced with appropriate levels of quality to meet the needs of customers.* From the perspective of operations, quality management deals with key issues relating to how goods and services are designed, created, and delivered to meet customer expectations. The Malcolm Baldrige Award Criteria described in Chapter 2 provide a comprehensive framework for building quality into organizational processes and practices.

16-1 Understanding Quality

Why is there so much emphasis on quality today? It helps review a bit of history. During the Industrial Revolution, the use of interchangeable parts and the separation of work into small tasks necessitated careful control of quality, leading to the dependence on inspection to identify and remove defects and reducing the role of the workers themselves in responsibility for quality. After World War II, two U.S. consultants, Dr. Joseph Juran and Dr. W. Edwards Deming, introduced statistical quality control techniques to the Japanese to aid them in their rebuilding efforts. While presenting to a group of Japanese industrialists (collectively representing about 80 percent of the nation's capital) in 1950, Deming emphasized the importance of consumers and suppliers, the interdependency of organizational processes, the usefulness of consumer research, and the necessity of continuous improvement of all elements of the production system.

Improvements in Japanese quality were slow and steady; some 20 years passed before the quality of Japanese products exceeded that of Western manufacturers. By the 1970s, primarily due to the higher quality levels of their products, Japanese companies had made significant penetration into Western markets. Most major U.S. companies answered the wake-up call by instituting extensive quality improvement campaigns, focused not only on conformance but also on improving design quality.

An interest in quality emerged in corporate boardrooms under the concept of *Six Sigma*, a customer-focused and results-oriented approach to business improvement. Six Sigma integrates many quality tools and techniques that have been tested and validated over the years with a bottom-line orientation that has high appeal to senior managers.

Motorola: Creating Quality Through Design and Manufacturing

Motorola places considerable emphasis on improving manufacturing quality by reducing defects through its product and process design activities. Motorola sets an ambitious goal of six sigma quality—a level of quality representing no more than 3.4 defects per million opportunities—for every process in the company. To reach this goal, Motorola knows that before it manufactures a product, it must first determine the product characteristics that will satisfy customers (marketing's role); decide whether these characteristics can be achieved through the product's design, the manufacturing process, or the materials used; develop design tolerances that will assure successful product performance; conduct measurements to determine process variations from existing specifications; and then hone the product design, manufacturing process, or both, in order to achieve the desired results.

What does quality mean? Many organizations use a simple definition: **Quality** *is meeting or exceeding customers' expectations.* Customers may be consumers, other businesses, or even the person to whom you report on the job. Providing goods and services that satisfy customers and meet their needs is essential for business sustainability.

From an operations perspective, however, the most useful definition of quality is how well the output of a manufacturing or service process conforms to the design specifications. **Quality of conformance** *is the extent to which a process is able to deliver output that conforms to the design specifications.* **Specifications** *are targets and tolerances determined by designers of goods and services.* Targets are the ideal values for which production is to strive; tolerances are the permissible variation. Specifications for physical goods are normally measured using some physical property such as length, weight, temperature, or pressure. For example, the specification for the diameter of a drilled hole might be 0.50 ± 0.02 cm. The target is 0.50 cm, and the tolerance is $\pm$ 0.02 cm; that is, the size of the hole is permitted to vary between 0.48 and 0.52 cm. This perspective of quality provides a clear way of measuring quality, thus providing managers and workers with the ability to make fact-based decisions.

Excellent service quality is achieved by the consistent delivery to the customer of a clearly defined customer benefit package, and associated process and service encounters, defined by many internal and external standards of performance. Performance standards are analogous to manufacturing specifications. For example, "on-time arrival" for an airplane might be specified as within 15 minutes of the scheduled arrival time. The target is the scheduled time, and the tolerance is specified to be 15 minutes. **Service quality** *is consistently meeting or exceeding customer expectations (external focus) and service-delivery system performance criteria (internal focus) during all service encounters.*

An established instrument for measuring customer perceptions of service quality is SERVQUAL.[2] The initial instrument identified 10 dimensions of service quality performance: (1) reliability, (2) responsiveness, (3) competence, (4) access, (5) courtesy, (6) communication, (7) credibility, (8) security, (9) understanding/knowing the customer, and (10) tangibles. These were reduced to five dimensions based on further research: *tangibles, reliability, responsiveness, assurance,* and *empathy*. Tangibles are what the customer sees, such as physical facilities, equipment, and the appearance of service employees. Reliability is the ability to provide what was promised, dependably and accurately. Responsiveness is the willingness to help customers

What Do Quality Managers Do?

A typical job ad often lists skills and competencies that a good quality manager should possess. Some key skills include:

- Work with other company managers toward meeting the goals and strategy of the organization.
- Design and implement quality control tools to ensure that all specifications are met.
- Find the root causes of product and process failures and develop corrective actions.
- Ensure that everyone in the company is aware of customer requirements.
- Maintaining the proper functioning of receiving, in-process and final inspection activities.
- Ensure that suppliers' performance is maintained for purchased materials, components, and services.
- Interface successfully with production, design engineering, manufacturing, supply chain, and sales functions.

ESB Professional/Shutterstock.com

- Help conduct experiments to improve product or process quality.

Quality managers must also possess strong interpersonal, communication, computer, leadership, problem-solving, negotiation, and decision-making skills; and be proficient in statistics and other technical areas such as blueprint reading. Doing all this requires excellent time management skills.

and provide prompt service. Assurance is the knowledge and courtesy of service providers and their ability to convey trust and confidence. Finally, empathy is caring, individual attention the firm provides its customers. These five dimensions of service quality are normally measured using a survey instrument with ordinal scales such as yes or no or a 5- or 7-point Likert scale. A typical 5-point Likert scale is 1 = Strongly disagree; 2 = Disagree; 3 = Neither agree nor disagree; 4 = Agree, 5 = Strongly agree. SERVQUAL is designed to apply to all service industries; however, dimensions specific to a certain industry or business or process may provide more accurate measures.

Quality is more than simply ensuring that goods and services consistently conform to specifications (see the box "What Do Quality Managers Do?"). Achieving high-quality goods and services depends on the commitment and involvement of everyone in the entire value chain. The principles of total quality are simple:

1. A focus on customers and stakeholders.
2. A process focus supported by continuous improvement and learning.
3. Participation and teamwork by everyone in the organization.

There is considerable evidence that investment in quality—not only in goods, services, and processes but in the quality of management itself—yields numerous benefits. Specific operational and financial results that Baldrige recipients have achieved include the following:

- Nestlé Purina PetCare Co. (NPPC) manufactures, markets, and distributes pet food and snacks for dogs and cats, as well as cat litter. NPPC ranks first in market share for pet-care products in North America, has twice the market share of its closest competitor, and has grown its market share by almost 10 percent over 10 years in a mature industry. It is also recognized as best in the industry for its outstanding safety performance.

- K&N Management is the licensed Austin, Texas–area developer for Rudy's "Country Store" & Bar-B-Q and the creator of Mighty Fine Burgers, Fries & Shakes, two fast-casual restaurant concepts. Guests rate their satisfaction with food quality, hospitality, cleanliness, and speed of service; overall customer satisfaction outperforms the best competitor. In 2010, the firm was named "the best place to work in Austin."
- Advocate Good Samaritan Hospital is an acute-care medical facility in Downers Grove, Illinois. Overall patient satisfaction levels for outpatient, emergency, ambulatory surgery, and convenient care exceed the top 10 percent nationally. Good Samaritan Hospital used Six Sigma methodology to pioneer improvement of "door-to-balloon" time, the critical period for assessing and diagnosing a heart attack and delivering the needed intervention, lowering the measure to 52 minutes, among the best in Illinois.

16-2 Influential Leaders in Modern Quality Management

Many individuals have made substantial contributions to quality management thought and applications. However, three people—W. Edwards Deming, Joseph M. Juran, and Philip B. Crosby—are regarded as "management gurus" in the quality revolution.

16-2a W. Edwards Deming

No individual has had more influence on quality management than Dr. W. Edwards Deming (1900–1993). Unlike other management gurus and consultants, Deming (pictured below) never defined or described quality precisely. In his last book, he stated, "A product or a service possesses quality if it helps somebody and enjoys a good and sustainable market."[3] The Deming philosophy focuses on bringing about improvements in product and service quality by reducing variability in goods and services design and associated processes. Deming professed that higher quality leads to higher productivity and lower costs, which in turn leads to improved market share and long-term competitive strength. In his early work in the United States, Deming preached his 14 Points, which provide guidance for building quality within organizations. These include the responsibility of top management to create a vision and commit to quality, continual improvement of products and processes, the importance of training and teams, and the creation of an environment that drives out fear and fosters pride in work. At that time (in the 1960s and 1970s), they represented a radical departure from management thinking and practice but still provide useful guidance today (see the box on Hillerich & Bradsby).

AP images/Richard Drew
W. Edwards Deming

Deming also advocated a process to guide and motivate improvement activities, which has become known as the *Deming cycle*. The Deming cycle is composed of four stages: *plan*, *do*, *study*, and *act* (PDSA). PDSA guides teams to develop an improvement plan, try it out, examine the results, and institute changes that lead to improved results—then repeat the process all over again.

16-2b Joseph Juran

Like Deming, Juran taught quality principles to the Japanese in the 1950s and was a principal force in their quality reorganization. Juran proposed a simple definition of quality: "fitness for use." Unlike Deming, however, Juran did not propose a major

Hillerich & Bradsby

Hillerich & Bradsby Co. (H&B) has been making the Louisville Slugger brand of baseball bat for more than 115 years. When the company faced significant challenges from market changes and competition, CEO Jack Hillerich decided to apply the philosophy of Deming's 14 Points to change the company. Managers and union officials talked about building trust and changing the system "to make it something you want to work in."

One of the first changes was the elimination of work quotas that were tied to hourly salaries, and a schedule of warnings and penalties for failures to meet quotas. Instead, a team-based approach was initiated. Although a few workers exploited the change, overall productivity actually improved as rework decreased because workers were taking pride in their work and producing things the right way the first time. H&B also eliminated performance appraisals and commission-based pay in sales. The company has also focused its efforts on training and education, resulting in an openness to change and a capacity for teamwork. Today, the Deming philosophy is still the core of H&B's guiding principles.[4]

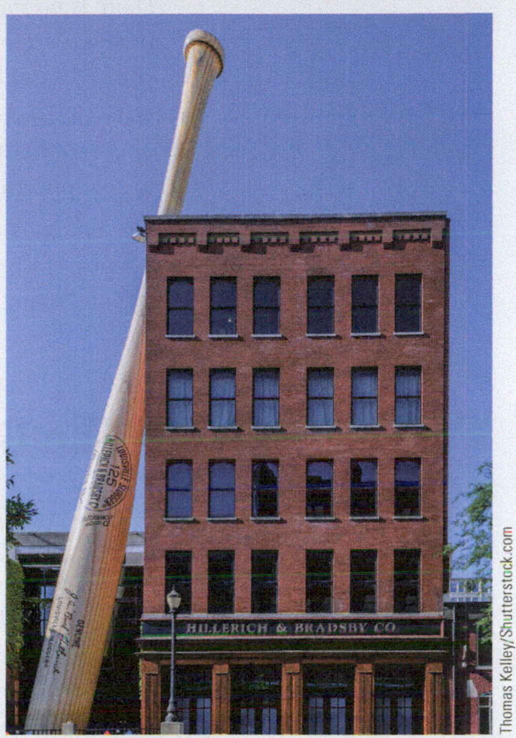

Thomas Kelley/Shutterstock.com

cultural change in the organization, but rather sought to improve quality by working within the system familiar to managers—plan, control, and improve. He argued that employees at different levels of an organization speak in their own "languages." Juran stated that top management speaks in the language of dollars; workers speak in the language of things; and middle management must be able to speak both languages and translate between dollars and things. To get the attention of top managers, quality issues must be cast in the language they understand—dollars. Hence, Juran advocated the use of quality cost measurement, discussed later in this chapter, to focus attention on quality problems. At the operational level, Juran focused on increasing conformance to specifications through elimination of defects, supported extensively by statistical tools for analysis. Thus, his philosophy fit well into existing management systems.

16-2c Philip B. Crosby

Philip B. Crosby authored several popular books. His first book, *Quality Is Free*, published in 1979, sold about 1 million copies and was greatly responsible for bringing quality to the attention of top corporate managers in the United States. The essence of Crosby's quality philosophy is embodied in what he calls the Absolutes of Quality Management and the Basic Elements of Improvement. A few key points of Crosby's Absolutes of Quality Management are as follows:

- *Quality means conformance to requirements, not elegance.* Requirements must be clearly stated so that they cannot be misunderstood.

- *There is no such thing as a quality problem.* Problems are functional in nature. Thus, a firm may experience accounting problems, manufacturing problems, design problems, front-desk problems, and so on.
- *There is no such thing as the economics of quality; doing the job right the first time is always cheaper.* Quality is free. What costs money are all actions that involve not doing jobs right the first time.
- *The only performance measurement is the cost of quality, which is the expense of nonconformance.* Quality cost data are useful to call problems to management's attention, to select opportunities for corrective action, and to track quality improvement over time.
- *The only performance standard is "Zero Defects"* (ZD). This simply represents the philosophy of preventing defects in goods and services rather than finding them after the fact and fixing them.

16-3 The Gap Model

Many people view quality by comparing features and characteristics of goods and services to a set of expectations, which may be promulgated by marketing efforts aimed at developing quality as an image variable in their minds. A framework for evaluating the quality of both goods and services, and identifying where to focus design and improvement efforts, is the GAP model.

The GAP model recognizes that there are several ways to mismanage the creation and delivery of high levels of quality. These "gaps" are shown in the model in Exhibit 16.1 and explained in the following list:

- ***Gap 1** is the discrepancy between customer expectations and management perceptions of those expectations.* Managers may think they understand why customers buy a good or service, but if their perception is wrong, then all subsequent design and delivery activities may be misdirected. Some organizations, for example, require senior managers to work in frontline jobs a few days every year so they keep in contact with customers and frontline employees.
- ***Gap 2** is the discrepancy between management perceptions of what features constitute a target level of quality and the task of translating these perceptions into executable specifications.* This represents a mismatch between management perceptions of what constitutes good performance and the actual job and process design specifications that we discussed in Chapter 5.
- ***Gap 3** is the discrepancy between quality specifications documented in operating and training manuals and plans and their implementation.* Gap 3 recognizes that the manufacturing and service delivery systems must execute quality specifications well. One way to improve day-to-day execution, for example, is by doing a better job at service management training.
- ***Gap 4** is the discrepancy between actual manufacturing and service-delivery system performance and external communications to the customers.* The customer should not be promised a certain type and level of quality unless the delivery system can achieve or exceed that level. Advertising, for example, can help establish customer expectations, and internal training and marketing materials can help set employee performance standards.
- ***Gap 5** is the difference between the customer's expectations and perceptions.* Gap 5 is where the customer judges quality and makes future purchase decisions. The fifth gap depends on the other four gaps. The theory of the GAP model is that if gaps 1 to 4 are minimized, higher customer satisfaction will result.

EXHIBIT 16.1 GAP Model of Quality

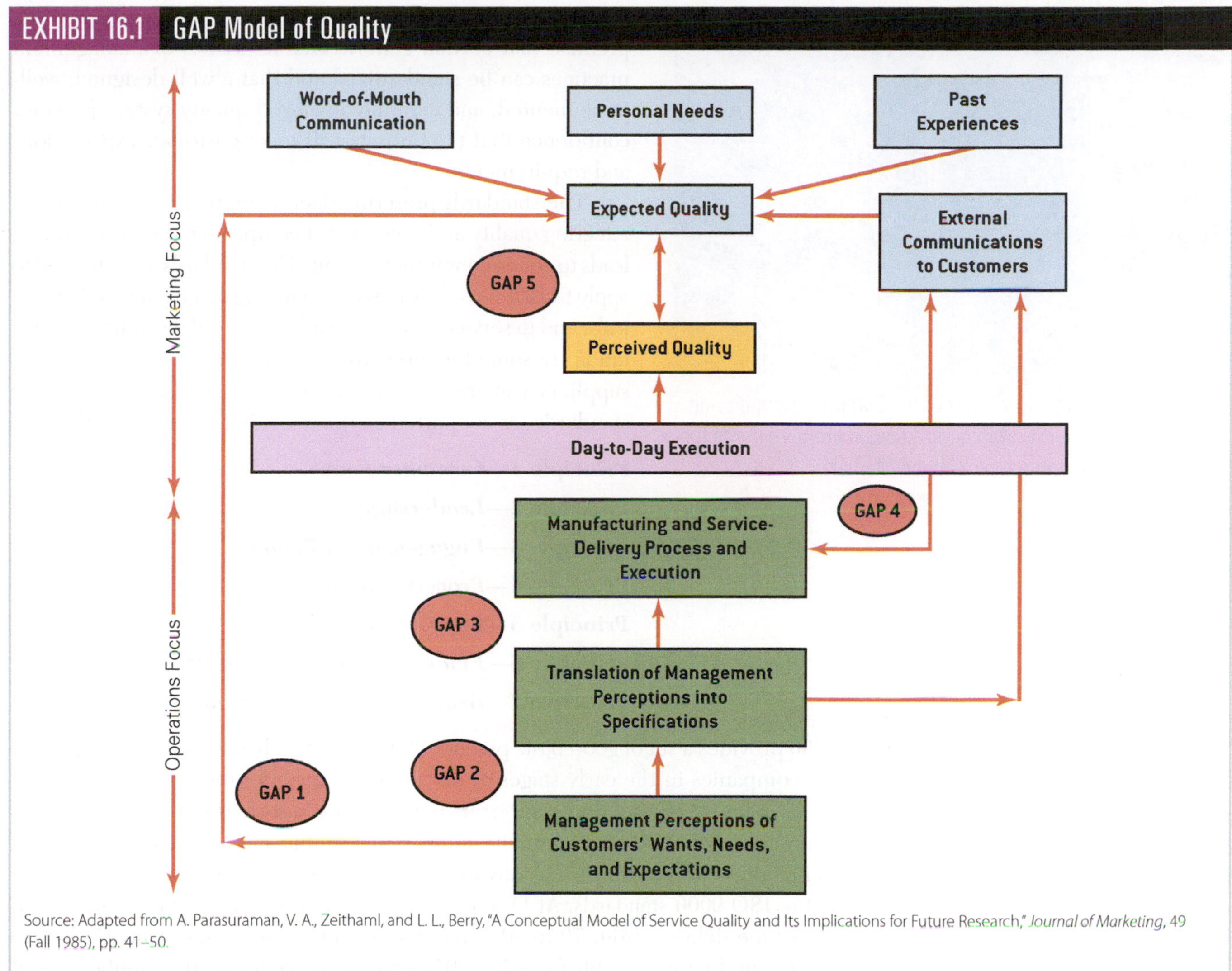

Source: Adapted from A. Parasuraman, V. A., Zeithaml, and L. L., Berry, "A Conceptual Model of Service Quality and Its Implications for Future Research," *Journal of Marketing*, 49 (Fall 1985), pp. 41–50.

Managers can use this model to analyze goods and services, and the processes that make and deliver them, to identify and close the largest gaps and improve performance. Failure to understand and minimize these gaps can seriously degrade the quality of a service and presents the risk of losing customer loyalty.[5]

16-4 ISO 9000

To standardize quality requirements for European countries within the Common Market and those wishing to do business with those countries, a specialized agency for standardization, the International Organization for Standardization (called ISO), founded in 1946 and composed of representatives from the national standards bodies of 91 nations, adopted a series of written quality standards in 1987 called the ISO 9000 family of standards. ISO took a unique approach in adopting the "ISO" prefix in naming the standards. ISO is a scientific term for equal (as in isotherm lines on a weather map, which show equal temperatures).Thus, the intent was to ensure that organizations certified under the ISO 9000 standards have quality equal to their peers. The standards were revised in 1994, and again (significantly) in 2000; another revision was released in 2015. The standards have been adopted in the United States by the American National Standards Institute (ANSI) with the endorsement and cooperation of the American Society for Quality (ASQ) and are recognized by about 100 countries.

Ugis Riba/Shutterstock.com

European Union flags fly in front of the European Commission in Brussels. In 1987, ISO standardized quality requirements for European nations within the Common Market.

ISO 9000 defines *quality system standards*, based on the premise that certain generic characteristics of management practices can be standardized and that a well-designed, well-implemented, and carefully managed quality system provides confidence that the outputs will meet customer expectations and requirements.

The standards prescribe documentation for all processes affecting quality and suggest that compliance through auditing leads to continuous improvement. The standards are intended to apply to all types of businesses, including electronics and chemicals, and to services such as health care, banking, and transportation. In some foreign markets, companies will not buy from suppliers who are not certified to the standards. The ISO 9000 standards are supported by the following seven principles:

Principle 1—*Customer Focus*

Principle 2—*Leadership*

Principle 3—*Engagement of People*

Principle 4—*Process Approach*

Principle 5—*Improvement*

Principle 6—*Evidence-based Decision Making*

Principle 7—*Relationship Management*

ISO 9000 provides a set of good basic practices for initiating a basic quality management system. For companies in the early stages of developing a quality program, the standards enforce the discipline of control that is necessary before they can seriously pursue continuous improvement. The requirements of periodic audits reinforce the stated quality system until it becomes ingrained in the company. Many organizations have realized significant benefits from using the ISO 9000 standards. At DuPont, for example, they have been credited with increasing on-time delivery from 70 to 90 percent, decreasing cycle time from 15 days to 1.5 days, increasing first-pass yields from 72 to 92 percent, and reducing the number of test procedures by one-third. Current information about ISO 9000 can be obtained from the ISO website (http://www.iso.org).

16-5 Six Sigma

Six Sigma *is a business improvement approach that seeks to find and eliminate causes of defects and errors in manufacturing and service processes by focusing on outputs that are critical to customers, resulting in a clear financial return for the organization.* The term "six sigma" is based on a statistical measure that equates to at most 3.4 errors or defects per million opportunities (we use *Six Sigma* to describe the approach, and *six sigma* for the statistical measure). An ultimate "stretch" goal of all organizations that adopt a Six Sigma philosophy is to have all critical processes, regardless of functional area, at a six-sigma level of capability—a level of near-zero defects. Robert Galvin, former Motorola CEO, stated back in 1987: "There is only one ultimate goal: zero defects—in everything we do." Six Sigma has garnered a significant amount of credibility over the last decade because of its acceptance at such major firms as Motorola, Allied Signal (now part of Honeywell), Texas Instruments, and General Electric (GE). It is facilitated through use of basic and advanced quality improvement and control tools by individuals and teams whose members are trained to provide fact-based decision-making information.

In Six Sigma terminology, *a* **defect** *is any mistake or error that is passed on to the customer. A* **unit of work** *is the output of a process or an individual process step.* We can measure output quality by defects per unit (DPU)

$$\text{Defects per unit} = \frac{\text{Number of defects discovered}}{\text{Number of units produced}} \quad [16.1]$$

Solved Problem 16.1 provides an example.

The Six Sigma concept characterizes quality performance by *defects per million opportunities (dpmo)*, computed as

$$\text{dpmo} = (\text{Number of defects discovered/opportunities for error}) \times 1{,}000{,}000 \quad [16.2]$$

(In service applications, we often use the term *errors per million opportunities—epmo*—instead of dpmo.)

A six-sigma quality level corresponds to a dpmo equal to 3.4 (this is derived from some advanced statistical calculations), which represents almost perfect quality.) Solved Problem 16.2 shows an example of calculating dpmo.

The use of dpmo allows us to define quality broadly. In the airline case, we might expand the concept to mean every opportunity for a failure to meet customer expectations from initial ticketing until bags are retrieved.

We noted that a six-sigma process has a dpmo of 3.4. We can translate any value of dpmo into a "sigma level" by using the Excel formulas below on a spreadsheet. Solved Problem 16.3 illustrates an example.

$$= \text{NORM.S.INV}(1 - \text{Number of Defects/Number of Opportunities}) + 1.5 \quad [16.3]$$

or equivalently,

$$= \text{NORM.S.INV}(1 - \text{dpmo}/1{,}000{,}000) + 1.5 \quad [16.4]$$

SOLVED PROBLEM 16.1: COMPUTING DPU

Suppose that a bank tracks the number of errors reported in customers' checking account statements. It discovered 12 errors in 1,000 statements. What is DPU?

Solution:

Using Formula [16.1],

DPU = 12/1000 = 0.012.

SOLVED PROBLEM 16.2: COMPUTING DPMO

An airline wishes to measure the effectiveness of its baggage handling system. It might measure nonconformances per unit by calculating the number of lost bags per customer. However, passengers may have different numbers of bags; thus, the number of opportunities for error differs with each passenger. Suppose that the average number of bags per passenger is 1.6, and the airline recorded three lost bags for 8000 passengers in one month. Compute the number of defects (errors) per million opportunities.

Solution:

The number of opportunities for a defect per passenger is 1.6; thus, the total number of opportunities for a defect is 8,000 x 1.6. Using Equation 16.2 we have

dpmo = 3/[(8,000)(1.6)] x 1,000,000 = 234.375

SOLVED PROBLEM 16.3: CALCULATING A SIGMA LEVEL

The dpmo for fulfilling customer orders is determined to be 35,256. What is the sigma level for this process?

Solution:

Using Excel formula 16.4 on a spreadsheet, we have

=NORM.S.INV(1 − 35256/1000000) + 1.5 = 3.31.

This is far from a six-sigma level of quality.

The value of 1.5 in these formulas stems from the mathematical calculation of six sigma. The developers of this concept allowed a process to shift by as much as 1.5 standard deviations from the mean, recognizing that it is not possible to control a process perfectly. Note that dpmo/1,000,000 is the same as defects per opportunity. Solved Problem 16.3 illustrates the use of this formula.

> Six Sigma has garnered a significant amount of credibility over the last decade because of its acceptance at such major firms as Motorola, Allied Signal (now part of Honeywell), Texas Instruments, and General Electric.

Although a six-sigma process has a dpmo of 3.4, we can also state that a three-sigma process has a dpmo of 66,807; a four-sigma process has dpmo = 6,210; and a five-sigma process has dpmo = 233. You can see that moving from a three- to a four-sigma level requires about a 10-fold improvement, and moving from a five- to a six-sigma level is almost a 70-fold improvement.

The difference between a four- and six-sigma quality level can be surprising. Put in practical terms, if your cellular phone system operated at a four-sigma level, you would be without service for more than four hours each month, whereas at six sigma, it would only be about nine seconds a month; a four-sigma process would result in one nonconforming package for every three truckloads, whereas a six-sigma process would have only one nonconforming package in more than 5,000 truckloads. And, if you play 100 rounds of golf each year, you would only miss one putt every 163 years at a six-sigma level! It isn't easy to reach six-sigma quality levels!

An Excel template, *Six Sigma,* is available in MindTap for performing six sigma calculations. Solved Problem 16.4 illustrates its use. Six Sigma has been applied in product development, new business acquisition, customer service, accounting, and many other business functions.

16-5a Implementing Six Sigma

Six Sigma has developed from simply a way of measuring quality to an overall strategy to accelerate improvements and achieve unprecedented performance levels. An organization does this by finding and organization does this by finding and eliminating causes of errors or

SOLVED PROBLEM 16.4: COMPUTING EPMO AND SIX SIGMA LEVEL

For the airline example in Solved Problem 16.2, find the value of dpmo and the sigma level at which this process is operating.

Solution:

Exhibit 16.2 shows the Excel *Six Sigma* template results. The airline recorded three lost bags among 8000 passengers, with each customer having an average of 1.6 bags, which is the number of defect opportunities per passenger.

The number of defects per unit (passenger) in cell B8 is 3/8000 = 0.000375. The total number of defect opportunities in cell B9 is 8000 × 1.6 = 12,800. Dpmo in cell B10 is found using Equation 16.2 and is equal to 234.375. This corresponds to a sigma level of approximately 5, which was computed using Excel formula 16.4 in cell B11.

EXHIBIT 16.2 Excel *Six Sigma* Template

	A	B	C	D
1	Six Sigma Calculations			
2	Enter data only in yellow-shaded cells.			
3				
4	Number of defects discovered	3		
5	Number of units	8000		
6	Number of defect opportunities/unit	1.6		
7				
8	Defects per unit (DPU)	0.000375		
9	Total number of defect opportunities	12800		
10	Defects per million opportunities (dpmo)	234.375		
11	Sigma level	4.99800633		

defects in processes by focusing on characteristics that are critical to customers.[6] The core philosophy of Six Sigma is based on some key concepts:[7]

1. Emphasizing dpmo or epmo as a standard metric that can be applied to all parts of an organization: manufacturing, engineering, administrative, software, and so on.
2. Providing extensive training followed by project team deployment to improve profitability, reduce non-value-added activities, and achieve cycle time reduction.
3. Focusing on corporate sponsors responsible for supporting team activities to help overcome resistance to change, obtain resources, and focus the teams on overall strategic objectives.
4. Creating highly qualified process improvement experts ("green belts," "black belts," and "master black belts") who can apply improvement tools and lead teams.
5. Ensuring that appropriate metrics are identified early in the process and that they focus on business results.
6. Setting stretch objectives for improvement.

The recognized benchmark for Six Sigma implementation is GE. GE's Six Sigma problem-solving approach (DMAIC) employs five phases:

1. ***Define (D)***
   - Identify customers and their priorities.
   - Identify a project suitable for Six Sigma efforts based on business objectives as well as customer needs and feedback.

- Identify CTQs (*critical-to-quality characteristics*) that the customer considers to have the most impact on quality.

2. ***Measure (M)***
   - Determine how to measure the process and how it is performing.
   - Identify the key internal processes that influence CTQs and measure the defects currently generated relative to those processes.
3. ***Analyze (A)***
   - Determine the most likely causes of defects.
   - Understand why defects are generated by identifying the key variables that are most likely to create process variation.
4. ***Improve (I)***
   - Identify means to remove the causes of the defects.
   - Confirm the key variables and quantify their effects on the CTQs.
   - Identify the maximum acceptable ranges of the key variables and a system for measuring deviations of the variables.
   - Modify the process to stay within the acceptable range.
5. ***Control (C)***
   - Determine how to maintain the improvements.
   - Put tools in place to ensure that the key variables remain within the maximum acceptable ranges under the modified process.

Using a structured process like the DMAIC approach helps project teams ensure that Six Sigma is implemented effectively (see the box on American Express).

All Six Sigma projects have three key characteristics: a problem to be solved, a process in which the problem exists, and one or more measures that quantify the gap to be closed and can be used to monitor progress. These characteristics are present in all business processes; thus, Six Sigma can easily be applied to a wide variety of transactional, administrative, and service areas in both large and small firms.

Taking Six Sigma out of the Factory

At DuPont, a Six Sigma project was applied to improve cycle time for an employee's application for long-term disability benefits.[8] Some examples of financial applications of Six Sigma include[9]

- reducing the average and variation of days outstanding of accounts receivable;
- closing the books faster;
- improving the accuracy and speed of the audit process;
- reducing variation in cash flow;
- improving the accuracy of journal entries (most businesses have a 3 to 4 percent error rate); and
- improving the accuracy and cycle time of standard financial reports.

The concepts and methods used in Six Sigma efforts have been around for a long time and may be categorized into seven general groups:

- elementary statistical tools (basic statistics, statistical thinking, hypothesis testing, correlation, simple regression);
- *advanced statistical tools* (design of experiments, analysis of variance, multiple regression);
- *product design and reliability* (quality function deployment, reliability analysis, failure mode and effects analysis);

- *measurement* (cost of quality, process capability, measurement systems analysis);
- *process control* (control plans, statistical process control, reducing variation);
- *process improvement* (process improvement planning, process mapping, mistake-proofing); and
- *implementation and teamwork* (organizational effectiveness, team assessment, facilitation tools, team development).

You may have covered some of these tools, such as statistics and teamwork, in other courses, and some, such as quality function deployment and statistical process control, are discussed in other chapters of this book.

In applying Six Sigma to services, there are four key measures of the performance: *accuracy*, as measured by correct financial figures, completeness of information, or freedom from data errors; *cycle time*, which is a measure of how long it takes to do something, such as pay an invoice; *cost*, the internal cost of process activities (in many cases, cost is largely determined by the accuracy and/or cycle time of the process—the longer it takes, and the more mistakes that have to be fixed, the higher the cost); and *customer satisfaction*, which is typically the primary measure of success.

16-6 Cost-of-Quality Measurement

The **cost of quality** *refers specifically to the costs associated with avoiding poor quality or those incurred as a result of poor quality.* Cost-of-quality analysis can help operations managers communicate with senior-level managers, identify and justify major opportunities for process improvements, and evaluate the importance of quality and improvement in operations.

Quality costs can be organized into four major categories: prevention costs, appraisal costs, internal failure costs, and external failure costs.

Prevention costs *are those expended to keep nonconforming goods and services from being made and reaching the customer.* They include

- *quality planning costs*—such as salaries of individuals associated with quality planning and problem-solving teams, the development of new procedures, new equipment design, and reliability studies;
- *process-control costs*—which include costs spent on analyzing processes and implementing process control plans;
- *information-systems costs*—which are expended to develop data requirements and measurements; and
- *training and general management costs*—which include internal and external training programs, clerical staff expenses, and miscellaneous supplies.

Appraisal costs *are those expended on ascertaining quality levels through measurement and analysis of data to detect and correct problems.* They include

- *test and inspection costs*—those associated with incoming materials, work-in-process, and finished goods, including equipment costs and salaries;
- *instrument maintenance costs*—those associated with the calibration and repair of measuring instruments; and
- *process-measurement and process-control costs*—which involve the time spent by workers to gather and analyze quality measurements.

SOLVED PROBLEM 16.5: ANALYZING THE COST OF QUALITY

D.B. Smith Company produces machine tools. The company conducted a cost-of-quality study and found the following:

Cost Category	Amount
Quality equipment design	$ 25,000
Scrap	330,000
Inspection and retest	340,000
Customer returns	90,000
Supplier quality surveys	8,000
Repair	80,000

What quality cost categories should each of these costs be associated with? What does a Pareto analysis reveal?

Cost Category	Amount	Quality Cost Category
Equipment maintenance	$ 25,000	Prevention
Machine downtime	330,000	Internal failure
Product inspection	340,000	Appraisal
Customer field repairs	90,000	External failure
Supplier quality audits	8,000	Prevention
Equipment repair	80,000	Internal failure

Solution:

The total costs in each category are as follows:

Prevention: $\$25,000 + \$8,000 = \$33,000$
Appraisal: $340,000
Internal failure: $\$330,000 + \$80,000 = \$410,000$
External failure: $90,000

Exhibit 16.3 shows a Pareto chart (one of the "Seven QC Tools" discussed in the next section) using the Excel *Pareto* template. This suggests that a very high amount of costs is spent on internal failure and appraisal. The company should probably invest more in activities focused on preventing internal failures, and seek to reduce the amount of inspection through better-quality processes.

EXHIBIT 16.3 Cost-of-Quality Analysis Using the Excel *Pareto* Template

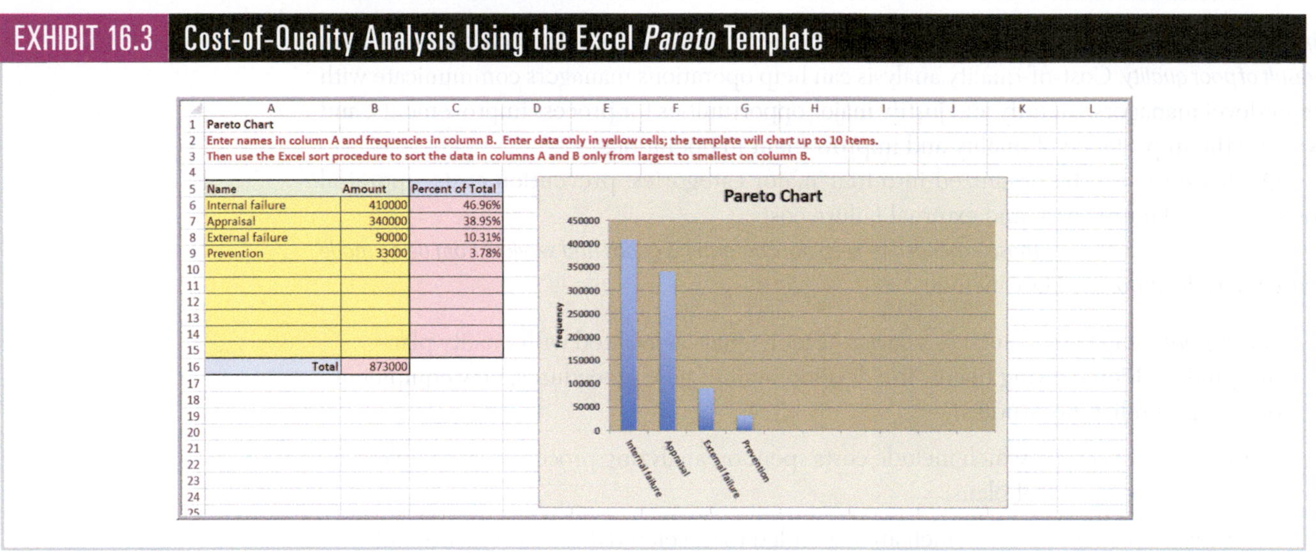

Internal failure costs *are costs incurred as a result of unsatisfactory quality that is found before the delivery of a good or service to the customer.* Examples include

- *scrap and rework costs*—including material, labor, and overhead;
- *costs of corrective action*—arising from time spent determining the causes of failure and correcting problems;
- *downgrading costs*—such as revenue lost by selling a good or service at a lower price because it does not meet specifications; and
- *process failures*—such as unplanned equipment downtime or service upsets or unplanned equipment repair.

External failure costs *are incurred after poor-quality goods or services reach the customer.* (Consider the cost that GM occurred because of its faulty ignition switches, as described at the beginning of this chapter.) They include

- *costs due to customer complaints and returns*—including rework on returned items, cancelled orders, discount coupons, and freight premiums;
- *goods and services recall costs and warranty and service guarantee claims*—including the cost of repair or replacement as well as associated administrative costs; and
- *product-liability costs*—resulting from legal actions and settlements.

By collecting and analyzing these costs, managers can identify the most important opportunities for improvement. Solved Problem 16.5 provides an example.

Food supply chains are under increasing quality risks due to global sourcing. For operations management, an important challenge is to manage the flow of each raw material and ingredient from its source, such as a small farm, to factories to distributors to retailers and ultimately to consumers to ensure a safe food supply. This includes monitoring possible contamination from bacteria, pesticides, carcinogens, and heavy metals, as well as the cleanliness of food processing and storage facilities. "It's a global information management problem," says Mr. Blissett, head of consumer products for IBM.

Chipotle, for instance, long enjoyed double-digit growth—until recently when several hundred people in the United States became sick from *Escherichia coli* (*E. coli*) and norovirus after eating Chipotle food. Sales declined 30 percent in December 2015. Consider how each of the four types of quality costs are relevant to Chipotle. When tainted food or ingredients enter supply chains, internal and external failure costs can increase dramatically. Monitoring requires increased appraisal. Suppliers, manufacturers, distributors, and retailers are adding more inspectors and inspection points in their supply chains. Better prevention through the design and control of food production processes can help reduce such costs.[10]

16-7 The "Seven QC Tools"

Seven simple tools—flowcharts, checksheets, histograms, Pareto diagrams, cause-and-effect diagrams, scatter diagrams, and control charts—termed the *Seven QC* (quality control) *Tools* by the Japanese, support quality improvement problem-solving efforts.[11] The Seven QC Tools are designed to be simple and visual so that workers at all levels can use them easily and provide a means of communication that is particularly well suited in group problem-solving efforts.

Flowcharts To understand a process, one must first determine how it works and what it is supposed to do. Flowcharting, or process mapping, identifies the sequence of activities or the flow of materials and information in a process. Once a flowchart is constructed, it can be used to identify quality problems as well as areas for productivity improvement. Questions such as the following help evaluate a process and identify areas for improvement: "What work activities can be combined, simplified, or eliminated?," "Are process capacities well planned?," and "How is quality measured at points of customer contact?"

> The Seven QC Tools are designed to be simple and visual so that workers at all levels can use them easily.

Run and Control Charts A *run chart* is a line graph in which data are plotted over time. The vertical axis represents a measurement; the horizontal axis is the time scale. Run charts show the performance and the variation of a process or some quality or productivity indicator over time. They can be used to track such things as production volume, costs, and customer satisfaction indexes. Run charts summarize data in a graphical fashion that is easy to understand and interpret, identify process changes and trends over time, and show the effects of corrective actions.

A *control chart* is simply a run chart to which two horizontal lines, called *control limits*, are added: the *upper control limit (UCL)* and *lower control limit (LCL)*, as illustrated in Exhibit 16.4. Control limits are chosen statistically so that there is a high probability (generally greater than 0.99) that points will fall between these limits if the process is in control. Control limits make it easier to interpret patterns in a run chart and draw conclusions about the state of control. The next chapter addresses this topic in much more detail.

Checksheets Checksheets are special types of data-collection forms in which the results may be interpreted on the form directly without additional processing. For example, in the checksheet in Exhibit 16.5, one can easily identify the most frequent causes of defects.

Histograms A histogram is a basic statistical tool that graphically shows the frequency or number of observations of a particular value or within a specified group. Histograms provide clues about the characteristics of the parent population from which a sample is taken. Patterns that would be difficult to see in an ordinary table of numbers become apparent. You are probably quite familiar with histograms from your statistics classes.

Pareto Diagrams The *Pareto principle* was observed by Joseph Juran in 1950. Juran found that most effects resulted from only a few causes. He named this technique after Vilfredo Pareto (1848–1923), an Italian economist who determined that 85 percent of the wealth in Milan was owned by only 15 percent of the people. Pareto analysis separates the vital few from the trivial many and provides direction for selecting projects for improvement.

An example of a Pareto diagram developed from the checksheet in Exhibit 16.5 is shown in Exhibit 16.6. The diagram shows that about 70 percent of defects result from the top two categories, Incomplete and Surface scars.

Pareto analysis is often used to analyze cost-of-quality data that we discussed in Section 16-6 of this chapter. Solved Problem 16.2 illustrates how this can be applied.

EXHIBIT 16.4 The Structure of a Control Chart

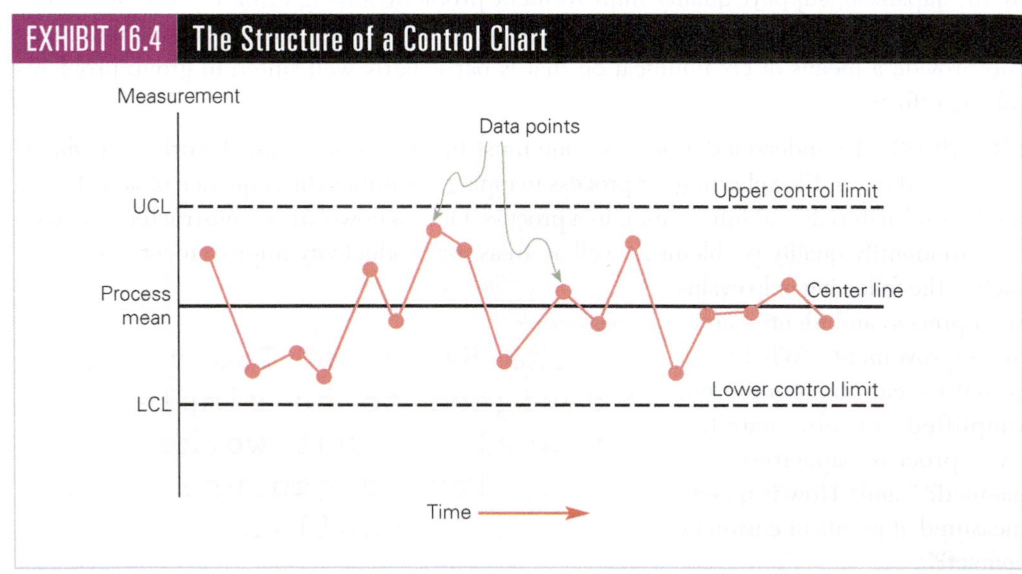

EXHIBIT 16.5 Defective Item Checksheet

Checksheet

Product:	Date:
	Factory:
Manufacturing stage: final insp.	Section:
	Inspector's name:
Type of defect: scar, incomplete, misshapen	Lot no.
	Order no.
Total no. inspected: 2530	
Remarks: all items inspected	

Type	Check	Subtotal
Surface scars	𝍸 𝍸 𝍸 𝍸 𝍸 𝍸 //	32
Cracks	𝍸 𝍸 𝍸 𝍸 ///	23
Incomplete	𝍸 𝍸 𝍸 𝍸 𝍸 𝍸 𝍸 𝍸 𝍸 ///	48
Misshapen	////	4
Others	𝍸 ///	8
	Grand total	115
Total rejects	𝍸 𝍸 𝍸 𝍸 𝍸 𝍸 𝍸 𝍸 𝍸 𝍸 𝍸 𝍸 𝍸 𝍸 𝍸 𝍸 𝍸 /	86

Source: Ishikawa, Kaoru. "Defective Item Checksheet," *Guide to Quality Control*. Asian Productivity Organization, 1982, p. 33. Reprinted with permission.

EXHIBIT 16.6 Pareto Diagram of Defective Items

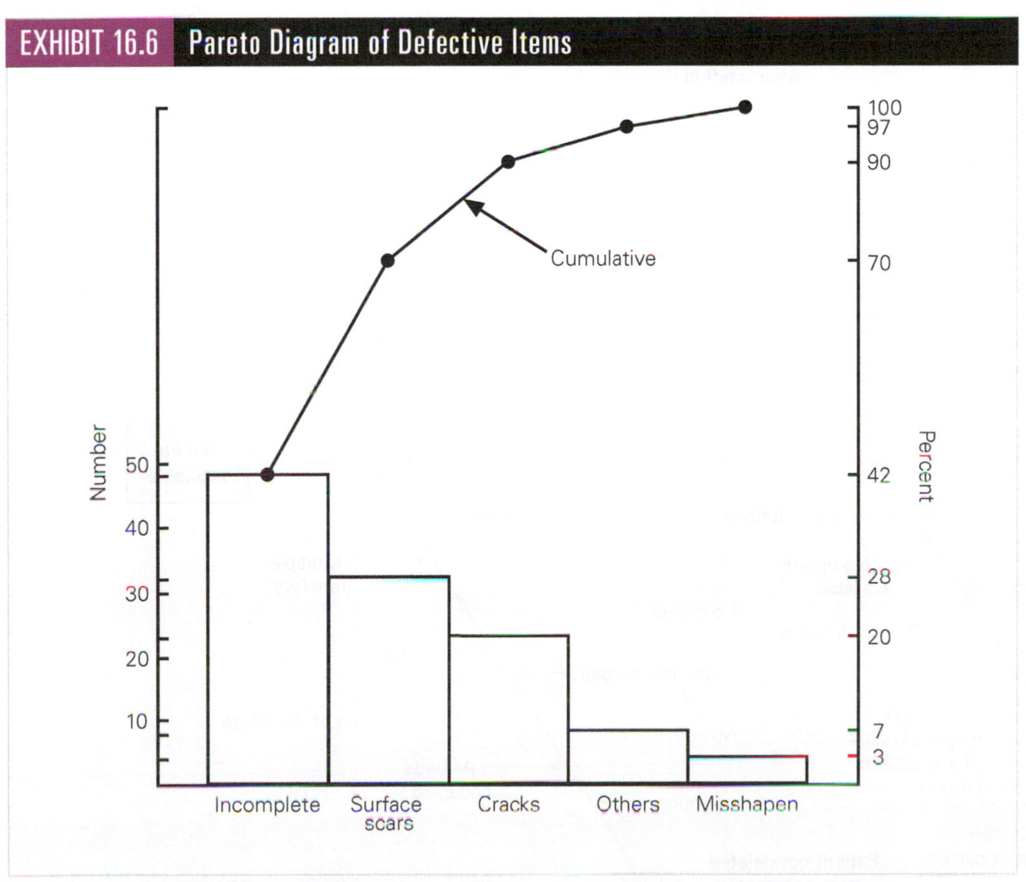

Cause-and-Effect Diagrams The cause-and-effect diagram is a simple, graphical method for presenting a chain of causes and effects and for sorting out causes and organizing relationships between variables. Because of its structure, it is often called a *fishbone diagram*. A cause-and-effect diagram is shown in Exhibit 16.7. At the end of the horizontal line, a problem is listed. Each branch pointing into the main stem represents a possible cause. Branches pointing to the causes are contributors to those causes. The diagram identifies the most likely causes of a problem so that further data collection and analysis can be carried out.

Scatter Diagrams Scatter Diagrams Scatter diagrams are the graphical component of regression analysis. Although they do not provide rigorous statistical analysis, they often point to important relationships between variables, such as the percentage of an ingredient in an alloy and the hardness of the alloy. Scatter diagrams are often used to verify possible causes and effects obtained from cause-and-effect diagrams.

16-7a Root Cause Analysis

The *root cause* is a term used to designate the source of a problem. Using the medical analogy, eliminating symptoms of problems provides only temporary relief; eliminating the root cause provides long-term relief. A useful approach to identify the root cause is called the *5-Why Technique*. This approach forces one to redefine a problem statement as a chain of causes and effects to identify the source of the symptoms by asking why, ideally five times. In a classic example at Toyota, a machine failed because a fuse blew. Replacing the fuse would have been the obvious solution; however, this action would have addressed only the symptom of the real

EXHIBIT 16.7 Cause-and-Effect Diagram for Hospital Emergency Admission

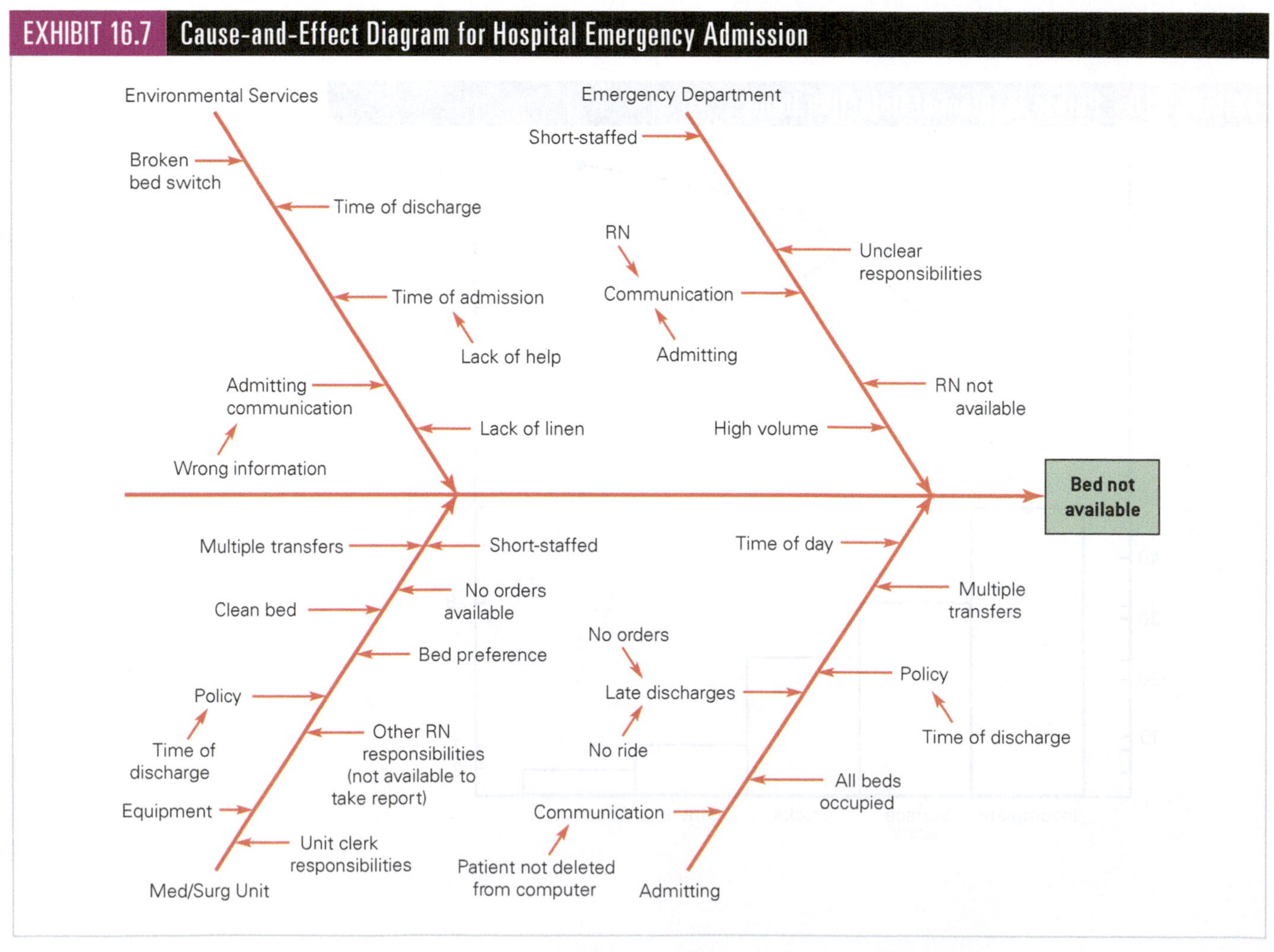

problem. Why did the fuse blow? Because the bearing did not have adequate lubrication. Why? Because the lubrication pump was not working properly. Why? Because the pump axle was worn. Why? Because sludge seeped into the pump axle, which was determined to be the root cause. Toyota attached a strainer to the lubricating pump to eliminate the sludge, thus correcting the problem of the machine failure.

Root cause analysis often uses the Seven QC Tools. For example, Pareto diagrams can also progressively help focus in on root causes. Exhibit 16.8 shows one example. At each step,

EXHIBIT 16.8 Use of Pareto Diagrams for Root Cause Analysis

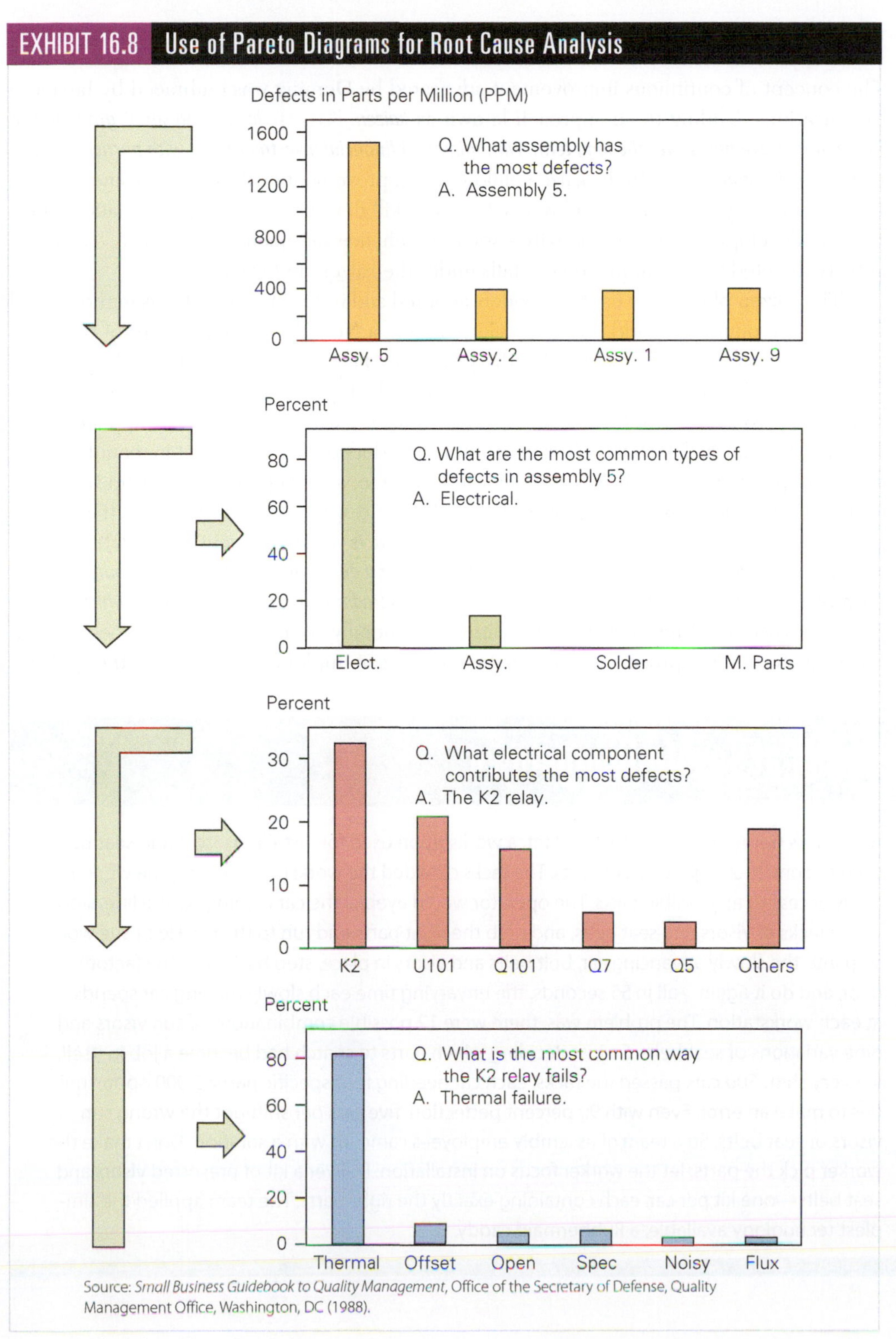

Source: *Small Business Guidebook to Quality Management*, Office of the Secretary of Defense, Quality Management Office, Washington, DC (1988).

the Pareto diagram stratifies the data to more detailed levels (or it may require additional data collection), eventually isolating the most significant issue.

16-8 Other Quality Improvement Strategies

Many other approaches to quality improvement have been developed and refined over the years. Two powerful approaches are kaizen and breakthrough improvement.

16-8a Kaizen

The concept of continuous improvement advocated by Deming was embraced by Japanese organizations, leading to an approach known as *kaizen*. **Kaizen** *focuses on small, gradual, and frequent improvements over the long term, with minimum financial investment and with participation by everyone in the organization.* In the kaizen philosophy, improvement in all areas of business—cost, meeting delivery schedules, employee safety and skill development, supplier relations, new product development, or productivity—serve to enhance the quality of the firm. Thus, any activity directed toward improvement falls under the kaizen umbrella.

The kaizen philosophy has been widely adopted and is used by many firms in the United States and around the world. At ENBI Corporation, a New York manufacturer of precision metal shafts and roller assemblies for the printer, copier, and fax machine markets, kaizen projects have resulted in a 48 percent increase in productivity, a 30 percent reduction in cycle time, and a 73 percent reduction in inventory. Kaizen has been successfully applied in the Mercedes-Benz truck factory in Brazil, resulting in reductions of 30 percent in manufacturing space, 45 percent in inventory, 70 percent in lead time, and 70 percent in set-up time over a three-year period. Sixteen employees have full-time responsibility for kaizen activities.[12]

A related approach to continuous improvement is a kaizen event. *A* **kaizen event** *is an intense and rapid improvement process in which a team or a department throws all its resources into an improvement project over a short time period, as opposed to traditional kaizen applications, which are performed on a part-time basis.* Kaizen event teams are generally comprised of employees from all areas involved in the process who understand it and can implement changes on the spot.[13]

Kaizen at Toyota Georgetown

At Toyota's Georgetown, Kentucky, plant, a workstation used for installing visors and seat belts used to consist of eight racks of parts. The racks crowded the workstation, giving the worker ready access to all possible parts. The operator would eyeball the car coming up the line, step to the racks of visors and seat belts, and grab the right parts and run to the car. He or she would step into the slowly advancing car, bolt belts and visors in place, step back onto the factory floor, and do it again—all in 55 seconds, the unvarying time each slowly moving car spends at each workstation. The problem was, there were 12 possible combinations of sun visors and nine variations of seat belts. So just deciding which parts to snatch had become a job in itself. In every shift, 500 cars passed the racks, each car needing four specific parts: 2,000 opportunities to make an error. Even with 99 percent perfection, five cars per shift got the wrong sun visors or seat belts. So a team of assembly employees came up with a solution. Don't make the worker pick the parts; let the worker focus on installation. Deliver a kit of presorted visors and seat belts—one kit per car, each containing exactly the right parts. The team applied the simplest technology available, a Rubbermaid caddy.

16-8b Breakthrough Improvement

Breakthrough improvement *refers to discontinuous change, as opposed to the gradual, continuous improvement philosophy of kaizen.* Breakthrough improvements result from innovative and creative thinking; often these are motivated by stretch goals, or breakthrough objectives. Stretch goals force an organization to think in a radically different way and to encourage major improvements as well as incremental ones. When a goal of 10 percent improvement is set, managers or engineers can usually meet it with some minor improvements. However, when the goal is 1,000 percent improvement, employees must be creative and think "outside of the box." The seemingly impossible is often achieved, yielding dramatic improvements and boosting morale. Motorola's Six Sigma thrust was driven by a goal of improving product and services quality ten times within two years, and at least 100-fold within four years.

The development and realization of improvement objectives, particularly stretch objectives, is often aided through the process of benchmarking. **Benchmarking** *is the search for industry best practices that lead to superior performance. The term* **best practices** *refers to approaches that produce exceptional results, are usually innovative in terms of the use of technology or human resources, and are recognized by customers or industry experts.* When GTE worked to improve eight core processes of its telephone operations, it examined the best practices of some 84 companies from diverse industries. By studying outside best practices, a company can identify and import new technology, skills, structures, training, and capabilities.

The concept of benchmarking is not new. Henry Ford created the assembly line after taking a tour of a Chicago slaughterhouse and watching carcasses, hung on hooks mounted on a monorail, move from one workstation to another. Toyota's just-in-time production system was influenced by the replenishment practices of U.S. supermarkets. Modern benchmarking was initiated by Xerox when it wanted to improve its spare parts distribution system. Xerox identified the warehousing and distribution practices of L. L. Bean as a best practice and adopted their approaches.

CHAPTER 16 LEARNING OBJECTIVE SUMMARIES

16.1 **Explain the concepts and definitions of quality.** Quality is meeting or exceeding customer's expectations. From an operations perspective, however, the most useful definition is how well the output of a manufacturing or service process conforms to the design specifications. Excellent service quality is achieved by the consistent delivery to the customer of a clearly defined customer benefit package and associated process and service encounters, defined by many internal and external standards of performance.

An established instrument for measuring the external customer perceptions of service quality is SERVQUAL, which identifies five key dimensions: tangibles, reliability, responsiveness, assurance, and empathy.

The principles of total quality are simple:

- a focus on customers and stakeholders,
- a process focus supported by continuous improvement and learning, and
- participation and teamwork by everyone in the organization.

16.2 **Describe the quality philosophies and principles of Deming, Juran, and Crosby.** The Deming philosophy focuses on bringing about improvements in product and service quality by reducing variability in goods and services design and associated processes. Deming professed that higher quality leads to higher productivity and lower costs, which in turn leads to improved market share and long-term competitive strength. In his early work in the United States, Deming preached his 14 Points, which provide guidance for building quality within organizations. These include the responsibility of top management to create a vision and commit to quality, continual improvement of products and processes, the importance of training and teams, and the creation of an environment that drives out fear and fosters pride in work. At that time (in the 1960s and 1970s), they represented a radical departure from management thinking and practice. However, they still convey important insights to all managers today. Juran proposed a simple definition of quality: "fitness for use." Unlike Deming, however, Juran did not propose a major cultural change in the organization, but rather sought to improve quality by working within the system familiar to managers. Juran stated that top management speaks in the language of dollars; workers speak in the language of things; and middle management must be able to speak both languages and translate between dollars and things. Thus, to get the attention of top managers, quality issues must be cast in the language they understand—dollars. Crosby's Absolutes of Quality Management include the following points:

- *Quality means conformance to requirements, not elegance.*
- *There is no such thing as a quality problem.*
- *There is no such thing as the economics of quality; doing the job right the first time is always cheaper.*
- *The only performance measurement is the cost of quality, which is the expense of nonconformance.*
- *The only performance standard is "Zero Defects (ZD)."*

16.3 **Explain the GAP model and its importance.** The GAP model (see Exhibit 15.1) recognizes that there are several ways to misspecify and mismanage the creation and delivery of high levels of quality.

- **Gap 1** *is the discrepancy between customer expectations and management perceptions of those expectations.*
- **Gap 2** *is the discrepancy between management perceptions of what features constitute a target level of quality and the task of translating these perceptions into executable specifications.*
- **Gap 3** *is the discrepancy between quality specifications documented in operating and training manuals and plans and their implementation.*
- **Gap 4** *is the discrepancy between actual manufacturing and service-delivery system performance and external communications to the customers.*
- **Gap 5** *is the difference between the customer's expectations and perceptions.*

16.4 **Describe the concepts and philosophy of ISO 9000.** ISO 9000 defines *quality system standards.* The ISO 9000:standards are supported by the following eight principles:

Principle 1—Customer Focus

Principle 2—Leadership

Principle 3—Engagement of People

Principle 4—Process Approach

Principle 5—Improvement

Principle 6—Evidence-Based Decision Making

Principle 7—Relationship Management

16.5 **Describe the philosophy and methods of Six Sigma.** The term *Six Sigma* is based on a statistical measure that equates to at most 3.4 errors or defects per million opportunities.

The core philosophy of Six Sigma is based on some key concepts:

- emphasizing dpmo or epmo as a standard metric that can be applied to all parts of an organization: manufacturing, engineering, administrative, software, and so on;
- providing extensive training followed by project team deployment to improve profitability, reduce non-value added activities, and achieve cycle time reduction;
- focusing on corporate sponsors responsible for supporting team activities to help overcome resistance to change, obtain resources, and focus the teams on overall strategic objectives;
- creating highly qualified process improvement experts ("green belts,"black belts,"and "master black belts" who can apply improvement tools and lead teams;
- ensuring that appropriate metrics are identified early in the process and that they focus on business results; and
- setting stretch objectives for improvement.

The Six Sigma problem-solving approach is Define, Measure, Analyze, Improve, and Control (DMAIC).

CHAPTER 16 LEARNING OBJECTIVE SUMMARIES

16.6 **Explain the categories of cost-of-quality measurement.** Quality costs can be organized into four major categories: prevention costs, appraisal costs, internal failure costs, and external failure costs. By collecting and analyzing these costs, managers can identify the most important opportunities for improvement.

16.7 **Describe how to apply the Seven QC Tools.** Seven simple tools—flowcharts, checksheets, histograms, Pareto diagrams, cause-and-effect diagrams, scatter diagrams, and control charts—termed the *Seven QC* (Quality Control) *Tools* by the Japanese, support quality improvement problemsolving efforts. The Seven QC Tools are designed to be simple and visual so that workers at all levels can use them easily and provide a means of communication that is particularly well suited in group problemsolving efforts. Root cause analysis often uses the Seven QC Tools. The root cause is a term used to designate the source of a problem.

16.8 **Explain the concepts of kaizen and breakthrough improvement.** The concept of continuous improvement is known as kaizen. In the kaizen philosophy, improvement in all areas of business—cost, meeting delivery schedules, employee safety and skill development, supplier relations, new product development, productivity—serve to enhance the quality of the firm. Breakthrough improvement refers to discontinuous change, as opposed to the gradual, continuous improvement philosophy of kaizen. Breakthrough improvements result from innovative and creative thinking; often these are motivated by stretch goals, or breakthrough objectives. The development and realization of improvement objectives, particularly stretch objectives, is often aided through the process of benchmarking. Benchmarking is the search for industry best practices that lead to superior performance. The term best practices refers to approaches that produce exceptional results, are usually innovative in terms of the use of technology or human resources, and are recognized by customers or industry experts.

KEY TERMS

- Appraisal costs
- Benchmarking
- Best practices
- Breakthrough improvement
- Cost of quality
- Defect
- External failure costs
- Internal failure costs
- Kaizen
- Kaizen event
- Prevention costs
- Quality
- Quality management
- Quality of conformance
- Service quality
- Six Sigma
- Specifications
- Unit of work

REVIEW QUESTIONS

16.1 1. Define quality management. Why is it important for every manager to understand?

16.1 2. What does the history of quality management suggest to today's managers?

16.1 3. How is quality defined from a customer perspective?

16.1 4. What is the most useful definition of quality from an operations perspective? How might an operations manager use this definition in making daily decisions?

16.1 5. How do you define service quality? Explain the five dimensions of service quality.

16.1 6. List and explain the three principles of total quality.

16.2 7. Describe the quality philosophies and principles of Deming, Juran, and Crosby.

16.3 8. Explain the five gaps in the GAP model. What can managers do to reduce these gaps?

16.4 9. Explain the purpose and structure of ISO 9000. What are the seven underlying principles?

16.5 10. What is Six Sigma? How is it measured?

16.5 11. Explain the key concepts used in implementing a Six Sigma quality initiative.

16.5 12. Summarize the DMAIC process for problem solving.

16.5 13. What tools and methods are used in Six Sigma projects?

16.5 14. How can Six Sigma be applied in services?

16.6 15. What does "cost of quality" mean? Why is it important?

16.6 16. Explain the classification of quality costs. Provide some specific examples in a fast-food operation and in the operation of your college or university.

16.7 17. Summarize the Seven QC Tools used for quality improvement, and provide an example of each.

16.7 18. What is a root cause? How can root causes be identified?

16.8 19. Explain the concept of kaizen. What must an organization do to successfully operate a kaizen initiative?

16.8 20. What is a kaizen event? How does it differ from the original notion of kaizen?

16.8 21. What is breakthrough improvement?

16.8 22. How do benchmarking and best practices support breakthrough improvement?

DISCUSSION QUESTIONS AND EXPERIENTIAL ACTIVITIES

16.1 23. Find two examples similar to the introductory example in this chapter that describe the economic consequences of poor quality.

16.1 24. Discuss how either good or poor quality affects you personally as a consumer. For instance, describe experiences in which your expectations were met, exceeded, or not met when you purchased goods or services. Did your experience change your regard for the organization and/or its product? How?

16.1 25. A top Ford executive stated "You can't have great value unless you have great quality." Comment on this statement. Do you agree? Why or why not?

16.1 26. Select a service activity with which you are familiar. If you were the manager of this activity, what "conformance to specifications" criteria would you use to monitor it?

16.1 27. Develop a portfolio of advertisements from the Internet, newspapers, and magazines, and illustrate how quality is used in promoting these products.

16.1 28. Examine the annual reports of one company over a period of years. Summarize how quality is discussed or implied in the company's statements and philosophy. Are any changes in the perspectives of quality evident over time?

16.1 29. Conduct some research on quality practices that is focused on a particular country or global region. Summarize your findings in a two- to three-page report.

16.1 30. How do you think that quality management concepts can support sustainability efforts? Find some sources or examples to support your beliefs.

16.2 31. Find the websites for the W. Edwards Deming Institute, the Juran Institute, and Philip Crosby Associates. What services do they offer? How do these organizations maintain the philosophies and legacies of these quality leaders?

16.2 32. Two of Deming's 14 Points are Point 8: Drive Out Fear (in the workplace) and Point 4: Stop Making Decisions Purely on the Basis of Cost. Discuss the importance of them to operations managers (as well as all managers) in today's business environment.

16.4 33. Identify an organization that has achieved ISO 9000 certification, and write a short paper (one page maximum) that summarizes the benefits and results that the organization has achieved using ISO 9000. See if you can find a service organization rather than a traditional manufacturing company.

16.5 34. Identify an organization that uses the Six Sigma DMAIC improvement approach. Describe in a short paper (maximum of two pages) some of the ways that this organization has applied DMAIC and the results it has achieved.

16.5 35. What types of defects or errors might the following organizations measure and improve as part of a quality or Six Sigma initiative?

a. A department store such as Walmart or Macy's
b. Walt Disney World or a regional amusement park such as Six Flags
c. Your college or university

16.6 36. Provide some specific examples of quality costs in a fast-food operation or in the operation of your college or university. Classify the costs into the four major categories described in the chapter.

16.7 37. Explain how each of the Seven QC Tools would be used in the five phases of the Six Sigma DMAIC problem-solving approach. For example, in which phase(s) (define, measure, analyze, improve, or control) would you expect to use flowcharts, check-sheets, and so on?

16.7 38. Which of the Seven QC Tools would be most useful in addressing each of the following situations?

Explain your reasoning. (You may decide more than one tool is useful.)

a. A copy machine suffers frequent paper jams, and users are often confused as to how to fix the problem.

b. The publication team for an engineering department wants to improve the accuracy of its user documentation but is unsure of why documents are not error-free.

c. A bank needs to determine how many teller positions, drive-through stations, and ATM machines it needs for a new branch bank in a certain busy location. Its information includes the average numbers and types of customers served by other similar facilities, as well as demographic information to suggest the level of customer traffic in the new facility.

d. A contracting agency wants to investigate why it had so many changes in its contracts. The company believes that the number of changes may be related to the dollar value of the original contract or the days between the request for proposal and the contract award.

e. A travel agency is interested in gaining a better understanding of how call volume varies by time of year in order to adjust staffing schedules.

16.8 39. Refer to the automobile repair flowchart in Exhibit 7.5 in Chapter 7. Identify three activities where a potentially serious service quality error may occur, and discuss how such errors might be reduced.

COMPUTATIONAL PROBLEMS AND EXERCISES

These exercises require you to apply the formulas and methods described in the chapter. The problems should be solved manually.

16.5 40. Leatherlike Manufacturing Company makes an artificial leather-like product for the fashion accessory market. The material is made in sheets and has the appearance of a thin rug. Each sheet is 36 inches wide, 100 feet long, and is wound into a roll. The quality manager has requested that 200 rolls be inspected. Twenty-six nonconformances were found. Calculate the nonconformances per unit (NPU).

16.5 41. Wellplace Insurance Company processes insurance policy applications in batches of 50. One day, they had ten batches to process and, after inspection, it was found that four batches had nonconforming policies. One batch had three nonconformances, another had five, another had two, and another had one nonconformance. What were (a) the proportion nonconforming for each batch and (b) the nonconformances per unit (NPU) in total for the ten batches?

16.5 42. Nighthawk Airlines measured their numbers of lost bags in one month and found that they had lost 35 bags for 10,000 customers. If the average number of bags per customer is 1.2, how many errors per million opportunities (epmo) does this represent? The worldwide rate of baggage mishandling reported by SITA (Société Internationale de Télécommunications Aéronautiques) in 2017 was 5.73 per 1,000 passengers. If the average number of checked bags per passenger is assumed to be 1.3, how many errors per million opportunities (epmo) does this represent? How does this compare with the error rate for Nighthawk—better or worse?

16.5 43. Boardwalk Electronics manufactures 300,000 circuit boards per month. A random sample of 3,000 boards is inspected every week for five characteristics. During a recent week, three defects were found for one characteristic, and two defects each were found for the other four characteristics. If these inspections produced defect counts that were representative of the population, what are the dpmo's for the individual characteristics and what is the overall dpmo for the boards?

16.6 44. Analyze the cost data below. What implications do these data suggest to managers?

	Product		
	A	B	C
Total sales	$537,280	$233,600	$397,120
External failure	42%	20%	20%
Internal failure	45%	25%	45%
Appraisal	12%	52%	30%
Prevention	1%	3%	5%

Note: Figures represent percentages of quality costs by product.

16.6 45. Given the cost elements in the table below, determine the total percentage in each of the four major quality-cost categories.

Cost Element	Amount ($)
Incoming test and inspection	7,500
Scrap	35,000
Quality training	0
Inspection	25,000
Test	5,000
Adjustment cost of complaints	21,250
Quality audits	2,500
Maintenance of tools and dies	9,200
Quality control administration	5,000
Laboratory testing	1,250
Design of quality assurance equipment	1,250
Material testing and inspection	1,250
Rework	70,000
Quality problem solving by product engineers	11,250
Inspection equipment calibration	2,500
Writing procedures and instructions	2,500
Laboratory services	2,500
Rework due to vendor faults	17,500
Correcting imperfections	6,250
Setup for test and inspection	10,750
Formal complaints to vendors	10,000

16.6 **46.** Classify the cost elements shown below for the Impressive Printing Company into the proper quality cost categories and find the total quality cost by category and percentage of total quality cost by category.

Cost Element	Amount
Customer complaint remakes	$24,300
Printing plate revisions	$25,200
Quality improvement projects	$11,700
Gauging	$90,000
Other waste	$34,200
Correction of typographical errors	$189,000
Proofreading	$405,000
Quality planning	$50,400
Press downtime	$256,400
Bindery waste	$45,900
Checking and inspection	$37,800

 **47.** Reship Solutions, Inc. has a distribution center in Cincinnati, where it receives and breaks down bulk orders from suppliers' factories and ships out products to retail customers. The different quality cost elements are shown in the table below. Classify these into the appropriate quality cost categories and compute the percentage of total quality cost for each category.

Cost Element	Amount
Checking outbound boxes for errors	$607,750
Quality planning	$10,625
Downtime due to conveyor/computer problems	$342,125
Packaging waste	$68,000
Incoming product inspection	$51,000
Customer complaint rework	$34,000
Correcting erroneous orders before shipping	$36,550
Quality training of associates	$25,925
Quality improvement projects	$17,425
Other waste	$36,125
Correction of typographical errors—pick tickets	$11,475

 **48.** The following list gives the number of defects found in 30 samples of 100 electronic assemblies taken on a daily basis over one month. Plot these data on a run chart, computing the average value (center line). How do you interpret the chart?

1	6	5	5	4	3	2	2	4	6
2	1	3	1	4	5	4	1	6	15
12	6	3	4	3	3	2	5	7	4

 **49.** Develop cause-and-effect diagrams for any one of the following problems:

a. Poor exam grade

b. No job offers

c. Too many speeding tickets

d. Late for work or school

EXCEL-BASED PROBLEMS

For these problems, you may use Excel or the spreadsheet templates in MindTap to assist in your analysis.

 **50.** Nighthawk Airlines measured their numbers of lost bags in one month and found that they had lost 35 bags for 10,000 customers. If the average number of bags per customer is 1.2, use the *Six Sigma* Excel template to find at what sigma level is the airline operating.

16.5 **51.** The worldwide rate of baggage mishandling reported by SITA (Société Internationale de Télécommunications Aéronautiques) in 2017 was 5.73 per 1,000 passengers. If the average number of checked bags per passenger is assumed to be 1.3, use the *Six Sigma* Excel template to determine what sigma level this represents.

 **52.** A bank has set a standard that mortgage applications be processed within eight days of filing. If, out of a sample of 1000 applications, 75 fail to meet this requirement, what is the epmo metric, and how does it compare with a six-sigma level? Use the *Six Sigma* Excel template for your analysis.

16.5 53. Over the last year, 1,200 injections were administered at a clinic. Quality is measured by the proper amount of dosage as well as the correct drug. In nine instances, the incorrect amount was given, and in two cases, the wrong drug was given. Use the *Six Sigma* Excel template to determine the value of the epmo metric and the sigma level it corresponds to.

16.6 54. Analysis of customer complaints at an e-commerce retailer revealed the following:

Billing errors: 1,421
Shipping errors: 845
Electronic charge errors: 650
Shipping delays: 3,016
Packing errors: 1,879

Use the Excel *Pareto* template to construct a Pareto chart, and discuss the conclusions you may draw from it.

16.6 55. The following cost-of-quality data were collected at the installment loan department of the Kenney Bank. Classify these data into the appropriate cost-of-quality categories, and analyze the results with a Pareto chart (use the Excel *Pareto* template). What suggestions would you make to management?

Loan Processing

1. Run credit checks: $2,675.01
2. Review documents: $3,000.63
3. Make document corrections; gather additional information: $1,032.65
4. Review all output: $2,243.62
5. Correct rejects and incorrect output: $425.00
6. Reconcile incomplete collateral report: $78.34
7. Handle dealer problem calls; address associate problems; research and communicate information: $2,500.00
8. Compensate for system downtime: $519.01
9. Conduct training: $1,500.00

Loan Payment

1. Receive, inspect, and process payments: $800.00
2. Respond to inquiries when no coupon is presented with payments: $829.65

Loan Payoff

1. Prepare tickler file; review and follow up on titles, insurance, second meetings: $ 155.75
2. Receive, inspect, and process payoff and release documents: $224.99
3. Research payoff problems: $15.35

16.7 56. One industry expert stated that software today has six errors for every 1,000 lines of code. Assuming that there is only one opportunity to make an error for each line of code, at what sigma level is the coding processing operating? If eight errors are discovered, use the *Six Sigma* Excel template to determine how many lines of code there must be for the process to be at a six-sigma level.

16.7 57. Use the Excel *Pareto* template to investigate the quality losses in a paper mill shown below. What conclusions do you reach?

Category	Annual Loss ($)
Downtime	38,000
Testing costs	20,000
Rejected paper	560,000
Odd lot	79,000
Excess inspection	28,000
Customer complaints	125,000
High material costs	67,000

Bonnie Blaine, Director of Hospital Operations

"The kid almost died! He's a diabetic! How did that patient get the wrong food tray?" said Bonnie Blaine, director of hospital operations, to Drew Owensboro, the director of dietary services. Bonnie Blaine, a woman in her early fifties, had worked in almost every area of the hospital. By going to school in the evenings for three years, she had earned a Master's in business administration. Owensboro had worked in the hospital for 19 years and had a high school education.

"Bonnie, I don't know! I'll try to find out but it may be impossible. The dietary department is really a very complex operation and it's very difficult to audit or trace anything," Owensboro said in frustration. "Drew, I've got enough problems trying to contain hospital costs without having to worry about patient lawsuits due to poor quality control on our part," Blaine continued. "The kid's family and family doctor are furious! Your employees are all blaming one another, but no one is really doing anything about it. Now fix it or maybe I'll have to get someone else in here to do the job," Blaine said as she turned to answer the telephone.

The Hospital's Dietary Department The dietary department provides food services to three basic groups: patients, employees, and visitors. The greatest demand for food services comes from the patients, and because of the many different diet requirements which must be fulfilled, this can be rather complex. Each day the patient fills out their required dietetic menu for all three meals for the following day and chooses from several different food items in each food group (entree, vegetable, fruit, dessert, beverage). Since the average patient stay is five days, the dietary department offers different daily menus for two weeks and then repeats the menu selection.

The dietary department, as shown in Exhibit 16.9, is a large department with a total of 124 full-time equivalent (FTE) employees, assuming two part-time employees equals one full-time position. The department has 10 managers (that is, directors, supervisors), 8 clinical dieticians, 9 administrative dieticians (7 of which are also managers), 89 full-time employees, and 30 part-time employees. The 89 direct full-time employees have an average education level of 10.8 years. The annual average salary for a part-time employee is $15,000, full-time food service employees excluding cooks earn $28,000, and clerk employees earn $31,000. Benefits for full-time employees average an additional 20 percent of their annual salary.

Clerical Support in Patient Services Eight full-time employees in the patient services area fill out diets for each patient, menus for tomorrow's meals, and last-minute changes for today's diets and menus. Central control is necessary due to the myriad of changes, which take place each day because of surgery, discharges, new admittances, or doctor-prescribed diet changes.

The clerks assemble the diets by room and floor and check to see that all menus are properly filled out. When patients are discharged, the clerks pull the patient's diet history from the room number of the floor and file it with the medical records. The prescribed diets of new admittances are to be checked by the clinical nutritionist in charge of the floor, but in the case of emergencies, the clerk calls the floor and speaks to the head nurse about what type of diet is to be presented. Besides the obvious patient health issues with regard to the accuracy of the prescribed diets, the patient and doctor expect the dietary department to "provide timely, neat meals with no errors."

Before each meal, the clerk's office gives the shift supervisor of tray assembly and production the updated list of menus for each patient's room. The clerks sequence the room numbers by floor for easy tray production and delivery. The clerks remain in the office during the day answering phones and messages about diet and menu changes. After each meal, the clerk's office distributes a patient census in terms of trays actually served. Then the process begins all over again for the next meal. Due to the short time between meals, some clerks are working on, say, the breakfast meal while others are working on the lunch meal.

Food Production The kitchen and patient tray assembly lines are located in the basement of the hospital. The kitchen is a beehive of activity for about 18 hours a day. The regular cooks, special diet cooks, kitchen workers, dieticians, and clerks from patient services are constantly visiting or calling the kitchen concerning patient meals. Meanwhile, food constantly arrives at the loading docks that had been ordered from the hospital's purchasing department or the hospital's food service manager.

Employees are assigned to one of three basic shifts—a breakfast shift that begins at 4 A.M., a lunch shift that arrives at staggered times from 6 A.M. until noon, and a dinner shift that begins at 3:30 P.M. Part-time employees help out during peak demand periods and when full-time employees are absent.

Purchasing The dietary department obtains its food and supplies from several sources. Bulk items are stored in the hospital's central warehouse and are delivered once a week. Many frozen items are delivered weekly from the state contracts warehouse. The remaining supplies, whether refrigerated, nonrefrigerated, or frozen, are delivered by private vendors at various frequencies during the week.

The hospital food service manager has five employees plus himself (see Exhibit 1.15) to coordinate the incoming food and supply orders. Dietary personnel are not responsible for the transportation of goods. However, they are responsible for receiving and accepting high-quality goods and maintaining that quality through the internal storage of food at the hospital.

Patient Tray Assembly The food is assembled on each patient tray on a large rotating oval track. Twelve employees staff the tray assembly line. The first position on the tray assembly line is the "caller," who places the patient's menu on a tray and puts the tray on a carrier with the necessary condiments. The second position puts the salad (tossed fruit, macaroni, cottage cheese, tuna, potato, chicken, bean, and chef's salad) and the ordered salad dressing on each tray. The third position puts the breads (white, wheat, rye) and butter on the tray along with jelly. The fourth position is responsible for the ordered cold beverage (soft drink, milk, buttermilk, orange juice, and so on).

Position five places the dessert (pie, fruit jello, and so on) on the tray. The sixth position serves the entrees and starch for each tray. The seventh position serves the

EXHIBIT 16.9 Dietary Department Organizational Chart

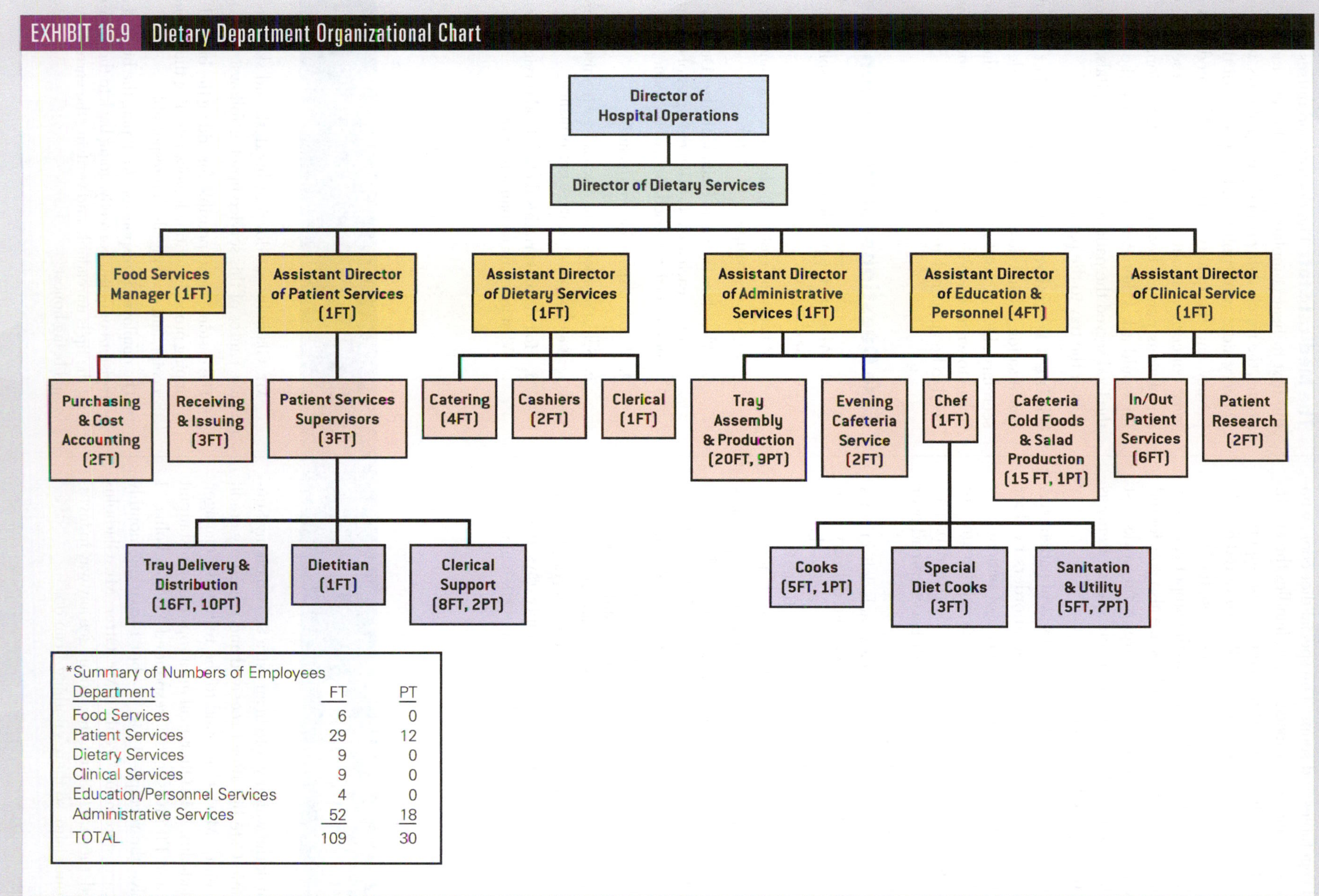

Department	FT	PT
Food Services	6	0
Patient Services	29	12
Dietary Services	9	0
Clinical Services	9	0
Education/Personnel Services	4	0
Administrative Services	52	18
TOTAL	109	30

ordered vegetables and soups. The special diet cook, who both prepares and serves special foods, handles the eighth position. The ninth position is reserved for the supervisor, who checks each menu to determine if the ordered food is on the proper patient tray. The tenth position, the "loader," covers the tray and loads the tray onto the proper cart, now ready for delivery. Two other workers are also considered to work on the line—the coffee pourer, who works just off the line, and the "runner," who gets special items as needed to keep the tray assembly line moving.

Patient Tray Delivery Once the clerks in patient services have sequenced the patient menu orders by floor and room numbers and a completed cart of patient trays is assembled in the basement, the tray delivery teams are responsible for the timely delivery and pickup of all patient meals. This particular hospital has 20 floors spread over three wings of the hospital.

Three teams of four delivery aides each deliver trays for each meal. Once the cart is loaded, the delivery team takes the cart and the appropriate hot beverage to the correct floor. After the cart is on the correct floor, the trays are "set up" by the team captain. A "setup" includes putting the correct hot beverage on the tray, checking the patient's name with the room number, and covering the tray. This procedure expedites service, as the other three delivery aides simply deliver trays from room to room. When eight trays are left, the team captain directs one of the aides to go back to the kitchen, get the next cart, and take it to the next floor for which the team is responsible. After delivering all trays to their assigned floors, the team goes back to the initial floor and begins picking up empty trays, putting them on carts, and returning the carts to the kitchen.

The Medical Staff The doctors and nurses are usually the first to hear complaints about the accuracy of menu orders, the timely delivery and pickup of trays, whether the delivery aides were polite and respectful of the patient's privacy, and the quality of the food. The medical staff is most concerned about the accuracy of prescribed diets for obvious patient health reasons. Occasionally, a doctor would ask a dietician to check or test the content of the food served the patient. At a few hospitals, the nurses deliver the tray to the patient.

Blaine's Decision After completing her telephone conversation, Blaine slowly got up from her desk, told her secretary she was not to be disturbed, shut the door, and began to write down a few notes. Some key questions that need to be answered are listed below.

Case Questions for Discussion:

1. What are the problems facing the hospital's dietary food service?
2. What is the cost to the hospital of a minor versus major service upset or failure?
3. What does the value chain look like? Describe features of each area. Provide examples of opportunities for errors at each stage of the value chain.
4. Who is responsible for quality?
5. Select a process and discuss how to mistake proof it and improve process performance.
6. How do we turn this dietary food service around? What are your recommendations?

Sunshine Enterprises

"I think the waiter wrote in an extra $25 tip on my Sunshine Café bill after I received and signed my credit card receipt," Mark Otter said to the restaurant manager, Brad Gladiolus. "Mr. Otter, mail me a copy of the restaurant receipt and I'll investigate," responded Mr. Gladiolus. "I don't have the receipt—I lost it—but I have my monthly credit card statement," replied Mr. Otter. Mr. Gladiolus hesitated, then said, "Mr. Otter, I don't see any way to investigate your claim, so there's nothing I can do."

Mr. Gladiolus sat down at his desk and sketched out possible causes of this service upset as follows:

- The customer is responsible for adding the bill and tipping properly, writing legibly, retaining the second receipt, and drinking alcohol responsibly.
- The employee is responsible for typing the bill in the register/computer correctly, going back to the customer if the tip is unreadable and verifying the correct amount, and being honest.

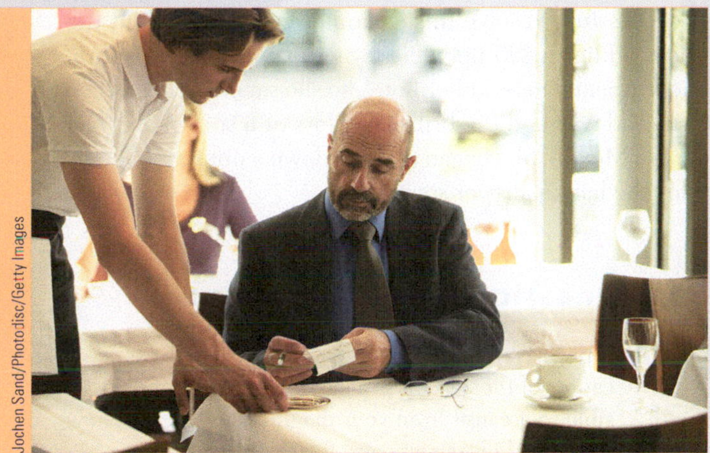
Jochen Sand/Photodisc/Getty Images

Sunshine restaurants average about one negative customer complaint per 100 customer comments.

- The restaurant manager is responsible for investigating the store's receipt history and finding this transaction; auditing the source of the error if possible, such as a mistyped decimal or extra zero; and contacting the credit card company and customer to resolve the issue.
- The credit card company, a third-party provider in this value chain, is responsible for providing records of the electronic transaction, helping resolve the issue, and issuing a debit or credit to the customer and/or restaurant if needed.

Company Background Abby Martin's parents came to Florida from Chicago in the 1960s. Her parents bought land in the Cape Coral area. Later they opened a hotel on Fort Myers Beach, and Abby was part of the housekeeping staff, her first job. By 17, she was running the hotel on her own. Today, she owns and operates six restaurants and a by-the-sea hotel. The restaurants are located in shopping centers next to high-traffic facilities such as movie theaters, groups of retail stores, and other clusters of restaurants. Abby uses four different restaurant concepts (facility décor, size, and layout; prices, menus; music and bands; wine list, lounge areas, etc.) for these six restaurants, depending on the location and local market demographics.

Abby has other investments but loves the challenge of managing restaurants. "I have a great passion for finding a need and meeting it," she said. "The secret to our restaurant success is customizing the business to local needs and being very consistent. Offer good food and service at the most reasonable price you can afford. And know that even if you offer all those things you can still fail. The hospitality business is the hardest business, period. You can never sit back and coast."

In her spare time, she is a prominent community figure involved in activities such as helping build the Ronald McDonald House, fund-raising for the hospital cancer foundation, and serving as chairperson of the local board for the Salvation Army. She likes the Salvation Army because it runs a lean operation, with only six cents spent on management for every one dollar in donations.

Day-to-Day Service Management Sunshine restaurants are normally open seven days a week from 11 a.m. to 10 p.m. Lunch prices are in the $10 to $20 range and include such entrees as a wood-grilled hamburger, seafood salad croissant, and sesame-crusted yellow fin tuna. Dinner prices range from $20 to $30 per person and include dishes such as shrimp and scallop scampi, red snapper picatta, and wood-grilled filet mignon. Each restaurant keeps about 20 to 30 popular wines in stock, such as a Cakebread Chardonnay. Wine, liquor, and some food items are ordered in bulk to take advantage of volume-price discounts and shipped directly from the suppliers to individual restaurants. All other items are ordered by the restaurant chef and general manager for each unique restaurant.

Abby, like most entrepreneurs, has her own approach to quality control. She notes that "I visit my restaurants every few days, and as I walk in I immediately begin to watch customer faces and behaviors. I try to see if they are happy, talking, smiling, and enjoying the food and surroundings. I look at their posture and facial expressions. I often talk with customers and ask if everything was to their liking. I ask my employees—waiters, bartenders, kitchen help, managers, and chef—if they have encountered any problems or service breakdowns. I look for untidy floors, tables, and restrooms. I try to learn from negative customer comments or complaints. My employees know that I will try to help them solve any problem—they trust me. I take the pulse of the restaurant in a short visit. I meet weekly with the restaurant chefs. I manage quality by observation and close contact with all of the people in the restaurant. At night I go over the financials and sales data."

A typical Sunshine restaurant has a core staff of about 12 employees, consisting of a manager, an assistant manager, chef, assistant chef, four waiters, two bartenders, and two helpers in the kitchen. During peak season each restaurant hires six to eight additional employees. Peak demand is when the "snow-birds" arrive in southwest Florida from November to April. During peak demand, the populations of Lee and Collier counties double to almost 2 million people.

Abby's entrepreneurial approach to managing the business results in about one negative customer complaint per 100 customer comments. The complaints are nearly equal in focusing on food or service quality. Contribution to profit and overhead per restaurant is 35 percent. The typical customer averages one visit every two months, and the customer defection rate is in the 5 to 10 percent range, but is difficult to estimate given the seasonal nature of the business.

Long-Term Strategic Issues Abby Martin has established a reputation in southwest Florida for superior service and food quality in her restaurants. She was considering expanding her restaurants to the Tampa and Orlando areas to leverage her expertise and grow the business for the family. She wondered whether she could maintain the proper financial and quality controls with more restaurants and whether to franchise or not. Due to the 2007–2009 credit crunch and high foreclosure rates, there were plenty of commercial properties in good locations for restaurants, and prices were at all-time lows. Abby thought it was now or never in terms of expanding up and down the west coast of Florida. She envisioned as many as 20 Sunshine restaurants in the next five years.

Decisions Abby wondered when she would ever get the time to analyze these issues. It was not easy keeping up with her businesses. She knew that superior, day-to-day food and service quality determines repeat business, so she had to successfully resolve this customer complaint about the waiter adding a $25 tip while trying to plan for the future. She happened to be at her hotel, so she sat down in a beach chair and watched the brilliant colors of a sunset over the Gulf of Mexico. She began to write down a number of questions she had to answer soon.

Case Questions for Discussion:

1. Draw a cause-and-effect diagram for the possible causes of the $25 tip service upset. Select one possible root cause from your diagram, and explain how you would investigate and fix it.
2. What is the average value of a loyal customer (VLC) at Abby's restaurants (see Chapter 2, Section 2-2b)? What is the best way to increase revenue given your VLC analysis?
3. Critique the current "informal" quality control system. What changes and improvements do you recommend if Sunshine expands to 20 restaurants?
4. What are your short- and long-term recommendations? Explain your rationale for these recommendations.

Integrative Case: Hudson Jewelers

The Hudson Jewelers case study found in MindTap integrates material found in each chapter of this book.

Case Question for Discussion:

1. What cost-of-quality criteria (i.e., prevention, appraisal, internal failure, and external failure costs) might be included in an analysis at the following stages of a global diamond supply chain—mining, cutting and polishing centers, and retail jewelry store? Explain and provide examples.

Quality Control and SPC | 17

Quality control is vital to hotels, and indeed, to all service industries.

iedmocha/Shutterstock.com

LEARNING OBJECTIVES

After studying this chapter, you should be able to:

17-1 Describe quality control systems and key issues in manufacturing and service.

17-2 Explain types of variation and the role of statistical process control (SPC).

17-3 Describe how to construct and interpret simple control charts for both continuous and discrete data.

17-4 Describe practical issues in implementing SPC.

17-5 Explain process capability, and calculate process capability indexes.

Marriott has become recognized for its obsessively detailed standard operating procedures (SOPs), which result in hotels that travellers either love for their consistently good quality or hate for their bland uniformity. "This is a company that has more controls, more systems, and more procedural manuals than anyone—except the government," says one industry veteran. "And they actually comply with them." Housekeepers work with a 114-point checklist. One SOP: Server knocks three times. After knocking, the associate should immediately identify herself or himself in a clear voice, saying, "Room service!" The guest's name is never mentioned outside the door. Although people love to make fun of such procedures, they are a serious part of Marriott's business, and SOPs are designed to protect the brand. Recently, Marriott has removed some of the rigid guidelines for owners of hotels it manages, empowering them to make some of their own decisions on details.[1]

WHAT DO YOU THINK?

What opportunities for improved quality control or use of SOPs can you think of at your college or university (e.g., bookstore, cafeteria)?

Quality control is vital in ensuring consistent service experiences and creating customer satisfaction, as the Marriott example illustrates. Simple control mechanisms such as checklists and standard operating procedures provide cost-effective means of doing this. Contacting customers after a poor service experience only uncovers the damage that has already occurred, requires extraordinary measures for service recovery, and often results in lost customers.

The task of **quality control** *is to ensure that a good or service conforms to specifications and meets customer requirements by monitoring and measuring processes and making any necessary adjustments to maintain a specified level of performance.* The consequences of a lack of effective quality control systems and procedures can be serious and potentially cause large financial losses or affect a company's reputation. Health care is one industry that has been highly criticized for its lack of effective quality control systems. For instance, a hospital in Philadelphia promised to evaluate and redesign its laboratory procedures after state investigators confirmed that faulty lab tests led to dozens of patients receiving overdoses of a blood-thinning medication, resulting in the deaths of two patients.[2] Many health care organizations are using contemporary manufacturing quality control methods and other quality improvement approaches, such as Six Sigma, in an effort to minimize such errors.

17-1 Quality Control Systems

Any control system has three components:

1. A performance standard or goal.
2. A means of measuring actual performance.
3. Comparison of actual performance with the standard to form the basis for corrective action.

Similar control measures are taken in services (we introduced service quality metrics in the previous chapter). Fast-food restaurants, for example, have carefully designed their processes for a high degree of accuracy and fast response time, using hands-free intercom systems, microphones that reduce ambient kitchen noise, and screens that display a customer's order. Timers at Wendy's count every segment of the order completion process to help managers control performance and identify problem areas.

Good control systems make economic sense. The importance of control is often explained by the *1:10:100 Rule:* If a defect or service error is identified and corrected at the design stage, it might cost $1 to fix. If it is first detected during the production process, it might cost $10 to fix. However, if the defect is not discovered until it reaches the customer, it might cost $100 to correct.

The dollar values and the exact ratios differ among firms and industries. However, the fact is that the cost of repair or service recovery grows dramatically the further that defects and errors move along the value chain. This rule clearly supports the need for control and a focus on prevention by building quality "at the source." **Quality at the source** *means the*

Leveling the Playing Field in Golf

antpkr/Shutterstock.com

Golf balls must meet five standards to conform to the *USPGA Rules of Golf:* minimum size, maximum weight, spherical symmetry, maximum initial velocity, and overall distance.[3] Methods for measuring such quality characteristics may be automated or performed manually. For instance, golf balls are measured for size by trying to drop them through a metal ring—a conforming ball sticks to the ring, whereas a nonconforming ball falls through; digital scales measure weight to one-thousandth of a gram; and initial velocity is measured in a special machine by finding the time it takes a ball struck at 98 mph to break a ballistic screen at the end of a tube exactly 6.28 feet away.

people responsible for the work control the quality of their processes by identifying and correcting any defects or errors when they first are recognized or occur. This requires that employees have good data-collection, observation, and analysis skills, as well as the proper tools, training, and support of management.

17-1a Quality Control Practices in Manufacturing

In manufacturing, control is generally applied at three key points in the supply chain: at the receiving stage from suppliers, during various production processes, and at the finished-goods stage.

Supplier Certification and Management If incoming materials are of poor quality, then the final manufactured good will certainly be no better. Suppliers should be expected to provide documentation and statistical evidence that they are meeting required specifications. If supplier documentation is done properly, incoming inspection can be completely eliminated. Many companies have formal supplier certification programs to ensure the integrity of incoming materials.

In-Process Control In-process quality control systems are needed to ensure that defective outputs do not leave the process and, more important, to prevent them in the first place. An organization must consider trade-offs between the explicit costs of detection, repair, or replacement and the implicit costs of allowing a nonconformity to continue through the production process. In-process control is typically performed by the people who run the processes on the frontlines; this is an example of quality at the source.

Finished-Goods Control Finished-goods control is often focused on verifying that the product meets customer requirements. For many consumer products, this consists of functional testing. For instance, a manufacturer of televisions might do a simple test on each unit to make sure it operates properly. Modern technology now allows for such tests to be conducted rapidly and costeffectively. For example, imaging scanners along food packaging lines reliably check for foreign particles.

17-1b Quality Control Practices in Services

Many of the same practices described in the previous section can be applied to quality control for back-office service operations such as check or medical insurance claim processing. Front-office services that involve substantial customer contact must be controlled differently. The day-to-day execution of thousands of service encounters is a challenge for any service-providing organization.

One way to control quality in services is to prevent sources of errors and mistakes in the first place by using the poka-yoke approach. Another way is to hire and train service providers in service management skills as part of a prevention-based approach to quality control.

Customer satisfaction measurement can provide the basis for effective control systems in services. Customer satisfaction instruments often focus on service attributes such as attitude, lead time, on-time delivery, exception handling, accountability, and technical support; product attributes such as reliability and price; and overall satisfaction measures. At FedEx, customers are asked to rate everything from billing to the performance of couriers, package condition, tracking and tracing capabilities, complaint handling, and helpfulness of employees.

Many organizations are more concerned with customer loyalty than customer satisfaction. Customers who are merely satisfied may often purchase from competitors because of convenience, promotions, or other factors. Loyal customers place a priority on doing business with a particular organization and will often go out of their way or pay a premium to stay with the company. Loyal customers spend more, are willing to pay higher prices, refer new clients, and are less costly to do business with.

Today, many firms use a metric called the *net promoter score (NPS)*, which was developed by (and is a registered trademark of) Fred Reichheld, Bain & Company, and Satmetrix, to measure customer loyalty. The metric is based on one simple question, "What is the likelihood that you would recommend us?," evaluated on a scale from 0 to 10. Scores of 9 or 10 are usually associated with loyal customers who will typically be repeat customers ("promoters"); scores of 7 or 8 are associated with customers who are satisfied but may switch to competitors ("passives"); and scores of 6 or below represent unhappy customers who may spread negative comments ("detractors"). Promoters are less price sensitive and are more profitable, whereas detractors are more price sensitive, defect at higher rates, and consequently are less profitable. NPS is the difference in the percentage of promoters and detractors, and is claimed to correlate strongly with market and revenue growth. Scores exceeding 50 percent are considered good, and outstanding companies often have scores in the 70 to 90 percent range. Solved Problem 17.1 illustrates how to calculate an NPS.

17-2 Variation and Statistical Process Control

Variation occurs for many reasons, such as inconsistencies in material inputs; changes in environmental conditions (temperature, humidity); machine maintenance cycles; customer participation and self-service; tool wear; and human fatigue. Some variation is obvious, such as inconsistencies in meal delivery times or food quantity at a restaurant; other variation—such as minute differences in physical dimensions of machined parts—is barely perceptible but can be determined through some type of measurement process.

Common cause variation *is the result of complex interactions of variations in materials, tools, machines, information, workers, and the environment.* Such variation is a natural part of the

SOLVED PROBLEM 17.1: CALCULATING A NET PROMOTER SCORE

A sample of 300 customers who responded to the question "What is the likelihood that you would recommend us?" resulted in the following:

The total number of promoters is 63 + 82 = 145; the total number of detractors is 21 + 12 + 6 + 7 + 3 + 0 + 1 = 50. As a percentage of the total, these are 48.3 percent and 16.7 percent, so the net promoter score is 48.3% − 16.7% = 31.6%.

Score	Frequency
10	63
9	82
8	64
7	41
6	21
5	12
4	6
3	7
2	3
1	0
0	1

technology and process design and cannot be controlled; that is, one cannot influence each individual output of the process. It appears at random, and individual sources or causes cannot be identified or explained. However, their combined effect is usually stable and can be described statistically.

Variation occurs for many reasons, such as inconsistencies in material inputs, changes in environmental conditions, machine maintenance cycles, customer participation and self-service, tool wear, and human fatigue.

Common causes of variation generally account for about 80 to 95 percent of the observed variation in a process. They can be reduced only if better technology, process design, or training is provided. This clearly is the responsibility of management.

Special (or assignable) cause variation *arises from external sources that are not inherent in the process, appear sporadically, and disrupt the random pattern of common causes.* Special cause variation occurs sporadically and can be prevented, or at least explained and understood. For example, a tool might break during a process step; a worker might be distracted by a colleague; or a busload of tourists might stop at a restaurant (resulting in unusual wait times). Special cause variation tends to be easily detectable using statistical methods because it disrupts the normal pattern of measurements. When special causes are identified, short-term corrective action generally should be taken by those who own the process and are responsible for doing the work, such as machine operators, order-fulfillment workers, and so on.

Keeping special cause variation from occurring is the essence of quality control. *If no special causes affect the output of a process, we say that the process is* **in control;** *when special causes are present, the process is said to be* **out of control.** A process that is in control does not need any changes or adjustments; an out-of-control process needs correction. However, employees often make two basic

Quality Control for Medical Prescriptions

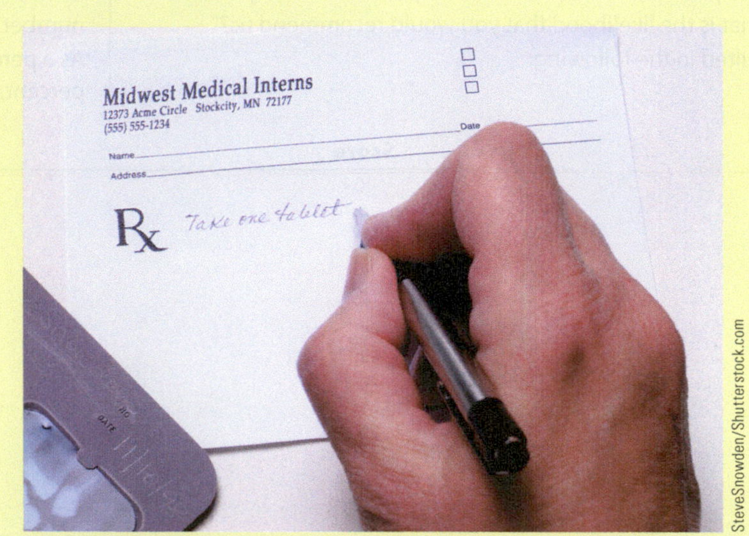

SteveSnowden/Shutterstock.com

Estimates are that at least 7,000 patients die each year from medication errors. Better process management and quality control, such as streamlining processes, building quality checks into every stage of the process, and using technology to eliminate handwritten prescriptions, can minimize such errors. Simple process changes, such as scanning drug containers and double-checking for the correct drug, strength, and quantity, can avoid serious errors. Sloppy handwriting is a major cause of medication errors. Electronic prescriptions avoid handwriting altogether, but although more than 85 percent of pharmacies have the technology to receive electronic prescriptions, only one-third of the nation's prescribers use such systems. However, one study found that as many as 12 percent of prescriptions sent electronically to pharmacies contain errors, matching the error rate of handwritten scrips.[4]

mistakes when attempting to control a process: adjusting a process that is already in control, or failing to correct a process that is out of control.

Although it is clear that a truly out-of-control process must be corrected, many workers mistakenly believe that whenever process output is off-target, some adjustment must be made. Actually, overadjusting a process that is in control will *increase* the variation in the output. Thus, employees must know when to leave a process alone to keep variation at a minimum.

17-2a Statistical Process Control

Statistical process control (SPC) *is a methodology for monitoring the quality of manufacturing and service-delivery processes to help identify and eliminate unwanted causes of variation.* Many customers require their suppliers to provide evidence of statistical process control. Thus, SPC provides a means by which a firm may demonstrate its quality capability, an activity necessary for survival in today's highly competitive markets. SPC is particularly effective for companies in the early stages of quality assurance. SPC helps workers to know when to take action, and more importantly, when to leave a process alone.

SPC relies on control charts. *A* **control chart** *is a run chart to which two horizontal lines, called control limits are added: the upper control limit (UCL) and lower control limit (LCL),* as illustrated in Exhibit 17.1

Control limits are calculated statistically to provide a high probability (generally greater than 0.99) that points will fall between these limits if the process is in control. Control limits make it easier to interpret patterns in a run chart and draw conclusions about the state of control. If special causes are present, the control chart will indicate them, and corrective action can be taken quickly. This will reduce the chances of producing nonconforming product.

EXHIBIT 17.1 Structure of a Control Chart

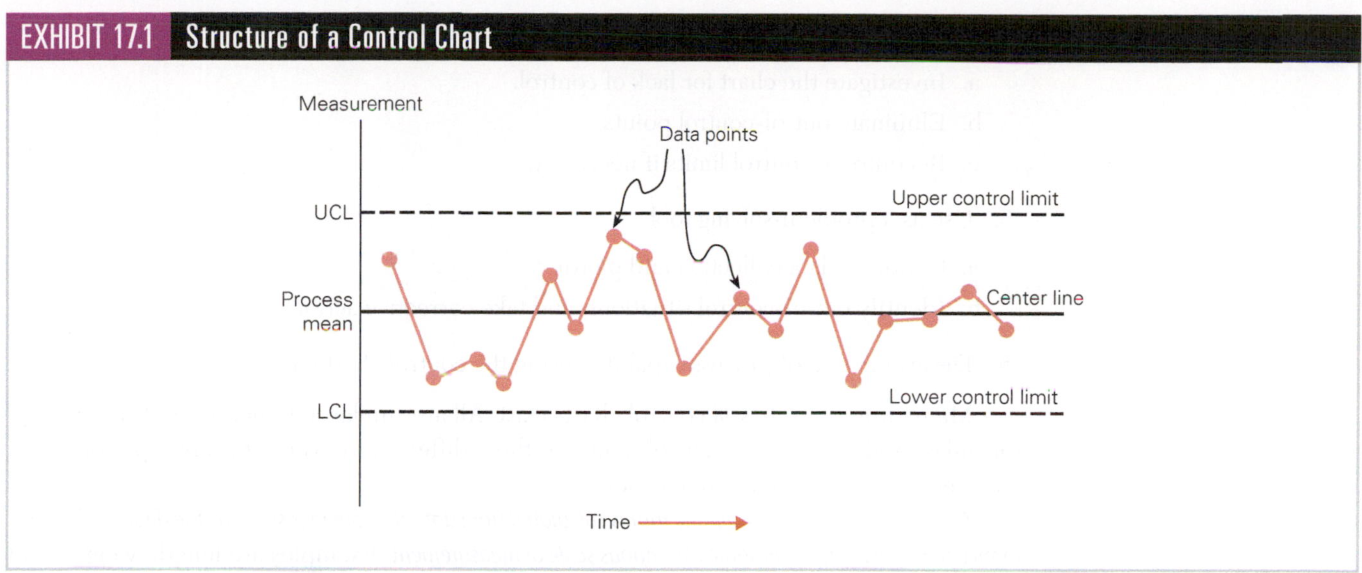

17-3 Constructing Control Charts

Control charts are quite simple to use; they were developed in the early twentieth century for use by shop floor workers (without computers or calculators!). Essentially, we take samples of output from a process at periodic intervals and measure the quality characteristic we wish to control, do some calculations, plot the data on a chart, and interpret the results.

The following is a summary of the steps required to develop and use control charts. Steps 1 through 4 focus on setting up an initial chart; in step 5, the charts are used for ongoing monitoring; and finally, in step 6, the data are used for process capability analysis.

1. Preparation

   a. Choose the metric to be monitored and controlled—for example, the diameter of a drilled hole, time to process an order, percentage of customer returns, or number of complaints per day, and determine the appropriate type of control chart.

   b. Determine the sample size (number of observations in each sample) and frequency of sampling (time between taking successive samples). We will discuss some practical issues related to these decisions later in this chapter.

   c. Set up the control chart. This can be done on a sheet of paper or, more efficiently, on a computer, using a spreadsheet or a commercial software package.

2. Data collection

   a. Record the data.

   b. Calculate relevant statistics: averages, ranges, proportions, and so on.

   c. Plot the statistics on the chart.

   These tasks may be done by hand or on a computer.

3. Determination of trial control limits

   a. Draw the center line (process average) on the chart.

   b. Compute the upper and lower control limits. Again, spreadsheets and computer software can automate these tasks.

4. Analysis and interpretation
   a. Investigate the chart for lack of control.
   b. Eliminate out-of-control points.
   c. Recompute control limits if necessary.
5. Use as a problem-solving tool
   a. Continue data collection and plotting.
   b. Identify out-of-control situations, and take corrective action.
6. Determination of process capability using the control chart data.

Many different types of control charts exist. All are similar in structure, but the specific formulas used to compute control limits for them differ. Moreover, different types of charts are used for different types of metrics.

A ***continuous metric*** *is one that is calculated from data that are measured as the degree of conformance to a specification on some continuous scale of measurement.* Examples are length, weight, and time. Customer waiting time and order lead time are other examples. Continuous data usually require $\overline{x}$- ("x-bar") and R-charts.

A ***discrete metric*** *is one that is calculated from data that are counted.* A dimension on a machined part is either within tolerance or out of tolerance, an order is either complete or incomplete, or a customer either made a complaint or did not about a service experience. We can count the percentage or number of parts within tolerance, the percentage or number of complete orders, and the percentage or number of complaints. These are examples of discrete metrics and usually require control charts that we call p- or c-charts.

To facilitate control chart calculations and to avoid the tedious task of either drawing control charts or constructing an Excel chart manually, we have created Excel templates for the control charts discussed in this chapter, which may be found in MindTap. These templates include automatic calculation of statistics and control limits and the charts themselves (on separate tabs in the workbook).

17-3a Constructing $\overline{x}$- and R-Charts

For continuous metrics, we use $\overline{x}$- and R-charts. *The* ***$\overline{x}$-chart*** *is used to monitor the centering of the process, and the* ***R-chart*** *is used to monitor the variation in the process.* The range is used as a measure of variation primarily for convenience, particularly when workers on the factory floor perform control chart calculations by hand, and works well for small samples.

The first step in developing $\overline{x}$- and R-charts is to gather data. Usually, about 25 to 30 samples are collected. Samples between size 3 and 10 are generally used, with 5 being the most common. The number of samples is indicated by k, and n denotes the sample size. For each sample i, the mean (denoted $\overline{x}_i$) and the range (R_i) are computed. These values are then plotted on their respective control charts. Next, the *overall mean* and *average range* calculations are made. These values specify the center lines for the $\overline{x}$- and R-charts, respectively. The overall mean (denoted $\overline{\overline{x}}$) is the average of the sample means

$$\overline{\overline{x}} = \frac{1}{k}\sum_{i=1}^{k} \overline{x}_i \qquad [17.1]$$

The average range $\overline{R}$ is similarly computed, using the formula

$$\overline{R} = \frac{1}{k}\sum_{i=1}^{k} R_i \qquad [17.2]$$

SOLVED PROBLEM 17.2: CONSTRUCTING AN $\bar{x}$ AND R-CHART

A tire manufacturer periodically tests its tires for tread wear under simulated road conditions. To study and control its manufacturing processes, the company uses $\bar{x}$- and R-charts. Twenty samples, each containing three radial tires, were chosen from different shifts over several days of operation. The data are shown in the $\bar{x}$&*R-Chart* Excel template in Exhibit 17.2. Because $n = 3$, the control limit factors for the R-chart are $D_3 = 0$ and $D_4 = 2.57$. Using Equations 17.1 and 17.2, $\bar{\bar{x}}$ is 31.88 and the average range is 10.8. The control limits are computed using Equations 17.3:

$$\text{UCL}_R = D_4\bar{R} = 2.57(10.8) = 27.8$$
$$\text{LCL}_R = D_3\bar{R} = 0$$

For the $\bar{x}$-chart, $A_2 = 1.02$; thus, the control limits are

$$\text{UCL}_{\bar{x}} = 31.88 + 1.02(10.8) = 42.9$$
$$\text{LCL}_{\bar{x}} = 31.88 - 1.02(10.8) = 20.8$$

In Exhibit 17.2, the Excel $\bar{x}$& *R-Chart* template calculates the control limits and plots the charts. We will discuss how to interpret these charts in section 17-3b.

EXHIBIT 17.2 Excel $\bar{x}$&*R-Chart* Template

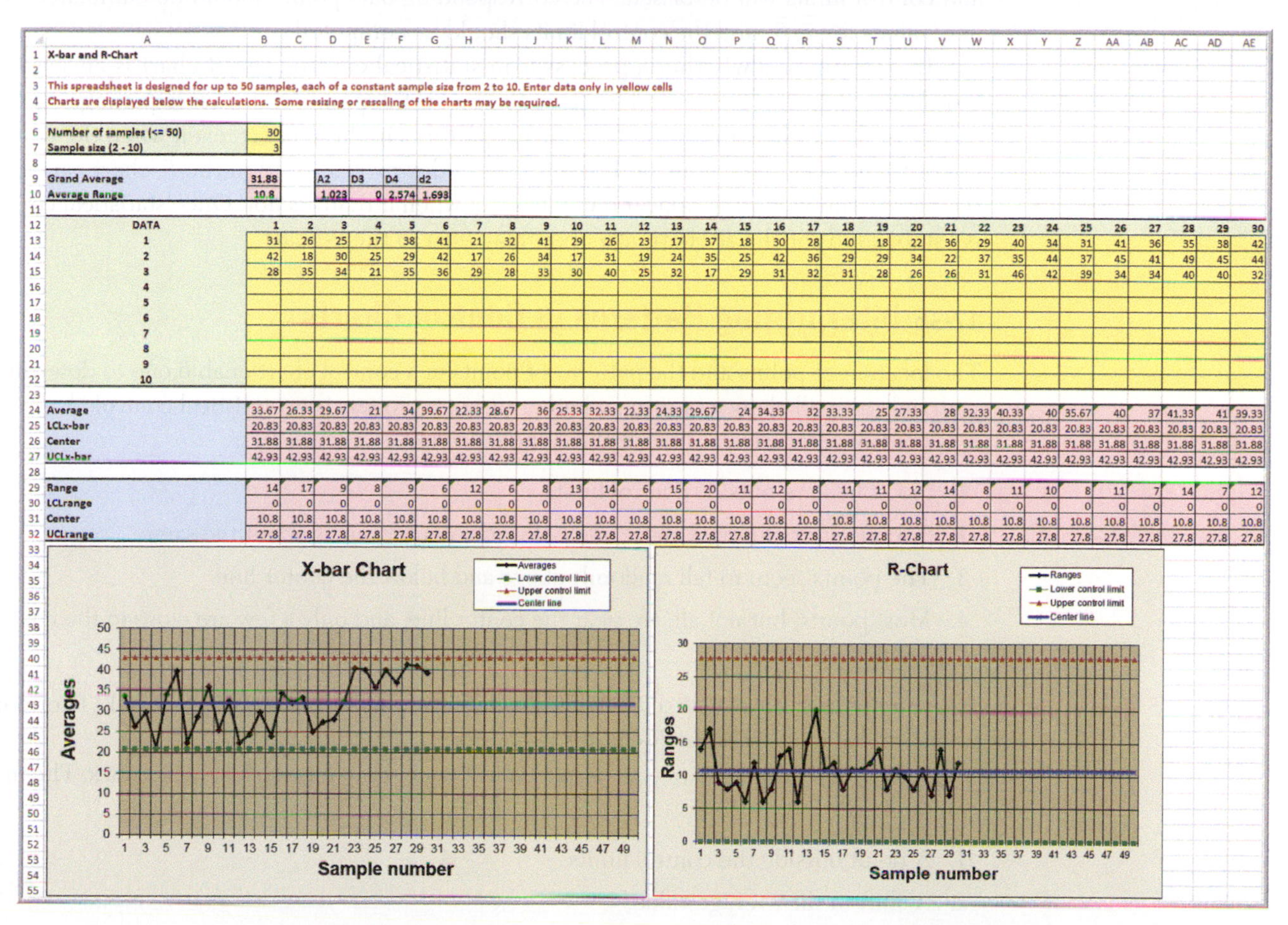

X-bar and R-Chart

This spreadsheet is designed for up to 50 samples, each of a constant sample size from 2 to 10. Enter data only in yellow cells
Charts are displayed below the calculations. Some resizing or rescaling of the charts may be required.

Number of samples (<= 50)	30
Sample size (2 - 10)	3

Grand Average	31.88
Average Range	10.8

A2	D3	D4	d2
1.023	0	2.574	1.693

DATA	1	2	3	4	5	6	7	8	9	10	11	12	13	14	15
1	31	26	25	17	38	41	21	32	41	29	26	23	17	37	18
2	42	18	30	25	29	42	17	26	34	17	31	19	24	35	25
3	28	35	34	21	35	36	29	28	33	30	40	25	32	17	29
4															
5															
6															
7															
8															
9															
10															
Average	33.67	26.33	29.67	21	34	39.67	22.33	28.67	36	25.33	32.33	22.33	24.33	29.67	24
LCLx-bar	20.83	20.83	20.83	20.83	20.83	20.83	20.83	20.83	20.83	20.83	20.83	20.83	20.83	20.83	20.83
Center	31.88	31.88	31.88	31.88	31.88	31.88	31.88	31.88	31.88	31.88	31.88	31.88	31.88	31.88	31.88
UCLx-bar	42.93	42.93	42.93	42.93	42.93	42.93	42.93	42.93	42.93	42.93	42.93	42.93	42.93	42.93	42.93
Range	14	17	9	8	9	6	12	6	8	13	14	6	15	20	11
LCLrange	0	0	0	0	0	0	0	0	0	0	0	0	0	0	0
Center	10.8	10.8	10.8	10.8	10.8	10.8	10.8	10.8	10.8	10.8	10.8	10.8	10.8	10.8	10.8
UCLrange	27.8	27.8	27.8	27.8	27.8	27.8	27.8	27.8	27.8	27.8	27.8	27.8	27.8	27.8	27.8

DATA	16	17	18	19	20	21	22	23	24	25	26	27	28	29	30
1	30	28	40	18	22	36	29	40	34	31	41	36	35	38	42
2	42	36	29	29	34	22	37	35	44	37	45	41	49	45	44
3	31	32	31	28	26	26	31	46	42	39	34	34	40	40	32
4															
5															
6															
7															
8															
9															
10															
Average	34.33	32	33.33	25	27.33	28	32.33	40.33	40	35.67	40	37	41.33	41	39.33
LCLx-bar	20.83	20.83	20.83	20.83	20.83	20.83	20.83	20.83	20.83	20.83	20.83	20.83	20.83	20.83	20.83
Center	31.88	31.88	31.88	31.88	31.88	31.88	31.88	31.88	31.88	31.88	31.88	31.88	31.88	31.88	31.88
UCLx-bar	42.93	42.93	42.93	42.93	42.93	42.93	42.93	42.93	42.93	42.93	42.93	42.93	42.93	42.93	42.93
Range	12	8	11	11	12	14	8	11	10	8	11	7	14	7	12
LCLrange	0	0	0	0	0	0	0	0	0	0	0	0	0	0	0
Center	10.8	10.8	10.8	10.8	10.8	10.8	10.8	10.8	10.8	10.8	10.8	10.8	10.8	10.8	10.8
UCLrange	27.8	27.8	27.8	27.8	27.8	27.8	27.8	27.8	27.8	27.8	27.8	27.8	27.8	27.8	27.8

The average range and average mean are used to compute upper and lower control limits (UCL and LCL) for the R- and $\bar{x}$-charts. Control limits are easily calculated using the following formulas:

$$\begin{aligned} \text{UCL}_R &= D_4\bar{R} \qquad \text{UCL}_{\bar{x}} = \bar{\bar{x}} + A_2\bar{R} \\ \text{LCL}_R &= D_3\bar{R} \qquad \text{LCL}_{\bar{x}} = \bar{\bar{x}} - A_2\bar{R} \end{aligned} \qquad [17.3]$$

where the constants D_3, D_4, and A_2 depend on the sample size (see Appendix B at the end of this book). Solved Problem 17.2 illustrates the use of the *$\bar{x}$&R-Chart* Excel template.

The control limits represent the range between which all points are expected to fall if the process is in statistical control. If any points fall outside the control limits or if any unusual patterns are observed, then some special cause has probably affected the process. The process should be studied to determine the cause. If special causes are present, then they are *not* representative of the true state of statistical control, and the calculations of the center line and control limits will be biased. The corresponding data points should be eliminated, and new values for $\bar{\bar{x}}$, $\bar{R}$, and the control limits should be computed.

In determining whether a process is in statistical control, the R-chart is always analyzed first. Because the control limits in the $\bar{x}$-chart depend on the average range, special causes in the R-chart may produce unusual patterns in the $\bar{x}$-chart, even when the centering of the process is in control. For example, a downward trend in the R-chart can cause the data in the $\bar{x}$-chart to appear out of control when it really is not. Once statistical control is established for the R-chart, attention may turn to the $\bar{x}$-chart.

17-3b Interpreting Patterns in Control Charts

The location of points and the patterns of points in a control chart enable one to determine, with only a small chance of error, whether or not a process is in statistical control. A process is in control when the control chart has the following characteristics:

1. No points are outside control limits.
2. The number of points above and below the center line is about the same.
3. The points seem to fall randomly above and below the center line.
4. Most points, but not all, are near the center line, and only a few are close to the control limits.

You can see that these characteristics are evident in the R-chart in Exhibit 17.1. Therefore, we would conclude that the R-chart is in control.

When a process is out of control, we typically see some unusual characteristics. The most common are:

1. A point outside the control limits.
2. A shift in the average value.
3. A gradual trend.
4. A cyclical pattern.

When a point falls outside the control limits, one should first check for the possibility that the control limits were miscalculated or that the point was plotted incorrectly. If neither is the case, this can indicate that the process average has changed.

An example of a shift in the average is shown in Exhibit 17.1; we see that the last eight points in the $\bar{x}$-chart are all above the center line, suggesting that the process mean has increased.

This might suggest that something is causing excessive tread wear in recent samples, perhaps a different batch of raw materials or improper mixing of the chemical composition of the tires. Some typical rules that are used to identify a shift include:

- 8 points in a row above or below the center line,
- 10 of 11 consecutive points above or below the center line,
- 12 of 14 consecutive points above or below the center line,
- 2 of 3 consecutive points in the outer one-third region between the center line and one of the control limits, and
- 4 of 5 consecutive points in the outer two-thirds region between the center line and one of the control limits.

These rules are derived from probability calculations; the chance of them occurring in a process that is in control is extremely small, so if they do occur, we would suspect a special cause.

An increasing or decreasing trend often results from tool wear, changes in temperature or other environmental conditions, general equipment deterioration, dirt buildup on fixtures, or operator fatigue. About six or seven consecutive points that increase or decrease in value usually signify a gradual change.

A cyclical pattern is also unusual and should be suspect. It might be a result of seasonal effects of material deliveries, temperature swings, maintenance cycles, or periodic rotation of operators. Whenever an unusual pattern in a control chart is identified, the process should be stopped until the problem has been identified and corrected. For example, in a drilling operation, if an $\bar{x}$-chart shows an increasing trend in the diameter of drilled holes, then the machinist would need to replace the worn drill bit. In a service operation, an upward shift in an R-chart signifies increased variation in performance, suggesting that additional training might be necessary.

17-3c Constructing *p*-Charts

Many quality characteristics assume only two values, such as good or bad, pass or fail, and so on. *A* ***p*-chart** *monitors the proportion of nonconforming items.* Often, it is also called a *fraction nonconforming* or *fraction defective* chart.

As with continuous data, a p-chart is constructed by first gathering 25 to 30 samples of the attribute being measured. The size of each sample should be large enough to have several nonconforming items. If the probability of finding a nonconforming item is small, a sample size of 100 or more items is usually necessary. Samples are chosen over time periods so that any special causes that are identified can be investigated.

Let us suppose that k samples, each of size n, are selected. If y_i represents the number nonconforming in sample i, the proportion nonconforming is $p_i = y_i/n$. The average fraction nonconforming for the group of k samples is

$$\bar{p} = \frac{y_1 + y_2 + \cdots + y_k}{nk} \qquad [17.4]$$

That is, add the number of nonconforming items in all samples and divide by n times k, the total number of items. Be careful not to confuse n and k. (Note that this formula applies only when all sample sizes are the same.) This statistic reflects the average performance of the process. One would expect a high percentage of samples to have a fraction nonconforming within 3 standard deviations of $\bar{p}$. An estimate of the standard deviation is given by

$$s_{\bar{p}} = \sqrt{\frac{\bar{p}(1-\bar{p})}{n}} \qquad [17.5]$$

Therefore, upper and lower control limits are given by

$$\begin{aligned} UCL_p &= \overline{p} + 3s_{\overline{p}} \\ LCL_p &= \overline{p} - 3s_{\overline{p}} \end{aligned} \quad [17.6]$$

If LCL_p is less than zero, a value of zero is used.

Analysis of a p-chart is similar to that of an $\overline{x}$- or R-chart. Points outside the control limits signify an out-of-control situation. Patterns and trends should also be sought to identify special causes. However, a point on a p-chart below the lower control limit or the development of a trend below the center line indicates that the process might have improved, based on an ideal target of zero defectives. Caution is advised before such conclusions are drawn, because errors may have been made in computation.

Solved Problem 17.3 shows the construction of a p-chart using the Excel *p-chart* template available in MindTap. The chart appears to be in control.

17-3d Constructing *c*-Charts

A p-chart monitors the proportion of nonconforming items, but a nonconforming item may have more than one nonconformance. For instance, a customer's order may have several errors, such as wrong item, wrong quantity, wrong price, and so on. To monitor the number of nonconformances per unit, we use a c-chart. These charts are used extensively in service applications because most managers of service processes are interested in the number of errors or problems that occur per customer (or patient, student, order), and not just the proportion of customers that experienced problems. ***A c-chart monitors the total number of nonconformances per unit when the size of the sampling unit or number of opportunities for errors is constant.*** The sampling unit could be a day, a unit of product, the area of a piece of fabric, and so on. Thus, for a c-chart, the size of each sample is one. We do not have multiple observations for each sample as we do with a p-chart. See the box *Choosing between p- and c-Charts*.

To construct a c-chart, we must first estimate the average number of nonconformances per unit, $\overline{c}$. This is done by taking a sample of at least 25 units, counting the number of nonconformances per unit, and finding the average by dividing the total number of nonconformances by the total number of units that were sampled. Then, control limits are given by

$$\begin{aligned} UCL_c &= \overline{c} + 3\sqrt{\overline{c}} \\ LCL_c &= \overline{c} - 3\sqrt{\overline{c}} \end{aligned} \quad [17.7]$$

Solved Problem 17.4 shows the construction of a c-chart using the Excel *c-chart* template in MindTap. The c-chart appears to be in control.

Choosing between *p*- and *c*-Charts

It can be difficult to choose correctly between a *p*- and a *c*-chart. One guideline to help decide is to think of what you wish to plot on the chart. On a *p*-chart, we plot the fraction of nonconforming units in a sample, where a sample consists of an equal size of *n* units, and each unit in the sample is either conforming or nonconforming.

In a *c*-chart we plot the number of nonconformances (defects or errors) per unit, where each unit can have more than one nonconformance. For a *c*-chart, a "unit" may be a single physical good; a service transaction such as a customer order; or even a time dimension, such as day, week, or month. Or a "unit" can be a sample of equal numbers of multiple items, each of which may have many possible types of nonconformances. For instance, a unit can be a sample of 50 shipments made each day. The *c*-chart would then monitor the number of nonconformances (wrong product, wrong quantity, wrong color, etc.) per 50 shipments. The key is defining what the unit is!

SOLVED PROBLEM 17.3: CONSTRUCTING A p-CHART

Automated sorting machines in a post office must read the ZIP code on letters and divert the letters to the proper carrier routes. Over a month's time, $k = 25$ samples of $n = 100$ letters were chosen, and the number of errors was recorded. Fifty-five errors were found. The average proportion defective, $\bar{p}$ is computed as $55/(25 \times 100) = 55/2500 = 0.022$.

The standard deviation is computed using formula [17.5] as

$$s_{\bar{p}} = \sqrt{\frac{0.022(1 - 0.022)}{100}} = 0.1467$$

Then, using formula [17.6], UCL = 0.022 + 3(0.01467) = 0.066, and LCL = 0.022 − 3(0.01467) = −0.022. Because the LCL is negative and the actual proportion nonconforming cannot be less than zero, the LCL is set equal to zero (see Exhibit 17.3).

EXHIBIT 17.3 Excel p-*Chart* Template

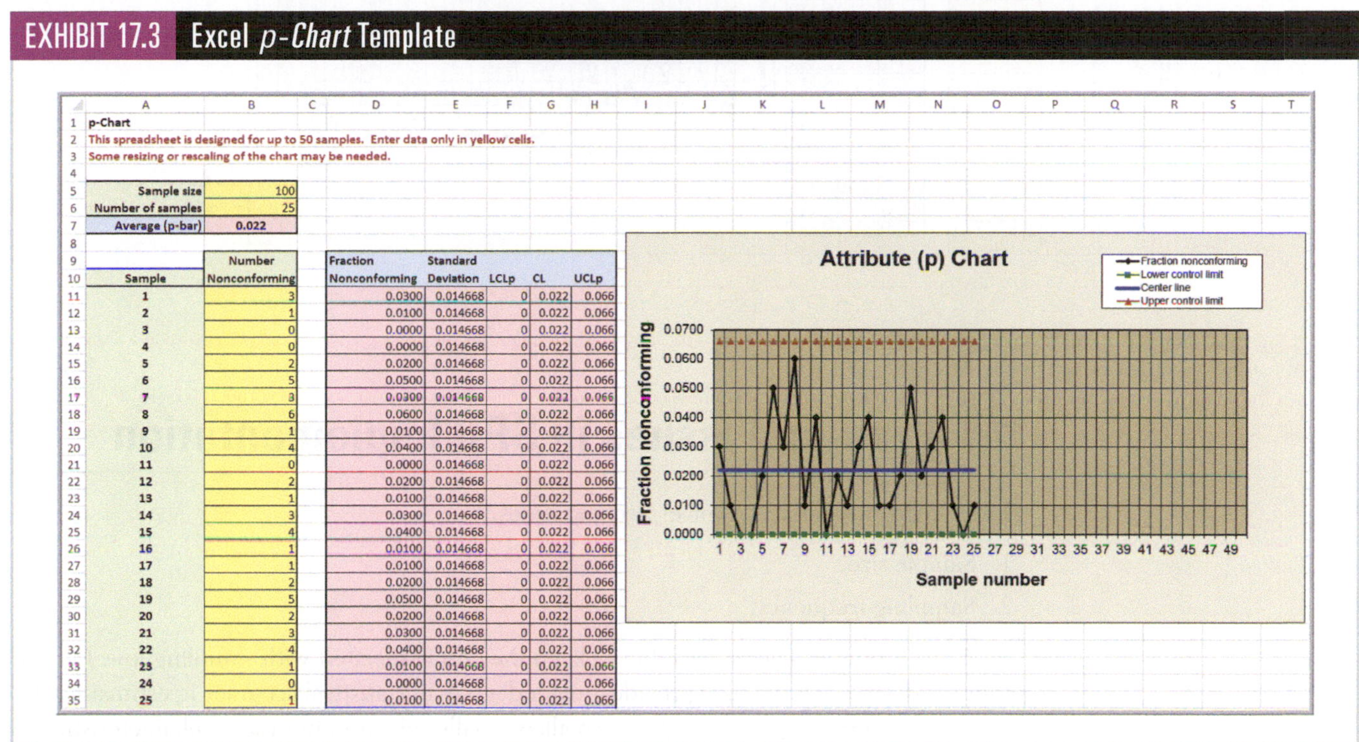
p-Chart

This spreadsheet is designed for up to 50 samples. Enter data only in yellow cells.

Some resizing or rescaling of the chart may be needed.

Sample size	100
Number of samples	25
Average (p-bar)	0.022

Sample	Number Nonconforming	Fraction Nonconforming	Standard Deviation	LCLp	CL	UCLp
1	3	0.0300	0.014668	0	0.022	0.066
2	1	0.0100	0.014668	0	0.022	0.066
3	0	0.0000	0.014668	0	0.022	0.066
4	0	0.0000	0.014668	0	0.022	0.066
5	2	0.0200	0.014668	0	0.022	0.066
6	5	0.0500	0.014668	0	0.022	0.066
7	3	0.0300	0.014668	0	0.022	0.066
8	6	0.0600	0.014668	0	0.022	0.066
9	1	0.0100	0.014668	0	0.022	0.066
10	4	0.0400	0.014668	0	0.022	0.066
11	0	0.0000	0.014668	0	0.022	0.066
12	2	0.0200	0.014668	0	0.022	0.066
13	1	0.0100	0.014668	0	0.022	0.066
14	3	0.0300	0.014668	0	0.022	0.066
15	4	0.0400	0.014668	0	0.022	0.066
16	1	0.0100	0.014668	0	0.022	0.066
17	1	0.0100	0.014668	0	0.022	0.066
18	2	0.0200	0.014668	0	0.022	0.066
19	5	0.0500	0.014668	0	0.022	0.066
20	2	0.0200	0.014668	0	0.022	0.066
21	3	0.0300	0.014668	0	0.022	0.066
22	4	0.0400	0.014668	0	0.022	0.066
23	1	0.0100	0.014668	0	0.022	0.066
24	0	0.0000	0.014668	0	0.022	0.066
25	1	0.0100	0.014668	0	0.022	0.066

SOLVED PROBLEM 17.4: CONSTRUCTING A c-CHART

Each day, a factory counts the number of machine failures and wants to plot the number of failures/day on a c-chart. A c-chart is appropriate, because each day there may be multiple machine failures (nonconformances). The data are shown in the *C-chart* Excel template in Exhibit 17.4. The total number of machine failures over a 25-day period is 45. Therefore, the average number of failures per day is

$$\bar{c} = \frac{45 \text{ failures}}{25 \text{ days}} = 1.8 \text{ failures/day}$$

Hence, control limits for a c-chart are given by

$$UCL_c = 1.8 + 3\sqrt{1.8} = 5.82$$

$$LCL_c = 1.8 - 3\sqrt{1.8} = -2.22, \text{ or zero}$$

EXHIBIT 17.4 Excel *c-Chart* Template

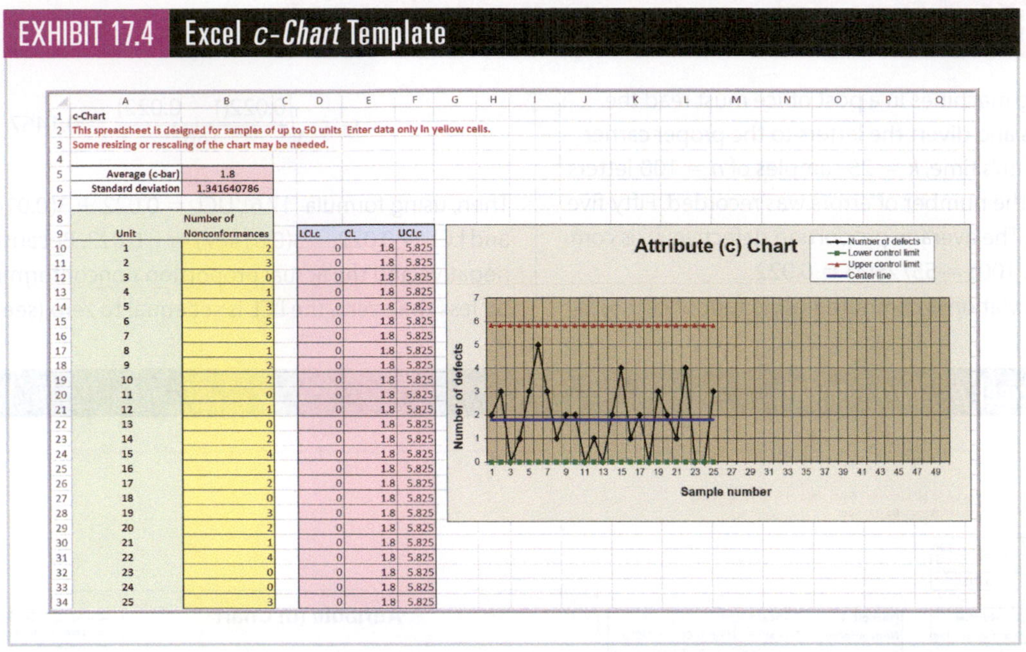

c-Chart

This spreadsheet is designed for samples of up to 50 units Enter data only in yellow cells.

Some resizing or rescaling of the chart may be needed.

Average (c-bar)	1.8
Standard deviation	1.341640786

Unit	Number of Nonconformances	LCLc	CL	UCLc
1	2	0	1.8	5.825
2	3	0	1.8	5.825
3	0	0	1.8	5.825
4	1	0	1.8	5.825
5	3	0	1.8	5.825
6	5	0	1.8	5.825
7	3	0	1.8	5.825
8	1	0	1.8	5.825
9	2	0	1.8	5.825
10	2	0	1.8	5.825
11	0	0	1.8	5.825
12	1	0	1.8	5.825
13	0	0	1.8	5.825
14	2	0	1.8	5.825
15	4	0	1.8	5.825
16	1	0	1.8	5.825
17	2	0	1.8	5.825
18	0	0	1.8	5.825
19	3	0	1.8	5.825
20	2	0	1.8	5.825
21	1	0	1.8	5.825
22	4	0	1.8	5.825
23	0	0	1.8	5.825
24	0	0	1.8	5.825
25	3	0	1.8	5.825

17-4 Practical Issues in SPC Implementation

Designing control charts involves two key issues:

1. Sample size.
2. Sampling frequency.

A small sample size is desirable to keep the cost associated with sampling low. On the other hand, large sample sizes provide greater degrees of statistical accuracy in estimating the true state of control. Large samples also allow smaller changes in process characteristics to be detected with higher probability. In practice, samples of about 5 have been found to work well in detecting process shifts of two standard deviations or larger. To detect smaller shifts in the process mean, larger sample sizes of 15 to 25 must be used.

For attributes data, too small of a sample size can make a p-chart meaningless. Even though many guidelines such as "use at least 100 observations" have been suggested, the proper sample size should be determined statistically, particularly when the true portion of non-conformances is small. If p is small, n should be large enough to have a high probability of detecting at least one nonconformance. For example, statistical calculations can show that if $p = 0.01$, then the sample size must be at least 300 to have at least a 95 percent chance of finding at least one nonconformance.

Managers must also consider the sampling frequency. Taking large samples on a frequent basis is desirable but clearly not economical. No hard-and-fast rules exist for the frequency of sampling. Samples should be close enough to provide an opportunity to detect changes in process characteristics as soon as possible and reduce the chances of producing a large amount of nonconforming output. However, they should not be so close that the cost of sampling outweighs the benefits that can be realized. This decision depends on the individual application and volume of output.

17-4a Controlling Six Sigma Processes

SPC is a useful methodology for processes that operate at a low sigma level; for example, the three sigma level or less. However, when the rate of defects is extremely low, standard control charts are not effective. For example, when using a p-chart for a process with a high sigma

IBM: Using Statistical Process Control (SPC)

At one IBM branch, preemployment physical examinations took too long and taxed the medical staff assigned to conduct them. The challenge IBM faced was to maintain the quality of the exam while reducing the time needed to perform it by identifying and eliminating waiting periods between the various parts of it.

Preliminary control charts revealed that the average time required for the examination was 74 minutes, but the range varied greatly. New equipment and additional training of the medical staff were suggested as means of shortening the average time. Initial charts indicated that the process was out of control, but continued monitoring and process improvements lowered the average time to 40 minutes, and both the average and range were brought into statistical control with the help of $\bar{x}$ and R-charts.[5]

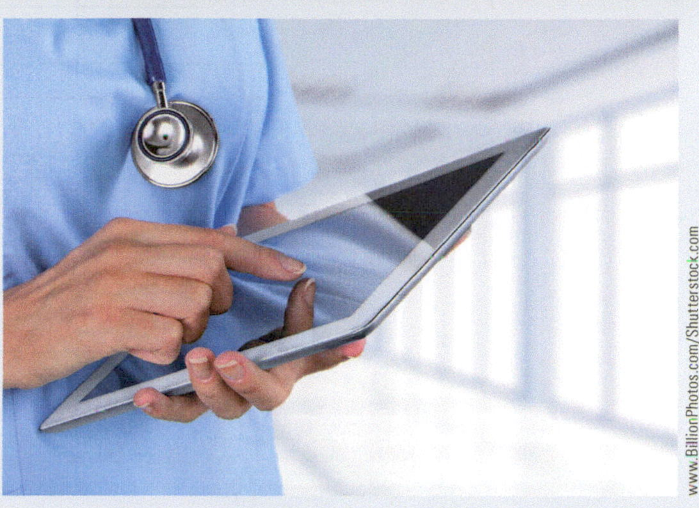
www.BillionPhotos.com/Shutterstock.com

level, few defects will be discovered even with large sample sizes. For instance, if $p = 0.001$, a sample size of 500 will have an expected number of only $500(0.001) = 0.5$ defects. Hence, most samples will have zero or only one defect, and the chart will provide little useful information for control. Using much larger sample sizes would only delay the timeliness of information and increase the chances that the process may have changed during the sampling interval. Small sample sizes will typically result in a conclusion that any observed defect indicates an out-of-control condition, thus implying that a controlled process will have zero defects, which may be impractical. In addition, conventional SPC charts will have higher frequencies of false alarms and make it difficult to evaluate process improvements. These issues are important for Six Sigma practitioners to understand in order not to blindly apply tools that may not be appropriate.

17-5 Process Capability

Process capability *refers to the natural variation in a process that results from common causes.* Knowing process capability allows one to predict, quantitatively, how well a process will meet specifications, and to specify equipment requirements and the level of control necessary. Process capability has no meaning if the process is not in statistical control because special causes will bias the mean or the standard deviation. Therefore, we should use control charts to first eliminate any special causes before computing the process capability.

A **process capability study** *is a carefully planned study designed to yield specific information about the performance of a process under specified operating conditions.* Typical questions that are asked in a process capability study are:

- Where is the process centered?
- How much variability exists in the process?
- Is the performance relative to specifications acceptable?
- What proportion of output will be expected to meet specifications?

EXHIBIT 17.5 Process Capability versus Design Specifications

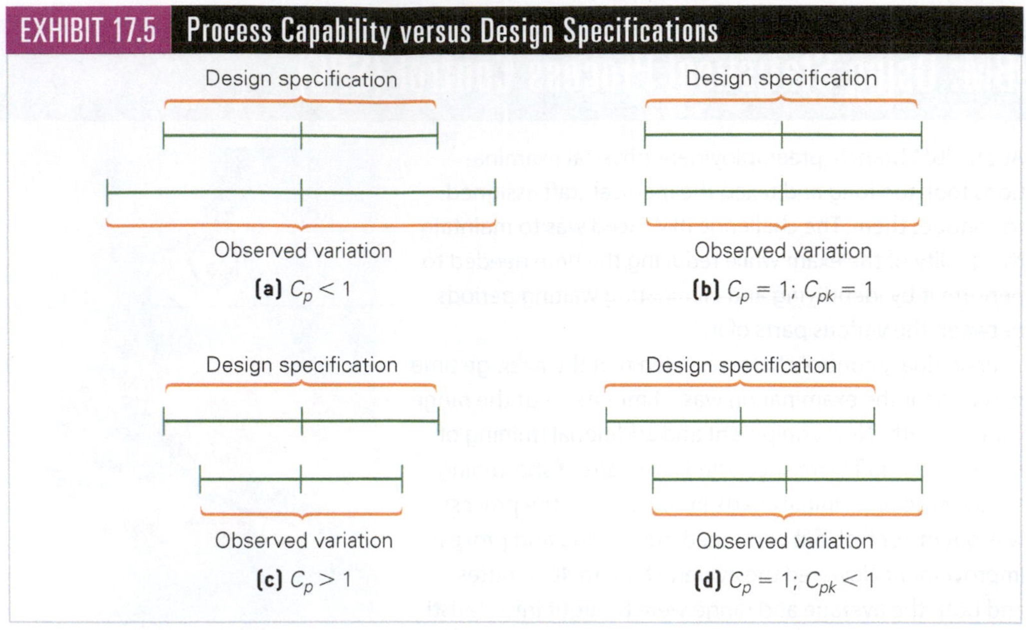

One of the properties of a normal distribution is that 99.73 percent of the observations will fall within three standard deviations from the mean. Thus, a process that is in control can be expected to produce a very large percentage of output between $\mu - 3\sigma$ and $\mu + 3\sigma$, where μ is the process average. Therefore, the natural variation of the process can be estimated by $\mu \pm 3\sigma$ and characterizes the capability of the process. One way of computing the standard deviation in this formula is to take a sample of data, compute the sample standard deviation, s, and use it as an estimate of σ. A second approach, often used in conjunction with an $\bar{x}$- and R-chart, is to estimate σ by dividing the average range by a constant, d_2, which can be found in Appendix B. That is,

$$\sigma = \frac{\bar{R}}{d_2} \qquad [17.8]$$

The process capability is usually compared to the design specifications to indicate the ability of the process to meet the specifications. Exhibit 17.5 illustrates four possible situations that can arise when the observed variability of a process is compared to design specifications. In part (a), the range of process variation is larger than the design specification; thus, it will be impossible for the process to meet specifications a large percentage of the time. Managers can either scrap or rework nonconforming parts (100 percent inspection is necessary), invest in a better process with less variation, or change the design specifications. In part (b), the process is able to produce according to specification, although it will require close monitoring to ensure that it remains in that position. In part (c), the observed variation is tighter than the specifications; this is the ideal situation from a quality control viewpoint, as little inspection or control is necessary. Finally, in part (d), the observed variation is the same as the design specification, but the process is off center; thus, some nonconforming product can be expected.

17-5a Process Capability Index

The relationship between the natural variation and specifications is often quantified by a measure known as the **process capability index.** The process capability index, C_p, is defined as the ratio of the specification width to the natural variation of the process. C_p relates the natural variation of the process with the design specifications in a single, quantitative measure. In numerical terms, the formula is

$$C_p = \frac{USL - LSL}{6\sigma} \tag{17.9}$$

where

USL = upper specification limit
LSL = lower specification limit
σ = standard deviation of the process (or an estimate based on the sample standard deviation, s)

C_p values less than 1 mean that a significant percentage of output (observed variation) will not conform to the design specifications (see Exhibit 17.4a). Note that when $C_p = 1$, the observed variation is the same as the design specification width, USL – LSL (as in Exhibit 17.4b). Values of C_p exceeding 1 indicate good capability (Exhibit 17.4c); in fact, many firms require that their suppliers demonstrate a high value of C_p.

The value of C_p does not depend on the mean of the process; thus, a process may be off-center, such as in Exhibit 17.4(d) and still show an acceptable value of C_p. To account for the process centering, one-sided capability indexes are often used:

$$C_{pu} = \frac{USL - \mu}{3\sigma} \text{ (upper one-sided index)} \tag{17.10}$$

$$C_{pl} = \frac{\mu - LSL}{3\sigma} \text{ (lower one-sided index)} \tag{17.11}$$

$$C_{pk} = \min(C_{pl}, C_{pu}) \tag{17.12}$$

For example, a high value of C_{pu} indicates that the process is very capable of meeting the upper specification. C_{pk} is the "worst case" and provides an indication of whether both the lower and upper specifications can be met regardless of where the process is centered. This is the value that most managers focus on.

SOLVED PROBLEM 17.5: COMPUTING PROCESS CAPABILITY INDEXES

One hundred and twenty measurements of the dimension of a manufactured part for an automobile were taken from a controlled process. Exhibit 17.6 shows a portion of the Excel *Process Capability* template available in MindTap, which computes the average and standard deviation of the data in rows 21 and 22, and the process capability indexes in cells G20:H23. We calculate C_p using Equation 17.9 as follows:

$$C_p = \frac{USL - LSL}{6\sigma} = \frac{(10.9 - 10.5)}{(6 \times 0.0868)} = 0.768 \tag{17.9}$$

$$C_{pu} = \frac{USL - \mu}{3\sigma} \text{ (upper one-sided index)} = \frac{(10.9 - 10.7171)}{(3 \times 0.0868)} = 0.702 \tag{17.10}$$

$$C_{pl} = \frac{\mu - LSL}{3\sigma} \text{ (lower one-sided index)} = \frac{(10.7171 - 10.5)}{(3 \times 0.0868)} = 0.833 \tag{17.11}$$

$$C_{pk} = \min(C_{pl}, C_{pu}) = \min(0.833, 0.702) = 0.702 \tag{17.12}$$

EXHIBIT 17.6 Portion of the Excel *Process Capability* Template

Process Capability Analysis

This template is designed to handle up to 150 observations. Enter data only in yellow cells.

Nominal specification	10.7
Upper specification limit	10.9
Lower specification limit	10.5

DATA	1	2	3	4	5	6	7	8	9	10	11	12	13	14	15
1	10.650	10.800	10.500	10.800	10.700	10.800	10.750	10.650	10.850	10.650	10.800	10.650			
2	10.750	10.850	10.800	10.800	10.700	10.700	10.850	10.700	10.800	10.550	10.700	10.850			
3	10.750	10.700	10.650	10.800	10.650	10.650	10.750	10.650	10.500	10.800	10.750	10.800			
4	10.600	10.650	10.650	10.700	10.600	10.750	10.800	10.850	10.650	10.650	10.700	10.600			
5	10.700	10.750	10.700	10.750	10.550	10.700	10.850	10.700	10.750	10.600	10.750	10.700			
6	10.600	10.900	10.850	10.750	10.650	10.650	10.600	10.750	10.750	10.600	10.650	10.650			
7	10.600	10.750	10.800	10.700	10.600	10.850	10.850	10.850	10.800	10.850	10.850	10.800			
8	10.750	10.750	10.700	10.700	10.700	10.600	10.650	10.850	10.750	10.650	10.700	10.650			
9	10.650	10.650	10.750	10.800	10.650	10.900	10.650	10.750	10.700	10.750	10.700	10.700			
10	10.600	10.600	10.750	10.800	10.750	10.850	10.750	10.750	10.700	10.650	10.600	10.650			

Process Capability Index Calculations

Average	10.7171
Standard deviation	0.0868

Cp	0.768
Cpl	0.833
Cpu	0.702
Cpk	0.702

EXHIBIT 17.7 Histogram Displayed in the Excel *Process Capability* Template

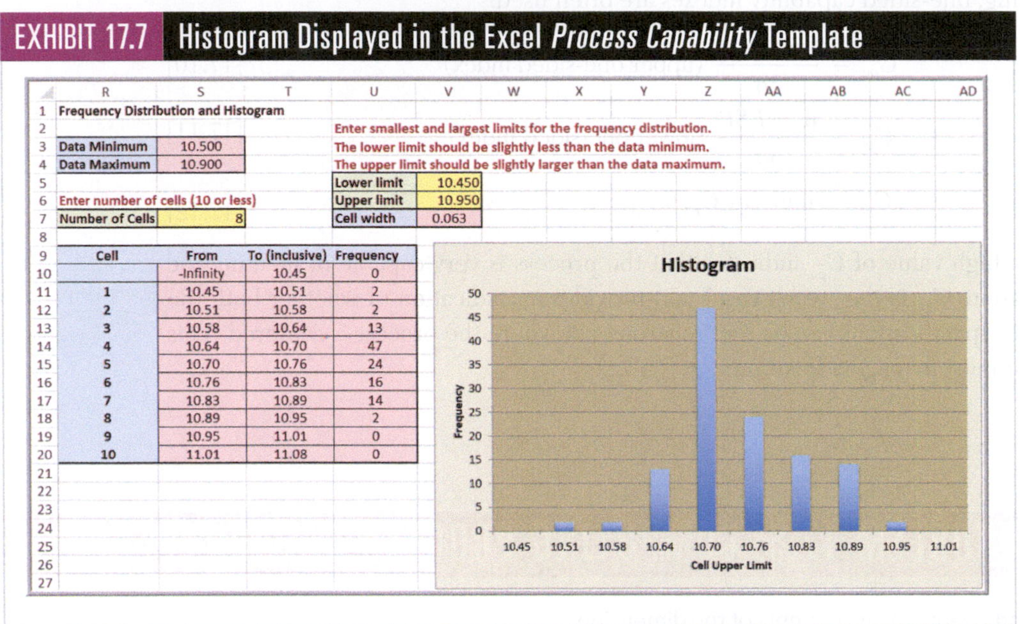

Frequency Distribution and Histogram

Data Minimum	10.500
Data Maximum	10.900

Enter number of cells (10 or less)

Number of Cells	8

Enter smallest and largest limits for the frequency distribution.
The lower limit should be slightly less than the data minimum.
The upper limit should be slightly larger than the data maximum.

Lower limit	10.450
Upper limit	10.950
Cell width	0.063

Cell	From	To (inclusive)	Frequency
	-Infinity	10.45	0
1	10.45	10.51	2
2	10.51	10.58	2
3	10.58	10.64	13
4	10.64	10.70	47
5	10.70	10.76	24
6	10.76	10.83	16
7	10.83	10.89	14
8	10.89	10.95	2
9	10.95	11.01	0
10	11.01	11.08	0

Because C_p is less than 1, the process is not capable of meeting the design specifications. The C_p and C_{pl} analyses indicate that the process is not centered because C_{pl} and C_{pu} are not equal, and that the process has more difficulty in meeting the upper specification limit. Finally, the fact that $C_{pk} = 0.702$ is less than 1 tells us that the actual process capability (including the off-centering of the mean) is not very good. Exhibit 17.7 shows the histogram displayed in the Excel *Process Capability* template. Only a few data points are actually outside the specification limits, but if the process should drift from the nominal specification, more defects will be produced.

Process capability is important to both product designers and process owners. If product specifications are too tight, the product will be difficult to manufacture. Employees who run the processes will be under pressure and will spend a lot of time adjusting the process and inspecting output.

CHAPTER 17 LEARNING OBJECTIVE SUMMARIES

17.1 **Describe quality control systems and key issues in manufacturing and service.** Any control system has three components:

1. a performance standard or goal,
2. a means of measuring actual performance, and
3. comparison of actual performance with the standard to form the basis for corrective action.

The importance of control is often explained by the 1:10:100 Rule: If a defect or service error is identified and corrected at the design stage, it might cost \$1 to fix. If it is first detected during the production process, it might cost \$10 to fix. However, if the defect is not discovered until it reaches the customer, it might cost \$100 to correct. In manufacturing, control is generally applied at three key points in the supply chain: at the receiving stage from suppliers, during various production processes, and at the finished-goods stage.

One way to control quality in services is to prevent sources of errors and mistakes in the first place by using the poka-yoke approaches. Another way is to hire and train service providers in service management skills as part of a prevention-based approach to quality control.

17.2 **Explain types of variation and the role of statistical process control (SPC).** Variation occurs for many reasons, such as inconsistencies in material inputs; changes in environmental conditions (temperature, humidity); machine maintenance cycles; customer participation and self-service; tool wear; and human fatigue. Common cause variation is the responsibility of management, whereas frontline employees focus more on special cause variation.

17.3 **Describe how to construct and interpret simple control charts for both continuous and discrete data.** The five steps required to develop and construct control charts are (1) preparation, such as choosing the metric to be monitored and determining sample size and the frequency; (2) collect the data and calculate basic statistics; (3) determine trial upper and lower control limits and center line; (4) investigate and interpret the control chart, eliminate out-of-control points, and recompute the control limits; and (5) use problem-solving tools and take corrective action(s).

Key formulas for an –*x*- and *R*-chart are

$$\bar{\bar{x}} = \frac{1}{k}\sum_{i=1}^{k}\bar{x}_i \quad [17.1]$$

$$\bar{R} = \frac{1}{k}\sum_{i=1}^{k}R_i \quad [17.2]$$

$$\text{UCL}_R = D_4\bar{R} \qquad \text{UCL}_{\bar{x}} = \bar{\bar{x}} + A_2\bar{R}$$
$$\text{LCL}_R = D_3\bar{R} \qquad \text{LCL}_{\bar{x}} = \bar{\bar{x}} - A_2\bar{R} \quad [17.3]$$

where *X* is the average of the *i*th sample.

Key formulas for a *p*-chart are

$$\bar{p} = \frac{y_1 + y_2 + \cdots + y_k}{nk} \quad [17.4]$$

$$s_{\bar{p}} = \sqrt{\frac{\bar{p}(1-\bar{p})}{n}} \quad [17.5]$$

$$\text{UCL}_p = \bar{p} + 3s_{\bar{p}}$$
$$\text{LCL}_p = \bar{p} - 3s_{\bar{p}} \quad [17.6]$$

where y_i is the number nonconforming in the *i*th sample, *k* is the number of samples, and n is the size of each sample.

Key formulas for a *c*-chart are

$$\text{UCL}_c = \bar{c} + 3\sqrt{\bar{c}}$$
$$\text{UCL}_c = \bar{c} - 3\sqrt{\bar{c}} \quad [17.7]$$

where $\bar{c}$ is the average number of nonconformances per unit. A process is in control when the control chart has the following characteristics:

1. No points are outside control limits.
2. The number of points above and below the center line is about the same.
3. The points seem to fall randomly above and below the center line.
4. Most points, but not all, are near the center line, and only a few are close to the control limits.

17.4 **Describe practical issues in implementing SPC.** Designing control charts involves two key issues:

1. sample size, and
2. sampling frequency.

A small sample size is desirable to keep the cost associated with sampling low. On the other hand, large sample sizes provide greater degrees of statistical accuracy in estimating the true state of control. Large samples also allow smaller changes in process characteristics to be detected with higher probability. In practice, samples of about 5 have been found to work well in detecting process shifts of 2 standard deviations or larger. To detect smaller shifts in the process mean, larger sample sizes of 15 to 25 must be used.

Taking large samples on a frequent basis is desirable, but clearly not economical. No hard-and-fast rules exist for the frequency of sampling. Samples should be close enough to provide an opportunity to detect changes in process characteristics as soon as possible and reduce the chances of producing a large amount of nonconforming output. However, they should not be so close that the cost of sampling outweighs the benefits that can be realized.

SPC is a useful methodology for processes that operate at a low sigma level—for example, the three-sigma level or lower. However, when the rate of defects is extremely low, standard control charts are not effective.

CHAPTER 17 LEARNING OBJECTIVE SUMMARIES

17.5 **Explain process capability, and calculate process capability indexes.** Knowing process capability allows one to predict, quantitatively, how well a process will meet specifications and to specify equipment requirements and the level of control necessary. Process capability has no meaning if the process is not in statistical control because special causes will bias the mean or the standard deviation. Therefore, we should use control charts to first eliminate any special causes before computing the process capability. Typical questions that are asked in a process capability study are:

- Where is the process centered?
- How much variability exists in the process?
- Is the performance relative to specifications acceptable?
- What proportion of output will be expected to meet specifications?

The process capability index, C_p, is defined as the ratio of the specification width to the natural tolerance of the process.

$$C_p = \frac{USL - LSL}{6\sigma} \qquad [17.9]$$

Values of C_p exceeding 1 indicate good capability. To account for the process centering, one-sided capability indexes are often used:

$$C_{pu} = \frac{USL - \mu}{3\sigma} \text{ (upper one-sided index)} \qquad [17.10]$$

$$C_{pl} = \frac{\mu - LSL}{3\sigma} \text{ (lower one-sided index)} \qquad [17.11]$$

$$C_{pk} = \min(C_{pl}, C_{pu}) \qquad [17.12]$$

KEY TERMS

- **c-chart**
- **Common cause variation**
- **Continuous metric**
- **Control chart**
- **Discrete metric**
- **In control**
- **Out of control**
- ***p*-chart**
- **Process capability**
- **Process capability index**
- **Process capability study**
- **Quality at the source**
- **Quality control**
- ***R*-chart**
- **Special (or assignable) cause variation**
- **Statistical process control (SPC)**
- **$\bar{x}$-chart**

REVIEW QUESTIONS

17.1 1. What is quality control? Why is it necessary in any organization?

17.1 2. Explain the three components of any control system and provide an example different from the text.

17.1 3. What is the 1:10:100 Rule? Why is it important for managers to understand?

17.1 4. What is "quality at the source"?

17.1 5. Describe the basic quality control practices used in manufacturing. In what service contexts can they be applied?

17.1 6. How does quality control in services involving customer contact differ from typical manufacturing practices?

17.1 7. How can customer satisfaction measurement provide useful information for control in services?

17.2 8. What is the difference between common and special causes of variation?

17.2 9. What do we mean when we say that a process is "in control" or "out of control"?

17.2 10. What is statistical process control?

17.3 11. What is a control chart and what benefits can control charts provide?

17.3 12. Explain the difference between a discrete and a continuous metric. Provide some examples different from those in the text.

17.3 13. Summarize the process used to apply SPC.

17.3 14. Describe the various types of control charts and their applications.

17.3 15. Discuss how to interpret control charts. What types of patterns indicate a lack of control?

17.4 16. Explain how to determine the appropriate sample size and sampling frequency for SPC.

17.5 17. What is process capability and why is it important to understand?

17.5 18. What is the purpose of a process capability study?

17.5 19. What is a process capability index? Explain how process capability indexes are computed and how to interpret the results.

DISCUSSION QUESTIONS AND EXPERIENTIAL ACTIVITIES

17.1 20. Think about the net promoter score question, "What is the likelihood that you would recommend a company such as a restaurant, airline, or online service?" What factors would drive you to give a 9 or 10 to this question? Base your answer on a specific product or service encounter that you have experienced.

17.1,3 21. Find a customer satisfaction survey from a restaurant or a hotel. How do the questions relate to the five dimensions of service quality introduced in Chapter 2? Discuss how the survey results could be used to control quality. What types of quality control charts might be used?

17.2 22. Provide some examples in business or daily life in which a controlled process is erroneously adjusted and an out-of-control process is ignored.

17.2 23. Discuss some examples of common and special causes of variation in your daily life (for example, at school or at home).

17.2,3 24. Develop a "personal quality checklist" on which you tally nonconformances in your personal life (being late for work or school, not completing homework on time, not getting enough exercise, and so on). What type of chart would you use to monitor your performance?

17.3 25. Hospital administrators wanted to understand and better control the waiting time of patients in the emergency department (ED). To do this, they constructed $\bar{x}$-chart and R-charts by sampling the waiting times of the first five patients admitted to the ED at the beginning of each shift (7 a.m., 3 p.m., and 11 p.m.). What do you think of this approach? Will it provide the information the hospital administrators seek? How might the sampling process be improved, and what would you recommend?

17.3 26. Suppose that you were monitoring the time it takes to complete order transactions at a call center. Discuss what might cause such out-of-control conditions as a trend, shift in the mean, or cycles in an $\bar{x}$-chart in this situation.

COMPUTATIONAL PROBLEMS AND EXERCISES

These exercises require you to apply the formulas and methods described in the chapter. The problems should be solved manually.

17.1 27. Bill & Becky Travel, Inc. is a full service travel agency. Data in the worksheet *C17 P27 Data* in MindTap shows results for the question "Would you recommend us to a friend?" from 200 customers who were sampled during one week. Count the number of responses at each level (1 through 10) and determine the number of and percentage of customers at the promoter, passive, and detractor levels.

17.3 28. Thirty samples of size 3 resulted in an overall mean of 16.51 and average range of 1.30. Compute control limits for $\bar{x}$- and R-charts.

17.3 29. Twenty-five samples of size 5 resulted in an overall mean of 5.42 and an average range of 20. Compute control limits for $\bar{x}$- and R-charts.

17.3 30. Thirty samples of size 4 of the customer waiting time at a call center for a health insurance company resulted in an overall mean of 14.7 minutes and average range of 0.9 minutes. Compute the control limits for $\bar{x}$- and R-charts.

17.3 31. Twenty-five samples, each consisting of 200 loan applications at a bank, resulted in a total of 40 applications that had some type of error. Compute the control limits for a p-chart.

17.3 32. Twenty-five samples of 100 items each were inspected and 68 were found to be defective. Compute control limits for a *p*-chart.

17.3 33. At a pizza restaurant, a 20-week study of 30 pizzas per week found a total of 18 pizzas made improperly. Compute control limits for a *p*-chart.

17.3 34. A fast food franchise tracked the number of errors that occurred in customers' orders. These included wrong menu item, wrong size drink, lack of condiments, wrong price total, and so on. Some orders may have more than one error. In one week, 1,500 orders were filled, and a total of 72 errors were discovered. Find the control limits for a *c*-chart to monitor the number of errors per order. Is order accuracy good or bad in your opinion?

17.3 35. Find control limits for a *c*-chart with $\bar{c} = 9$.

17.3 36. Consider the following data showing the number of errors per thousand lines of code for a software development project. Find the control limits for a *c*-chart for monitoring errors per thousand lines of code.

Sample	1	2	3	4	5	6	7	8	9	10
Number of Errors	4	15	13	20	17	22	26	17	20	22

17.3 37. The worksheet *C17 P37 Data* in MindTap provides five examples of control charts. Interpret the patterns in each and determine if the processes are in control. If not, state the type of out-of-control condition that you identify (for example, points outside of the control limits, shifts, trends, and so on).

17.5 38. Suppose that a specification calls for LTL = 2.0 and UTL = 6.0. A sample of 100 parts found $\mu = 4.5$ and $\sigma = 0.5$. Compute C_p, C_{pl}, C_{pu}, and C_{pk}. Should the manager consider any action based on these results?

17.5 39. A specification for a spacer plate used in a machine tool has specifications LSL = 0.05 and USL = 0.10 cm in thickness. A sample of 100 parts found $\mu = 0.067$ and $\sigma = 0.021$. Compute and interpret the process capability indexes C_p, C_{pl}, C_{pu}, and C_{pk}.

EXCEL-BASED PROBLEMS

For these problems, you may use Excel or the spreadsheet templates in MindTap to assist in your analysis.

17.3 40. Thirty samples of size 3, available in the worksheet *C17 Excel P40 Data* in MindTap were taken from a machining process over a 15-hour period. Construct control charts using the Excel template *$\bar{x}$&R-Chart*. Verify the Excel calculations of the control limits by hand using the formulas in the chapter. Does the process appear to be in statistical control? Why or why not?

17.3 41. Tri-State Bank is investigating the processing time for loan applications. Samples were taken for 25 random days from four branches. These data can be found in the worksheet *C17 Excel P41 Data* in MindTap. Construct control charts using the Excel template *$\bar{x}$&R-Chart*. Verify the Excel calculations of the control limits by hand using the formulas in the chapter. Does the process appear to be in statistical control? Why or why not?

17.3 42. Eighty insurance claim forms are inspected daily for 25 working days, and the number of forms with errors are recorded in the worksheet *C17 Excel P42 Data* in MindTap. Construct a *p*-chart using the Excel template *p-Chart*. Verify the Excel calculations of the control limits by hand using the formulas in the chapter. If any special causes are identified, remove them from the data and construct a revised control chart.

17.3 43. An Internet service provider (ISP) measures the proportion of peak period time when a customer is likely to receive busy signals. Data on the number of busy signals received from samples of 500 calls over a 30-day period can be found in the worksheet *C17 Excel P3 Data* in MindTap. Construct and interpret a *p*-chart for these data.

17.3 44. Data showing the number of errors per thousand lines of code for a software development project are given in the worksheet *C17 Excel P44 Data* in MindTap. Construct a *c*-chart and interpret the results.

17.3 45. A mail-order prescription drug vendor measured the number of errors per standard order being picked in their distribution center. Data can be found in the worksheet *C17 Excel P45 Data* in MindTap. Construct a *c*-chart and interpret the results. What practical implications do these results have?

17.5 46. Use the data from the machining process in Problem 40 (worksheet *C17 Excel P40 Data* in MindTap) to calculate C_p, C_{pl}, C_{pu}, and C_{pk}, assuming that the specifications are 3.75 ± 1.25. Interpret the results for the manager of this process.

17.5 47. The worksheet *C17 Excel P47 Data* in MindTap provides sample times in hours for processing and shipping orders from a web-based retailer. The retailer advertises that orders are shipped within four hours of receipt. What is the capability of the process to achieve this standard? Explain your conclusions.

Eckhardt Hospital

The Joint Commission on Accreditation of Healthcare Organizations (JCAHO) monitors and evaluates health care providers according to strict standards and guidelines. Improvement in the quality of care is a principal concern. Hospitals are required to identify and monitor important quality indicators that affect patient care and establish "thresholds for evaluation" (TFEs), which are levels at which a special investigation of problems should occur. TFEs provide a means of focusing attention on nonrandom errors (that is, special causes of variation). A logical way to set TFEs is through control charts.

Eckhardt Hospital collected data on the number of infections that occurred for samples of 200 surgeries each month over a three-year period. These data are shown in Exhibit 17.8 and are available in the worksheet *Eckhardt Hospital Case Data* in MindTap. Hospital administrators are concerned about whether a high number of infections (such as in month 12) are caused by factors other than randomness.

Case Questions for Discussion:

1. Using the data in Exhibit 17.8, what is the average percentage of infections?
2. Construct an appropriate control chart, compute the upper and lower control limits, plot the data on the chart, and determine if the process is in statistical control. Based on your analysis, what action, if any, should management take?
3. What threshold for evaluation should management use to monitor future samples as a basis for taking action?

EXHIBIT 17.8 Monthly Data on Number of Infections

Month	Number of Infections Per 200 Surgeries
1	1
2	3
3	3
4	1
5	3
6	1
7	1
8	1
9	1
10	0
11	2
12	4
13	2
14	1
15	2
16	0
17	1
18	1
19	1
20	2
21	1
22	0
23	2
24	2
25	1
26	2
27	1
28	0
29	3
30	1
31	2
32	1
33	3
34	1
35	3
36	1

Goodman Tire and Rubber Company

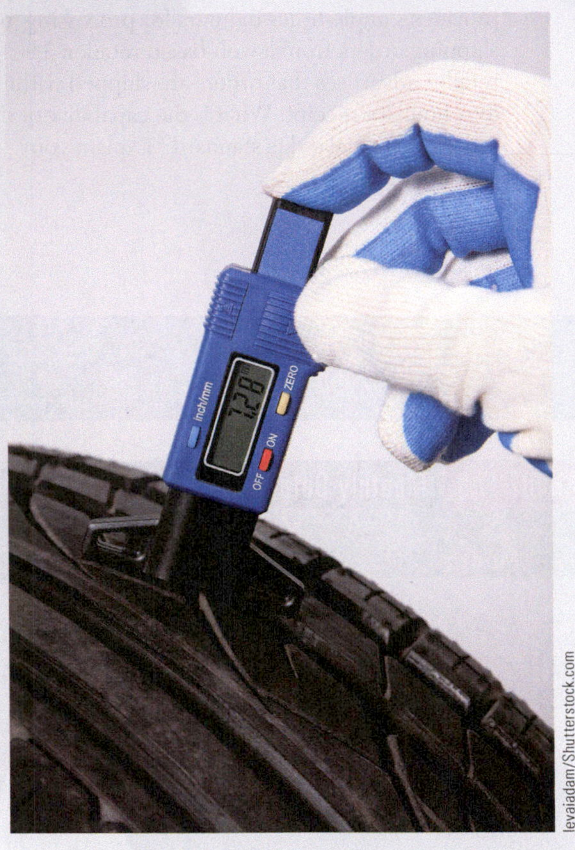

levaiadam/Shutterstock.com

EXHIBIT 17.9 Goodman Tire

Sample	Tread Wear		
1	31	42	28
2	26	18	35
3	25	30	34
4	17	25	21
5	38	29	35
6	41	42	36
7	21	17	29
8	32	26	28
9	41	34	33
10	29	17	30
11	26	31	40
12	23	19	25
13	17	24	32
14	43	35	17
15	18	25	29
16	30	42	31
17	28	36	32
18	40	29	31
19	18	29	28
20	22	34	26
21	18	24	30
22	24	28	19
23	27	32	20
24	39	26	19
25	17	32	27

The U.S. National Highway Traffic Safety Administration (NHTSA) independently tests over 2,400 types of tires annually. In 2015, they issued over 900 recalls, affecting 51 million vehicles nationwide. Obviously, tire failure is a leading cause of accidents, injury, and death. The cost of poor quality can be in the hundreds of millions of dollars to the tire manufacturer due to lawsuits, liability claims, and the cost of recalls to fix the problem. Your safety depends on a high level of tire quality and performance.

Therefore, the Goodman Tire and Rubber Company periodically tests its tires for tread wear under simulated road conditions. To study and control its manufacturing processes, the company uses x- and R-charts. Twenty-five samples, each containing three radial tires, were chosen from different shifts over several days of operation. Exhibit 17.7 shows data for 25 samples of three observations of tread wear in hundredths of millimeters. (These data are available in the worksheet *Goodman Tire Case Data* in MindTap.) Lower numbers in Exhibit 17.9 represent better performance. Engineers have determined that, over the time in which the tires were tested, the design specifications are 28 ± 6 millimeters, in order to provide the 60-month lifetime the tires are designed to achieve.

Case Questions for Discussion:

1. Draw a histogram of these data. What can you conclude (if anything) about the distribution of the tread wear?
2. Construct $\bar{x}$- and R-charts for these data. Is the production process in control?
3. Provide two examples of each of the four major categories of quality costs applicable to this situation (i.e., prevention, appraisal, internal and external failure costs).
4. What are the process capability indexes for this process to meet design specifications? What do you recommend?

Integrative Case: Hudson Jewelers

The Hudson Jewelers case study found in MindTap integrates material found in each chapter of this book.

Case Questions for Discussion:

1. Research and acquire the criteria for diamond appraisals and critique these criteria in terms of objectivity, measurement, and overall accuracy. Are diamond quality criteria as specific and measureable as for manufactured parts? Explain.
2. Develop p-charts for the diamond blemish and inclusion data found in the worksheet *Hudson Jeweler Blemish and Inclusion Data* in MindTap, which documents the quality of the diamonds on "clarity and defects" coming from two different diamond mines (suppliers)—one in Asia and one in Africa. What do you conclude?

18 Lean Operating Systems

LEARNING OBJECTIVES

After studying this chapter, you should be able to:

18-1 Explain the four principles of lean operating systems and common types of waste.

18-2 Describe the basic lean tools and approaches.

18-3 Explain the concept of Lean Six Sigma and how it is applied to improving operations performance.

18-4 Explain how lean principles are used in manufacturing and service organizations.

18-5 Describe the concepts and philosophy of just-in-time operating systems.

Lean principles improve the efficiency of hospital pharmacies and many other processes.

BSIP/Universal Images Group/Getty Images

"Our hospital pharmacy processes are out of control. Patient health is at stake," noted a Michigan hospital manager. A study of pharmacy outcomes revealed that technicians were spending 77.4 percent of their time locating products; medication errors were high; and the current, 14-stage process had some unnecessary steps, resulting in a total lead time of 166 minutes to fill a hospital prescription. Teams with names like "Paper Pushers" and "Zip Scripts" were formed and trained in lean operating methods and principles. Their objective was to apply lean principles to enhance the ability to deliver medications safely to hospital patients. After redesigning the system, the pharmacy realized a 33 percent reduction in time to get medications to patients, and reduced the number of process steps from 14 to 9 simply by removing non-value-added steps. Patients have experienced a 40 percent reduction in pharmacy-related medication errors, and the severity of those errors has decreased.[1]

WHAT DO YOU THINK?

Can you cite any personal experiences in your work or around your school where you have observed similar inefficiencies (how about your dorm or bedroom)?

Lean thinking *refers to approaches that focus on the elimination of waste in all forms, and smooth, efficient flow of materials and information throughout the value chain to obtain faster customer response, higher quality, and lower costs. Manufacturing and service operations that apply the principles of lean enterprise are often called* **lean operating systems.** Lean concepts were initially developed and implemented by the Toyota Motor Corporation, and lean operating systems are often benchmarked with the Toyota Production System (TPS).

In the opening scenario, the lean teams greatly improved hospital pharmacy processes, enhanced patient health, and reduced liability risk to the hospital. For example, with only one printer for prescription labels in the pharmacy, labels were not always printed in the same order that the physical goods were available. This created confusion, and pharmacy technicians occasionally placed labels on the wrong bottles and bags. After applying lean thinking and methods, processing time and quality were greatly improved.

Lean thinking is playing a large role in making supply chains more efficient and in sustainability efforts. Lean thinking helps to drive a culture of waste elimination. At a recent conference of the Association for Manufacturing Excellence, Interface Americas, a LaGrange, Georgia, manufacturer of commercial carpet, tile, and interior fabrics, cited numerous examples of waste elimination activities that resulted from lean thinking, including over $300 million in cost avoidance from waste elimination, a 70 percent reduction of manufacturing waste sent to landfills, a 60 percent reduction in greenhouse gas emissions, and over 1 million pounds of carpet diverted from landfills.[2]

Any activity, material, or operation that does not add value in an organization is considered waste.

18-1 Principles of Lean Operating Systems

Lean operating systems have four basic principles:

1. Elimination of waste.
2. Increased speed and response.
3. Improved quality.
4. Reduced cost.

As simple as these may seem, organizations require disciplined thinking and application of good operations management tools and approaches to achieve them.

Eliminate Waste Lean, by the very nature of the term, implies doing only what is necessary to get the job done. Any activity, material, or operation that does not add value in an organization is considered waste. The goal is zero waste in all value-creation and support processes in the entire value chain. Exhibit 18.1 shows a variety of specific examples. The Toyota Motor Company classified waste into seven major categories:

1. *Overproduction*: For example, making a batch of 100 when there are orders for only 50 in order to avoid an expensive setup, or making a batch of 52 instead of 50 in case there are rejects. Overproduction ties up production facilities, and the resulting excess inventory simply sits idle.

D'Addario & Co. Exploits Lean Thinking

D'Addario & Co. manufactures strings found on all sorts of musical instruments, from cellos to electric guitars. The company has invested in technology that makes it lean, boosting output with fewer workers and smarter production. It's an example of a company that's managed to grow despite a shrinking marketplace, partly by freeing up more than 70,000 square feet of space for manufacturing and warehousing, and investing in technology and automation that also has allowed it to bring back jobs from abroad.

"Manufacturers have learned to be a lot more lean, do a lot more with less," said the chief economist for the National Association of Manufacturers. "In kind of a twist, those efforts to increase productivity have made the U.S. a lot more attractive (for investment) on a global scale. Those investments in technology and innovation... have also helped to increase U.S. viability in terms of manufacturing."[3]

homydesign/Shutterstock.com

2. *Waiting time*: For instance, allowing queues to build up between operations, resulting in longer lead times and more work-in-process.
3. *Transportation*: The time and effort spent in moving products around the factory as a result of poor layout.
4. *Processing*: The traditional notion of waste, as exemplified by scrap that often results from poor product or process design.
5. *Inventory*: Waste associated with the expense of idle stock and extra storage and handling requirements needed to maintain it.
6. *Motion*: As a result of inefficient workplace design and location of tools and materials.
7. *Production defects*: The result of not performing work correctly the first time.

Increase Speed and Response Lean operating systems focus on quick and efficient response in designing and getting goods and services to market, producing to customer demand and delivery requirements, responding to competitors' actions, collecting payments, and addressing customer inquiries or problems. Perhaps the most effective way of increasing speed and response is to synchronize the entire value chain. By this we mean that not only are all elements of the value chain focused on a common goal, but that the transfer of all physical materials

EXHIBIT 18.1 Common Examples of Waste in Organizations

Excess capacity	Excess inventory	Spoilage
Inaccurate information	Long changeover and setup times	Excessive energy use
Clutter	Scrap	Unnecessary movement of materials, people, and information
Planned product obsolescence	Rework and repair	Equipment breakdowns
Excessive material handling	Long, unproductive meetings	Knowledge bottlenecks
Overproduction	Poor communication	Non-value-added process steps
Producing too early	Waiting time	Misrouting jobs
Long distance traveled	Accidents	Wrong transportation mode
Retraining and relearning time and expense	Too much space	

and information is coordinated to achieve a high level of efficiency. A champion of lean practices would argue "be fast or last" and "synchronize value chain operations."

Improve Quality Lean operating systems cannot function if raw materials are bad; processing operations are not consistent; materials and tools are not located in the correct place; or machines break down. Poor quality disrupts work schedules and reduces yields, requiring extra inventory, processing time, and space for scrap and parts waiting for rework. All these are forms of waste and increase costs to the customer. Eliminating the sources of defects and errors in all processes in the value chain greatly improves speed, reduces variability, and supports the notion of continuous flow. All of the concepts and methods of quality management, such as product and process design simplification, root cause analysis, mistake-proofing, and statistical process control, are employed to improve quality.

Reduce Cost Certainly, reducing cost is an important objective of lean enterprise. Anything that is done to reduce waste and improve quality often reduces cost at the same time. More efficient equipment, better preventive maintenance, and smaller inventories reduce costs in manufacturing firms. Simplifying processes, such as using customer labor via self-service in a fast-food restaurant, depositing a check using an automatic teller machine, and completing medical forms online before medical service, are ways for service businesses to become leaner and reduce costs.

The Benefits of 5S

Jeff Frushtick, CEO of industrial equipment maker Leonard Automatics, discovered through a consultant that his team spent hours each week hunting for missing tools at the Denver, North Carolina, firm. They turned up in places like "someone's tool belt or a work bucket at a different assembly job," Frushtick says. By storing all tools for each operation on its own cart located in its own space (i.e., sort and set in order)—and addressing dozens of other comparable operational hiccups—he has raised profits fivefold since 2013 at the 35-employee firm.[4]

18-2 Lean Tools and Approaches

Meeting the objectives of lean enterprise requires disciplined approaches for designing and improving processes. Organizations use several tools and approaches to create a lean organization. We describe some of these here.

18-2a The 5Ss

Workers cannot be efficient if their workplaces are messy and disorganized. Efficient manufacturing plants are clean and well organized. Firms use the "5S" principles to create this work environment. *The **5Ss** are derived from Japanese terms: seiri (sort), seiton (set in order), seiso (shine), seiketsu (standardize), and shitsuke (sustain).*

- *Sort* refers to ensuring that each item in a workplace is in its proper place or identified as unnecessary and removed.
- *Set in order* means to arrange materials and equipment so that they are easy to find and use.
- *Shine* refers to a clean work area. Not only is this important for safety, but as a work area is cleaned, maintenance problems such as oil leaks can be identified before they cause problems.
- *Standardize* means to formalize procedures and practices to create consistency and ensure that all steps are performed correctly.
- Finally, *sustain* means to keep the process going through training, communication, and organizational structures.

18-2b Visual Controls

Visual controls *are indicators for operating activities that are placed in plain sight of all employees so that everyone can quickly and easily understand the status and performance of the work system.* Visual signaling systems are known as *andon*, drawing from the Japanese term from which the concept first originated. For example, if a machine fails or a part is defective or manufactured incorrectly, a light might turn on or a buzzer might sound, indicating that immediate action should be taken. Many firms have cords that operators can pull that tell supervisors and other workers that a problem has occurred. Some firms, such as Honda (on the manufacturing floor) and JPMorgan Chase (at its call centers), use electronic "scoreboards" to keep track of daily performance. These scoreboards are located where everyone can see them and report key metrics such as volume, quality levels, speed of service, and so on.

18-2c Single Minute Exchange of Dies (SMED)

Long setup times waste manufacturing resources. Short setup times, on the other hand, enable a manufacturer to have frequent changeovers and move toward single-piece flow, thus achieving high flexibility and product variety. Reducing setup time also frees up capacity for other productive uses. **Single Minute Exchange of Dies (SMED)** *refers to the quick setup or changeover of tooling and fixtures in processes so that multiple products in smaller batches can be run on the same equipment.* SMED was pioneered by Toyota and other Japanese manufacturers and has been adopted by companies around the world.

18-2d Batching and Single-Piece Flow

One of the practices that inhibits increasing speed and response in manufacturing or service processing of discrete parts such as a manufactured part, invoices, medical claims, or home loan mortgage approvals is **batching**—*the process of producing large quantities of items as a group before they are transferred to the next operation.* Batching is often necessary when producing a broad goods or service mix with diverse requirements on common equipment. When making different goods, manufacturers often need to change dies, tools, and fixtures on equipment, resulting in expensive time-consuming setups and teardowns. For services, preprinted forms or software may have to be changed or modified. By running large batches, setups and teardowns are reduced, providing economies of scale. However, this often builds up inventory that might not match market demand, particularly in highly dynamic markets.

A better strategy would be to use small batches or single-piece flow. Moving a portion of a completed batch before the entire batch is finished is called a **transfer batch**. *A* **transfer batch** *is a portion of the original lot size that is completed at one workstation and moved to the next downstream workstation.* **Single-piece flow** *is the concept of ideally using batch sizes of one.* That is, as one part is completed at a workstation, it moves immediately to the next. However, to do this economically requires the ability to change between products quickly and inexpensively. Solved Problem 18.1 provides a numerical example of batching and single-piece flow logic.

Quality at the source requires doing it right the first time, and therefore eliminates the opportunities for waste.

Batching is often necessary when producing a broad goods or service mix with diverse requirements on common equipment. When making different goods, manufacturers often need to change dies, tools, and fixtures on equipment, resulting in expensive and time-consuming setups and teardowns. For services, preprinted forms or software may have to be changed or modified. By running large batches, setups and teardowns are reduced, providing economies of scale. However, this often builds up inventory that might not match market demand, particularly in highly dynamic markets. A better strategy would be to use small transfer batches or single-piece flow. However, to do this economically requires the ability to change setups between products quickly and inexpensively. Many companies have made remarkable improvements in reducing product setup times, making small-batch or single-piece flow a reality in job shop environments.

SOLVED PROBLEM 18.1: BATCHING AND SINGLE-PIECE FLOW

A product is assembled on three workstations using a batch size of 100. Each item must be processed sequentially on each workstation. Exhibit 18.2 shows the processing time per item and total time per batch at each workstation. The entire lot size of 100 is produced at workstation A, it is moved to workstation B, and so on; this is visualized in Exhibit 18.3. Therefore, the time it takes to process a batch of 100 items through the three workstations is 500 + 2,000 + 1,000 = 3,500 seconds.

Next, consider a transfer batch of 20 items. It takes 20 × 5 seconds = 100 seconds to process the first batch of 20 items at workstation A. This batch begins processing at workstation B at time 100 and takes 20 × 20 seconds = 400 seconds to process, being completed at time 500. Then it moves to workstation C and takes 20 × 10 seconds = 200 seconds to process, and it is finished at time 700. The second batch arrives at workstation B at time 200 but must wait until time 500 to begin processing, and it is completed at time 900. When it moves to workstation C, it immediately begins processing because the first batch has already been completed and is finished at time 1,100. Note that workstation B is the bottleneck; batches arrive for processing at B faster than B is capable of processing them. The table below summarizes the completion times at each workstation for the five batches of 20 items.

	Completion time at workstation		
Batch	**A**	**B**	**C**
1	100	500	700
2	200	900	1,100
3	300	1,300	1,500
4	400	1,700	1,900
5	500	2,100	2,300

We see that using a smaller batch has reduced the time to process all 100 items from 3,500 to 2,300 seconds.

Finally, consider single-piece flow as illustrated in Exhibit 18.4. The first item is processed at workstation A in five seconds, and then immediately moves to workstation B (we assume zero delay time in moving from one workstation

EXHIBIT 18.2 Batch versus Single-Piece Flow Processing

Workstation	Batch Size (Q)	Processing Time per Item	Total Time per Batch (Seconds)
A	100	5 seconds	500
B	100	20 seconds	2,000
C	100	10 seconds	1,000

EXHIBIT 18.3 Illustration of Batch Processing

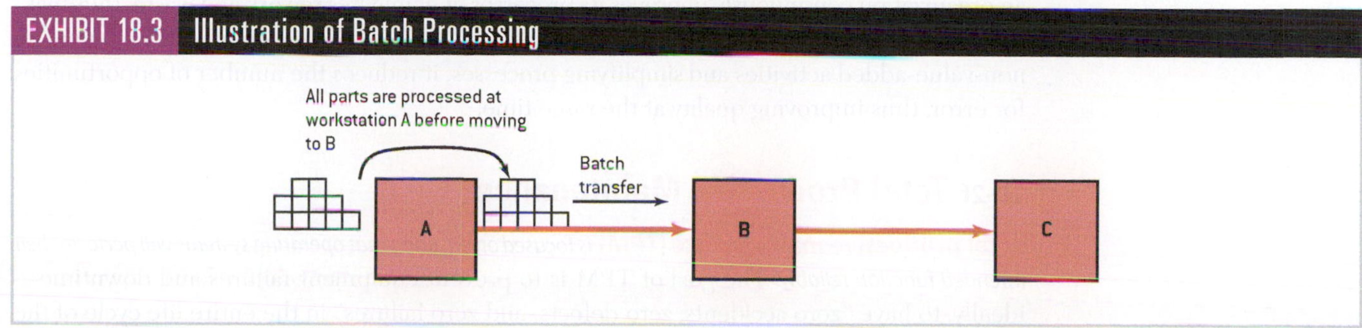
All parts are processed at workstation A before moving to B
Batch transfer
A
B
C

to another). At this time, the second item begins processing at workstation A and will be moved to workstation B at time 10. However, the first item requires 20 seconds to process at workstation B. Therefore, the first item completes processing at workstation B in a total of 25 seconds; then moves on to workstation C, taking 10 seconds; and finishes in a total of 35 seconds. The table below shows the completion times for the first three items at each workstation.

	Completion time at workstation		
Item	**A**	**B**	**C**
1	5	25	35
2	10	45	55
3	15	65	75

You can see that items 2, 3, and so on are completed at workstation C every 20 seconds after the completion of item 1. Thus, the total time to complete the entire batch of 100 items will be $35 + 99 \times 20 = 2{,}015$ seconds. Single-piece flow reduces the total processing time from 3,500 seconds to 2,015 seconds, or about 42 percent.

EXHIBIT 18.4 Single-piece Flow

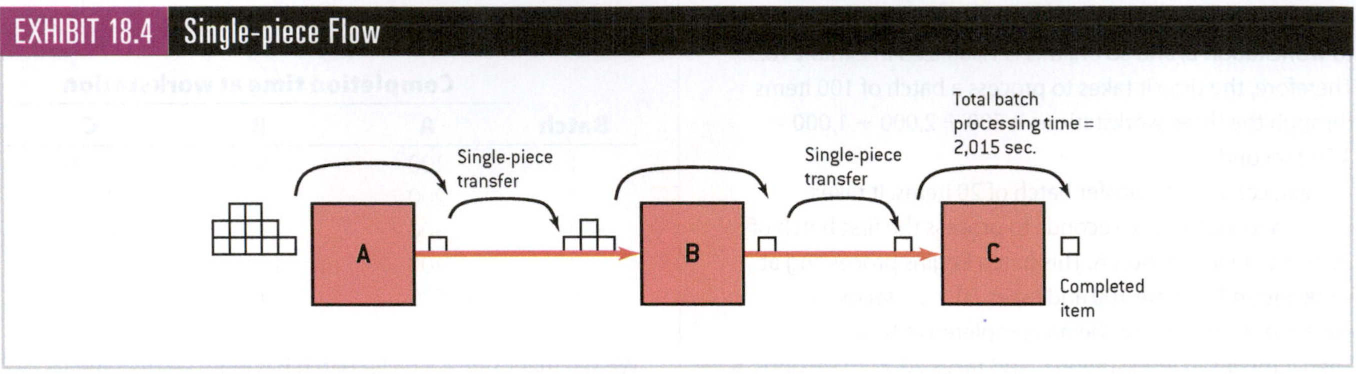

18-2e Quality and Continuous Improvement

Quality at the source requires doing it right the first time, and therefore eliminates the opportunities for waste. Employees inspect, analyze, and control their own work to guarantee that the good or service passed on to the next process stage conforms to specifications. Continuous improvement initiatives are vital in lean environments, as is teamwork among all managers and employees.

An important synergy exists between quality improvement and lean thinking. Clearly, as an organization continuously improves its processes, it eliminates rework and waste, thus making the processes leaner. Moreover, as an organization tries to make itself leaner by eliminating non-value-added activities and simplifying processes, it reduces the number of opportunities for error, thus improving quality at the same time.

18-2f Total Productive Maintenance

Total productive maintenance (TPM) *is focused on ensuring that operating systems will perform their intended function reliably.* The goal of TPM is to prevent equipment failures and downtime—ideally, to have "zero accidents, zero defects, and zero failures" in the entire life cycle of the operating system.[5] TPM seeks to

- maximize overall equipment effectiveness and eliminate unplanned downtime,
- create worker "ownership" of the equipment by involving employees in maintenance activities, and
- foster continuous efforts to improve equipment operation through employee involvement activities.

Setup Time Reduction from 9.2 Hours to 9 Minutes

Many companies have made remarkable improvements in reducing product setup times, making small-batch or single-piece flow a reality in job shop environments. Yammar Diesel reduced a machining line tool setting from 9.2 hours to 9 minutes; a U.S. chainsaw manufacturer reduced setup time on a punch press from more than 2 hours to 3 minutes; and a midwestern manufacturer was able to cut equipment setup time on a 60-ton press from 45 minutes to 1 minute.

The cost of maintenance and prevention can be evaluated using basic statistics as shown in Solved Problem 18.2. We suggest that you review Supplement A: Probability and Statistics to understand how to compute the expected value of a discrete probability distribution.

SOLVED PROBLEM 18.2: EVALUATING THE ECONOMICS OF PREVENTIVE MAINTENANCE

Hospital laboratory equipment must often be recalibrated to avoid costly errors in lab tests. Errors can endanger patient's health, cause retesting and rework, delay testing and lab results, and increase costs. The gas chromatography equipment analyzes the mixture of chemicals in a sample of gas or liquid. Patient samples of blood, saliva, and urine can be analyzed for a host of reasons ranging from food additives to signs of disease.

The unit is expensive, used 365 days per year, and the hospital has only one gas chromatography unit. The imputed cost of an equipment failure is \$1,500 per day because doctors, and patients would have to wait until the unit is repaired. The cost of preventative maintenance (daily recalibration and testing of the equipment including replacing certain filters and parts) is \$1,200 per day. If preventive maintenance is performed daily, the probability that the unit will fail is zero. The probability of gas chromatography failures per day are as follows:

Number of failures per 24-hour work day	0	1	2	3
Probability of failure	0.3	0.3	0.25	0.15

What are the economics of the situation? What do you recommend?

Solution:

The expected number of failures per day without preventive maintenance can be computed using formula [A.10] in Supplement A:

$$E[X] = \sum_{i=1}^{\infty} x_i f(x_i)$$
$$= (0 \times 0.3 + 1 \times 0.3 + 2 \times 0.25 + 3 \times 0.15)$$
$$= 1.25 \text{ failures per day.}$$

The expected cost per day of a failure is $1.25 \times \$1{,}500 = \$1{,}875$ per day. Because the preventive maintenance cost is only \$1,200 per day, the hospital saves \$675 per day or \$246,375 per year by adopting a preventive maintenance plan of action.

Dmitry Kalinovsky/Shutterstock.com

Because of its importance in lean thinking, TPM has been called "lean maintenance." Lean maintenance is more than preventing failures of equipment and processes; it now includes maintenance and backup systems for software and electronic network systems such as the Internet or wireless networks.

18-3 Lean Six Sigma

Six Sigma is a useful and complementary approach to lean production. For example, a cycle-time-reduction project might involve aspects of both. Lean tools might be applied to streamline an order entry process. This application leads to the discovery that significant rework occurs because of incorrect addresses, customer numbers, or shipping charges, and results in high variation of processing time. Six Sigma tools might then be used to drill down to the root cause of the problems and identify a solution. Because of these similarities, many practitioners have begun to focus on *Lean Six Sigma*, drawing upon the best practices of both approaches. Both are driven by customer requirements, focus on real dollar savings, have the ability to make significant financial impacts on the organization, and can easily be used in nonmanufacturing environments. Both use basic root cause, process, and data analysis techniques.

However, some differences clearly exist between lean production and Six Sigma. First, they attack different types of problems. Lean production addresses visible problems in processes; for example, inventory, material flow, and safety. Six Sigma is more concerned with less visible problems; for example, variation in performance. In essence, lean is focused on efficiency by reducing waste and improving process flow, whereas Six Sigma is focused on effectiveness by reducing errors and defects. Another difference is that lean tools are more intuitive and easier to apply by anybody in the workplace, whereas many Six Sigma tools require advanced training and expertise of specialists, particularly in statistical analyses, commonly called Black Belts and Master Black Belts. For example, most workers can easily understand the concept of the 5Ss, but may have more difficulty with statistical methods. Thus, organizations might be well advised to start with basic lean principles and evolve toward more sophisticated Six Sigma approaches. However, it is important to integrate both approaches with a common goal—improving business results. Lean Six Sigma often is an important part of implementing a strategy built upon sustainability.

Science and Society/Superstock

18-4 Lean Manufacturing and Service Tours

Lean manufacturing plants look significantly different from traditional plants. They are clean and organized, devoid of long and complex production lines and high levels of work-in-process, have efficient layouts and work area designs, use multiskilled workers who perform both direct and indirect work such as maintenance, and have no incoming or final inspection stations. Next, we "tour" a manufacturing firm to examine how it focuses on the four major lean objectives.

18-4a Timken Company

The Timken Company (www.timken.com) is a leading global manufacturer of highly engineered bearings and alloy steels and related products and services for three major markets—industrial, automotive, and steel. Timken employs about

18,000 employees in over 50 factories and more than 100 sales, design, and distribution centers located throughout the world. Timken places increasing emphasis on pre- and post-production services such as integrated engineering solutions to customer requirements.

Like most manufacturers, Timken faced intense, survival-threatening, global competition. A key Timken initiative was to increase productivity through lean manufacturing operating principles and technologies, some of which we highlight next.

Eliminate Waste Timken's automotive business uses a "boot camp" in which a certain factory identifies several improvement opportunities, and Timken employees and managers from other sites then try to solve these specific problems at the host factory. The problems often focus on removing non-value-added steps from processes, reducing process and equipment variation, and eliminating waste. The boot camp approach allows "fresh eyes" to evaluate improvement opportunities and present solutions to host plant management.

Increase Speed and Response Timken has focused on improving its product development process—a nonmanufacturing, information-intensive process—with the objective to radically reduce the total cycle time for new product development with fewer errors and to be more responsive to customer requests, competitor capabilities, and marketplace changes.

Timken developed flexible manufacturing systems to facilitate rapid, cost-effective changeover from one product to another, combining the advantages of batch and mass production. Lean manufacturing's most distinguishing characteristic at Timken, however, was the authority and responsibility it gave to people on the shop floor. Initiatives aimed at empowering shop floor employees included more open communication, enhanced training, widespread adoption of a team approach to problem solving and decision making, and changes in measures of performance and rewards.

Improve Quality Total quality and continuous improvement have long been areas of focus for Timken. Through programs like Breakthrough and Accelerated Continuous Improvement, thousands of improvement ideas have been implemented, saving millions of dollars. Quality standards are determined for all manufacturing processes, and worldwide quality audits make sure that these standards are being met. Each plant is certified to ISO 9000 or other quality certifications. Timken has applied Six Sigma tools to minimize process variation. One initiative was to improve machine operator efficiency and reduce variability. Workstation processes were standardized, and machine operator walking and movement time were eliminated or reduced. The result was improved quality and reduced scrap.

Reduce Cost Timken redefined its mission statement in 1993 to be "the best performing manufacturing company in the world as seen through the eyes of our customers and shareholders." Timken factories, suppliers, and customers share information using the Internet. Purchasing, order fulfillment, manufacturing strategy implementation, Lean Six Sigma, and logistics have been brought together to create an "integrated supply chain model." The purpose of this focus is to reduce asset intensity, improve customer service and systems support, respond faster to customer needs, and better manage inventory levels.

Timken uses Lean Six Sigma to reduce waste and variation in production. All manufacturing processes are flowcharted, and the DMAIC problem-solving framework is used to generate process improvements. The automotive business achieved a net documented savings of $7 million from Lean Six Sigma projects in one year alone.

Service organizations can benefit significantly from applying lean principles, especially to back room operations. Lean principles are not always transferable to "front-office" services that involve high

> Service organizations can benefit significantly from applying lean principles, especially to back room operations.

customer contact and service encounters. In these situations, the service provider and firm do not have complete control over creating the service. However, back-office service processes such as hospital laboratory testing, check processing, and college application processing, are nearly identical to many manufacturing processes. Time, accuracy, and cost are all important to their performance, and therefore they can clearly benefit from the application of lean principles. The following discussion shows how lean concepts have been used at Southwest Airlines.[6]

18-4b Southwest Airlines

Since its inception, Southwest Airlines has shown lean performance when compared to other major airlines. It has consistently been profitable while other major airlines have not. The vast majority of total airline cost focuses on operations management activities: traffic servicing (13 percent), aircraft servicing (7 percent), flight operations (47 percent), reservations and sales (10 percent), and passenger in-flight service (7 percent). Note that the first three are low-contact (back-office) operations, whereas passenger in-flight service and reservations and sales are high-contact, service management functions. Therefore, taking a lean approach to all operations is vital to airline performance. Southwest is clearly a lean airline—it does more with less than any other airline competitor. Let us examine some of the reasons.

Chris Parypa Photography/Shutterstock.com

Eliminate Waste In the airline industry, idle time is the largest form of waste. Southwest locates its planes at noncongested airports to help it minimize airplane turnaround time. Fewer ancillary services reduce the opportunity for waste and inefficiencies. Southwest also enjoys a much lower employee turnover rate than its competitors, resulting in lower training costs.

All the resources at Southwest work to keep the airplanes in the air earning revenue—the primary focus of its strategy. The more time spent on the ground, the less revenue. It relies on motivated employees, a culture focused on the customer, and teamwork to accomplish this strategy. Southwest employees are cross-trained and organized into teams to accomplish all key operational activities. For example, all employees cooperate to ensure timely takeoffs and landings; it is not unusual to see pilots helping load baggage if this will get the plane off on time. This maintains smooth system schedules and reduces the need for reschedules and reticketing, both of which are a form of rework. As one example, in as little as 15 minutes, Southwest can change the flight crew; deplane and board 137 passengers; unload 97 bags, 1,000 pounds of mail, and 25 pieces of freight; load another 123 bags and 600 pounds of mail; and pump 4,500 pounds of jet fuel into the aircraft.[7]

Increase Speed and Response Southwest uses a much simpler structure and operating system than its competitors. It uses only one type of aircraft—the Boeing 737—making it easier to schedule and train crews, perform maintenance, manage airplane parts inventory, and standardize such activities as boarding, baggage storage and retrieval, and cabin operations. For example, if Southwest can turn its planes around on average in at most half an hour, whereas competitors take one hour, then, assuming a 90-minute flight, approximately one to two more flights per day per plane can be made. This can be a significant economic and strategic advantage.

Southwest was the first airline to introduce ticketless travel. Customers simply get a confirmation number and show up on time. A significant proportion of customers book their flights directly on Southwest.com. If a customer misses a flight, he or she can use the ticket for a future flight with no penalty; this reduces paperwork and processing, contributing to a leaner operation.

Improve Quality Simplified processes reduce variability in flight schedules—a major source of customer complaints—and therefore improve customers' perceptions of quality and satisfaction. Southwest encourages carry-on baggage; hence, there is less opportunity for losing, misrouting, or damaging baggage. People-oriented employees are carefully chosen and empowered to both serve and entertain passengers.

Reduce Cost Short setup and turnaround time translates into higher asset utilization and reduces the need for costly inventories of aircraft. Southwest does not have assigned seating; customers wait on a first-come, first-served basis and board in zones. This lowers costs, and only a few employees are needed to coordinate passenger boarding. In addition, rather than carry the high overhead costs of airplane maintenance and repair, Southwest outsources these tasks to third parties.

18-5 Just-in-Time Systems

Just-in-time (JIT) was introduced at Toyota during the 1950s and 1960s to address the challenge of coordinating successive production activities. An automobile, for instance, consists of thousands of parts. It is extremely difficult to coordinate the transfer of materials and components between production operations. Traditional factories use a **push system,** *which produces finished-goods inventory in advance of customer demand using a forecast of sales.* Parts and subassemblies are "pushed" through the operating system based on a predefined schedule that is independent of actual customer demand. In a push system, a model that might not be selling well is still produced at the same predetermined production rate and held in finished-goods inventory for future sale, whereas enough units of a model in high demand might not get produced.

Another problem was that traditional automobile production systems relied on massive and expensive stamping press lines to produce car panels. The dies in the presses weighed many tons, and specialists needed up to a full day to switch them for a new part. To compensate for long setup times, large batch sizes were produced so that machines could be kept busy while others were being set up. This resulted in high work-in-process inventories and high levels of indirect labor and overhead.

Toyota created a system based on a simple idea: produce the needed quantity of required parts each day. This concept characterizes a **pull system,** *in which employees at a given operation go to the source of required parts, such as machining or subassembly, and withdraw the units as they need them.* Then just enough new parts are manufactured or procured to replace those withdrawn. As the process from which parts were withdrawn replenishes the items it transferred out, it draws on the output of its preceding process, and so on. Finished goods are made to coincide with the actual rate of demand, resulting in minimal inventories and maximum responsiveness.

JIT systems are based on the concept of pull rather than push. In a JIT system, a key gateway workstation (such as final assembly) withdraws parts to meet demand and therefore provides real-time information to preceding workstations about how much to produce and when to produce to match the sales rate. By pulling parts from each preceding workstation, the entire manufacturing process is synchronized to the final assembly schedule. JIT operating systems prohibit all process workstations from pushing inventory forward only to wait idle if it is not needed.

A JIT system can produce a steady rate of output to meet the sales rate in small, consistent batch sizes to level loads and stabilize the operating system. This dramatically reduces the

Using JIT in a Supply Chain

Traditionally, the supply chain for books has been a "push" system—physical goods produced and delivered to bookstores for sale to consumers. Despite the promulgation of e-books and the demise of traditional bookstores such as Borders, many people still like to turn pages. As bookstores become leaner, many books are not available. For example, HarperCollins Publishers estimates that 25 to 80 percent of its paperback titles are not available in bookstores because of space considerations. However, the publisher is leveraging the JIT concept by using the Espresso Book Machine, distributed by On Demand Books LLC. This is a desk-sized machine that can custom print a book in only a few minutes. HarperCollins is using this technology to make about 5,000 paperback books available to bookstores.

inventory required between stages of the production process, thus greatly reducing costs and physical capacity requirements.

Many suppliers are asked to provide materials on a JIT basis to reduce inventories. Arriving shipments are sent directly to production. To accomplish this, suppliers often locate their parts warehouses close to final assembly factories. At the other end of the supply chain, distribution centers and retail stores are located close to their customers to speed up delivery.

18-5a Operation of a JIT System

A simple, generic JIT system with two process cycles—one for the customer and a second for the supply process—is shown in Exhibit 18.5. Conceptually, the customer can be an internal or external customer, and the customer-supply configuration in Exhibit 18.5 can be chained together to model a more complex sequence of production or assembly operations. In this process, the customer cycle withdraws what is needed at the time it is needed according to sales. The supply cycle creates the good to replenish only what has been withdrawn by the customer. The storage area is the interface and control point between the customer and supply cycles.

EXHIBIT 18.5 A Two-Card Kanban JIT Operating System

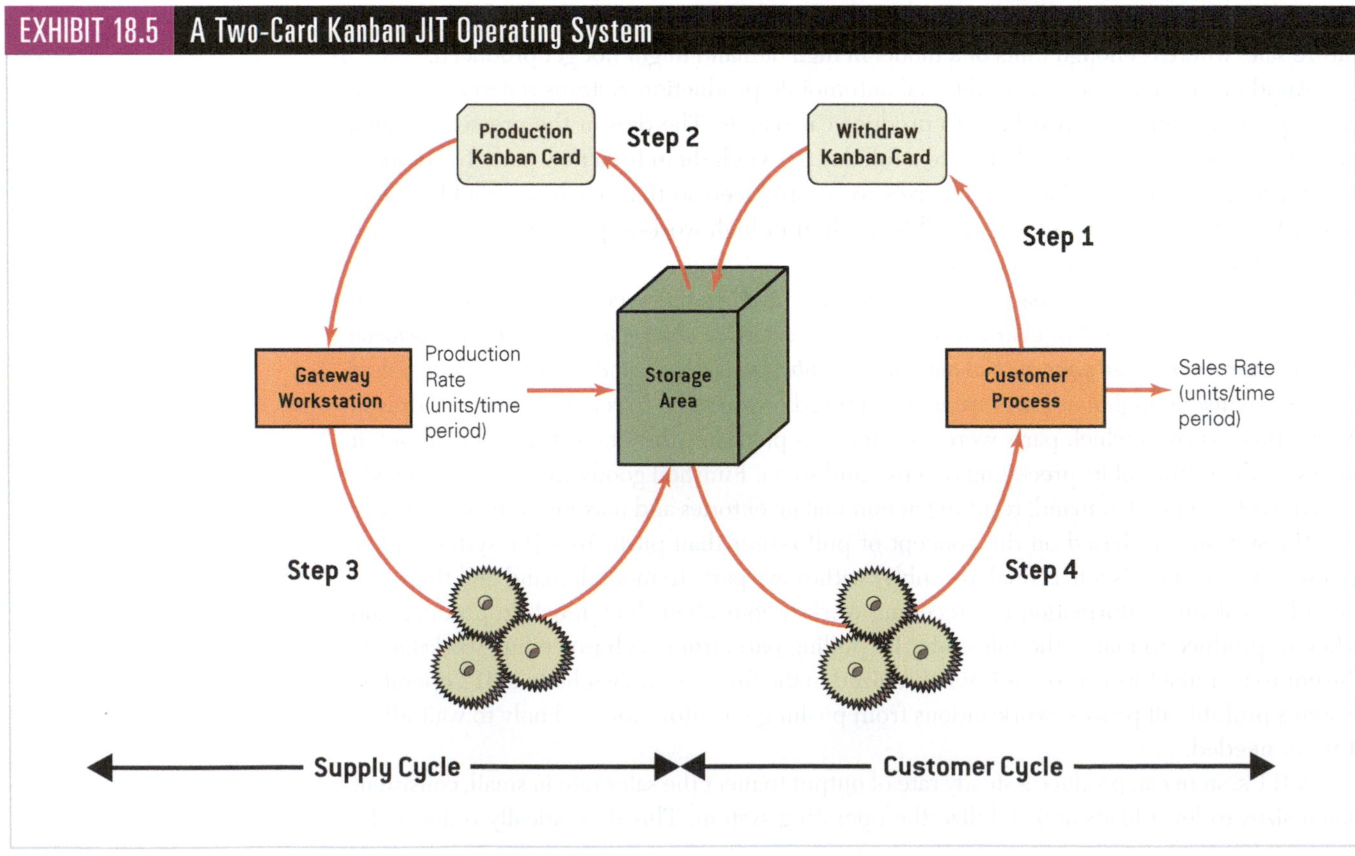

Slips, called Kanban cards (*Kanban* is a Japanese word that means "visual record" or "card"), are circulated within the system to initiate withdrawal and production items through the production process. *A* **Kanban** *is a flag or a piece of paper that contains all relevant information for an order: part number, description, process area used, time of delivery, quantity available, quantity delivered, production quantity, and so on.* Because of this, a JIT system is sometimes called a Kanban system.

The Kanban system begins when the customer buys or uses the good, and an empty container is created. The withdraw Kanban (step 1) authorizes the material handler to transfer empty containers to the storage area. Withdraw Kanbans trigger the movement of parts. The material handler detaches the withdraw-ordering Kanban that was attached to the empty container and places the Kanban card in the storage area or on the Kanban receiving post, leaving the empty container(s) (step 1). A material handler for the supply cycle places a production Kanban on the empty container, and this authorizes the gateway workstation to produce parts (step 2). Production Kanbans trigger the production of parts. The container holds a small lot size of parts. Without the authorization of the production Kanban, the gateway workstation and all other workstations may be idle. The gateway workstation must be scheduled to meet the sales rate, and it pulls parts from all other workstations. The other workstations in the process do not need to be scheduled because they get their production orders from the production Kanban that pulls parts through the supply process. The supply process returns a full container of parts to the storage area, with the production Kanban attached (step 3). The Kanban process is complete when the material handler for the customer process picks up a full container of parts and takes the production Kanban card off the container. Normally, the material handler drops off a withdrawal Kanban and empty container when picking up a full container of parts.

JIT practice is to set the lot size or container size equal to about 5 to 20 percent of a day's demand, or between 20 to 90 minutes, worth of demand. The number of containers in the system determines the average inventory levels. The following equation is used to calculate the number of Kanban cards (K) required:

$$K = \frac{\text{Average daily demand during lead time plus a safety stock}}{\text{Number of units per container}} = \frac{d(p+w)(1+\alpha)}{C} \quad [18.1]$$

where K = the number of Kanban cards in the operating system.

d = the average daily production rate as determined from the master production schedule.

w = the waiting time of Kanban cards in decimal fractions of a day (i.e., the waiting time of a part).

p = the processing time per part, in decimal fractions of a day.

C = the capacity of a standard container in the proper units of measure (parts, items, etc.).

α = a policy variable determined by the efficiency of the process and its workstations and the uncertainty of the workplace, and therefore a form of safety stock usually ranging from 0 to 1. However, technically, there is no upper limit on the value of α.

The number of Kanban cards is directly proportional to the amount of work-in-process inventory. Managers and employees strive to reduce the number of cards in the system through reduced lead time (p or w), lower α values, or through other improvements. The maximum authorized inventory in the operating system is $K \times C$. Solved Problem 18.3 illustrates kanban calculations and logic.

SOLVED PROBLEM 18.3: EVALUATING A KANBAN SYSTEM

Babbitt Manufacturing uses a Kanban system for a component part. The daily demand is 800 brackets. Each container has a combined waiting and processing time of 0.34 days. The container size is 50 brackets, and the safety factor (α) is 9 percent.

a. How many Kanban card sets should be authorized?
b. What is the maximum inventory of brackets in the system of brackets?
c. What are the answers to (a) and (b) if waiting and processing time is reduced by 25 percent?
d. If we assume one-half the containers are empty and one-half full at any given time, what is the average inventory in the system for the original problem?

Solution:

a. Using Equation 18.1:

$$K = \frac{d(p+w)(1+\alpha)}{C}$$

$$= \frac{(800\,\text{units})(0.34)(1+0.09)}{50} = 5.93$$

$$\cong 6\,(\text{rounded up to } 6)$$

Thus, six containers and six Kanban card sets are necessary to fulfill daily demand.

b. The maximum authorized inventory is $K \times C = 6 \times 50 = 300$ brackets.

c. $$K = \frac{d(p+w)(1+\alpha)}{C}$$

$$= \frac{(800\,\text{units})(0.255)(1+0.09)}{50} = 4.45$$

$$\cong 5\,(\text{rounded up to } 5)$$

Thus, five containers and five Kanban card sets are necessary to fulfill daily demand. The maximum authorized inventory is now $K \times C = 5 \times 50 = 250$ brackets.

d. The average inventory under this assumption is $300/2 = 150$ brackets. Many variables in the JIT system determine whether this assumption is valid or not. For example, for a given combination of daily demand, processing and waiting times, and other process inefficiencies and uncertainties, it is possible for more or fewer containers to be empty (full).

JIT systems produce according to the rate of sales. **Takt time** *is the production rate for one good or service based on the rate of sales.* Takt time is a term widely used in lean operating systems and value stream mapping. Takt is a German word for the baton that an orchestra conductor uses to regulate the tempo of the music. Takt time sets the pace of the process and its workstations, and it is often referred to as the "heartbeat" of a JIT and lean operating system.

The objective of takt time is to match the production and sales rate. Ideally, this approach results in zero work-in-progress inventory and no extra finished goods inventory. We make what we can sell and no more. Lean systems work best when the production schedule creates uniform loads on workstations. Takt time is computed using Equation 18.2.

$$\text{Takt time} = \frac{\text{Available time per time period}}{\text{Market demand rate per time period}} \qquad [18.2]$$

For example, an 8-hour workday that includes one hour for lunch and breaks effectively has 25,200 seconds per workday (7 hours/day × 3,600 seconds/hour). If the rate of sales is 400 units per day then the takt time is 25,200 seconds/day × 400 units/day = 63 seconds/unit. If the production process pulls units through the system at the rate of 63 seconds/unit, the pace of production will match the pace of sales.

Takt time is equivalent to cycle time (CT) for assembly line balancing as described in Chapter 8 and Equation 8.2. Equation 8.2 is $CT = A/R$, where A is the available time to produce the output and R is the demand sales forecast. Solved Problem 18.4 provides an example of computing takt and cycle time.

SOLVED PROBLEM 18.4: TAKT TIME AND CYCLE TIME COMPUTATIONS

TAC Manufacturing is implementing lean ideas and methods in its factory. It wants to compute the takt time based on its gateway assembly workstation that pulls parts from preceding workstations. The assembly workstation is available 9 hours a day with one hour for lunch and breaks, so it's available 8 hours per day. Daily demand is 1,000 units per day.

a. What is the takt time?
b. Show that cycle time used in balancing an assembly line is the same as Takt time used by lean practitioners.

Solution:

a. Using Equation 18.2,

Assembly Workstation Takt Time

$$= \frac{8 \text{ hours/day} \times 60 \text{ minutes/hour} \times 60 \text{ seconds/minute}}{1{,}000 \text{ parts/day}}$$

$$= \frac{28{,}800 \text{ seconds/day}}{1{,}000 \text{ parts/day}}$$

$$= 28.8 \text{ seconds/part}$$

b. From Chapter 8 and Equation 8.2, cycle time is related to the output rate (R) by the following equation:

$$CT = A/R \qquad [8.2]$$

where A = available time to produce the output and R = output rate. By definition they are the same, so cycle time = takt time = 28.8 seconds/part.

18-5b JIT in Service Organizations

Although JIT has had its biggest impact in manufacturing, many service organizations are increasingly applying it. At the Nashua Corporation, for example, a JIT-oriented study of administrative operations reduced order-cycle time from three days to one hour, office space requirements by 40 percent, and errors by 95 percent, and increased productivity by 20 percent.[8] One overnight package-delivery service saw its inventory investment climb from $16 million to $34 million with conventional inventory management techniques.[9] Implementing JIT reduced its inventory investment, but the company's major objective was to increase profits by providing a 99.9 percent level of service to its customers. Before JIT implementation, its service level—computed by dividing the number of items filled weekly by the number of items requested—was 79 percent. After JIT, the level was 99 percent, and the firm looked forward to meeting its goal. Baxter International is another service company that has experienced the benefits of a JIT system. Some of the characteristics of a well-designed JIT system are summarized in Exhibit 18.6.

EXHIBIT 18.6 Example JIT Characteristics and Best Practices

- Setup/changeover time minimized
- Excellent preventive maintenance
- Mistake-proof job and process design
- Stable, level, repetitive master production schedule
- Phantom bill of materials with zero lead time
- Fast processing times
- Clean and uncluttered workspaces
- Very little inventory to hide problems and inefficiencies
- Use production cells with no wasted motion
- May freeze the master production schedule
- Use reusable containers
- Outstanding communication and information sharing
- Keep it simple and use visual controls
- High-quality, approaching zero defects
- Small repetitive order/lot sizes
- Minimize the number of parts/items
- Minimize the number of bill of materials levels
- Facility layout that supports continuous or single-piece flow
- Minimize distance traveled and handling
- Clearly defined performance metrics
- Minimize the number of production, inventory, and accounting transactions
- Good calibration of all gauges and testing equipment
- Employees trained in quality management concepts and tools
- Excellent employee recognition and reward systems
- Employee cross-training and multiple skills
- Empowered and disciplined employees

However, lean principles can't be blindly implemented in services without considering their effects on customers, as Starbucks discovered. Starbucks initiated a "lean team" that goes around the country with a Mr. Potato Head toy used in a lean training program for Starbucks managers. Managers learn how to assemble the toy in less than 45 seconds and apply the learnings to their store processes. However, customer service encounters may have suffered, as one customer wrote: "Customers come into Starbucks—at least they did—to experience something that could only happen without lean—friendly banter with the barista, sampling coffee or a pastry, etc. Lean is best suited to assembly lines and factories, not so for managing human interaction, which is never a repeatable routine."[10]

18-6 Comparing Six Sigma, Lean, and the Theory of Constraints

Lean thinking, quality management (Chapters 16 and 17), and the Theory of Constraints (Chapter 11) are somewhat similar in that each are focused on improvement, yet each use different theories, methods, and ways of thinking. In this section, we contrast these approaches. Exhibit 18.7 summarizes key differences between the three improvement strategies.

As we discussed in this chapter, lean thinking is focused on reducing waste using tools such as the 5Ss, visual controls, SMED, batching and single-piece flow, continuous improvement, total productive maintenance, and just-in-time systems. Lean results in improved process flow, less variation, and minimal inventory by producing only what you sell. Quality management focuses on reducing variation and eliminating defects and errors using tools and approaches such as ISO 9000, Six Sigma and its DMAIC problem solving approach, cost-of-quality analysis, kaizen, and statistical process control. The Theory of Constraints seeks to maximize throughput in processes. This is accomplished by using process and value stream maps, financial metrics, identifying constraints, and managing bottleneck activities. This results in improved process flow, reduced waste, and improved quality.

We see that although the focus of each of these approaches are different, the goals and benefits are quite similar. Thus, these approaches support and complement one another. For instance, quality improvement is needed to accomplish lean objectives; applying TOC leads to a better understanding of processes and financial implications that can be used in quality efforts, and lean approaches help improve processes that can make TOC more effective. In each of these approaches, the tools and methods are synergistic; that is, the tools and methods work together to produce benefits greater than the sum of their individual applications. While some organizations may use only one of these approaches, it is important to understand and consider how all three can work together from a systems perspective.

EXHIBIT 18.7 Comparing Lean, Six Sigma, and the Theory of Constraints

Improvement Approach	Lean Thinking	Quality Management	Theory of Constraints
Focus	Reduce waste	Reduce variation and eliminate defects and errors	Maximize throughput and cash flow
Tools and methods	5Ss, visual controls, SMED, batching and single-piece flow, continuous improvement, TPM, JIT	ISO 9000, Six Sigma and DMAIC, cost of quality, kaizen, SPC	Process and value stream maps, financial metrics, constraint identification, bottleneck management
Goals and benefits	Improved process flow, less variation, smaller inventory requirements, higher productivity	Lower costs, higher yields, less scrap, higher productivity, higher customer satisfaction	Improved process flow, reduced waste, improved quality, higher productivity

It is also important to understand that using any of these approaches requires training, discipline, and cultural change. Not all of them are appropriate to every organization, nor will they always be easy to implement. Six Sigma, for example, requires a more analytical, measurement-driven approach. Traditional quality management can be implemented in small teams and by individuals in a kaizen approach. Lean approaches often require external consultants or additional training for internal staff. TOC requires a process-driven organization and is more complex to understand and implement. As noted in this chapter, Starbucks implemented lean thinking and practices in 2009. However, while this venture improved speed and efficiency, the CEO admitted that it diminished the product and service experience of customers.[11] For organizations that are customer- and process-focused, all three approaches can provide substantial benefits.

CHAPTER 18 LEARNING OBJECTIVE SUMMARIES

18.1 **Explain the four principles of lean operating systems and common types of waste.** Lean operating systems have four basic principles:

1. elimination of waste,
2. increased speed and response,
3. improved quality, and
4. reduced cost.

The Toyota Motor Company classified waste into seven major categories:

1. *Overproduction:* For example, making a batch of 100 when there are orders for only 50 in order to avoid an expensive setup, or making a batch of 52 instead of 50 in case there are rejects. Overproduction ties up production facilities, and the resulting excess inventory simply sits idle.
2. *Waiting time:* For instance, allowing queues to build up between operations, resulting in longer lead times and more work-in-process.
3. *Transportation:* The time and effort spent in moving products around the factory as a result of poor layout.
4. *Processing:* The traditional notion of waste, as exemplified by scrap that often results from poor product or process design.
5. *Inventory:* Waste associated with the expense of idle stock and extra storage and handling requirements needed to maintain it.
6. *Motion:* As a result of inefficient workplace design and location of tools and materials.
7. *Production defects:* The result of not performing work correctly the first time. Lean operating systems focus on quick and efficient response in designing and getting goods and services to market, producing to customer demand and delivery requirements, responding to competitors' actions, collecting payments, and addressing customer inquiries or problems.

18.2 **Describe the basic lean tools and approaches.** The 5Ss are derived from Japanese terms: *seiri (sort), seiton (set in order), seiso (shine), seiketsu (standardize),* and *shitsuke (sustain).*

- *Sort* refers to ensuring that each item in a workplace is in its proper place or identified as unnecessary and removed.
- *Set in order* means to arrange materials and equipment so that they are easy to find and use.
- *Shine* refers to a clean work area. Not only is this important for safety, but as a work area is cleaned, maintenance problems such as oil leaks can be identified before they cause problems.
- *Standardize* means to formalize procedures and practices to create consistency and ensure that all steps are performed correctly.
- Finally, *sustain* means to keep the process going through training, communication, and organizational structures.

Visual signaling systems are known as *andon*, drawing from the Japanese term from which the concept first originated. For example, if a machine fails or a part is defective or manufactured incorrectly, a light might turn on or a buzzer might sound, indicating that immediate action should be taken. Many firms have cords that operators can pull that tell supervisors and other workers that a problem has occurred. Single minute exchange of dies (SMED), pioneered by Toyota and other Japanese manufacturers, refers to quickly changing tooling and fixtures to reduce setup time and achieve higher flexibility and productivities. Batching is often necessary when producing a broad goods or service mix with diverse requirements on common equipment. By running large batches, setups and teardowns are reduced, providing economies of scale. However, this often builds up inventory that might not match market demand, particularly in highly dynamic markets. A better strategy would be to use small batches or single-piece flow. However, to do this economically requires the ability to change between products quickly and inexpensively. Quality at the source eliminates opportunities for waste and is a fundamental approach in lean thinking. The goal of total productive maintenance is to prevent equipment failures and downtime—ideally, to have "zero accidents, zero defects, and zero failures" in the entire life cycle of the operating system. Many companies are actively recovering and recycling parts (sometimes called green manufacturing).

18.3 **Explain the concept of Lean Six Sigma and how it is applied to improving operations performance.** Six Sigma is a useful and complementary approach to lean production. Lean Six Sigma draws upon the best practices of both approaches; however, they attack different types of problems. Lean production addresses visible problems in processes, for example, inventory, material flow, and safety. Six Sigma is concerned with less visible problems, for example, variation in performance.

18.4 **Explain how lean principles are used in manufacturing and service organizations.** Lean manufacturing plants look significantly different from traditional plants. They are clean and organized, devoid of long and complex production lines and high levels of work-in-process, have efficient layouts and work area designs, use multiskilled workers that perform both direct and indirect work such as maintenance, and have no incoming or final inspection stations. Lean principles are not always transferable to front-office services that involve high customer contact and service encounters. Different customers, service-encounter situations, and customer and employee behaviors cause the creation and delivery of the service to be much more variable and uncertain than producing a manufactured good in the confines of a factory. However,back-office service processes such as hospital laboratory testing, check processing, and college application processing are nearly identical to many manufacturing processes.

CHAPTER 18 LEARNING OBJECTIVE SUMMARIES

18.5 **Describe the concepts and philosophy of just-in-time operating systems.** Just-in-time (JIT) was introduced at Toyota during the 1950s and 1960s to address the challenge of coordinating successive production activities. Toyota created a system based on a simple idea: Produce the needed quantity of required parts each day. Then just enough new parts are manufactured or procured to replace those withdrawn. As the process from which parts were withdrawn replenishes the items it transferred out, it draws on the output of its preceding process, and so on. Finished goods are made to coincide with the actual rate of demand, resulting in minimal inventories and maximum responsiveness.

A JIT system can produce a steady rate of output to meet the sales rate in small, consistent batch sizes to level loads and stabilize the operating system. This dramatically reduces the inventory required between stages of the production process, thus greatly reducing costs and physical capacity requirements. In a JIT process, the customer cycle withdraws what is needed at the time it is needed according to sales. The supply cycle creates the good to replenish only what has been withdrawn by the customer. The storage area is the interface and control point between the customer and supply cycles. Slips, called Kanban cards (*Kanban* is a Japanese word that means "visual record" or "card"), are circulated within the system to initiate withdrawal and production items through the production process. The number of Kanban cards is directly proportional to the amount of work-in-process inventory (see Equation 18.1). Exhibit 18.7 summarizes key characteristics and best practices for JIT systems.

Takt time is a term widely used in lean operating systems and value stream mapping. Takt time is the production rate for one good or service based on the rate of sales, computed as:

$$\text{Takt time} = \frac{\text{Available time per time period}}{\text{Market demand rate per time period}} \quad [18.2]$$

The objective of Takt time is to match the production and sales rate. Ideally, this approach results in zero work-in-progress inventory and no extra finished goods inventory.

KEY TERMS

- 5Ss
- Batching
- Kanban
- Lean operating systems
- Lean thinking
- Pull system
- Push system
- Single Minute Exchange of Dies (SMED)
- Single-piece flow
- Takt time
- Total productive maintenance (TPM)
- Transfer batch
- Visual controls

REVIEW QUESTIONS

1. What is lean enterprise?

2. Explain the four fundamental objectives of lean operating systems.

3. What are the benefits of adopting lean operating systems?

4. What are the "5Ss"? Why are they important to becoming lean?

5. What benefits do visual controls have for lean operating systems?

6. Explain the importance of short setup times in a lean environment. What approach is used to reduce setup times?

18.2 7. Define a transfer batch and single-piece flow. Why are they important?

8. How does quality improvement support lean enterprise?

9. Explain the role of total productive maintenance in lean operating systems.

10. What is Lean Six Sigma? Why are lean and Six Sigma concepts highly complementary?

11. Explain the difference between push and pull systems. What advantages do pull systems have over push systems?

18.5 12. What is a Kanban? Explain how a Kanban system operates.

18.5 13. Describe some of the key features of good JIT systems.

18.5 14. What is the role of suppliers in JIT systems?

18.5 15. Does a high alpha value (say $\alpha = 2$ or 3) in Equation 18.12 negate the benefits of a Kanban/JIT operating system? Explain.

18.5 16. Define Takt time and explain why it is important?

DISCUSSION QUESTIONS AND EXPERIENTIAL ACTIVITIES

18.1 17. Provide some examples of different types of waste in an organization with which you are familiar, such as an automobile repair shop or a fast-food restaurant.

18.1 18. Some companies use a technique called *heijunka*, which is a Japanese term that refers to production smoothing in which the total volume of parts and assemblies are kept as constant as possible. Research and write a short paper (two pages max) about this technique and how it relates to lean principles. Try to illustrate a case study of a company that has used it.

18.2 19. Search the Internet for images of visual controls. Select five of them and explain how they contribute to achieving one of the four principles of lean operating systems.

18.2 20. What types of "setups" do you perform in your work or school activities? How might you reduce the setup times?

18.2 21. Choose one of the lean tools and approaches from Section 18-2 and research and write a short paper (two pages maximum) on how organizations use this tool, and provide specific examples.

18.2 22. A catalog order-filling process can be described as follows:[12] Telephone orders are taken over a 12-hour period each day. Orders are collected from each person at the end of the day and checked for errors by the supervisor of the phone department, usually the following morning. The supervisor does not send each one-day batch of orders to the data processing department until after 1:00 p.m. In the next step—data processing—orders are invoiced in the one-day batches. Then they are printed and matched back to the original orders. At this point, if the order is from a new customer, it is sent to the person who did the customer verification and setup of new customer accounts. This process must be completed before the order can be invoiced. The next step—order verification and proofreading—occurs after invoicing is completed. The orders, with invoices attached, are given to a person who verifies that all required information is present and correct to permit typesetting. If the verifier has any questions, they are checked by computer or by calling the customer. Finally, the completed orders are sent to the typesetting department of the print shop.

a. Develop a flowchart for this process (see Chapter 7).

b. Identify opportunities for improving the process using lean principles.

18.2 23. A team at a hospital studied the process of performing a diagnostic CT scan. The current process can be described as follows.

The CT tech enters a "send for patient" request into a computer when the CT is available for the next patient. The computer prints a request for transport and an orderly is assigned to take the patient for the scan. The orderly walks to radiology and gets the ticket and patient information. The orderly takes the elevator to the patient's unit and goes to the nurse's station, locates the nurse in charge and obtains the patient's chart. He or she signs out the patient and walks to the patient's room and waits for a nurse to help transfer the patient. The patient is transferred to a mobile bed and then taken to the elevator and brought to radiology. The chart is given to the CT technician while the patient waits in the hall. When the CT is ready, the patient is moved to the CT machine and the scan is performed. The orderly is called back to take the patient back to his or her room.

Draw a flowchart of this process, identify the value-added and non-value added activities, and describe how lean thinking can be applied to shorten the throughput time to perform the CT scan.

18.4 24. Compare the lean service system of Southwest Airlines to a full service airline such as United Airlines or British Airways on the following: (a) airplane boarding process, (b) cabin service, (c) ticket transfer to other Southwest flights, (d) frequent flyer program, (e) baggage handling, (f) seat assignment system, and (g) service encounters.

18.4 25. Do you think applying operations management concepts and methods such as Six Sigma and lean principles can reduce U.S. health care costs? Explain. Provide examples that show how OM can help the U.S. health care industry.

18.4 26. Research and write a short paper (two pages maximum) on applications of the 5S principles in service organizations, such as a hospital. If possible, provide some pictures that illustrate the results of using the 5S principles.

18.4 27. Search the Internet for manufacturing or service tours similar to the ones in this chapter. Classify their practices according to the four lean principles in a manner similar to the examples.

18.4 28. Research and briefly describe one or two lean initiatives in service organizations and then make an argument for or against adopting lean principles in service businesses. What is different about applying lean in a factory versus a service situation? Describe your findings in a two-page paper.

18.5 29. Interview a manager at a local company that uses JIT. Report on how it is implemented and the benefits the company has realized.

18.5 30. Research JIT practices and how they impact purchasing. How do you think JIT systems affect purchasing functions and practices? Answer this question in a short paper of no more than two typed pages.

18.5 31. Research and write a short paper on the impact of global supply chains on JIT.

COMPUTATIONAL PROBLEMS AND EXERCISES

These exercises require you to apply the formulas and methods described in the chapter. The problems should be solved manually.

18.2 32. Esplanade Marine Parts Inc. wants to produce parts in batches of 100 parts. Each part must be processed sequentially from workstation A to B.

Workstation	Batch Size (Q)	Processing time per part
A	100	20 seconds
B	100	15 seconds

a. How many seconds is required to produce the batch under the assumptions of batch processing?

b. How many seconds is required to produce the batch under the assumptions of single-piece flow processing?

c. Compare the two solutions in terms of time saved and any other issue(s) you think important.

18.2 33. CDC Discrete Fabricators wants to produce parts in batches of 300 parts. Each part must be processed sequentially from workstation A to B to C to D.

Workstation	Batch Size (Q)	Processing time per part
A	300	20 seconds
B	300	15 seconds
C	300	10 seconds
D	300	25 seconds

a. How many seconds is required to produce the batch under the assumptions of batch processing?

b. How many seconds is required to produce the batch under the assumptions of single-piece flow processing?

c. Compare the two solutions in terms of time saved and any other issue(s) you think important.

18.2 34. A Florida lottery machine and printer at Store #8302 operates 360 days a year. If the machine does not work and breaks down, it costs the Florida Lottery Commission $2,000 per day. If store employees are trained to perform local tests on the machine each day plus the costs of machine repairpersons, these preventive maintenance costs average $670 per day. If preventive maintenance is performed daily, the probability the equipment fails is zero. The probability of store lottery machine breakdown is as follows. What are the economics of the situation? What do you recommend?

Number of lottery machine breakdowns per day	0	1	2
Probability of a breakdown	0.333	0.333	0.333

18.2 35. A plastic injection molding machine operates 348 days a year. It is the bottleneck workstation in a process that produces plastic housed wall clocks.

Industrial engineers collected data on the probability of machine breakdowns, the costs of preventive maintenance, and the cost of a breakdown.

Number of molding machine breakdowns per day	0	1	2	3	4
Probability of a breakdown	0.32	0.28	0.22	0.13	0.05

The cost of preventive maintenance is high due to performing it between 1 and 4 a.m. each day by two machine experts. The preventive maintenance cost is $1,980 per day including replacement parts, cleaning, and software upgrades. The cost of a breakdown of $1,850 is also high because the downstream workstations can only work until all work-in-progress inventory is completed; then the entire process must stop.

18.5 36. Bracket Manufacturing uses a Kanban system for a component. Daily demand is 1,000 units. Each container has a combined waiting and processing time of .85 days. If the container size is 70 and the alpha value (α) is 13%, how many Kanban card sets should be authorized? What is the maximum authorized inventory?

18.5 37. Tooltron Manufacturing uses a Kanban system for a component. Daily demand is 425 units. Each container has a combined waiting and processing time of 1.5 days. If the container size is 35 and the alpha value (α) is 12 percent, how many Kanban card sets should be authorized? What is the maximum authorized inventory?

18.5 38. Lou's Bakery has established that JIT should be used for chocolate chips due to the high probability of the kitchen heat melting the chips. The average demand is 150 cups of chocolate chips per week. The average setup and processing time is ¼ day. Each container holds exactly two cups. The current safety stock factor is 5 percent. The baker operates six days per week.

a. How many *Kanbans* are required for the bakery?
b. What is the maximum authorized inventory?
c. If the average setup and processing time is increased to ⅜ of a day due to a process change, what are the answers to (a) and (b)?

18.5 39. Due to rapid changes in technology, a telecommunications manufacturer decides to produce a router using JIT methods. Daily demand for the router is 17 units per day. The routers are built on racks that hold four at a time (i.e., the container size). Total processing and waiting time is 3.75 days. The process manager wants a safety factor of only 5 percent.

a. How many Kanbans are required?
b. What is the maximum authorized router inventory?
c. If you assume that one-half of the racks are empty and one-half full at any given time, what is the average inventory of routers?
d. What are the answers to a to c if due to process improvements the total processing and waiting time is reduced from 3.75 to 2.75 days?

18.5 40. An automobile transmission manufacturer is considering using a JIT approach to replenishing its stock of transmissions. Daily demand for transmission #230 is 55 transmissions per day and they are built in groups of six transmissions. Total assembly and waiting time is two days. The supervisor wants to use an alpha value (α) of 1, or 100 percent.

a. How many *Kanbans* are required?
b. What is the maximum authorized inventory?
c. What are the pros and cons of using such a high alpha value (α)?

18.5 41. A pillow assembly line consists of five stages arranged in series. The first workstation stuffs the pillow with filler material. The second workstation sews the pillow case and the third stage places the pillow in a clear plastic sleeve. The fourth workstation places the pillow in a box of three for shipping and seals the box. The fifth workstation places labels on the box for shipping. Pillows are low value yet high cubic volume, so inventory holding cost is high. In fact, the operations managers use a JIT lean assembly line and attempt to only produce what they can sell. The assembly line works two shifts/day, 8 hours/shift minus 1 hour for breaks and food, and 330 days per year. Annual demand is 1,000,000 pillows. What is the Takt time in seconds? How is your answer used?

Kempfer Furniture, Inc.

Marta Tompkins, a graduate in industrial engineering from Purdue University, was excited. She had accepted a new job in South Carolina as the Operations & Logistics manager at Kempfer Furniture, Incorporated. Marta had work for Honda Manufacturing in Marysville, Ohio for twelve years as the director of Lean Operations. Her resume documented extensive experience with lean manufacturing and Six Sigma strategies and methodologies. Many of her improvement initiatives created fast throughput, and less waste and inventory. She had also led projects on new environmental quality standards outlined by ISO 14000. Kempfer hired her to be the factory manager at their South Carolina facility.

During her first two weeks on the job, Marta learned the processes that produced some standard and some customized furniture orders. Kempfer manufactured wood furniture, such as kitchen and dining room tables and chairs, beds, and bedroom dressers and night stands. They specialized in specialty hardwoods, such as cherry and red oak. The firm was known for producing high-quality furniture at low to moderate prices. Delivery time was a problem.

Kempfer was one of a handful of American based furniture manufacturers because most furniture was built in Asian factories. But Kempfer Furniture had not been profitable for two years. The owner, Mr. Tomas Luke, hired Ms. Audubon to help turn the business around and make it profitable. His mandate to the 156 factory employees was if the business didn't make a profit in two of the next three years, he would close the business and declare bankruptcy.

Marta keep notes on all that she heard and saw. A sample of her notes are shown in Exhibit 18.8. She also noted that work center, loading dock, and shipping managers often missed her meetings because they were too busy getting the product out the door.

Case Questions for Discussion:

1. Identify three lean tools that you would recommend Kempfer Furniture use. Explain the benefits of using them.
2. Recommend three Six Sigma or Theory of Constraints methods and tools that would help turn this firm around. Explain your reasoning for choosing them.
3. Develop a ten-step improvement implementation plan to be completed and led by Marta Tompkins in the first six months. Justify this plan based on the facts of the case.
4. Recommend three longer-term improvement initiatives to be accomplished after the first six months. Describe each initiative in no more than three sentences (i.e., a short paragraph).

EXHIBIT 18.8 Marta's Notes During Factory Walk-Arounds and Meetings

1. Sawdust was everywhere. The factory was not clean. The air smelled of dust and wood finishing varnishes. Varnish spray booths were not fully enclosed with adequate exhaust systems.
2. The factory layout was best described as a process layout to accommodate a job shop structure.
3. Our selling price is 20 percent above our manufactured cost, we think.
4. The cash flow of the factory was not sufficient to fully fund the factory and leased public warehouse. Mr. Thomas Luke acquired a promissory note from a regional bank to fund operations.
5. Customer orders ranged from one unit to thirty units but factory practice is to build one unit at a time. One work center manager said, "We setup way too many times for a single customer order."
6. Inventory was scattered throughout the factory. Some component inventory and finished products were stored in heavy canvas tents outside.
7. Third party contract truckers often showed up at the loading docks with their orders not ready. This happened 15 percent of the time and many truck drivers avoided working for Kempfer Furniture, Inc.
8. A shop foreman said that "two old planing machines often breakdown."
9. Customer orders were often changed but these changes didn't get to the factory floor about one-third of the time resulting in rework and starting the order anew.
10. Wood saws blades were dull and seldom sharpened.
11. All work centers, employees, and equipment were utilized 100 percent of the time, six days a week.
12. Last year, three accidents happened at the factory. One employee was hit by a forklift truck out of its lane on the loading dock, another employee tripped on scrap wood and broke his wrist, and a third employee slipped on the sawdust on the floor and had a severe concussion.
13. Kiln drying capacity held up about one-half of all jobs.
14. $3 million dollars of finished furniture was stored in a leased public warehouse four miles away from the factory. It was unsold due to overproduction or cancelled customer orders.

Community Medical Associates

Community Medical Associates (CMA) is a large health care system with 2 hospitals, 25 satellite health centers, and 56 outpatient clinics. CMA had 1.5 million outpatient visits and 60,000 inpatient admissions the previous year. Just a few years ago, CMA's health care delivery system was having significant problems with quality of care. Long patient waiting times, uncoordinated clinical and patient information, and medical errors plagued the system. Doctors, nurses, lab technicians, managers, and medical students in training were very aggravated with the labyrinth of forms, databases, and communication links. Accounting and billing were in a situation of constant confusion and constantly correcting medical bills and insurance payments. The complexity of the CMA information and communication system overwhelmed its people.

Prior to redesigning its systems, physicians were faced with a complex array of appointments and schedules in order to see patients in the hospital, centers, and clinics. For example, an elderly patient with shoulder pain would get an X-ray at the clinic but have to set up an appointment for a CAT scan in the hospital. Furthermore, the patient's blood was sent to an off-site lab, and physician notes were transcribed from tape recorders. Radiology would read and interpret the X-rays and body scans in a consultant report. Past and present medication records were kept in the hospital and off-site pharmacies. Physicians would write paper prescriptions for each patient. Billing and patient insurance information was maintained in a separate database. The patient's medical chart was part paper based and part electronic. The paper medical file could be stored at the hospital, centers, or clinics. Nurses handwrote their notes on each patient, but their notes were seldom input into the patient's medical records or chart.

"We must access one database for lab results, then log off and access another system for radiology, then log off and access the CMA pharmacy system to gain an integrated view of the patient's health. If I can't find the patient's records within five minutes or so, I have to abandon my search and tell the patient to wait or make another appointment," said one doctor. The doctor continued, "You have to abandon the patient because you have to move on to patients you truly can diagnose and help. If you don't abandon the patient, you might make clinical decisions about the patient's health without having a complete set of information. Not having all the medical information fast has a direct impact on quality of care and patient satisfaction."

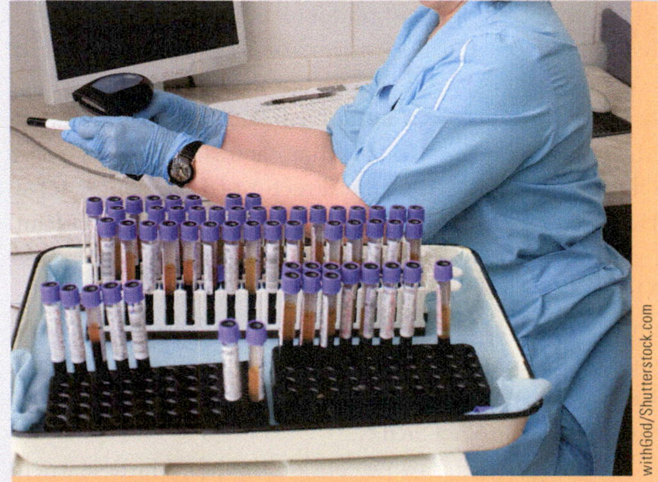
withGod/Shutterstock.com

Today, CMA uses an integrated operating system that consolidates over 50 CMA databases into one.

Today, CMA uses an integrated operating system that consolidates over 50 CMA databases into one. Health care providers in the CMA system now have access to these records through 7,000 computer terminals. Using many levels of security and some restricted databases, all patient information is accessible in less than two minutes. For example, sensitive categories of patient records such as psychiatric and AIDS problems were kept in super-restricted databases. It cost CMA $4.46 to retrieve and transport a single patient's paper-based medical chart to the proper location, whereas the more complete and quickly updated electronic medical record costs $1.32 to electronically retrieve and transport once. A patient's medical records are retrieved on average 1.4 times for outpatient services and 4.8 times for inpatient admissions. In addition, CMA has spent more money on database security, although it has not been able to place a dollar value on this. Electronic security audit trails show who logs on, when, how long he or she views a specific file, and what information has been viewed.

The same doctor who made the previous comments two years ago now said, "The speed of the system is what I like. I can now make informed clinical decisions for my patients. Where it used to take several days and sometimes weeks to transcribe my patient medical notes, it now takes no more than 48 hours to see them pop up on the CMA system. Often my notes are up on the system the same day. I'd say we use about one-half the paper we used with the old system. I also find myself editing and correcting transcription errors in the database—so it is more accurate now."

The next phase in the development of CMA's integrated system is to connect it to suppliers, outside labs and pharmacies, other hospitals, and to doctors' home computers.

Case Questions for Discussion:

1. Explain how CMA used the four principles of lean operating systems to improve performance.
2. Using the information from the case, sketch the original, paper-based value chain and compare it to a sketch of the modern, electronic value chain, which uses a common database. Explain how the performance of both systems might compare.
3. What is the total annual record retrieval cost savings with the old (paper-based) versus new (electronic) systems?
4. Does this CMA improvement initiative have any effect on sustainability? If so, how? If not, why?
5. Using lean principles, can you simultaneously improve speed and quality while reducing waste and costs? What are the trade-offs? Explain your reasoning.

Integrative Case: Hudson Jewelers

The Hudson Jewelers case study found in MindTap integrates material found in each chapter of this book.

Case Questions for Discussion:

1. Write a short paper (maximum of two pages) on how the four principles of lean operating systems are applied to diamond mining.
2. If you were to design a jewelry store based only upon the four principles of lean operating systems—elimination of waste, increased speed and response, improved quality, and reduced cost—what would it look like? Incorporate OM concepts and methods used throughout this textbook, such as mission and strategy, competitive priorities, process type, service guarantees, supply chain, and so on as appropriate, into your discussion.

19 Project Management

LEARNING OBJECTIVES

After studying this chapter, you should be able to:

- 19-1 Explain the key issues associated with project management.
- 19-2 Describe how to apply the Critical Path Method (CPM).
- 19-3 Explain how to make time/cost trade-off decisions in projects.
- 19-4 Describe how to calculate probabilities for project completion time using the Project Evaluation and Review Technique (PERT).

Despite construction delays and budget overruns, the venues were ready for the 2004 Olympic Games in Athens, Greece.

GERARD JULIEN/AFP/Getty Images

The Olympic Games were established over 2,500 years ago. Athens, Greece, was chosen in 1997 to host the 2004 Games, but organizers badly underestimated the cost and overestimated the city's ability to meet construction and preparation schedules. Organizers were plagued with construction delays and budget overruns, forcing them to complete seven years' worth of work in just four years. Delays in the main stadium's glass-and-steel room pushed back delivery of the entire complex to the end of July, immediately preceding the August 13, 2004, opening ceremonies. The International Olympic Committee had even considered asking the Athens organizers to cancel the Games.[1] Problems also occurred with other venues. Construction delays had consequences for Greece's own athletes, forcing them out of their own training centers. Even the famed Parthenon, which was to have been restored for the Games, was still shrouded with scaffolding when tourists began arriving. Despite all this, the venues were ready—although some at the last minute—and the Games were successfully completed.

WHAT DO YOU THINK?

Think of a project in which you have been involved, perhaps at work or in some student activity. What factors made your project either difficult or easy to accomplish?

A **project** *is a temporary and often customized initiative that consists of many smaller tasks and activities that must be coordinated and completed to finish the entire initiative on time and within budget.* Suppose that a small business is considering expanding its facility. Some of the major tasks in planning for expansion are hiring architects, designing a new facility, hiring contractors, building the facility, purchasing and installing equipment, and hiring and training employees. Each of these major tasks consists of numerous subtasks that must be performed in a particular sequence, on time, and on budget. Taken together, these activities constitute a project.

In many firms, projects are the major value-creation process, and the major activities in the value chain revolve around projects. Some examples are market research studies, construction, movie production, software development, book publishing, and wedding planning. In other firms, projects are used on an infrequent basis to implement new strategies and initiatives or for supporting value chain design and improvement activities. Some examples are preparation of annual reports, installing an automated materials-handling system, or training employees to learn a new computer-support system. Even U.S. courts use projects to help resolve construction claim litigations. Exhibit 19.1 lists a variety of examples of projects in many different functional areas of business.

> In many firms, projects are the major value-creation process, and the major activities in the value chain revolve around projects. Some examples are market research studies, construction, and movie production.

In all project situations, projects require systematic management. **Project management** *involves all activities associated with planning, scheduling, and controlling projects.* The 2004 Olympic Games provides a good example of the importance of project management. The London 2012 Olympic Organizing Committee advertised for a variety of job opportunities, including project management, and a post at blogspot.com observed "Students of project management should train their binoculars on east London and watch what is going to be a lively and living case study. The London Olympics is a project that will unfold before our very eyes, and what we will see, at least for the project management geeks among us, is going to be a lot more amusing and instructive than the games themselves."[2] Every four years, another city faces similar project management issues!

Good project management ensures that an organization's resources are used efficiently and effectively. This is particularly important, because projects generally cut across organizational boundaries and require the coordination of many different departments and functions, and sometimes companies. In addition, most projects are unique, requiring some customization and response to new challenges.

The Project Management Institute reports that effective project management decreased failed projects by 31 percent, delivered 30 percent of projects under budget, and delivered 19 percent of projects ahead of schedule.

Project management is becoming more important in achieving environmental, social, and economic sustainability. New jobs are emerging, having titles such as environmental project manager, health and safety manager, environmental auditor, and sustainability compliance manager. In the last decade, millions of project manager jobs have been created across the globe. The Bureau of Labor Statistics in the U.S. Department of labor now recognizes "project manager" as an occupational category and will measure the economic contribution of project management professionals. Each of these requires project management skills. Green activities are becoming more common in construction, waste management, procurement, recycling, and energy conservation projects. Project management skills are also essential to coordinate the multiple project disciplines needed to successfully accomplish a project with complete or partial sustainability objectives and desired outcomes.

EXHIBIT 19.1 Example Projects in Different Functional Areas that Impact the Value Chain

Functional Areas	Example Projects
Marketing	Point-of-sale system installation New product introduction Market research studies
Accounting and Finance	Auditing a firm's accounting and financial systems Planning a firm's initial public offering (IPO) Auditing a firm's procedures and stock trading rules for compliance with the Securities & Exchange Commission
Information Systems	Software development Software upgrades throughout a firm Hardware installation
Human Resource Management	Launching and coordinating training programs Annual performance and compensation review Implementing new benefits plans
Engineering	Designing new manufactured parts Implementing a new computer-aided design system Installing factory automation
Logistics	Installing an automated warehouse system Implementing an order-tracking system Building a transportation hub
Operations	Planning preventive maintenance for an oil refinery Implementing enterprise resource planning (ERP) software and systems Installing a revenue management system

19-1 The Scope of Project Management

Most projects go through similar stages from start to completion. These stages characterize the project life cycle and form the basis for effective project management.

1. *Define*: Projects are implemented to satisfy some need; thus, the first step in managing a project is to clearly define its goal, its responsibilities and deliverables, and when it must be accomplished. A common way to capture this information is with a specific and measurable *statement of work*. For example, the goal of an accounting audit might be; "Audit the firm's accounting and financial statements and submit a report by December 1 that determines statement accuracy in accordance with generally accepted accounting principles in the United States of America. The audit fee shall not exceed $200,000."
2. *Plan*: In this stage, the steps needed to execute a project are defined; it is determined who will perform these steps; and the start and completion dates are developed. Planning entails breaking down a project into smaller activities and developing a project schedule by estimating the time required for each activity and scheduling them so they meet the project due date.
3. *Organize*: Organizing involves such activities as forming a team, allocating resources, calculating costs, assessing risk, preparing project documentation, and ensuring good communications. It also requires identifying a project manager who provides the leadership to accomplish the project goal.

4. *Control*: This stage assesses how well a project meets its goals and objectives and makes adjustments as necessary. Controlling involves collecting and assessing status reports, managing changes to baselines, and responding to circumstances that can negatively impact the project participants.
5. *Close*: Closing a project involves compiling statistics, releasing and/or reassigning people, and preparing a "lessons learned" list.

19-1a Roles of the Project Manager and Team Members

Project managers have significant responsibilities. It is their job to build an effective team, motivate them, provide advice and support, align the project with the firm's strategy, and direct and supervise the conduct of the project from beginning to end. In addition to managing the project, they must manage the relationships among the project team, the parent organization, and the client. The project manager must also have sufficient technical expertise to resolve disputes among functional specialists.

Good project managers recognize that people issues are as important as technical issues. Several principles can help project managers be successful:[3]

- Manage people individually and as a project team.
- Reinforce the commitment and excitement of the project team.
- Keep everyone informed.
- Build agreements and consensus among the team.
- Empower the project team.

19-1b Organizational Structure

How a project fits into a firm's organizational structure impacts its effectiveness. Some organizations use a pure project organizational structure whereby team members are assigned exclusively to projects and report only to the project manager. This approach makes it easier to manage projects because project teams can be designed for efficiency by including the right mix of skills. However, it can result in inefficiencies because of duplication of resources across the organization; for example, having a different information technology support person on each project.

A pure functional organizational structure charters projects exclusively within functional departments, such as manufacturing or research and development. Although this approach allows team members to work on different projects simultaneously and provides a "home" for the project, it ignores an important reality: In a typical functional organization, a project cuts across organizational boundaries. Assigning projects exclusively to functional areas makes communication across the organization difficult and can limit the effectiveness of projects that require a systems perspective.

A practical solution to this dilemma is a matrix organizational structure, which "lends" resources to projects while still maintaining control over them. Project managers coordinate the work across the functions. This minimizes duplication of resources and facilitates communication across the organization but requires that resources be negotiated. Functional managers may be reluctant to provide

The Penalties of Poor Project Management

Not completing projects on time can have severe consequences. For example, the construction of the Matlacha Bridge in Florida was finished 10 months later than its original project schedule indicated. The contract provisions call for penalties of over $8,000 per day! This shows just how important all steps of project management are, from defining the project, its budget, and possible penalties, through planning, execution, and control.

Custom Research Inc.: Project Management in Marketing Research

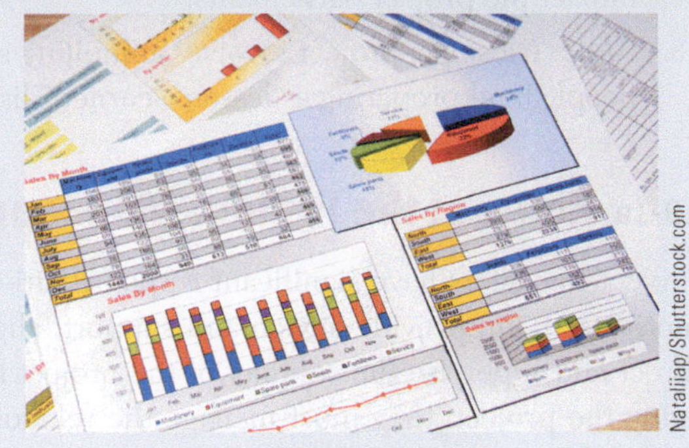

Founded in 1974 and based in Minneapolis, privately owned Custom Research Inc. (CRI) conducts survey marketing research for a wide range of firms. The bulk of its projects assist clients with new product development in consumer, medical, and service businesses. Marketing research projects consist of numerous processes, and although each project is custom-designed, all projects essentially require the same processes, such as project definition, data collection, report generation, and so on. CRI measures project performance at each step. CRI's steering committee distilled requirements for each research project to four essentials: accurate, on time, on budget, and meeting or exceeding client expectations. At the end of each project, clients are surveyed to solicit an overall satisfaction rating based on the customers' expectations. Each month the results of the client feedback are summarized and distributed to all employees. Internally, end-of-project evaluations also are conducted for CRI support teams and key suppliers.[4]

> In a typical functional organization, a project cuts across organizational boundaries.

the resources, and employees assigned to projects might relegate a project to a lower priority than their daily functional job, making it difficult for the project manager to control the project.

19-1c Factors for Successful Projects

Projects are not always successful. Information technology projects have a notorious rate of failure. One study in the United States found that over 30 percent of software projects are canceled before completion, and more than half cost almost double their original estimates. Exhibit 19.2 summarizes the principal factors that help or hinder project management.

Ensuring project success depends on having well-defined goals and objectives, clear reporting relationships and channels of communication, good procedures for estimating time and other resource requirements, cooperation and commitment among all project team members, realistic expectations, effective conflict resolution, and top management sponsorship.

19-2 Techniques for Planning, Scheduling, and Controlling Projects

All project management decisions involve three factors: *time*, *resources*, and *cost*. Various techniques have long been used to help plan, schedule, and control projects. The key steps involved are the following:

1. *Project definition*: Identifying the activities that must be completed and the sequence required to perform them.
2. *Resource planning*: For each activity, determining the resource needs: personnel, time, money, equipment, materials, and so on.

EXHIBIT 19.2 Contributors and Impediments to Project Success

Contributors to Project Success	Impediments to Project Success
Well-defined and agreed-upon objectives	Ill-defined project objectives
Top management support	Lack of executive champion
Strong project manager leadership	Inability to develop and motivate people
Well-defined project definition	Poorly defined project definition
Accurate time and cost estimates	Lack of data accuracy and integrity
Teamwork and cooperation	Poor interpersonal relations and teamwork
Effective use of project management tools	Ineffective use of project management tools
Clear channels of communication	Poor communication among stakeholders
Adequate resources and reasonable deadlines	Unreasonable time pressures and lack of resources
Constructive response to conflict	Inability to resolve conflicts

3. *Project scheduling*: Specifying a time schedule for the completion of each activity.
4. *Project control*: Establishing the proper controls for determining progress and developing alternative plans in anticipation of problems in meeting the planned schedule.

Several software packages, such as Microsoft Project™, are available to help project managers plan and manage projects. Although we will not discuss such software in detail, we will introduce the underlying techniques that are used in modern project management software.

To illustrate how these steps are applied in project management, we will use a simple example. Wildcat Software Consulting Inc. helps companies implement software integration projects. Raj Yazici has been named the project manager in charge of coordinating the design and installation of the new software system. In the following sections, we address the various tasks involved in project definition, resource planning, project scheduling, and project control that he will face in his role as project manager.

19-2a Project Definition

The first step is to define the project objectives and deliverables. Mr. Yazici and his project team decided on the following statements:

- **Project objective:** To develop an integrative software package within a predetermined budget and promised project completion date that meets all system requirements while providing adequate interfaces with legacy systems.
- **Deliverables:** (1) New software package, (2) successful implementation of the package, and (3) pretraining of sales force and PC system operators.

Next, Mr. Yazici needed to identify the specific activities required to complete the project and the sequence in which they must be performed. **Activities** *are discrete tasks that consume resources and time.* **Immediate predecessors** *are those activities that must be completed immediately before an activity may start.* Precedence relationships ensure that activities are performed in the proper sequence when they are scheduled.

The initial list of activities and precedence relationships associated with the software integration project is summarized in Exhibit 19.3. For instance, activities A and B can be started at any time because they do not depend on the completion of prior activities. However, activity C cannot be started until both activities A and B have been completed. Mr. Yazici and his team reviewed and discussed the list several times to be sure that no activities were omitted from the project definition.

Defining the list of activities in a project is often facilitated by creating a work breakdown structure, which breaks a project down into manageable pieces, or items, to help ensure that all of the work elements needed to complete the project are identified. *The*

EXHIBIT 19.3 Project Activities and Precedence Relationships

Activity	Activity Description	Immediate Predecessors
A	Define software project objectives, budget, due date, and possible staff	None
B	Inventory new and old software interfaces and features	None
C	Assemble teams and allocate work	A, B
D	Design and develop code from old to new databases	C
E	Design and develop code for PC network	C
F	Test and debug PC network code	E
G	Design and develop code for off-site sales force	C
H	New complete system test and debug	D, G, F
I	Train PC system and database operators	D, F
J	Train off-site sales force	H
K	Two-week beta test of new system with legacy backup system	I, J

work breakdown structure *is a hierarchical tree of end items that will be accomplished by the project team during the project.*[5] A work breakdown structure allows project teams to drill down to the appropriate level of detail in defining activities. For example, activity A might be broken down into the individual tasks of defining the objectives, developing the budget, determining the due date, and identifying staff. Deciding on the appropriate work breakdown structure depends on how responsibility and accountability for accomplishing the tasks are viewed, and the level at which the project team wants to control the project budget and collect cost data.

The activities and their sequence are usually represented graphically using a project network. *A* **project network** *consists of a set of circles or boxes called* **nodes,** *which represent activities, and a set of arrows called* **arcs,** *which define the precedence relationships between activities.* This is called an activity-on-node (AON) network representation. The project network for the software integration project is shown in Exhibit 19.4. You should be able to match the information in Exhibit 19.3 with the network.

19-2b Resource Planning

Resource planning includes developing time estimates for performing each activity, other resources that may be required, such as people and equipment, and a realistic budget. Activity times can be estimated from historical data of similar work tasks or by the judgment and experience of managers and employees who perform the tasks. Cost control is a vital part of project management. This requires good budgeting, which in turn first requires estimating the costs of completing the activities. Exhibit 19.5 shows the estimated times and costs for the activities in the software integration project. We'll make use of these costs later in the chapter.

EXHIBIT 19.4 Project Network for the Software Integration Project

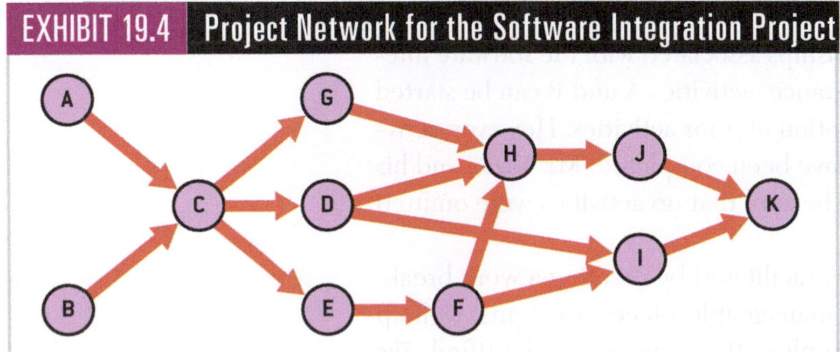

19-2c Project Scheduling with the Critical Path Method

The *Critical Path Method (CPM)* is an approach to scheduling and controlling project activities. *The* **critical path** *is the sequence of activities that takes the longest time and defines the total project completion time.* Understanding the critical path is vital to

EXHIBIT 19.5 Wildcat Software Consulting Inc. Project Work Activities Times and Costs

Activity Letter	Activity Description	Immediate Predecessors	Normal Time (in weeks)	Normal Cost Estimate ($)
A	Define software project objectives, budget, due date, and possible staff	None	3	1,200
B	Inventory new and old software interfaces and features	None	5	2,500
C	Assemble teams and allocate work	A, B	2	500
D	Design and develop code from old to new databases	C	6	300
E	Design and develop code for PC network	C	5	6,000
F	Test and debug PC network code	E	3	9,000
G	Design and develop code for off-site sales force	C	4	4,400
H	New complete system test and debug	D, G, F	3	3,000
I	Train PC system and database operators	D, F	4	4,000
J	Train off-site sales force	H	2	3,200
K	Two-week beta test of new system with legacy backup system	I, J	2	1,800

managing a project because any delays of activities on the critical path will delay the entire project. CPM assumes the following:

- The project network defines a correct sequence of work in terms of technology and workflow.
- Activities are assumed to be independent of one another, with clearly defined start and finish dates.
- The activity time estimates are accurate and stable.
- Once an activity is started, it continues uninterrupted until it is completed.

To understand CPM, we need to define several terms. We will replace the simple circled nodes in the project network with boxes that provide other useful information, as shown in Exhibit 19.6.

For each activity we first compute the earliest possible times that the activity can start and finish without violating any precedence relationships. Earliest start (ES) and earliest finish (EF) times are computed by moving through the project network in a forward direction from start to finish, sometimes called the *forward pass*, through the network. We begin at the start of the project by assigning all nodes without any immediate predecessors an earliest starting time of 0. Two rules are used to guide the calculations of ES and EF during this step:

Rule 1: $EF = ES + T$. That is, the earliest time that an activity can be completed is equal to the earliest time it can begin plus the time to perform the activity.

Rule 2: The ES time for an activity equals the largest EF time of all immediate predecessors. Therefore, whenever an activity is preceded by two or more activities, we must first compute the EF times of the preceding activities, using Rule 1. Of course, if an activity has only one immediate predecessor, the ES time is simply equal to the EF time of the immediate predecessor.

Solved Problem 19.1 illustrates the use of these rules to compute ES and EF for each activity in the Wildcat Software Consulting project.

After ES and EF times are calculated, we compute the latest possible start and finish times for each activity. Latest start (LS) and latest finish (LF) times are computed by making a *backward pass* through the network, beginning with the ending project activity or activities. First set the LF time for all terminal activities to be the project completion time and use the following rules:

EXHIBIT 19.6 Activity-on-Node Format and Definitions

ES	N	EF
ST		ST
LS	T	LF

- Identification number (N) of the activity
- Normal time (T) to complete the activity
- Earliest start (ES) time
- Earliest finish (EF) time
- Latest start (LS) time
- Latest finish (LF) time
- Slack time (ST)—the length of time an activity can be delayed without affecting the competition date for the entire project, computed as $ST = LS - ES = LF - EF$

SOLVED PROBLEM 19.1: COMPUTING EARLY START AND EARLY FINISH TIMES

Compute the early start (ES) and early finish (EF) times for the Wildcat Software Consulting project.

Solution:

Exhibit 19.7 shows the software integration project network after all of the ES and EF times have been computed. Refer to this exhibit to help follow the process. (Solved Problem 19.2 illustrates how the LS and LF times are calculated).

To begin, activities A and B have no immediate predecessors and may begin at time zero; thus their ES times are 0. For activity A, we use Rule 1 to compute the EF time as

$$\text{EF} = \text{ES} + T = 0 + 3 = 3.$$

For activity B, the EF time is

$$\text{EF} = \text{ES} + T = 0 + 5 = 5.$$

Next, we see that both A and B are immediate predecessors to activity C. Thus, we use Rule 2 to find the ES time for activity C as the largest of the EF times for activities A and B, or max(3, 5) = 5. Then the EF time for activity C is computed using Rule 1 as

$$\text{EF} = \text{ES} + T = 5 + 2 = 7.$$

Next, activities G, D, and E have only one immediate predecessor—activity C. Thus, the EF time of activity C, 7, becomes the ES time for activities G, D, and E. From the structure of the network, you cannot compute the ES time for activity H until the EF time for activity F is found. Because activity E is the only immediate predecessor for activity F, the ES time for activity F is the EF time for activity E, or 12. Then the EF time for activity F is 12 + 3 = 15. Now, the ES time for activity H is the largest EF time of all immediate predecessors, or max (11, 13, 15) = 15.

We suggest that you work through the remaining calculations for the ES and EF times to ensure your understanding of this process. The EF time of the last activity specifies the earliest time that the entire project can be completed. For our example, this is 22 weeks. If a project has more than one terminal activity, the earliest project completion time is the largest EF time among these activities.

Rule 3: LS = LF − T. That is, the latest start time for an activity is equal to its LF time minus the activity time.

Rule 4: The LF time for an activity is the smallest LS time of all immediate successors. Therefore, the LS times of all successors must be computed before moving to a preceding node. If an activity has only one immediate successor, the LF time is simply equal to the LS time of that immediate successor.

Solved Problem 19.2 shows how to compute LS and LF times using these rules for the Wildcat Software Consulting project.

SOLVED PROBLEM 19.2: COMPUTING LATEST START AND LATEST FINISH TIMES

Compute the latest start (LS) and latest finish (LF) times for the activities in the Wildcat Software Consulting project.

Solution:

Refer to Exhibit 19.7, which shows the LS and LF times for all activities. To illustrate the backward pass procedure, we begin with the last activity, K. Set LF = 22, which is the project completion time. The LS time for activity K is found using Rule 3:

$$\text{LS} = \text{LF} - T = 22 - 2 = 20.$$

Because activity K is the only successor to activities J and I, the LF times for both J and I are set equal to 20, and their LS times are computed using Rule 3. So, LS for activity I = 20 − 4 = 16, and LS for activity J is 20 − 2 = 18. However, consider activity F. Activity F has two successors, H and I. The ES time for H is 15, and the ES time for I is 16. Using Rule 4, we set the EF time for activity F to be the smallest of the ES times for activities H and I, or min(15, 16) = 15. Then use Rule 3 to find the LS time for activity F, which is 15 − 3 = 12.

We encourage you to work through the remaining calculations of this backward pass procedure to better understand how to apply these rules.

EXHIBIT 19.7 Wildcat Software Consulting Activity-on-Node Project Network

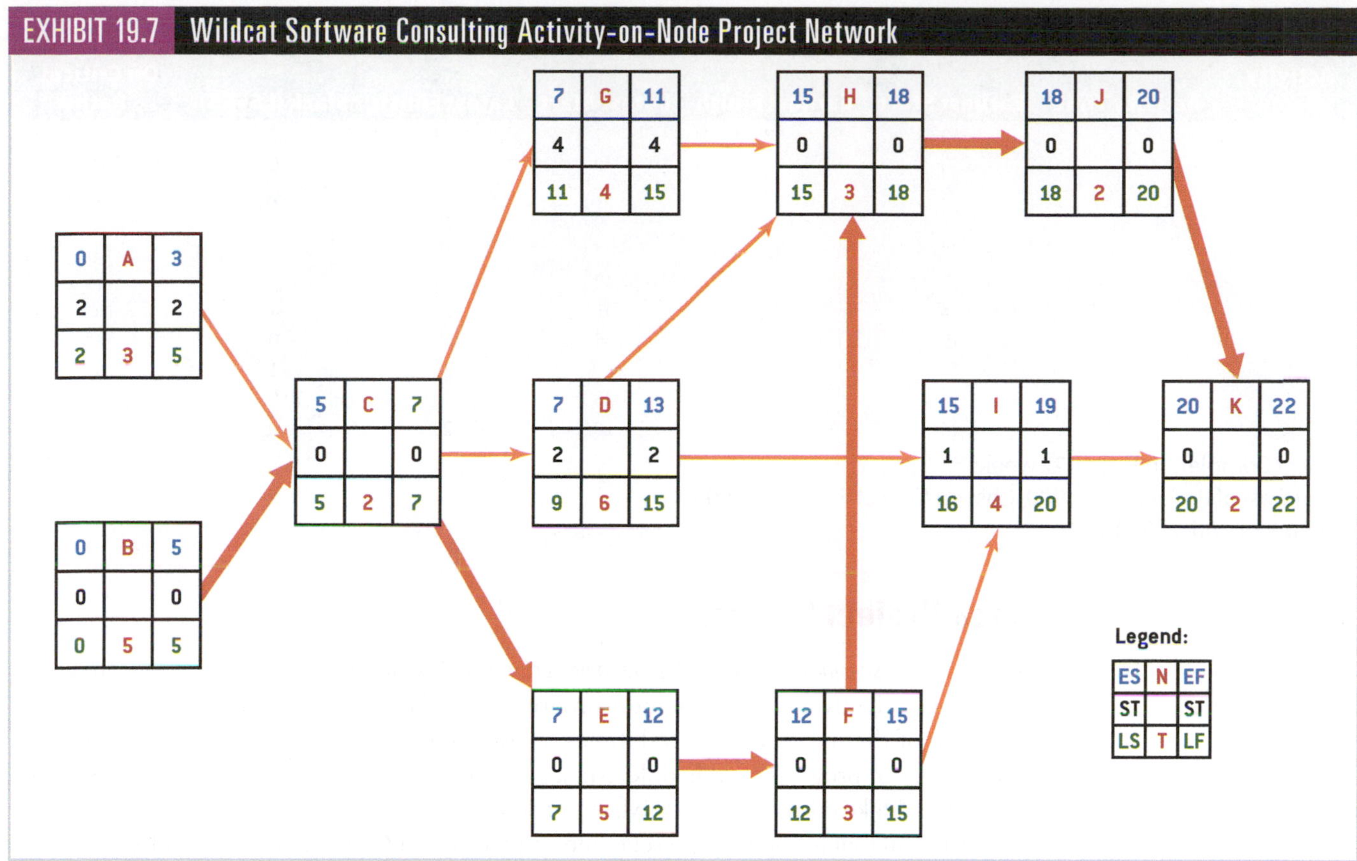

> If you work on an activity on the critical path, it must be completed on time; otherwise, you and your team might receive some unwanted attention.

After all ES, EF, LS, and LF times of all project activities are computed, we can compute slack time (ST) for each activity. Slack time is computed as ST = LS − ES = LF − EF (note that either one can be used). For example, the slack time for activity A is 5 − 3 = 2 − 0 = 2, and the slack time for activity B is 5 − 5 = 0 − 0 = 0. Note that although the earliest start time for activity A is 3, the activity need not begin until time LS = 5 and will not delay the completion of the entire project. However, activity B must start exactly on schedule at time 0, or else the project will be delayed.

After all slack times are computed, we may find the critical path. The critical path (CP) is the longest path(s) through the project network; activities on the critical path have zero slack time (ST = 0) and, if delayed, will cause the total project to be delayed. The critical path for the software development project is B–C–E–F–H–J–K, and is denoted by the heavy arrows in Exhibit 19.7. If any activity along the critical path is delayed, the total project duration will be longer than 22 weeks.

There are many ways to display the information in Exhibit 19.7; a summary is given in the table in Exhibit 19.8. Using the cost information in Exhibit 19.5, the total cost to complete the project in 22 weeks is $35,900. The cost of all activities along the critical path is $26,000, or 72.4 percent of total project cost. If you work on an activity on the critical path, it must be completed on time; otherwise, you and your team assigned to this work activity might receive some unwanted attention. If you were a "slacker," however, where would you want to work? Probably on activity G because it has four weeks of slack time!

EXHIBIT 19.8 CPM Tabular Analysis for Wildcat Software Consulting Using Normal Time

Activity Name	Activity Time	Earliest Start	Earliest Finish	Latest Start	Latest Finish	Slack (LS–ES)	On Critical Path
A	3	0	3	2	5	2	No
B	5	0	5	0	5	0	Yes
C	2	5	7	5	7	0	Yes
D	6	7	13	9	15	2	No
E	5	7	12	7	12	0	Yes
F	3	12	15	12	15	0	Yes
G	4	7	11	11	15	4	No
H	3	15	18	15	18	0	Yes
I	4	15	19	16	20	1	No
J	2	18	20	18	20	0	Yes
K	2	20	22	20	22	0	Yes

Project Completion Time = 22 weeks
Total Cost of Project = $35,900 (Cost on Critical Path = $26,000)
Number of Critical Paths = 1

19-2d Project Control

A **schedule** *specifies when activities are to be performed.* A schedule enables a manager to assign resources effectively and to monitor progress and take corrective action when necessary. Because of the uncertainty of task times, unavoidable delays, or other problems, projects rarely, if ever, progress on schedule. Managers must therefore monitor performance of the project and take corrective action when needed.

A useful tool for depicting a schedule graphically is a Gantt chart, named after Henry L. Gantt, a pioneer of scientific management. Gantt charts enable the project manager to know what activities should be performed at a given time and, more importantly, to monitor daily progress of the project so that corrective action can be taken when necessary.

To construct a Gantt chart, we list the activities on a vertical axis and use a horizontal axis to represent time. The following symbols are commonly used in a Gantt chart:

Symbol	Description
⌐	Scheduled starting time for activity
¬	Scheduled completion time for activity
▬	Completed work for an activity
⋈	Scheduled delay or maintenance
∨	Current date for progress review

Free Project Management Software

Project management software provides easy means of managing projects. Some of them, such as Wrike and Producteev, are free. Wrike comes in both online and app form. It allows you to track a project's status, run workload reports, meet deadlines, and keep account of time and money spent. You can also connect Wrike with programs such as Outlook, Dropbox, and Google Drive. Producteev is easy to maneuver around and offers simple, real-time communication, task listing, and progress tracking. However, several features—such as time tracking and billing software—are not available; but if those are not essential to you, Producteev is a great option.[6]

Solved Problem 19.3 shows how to construct a Gantt chart for the Wildcat Software Consulting project. Using this early start schedule, the project is scheduled to be completed in 22 weeks. What happens if an activity on the critical path is delayed? Suppose, for example, that activity E takes six weeks instead of five weeks. Because E is a predecessor of F, and the starting time of F is the same as the completion time of E, F is forced to begin one week later. This forces a delay in activity H that is also on the critical path, and in turn delays activities J and K. In addition, activity I is also delayed one week. Now it would take 23 weeks to complete the project, as shown by the Gantt chart in Exhibit 19.11.

Gantt charts work well for small projects and subsets of larger projects because they are easy to read and visualize, and provide a summary of project activities. However, for larger and more complex projects, Gantt charts are limited and do not clearly show the interdependencies among multiple activities, or other details such as activity slack and costs. In addition, they do not consider limited resources such as labor and equipment that must be shared among the activities. Determining how to allocate limited resources is often a very challenging task. Fortunately, project management software packages such as Microsoft Project™ provide these capabilities.

SOLVED PROBLEM 19.3: CONSTRUCTING A GANTT CHART

Construct a Gantt chart for the Wildcat Software Consulting project.

Solution:

We will assume that each activity will be scheduled at its early start time. Exhibit 19.9 shows a Gantt chart for the early start schedule for the Wildcat Software project using the information in Exhibit 19.8. To construct the chart, simply place a bar starting that the ES time and ending at the EF time for each activity. For instance, activities A and B can begin at time 0 and have durations of three and five weeks, respectively. So we place a bar along the timeline for activity A that starts at time 0 and ends at time 3, and another on the timeline for activity B that starts at time 0 and ends at time 5. Activity C is scheduled to begin at time 5 and end at time 7, and so on. The resulting schedule will be an "early start" or "left-shifted" schedule.

If you compare the Gantt chart in Exhibit 19.9 with the project network in Exhibit 19.7, you will see that they portray the same information, just in a different format. An Excel template, *Gantt Chart*, available in MindTap automatically constructs a Gantt chart for an early start schedule. This is shown in Exhibit 19.10.

EXHIBIT 19.9 Early Start Schedule for Wildcat Software Project

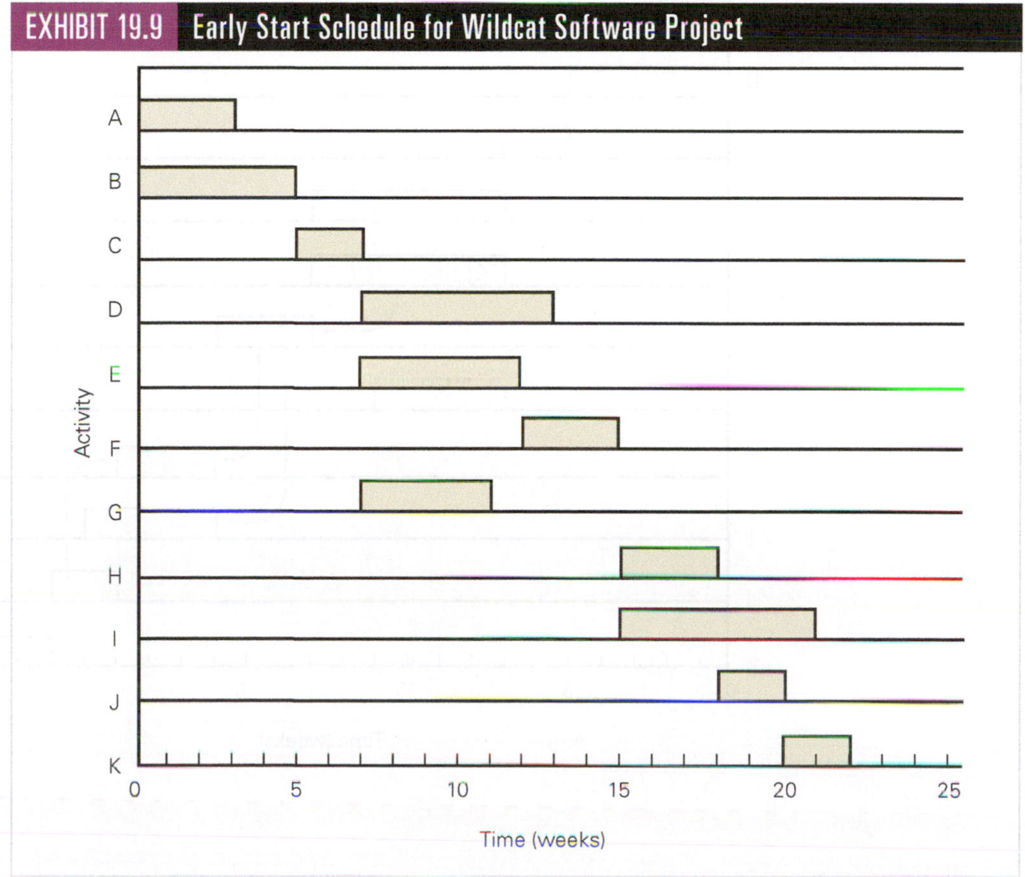

EXHIBIT 19.10 Spreadsheet Template for Early Start Gantt Chart Schedule

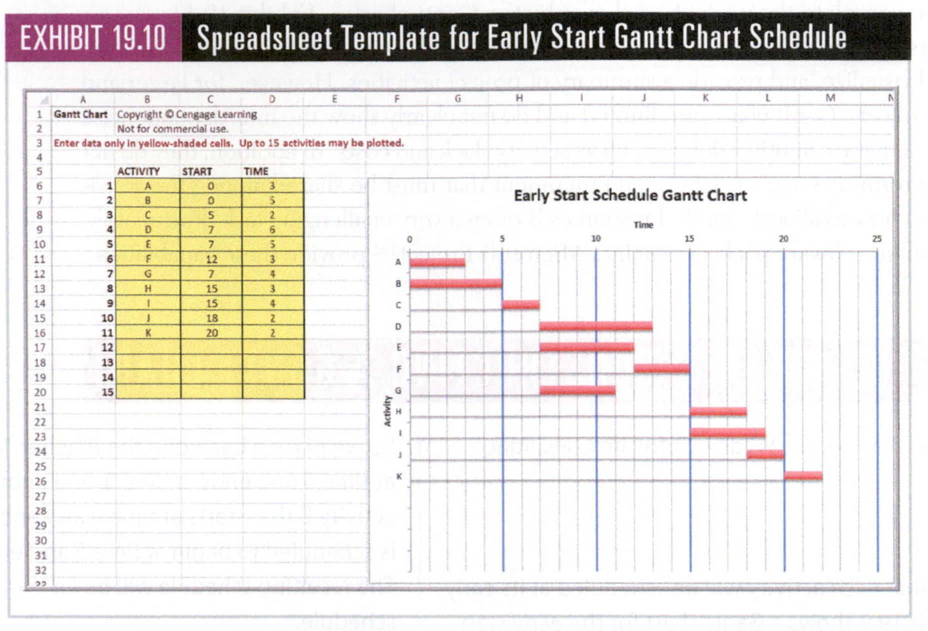

	ACTIVITY	START	TIME
1	A	0	3
2	B	0	5
3	C	5	2
4	D	7	6
5	E	7	5
6	F	12	3
7	G	7	4
8	H	15	3
9	I	15	4
10	J	18	2
11	K	20	2
12			
13			
14			
15			

EXHIBIT 19.11 Example Gantt Chart of Wildcat Software with Activity E Delayed

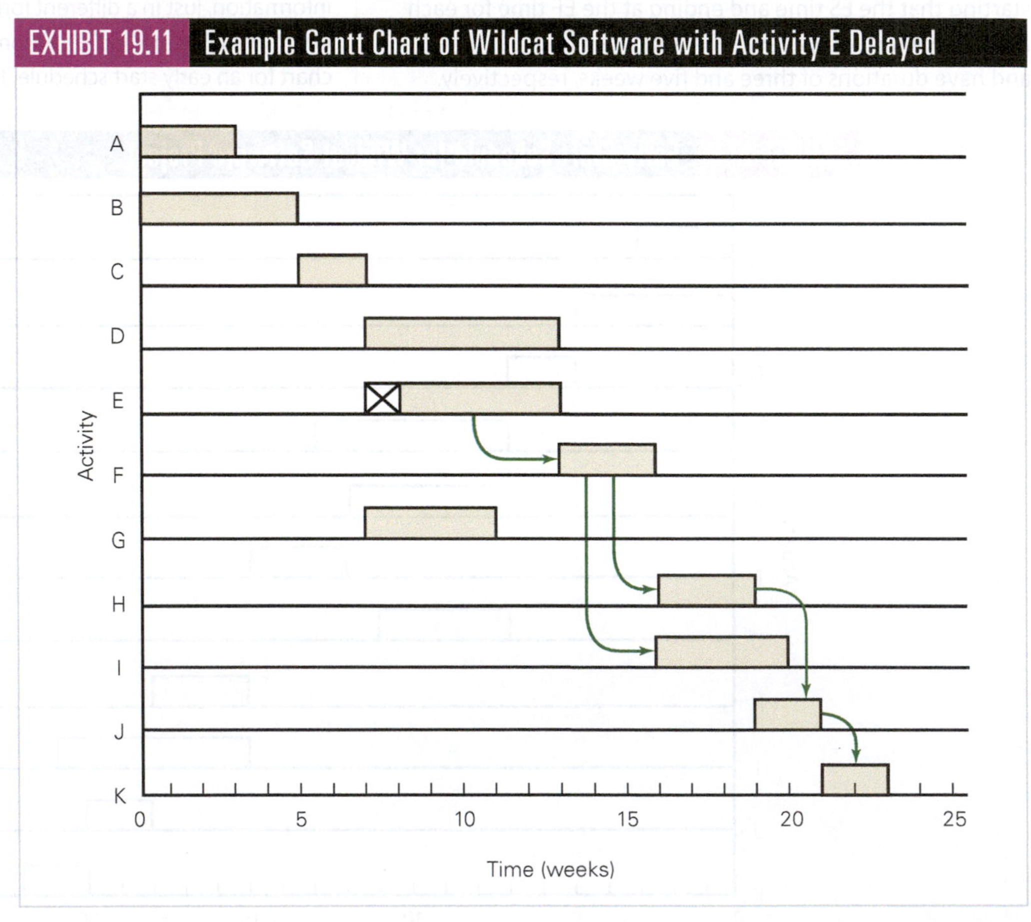

19-3 Time/Cost Trade-Offs

One of the benefits of the Critical Path Method is the ability to consider shortening activity times by adding additional resources to selected activities and thereby reducing the overall project completion time. This is often referred to as "crashing." **Crashing a project** *refers to reducing the total time to complete the project to meet a revised due date.* However, doing so does not come without a cost. Therefore, it is necessary to evaluate the trade-offs between faster completion times and additional costs.

The first step is to determine the amount of time by which each activity may be reduced and its associated cost, as shown in Exhibit 19.12. **Crash time** *is the shortest possible time in which the activity can realistically be completed. The* **crash cost** *is the total additional cost associated with completing an activity in its crash time rather than in its normal time.* We assume that the normal times and costs are based on normal working conditions and work practices and therefore are accurate estimates. Some activities cannot be crashed because of the nature of the task. In Exhibit 19.12, this is evident when the normal and crash times, as well as the normal and crash costs, are equal. For example, activities F, H, J, and K cannot be crashed. If you examine the content of these activities, you see that activities H and K are related to testing and debugging the new system software, and activities I and J are related to training people to use this new software. In the judgment of the project managers, these work activities could not be expedited by adding any additional resources.

For example, in the software development project, activity A can be completed in one week at a cost of $2,000 instead of the normal time of three weeks at a cost of $1,200. A key assumption with crashing is that the time can be reduced to any proportion of the crash time at a proportional increase in cost; that is, the relationship between time and cost is linear, as shown in Exhibit 19.13 for activity A. The slope of this line is the crash cost per unit of time and is computed by Equation 19.1.

$$\text{Crash cost per unit of time} = \frac{\text{Crash cost} - \text{Normal cost}}{\text{Normal time} - \text{Crash time}} \qquad [19.1]$$

EXHIBIT 19.12 Wildcat Software Project Data Including Crash Times and Costs

Activity Letter	Activity Description	Immediate Predecessors	Normal Time (in weeks)	Crash Time (in weeks)	Normal Cost Estimate ($)	Crash Cost Estimate ($)
A	Define software project objectives, budget, due date, and possible staff	none	3	1	1,200	2,000
B	Inventory new and old software interfaces and features	none	5	3	2,500	3,500
C	Assemble teams and allocate work	A, B	2	1	500	750
D	Design and develop code from old to new databases	C	6	3	300	450
E	Design and develop code for PC network	C	5	3	6,000	8,400
F	Test and debug PC network code	E	3	3	9,000	9,000
G	Design and develop code for off-site sales force	C	4	3	4,400	5,500
H	New complete system test and debug	D, G, F	3	3	3,000	3,000
I	Train PC system and database operators	D, F	4	2	4,000	6,000
J	Train off-site sales force	H	2	2	3,200	3,200
K	Two-week beta test of new system with legacy backup system	I, J	2	2	1,800	1,800

EXHIBIT 19.13 Normal Versus Crash Activity Analysis

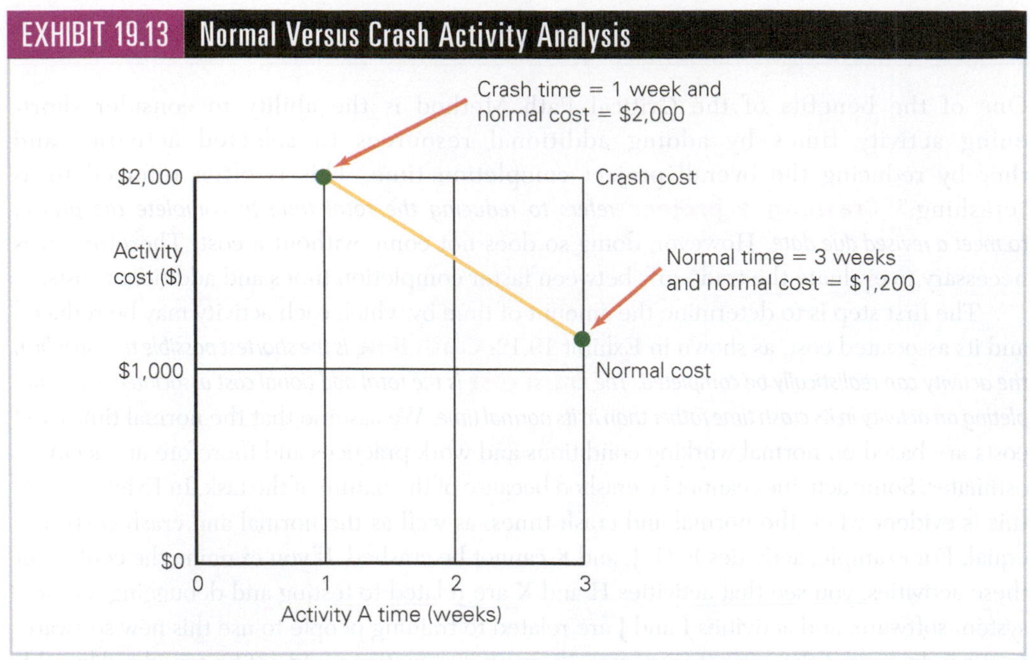

Crashing an activity *refers to reducing its normal time, possibly up to its limit—the crash time.* For example, we can crash activity A from its normal time of three weeks down to one week or anywhere in between. Because the crash cost per unit of time for activity A is ($2,000 − $1,200) / (3 − 1) = $400 per week, crashing the activity from three weeks to two weeks will result in an additional cost of $400. Likewise, crashing from three to one and a half weeks will result in an additional cost of 1.5($400) = $600. Managers can crash a project and ignore the cost implications, or they can search for the minimum cost crash schedule to meet the revised due date. Solved Problem 19.4 shows how to make crashing decisions for the Wildcat Software Consulting project. Solved Problem 19.5 illustrates crashing for a smaller example.

SOLVED PROBLEM 19.4: MAKING CRASHING DECISIONS

Suppose the client asks Wildcat Software Consulting Inc., first, how much it would cost to complete the project in 20 weeks instead of the current 22 weeks, and second, how much it would cost to finish the project in the fastest possible time.

To address the first question, we need to determine the crash cost per unit of time for each activity, using Equation 19.1. These are: A—$400 per week, B—$500 per week, C—$250 per week, D—$50 per week, E—$1,200 per week, G—$1,100 per week, and I—$1,000 per week. Activities F, H, J, and K cannot be crashed. Note that the only way the project completion time can be reduced is by crashing activities on the critical path. When we do this, however, another path in the network might become critical, so this must be carefully watched.

In this example, several options exist for completing the project in 20 weeks:

Crashing Option #1

Crash B by one week = $500

Crash C by one week = $250

Additional cost = $750

The least-expensive option is the first. The critical path remains the same, namely, B–C–E–F–H–J–K. Exhibit 19.14 summarizes the results for this option. Notice that although activity D costs only $50 per week to crash, it is not on the critical path—crashing it would not affect the completion time.

EXHIBIT 19.14 CPM Tabular Analysis for Wildcat Software Consulting for Target 20-Week Completion Time

Activity Name	On Critical Path	Activity Time	Earliest Start	Earliest Finish	Latest Start	Latest Finish	Slack (LS – ES)
A	No	3	0	3	1	4	1
B	Yes	4	0	4	0	4	0
C	Yes	1	4	5	4	5	0
D	No	6	5	11	7	13	2
E	Yes	5	5	10	5	10	0
F	Yes	3	10	13	10	13	0
G	No	4	5	9	9	13	4
H	Yes	3	13	16	13	16	0
I	No	4	13	17	14	18	1
J	Yes	2	16	18	16	18	0
K	Yes	2	18	20	18	20	0

Project Completion Time = 20 weeks
Total project cost = \$36, 650 (cost on CP = \$26,750)
Number of critical paths = 1

The second question seeks to find the crash schedule that minimizes the project completion time. Again, we will address this using a trial-and-error approach. From the previous crashing solution of 20 weeks, we can identify two crashing options to shorten the project to 19 weeks:

Crashing Option #2

Crash B by two weeks = \$1,000
Additional cost = \$1,000

Crashing Option #3

Crash C by one week = \$500
Crash E by one week = \$1,200
Additional cost = \$1,700

Crashing Option #4

Crash B by a second week = \$500
Additional cost = \$500

Crashing Option #5

Crash E by one week = \$1,200
Additional cost = \$1,200

The cheapest way to achieve a project completion date of 19 weeks is Option #4, by crashing B by two weeks and C by one week. The critical path for a 19-week project completion date is still B–C–E–F–H–J–K. The total project cost is now $\$37,150$ $(\$35,900 + \$1,000 + \$250)$. Activities B and C have reached their crash time limits; therefore, to try to find an 18-week completion date, we must examine other activities. Only one option is available because activities B, C, F, H, J, and K cannot be crashed further:

Crashing Option #6

Crash E by one week = \$1,200
Additional cost = \$1,200

At this point, there are two critical paths: A–C–E–F–H–J–K and B–C–E–F–H–J–K. All other paths through the network are less than 18 weeks. The total project cost is now $\$38,350$ $(\$35,900 + \$1,000 + \$250 + \$1,200)$.

The only way to achieve a 17-week project completion time is to crash activity E a second week. The total project cost for a 17-week completion time is now $\$39,550$ $(\$35,900 + \$1,000 + \$250 + \$1,200 + \$1,200)$, and four critical paths now exist:

CP Path 1: B–C–E–F–H–J–K

CP Path 2: A–C–E–F–H–J–K

CP Path 3: A–C–D–H–J–K

CP Path 4: B–C–D–H–J–K

All other paths are not critical. Exhibit 19.15 summarizes the results for this 17-week minimum crash cost schedule. We cannot crash any other activities to reduce the project completion time further.

EXHIBIT 19.15 Wildcat Software Consulting 17-Week Project Schedule at Total Project Cost = $39,550

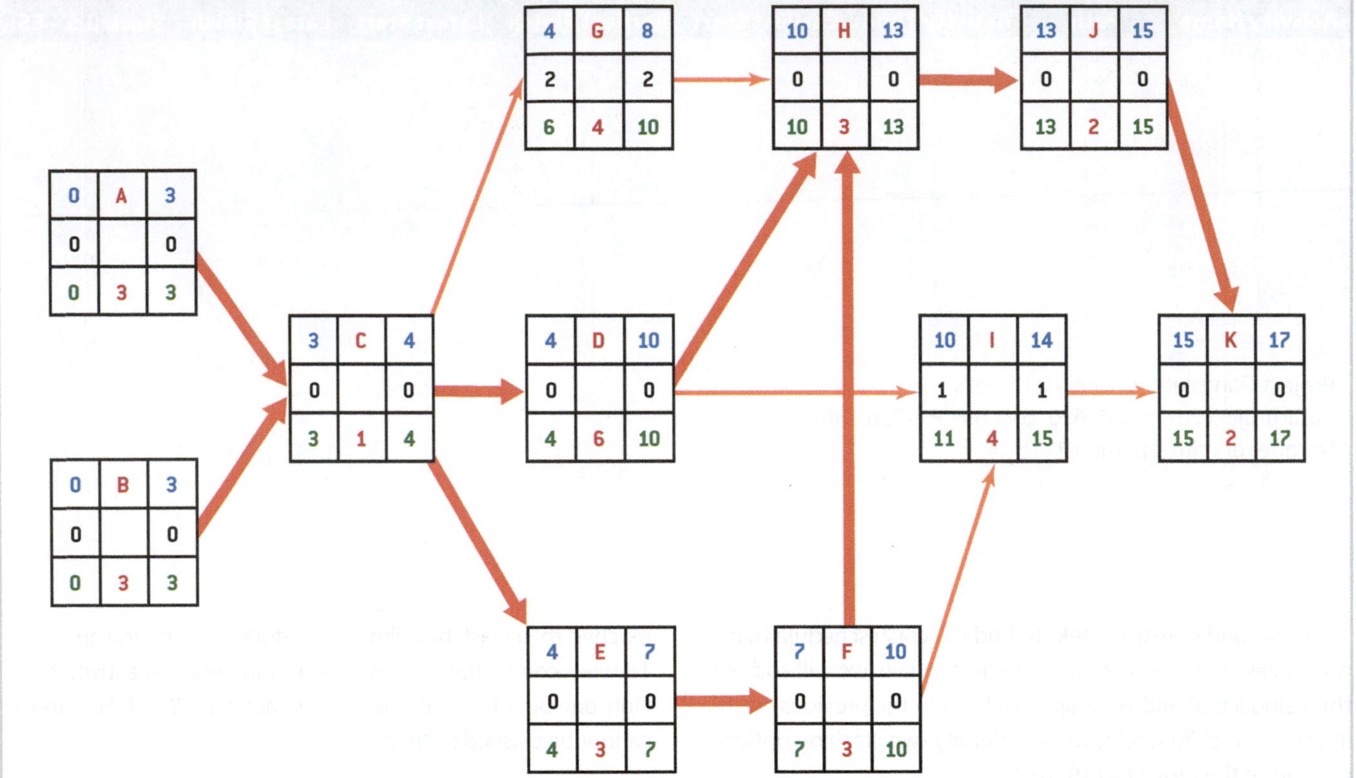

SOLVED PROBLEM 19.5: A SIMPLE CRASHING PROBLEM

The critical path calculations for a project network are shown in the accompanying figure. Using the information in the table below, find the best crashing option to reduce the project completion time to 17 weeks.

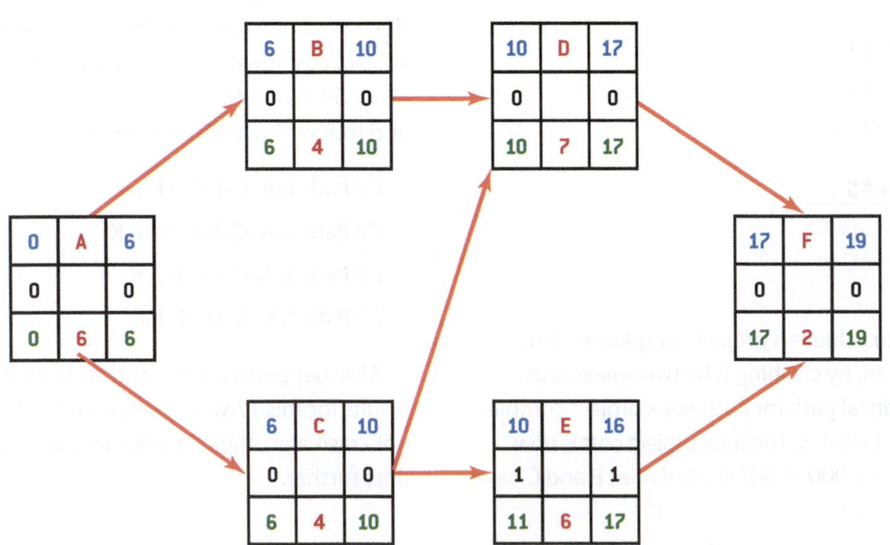

Activity	Normal Duration	Normal Cost	Crash Duration	Total Crash Cost	Crash Cost Per Week
A	6	$ 500	4	$1,300	$400
B	4	300	2	1,000	350
C	4	900	3	1,200	300
D	7	1,600	5	2,000	200
E	6	200	4	300	50
F	2	400	1	900	500

One-Week Crash Options

We might first look at activities common to both critical paths (A–B–D–F and A–C–D–F), namely A and D, and consider crashing each of them individually. Other options are to crash activities B and C together, activity F, and activities A and D together. The lowest-cost option is to crash activity D by one week, costing $200. Now all three paths through the network are critical paths with a total duration of 18 weeks.

Crashing Option #1
Crash A by one week = $400

Crashing Option #2
Crash D by one week = $200

Crashing Option #3
Crash B by one week = $350
Crash C by one week = $300
Total cost = $650

Crashing Option #4
Crash F by one week = $500

Crashing Option #5
Crash A by one week = $400
Crash D by one week = $200
Total cost = $600

Second-Week Crash Options

All other crash options cost more than Option #2. Therefore, we should recommend that we crash D by a second week and E by one week, for a total cost of $250. All three network paths take 17 weeks to complete.

The total normal costs are $3,900 plus crashing D by two weeks (+$400) and E by one week (+$50), so the total cost of a 17-week project-completion schedule is $4,350.

Crashing Option #1
Crash A by one week = $400

Crashing Option #2
Crash D by one week = $200
Crash E by one week = $ 50
Total cost = $250

Crashing Option #3
Crash B by one week = $350
Crash C by one week = $300
Total cost = $650

Crashing Option #4
Crash F by one week = $500

19-4 Uncertainty in Project Management

Another approach to project management that was developed independently of CPM is called **PERT (Project Evaluation and Review Technique)**. PERT was introduced in the late 1950s specifically for planning, scheduling, and controlling the Polaris missile project. Because many activities associated with that project had never been attempted previously, it was difficult to predict the time needed to complete the various tasks. PERT was developed as a means of handling the uncertainties in activity completion times. In contrast, CPM assumes that activity times are constant.

PERT was developed as a means of handling the uncertainties in activity completion times. In contrast, CPM assumes that activity times are constant.

Any variation in critical path activities can cause variation in the project completion date. Also, if a noncritical activity is delayed long enough to expend all of its slack time, that activity will become part of a new critical path, and further delays there will extend the project completion date. The PERT procedure uses the variance in the critical path activities to understand the risk associated with completing the project on time.

When activity times are uncertain, they are often treated as random variables with associated probability distributions. Usually three time estimates are obtained for each activity:

1. **Optimistic time** (a)—the activity time if everything progresses in an ideal manner.
2. **Most probable time** (m)—the most likely activity time under normal conditions.
3. **Pessimistic time** (b)—the activity time if significant breakdowns and/or delays occur.

Exhibit 19.16 shows an assumed probability distribution for activity B in the Wildcat project. Note that this is a positively skewed distribution, allowing for a small chance of a large activity time. Different values of a, m, and b provide different shapes for the probability distribution of activity times. Technically, this characterizes a *beta probability distribution*. The beta distribution is usually assumed to describe the inherent variability in these three time estimates. This approach is quite practical because managers can usually identify the best case, worst case, and most likely case for activity times, and it provides much flexibility in characterizing the distribution of times, as opposed to forcing times to a symmetric normal probability distribution. However, with today's software, any type of distribution can be used.

The expected time is computed using the following formula:

$$\text{Expected time} = (a + 4m + b)/6 \quad [19.2]$$

Note that the expected times correspond to the normal times we used in the CPM example. We can also show that the variance of activity times is given by the following:

$$\text{Variance} = (b - a)^2/36 \quad [19.3]$$

The critical path is found using the expected times in the same fashion as in the Critical Path Method. PERT allows us to investigate the effects of uncertainty of activity times on the project completion time. The expected project completion time is the sum of the expected times for activities on the critical path. The variance of the project completion time is given by the sum of the variances of the critical path activities. These formulas are based on the assumption that all the activity times are independent. With this assumption, we can also assume that the distribution of the project completion time is normally distributed (see Supplement A: Probability and Statistics for a review of the normal probability distribution). The use of the normal probability distribution as an approximation is based on the central limit theorem of statistics, which states that the sum of independent activity times follows a normal distribution as the number of activities becomes large. We can use this information to compute the probability of meeting a specified completion date. Solved Problems 19.6 and 19.7 illustrate the use of PERT to analyze project networks with uncertain activity times.

EXHIBIT 19.16 Activity Time Distribution for Activity B of Wildcat Software Project

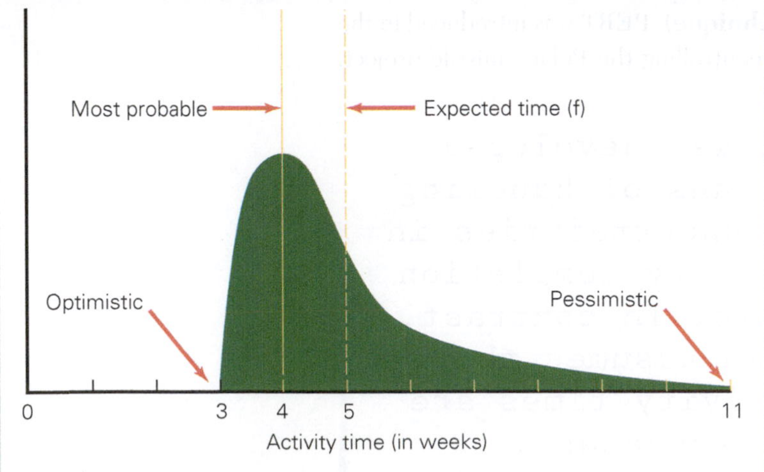

SOLVED PROBLEM 19.6: COMPUTING THE PROBABILITY OF PROJECT COMPLETION TIME

For the Wildcat Software integration project, we will assume that the project manager has developed estimates for the optimistic, most probable, and pessimistic times for each activity, as shown in Exhibit 19.17. Using formulas 19.2 and 19.3, the expected times and variances are also shown. Find the probability of completing the project within 25 weeks.

Solution:

For the Wildcat project, the critical path is B–C–E–F–H–J–K. The expected completion time is the sum of the expected times along this critical path, or 22 weeks. The variance (σ^2) of the project duration is given by the sum of the variances of the critical path activities. From Exhibit 19.17, this is 2.77.

Therefore, we can say that the project completion time for the Wildcat example is normal with a mean of 22 weeks and a standard deviation of $\sqrt{2.77} = 1.66$. Because of uncertainty in the activity times, the project may not be completed in 22 weeks. Exhibit 19.18 shows the normal distribution for the project completion time. The shaded area represents the probability that the project will be completed by 25 weeks. The z-value for the normal distribution at $T = 25$ is:

$$z = (25 - 22)/1.66 = 1.81$$

Using $z = 1.81$ and the tables for the standard normal distribution (see Appendix A), we find that the probability of the project meeting the 25-week deadline is $P(z \le 1.81) =$ P(completion time $\le$ 25) = 0.965. This can also be found using the Excel function =NORM.DIST(*x, mean, standard deviation, TRUE*), which finds the probability to the left of *x* in a normal distribution with a given mean and standard deviation. Thus, =NORM.DIST(25, 22, 1.66, TRUE) = 0.965. Thus, while variability in the activity time may cause the project to exceed the 22-week expected duration, there is an excellent chance that the project will be completed before the 25-week deadline.

EXHIBIT 19.17 Activity Time Estimates for the Wildcat Software Integration Project

Activity	Optimistic Time (*a*)	Most Probable Time (*m*)	Pessimistic Time (*b*)	Expected Time	Variance
A	2	3	4	3	0.11
B	3	4	11	5	1.78
C	1	2	3	2	0.11
D	4	5	12	6	1.78
E	3	5	7	5	0.44
F	2	3	4	3	0.11
G	2	3	10	4	1.78
H	2	3	4	3	0.11
I	2	3	10	4	1.78
J	1	2	3	2	0.11
K	1	2	3	2	0.11

EXHIBIT 19.18 Probability of Completing the Wildcat Software Project within 25 Weeks

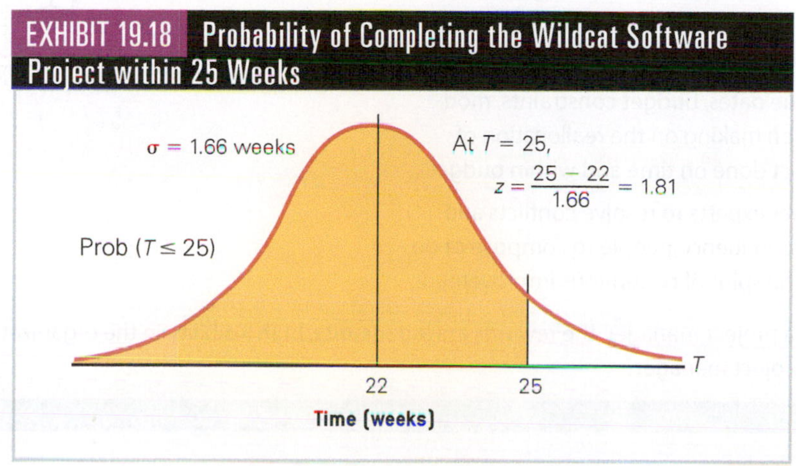

SOLVED PROBLEM 19.7: APPLYING PERT TO A SMALL PROJECT

Consider the following simple PERT network used to remodel the kitchen at Rusty Buckets restaurant:

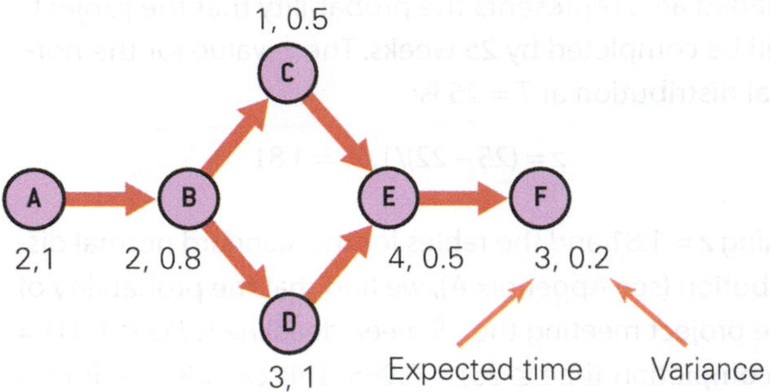

a. What is the expected completion time and variance for the project?

b. What is the probability that the project will meet a 12-day deadline? What about the probability for a 15-day deadline?

Solution:

a. There are two paths through the network—A-B-C-E-F with an expected completion time of 12 days, and A-B-D-E-F with an expected completion time of 14 days. The critical path is A-B-D-E-F. The variance of the project time is the sum of the activity variances on the critical path, or $1 + 0.8 + 1 + 0.5 + 0.2 = 3.5$ days.

b. To find the probability of meeting a 12-day deadline, compute $z = (12 - 14)/\sqrt{3.5} = -2/1.871 = -1.07$. From Appendix A, the probability from $-\infty$ to $z = -1.07$ is $P(z \leq -1.07) = 0.14231$. Therefore, $P(\text{completion time} \leq 12) = 0.14231$. Also, note that there is only a 50 percent chance of completing the project within the expected time of 14 days (i.e., $z = (14 - 14)/1.871 = 0$ and $P(\text{completion time} \leq 14 \text{ days}) = 0.5000$.

The probability of meeting a 15-day completion time is found by computing $z = (15 - 14)/\sqrt{3.5} = 1/1.871 = +0.53$. From Appendix A, the probability from $-\infty$ to $z = 0.53 = P(z \leq 0.53) = 0.70194$, and therefore, $P(\text{completion time} \leq 15 \text{ days}) = 0.70194$. (Using the Excel function =NORM.DIST(15, 14, 1.871, TRUE), we find the probability equal to 0.7035, the difference due to rounding in Appendix A.)

Project Managers Need Many Skills

To be successful, project managers need many skills, including:

- Technical knowledge and multidisciplinary skills to interact well with a broad range of experts to accomplish a common goal given resource and budget constraints.
- Leadership and good human interaction skills to work with people in many different functional areas who may be scattered around the globe.
- The ability to handle conflicting deadlines, multiple projects, changing priorities and due dates, budget constraints, modeling mistakes, and decision making on the reallocation of resources to get the project done on time and within budget.
- The ability to listen to other experts to resolve conflicts and differences of opinion, and influence people to comprise or do things a different way in the spirit of continuous improvement.

Sergey Nivens/Shutterstock.com

If you are good at being a project manager, the rewards are job security, high visibility in the organization, and high pay. Do you have what it takes to be a project manager?

CHAPTER 19 LEARNING OBJECTIVE SUMMARIES

19.1 **Explain the key issues associated with project management.** In many firms, projects are the major value-creation process, and the major activities in the value chain revolve around projects. In other firms, projects are used on an infrequent basis to implement new strategies and initiatives, or for supporting value chain design and improvement activities.

Most projects go through similar stages from start to completion:

1. *Define:* The first step in managing a project is to clearly define the goal of the project, responsibilities, deliverables, and when it must be accomplished.
2. *Plan:* In this stage, the steps needed to execute a project are defined; it is determined who will perform these steps; and the start and completion dates are developed.
3. *Organize:* Organizing involves such activities as identifying a project manager, forming a team, allocating resources, calculating costs, assessing risk, preparing project documentation, and ensuring good communications.
4. *Control:* This stage assesses how well a project meets its goals and objectives, and makes adjustments as necessary.
5. *Control:* Closing a project involves compiling statistics, releasing and/or reassigning people, and preparing "lessons learned."

The job of project managers is to build an effective team, motivate team members, provide advice and support, align the project with the firm's strategy, and direct and supervise the conduct of the project from beginning to end. In addition to managing the project, they must manage the relationships among the project team, the parent organization, and the client. The project manager must also have sufficient technical expertise to resolve disputes among functional specialists. A matrix organizational structure that "lends" resources to projects while still maintaining control over them is an effective structure for projects. Project managers coordinate the work across the functions. This minimizes duplication of resources and facilitates communication across the organization but requires that resources be negotiated. Ensuring project success depends on having well-defined goals and objectives, clear reporting relationships and channels of communication, good procedures for estimating time and other resource requirements, cooperation and commitment among all project team members, realistic expectations, effective conflict resolution, and top management sponsorship.

19.2 **Describe how to apply the Critical Path Method (CPM).** All project management decisions involve three factors: *time*, *resources*, and *cost*. Various techniques have long been used to help plan, schedule, and control projects. The key steps involved are the following:

1. *Project definition:* Identifying the activities that must be completed and the sequence required to perform them.
2. *Resource planning:* For each activity, determining the resource needs: personnel, time, money, equipment, materials, and so on.
3. *Resource scheduling:* Specifying a time schedule for the completion of each activity.
4. *Project control:* Establishing the proper controls for determining progress and developing alternative plans in anticipation of problems in meeting the planned schedule.

The **critical path method (CPM)** is an approach to scheduling and controlling project activities. CPM assumes:

- The project network defines a correct sequence of work interms of technology and workflow.
- Activities are assumed to be independent of one an other, with clearly defined start and finish dates.
- The activity time estimates are accurate and stable.
- Once an activity is started, it continues uninterrupted until it is completed.

Earliest start (ES) and earliest finish (EF) times are computed by moving through the project network in a forward direction from start to finish, sometimes called the *forward pass*, through the network.

Rule 1: The earliest time that an activity can be completed is equal to the earliest time it can begin plus the time to perform the activity.

Rule 2: The ES time for an activity equals the largest EF time of all immediate predecessors. *Latest start (LS) and latest finish (LF) times* are computed by making a *backward pass* through the network, beginning with the ending project activity or activities.

Rule 3: The latest start time for an activity is equal to its LF time minus the activity time.

Rule 4: The LF time for an activity is the smallest LS time of all immediate successors.

Slack time is computed as ST = LS − ES or LF − EF. The critical path (*CP*) is the longest path(s) through the project network; activities on the critical path have zero slack time (ST = 0) and, if delayed, will cause the total project to be delayed. Because of the uncertainty of task times, unavoidable delays, or other problems, projects rarely, if ever, progress on schedule. Managers must therefore monitor performance of the project and take corrective action when needed. Gantt charts are often used for this purpose.

19.3 **Explain how to make time/cost trade-off decisions in projects.** The first step is to determine the amount of time by which each activity may be reduced and its associated cost. Then determine the crash cost per unit of time for each activity. To find the crash schedule that minimizes the project completion time, use a trial-and-error approach.

19.4 **Describe how to calculate probabilities for project completion time using the Project Evaluation and Review Technique (PERT).** PERT was developed as a means of handling the uncertainties in activity completion times. The PERT procedure uses the variance in the critical path activities to understand the risk associated with completing the project on time. When activity times are uncertain, they are often treated as random variables with associated probability distributions. Usually three time estimates are obtained for each activity: optimistic, most probable, and pessimistic times. The expected project completion time is the sum of the expected times for the activities on the critical path.

The variance in project duration is given by the sum of the variances of the critical path activities.

$$\text{Expected time} = (a + 4m + b)/6 \quad [19.2]$$

$$\text{Variance} = (b - a)^2/36 \quad [19.3]$$

Using this information, we can compute the probability of meeting a specified completion date.

KEY TERMS

- **Activities**
- **Arcs**
- **Crash cost**
- **Crashing a project**
- **Crashing an activity**
- **Crash time**
- **Critical path**
- **Immediate predecessors**
- **Nodes**
- **Project**
- **Project management**
- **Project network**
- **Schedule**
- **Work breakdown structure**

REVIEW QUESTIONS

19.1 1. Define a project and provide a non-manufacturing or non-construction example.

19.1 2. Discuss the three key factors of the project-planning process.

19.1 3. What are the four major steps in the project-planning process?

19.1 4. Describe the role of the project manager. What skills should he or she possess?

19.1 5. Identify and discuss three contributors and impediments to project success.

19.2 6. Define and give an example of an immediate predecessor.

19.2 7. What do arcs and nodes represent in a project network?

19.2 8. What information do you need to collect to conduct a basic CPM model and analysis?

19.2 9. Define *critical path*. Describe, in your own words, the procedure for finding a critical path.

19.2 10. Define and explain the following terms: *normal time, crash time, earliest start time, earliest finish time, latest start time, and latest finish time.*

19.2 11. Define *slack time* and how is it computed. How is it used in project scheduling and why is it important?

19.2 12. Discuss the importance of project control and monitoring.

19.2 13. Explain the usefulness of Gantt charts to a manager.

19.2 14. How do you construct a left- or right-shifted Gantt chart?

19.3 15. Explain the concept of crashing in project management. What issues must a project manager wrestle with in making crashing decisions?

19.3 16. Explain how to compute the crash cost per unit of time.

19.4 17. Explain how to evaluate the effect of uncertainty of activity times on the total project completion time.

19.4 18. Explain the PERT concepts of optimistic time, most probable time, and pessimistic time estimates. How would you estimate these times for a specific activity?

19.4 19. How is the expected time and variance of each activity computed using PERT?

19.4 20. Describe the logic of computing the probability of completing a project.

DISCUSSION QUESTIONS AND EXPERIENTIAL ACTIVITIES

19.1 21. Prepare a job profile for a newspaper or on-line advertisement for a project manager.

19.1 22. Identify at least five additional examples of projects that are not cited in this chapter.

19.1 23. Exhibit 19.2 lists a number of impediments to project success. How might you minimize or eliminate these impediments?

19.1 24. Research and write a short paper (two pages maximum) on the skills needed to be a successful project manager.

19.1 25. The local chapter of the *Project Management Institute* is planning a dinner meeting with a nationally known speaker, and you are responsible for organizing it. How could the methodology discussed in this chapter help you?

19.1 26. Perhaps the most well-known software for project management is Microsoft Project™. Investigate its capabilities and write a short paper (two pages maximum) that describes its features.

19.2 27. Develop a small example consisting of no more than ten activities and illustrate the ideas, rules, and mechanics of forward and backward passes through the project network to compute the critical path.

19.2 28. Find an application of project management in your own life (e.g., in your home, fraternity, or business organization). List the activities and events that comprise the project, and draw the precedence network. What problems did you encounter in doing this?

19.3 29. Crashing in the Critical Path Method (CPM) assumes that the cost of crashing an activity is linearly proportional to the amount of time the activity is crashed; that is, the rate of cost increase is constant (see Exhibit 19.12). Is this a reasonable assumption? Why or why not? How might the concepts of economies and diseconomies of scale help to address this issue?

19.4 30. The calculations in PERT allow you to determine the probability that as project will be completed. Suppose you calculate that the probability a project will be completed by a target deadline is only 0.25. What steps might you take if you were the project manager? Would your decisions be different if the probability was calculated as 0.75? Would you be willing to take a 25% risk of failing to complete the project on time?

COMPUTATIONAL PROBLEMS AND EXERCISES

These exercises require you to apply the formulas and methods described in the chapter. The problems should be solved manually.

19.2 31. The county government has decided to redo the street you live on and plans to block the street off, which causes you and your neighbors considerable inconvenience. The project has three parallel paths defined as follows: (i) path A-B-C-H to install street lights and electrical wiring that takes 22 days, (ii) path A-D-E-H to install sidewalks with handicap capabilities that takes 30 days, and (iii) path A-F-G-H to repave the street including storm drains that takes 36 days. What path through the project network is the critical path?

19.2 32. The Mohawk Discount Store chain is designing a management-training program for individuals at its corporate headquarters. The company would like to design the program so that the trainees can complete it as quickly as possible. There are important precedence relationships that must be maintained between assignments or activities in the program. For example, a trainee cannot serve as an assistant store manager until after she or he has had experience in the credit department and at least one sales department. The data below shows the activity assignments that must be completed by each trainee:

Activity	Immediate Predecessors
A	—
B	—
C	A
D	A, B
E	A, B
F	C
G	D, F
H	E, G

Construct an activity-on-node project network for this problem. Do not attempt to perform any further analysis.

19.2 33. Construct a project network for the activities listed below. Do not attempt to perform any further analysis.

Activity	Immediate Predecessors
A	—
B	—
C	A
D	A, B
E	C, D
F	C, D
G	E
H	F

19.2 34. You are in charge of a new initial public offering (IPO) on the NASDAQ stock exchange for a major bank. You have defined the project with the following characteristics. You expect to be promoted if this project and offering goes well.

Activity	Immediate Predecessor(s)	Activity Time in Weeks
A	—	1
B	A	2
C	A	3
D	A, B	4
E	C, D	3
F	D, E	2

a. Draw the project network.
b. What is the earliest completion time for this project?
c. What is the largest amount of slack that any activity in this project has? Why is slack important?

19.2 35. You are in charge of the advertising program for the Boston Red Sox baseball team during their spring training season in Fort Myers, Florida. You have defined the advertising program as a project with the following characteristics. The goal is to fill all stadium seats during the spring training season or you may not have this job next year—the pressure is on!

Activity	Immediate Predecessor(s)	Activity Time in Weeks
A	—	2
B	—	1
C	A	4
D	A, B	3
E	C, D	2
F	D, E	4

a. Draw the project network.
b. What is the earliest completion time for this advertising project?
c. What activity has the largest amount of slack? How many weeks is it?
d. If activity D is delayed two weeks, what is the revised earliest completion time?
e. If activity C in the original problem is crashed from four to two weeks, what is the revised critical path and project completion time?

19.2 36. Mary is planning her wedding and develops the following preliminary information.

Activity	Immediate Predecessor(s)	Estimated Normal Time
A (select wedding date)	—	3 weeks
B (select wedding location)	—	4 weeks
C (guest list, who's attending)	A, B	4 weeks
D (select entertainment)	A	3 weeks
E (choose catering)	A, C	2 weeks
F (wedding day)	D, E	0 weeks

a. Draw the network for this project.
b. Identify the critical path(s)?
c. What is the project completion time?
d. Construct an early start date Gantt chart.
e. As a project manager, where would you focus your attention given your analysis?

19.2 37. A computer-system installation project consists of eight activities. The immediate predecessors and activity times in weeks are shown below.

Activity	Immediate Predecessor(s)	Activity Time
A	—	3
B	—	6
C	A	2
D	B, C	5
E	D	4
F	E	3
G	B, C	9
H	F, G	3

a. Draw the network for this project.
b. Identify the critical path(s).
c. What is the project completion time?
d. Construct an early-start date Gantt chart.
e. As a project manager, where would you focus your attention given your analysis?

19.2 38. Colonial State College is considering building a new athletic complex on campus. The complex would provide a new gymnasium for intercollegiate basketball games, expanded office space, classrooms, and intramural facilities. The activities that would have to be completed before beginning construction are listed below.

Activity	Description	Immediate Predecessor(s)	Time (weeks)
A	Survey building site	—	6
B	Develop initial design	—	8
C	Obtain board approval	A, B	12
D	Select architect	C	4
E	Establish budget	C	6
F	Finalize design	D, E	15
G	Obtain financing	E	12
H	Hire contractor	F, G	8

a. Develop a network for this project.
b. Identify the critical path(s).
c. Construct an early-state date Gantt chart.
d. Does it appear reasonable that construction could begin one year after the decision to begin the project? What is the project completion time?

19.2 **39.** A computer-system installation project consists of eight activities. The immediate predecessors and activity times in weeks are shown below.

Activity	Immediate Predecessor	Activity Time
A	—	6
B	—	3
C	A	2
D	B, C	3
E	C, D	6
F	E	3
G	B	9
H	F, G	3

a. Draw the network for this project.

b. Identify the critical path(s).

c. What is the project completion time?

19.2 **40.** Environment Recycling, Inc. must clean up a large automobile tire dump under a state environmental cleanup contract. The tasks, durations (in weeks), costs, and predecessor relationships are shown as follows:

Activity	Immediate Predecessor	Time
A	—	5
B	A	8
C	A	7
D	—	6
E	B, D, C	8
F	D	3
G	D	3
H	E	4
I	F, G, H	6

a. Draw the project network.

b. Identify the critical path(s).

c. What is the total project completion time?

19.2 **41.** Rozales Manufacturing Co. is planning to install a new flexible manufacturing system. The activities that must be performed, their immediate predecessors, and estimated activity times are shown below. Draw the project network and find the critical path computing early and late start days, early and late finish days, and activity slack.

Activity	Description	Immediate Predecessors	Estimated Activity Time (days)
A	Analyze current performance	—	4
B	Identify goals	A	2
C	Conduct study of existing operation	A	6
D	Define new system capabilities	B	7
E	Study existing technologies	B	8
F	Determine specifications	D	7
G	Conduct equipment analyses	C, F	12
H	Identify implementation activities	C	9
I	Determine organizational impacts	H	8
J	Prepare report	E, G, I	2
K	Establish audit procedure	H	3
L	Dummy ending activity	J, K	0

19.2 **42.** Two international banks are integrating two financial processing software systems as a result of their merger. Preliminary analysis and interviews with all parties involved resulted in the following project information. The "systems integration team" for this project plans to define and manage this project on two levels. The following activities represent an aggregate view, and within each activity is a more detailed view with subtasks and project networks defined. All times are in weeks.

Activity	Immediate Predecessor	Time
A	—	3
B	A	1
C	A	2
D	B, C	3
E	C	5
F	C	3
G	E	7
H	E, F	5
I	D, G, H	8

a. Draw the project network.

b. Identify the critical path(s).

c. What is the total project completion time and total cost?

19.3 43. You are assigned your first project and if things go well you should get promoted. The CEO is aware of this project, so you have a chance for high visibility. You want to do a good job! Your first task is to define the *work break down structure* by interviewing project activity managers and the firm's friendly, yet boring, accountants to get "good estimates" of project activity times and costs. For one of the activities, the normal time is five weeks, crash time is two weeks, the normal cost is $7,560, and the crash cost is $17,365. What is the crash cost per week?

 44. You have collected the information in the table below for the project you are leading on web page design and development. The times are in weeks.

a. What is the total time of this project?
b. What is the total normal cost of the project?
c. If you need to crash the project by one week, what activity would you crash to minimize project costs and what is the revised completion time?

Activity	Immediate Predecessor	Normal Time	Crash Time	Normal Cost	Crash Cost
A	None	3	2	$200	$400
B	A	4	3	$300	$600
C	A	1	1	$200	$200
D	B and C	3	2	$500	$550
E	D	2	1	$500	$900

19.3 45. You are a marketing major and have been working at a major consumer products company for the past three years. Today, your boss walked into your office and said, "Polly, I want you to be the Project Leader for our launch of Perfect Clean Home System. It must be successful; we have invested over $100 million in its development." After discussing the project for an hour, your boss left the room. After several days of thinking about the project, panic began to overwhelm you. You realized you should have paid more attention to your operations management course, and especially the lecture on the critical path method. All of your work colleagues said without it, you will fail on such a complicated project. During the next week you reviewed the project management material in your old OM text and feel confident that you can handle this task. Basic project information is as follows.

a. Draw the project network.
b. What is the critical path(s) and expected completion time for this project?
c. What activity has the largest amount of slack?
d. If activity D is delayed by two weeks, what are the revised critical path(s)?
e. What activity or activities would you crash to reduce the original project completion time by two weeks at minimum crash costs?
f. What is the total project (normal plus crash) costs given your answer to the previous question?

Activity	Immediate Predecessor(s)	Normal Time (Weeks)	Crash Time (Weeks)	Normal Cost ($)	Crash Cost ($)
A	None	3	2	$14,000	$16,500
B	None	6	6	$ 5,500	$ 5,500
C	None	2	1	$ 6,000	$ 8,000
D	A	5	3	$ 7,500	$14,500
E	C	2	1	$ 9,000	$10,500
F	A	7	6	$15,000	$18,000
G	B, D, E, F	4	3	$ 8,400	$10,000

19.3 46. Office Automation, Inc. has developed a proposal for introducing a new computerized office system that will improve word processing and interoffice communications for a particular company. Contained in the proposal is a list of activities that must be accomplished to complete the new office-system project. Information about the activities is shown below.

a. Draw the network for this project.
b. Develop a schedule for the project using normal times.
c. What is the critical path and the expected project-completion time?
d. Assume the company wants to complete the project in 26 weeks. What crashing decisions would you recommend for meeting the completion date at the least possible cost? What is the added project cost to meet the 26-week completion time?
e. Develop an activity schedule for the crashed project using early and late start times, early and late finish times and slack.

Activity	Description	Immediate Predecessor(s)	Normal Time	Crash Time	Normal Cost	Crash Cost
A	Plan needs	—	10	8	$ 30	$ 70
B	Order equipment	A	8	6	120	150
C	Install equipment	B	10	7	100	160
D	Set up training lab	A	7	6	40	50
E	Training course	D	10	8	50	75
F	Test system	C, E	3	3	60	—

Times are in weeks and costs are in thousands of dollars.

19.3 47. You are in charge of the purchasing, installing, and testing a new 30-ton stamping machine for a major automobile assembly line. It stamps out metal fenders and hoods for vehicles prior to painting them. The goal is to complete the project on time and within budget or you may not have this job next year—the pressure is on! The activities listed are for installing and testing the machine, not the purchase price.

Activity	Immediate Predecessor(s)	Normal Time in days	Crash Time in days	Normal Cost	Crash Cost
A	—	2	2	$15,000	$15,000
B	—	1	1	$12,000	$12,000
C	A,B	5	3	$18,000	$24,000
D	A, B	4	2	$12,000	$16,000
E	C, D	2	1	$22,000	$23,500
F	D	4	3	$32,000	$36,000
G	E,F	3	2	$19,000	$20,000

a. Draw the project network.
b. What is the earliest completion time for this project?
c. What is the largest amount of slack that any activity has in this project?
d. What is the total normal cost of the project?
e. If your boss gives you $5,000 to speed up the original completion time (i.e., project improvement dollars), what activity would you spend the improvement dollars on first?
f. What activity or activities would you crash to complete the project two weeks early from the original project completion time to minimize total crash costs?

48. Suppose that some of the activities in the Environment Recycling, Inc. project (problem 40) can be crashed. The table below shows the crash times and costs associated with performing the activities at their original (normal) times and also for the crash times (all times are in weeks). Find the total project completion time and lowest cost solution if the state wants to complete the project three weeks early.

Activity	Predecessor(s)	Normal Time	Crash Time	Normal Cost	Crash Cost
A	—	5	4	$ 400	$ 750
B	A	8	6	1,800	2,200
C	A	7	6	800	1,100
D	—	6	5	600	1,000
E	B, D, C	8	6	1,700	2,200
F	D	3	2	800	1,000
G	D	3	2	500	650
H	E	4	3	400	600
I	F, G, H	6	5	900	1,300

19.3 49. The table below shows the crash times, and normal and crash costs for the international bank systems integration project. What is the total project completion time and lowest-cost solution if the bank wants to complete the project two weeks early?

Activity	Predecessor(s)	Normal Time	Crash Time	Normal Cost	Crash Cost
A	—	3	1	$1,000	$ 6,000
B	A	1	1	4,000	4,000
C	A	2	2	2,000	2,000
D	B, C	3	1	5,000	6,000
E	C	5	4	2,500	3,800
F	C	3	2	2,000	3,000
G	E	7	5	4,500	8,500
H	E, F	5	4	3,000	3,800
I	D, G, H	8	5	8,000	17,000

19.4 50. Estimates of activity times in (weeks) for a project are as follows.

Activity	Optimistic Time	Most Probable Time	Pessimistic Time
A	4	5	6
B	2.5	3	3.5
C	6	7	8
D	5	5.5	9
E	5	7	9
F	2	3	4
G	8	10	12
H	6	7	14

Suppose that the critical path is A-D-F-H. What is the probability that the project will be completed within

a. 20 weeks?
b. 22 weeks?
c. 24 weeks?

19.4 51. The table below shows estimates of activity times in (weeks) for a project:

Activity	Optimistic Time	Most Probable Time	Pessimistic Time
A	4	5	6
B	2.5	3	3.5
C	6	7	8
D	5	5.5	9
E	6	7	8
F	1	3	5
G	8	10	12

Suppose that the critical path is A-C-E-F-G. What is the probability that the project will be completed

a. within 33 weeks?
b. within 30 weeks?
c. in more than 31 weeks?
d. in 32 weeks?

19.4 52. You are responsible for wiring a smart 12-story building in downtown Chicago. The project network and basic information are shown in the following table. The time is in weeks. Your promotion depends on the successful completion of this project in 20 weeks.

a. Draw the project network and compute expected times and variances for each activity.
b. What is the critical path and expected time of completion?
c. What activity has the largest slack time and how much is it?
d. What is the probability of completing the project in 20 weeks using PERT?

Project Activity	Immediate Predecessor(s)	Optimistic Time	Most Likely Time	Pessimistic Time
A	None	2	5	14
B	None	8	11	14
C	A	5	7	9
D	A	6	9	12
E	B, C, D	1	3	5

19.4 53. A competitor of Kozar International, Inc. has begun marketing a new instant-developing film project. Kozar has had a similar product under study in its R&D department but has not yet been able to begin production. Because of the competitor's action, top managers have asked for a speedup of R&D activities so that Kozar can produce and market instant film at the earliest possible date. The predecessor information and activity time estimates in months are shown in the following columns.

a. Draw the project network and compute expected times and variances for each activity.
b. Develop an activity schedule for this project, compute activity slack time, and define the critical activities.
c. What is the probability of completion in 20, 21, and 22 weeks?

Activity	Immediate Predecessor(s)	Optimistic Time	Most Probable Time	Pessimistic Time
A	—	1	1.5	5
B	A	3	4	5
C	A	1	2	3
D	B, C	3.5	5	6.5
E	B	4	5	12
F	C, D, E	6.5	7.5	11.5
G	E	5	9	13

19.4 54. LCD Software must complete the project defined by the following network in 22 weeks. The expected times and the activity variances are shown in the table below.

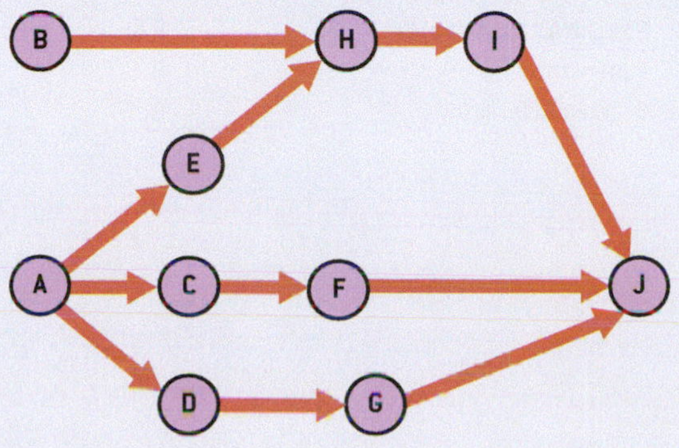

B → H → I → J; A → E → H; A → C → F → J; A → D → G → J

Activity	Expected time	Variance
A	7	1.78
B	3	0.44
C	3	0.11
D	8	1.78
E	3	0.11
F	3	0.03
G	4	0.25
H	6	0.69
I	2	0.11
J	2	0.11

a. Find the critical path(s) and compute the probability of completing the project by week 18.
b. Draw a Gantt chart for the project.

EXCEL-BASED PROBLEMS

For these problems, you may use Excel or the templates in MindTap to assist in your analysis.

 55. Use the Excel template *Gantt Chart* to develop a Gantt chart for the early start schedule for the wedding project in problem 36. Explain and trace the project's critical path(s).

 56. Use the Excel template *Gantt Chart* to construct an early-start Gantt chart for the computer-system installation project described in problem 39. As a project manager, where would you focus your attention, given your analysis?

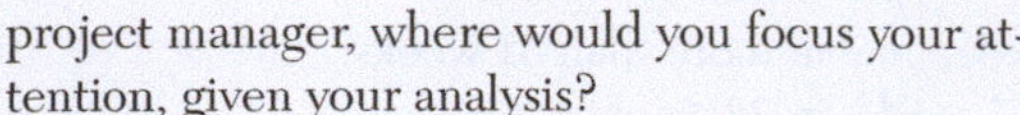

 57. Use the Excel template *Gantt Chart* to construct a Gantt chart for the early-start schedule found in problem 41, Rozales Manufacturing Co. Explain and trace the project's critical path(s).

University Medical Center

University Medical Center needs to move from its existing facility to a new and larger facility five miles away from its current location. Due to construction delays, however, much of the new equipment ordered for installation in the new hospital was delivered to the old hospital and put into use. As the new facility is being completed, all this equipment has to be moved from the old facility to the new one. This requires a large number of planning considerations: National Guard vehicles and private ambulances are being contracted to move patients, local merchants would be affected by the move, police assistance would be required, and so on. Exhibit 19.19 shows the activities, their predecessors, and estimated activity times.

EXHIBIT 19.19 University Medical Center Relocation Project Information

Activity	Description	Immediate Predecessor(s)	Activity Time (weeks)
A	Meet with department heads	None	3
B	Appoint move advisory committee	None	2
C	Plan public relations activities	None	5
D	Meet with police department	None	1
E	Meet with city traffic engineers	A	2
F	Develop preliminary move plan	A	6
G	Develop final move plan	E, F, N	2
H	Establish move admissions policies	B	2
I	Plan dedication	C	3
J	Develop police assistance plan	D	2
K	Consult with contractor	G	1
L	Decide move day	K	4
M	Prepare final move tags	G	3
N	Develop patient forms	H	4
O	Publish plans	L	2
P	Modify plans	O	5
Q	Tag equipment	M	2
R	Implement pre-move admission policies	N	2
S	Dedication	I	1
T	Prepare for patient move	P, Q	1
U	Patient move	R, S, T	1
V	Secure old facility	U, J	3

Case Questions for Discussion:

1. Develop a network for this project.
2. It is important to realize that the activities shown in Exhibit 19.19 need to be broken down into more detail for actual implementation. For example, for the activity "patient move," managers have to determine which patients to move first (e.g., intensive care), the equipment that would have to be in place to support each class of patient, and so on. Discuss what types of sub-activities might have to be accomplished in an expanded network. You need not draw this expanded network, however.
3. Use the case information to find the critical path and the project completion time. Summarize your findings in a report to the hospital administrator.

Alternative Water Supply

Gordon Rivers, the city manager of Saratoga, Florida, pitched the proposed design schedule back at Jay Andrews. Jay Andrews is the project manager for Major Design Corporation (MDC). The city of Saratoga selected MDC for this project. As project manager, it is Jay's responsibility to assemble the technical team necessary to complete the project, develop and track the budget, establish and maintain the schedule, allocate resources as required, and manage the project until completion.

"We need the intake and transmission main designed, bid, and completed in 35 weeks. The city of Saratoga has a future $2 million dollar federal grant riding on the project getting done on time," Mr. Rivers said. Jay nodded in agreement. Mr. Rivers continued by saying, "Jay, the project needs to come in on schedule and within the budget. Now take this schedule back and figure out how we are going to do it."

Background Major Design Corporation is a 3,500-employee firm with annual revenues of more than $1 billion. The firm is divided into five geographically based global sales divisions, an engineering/technical services division based in the United States, and a wholly owned construction company. MDC offers full services—consulting, engineering, construction, and operations—across the "project life cycle" for water, environment, transportation, energy, and facility resources.

MDC was selected by the city of Saratoga to design a new, 10-million-gallon-per-day surface water intake and transmission main. The intake withdraws water from a canal and pumps it more than two miles to the city's wastewater treatment plant. There, the canal water is blended with reclaimed water (i.e., treated sewage water) and distributed back to customers for irrigation purposes. This project is touted as an "alternative" water supply project because the water source is not a historically used source. The project will increase the long-term sustainability of the city because it will diversify the city's water supply portfolio and recycle water. The project will also minimize the need for additional withdrawals from historic water sources, which have become less productive and more highly regulated in the past 10 years, as the city's population continues to grow. Other green benefits of the project include reduced environmental impacts on the historic water sources and a reduced carbon footprint, as the irrigation water requires less energy-intensive treatment than the city's other drinkable water sources.

Project Description The objective of the project is to design a fully functional surface water intake that is protective of the environment, will last at least 30 years, and will have a low life-cycle cost (i.e., capital, maintenance, and energy consumption). For this type of project, engineering design accounts for 20 percent of total project cost. The design stage is also important because the decisions made during design lock in 80 percent or more of the life-cycle costs of the project. As a result, engineers take a holistic approach when selecting equipment and features for projects. A piece of equipment, for example, that is inexpensive upfront may have significant, long-term maintenance costs.

The following narrative describes the main activities required to complete the AWS project. Exhibit 19.20 provides project work activities, precedence relationships, and costs.

The project will begin with the development of a conceptual design (activity A). During the conceptual design, engineers confirm the applicable regulations and laws for the project, including sustainability criteria; perform evaluations of alternative equipment; identify site conditions and constraints; and develop initial facility and equipment layouts.

Once the conceptual design is complete and MDC has received feedback on it from the city of Saratoga, preliminary design (B) begins. Preliminary design expands the design based on the preferences and constraints identified during the conceptual design. The preliminary design finalizes the project design criteria (e.g., sizing, operational capacity, reliability, and sustainability) and incorporates them (along with additional geotechnical, survey, and environmental findings) into preliminary drawings and written specifications. Drawings and specifications are the key information-intensive products that come out of this work. The drawings show how the project will look when constructed, and the specifications provide detailed guidance and criteria by which the construction is to proceed.

For this project, the completion of the preliminary design allows three other parallel tasks to begin: final design (C), environmental permit application preparation (D), and property acquisition (H). Final design is a continuation of the preliminary design stage. In final design, additional information is added to the specifications.

Environmental permit application preparation (D) involves taking certain drawings from the preliminary design and modifying them to illustrate the controls included in the project to minimize environmental impacts. To receive a permit, the engineers must demonstrate that the project will have little to no impact on the environment and be constructed in accordance with applicable laws. Typical impacts engineers try to prevent include storm water runoff from the site, pollutant discharges from the site, uncontrolled emissions from equipment, destruction of natural habitats, and displacement of endangered species. Once the environmental permit application is complete, it is submitted to a regulatory agency for review. This activity, identified as environmental permit review and approval (E), does not require any work on the part of the MDC engineers, but cannot be crashed because an outside entity is responsible for it.

Property acquisition (H) starts with the identification of all properties on which the project sits or passes through. For the properties identified that the city doesn't currently own, the city must acquire rights to use the properties. There are two ways the city can obtain these rights. The first is to find a willing seller—a property owner who, for a price, will turn over certain property rights to the city. The second is through condemnation. Condemnation is a lengthy legal process by which the city can take the property rights from the owner by demonstrating to a court that the project serves the public good and that there are no other viable alternatives.

Upon approval of the environmental permit, the engineers can begin work on preparing the building permit application (F). This task involves filling out the application form and compiling the necessary sheets from the drawing set to illustrate that the project will be constructed to the latest local, state, and federal building codes. When the application has been completed, it is submitted to the appropriate government entities for building permit review and approval (G). During the review, the MDC engineer is not required to do any work, but, similar to the environmental permit, nothing can be done to make the review go quicker because it is done by an outside party.

When the final design is complete and the building permit issued, the city can bid the project (I). Bidding the project involves advertising the project in the local newspaper and online. Contractors interested in building the project obtain a copy of the project drawings and specifications from the city. Based on what they see in the drawings and how they interpret the specifications, each interested contractor then develops a bid that will be low enough to win the project while still allowing for a reasonable profit. During the bidding stage, MDC will assist the city by responding to contractor questions, holding a meeting to discuss the project with potential contractors (known as pre-bid meetings), and holding site visits of the actual construction site so the contractors can get a better understanding of the conditions they will face if they win the job. At the end of the bidding period, the contractors submit their bids in sealed envelopes to the city of Saratoga.

The city opens the bids and compares the submissions. The apparent low bid will be sent to MDC for review. MDC will review both the dollar amount of the bid and the other documents (e.g., drawings, references, insurance, specifications, and bonds) included in the submittal. If a low bidder has not completed the other documents properly, it is deemed nonresponsive, and the engineer begins review of the next lowest bid. This process continues until the lowest responsive bidder is identified. The bid phase ends with MDC's recommendation to the city as to which qualified contractor should be awarded the job.

Immediately following the bid phase, as long as the building permit has been issued, construction can start (J). This dummy activity has an activity time of zero. The construction start is a milestone that designates the end of the engineering design phase of the project and the beginning of the construction phase (another project).

EXHIBIT 19.20 Alternative Water Supply (AWS)

Activity ID	Description	Immediate Predecessor(s)	Regular Time (weeks)	Crash Time (weeks)	Normal Cost Estimate	Crash Cost Estimate
A	Conceptual design	—	4	3	$ 30,000	$ 33,500
B	Preliminary design	A	12	10	$ 52,000	$ 58,000
C	Final design	B	19	16	$ 59,000	$ 76,000
D	Environmental permit application preparation	B	8	5	$ 48,000	$ 58,200
E	Environmental permit review and approval	D	4	4	$ 38,000	$ 38,000
F	Building permit application preparation	E	2	1	$ 35,000	$ 38,000
G	Building permit review and approval	F	4	4	$ 6,000	$ 6,000
H	Property acquisition	B	20	18	$ 90,000	$115,000
I	Bid project	C, H	4	4	$ 6,000	$ 6,000
J	Construction start (dummy activity	G,I	0	0	$ 0	$ 0

calldanai/Shutterstock.com

MDC was selected by the city of Saratoga to design a new, 10-million-gallon per day surface water intake and transmission main.

Decisions Jay manages about six engineering projects at any one time, so he asks you to analyze this project for ways to complete it in 35 weeks. Jay would like to meet with you tomorrow to discuss the results of your analysis.

Case Questions for Discussion:

1. Draw the project network, and determine the normal time to complete the project, activity slack times, the critical path(s), and total project costs (i.e., baseline your project), using the Critical Path Method.
2. Determine the best way to crash the project to complete it in 35 weeks with *revised* activity slack times, critical path(s), and total project costs. Provide reasoning as to how all crashing decisions were made.
3. Activity times with the greatest uncertainty are activities D, E, and H. Describe conceptually how you could model this uncertainty in activity times. (You do not have the necessary data to actually do this numerically.)
4. What are your final recommendations?

Integrative Case: Hudson Jewelers

The Hudson Jewelers case study found in MindTap integrates material found in each chapter of the book.

Case Question for Discussion:

1. Exhibit 19.21 shows the project work activities for designing custom jewelry using computer aided design (CAD). Draw the network diagram, determine the project completion time, critical path(s), activity slack times, and create a Gantt chart for the project. Summarize your insights. What other types of work activities might be included in a more comprehensive work breakdown structure?

EXHIBIT 19.21 Hudson Jewelers Case Work Breakdown Structure

Activity	Immediate Predecessor(s)	Activity Times (Days)
START		
Codesign		
A. Conceptualize Design	–	3;
B. Deposit Made	–	2
C. CAD Program	A	2
D. CAM Process	A	2
Payment		
E. Payment Balance	B	3
Manufacturing		
F. Lost-Wax Casting Process	C, D	6
G. Finishing By Hand	D, E	2
H. Final Polish	G	2
Deliver		
I. Quality Control & Inspection	F	3
J. Packaging	I	2
K. End Costumer Delivery	H, J	1

SUPPLEMENT A
Probability and Statistics

Statistics is a science concerned with the collection, organization, analysis, interpretation, and presentation of data. Statistics provides the means of gaining insight—both numerically and visually—into large quantities of data, understanding uncertainty and risk in making decisions, and drawing conclusions from sample data that come from very large populations. Statistics is essential for operations and supply chain management, and helps managers make sense of data and gain better insight about the processes they manage in manufacturing and service operations and supply chains. Operations managers use statistics to gauge production and quality performance to determine process and design improvements. Probability is the foundation of statistics and is essential to many analytical methods in operations and supply chain management, such as reliability, queueing, inventory, and simulation.

Descriptive Statistics

Descriptive statistics summarize the numerical characteristics of populations or samples. A **population** is a complete set or collection of objects of interest; a **sample** is a subset of objects taken from the population. In nearly all applications of statistics, we deal with sample data. The most important types of descriptive statistics and formulas are summarized below.

Mean

The mean of a sample of n observations, $x_1, x_2, \ldots, x_n$, is denoted by $\bar{x}$ ("x-bar") and is calculated as:

$$\bar{x} = \frac{\sum_{i=1}^{n} x_i}{n} \tag{A.1}$$

We may calculate the mean in Excel using the function AVERAGE(*data range*).

Median

The median specifies the middle value (or 50th percentile) when the data are arranged from smallest to largest. Half the data are below the median, and half the data are above it. For an odd number of observations, the median is the middle of the sorted numbers. For an even number of observations, the median is the mean of the two middle numbers. We may find the median using the Excel function MEDIAN(*data range*).

Range

The range is the simplest measure of dispersion, or variation, and is computed as the difference between the maximum value and the minimum value in the data set. Although Excel does not provide a function for the range, it can be computed easily by the formula =MAX(*data range*) −MIN(*data range*).

Variance

The variance is a measure of dispersion that depends on all the data. The larger the variance, the more the data are "spread out" from the mean, and the more variability one can expect in the observations. The formula for the variance of a sample is calculated using the formula:

$$s^2 = \frac{\sum_{i=1}^{n}(x_i - \overline{x})^2}{n - 1} \tag{A.2}$$

where n is the number of items in the sample, and $\overline{x}$ is the sample mean. The Excel function VAR.S(*data range*) may be used to compute the sample variance.

Standard Deviation

The standard deviation is the square root of the variance. For a sample, it is

$$\sigma = \sqrt{\frac{\sum_{i=1}^{N}(x_i - \mu)^2}{N}} \tag{A.3}$$

The Excel function STDEV.S(*data range*) calculates this.

Frequency Distributions and Histograms

A **frequency distribution** is a table that shows the number of observations in each of several nonoverlapping groups, or cells. A graphical depiction of a frequency distribution for numerical data in the form of a column chart is called a **histogram**. For numerical data that have a many different discrete values with little repetition or are continuous, define the cells by specifying

1. the number of cells,
2. the width of each cell, and
3. the upper and lower limits of each cell.

It is important to remember that the cells may not overlap so that each value is counted in exactly one group.

You should define the cells after examining the range of the data. Generally, you should choose between 5 to 15 cells, and the range of each should be of equal width. Sometimes you need to experiment to find the best number of cells that provide a useful visualization of the data. Choose the lower limit of the first cell (LL) as a whole number smaller than the minimum data value, and the upper limit of the last cell (UL) as a whole number larger than the maximum data value. Generally, it makes sense to choose nice, round whole numbers. Then you may calculate the cell width as

$$\text{Cell width} = (\text{UL} - \text{LL})/\text{Number of cells} \tag{A.4}$$

Spreadsheet Template for Statistical Analysis

MindTap provides a template, *Statistical Analysis*, which allows you to compute basic descriptive statistics and create a frequency distribution and histogram for up to 150 observations.

Example: Descriptive Statistics for Manufacturing Data

Exhibit A.1 shows a portion of the *Statistical Analysis* template with 120 observations of part dimensions from a manufacturing process. Simply enter the data in the data matrix. Columns M and N provide the basic descriptive statistical measures (mean, median, and standard deviation) as well as the number of observations and minimum and maximum values. Exhibit A.2 shows the second portion of the template for finding a frequency distribution and histogram. Enter the number of cells and the lower and upper limits for the histogram in the yellow cells in column S. The spreadsheet will automatically create the frequency distribution and histogram. Exhibit A.3 shows the results for changing the number of cells to 10 in Q7 of the spreadsheet. As we noted, some experimentation is necessary to provide a good visual histogram.

EXHIBIT A.1 First Portion of Spreadsheet Template for Statistical Analysis

	A	B	C	D	E	F	G	H	I	J	K	L	M	N	O
1	Statistical Analysis												Copyright © Cengage Learning		
2	This template is designed to handle up to 500 observations. Enter data only in yellow cells.												Not for commercial use.		
3															
4	DATA	1	2	3	4	5	6	7	8	9	10		Mean	10.717	
5	1	10.65	10.85	10.65	10.70	10.55	10.65	10.85	10.75	10.70	10.65		Median	10.700	
6	2	10.75	10.70	10.65	10.75	10.65	10.85	10.65	10.75	10.70	10.80		Standard Deviation	0.087	
7	3	10.75	10.65	10.70	10.75	10.60	10.60	10.65	10.85	10.65	10.70		Count	120	
8	4	10.60	10.75	10.85	10.70	10.70	10.90	10.75	10.85	10.55	10.75		Minimum	10.500	
9	5	10.70	10.90	10.80	10.70	10.65	10.85	10.65	10.80	10.80	10.70		Maximum	10.900	
10	6	10.60	10.75	10.70	10.80	10.75	10.75	10.70	10.50	10.65	10.75				
11	7	10.60	10.75	10.75	10.80	10.80	10.85	10.65	10.65	10.60	10.65				
12	8	10.75	10.65	10.75	10.70	10.70	10.75	10.85	10.75	10.60	10.85				
13	9	10.65	10.60	10.80	10.70	10.65	10.80	10.70	10.75	10.85	10.70				
14	10	10.60	10.50	10.80	10.65	10.75	10.85	10.75	10.80	10.65	10.70				
15	11	10.80	10.80	10.80	10.60	10.70	10.60	10.85	10.75	10.75	10.60				
16	12	10.65	10.85	10.80	10.60	10.70	10.65	10.80	10.65	10.70	10.65				

EXHIBIT A.2 Frequency Distribution and Histogram Using 5 Cells

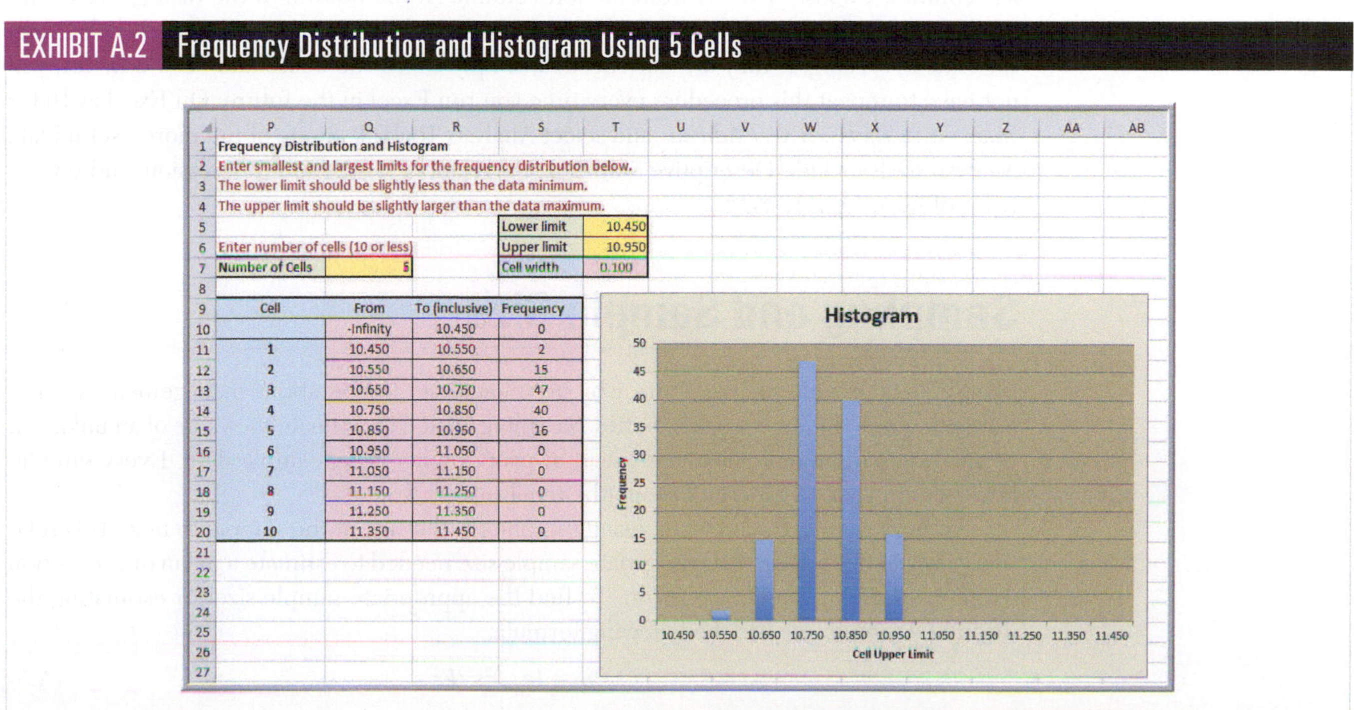

	P	Q	R	S	T
1	Frequency Distribution and Histogram				
2	Enter smallest and largest limits for the frequency distribution below.				
3	The lower limit should be slightly less than the data minimum.				
4	The upper limit should be slightly larger than the data maximum.				
5				Lower limit	10.450
6	Enter number of cells (10 or less)			Upper limit	10.950
7	Number of Cells	5		Cell width	0.100
8					
9	Cell	From	To (inclusive)	Frequency	
10		-Infinity	10.450	0	
11	1	10.450	10.550	2	
12	2	10.550	10.650	15	
13	3	10.650	10.750	47	
14	4	10.750	10.850	40	
15	5	10.850	10.950	16	
16	6	10.950	11.050	0	
17	7	11.050	11.150	0	
18	8	11.150	11.250	0	
19	9	11.250	11.350	0	
20	10	11.350	11.450	0	

EXHIBIT A.3 Frequency Distribution and Histogram Using 10 Cells

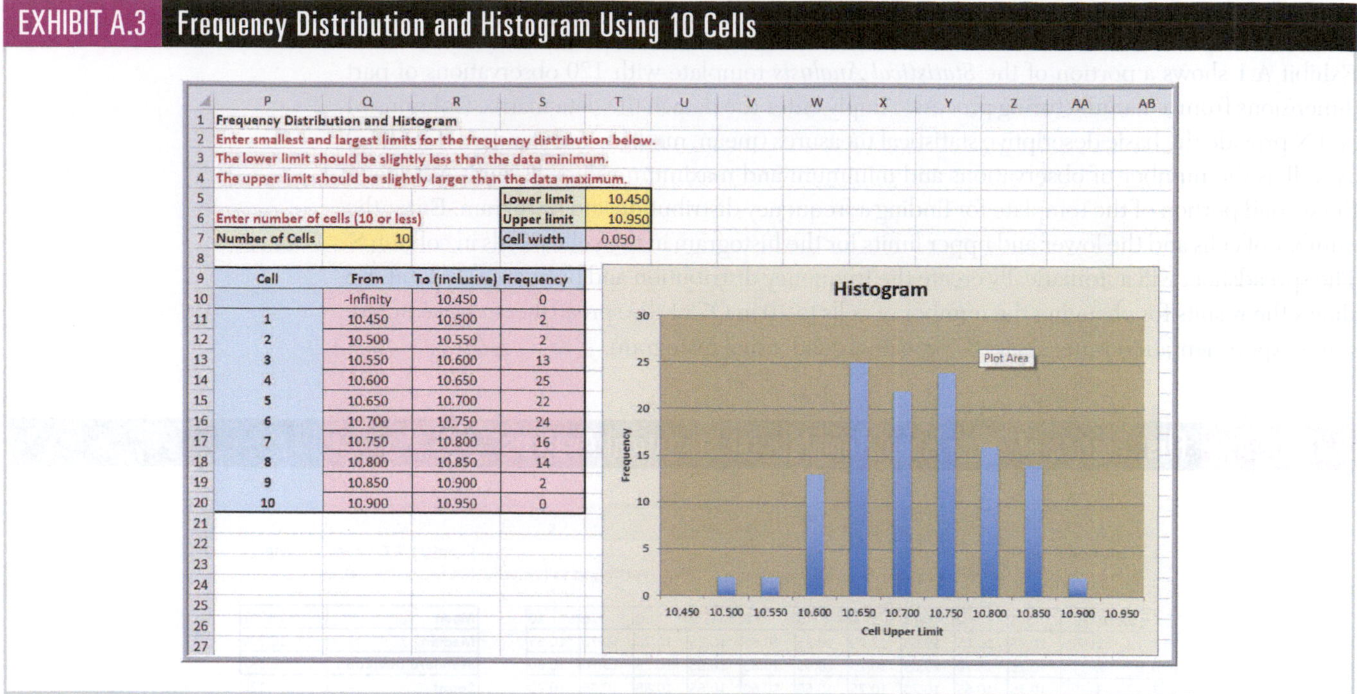

Frequency Distribution and Histogram
Enter smallest and largest limits for the frequency distribution below.
The lower limit should be slightly less than the data minimum.
The upper limit should be slightly larger than the data maximum.

Lower limit	10.450
Upper limit	10.950
Cell width	0.050

Enter number of cells (10 or less)

Number of Cells	10

Cell	From	To (inclusive)	Frequency
	-Infinity	10.450	0
1	10.450	10.500	2
2	10.500	10.550	2
3	10.550	10.600	13
4	10.600	10.650	25
5	10.650	10.700	22
6	10.700	10.750	24
7	10.750	10.800	16
8	10.800	10.850	14
9	10.850	10.900	2
10	10.900	10.950	0

Excel Data Analysis Tools

Excel also provides a variety of functions and data analysis tools for performing statistical calculations it its Data Analysis Toolpak. This can be found in the *Data* tab in Excel. If it is not there, you can activate it easily. In Windows, click the *File* tab and then *Options* in the left column. Choose *Add-Ins* from the left column. At the bottom of the dialog, make sure Analysis Toolpak and Analysis Toolpak VBA are selected in the *Manage:* box and click *Go*. In the *Add-Ins* dialog, if they are not checked, simply check the boxes and click *OK*. You will not have to repeat this procedure every time you run Excel in the future. On Excel 2016 for Mac, go to *Tools > Excel Add-ins* and select Analysis Toolpak. Some of the more useful Data Analysis tools include Descriptive Statistics, Correlation, Histogram, Regression, and several types of hypothesis tests.

Sampling and Sample Size

Sample data provide the basis for many useful analyses in operations management, such as estimating task times for work activities. Sampling is used to estimate the value of an unknown population parameter—such as a mean or proportion—using sample data. Every sample, however, is prone to error and cannot be totally avoided.

An important question when using sampling is the size of the sample to take. It is relatively easy to determine the appropriate sample size needed to estimate a mean or proportion within a specified level of precision. To find the appropriate sample size for estimating the mean of a sample, we use the following formula:

$$n = (z_{\alpha/2})^2 s^2 / E^2 \qquad \text{(A.5)}$$

where $z_{\alpha/2}$ is the value of the standard normal distribution having an area of $\alpha/2$ in the upper tail, s is an estimate of the standard deviation, and E is the desired sampling error. The sample size (n) should be rounded up to the next integer value.

Example: Finding a Sample Size for Estimating a Mean

Suppose that a production supervisor wants to estimate the time that a worker takes to perform an assembly task, and desires a 90 percent probability that the value of the sample mean provides a sampling error of 0.01 minute or less. A preliminary sample estimated the standard deviation of the task time to be 0.019. Therefore, $\alpha = 0.10$, $z_{.05} = 1.645$, and $E = 0.01$. Using formula A.5, we compute

$$n = (1.645)^2(0.019)^2/(0.01)^2 = 9.8$$

Rounding this up, the supervisor should take a sample size of 10 to provide the required precision.

To find the appropriate sample size for estimating a proportion in a sample, we use the following formula:

$$n = (z_{\alpha/2})^2\pi(1 - \pi)/E^2 \qquad \text{(A.6)}$$

where π is the true population proportion. Of course, we won't know this, so the most conservative estimate is to set $\pi = 0.5$. This will result in the sample size that will guarantee the required precision no matter what the true proportion is.

Example: Finding a Sample Size for Estimating a Proportion

Suppose we want to estimate the proportion of time that an office worker spends on budgeting to within ± 5 percent with a 95 percent probability. We use formula A.6 with $E = 0.05$, $z_{\alpha/2} = 1.96$, and $\pi = 0.5$. Then the required sample size is

$$n = (1.96)^2 0.5(1 - 0.5)/0.05^2 = 384.16$$

Therefore, at least 385 observations should be taken.

Probability

Probability is the likelihood that an outcome occurs. In statistical terminology, an **experiment** is a process that results in some outcome. Two examples would be taking a sample of 10 parts from a production process or burning a light bulb until it fails. The outcome of an experiment is a result that we observe; it might be number of defective parts in the sample or the length of time until the bulb fails.

A **random variable** is a numerical description of the outcome of an experiment. For example, suppose an experiment consists of sampling 10 parts and counting the number of defectives. We might define the random variable X to be the number of defective parts in the sample. If the experiment consists of testing a product after final assembly, the outcomes would be pass or fail. We might define a random variable Y to be 1 if the outcome is pass, and 0 if the outcome is fail. A random variable can be either discrete or continuous, depending on the specific numerical values it may assume.

A **probability distribution** is a characterization of the possible values that a random variable may assume along with the probability of assuming these values. For a random variable X, the probability distribution of X is denoted by a mathematical function $f(x)$. A probability distribution can be either discrete or continuous, depending on the nature of the random variable it models.

Discrete Probability Distributions

For a discrete distribution, the symbol x_i represents the ith value of the random variable X and $f(x_i)$ its probability. The **cumulative distribution function**, $F(x)$, specifies the probability that the random variable X will assume a value less than or equal to a specified value, x.

This is also denoted as $P(X \leq x)$, and read as "the probability that the random variable X is less than or equal to x."

Example: A Discrete Probability Distribution

Based on historical data, the hourly demand for a product (the random variable X) varies from 0 to 3 units with the following probabilities:

Demand, x	Probability, f(x)	Cumulative Probability, P(X ≤ x)
0	0.12	0.12
1	0.23	0.35
2	0.38	0.73
3	0.27	1.00

Thus, $f(0) = 0.12$, $f(1) = 0.23$, $f(2) = 0.38$, and $f(3) = 0.27$. The probability that the demand is 2 or less is $P(X \leq 2) = f(2) = f(0) + f(1) + f(2) = 0.73$.

Continuous Probability Distributions A continuous random variable is defined over one or more intervals of real numbers, and has an infinite number of possible outcomes. A curve that characterizes outcomes of a continuous random variable is called a **probability density function**, and it is described by a mathematical function $f(x)$, which has the properties that (1) $f(x) \geq 0$ for all values of x, and (2) the total area under the density function is 1.0. For continuous random variables, it does not make mathematical sense to attempt to define a probability for a specific value of x because there are an infinite number of values. Probabilities are only defined over intervals. Thus, we may calculate probabilities between two numbers a and b, $P(a \leq X \leq b)$, or to the left or right of a number c, for example, $P(X \leq c)$ or $P(X \geq c)$. $P(a \leq X \leq b)$ is the area under the density function between a and b.

The cumulative distribution function for a continuous random variable is denoted the same way as for discrete random variables, $F(x)$, and represents the probability that the random variable X is less than or equal to x, $P(X \leq x)$. $F(x)$ represents the area under the density function to the left of x. Knowing $F(x)$ makes it easy to compute probabilities over intervals for continuous distributions. The probability that X is between a and b, $P(a \leq X \leq b)$, is equal to the difference of the cumulative distribution function evaluated at these two points; that is

$$P(a \leq X \leq b) = P(X \leq b) - P(X \leq a) = F(b) - F(a) \quad \text{(A.7)}$$

The Uniform Distribution The simplest continuous distribution is the uniform distribution. The uniform distribution characterizes a continuous random variable for which all outcomes between some minimum value, a, and maximum value, b, are equally likely. The uniform distribution is often used in applications when little is known about a random variable other than reasonable estimates for minimum and maximum values. The parameters a and b are chosen judgmentally to reflect a modeler's best guess about the range of the random variable.

The probability density function is

$$f(x) = \begin{cases} \dfrac{1}{b-a}, & \text{for } a \leq x \leq b \\ 0, & \text{otherwise} \end{cases} \quad \text{(A.8)}$$

Exhibit A.4 shows the uniform density function for $a = 1$ and $b = 10$.

EXHIBIT A.4 Uniform Distribution for $a = 1$ and $b = 10$

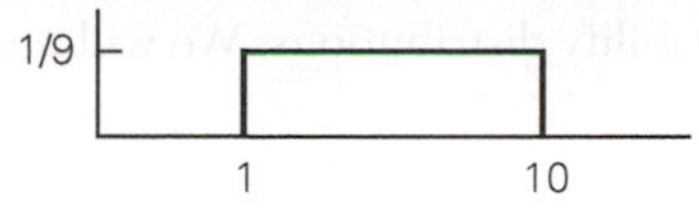

The cumulative distribution function is

$$F(x) = \begin{cases} 0, & \text{if } x < a \\ \dfrac{x-a}{b-a}, & \text{if } a \le x \le b \\ 1, & \text{if } b < x \end{cases} \quad \text{(A.9)}$$

Excel does not provide a function to compute uniform probabilities; however, the formulas are simple enough to incorporate into a spreadsheet.

Example: A Uniform Distribution

The time to complete a project task is estimated to be somewhere between $a = 5$ and $b = 12$ days. Then $F(x) = (x - 5)/(12 - 5) = (x - 5)/7$ for values of x between 5 and 12. Using formula (A.7), the probability that the project task would be completed between 5 and 8 days is

$$P(5 \leq X \leq 8) = P(X \leq 8) - P(X \leq 5) = F(8) - F(5) = (8 - 5)/7 - (5 - 5)/7 = 3/7, \text{ or } 0.43.$$

Expected Value

The **expected value** of a random variable corresponds to the notion of the mean, or average, for a sample. For a discrete random variable X, the expected value, denoted $E[X]$, is the weighted average of all possible outcomes, where the weights are the probabilities:

$$E[X] = \sum_{i=1}^{\infty} x_i f(x_i) \quad \text{(A.10)}$$

Example: Computing an Expected Value

Based on historical data, the hourly demand for a product (the random variable X) varies from 0 to 3 units with the following probabilities:

Demand, x	Probability, $f(x)$
0	0.12
1	0.23
2	0.38
3	0.27

the expected value is $E[X] = 0(0.12) + 1(0.23) + 2(0.38) + 3(0.27) = 1.8$. This means that we can expect an average demand of 1.8 units per hour.

The definition of expected value for a continuous random variable is similar to those for a discrete random variable; however, to understand it, we must rely on notions of calculus, which we will not discuss.

Useful Probability Distributions

There are many different probability distributions. We will review the most useful ones that are used in this book.

Poisson Distribution

The Poisson distribution is a discrete distribution that is often used in waiting line (queuing) models. The Poisson probability distribution is given by

$$f(x) = \frac{e^{-\lambda}\lambda^{x}}{x!} \tag{A.11}$$

where λ = expected value or mean number of occurrences, x = 0, 1, 2, 3, . . ., and e = 2.71828, a constant. Exhibit A.5 shows a Poisson distribution with $\lambda = 12$.

Poisson probabilities are cumbersome to compute by hand. Probabilities can easily be computed in Excel using the function POISSON.DIST(*x, mean, cumulative*). If cumulative is set to TRUE, then this function will provide the cumulative probability function $F(x) = P(X \leq x)$; otherwise the default is FALSE, and it provides values of the probability mass function, $f(x) = P(X = x)$.

Example: Using the Poisson Distribution

Customers arrive at a cafeteria for lunch at a rate of 20 per hour. The probability that exactly 15 customers will arrive during one hour is f(15), which can be found in Excel with the function = POISSON.DIST(*15, 20, FALSE*) = 0.052. The probability that more than 15 customers will arrive is $1 - F(15)$. $F(15)$—the probability that 15 or less customers will arrive—can be found using the Excel function POISSON.DIST(*15, 20, TRUE*) = 0.157. Thus, the probability that more than 15 customers will arrive is 1 − 0.157 = 0.843.

EXHIBIT A.5 Poisson Distribution with $\lambda = 12$

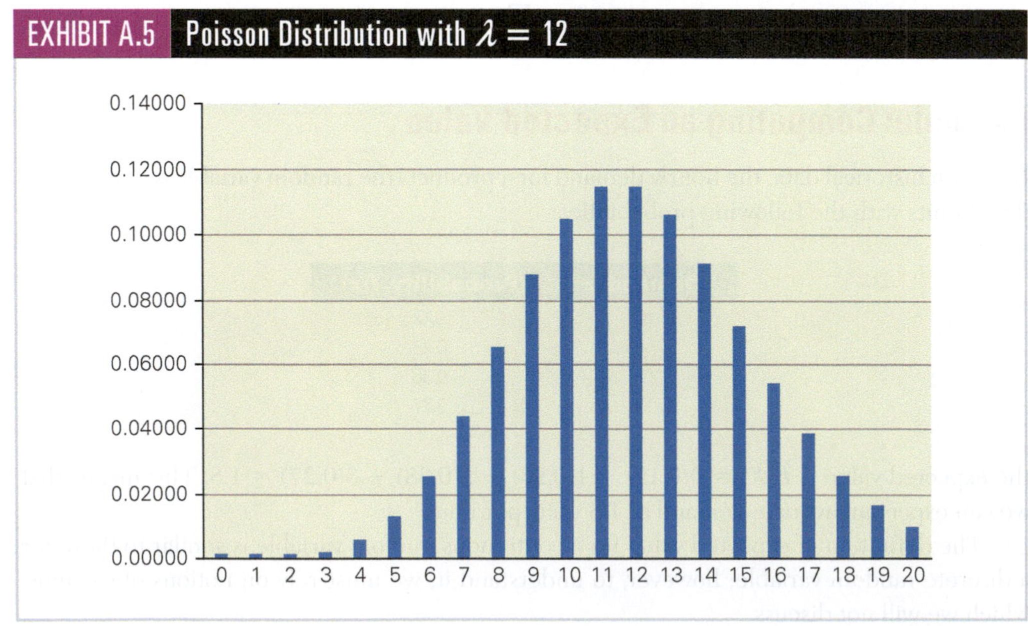

EXHIBIT A.6 Examples of Normal Distributions

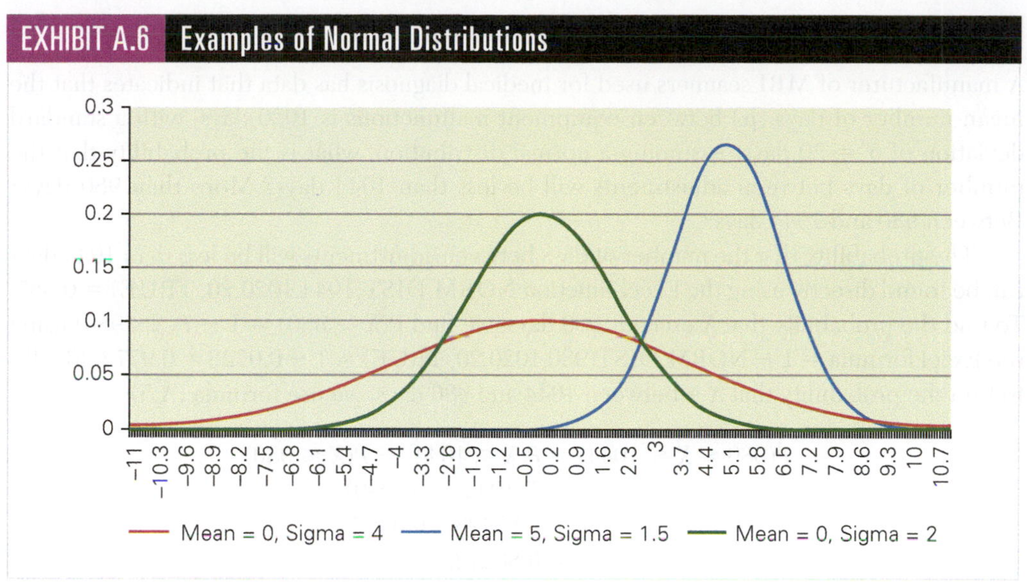

Normal Distribution

The probability density function of the normal distribution is represented graphically by the familiar bell-shaped curve and is defined by its mean and standard deviation. Exhibit A.6 shows some examples for different means and standard deviations. However, not every symmetric, unimodal curve is a normal distribution, nor can all data from a sample be assumed to fit a normal distribution. However, data are often assumed to be normally distributed to simplify certain calculations. In most cases, this assumption makes little difference in the results but is important from a theoretical perspective.

The probability density function for the normal distribution is as follows:

$$f(x) = \frac{1}{\sqrt{2\pi\sigma^2}} e^{-(x-\mu)^2/2\sigma^2} \quad \text{for } -\infty < x < \infty \tag{A.12}$$

where

μ = the mean of the random variable x
σ^2 = the variance of x
e = 2.71828 . . .
π = 3.14159 . . .

If a normal random variable has a mean $\mu = 0$ and a standard deviation $\sigma = 1$, it is called a **standard normal distribution**. The letter z is usually used to represent this particular random variable. Fortunately, if x is any value from a normal distribution with mean μ and standard deviation σ, we may easily convert it to an equivalent value from a standard normal distribution using the following formula:

$$z = \frac{x - \mu}{\sigma} \tag{A.13}$$

The Excel function NORM.DIST(x, *mean, standard deviation, TRUE*) calculates the cumulative probability $F(x) = P(X \leq x)$ for a specified mean and standard deviation. The Excel function NORM.S.DIST(z) calculates the cumulative probability for any value of z for the standard normal distribution.

Example: Applying the Normal Distribution

A manufacturer of MRI scanners used for medical diagnosis has data that indicates that the mean number of days (μ) between equipment malfunctions is 1020 days, with a standard deviation of $\sigma = 20$ days. Assuming a normal distribution, what is the probability that the number of days between adjustments will be less than 1044 days? More than 980 days? Between 980 and 1044 days?

The probability that the number of days between adjustments will be less than 1044 days can be found directly using the Excel function NORM.DIST(1044,1020,20, TRUE) = 0.885. To find the probability that X exceeds 980 days, we find $P(X > 980) = 1 - P(X \leq 980)$ using the Excel formula = 1 − NORM.DIST(980,1020,20, TRUE) = 1 − 0.0228 = 0.9772. Finally, to find the probability that X is between 1044 and 980 days, we use formula (A.5):

$$\begin{aligned} P(980 \leqslant X \leqslant 1044) &= P(X \leqslant 1044) - P(X \leqslant 980) \\ &= F(1044) - F(980) \\ &= 0.88493 - 0.02275 \\ &= 0.86218. \end{aligned}$$

Exponential Distribution

The exponential distribution models the time between randomly occurring events, such as the time between arrivals of customers in a service system, jobs in a manufacturing system, or the time to or between failures of mechanical or electrical components. The exponential distribution is related to the Poisson distribution: If the distribution of the time between events is exponential, then the number of events occurring during an interval of time is Poisson. For example, if the average time between failures of a machine is exponential with a mean of 500 hours, then the average number of failures per hour is Poisson with a mean of 1/500 failures/hour. The exponential density function has the shape of a "decay" curve as shown in Exhibit A.7.

The probability density function is

$$f(x) = \lambda e^{-\lambda x} \qquad \text{for } x \geqslant 0 \tag{A.14}$$

EXHIBIT A.7 Exponential Distribution with $\lambda = 1$

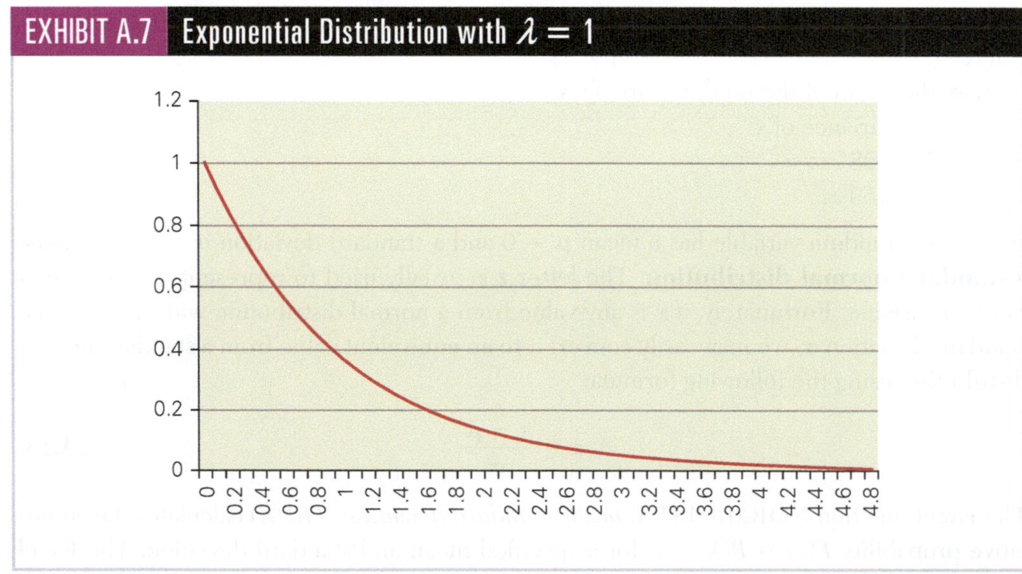

where

$1/\lambda$ = mean of the exponential distribution (note that λ is the mean of the corresponding Poisson distribution),

x = time or distance over which the variable extends, and

e = 2.71828 . . . (the base of natural logarithms).

The cumulative distribution function is

$$F(x) = 1 - e^{-\lambda x} \tag{A.15}$$

The exponential distribution has the properties that it is bounded below by 0, it has its greatest density at 0, and the density declines as x increases. The Excel function EXPON.DIST(*x, lambda, TRUE*) can be used to compute cumulative exponential probabilities.

Example: Applying the Exponential Distribution

A company manufacturer's electronic components for tablet devices. It tested a large number of these components and found the average time to failure is $1/\lambda = 4000$ hours. What is the probability that a component will fail within 4000 hours? The mean rate of failure is $\lambda = 1/4000 = 0.00025$ failures/hour. Therefore, the probability of failure within 4000 hours is

$$F(4000) = 1 - e^{-(0.00025)(4000)} = 0.6321$$

This can also be found using the Excel function EXPON.DIST(500, 0.00025, TRUE). Note that 4000 hours is the average (mean) time to failure; however, the probability of failing before 4000 hours is not one half, which is a common misconception. The mean is not the same as the median, as this example clearly illustrates.

Regression and Correlation

Regression analysis is a tool for building statistical models that characterize relationships between a dependent variable and one or more independent variables, all of which are numerical. A regression model that involves a single independent variable is called *simple regression*. A regression model that involves several independent variables is called *multiple regression*. Linear regression—which assumes a linear relationship between the independent and dependent variables—is the most common application. To verify linearity, we recommend that you first plot the data on a scatter chart to determine if linear regression applies.

Correlation is a measure of a linear relationship between two variables, X and Y, and is measured by the (population) correlation coefficient. Correlation coefficients will range from -1 to $+1$. A correlation of 0 indicates that the two variables have no linear relationship to each other. Thus, if one changes, we cannot reasonably predict what the other variable might do by using a linear equation (we might, however, have a well-defined nonlinear relationship). A correlation coefficient of $+1$ indicates a perfect positive linear relationship; as one variable increases, the other will also increase. A correlation coefficient of -1 also shows a perfect linear relationship, except that as one variable increases, the other decreases. The square of the correlation coefficient, R^2, is called the **coefficient of determination**, and measures the proportion of the variation in the dependent variable that is explained by the independent variable(s).

Regression is a complex topic, and we assume that you have prior familiarity with the basic concepts and theory. Microsoft Excel has a Data Analysis tool for conducting simple or multiple linear regression. We will illustrate a simple application in operations management.

Example: Using Regression Analysis for Time Estimation

Regression analysis can be used to estimate the time required to do a particular job or work activity. Using regression to estimate standard times can be advantageous because it avoids the assumption of additive task times when this might not hold; statistically significant variables can be determined; confidence intervals for the prediction can be developed; and finally, it may cost less than a detailed work study.

An electric power company wishes to determine a standard time estimating formula for installing power lines. A good formula would help them plan capacity and staffing needs. The following data has been collected.

Total Time (hours)	Number of Poles	Wire (100 feet)	No. Cross Arms	No. of Insulators	No. of Guy wires
8.0	1	4	1	2	1
14.0	2	10	2	4	0
17.5	3	6	3	6	1
7.0	1	2.5	2	3	0
16.0	2	10	4	6	0
37.5	4	24	8	12	2
39.5	4	33	7	11	1
10.5	1	3	2	4	2
17.0	2	8	4	8	1
23.5	3	12	6	12	0
16.5	2	12	2	4	1
22.0	3	18	3	6	0
8.5	1	5	2	3	0
28.5	4	12	8	12	0

Exhibit A.8 shows the results using Excel's Data Analysis Regression tool (the data and regression output can be found in in MindTap. The model obtained from this analysis is

$$\text{Time} = 0.237 + 2.804 \times \text{Poles} + 0.514 \times \text{Wire} + 1.09 \times \text{Cross Arms} + 0.170 \times \text{Insulators} + 1.50 \times \text{Guy Wires}$$

The regression analysis shows a high R^2 value, showing a strong fit to the data. Moreover, the p-values for the regression coefficients are significant, meaning that each of the variables contributes to predicting time. If the utility faces a situation in which they estimate installation of 4 poles, 1500 feet of wire, 7 cross arms, 12 insulators, and no guy wires, the predicted time for the job would be

$$\text{Time} = 0.237 + 2.804 \times 4 + 0.514 \times 1500 + 1.09 \times 7 + 0.170 \times 12 + 1.50 \times 0 = 792{,}123 \text{ hours}$$

EXHIBIT A.8 Results of Regression Analysis for Electric Power Line Installation

	A	B	C	D	E	F	G	H	I
1	SUMMARY OUTPUT								
2									
3	*Regression Statistics*								
4	Multiple R	0.999883766							
5	R Square	0.999767546							
6	Adjusted R Square	0.999622263							
7	Standard Error	0.199955077							
8	Observations	14							
9									
10	ANOVA								
11		*df*	*SS*	*MS*	*F*	*Significance F*			
12	Regression	5	1375.680144	275.1360287	6881.491748	2.63388E-14			
13	Residual	8	0.319856262	0.039982033					
14	Total	13	1376						
15									
16		*Coefficients*	*Standard Error*	*t Stat*	*P-value*	*Lower 95%*	*Upper 95%*	*Lower 95.0%*	*Upper 95.0%*
17	Intercept	0.237091444	0.142812253	1.660161786	0.135462338	-0.092234414	0.566417302	-0.092234414	0.566417302
18	Poles	2.804085742	0.128023003	21.90298367	1.99219E-08	2.508863977	3.099307507	2.508863977	3.099307507
19	Wire	0.513567216	0.011168094	45.98521515	5.52546E-11	0.487813528	0.539320904	0.487813528	0.539320904
20	Cross Arms	1.090405281	0.096996889	11.24165209	3.52015E-06	0.866729909	1.314080653	0.866729909	1.314080653
21	Insulators	0.170334993	0.065023566	2.619588596	0.030670058	0.020390283	0.320279703	0.020390283	0.320279703
22	Guy Wires	1.500986653	0.076361055	19.65644214	4.66801E-08	1.324897632	1.677075675	1.324897632	1.677075675

SUPPLEMENT B
Decision Analysis

Decision analysis *is the formal study of how people make decisions, particularly when faced with uncertain information, as well as a collection of techniques to support the analysis of decision problems*. For example, the manufacturer of a new style or line of seasonal clothing would like to manufacture large quantities of the product if consumer acceptance and, consequently, demand for the product are going to be high. Unfortunately, the seasonal clothing items require the manufacturer to make a production-quantity decision before the actual demand is known. Most decisions that we face in business and in our personal lives require a choice in the face of an uncertain future. Decision analysis has many applications in product selection, facility capacity expansion and location, inventory analysis, technology and process selection, and other areas of operations management.

Decision analysis tools should not be used in every decision situation. Characteristics of management decisions where decision analysis techniques apply are summarized as follows:[1]

- *They must be important*. Decision analysis techniques would not be appropriate for minor decisions where the consequences of a mistake are so small that it is not worth our time to study the situation carefully. The consequences of many decisions, such as building a major facility, are not felt immediately but may cover a long period of time.
- *They are probably unique*. Decisions that recur can be programmed and then delegated. But the ones that are unusual and perhaps occur only one time cannot be handled this way.
- *They allow some time for study*. For example, decision analysis techniques would not be useful in making a decision in the emergency room or when a jet fighter flames out during takeoff.
- *They are complex*. Practical decision problems involve multiple objectives, requiring the evaluation of tradeoffs among the objectives. For example, in evaluating routes for proposed pipelines, a decision maker would want to minimize environmental impact, minimize health and safety hazards, maximize economic benefit, and maximize social impact. Decisions involve many intangibles, such as the goodwill of a client, employee morale, and governmental regulations, and may involve several stakeholders. For instance, to build a plant in a new area, corporate management may require approval from stockholders, regulatory agencies, community zoning boards, and perhaps even the courts. Finally, most decisions are closely allied to other decisions. Choices today affect both the alternatives available in the future and the desirability of those alternatives. Thus, a sequence of decisions must often be made.
- *They involve uncertainty and risk*. Uncertainty refers to not knowing what will happen in the future. An advertising campaign may fail, a reservoir may break, or a new product may be a complete failure. Uncertainty is further complicated when little or no data are available, or some data are very expensive or time-consuming to obtain. Faced with such uncertainties, different people view the same set of information in different ways. Risk is the uncertainty associated with an undesirable outcome, such as financial loss. To appreciate the importance of risk, consider the fact that it takes hundreds of millions of dollars and about 10 years for a pharmaceutical company to bring a drug to market. Once there, seven of ten products fail to return the company's cost of capital. Decisions involving capital investment and continuation of research over the long development cycle do not lend themselves to traditional financial analysis.

Structuring Decision Problems

To illustrate the process of defining a decision problem, we present an example of a medium-size producer of industrial chemical products, Commonwealth Chemicals Company, who is facing a decision about capacity expansion. The company has recently developed a new synthetic industrial lubricant that will increase tool life for machining operations in metal-fabrication industries. A new factory would be necessary to produce the lubricant on a large scale, but expanding the existing facilities would allow production on a smaller scale.

Managers are uncertain which decision to choose. Clearly, the best decision depends on future demand. If the demand for the product is high, the expansion alternative will not provide enough capacity to meet all the demand and profits will be lost. If demand is low, and a new factory is built, the excess capacity will substantially reduce the return on investment. With an unstable economy, it is difficult to predict actual demand for the product.

The first step in structuring a decision problem is to define the decision alternatives. Decision alternatives represent the choices that a decision maker can make. In this case, the alternatives are whether to expand the existing plant or to build a new factory. Let

d_1 = decision to expand the existing plant.
d_2 = decision to build a new plant.

The second step is to define the events that might occur after a decision is made. Events represent the future outcomes that can occur after a decision is made and which are not under the control of the decision maker.

An Example of Structuring a Decision Problem

In deciding to expand an existing plant or build a new one, Commonwealth Chemicals needs to consider the future demand for the product. Demand might be expressed quantitatively in sales units or dollars. In this example, events might be designated as "high demand," "medium demand," and "low demand." Alternatively, they might be quantified as "demand estimated as 15,000 units," "demand estimated as 10,000 units," and "demand estimated as 5,000 units." Thus, for the Commonwealth Chemicals decision problem, we will define the events as:

s_1 = low product demand.
s_2 = high product demand.

For each combination of production-volume decision and subsequent event, a payoff can be computed. For instance, if the manufacturer decides to produce 10,000 units, but demand is low, the manufacturer will incur the cost of producing the 10,000 units but will receive revenue for sales of only 5,000; the remaining units will have to be disposed of at a loss. On the other hand, if sales are medium or high, all 10,000 units will be sold, and the net profit can be computed. The payoff would be the net profit. Next, we need well-defined decision criteria on which to evaluate potential options. Decision criteria might be net profit, customer service, cost, social benefits, or any other measure of output that may be appropriate for the particular situation being analyzed. A numerical value associated with a decision coupled with some event is called a payoff. Using the best information available, the managers of Commonwealth Chemicals have estimated the payoffs, expressed as profits, shown in Exhibit B.1. A table of this form is referred to as a payoff table. The notation we use for the entries in the payoff table is $V(d_i, s_j)$, which denotes the payoff, V, associated with decision alternative d_i and event s_j. Using this notation, we see that $V(d_2, s_1)$ = \$100,000.

In many decision problems, the probabilities of events can be estimated, either from historical data or managerial judgment. Knowing the likelihood of the occurrence of events helps to assess risk when making a decision. In some cases, however, event probabilities may not be available or appropriate to try to assess. We will provide examples of both situations

EXHIBIT B.1 Payoff Table for Commonwealth Chemicals

	Possible Future Events	
Decision Alternative	**Low Product Demand (s_1)**	**High Product Demand (s_2)**
Expand existing plant (d_1)	$200,000	$300,000
Build new plant (d_2)	$100,000	$450,000

in the following sections. In summary, the elements of a decision problem are (1) decision alternatives, (2) events, (3) estimated payoffs for each combination of decision alternatives and events, and possibly (4), probabilities of the events.

Selecting Decision Alternatives

Making decisions with uncertain future consequences is a source of anxiety for individuals and managers alike. Managers run the risk that any decision they choose may result in undesirable consequences once they see what the future holds. There are two principal ways of viewing a decision strategy, and these depend on the frequency with which the decision will be made. For one-time decisions, managers must take into account the risk associated with making the wrong decision. However, for decisions that are repeated over and over, managers can choose decisions based on the expected payoffs that might occur.

One Time Decisions Without Event Probabilities

The Commonwealth Chemicals decision is clearly a one-time decision. So how should the choice be made? Different criteria can be used to reflect different attitudes toward risk, and they may result in different decision recommendations. For a problem in which the payoff is profit, as it is in the Commonwealth Chemicals problem, three common criteria are:

1. *Maximax*—choose the decision that will maximize the maximum possible profit among all events. This is an aggressive, or risk-taking, approach.
2. *Maximin*—choose the decision that will maximize the minimum possible profit among all events. This is a conservative, or risk-averse, approach.
3. *Minimax regret*—choose the decision that will minimize the maximum opportunity loss associated with the events. Opportunity loss represents the regret, or ill-feeling, that people often have after making a non-optimal decision ("I should have bought that stock years ago…") This approach is neither aggressive nor conservative, but focuses on not erring too much in either direction.

Example: Applying Decision Criteria to the Commonwealth Chemicals Problem

We will apply these criteria for the Commonwealth Chemicals problem. For the *maximax criterion*, we see that if d_1 is selected, the maximum payoff is $300,000, and it occurs for s_2. If d_2 is selected, the maximum payoff is $450,000, also for s_2. The decision maker should choose d_2, build a new plant, because it results in the largest possible payoff. For the *maximin criterion*, we see that if d_1 is chosen, the minimum payoff is $200,000, whereas if d_2 is selected, the minimum payoff is $100,000. Thus, to maximize the minimum payoff, the decision maker should choose d_1, expand the existing plant.

To apply the *minimax-regret criterion*, we must first construct a regret or opportunity-loss matrix. The opportunity loss associated with a particular decision, d_i, and state of nature, s_j,

EXHIBIT B.2 Opportunity Loss Matrix for Commonwealth Chemicals

Decision	Low Product Demand (s_1)	High Product Demand (s_2)	Maximum Opportunity Loss
Expand existing plant (d_1)	0	$150,000	$150,000
Build new plant (d_2)	$100,000	0	$100,000

is the difference between the best payoff that the decision maker can receive by making the optimal decision d^* corresponding to s_j, $V(d^*, s_j)$, and the payoff for choosing any arbitrary decision di and having sj occur, $V(d_i, s_j)$. For example, if we know that s_1 will occur, the best decision is to choose $d^* = d_1$ and receive a payoff of $200,000: the opportunity loss will be zero because we chose the best decision. If we choose d_2, we will receive only $100,000 and will lose the opportunity to receive $200,000 – $100,000 = $100,000. Similarly, if we know that s_2 will occur, the best decision is $d^* = d_2$; an opportunity loss of $450,000 − $300,000 = $150,000 will occur if we choose d_1.

Exhibit B.2 shows the complete opportunity loss matrix for this situation. We see that the smallest maximum opportunity loss occurs for d_2, so using this criterion, Commonwealth should build the new plant.

We see that different criteria can result in different decisions; which to use is purely a judgment call on the part of the decision maker and reflects the firm's and decision maker's values and attitudes toward risk.

Decisions with Event Probabilities

When probabilities of events are known or can be estimated, we can use expected value to identify the best decision. In many situations, good probability estimates can be developed from historical data or judgmentally. *The* ***expected value approach*** *computes the expected value for each decision and selects the decision alternative with the best expected payoff.* Let

$$P(s_j) = \text{probability of occurrence for event } s_j.$$
$$N = \text{number of events.}$$

Because one and only one of the N events can occur, the associated probabilities must satisfy these two conditions.

$$P(s_j) \geq 0 \text{ for all } j$$
$$P(s_j) = P(s_1) + P(s_2) + \cdots + P(s_N) = 1$$

The expected value for decision alternative d_i is given by

$$EV(d_i) = \Sigma_j\, P(s_j)V(d_i, s_j). \qquad \text{(B.1)}$$

Example: Expected Value Decision-Making in Revenue Management

The EV criterion is used in revenue management applications. Most airlines, for example, offer discount fares for advanced purchase. Assume that only two fares are available: full and discount. The airline must make the decision of whether or not to accept the next request for a discount seat. If it accepts the discount request, the revenue it earns is the discount fare. If it rejects the discount request, two outcomes are possible. First, the seat may remain empty and the airline will not realize additional revenue. Alternatively, the remaining seat may be filled by a full-fare passenger, either because full-fare passenger demand is sufficient to fill the seats or because discount-fare passengers choose to pay full-fare when told the discount fare is not available.

EXHIBIT B.3 Airline Discount-Fare Request Decision

	Events		
Decision	**Sell Full-Fare Ticket**	**Do Not Sell Full-Fare Ticket**	**Expected Value**
Reject request (d_1)	\$560	\$0	\$560 × 0.75 + \$0 × 0.25 = \$420
Accept request (d_2)	\$400	\$400	\$400 × 0.75 + \$400 × 0.25 = \$400
Probability of Event	0.75	0.25	

This decision situation is illustrated by an example in Exhibit B.3. Suppose that a full-fare ticket is \$560 and the discount fare is \$400. The decision depends on the probability p of getting a full-fare request when a discount request is rejected. The expected value of rejecting the discount seat request is \$560 × 0.75 + \$0 × 0.25 = \$420. The expected value of accepting the request is \$400 × 0.75 + \$400 × 0.25 = \$400. The expected value of d_1 is higher than that of d_2, so the discount request should be rejected. Because an airline makes hundreds or thousands of such decisions each day, the expected value criterion is appropriate.

Caution must be taken when using the EV criterion. If an individual or business faces the same decision problem repeatedly, then over the long run, the decision can be made based on expected value. However, for one-time decisions, we must realize that the expected value will never occur; you will only achieve the payoff associated with one of the events.

Expected Value of Perfect Information

By perfect information, we mean knowing in advance what state of nature will occur. Although we never have perfect information in practice, it is worth knowing how much we could improve the value of our decision if we had such information. This is called the expected value of perfect information, or EVPI. **EVPI** *is the difference between the expected payoff under perfect information and the expected payoff of the optimal decision without perfect information.* We compute EVPI by asking the following question: If each event occurs, what would be the best decision and payoff? Then we weight these payoffs by the probabilities associated with the events to obtain the expected payoff under perfect information.

Example: Finding the Expected Value of Perfect Information (EVPI)

In the previous example, suppose the airline somehow knew in advance that it could not sell the full-fare ticket to a particular customer (perhaps based on demographic profiles and analysis of past behavior). Then clearly the best decision would be to accept the discount request and receive revenue of \$400. On the other hand, if it knows that it can sell the full-fare ticket, then obviously, it should reject the request and receive \$560. However, on average, we know that only 75 percent of customers will buy the full-fare ticket if the request is rejected and 25 percent will not. So, the expected value of having perfect information would be (0.75)(560) + (0.25)(400) = \$520.

Recall that without the perfect information, the best decision is to always choose d_1, which has an expected value of \$420. By having perfect information about what a particular customer might do, we see that the value of the expected payoff can be increased by

$$\text{EVPI} = \$520 - \$420 = \$100.$$

This difference is the expected value of perfect information (EVPI), and it represents the maximum amount the company should be willing to pay for any information about the events,

EXHIBIT B.4 Airline Discount-Fare Opportunity Loss Matrix

	Events		
Decision	**Sell Full-Fare Ticket**	**Do Not Sell Full-Fare Ticket**	**Expected Value**
Reject request (d_1)	\$0	\$400	\$0 × 0.75 + \$400 × 0.25 = \$100
Accept request (d_2)	\$160	\$0	\$160 × 0.75 + \$0 × 0.25 = \$120
Probability of Event	0.75	0.25	

no matter how good it is. It this case, we might interpret it as the maximum incentive that the airline might give to a customer that is unwilling to purchase the full-fare ticket.

A simple way to compute the EVPI is to find the expected value of the opportunity loss (EOL) associated with the expected value decision. First, construct the opportunity loss matrix and then find the expected value of the opportunity loss for the original expected value decision.

Example: Finding EVPI Using the Expected Opportunity Loss Criterion

Exhibit B.4 shows the opportunity loss matrix for the airline revenue management example. The expected values are computed in the last column. Because the best expected value decision was to choose d_1, EVPI is \$100.

Excel Template For Decision Analysis

MindTap contains a template for decision analysis. The completed *Decision Analysis* template for the Commonwealth Chemicals example is shown in Exhibit B.5. Enter the data only in the yellow cells; other cells are locked so that you cannot inadvertently change a formula. The decisions without event probabilities are shown in rows 23–25.

EXHIBIT B.5 Decision Analysis Template for Commonwealth Chemicals Example

	A	B	C	D	E	F	G	H	I
1	Decision Analysis					Copyright © Cengage Learning			
2	Enter the data only in the yellow cells.					Not for commercial use.			
3	This template is designed to allow up to 5 decision alternatives and future events.								
4	Enter names of decision alternatives and future events in the appropriate cells in column A or K and row 7. Probabilities are optional.								
5									
6	*Payoff Table*	Future Events							
7	Decision Alternative	Low Product Demand	High Product Demand				Maximum	Minimum	Expected Value
8	Expand existing plant	\$200,000.00	\$300,000.00				\$300,000.00	\$200,000.00	
9	Build new plant	\$100,000.00	\$450,000.00				\$450,000.00	\$100,000.00	
10									
11									
12									
13	Probability						Maximum Expected Value		\$0.00
14									
15	Opportunity Loss Matrix	Future Events							
16	Decision Alternative	Low Product Demand	High Product Demand				Maximum		
17	Expand existing plant	\$0.00	\$150,000.00				\$150,000.00		
18	Build new plant	\$100,000.00	\$0.00				\$100,000.00		
19									
20									
21									
22									
23	Maximax Decision	Build new plant							
24	Maximin Decision	Expand existing plant							
25	Opportunity Loss Decision	Build new plant							
26	Expected Value Decision	#N/A							
27	EVPI	#N/A							

EXHIBIT B.6 Decision Analysis Template for Airline Revenue Management Example

	A	B	C	D	E	F	G	H	I
1	Decision Analysis					Copyright © Cengage Learning			
2	Enter the data only in the yellow cells.					Not for commercial use.			
3	This template is designed to allow up to 5 decision alternatives and future events.								
4	Enter names of decision alternatives and future events in the appropriate cells in column A or K and row 7. Probabilities are optional.								
5									
6	*Payoff Table*	Future Events							
7	Decision Alternative	Low Product Demand	High Product Demand				Maximum	Minimum	Expected Value
8	Expand existing plant	$560.00	$0.00				$560.00	$0.00	$420.00
9	Build new plant	$400.00	$400.00				$400.00	$400.00	$400.00
10									
11									
12									
13	Probability	0.75	0.25				Maximum Expected Value		$420.00
14									
15	Opportunity Loss Matrix	Future Events							
16	Decision Alternative	Low Product Demand	High Product Demand				Maximum		
17	Expand existing plant	$0.00	$400.00				$400.00		
18	Build new plant	$160.00	$0.00				$160.00		
19									
20									
21									
22									
23	Maximax Decision	Expand existing plant							
24	Maximin Decision	Build new plant							
25	Opportunity Loss Decision	Build new plant							
26	Expected Value Decision	Expand existing plant							
27	EVPI	$100.00							

When event probabilities apply, the template computes expected value for each decision in column I and also finds the expected value decision and expected value of perfect information in rows 26 and 27. Exhibit B.6 shows the completed template for the airline revenue management example. EVPI in cell C27 is found using the expected opportunity loss criterion.

The template may also be used when payoffs are cost; however, they must be entered as negative values.

SUPPLEMENT C
Break-Even Analysis

Break-even analysis (BEA) *is a simple approach to analyze profit or loss, or to make an economical choice between two options that vary with volume.* Operations managers use BEA as a decision support tool. The BEA helps them analyze decisions such as:

- Analyze the profitability of goods or services based on anticipated sales volumes
- Whether to produce a manufactured good in-house or purchase (outsource) it from a supplier based on required production quantities
- Choosing between alternative technologies that have different cost structures

We illustrate the use of break-even analysis for applications to each of these types of decisions.

Profitability Analysis

For new or existing goods or services, we are often interested in understanding what the net profit or loss would be for a forecast of sales volume or determining how many units must be sold to recover the cost associated with producing the good or delivering the service. Costs typically include both fixed cost and variable cost. **Fixed cost** *is that portion of total cost that does not vary with the amount produced.* **Variable cost** *is the portion of total cost varies with the level of output or quantity*. Therefore, the variable cost is cost per unit times the quantity produced. The total cost can be computed by formula C.1:

$$\begin{aligned}\text{Total cost (TC)} &= \text{Fixed cost (FC)} + \text{Unit cost (C)} \times \text{Quantity (Q)} \\ &= \text{FC} + \text{C} \times \text{Q} \qquad \text{(C.1)}\end{aligned}$$

Revenue is simply the price times the quantity sold, which can be found using formula C.2:

$$\begin{aligned}\text{Total revenue (R)} &= \text{Price (P)} \times \text{Quantity (Q)} \\ &= \text{P} \times \text{Q} \qquad \text{(C.2)}\end{aligned}$$

We will assume that all units produced can be sold; thus, the sales volume is the same as the production quantity in our calculations. Finally, we can compute the net profit using formula C.3:

$$\begin{aligned}\text{Net Profit (NP)} &= \text{Total revenue (R)} - \text{Total cost (TC)} \\ &= \text{R} - \text{TC} \qquad \text{(C.3)}\end{aligned}$$

Thus, for any forecast of sales, Q, we may determine if the firm will achieve a profit or incur a loss.

A related question is determining how many units must be produced and sold to break even. The break-even point is amount of sales at which the net profit is zero—or equivalently, the point where total cost equals total revenue. We can find the break-even point by setting total revenue equal to total cost (or equivalently, setting net profit equal to zero), and solving for Q. Let Q* = be the quantity at the break-even point. Using formulas C.1–C.3 we have

$$\begin{aligned}\text{Total revenue (R)} &= \text{Total cost (TC)} \\ \text{P} \times \text{Q}^* &= \text{FC} + \text{C} \times \text{Q}^* \\ \text{P} \times \text{Q}^* - \text{C} \times \text{Q}^* &= \text{FC} \\ \text{Q}^* \times (\text{P} - \text{C}) &= \text{FC}\end{aligned}$$

or,

$$\text{Break-even quantity} = Q^* = \frac{FC}{P - C} \qquad (C.4)$$

Example: Profitability Analysis

An industrial electronics manufacturer is considering expanding its production facility to manufacture an electrical component. The cost for new equipment and installation is $100,000. Each unit produced would have a variable cost of $12 per unit and sell for $20. Currently, the forecast is for 10,000 units. For this forecast, would the expansion be profitable or not? How many units would have to be produced and sold in order to break even?

If 10,000 units are produced and sold, the total cost would be

$$\begin{aligned} TC &= FC + C \times Q \\ &= \$100{,}000 + \$12(10{,}000) = \$220{,}000 \end{aligned}$$

The revenue received from selling 10,000 units would be

$$\begin{aligned} R &= P \times Q \\ &= \$20(10{,}000) = \$200{,}000 \end{aligned}$$

At this sales level, the net profit would be

$$\begin{aligned} NP &= R - TC \\ &= \$200{,}000 - \$220{,}000 = -\$20{,}000 \end{aligned}$$

Therefore, the firm would incur a loss.

Next, we will find the break-even point. The total cost and revenue formulas are

$$\begin{aligned} TC &= \$100{,}000 + \$12 \times Q^* \\ R &= \$20 \times Q^* \end{aligned}$$

Setting total cost equal to total revenue and solving for Q*, we have

$$\begin{aligned} \$20 \times Q^* &= \$100{,}000 + \$12 \times Q^* \\ 8 \times Q^* &= \$100{,}000 \\ Q^* &= 12{,}500 \text{ units} \end{aligned}$$

Alternatively, using Equation C.4:

$$\text{Break-even quantity} = Q^* = FC/(P - C) = \$100{,}000/(\$20 - \$12) = 12{,}500 \text{ units} \qquad (C.4)$$

If sales are less than 12,500 units, the firm will incur a loss; if sales are more than 12,500, it will realize a profit. Such information, when combined with sales forecasts, can assist the manager in deciding whether or not to pursue the expansion.

Outsourcing Decisions

A second application of break-even analysis is determining whether to make a manufactured part in-house or outsource production to a supplier based on the forecasted volume needed (often this is called a *make-or-buy decision*). If a company decides to make a part, it typically incurs fixed costs associated with purchasing equipment or setting up a production line, as well as a variable cost per unit. Fixed costs do not vary with volume and often include costs of a building, buying or leasing equipment, and administrative costs. Variable costs are a function of the quantity produced and might include labor, transportation, utilities, and materials costs. However, the cost per unit will normally be more if the work is outsourced to some external supplier. A fixed cost for outsourcing may also apply. Outsourcing decisions can also be applied to services. Service examples are photocopying in-house or using an external company such as FedEx Office, managing a recycling process in-house or using an outside recycler, and screening job applications in-house or sending them to a specialized human resources firm.

We can apply break-even analysis in a similar fashion by modifying formulas C.1–C.3:

Total cost in-house (TCI)
$$= \text{Fixed cost in-house (FCI)} + \text{Unit cost in-house (CI)} \times \text{Quantity (Q)} \qquad \text{(C.5)}$$

Total cost to outsourcing (TCO)
$$= \text{Fixed cost outsourcing (FCO)} + \text{Unit cost outsourcing (CO)} \times \text{Quantity (Q)} \qquad \text{(C.6)}$$

$$\text{Cost difference (D)} = \text{Total cost in-house (TCI)} - \text{Total cost outsourcing (TCO)} \qquad \text{(C.7)}$$

If the cost difference is negative, then TCI < TCO, and it is more economical to produce in-house; if the cost difference is positive, then TCI > TCO and it is more economical to outsource. The break-even point is the quantity where TCI = TCO, or

$$FCI + CI \times Q^* = FCO + CO \times Q^*$$
$$(CI - CO) \times Q^* = FCO - FCI$$
$$Q^* = \frac{FCO - FCI}{CI - CO} \qquad \text{(C.8)}$$

Example: Make or Buy Decision

Fisher Manufacturing needs to produce a custom aluminum housing for a special customer order. Because it currently does not have the equipment necessary to make the housing, it would have to acquire machines and tooling at a fixed cost (net of salvage value after the project is completed) of $250,000. The variable cost of production is estimated to be $20 per unit. The company can outsource the housing to a metal fabricator at a cost of $35 per unit (note that there is not fixed cost for outsourcing). The customer order is for 12,000 units. What should it do? What is the break-even point?

Using formula C.5, we find that the total cost of production in-house is

$$\text{Total cost in-house (TCI)} = FCI + CI \times Q = \$250{,}000 + (\$20)(12{,}000) = \$490{,}000$$

Using formula C.6, the total cost of outsourcing is

$$TCO = FCO + CO \times Q = \$0 + (\$35)(12{,}000) = \$420{,}000$$

From formula C.7, the cost difference (in-house minus outsourced cost) is

$$D = TCI - TCO = \$490{,}000 - \$420{,}000 = \$70{,}000$$

Therefore, outsourcing is less expensive and the firm saves $70,000.

We may find the break-even point using formula C.8:

$$\text{Break-even quantity } (Q^*) = \frac{FCO - FCI}{CI - CO}$$
$$= (0 - \$250{,}000)/(\$20 - \$35) = 16{,}667 \text{ units}$$

Thus, whenever the order quantity is 16,667 units or less, it is more economical to outsource. If the order quantity exceeds 16,667 units, then it is more economical to produce in-house.

Technology Choice Decisions

Many decisions revolve around choosing between two technology options, for example, machine tools from different vendors, or service options such as paper shredding or office housekeeping. From a break-even analysis perspective, these are similar to outsourcing decisions.

Example: A Technology Choice Decision

CDC Hospital must decide between two slightly different types of technology and vendors for their X-ray equipment. The expected demand for either of these machines is 11,000 X-rays per year. Vendor A offers a fixed X-ray machine with an upfront one-time fee (or fixed cost) of $200,000 and a variable cost per X-ray of $18.60. Vendor B offers a mobile X-ray machine with a one-time fee of $100,000 and a variable cost per X-ray of $21.00.

Using formulas C.1 and C.7, we compute the total cost for each vendor and the cost difference between the two options:

$$\text{Total cost (TC)} = \text{Fixed cost (FC)} + \text{Unit cost (C)} \times \text{Quantity (Q)} \tag{C.9}$$

$$\text{TCA} = \text{FCA} + \text{CA} \times \text{Q} = \$200{,}000 + \$18.60(11{,}000) = \$404{,}600$$

$$\text{TCB} = \text{FCB} + \text{CB} \times \text{Q} = \$100{,}000 + \$21.00(11{,}000) = \$331{,}000$$

$$\text{Cost difference (D)} = \text{Total cost vendor A (TCA)} - \text{Total cost vendor B (TCB)} \tag{C.10}$$

$$\text{D} = \text{TCA} - \text{TCB} = \$404{,}600 - \$331{,}000 = \$73{,}600$$

The cost of vendor A is $73,600 higher than vendor B for the expected demand of 11,000 X-rays, so choosing vendor B would be the economical decision. This type of analysis can be helpful in negotiating with both vendors.

To find the break-even point, set TCA = TCB and solve for Q*:

$$\text{FCA} + \text{CA} \times \text{Q}^* = \text{FCB} + \text{CB} \times \text{Q}^*$$

$$\$200{,}000 + \$18.60\text{Q}^* = \$100{,}000 + \$21.00\text{Q}^*$$

$$\$100{,}000 = \$2.40\text{Q}^*$$

$$\text{Q}^* = 41{,}667 \text{ X-rays}$$

Formula C.8 finds this directly:

$$\text{Q}^* = \frac{\text{FCB} - \text{FCA}}{\text{CA} - \text{CB}} \tag{C.11}$$

$$= \frac{\$100{,}000 - \$200{,}000}{\$18.6 - \$21.00}$$

$$= 41{,}667 \text{ X-rays}$$

Excel *Break-Even* Template

MindTap contains a template, *Break-Even*, that can be used for profitability analysis, outsourcing decisions, and technology choice decisions. Exhibit C.1 shows the use of this template for the three examples we illustrated in this supplement. Enter the input values in the yellow cells (the remaining cells are locked so you cannot inadvertently change any formulas). In row 18, the template shows the outcome (Profit, Loss, or Break-Even for profitability analysis; In-house, Outsource, or Break-Even for outsourcing decisions; and Option A, Option B, or Break-Even for technology choice decisions).

Using the Excel Goal Seek Tool to Find the Break-Even Point

The Excel Goal Seek tool may be used to find the break-even point. We will use the profitability analysis example. You can use any value for the quantity in cell B5. For the break-even point, we want to find the quantity in cell B5 that results in a net profit of zero in cell B17.

EXHIBIT C.1 Break-Even Excel Template

	A	B	C	D	E	F	G	H
1	Break-Even Analysis	Copyright © Cengage Learning. Not for commercial use.						
2	Enter data only in yellow cells.							
3								
4	Profitability Analysis			Outsourcing Decision			Technology Choice Decision	
5	Quantity	10,000		Quantity	12,000		Quantity	11,000
6								
7	Cost			Produce In-House			Option A	
8	Fixed cost	$100,000.00		Fixed cost	$250,000.00		Fixed cost	$200,000.00
9	Unit cost	$12.00		Unit cost	$20.00		Unit cost	$18.60
10								
11				Outsource			Option B	
12	Revenue			Fixed cost			Fixed cost	$100,000.00
13	Unit revenue	$20.00		Unit cost	$35.00		Unit cost	$21.00
14								
15	Total Cost	$220,000.00		Total In-House Production Cost	$490,000.00		Total Cost Option A	$404,600.00
16	Total Revenue	$200,000.00		Total Outsourced Cost	$420,000.00		Total Cost Option B	$331,000.00
17	Net Profit	-$20,000.00		Cost difference (In-House - Outsourced)	$70,000.00		Cost difference (Option A - Option B)	$73,600.00
18	Profit or Loss	Loss		Economical Decision	Outsource		Economical Decision	Option B

EXHIBIT C.2 Goal Seek Dialog

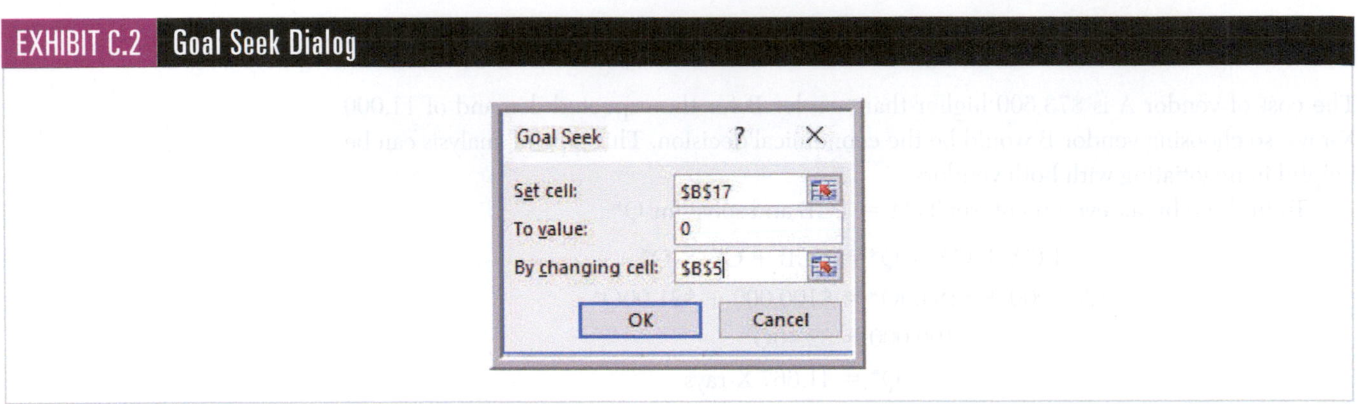

EXHIBIT C.3 Result of Using the Goal Seek tool to Find the Break-Even Point

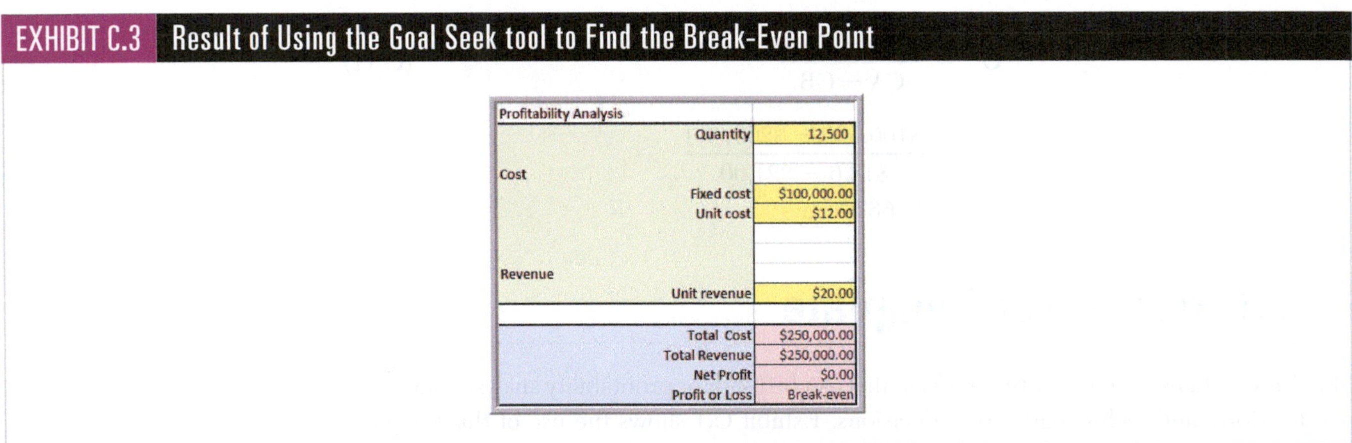

Profitability Analysis	
Quantity	12,500
Cost	
Fixed cost	$100,000.00
Unit cost	$12.00
Revenue	
Unit revenue	$20.00
Total Cost	$250,000.00
Total Revenue	$250,000.00
Net Profit	$0.00
Profit or Loss	Break-even

1. Select *Goal Seek* from *What-If Analysis* menu in the Excel *Data* tab. A small dialog box will appear. See Exhibit C.2.
2. In the "Set Cell" field, enter B17 (or simply click on this cell); this is the output cell that the *Goal Seek* tool seeks to find. In the "To Value" field, enter 0; this is the value of net profit that we seek. Finally, in the "By changing cell" field, enter B5 (or again, simply click on the cell); this the cell that *Goal Seek* will change that results in a net profit of zero.
3. When you click *OK*, Excel will find the break-even quantity in cell B5 that results in a cost difference of 0 for the net profit in cell B17 as shown in Exhibit C.3.

SUPPLEMENT D
Linear Optimization

Analytical models that seek to maximize or minimize some objective function while satisfying a set of constraints are called **optimization models**. An important category of optimization models is **linear optimization**—often called linear programming (LP)—models, which are widely used for many types of operations design and planning problems that involve allocating limited resources among competing alternatives. They are also used for many distribution and supply chain management designs and operations.

A linear optimization model has two basic properties:

1. All mathematical relationships are linear functions. A linear function is simply a sum of terms, each of which is a constant multiplied by a variable, such as $10x + 3y$. Terms such as $5x^2$, $1/x$, and so on are not linear functions and are not allowed for linear optimization.
2. All variables are continuous, meaning that they may assume any real value (typically, nonnegative, that is, greater than or equal to zero). Of course, this assumption may not be realistic for a practical business problem (you cannot produce half a television). However, this assumption simplifies the solution method and analysis, and we often apply it in many situations where the solution would not be seriously affected.

We first introduce the basic concepts of optimization modeling, then present some OM applications of LP, and finally discuss the use of Excel Solver to solve LP models. We will see several applications of linear optimization models in operations and supply chain management in various chapters of this book.

Developing Linear Optimization Models

Any optimization model has three elements:

1. Decision variables
2. An objective to maximize or minimize
3. Constraints

Decision variables *are the unknown values that the model seeks to determine.* Depending on the application, decision variables might be the quantities of different products to produce, the amount to ship from a warehouse to a customer, allocating production among different manufacturing processes, and so on. *The* **objective function** *is the quantity we seek to minimize or maximize.* For example, we might wish to maximize profit or revenue, or to minimize cost.

Constraints *are limitations, requirements, or other restrictions that are imposed on any solution, either from practical or technological considerations or by management policy. Any values of decision variables that satisfy all constraints are referred to as* **feasible solutions**. *Any feasible solution that minimizes or maximizes the objective function is called an* **optimal solution**.

We will approach optimization models in the following fashion:

1. Identify the decision variables, the objective, and all appropriate constraints.
2. Write the objective and constraints as mathematical expressions to create a mathematical model of the problem.
3. Implement the mathematical model on a spreadsheet and use Excel Solver to find an optimal solution.

Example: A Production Planning Problem

Florida Chemical Supply (FCS) manufactures and sells a variety of products used in purifying and softening water. One of its products is a pellet that is produced and sold in 40- and 80-pound bags. A common production line packages both products, although the fill rate is slower for 80-pound bags. FCS is currently planning its production schedule and wants to develop a linear optimization model that will assist in its production-planning effort.

The company has orders for 20,000 pounds over the next week. Currently, it has 4,000 pounds in inventory. Thus, it should plan on an aggregate production of at least 16,000 pounds. FCS has a sufficient supply of pellets to meet this demand but has limited amounts of packaging materials available as well as a limited amount of time on the packaging line. FCS has 6,000 square feet of packaging materials available; each 40-pound bag requires 6 square feet and each 80-pound bag requires 10 square feet of these materials. In a normal workweek, the packaging line operates 1,500 minutes. The 40-pound bags, for which the line was designed, each require 1.2 minutes of packaging time; the 80-pound bags require 3 minutes per bag. FCS nets \$2 for each 40-pound bag produced and sold and \$4 for each 80-pound bag produced and sold. The problem is to determine how many 40- and 80-pound bags to produce in order to maximize profit, given limited materials and time on the packaging line.

Decision Variables For the FCS problem, the manager needs to determine the number of 40- and 80-pound bags to produce. We denote these by the variables x_1 and x_2, respectively:

$$x_1 = \text{amount of 40-pound bags to produce}$$
$$x_2 = \text{amount of 80-pound bags to produce}$$

Using subscripted variables like this is useful when developing mathematical models. However, using more descriptive names, such as Amount40 and Amount80 is often better when implementing the model on a spreadsheet.

Objective Function For FCS, the objective is to maximize profit. If the company makes \$2 for every 40-pound bag produced, it will make $2x_1$ dollars if it produces x_1 40-pound bags. Similarly, if it makes \$4 for every 80-pound bag produced, it will make $4x_2$ dollars if it produces x_2 80-pound bags. Thus:

$$\text{Total Profit} = 2x_1 + 4x_2$$

The constant terms in the objective function are called objective function coefficients. Thus, in this example, the objective function coefficients are \$2 (associated with x_1) and \$4 (associated with x_2). FCS must determine the values for the variables x_1 and x_2 that will yield the highest possible value of profit. Therefore, the objective function is

$$\text{Maximize Total Profit} = 2x_1 + 4x_2$$

Suppose that FCS decided to produce 200 40-pound bags and 300 80-pound bags. Then the total profit would be

$$\begin{aligned}\text{Total Profit} &= 2(200) + 4(300)\\ &= 400 + 1{,}200\\ &= \$1{,}600\end{aligned}$$

Alternatively, if they produce 400 40-pound bags and 400 80-pound bags, the profit would increase to:

$$\begin{aligned}\text{Total Profit} &= 2(400) + 4(400)\\ &= 800 + 1{,}600\\ &= \$2{,}400\end{aligned}$$

However, it may not be possible for FCS to produce that many bags. For instance, there might not be enough materials or enough time available on the packaging line to produce those quantities. This requires us to first identify all the constraints of the problem.

Constraints Because each 40-pound bag requires 1.2 minutes on the packaging line, and each 80-pound bag requires 3 minutes, the total packaging time used for the production of x_1 40-pound bags and x_2 80-pound bags is given by

$$\text{Total packaging time used} = 1.2x_1 + 3x_2$$

Because only 1,500 minutes of packaging time are available, it follows that the production combination we select must satisfy the constraint:

$$\text{Total packaging time used} = 1.2x_1 + 3x_2 \leq 1{,}500 \text{ minutes}$$

This constraint states that the total packaging time used cannot exceed the amount available. Similarly, because the amount of packaging materials used cannot exceed what is available, the constraint for the packaging materials limitation is

$$\text{Total packaging materials used} = 6x_1 + 10x_2 \leq 6{,}000 \text{ square feet}$$

Next, we must ensure that the aggregate production of softening pellets each week is at least 16,000 pounds. We have the constraint:

$$\text{Aggregate production} = 40x_1 + 80x_2 \geq 16{,}000 \text{ pounds}$$

Finally, we must prevent the decision variables x_1 and x_2 from having negative values. Thus, the two constraints:

$$x_1 \geq 0 \text{ and } x_2 \geq 0$$

must be added. These constraints are referred to as the *nonnegativity constraints*. Nonnegativity constraints are a general feature of all linear optimization problems and are written in this abbreviated form:

$$x_1, x_2 \geq 0$$

FCS Optimization Model The complete mathematical model for the FCS problem follows:

$$\text{Maximize Total Profit} = 2x_1 + 4x_2$$

subject to the constraints:

$1.2x_1 + 3x_2 \leq 1{,}500$ (packaging line)
$6x_1 + 10x_2 \leq 6{,}000$ (materials availability)
$40x_1 + 80x_2 \geq 16{,}000$ (aggregate production)
$x_1, x_2 \geq 0$ (nonnegativity)

Our task now is to find the product mix (i.e., the combination of x_1 and x_2) that satisfies all the constraints and, at the same time, yields a value for the objective function that is greater than or equal to the value given by any other feasible solution. Once this is done, we will have found the optimal solution to the problem.

Solving Linear Optimization Models with Excel Solver

In this section, we illustrate how to use Excel Solver to solve linear optimization models. Solver is an add-in packaged with Excel that was developed by Frontline Systems, Inc. (www.solver.com), and can be used to solve many different types of optimization problems. Solver can be found in the *Data* tab in Excel. If it is not there, you can activate it easily. in Windows, click the *File* tab and then *Options* in the left column. Choose *Add-Ins* from the left column. At the bottom of the dialog, make sure *Excel Add-ins* is selected in the *Manage:* box and click *Go*. In the *Add-Ins* dialog, if *Solver Add-in* is not checked, simply check the boxes and click *OK*. You will not have to repeat this procedure every time you run Excel in the future. On Excel 2016 for Mac, go to *Tools* > *Excel Add-ins* and select Solver.

We will illustrate Solver using the FCS example. The first step is to construct a spreadsheet model for the problem, such as the one shown in Exhibit D.1 (available in MindTap as FCS *Spreadsheet Model*). The problem data are given in the range of cells A4:E8 in the same way that we write the mathematical model. Cells B12 and C12 provide the values of the decision variables. Cells B16:B18 provide the left-hand side values of the constraints (called *constraint functions*). For example, the formula for the left side of the packaging constraint in cell B16 is =B6*B12+C6*C12. The value of the objective function, =B5*B12+C5*C12, is entered in cell B20.

The spreadsheet model is designed to exploit the way that Solver creates names in its output reports. Solver assigns names to the objective, decision variable, and constraint function cells by concatenating (joining) the text in the first cell containing text to the left of the cell with the first cell containing text above it. For example, in the FCS model, the objective cell is B19. The first cell containing text to the left of B20 is "Profit" in cell A20, and the first cell containing text above B20 is "Total" in cell B19. Concatenating these text strings yields the objective cell name "Profit Total," which is found in the Solver reports. The constraint functions are calculated in cells B16 to B18. The names assigned to these cells would be "Packaging Line Amount," "Materials Amount," and "Aggregate production Amount." Finally, the decision variable cells in B12 and C12 have the names "Amount produced 40-lb bag" and "Amount produced 80-lb bag."

EXHIBIT D.1 Excel Model for the FCS Problem

	A	B	C	D	E	F
1	Florida Chemical Supply					
2						
3	Problem Data					
4	Product	40-lb bag	80-lb bag			
5	Profit/unit	$2.00	$4.00		Limitations	
6	Packaging line	1.2	3	<=	1,500	minutes
7	Materials availability	6	10	<=	6,000	square feet
8	Aggregate production	40	80	>=	16,000	pounds
9						
10	Decision Variables					
11	Product	40-lb bag	80-lb bag			
12	Amount produced	0	0			
13						
14	Constraints					
15		Amount used				
16	Packaging line	0				
17	Materials availability	0				
18	Aggregate production	0				
19						
20		Total				
21	Profit	$0.00				

EXHIBIT D.2 Completed Solver Parameters Dialog

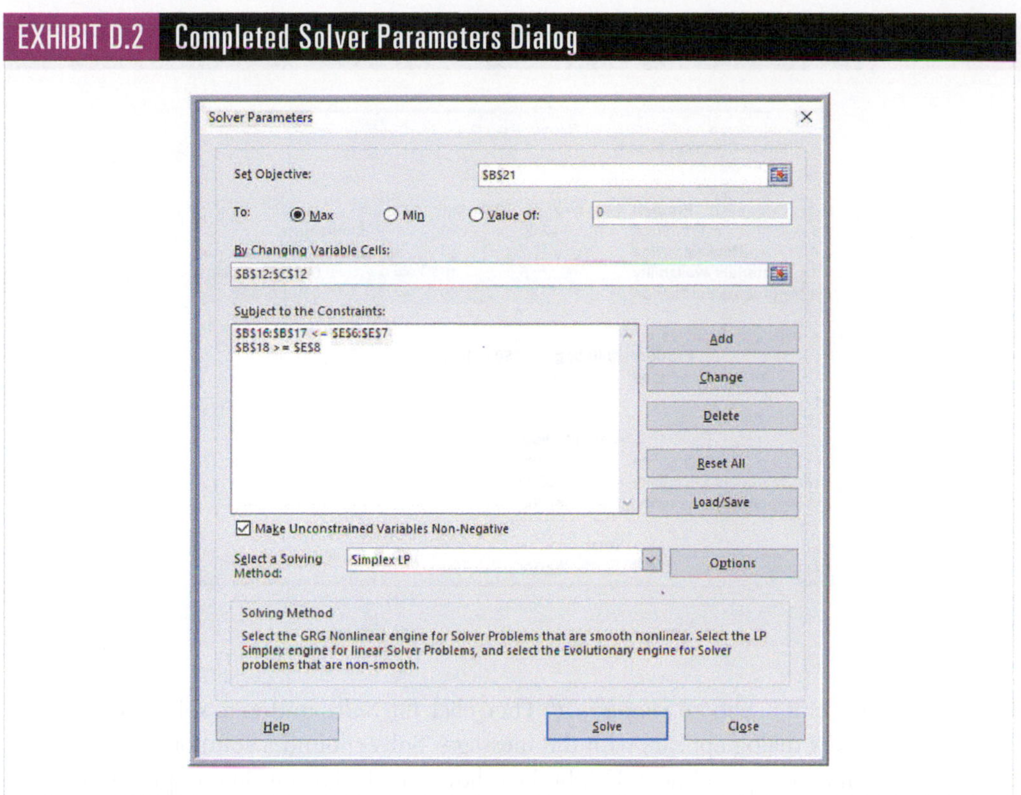

Solver can be found in the *Data* tab in Excel. When Solver is selected, the *Solver Parameters* dialog appears. You use this dialog to define the objective, decision variables, and constraints from your spreadsheet model within Solver. Exhibit D.2 shows the completed *Solver Parameters* dialog for the FCS model. The *Set Objective* cell is the one that contains the objective function value. Click the appropriate radio button for the objective: *Max* or *Min*. *Changing Variable Cells* are those that contain the decision variables. Constraints are constructed in the constraint box or edited by using the *Add*, *Change*, or *Delete* buttons. To enter a constraint, click the *Add* button. A new dialog, *Add Constraint*, appears (see Exhibit D.3). In the left field, *Cell Reference*, enter the cell that contains the left-hand side of the constraint. For example, the left-hand sides of the constraints are in cell B16 through B18. Select the correct type of constraint (<=, = or >=) in the drop-down box in the middle of the dialog. Enter the cell reference for the right-hand side of the constraint in the *Constraint* box on the right. In this example, the right-hand sides of the constraints are in cells E6 through E8. You may define a group of constraints that all have the same algebraic form (all >=, all =, or all <=) and enter them together as a range. For example, both the packaging line and materials availability constraints are <= types. Notice in Exhibit D.3, we entered these together as $B$16:$B$17 <= $E$6:$E$7.

Excel does *not* assume nonnegativity; thus, this must be added to the model by checking the box *Make Unconstrained Variables Non-Negative*. Solver provides three options in the field *Select a Solving Method* for choosing the algorithmic method to solve the problem:

1. *GRG Nonlinear*—used for solving nonlinear optimization problems
2. *Simplex LP*—used for solving linear and linear integer optimization problems
3. *Evolutionary*—used for solving complex nonlinear and nonlinear integer problems

EXHIBIT D.3 *Add Constraint* Dialog

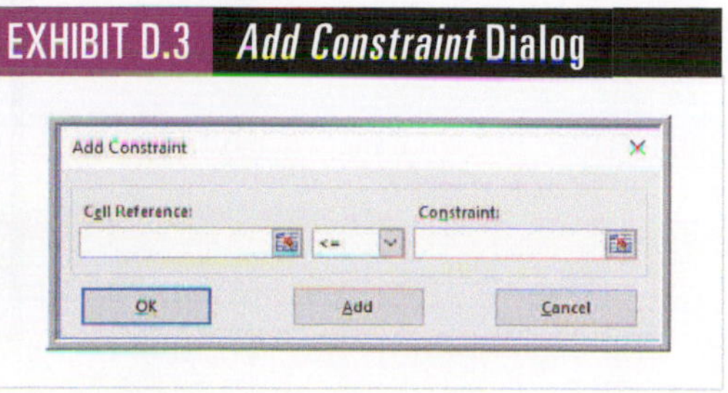

EXHIBIT D.4 Solver Solution for FCS

	A	B	C	D	E	F
1	**Florida Chemical Supply**					
2						
3	*Problem Data*					
4	**Product**	**40-lb bag**	**80-lb bag**			
5	**Profit/unit**	$2.00	$4.00		**Limitations**	
6	**Packaging line**	1.2	3	<=	1,500	minutes
7	**Materials availability**	6	10	<=	6,000	square feet
8	**Aggregate production**	40	80	>=	16,000	pounds
9						
10	*Decision Variables*					
11	**Product**	**40-lb bag**	**80-lb bag**			
12	**Amount produced**	500	300			
13						
14	*Constraints*					
15		**Amount used**				
16	**Packaging line**	1500				
17	**Materials availability**	6000				
18	**Aggregate production**	44000				
19						
20		**Total**				
21	**Profit**	$2,200.00				

For linear optimization, choose *Simplex LP*. Then click the *Solve* button to solve the problem. The *Solver Results* dialog appears with the message "Solver found a solution." Click OK to save the solution in the spreadsheet. Exhibit D.4 shows the final results in the spreadsheet. If a solution could not be found, Solver would notify you with a message to this effect. This generally means that you have an error in your model or you have included conflicting constraints that no solution can satisfy. In such cases, you need to reexamine your model.

After a solution is found, Solver allows you to generate three reports—an Answer Report, a Sensitivity Report, and a Limits Report—from the *Solver Results* dialog. Click on the ones you want before clicking *OK*. (Do not check the box *Outline Reports*; this is an Excel feature that produces the reports in "outlined format."). These reports are placed in separate sheets in the Excel workbook. The Answer Report (Exhibit D.5) provides basic information about the solution. (Note the names used, which we described earlier.) The Constraints section requires further explanation. "Cell Value" refers to the left side of the constraint if we substitute the optimal values of the decision variables:

$$
\begin{aligned}
&\text{Packaging line: } 1.2(500) + 3(300) = 1{,}500 \text{ minutes}\\
&\text{Materials: } 6(500) + 10(300) = 6{,}000 \text{ square feet}\\
&\text{Production: } 40(500) + 80(300) = 44{,}000 \text{ pounds}
\end{aligned}
$$

EXHIBIT D.5 Solver Answer Report for FCS

	A	B	C	D	E	F	G
14	Objective Cell (Max)						
15		**Cell**	**Name**	**Original Value**	**Final Value**		
16		$B$21	Profit Total	$0.00	$2,200.00		
17							
18							
19	Variable Cells						
20		**Cell**	**Name**	**Original Value**	**Final Value**	**Integer**	
21		$B$12	Amount produced 40-lb bag	0	500	Contin	
22		$C$12	Amount produced 80-lb bag	0	300	Contin	
23							
24							
25	Constraints						
26		**Cell**	**Name**	**Cell Value**	**Formula**	**Status**	**Slack**
27		$B$16	Packaging line Amount used	1500	$B$16<=$E$6	Binding	0
28		$B$17	Materials availability Amount used	6000	$B$17<=$E$7	Binding	0
29		$B$18	Aggregate production Amount used	44000	$B$18>=$E$8	Not Binding	28000

EXHIBIT D.6 Solver Sensitivity Report for FCS

	A	B	C	D	E	F	G	H
6	Variable Cells							
7				Final	Reduced	Objective	Allowable	Allowable
8		Cell	Name	Value	Cost	Coefficient	Increase	Decrease
9		$B$12	Amount produced 40-lb bag	500	0	2	0.4	0.4
10		$C$12	Amount produced 80-lb bag	300	0	4	1	0.666666667
11								
12	Constraints							
13				Final	Shadow	Constraint	Allowable	Allowable
14		Cell	Name	Value	Price	R.H. Side	Increase	Decrease
15		$B$16	Packaging line Amount used	1500	0.666666667	1500	300	300
16		$B$17	Materials availability Amount used	6000	0.2	6000	1500	1000
17		$B$18	Aggregate production Amount used	44000	0	16000	28000	1E+30

We see that the amount of time used on the packaging line and the amount of materials used are at their limits. We call such constraints *binding*. However, the aggregate production has exceeded its requirement by 44,000 − 16,000 = 28,000 pounds. This difference is referred to as the *slack* in the constraint. In general, slack is the absolute difference between the left and right sides of a constraint.

The Variable Cells portion of the Sensitivity Report (Exhibit D.6) tells us how much the objective-function coefficients can vary without changing the optimal values of the decision variables. They are given in the "Allowable Increase" and "Allowable Decrease" columns. Thus, the profit coefficient on 40-pound bags may vary between 2 − 0.4 = 1.6 and 2 + 0.4 = 2.4 without changing the optimal product mix. If the coefficient is changed beyond these ranges, the problem must be re-solved. The Constraints section provides information about changes in the right side values of the constraints. *The* ***shadow price*** *is the change in the objective function value as the right side of a constraint is increased by one unit*. Thus, for the packaging line constraint, an extra minute of line availability will improve profit by approximately 67 cents. Similarly, one fewer minute in line availability will reduce profit by about 67 cents. This will hold for increases or decreases within the allowable ranges in the last two columns; if the change in the right-hand side of a constraint exceeds these limits, the problem must be re-solved. For instance, the packaging line limitation can be increased by 300 (the Allowable Increase) or decreased by 300 (the Allowable Decrease), and the profit will change by approximately 67 cents for each unit. If the packaging limitation were increased by 100 to 1600 minutes, then profit would increase by $0.6667(100) = $66.67. If the packaging limitation were decreased by 50 to 1450 minutes, then the profit will decrease by $0.6667(50) = $33.34.

The Limits Report generally does not provide much useful information, and we will not discuss it.

SUPPLEMENT E
The Transportation and Assignment Problems

The **transportation problem** is a special type of linear optimization problem (see Supplement D: Linear Optimization) that arises in planning the distribution of goods and services from several supply points (factories, warehouses, etc.) to several demand locations (warehouses, customers, etc.). This involves determining how much to ship from the supply points to the demand locations at minimum cost. The transportation problem is the basis for advanced optimization models in supply chain management that are used extensively. A special case of the transportation problem is the **assignment problem**. In this supplement, we show how to model transportation and assignment problems, implement them on spreadsheets, and solve them using Excel Solver.

Modeling the Transportation Problem

To develop a linear optimization model, we first define the decision variables as the amount to ship between each supply point and demand location. We will assume that we have *m* supply points and *n* demand locations. For a mathematical model, we use double-subscripted variables to simplify the formulation. Define X_{ij} to be the amount shipped from supply point *i* to demand location *j*. Therefore, we have *m* x *n* variables, $X_{11}, X_{12}, \ldots, X_{mn}$. Define C_{ij} be the cost to ship one unit from supply point *i* to demand location *j*. Thus, $C_{ij} X_{ij}$ is the total cost of shipping from supply point i to demand location *j*. If we sum these terms over all supply points and demand locations, we have the objective function that we wish to minimize:

$$\text{Minimize Total Cost} = C_{11} X_{11} + C_{12} X_{12} + \cdots + C_{mn} X_{mn} \qquad \text{(E.1)}$$

Usually, the quantity of goods available at each supply point is limited, and a specified quantity of goods is needed at each demand location. Let S_i be the supply available at supply point *i*, and D_j be the demand required at demand location *j*. Therefore, the constraints in the model must ensure that we cannot ship more than the amount available at each supply point, and that we ship the required amount from the supply points to each demand location. Mathematically, we have a supply constraint for each supply point and a demand constraint for each demand location:

Supply Constraints

$$\begin{aligned} X_{11} + X_{12} + \cdots + X_{1n} &\leq S_1 \\ X_{21} + X_{22} + \cdots + X_{2n} &\leq S_2 \\ &\cdots \\ X_{m1} + X_{m2} + \cdots + X_{mn} &\leq S_m \end{aligned} \qquad \text{(E.2)}$$

Demand Constraints

$$\begin{aligned} X_{11} + X_{21} + \cdots + X_{m1} &= D_1 \\ X_{12} + X_{22} + \cdots + X_{m2} &= D_2 \\ &\cdots \\ X_{1n} + X_{2n} + \cdots + X_{mn} &= D_n \end{aligned} \qquad \text{(E.3)}$$

Finally, all variables must be nonnegative:

$$X_{ij} \geq 0 \text{ for } i = 1,\ldots,m \text{ and } j = 1,\ldots,n$$

Transportation Model Example

Let us consider the problem faced by Foster Manufacturing, Inc., which produces commercial generators. Currently Foster has three plants: one in Cleveland, Ohio; one in Bedford, Indiana; and one in York, Pennsylvania. Generators produced at the plants (supply points) are shipped to distribution centers (demand locations) in Boston, Chicago, St. Louis, and in Lexington, Kentucky. The question is how to best allocate production among the distribution centers at minimum cost.

Using a typical one-month planning period, the production capacities at the three plants are shown in Exhibit E.1. Forecasts of monthly demand at the four distribution centers are shown in Exhibit E.2. The transportation cost per unit for each route is shown in Exhibit E.3.

A convenient way of summarizing the transportation-problem data is with a table such as the one shown in Exhibit E.4. Note that the 12 cells in the table correspond to the 12 possible shipping routes from the three plants to the four distribution centers. The entries in the column at the right of the table represent the supply available at each plant, and the entries at the bottom represent the required demand at each distribution center. In order for the problem to be feasible the total supply must be at least as large as the total demand; in this case, they are equal. The entry in the upper-right corner of each cell represents the per-unit cost of shipping over the corresponding route.

If we ship X_{11} units from Cleveland to Boston, we incur a total shipping cost of $3X_{11}$. By summing the costs associated with each shipping route, we have the total cost expression that we want to minimize.

$$\text{Total cost} = 3X_{11} + 2X_{12} + 7X_{13} + 6X_{14} + 7X_{21} + 5X_{22} + 2X_{23} + 3X_{24} + 2X_{31} + 5X_{32} + 4X_{33} + 5X_{34}.$$

EXHIBIT E.1 Foster Manufacturing Production Capacities

Origin	Plant	Production Capacity (units)
1	Cleveland	5,000
2	Bedford	6,000
3	York	2,500
	Total	13,500

EXHIBIT E.2 Foster Manufacturing Monthly Forecast

Destination	Distribution Center	Demand Forecast (units)
1	Boston	6,000
2	Chicago	4,000
3	St. Louis	2,000
4	Lexington	1,500
	Total	13,500

EXHIBIT E.3 Foster Manufacturing Transportation Cost per Unit

	Destination			
Origin	Boston	Chicago	St. Louis	Lexington
Cleveland	$3	$2	$7	$6
Bedford	7	5	2	3
York	2	5	4	5

EXHIBIT E.4 Foster Manufacturing Transportation Table

Plant	Distribution Center: 1. Boston	2. Chicago	3. St. Louis	4. Lexington	Origin Supply
1. Cleveland	3 X_{11}	2 X_{12}	7 X_{13}	6 X_{14}	5,000
2. Bedford	7 X_{21}	5 X_{22}	2 X_{23}	3 X_{24}	6,000
3. York	2 X_{31}	5 X_{32}	4 X_{33}	5 X_{34}	2,500
Destination Demand	6,000	4,000	2,000	1,500	13,500

Cell corresponding to shipments from Bedford to Boston

Total supply and total demand

Looking across the first row of this table, we see that the amount shipped from Cleveland to all destinations must not exceed 5,000, or $X_{11} + X_{12} + X_{13} + X_{14} \leq 5{,}000$. Similarly, the amount shipped from Bedford to all destinations must not exceed 6,000 or $X_{21} + X_{22} + X_{23} + X_{24} \leq 6{,}000$. Finally, the amount shipped from York to all destinations must not exceed 2,500 or $X_{31} + X_{32} + X_{33} + X_{34} \leq 2{,}500$.

We also must ensure that each destination receives the required demand. Thus, the amount shipped from all origins to Boston must equal 6,000 or $X_{11} + X_{21} + X_{31} = 6{,}000$. For Chicago, St. Louis, and Lexington we have similar constraints.

$$\begin{aligned} &\text{Chicago:} && X_{12} + X_{22} + X_{32} = 4{,}000 \\ &\text{St. Louis:} && X_{13} + X_{23} + X_{33} = 2{,}000 \\ &\text{Lexington:} && X_{14} + X_{24} + X_{34} = 1{,}500 \end{aligned}$$

By including nonnegativity restrictions, $x_{ij} \geq 0$ for all variables, we have the linear optimization model.

Solving the Transportation Problem Exhibit E.5 is a spreadsheet model of the Foster Manufacturing transportation problem (available in MindTap as *Foster Manufacturing*). Cells in the range A3:F7 provide the model data. In Exhibit E.5, the range B12:E14 corresponds to the decision variables (amount shipped) in the problem. The amount shipped out if each supply point (Cleveland, Bedford, and York) in cells B17:D17 is the sum of the decision variables for that supply point. For example, the formula in cell B17 is =SUM(B12:E12). These values cannot exceed the supplies in cells F4:F6. For distribution centers (Boston, Chicago, St. Louis, and Lexington), the amount shipped into each is the sum of the decision variable cells for that distribution center (cells B20:E20). For example, the formula for cell B20 is =SUM(B12:B14). These values must be equal to the demands in cells B7:E7. The objective to be minimized is the total cost, which is computed in cell B23 as =SUMPRODUCT(B4:E6,B12:E14). The Solver model is shown in Exhibit E.6, and the solution to the transportation problem is shown in Exhibit E.7. Exhibit E.8 provides a summary of the solution. One useful property of the transportation model is that if all supplies and demands are whole numbers, then the optimal values of the decision variables will also be whole numbers.

EXHIBIT E.5 Spreadsheet Model for Foster Manufacturing Transportation Problem

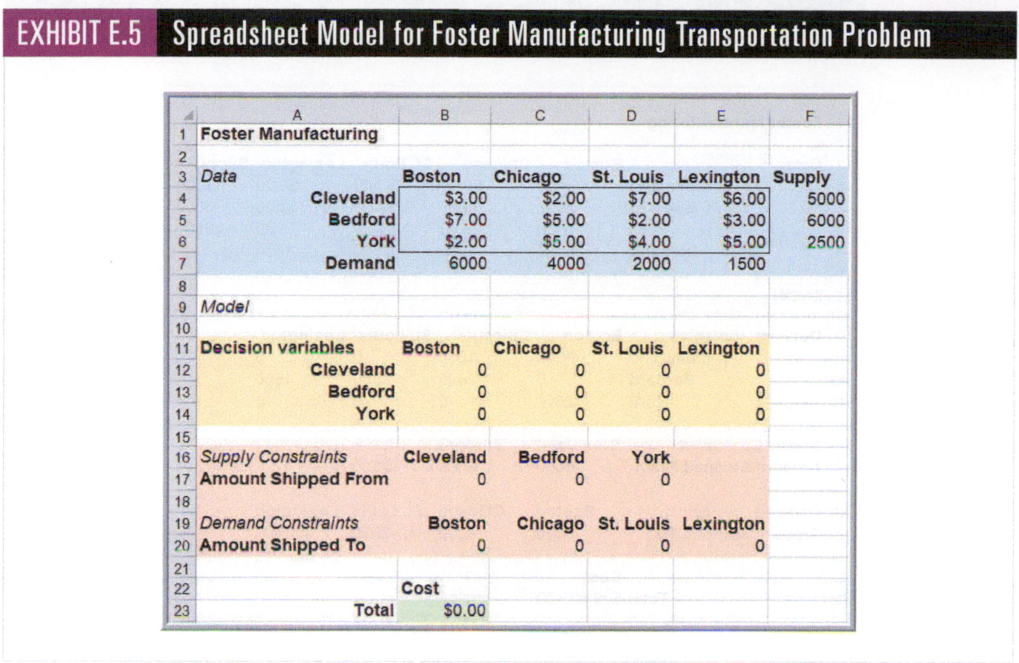

	A	B	C	D	E	F
1	**Foster Manufacturing**					
2						
3	*Data*	**Boston**	**Chicago**	**St. Louis**	**Lexington**	**Supply**
4	**Cleveland**	$3.00	$2.00	$7.00	$6.00	5000
5	**Bedford**	$7.00	$5.00	$2.00	$3.00	6000
6	**York**	$2.00	$5.00	$4.00	$5.00	2500
7	**Demand**	6000	4000	2000	1500	
8						
9	*Model*					
10						
11	**Decision variables**	**Boston**	**Chicago**	**St. Louis**	**Lexington**	
12	**Cleveland**	0	0	0	0	
13	**Bedford**	0	0	0	0	
14	**York**	0	0	0	0	
15						
16	*Supply Constraints*	**Cleveland**	**Bedford**	**York**		
17	**Amount Shipped From**	0	0	0		
18						
19	*Demand Constraints*	**Boston**	**Chicago**	**St. Louis**	**Lexington**	
20	**Amount Shipped To**	0	0	0	0	
21						
22		**Cost**				
23	**Total**	$0.00				

EXHIBIT E.6 Solver Parameters Dialog

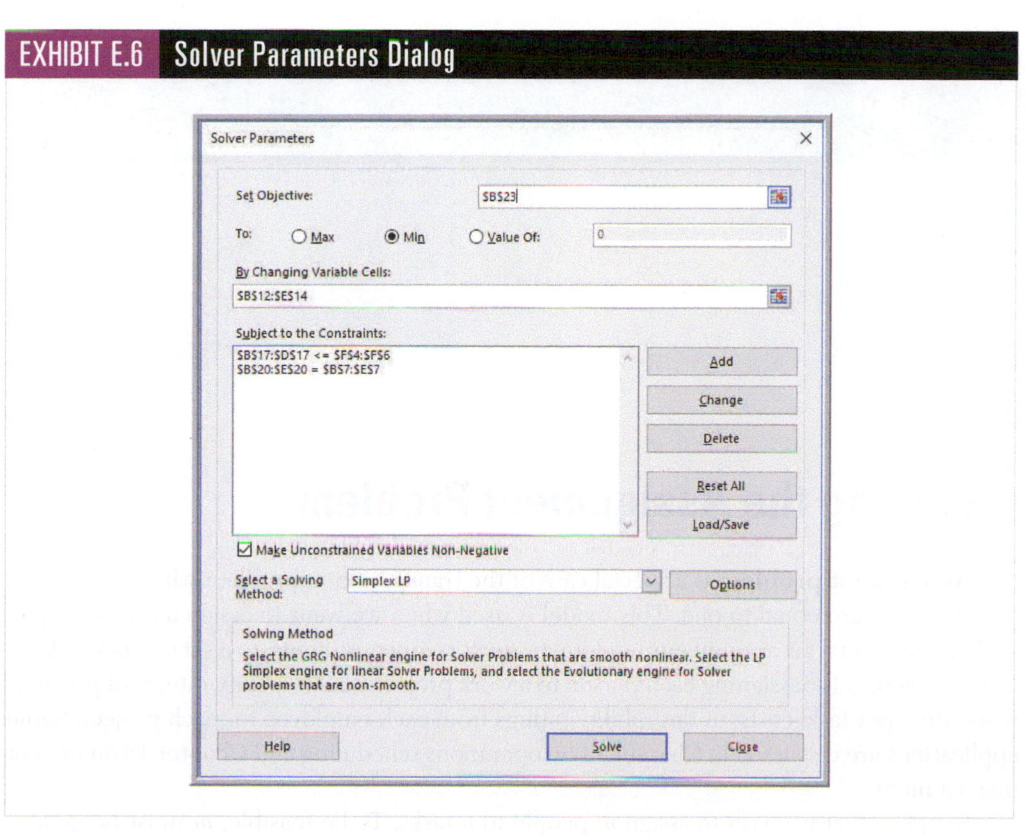

EXHIBIT E.7 Foster Manufacturing Transportation Optimal Solution

	A	B	C	D	E	F
1	Foster Manufacturing					
2						
3	*Data*	Boston	Chicago	St. Louis	Lexington	Supply
4	Cleveland	$3.00	$2.00	$7.00	$6.00	5000
5	Bedford	$7.00	$5.00	$2.00	$3.00	6000
6	York	$2.00	$5.00	$4.00	$5.00	2500
7	Demand	6000	4000	2000	1500	
8						
9	*Model*					
10						
11	Decision variables	Boston	Chicago	St. Louis	Lexington	
12	Cleveland	3500	1500	0	0	
13	Bedford	0	2500	2000	1500	
14	York	2500	0	0	0	
15						
16	*Supply Constraints*	Cleveland	Bedford	York		
17	Amount Shipped From	5000	6000	2500		
18						
19	*Demand Constraints*	Boston	Chicago	St. Louis	Lexington	
20	Amount Shipped To	6000	4000	2000	1500	
21						
22		Cost				
23	Total	$39,500.00				

EXHIBIT E.8 Foster Manufacturing Solution Summary

Route					
From	*To*	Units Shipped	Unit Cost ($)		Total Cost ($)
Cleveland	Boston	3,500	3		10,500
Cleveland	Chicago	1,500	2		3,000
Bedford	Chicago	2,500	5		12,500
Bedford	St. Louis	2,000	2		4,000
Bedford	Lexington	1,500	3		4,500
York	Boston	2,500	2		5,000
				Total	39,500

Modeling the Assignment Problem

The **assignment problem** is a special case of the transportation problem when all supplies and demands are equal to one. This model is used when we want to assign a set of people, such as engineers, tax accountants, architects, doctors, or consultants, to a set of work tasks or projects. Scores for assigning each person to a work project can be quality ratings of previous work, time per task, costs, or desirability ratings from each employee for each project. Some applications are discussed in Chapter 14 on operations scheduling and Chapter 18 on project management.

Suppose that we wish to assign m people to n tasks. To be feasible, m must be greater than or equal to n. Define $X_{ij} = 1$ if person i is assigned to task j. Mathematically, the model is virtually identical to the transportation problem, except that the supplies and demands are all 1. The objective is to minimize total cost or maximize total benefit:

$$\text{Minimize Total Cost (or Maximize Total Benefit)} = C_{11}X_{11} + C_{12}X_{12} + \cdots + C_{mn}X_{mn} \quad \text{(E.4)}$$

where C_{ij} = cost or benefit of assigning person i to task j.

The constraints have the same form as those in the transportation model. First, each person must be assigned to at most one task:

Supply (People) Constraints

$$X_{11} + X_{12} + \cdots + X_{1n} \leq 1$$
$$X_{21} + X_{22} + \cdots + X_{2n} \leq 1$$
$$\cdots$$
$$X_{m1} + X_{m2} + \cdots + X_{mn} \leq 1 \qquad \text{(E.5)}$$

Second, each task must have one person assigned to it:

Demand (Task) Constraints

$$X_{11} + X_{21} + \cdots + X_{m1} = 1$$
$$X_{12} + X_{22} + \cdots + X_{m2} = 1$$
$$\cdots$$
$$X_{1n} + X_{2n} + \cdots + X_{mn} = 1 \qquad \text{(E.6)}$$

Finally, all variables must be nonnegative:

$$X_{ij} \geq 0 \text{ for } i = 1, \ldots, m \text{ and } j = 1, \ldots, n$$

Like the transportation model, a property of the assignment model is that all variables will have integer values if the model is solved using ordinary linear optimization.

Example: Assigning Janitorial Crews to Buildings

Esplanade Janitorial Service cleans six different office buildings each day with six different crews. Each building has similar cleaning requirements, but due to differences such as crew skill mix and building square footage, each crew has different total costs as shown in Exhibit E.9. The objective is to assign crews to buildings to minimize total daily cost.

Each crew can be assigned to at most one building, and each building must have exactly one crew assigned to it. In this example, we have six buildings and six crews, so every crew will be assigned. However, in some applications, we might have more crews than buildings, and some crews will not be assigned.

Define $X_{ij} = 1$ if crew i is assigned to building j, and 0 otherwise. Note that we have 36 decision variables. Using the model developed in formulas (E.4)–(E.6), we have

$$\text{Minimize Total Cost} = 7210X_{1A} + 7060X_{2A} + 6510X_{3A} + \cdots + 6340X_{4F} + 6700X_{5F} + 5820X_{6F}$$

EXHIBIT E.9 Costs to Clean Each Building

	Crew					
Building	**1**	**2**	**3**	**4**	**5**	**6**
A	$7,210	$7,060	$6,510	$7,740	$5,970	$5,390
B	$5,970	$6,030	$6,300	$7,810	$5,690	$6,990
C	$5,280	$7,440	$6,290	$7,710	$7,380	$6,480
D	$6,310	$7,220	$6,390	$6,820	$7,360	$6,880
E	$5,340	$5,610	$5,790	$5,880	$5,680	$5,050
F	$6,440	$5,820	$7,620	$6,340	$6,700	$5,820

Supply (Crew) Constraints

$$X_{1A} + X_{1B} + X_{1C} + X_{1D} + X_{1E} + X_{1F} \leq 1$$
$$X_{2A} + X_{2B} + X_{2C} + X_{2D} + X_{2E} + X_{2F} \leq 1$$
$$X_{3A} + X_{3B} + X_{3C} + X_{3D} + X_{3E} + X_{3F} \leq 1$$
$$X_{4A} + X_{4B} + X_{4C} + X_{4D} + X_{4E} + X_{4F} \leq 1$$
$$X_{5A} + X_{5B} + X_{5C} + X_{5D} + X_{5E} + X_{5F} \leq 1$$
$$X_{5A} + X_{5B} + X_{5C} + X_{5D} + X_{5E} + X_{5F} \leq 1$$

Demand (Building) Constraints

$$X_{1A} + X_{2A} + X_{3A} + X_{4A} + X_{5A} + X_{6A} = 1$$
$$X_{1B} + X_{2B} + X_{3B} + X_{4B} + X_{5B} + X_{6B} = 1$$
$$X_{1C} + X_{2C} + X_{3C} + X_{4C} + X_{5C} + X_{6C} = 1$$
$$X_{1D} + X_{2D} + X_{3D} + X_{4D} + X_{5D} + X_{6D} = 1$$
$$X_{1E} + X_{2E} + X_{3E} + X_{4E} + X_{5E} + X_{6E} = 1$$
$$X_{1F} + X_{2F} + X_{3F} + X_{4F} + X_{5F} + X_{6F} = 1$$

Nonnegativity

$$X_{ij} \geq 0 \text{ for } i = 1, \ldots, 6 \text{ and } j = A, \ldots, F$$

Exhibit E.10 shows the spreadsheet model and Solver solution (*Esplanade Janitorial Service* in MindTap). The minimum cost solution is to assign building A to crew 6, building B to crew 5, building C to crew 1, building D to crew 3, building E to crew 4, and building F to crew 2 at a total cost of $34,450.

EXHIBIT E.10 Spreadsheet Model and Solver Solution for the Esplanade Janitorial Service Assignment Problem

	A	B	C	D	E	F	G	H
1	Assignment Model							
2								
3				Building				
4	Crew A		B	C	D	E	F	Supply
5	1	$7,210	$5,970	$5,280	$6,310	$5,340	$6,440	1
6	2	$7,060	$6,030	$7,440	$7,220	$5,610	$5,820	1
7	3	$6,510	$6,300	$6,290	$6,390	$5,790	$7,620	1
8	4	$7,740	$7,810	$7,710	$6,820	$5,880	$6,340	1
9	5	$5,970	$5,690	$7,380	$7,360	$5,680	$6,700	1
10	6	$5,390	$6,990	$6,480	$6,880	$5,050	$5,820	1
11	Demand	1	1	1	1	1	1	
12								
13	*Model*							
14								
15	Decision variables A	B	C	D	E	F		
16	1	0	0	1	0	0	0	
17	2	0	0	0	0	0	1	
18	3	0	0	0	1	0	0	
19	4	0	0	0	0	1	0	
20	5	0	1	0	0	0	0	
21	6	1	0	0	0	0	0	
22								
23	Crew Constraints	1	2	3	4	5	6	
24	Building assigned	1	1	1	1	1	1	
25								
26	Building Constraint A	B	C	D	E	F		
27	Crew assigned	1	1	1	1	1	1	
28								
29		Cost						
30	Total	$34,450.00						

SUPPLEMENT F
Queuing Models

This supplement introduces basic concepts and methods of queuing models that have wide applicability in manufacturing and service organizations. We focus only on simple models; other textbooks devoted exclusively to management science develop more complex models.

Queuing Systems

A **queuing system** consists of customers (e.g., people, machines to be repaired, jobs to be processed, etc.) that arrive for service, one or more servers (e.g., grocery store checkout facilities, repairpersons, machines) that provide the service, and a queue of customers that wait for service if the server is busy.

Customer Characteristics

Customers arrive to the system according to some arrival process. The arrival process can be deterministic or probabilistic. Examples of deterministic arrivals would be parts feeding from an automated machine to an assembly line or patients arriving at appointed times to a medical facility. Most arrival processes, such as people arriving at a supermarket, are random. We can model this behavior with a probability distribution representing the number of arrivals during a specific time interval or by a distribution that represents the time between successive arrivals.

The arrival rate may be constant or may vary with time. For instance, the demand for service at a quick-service restaurant is low in the mid-morning and mid-afternoon but peaks during the breakfast, lunch, and dinner hours. Individual customers may arrive singly and independently (telephone calls to a mail order company) or in groups (a pallet-load of parts arriving at a machine center or patrons at a movie theater).

The calling population is the set of potential customers. In many applications, the calling population is assumed to be infinite; that is, an unlimited number of possible customers can arrive to the system. This would be the case with telephone calls to a mail order company or shoppers at a supermarket. In other situations, the calling population is finite. One example would be a factory in which broken-down machines await repair.

Service Characteristics

Service occurs according to some *service process*. The time it takes to serve a customer may be deterministic or probabilistic. In the probabilistic case, the service time is described by some probability distribution. The average service time might vary during the day (taking orders and serving dinner might be longer than for breakfast). Service times might depend on the type of customer. The service process may include one or several servers. The service characteristics of multiple servers may be identical or different. In some systems, certain servers may only service specific types of customers. In many systems, such as restaurants and department stores, managers vary the number of servers to adjust to busy or slack periods.

Queue Characteristics

The order in which customers are served is defined by the *queue discipline*. The most common queue discipline is first-come, first-served (FCFS). In some situations, a queue may be structured as last-come, first-served (LCFS); just think of the in-box on a clerk's desk. In many situations, such as repairing electrical lines after a major storm, work is prioritized according to criticality.

System Configuration

The customers, servers, and queues in a queuing system can be arranged in various ways. Three common queuing configurations are as follows:

1. *One or more parallel servers fed by a single queue*. This is the typical configuration used by many banks and airline ticket counters, as well as quick-service restaurants like Wendy's.
2. *Several parallel servers fed by their own individual queues*. Most supermarkets and discount retailers use this type of system.
3. *A combination of several queues in series*. This structure is common when multiple processing operations exist, such as in manufacturing facilities or hospitals. Some service systems have this configuration. For example, in a voting facility, one might first wait to sign in and then wait for an open voting machine.

Queue Discipline

A **queue discipline** *is the manner in which new arrivals are ordered or prioritized for service*. For the airport problem, and in general for most customer-oriented waiting lines, the waiting units are ordered on a first-come, first-served (FCFS) basis, referred to as a FCFS queue discipline. Other types of queue disciplines are also prevalent. These include the following:

- *Shortest processing time*, which is discussed in Chapter 14. SPT tries to maximize the number of units processed, but units with long processing times must wait long periods of time to be processed, if at all.
- A *random queue discipline* provides service to units at random regardless of when they arrived for service. In some cultures, a random queue discipline is used for serving people instead of the FCFS rule.
- *Triage* is used by hospital emergency rooms based on the criticality of the patient's injury as they arrive. That is, a patient with a broken neck receives top priority over another patient with a cut finger.
- *Preemption* is the use of a criterion that allows new arrivals to displace members of the current queue and become the first to receive the service. This criterion could be wealth, society status, age, government official, and so on. Triage is a form of preemption based on the patient's degree and severity of medical need.
- *Reservations and appointments* allocate a specific amount of capacity at a specific time for a specific customer or processing unit. Legal and medical services, for example, book their day using appointment queuing disciplines.

Queuing models can represent many of these situations, but simulation is often required to analyze complex systems, servers, and customer behavior.

Queuing Behavior

People's behavior in queues and service encounters is often unpredictable. **Reneging** *is the process of a customer entering the waiting line but later decides to leave the line and server system.* **Balking** *is the process of a customer evaluating the waiting line and server system and decides not to enter the queue.* In both situations, the customer leaves the system, may not return, and a current sale or all future sales may be lost. Most analytical models assume the customer's behavior is patient and steady and they will not renege or balk; such situations are difficult to model without simulation.

QUEUING MODEL PERFORMANCE METRICS

Queuing models translate the customer, service, and queue characteristics into measures of system performance. Thus, queuing models are descriptive in nature. The two basic measures by which we evaluate the performance of a queuing system are as follows:

1. The quality of the service provided to the customer.
2. The efficiency of the service operation and the cost of providing the service.

Various numerical measures of performance can be used to evaluate the quality of the service provided to the customer. These include the following:

- Waiting time in the queue
- Time in the system (waiting time plus service time)
- Completion by a deadline

The efficiency of the service operation can be evaluated by computing such measures as the following:

- Average queue length
- Average number of customers in the system (queue plus in service)
- Throughput—the rate at which customers are served
- Server utilization—percentage of time servers are busy
- Percentage of customers who balk or renege

Usually we can use these measures to compute an operating cost in order to compare alternative system configurations.

The most common measures of queuing system performance and the symbols used to denote them are given in Exhibit F.1. These measures are called the *operating characteristics* of the queuing system.

Many different queuing models exist, each based on unique assumptions about the nature of arrivals, service times, and other aspects of the system. The simplest and most common model is for a single- or multiple-channel queue with Poisson arrivals and exponential service times.

Single Server Queuing Model

The queuing model presented in this section can be applied to waiting line situations that meet these assumptions or conditions:

1. The waiting line has a single server.
2. The pattern of arrivals follows a Poisson probability distribution with a mean arrival rate, λ. This is the average number of customers arriving each time period.

EXHIBIT F.1 Measures of Queuing System Performance

Measure	Symbol
Average number in the system (queue plus in-service)	L
Average number in the queue	L_q
Average waiting time in the system (queue plus in-service)	W
Average time in the queue	W_q
Probability that the system is empty (servers are idle)	P_0

3. The service times follow an exponential probability distribution with a mean service rate, μ. This is the average number of customers that are serviced each time period.
4. The queue discipline is first-come, first-served (FCFS).
5. No balking or reneging is allowed.

Using the assumptions of Poisson arrivals and exponential service times, analysts have developed the following expressions to define the operating characteristics of a single-channel waiting line.

1. The probability that the system is empty (i.e., the probability of 0 units in both the queue and in service):

$$P_0 = (1 - \lambda/\mu) \tag{F.1}$$

2. The average number of units waiting for service in the queue:

$$L_q = \frac{\lambda^2}{\mu(\mu - \lambda)} \tag{F.2}$$

3. The average number of units in the system (queue and in service):

$$L = L_q + \lambda/\mu \tag{F.3}$$

4. The average time a unit spends waiting for service (time in queue):

$$W_q = L_q/\lambda \tag{F.4}$$

5. The average time a unit spends in the system (waiting time plus service time):

$$W = W_q + 1/\mu \tag{F.5}$$

6. The probability that an arriving unit has to wait for service:

$$P_w = \lambda/\mu \tag{F.6}$$

7. The probability of n units in the system (queue and in service):

$$P_n = (\lambda/\mu)^n P_0 \tag{F.7}$$

The values of the mean arrival rate, λ, and the mean service rate, μ, are clearly important components in these formulas. From formula F.7, we see that the ratio of these two values, λ/μ, is simply the probability that an arriving unit must wait because the server is busy. Thus, λ/μ is often referred to as the *utilization factor* for the waiting line. The formulas for determining the operating characteristics of a single server waiting line are applicable only when the utilization factor, λ/μ, is less than 1. This condition occurs when the mean service rate, μ, is greater than the mean arrival rate, λ, and hence when the service rate is sufficient to process or service all arrivals.

Example: A Queuing Model For An Airport Check-In Process

We will consider the problem of designing an automated check-in kiosk for passengers at an airport. Most major airlines now use automated kiosks to speed up the process of obtaining a boarding pass with an electronic ticket. Passengers either enter a confirmation number or scan their electronic ticket to print a boarding pass. A queuing analysis of the system will help to determine if the systems will provide adequate service to the airport passengers.

To develop a queuing model, we first need to quantify the arrival and service time characteristics.

Arrival Distribution Defining the arrival distribution for a waiting line consists of determining how many customers arrive for service in given periods of time, for example, the number of passengers arriving at the check-in kiosk during each one-, ten-, or 60-minute period. Because the number of passengers arriving each minute is not a constant, we need to define a probability distribution that will describe the passenger arrivals. The choice of time period is arbitrary—as long as the same time period is used consistently—and is often determined based on the rate of arrivals and the ease by which the data can be collected. Generally, the slower the rate of arrivals, the longer the time period chosen.

For many waiting lines, the arrivals occurring in a given period of time appear to have a random pattern—that is, although we may have a good estimate of the total number of expected arrivals, each arrival is independent of other arrivals, and we cannot predict when it will occur. In such cases, a good description of the arrival pattern is obtained from the Poisson probability distribution:

$$P(x) = \frac{\lambda^x e^{-\lambda}}{x!} \quad \text{for } x = 0, 1, 2, \ldots \tag{F.8}$$

where:

x = number of arrivals in a specific period of time,
λ = average number of arrivals for the specific period of time, and
$e \approx 2.71828$.

For more information on the Poisson distribution see Supplement A: Probability and Statistics.

Airport planners have projected passenger volume through the year and estimate that passengers will arrive at an average rate of nine passengers per ten-minute periods during the peak activity times. Note that the choice of time period is arbitrary. We could have used an equivalent rate of 54 passengers per hour or 0.9 passengers per minute—as long as we are consistent in using the same time period in our analysis. Therefore, in the Poisson distribution, the mean arrival rate is $\lambda = 9$. We can use formula F.8 to compute the probability of x passenger arrivals in a ten-minute period.

$$P(x) = \frac{9^x e^{-9}}{x!} \quad \text{for } x = 0, 1, 2, \ldots$$

Sample calculations for $x = 0$, 5, and 10 passenger arrivals during a one-minute period follow.

$$P(0) = \frac{9^0 e^{-9}}{0!} = 0.0001$$

$$P(5) = \frac{9^5 e^{-9}}{5!} = 0.0607$$

$$P(10) = \frac{9^{10} e^{-9}}{10!} = 0.1186$$

Using the Poisson probability distribution, we expect it to be very rare to have a ten-minute period in which no passengers ($x = 0$) arrive for screening, because $P(0) = .0001$. Five passenger arrivals occur with a probability $P(5) = .0607$, and 10 with a probability of $P(10) = 0.1186$. The probabilities for other numbers of passenger arrivals can also be computed.

Service Time Distribution A service-time probability distribution is needed to describe how long it takes to check in a passenger at the kiosk. This length of time is referred to as the service time for the passenger. Although many passengers will complete the check-in process in a relatively short time, others might take a longer time because of unfamiliarity with the kiosk operation, ticketing problems, flight changes, and so on. Thus, we expect service times to vary from passenger to passenger. In the development of waiting-line models, operations researchers have found that the exponential probability distribution can often be used to describe the service-time distribution. Formula F.9 defines the exponential probability distribution:

$$f(t) = \mu e^{-\mu t} \quad \text{for } t \geq 0. \tag{F.9}$$

where:

t = service time (expressed in number of time periods),
μ = average number of customers that the service facility can handle in a specific period of time, and
$e \approx 2.71828$.

For more information on the exponential distribution see Supplement A: Probability and Statistics.

It is important to use the same time period used for defining arrivals in defining the average service rate! If we use an exponential service-time distribution, the probability of a service being completed within t time periods is given by:

$$P(\text{service time} \leq t \text{ time periods}) = 1 - e^{-\mu t} \tag{F.10}$$

By collecting data on service times for similar check-in systems in operation at other airports, we find that the system can handle an average of 10 passengers per ten-minute period. Using a mean service rate of $\mu = 10$ customers per ten-minute period in formula F.10, we find that the probability of a check-in service being completed within t ten-minute periods is

$$P(\text{service time} \leq t \text{ ten-minute time periods}) = 1 - e^{-10t}$$

Now we can compute the probability that a passenger completes the service within any specified time, t. For example, for one minute, we set t = 0.1 (as a fraction of a ten-minute period). Some example calculations are

$$P(\text{service time} \leq 1 \text{ minute}) = 1 - e^{-10(0.1)} = 1 - e^{-1} = 0.6321.$$
$$P(\text{service time} \leq 2.5 \text{ minutes}) = 1 - e^{-10(0.25)} = 1 - e^{-2.5} = 0.9179.$$

Thus, using the exponential distribution, we would expect 63.21 percent of the passengers to be serviced in one minute or less, and 91.79 percent in 2.5 minutes or less.

Applying the Single Server Queuing Model Using the mean arrival rate of $\lambda = 9$ passengers per ten-minute period and the mean service rate of $\mu = 10$ passengers per ten-minute period, we can use formulas (F.1) through (F.6) to determine the operating characteristics of the airline check-in process:

1. The probability that the system is empty:

$$P_0 = (1 - \lambda/\mu) = (1 - 9/10) = 0.10$$

2. The average number of customers waiting for service:

$$L_q = \frac{\lambda^2}{\mu(\mu - \lambda)} = \frac{9^2}{10(10 - 9)} = \frac{81}{10} = 8.1 \text{ passengers}$$

3. The average number of customers in the system:

$$L = L_q + \lambda/\mu = 8.1 + 9/10 = 9.0 \text{ passengers}$$

4. The average time a customer spends waiting for service:

$W_q = L_q/\lambda = 8.1/9 = 0.9$ ten-minute periods, or equivalently, 9 minutes per passenger

5. The average time a customer spends in the system:

$$W = W_q + 1/\mu$$
$$= 0.9 \text{ ten-minute periods} + 0.1 \text{ ten-minute periods}$$
$$= 1 \text{ ten-minute period, or equivalently 10 minutes per passenger}$$

6. The probability that an arriving customer has to wait for service:

$$P_w = \lambda/\mu = 9/10 = 0.9$$

7. The probability of n units in the system (queue and in service). We could use formula E.7 to tabulate the probability of n customers in the system (however, it is much easier to use the Excel template). For example:

$$P_1 = (\lambda/\mu)^n P_0 = (9/10)^1(0.1) = 0.0900$$
$$P_2 = (\lambda/\mu)^n P_0 = (9/10)^2(0.1) = 0.0810$$
$$P_3 = (\lambda/\mu)^n P_0 = (9/10)^3(0.1) = 0.0729$$
$$P_4 = (\lambda/\mu)^n P_0 = (9/10)^4(0.1) = 0.0656$$

Using this information, we can learn several important things about the check-in operation. In particular, we see that passengers wait an average of $W_q = 9$ minutes at the kiosk. With this as the average, many passengers wait even longer. In airport operations with passengers rushing to meet plane connections, this waiting time might be judged to be undesirably high. In addition, the facts that the average number of passengers waiting in line is $L_q = 8.1$ and that 90 percent of the arriving passengers must wait to check-in might suggest to the operations manager that something should be done to improve the efficiency of the process.

Excel Template for Single Server Queuing

The templates in MindTap include one, *Single Server Queue*, for the single server queuing model, shown in Exhibit F.2, using the airline kiosk example.

The template may be used to examine what-if scenarios. For example, we assumed an arrival rate of 9 and a service rate of 10 per ten-minute period. As the figures are based on airport planners' estimates, they are subject to forecasting errors. We might examine the effect of changes in the mean arrival rate from 7 to 10 passengers per period. Such a summary is shown in Exhibit F.3. Note that this cannot be done in the student-protected template.

EXHIBIT F.2 ***Single Server Queue*** **Excel Template**

	A	B
1	Single Server Queueing Model	
2	Enter the data only in the yellow cells.	
3		
4	Lambda	9
5	Mu	10
6		
7	Probability system is empty	0.100
8	Average number waiting for service in the queue	8.100
9	Average number in system (queue and in service)	9.000
10	Average time waiting for service (time in queue)	0.900
11	Average waiting time in system (waiting time plus service time)	1.000
12	Probability arrival has to wait	0.900
13	n =	3
14	Probability of n units in the system (queue and in service)	0.073

EXHIBIT F.3 What-if Analysis of Changing the Arrival Rate

Lambda	7	8	9	10
Mu	10	10	10	10
Probability system is empty	0.300	0.200	0.100	0.000
Average number waiting for service in the queue	1.633	3.200	8.100	#DIV/0!
Average number in system (queue and in service)	2.333	4.000	9.000	#DIV/0!
Average time waiting for service (time in queue)	0.233	0.400	0.900	#DIV/0!
Average waiting time in system (waiting time plus service time)	0.333	0.500	1.000	#DIV/0!
Probability arrival has to wait	0.700	0.800	0.900	1.000

These results tell us that if the mean arrival rate is seven passengers per period, the system functions acceptably. On the average, only 1.63 passengers are waiting and the average waiting time of 0.23(10 minutes) = 2.3 minutes appears acceptable. However, we see that the mean arrival rate of nine passengers per period provides undesirable waiting characteristics, and if the rate increases to 10 passengers per period, the system as proposed is completely inadequate. When $\lambda = \mu$, the operating characteristics are not defined, meaning that these times and numbers of passengers grow infinitely large (i.e., when $\lambda = \mu \rightarrow \infty$). These results show that airport planners need to consider design modifications that will improve the efficiency of the check-in process.

If a new process can be designed that will increase the passenger-service rate, the system performance will improve. One way is to improve the technology so that more customers can be served within the ten-minute period (e.g., increasing the mean service rate, μ from 10 passengers per ten-minute period to 11 or 12). A more practical option is to add additional kiosks. By having more than one server, the check-in process can be dramatically improved.

Multiple Server Queuing Model

In a multiple server queuing model, customers wait in a single line, and move to the next available server, as illustrated in Exhibit F.4. Note that this is a different situation from one in which each server has a distinct queue, such as with highway tollbooths, bank teller windows, or supermarket checkout lines.

EXHIBIT F.4 A Two Server Queuing System

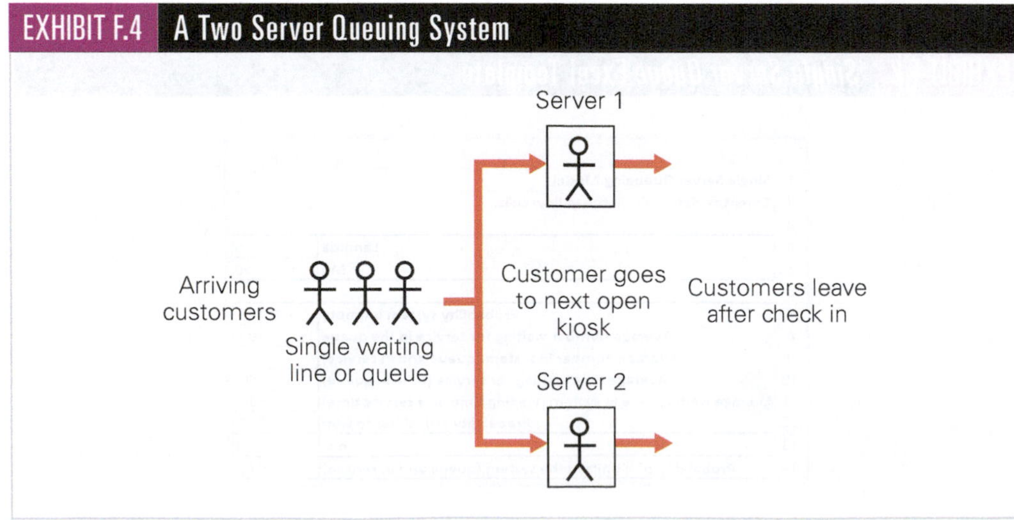

In this section we present formulas that can be used to compute various operating characteristics for a multiple-server waiting line. The model we will use can be applied to situations that meet these assumptions:

1. The waiting line has two or more identical servers.
2. The arrivals follow a Poisson probability distribution with a mean arrival rate of λ.
3. The service times have an exponential distribution.
4. The mean service rate, μ, is the same for each server.
5. The arrivals wait in a single line and then move to the first open server for service.
6. The queue discipline is first-come, first-served (FCFS).
7. No balking or reneging is allowed.

Using these assumptions, we can determine the operating characteristics of the multiple-server waiting line mathematically. Let

k = number of servers,
λ = mean arrival rate for the system, and
μ = mean service rate for each server.

The following equations apply to multiple-server waiting lines for which the overall mean service rate, $k\mu$, is greater than the mean arrival rate, λ. In such cases, the service rate is sufficient to process all arrivals.

1. The probability that all k service channels are idle (i.e., the probability of zero units in the system):

$$P_0 = \frac{1}{\left[\sum_{n=0}^{k-1} \frac{(\lambda/\mu)^n}{n!}\right] + \frac{(\lambda/\mu)^k}{(k-1)!}\frac{\mu}{k\mu - \lambda}} \tag{F.11}$$

2. The probability of n units in the system:

$$P_n = \frac{(\lambda/\mu)^n}{k!k^{n-k}} P_0 \quad \text{for } n > k$$
$$P_n = \frac{(\lambda/\mu)^n}{n!} P_0 \quad \text{for } 0 \leq n \leq \text{k} \tag{F.12}$$

3. The average number of units waiting for service:

$$L_q = \frac{(\lambda/\mu)^k \lambda\mu}{(k-1)!(k\mu - \lambda)^2} P_0 \tag{F.13}$$

4. The average number of units in the system:

$$L = L_q + \lambda/\mu \tag{F.14}$$

5. The average time a unit spends waiting for service:

$$W_q = L_q/\lambda \tag{F.15}$$

6. The average time a unit spends in the system (waiting time plus service time):

$$W = W_q + 1/\mu \tag{F.16}$$

7. The probability that an arriving unit must wait for service:

$$P_w = \frac{1}{k!}\left(\frac{\lambda}{\mu}\right)^k \frac{k\mu}{k\mu - \lambda} P_0 \tag{F.17}$$

Although the equations describing the operating characteristics of a multiple-server queuing model with Poisson arrivals and exponential service times are somewhat more complex than the single server equations, they provide the same information and are used exactly as we used the results from the single-channel model. They are best computed on a spreadsheet.

Excel Template for Multiple Server Queuing

Exhibit F.5 shows the *Multiple Server Queue* template in MindTap, which is designed to compute operating characteristics for up to eight servers in the multiple-server queuing model using the arrival and service rates for the airline kiosk example.

We see that the performance of the system improves as additional kiosks are added. With three servers, we see a significant improvement over two servers in the operating characteristics; beyond this, the improvement is negligible. Although we noted that the queue will grow indefinitely when $\lambda \geqslant \mu$ in the single server queuing model (see Exhibit F.3), we can use the spreadsheet to show that even if the mean arrival rate for passengers exceeds the estimated nine passengers per hour, the two-channel system should operate well up to values of $\lambda < 20$.

EXHIBIT F.5 Multiple Server Queue Excel Template

	A	B	C	D	E	F	G	H
1	Multiple Server Queueing Model			Copyright © Cengage Learning				
2	Enter the data only in the yellow cells.			Not for commercial use.				
3								
4	Lambda	9						
5	Mu	10						
6								
7	Number of servers	2	3	4	5	6	7	8
8	Probability system is empty	0.379	0.403	0.406	0.407	0.407	0.407	0.407
9	Average number waiting for service in the queue	0.229	0.030	0.004	0.001	0.000	0.000	0.000
10	Average number in system (queue and in service)	1.129	0.930	0.904	0.901	0.900	0.900	0.900
11	Average time waiting for service (time in queue)	0.025	0.003	0.000	0.000	0.000	0.000	0.000
12	verage waiting time in system (waiting time plus service time)	0.125	0.103	0.100	0.100	0.100	0.100	0.100
13	Probability arrival has to wait	0.279	0.070	0.014	0.002	0.000	0.000	0.000

SUPPLEMENT G
Simulation

Many practical problems are so complex that it is difficult to compute performance measures analytically or incorporate uncertainty. Simulation modeling can overcome many of these difficulties. **Simulation** *is the process of developing and analyzing a logical model of a system, process, or management decision, and conducting computer-based experiments with the model to describe, explain, and predict the behavior of the system or outcomes associated with the decision.* In this supplement, we introduce the basic concepts of computer simulation.

Simulation has many advantages. One advantage is that the simulation model provides a convenient experimental laboratory. Simulation models allow us to draw conclusions about the behavior of a real system by studying the behavior of a model of the system, usually with random sequences of events similar to what we might observe in the real system. An analyst can perform "what if" studies, that is, change the design characteristics or operating rules to determine their impact without changing the actual system. For instance, the number of jobs entering a manufacturing process can be changed to learn the effect of greater demand on waiting times. Another advantage is the modeler does not have to disrupt the current process to examine alternative equipment, material and information flows, decision rules, and configurations.

However, disadvantages also exist. These include the difficulty of modeling real systems and their performance relationships, collecting the appropriate input data, selection of the correct probability distributions to model uncertainty, and accuracy of outputs. Another challenge with simulation is designing good experiments to test for statistically significant differences in various scenarios and changes in decision variables. It is easy to make mistakes in programming and structuring the simulation model. Finally, sometimes the results of the simulation are not very traceable so it is hard to clearly determine cause and effect.

Some simulation models, called *Monte-Carlo simulation models*, are based on repeated sampling of uncertain inputs in spreadsheets and are used to evaluate risks in management decisions. These models often arise in finance and marketing applications. *Dynamic*, or *system simulation models* are more prevalent in operations management. Dynamic systems involve processes that consist of interacting events occurring over time. For example, nearly everyone experiences waiting lines, or queues, at supermarkets, banks, toll booths, telephone call centers, restaurants, and amusement parks. Many other waiting line systems involve "customers" other than people—for example, messages in communication systems, trucks waiting to be unloaded at a warehouse, work in process at a manufacturing plant, and photocopying machines awaiting repair by a traveling technician. In these systems, customers arrive at random times, and service times are rarely predictable. Managers of these systems would be interested in knowing how long customers have to wait, the length of waiting lines, the utilization of the servers, and other measures of performance. Another example of a dynamic system is an inventory management system. Managers would be interested in knowing inventory levels, numbers of lost sales or backorders incurred, and the costs of operating the system. More complex examples of dynamic systems include entire production systems, which might incorporate aspects of both waiting lines and inventory systems, as well as material movement, information flow, and so on.

Simulation has the advantage of being able to incorporate nearly any practical assumption and thus is the most flexible tool for dealing with dynamic systems. Dynamic simulation models trace the detailed logic or actions that occur in the system in a step-by-step fashion over time. The model is usually described by a logical flowchart detailing the sequence of steps performed.

For example, in simulating a manufacturing process, the program would track each job as it moves from one workstation to another and maintain statistics on how long the job may have waited for processing and the total time taken to complete the job. Probability distributions are used to characterize the uncertainty in processing or transit times through the system, and the model samples from these distributions to generate randomness in system behavior to show the variation in system performance that might occur under real conditions. Other factors such as equipment breakdowns or delays can be included in the simulation to add realism to the model. In practice, simulating dynamic systems is best accomplished using powerful commercial software; however, we can use Excel quite easily for simple applications to illustrate the concepts.

Using Probability Distributions in Simulation

In simulation, we model uncertainty using probability distributions. (See Supplement A for a review of probability distributions.) Determining the appropriate probability distributions is crucial to building good simulation models. In many cases, historical data may be available that will characterize the uncertainty. For example, maintenance records might provide data on machine failure rates and repair times, or observers might collect data on service times in a bank or post office. This provides a factual basis for choosing the appropriate probability distribution to model the input variable. We can draw upon the properties of well-known probability distributions to help choose a representative distribution. For example, a normal distribution is symmetric, with a peak in the middle. Exponential data are very positively skewed, with no negative values. Thus, if a histogram of the data resembles the shape of some common probability distribution, we could use that distribution in the simulation. If the data do not seem to correspond to any common distribution, we simply might use the frequency distribution of the data (i.e., often called an empirical distribution). When historical data are not available, we simply have to use judgment and experience to choose a distribution. For example, we might use a uniform distribution when all we know is the smallest and largest value that the uncertain variable might assume.

Random Numbers and Random Variates

The basis for generating random samples from probability distributions—which underlies simulation—is the concept of a random number. In the context of simulation, *a* **random number** *is a number that is uniformly distributed between 0 and 1.* Technically speaking, computers cannot generate truly random numbers because they must use a predictable algorithm. However, the algorithms are designed to generate a sequence of numbers that appear to be random. In Excel, we may generate a random number that is greater than or equal to 0 and less than 1 within any cell using the function RAND( ). This function has no arguments; therefore, nothing should be placed within the parentheses (but the parentheses are required). You should be aware that unless the automatic recalculation feature is suppressed, whenever any cell in the spreadsheet is modified, the values in any cell containing the RAND( ) function will change. Automatic recalculation can be changed to manual by choosing *Calculation Options* under the *Formulas* tab in Excel. Under manual recalculation mode, the worksheet is recalculated only when the F9 key (in Excel for Windows) is pressed, or the *Calculate Now* button in the *Formulas* tab is clicked.

A value randomly generated from a specified probability distribution is called a **random variate**. Most techniques for generating random variates involve transforming random numbers into outcomes from a probability distribution. Excel functions and formulas are available to do this for some common probability distributions. For instance, to generate a random variate from a uniform distribution between a and b, consider the following formula:

$$U = a + (b - a) * \text{RAND( )} \tag{G.1}$$

If RAND( ) = 0, then $U = a$, and if RAND( ) = 1, then $U = b$. As RAND( ) varies between 0 and 1, U will vary between a and b. If you want to generate whole numbers from a uniform distribution between a and b (called a **discrete uniform distribution**), use the Excel function RANDBETWEEN(a, b). Exponential random variates can be generated easily using the Excel formula $= -(1 > \lambda)$°LN(RAND( )), where $1/\lambda = \mu$ is the mean of the exponential distribution and LN is the Excel function for the natural logarithm.

Normal random variates can be generated in Excel using inverse functions. Inverse functions find the value for a distribution that has a specified cumulative probability. For normal distributions, we may use the function NORM.INV(*probability, mean, standard_deviation*). To use this function to generate random variates, simply enter RAND( ) in place of *probability* in the function. Thus, NORM.INV(RAND( ), *mean, standard_deviation*) generates a random variate from a normal distribution with a specified mean and standard deviation. This function may be embedded in cell formulas and will generate new values whenever the worksheet is recalculated.

Generating a random variate from a discrete probability distribution is quite easy. Suppose that we wish to generate random values of demand in a simulation model from the following frequency distribution:

Demand	Frequency
5	12
10	23
15	38
20	27

Convert the frequencies into probabilities by dividing each frequency by the total (100), and then find the cumulative probabilities.

Demand	Probability	Cumulative Probability
5	0.12	0.12
10	0.23	0.35
15	0.38	0.73
20	0.27	1.00

Note that the values of the cumulative probability divide the interval from 0 to 1 into smaller intervals that correspond to the probabilities of the demands. For example, the interval from 0 up to but not including 0.12 has a probability of $0.12 - 0 = 0.12$ and corresponds to a demand of 5; the interval from 0.12 up to but not including 0.35 has a probability of $0.35 - 0.12 = 0.23$ and corresponds to a demand of 10—and so on as summarized below:

Random Number Interval	Demand
≥ 0 and < 0.12	5
≥ 0.12 and < 0.35	10
≥ 0.35 and < 0.73	15
≥ 0.73 and < 1.0	20

Now, if we generate a random number, it must fall within one of these intervals. Choosing the corresponding value of demand provides a random outcome of the demand in the simulation model.

EXHIBIT G.1 Generating Outcomes from a Discrete Probability Distribution

	A	B	C	D	E	F
1	Demand	Probability	Cumulative Probability		Random Number	Demand
2	5	0.12	0.12		0.924958157	20
3	10	0.23	0.35		0.147980113	10
4	15	0.38	0.73		0.996568244	20
5	20	0.27	1		0.706102893	15
6					0.698783497	15
7	Random Number Interval		Demand		0.105473195	5
8	0	0.12	5		0.744952461	20
9	0.12	0.35	10		0.000172984	5
10	0.35	0.73	15		0.199649326	10
11	0.73	1	20		0.657179804	15

We may implement this easily in Excel using the VLOOKUP function. Exhibit G.1 shows a spreadsheet that does this. The random number intervals and demand outcomes are specified in the range A8:C11. In column E, we generated 10 random numbers. In cell F2, we enter the formula: =VLOOKUP(E2, $A$8:$C$11, 3) and copy it down the column. This function takes the value of the random number in cell E2, finds the last number in the first column of the table range ($A$8:$C$11) that is less than the random number, and returns the value in the third column of the table range. For example, the first random number is 0.45, which falls between 0.35 and 0.73; thus, the corresponding demand is 15. You should check several others to understand how the demands were generated. An alternative way to generate outcomes in this fashion is simply to embed RAND( ) within the VLOOKUP function, for instance, =VLOOKUP(RAND(), $A$8:$C$11, 3). This is useful when we need to generate uncertain inputs within spreadsheet models. We will see this used in the following example.

Example: A Simulation Model For A Production-Inventory Decision

Hill Manufacturing supplies various engine components to manufacturers of motorcycles on a just-in-time basis. Planned production capacity for one component is 100 units per shift, and the plant operates one shift per day. Because of fluctuations in customers' assembly operations, however, demand fluctuates and is historically between 80 and 130 units per day. To maintain sufficient inventory to meet its just-in-time commitments, the operations manager is considering a policy to run a second shift the next day if inventory falls to 50 or below at the end of a day (after the daily demand is known). For the annual budget planning process, he needs to know how many additional shifts will be needed.

The fundamental equation that governs this process each day is

$$\text{Ending Inventory} = \text{Beginning Inventory} + \text{Production} - \text{Demand} \qquad (G.2)$$

Exhibit G.2 shows a portion of a spreadsheet model (Excel file *Hill Manufacturing*) that simulates 260 working days (one year) and count the number of additional shifts that are required. We assume that on day 1, the initial inventory and production are 100 units. The Excel function =RANDBETWEEN(80, 130) is used in column C to generate discrete uniform random variates for the demand. In column D, we use an IF function to determine whether an additional production shift is scheduled based on the beginning inventory in column B. For example, the formula in cell D6 is =100+IF(B6<50, 100). Then in column E, the ending inventory is calculated using equation (G.1); this is copied to the beginning inventory for the next day. The chart shows the ending inventory and production each day. The spikes in the production series show when additional shifts were scheduled. If you recalculate the spreadsheet, the results will change.

EXHIBIT G.2 Portion of Excel Simulation of Hill Manufacturing Problem

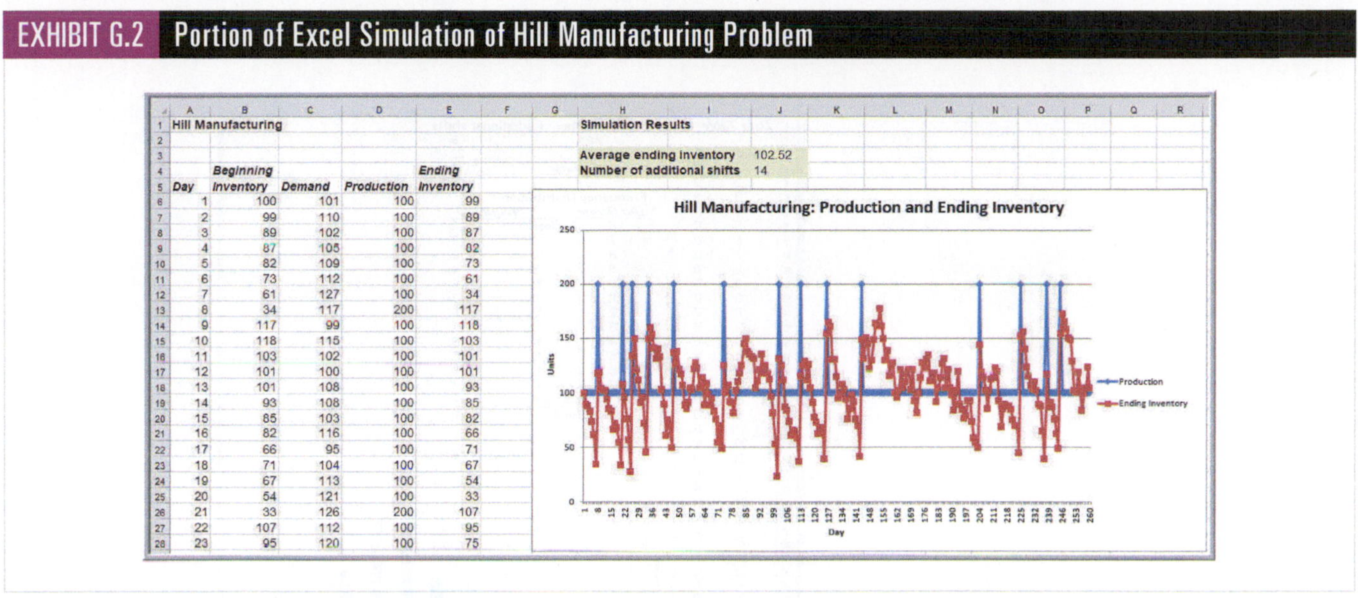

Hill Manufacturing

Day	Beginning Inventory	Demand	Production	Ending Inventory
1	100	101	100	99
2	99	110	100	89
3	89	102	100	87
4	87	105	100	82
5	82	109	100	73
6	73	112	100	61
7	61	127	100	34
8	34	117	200	117
9	117	99	100	118
10	118	115	100	103
11	103	102	100	101
12	101	100	100	101
13	101	108	100	93
14	93	108	100	85
15	85	103	100	82
16	82	116	100	66
17	66	95	100	71
18	71	104	100	67
19	67	113	100	54
20	54	121	100	33
21	33	126	200	107
22	107	112	100	95
23	95	120	100	75

Simulation Results

Average ending inventory	102.52
Number of additional shifts	14

The model shown in Exhibit G.2 represents a simulation of one year. If we repeat the simulation (by recalculating the spreadsheet), the results, such as the average ending inventory and number of additional shifts, will change. To make a rational decision, the operations manager at Hill Manufacturing needs to understand the variability in the number of possible shifts because of the uncertainty in the model. Of course, we can recalculate the spreadsheet numerous times and record the results; however, there is a much easier way to do this automatically in Excel using a data table.

First, construct a one-way data table by listing the number of trials down a column and referencing the cell associated with the number of shifts (cell J4) in the cell above and to the right of the list (cell U3). This is shown in Exhibit G.3, and we used 100 trials, extending from cell T4 to cell T103. Select the range of the table (T4:U103), and then from the *Data* tab in Excel, select *Data Table* under the *What-If Analysis* menu. In the *Data Table* dialog (see Exhibit G.4)—and here's the trick—enter any *blank* cell in the spreadsheet in the *Column Input Cell* field. Make sure that this is one you will not use. When you click *OK* in the *Data Table* dialog, the values in column U will display the simulation results for the number of additional shifts.

Why does this work? When you create a data table, the *Column Input Cell* generally refers to some parameter in the model. The data table simply takes these values, replaces them in the model, and then displays the output. Because we used a blank cell for the *Column Input Cell*, the trial numbers do not affect the model. However, for each trial, the spreadsheet is recalculated. Because we used the RAND function to generate random variates, each recalculation uses different values for the uncertain inputs. Because you may want to preserve the results for subsequent analysis, we suggest setting the *Calculations Options* in the *Formulas* tab to *Automatic Except for Data Tables*.

The last step in the simulation process is to analyze the results using various statistical tools such as summary statistics, percentiles, confidence intervals, and frequency distributions and histograms. We don't recommend using Excel *Data Analysis* tools because if you wish to recalculate the spreadsheet and run a new simulation, the results will not update. Instead, use Excel functions. An easy way to compute a frequency distribution is to use the Excel function FREQUENCY(*data array, bin array*). This is an "array" function and returns values in a range of cells. When you enter an array formula, you must first select the range in which to place the results. Then, after entering the formula, you must press Ctrl+Shift+Enter in Windows or

EXHIBIT G.3 Data Table Replication of the Hill Manufacturing Simulation Model

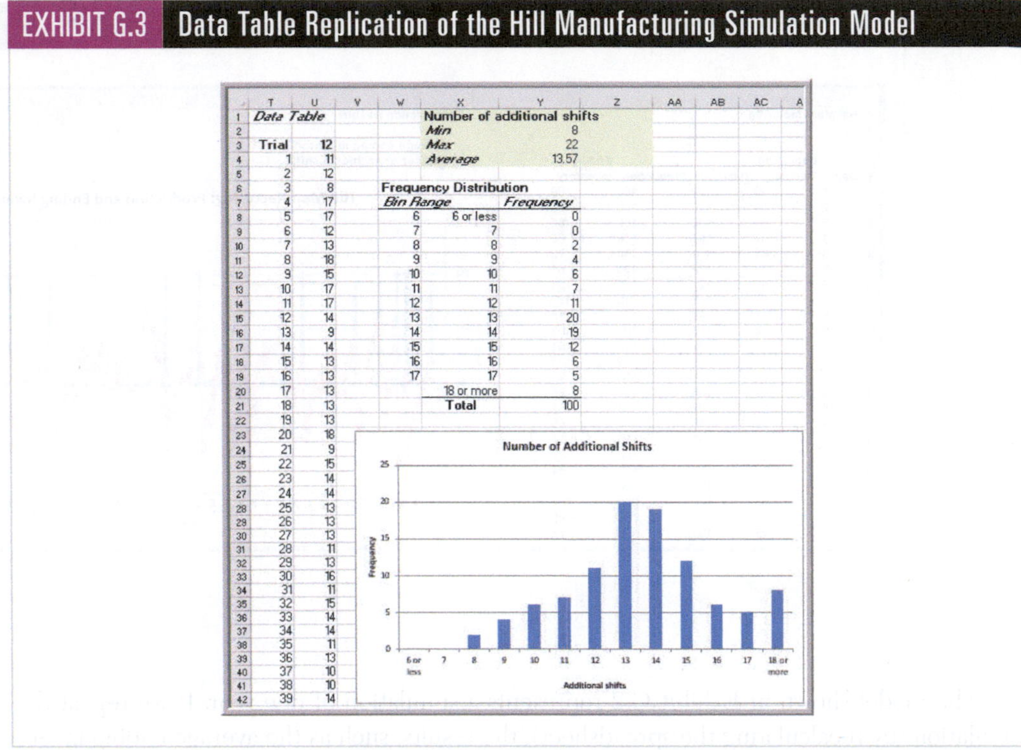

	T	U	V	W	X	Y
1	*Data Table*				Number of additional shifts	
2					*Min*	8
3	Trial	12			*Max*	22
4	1	11			*Average*	13.57
5	2	12				
6	3	8		Frequency Distribution		
7	4	17		*Bin Range*		*Frequency*
8	5	17		6	6 or less	0
9	6	12		7	7	0
10	7	13		8	8	2
11	8	18		9	9	4
12	9	15		10	10	6
13	10	17		11	11	7
14	11	17		12	12	11
15	12	14		13	13	20
16	13	9		14	14	19
17	14	14		15	15	12
18	15	13		16	16	6
19	16	13		17	17	5
20	17	13			18 or more	8
21	18	13			Total	100
22	19	13				
23	20	18				
24	21	9				
25	22	15				
26	23	14				
27	24	14				
28	25	13				
29	26	13				
30	27	13				
31	28	11				
32	29	13				
33	30	16				
34	31	11				
35	32	15				
36	33	14				
37	34	14				
38	35	11				
39	36	13				
40	37	10				
41	38	10				
42	39	14				

EXHIBIT G.4 Data Table Dialog

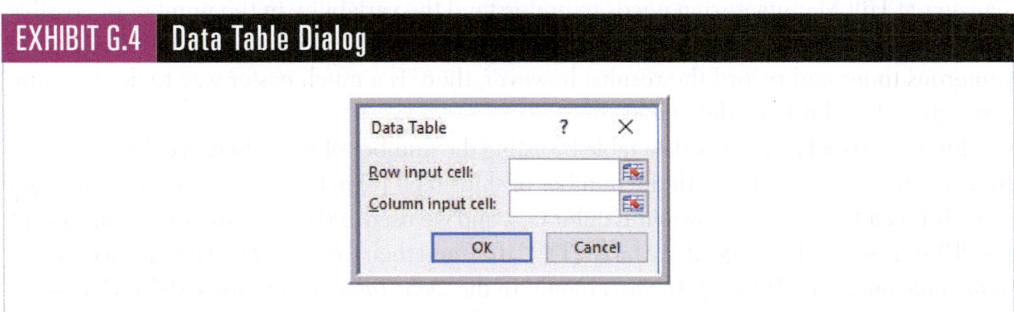

Command+Shift+Enter on a Mac simultaneously. For example, in Exhibit G.3, we selected the range Y8:Y20, then entered =FREQUENCY(U4:U103, W8W20), and pressed Ctrl(or Command)+Shift+Enter. This enters the frequencies of the number of additional shifts in column Y. Then simply chart the frequencies in an Excel column chart to create a histogram.

From Exhibit G.3, we see that while the average number of additional shifts is around 13 or 14, considerable variation exists among simulation runs. The histogram shows that they may vary from as low as 6 to more than 18. To be safe, the budget should plan on a higher number of shifts than the average.

Simulation models are costly to build and maintain and they take a long time to create. Teams of experts and programmers can work years on some supply chain simulation models. Nike, for example, spent over $500 million over decades on developing a global supply chain system with the help of SAP's Enterprise Resource Planning (ERP) software and Llamasoft, Inc. logistic system. Nike has hundreds of contract manufacturers around the world producing a wide assortment of shoes, clothing, and sports apparel. Their products are sold in over 290 countries using hundreds of distribution centers and 140,000 retail stores. Simulation coupled with analytical models is the only way to truly capture the scale and complexity of Nike's global supply chain. Ultimately, simulation is another tool to support better management decision making.

APPENDIX A

Areas for the Cumulative Standard Normal Distribution

Entries in the table below give the area under the standard normal distribution to the left of z. This table applies to negative values of z. For example, for $z = -1.25$, the area to the left of z is 0.10565.

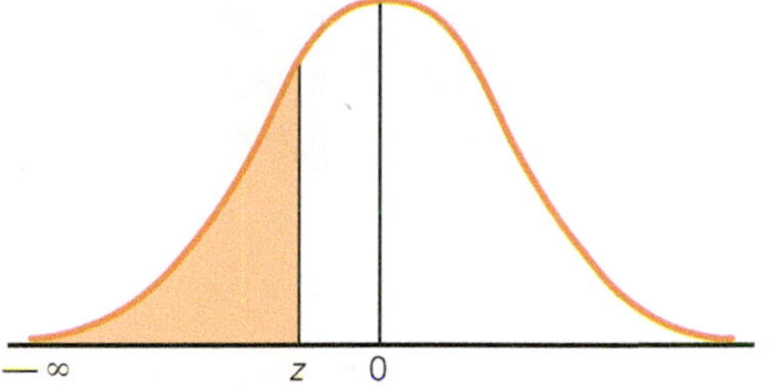

z	0	0.01	0.02	0.03	0.04	0.05	0.06	0.07	0.08	0.09
−3.9	0.00005	0.00005	0.00004	0.00004	0.00004	0.00004	0.00004	0.00004	0.00003	0.00003
−3.8	0.00007	0.00007	0.00007	0.00006	0.00006	0.00006	0.00006	0.00005	0.00005	0.00005
−3.7	0.00011	0.00010	0.00010	0.00010	0.00009	0.00009	0.00008	0.00008	0.00008	0.00008
−3.6	0.00016	0.00015	0.00015	0.00014	0.00014	0.00013	0.00013	0.00012	0.00012	0.00011
−3.5	0.00023	0.00022	0.00022	0.00021	0.00020	0.00019	0.00019	0.00018	0.00017	0.00017
−3.4	0.00034	0.00032	0.00031	0.00030	0.00029	0.00028	0.00027	0.00026	0.00025	0.00024
−3.3	0.00048	0.00047	0.00045	0.00043	0.00042	0.00040	0.00039	0.00038	0.00036	0.00035
−3.2	0.00069	0.00066	0.00064	0.00062	0.00060	0.00058	0.00056	0.00054	0.00052	0.00050
−3.1	0.00097	0.00094	0.00090	0.00087	0.00084	0.00082	0.00079	0.00076	0.00074	0.00071
−3	0.00135	0.00131	0.00126	0.00122	0.00118	0.00114	0.00111	0.00107	0.00104	0.00100
−2.9	0.00187	0.00181	0.00175	0.00169	0.00164	0.00159	0.00154	0.00149	0.00144	0.00139
−2.8	0.00256	0.00248	0.00240	0.00233	0.00226	0.00219	0.00212	0.00205	0.00199	0.00193
−2.7	0.00347	0.00336	0.00326	0.00317	0.00307	0.00298	0.00289	0.00280	0.00272	0.00264
−2.6	0.00466	0.00453	0.00440	0.00427	0.00415	0.00402	0.00391	0.00379	0.00368	0.00357
−2.5	0.00621	0.00604	0.00587	0.00570	0.00554	0.00539	0.00523	0.00508	0.00494	0.00480
−2.4	0.00820	0.00798	0.00776	0.00755	0.00734	0.00714	0.00695	0.00676	0.00657	0.00639
−2.3	0.01072	0.01044	0.01017	0.00990	0.00964	0.00939	0.00914	0.00889	0.00866	0.00842
−2.2	0.01390	0.01355	0.01321	0.01287	0.01255	0.01222	0.01191	0.01160	0.01130	0.01101
−2.1	0.01786	0.01743	0.01700	0.01659	0.01618	0.01578	0.01539	0.01500	0.01463	0.01426
−2	0.02275	0.02222	0.02169	0.02118	0.02068	0.02018	0.01970	0.01923	0.01876	0.01831
−1.9	0.02872	0.02807	0.02743	0.02680	0.02619	0.02559	0.02500	0.02442	0.02385	0.02330
−1.8	0.03593	0.03515	0.03438	0.03362	0.03288	0.03216	0.03144	0.03074	0.03005	0.02938
−1.7	0.04457	0.04363	0.04272	0.04182	0.04093	0.04006	0.03920	0.03836	0.03754	0.03673
−1.6	0.05480	0.05370	0.05262	0.05155	0.05050	0.04947	0.04846	0.04746	0.04648	0.04551
−1.5	0.06681	0.06552	0.06426	0.06301	0.06178	0.06057	0.05938	0.05821	0.05705	0.05592
−1.4	0.08076	0.07927	0.07780	0.07636	0.07493	0.07353	0.07215	0.07078	0.06944	0.06811
−1.3	0.09680	0.09510	0.09342	0.09176	0.09012	0.08851	0.08691	0.08534	0.08379	0.08226
−1.2	0.11507	0.11314	0.11123	0.10935	0.10749	0.10565	0.10383	0.10204	0.10027	0.09853
−1.1	0.13567	0.13350	0.13136	0.12924	0.12714	0.12507	0.12302	0.12100	0.11900	0.11702
−1	0.15866	0.15625	0.15386	0.15151	0.14917	0.14686	0.14457	0.14231	0.14007	0.13786
−0.9	0.18406	0.18141	0.17879	0.17619	0.17361	0.17106	0.16853	0.16602	0.16354	0.16109
−0.8	0.21186	0.20897	0.20611	0.20327	0.20045	0.19766	0.19489	0.19215	0.18943	0.18673

z	0	0.01	0.02	0.03	0.04	0.05	0.06	0.07	0.08	0.09
−0.7	0.24196	0.23885	0.23576	0.23270	0.22965	0.22663	0.22363	0.22065	0.21770	0.21476
−0.6	0.27425	0.27093	0.26763	0.26435	0.26109	0.25785	0.25463	0.25143	0.24825	0.24510
−0.5	0.30854	0.30503	0.30153	0.29806	0.29460	0.29116	0.28774	0.28434	0.28096	0.27760
−0.4	0.34458	0.34090	0.33724	0.33360	0.32997	0.32636	0.32276	0.31918	0.31561	0.31207
−0.3	0.38209	0.37828	0.37448	0.37070	0.36693	0.36317	0.35942	0.35569	0.35197	0.34827
−0.2	0.42074	0.41683	0.41294	0.40905	0.40517	0.40129	0.39743	0.39358	0.38974	0.38591
−0.1	0.46017	0.45620	0.45224	0.44828	0.44433	0.44038	0.43644	0.43251	0.42858	0.42465
0	0.50000	0.49601	0.49202	0.48803	0.48405	0.48006	0.47608	0.47210	0.46812	0.46414

Entries in the table below give the area under the standard normal distribution to the left of z. This table applies to positive values of z. For example, for $z = 2.33$, the area to the left of z is 0.99010.

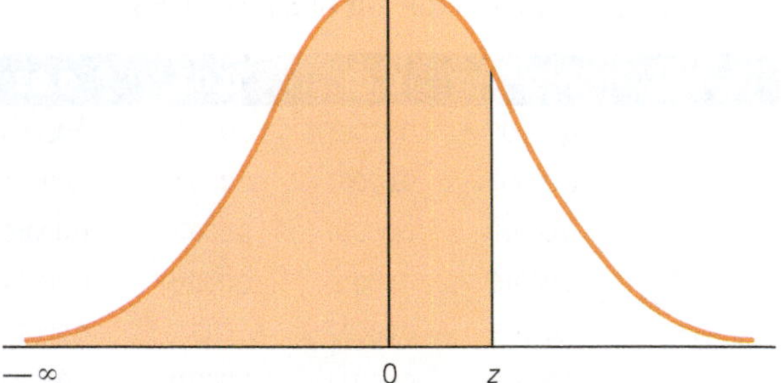

z	0	0.01	0.02	0.03	0.04	0.05	0.06	0.07	0.08	0.09
0	0.50000	0.50399	0.50798	0.51197	0.51595	0.51994	0.52392	0.52790	0.53188	0.53586
0.1	0.53983	0.54380	0.54776	0.55172	0.55567	0.55962	0.56356	0.56749	0.57142	0.57535
0.2	0.57926	0.58317	0.58706	0.59095	0.59483	0.59871	0.60257	0.60642	0.61026	0.61409
0.3	0.61791	0.62172	0.62552	0.62930	0.63307	0.63683	0.64058	0.64431	0.64803	0.65173
0.4	0.65542	0.65910	0.66276	0.66640	0.67003	0.67364	0.67724	0.68082	0.68439	0.68793
0.5	0.69146	0.69497	0.69847	0.70194	0.70540	0.70884	0.71226	0.71566	0.71904	0.72240
0.6	0.72575	0.72907	0.73237	0.73565	0.73891	0.74215	0.74537	0.74857	0.75175	0.75490
0.7	0.75804	0.76115	0.76424	0.76730	0.77035	0.77337	0.77637	0.77935	0.78230	0.78524
0.8	0.78814	0.79103	0.79389	0.79673	0.79955	0.80234	0.80511	0.80785	0.81057	0.81327
0.9	0.81594	0.81859	0.82121	0.82381	0.82639	0.82894	0.83147	0.83398	0.83646	0.83891
1	0.84134	0.84375	0.84614	0.84849	0.85083	0.85314	0.85543	0.85769	0.85993	0.86214
1.1	0.86433	0.86650	0.86864	0.87076	0.87286	0.87493	0.87698	0.87900	0.88100	0.88298
1.2	0.88493	0.88686	0.88877	0.89065	0.89251	0.89435	0.89617	0.89796	0.89973	0.90147
1.3	0.90320	0.90490	0.90658	0.90824	0.90988	0.91149	0.91309	0.91466	0.91621	0.91774
1.4	0.91924	0.92073	0.92220	0.92364	0.92507	0.92647	0.92785	0.92922	0.93056	0.93189
1.5	0.93319	0.93448	0.93574	0.93699	0.93822	0.93943	0.94062	0.94179	0.94295	0.94408
1.6	0.94520	0.94630	0.94738	0.94845	0.94950	0.95053	0.95154	0.95254	0.95352	0.95449
1.7	0.95543	0.95637	0.95728	0.95818	0.95907	0.95994	0.96080	0.96164	0.96246	0.96327
1.8	0.96407	0.96485	0.96562	0.96638	0.96712	0.96784	0.96856	0.96926	0.96995	0.97062
1.9	0.97128	0.97193	0.97257	0.97320	0.97381	0.97441	0.97500	0.97558	0.97615	0.97670
2	0.97725	0.97778	0.97831	0.97882	0.97932	0.97982	0.98030	0.98077	0.98124	0.98169
2.1	0.98214	0.98257	0.98300	0.98341	0.98382	0.98422	0.98461	0.98500	0.98537	0.98574
2.2	0.98610	0.98645	0.98679	0.98713	0.98745	0.98778	0.98809	0.98840	0.98870	0.98899
2.3	0.98928	0.98956	0.98983	0.99010	0.99036	0.99061	0.99086	0.99111	0.99134	0.99158

z	0	0.01	0.02	0.03	0.04	0.05	0.06	0.07	0.08	0.09
2.4	0.99180	0.99202	0.99224	0.99245	0.99266	0.99286	0.99305	0.99324	0.99343	0.99361
2.5	0.99379	0.99396	0.99413	0.99430	0.99446	0.99461	0.99477	0.99492	0.99506	0.99520
2.6	0.99534	0.99547	0.99560	0.99573	0.99585	0.99598	0.99609	0.99621	0.99632	0.99643
2.7	0.99653	0.99664	0.99674	0.99683	0.99693	0.99702	0.99711	0.99720	0.99728	0.99736
2.8	0.99744	0.99752	0.99760	0.99767	0.99774	0.99781	0.99788	0.99795	0.99801	0.99807
2.9	0.99813	0.99819	0.99825	0.99831	0.99836	0.99841	0.99846	0.99851	0.99856	0.99861
3	0.99865	0.99869	0.99874	0.99878	0.99882	0.99886	0.99889	0.99893	0.99896	0.99900
3.1	0.99903	0.99906	0.99910	0.99913	0.99916	0.99918	0.99921	0.99924	0.99926	0.99929
3.2	0.99931	0.99934	0.99936	0.99938	0.99940	0.99942	0.99944	0.99946	0.99948	0.99950
3.3	0.99952	0.99953	0.99955	0.99957	0.99958	0.99960	0.99961	0.99962	0.99964	0.99965
3.4	0.99966	0.99968	0.99969	0.99970	0.99971	0.99972	0.99973	0.99974	0.99975	0.99976
3.5	0.99977	0.99978	0.99978	0.99979	0.99980	0.99981	0.99981	0.99982	0.99983	0.99983
3.6	0.99984	0.99985	0.99985	0.99986	0.99986	0.99987	0.99987	0.99988	0.99988	0.99989
3.7	0.99989	0.99990	0.99990	0.99990	0.99991	0.99991	0.99992	0.99992	0.99992	0.99992
3.8	0.99993	0.99993	0.99993	0.99994	0.99994	0.99994	0.99994	0.99995	0.99995	0.99995
3.9	0.99995	0.99995	0.99996	0.99996	0.99996	0.99996	0.99996	0.99996	0.99997	0.99997

APPENDIX B
Factors for $\bar{x}$- and R-Control Charts

Sample Size	$\bar{x}$-charts	R-charts	
n	A_2	D_3	D_4
2	1.880	0	3.267
3	1.023	0	2.574
4	0.729	0	2.282
5	0.577	0	2.114
6	0.483	0	2.004
7	0.419	0.076	1.924
8	0.373	0.136	1.864
9	0.337	0.184	1.816
10	0.308	0.223	1.777
11	0.285	0.256	1.744
12	0.266	0.283	1.717
13	0.249	0.307	1.693
14	0.235	0.328	1.672
15	0.223	0.347	1.653
16	0.212	0.363	1.637
17	0.203	0.378	1.622
18	0.194	0.391	1.608
19	0.187	0.403	1.597
20	0.180	0.415	1.585
21	0.173	0.425	1.575
22	0.167	0.434	1.566
23	0.162	0.443	1.557
24	0.157	0.451	1.548
25	0.153	0.459	1.541

Source: Adapted from Table 27 of ASTM STP 15D ASTM Manual on Presentation of Data and Control Chart Analysis. © 1976 American Society for Testing and Materials, Philadelphia, PA.

ENDNOTES

1

1. T. Wailbum, "Study: Apple, Nokia, Dell Tops Among Global Supply Chains," May 29, 2008, http://www.cio.com/article/373563/Study_Apple_Nokia_Dell_Tops_Among_Global_Supply_Chains; A. Satariano and P. Burrows, "Apple's Supply-Chain Secret? Hoard Lasers," *Business-Week Technology*, November 3, 2011, http://www.businessweek.com/magazine/apples-supplychain-secret-hoard-lasers-11032011.html.

2. D. A. Collier, *The Service/Quality Solution: Using Service Management to Gain Competitive Advantage*, Milwaukee, WI: ASQC Quality Press and Burr Ridge, IL: Irwin Professional Publishing, 1994, pp. 16, 63–64, 167.

3. These differences between goods and services were first defined by W. E. Sasser, R. P. Olsen, and D. D. Wyckoff, *Management of Service Operations*, Boston: Allyn and Bacon, 1978, pp. 8–21, and later improved and expanded by J. A. Fitzsimmons and R. S. Sullivan, *Service Operations Management*, New York: McGraw-Hill, 1982; D. A. Collier, "Managing a Service Firm: A Different Management Game," *National Productivity Review* (Winter 1983–1984), pp. 36–45.

4. D. A. Collier, "New Orleans Hilton & Hilton Towers," *Service Management: Operating Decisions*, Englewood Cliffs, NJ: Prentice Hall, Inc., 1987, p. 120.

5. Jan Carlzon, CEO of Scandinavian Airlines Systems, first defined a moment of trust or truth. See T. J. Peters and N. Austin, *A Passion for Excellence: The Leadership Difference*, New York: Warner Books, 1985, pp. 58, 78.

6. Reprinted from Business Horizons, "Using 'biztainment' to gain competitive advantage," by Mi Kyong Newsom, David A. Collier, and Eric O. Olsen, 52:2, 167–176, 2009 with permission from Elsevier.

7. D. A. Collier, *The Service/Quality Solution: Using Service Management to Gain Competitive Advantage*, Milwaukee, WI: ASQC Quality Press and Burr Ridge, IL: Irwin Professional Publishing, 1994, pp. 63–96.

8. K. O'Sullivan and D. Durfee, "Offshoring by the Numbers," *CFO Magazine*, June 2004, p. 53.

9. *AT&T's Total Quality Approach*, AT&T Corporate Quality Office, 1992, p. 6.

10. H. Forcinio, "Supply Chain Mastery: HP," *Managing Automation*, November 3, 2006, http://www.managingautomation.com/maonline/magazine/read/view/Supply_Chain_Mastery_HP_2588698.

11. M. J. Liberatore and W. Luo, "The Analytics Movement: Implications for Operations Research," *Interfaces*, 40, 4 (July–August 2010), pp. 313–324.

12. James Manyika, Michael Chui, Brad Brown, Jacques Bughin, Richard Dobbs, Charles Roxburgh, and Angela Hung Byers, "Big Data: The Next Frontier for Innovation, Competition, and Productivity," McKinsey & Company, May 2011.

13. Geoff Colvin, "Every Aspect of Your Business Is About to Change," *Fortune.com*, November 1, 2015, pp. 103–112.

14. Facts in this case adapted from J. M. O'Brien, "Zappos Knows How to Kick It," *Fortune*, January 15, 2009, http://www.fortune.com; and "Zappos," *Fast Company*, March 2009, pp. 75–76.

2

1. Malcolm Baldrige National Quality Award, Profiles of Winners, National Institute of Standards and Technology, Department of Commerce, http://www.nist.gov/baldrige/award_recipients/index.cfm.

2. Private communication from Stephen D. Webb, manager of quality control, ground operations, American Airlines.

3. Adapted from A. Lashinsky, "Meg and the Machine," *Fortune*, September 1, 2003, pp. 68–78.

4. A. Parasuraman, V. A. Zeithaml, and L. L. Berry, "SERVQUAL: A Multiple-Item Scale for Measuring Consumer Perceptions of Service Quality," *Journal of Retailing*, 64, Spring 1988, pp. 12–40; S. Davis, *Future Perfect*, New York: Addison-Wesley, 1987, p. 108.

5. "Are You Built for Speed?," *Fast Company*, June 2003, p. 85.

6. D. A. Collier, *The Service/Quality Solution*, Milwaukee, WI: ASQC Quality Press, and Burr Ridge, IL: Irwin Professional Publishing, pp. 235–260. Also, see, for example, D. A. Collier, "A Service Quality Process Map for Credit Card Processing," *Decision Sciences*, 22, 2, 1991, pp. 406–420; or D. D. Wilson and D. A. Collier, "The Role of Automation and Labor in Determining Customer Satisfaction in a Telephone Repair Service," *Decision Sciences*, 28, 3, 1997, pp. 1–21.

7. S. Hoisington and E. Naumann, "The Loyalty Elephant," *Quality Progress*, February 2003, pp. 33–41.

8. R. S. Kaplan and D. P. Norton, *The Balanced Scorecard*, Boston, MA: Harvard Business School Press, 1996, p. 1.

9. 2007 Malcolm Baldrige Application Summary.

10. J. L. Heskett, T. O. Jones, et al., "Putting the Service-Profit Chain to Work," *Harvard Business Review*, 72, 1994, pp. 164–174.

3

1. V. A. Zeithaml, "How Consumer Evaluation Processes Differ Between Goods and Services," in J. H. Donnelly and W. R. George, eds., *Marketing in Services*, Chicago, IL: American Marketing Association, 1981, pp. 186–199.

2. D. H. Pink, "Out of the Box," *Fast Company*, October 2003, pp. 104–106; P. Sellers, "Gap's New Guy Upstairs," *Fortune*, April 14, 2003, pp. 110–116; and "How to Listen to Consumers," *Fortune*, January 11, 1993, p. 77.

3. "Southwest Sets Standards on Costs," *The Wall Street Journal*, October 9, 2002, p. A2.

4. *The PIMS Letter on Business Strategy*, Cambridge, MA: The Strategic Planning Institute, Number 4, 1986.

5. G. B. Lafamore, "The Burden of Choice," *APICS—The Performance Advantage*, January 2001, pp. 40–43.

6. B. Horovitz, "Drive-thru Times Slow to a Crawl," http://www.usatoday.com/story/money/business/2014/10/06/fast-food-drive-thru-times-restaurants-mcdonalds-taco-bellwendys/16644673/.

7. J. B. Quinn, *Strategies for Change: Logical Incrementalism*, Homewood IL: Richard D. Irwin, 1980.

8. Beth Kowitt, "The World According to WalMart," *Fortune*. 10/1/2018, Vol. 178 Issue 4, 70–76.

9. Adapted in part from R. Kauffeld, A. Malhotra, and S. Higgins, "Green Is a Strategy: Five Steps to 'Differentiated' Sustainability for a Full Embrace of Environmentalism," *Strategy + Business*, December 21, 2009, http://www.strategy-business.com/article/00013?pg=all.

10. T. Laseter, A. Ovchinnikov, and G. Raz, "Reduce, Reuse, Recycle . . . or Rethink," *Strategy + Business*, 61, Winter 2010, pp. 30–34.

11. T. Hill, *Manufacturing Strategy: Text and Cases*, 2nd ed., Burr Ridge, IL: Irwin Publishers, 1994.

12. http://www.mcdonalds.com/corporate/info/vision/index.html. This example is the book author's interpretation of McDonald's public information with the objective of illustrating Professor Terry Hill's generic strategy development framework. It may or may not be perfectly accurate and it is only partially complete due to space limitations.

4

1. S. Amyx, "6 Ways Analytics and 'The Internet of Things' Will Transform Business," November 17, 2015, http://readwrite.com/2015/11/17/analytics-ibm-insight; J. Wiecaner, "The New Geek Squad (That's Fixing Best Buy)," *Fortune*, November 1, 2015, pp. 143–148; McKinsey Quarterly, "The Internet of Things," http://www.mckinsey.com/insights/high_tech_telecoms_internet/the_internet_of_things; and L. S. Gould, "The Internet of Things," *Automotive Design and Production*, May 1, 2015, http://www.autofieldguide.com/articles/the-internet-of-things(2).

2. *Award, The Newsletter of Baldrigeplus*, May 7, 2000, http://www.baldrigeplus.com.

3. M. Dusharme, "RFID Tunes into Supply Chain Management," *Quality Digest*, October 18, 2007, http://www.qualitydigest.com.

4. *Bloomberg Businessweek*, June 26, 2017, "500,000 Tons of Steel. 14 Jobs," Thomas Biesheuvel, p. 16–17.

5. *BusinessWeek*, Online Extra: "The Quickening at Nissan," March 27, 2006.

6. L. Braverman, "Kroger Testing Faster Self-Checkout Machine," *The Cincinnati Enquirer*, September 30, 2010, pp. B1, B2.

7. B. Geier, "Using 3-D Printing to Make Jet Engines," http://fortune.com/2014/11/13/3-d-printing-jet-engines-alcoa/.

8. "Great Examples of New Manufacturing Technology," http://www.nebraskamanufacturing.com/2013/07/4-great-examples-of-american-manufacturing-technology/.

9. "Sweeping Manufacturing Technology Trends to Change Paradigms Forever," http://cerasis.com/2015/01/13/manufacturing-technology/.

10. M. Garry, "Stop & Shop Completes Rollout of Portable EasyShop Shopping Device," *Supermarket News*, December 12, 2007, http://supermarketnews.com/technology_logistics/stopshop_easyshop/.

11. N. McManus, "Robots at Your Service," *Wired*, January 2003, pp. 58–59.

12. "Honda All Set to Grow," *The Columbus Dispatch*, September 18, 2002, pp. B1–B2.

13. T. H. Davenport and J. G. Harris, *Competing on Analytics: The New Science of Winning*, Boston, MA: Harvard Business School Press, 2007.

14. M. V. Copeland, "Reed Hastings: Leader of the Pack," *Fortune*, December 6, 2010, pp. 121–130; Netflix Consumer Press Kit; Netflix Investor Press Kit.

15. T. Omer, "From Business Intelligence to Analytics," *Analytics*, January/February, 2011, p. 20, analyticsmagazine.com.

16. "Florida Courses on Leading Edge of Water Conservation Technology," http://www.visitflorida.com/experts/golf/action.blog/id.1977, April 26, 2010.

17. "Advancing Global Sustainability Through Technology," Intel White Paper, 2007.

18. T. Gaskill, "Turning the Tables," *Quality Progress*, August 2015, pp. 10–12.

5

1. Adapted and reprinted with permission from "Building Cars by Design" by Vikas Sehgal, Robert Reppa, and Kazutoshi Tominaga from the strategy+business website, published by Booz & Company, Inc. (http://www.strategy-business.com/article/li00107?gko=7b465). Copyright © 2009. All rights reserved.

2. Charles Fishman, "To The Moon! (In a Minivan)," *Fast Company*, December 2007/January 2008.

3. Eric Fish, "Rapid Prototyping: How It's Done at GM," *Automotive Design and Production*, 123(5), September/October 2011, pp. 46–47.

4. Douglas Daetz, "The Effect of Product Design on Product Quality and Product Cost," *Quality Progress*, June 1987, pp. 63–67.

5. "Venza Revealed," *Automotive Design and Production*, December 2008, pp. 30–32.

6. *BusinessWeek: Quality 1991* (special issue), October 25, 1991, p. 73.

7. Early discussions of this topic can be found in Bruce Nussbaum and John Templeton, "Built to Last—Until It's Time to Take It Apart," *BusinessWeek*, September 17, 1990, pp. 102–106. A more recent reference is Michael Lenox, Andrew King, and John Ehrenfeld, "An Assessment of Design-for-Environment Practices in Leading US Electronics Firms," *Interfaces* 30, 3, May–June 2000, pp. 83–94.

8. "Pepsi Makes Bottles from Plants," *USA Today*, Money, March 16, 2011, p. 1B; "Pepsi Bottles: No More Plastic," *The Christian Science Monitor*, http://www.csmonitor.com/Business/Latest-News-Wires/2011/0315/Pepsi-bottles-no-more-plastic.

9. M. J. Bitner, "Servicescapes: The Impact of Physical Surroundings on Customers and Employees," *Journal of Marketing*, 56, 2, 1994, pp. 57–71; M. J. Bitner, "Managing the Evidence of Service," in F. F. Scheuing and W. F. Christopher, eds., *The Service Quality Handbook*, New York: American Management Association (AMACOM), 1993, pp. 358–370.

10. Ibid.

11. Ibid.

12. Sarah Anne Wright, "Putting Fast-Food to the Test," *The Cincinnati Enquirer*, July 9, 2000, pp. F1, 2.

13. http://www.emirates.com/us/english/flying/cabin_features/first_class/first_class.aspx.

14. R. B. Chase, "Where Does the Customer Fit in a Service Operation?" *Harvard Business Review*, November–December 1978, pp. 137–142.

15. R. B. Chase, 1983, op. cit., pp. 1037–1050. "The Customer Contact Model for Organizational Design," *Management Science*, 29, 9, 1983, pp. 1037–1050.

16. The Disney Institute, *Be Our Guest*, Disney Enterprises, Inc., 2001, p. 86.

17. http://www.llbean.com/customerService/aboutLLBean/guarantee.html, accessed June 6, 2010.

18. D. A. Collier and T. K. Baker, "The Economic Payout Model for Service Guarantees," *Decision Science*, 36, 2, 2005, pp. 197–220. Also, see D. A. Collier, "Process Moments of Trust: Analysis and Strategy," *The Service Industry Journal*, 9, 2, April 1989, pp. 205–222.

19. http://www.lenscrafter.com/al_mission.html, accessed December 2, 2002.

6

1. http://www.gapinc.com.

2. Deborah Abrams Kaplan, How Johnson & Johnson overhauled its baby care supply chain, SUPPLYCHAINDIVE, September 25, 2018.

3. Bernard Marr, "How Blockchain Will Transform The Supply Chain And Logistics Industry," March 23, 2018, https://www.forbes.com/sites/bernardmarr/2018/03/23/how-blockchain-will-transform-the-supply-chain-and-logistics-industry/#d3fa1555fecd

4. Wal-Mart using tech for food safety," *The Naples Daily News*, Naples, Florida, November 19, 2016, pp. B1–B2.

5. "Is Your Job Next?" *BusinessWeek*, February 3, 2003, pp. 50–60.

6. "The UPS Green Dream," *Fortune*, December 27, 2010, pp. 44–51.

7. "A Key Link in the Supply Chain," advertisement in *Fortune* magazine, September 6, 2010, http://www.fortune.com/adsections.

8. "It's All About the Shoes," *Fast Company*, 2004, p. 85, http://pf.fastcompany.com/magazine/86/stollenwerk.html.

9. Read about the company history at http://www.allenedmonds.com.

10. B. Kane, "Outsourced Manufacturing Coming Back?," hartfordbusiness.com, October 3, 2011.

11. C. Giammona, "Homemade Cotton Cloth," *Fortune*, January 13, 2014, pp. 11–12.

12. Boris Ladwig, Lessons in reshoring; The turnaround at GE's Appliance Park, Insider Louisville, Feb. 27, 2019, https://insiderlouisville.com/economy/reshoring-turnaround-ge-appliance-park/.

13. J. L. Graham and N. M. Lam, "The Chinese Negotiation," *Harvard Business Review*, October, 2003, pp. 19–28. We highly recommend reading this article.

14. http://www.inditex.com/en/downloads/annual_report_2012.pdf.

15. Jen A. Miller, Why Amazon picked Nashville, Tennessee. SUPPLYCHAINDIVE, Nov 20, 2018. https://www.supplychaindive.com/news/why-Amazon-Nashville-supply-chain-operations/542621/.

16. T. Stank, Ph.D., M. Burnette, and P. Dittmann, Ph.D. University of Tennessee Knoxville Global Supply Chain Institute, Global Supply Chains, November 2014.

7

1. Chris Woodyard, "Ford Focuses on Flexibility at Its Factories," http://www.usatoday.com/cleanprint/?1298911481142; "Flexibility, Quality in Focus at New Ford Plant," *Targeted News Service*, March 18, 2011, http://asq.org/qualitynews/qnt/execute/displaySetup?newsIDv10869. Copyright © 2005–2008 American Society for Quality.

2. This discussion is adapted from Charles A. Horne, "Product Strategy and the Competitive Advantage," P&IM Review with *APICS News*, 7, 12, December 1987, pp. 38–41.

3. Alfa Laval Business Principles Progress Report, 2009, published March 31, 2010, p. 4, http://www.alfalaval.com/about-us/sustainability/reports/Documents/Progress_report_2009.pdf.

4. A. Phillips, "Boeing Rolls Out 'Toyota-style' Lean Production Methodology for Aeroplanes," *Lean*, April 29, 2015, http://www.manufacturingglobal.com/lean/436/Boeing-rolls-out-Toyotastyle-lean-production-methodology-for-aeroplanes; E. A. Carlson, "Boeing Gets Lessons in Lean form Toyota and UK," http://bizlex.com/2012/03/boeing-gets-lessons-in-lean-from-toyota-and-uk/2/.

5. R. H. Hayes and S. C. Wheelwright, "Linking Manufacturing Process and Product Life Cycles," *Harvard Business Review* 57, 1, 1979, pp. 133–140; R. H. Hayes and S. C. Wheelwright, "The Dynamics of Process-Product Life Cycles," *Harvard Business Review* 57, 2, 1979, pp. 127–136; and R. H. Hayes and S. C. Wheelwright, *Restoring Our Competitive Edge*, New York: John Wiley & Sons, 1984.

6. H. Noori, *Managing the Dynamics of New Technology: Issues in Manufacturing Management*, Englewood Cliffs, NJ: Prentice Hall, 1989.

7. D. A. Collier and S. M. Meyer, "A Service Positioning Matrix," *International Journal of Production and Operations Management*, 18, 12, 1998, pp. 1123–1244.

8. D. A. Collier and S. Meyer, "An Empirical Comparison of Service Matrices," *International Journal of Operations and Production Management*, 20, 5–6, 2000, pp. 705–729.

9. Prince McLean, "Apple Details New MacBook Manufacturing Process, *AppleInsider*, October 14, 2008, http://www.appleinsider.com/articles/08/10/14/.

10. Alaska Airlines, "Our Baggage Guarantee," http://www.alaskaair.com/content/travel-info/baggage/baggage-service-guarantee/20-minutes-or-less.aspx; *USA TODAY*, "Delta tests 20-minute 'guarantee' for checked bags," February 23, 2015, http://www.usatoday.com/story/todayinthesky/2015/02/19/delta-rolls-out-20-minute-guarantee-for-checked-bags/23699575/.

11. http://www.autofieldguide.com.

12. Richard B. Chase and Douglas M. Stewart, "Make Your Service Fail-Safe," *Sloan Management Review* 35, no. 3 (Spring 1994), 35–44.

13. Michael A. Prospero, "Top Scalpel," *Fast Company*, April 2006, 31.

14. Michael Hammer and James Champy, *Reengineering the Corporation*, New York: HarperBusiness, 1993, pp. 177–178.

15. Michael Hammer and James Champy, *Reengineering the Corporation*, New York: Harper Business, 1993.

16. Patricia Houghton, "Improving Pharmacy Service," *Quality Digest*, October 18, 2007.

8

1. P. C. Bell and J. Van Brenk, "Vytec Corporation: Warehouse Layout Planning," *The European Case Clearing House*, England, Case # 9B03E013. (http://www.ecch.cranfield.ac.uk.)

2. Marty Lariviere, "Lean Operations for Luxury Bags," The Operations Room, June 28, 2011, http://operationsroom.wordpress.com/2011/06/28/lean-operation; "At Vuitton, Growth in Small Batches," *The Wall Street Journal*, June 27, 2011.

3. "GM Plans to Lay Off 1,600 Workers," *The News-Press*, Fort Myers, FL, October 17, 2008, p. D2.

4. Profiles of Winners, Malcolm Baldrige National Quality Award, and Sunny Fresh Foods Baldrige Application Summary, 1999.

5. P. Johnson, V. Heimann, and K. O'Neill, "The Wonderland of Virtual Teams," *Journal of Workplace Learning*, 13, 1, 2001, pp. 24–29.

6. "Dilbert Is Right, Says Gallup Study," *Gallup Management Journal*, April 13, 2006.

7. V. Harnish, "5 Ways to Tap Nature to Build a Better Business," *Fortune*, August 1, 2015, p. 40.

8. http://www.dnb.com/lc/supply-management-education/ethical-supply-chain.html.

9. http://www.ethicaltrade.org/eti-base-code/.

9

1. Pete Buczkowski and Hai Chu, "Corporate Profile: How analytics enhance the guest experience at Walt Disney World," *Analytics Magazine*, September/October 2012.

2. Frank M. Bass, Kent Gordon, Teresa L. Ferguson, and Mary Lou Githens, "DIRECTV: Forecasting Diffusion of a New Technology Prior to Product Launch," *Interfaces*, 31, 3, Part 2 of 2, May–June 2001, pp. S82–S93.

3. Robert Fildes and Paul Goodwin, "Against Your Better Judgment? How Organizations Can Improve Their Use of Management Judgment in Forecasting," *Interfaces*, 37, 6, November–December 2007, pp. 570–576.

10

1. *Fortune*, April 19, 2011, http://money.cnn.com/2011/04/19/news/companies/jeff_smisek_united_continental.fortune/index.htm.

2. http://articles.baltimoresun.com/2000-07-14/news/0007140079_1_district-court-criminal-justice-system-indigent-defendants.

3. "Strategy: European Auto Union," *Bloomberg BusinessWeek*, April 19, 2010, p. 8.

4. Philip Walzer, "Analysts: Slumping Demand Why Franklin Paper Mill Closing," *The Virginian-Pilot*, April 11, 2010.

5. http://www.briggsandstratton.com.

6. "Disney Restaurant No-Shows Will Pay," *USA Today*, October 21, 2011, p. 4D.

7. http://www.usatoday.com/story/travel/hotels/2014/10/26/how-hotels-come-up-with-rates/17792537/.

8. W. Liberman, "Implementing Yield Management," ORSA/TIMS National Meeting Presentation, San Francisco, November 1992.

9. M. Geraghty and M. Johnson, "Revenue Management Saves National Car Rental," *Interfaces*, 12, 7, 1997, pp. 107–127.

10. Eliyahu M. Goldratt and Jeff Cox, *The Goal*, 2nd rev. ed. Croton-on-Hudson, NY: North River Press, 1992; and Eliyahu M. Goldratt, *The Theory of Constraints*, Croton-on-Hudson, NY: North River Press, 1990.

11. Jeremy Pastore, Sekar Sundararajan, and Emory W. Zimmers, "Innovative Application," *APICS—The Performance Advantage*, 14, 3, March 2004, pp. 32–35.

12. http://www.goldratt.com/kreisler.htm.

11

1. Gregory Korte, "473 Steps," *The Cincinnati Enquirer*, October 30, 2002, A1, A10.

2. Goedert, J., "Hospital Realizes Benefits, ROI with Automated Patient Tracking," *Health Data Management*, November 2004, pp. 12, 18.

3. Gibson, Richard, "Merchants Mull the Long and the Short of Lines," *The Wall Street Journal*, September 3, 1998, p. B1.

4. Goldratt, Eliyahu M., and Cox, Jeff, *The Goal*, Second Revised Edition, Croton-on-Hudson, NY: North River Press, 1992; and Goldratt, Eliyahu M., *The Theory of Constraints*, Croton-on-Hudson, NY: North River Press, 1990.

5. http://www.goldratt.com/kreisler.htm.

12

1. https://www.renttherunway.com/pages/about.

2. V. W. Slaugh, B. Biller, and S. R. Tayur, "Managing Rentals with Usage-Based Loss," *Manufacturing & Service Operations Management* (accepted January 2016). We thank Dr. Slaugh for providing the inspiration and the information for this example.

3. http://orf.od.nih.gov/Environmental+Protection/Green1Purchasing/.

4. Fit for the future by Phil Wahba http://fortune.com/2014/10/09/bloomingdales-smart-dressing-room/.

5. A more complete technical classification and survey of inventory problems is given in E. A. Silver, "Operations Research in Inventory Management," *Operations Research*, 29, 1981, pp. 628–645.

6. http://www.themanager.org/Strategy/Out-Of-Stock_Situations.htm.

7. Hau L. Lee, Corey Billington, and Brent Carter, "Hewlett-Packard Gains Control of Inventory and Service Through Design for Localization," *Interfaces*, 23, 4, July–August, 1993, pp. 1–11.

13

1. S. Fourtané, "Supply Chain Agility: Nokia's Supply Chain Management Success," June 4, 2014, http://www.ebnonline.com/author.asp?section_id=1364&doc_id=273562.

2. J. L. Schiff, "4 Ways Retailers Can Improve Supply Chain Management," CIO, June 18, 2015, http://www.cio.com/article/2932207/supply-chain-management/4-ways-retailers-can-improve-supply-chain-management.html.

3. "Supply Chain Excellence," Special Advertising Section, *BusinessWeek*, April 25, 2005.

4. The Supply Chain Council was formed in 1996–1997 as a grassroots initiative by firms including AMR Research, Bayer, Compaq Computer, Pittiglio Rabin Todd & McGrath (PRTM), Procter & Gamble, Lockheed Martin, Nortel, Rockwell Semiconductor, and Texas Instruments. See http://www.supply-chain.org/ for information on the Supply Chain Council and development of the SCOR model.

5. *USA Today*, March 6, 2016 p. 6B.

6. Robot delivery trucks to test in Detroit, China," by Mark Phelan, Detroit Free Press and USA Today Network, The Naples Daily News, February 11, 2019, pp. 4B and 5B.

7. G. Callioni and C. Corey, "Effective Collaboration," *OR/MS Today*, 28, no. 5, October 2001, pp. 34–39.

8. Facts in this example were drawn from P. Gallagher, "*Value Pricing for Profits*," *Cincinnati Enquirer*, December 21, 1992, pp. D-1, D-6; "Procter & Gamble Hits Back," *BusinessWeek*, July 19, 1993, pp. 20–22; and B. Sapority, "Behind the Tumult at P&G," *Fortune*, March 7, 1994, pp. 75–82.

9. "Quake Stirs Unease About Global Supply Chain," Associated Press March 31, 2011; C-R. Kim, "Toyota Aims for Quake-Proof Supply Chain," baltimoresun.com, September 6, 2011.

10. Cited in T. Stank, M. Burnette, and P. Dittmann, University of Tennessee Knoxville Global Supply Chain Institute, Global Supply Chains, November 2014.

11. https://www.prosancons.com/tax/pros-cons-tariffs/, June 4, 2019

12. L. Kishpaugh, "Process Management and Business Results," presentation at the 1996 Regional Malcolm Baldrige Award Conference, Boston, Massachusetts.

13. W. H. Murphy, "An Inside Look at How Target Ensures Quality in a Complex Supply Chain," *Quality Progress*, June 2010.

14. K. Parks and T. Connor, "An Inside Look at How Boeing's Supplier Rating System Keeps the Aviation Giant Focused on Continuous Improvement," *Quality Progress*, April 2011.

15. Charles Dominick, "Green Procurement: Let's Get Started," April 18, 2010, http://www.nextlevelpurchasing.com/articles/green-procurement.html.

16. D. Joseph, "Score Two for Sustainability," *FastCompany*, November 2010, p. 54.

17. Patrick Penfield, "The Green Supply Chain: Sustainability Can Be a Competitive Advantage," August 7, 2007, http://www.mhia.org/news/industry/7056/the-green-supply-chain.

18. "Apple's Quest for a 100% Renewably Powered Supply Chain," GreenBiz, https://www.greenbiz.com/article/apples-quest-renewably-powered-supply-chain.

19. http://www.ups.com/content/us/en/bussol/browse/leadership-nvironment.html?srch_pos=1&srch_phr=environmental+impact.

20. http://about.van.fedex.com/conservation.

14

1. S. Delurgio, B. Denton, R. Cabanela, S. Bruggeman, N. Groves, A. Williams, S. Ward, and J. Osborn, "Planning and Forecasting Weekly Outpatient Demands for a Large Medical Center," *Production & Inventory Management*, 45, 2, 2009, pp. 35–46, 44–51.

2. Adapted from Martin S. Visagie, "Production Control on a Flow Production Plant," *APICS 1975 Conference Proceedings*, pp. 161–166.

3. E. Steinberg, B. Khumawala, and R. Scamell, "Requirements Planning Systems in the Healthcare Environment," *Journal of Operations Management* 2, 4, 1982, pp. 251–259.

15

1. G. M. Campbell, "Overview of Workforce Scheduling Software," *Production and Inventory Management*, 45, 2, pp. 7–22.

2. http://www.abs-usa.com.

3. This approach is suggested in R. Tibrewala, D. Phillippe, and J. Browne, "Optimal Scheduling of Two Consecutive Idle Periods," *Management Science*, 19, 1, September 1972, pp. 71–75.

4. http://www.cbsnews.com/news/airlines-try-to-save-time-with-speedier-boarding/.

5. S. M. Johnson, "Optimal Two- and Three-Stage Production Schedules with Setup Times Included," *Naval Research Logistics Quarterly*, 1, 1, March 1954, pp. 61–68.

6. Randolpgh Hall and Janice Partyka, "Higher expectations drive transformation," Analytics-Magazine.org, March/April 2016, 66–72.

16

1. http://money.cnn.com/2015/05/12/autos/gm-ignition-switch-recall-100-deaths/index.html.

2. A. Parasuraman, V. Zeithaml, and L. Berry, "A Conceptual Model of Service Quality and Its Implications for Future Research," *Journal of Marketing*, 49, 4, 1985, pp. 41–50; A. Parasuraman, V. Zeithaml, and L. Berry, "SERVQUAL: A Multiple-Item Scale for Measuring Consumer Perceptions of Service Quality," *Journal of Retailing*, 64, 1, 1988, pp. 29–40; A. Parasuraman, V. A. Zeithaml, and L. L. Berry, "Refinement and Reassessment of the SERVQUAL instrument," *Journal of Retailing*, 67, 4, 1991, pp. 420–450.

3. W. Edwards Deming, *The New Economics for Industry, Government, Education*, Cambridge, MA: MIT Center for Advanced Engineering Study, 1993.

4. Adapted from March Laree Jacques, "Big League Quality," *Quality Progress*, August 2001, pp. 27–34.

5. A. Parasuraman, V. A. Zeithaml, and L. L. Berry, "A Conceptual Model of Service Quality and Its Implications for Future Research," *Journal of Marketing*, 49, Fall 1985, pp. 41–50.

6. Ronald D. Snee, "Why Should Statisticians Pay Attention to Six Sigma?" *Quality Progress*, September 1999, pp. 100–103.

7. Stanley A. Marash, "Six Sigma: Business Results Through Innovation," in *ASQ's 54th Annual Quality Congress Proceedings*, 2000, pp. 627–630.

8. Lisa Palser, "Cycle Time Improvement for a Human Resources Process," in *ASQ's 54th Annual Quality Congress Proceedings*, 2000 (CD-ROM).

9. Roger Hoerl, "An Inside Look at Six Sigma at GE," *Six Sigma Forum Magazine*, 1, 3, May 2002, pp. 35–44.

10. A. V. Roth, A. A. Tsay, M. E. Pullman, and J. V. Gray, "Unraveling the Food Supply Chain: Strategic Insights from China and the 2007 Recalls," *Journal of Supply Chain Management*, 44, 1, January 2008, pp. 22–39.

11. *Reports of Statistical Application Research, Japanese Union of Scientists and Engineers*, 33, 2, June 1986.

12. Lea A. P. Tonkin, "Kaizen BlitzSM 5: Bottleneck-Bashing Comes to Rochester, NY," *Target* 12, no. 4 (September–October 1996), 41–43; and Mark Oakeson, "Makes Dollars & Sense for Mercedes-Benz in Brazil," *IIE Solutions* (April 1997), 32–35.

13. Davis R. Bothe, "Improve Service and Administration," *Quality Progress*, September 2003, pp. 53–57.

17

1. Eryn Brown, "Heartbreak Hotel?" *Fortune*, November 26, 2001, pp. 161–165.

2. "Hospital to Revise Lab Procedures After Faulty Tests Kill 2," *The Columbus Dispatch*, Columbus, OH, August 16, 2001, p. A2.

3. "Testing for Conformity: An Inside Job," *Golf Journal*, May 1998, pp. 20–25.

4. http://www.kevinmd.com/blog/2010/12/medical-errors-involve-handwritten-prescriptions.html and http://www.pharmalot.com/2011/07/e-prescribing-handwritten-error-rates-are-similar/.

5. W. J. McCabe, "Improving Quality and Cutting Costs in a Service Organization," *Quality Progress*, June 1985, pp. 85–89.

18

1. P. Houghton, "Improving Pharmacy Service," *Quality Digest*, October 18, 2007.

2. "Lean + Sustainability = Good Business," http://leaninsider.productivitypress.com/2007/12/leansustainability-good-business.html.

3. K. G. Hall, "'Lean' Manufacturing Bringing Industry Back from Depths," http://www.mcclatchydc.com/news/nation-world/national/economy/article24760876.html.

4. V. Harnish, "5 Ways to Tone Your Operations," October 9, 2014, Fortune.com, http://fortune.com/2014/10/09/5-ways-to-tone-your-operations/.

5. S. Nakajima, "Explanation of New TPM Definition," *Plant Engineer*, 16, 1, pp. 33–40.

6. R. Ellis and K. Hankins, "The Timken Journey for Excellence," presentation for the Center of Excellence in Manufacturing Management, Fisher College of Business, The Ohio State University, Columbus, OH, August 22, 2003. Also see Timken's 2003 Annual Report and "From Missouri to Mars—A Century of Leadership in Manufacturing," http://www.timken.com.

7. "Lean and Pharmacies," *Quality Digest*, October 2006, http://www.qualitydigest.com.

8. P. E. Dickinson, E. C. Dodge, and C. S. Marshall, "Administrative Functions in a Just-in-Time Setting," *Target*, Fall 1988, pp. 12–17.

9. R. Inman and S. Mehra, "JIT Implementation Within a Service Industry: A Case Study," *International Journal of Service Industry Management*, 1, 3, 1990, pp. 53–61.

10. http://www.qualitydigest.com/print/8704, August 11, 2009.

11. Modeled after an example in Soren Bisgaard and Johannes Freiesleben. "Six Sigma and the Bottom Line," *Quality Progress*, Vol. 37, No. 9, September 2004, 57–62.

19

1. http://sportsillustrated.cnn.com/2004/olympics/2004/06/28/bc.oly.athensnotebook.ap/index.html.

2. http://ijourneys.blogspot.com/2008/01/london-olympics-is-live-project.html.

3. W. Alan Randolph and Barry Z. Posner, "What Every Manager Needs to Know About Project Management," *Sloan Management Review*, Summer 1988, pp. 65–73.

4. Baldrige Award Recipient Profile, Custom Research Inc., National Institute of Standards and Technology, 1996, http://baldrige.nist.gov/Custom_Research_96.htm.

5. Jack Gido and James P. Clements, *Successful Project Management*, 2nd ed., Mason, OH: Thomson South-Western, 2003, p. 103.

6. D. Hendricks, "How Technology Has Revitalized Project Management," Tech.Co, March 25, 2015, http://tech.co/technology-revitalized-project-management-2015-03.

5Ss - are derived from Japanese terms: *seiri* (sort), *seiton* (set in order), *seiso* (shine), *seiketsu* (standardize), and *shitsuke* (sustain).

A

Action bucket - is the current time period.

Actionable measures - provide the basis for decisions at the level at which they are applied.

Activities - discrete tasks in a project that consume resources and time.

Activity - a group of tasks needed to create and deliver an intermediate or final output.

Aggregate planning - the development of a long-term output and resource plan in aggregate units of measure.

Aggregate production plan - specifies the production level for each time period within the horizon, such as a week or month.

Allowances - include time for labor fatigue and personal needs, equipment breakdowns, rest periods, information delays, and so on.

Appraisal costs - are those expended on ascertaining quality levels through measurement and analysis of data to detect and correct problems.

Arcs - arrows in a project network that represent activities.

Assembly line - is a product layout dedicated to combining the components of a good or service that has been created previously.

Assembly-line balancing - technique to group tasks among workstations so that each workstation has—in the ideal case—the same amount of work.

B

Backhaul - when a truck delivers its load and also carries freight on the return journey.

Backorder - occurs when a customer is willing to wait for the item.

Backward integration - refers to acquiring capabilities toward suppliers.

Balking - is the process of a customer evaluating the waiting line and server system and decides not to enter the queue.

Batching - is the process of producing large quantities of items as a group before they are transferred to the next operation.

Benchmarking - the search for industry best practices that lead to superior performance.

Best practices - refers to approaches that produce exceptional results, are usually innovative in terms of the use of technology or human resources, and are recognized by customers or industry experts.

Bias - the tendency of forecasts to consistently be larger or smaller than the actual values of the time series.

Bill of labor (BOL) - a hierarchical record analogous to a BOM that defines labor inputs necessary to create a good or service

Biztainment - the practice of adding entertainment content to a bundle of goods and services in order to gain competitive advantage.

Blockchain - a distributed database network that holds records of digital data and events in a way that makes them tamper-resistant.

Bottleneck - the work activity that effectively limits the throughput of the entire process.

Break-even analysis - a simple approach to analyze profit or loss, or to make an economical choice between two options that vary with volume.

Breakthrough improvement - refers to discontinuous change, as opposed to the gradual, continuous improvement philosophy of kaizen.

Business analytics - is a process of transforming data into actions through analysis and insights in the context of organizational decision making and problem solving.

C

CAD/CAE - enables engineers to design, analyze, test, simulate, and "manufacture" products before they physically exist, thus ensuring that a product can be manufactured to specifications when it is released to the shop floor.

CAM - involves computer control of the manufacturing process, such as determining tool movements and cutting speeds.

Capacity requirements planning (CRP) - the process of determining the amount of labor and machine resources required to accomplish the tasks of production on a more detailed level, taking into account all component parts and end items in the materials plan

Capacity - the capability of a manufacturing or service system, such as a facility, process, workstation, or piece of equipment, to accomplish its purpose or to produce output in a period of time.

c-chart - monitors the total number of nonconformances per unit when the size of the sampling unit or number of opportunities for errors is constant.

Cellular layout - a layout that is not according to the functional characteristics of equipment, but rather is based on self-contained groups of equipment (called cells) needed for producing a particular set of goods or services.

Center-of-gravity method - the process by which x- and y-coordinates (location) for a single facility are determined.

Certified supplier - is one that, after extensive investigation, is found to supply material of such quality that routine testing on each lot received is unnecessary.

Chase demand production strategy - sets the production rate equal to the demand in each time period.

Common cause variation - is the result of complex interactions of variations in materials, tools, machines, information, workers, and the environment.

Competitive advantage - denotes a firm's ability to achieve market and financial superiority over its competitors.

Competitive priorities - represent the strategic emphasis that a firm places on certain performance measures and operational capabilities within a value chain.

Complementary goods and services - goods and services that can be produced or delivered using the same resources available to the firm, but whose seasonal demand patterns are out of phase with each other.

Components - are any items (raw materials, manufactured parts, purchased parts) other than an end item that goes into a higher-level parent item(s).

Computer numerical control (CNC) - NC machines whose operations are driven by a computer.

Computer-integrated manufacturing systems (CIMSs) - represent the union of hardware, software, database management, and communications to automate and control production activities, from planning and design to manufacturing and distribution.

Constraint (TOC) - is anything in an organization that limits it from moving toward or achieving its goal.

Constraints (optimization) - are limitations, requirements, or other restrictions that are imposed on any solution, either from practical or technological considerations or by management policy.

Continuous flow processes - create highly standardized goods or services, usually around the clock in very high volumes.

Continuous metric - is one that is calculated from data that are measured as the degree of conformance to a specification on some continuous scale of measurement.

Continuous timing - involves starting the clock at the beginning of each observation and recording the cumulative time at the completion of each work task

Contract manufacturer - is a firm that specializes in certain types of goods-producing activities, such as customized design, manufacturing, assembly, and packaging, and works under contract for end users.

Control chart - is a run chart to which two horizontal lines, called control limits are added: the upper control limit (UCL) and lower control limit (LCL).

Core competencies - which are the strengths that are unique to that organization.

Cost of quality - refers specifically to the costs associated with avoiding poor quality or those incurred as a result of poor quality.

Crash cost - is the total additional cost associated with completing an activity in its crash time rather than in its normal time.

Crash time - is the shortest possible time in which the activity can realistically be completed.

Crashing a project - refers to reducing the total time to complete the project to meet a revised due date.

Crashing an activity - refers to reducing its normal time, possibly up to its limit—the crash time.

Credence attributes - any aspects of a good or service that the customer must believe in but cannot personally evaluate even after purchase and consumption.

Critical path - is the sequence of activities that takes the longest time and defines the total project completion time.

Custom, or make-to-order, goods and services - generally produced and delivered as one of a kind or in small quantities, and designed to meet specific customers' specifications.

Customer benefit package (CBP) - a clearly defined set of tangible (goods-content) and intangible (service-content) features that the customer recognizes, pays for, uses, or experiences.

Customer contact - refers to the physical or virtual presence of the customer in the service-delivery system during a service experience.

Customer relationship management (CRM) - a business strategy designed to learn more about customers' wants, needs, and behaviors in order to build customer relationships and loyalty, and ultimately enhance revenues and profits.

Customer-contact requirements - measurable performance levels or expectations that define the quality of customer contact with representatives of an organization.

Customer-routed services - those that offer customers broad freedom to select the pathways that are best suited for their immediate needs and wants from many possible pathways through the service delivery system.

Customer-satisfaction measurement system - provides a company with customer ratings of specific goods and service features and indicates the relationship between those ratings and the customer's likely future buying behavior.

Cycle inventory - (also called **order** or **lot size inventory**) is inventory that results from purchasing or producing in larger lots than are needed for immediate consumption or sale.

Cycle time - the interval between successive outputs coming off the assembly line.

Cyclical patterns - are regular patterns in a data series that take place over long periods of time.

Decision analysis - the formal study of how people make decisions, particularly when faced with uncertain information, as well as a collection of techniques to support the analysis of decision problems.

Decision variables - are the unknown values that the model seeks to determine.

Defect - any mistake or error that is passed on to the customer.

Delphi method - consists of forecasting by expert opinion by gathering judgments and opinions of key personnel based on their experience and knowledge of the situation.

Dependent demand - is a demand that is directly related to the demand of other SKUs and can be calculated without needing to be forecasted.

Descriptive statistics - refers to the methods of describing and summarizing data using tabular, visual, and quantitative techniques.

Design for environment (DfE) - is the explicit consideration of environmental concerns during the design of goods, services, and processes, and includes such practices as designing for recycling and disassembly.

Design for manufacturability (DFM) - is the process of designing a product for efficient production at the highest level of quality.

Disaggregation - is the process of translating aggregate plans into short-term operational plans that provide the basis for weekly and daily schedules and detailed resource requirements.

Discrete metric - is one that is calculated from data that are counted.

Diseconomies of scale - occur when the average unit cost of the good or service begins to increase as the capacity and/or volume of throughput increases.

Dispatching - is the process of selecting jobs for processing and authorizing the work to be done.

Distribution centers (DCS) - warehouses that act as intermediaries between factories and customers, shipping directly to customers or to retail stores where products are made available to customers.

Durable good - is one that does not quickly wear out and typically lasts at least three years.

Dynamic demand - demand that varies over time

Economic order quantity (EOQ) - is a classic economic model developed in the early 1900s that minimizes the total cost, which is the sum of the inventory-holding cost and the ordering cost.

Economic sustainability - an organization's commitment to address current business needs and economic vitality, and to have the agility and strategic management to prepare successfully for future business, markets, and operating environments.

Economies of scale - are achieved when the average unit cost of a good or service decreases as the capacity and/or volume of throughput increases.

Effective capacity - is the actual capacity that can reasonably be expected to be achieved in the long run under normal operating conditions.

Efficient supply chains - are designed for efficiency and low cost by minimizing inventory and maximizing efficiencies in process flow.

Elaborate servicescape environments - provide service using more complicated designs and service systems (e.g., hospitals, airports, and universities).

Empowerment - means giving people authority to make decisions based on what they feel is right, to have control over their work, to take risks and learn from mistakes, and to promote change.

End items - finished goods scheduled in the MPS or FAS that must be forecasted.

Environmental sustainability - an organization's commitment to the long-term quality of our environment.

Environmentally preferable purchasing (EPP) - is the affirmative selection and acquisition of products and services that most effectively minimize negative environmental impacts over their life cycle of manufacturing, transportation, use, and recycling or disposal.

Ergonomics - is concerned with improving productivity and safety by designing workplaces, equipment, instruments, computers, workstations, and so on that take into account the physical capabilities of people.

ERP systems - integrate all aspects of a business—accounting, customer relationship management, supply chain management, manufacturing, sales, human resources—into a unified information system, and they provide more timely analysis and reporting of sales, customer, inventory, manufacturing, human resource, and accounting data.

E-service - refers to using the Internet and technology to provide services that create and deliver time, place, information, entertainment, and exchange value to customers and/or support the sale of goods.

EVPI the difference between the expected payoff under perfect information and the expected payoff of the optimal decision without perfect information.

Execution - refers to moving work from one workstation to another, assigning people to tasks, setting priorities for jobs, scheduling equipment, and controlling processes.

Expected value approach - computes the expected value for each decision and selects the decision alternative with the best expected payoff.

Experience attributes - those that can be discerned only after purchase or during consumption or use.

Experience curve - states that the cost of doing any repetitive task, work activity, or project decreases as the accumulated experience of doing the job increases.

External failure costs - are incurred after poor-quality goods or services reach the customer.

F

Facility layout - refers to the specific arrangement of physical facilities.

Feasible solutions - any values of decision variables that satisfy all constraints.

Final assembly schedule (FAS) - defines the quantity and timing for assembling subassemblies and component parts into a final finished good

Finished-goods inventory - is completed products ready for distribution or sale to customers.

Fixed cost - that portion of total cost that does not vary with the amount produced.

Fixed-order-quantity (FOQ) - rule uses a fixed order size for every order or production run

Fixed-period system (FPS) - a periodic review system— is one in which the inventory position is checked only at fixed intervals of time, *T*, rather than on a continuous basis.

Fixed-position layout - consolidates the resources necessary to manufacture a good or deliver a service, such as people, materials, and equipment, in one physical location.

Fixed-quantity system (FQS) - the order quantity or lot size is fixed; that is, the same amount, Q, is ordered every time.

Fixed-time simulation model - a simulation model that increments time in fixed intervals.

Flexibility - the ability to adapt quickly and effectively to changing requirements.

Flexible manufacturing systems (FMSs) - consists of two or more computer-controlled machines or robots linked by automated handling devices such as transfer machines, conveyors, and transport systems. Computers direct the overall sequence of operations and route the work to the appropriate machine, select and load the proper tools, and control the operations performed by the machine.

Flow shop processes - organized around a a fixed sequence of activities and process steps, such as an assembly line, to produce a limited variety of similar goods or services.

Flow time (cycle time) - the average time it takes to complete one cycle of a process.

Flow time - the amount of time a job spends in the shop or factory.

Flow-blocking delay (or blocking delay) - when a work center completes a unit but cannot release it because the in-process storage at the next stage is full.

Focused factory - is a way to achieve economies of scale, without extensive investments in facilities and capacity, by focusing on a narrow range of goods or services, target market segments, and/or dedicated processes to maximize efficiency and effectiveness.

Forecast error - is the difference between the observed value of the time series and the forecast, or $A_t - F_t$.

Forecasting - the process of projecting the values of one or more variables into the future.

Forward integration - refers to acquiring capabilities toward distribution, or even customers.

G

Good - a physical product that you can see, touch, or possibly consume.

Goods and service design flexibility - the ability to develop a wide range of customized goods or services to meet different or changing customer needs.

Goods quality - relates to the physical performance and characteristics of a good.

Grassroots forecasting - asking those who are close to the end consumer, such as salespeople, about the customers' purchasing plans.

Green purchasing - the affirmative selection and acquisition of products and services that most effectively minimize negative environmental impacts over their life cycle of manufacturing, transportation, use, and recycling or disposal.

Green sustainable supply chain - one that uses environmentally friendly inputs and transforms these inputs through change agents—whose byproducts can improve or be recycled within the existing environment.

Gross requirements (GR) - the total demand for an item derived from all of its parents.

H

Hard technology - refers to equipment and devices that perform a variety of tasks in the creation and delivery of goods and services.

High scalability - the capability to serve additional customers at zero or extremely low incremental costs.

High-contact systems - systems in which the percentage of customer contact is high.

I

Immediate predecessors - those activities that must be completed immediately before an activity may start.

In control - when no special causes affect the output of a process.

Independent demand - is demand for an SKU that is unrelated to the demand for other SKUs and needs to be forecasted.

Infrastructure - focuses on the nonprocess features and capabilities of the organization and includes the workforce, operating plans and control systems, quality control, organizational structure, compensation systems, learning and innovation systems, and support services.

Innovation - refers to the ability to create new and unique goods and services that delight customers and create competitive advantage.

Interlinking - the quantitative modeling of cause-and-effect relationships between external and internal performance criteria.

Intermediary - any entity—real or virtual—that coordinates and shares information between buyers and sellers.

Internal failure costs - the costs incurred as a result of unsatisfactory quality that is found before the delivery of a good or service to the customer.

Inventory management - involves planning, coordinating, and controlling the acquisition, storage, handling, movement, distribution, and possible sale of raw materials, component parts and subassemblies, supplies and tools, replacement parts, and other assets that are needed to meet customer wants and needs.

Inventory position (IP) - the on-hand quantity (OH) plus any orders placed but which have not arrived (called scheduled receipts, SR), minus any backorders (BO).

Inventory - raw materials, work-in-process, or finished goods that are maintained to support production or satisfy customer demand.

Inventory-holding - the expenses associated with carrying inventory.

Irregular variation - is a one-time variation that is explainable.

J

Job design - involves determining the specific job tasks and responsibilities, the work environment, and the methods by which the tasks will be carried out to meet the goals of operations.

Job enlargement - the horizontal expansion of the job to give the worker more variety—although not necessarily more responsibility.

Job enrichment - vertical expansion of job duties to give the worker more responsibility.

Job shop processes - organized around particular types of general-purpose equipment that are flexible and capable of customizing work for individual customers.

Job - the set of tasks an individual performs.

Judgmental forecasting - relies upon opinions and expertise of people in developing forecasts.

K

Kaizen event - an intense and rapid improvement process in which a team or a department throws all its resources into an improvement project over a short time period, as opposed to traditional kaizen applications, which are performed on a part-time basis.

Kaizen - focuses on small, gradual, and frequent improvements over the long term, with minimum financial investment and with participation by everyone in the organization.

Kanban - is a flag or a piece of paper that contains all relevant information for an order: part number, description, process area used, time of delivery, quantity available, quantity delivered, production quantity, and so on.

L

Lack-of-work delay - occurs whenever one stage completes work and no units from the previous stage are awaiting processing.

Lateness - the difference between the completion time and the due date (either positive or negative).

Lead time - is the time between placement of an order and its receipt.

Lean operating systems - manufacturing and service operations that apply the principles of lean enterprise.

Lean servicescape environments - provide service using simple designs (e.g., online outlets or FedEx kiosks).

Lean thinking - refers to approaches that focus on the elimination of waste in all forms, and smooth, efficient flow of materials and information throughout the value chain to obtain faster customer response, higher quality, and lower costs.

Learning curve - is that direct labor unit cost decreases in a predictable manner as the experience in producing the unit increases

Learning - refers to creating, acquiring, and transferring knowledge, and modifying the behavior of employees in response to internal and external change.

Level production strategy - plans for the same production rate in each time period.

Little's law - a simple equation that explains the relationship among flow time (T), throughput (R), and work-in-process (WIP).

Logistics - is the discipline of managing the flow of materials and transportation activities to ensure adequate customer service at reasonable cost.

Lost sale when a customer is unwilling to wait and purchases the item elsewhere.

Lot sizing - is the process of determining the appropriate amount and timing of ordering to reduce costs.

Lot-for-lot (LFL) - an ordering schedule that covers the gross requirements for each week.

Low scalability - when serving additional customers requires high incremental variable costs.

Low-contact systems - systems in which the percentage of customer contact is low.

M

Makespan - is the time needed to process a given set of jobs.

Mass customization - being able to make whatever goods and services the customer wants, at any volume, at any time for anybody, and for a global organization, from any place in the world.

Master production schedule (MPS) - is a statement of how many finished items are to be produced and when they are to be produced.

Materials requirements planning (MRP) - is a forward-looking, demand-based approach for planning the production of manufactured goods and ordering materials and components to minimize unnecessary inventories and reduce costs.

Measurement - the act of quantifying the performance of organizational units, goods and services, processes, people, and other business activities.

Moments of truth - any episodes, transactions, or experiences in which a customer comes into contact with any aspect of the delivery system, however remote, and thereby has an opportunity to form an impression.

Moving average (MA) forecast - an average of the most recent "*k*" observations in a time series.

MRP explosion - is the process of using the logic of dependent demand to calculate the quantity and timing of orders for all subassemblies and components that go into and support the production of the end item(s).

Multinational enterprise - an organization that sources, markets, and produces its goods and services in several countries to minimize costs, and to maximize profit, customer satisfaction, and social welfare.

Multiple linear regression model - a linear regression model with more than one independent variable.

Multisite management - the process of managing geographically dispersed service-providing facilities.

N

Nodes - a set of circles or boxes in a project network.

Non-bottleneck work activity - is one in which idle capacity exists.

Nondurable good - one that is no longer useful once it's used, or lasts for less than three years.

Nonphysical constraint - is environmental or organizational, such as low product demand or an inefficient management policy or procedure.

Numerical control (NC) - machine tools, which enable the machinist's skills to be duplicated by a programmable device (originally punched paper tape) that controls the movements of a tool used to make complex shapes.

O

Objective function - the quantity we seek to minimize or maximize in an optimization model.

Offshoring - the building, acquiring, or moving of process capabilities from a domestic location to another country location while maintaining ownership and control.

Operational efficiency - the ability to provide goods and services to customers with minimum waste and maximum utilization of resources.

Operational structure - is the configuration of resources, such as suppliers, factories, warehouses, distributors, technical support centers, engineering design and sales offices, and communication links.

Operations design choices - the decisions management must make as to what type of process structure is best suited to produce goods or create services.

Operations management (OM) - the science and art of ensuring that goods and services are created and delivered successfully to customers.

Operations strategy - the set of decisions across the value chain that supports the implementation of higher-level business strategies.

Optimal solution - any feasible solution that minimizes or maximizes the objective function.

Option, or assemble-to-order, goods and services - configurations of standard parts, subassemblies, or services that can be selected by customers from a limited set.

Optimization Models - models that seek to minimize or maximize an objective function subject to a set of constraints.

Order amplification - a phenomenon that occurs when each member of a supply chain "orders up" to buffer its own inventory.

Order qualifiers - basic customer expectations are generally considered the minimum performance level required to stay in business.

Order winners - goods and service features and performance characteristics that differentiate one customer benefit package from another and win the customer's business.

Ordering costs - the work involved in placing orders with suppliers or configuring tools, equipment, and machines within a factory to produce an item.

Out of control - when special causes are present.

Outsourcing - the process of having suppliers provide goods and services that were previously provided internally.

P

Parent item - is manufactured from one or more components.

Pathway - a unique route through a service system.

p-chart - a control chart that monitors the proportion of nonconforming items.

Periodic-order quantity (POQ) - orders a quantity equal to the gross requirement quantity in one or more predetermined time periods minus the projected on-hand quantity of the previous time period

Peripheral goods or services - those that are not essential to the primary good or service, but enhance it.

Physical constraint - is associated with the capacity of a resource such as a machine, employee, or workstation.

Pipeline inventory - is inventory that has been ordered but is in transit.

Planned order receipt (PORec) - specifies the quantity and time an order is to be received.

Planned order release (PORel) - specifies the planned quantity and time an order is to be released to the factory or a supplier.

Planning horizon - the length of time on which a forecast is based.

Poka-yoke - an approach for mistake—proofing processes, using automatic devices or simple methods to avoid human error.

Postponement - is the process of delaying product customization until the product is closer to the customer at the end of the supply chain.

P-percent learning curve - characterizes a process in which the time of the $2x^{th}$ unit is p percent of the time of the xth unit.

Prevention costs - are those expended to keep nonconforming goods and services from being made and reaching the customer.

Primary good or service - the "core" offering that attracts customers and responds to their basic needs.

Process boundary - the beginning or end of a process.

Process capability index - the relationship between the natural variation and specifications is often quantified by a measure.

Process capability study - is a carefully planned study designed to yield specific information about the performance of a process under specified operating conditions.

Process capability - refers to the natural variation in a process that results from common causes.

Process layout - consists of a functional grouping of equipment or activities that do similar work.

Process map (flowchart) - describes the sequence of all process activities and tasks necessary to create and deliver a desired output or outcome.

Process - a sequence of activities that is intended to create a certain result.

Processing time - the time it takes to perform some task.

Product layout - an arrangement based on the sequence of operations that is performed during the manufacturing of a good or delivery of a service.

Product life cycle - is a characterization of product growth, maturity, and decline over time.

Product simplification - the process of trying to simplify designs to reduce complexity and costs and thus improve productivity, quality, flexibility, and customer satisfaction.

Productivity - the ratio of the output of a process to the input.

Product-process matrix - a model that describes the alignment of process choice with the characteristics of the manufactured good.

Project management - involves all activities associated with planning, scheduling, and controlling projects.

Project network - a graphical representation of a project consisting of a set of circles or boxes called **nodes** which represent activities, and a set of arrows called **arcs,** which define the precedence relationships between activities.

Project - is a temporary and often customized initiative that consists of many smaller tasks and activities that must be coordinated and completed to finish the entire initiative on time and within budget.

Projected on-hand inventory (POH) - is the expected amount of inventory on hand at the beginning of the time period considering on-hand inventory from the previous period plus scheduled receipts or planned order receipts minus the gross requirements.

Projects - are large-scale, customized initiative that consists of many smaller tasks and activities that must be coordinated and completed to finish the entire initiative on time and within budget.

Prototype testing - the process by which a model (real or simulated) is constructed to test the product's performance under actual operating conditions, as well as consumer reactions to the prototypes.

Provider-routed services - services in which customers follow a very small number of possible and predefined pathways through the service system.

Pull system - in which employees at a given operation go to the source of required parts, such as machining or subassembly, and withdraw the units as they need them.

Pull system - produces only what is needed at upstream stages in the supply chain in response to customer demand signals from downstream stages.

Purchasing (procurement) - the function responsible for acquiring raw materials, component parts, tools, services, and other items required from external suppliers.

Push system - produces goods in advance of customer demand using a forecast of sales and moves them through the supply chain to points of sale, where they are stored as finished-goods inventory.

Push–pull boundary - the point in the supply chain that separates the push system from the pull system.

Q

Quality at the source - means the people responsible for the work control the quality of their processes by identifying and correcting any defects or errors when they first are recognized or occur.

Quality control - is to ensure that a good or service conforms to specifications and meets customer requirements by monitoring and measuring processes and making any necessary adjustments to maintain a specified level of performance.

Quality function deployment (QFD) - an approach to guide the design, creation, and marketing of goods and services by integrating the voice of the customer into all decisions.

Quality management - refers to systematic policies, methods, and procedures used to ensure that goods and services are produced with appropriate levels of quality to meet the needs of customers.

Quality of conformance - the extent to which a process is able to deliver output that conforms to the design specifications.

Quality - measures the degree to which the output of a process meets customer requirements, or meeting or exceeding customers' expectations.

Queue discipline - the manner in which new arrivals are ordered or prioritized for service.

Queue time - a fancy word for wait time.

Queue a waiting line.

Queueing system - consists of customers that arrive for service, one or more servers that provide the service, and a queue (waiting line) of entities that wait for service if the server is busy.

Queueing theory - the analytical study of waiting lines.

R

Random number - is a number that is uniformly distributed between 0 and 1.

Random variate - a value randomly generated from a specified probability distribution.

Random variation - (sometimes called **noise**) is the unexplained deviation of a time series from a predictable pattern such as a trend, seasonal, or cyclical pattern.

Raw materials, component parts, subassemblies, and supplies - are inputs to manufacturing and service-delivery processes.

***R*-chart** - a control chart to monitor the variation in the process.

Reengineering - has been defined as the fundamental rethinking and radical redesign of business processes to achieve dramatic improvements in critical, contemporary measures of performance, such as cost, quality, service, and speed.

Regression analysis - is a method for building a statistical model that defines a relationship between a single dependent variable and one or more independent variables, all of which are numerical.

Reliability - the probability that a manufactured good, piece of equipment, or system performs its intended function for a stated period of time under specified operating conditions.

Reneging - the process of a customer entering the waiting line but later decides to leave the line and server system.

Reorder point - the value of the inventory position that triggers a new order.

Reservation - a promise to provide a good or service at some future time and place.

Reshoring - the process of moving operations back to a company's domestic location.

Resource management - deals with the planning, execution, and control of all the resources that are used to produce goods or provide services in a value chain.

Responsive supply chains - focus on flexibility and responsive service and ability to react quickly to changing market demand and requirements.

Return facilitators - specialize in organizations that handle all aspects of customers returning a manufactured good or delivered service and requesting their money back, repair the manufactured good and return it to the customer, and/or invoke the service guarantee.

Revenue management system (RMS) - consists of dynamic methods to forecast demand, allocate perishable assets across market segments, decide when to overbook and by how much, and determine what price to charge different customer (price) classes.

Reverse logistics - refers to managing the flow of finished goods, materials, or components that may be unusable or discarded through the supply chain from customers toward either suppliers, distributors, or manufacturers for the purpose of reuse, resale, or disposal.

Risk management - involves identifying risks that can occur, assessing the likelihood that they will occur, determining the impact on the firm and its customers, and identifying steps to mitigate the risks.

Robot - a programmable machine designed to handle materials or tools in the performance of a variety of tasks.

S

Safety capacity - an amount of capacity reserved for unanticipated events such as demand surges, materials shortages, and equipment breakdowns.

Safety stock inventory - is an additional amount that is kept over and above the average amount required to meet demand.

Safety stock - additional, planned on-hand inventory that acts as a buffer to reduce the risk of a stockout.

Scalability - a measure of the contribution margin (revenue minus variable costs) required to deliver a good or service as the business grows and volumes increase.

Schedule - a sequence of activities that are to be performed.

Scheduled or planned receipts (S/PR) - are orders that are due or planned to be delivered.

Scheduling - refers to the assignment of start and completion times to particular jobs, people, or equipment.

Search attributes - those that a customer can determine prior to purchasing the goods and/or services.

Seasonal patterns - are characterized by repeatable periods of ups and downs over short periods of time.

Sequencing - refers to determining the order in which jobs or tasks are processed.

Service encounter - an interaction between the customer and the service provider.

Service guarantee - a promise to reward and compensate a customer if a service upset occurs during the service experience.

Service level - the desired probability of not having a stockout during a lead-time period.

Service management - integrates marketing, human resources, and operations functions to plan, create, and deliver goods and services, and their associated service encounters.

Service process design - the activity of developing an efficient sequence of activities to satisfy both internal and external customer requirements.

Service quality - consistently meeting or exceeding customer expectations (external focus) and service-delivery system performance criteria (internal focus) during all service encounters.

Service recovery - the process of correcting a service upset and satisfying the customer.

Service upset any problem a customer has—real or perceived—with the service-delivery system and includes terms such as service failure, error, defect, mistake, and crisis.

Service upsets, or Service failures errors in service creation and delivery.

Service - is any primary or complementary activity that does not directly produce a physical product.

Service-delivery system design - includes facility location and layout, the service-scape, service process and job design, technology and information support systems.

Service-encounter activity sequence - consists of all the process steps and associated service encounters necessary to complete a service transaction and fulfill a customer's wants and needs.

Service-encounter design - focuses on the interaction, directly or indirectly, between the service provider(s) and the customer.

Servicescape - all the physical evidence a customer might use to form an impression. It also provides the behavioral setting when service encounters take place.

Shadow price - is the change in the objective function value as the right side of a constraint is increased by one unit.

Shortage or stockout costs - are costs associated with inventory being unavailable when needed to meet demand.

Simulation - is the process of developing and analyzing a logical model of a system, process, or management decision, and conducting computer-based experiments with the model to describe, explain, and predict the behavior of the system or outcomes associated with the decision.

Single exponential smoothing (SES) - a forecasting technique that uses a weighted average of past time-series values to forecast the value of the time series in the next period.

Single Minute Exchange of Dies (SMED) - refers to the quick setup or changeover of tooling and fixtures in processes so that multiple products in smaller batches can be run on the same equipment.

Single-piece flow - is the concept of ideally using batch sizes of one.

Six sigma - a business improvement approach that seeks to find and eliminate causes of defects and errors in manufacturing and service processes by focusing on outputs that are critical to customers, resulting in a clear financial return for the organization.

Social sustainability - an organization's commitment to maintain healthy communities and a society that improves the quality of life.

Soft technology - refers to the application of the Internet, computer software, and information systems to provide data, information, and analysis and to facilitate the creation and delivery of goods and services.

Special (or assignable) cause variation - arises from external sources that are not inherent in the process, appear sporadically, and disrupt the random pattern of common causes.

Specifications - are targets and tolerances determined by designers of goods and services.

Standard, or make-to-stock, goods and services made according to a fixed design, and the customer has no options from which to choose.

Standard time - is a reasonable estimate of the amount of time needed to perform a task based on an analysis of the work by a trained industrial engineer or other operations expert.

Static demand - the unchanging demand over time.

Statistical forecasting - based on the assumption that the future will be an extrapolation of the past.

Statistical process control (SPC) - a methodology for monitoring the quality of manufacturing and service-delivery processes to help identify and eliminate unwanted causes of variation.

Statistics - involves collecting, organizing, analyzing, interpreting, and presenting data.

Stock-keeping unit (SKU) - a single item or asset stored at a particular location.

Stockout - the inability to satisfy the demand for an item.

Strategy - a pattern or plan that integrates an organization's major goals, policies, and action sequences into a cohesive whole.

Subassembly - a part of a product that has at least one immediate parent and also has at least one immediate component.

Supply chain integration - is the process of coordinating the physical flow of materials to ensure that the right parts are available at various stages of the supply chain, such as manufacturing and assembly plants.

Supply chain management (SCM) - the management of all activities that facilitate the fulfillment of a customer order for a manufactured good to achieve customer satisfaction at reasonable cost.

Supply Chain Operations Reference (SCOR) model - a framework for understanding the scope of supply chain management (SCM) that is based on five basic functions involved in managing a supply chain: plan, source, make, deliver, and return.

Supply chain optimization - is the process of ensuring that a supply chain operates at the highest levels of efficiency and effectiveness.

Supply chain - the portion of the value chain that focuses primarily on the physical movement of goods and materials, and supporting flows of information and financial transactions through the supply, production, and distribution processes.

Sustainability - refers to an organization's ability to strategically address current business needs and successfully develop a long-term strategy that embraces opportunities and manages risk for all products, systems, supply chains, and processes to preserve resources for future generations.

T

Takt time - is the production rate for one good or service based on the rate of sales.

Tardiness - is the amount of time by which the completion time exceeds the due date.

Task - a specific unit of work required to create an output.

Theoretical capacity - the maximum rate of output that can be produced in a period of time under ideal operating conditions.

Theory of Constraints (TOC) - is a set of principles that focuses on increasing total process throughput by maximizing the utilization of all bottleneck work activities and workstations.

Third-party logistics (3PL) providers - businesses that provide integrated services that might include packaging, warehousing, inventory management, and transportation.

Throughput - the number of units or tasks that are completed per unit time from a process.

Time buckets - the time-period size used in the MRP explosion process and usually are one week in length.

Time series - is a set of observations measured at successive points in time or over successive periods of time.

Time study - the development of a standard time by observing a task with the use of a stopwatch and analyzing the data.

Total productive maintenance (TPM) - focused on ensuring that operating systems will perform their intended function reliably.

Transfer batch - portion of the original lot size that is completed at one workstation and moved to the next downstream workstation.

Transportation model - a linear optimization model that seeks to minimize the cost of shipping from sources such as factories to destinations such as warehouses or customer zones.

Trend - is the underlying pattern of growth or decline in a time series.

Triple bottom line (TBL or 3BL) - refers to the measurement of environmental, social, and economic sustainability.

U

Unit cost - is the price paid for purchased goods or the internal cost of producing them.

Unit of work - the output of a process or an individual process step.

Utilization - is the fraction of time a workstation or individual is busy over the long run.

V

Value chain integration - the process of managing information, physical goods, and services to ensure their availability at the right place, at the right time, at the right cost, at the right quantity, and with the highest attention to quality.

Value chain - a network of facilities and processes that describes the flow of materials, finished goods, services, information, and financial transactions from suppliers, through the facilities and processes that create goods and services, and those that deliver them to the customer.

Value of a loyal customer (VLC) - a model that quantifies the total revenue or profit each target market customer generates over the buyer's life cycle.

Value stream - refers to all value-added activities involved in designing, producing, and delivering goods and services to customers.

Value - the perception of the benefits associated with a good, service, or bundle of goods and services in relation to what buyers are willing to pay for them.

Variable cost - the portion of total cost varies with the level of output or quantity.

Variant - a CBP feature that departs from the standard CBP and is normally location or firm specific.

Vendor-managed inventory (VMI) - is where the vendor (supplier) monitors and manages inventory for the customer.

Vertical integration - refers to the process of acquiring and consolidating elements of a value chain to achieve more control.

Visual controls - are indicators for operating activities that are placed in plain sight of all employees so that everyone can quickly and easily understand the status and performance of the work system.

Voice of the customer - customer requirements, as expressed in the customer's own words.

Volume flexibility - the ability to respond quickly to changes in the volume and type of demand.

W

Wait time - the time spent waiting.

Work breakdown structure - is a hierarchical tree of end items that will be accomplished by the project team during the project.

Work measurement - a systematic procedure for the analysis of work, and determination of standard times required to perform key tasks in a process.

Work order - a specification of work to be performed for a customer or a client.

Work-in-process (WIP) inventory - consists of partially finished products in various stages of completion that are awaiting further processing.

X

$\bar{x}$-chart - a control chart that monitor the centering of the process.

D

E

F

G

H

I

N

O

P

Q

R

S

T

U

V

W

X

Y

Z

Non Returnable if Shrinkwrap is Broken

ISBN-13: 978-0357131732
ISBN-10: 0357131738